THE ROUGH GUIDE TO

Ireland

This eleventh edition updated by

Paul Clements, Paul Gray, Ciara Kenny, Norm Longley
and Ally Thompson

ROUGH
GUIDES

roughguides.com

Contents

Introduction to
Ireland

Over the past three decades, Ireland has transformed itself with quiet determination. Gone – or certainly on its way out – is the image of a conservative, introspective, dourly rural nation, while the infamous unrest and violence have, mercifully, faded away. An outward-looking Ireland has stepped forward, energized by rejuvenated cities no longer weighed down by the Troubles, where the fresh ideas introduced by immigrants and returnees during the Celtic Tiger years of the 1990s are maturing nicely. Of course, it's not called the Emerald Isle for nothing and Ireland's physical appeal endures clear and true as a jewel – but it's by no means a blanket of green. From the Burren's grey limestone pavement and the black peat bogs of the Midlands (where some of the prehistoric gold ornaments on show in Dublin's National Museum were dug up) to Connemara's gold- and purple-tinged mountains, Ireland's smouldering – even unnerving – good looks can send a shiver down your spine. And when the sun is shining the sky throbs bluer than anywhere else on earth – or so the Irish would have you believe.

While Dublin, Belfast and the other cities are cranking up the cosmopolitan – from hipster coffee shops to edgy, internationally relevant arts scenes – their on-message worldliness is not the be all and end all: **traditional culture** is cherished by even the most city-slicking of the Irish. Moreover, as Northern Irish historian J. C. Beckett (1912–96) noted, his homeland "has no natural focal point, no great crossing-place of routes, no centre from which influence spreads naturally." The lay of the land and the **road network** lend themselves to a democratic exploration, with each part of the country fair game, and you're unlikely to feel swallowed up by the cities' gravitational pull. In **rural areas**, switch modes to walking boots or two wheels (motorized or otherwise) and you'll be in no great hurry to return to the urban sprawl, however vibrant.

ABOVE LOUGH INAGH, CONNEMARA, CO. GALWAY **OPPOSITE** DUBLIN

In some areas **public transport** coverage fades to black, and you have no choice but to feel your way – the perfect opportunity to get to grips with Ireland's rich textures. The **west coast** is famous for its long beaches and windswept cliffs with views of the western islands; the drama of the landscape here is awe-inspiring, not least to the surfers who flock to Donegal and Galway. In the **east**, outside Dublin, the crumpled granite of the Wicklow Hills sits in stark contrast to the lush central plain just a few kilometres away. Cross the border into **Northern Ireland** and it is a short journey through rolling hills – known locally as drumlins – to the spectacular coast road that leads to the geological wonder of the **Giant's Causeway**.

Scattered across these landscapes is an abundance of **historic sites**. The very earliest of these include enigmatic prehistoric tombs, stone circles and hill forts. It is possible to trace the history of successive waves of immigration, whether Christian pilgrims, Viking raiders or Norman settlers, through the stone churches, distinctive **round towers** and high crosses strewn across the landscape.

FACT FILE

• Ireland is the third largest island in Europe. The **landmass** has a total area of 84,412 square kilometres, with its **coastline** stretching for 3152km.
• Its longest **river** is the Shannon (358km), largest **lake** Lough Neagh (387 square kilometres), **highest point** Carrauntoohil in Kerry (1038m) and its deepest **cave** is Reyfad Pot in Fermanagh (193m).
• The Newgrange Passage Tomb in County Meath dates back to **3200 BC**, making it around 1000 years older than Stonehenge.
• The island is made up of the Republic of Ireland, consisting of 26 **counties**, and Northern Ireland, subject to devolved British rule, which comprises six counties.
• The Republic's **population** is roughly 4.4 million, with 1.7 million residing in the Greater Dublin area. Northern Ireland's population is approximately 1.8 million, with some 650,000 occupying the Greater Belfast area.
• Irish is the **national language** of the Republic, according to the constitution, with English recognized as a second official language. However, only around fifteen percent of the population has a good competence in Irish.
• Ireland is the only country in the world with a musical instrument, the Irish harp, as its **national emblem**.

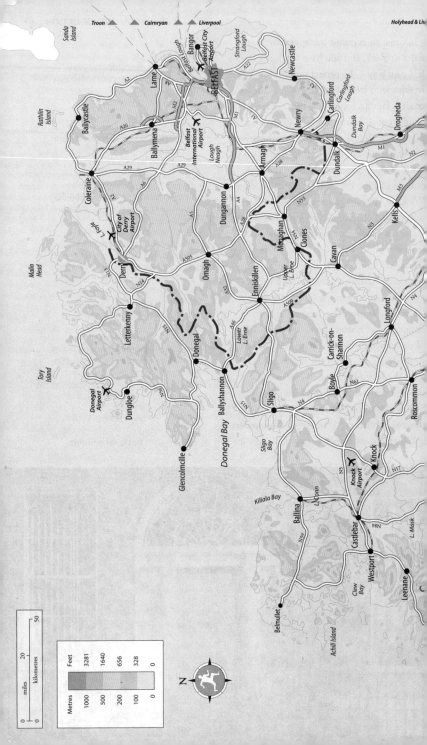

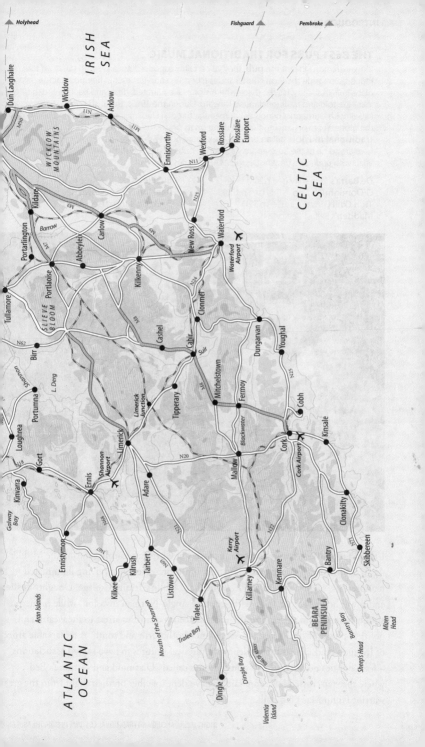

THE BEST PUBS FOR TRADITIONAL MUSIC

If the Irish didn't invent the **pub**, they've certainly espoused its cause with great vigour. Indeed, alongside the local church and the betting shop (for men), the pub retains a pivotal place in Irish society. It's the place where stories are narrated, deals and pacts are made, jokes are told and traditional music is heard. During the 1990s, the "Irish pub" concept (albeit with "authentic" period decor manufactured in Dublin) spread to far-flung points of the globe. Yet experiencing the real thing on its home turf to a live soundtrack of **traditional music** is still an unbeatable experience. With a pint of the black stuff in hand, here are some of the best, entirely authentic pubs to get you started on a lifelong love affair with *bodhráns*, tin whistles, pipes and fiddles:

De Barra's Clonakilty (see p.254)
O'Donoghue's Dublin City (see p.106)
Tigh Coili Galway City (see p.351)
Madden's Belfast (see p.484)

Buckley's Killarney (see p.281)
Reel Inn Donegal Town (see p.431)
Seán Og's Tralee (see p.304)

Ireland's **monasteries** were important centres of Christian learning during the Middle Ages, and the monks' elaborate craftsmanship is preserved in surviving illuminated manuscripts, such as the *Book of Kells*, held at Dublin's Trinity College. Doughty **castles** and tower houses record the twelfth-century Anglo-Norman invasion, while numerous **stately homes** from the eighteenth and nineteenth centuries attest to the wealth and political power of the Protestant Ascendancy both north and south. A remarkable aspect of Ireland's landscape is the tendency for physical features to have **sacred associations** – few counties do not shelter a pile of stones called "Diarmuid and Gráinne's Bed", where the star-crossed lovers are said to have slept together on their flight from the great warrior Fionn Mac Cumhaill.

RIGHT IRISH DANCING AND TRADITIONAL COSTUME IN BIRR, THE MIDLANDS

Inseparable from Ireland's history is its cultural heritage, a happy coming together of millennia and myriad influences from home and abroad. Here you have the richest store of **mythological traditions** in northern Europe, folkloric associations at every turn and world-famous literature and poetry. But there are a couple of elements you'll likely encounter in vivid form on a daily basis – particularly if you're a pub goer. First you have **traditional music**, with its ballads and *sean-nós* ("old-style" Irish-language singing) recounting tales of love, history and humour. Then there's the *craic*, the talking therapy of Ireland's pubs, a combination of unlikely yarns, surreal comedy and plain old chatter and gossip. **Dublin**, which has long enjoyed a reputation as a culturally rich city, remains the epicentre of artistic activity. The Republic's capital is justifiably proud of its literary tradition, which takes in (among countless other luminaries) Oscar Wilde, Flann O'Brien and James Joyce, whose famously complex and experimental *Finnegans Wake* is – besides its many other triumphs – a worthy encapsulation of the sheer weightiness of Irish culture.

Ireland is rightly renowned for the **welcome** extended to visitors, and the tourist sector is, unsurprisingly, at the centre of its plans for lasting economic recovery. Northern Ireland and Belfast, in particular, have taken full advantage of the sudden influx of visitors previously deterred by the Troubles. What they will encounter is an Ireland where, finally, the past is significant for its **cultural riches** rather than the shadow it casts – and where the future is all about that big blue sky.

Where to go

Dublin is the Republic's main entry-point, a confident capital whose raw, modern energy is complemented by rich cultural traditions, and which boasts outstanding **medieval monuments** and the richly varied exhibits of the **National Gallery** and **National Museum**. South of the city, the desolate **Wicklow Mountains** offer a breathtaking contrast to city life.

If you arrive on the **west coast** at Shannon Airport in County Clare, Ireland's most spectacular landscapes are within easy reach. **Clare**'s coastline rises to a head at the vertiginous **Cliffs of Moher**, while inland lies **the Burren**, a barren limestone plateau at odds with the lush greenery characteristic of much of Ireland. To Clare's south, Limerick's **Hunt Museum** houses one of Ireland's most diverse and fascinating collections. The **Wild Atlantic Way**, meanwhile, is a scenic west coast driving route launched in 2014 that encourages exploration on this side of the island.

County Kerry, south of Limerick, features dazzling scenery, an intoxicating brew of seascapes, looming mountains and sparkling lakes. Though the craggy coastline traversed by the **Ring of Kerry** is a major tourist attraction, it's still relatively easy to find seclusion. In County Galway, to Clare's north, lies enthralling **Connemara**, untamed bogland set between sprawling beaches and a muddle of quartz-gleaming mountains; in contrast, university cities such as **Galway** and **Limerick** provide year-round festivals and buzzing nightlife. Further north, **Donegal** offers a dramatic mix of rugged peninsulas and mountains, glistening beaches and magical lakes.

Dotted around the west coast are numerous **islands**, providing a glimpse of the harsh way of life endured by remote Irish-speaking communities. The **Arans** are the most famous – windswept expanses of limestone supporting extraordinary prehistoric sites – but the savagely beautiful landscape of the **Blasket Islands**, off Kerry's coast, is equally worthy of exploration. **Achill Island**, the largest and accessible by bridge, is home to five spectacular blue flag beaches.

On Ireland's southern coast, **Cork**'s shoreline is punctuated by secluded estuaries, rolling headlands and historic harbours, while **Cork city** itself is the region's hub, with a vibrant cultural scene and nightlife. Nearby, the pretty seaside town of **Cobh** (previously called Queenstown) is renowned as the departure point for over 2.5 million Irish immigrants bound for North America after the Great Famine, and as a port of call for the ill-fated RMS *Titanic* in 1912. To Cork's east, **Waterford city** houses the wondrous Viking and medieval collections of Waterford Treasures, while, in Ireland's southeastern corner, **Wexford**'s seashore features broad estuaries teeming with bird life and expansive dune-backed beaches.

Inland, the Republic's scenery is less enchanting, its **Midland** counties characterized by fertile if somewhat drab agricultural land, as well as broad expanses of **peat bog**, home to endangered species of rare plants. However, there is gentle appeal in Ireland's great watercourse, the **Shannon**, with its succession of vast loughs, and the quaint river valleys of the southeast.

CLOCKWISE FROM TOP LEFT KILKENNY CITY; BRIDGE TO CARRICK-A-REDE ISLAND; TRINITY COLLEGE, DUBLIN; MALIN HEAD

Numerous **historic** and **archeological sites** provide fine alternative attractions. The prehistoric tomb at Meath's **Newgrange** and the fortress of **Dun Aengus** on Inishmore are utterly mesmerizing; County Cork features many **stone circles**; and there's a multitude of **tombs** and **ring forts** across the west coast counties. Stunning early **Christian monuments** abound, too, including those located on **Skellig Michael** and the **Rock of Cashel** and atmospheric sites at **Clonmacnois**, **Glendalough** and **Monasterboice**. Of more recent origin, the Anglo-Irish nobility's planned **estates**, developed during the eighteenth and nineteenth centuries around impressive Neoclassical mansions, are visible across Ireland.

Much of **Northern Ireland's** countryside is intensely beautiful and unspoiled. To the north are the green **Glens of Antrim** and a coastline as scenic as anywhere in Ireland, with, as its centrepiece, the bizarre basalt geometry of the **Giant's Causeway**. The **Antrim Coast Road**, meanwhile, is one of Ireland's most scenic drives. In the southeast, **Down** offers the contrasting beauties of serene **Strangford Lough** and the brooding presence of the **Mourne Mountains**, while, to the west, **Fermanagh** has the peerless lake scenery of **Lough Erne**, a fabulous place for watersports, fishing and exploring island monastic remains. Evidence of the Plantation is also provided by planned towns and various grand **mansions**, often set in sprawling, landscaped grounds.

To get to grips with the North's history, a visit to its **cities** is essential, not least for their tremendous museums: **Belfast**, with its ship-building past and grand public buildings, built on the profits of industry; **Derry**, which grew around the well-preserved walls of its medieval antecedent; and the cathedral town of **Armagh** where St Patrick established Christianity in Ireland.

When to go

Whenever you visit Ireland it's wise to come prepared for wet and/or windy conditions, especially along the west coast which faces the Atlantic, the source of much of Ireland and Britain's weather. On average (see box, p.43), it **rains** around 150 days a year along the east and southeast coasts, and up to as many as 225 days a year in parts of the west and southwest. April is the driest time across most of the island, while December and January are the wettest. Whatever the case, the weather is very changeable and you'll often find a soggy morning rapidly replaced by brilliant sunshine in the afternoon. Most years also see long periods of gorgeous weather, though predicting their occurrence is often well nigh impossible. Generally, the **sunniest months** (see box, p.43) are April, May and June, while July and August are the warmest with temperatures sometimes reaching as high as 25°C. Overall, the southeast gets the best of the sunshine.

Author picks

Our authors scoured every inch of the Emerald Isle to bring you these hand-picked gems, from dolphin spotting to champagne supping.

Ticking off Dublin's pubs In Joyce's *Ulysses*, Leopold Bloom queried whether it would be possible to cross Dublin without passing a pub – and with more than 700 dotted around the city, it would be a mean feat indeed. A cliché it may be, but there's something very special about a perfect pint of Guinness in a Dublin pub – *The Palace Bar* (p.104) offers you this and gorgeous interiors to boot.

Twitching on Rathlin Island Hop on board the Rathlin ferry from Ballycastle (p.501) for the short crossing to Northern Ireland's only inhabited island. It's home to a colony of seals and an RSPB nature reserve attracting guillemots, puffins, razorbills and the red-billed chough.

Go on dolphin watch On a summer's day, set sail from Carrigaholt in South Clare for a two-hour boat trip in the Shannon estuary (p.330) – you'll be rewarded with views of the delectable Loop Head peninsula and Ireland's only resident bottlenose dolphins.

Join the seafaring gentry Set aside an hour or two on a Sunday to enjoy a decadent afternoon tea at the foot of the iconic RMS *Titanic*'s Grand Staircase. The replica stands tall in Titanic Belfast (p.470) and a live jazz band accompanies proceedings, setting the scene as champagne-quaffing guests nibble on tasty delicacies.

Cycle the Great Western Greenway Opened in 2011, this glorious 42km route (p.384), along a former railway track in Mayo, is the longest off-road walking and cycling trail in Ireland. Broken down into three easy-to-manage sections, it's a favourite with families: Achill to Mulranny (13km), Mulranny to Newport (18km) and Newport to Westport (11km).

Our author recommendations don't end here. We've flagged up our favourite places – a perfectly sited hotel, an atmospheric café, a special restaurant – throughout the guide, highlighted with the ★ symbol.

FROM TOP AFTERNOON TEA AT TITANIC BELFAST; DOLPHINS IN THE SHANNON ESTUARY; *THE PALACE BAR*, DUBLIN

25

things not to miss

It's not possible to see everything that Ireland has to offer in one trip – and we don't suggest you try. What follows, in no particular order, is a selective and subjective taste of the country's highlights: from geological wonders and ancient ruins to activities and experiences both on land and at sea. Each entry has a page reference to take you straight into the Guide, where you can find out more. Coloured numbers refer to chapters in the Guide section.

1

1 KYLEMORE ABBEY, CONNEMARA

Page 376

One of Connemara's most historic sites, the spectacular Kylemore Abbey comes with a beautifully restored walled garden and Neogothic church.

2 TRINITY COLLEGE, DUBLIN

Page 58

Wonder at the ninth-century *Book of Kells*, housed in the Old Library, before wandering through the city-centre campus, taking in the best of Dublin's architecture.

3 TITANIC BELFAST

Page 470

Taking pride of place in the heart of Belfast's newly developed Titanic Quarter, this interactive museum takes visitors on a fascinating journey through the city's maritime heritage and the story of the ill-fated RMS *Titanic*.

4

5

6

7

8

4 TRADITIONAL MUSIC
Pages 600–604

Often loud, often raucous and always fun, traditional Irish music can be heard in many pubs and at dedicated festivals such as the Willie Clancy Festival in Miltown Malbay every July.

5 SURFING AT BUNDORAN
Page 426

Thunderous waves roll in at Ireland's surfing capital, attracting fans from around the globe.

6 BRÚ NA BÓINNE
Page 141

This extraordinary ritual landscape is simply one of the world's most important prehistoric sites.

7 GARINISH ISLAND
Page 265

Sail across from Glengarriff Pier, past the basking seals, to discover these magical, otherworldly gardens.

8 BANTRY HOUSE
Page 262

A magnificent setting for some lavish artworks, among formal gardens overlooking Bantry Bay.

9 SKELLIG MICHAEL
Page 285

A remarkable and inspiring early Christian hermitage clinging to a mountain summit on a wild, bleak island.

9

13

14

21

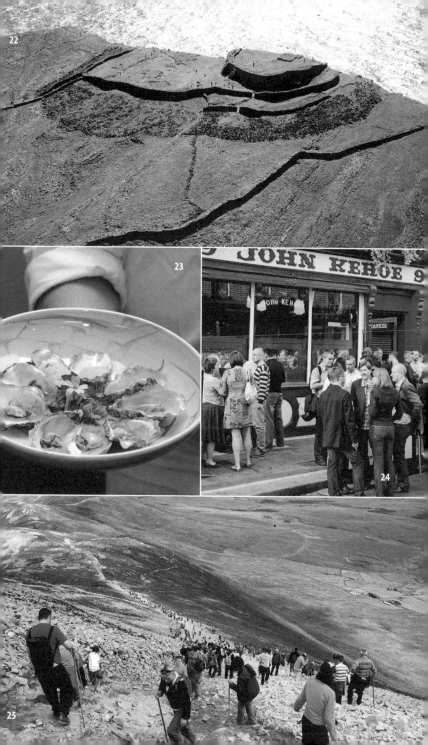

Itineraries

Ireland is compact but it packs an awful lot in. Five days on the Wild Atlantic Way guarantees a host of unforgettable vistas, while a few days in the southwest will introduce foodies to a feast of local delicacies. The coastline around the Giant's Causeway in the North is simply one of the world's great road trips – at 120 miles (190km) it can easily be driven in a day, though you're bound to want to slow down and savour the ride.

A SOUTHWEST FOODIE TRIP

Allow three to four days to cover these 140km, sampling some of the finest produce the island has to offer, from seafood to superb cheeses.

❶ Kinsale The southwest's culinary honeypot boasts a beautiful harbour setting. For seafood lovers, the pick of the crop is the *Fishy Fishy Café and Restaurant*, serving up the freshest catch from the morning's haul. **See p.250**

❷ Clonakilty Heading west, you'll come to the source of the famous Clonakilty Black Pudding, sold at traditional butcher's Twomey's. Enjoy fine local produce for dinner at the *Inchydoney Island Lodge and Spa*, which overlooks the beach just outside of town. **See p.252**

❸ Baltimore Further southwest lies the small harbour village of Baltimore where the award-winning *Rolf's* makes a perfect leisurely lunch stop – it serves delicious local and organic lunches during the summer months. **See p.257**

❹ Schull Continue onto Schull where the Ferguson family produce their excellent Gubbeen cheese and meats. They sell at various local markets, including the Sunday morning Schull Market (Easter to Sept). **See p.259**

❺ Durrus The beautiful village of Durrus has two excellent options. For lunch try *Good Things Café*, run by renowned chef Carmel Somers. In

the evening head to the fabulous *Blairscove House & Restaurant*, with its impressive choice of Irish meats cooked over a roaring fire. **See p.261**

❻ Bantry Finish off your gastronomic gallivanting with a trip to Bantry Market, one of West Cork's largest. Located in the main square, it runs every Friday morning from 9.30am–1pm. **See p.262**

CAUSEWAY COASTAL ROUTE

The distances are short but the views immense on this spectacular road trip.

❶ Carrickfergus From Belfast, head north on the M2 to Carrickfergus, home to a twelfth-century Anglo-Norman castle, complete with cannons, portcullis and ramparts. **See p.492**

❷ The Glens of Antrim A drive through the Glens of Antrim guarantees waterfalls, forests, glacier-gouged valleys and the pretty villages of Carnlough, Cushendall and Cushendun – *Game of Thrones* fans might recognize some of the location backdrops en route. **See p.496**

❸ Rathlin Island Explore the market town of Ballycastle before hopping on the ferry to craggy Rathlin Island, which offers fantastic bird-watching and nature walks. Get some rest at the *Manor House*, a charming, National Trust-owned B&B. **See p.501**

ABOVE CARRICKFERGUS CASTLE; *FISHY FISHY CAFÉ AND RESTAURANT*; OLD BUSHMILLS DISTILLERY

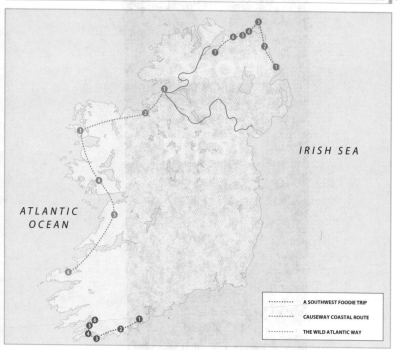

4 The Giant's Causeway Channel your inner Indiana Jones at Carrick-a-rede rope bridge before continuing on to the Causeway, with its world-famous rock formations. **See p.503**

5 Bushmills Continue along the coastline to Bushmills for a tour (and a dram) at its famed whiskey distillery before booking in to the cosy *Bushmills Inn*. **See p.505**

6 Portstewart Explore ruined Dunluce Castle (believed to have been the inspiration for Cair Paravel in C. S. Lewis' *The Chronicles of Narnia*) then continue, via the classic seaside town of Portrush, to picturesque Portstewart, with its two-mile stretch of golden sand. **See p.507**

7 Roe Valley Country Park Sample Roe Valley Country Park's riverside walks, ending your trip at the luxurious *Roe Park Resort*. **See p.510**

THE WILD ATLANTIC WAY

This spectacular driving tour (see p.31) features some of Ireland's finest cliffs, beaches, peninsulas, and panoramic land- and seascapes.

1 Rossnowlagh Donegal has a wealth of natural riches, including nearly thirty percent of Ireland's beaches; one of the best for watching

the surfers is at Rossnowlagh. **See p.426**

2 Strandhill Sligo's coastline is filled with short detours. The road out to Strandhill is worth a diversion to sample a cute, old-school seaside resort and some superb sunsets. **See p.401**

3 Achill Island County Mayo highlights include the Céide Fields and Erris, but the pick is Achill Island, where you can climb Slievemore for views across some of the country's most rugged landscape. **See p.387**

4 Connemara After taking in the majesty of Killary harbour and Ireland's only fjord, the indented Connemara coastline has many attractions in store. From Clifden and Roundstone, to Carna and Barna, you can survey the great theatre of Galway Bay. **See p.368**

5 The Burren The Burren area has some of the most dramatic stretches of the way, particularly the road out to Ballyvaughan - be sure to venture inland too. **See p.334**

6 The Dingle Peninsula The Dingle Peninsula boasts stunning beaches such as Inch Strand and Castlegregory (home to natterjack toads). You can also hike in the footsteps of ancient pilgrims to the summit of Mount Brandon. **See p.291**

GREEN-PAINTED LETTERBOX

Basics

Getting there

Dublin is the Republic of Ireland's main point of arrival, Belfast that of the North, while Shannon, near Limerick city in Co. Clare, is the major airport giving direct access to the west coast. There's an ever-changing route map of flights between Britain and Ireland – book early to get the best price. Train–ferry and bus–ferry combinations are kinder to the environment and generally take longer, though of course they take longer. For those bringing their own car, there's a wide range of ferry routes from southwest Scotland, northwest England and Wales to Northern Ireland, Dublin and Wexford. North American visitors can fly direct to Shannon, Dublin or Belfast, but those from South Africa, Australia and New Zealand have to travel via Britain, Europe or the Gulf. If you're thinking of booking an organized tour, there are plenty of interesting options based in Ireland that have an online presence.

Flights from Britain

It's never been easier or cheaper to fly from Britain to Ireland. There are dozens of **routes** available, with new destinations regularly appearing and unsuccessful routes being phased out. With so much competition, **prices** can be ridiculously cheap, especially if you book online. The secret is to book as early as possible: the biggest carrier, Ryanair, for example, offers fares of under £20 one-way if booked well in advance, but these can rise to over £150 one-way if left till the last minute. Flight time between London, for example, and any airport in Ireland is between one hour and one hour thirty minutes.

Flights from the US and Canada

From the US and Canada, Aer Lingus, the national airline of the Republic, offers the widest choice of routes, including nonstop flights from Boston, Chicago, New York, Orlando, San Francisco, Toronto and Washington to Dublin, and from Boston and New York to Shannon. If booked well in advance, their low-season fares from New York (JFK) to Dublin start at around US$600 return (including taxes), from San Francisco around US$950 and Can$660 from Toronto. In high season fares rise to US$1070 from New York, US$1400 from San Francisco, Can$1110 from Toronto. Flying time to Dublin, for example, is around six hours thirty minutes from New York and Toronto and ten hours fifteen minutes from San Francisco.

Flights from Australia, New Zealand and South Africa

Travel from Australia, New Zealand and South Africa is generally via London, or one of the other European or Gulf cities such as Frankfurt or Abu Dhabi which have nonstop flights to Ireland. From Australia and New Zealand, it takes over twenty-four hours to reach Ireland, from South Africa at least thirteen hours. **Fares** (including taxes) to Dublin from Sydney start at around A$1500, from Auckland around NZ$1750, and from Johannesburg around R6000.

Ferries

Ferry **routes** to Ireland are detailed below, along with the length of each voyage; Ⓦ ferrybooker.com will give you an overview of what's currently available and allow you to compare prices. High-speed catamarans (which also take cars) operate on some of these routes (see p.28), though some don't run in the winter and in bad weather they're more likely to be cancelled than regular ferries.

Prices vary hugely according to the time of year, and even the day and hour you travel. Most ferry companies have peak seasons of July and August and may charge higher fares around public holidays; generally, it's cheaper to travel midweek, and to book online and in advance. As an example of prices, Stena Line's single fares for a car and driver

---

A BETTER KIND OF TRAVEL

At Rough Guides we are passionately committed to travel. We believe it helps us understand the world we live in and the people we share it with – and of course tourism is vital to many developing economies. But the scale of modern tourism has also damaged some places irreparably, and climate change is accelerated by most forms of transport, especially flying. All Rough Guides' flights are carbon-offset, and every year we donate money to a variety of environmental charities.

from Holyhead to Dublin Port cost from around £70 off-peak (Tues & Wed) to around £150 at peak times (weekends); additional passengers cost £30 per adult, while foot passengers are charged £32 per adult, plus £10 per bicycle.

Trains

Combined train and boat journeys from Britain generally use one of three **routes** across the Irish Sea: Cairnryan to Belfast, Holyhead to Dublin/Dún Laoghaire or Fishguard to Rosslare. Journey times are generally quicker than by coach: London to Dublin, for example, takes around eight hours, Glasgow to Belfast as little as four hours fifty minutes.

Ticket prices are **calculated** partly on a zonal basis, but also depend on which boat you take and whether you book in advance. For Dublin, they range from £31 single from Manchester, for example, including the cost of a boat from Holyhead, while from London they start at £36; add around £18 one-way if you're continuing by train to Cork, for example. Online, you can **book** train–boat tickets through the Man in Seat 61, or direct with Raileasy. Otherwise, you can book tickets in person at most railway stations in Britain, including through-tickets to other places in Ireland.

Buses

The main bus services to Ireland are provided by National Express and Bus Éireann, under the brand name **Eurolines**, crossing the Irish Sea via Cairnryan, Holyhead and Pembroke. They can be cheaper than travelling by train if booked well in advance, but take far longer. The daily through-service from London to Dublin, for example, takes around twelve hours thirty minutes and **costs** £69 for a standard return. Direct coaches also run between other major cities in Britain and Ireland; a standard return ticket from London to Cork costs £90, for example. Cheap advance offers, known as "funfares", can be accessed online, and reductions are also available for anyone under 26 or over 59. Tickets can be **booked** at any National Express agent, by phoning ☎ 08717 818178, or online at ⓦ eurolines.co.uk.

AIRLINES

FROM BRITAIN

Aer Lingus ⓦ aerlingus.com
BMI ⓦ bmiregional.com
British Airways ⓦ britishairways.com
Cityjet ⓦ cityjet.com

easyJet ⓦ easyjet.com
Flybe ⓦ flybe.com
Jet2.com ⓦ jet2.com
Ryanair ⓦ ryanair.com

FROM THE US AND CANADA

Aer Lingus ⓦ aerlingus.com
Air Canada ⓦ aircanada.com
Air Transat ⓦ airtransat.com
American Airlines ⓦ aa.com
Delta ⓦ delta.com
Lufthansa ⓦ lufthansa.com
United ⓦ united.com
US Airways ⓦ usairways.com

FROM AUSTRALIA, NEW ZEALAND AND SOUTH AFRICA

Air New Zealand ⓦ airnewzealand.com
British Airways ⓦ britishairways.com
Emirates ⓦ emirates.com
Etihad Airways ⓦ etihadairways.com
Lufthansa ⓦ lufthansa.com
Qantas ⓦ qantas.com
Singapore Airlines ⓦ singaporeair.com
South African Airways ⓦ flysaa.com

FERRY AND CATAMARAN CONTACTS

Irish Ferries ☎ 08717 300 400, ⓦ irishferries.com. Holyhead to Dublin Port (3hr 15min, catamaran 1hr 50min); and Pembroke to Rosslare (4hr).
P&O ☎ 0871 664 2121, ⓦ poferries.com. Cairnryan to Larne (2hr); Troon to Larne (catamaran 2hr 15min); Liverpool to Dublin (8hr).
Stena Line ☎ 08447 70 70 70, ⓦ stenaline.co.uk. Fishguard to Rosslare (3hr 30min); Liverpool to Belfast (8hr); Holyhead to Dublin Port (3hr 15min) and Dún Laoghaire (catamaran 2hr 20min); and Cairnryan to Belfast (2hr 15min).

RAIL CONTACTS

The Man in Seat 61 ⓦ seat61.com
Raileasy ⓦ raileasy.co.uk

AGENTS AND OPERATORS

Bunk Campers Northern Ireland ☎ 028 9081 3057, ⓦ bunkcampers.com. Campervan rental in Belfast and Dublin.
Extreme Ireland Republic of Ireland ☎ 01 410 0700, ⓦ extremeireland.ie. Hiking and adventure multi- and one-day tours all around Ireland; activities include kayaking, horse riding, mountain-climbing and cycling.
Go Visit Ireland Republic of Ireland ☎ 066 976 2094, ⓦ govisitireland.com. Small-group, customized and self-guided walking, cycling and hike-and-bike tours mostly on the west coast, as well as horse riding and kayaking.
Inroads Ireland US ☎ 1 888 220 7711, ⓦ inroadsireland.com. Irish-American company offering well-received seven-day small-group tours, staying mostly in B&Bs.

Irish Boat Rental Association Republic of Ireland

Ⓦ boatholidaysireland.com. Umbrella association of companies who rent out cruisers for holidays on the Shannon. See Ⓦ iwai.ie or Ⓦ waterwaysireland.org for fuller listings across the country.

Irish Cycling Safaris and **Irish Ways** Republic of Ireland ☎ 01 260 0749, Ⓦ cyclingsafaris.com and Ⓦ irishways.com. Long-established and well-regarded companies, based at University College Dublin, offering guided and self-led cycling and walking tours all over the country, with accommodation and luggage transfer covered.

Irish Horse-Drawn Caravans Federation

Ⓦ irishhorsedrawncaravans.com. Companies in Wicklow, Laois, East Galway and Mayo offering horse-drawn caravan holidays, driving and sleeping in traditional, wooden covered wagons.

Naturetrek UK ☎ 01962 733051, Ⓦ naturetrek.co.uk. Wildlife specialist offering four-day botanical tours of the Burren and four-day tours of the Northern Ireland coast.

North South Travel UK ☎ 01245 608 291, Ⓦ northsouthtravel .co.uk. Friendly, competitive travel agency, offering discounted fares worldwide. Profits are used to support projects in the developing world, especially the promotion of sustainable tourism.

South West Walks Ireland Republic of Ireland ☎ 066 718 6181, Ⓦ southwestwalksireland.com. Guided and self-guided walking holidays on the west coast, in Antrim and in Wicklow, as well as self-guided cycling holidays.

STA Travel UK ☎ 0333 321 0099, US ☎ 1800 781 4040, Australia ☎ 134 782, New Zealand ☎ 0800 474 400, South Africa ☎ 0861 781 781, Ⓦ statravel.co.uk. Worldwide specialists in independent travel; also student IDs, travel insurance, car rental, rail passes, and more. Good discounts for students and under-26s.

Trailfinders UK ☎ 0207 368 1200, Ⓦ trailfinders.com. One of the best-informed and most efficient agents for independent travellers.

Travel CUTS Canada ☎ 1800 667 2887, US ☎ 1800 592 2887, Ⓦ travelcuts.com. Canadian youth and student travel firm.

USIT Australia ☎ 1800 092 499, Ⓦ usit.ie. Branch of Ireland's main student and youth travel specialists.

Getting around

It's easy to travel between the Republic's larger towns and cities by public transport. However, it's common for small towns and villages to have just one or two bus services per week, often geared towards market days. Transport in Northern Ireland is equally sparse in rural areas, with just a few train lines across the region, though the bus network is pretty comprehensive. Renting a car is perhaps the easiest way to explore rural and remote areas across Ireland, though traffic has become increasingly heavy on major routes. Picturesque areas are particularly enjoyable on a bike, though you may need to bring your own as rental outlets have dried up in rural areas. If you want to travel quickly from Dublin or Belfast to outlying areas, it's also worth considering the internal flights available.

By rail

Train services in the **Republic** are operated by Iarnród Éireann (Irish Rail; Ⓦ irishrail.ie). Prices are usually higher than taking a coach, though journeys are often much quicker – for example, the train from Dublin to Killarney can take at least two and a half hours less than the bus. Most of the lines fan out from Dublin towards the southern and western coasts, but there are few links between them, and some counties (such as Donegal and Cavan) have no rail links at all.

Tickets come in a variety of formats – single, day return, open return, family day and open returns, and student tickets. However, bear in mind that a standard single is much more than half the cost of an open return ticket – for example, a standard single from Dublin to Killarney is €66.50, a return €84.70. Tickets booked online in advance for specific trains are generally much cheaper – as little as €24 for a Dublin–Killarney single; if you miss your train, you can pay an extra €10 at the ticket office to get on a later service, if seats are available.

The only line operating **between the Republic and the North** is the Dublin–Belfast Enterprise service. The **North**'s rail service is operated by Translink (Ⓦ translink.co.uk) and restricted to just a few lines running out of Belfast. Services are generally efficient and the rolling stock has been recently updated. Fares are pretty reasonable – for example, travelling from Belfast to Derry costs £11.50 single and £17.50 day return – and often comparable with bus services.

You can also **transport bikes** on trains (see p.31).

Rail and bus passes

Although rail passes for travel within the Republic represent reasonably good value, a combined bus and rail pass, such as the Irish Explorer, is probably more useful owing to the limitations of the rail network. Passes are available at all major train and bus stations.

The Trekker ticket (€110) allows unlimited travel over the Republic's rail network for four consecutive days. The **Irish Explorer** pass (€160) covers five days' rail travel out of fifteen consecutive days, though you can extend this to cover both rail travel and bus travel on Bus Éireann services for eight days out of fifteen days (€245).

Bus Éireann offers an **Open Road** pass for travel on buses within the Republic, which can be purchased in a wide variety of combinations: three days' travel out of six, for example, costs €57, while the maximum of fifteen days out of thirty costs €249.

In the North, Translink's Rambler ticket (£9) provides unlimited travel around the bus network after 9.15am on Sundays and during school holidays (including July and August). Families can take advantage of a variety of day passes for trains and/or buses.

If your visit to Ireland is just part of a grander European trip, it's well worth investigating the range of different passes on offer, such as InterRail (Ⓦ interrail.eu) and Eurail (Ⓦ eurail.com).

By bus

Bus Éireann (Ⓦ buseireann.ie) runs express coach and slower local services throughout the Republic. Ticket prices are generally far more reasonable than trains and you can often snap up cheap deals, especially between Dublin and Cork. Timetables and fares (including special deals) for the major routes can be found on the website. The majority of buses show destinations in both Irish and English, but some in rural areas may only display the former.

A vast number of **private bus companies** also operate in the Republic, running services on major routes, as well as areas not covered by the Bus Éireann network (especially Co. Donegal). The names, contact details and routes of these companies are listed in the *Guide*, where applicable. These can sometimes be cheaper and quicker than Bus Éireann, but are usually very busy at weekends, when advance booking is advisable.

In **Northern Ireland**, Metro (Belfast city buses), **Ulsterbus** (local buses) and **Goldline** (long-distance), all part of Translink (see p.29), run a pretty comprehensive network of regular and reliable services across Northern Ireland.

You can also **transport bikes** on buses (see opposite).

By car and motorcycle

Travelling by **car** or **motorbike** is the ideal way to explore at your leisure, especially in remote areas. You might be tempted to take on the Wild Atlantic Way, a signposted route around the west coast all the way from west Cork to Donegal (see box opposite) – and if you enjoy that, you could keep going along the Causeway Coastal Route, which runs from Derry to Belfast for over 300km, mostly along the N2. If you bring your own vehicle, it's essential to carry its registration document and certificate of **insurance** – and make sure that your existing policy covers you for driving in Ireland. Whether bringing your own vehicle or renting one on arrival, you'll need to be in possession of a valid **driving licence** (and should carry it with you – a photocopy is insufficient). A driving licence from any EU country is treated like an Irish licence, while all other visitors are allowed to drive on a valid non-EU licence for a stay of up to 12 months.

In the Republic, unleaded **petrol** costs around €1.55 a litre – cheaper than the North where the equivalent price is about £1.30.

Rules of the road

The fundamental rule of the road in Ireland, both North and South, is to **drive on the left**. Wearing **seat belts** is compulsory for drivers and passengers, as is the wearing of helmets for motorcyclists and their pillion riders. The Republic's **speed limits** are 50–60km/h in built-up areas (though in some parts of inner-city Dublin it's 30km/h), 80km/h on rural roads (denoted by the letter "R" on maps and signposts), 100km/h on national roads (denoted by an "N", and a green colour scheme on signposts) and 120km/h on motorways ("M" roads, with a blue colour scheme on signposts). Maximum speeds in Northern Ireland are 20–40mph in built-up areas, 70mph on motorways and 60mph on most other main roads. Minor rural roads in the Republic are generally poor in quality, often potholed and sometimes rutted – a situation notably different from the North where the overwhelming majority of roads, of all categories, are well maintained. **Signposts** in the Republic generally provide place names in both Irish and English, though in the Gaeltacht (Irish-speaking areas) you'll generally only encounter signposts in Irish. Virtually all signposts in the Republic provide distance information in kilometres; in the North distances are given in miles.

Parking

Throughout Ireland many town centres require payment for on-street **parking**, either using ticket machines or a disc or card parking scheme (discs or cards can be purchased in adjacent shops). If you don't display a ticket or disc you may end up with a parking fine or, particularly in Dublin, Cork and Galway, your car being clamped or towed away. Some Dublin streets still have parking meters, but since the city suffers from high rates of **theft** and vandalism, it's always advisable to use a secure car park.

Car rental

Outlets of multinational **car-rental companies**, such as Avis and Hertz, can be found at airports, in the cities and in some tourist towns. Rental charges are high – expect to pay around €30/£25 per day plus insurance – though prices are often much cheaper in the Republic than in the North, with the best offers garnered if you book well in advance, especially via the internet. Sometimes smaller local firms can undercut the big names.

In most cases, you'll need to be 23 or over (though some companies may accept younger drivers with a price hike) and able to produce a full and valid driving licence, with no endorsements incurred during the previous two years. Considering the nature of Ireland's roads, it's always advisable to pay for extra collision damage waiver (CDW). The daily rate for this from the car-rental companies is usually at least €10/£7, or you can buy it more cheaply in advance from specialist insurance agencies (such as W icarhireinsurance.com), but it guarantees that you won't be liable for a hefty bill if you suffer an accident or any other damage. If you're planning to cross the border, ensure that your rental agreement provides full insurance; in some cases, you may need to pay extra.

Booking a car prior to your journey saves time when you arrive in Ireland and provides the chance to shop around on the web for the best deals. We've listed the main brokers and agencies below.

CAR-RENTAL AGENCIES

Argus W arguscarhire.com
Atlas W atlascarhire.com
Auto Europe W autoeurope.com
Avis W avis.com
Budget W budget.com
Dan Dooley W dan-dooley.ie
Europcar W europcar.com
Great Island W greatislandcarrentals.com
Hertz W hertz.com
Holiday Autos W holidayautos.co.uk

Nova W novacarhire.com
Thrifty W thrifty.com

By bike

Apart from some steep ascents, occasional poor road surfaces and an unpredictable climate, Ireland provides ideal territory for **cycling**, one of the most enjoyable ways to explore the country's often stunning scenery. The tourist board's website, W ireland.com, details waymarked **trails across the island** (see p.40), as well as specialist cycling-tour operators.

If you plan to **bring your own bike**, note that some airlines will transport bicycles for free as long as you keep within your weight allowance, but it's always worth checking with them well in advance.

Across the island, minor roads in rural areas are generally quiet, but major roads are well worth avoiding due to heavy traffic. Bikes are easy to **transport** over long distances by train, but less so by bus. In the Republic, the cost of taking a bike on a main-line train generally starts at €2.50 (free on Dublin–Belfast trains) and is most easily booked online, for €6. On DART and commuter services you can take bikes with you for free but only **at off-peak hours**. Folding bicycles incur no charge and can be carried on any service.

Bus companies will generally allow bikes to be carried, as long as there is room in the luggage compartment. In the Republic, prices vary according to the company but can come to over €10 for a long journey. In the **North** carrying a bike is free on Ulsterbus and Goldline services and on the trains, but is only permitted on the latter at off-peak hours.

Bike rental

Thanks to a rise in insurance premiums, far fewer places in the Republic now **rent out** bikes – though **Dublin** now has a city bike scheme (see p.94) – and there are still just a small number of outlets in the

---

THE WILD ATLANTIC WAY

The Atlantic crashes fiercely against headlands and inlets all the way down the west coast of Ireland. Alongside it run roller-coaster roads and winding, single-track boreens (rural roads), now packaged by marketing gurus as the Wild Atlantic Way (W ireland.com/en-gb/wild-atlantic-way), a long-distance driving route launched in 2014. Made up of loops and detours to islands, the Way runs from the Inishowen peninsula in north Donegal to Kinsale in west Cork, a distance of some 2500km, some of which is covered as a driving tour in itineraries (see p.25). Signposts with a distinctive zigzag wave logo direct you to key attractions and 159 "Discovery Points", where storyboards outline heritage, history and culture, opening up little-known locations.

North, meaning that it's always wise to book your wheels well ahead. Raleigh (Ⓦ raleigh.ie) is the largest distributor of bikes in Ireland and its website lists a number of its agents offering rental. It's best to contact one of these directly, and bear in mind that local dealers, including some hostels, may often be cheaper. Rental rates are generally around €20 per day, €120 per week, with an extra charge of €5 per day or €20 per week for hiring panniers, though a helmet is usually included free. A deposit of anything from €100 to €200 is also required. When collecting your bike, check that its brakes and tyres are in good condition, and make sure that it comes equipped with a pump and repair kit. If you're planning on cycling in upland areas it makes sense to rent a bike with at least sixteen gears and preferably 24.

By air

Easily the quickest way to reach outlying areas is to take a scheduled flight to one of the **regional airports** dotted around the country. Aer Lingus operates the largest network. Prices can be as little as €20 one-way, if booked online well in advance, and much time can be gained; for instance, the flight from Dublin to Donegal takes only an hour, compared with at least four hours on the bus.

DOMESTIC AIRLINES

Aer Lingus Ⓦ aerlingus.com
Ryanair Ⓦ ryanair.com

Accommodation

You'll find accommodation to suit most budgets across Ireland, from swish city hotels and luxurious converted castles to historic country houses and B&Bs. There are also plenty of hostels, varying hugely in quality and atmosphere, but all providing a bed and usually a kitchen; lots offer much more. Finally, there are well-run campsites and, for the hardy, the chance to pitch a tent in a farmer's field or on common land.

You'll need to book your accommodation well in advance over **St Patrick's Day**, **Easter**, summer **public holidays** (see p.46), and during all of **July** and **August**. Accommodation is at a premium in Dublin throughout the year, especially at weekends, and may be booked out in places such as the **Aran Islands**, **Belfast**, **Cork**, **Derry**, **Dingle**, **Galway city**, **Kilkenny** and **Killarney**, and during major festivals

elsewhere (see pp.37–38). Many establishments close over the Christmas period.

ACCOMMODATION CONTACTS

Adams & Butler Ⓦ adamsandbutler.com. A selection of mostly rural and historic houses and castles across Ireland for self-catering.

Authentic Northern Ireland Ⓦ authenticnorthernireland.com. Official Northern self-catering association with over a thousand holiday homes, cottages and apartments.

B&B Ireland Ⓦ bandbireland.com. The major B&B association in the Republic (plus a few members in the North), with over a thousand tourist-board-approved members and booking available on its website.

Family Homes of Ireland Ⓦ familyhomes.ie. B&B association, both South and North, now with some self-catering options.

Good Food Ireland Ⓦ goodfoodireland.ie. This network of high-quality food purveyors includes a large number of good hotels where the emphasis is on cuisine.

Hidden Ireland Ⓦ hiddenireland.com. Over thirty B&Bs in private homes, mainly in the Republic, most of which are selected for their historic nature or architectural merit, as well as a similar number of self-catering properties.

Ireland's Blue Book Ⓦ irelandsbluebook.com. Upmarket country-house hotels and B&Bs, as well as restaurants, both North and South.

Irish Farmhouse Holidays Ⓦ irishfarmholidays.com. More than 300 farmhouse B&Bs, some in exquisite rural locations.

Irish Hotels Federation Ⓦ irelandhotels.com. Covering numerous hotels and guesthouses across Ireland, with a comprehensive listing, direct booking and special offers available on the website.

Irish Self Catering Federation Ⓦ letsgoselfcatering.com. Tourist-board-approved site, a good starting point for finding your preferred holiday home.

Northern Ireland Hotels Federation Ⓦ nihf.co.uk. Smaller than its equivalent in the Republic, but still offering an extensive range of around a hundred hotels and guesthouses.

B&Bs and guesthouses

The overwhelming majority of **B&Bs** and **guesthouses** across Ireland are welcoming family homes and provide clean and cosy rooms, usually with en-suite facilities. Most B&Bs in the Republic, and virtually all in Northern Ireland, are registered with the official tourist board, but many other places open their doors during local festivals or high season. Registration is usually a guarantee of well-maintained standards and good service, though non-registered places are not necessarily of lower quality. Most B&Bs and guesthouses serve mammoth **breakfasts** (see p.36).

Hotels

In most areas **hotels** are usually the most expensive option, particularly in cities such as Dublin, Galway

ACCOMMODATION PRICES

Throughout this book, for hotels, guesthouses and B&Bs, we've noted how much you can expect to pay for a double room in high season. Unless otherwise indicated, breakfast is included, but do check this at the time of booking. For hostels, we've given a per-adult price for dorms in high season and, where appropriate, a per-room price for double or twin rooms. For campsites, we've noted the price for two adults and a tent in high season.

Some establishments provide **single rooms**, but, in most cases, single travellers will occupy a double room. In hotels, there may be no discount on the room price at all for single occupation. You're more likely to get a good deal at traditional B&Bs, where the single rate may be around 25 percent higher than the cost of a double per person.

and Belfast which provide high-end "boutique" accommodation as well as the big chains such as Sheraton and Radisson. Offering more character are Ireland's country houses, mansions and castles, offering sumptuous rooms in astonishingly scenic locations. Aimed at weekend breakers, these often also provide spa facilities and gourmet restaurants.

Away from the main tourist areas, it's still possible to find real bargains. Most hotels in the Republic offer reductions mid-week, but in the North, especially in Belfast or Derry, you're far more likely to get a good deal at the weekend. Budget chains Jury's Inn, Premier Inn and Travelodge also have a growing presence in the major cities and can offer very competitive deals if booked in advance.

Hostels

Well-run, good-quality **hostels** can be found across all of Ireland, often in lovely, off-the-beaten-track locations. Meals, bike rental and other facilities are also sometimes provided, as detailed within the *Guide*. Booking ahead is advisable, especially in Dublin and Galway at all times, and elsewhere during high season or local festivals.

Independent hostels

There are dozens of **independently run hostels** across Ireland, many belonging to the Holiday Hostels of Ireland association (IHH; **W** hostels-ireland.com) or the Independent Hostel Owners organization (IHO; **W** independenthostelsireland .com). All IHH hostels are approved by either Fáilte Ireland or the NITB (see p.46), meaning that their facilities meet certain standards. Some IHO hostels are also approved, but those that aren't usually provide equivalent facilities. Most hostels offer dorms of varying sizes, as well as smaller private and family rooms, and are open year-round.

The character of independent hostels varies enormously, from the serene and bucolic to the urban and noisy. Though most hostels are

efficiently run, there's generally a relaxed atmosphere, often with no curfews. In the most popular tourist areas, however, they can be crammed to the rafters at busy times. The vast majority provide free bedding, but some may charge a fee for a sheet sleeper, and many will charge for a towel. In high season expect to pay €20–30 for a dorm bed in Dublin, and around €15–25 elsewhere; in Northern Ireland you'll usually pay £10–20.

An Óige and HINI hostels

The Republic's Youth Hostel Association, **An Óige** (centralized booking on **T** 01 830 4555, or at **W** anoige.ie; annual membership €20, under-18s €10, family €40, one-adult family €20), has 21 hostels concentrated mainly in popular tourist spots. Most offer smaller dorms or private rooms, usually with very good facilities, especially in some of the urban hostels or the new-builds at Errigal in Donegal and Knockree in Wicklow. Rates are around €12–25 per night depending on season and room. **Hostelling International Northern Ireland** (HINI; **T** 028 9032 4733, **W** hini.org.uk; annual membership £15, under-25s £10, family £30, one-adult family £15) has just five hostels, most of which are recently built or refurbished. Prices are around £10–20 per night.

Membership of either organization or the umbrella **Hostelling International** (HI) is not needed to stay in an An Óige or HINI hostel, but it does give you ten percent off accommodation at most hostels, as well as providing numerous **discounts**, ranging from travel to entry to attractions. So, if you're planning to use the An Óige/HINI network a lot, it's worth joining your own country's HI-affiliated association in advance.

HOSTELLING INTERNATIONAL AFFILIATED ASSOCIATIONS

Youth Hostel Association England and Wales **W** yha.org.uk
Scottish Youth Hostel Association **W** syha.org.uk
Hostelling International USA **W** hiusa.org

Hostelling International Canada Ⓦ hihostels.ca
YHA Australia Ⓦ yha.com.au
YHA New Zealand Ⓦ yha.co.nz
Hostelling International South Africa Ⓦ hisouthafrica.com

Camping

The website of the **Irish Caravan and Camping Council** (Ⓦ camping-ireland.ie) gives details of around a hundred sites all over Ireland. The price of a night's stay at a campsite depends on the area's popularity, facilities and tent size. Usually it will cost around €20/£16 for two adults to pitch a tent in high season. Some hostels also allow camping on their land for around €5–10/£4–8 per person per night, with use of a kitchen and showers.

Camping rough is possible in many parts of Ireland, though the likelihood of rain coupled with the lack of proper facilities may prove a deterrent. Some of the terrain in Ireland's windy west, often boggy or rocky, may make pitching a tent difficult too. Off the beaten track, many farmers in the Republic will allow camping in one of their fields, usually for a few euros. It's permissible to camp in some state forests in the North, but not in the Republic.

Food and drink

Few visitors come to Ireland just for the food (though plenty come to drink). However, the quality and choice on offer have improved markedly in the last twenty years. A new generation of small-scale artisan producers has emerged, be they cheese-makers, organic farmers, fish-smokers or bakers, and the best Irish chefs seek out this local produce to re-create and adapt traditional dishes using global techniques. It's well worth looking out for Good Food Ireland signs (or checking out Ⓦ goodfoodireland.ie), a network of high-quality restaurants, cafés, hotels, producers and cookery schools, who are committed to using local, seasonal, artisan ingredients wherever possible.

Food

Irish meat is internationally renowned, especially Aberdeen Angus beef and lamb from the west coast, the latter appearing in **Irish stew**, a classic

---

TRADITIONAL DISHES

Bacon and cabbage Shoulder of pork boiled with cabbage.
Boxty Potato pancakes.
Carrageen Edible seaweed, used to make a blancmange-like dessert.
Champ Northern Irish version of colcannon, with spring onions.
Colcannon Mashed potato mixed with cabbage and often leeks.
Crubeen Boiled pig's trotters.
Drisheen Sausage of sheep and beef blood with oatmeal and pepper.
Fadge Northern fried potato bread.
Soda bread Bread baked with bicarbonate of soda, buttermilk and flour.

---

broth with potatoes, onions and carrots. Variants to look out for include Achill lamb, what the French call pré-salé: as the animals graze on seaside meadows, the meat is naturally salty and a little sweet; and air-dried Connemara lamb from Oughterard, a little like Italian Parma ham. Beef, pork and lamb of course crop up in excellent sausages, which may be accompanied for breakfast by **black pudding**, a sausage of pig's blood, and **white pudding**, made from pig's offal and cereals (butchers in Clonakilty specialize in these puddings).

Seafood

Fresh **fish** and **seafood** such as prawns, lobsters, crabs and mussels, particularly from the west coast, Dublin Bay and Carlingford Lough, Dundrum Bay and Strangford Lough in the North, are also generally excellent. Among Ireland's many seafood festivals, the most famous are at Clarinbridge and nearby Galway city celebrating Galway Bay's **oysters**. These large, silky European flat oysters are some of the best in the world, having matured for about three years in anticipation of a season that runs from September until April. Ireland is also home to dozens of excellent **smokehouses**, which smoke not only delicately flavoured, satiny salmon but also mussels, eels, bacon and chicken.

Cheese

Cheese-making in Ireland entirely died out during the eighteenth century, partly because of the plantations and the rise of the international butter trade. However, legend has it that Irish monks had exported the secrets of cheese-making to Europe in the sixth century, while many kinds of Irish cheese

---

TOP FIVE CHEESES

Ardrahan From Kanturk, Co. Cork, with powerful, complex flavours of milk and mustard.

Desmond Piquant, long-matured, Swiss-style cheese from Co. Cork; also Gabriel, a hard, aromatic and full-bodied Gruyère-like cheese from the same makers.

Durrus Semi-soft, washed-rind, raw milk cheese from west Cork.

Kilshanny Type of Gouda, sweet, hard and milky, made in Lahinch, Co. Clare; sometimes flavoured with garlic, cumin or nettles.

St Tola Fine range of goat's cheeses from Inagh, Co. Clare.

---

are recorded in early texts – notably the twelfth-century *Aislinge Meic Conglinne*, a brilliantly satirical tale about a king possessed by a demon of gluttony, and an underfed monk who tries to tempt the demon out with a vision of a foodie's paradise. Since the 1970s, cheese-making has blossomed once again, especially in Munster, often handmade by farmers.

Drink

Dark, creamy **stout** has long been Ireland's most popular drink. It's always granted two minutes' settling time halfway through pouring and you should let it settle again once it's fully poured. Brewed in Dublin, Guinness is the market leader, but Beamish and Murphy's from Cork are also worth trying, as are microbrewery-produced stouts and beers.

The other indigenous tipple is **whiskey** (from *uisce beatha*, "water of life"). Apart from an inexplicable change in spelling, the main differences with Scotch whisky is that the Irish versions generally don't have the smoky, peaty flavour found in many Scotches, as the malt is dried in smokeless kilns rather than over peat fires; they are often smoother too, being triple-distilled whereas Scotch only goes round twice. The main brands are Jameson's, Power's, Paddy's – all three of which are now distilled in Midleton, Co. Cork – and Bushmills, made in Co. Antrim and the preferred drop in the North.

Restaurants

The widest array of **restaurants** is concentrated in the big cities – where, alongside Dublin and Belfast, Cork has a particularly vibrant scene – and in gourmet hotspots such as Kilkenny, Kinsale, Kenmare and Dingle, but good places can be found all over the country, sometimes in quite unexpected locales, as detailed throughout the *Guide*. Off the beaten track, it's usually worth phoning ahead, as opening hours can be erratic and, in winter, some establishments in tourist areas close down entirely. There's no getting away from the fact that dining out in Ireland is expensive, particularly when you factor in the high price of wine, but many fine restaurants offer cheaper, simpler menus at lunch time, and plenty also lay on good-value **early-bird menus** in the evening – two or three courses for a set price, usually available until 7 or 7.30pm, though often not at weekends. Found in small towns across the country, though sometimes takeaway only, the most widespread ethnic restaurants are Chinese, Indian and Italian, followed by Thai; reflecting recent immigration patterns, you'll find Eastern European delis in many large towns and restaurants.

Pubs and cafés

Most **pubs** across the country will be able to rustle you up a simple sandwich or toastie and a cup of tea or coffee, and many offer a substantial **lunch**. This is often based around a carvery, serving slices of roast meat, potatoes and veg, as well as

---

SPECIALITY DRINKS

Black and Tan Stout and ale.

Black velvet Stout and champagne.

Hot port Winter warmer, made with port, hot water, lemon and cloves.

Hot whiskey As above, with whiskey instead of port.

Irish coffee Invented in Foynes, Co. Limerick, in the 1940s to warm up miserable transatlantic flying-boat passengers; whiskey, coffee, sugar and cream.

Poteen (poitín, "little pot") Subject of many a song, a powerful, usually illicitly distilled whiskey that varies enormously in quality – some being fit only to strip paint.

> ## THE FULL IRISH
> Big **breakfasts** are an Irish tradition and are generally available at old-style cafés, often all day long; however, visitors are most likely to come across them at their hotel or B&B, where they're invariably included in the price. The "full Irish" or "Ulster fry" typically consists of bacon, sausage, eggs and tomatoes, sometimes stretching to mushrooms, black pudding and white pudding, though many hotels and B&Bs now offer less heart-stopping alternatives such as smoked salmon and fruit salad.

sandwiches and salads – which regularly feature crab and other seafood in coastal areas – and hot staples such as Irish stew and soups. An increasing number of Irish pubs now also serve meals in the evening. Similar fare is also available in traditional daytime **cafés**, alongside cakes and scones, which are now augmented in some towns by deli-cafés, offering a more interesting array of food.

Markets

If you fancy trying your hand at preparing a few dishes yourself, head for one of the country's many food **markets** – virtually every sizeable town now hosts a farmers' market, often on a Saturday. The best markets – colourful, vibrant affairs that are worth a visit in their own right – are the permanent English Market in Cork city; the Temple Bar Food Market in Dublin, the Galway city market and the Midleton market in east Cork, all on Saturdays; and St George's Market in Belfast, on Fridays and Saturdays. For a full list of farmers' markets around the country, go to the Irish Food Board's website, ⓦ bordbia.ie/consumer/aboutfood/farmersmarkets, and, for the north, ⓦ discovernorthernireland.com/Ulster-Farmers-Markets-A1930.

The media

Both the Republic and the North have a wide range of daily and weekly newspapers, the latter often county-based in their coverage. The choices for Ireland-based TV are more limited both sides of the border, but there's an abundance of local radio stations, together with several national stations in the Republic.

Newspapers and magazines

The Republic's most popular middlebrow **newspapers** are the *Irish Times* and the more populist *Irish Independent*. Though generally liberal, if sometimes tinged by old-fashioned Ascendancy attitudes, the *Times* offers comprehensive news coverage of events both at home and abroad and often excellent features (ⓦ irishtimes.com). The *Independent* (ⓦ independent.ie) has a more right-of-centre outlook, while the *Irish Examiner* (formerly the *Cork Examiner*; ⓦ irishexaminer.com) has a Munster-based focus and generally less analytical coverage of news. British newspapers are commonly available in Dublin and other cities and some produce Irish editions.

Every county has at least one weekly newspaper, often conservative and usually crammed with local stories of little interest to outsiders. However, some, such as the *Kerryman*, the *Kilkenny People* and the *Donegal Democrat*, often provide good coverage of local events and very readable features. To delve deeper into the seamy world of Irish politics, turn to the monthly *Village* (ⓦ villagemagazine.ie) or the satirical fortnightly **magazine** *Phoenix* (ⓦ thephoenix.ie).

The **North**'s two morning dailies are the Nationalist *Irish News* (ⓦ irishnews.com) and the Unionist *News Letter* (ⓦ newsletter.co.uk), but the widest circulation belongs to the evening *Belfast Telegraph* (ⓦ belfast-telegraph.co.uk), whose Unionist stance has become progressively more liberal over the years. All UK national papers are also available in the North.

Television and radio

In the **Republic**, the three main **TV channels** are operated by the state-sponsored Radio Telefis Éireann (RTÉ; ⓦ rte.ie). As well as imported shows, the main news and current affairs channel, RTÉ 1 also features the popular home-grown Dublin-based soap, *Fair City*, and Friday's *Late Late Show*, a long-standing chat and entertainment institution. RTÉ 2 is a little more bubbly, with a smattering of locally produced programmes, though still swamped by imported tat and overburdened by sporting events. Some of the most innovative viewing is provided by the Irish-language channel TG4 (which provides English subtitles; ⓦ tg4.ie) including excellent traditional-music shows and often incisive features on the culture of Irish-speaking areas. In most of the Republic, the four major British terrestrial TV channels are available on cable or satellite.

RTÉ also operates four **radio stations**, three of which are English-language: the mainstream RTÉ Radio 1 (FM 88–89), whose morning shows are largely devoted to current affairs and chat; RTÉ 2FM (FM 90–92), which is more music- and youth-oriented; and Lyric FM (FM 96–99), which mixes popular classics with jazz and occasionally inspiring world-music shows. Raidió na Gaeltachta (FM 93) is the national Irish-language station, with broadcasts including much traditional music.

Northern Ireland receives television and radio programmes from the BBC (W bbc.co.uk) and has a limited, if often keenly followed, number of locally produced current-affairs productions. On BBC Radio Ulster (FM 92.4–95.4), *Talkback* (Mon–Fri noon–1.30pm) offers lively discussions on the North's political situation. The BBC's main commercial rival, Ulster Television (W u.tv), relies on the standard ITV diet of soaps and drama. In most parts of the North you can also watch or listen to RTÉ programmes.

Festivals and events

Ireland has a plethora of annual festivals, ranging from small local affairs to major international occasions and significant events in the sporting calendar. For more on the big events in Belfast, Cork, Derry, Dublin, Galway and Kilkenny, see the appropriate chapter sections or boxes.

FEBRUARY–APRIL

Tedfest W tedfest.org. A long weekend of wackiness in the Aran Islands at the end of February, celebrating the characters and storylines of the hugely popular sitcom *Father Ted*.

St Patrick's Day March 17; W stpatricksday.ie. Almost every Irish town and village commemorates the national patron saint's day, though the most significant celebration is the week-long festival held in Dublin.

Irish Grand National W fairyhouse.ie. The biggest event of the National Hunt horse-racing season takes place at Fairyhouse, Co. Meath, on Easter Monday.

MAY

North West 200 W northwest200.org. Major international motorcycle road-racing event held in Portstewart, Co. Derry, in the middle of the month.

Fleadh Nua W fleadhnua.com. One of the country's biggest traditional-music festivals, held in Ennis, Co. Clare, over a week in late May.

JUNE

Writers' Week W writersweek.ie. Ireland's biggest literary festival, five days of workshops and events in Listowel, Co. Kerry, over the bank-holiday weekend at the beginning of June.

The Cat Laughs W thecatlaughs.com. Four-day comedy festival featuring an array of renowned and lesser-known acts, staged in Kilkenny in early June.

Bloomsday W jamesjoyce.ie. A week of Dublin-based James Joyce-related events leading up to June 16, the day on which his masterwork *Ulysses* is set.

Irish Derby W curragh.ie. The major event in the Irish flat-racing season, held at the Curragh, Co. Kildare, in late June or early July.

JULY

Willie Clancy Summer School W scoilsamhraidhwillieclancy.com. Hugely popular, week-long traditional-music event with a host of pub sessions and several concerts, hosted in Miltown Malbay, Co. Clare, at the beginning of July.

Orange Order Parades July 12. Unionists and Loyalists commemorate the Battle of the Boyne and close down much of Northern Ireland in the process.

Galway International Arts Festival W giaf.ie. Massive festival of music, drama and general revelry over a fortnight from the middle of the month.

Mary from Dungloe W maryfromdungloe.com. Ten days of entertainment in Co. Donegal, often featuring Daniel O'Donnell and culminating in a beauty contest (where one of the prizes is sometimes a date with the man himself); runs from late July.

Yeats International Summer School W yeatssociety.com. Sligo-based late-July to August literary festival focusing on the life of the poet.

Galway Races W galwayraces.com. The west of Ireland's biggest horse-racing event, long celebrated in the song of the same name; held over a week at the end of the month.

AUGUST

Kilkenny Arts Festival W kilkennyarts.ie. All manner of musical and literary events, recitals and exhibitions staged in the city over ten days in mid-August.

Puck Fair W puckfair.ie. Three days of mayhem in Killorglin, Co. Kerry, culminating in the crowning of a goat as King Puck; takes place in the middle of the month.

Rose of Tralee International Festival W roseoftralee.ie. Tremendously popular event, focused on a beauty contest, but offering an enormous range of other entertainment; late August.

Fleadh Cheoil na hÉireann W comhaltas.ie. Competitive traditional-music festival, drawing hundreds of participants and big crowds – different towns bid for the mid- to late-August event each year.

Ould Lammas Fair More than 400 years old, Ballycastle's traditional market fair remains a huge draw, featuring livestock sales, and bucket-loads of music, dancing and entertainment on the last Monday and Tuesday of the month.

SEPTEMBER

Electric Picnic W electricpicnic.ie. Hugely popular rock and dance festival held at Stradbally Hall, Laois, over the first weekend.

All-Ireland Senior Hurling and Football Finals W gaa.ie. The zenith of the sporting year for Gaelic games, with the hurling on the first or second Sunday and the football on the third or fourth Sunday, in Dublin's Croke Park.

Lisdoonvarna Matchmaking Festival W matchmakerireland .com. A month-long date-athon which attracts hopeful suitors from all over the world, and there's plenty of traditional entertainment too.

Dublin Fringe Festival W fringefest.com. Lively programme of theatre, dance, performance arts and comedy, featuring hundreds of events spread over more than a fortnight.

Dublin Theatre Festival W dublintheatrefestival.com. Ireland's most prestigious drama festival, commencing late in the month and running for more than a fortnight.

Galway Oyster Festival W galwayoysterfest.com. Boisterous four-day festival to kick off the annual oyster season.

OCTOBER

Wexford Opera Festival W wexfordopera.com. Prestigious and massively popular international festival now lasting for a fortnight commencing in mid-October.

Belfast Festival at Queen's W belfastfestival.com. Major arts festival, running for two weeks from the middle of the month.

Cork Jazz Festival W guinnessjazzfestival.com. Four days of jazz in all its forms at the end of the month.

Banks of the Foyle Halloween Carnival W derrycity.gov.uk/ halloween. Street theatre, music and mayhem, especially during the fireworks display on October 31.

NOVEMBER

Cork Film Festival W corkfilmfest.org. Established in 1956 and still going strong with a broad-ranging programme of big-budget and international cinema staged early in the month or in late Oct.

DECEMBER

Wren Boys. On St Stephen's Day (December 26), it was traditional for men and children carrying the corpse of a wren to go around the neighbourhood knocking on doors, asking for money to bury the bird while singing songs and telling jokes – the money, of course, would be spent on a party. The tradition can still be found in a few places, such as Dublin's Sandymount and Dingle in Co. Kerry.

Culture and etiquette

Ireland likes to describe itself as the land of Cead Míle Fáilte ("a hundred thousand welcomes"), which you'll often see inscribed on pubs, and that's essentially true for most visitors. In terms of general etiquette, wherever you go, you'll encounter the standard Irish greeting – an enquiry about your health ("How are you?" sometimes just abbreviated to "About you?" in parts of the North) – and it's reasonable to return the compliment. Also, if someone buys you a pint in a pub, then an even-handed gesture is to pay for the next round.

Children

Children are very well received, though few places including cafés, hotels and many key attractions, are actually designed with them in mind. Baby supplies are readily available and most B&Bs and hotels welcome children, and an increasing number have cots. It's usually fine to take a child into a pub during the daytime, though definitely not so legally in the Republic after 9pm.

Women

Irish women's economic and social status has much improved over the last couple of decades, with the Republic even outranking Germany and the Netherlands in terms of gender equality. Whether this progress has extended beyond the major cities is debatable, though, as rural areas often preserve entrenched sexist attitudes.

In terms of the travel experience, **female visitors** are unlikely to encounter problems. For all their charm and prodigious drinking, Irish men tend to be remarkably polite around women, and the most you can expect is the odd cat call or drunken chat-up line. However, as with anywhere, if you're travelling alone or to an unfamiliar area, it's worth adopting a cautionary attitude, particularly when enjoying pubs and nightlife. In the rare case of experiencing a serious personal assault, contact either a rape crisis centre (see p.43) or the Tourist Assistance Service (see p.43), as local police forces are unlikely to be experienced in these situations.

Racism

The arrival of refugees and, latterly, large number of migrant workers over the last decade or so has undoubtedly shifted attitudes in the Republic towards those from other cultures and has had a significant effect upon the population's long-standing homogeneity. That being said, it's still possible that black visitors will encounter **racist attitudes** at some point in their travels, especially in rural areas, but these are generally not threatening and usually the result of ignorance rather than intended to cause deliberate offence.

The situation is less optimistic in Northern Ireland where, especially in Belfast, Loyalist gangs have attempted to "cleanse" the city's ethnic population, targeting mainly the Chinese and other Asian communities, and there have been several reported attacks on migrant workers across the region. Tourists, of whatever culture, are very rarely the victims of assaults.

Ireland also has its own recognized ethnic minority, the **Travellers** (widely known by a range of insulting epithets), against whom discrimination remains widespread, both North and South.

Gays and lesbians

Despite legal advances towards equality, attitudes to **gays and lesbians** remain largely discriminatory among the general population (especially Northern Irish Protestants), and the gay community in Ireland keeps a low profile, the only "scene" largely concentrated on the nightlife of Belfast and Dublin. Though private same-sex activity is legal across Ireland, away from the larger cities, public displays of affection may produce hostile verbal reactions, and many small-town and rural B&Bs will look askance at a pair of men wanting to share a bed for the night. Be aware that known cruising areas, such as Belfast's Cave Hill and Dublin's Phoenix Park, are often patrolled by the police.

Alcohol

The pub (see p.8) has long been at the centre of Irish society and the ready availability of alcohol has played a major part in the development of the national psyche and as a Muse to some of the country's greatest writers (O'Brien, Kavanagh, Behan) and actors (Richard Harris and Peter O'Toole).

Consumption is gradually falling but the Irish are still among Europe's heaviest drinkers, imbibing as a whole on average some twenty percent more than their continental European neighbours, and that's despite the government's heavy excise duties on drink. According to Alcohol Action Ireland, more than half of the population have harmful drinking patterns (40 percent of women and 70 percent of men) and binge-drinking, especially among the 18–25 age group, is a significant problem. Contrastingly, thanks to movements such as the Pioneer Total Abstinence Association, around a fifth of the Irish population are teetotal.

Sports

Hurling and Gaelic football are among the fastest and most physical sports in the world, and well worth catching on your travels, whether on TV or, preferably, live. Rugby and soccer are also widely followed, while going to the races is a great day out, with less of the snobbery sometimes found in Britain. Golf (see p.41) is also hugely popular north and south of the border.

Hurling and Gaelic football

Both Gaelic football and hurling (see also p.55), Ireland's two main indigenous sports, are played at a rollicking pace on huge pitches, 140m long and 80m wide, between teams of fifteen; goalposts are H-shaped, with three points awarded for a goal, when the ball goes under the crossbar into the net, and a point when it goes over the crossbar. Over two thousand clubs in villages and parishes all over Ireland vie for the privilege of reaching the club finals, held on St Patrick's Day at 80,000-seater Croke Park in Dublin, one of the largest stadiums in Europe (see p.87), while the more popular and prestigious intercounty seasons begin with provincial games in the early summer, reaching their climax in the All-Ireland County Finals in September, also at Croke Park. Details of all fixtures for hurling and Gaelic football can be obtained from the Gaelic Athletic Association (Ⓦ gaa.ie).

Hurling is played with a leather *slíothar*, similar in size to a hockey ball, and a hurley (or *camán*), a broad stick made of ash that is curved outwards at the end. The *slíothar* is belted prodigious distances, caught and carried on the flattened end of the player's hurley. It's a highly skilled game of constant movement and aggression that does not permit a defensive, reactive style of play. Cork, Kilkenny and Tipperary are the most successful counties, while Clare, Galway, Offaly and Wexford have emerged in the modern era. No county from the North has ever won an All-Ireland Final, though the sport is very popular in the Glens of Antrim and parts of the Ards Peninsula in Co. Down. **Camogie**, the women's version of hurling, is becoming increasingly popular, and is also well worth watching. Dublin has won the most camogie All-Irelands, though they haven't prevailed since 1984 and the most successful team in the modern era has been Cork.

Gaelic football has similarities with both rugby and association football, but its closest relation is

Australian Rules Football; indeed every autumn, Australia play Ireland in a hurly-burly series of "international rules" matches that are known for their frequent brawling. The round Gaelic ball, which is slightly smaller than a soccer ball, can be both kicked and caught. However, running with the ball is only permitted if a player keeps control by tapping it from foot to hand or by bouncing it, and throwing is not allowed – the ball must be "hand-passed", volleyball-style. Whereas hurling's strongholds are in the southern counties of the island, footballing prowess is more widely spread – Kerry is the most successful county, followed by Dublin, but there are plenty of strong teams in Northern Ireland at the moment, notably Donegal.

Rugby union and soccer

Rugby union and **soccer** are very popular in Ireland and tickets for international matches, especially for rugby, can be hard to come by. The Republic's home soccer matches (Ⓦ fai.ie) and Ireland's rugby matches (Ⓦ irishrugby.ie) are played at Dublin's recently rebuilt Aviva Stadium (formerly Lansdowne Road). Northern Ireland's soccer matches (Ⓦ irishfa .com) are played at Windsor Park, Belfast (see p.488). For the international rugby team, which is a joint Republic–Northern Ireland side, the main event of the year is the Six Nations Championship, a series of international games played in February and March against England, France, Wales, Scotland and Italy. You're more likely to get tickets, however, for matches featuring the four provinces, Munster (which includes Irish rugby's natural heartland, Limerick), Leinster, Connacht and Northern Ireland, in the European Rugby Champions or Challenge Cups or in the Pro 12 League.

Soccer is played semiprofessionally in both the North and the Republic, organized into the Danske Bank Premiership and the Airtricity Premier Division respectively. Both international teams field most of their players from the English leagues; Manchester United and Liverpool are the most popular clubs among Irish fans. Glasgow Celtic are also popular both north and south, Rangers in the North, with support following Catholic and Protestant divisions, respectively.

Racing

Going to the **races** is a hugely popular and enjoyable day out in Ireland. A good place to get a sense of the Irish passion for horses is the National Stud in Kildare (see p.130), while for details of all meetings, go to Horse Racing Ireland's website Ⓦ goracing.ie. The Irish Grand National is run at Fairyhouse in Co. Meath on Easter Monday (see p.107), followed in April by the five-day Irish National Hunt Festival at Punchestown in Co. Kildare (see box, p.131); at the Curragh, the classic flat-racecourse in Kildare (see box, p.131), the Irish 1000 Guineas and 2000 Guineas are held in May, the Irish Derby in late June or early July, the Irish Oaks in July and the Irish St Leger in September. Dublin's racecourse (see p.107) plus notable local meetings, such as those at Galway, Killarney, Listowel, Sligo and Downpatrick, are described in the *Guide*. One local oddity worth mentioning is the meeting at Laytown in Co. Meath, the last remaining beach racing under Jockey Club rules, held once a year when the tides are at their lowest (Ⓦ laytownstrandraces.ie).

Outdoor activities

Despite the weather, Ireland is a great place for getting out and about. Cycling is one of the best ways to appreciate the quiet pleasures of the Irish countryside, while walkers can take advantage of generally free access across much of the countryside and a number of waymarked trails. With over 120 sailing and yacht clubs, plenty of lakes, rivers and sheltered coastline to explore and some great beaches for surfers, there are many opportunities for watersports enthusiasts, too. The North is covered by Ⓦ outdoorni.com, a comprehensive guide to outdoor activities and adventure sports.

Cycling

Signposted **cycling trails** in the Republic include the Beara Way (see p.263) and the Sheep's Head Cycling Route (see p.261) in Cork, and the Kerry Way (p.276). On- and off-road routes are detailed on Ⓦ irishtrails.ie, but trails in the North are better documented and promoted: for detailed information on the many routes here, the best places to start are Ⓦ cycleni.com and Ⓦ sustrans.org.uk. They include the Kingfisher Trail (see p.571), which also stretches into Leitrim and Cavan. Other cross-border routes include the 326km North West Trail, mainly on quiet country roads through Donegal, Tyrone, Fermanagh, Leitrim and Sligo. Getting around the country by bike is a great option (see p.31).

Fishing

There are plenty of opportunities for sea **angling** and dozens of rivers and lakes for fly- and game-fishing. For information, the best places to start are Inland Fisheries Ireland's website, ⓦfishinginireland.info, and the tourist-board site, ⓦireland.com. Great Fishing Houses of Ireland (ⓦirelandflyfishing.com) covers a dozen or so specialist hotels and B&Bs.

Golf

Golf, which was probably first brought to Ireland by the Ulster Scots, attracts huge numbers of visitors every year; the Golfing Union of Ireland, based in Kildare (ⓦgui.ie), provides details of over four hundred clubs, north and south, with online booking.

Horse riding

Horse riding, whether over the hills or along the beaches, is also a popular pastime, for both novices and experienced riders, who also have the option of multi-day trails rides. Stables in popular locations are listed throughout the *Guide*, including Killarney and Clifden. The Association of Irish Riding Establishments (ⓦaire.ie) maintains standards among riding centres in the Republic and the North and publishes details on its website; for information on horse-riding holidays, go to ⓦehi.ie.

Walking and mountain climbing

There are dozens of waymarked long-distance **walking trails** in the Republic, ranging from routes through or around mountain ranges, such as the Wicklow Way (see p.121), the Táin Way (see p.154), the Slieve Bloom Way (see p.176) and the Western Way (p.369), to walks around entire peninsulas, like the Sheep's Head Way (p.261), the Beara Way (p.263), the Kerry Way (p.276) and the Dingle Way (p.303). The Ulster Way (see also p.279) in the North, the oldest and longest waymarked walking trail in Ireland, has recently been redeveloped as a 625-mile circuit of the whole province, taking in the Giant's Causeway, the Sperrins and the Mournes; it's now divided into link sections, which can be skipped by taking public transport, and quality sections. For information on these trails in the Republic, go to ⓦirishtrails.ie, which also has details of hundreds of looped day walks; in the *Guide*, we list the very useful websites on the Wicklow, Kerry and Dingle Ways, which include details of walker-friendly accommodation. In the

> ## A NOTE ON ACCESS
>
> Unlike the North, the Republic has no public "rights of way", but there is a tradition of relatively free access to privately owned countryside. In recent years, the growing numbers and occasional carelessness of walkers, as well as insurance worries, have led some farmers to bar access to their land, and, in response, the government has begun to pay farmers who maintain popular walks across their land under the National Walks Scheme. In general, the majority of landowners do not object to walkers crossing their property. For detailed advice on **access**, including a Good Practice Guide, have a look at ⓦmountaineering.ie or and ⓦleavenotraceireland.org.

North, ⓦwalkni.com has comprehensive information on all aspects of walking. Some councils and local tourist offices have produced helpful map guides for the main routes too, but you should always get hold of the relevant Ordnance Survey map and carry a compass.

Other **walking highlights** include the ascents of Croagh Patrick in Co. Mayo (see p.382) and of Carrauntoohil, for more experienced walkers, in Co. Kerry (see p.276), the easily accessible Bray–Greystones walks in Co. Wicklow (see p.118) and just about anywhere in Connemara (see p.369), notably the excellent Diamond Hill trail in the national park; not to mention walks in the Wicklow (see p.124) and Killarney (see p.275) national parks.

Mountaineering Ireland, an organization that covers hill-walking and rambling, as well as climbing, maintains a compendious website (ⓦmountaineering.ie). Particularly useful walking guidebooks are listed in Contexts, p.622. Some guided walking tour operators are detailed on p.28, while more complete lists are available on ⓦireland.com.

If you need help in a real emergency on the mountains, call ☎999 or ☎112 and ask for **mountain rescue** (ⓦmountainrescue.ie).

Watersports

Sailing

Ireland's many **sailing** clubs include the Royal Cork Yacht Club, established in Cobh in 1720, which is thought to be the oldest in the world. Dozens of regattas, such as Calves Week in Schull,

> ## BIRDWATCHING
>
> With a wide variety of migrating flocks, including a large number of rare species, visiting its shores, Ireland is a great place for **birdwatching**; Wexford Wildfowl Reserve (see p.194), where thousands of Greenland white-fronted geese and pale-bellied brent geese spend the winter, Cape Clear (see p.258), famous for spotting rare migratory birds in October, and the wetlands at Castle Espie (see p.536) are especially fruitful hunting grounds. The best general contacts are Ⓦirishbirding.com, Birdwatch Ireland in the Republic (Ⓦbirdwatchireland.ie) and, in the North, the Royal Society for the Protection of Birds (Ⓦrspb.org.uk).

and traditional boat festivals, such as the Wooden Boat Festival in Baltimore and Cruinniú na mBád in Kinvarra, are held every year. The most popular areas for sailing are the relatively sheltered waters of the east coast, especially in Dublin Bay; Cork Harbour and west Cork; Lough Swilly on the north coast of Donegal; Strangford Lough in Co. Down; and some of the larger lakes, such as Lough Derg in Co. Clare. Popular sailing clubs are listed in the *Guide*; for further information contact the Irish Sailing Association (Ⓦsailing.ie).

Canoeing and kayaking

Inland waterways and sheltered coasts – notably in west Cork (see p.254), Dingle (see p.291) and Waterford (see p.211) – offer **canoeing** and **kayaking** opportunities, ranging from day-trips and touring to rough- and white-water racing. We've detailed rental and guided trip providers in the Guide; the Irish Canoe Union's website covers courses and clubs in the South (Ⓦcanoe.ie), while the North has a more comprehensive website, Ⓦcanoeni.com, that includes canoe trails for multi-day touring. Another useful website is Ⓦirishseakayakingassociation.org.

Surfing, wind-surfing and kite-surfing

There are some superb beaches for **surfing** (Ⓦisasurf.ie) and its spin-offs, **wind-surfing** (Ⓦwind-surfing.ie) and **kite-surfing** (Ⓦiksa.ie). For kite- and wind-surfing, some of the best spots are: Rosslare, Co. Wexford; Tramore, Co. Waterford; Castlegregory, Kerry; Rusheen Bay, Co. Galway; Keel Strand, Achill and Elly Bay, Belmullet, in Mayo; Lough Allen, Leitrim; and Rossnowlagh, Co. Donegal. Surfers head for: Garrettstown and Inchydoney, Co. Cork; Inch and Brandon Bay, Kerry; Lahinch, Clare; Easkey, Mullaghmore and Strandhill, Co. Sligo; Bundoran and Rossnowlagh, Co. Donegal; Portrush, Antrim; and Tramore, Co. Waterford.

Scuba diving

Right in the path of the warm North Atlantic Drift current, Ireland offers some of the best **scuba diving** in Europe, notably off the rocky west coast. We've listed dive centres throughout the *Guide*, and you can get further information from the Irish Underwater Council (Ⓦdiving.ie) and Ⓦukdiving.co.uk.

Travel essentials

Costs

Though it's still possible to get a main **meal** in cafés and pubs for around €10, a three-course restaurant dinner will usually cost at least €30, with a bottle of wine setting you back around €20, though some offer "early bird" menus and midweek set menus at reduced rates. The price of a pint in a pub is around €4–5, significantly higher in some city-centre clubs.

The cheapest **accommodation** is a hostel dorm bed, which will cost around €12–20, rising to as much as €30 at peak periods in Dublin. Alternatively, it's also possible to get a decent bed and breakfast from around €35 per person sharing or €45 in Dublin. So, even if you count the cents, you're likely to spend a daily minimum of around €35, and more than double this if you're eating out and staying in a B&B.

The main change in the **North** over the last two decades has been the fall in the value of the pound against the euro. This has meant that while quoted prices are roughly the same as their euro equivalents in the Republic, they are comparatively cheaper.

Crime and personal safety

Crime in Ireland is largely an urban affair and generally at a low level compared with other European countries. However, thieves do target popular tourist spots, so don't leave anything of value visible in your car and take care of your bags while visiting bars and restaurants. It's sensible to seek advice from your accommodation provider about safety in the local area and take as much care as you would anywhere else.

Crimes against the person are relatively rare, except in certain inner-city areas, and seldom involve tourists. The **Republic**'s police force is An Garda Síochána (☎112 or ☎999 for emergencies, ⓦgarda.ie), more commonly referred to as the guards or **Gardaí**, whom you'll find generally helpful when it comes to reporting a crime. The Irish Tourist Assistance Service (☎1890 365700, ⓦitas.ie) offers support to tourist crime victims. Rape crisis support is available from the Dublin Rape Crisis Centre (☎1800 778888, ⓦdrcc.ie), which can also direct you to similar agencies across Ireland.

Away from the sectarian hotspots, crime in **Northern Ireland** is very low. In the unlikely event that your person or property is targeted, contact the Police Service of Northern Ireland (☎999 for emergencies, ⓦpsni.police.uk). The presence of the British army has diminished almost to invisibility, though it is just possible you might encounter police or army security checks on the rare occasion of a major incident.

Discount cards

For all attractions in the *Guide*, we've given the adult entry price. The majority of sites offer reduced rates for children (under-5s usually get in free), students (for which you'll need ID such as an International Student Identity Card, ⓦisic.org) and senior citizens.

An annual **Heritage Card** (€21, senior citizens €16, children/students €8, family €55; ⓦheritageireland .ie) is worth considering if you're planning to visit many historic sites and monuments in the Republic. It provides unlimited entry to attractions run by the Office of Public Works (sites are detailed throughout the *Guide*) and is mostly easily purchased at the first OPW site that you visit.

Members of **An Óige/YHA/HINI** (see p.33) also receive discounts on entry to certain sites. A number of historic buildings and sites in the North are operated by the **National Trust**. Membership (£58; under-26s £27, family £98, one-adult family £60.50; ⓦnationaltrust.org.uk) provides free and unlimited entry to these and all National Trust–run sites in Britain too. More than eighty sites across Ireland are members of the independent **Heritage Island** organization (ⓦheritageisland.com) whose booklet (€6.99) provides discounted admission prices or other special offers.

Electricity

The standard **electricity** supply is 220V AC in the Republic and 240V AC in the North. Most sockets require three-pin plugs. To operate North American appliances you'll need to bring or buy a transformer

CLIMATE

AVERAGE MAXIMUM AND MINIMUM DAILY TEMPERATURES (°C/°F) AND MONTHLY RAINFALL (MM)

	Feb	Apr	Jun	Aug	Oct	Dec
BELFAST						
Max/min (°C)	7/5	10/6	15/11	17/12	11/8	7/5
Max/min (°F)	45/41	50/43	59/52	63/54	52/46	45/41
Rainfall (mm)	77	66	72	101	106	106
CORK						
Max/min (°C)	9/3	13/5	19/10	20/12	14/7	9/3
Max/min (°F)	48/37	55/41	66/50	68/54	57/45	48/37
Rainfall (mm)	79	57	57	71	99	122
DUBLIN						
Max/min (°C)	8/2	13/4	18/9	19/11	14/6	8/3
Max/min (°F)	46/36	55/39	64/48	66/52	57/43	46/37
Rainfall (mm)	55	45	57	74	70	74
LIMERICK						
Max/min (°C)	8/3	13/6	18/11	20/13	14/7	8/4
Max/min (°F)	46/37	55/43	64/52	68/55	57/45	46/40
Rainfall (mm)	72	58	64	84	96	106

and an adapter; only the latter is needed for equipment made in Australia or New Zealand.

Entry requirements

UK nationals do not need a passport to enter the Republic, but it's a good idea to carry one – and note that airlines generally require official **photo ID** on flights between Britain and Ireland. Under EU regulations, British passport holders are entitled to stay in the Republic for as long as they like.

Travellers from the US, Canada, Australia, New Zealand and South Africa can enter the **Republic** for up to three months with just a passport. For further information on immigration and visas, contact the Irish Naturalization and Immigration Service, 13–14 Burgh Quay, Dublin (☎ 1890 551500, ⊛ inis.gov.ie). A full list of Irish consulates and embassies is available on the Department of Foreign Affairs website, ⊛ dfa.ie.

US, Canadian, Australian, South African and New Zealand citizens can enter **Northern Ireland** for up to six months with just a passport. Full details of British diplomatic representatives overseas are available on the Foreign Office's website, ⊛ fco.gov .uk. For further information on immigration and visas, go to ⊛ gov.uk/government/organisations/ uk-visas-and-immigration.

The **border** between Northern Ireland and the Republic has no passport or immigration controls.

IRISH EMBASSIES ABROAD

Australia 20 Arkana St, Yarralumla, Canberra, ACT 2600 ☎ 02 6214 0000, ⊛ embassyofireland.au.com.
Canada 130 Albert St, Suite 1105, Ottawa, ON K1P 5G4 ☎ 613 233 6281, ⊛ embassyofireland.ca.
New Zealand Handled by the embassy in Australia.
South Africa 2nd Floor, Parkdev Building, Brooklyn Bridge Office Park, 570 Fehrsen St, Brooklyn 0181, Pretoria ☎ 012 452 1000.
UK 17 Grosvenor Place, London SW1X 7HR ☎ 020 7235 2171.
US 2234 Massachusetts Ave NW, Washington, DC 20008 ☎ 202 462 3939.

BRITISH EMBASSIES AND HIGH COMMISSIONS ABROAD

Australia Commonwealth Ave, Yarralumla, ACT 2600 ☎ 02 6270 6666.
Canada 80 Elgin St, Ottawa, ON K1P 5K7 ☎ 613 237 1530.
New Zealand 44 Hill St, Wellington 6011 ☎ 04 924 2888.
South Africa 255 Hill Street, Arcadia 0028, Pretoria ☎ 012 421 7500.
US 3100 Massachusetts Ave NW, Washington, DC 20008 ☎ 202 588 6500.

Emergencies

Across Ireland, in the case of an **emergency** call either ☎ 999 or ☎ 112.

Health and insurance

Visitors from the UK are entitled to **medical treatment** in the Republic under a reciprocal agreement between the two countries. This will give access only to state-provided medical treatment in the Republic, which covers emergency hospital treatment but not all GPs' surgeries – check that the doctor you're planning to use is registered with the local Health Board Panel. Citizens of some other countries also enjoy reciprocal agreements – in Australia, for example, Medicare has such an arrangement with Ireland and Britain.

None of these arrangements covers all the medical costs you may incur or repatriation, so it's advisable for all travellers to take out some form of **travel insurance**. Most travel insurance policies exclude so-called dangerous sports unless an extra premium is paid; in Ireland this could mean, for example, horse riding, scuba diving, wind-surfing, mountaineering and kayaking.

Internet

With the arrival of 3G and free wi-fi, there's less and less need for **internet cafés**; if you do find one,

---

ROUGH GUIDES TRAVEL INSURANCE

Rough Guides has teamed up with WorldNomads.com to offer great travel insurance deals. Policies are available to residents of over 150 countries, with cover for a wide range of adventure sports, 24hr emergency assistance, high levels of medical and evacuation cover and a stream of travel safety information. Roughguides.com users can take advantage of their policies online 24/7, from anywhere in the world – even if you're already travelling. And since plans often change when you're on the road, you can extend your policy and even claim online. Roughguides.com users who buy travel insurance with WorldNomads.com can also leave a positive footprint and donate to a community development project. For more information, go to ⊛ roughguides.com/travel-insurance.

you'll typically pay around €4/£4 per hour. Nearly all hotels, hostels and B&Bs in Ireland, as well as many restaurants, pubs and cafés, now offer free wi-fi. Otherwise, some B&Bs, hotels and hostels will let you access the internet on their computer.

Mail

In the **Republic**, post is handled by An Post (the national postal service; ⓦ anpost.ie); allow two days (or more) for a letter to reach Britain, for example. Small letters and postcards to any destination overseas cost €1. Main post offices are usually open Monday to Friday 9am to 5.30pm, Saturday 9am to 1pm (in cities sometimes until 5.30pm on Saturday). From **the North** with the Royal Mail (ⓦ royalmail .com), postcards and the smallest letters cost 97p to airmail abroad. Main post offices are generally open Monday to Friday 9am–5.30pm, Saturday 9am to 12.30pm.

Maps

The **maps** in this guide will provide you with sufficient detail to navigate your way around cities, towns and counties. For more detail, there's the Ordnance Survey of Ireland's (ⓦ osi.ie) four *Holiday* maps at 1:250,000 scale (€7.33), dividing the country into quadrants, and its *Official Road Atlas of Ireland* (1:210,000; €9.99), produced in conjunction with the Ordnance Survey of Northern Ireland, is extremely useful if you're driving.

The majority of tourist offices will provide free local maps, but, if you're planning on walking or exploring a locality fully, then the OSI's *Discovery* 1:50,000 scale series of maps (€7.57 each) is the best bet for the Republic. The Ordnance Survey of Northern Ireland (ⓦ osni.gov.uk) produces a similar *Discoverer* series (£6.50).

If you're walking or cycling, the OSI/OSNI also produce special-interest 1:25,000-scale maps covering areas such as the Aran Islands, Killarney National Park, Lough Erne, Macgillycuddy's Reeks, and the Mourne and Sperrin mountain ranges. All of these maps can be purchased via the internet.

Money and cards

The **currency** of the Republic is the euro (€), divided into 100 cents (c). Northern Ireland's currency is the pound sterling (£), though notes are printed by various local banks and are different from those found in Britain; however, standard British banknotes can still be used in Northern Ireland.

Exchange rates fluctuate, but, at the time of writing, £1 sterling was equivalent to around €1.27 and US$1.59, €1 was worth £0.78 and US$1.24. The best exchange rates are provided by banks, though it's easiest to use an ATM, for which your own bank or credit card company may charge a fixed-rate or percentile fee. Unless you're absolutely stuck, avoid changing money in hotels, where the rates are often very poor. In areas around the border between the Republic and the North many businesses accept both currencies.

Credit and debit cards

The handiest means of obtaining cash is to use a **debit or credit card**. ATMs are very common throughout Ireland except in remote rural areas (where you're likeliest to find one in a supermarket), with most accepting Visa/Plus, MasterCard and Cirrus/Maestro. Major credit cards, such as Visa/Plus and MasterCard, and all cards bearing the Eurocard symbol, are widely accepted, though in rural areas you'll find that they're not accepted by some B&Bs.

Opening hours and public holidays

Shops and businesses across Ireland usually open 9am to 5.30pm, Monday to Saturday, though newsagents and petrol stations (many of which also have grocery stores) are often open earlier and later. Most large towns generally have a day when all shops open late (until 8pm or 9pm), usually Thursdays, and some also open on Sundays from around noon (1pm in Northern Ireland) until 6pm. Lunch-time closing still applies in some smaller towns, where also some businesses (except pubs) close for a half-day midweek. In rural areas opening times are far more variable.

Banks in the Republic are generally open from Monday to Friday between 10am and 4pm, and until 5pm one day a week, usually Wednesday or Thursday, sometimes closing for lunch in remoter areas. In the North, they open Monday to Friday 9.30am to 4.30pm, with some opening for longer hours and on Saturdays, though others may close for lunch. Post offices are also closed on Sunday (see above).

Throughout Ireland **cafés** tend to open in the daytime, Monday to Saturday. **Restaurants** usually open for lunch and again for dinner every day, though, away from the major towns and popular tourist areas, many may be closed at lunch times or all day on certain days of the week (especially out of season).

PUBLIC HOLIDAYS

Holiday	Republic	N Ireland
New Year's Day	√	√
St Patrick's Day – March 17	√	√
Good Friday	√	√
Easter Monday	√	√
May – first Mon	√	√
May – last Mon	×	√
June – first Mon	√	×
Orange Day – July 12	×	√
Aug – first Mon	√	×
Aug – last Mon	×	√
Oct – last Mon	√	×
Christmas Day	√	√
St Stephen's Day /Boxing Day – Dec 26	√	√

The law in the Republic states that **pubs are allowed to open** Monday to Thursday 10.30am–11.30pm, Friday and Saturday 10.30am–12.30am, Sunday 12.30–11pm. In the North the hours are Monday to Saturday 11.30am–11pm and Sunday 12.30–10pm. Some pubs apply for late licences, usually at weekends, while across Ireland **clubs** have variable opening days, though the majority are open from Thursday to Sunday and hours tend to be from around 10pm to 2am (or later in the major cities). Note that in the Republic all pubs and clubs are closed on Good Friday and Christmas Day.

On **public holidays**, away from the cities, most businesses will be closed, apart from pubs, newsagents, some supermarkets, grocers and petrol stations. If St Patrick's Day, Orange Day, Christmas Day or St Stephen's Day falls at the weekend, then a substitute holiday is taken at the beginning of the following week.

Phones

The international **dialling code** for the Republic is +353, and for Northern Ireland, as part of the UK, it's +44. If you're calling the North from the Republic, however, knock off the 028 area code and instead dial 048 followed by the eight-digit subscriber number.

Mobile phones

Both the UK and Ireland use the GSM system for **mobile phones**, so British travellers only need worry about the high roaming charges for making calls, texting, receiving calls and data usage in the Republic. Travellers from other parts of the world will need to check whether their phone is multi-band GSM, and will probably also want to find out from their provider what the roaming charges are. The cheapest way to get round roaming charges is to get hold of a UK or Irish pay-as-you-go SIM card to insert in your phone, which will give you a local number and eliminate charges for receiving calls. Vodafone in the Republic (Ⓦvodafone.ie), for example, are currently offering a €30 thirty-day package (plus €10 for a SIM card), which includes 100 minutes of international calls and 500mb of data, as well as free calls and texts to other Vodafone numbers.

Smoking

Smoking is illegal in all public buildings and places of employment across Ireland. Some hotels, but increasingly few B&Bs, have bedrooms available for smokers. Many pubs in cities and large towns have outdoor areas allocated for smokers, some covered and heated.

Time

Ireland is on **GMT**, eight hours ahead of US Pacific Standard Time and five hours ahead of Eastern Standard Time. Clocks are advanced one hour at the end of March and back again at the end of October.

Tipping

Though discretionary, **tipping** restaurant staff or taxi drivers is the expected reward for satisfactory service; ten to fifteen percent of your tab will suffice.

Toilets

Public toilets are usually only found in the big towns in the Republic (especially in shopping malls), though in the North are much more common and generally well maintained. Toilet doors often bear the indicator *Fir* (men) and *Mná* (women).

Tourist information

The Irish tourist development agency, **Fáilte Ireland** (Ⓦdiscoverireland.ie), as well as the the **Northern Ireland Tourist Board** (NITB; Ⓦdiscover northernireland.com) both provide a wealth of area-specific information on their websites. Abroad, the two boards combine as **Tourism Ireland**, with their main point of contact for the public at Ⓦ ireland.com. There are also plenty of local and regional tourism websites, and we have listed the best of these in the relevant sections of the Guide.

Both Fáilte Ireland and the NITB provide an extensive network of **tourist offices**, covering every city, many major towns and almost all the popular tourist areas. Additionally, some local councils provide their own offices. Tourist offices offer plenty of information on local attractions and can book accommodation. Bear in mind, though, that the opening hours of tourist offices are especially volatile, depending on budgets and staffing levels and varying from year to year and often from month to month.

Travellers with disabilities

Disabled travellers should glean as much information as possible before travelling since facilities in Ireland are generally poor – the best place to start looking is on the joint tourist board website, Ⓦ ireland.com/en-us/about-ireland/once-you-are-here/accessibility. For example, older buildings, including most B&Bs, may lack lifts and their entrances may not have been converted to allow easy wheelchair access.

All new buildings and many hotels, however, now have wheelchair access. Go to Ⓦ accessibleireland .com for island-wide listings of hotels with disabled facilities, as well as visitor attractions.

The main **transport** companies (see pp.29–30) have considerably improved their facilities for disabled travellers, with, for example, low-floor buses in many cities and kneeling coaches on some long-distance routes. Disabled drivers travelling with their cars from Britain can usually obtain reduced rates for ferry travel, depending on the time of year. Motability Ireland near Dublin (❶01 835 9173, Ⓦ motabilityireland.com) offer vehicle rental all over Ireland.

Dublin

TRINITY COLLEGE

1

Dublin

Set beside the shores of curving Dublin Bay, Ireland's capital city, Dublin, is a vibrant, dynamic place, which despite its size remains utterly beguiling and an essential part of any visit to the country. Much of Dublin's centre has been redeveloped over the last few decades, so alongside the city's historic buildings – its cathedrals and churches, Georgian squares and town houses, castles, monuments and pubs – you'll discover grand new hotels and shopping centres, stunning new street architecture and a state-of-the-art tramway system.

More than a quarter of the Republic of Ireland's population of four and a half million lives within the Greater Dublin area. Most Dubliners are intensely proud of their city, its heritage and powerful literary culture, and can at times exhibit a certain snobbishness towards those living in Ireland's rural backwaters (often termed "culchies"). Locals are noted for their often caustic, but engaging, brand of humour, as shown in the numerous and sometimes bawdy nicknames given to many of the city's landmarks (the Dublin Spire, for instance, has all manner of sobriquets including "the eyeful tower" and "the stiffy by the Liffey"), but there is also a warmth in their welcome – it's easy to find yourself drawn into conversation or debates in bars and cafés (or, if you smoke, outside them). Dubliners are also increasingly style-conscious; where once the city looked inward for inspiration, today it glances both east and west, to Europe and America, catching new trends and bringing a decidedly Irish slant to bear upon them.

Most of Dublin's attractions are contained within a relatively compact area, spreading either side of the many-bridged **River Liffey**, which divides the city between its **northside** and **southside**. These have very distinct characters, defined over the city's historical development: stereotypically, the south is viewed in terms of its gentility while the north is seen as brash and working class, home of the true Dub accent. Certainly, the southside is regarded as more fashionable and fashion-conscious, thanks to its **Grafton Street** shopping area and the rejuvenated **Temple Bar** arts quarter, yet the north possesses Ireland's two most renowned theatres and its own increasingly lively nightlife. On either side of the river it's easy to escape the city's bustle, to relax or picnic in its numerous green spaces; or visitors can head to the shoreline for seaside strolls and blustery cliff-top walks.

West of the centre is the green expanse of **Phoenix Park**, while across the river to the south lies the grim memorial of **Kilmainham Gaol** and, to the east, is the more obviously appealing **Guinness Brewery and Storehouse**. In the city's **suburbs**, the attractions of the northside have a definite edge over those to the south of the river: most compelling are the national **cemetery at Glasnevin**; the splendid stadium home of the Gaelic Athletic Association, **Croke Park**, which contains a fine museum; and the architectural wonders of the **Casino at Marino**. For a scenic breather from the city, take the southerly branch of the DART to panoramic **Dalkey and Killiney Hills**.

NATIONAL GALLERY

Highlights

❶ Trinity College Admire the illuminated *Book of Kells* and the magnificent Long Room, or just enjoy the architecture. **See p.58**

❷ The National Museum – Archaeology Prehistoric gold and Christian treasures are the highlights of this collection. **See p.63**

❸ The National Gallery A graceful showcase, especially for Irish art and the vibrant Yeats collection. **See p.64**

❹ The Chester Beatty Library An elegant, world-renowned display of manuscripts, prints and objets d'art. **See p.71**

❺ Dublin Spire The 121m pin-like monument is also called the Monument of Light for the

way it catches the sun. **See p.77**

❻ Bloomsday Follow Joyce's *Ulysses* journey on this annual pilgrimage through Dublin. See p.80

❼ Kilmainham Gaol Tour the city's most historic prison and visit the museum for fascinating insights into Republican history. **See p.85**

❽ Croke Park Catch an inter-county hurling or football match at the stadium home of Gaelic games, which also houses one of Ireland's best museums. **See p.87**

❾ The Cobblestone A magnet for traditional-music fans and an atmospheric pub to boot. See p.105

HIGHLIGHTS ARE MARKED ON THE MAP ON PP. 56–57

A DECADE OF CENTENARIES

The decade between 1912 and 1922 was one of the most eventful in Irish history. The passing of Home Rule, to the beginning of World War One, the growth of militant Ulster Unionism, the Easter Rising of 1916, the War of Independence and Civil War, as well as the rise of the labour and suffrage movements, were among the many momentous events which radically reshaped the political and social fabric of Ireland and its relationship with Britain during that period.

The programme A Decade of Centenaries (Ⓦ decadeofcentenaries.com) began in 2012 to mark the 100th anniversary of these events at a local and national level, with exhibitions, public discussions, and other commemorative initiatives. The programme focuses on the everyday experience of ordinary people, as well as the leaders and key actors.

The biggest event will be "Ireland 2016" (Ⓦ ireland.ie), a year-long programme to remember those who fought and died in the 1916 Rising, and reflecting on the legacy of that period. A number of formal state events will be held over Easter weekend, including a military ceremony, a reception for relatives, and a parade. Historical and cultural events are planned for throughout the year. Construction of a new interpretive centre at the General Post Office (GPO), which will tell the story of the 1916 Rising, began in late 2014, and should be ready for the centenary commemorations. A sculptured garden in the courtyard, which has been closed to the public since the GPO was rebuilt after 1916, will feature a memorial to the 38 children killed during the Rising. A new culture and heritage centre is also due to be completed by 2016 at the Bank of Ireland building on College Green.

Brief history

Dublin's origins date back to ninth-century **Viking** times when the Norsemen saw the strategic potential of Dublin Bay and established a trading post on the Liffey's southern bank. They adopted the location's Irish name, Dubh Linn ("dark pool"), for their new home, soon amalgamating with an Irish settlement on the northern bank called Baile Atha Cliath ("place of the hurdle ford"), which remains the Irish name for the city.

The twelfth century saw Dublin conquered by the **Anglo-Normans** when Dermot MacMurrough, the deposed King of Leinster, sought help from Henry II to regain his crown. In return for Dermot's fealty, Henry sent Strongbow (see p.583) and a contingent of Welsh knights to restore MacMurrough's power. Strongbow conquered Dublin in the process and, concerned at this threat to his authority, Henry came over to Ireland to assert control, establishing Dublin as the focus for British sway over Ireland. This became the centre of the "English Pale" (from the Latin *palum*, meaning originally a "stake", though later a "defined territory"), ruling over the areas of Anglo-Norman settlement in Ireland; since Irish resistance to conquest was so strong in other parts of the country, the pejorative phrase "beyond the pale" evolved as a means of signifying (at least in English terms) a lack of civilized behaviour.

Only a few buildings have survived from before the seventeenth century, mainly in the area encompassing Dublin Castle and the two cathedrals, and much of the city's layout is **Georgian**. During this period, Dublin's Anglo-Irish nobility and its increasingly wealthy mercantile class used their money (often, in the aristocracy's case, derived from confiscated land granted as a reward for services to the Crown) to showcase their wealth in the form of grandiose houses, public buildings and wide thoroughfares. Wealthy members of the elite revelled in their new-found opulence, filling their houses with works by the latest artists and craftsmen, and seeking to enhance their own cachet by patronizing the arts; Handel conducted the first performance of his *Messiah* in the city, for example. Increasing political freedom resulted in demands for self-government, inspired by the American and French revolutions. The legislative independence achieved during "Grattan's Parliament" in 1782 was to be short-lived, however, and the failure of the **1798 Rebellion** (see p.586),

1

FESTIVALS AND EVENTS

JANUARY

Temple Bar Trad Festival ☎ 01 677 2397, ⊛ templebartrad.com. Five days and nights of traditional-music pub sessions, concerts, instrument workshops and more in the heart of the city.

FEBRUARY

Jameson Dublin International Film Festival ☎ 01 687 7974, ⊛ jdiff.com. Held at cinemas and other venues across the city centre for eleven days in mid-February. While screening the latest in new Irish cinema, the festival also has a decidedly international flavour and its hundred or so films include special themes and retrospectives.

MARCH

Easter Rising Commemorations take place on Easter Sunday, featuring speeches and a march from the General Post Office to Glasnevin Cemetery.

St Patrick's Festival ☎ 01 676 3205, ⊛ stpatricksfestival.ie. Running for five days on and around St Patrick's Day (March 17), this city-wide festival includes a parade, light shows, concerts, funfair, films, exhibitions and a *céilí mór*, in which thousands of locals and visitors fill the streets in a traditional danceathon.

Poetry Now Festival ☎ 01 231 2929, ⊛ poetrynow.ie. A major four-day event, held over the last weekend in March at The Pavilion Theatre, Dún Laoghaire, the festival features readings by well-known Irish and international poets, master classes, exhibitions and children's events.

MAY

International Dublin Gay Theatre Festival ☎ 01 677 8511, ⊛ gaytheatre.ie. A fortnight of LGBT-focused drama, comedy, cabaret and musical theatre with international and Irish casts taking place at a variety of city-centre locations.

Dublin Writers Festival ☎ 01 222 7848, ⊛ dublinwritersfestival.com. Major Irish and international writers and poets take part in six days of readings, discussions and other events around the city centre.

JUNE

Docklands Maritime Festival ☎ 01 818 3300, ⊛ www.dublindocklands.ie. Tall ships open their decks to visitors over the first weekend in June at North Wall Quay, plus there's a market, street theatre, trips along the Liffey and a variety of events for children.

Bloomsday ☎ 01 878 8547, ⊛ jamesjoyce.ie. The James Joyce Centre organizes a week of events in mid-June, culminating in Bloomsday itself (June 16), the day on which Joyce's *Ulysses* is set.

Dublin Pride ⊛ dublinpride.ie. A week of celebration by the city's gay, lesbian, bi-and transsexual communities, featuring all manner of events, culminating in a vibrant and entertaining street parade.

---

led largely by members of the Protestant Anglo-Irish Ascendancy, inevitably led to the 1801 **Act of Union** and the removal of Dublin's independent powers.

With Ireland now governed by a British vice-regent, Dublin sank into a period of **economic decline**, brought about by its inability to compete with Britain's flourishing industries. The city remained the focus of agitation for self-rule, and by the end of the nineteenth century had also become the centre for efforts to form a sense of Irish national consciousness via the foundation of the **Gaelic League** in 1893. This sought to revive both the Irish language and traditional culture, and set the scene for the **Celtic literary revival**, led by W.B. Yeats and Lady Gregory, who established the Abbey Theatre in 1904. The political struggle for independence remained a live issue and events came to a head with the **Easter Rising** of 1916 (see box, p.78). The city's streets saw violence again during the **civil war**, which followed the establishment of the Irish Free State in 1921.

Austerity and much **emigration** followed Independence and it was not until the 1950s that Dublin began to emerge from its colonial past. The city's infrastructure was

JULY

Vodafone Comedy Festival Ⓦvodafonecomedy.com. A stellar line-up of mostly Irish comedians in the stunning surrounds of the Iveagh Gardens over four days.

Gaze LGBT Film Festival Ⓦgaze.ie. A strong bill of Irish and international LGBT films screened over five days towards the end of the month at the Light House Cinema in Smithfield (see p.107).

AUGUST

Dublin Horse Show Ⓣ01 485 8010, Ⓦdublinhorseshow.com. Five-day festival of equestrian events in early August at the RDS arena in Ballsbridge, featuring major international showjumpers participating in the Nations' Cup.

Dublin Viking Festival Ⓣ01 222 2242, Ⓦdublinia.ie. The last weekend in August sees a re-created Viking village established off Wood Quay, which features plenty of wandering inhabitants and the chance to watch re-enacted combats.

SEPTEMBER/OCTOBER (DUBLIN FESTIVAL SEASON)

Culture Night Ⓦculturenight.ie. Hundreds of arts and cultural organizations around the city open their doors until late for one Friday in mid-September, with free events, tours, talks and performances.

All-Ireland Senior Hurling and Gaelic Football finals Two of Ireland's major sporting events are staged at Croke Park (see p.87) in September: the hurling final on the first or second Sunday and the football final on the third or fourth Sunday.

Dublin Fringe Festival Ⓣ1850374643, Ⓦfringefest.com. Ireland's biggest performing-arts festival takes place over more than two weeks from mid-September and features all manner of music, dance, street theatre, comedy and children's events.

Dublin Theatre Festival Ⓣ01 677 8899, Ⓦdublintheatrefestival.com. A major celebration of theatre, held during the last few days of September and the first two weeks in October, this includes performances of new and classic drama at various city-centre venues.

Dublin City Marathon Ⓣ01 623 2250, Ⓦdublinmarathon.ie. Featuring 10,000 entrants, the race takes place on the last Monday in October and involves a roughly circular course starting from Fitzwilliam Street Upper, heads north across O'Connell Bridge, and takes in Phoenix Park and some southern suburbs before the finish at Merrion Square North.

Oktoberfest Ⓦoktoberfest-dublin.de. A fest of German food, music and tankards of Bavarian beer for two weeks in the Dublin Docklands, with stalls and entertainment for all the family.

DECEMBER

NYE Dublin Ⓦnye.visitdublin.com. Four days of festivities to ring in the New Year, with a "procession of light" through the city centre culminating in a big countdown concert on College Green.

---

ravaged by ill-conceived redevelopment in the 1960s which saw the demolition of many Georgian edifices, as well as the creation of poorly planned "sink" estates to replace dilapidated tenements. A couple of decades later city planners began to address the issue of inner-city depopulation, constructing apartment blocks to house Dublin's wealthy middle classes. The most obvious evidence of reinvigoration in the city centre is the Temple Bar area, though the original intention to develop a Parisian-style quarter of *ateliers* and arts centres soon fell foul of the moneygrubbers, and the area is now home to a plethora of kitch tourist bars and fast-food chains. East of the centre, reconstruction continues in the city's docklands.

The so-called Celtic Tiger years of the late 1990s and early 2000s saw the wealth of the city grow exponentially, as a property boom drove the demolition of derelict or vacant buildings to make way for new apartments and offices.

Another legacy of the boom was the arrival of **migrants**, particularly from Africa and Eastern Europe, which, together with the city's longer-standing Chinese community, saw Dublin gradually inch towards multiculturalism.

1

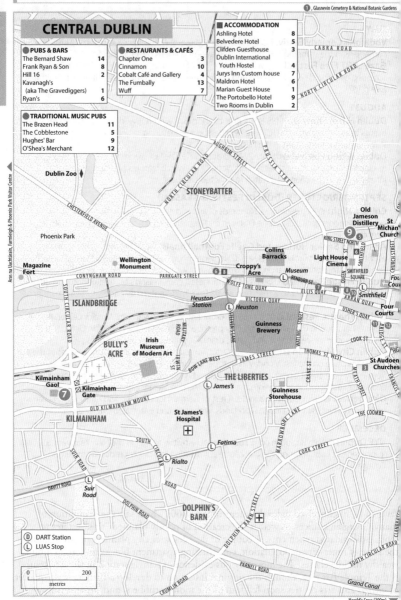

CENTRAL DUBLIN

● PUBS & BARS

The Bernard Shaw	14
Frank Ryan & Son	8
Hill 16	2
Kavanagh's (aka The Gravediggers)	1
Ryan's	6

● TRADITIONAL MUSIC PUBS

The Brazen Head	11
The Cobblestone	5
Hughes' Bar	9
O'Shea's Merchant	12

● RESTAURANTS & CAFÉS

Chapter One	3
Cinnamon	10
Cobalt Café and Gallery	4
The Fumbally	13
Wuff	7

■ ACCOMMODATION

Ashling Hotel	8
Belvedere Hotel	5
Clifden Guesthouse	3
Dublin International Youth Hostel	4
Jurys Inn Custom house	7
Maldron Hotel	6
Marian Guest House	1
The Portobello Hotel	9
Two Rooms in Dublin	2

The financial crisis of 2008 called a halt to the dizzying pace of development. Many new buildings were left half-finished, while shops and office blocks on some of the city's most prestigious streets were without tenants for years at a time. But the downturn has had an upside; cheaper rents have allowed more creative businesses to open, with new galleries, performing spaces and places to eat popping up seemingly every week. Many of the city's overpriced, overly pretentious restaurants that

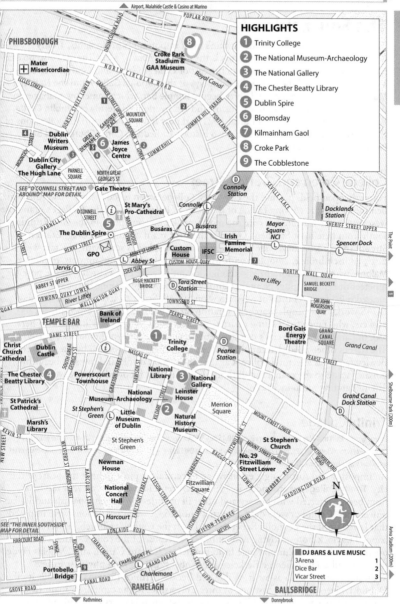

Airport, Malahide Castle & Casino at Marino

POPLAR ROW

PHIBSBOROUGH

HIGHLIGHTS

1 Trinity College
2 The National Museum–Archaeology
3 The National Gallery
4 The Chester Beatty Library
5 Dublin Spire
6 Bloomsday
7 Kilmainham Gaol
8 Croke Park
9 The Cobblestone

Mater Misericordiae

Croke Park Stadium & GAA Museum

NORTH CIRCULAR ROAD

Royal Canal

ECCLES STREET

MOUNTJOY SQUARE

Dublin Writers Museum

Dublin City Gallery The Hugh Lane

James Joyce Centre

SUMMERHILL

SUMMER HILL PARADE

PORTLAND ROW

PARNELL SQUARE

NORTH GREAT GEORGE'S ST

GREAT DENMARK ST

SEE "O'CONNELL STREET AND AROUND" MAP FOR DETAIL

Gate Theatre

Connolly Station

SEVILLE PLACE

O'CONNELL STREET

St Mary's Pro-Cathedral

Connolly

Docklands Station

SHERIFF STREET UPPER

PARNELL ST

The Dublin Spire

Busáras

Busáras

Irish Famine Memorial

Mayor Square NCI

Spencer Dock

HENRY STREET

GPO

Abbey St

Custom House

CUSTOM HOUSE QUAY

IFSC

NORTH WALL QUAY

Jervis

Tara Street Station

River Liffey

SAMUEL BECKETT BRIDGE

SIR JOHN ROGERSON'S QUAY

ABBEY ST UPPER

ORMOND QUAY LOWER

River Liffey

WELLINGTON QUAY

ROSIE HACKETT BRIDGE

TOWNSEND ST

PEARSE STREET

QUAY

TEMPLE BAR

DAME STREET

Bank of Ireland

Trinity College

Pearse Station

Bord Gais Energy Theatre

GRAND CANAL SQUARE

Grand Canal

Christ Church Cathedral

Dublin Castle

Powerscourt Townhouse

National Library

National Gallery

Leinster House

PEARSE STREET

The Chester Beatty Library

National Museum–Archaeology

Merrion Square

Grand Canal Dock Station

St Patrick's Cathedral

St Stephen's Green

Little Museum of Dublin

Natural History Museum

Marsh's Library

St Stephen's Green

MOUNT STREET LOWER

St Stephen's Church

No. 29 Fitzwilliam Street Lower

KEVIN ST

CUFFE ST

Newman House

Fitzwilliam Square

National Concert Hall

Harcourt

SEE "THE INNER SOUTHSIDE" MAP FOR DETAIL

HARCOURT ROAD

ADELAIDE ROAD

WILTON TERRACE

HADDINGTON ROAD

N

Anna Stadium (200m)

HARCOURT STREET

Portobello Bridge

Charlemont

GRAND PARADE

CANAL ROAD

GROVE ROAD

RANELAGH

Rathmines

BALLSBRIDGE

Donnybrook

Shelbourne Park (200m)

The Point

■ **DJ BARS & LIVE MUSIC**
3Arena	1
Dice Bar	2
Vicar Street	3

prevailed during the boom have withered, clearing the way for a plethora of excellent new cafés, restaurants and bars offering much more innovative dishes and better value for money.

As the economy begins to recover, the cranes are returning to the Dublin skyline. Its inhabitants can only hope that the city's planners and developers have learned from the mistakes of the past.

1 The Southside

The southside is home to one of Dublin's most important historic sights, **Trinity College**, whose main draw for visitors is the glorious *Book of Kells*. The area also boasts stylish Georgian streets, which lie to the east of College Green and Grafton Street, and are where you'll find the compelling displays of the **National Gallery** and the **National Museum**. On the west side of Trinity begins **Temple Bar**, which somehow manages to remain the city's hub for both carousing and art, overlooked sternly by **Dublin Castle**, British headquarters in Ireland until 1921 and now home to the glorious collections of the **Chester Beatty Library**. Dublin's two historic cathedrals, **Christ Church** and **St Patrick's**, stand to the west of here.

College Green and Grafton Street

Formerly open fields beyond the city walls, **College Green** is today just a road junction, hemmed in by the curving façade of the Bank of Ireland and Trinity College's grandiose west front, whose main gates are the most popular meeting place in the city. Running south from here to St Stephen's Green is the city's main commercial drag, **Grafton Street**. This pedestrianized street gets off to an inauspicious start with "the tart with the cart", a kitsch bronze, complete with wheelbarrow of cockles and mussels, of **Molly Malone**, who was immortalized – though it's unlikely she ever existed – in the popular nineteenth-century song. Note that until 2017, the Molly Malone statue will be located outside the church of St Andrew on Suffolk Street to accommodate the new LUAS works. For people-watchers, Grafton Street is a must, noted especially for its buskers, who range from string quartets to street poets. Shoppers will be drawn here, too, in particular to the city's flagship department store, **Brown Thomas** (see p.109). The street's other major landmark, **Bewley's** (see p.99), was founded by the Quaker Bewley family as a teetotal bulwark against the demon drink, and owes its beautiful mosaic façade to the mania for all things Egyptian that followed the discovery of Tutankhamun's tomb in 1922.

Trinity College

College Green • Tours mid-May to Sept 14 every 20min 10.15am–3.40pm; see website for schedule during the rest of the year • Free campus access to visitors; tours €5, or €12 including admission to the Old Library – if there are any queues there, this combination ticket will allow you to jump them • ⓦ tcd.ie

An'imposing and surprisingly extensive architectural set piece right at the heart of the city, **Trinity College** was founded in 1592 by Queen Elizabeth I to prevent the Irish from being "infected with popery and other ill qualities" at French, Spanish and Italian universities. Catholics were duly admitted until 1637, when restrictions were imposed that lasted until the Catholic Relief Act of 1793; the Catholic Church, however, banned its flock from studying here until 1970 because of the college's Anglican orientation. Famous alumni range from politicians Edward Carson and Douglas Hyde, through philosopher George Berkeley and Nobel Prize-winning physicist Ernest Walton, to writers such as Swift, Wilde and Beckett. Trinity, though it also calls itself Dublin University, is now just one of three universities in the capital: its main rival, University College Dublin (UCD), part of the National University of Ireland, is based at Belfield in the southern suburbs; while Dublin City University is in Glasnevin.

From just inside the main gates, Trinity students lead thirty-minute **walking tours** of the college. The gates give onto eighteenth-century **Front Square**, flanked, with appealing symmetry, by the Chapel and the Examination Hall, which is the elegant, stuccoed setting for occasional concerts. On the east side of adjoining Library Square is the college's oldest surviving building, the **Rubrics**, a red-brick student dormitory dating from around 1701, though much altered in the nineteenth century. In New

Square beyond, the School of Engineering occupies the old **Museum Building** (1852), designed in extravagant Venetian Gothic style by Benjamin Woodward under the influence of his friend, John Ruskin, and awash with decorative stone-carving of animals and floral patterns.

Science Gallery

Pearse St • Tues–Fri noon–8pm, Sat & Sun noon–6pm; café and shop open 8am–8pm; closed for 2 weeks over Christmas and New Year • Free • Ⓦ dublin.sciencegallery.com

In the northeastern corner of the college at the Pearse Street entrance (handy for Pearse DART Station) is the excellent **Science Gallery**. Both thoughtful and thought-provoking, it hosts high-tech and interactive temporary exhibitions on all aspects of science, from how the body uses fat to the causes of extreme weather events, as well as interesting one-off lectures.

Douglas Hyde Gallery

Nassau St entrance • Mon–Wed & Fri 11am–6pm, Thurs 11am–7pm, Sat 11am–4.45pm • Free • ❶ 01 896 1116, Ⓦ douglashydegallery.com

In Fellows' Square on the south side of Library Square, the modern Arts Block is home to the **Douglas Hyde Gallery**, one of Ireland's most important galleries of modern art. Temporary exhibitions focus on Irish and international artists whose work is not yet well known, or has been previously overlooked. Gallery 2 regularly hosts exhibitions of ethnographic and craft artefacts.

The Old Library and the Book of Kells

Fellows' Square • May–Sept Mon–Sat 9.30am–5pm, Sun 9.30am–4.30pm; Oct–April Mon–Sat 9.30am–5pm, Sun noon–4.30pm; closed for 10 days over Christmas and New Year • €9 • Ⓦ tcd.ie/library

Trinity's most compelling tourist attraction is the **Book of Kells**, kept in the eighteenth-century **Old Library**. On the library's ground floor, beautiful pages are displayed not just from the *Book of Kells* (around 800 AD), but from other works such as the *Book of Armagh* (early ninth century) and the *Book of Mulling* (late eighth century). The books themselves are preceded by a fascinating exhibition, **Turning Darkness into Light**, which sets Irish illuminated manuscripts in context – ranging from ogham (the earlier, Celtic writing system of lines carved on standing stones) to Ethiopian books of devotions.

Pre-eminent for the scale, variety and colour of its decoration, the *Book of Kells* probably originated at the monastery on Iona off the west coast of Scotland, which had been founded around 561 by the great Irish scholar, bard and ruler St Colmcille (St Columba in English). After a Viking raid in 806 the Columbines moved to the monastery of Kells in County Meath, which in its turn was raided four times between 920 and 1019. Although they looted the book's *cumdach* or metal shrine cover, the pagan Norsemen did not value the book itself, however, and despite spending some time buried underground and losing thirty folios, it survived at Kells up to the seventeenth century when it was taken to Dublin for safekeeping during the Cromwellian Wars. The 340 calfskin folios of the *Book of Kells* contain the four New Testament Gospels along with preliminary texts, all in Latin. It's thought that three artists created the book's lavish decoration, which shows Pictish, Germanic and Mediterranean, as well as Celtic, influences. Not only are there full-page illustrations of Christ and the Virgin and Child, but an elaborate decorative scheme of animals and spiral, roundel and interlace patterns is employed throughout the text, on the initials at the beginning of each Gospel and on full-length "carpet pages".

Upstairs is the library's magnificent **Long Room**, built by Thomas Burgh between 1712 and 1732 and enlarged, with a barrel-vaulted ceiling, in 1860. As a copyright library, Trinity has had the right to claim a free copy of all British and Irish publications since 1801; of its current stock of four million titles, 200,000 of the oldest are stored in the Long Room's oak bookcases. Besides interesting temporary exhibitions of books and prints from the library's collection, the Long Room also displays a gnarled

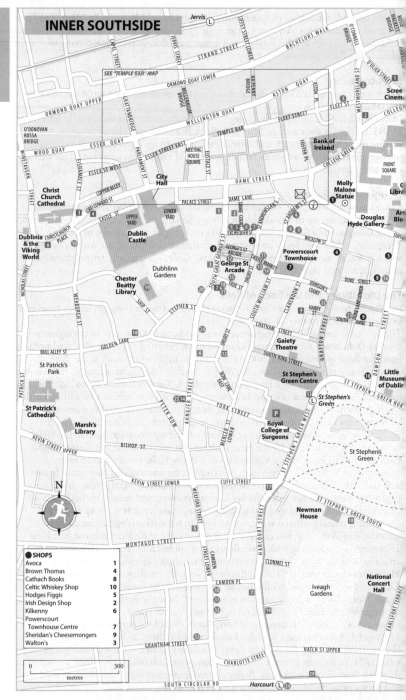

INNER SOUTHSIDE

SHOPS

Avoca	1
Brown Thomas	4
Cathach Books	8
Celtic Whiskey Shop	10
Hodges Figgis	5
Irish Design Shop	2
Kilkenny	6
Powerscourt Townhouse Centre	7
Sheridan's Cheesemongers	9
Walton's	3

0 ————— 300
metres

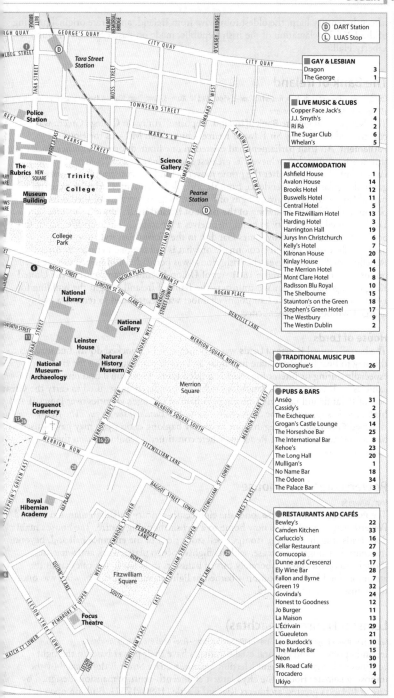

1

fifteenth-century harp, the oldest to survive from Ireland, and a rare original printing of the 1916 Proclamation of the Irish Republic, made on Easter Sunday in Dublin's Liberty Hall.

The Bank of Ireland

College Green • House of Lords: Mon, Tues & Fri 10am–3.45pm, Wed 10.30am–3.45pm, Thurs 10am–4.45pm; guided tours Tues 10.30am, 11.30am & 12.30pm • Entry and tours free

The Neoclassical granite **Bank of Ireland**, opposite Trinity on College Green, was constructed in 1729 by Sir Edward Pearce – himself an MP – as the **House of Parliament**. An Irish parliament had existed in one limited form or another since the thirteenth century, but achieved its greatest success here in 1782, when "Grattan's Parliament" (so named after the prime mover behind the constitutional reform) was granted legislative independence from the British Parliament. Catholics were still barred from sitting, but many signs of Irish sovereignty were established during this period, including the founding of the Bank of Ireland itself. Around this time, the Lords deemed it necessary to build themselves a separate entrance on Westmoreland Street, designed in 1785 by James Gandon in the Corinthian style in order to distinguish it from the Ionic colonnade of what is still the main entrance. After the Rebellion of 1798, however, the Irish House was persuaded and bribed to vote itself out of existence, and with the 1801 Act of Union Ireland became part of the United Kingdom, governed from Westminster. The Bank of Ireland bought the building for £40,000 in 1802, and the Commons chamber was demolished to remove a highly charged symbol of independence.

House of Lords

The barrel-vaulted **House of Lords** was also meant to be knocked down, but survives to this day to host high-level state functions and as the main attraction for visitors, especially during its interesting, weekly guided tours. Here you'll find one or two exhibits such as the Lord Chancellor's richly embroidered purse, used to carry the Great Seal of Ireland, and tapestries showing William of Orange's victories over James II and his Catholic supporters, the *Siege of Derry* and the *Battle of the Boyne*. The richly stuccoed **Cash Hall** – an elegant spot to do any banking chores you may have – used to be the Parliament's Hall of Requests, where constituents would petition their representatives.

Powerscourt Townhouse

South William St

The **Powerscourt Townhouse**, once the eighteenth-century Palladian mansion of Lord Powerscourt (see p.121), is now home to a stylish shopping centre. The house's main door leads straight onto the trompe l'oeil stone floor of the entrance hall and, beyond, the central mahogany staircase, with its flighty rococo plasterwork and what are thought to be the most elaborately carved balusters in Ireland. The café-bar in the atrium is notable for its location – bathed in light on sunny days – in what was once the mansion's inner courtyard.

Leinster House (Oireachtas)

Kildare St • Entrance by guided tour only, Mon–Fri 10.30am & 2.30pm • Free • ☎ 01 618 3271, ⊕ oireachtas.ie

Ireland's political and cultural establishments have their power bases in the tight confines of Kildare Street and Merrion Square. Kildare Street is dominated by the imposing **Leinster House**, the city's largest eighteenth-century mansion, designed by one of Ireland's greatest architects Richard Castle (1690–1751). Built on open fields in1745 for the Earl of Kildare James FitzGerald, the town house started a trend among the gentry and wealthy, who eschewed traditionally fashionable parts of the city to build new homes in the surrounding area. Originally called Kildare House, it was renamed when the earl became Duke of Leinster in 1766. Dublin's largest Georgian-style district grew up around Leinster House, and still survives today.

After the formation of the Irish Free State in 1922, the building was acquired by the newly formed government. It has since been home to the Irish parliament, the Oireachtas (pronounced something like "a-ruck-tas"), which is divided into Dáil Éireann (House of Representatives) and Seannad Eireann (the Senate). Portraits of two of the leading members of the first Dáil, Cathal Brugha and Michael Collins, hang opposite each other in the entrance hall, alongside paintings of past Irish presidents and an original copy of the 1916 Proclamation.

Natural History Museum

Merrion St • Tues–Sat 10am–5pm, Sun 2–5pm • Free • ☎ 01 677 7444, Ⓦ museum.ie

The charmingly unreconstructed displays of the **Natural History Museum** have been impressing visitors since the "Dead Zoo" first opened its doors to the public in 1857. Recent conservation work has improved access and provided new learning opportunities – including a discovery zone where visitors can handle taxidermy and open drawers to see what is lurking inside – but overall, the exhibition style and furnishings have changed little in 150 years.

The ground floor is dedicated to native Irish species, and includes the skeleton of an 11,000-year-old deer alongside a variety of mammals, birds and fish. The upper floors feature animals from around the world, laid out in the nineteenth century by taxonomic group, which aimed to demonstrate the evolution of animal life.

The National Museum – Archaeology

Kildare St • Tues–Sat 10am–5pm, Sun 2–5pm • Free • ☎ 01 677 7444, Ⓦ museum.ie

The **National Museum – Archaeology** is the finest of a portfolio of jointly run museums – including Collins Barracks (see p.81), which focuses on the decorative arts, and the National Museum of Country Life in Castlebar (see p.386) – and a must-see for visitors to Dublin. Undoubtedly the stars of the show here are a stunning hoard of prehistoric gold and a thousand years' worth of ornate ecclesiastical treasures, but the whole collection builds up a fascinating and accessible story of Irish archaeology and history. The shop in the beautiful entrance rotunda sells a range of high-quality crafts inspired by works in the museum, and there's a small café.

Prehistoric gold, much of it discovered during peat-cutting, takes pride of place on the ground floor of the main hall. From the Earlier Bronze Age (c.2500–1500 BC) come *lunulae*, thin sheets of gold formed into crescent-moon collars. After around 1200 BC, when new sources of the metal were apparently found, goldsmiths could be more extravagant, fashioning chunky torcs, such as the spectacular Gleninsheen Collar and the Tumna Hoard of nine large gold balls, which are perforated, suggesting that when joined together they formed a huge necklace. Further prehistoric material is arrayed around the walls of the main hall, including the 15m-long Lurgan Logboat, dating from around 2500 BC, which was unearthed in a Galway bog in 1902.

The adjacent **Treasury** holds most of the museum's better-known ecclesiastical exhibits, notably the ornate eighth-century Ardagh Chalice, the Tara Brooch, decorated with beautiful knot designs, and the Cross of Cong, created to enshrine a fragment of the True Cross given to the King of Connacht by the Pope in 1123. Also on the ground floor is **Kingship and Sacrifice**, showcasing the leathery bodies of four Iron Age noblemen that were preserved and discovered in various bogs around Ireland.

1

Upstairs, **Viking-age Ireland** (c.800–1150) features models of a house and the layout of Dublin's Fishamble Street, while **Medieval Ireland** (1150–1550) moves on to cover the first English colonists, their withdrawal to the fortified area around Dublin known as "the Pale" after 1300, and the hybrid culture that developed all the while – you can listen to recordings of poetry written in Ireland in Middle Irish, Middle English and Norman French. Unmissable here is a host of strange, ornate portable shrines, made to hold holy relics or texts, including examples for all three of Ireland's patron saints: the Shrine of St Patrick's Tooth, the Shrine of St Brigid's Shoe (see p.129) and the Shrine of the Cathach, containing a manuscript written by St Colmcille (St Columba), legendary bard, scholar, ruler and evangelizer of Scotland.

The National Library

Kildare St • **National Library** Mon–Wed 9.30am–7.45pm, Thurs & Fri 9.30am–4.45pm, Sat 9.30am–4.30pm • Free • **Genealogy Room** Mon–Fri 9.30am–5pm • Free • ⓦ www.nli.ie

The **National Library** was opened on Kildare Street in 1890, shortly after the National Museum, whose design it mirrors across the courtyard of Leinster House. Besides prestigious public talks and readings, its main draws are its long-term temporary exhibitions on subjects such as W.B. Yeats, which are mounted in a beautiful, high-tech space on the lower ground floor. Visitors are also allowed up to the hushed domed **Reading Room** on the first floor, decorated with ornate bookcases and an incongruously playful frieze of cherubs. It is in the office here that Stephen Dedalus engages the librarians – who appear under their real names – in literary talk in the "Scylla and Charybdis" episode of *Ulysses*.

In the **Genealogy Room**, library staff can give advice to anyone researching their family history on how to access the records here and elsewhere in Dublin, as well as in Belfast.

The National Gallery

Merrion Square West • Mon–Sat 9.30am–5.30pm, Thurs 9.30am–8.30pm, Sun noon–5.30pm, public holidays 10am–5.30pm; guided tours Sat 12.30pm, Sun 12.30pm & 1.30pm • Entry and tour free • ☎ 01 661 5133, ⓦ nationalgallery.ie

The **National Gallery** hosts a fine collection of Western European art dating from the Middle Ages to the twentieth century, which will happily engage you for hours. The gallery's old buildings, the Milltown and Dargan wings, are undergoing extensive refurbishment and will remain closed until 2016. In the meantime, entrance to the gallery is via the **Millennium Wing** on Clare Street, which hosts major temporary exhibitions around its striking sky-lit atrium. The gallery also offers classical and contemporary concerts, lectures and workshops, which are detailed in the quarterly *Gallery News* (available in the information desk, along with free floor-plan leaflets).

Level 1 is chiefly given over to **Irish art** from the seventeenth century onwards. The highlight is the collection of paintings by Jack B. Yeats (1871–1957), younger brother of the writer W.B. Yeats, which traces the artist's development from an unsentimental illustrator of everyday scenes to an expressive painter in abstract, unmixed colours. Other works include early twentieth-century portraits by William Orpen (1878–1931) and John Lavery (1856–1941), as well as more modern Irish landscapes by Gerard Dillon (1916–71).

Watercolours by Turner are exhibited every January, when the light is low enough for these delicate works.

Highlights of the European collection include *Kitchen Maid with the Supper at Emmaus*, the earliest known picture by **Velázquez** (1599–1660); **Vermeer**'s *Woman Writing a Letter, with her Maid*, one of only 35 accepted works by the artist, with his characteristic use of white light from the window accentuating the woman's heated

CLOCKWISE FROM TOP BLOOMSDAY (P.80); THE SPIRE (P.77); KILMAINHAM GAOL (P.85) >

1

emotions; and **Caravaggio**'s dynamic *The Taking of Christ*, in which the artist portrayed himself as a passive spectator on the right of the picture, holding a lamp.

Merrion Square

Begun in 1762, **Merrion Square** represents Georgian town planning at its grandest. Its long, graceful terraces of red-brown brick sport elaborate doors, knockers and fanlights, as well as wrought-iron balconies (added in the early nineteenth century) and tall windows on the first floor, where the main reception rooms would have been; the north side of the square was built first and displays the widest variety of design.

The broad, manicured lawns of the square's gardens themselves are a joy, quieter than St Stephen's Green, and especially agreeable for picnics on fine days. Revolutionary politician Michael Collins is commemorated with a bronze bust on the gardens' south side, near a slightly hapless stone bust of Henry Grattan (see p.586), while writer, artist and mystic George Russell ("AE") stands gravely near the southwest corner and his former home at no. 74. But the square's most remarkable and controversial statue is at the northwest corner, where **Oscar Wilde** reclines on a rock facing his childhood home at no. 1 (now the American College Dublin), in a wry, languid pose that has earned the figure the nickname "the fag on the crag". In front of him, a male torso and his wife Constance, pregnant with their second child, stand on plinths inscribed with Wildean witticisms: "This suspense is terrible. I hope it will last", "I drink to keep body and soul apart." Nearby on the railings around the square's gardens, dozens of artists hang their paintings for sale every Sunday (and some Sats, depending on the weather).

The Merrion Square South terrace has the greatest concentration of famous former residents, giving a vivid sense of the history of the place: politician Daniel O'Connell bought no. 58 in 1809; the Nobel Prize-winning Austrian physicist, Erwin Schrödinger, occupied no. 65; Gothic novelist Joseph Sheridan Le Fanu died at no. 70, which is now the Arts Council; and W.B. Yeats lived at no. 82 from 1922 to 1928. At no. 39 stood the British Embassy, which was burnt down by a crowd protesting against the Bloody Sunday massacre in Derry in 1972.

No. 29 Fitzwilliam Street Lower

Fitzwilliam Street lower • Mid-Feb to mid-Dec Tues–Sat 10am–5pm, Sun noon–5pm • Guided tours 11am (for groups only, must be pre-booked) and 3pm • €6 • ⓦ esb.ie/no29

This **town house** at the southeast corner of Merrion Square has been carefully reconstructed in the style of a middle-class home of the period 1790–1820 by the Electricity Supply Board, using furniture from the National Museum's collection. The ESB may sound like a strange curator for such a venture, but the house was rebuilt as an act of homage after the Board had knocked down 26 Georgian houses here to build its adjoining offices in the 1960s. Entertaining guided tours bring to life the details of bourgeois Georgian life, both below stairs and in the elegant living rooms upstairs, which benefited from such gadgets as a lead-lined wine cooler and a belly-warmer for soothing gastric complaints. From this corner of the square there's a fine view down Mount Street Upper of the "peppercanister" church of **St Stephen's**, a Greek Revival work dating from 1824.

St Stephen's Green

As well as being a major landmark and transport hub for buses, taxis and the LUAS **St Stephen's Green** is central Dublin's largest and most varied park, whose statuary provides a poignant history lesson in stone, wood and bronze. The Green preserves its distinctive Victorian character with a small lake, bandstand, arboretum and well-tended flower displays. It was originally open common land, a notoriously dirty and dangerous spot and the site of public hangings until the eighteenth century. In 1880, however, it was turned into a public park with funding from the brewer Lord Ardilaun (Arthur Guinness), who now boasts the grandest of the Green's many statues, seated at his leisure on the far western side. Over at the northeast corner, a row of huge granite monoliths – nicknamed "Tonehenge" – has been erected in honour of eighteenth-century nationalist **Wolfe Tone**, behind which stands a moving commemoration of the **Great Famine**. Meanwhile, on the west side of the central flower display, a tiny plaque inlaid in a wooden park bench commemorates the so-called "fallen women" – mostly unmarried mothers or abused girls – who were forced to live and work in severe conditions in Ireland's **Magdalen laundries**; the last of them, in Dublin, wasn't closed down until 1996. From the Green's northwest corner, by the top of Grafton Street, you can hire a **horse and carriage**, either as a grandiose taxi or for a tour of the sights, which will typically set you back €40–50 for thirty minutes.

The main sightseeing draws in the area date from the Georgian period: the splendid stuccowork of **Newman House** and the elegant streets and squares to the east of the Green, as well as the excellent **Little Museum of Dublin**.

Termed in the eighteenth century "Beau Walk", **St Stephen's Green North** is still the most fashionable side of the square. The **Shelbourne Hotel** here claims to have been "the best address in Dublin" since its establishment in 1824 (see p.96). Beyond the hotel at the start of Merrion Row, the tiny, tree-shaded **Huguenot Cemetery** was opened in 1693 for Protestant refugees fleeing religious persecution in France. A large plaque inside the gates gives a roll call of Huguenot Dubliners, among whom the most famous have been writers Dion Boucicault and Sheridan Le Fanu.

Newman House

85–86 St Stephen's Green South • Guided tours only: June–Aug Tues–Fri 2pm, 3pm & 4pm • €5

Newman House boasts probably the finest Georgian interiors in Dublin, noted especially for their decorative plasterwork. The place is named after John Henry Newman, the famous British convert from Anglicanism, who was invited to found the Catholic University of Ireland here in 1854 as an alternative to Anglican Trinity College and the recently established "godless" Queen's Colleges in Belfast, Cork and Galway. James Joyce and Éamon de Valera were educated at what became University College Dublin (UCD), which now occupies a large campus in the southern suburbs.

Newman House began life as two houses. **No. 85** is a Palladian mansion built by Richard Castle in 1738 and adorned with superb Baroque stuccowork by the Swiss Lafranchini brothers, notably in the ground-floor **Apollo Room**, where the god himself appears majestically over the fireplace, attended by the nine muses on the surrounding walls. The much larger **no. 86**, with flowing rococo plasterwork by Robert West, the notable Dublin-born imitator of the Lafranchinis, was added in 1765. On the top floor of the latter are a lecture room, done out as in Joyce's student days (1899–1902), and the bedroom of the English poet **Gerard Manley Hopkins**. Having converted from Anglicanism, Hopkins became a Jesuit priest and then Professor of Classics here in 1884; after five wretched years in Dublin, he died of typhoid and was buried in an unmarked grave in Glasnevin Cemetery.

Little Museum of Dublin

15 St Stephen's Green North • Mon–Wed & Fri–Sun 9.30am–5pm, Thurs 9.30am–8pm • Guided tour on the hour every hour • €7 • 01 661 1000, ⓦ littlemuseum.ie

Crammed into two floors of a Georgian house, the **Little Museum of Dublin** displays more than 5,000 artefacts and curios telling the social history of twentieth-century Dublin. Beginning with a photograph of Queen Victoria arriving in Dún Laoghaire in 1900, the exhibition traces the transformation of the city over 100 years, using

1

newspaper clippings, old photographs, children's toys, ticket stubs, posters, letters and other bric-a-brac on loan from the people of Dublin since the museum opened in 2011.

Temporary exhibitions cover subjects ranging from Irish emigration to America and the challenges of tenement living in 1913, to the early days of U2 and Dublin street style through the decades. Regular lectures are held on Dublin-themed topics, spanning literature, art, history, music and more.

Visitors looking to meet Dubliners and learn more about the city first-hand over a free drink can sign up online for the museum's excellent "City of a Thousand Welcomes" greeting service, which matches local volunteers with tourists.

Fitzwilliam Square

The area to the east of St Stephen's Green is the best in the city for a Georgian architectural tour, where an aimless wander will reveal plenty of wrought-iron balconies and much-photographed doorways sporting elegant knockers and fanlights. At its centre lie the still-private lawns of the small but well-preserved **Fitzwilliam Square** (1825), where, at no. 42, W.B. Yeats lived from 1928 to 1932. His brother, the painter Jack B., had a house and studio round the corner at no. 18 Fitzwilliam Place, which together with its continuation Fitzwilliam Street forms a – now much-interrupted – kilometre-long terrace of Georgian houses, marching off towards the magnificent backdrop of the Wicklow Mountains.

GEORGE BERNARD SHAW

Born in Dublin in 1856, **George Bernard Shaw** grew up among a Protestant family fallen on hard times. His father was an unsuccessful grain merchant and alcoholic – prompting Shaw to become a lifelong abstainer – and there was no money to pay for his education. At 15 he started work as a junior clerk for a land agency, but five years later went to London to join his mother who had moved there to further the musical career of one of his sisters. Reliant on what little income his mother earned as a music teacher, Shaw set about educating himself by spending his afternoons in the reading room of the British Museum. He hoped to become a novelist, but, following the rejection of no fewer than five novels, turned his hand to journalism instead, contributing music and drama criticism to London newspapers.

Shaw was a devout socialist, joining the Fabian Society in 1884, writing pamphlets and gaining a reputation as a natural orator. He espoused numerous causes, including electoral reform, vegetarianism and the abolition of private property. His **theatrical career** began in the 1890s when, influenced by Ibsen, he began to compose plays focusing on social and moral matters, rather than the romantic and personal subjects which then dominated British theatre.

In 1898 he married the heiress Charlotte Payne-Townshend and the same year saw the production of his first successful play, *Candida*. A stream of equally lauded comedy-dramas followed – including *The Devil's Disciple, Arms and the Man, Major Barbara* and *Pygmalion* – though he later turned to more serious drama, such as *Heartbreak House* and *Saint Joan*. Simultaneously, he maintained an active career as a **critic**, journalist and essayist, his often bitterly ironic wit ("England and America are two countries separated by a common language") becoming legendary. In 1925 he was awarded the Nobel Prize for Literature, but initially rejected the honour before relenting and giving his prize money to a newly established Anglo-Swedish Literary Foundation.

Shaw's attitude to Ireland was ever ambivalent – he once commented "I am a typical Irishman; my family came from Yorkshire" – and, though he remained interested in Irish affairs and became a personal friend of Michael Collins, his brand of democratic socialism would have been antipathetic to the austere Catholic and anti-British state that emerged post-independence. Shaw died in 1950 at Ayot St Lawrence, Hertfordshire.

A plaque outside 33 Synge Street marks Shaw's birthplace, closed to the public at the time of writing.

Royal Hibernian Academy

15 Ely Place • Mon–Sat 11am–5pm, Sun noon–5pm • Free • ☎ 01 661 2558, ⓦ rhagallery.ie

The **Royal Hibernian Academy** is one of the country's leading contemporary art venues. Hosting major temporary shows by Irish and international artists, its well-designed viewing spaces are also home to the RHA Annual Exhibition, usually from May to July.

Temple Bar

Sandwiched between the busy thoroughfare of Dame Street and the Liffey, **Temple Bar** is marketed, with a fair dose of artistic licence, as Dublin's "Left Bank" (inconveniently, it's on the right bank as you face downstream). Its transformation into the city's main cultural and entertainment district came about after a 1960s plan for a new central bus terminal here was abandoned after much procrastination. Instead, the area's narrow cobbled streets and old warehouses, by now occupied by short-lease studios, workshops and boutiques, began to be sensitively redeveloped as an artistic quarter in the 1980s. Nowadays, as well as more galleries and arts centres than you can shake a paintbrush at – even the helpful information centre on Essex Street East (March–Oct Mon–Fri 9am–5.30pm, Sat 10am–5.30pm, Sun noon–3pm; Nov–April Mon–Fri 9am–5.30pm, Sat 10am–5.30pm; ☎01 677 2255, ⓦtemplebar.ie) houses a small exhibition space for independent, "no-grants" artists – Temple Bar shelters a huge number of hotels, restaurants, pubs and clubs, engendering a notoriously raucous nightlife scene that attracts more outsiders than Dubliners.

Most people enter Temple Bar from Dame Street, past the unusual and highly controversial 1970s **Central Bank**, whose floors are suspended from the roof by external cables. The main access from the northside is the cast-iron **Ha'penny Bridge**, Dublin's oldest and most renowned pedestrian river crossing, with great views of the river along the quays in both directions. It began life in 1816 as the Wellington Bridge but soon acquired its nickname thanks to a halfpenny toll, which was levied until 1919. The central **Temple Bar Square** is a popular spot for people-watching, with several open-air cafés. It hosts a small book market on Saturdays and Sundays (11am–6pm), while the

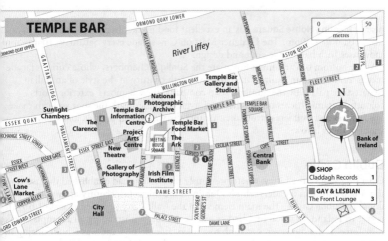

1

TEMPLE BAR GALLERIES AND ART CENTRES

THE ARK

11A Eustace St • ☎ 01 670 7788, ⓦ ark.ie

Europe's first custom-built cultural centre for children, hosting plays, exhibitions, workshops, festivals, concerts and multimedia programmes for 2- to 12-year-olds.

GALLERY OF PHOTOGRAPHY

Meeting House Square • Tues–Sat 11am–6pm, Sun 1–6pm • Free • ☎ 01 671 4654, ⓦ galleryofphotography.ie

Stages some great shows of contemporary photographs from Ireland and around the world in smart, well-lit rooms above a good photographic bookshop.

IRISH FILM INSTITUTE

6 Eustace St • ⓦ ifi.ie

An eighteenth-century Quaker meeting house (see p.107), which has been converted into an art-house cinema, with a fashionable bar-restaurant (see p.99).

NATIONAL PHOTOGRAPHIC ARCHIVE

Meeting House Square • Mon–Fri 10am–5pm, Sat 10am–2pm • Free • ☎ 01 603 0374, ⓦ www.nli.ie

Mounts a series of often fascinating temporary exhibitions, mostly on Irish historical subjects, from the 5.2 million photographs in the National Library's collection.

PROJECT ARTS CENTRE

39 East Essex St • ☎ 01 881 9613, ⓦ projectartcentres.ie

One of Dublin's most renowned contemporary performance art spaces, hosting theatre, dance, film and music shows (see p.107).

TEMPLE BAR GALLERY AND STUDIOS

5–9 Temple Bar • Tues–Sat 11am–6pm, Thurs 11am–7pm • ☎ 01 671 0073, ⓦ templebargallery.com

This publicly funded gallery, purpose-built in the 1990s with thirty artists' studios attached, exhibits cutting-edge Irish and international artists working in a wide range of media.

nearby **Meeting House Square** has an excellent food market (see p.109) on Saturdays from 10am to 4.30pm. The Designer Mart on Cow's Lane every Saturday (10am–5pm showcases Irish handmade craft and design.

At the bottom of Parliament Street are the **Sunlight Chambers**, whose curious façade merits a short detour. Built in the early twentieth century in the style of an Italian Renaissance palace by the Sunlight soap company, the Chambers' exterior sports colourful ceramic friezes on the theme of hygiene; underneath the soot you can make out farmers and builders getting their clothes dirty on the upper tier, and women washing them below.

Dublin Castle

On a ridge above the Liffey, where previously the Vikings had established themselves, the Anglo-Norman invaders rebuilt Dublin in the thirteenth century around the doughty **Dublin Castle**. The main element of the walled city became the seat of British power in Ireland for seven hundred years, successfully withstanding all attempts to take it by force. It did, however, succumb to a major fire in 1684 and was rebuilt during the eighteenth century as a complex of residential and administrative buildings over two quadrangles, giving a sedate collegiate appearance. The outline of the medieval castle is traced by the **Upper Yard**; above its original main gate, the Cork Hill State Entrance, stands a statue of *Justice*, wearing no blindfold and turning her back on the city – a fitting symbol of British rule, locals reckon. Visitors are free to walk around the courtyards, now home to police and tax offices, before visiting the **State Apartments** or the world-class collection of books and objets d'art from around the globe in the **Chester Beatty Library**.

The State Apartments

Mon–Sat 10am–4.45pm, Sun noon–4.45pm; it's advisable to ring ahead as the apartments are sometimes closed for state occasions; a number of guided tours run daily, but it is advisable to arrive early to book a place • €4.50; Heritage Card • ☎ 01 645 8813, Ⓦ dublincastle.ie

The State Apartments were built as the residence of the English viceroy and are entered from the Upper Yard. Inside the apartments, the Grand Staircase leads up to the east wing of bedrooms and drawing rooms, refurbished to their eighteenth- and nineteenth-century style after a major fire in 1941. The brass chandelier in the Throne Room, with its shamrock, rose and thistle emblems, commemorates the 1801 Act of Union, while the Picture Gallery beyond is lined with viceroys, including – hiding ignominiously behind the door – the First Marquis of Cornwallis, who not only lost the American colonies, but also faced rebellions as viceroy, first of India, then of Ireland (1798). St Patrick's Hall, formerly a ballroom that hosted investitures of the Knights of St Patrick, is now used for the inaugurations and funerals of Irish presidents. Its overblown, late eighteenth-century ceiling paintings show St Patrick converting the Irish, Henry II receiving the submission of the Irish chieftains, and George III's coronation.

Public access also includes the **Chapel Royal** in the Lower Yard, an ornate Gothic Revival gem, and the excavations of the **Undercroft**, which have revealed the base of the gunpowder tower of the medieval castle and steps leading down to the moat (fed by the old River Poddle on its way down to the Liffey), as well as part of the original Viking ramparts.

The Chester Beatty Library

Oct–April Tues–Fri 10am–5pm, Sat 11am–5pm, Sun 1–5pm; May–Sept Mon 10am–5pm, Tues–Fri 10am–5pm, Sat 11am–5pm, Sun 1–5pm • Free; free guided tours Wed 1pm & Sun 3pm & 4pm • ☎ 01 407 0750, Ⓦ cbl.ie

To the south of the Chapel Royal lies the pretty **castle garden**; now adorned with a swirling motif taken from the passage grave at Newgrange, it marks the site of the "black pool" (*dubh linn*) from which the city derives its name. Overlooking the garden from the renovated eighteenth-century Clock Tower Building, the **Chester Beatty Library** preserves a dazzling collection of books, manuscripts, prints and objets d'art from around the world. Superlatives come thick and fast here: as well as one of the finest Islamic collections in existence, containing some of the earliest manuscripts from the ninth and tenth centuries, the library holds important biblical papyri, including the earliest surviving examples in any language of Mark's and Luke's Gospels, St Paul's Letters and the Book of Revelation. Elegantly displayed in high-tech galleries, the artefacts are used to tell the story of religious and artistic traditions across the world with great ingenuity. It's well worth timing your visit to coincide with lunch at the excellent *Silk Road Café* (see p.100).

The collection was painstakingly put together by the remarkable **Sir Alfred Chester Beatty**, an American mining magnate who moved himself and his works to Dublin in the early 1950s, after cutting a deal with the Irish government on import taxes and estate duties. In 1957 he was made the first honorary citizen of Ireland, and, when he died in 1968, he bequeathed his collection to the state and was given a state funeral.

Most of the Chester Beatty Library's vast holding is accessible only to scholars via the reference library, with less than two percent on show in the public galleries at any one time – though that's more than enough to keep you occupied for a few hours. It makes sense to start with the second-floor gallery, which covers "Sacred Traditions", while the first floor deals with "the Arts of the Book" (alongside a space for fascinating temporary exhibitions), with each divided into Western, Islamic and Eastern sections; exhibits

1

range from sixteenth-century biblical engravings by Albrecht Dürer to books carved in jade for the Chinese emperors, and from gorgeously illustrated collections of Persian poetry to serene Burmese statues of the Buddha.

City Hall

Dame St • Mon–Sat 10am–5.15pm, Sun 11–5pm • Free • ⓦ dublincity.ie

In front of the castle stands the gleamingly restored rotunda of **City Hall**, where creamy Portland-stone columns, interspersed with statues of notables, including Daniel O'Connell (the city's first Catholic Lord Mayor), are bathed in wonderful natural light from the dome. The sumptuous Neoclassical building was constructed between 1769 and 1779 as the Royal Exchange, but fell into disuse after the Act of Union of 1801 passed governance of Ireland back to London; Dublin Corporation bought it in 1851, and it's still the venue for city council meetings. Arts and crafts murals under the dome trace Dublin's history, while the colourful floor mosaic shows the civic coat of arms, three castles topped by flames, which apparently represent the zeal of the citizens to defend Dublin – reinforced by the city motto *Obedientia Civium Urbis Felicitas* ("Happy the City whose Citizens Obey").

Christ Church Cathedral

Christchurch Place • Mon–Sat March–May 9am–6pm, June–Sept 9am–7pm, Oct–April 9am–5pm; Sun March–Sept 12.30–2.30pm & 4.30–6pm, Oct–Feb 12.30–2.30pm • €6, combined ticket with Dublinia €13.25 • ⓦ christchurchdublin.ie

Occupying the highest point of the old city, **Christ Church Cathedral** sits above Wood Quay, the location of a Viking settlement of more than two hundred houses over which the Dublin Corporation controversially built its Civic Offices in the early 1980s.

The Gothic cathedral is now hemmed in by buildings and traffic, but inside you'll find some fascinating remnants from its long history as the seat of the (now Anglican) Archbishop of Dublin and Glendalough. From as early as the seventh century, there may have been a small Celtic church on these grounds, and in about 1030, the recently converted Viking king of Dublin, Sitric Silkenbeard, built a wooden cathedral here. This in turn was replaced by the Normans, who between 1186 and 1240 erected a magnificent stone structure to mark their accession to power. Of this, the crypt (which is Dublin's oldest functioning structure), two transepts (which retain many original Romanesque carvings) and the remarkable **leaning north wall** can still be seen. The weight of the original vaulted stone ceiling caused the roof to collapse in 1562, bringing down the south wall and pulling the north side of the nave half a metre out of the perpendicular. In the 1870s, distiller Henry Roe lavished the equivalent of €30 million on the heavy-handed restoration you can see today, and bankrupted himself.

Tomb of Strongbow

Near the main entrance at the southwest corner you'll come across the strange **tomb of Strongbow**, the Norman leader who captured Dublin in 1170 and was buried here six

---

THE STORY OF THE CAPITAL

The vaults beneath City Hall now shelter **The Story of the Capital** (Mon–Sat 10am–5.15pm, Sun 2–5pm; last admission 1hr before closing; €4), a fascinating multimedia journey through Dublin's history and politics – with occasional hints of self-promotion for the exhibition's sponsors, the city council. The story is told through exhaustive display panels, slick interactive databases and a series of videos, complemented by an entertaining audio-guide narrated by Irish actress Sinead Cusack with snippets from leading historians. There are few exhibits as such, though a notable exception is the intricate city seal and its safe, which was instituted after the seal was stolen in 1305 and required the presence of all six keyholders.

DUBLIN AND THE MESSIAH

Opposite the cathedral on Fishamble Street once stood **Neal's Music Hall**, where **Handel** conducted the combined choirs of Christ Church and St Patrick's cathedrals in the first performance of his *Messiah* in 1742. As the takings were going to charity, ladies were requested not to wear hoops in their crinolines, to get more bums on seats. Jonathan Swift exclaimed, "Oh, a German, a genius, a prodigy." In a private garden on the site, the composer's reward is a statue of himself conducting in the nude, perched on a set of organ pipes. Every April 13, on the anniversary of the first performance, Our Lady's Choral Society gives a sing-along performance of excerpts from the *Messiah* here.

years later. The original, around which the landlords of Dublin had gathered to collect rents, was destroyed by the sixteenth-century roof collapse, and had to be replaced with a fourteenth-century effigy of one of the earls of Drogheda so that business could proceed as usual. The small half-figure alongside is probably a fragment of the original tomb, though legend maintains that it's an effigy of Strongbow's son, hacked in two by his own father for cowardice in battle.

The chapels

The chapels off the choir show the Anglo-Normans celebrating their dual nationality. To the left stands the **Chapel of St Edmund**, the ninth-century king of East Anglia who was martyred by the Vikings, while on the right is the **Chapel of St Laud**, the sixth-century bishop of Coutances in Normandy. The floor tiles here are original – those in the rest of the cathedral are 1870s replicas – while on the wall there's an iron cage with some of the bars removed, which used to contain the embalmed heart of twelfth-century St Laurence O'Toole, Dublin's only canonized archbishop, before it was stolen in 2012.

The crypt

If you descend the stairs by the south transept, you'll reach the **crypt**, the least changed remnant of the twelfth-century cathedral; formerly a storehouse for the trade in alcohol and tobacco, it's one of the largest crypts in Britain and Ireland, extending under the entire cathedral for 55m. Here you'll find the **Treasures of Christ Church** exhibition, which includes an interesting twenty-minute audiovisual on the history of the cathedral, as well as a miscellany of manuscripts and church silverware, and a mummified cat and rat, which were frozen in hot pursuit in an organ pipe in the 1860s. Look out also for a ropey tabernacle and pair of candlesticks made for James II on his flight from England in 1689, when, for three months only, Latin Mass was again celebrated at Christ Church (the existing cathedral paraphernalia was hidden by quick-thinking Anglican officials under a bishop's coffin). In extravagant contrast is a chunky silver-gilt plate, around a metre wide, presented by King William III in thanksgiving for his victory at the Battle of the Boyne in 1690.

Dublinia & the Viking World

St Michael's Hill • Daily: March–Sept 10am–6.30pm; Oct–Feb 10am–4.30pm • €8.50, children €5.50, family ticket €24; combined ticket with Christ Church Cathedral €13.25 • ☎ 01 679 4611, ⓦ dublinia.ie

Housed in the former Synod Hall of the Church of Ireland, **Dublinia & the Viking World** provides a lively, hands-on portrait of Viking and medieval Dublin that's especially good fun for kids (see website for details of special activities during the summer months). Themes such as the plague and the medieval fair are explored via walk-through tableaux of streets and houses, sound effects and lots of fun interactive displays. An archaeology room explores how the city's past has been unearthed, with a re-created excavation site and lab where visitors can examine medieval bugs under a microscope.

1

On the second floor, the Great Hall, where the Anglican bishops met until 1982, is now the home of Viking World, which uses a near-life-size ship, audiovisuals on the sagas and the chance to try on slave chains to convey Viking life. Before crossing the graceful, much-photographed bridge over to Christ Church Cathedral, it's worth climbing **St Michael's Tower**, a remnant of the seventeenth-century Church of St Michael and All Angels, for fine views over the city.

St Audoen's

Corn Market • May–Oct daily 9.30am–5.30pm, last admission 4.45pm • Free

Just to the west of Dublinia, on the corner of Bridge Street, stand two churches dedicated to St Audoen (in French, Ouen, seventh-century bishop of Rouen and the patron saint of Normandy). The monumental but largely uninteresting nineteenth-century Catholic version overshadows its neighbour, **Protestant St Audoen's**, which was built around 1190 and is now an intriguing tourist site. There are still services every Sunday, however, at 10.15am – the church has been continuously used for worship for over eight centuries, longer than any other in Dublin.

The most fascinating aspect of a visit is seeing the physical evidence of how the church's fortunes waxed and waned over the centuries. As it prospered through close association with the city's guilds, St Audoen's expanded in stages around its original single-naved church, including the addition, in 1431, of **St Anne's Guild Chapel**, making a two-aisled nave. The latter is now the main exhibition area, with informative displays on the parish and the guilds.

Until the Reformation, St Audoen's was the most prestigious parish church among Dublin's leading families. Afterwards, however, many members of the all-important Guild of St Anne refused to become Protestant and the congregation declined. By the nineteenth century St Audoen's had retreated to its original single nave, by the simple expediency of removing the roofs from the other parts of the church and letting them rot. You can now poke around the open-air **chancel** and **Portlester Chapel**, where, before the building was declared a national monument, locals would hang their washing out to dry.

Behind the Protestant church, steps descend to thirteenth-century **St Audoen's Arch**, the only remaining gate in the **Norman city walls** – a dramatic, though heavily restored, remnant stretching for 200m along Cook Street, 7m high and tipped with battlements.

St Patrick's Cathedral

Patrick St • Mon–Sat 9am–5pm, Sun 9am–10.30am & 12.30–2.30pm • €5.50 • ⓦ stpatrickscathedral.ie

The history of **St Patrick's Cathedral** is remarkably similar to that of its fellow Anglican rival Christ Church up the road. It was built between 1220 and 1270 in Gothic style, but its roof collapsed in 1544, leading to a decline that included its use as a stable by Cromwell's army in 1649. Its Victorian restoration, however, by Sir Benjamin Guinness in the 1860s, was more sensitive than at Christ Church, and it has a more appealing, lived-in feel, thanks largely to its clutter of quirky funerary monuments. Dublin has two Church of Ireland cathedrals because, in the 1190s, Archbishop John Comyn left the clergy of Christ Church and built his own palace and church here outside the city walls, and therefore beyond the jurisdiction of the city provosts.

To the right of the entrance in the harmoniously proportioned nave are diverse memorials to **Jonathan Swift**, the cathedral's dean for 32 years, including his and his long-term partner Stella's graves, his pulpit and table, and a cast of his skull – both his and Stella's bodies were dug up by Victorian phrenologists, studying the skulls of the famous. The **Door of Reconciliation** by the north transept recalls a quarrel between the earls of Kildare and Ormond in 1492. Ormond fled and sought sanctuary in the

JONATHAN SWIFT

"Here is laid the body of Jonathan Swift…where fierce indignation can no longer rend the heart. Go, traveller, and imitate if you can this earnest and dedicated champion of liberty."

Swift's epitaph in St Patrick's Cathedral, penned by himself and translated here from the Latin, conveys not only his appetite for political satire and campaigning, but also perhaps a certain prescience about the longevity of his fame. Born in Dublin in 1667 and educated at Trinity College, Swift went to England in 1689 to work as secretary to the retired diplomat Sir William Temple. Here he met Esther Johnson, nicknamed **Stella**, the daughter of Temple's housekeeper, who became his close companion – whether platonic or sexual, no one knows – until her death in 1728. Swift was ordained in the Church of Ireland in 1695, and wrote his first major work, **A Tale of a Tub**, anonymously in 1704, satirizing the official churches and the unscrupulous "modern" writers of his day. Sent to London to lobby the government for the relief of church taxes, from 1710 he was at the centre of England's political and literary life, a friend of Tory ministers as well as of Alexander Pope and John Gay. When the Tories fell from power, however, instead of the English bishopric he had hoped for, he was made Dean of St Patrick's, in 1713. Here he turned his caustic wit on Irish injustices, writing a series of pamphlets in the 1720s and 1730s including **A Modest Proposal**, one of the most admired works of irony in the English language, which suggests that the Irish poor sell off their children to the rich as "a most delicious, nourishing and wholesome food". At this time, too, he wrote his most famous work, the gloriously imaginative satirical novel, **Gulliver's Travels** (1726). Swift's later years were blighted by a progressive mental illness, and when he died, in 1745, he left his estate to build St Patrick's on James's Street, the first psychiatric hospital in Ireland.

cathedral's chapterhouse, but Kildare, eager to make peace, cut a hole in the door and stretched his arm through to shake Ormond's hand – so giving us the phrase "chancing your arm". Nearby in the north aisle of the choir, a simple black slab commemorates **Duke Frederick Schomberg**, who advised William of Orange to come to Ireland in 1686 but had the misfortune to be slain at the ensuing Battle of the Boyne. His family didn't bother to erect a memorial for him, so it was left to Dean Swift to do the honours here in 1731; in Swift's words, "The renown of his valour had greater power among strangers than had the ties of blood among his kith and kin."

In the northwest corner of the nave you'll find a slab carved with a Celtic cross that once marked the site of a well next to the cathedral, where **St Patrick** baptized converts in the fifth century. Back near the entrance, you can't miss the extravagant **Boyle monument**, which Richard Boyle, Earl of Cork, erected in 1632 in memory of his wife Katherine who had borne him fifteen children, including the famous chemist Robert Boyle (shown in the bottom-centre niche). Viceroy Wentworth, objecting to being forced to kneel before a Corkman, had the monument moved here from beside the altar, but Boyle exacted revenge in later years by engineering Wentworth's execution.

Marsh's Library

St Patrick's Close • Mon & Wed–Fri 9.30am–5pm, Sat 10am–5pm; closed for 10 days over Christmas and New Year • €3 • ⓦ marshlibrary.ie

Behind St Patrick's Cathedral lies the oldest public library in Ireland, **Marsh's Library**, which has remained delightfully untouched since it was built by Sir William Robinson, the architect of Kilmainham Hospital, in 1701, and still functions as a research and conservation library. Its founder, Archbishop Narcissus Marsh, was particularly interested in science, mathematics and music, and oversaw the first translation of the Old Testament into Irish. His books form one of the library's four main collections, totalling 25,000 works, relating to the sixteenth, seventeenth and early eighteenth centuries. They're housed in beautiful rows of dark-oak bookcases, each with a carved and lettered gable (for cataloguing purposes) topped by a bishop's mitre, and three screened alcoves, or "cages",

1

where readers were locked in with rare books. The library mounts regular exhibitions from its collections on subjects such as astronomy, and displays a death mask of its former governor, Jonathan Swift, as well as a cast of his companion Stella's skull.

The Northside

Running due north from O'Connell Bridge, broader than it is long, to Parnell Square, **O'Connell Street** is the main artery of Dublin's northside. This bustling thoroughfare was originally laid out in the fashion of the grand Parisian boulevards, but poor redevelopment since the damage caused by the 1916 Rising means there are few vestiges of its former grandeur.

Nowadays, the street is lined with fast-food outlets and ugly modern shop frontages, but the historic GPO remains a central focal point, opposite which soars the remarkable stainless-steel **Dublin Spire**. A number of other important monuments also remain, mostly positioned in the street's broad central reservation. Just north of O'Connell Bridge, you'll encounter first the imposing figure of the politician **Daniel O'Connell**, "The Liberator", who played a major role in nineteenth-century political campaigns to secure independence. The winged figures by his side represent O'Connell's bravery, patriotism, fidelity and eloquence, while the smaller female figure nearby symbolizes Ireland unchained. At the Abbey Street junction is a statue of the trade unionist **Jim Larkin**, who led the workers of Dublin in the 1913 Lockout, caught in the act of addressing a crowd.

At the very top of O'Connell Street stands an imposing statue of **Charles Stewart Parnell**, the leading late nineteenth-century advocate of Irish Home Rule. The plinth records his famous declaration:

No man has a right to fix the boundary to the march of a nation. No man has a right to say to his country, "Thus far shalt thou go and no further."

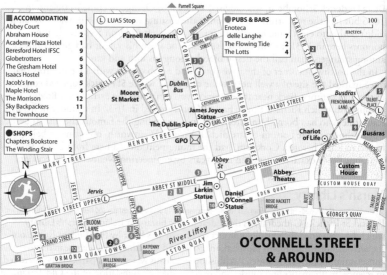

1

The streets around represent a consumer's paradise and, particularly on Liffey Street Lower and in the burgeoning **Italian quarter** centred on Bloom Lane (the result of a local developer's fascination with all things Tuscan), you'll find plenty of stylish bars and cafés. Notable cultural landmarks east of O'Connell Street include the **Abbey Theatre**, centre of the twentieth-century revival in Irish theatre, and, along The Quays, the opulent eighteenth-century **Custom House**.

Parnell Square, at the top of O'Connell Street, might lack the allure of its southside Georgian equivalents, but it still has a certain grace. The Square's north side hosts one of Dublin's premier galleries, the **Hugh Lane**, as well as the **Dublin Writers Museum**, an excellent place to learn about the city's literary history, while nearby is a centre devoted to the works of the acclaimed writer **James Joyce**.

To the west lie the **Old Jameson Distillery**, in the historic **Smithfield** area, and **Collins Barracks**, home to the National Museum's collection of decorative arts.

Dublin Spire

By the junction with Earl Street North stands the northside's most remarkable landmark on the spot where Nelson's Pillar stood until it was blown up by Republicans in 1966 – the frankly astonishing **Dublin Spire** or "Spike" as it's colloquially known. Designed by Ian Ritchie, this 120m-high stainless-steel needle, surmounted by a beacon, is easily the tallest structure in the city centre. Three metres wide at its base, it tapers to a mere 15cm at its summit. In the early morning or at dusk its surface takes on an ethereal blue colour, while at night it seems to loom ominously over the city. What the ghost of **James Joyce**, whose adjacent and somewhat rakish statue stands just down Earl Street North, would make of it is open to question.

The General Post Office

O'Connell St · **GPO** Mon–Sat 8.30am–6pm · Free · **Museum** Mon–Sat 10am–5pm · €2

Just to the left of the Spire stands one of O'Connell Street's few remaining buildings of major historical importance, the **General Post Office**, whose significance lies in its role as the rebels' headquarters during the Easter Rising of 1916 (see box, p.78). The building was constructed in 1818 but only its Ionic portico survived the fighting – and still bears the marks of gunfire. Following restoration, the GPO reopened in 1929 and inside its marble halls you'll find Oliver Sheppard's intricately wrought bronze statue *The Death of Cúchulainn*, representing a key moment in the Irish legend *Táin Bó Cúailnge* (see box, p.155).

A small museum in the corner of the building explores the influence of the post office on Irish society. The exhibition includes an extensive collection of stamps, one of the few surviving copies of the 1916 Proclamation – read by Pearse under the GPO portico on Easter Monday, declaring Ireland a sovereign independent Republic – and a display on the involvement of postal staff who were in the GPO during the Rising.

The Abbey Theatre

26–27 Lower Abbey St · Tours Mon–Fri 4pm, Sat 11.30am · €8 · ☎ 01 887 2200, ⓦ abbeytheatre.ie

Just east of O'Connell Street's southern end stands the **Abbey Theatre**, focal point for Ireland's twentieth-century cultural revival. It first opened its doors in December 1904 to present three plays, two by the poet and dramatist W.B. Yeats and the other by his patron Lady Gregory. The theatre's company turned professional in 1906 and Yeats and Gregory along with J.M. Synge became its first directors. The staging of Synge's own tragicomic *Playboy of the Western World*, with its frank language and suggestion that Irish peasants would condone a murder, provoked riots on its opening night, while later, in 1926, Seán O'Casey's *The Plough and the Stars* incited bitter outrage, the

1

THE EASTER RISING

The initial impact of some historical events often runs counter to their long-term effects, and such was the case with the **Easter Rising** of 1916. Truth be told, this inherently idealistic rebellion was a bungled affair from start to finish, and it was only the repressive response of the British Army, whose political overlords were unsurprisingly sidetracked by the seemingly more pressing affairs taking place in the fields of Flanders, that gave the event its pivotal role in attaining Ireland's independence.

The Rising was organized by the **Irish Republican Brotherhood** (IRB), a Republican grouping founded in 1858, led by educationalist and Gaelic cultural revivalist **Patrick Pearse**, with the support of the Irish Citizen Army's Dublin Brigade under socialist and trades union activist **James Connolly**. Impelled by the continuing failure of democratic means to achieve the goal of independence, they concocted a plan to take over by force, aided by the much larger **Irish Volunteers**, a Nationalist corps founded in 1913, and using arms acquired from Germany. The armaments were however intercepted by the British, and though the Volunteers' leader withdrew his support, the Rising still went ahead.

On the morning of Easter Monday, the rebels took control of a number of key buildings in the city centre and further afield (see p.590). They made the **General Post Office** on O'Connell Street their base, and it was from here that Pearse emerged to make his Proclamation of the Irish Republic. The British response was initially guarded, but a full-scale battle soon ensued, destroying much of the surrounding area and heavily damaging rebel-held buildings elsewhere in the city.

It took five days for the rebellion to be suppressed and its leaders captured. Dubliners decried the uprising at its outset, dismayed by the devastation ravaged upon their city by the fighting. Had the British simply imprisoned the IRB's leaders, it's extremely unlikely later political developments would have occurred as quickly as they did, but the draconian decision was made to execute all of them (with the exception of Éamon de Valera, who had US citizenship). In the process, the British created national martyrs, transforming the situation irrevocably and ultimately leading to a bitter war of independence.

audience regarding its view of the Easter Rising as derisive not least because the theatre had begun to receive state funding the previous year.

The original Abbey burnt to the ground in 1951 and its more modern, outwardly grim replacement opened in 1966. Informative guided tours – a must for anyone interested in the link between Ireland's culture and politics – take in both back- and front-stage areas and recount key moments in the Abbey's history. Its programme continues to include a range of drama, blending revivals of Irish classics with works by established writers such as Brian Friel and younger dramatists, while the much smaller Peacock Theatre in the basement is devoted to new experimental works. During the first years of the twenty-first century the theatre suffered disastrous financial mismanagement and was bailed out in 2006 by the largest grant ever awarded by the Arts Council of Ireland.

Backstage tours offer an insight into the history and behind-the-scenes work of the theatre; tours take place while plays are running on the Abbey stage.

The Custom House

The building and grounds are closed to the public

Opened in 1791, the imposing **Custom House** is one of several notable Dublin landmarks designed by the English architect James Gandon (others include the Four Courts and O'Connell Bridge). The Custom House cost the then unearthly sum of £500,000 sterling to construct, owing to its bulk and the intricacy of Gandon's architectural detail – and because it was constructed on a submerged mudflat which required covering by a layer of solid pine planks. Such cost proved even more extravagant when the Act of Union transferred customs and excise to London in 1800.

The building's grandiose Neoclassical exterior, more than 100m long, features heads sculpted by Gandon's contemporary Edward Smyth, with cattle heads symbolizing Ireland's beef trade and the others representing Ireland's rivers (including the Liffey above the main entrance). Its 35m-high-dome was based upon Christopher Wren's Greenwich Hospital.

After 1801, the Custom House became the administrative centre for the city's work on public hygiene and Poor Law relief, the latter demonstrated by an enormous Famine pot. The building suffered a major fire in 1833 and was completely gutted in 1921 after being set alight by the IRA. Subsequently restored, though with significant changes to its internal structure and façade, it housed various government departments and some of its more illustrious employees, including Brian O'Nolan, better known as the comic novelist Flann O'Brien, and the songwriter Percy French.

The Irish Famine Memorial

To the Custom House's east, and set between the looming presence of the International Financial Services Centre and the Liffey, is the **Irish Famine Memorial**. These six life-sized bronze figures were designed and cast by the Dublin sculptor Rowan Gillespie to mark the 150th anniversary of the worst year of the Great Famine (see p.587). That these stark, beseeching figures are staring eastwards towards Britain is not coincidental.

Dublin City Gallery – The Hugh Lane

Parnell Square North • Tues–Thurs 10am–6pm, Fri & Sat 10am–5pm, Sun 11am–5pm; tours Sun 2pm • Entry and tour free, but €2 donation suggested • ⓦ hughlane.ie

The elegant, Georgian, stone-clad Charlemont House, with its curved outer and inner walls and Neoclassical interior, has provided a permanent home for the **Dublin City Gallery – The Hugh Lane** since 1933. Sir Hugh, a nephew of Lady Gregory (see p.354), wanted Dublin to house a major gallery of Irish and international art. He amassed a considerable collection by persuading native artists to contribute their work and purchasing many other paintings himself, particularly from the French Impressionist school and Italy.

The gallery holds around half of the Lane collection (the rest is in London's National Gallery) and only a fraction is on display here at any one time, though you're likely to see works by Renoir, Monet and Degas, as well as Pissarro and the Irish painters Jack B. Yeats, Roderic O'Connor and Louis le Brocquy, and there are also stained-glass pieces by Evie Hone and Harry Clarke. The gallery usually hosts temporary exhibitions of more modern artworks.

Part of the gallery is devoted to a re-creation of Dublin-born painter **Francis Bacon's studio**, transported from its original location at Reece Mews in South Kensington, London, where the artist lived and worked for the last thirty years of his life. After his death in 1992, his studio was donated to the gallery by his heir, John Edwards, and reconstructed here with astonishing precision – more than seven thousand individual items were catalogued and placed here with verisimilitude in the reconstruction. The studio can only be viewed through the window glass, but among the apparent debris are an old Bush record-player, empty champagne boxes and huge tins of the type of matt vinyl favoured by Bacon, the fumes of which exacerbated his asthma. The surrounding rooms hold displays of memorabilia, such as photographs and correspondence, as well as a detailed database of every item found in the studio (accessible via touchscreen consoles) and large canvases from the painter's last years.

The gallery runs guided **tours** of the exhibits, a programme of **lectures and films** related to its current shows (various times; €5) and very popular classical-music **concerts** (Sun noon; free).

1

Dublin Writers Museum

18 Parnell Square • Mon–Sat 10am–5pm, Sun & public hols 11am–5pm • €7.50 • ⓦ writersmuseum.com

The **Dublin Writers Museum** highlights Ireland's literary history, featuring not just giants such as Wilde, Shaw, Joyce and Beckett, but also lesser-known figures like Sheridan Le Fanu and Oliver St John Gogarty. The ground floor contains a plethora of displays on particular writers or literary schools, and it is well worth picking up the free and entertaining audio-guide to receive background information on the authors. The hall downstairs, hung with modern paintings of writers, leads to an outdoor Zen garden where you can contemplate works you've purchased in the museum's bookshop.

On the first floor is the Gallery of Writers, an elegant salon with plasterwork by Michael Stapleton, which features James Joyce's piano and more paintings, of which the most impressive is John B. Yeats's portrait of George Moore. Beside this is the Gorham Library, which features numerous rare editions.

The museum's basement houses one of the northside's best restaurants, *Chapter One* (see p.101).

The James Joyce Centre

35 North Great George's St • Tues–Sat 10am–5pm, Sun noon–5pm • €5 • ⓦ jamesjoyce.ie

Occupying a grand eighteenth-century town house restored in the 1980s, the **James Joyce Centre** celebrates the work of perhaps Ireland's most imaginative yet most complex writer. Joyce spent part of his life living in the inner northside, and drew upon his experiences in the creation of his characters and the settings for his works. The building features decorative stucco mouldings by Michael Stapleton. The ground floor houses a small shop full of Joyceiana, such as books and prints, and an airy courtyard which includes the actual period door of 7 Eccles St, the fictional home of Leopold and Molly Bloom, two of the main protagonists in *Ulysses*, as well as a somewhat enigmatic, modernist Joyce-inspired sculpture of a cow.

BLOOMSDAY

Perhaps no other writer has so encapsulated the life, lore and mores of his native city as **James Joyce** so successfully achieved in his remarkable novels, most notably **Ulysses** (1922). So precise are the author's descriptions of the locales visited by the book's protagonists on the date of the book's setting, June 16, that it is possible literally to follow in their footsteps. This annual pilgrimage undertaken by Joycean aficionados across the city has become known as Bloomsday. Though you can undertake to cover the **Bloomsday** route independently (a *Ulysses* map is available from the Visit Dublin Centre on Suffolk St), guided walks are organized by the James Joyce Centre (see above). There are plenty of other associated events, including re-creations by actors of some of the book's central passages and concerts devoted to music referenced in the novel.

Strangely, for someone who documented his native city's life with such pride, Joyce came to loathe Dublin, once describing the place in a letter as a "city of failure, of rancour and of unhappiness", and concluding "I long to be out of it." Though his early works, such as the short-story collection **Dubliners** and the semi-autobiographical novel **A Portrait of the Artist as a Young Man**, draw heavily upon his upbringing, Catholic education and Dublin experiences, by the time of the latter's publication in 1916, Joyce had long abandoned Ireland. Not long after meeting a Connemara-born chambermaid, Nora Barnacle, having first dated her on June 16, 1904, the pair eloped to Europe. Other than two brief visits to Ireland, Joyce spent the rest of his life in exile living in cities across Europe – in Pola (now Pula) in Istria, Trieste, Zurich and, notably, Paris, where *Ulysses* was published in 1922 and where he finally wed Nora in 1931. Joyce's only subsequent published work was the convoluted **Finnegans Wake** (1939). When he died in 1941, *Ulysses* was still unavailable in Ireland (though it never officially fell foul of Ireland's censorship laws, booksellers were loath to stock copies), and was not published in the country until the 1960s.

The building's upper floors house a re-creation of the tiny room occupied by Joyce in Trieste, featuring various books, pianola music-rolls and a splendid collection of hats, as well as photographs of people and places associated with *Ulysses*, and touchscreen consoles tracing the development of the novel's plot and its variety of characters. Three short documentary films on the writer's life can also be viewed. The centre's **walking tour** (April–Sept Tues, Thurs & Sat 11am & 2pm, Oct–March Sat 11am; €10; 1hr), which begins here, is well worth taking if you want to learn more about Joycean connections with the surrounding area.

Smithfield

The area christened **Smithfield Village** by developers is more an ongoing process of urban renewal than an identifiable community, but at its centre lies the city's largest civic open space, cobbled **Smithfield**. Surrounded by rising blocks of executive flats, shops and restaurants, Smithfield still manages to host one of the city's major sights – the 300-year-old **Dublin Horse Fair**, which takes place from around 9am or so until noon on the first Sunday of each month and draws a number of traders and other horse-lovers from the city and outlying rural areas.

Collins Barracks

Benburb St • Tues–Sat 10am–5pm, Sun 2–5pm • Free • Ⓦ museum.ie

The **National Museum of Decorative Arts and History** is housed in the eighteenth-century **Collins Barracks**, which surrounds Europe's largest regimental drilling square. The buildings set around this quadrangle contain a wonderful series of galleries devoted to the fine arts of Ireland and selected works from abroad. Unquestionably, the best of these is Curator's Choice, on the first floor of the west block, which is selected by museum curators from all over Ireland. Among its draws are a medieval oak carving of St Molaise; the extravagant cabinet presented by Oliver Cromwell to his daughter Bridget in 1652; and the remarkable fourteenth-century Chinese porcelain Fonthill Vase. The Out of Storage section is another highlight, bringing together everything from decorative glassware to a seventeenth-century suit of Samurai armour. There are also displays on Celtic art, coinage, silverware, period furniture, costumes and scientific instruments, and there are usually plenty of temporary exhibits.

On the ground floor is a chain of thematically interconnected galleries, Soldiers and Chiefs, devoted to almost five hundred years of Irish military history. Apart from an array of helmets and weaponry, there's the remarkable Stokes tapestry, created by one Stephen of that ilk, a British soldier who devoted his spare time to the depiction of contemporary garrison life and was honoured to have his work shown to Queen Victoria on a royal visit to Ireland in 1849. Other exhibits trace the Irish involvement in the US Civil War and World War I with later examples of tanks and a de Havilland Vampire fighter plane, while, contrastingly, there's the 200-year-old Bantry Boat, captured from the French frigate *La Résolue* during the abortive invasion of 1796.

Croppy's Acre

Benburb St

Croppy's Acre marks the location where many of those executed for their part in the 1798 Rebellion are buried ("croppy" being a derogatory term for the rebels on account of many of them sporting closely cropped hair in the style of some French revolutionaries, an act in itself considered seditious) – a Wicklow-granite monument marks the precise location of their graves. The park is also home to Éamonn O'Doherty's *Anna Livia* sculpture, a bronze embodiment of her namesake the River Liffey.

1

The Four Courts

Inn's Quay • Mon–Fri 10am–4pm

The imposing riverside structure of the **Four Courts**, fronted by Corinthian columns and surmounted by an impressive dome, has seen many a legal hearing since it first opened its doors in 1802. Like the Custom House (see p.78), it was designed by James Gandon, and took some sixteen years to complete at a cost of £200,000 sterling. The Four Courts was seized by Republicans opposed to the Anglo-Irish Treaty in 1921, and heavily bombarded by Free State forces during the subsequent Civil War using, ironically, howitzers borrowed from the British. However, before the siege came to its inevitable end, the rebels accidentally set off explosives inside the building, destroying the Public Records Office and innumerable irreplaceable historic documents in the process. After rebuilding, the Four Courts reopened in 1931 and nowadays houses the High Court of Justice and, following the construction of the new Criminal Court of Justice on Parkgate Street, now only hears civil cases.

St Michan's Church

Church St • Guided tours mid-March to Oct Mon–Fri 10am–12.45pm & 2–4.45pm, Sat 10am–12.45pm; Nov–Feb Mon–Fri 12.30–3.30pm, Sat 10am–12.45pm • €5 • ⓦ stmichans.com

Constructed in 1095 by the Vikings in honour of a Danish bishop, **St Michan's Church** was substantially rebuilt some six hundred years later. Next to the church organ, reputedly once played by Handel, is the unusual Penitents' Pew, in which parishioners knelt facing the congregation to confess their errant ways. It is the church's **vaults**, however, that hold the most fascination. Guided **tours** descend an almost sheer staircase to view the contents of tiny crypts, which contain a dozen bodies, some dating back more than seven hundred years. These have been mummified by a process that involves two factors: the vaults' limestone walls, which absorb the air's natural moisture, and the methane produced by vegetation decaying below the floor. One of the mummies is believed to have been a Crusader, another a nun, and a third, which lacks a hand, may have been a repentant thief. Another crypt contains John and Henry Sheares, executed for their role in the 1798 Rebellion, as well as the death mask of one of its leaders, Wolfe Tone. Two other rebels, Oliver Bond and the Reverend William Jackson, are buried in the church's graveyard, and some reckon an unmarked grave to the rear houses the body of Robert Emmet, leader of the 1803 rising.

Old Jameson Distillery

Bow St, Smithfield • Daily 9.30am–6pm; last tour 5.30pm • €13.50 • ⓦ jamesonwhiskey.com

The buildings of the **Old Jameson Distillery**, where John Jameson set up his whiskey company, have long been turned over to a touristy but popular shrine to "the hard stuff". Guided **tours** whirl visitors through the process itself, from milling and mashing to the essential distillation element; while the separation of water from alcohol only occurs once in bourbon and twice in Scotch, the production of *uisce beatha* (Irish for "water of life", anglicized to "whiskey") involves a three-stage process. The tour ends with a tasting.

West of the centre

Unless you're a keen walker, you'll want to take a bus or LUAS tram to reach some of the city's western attractions. Highlights on the north side of the river include the vast grounds of **Phoenix Park**, with the dazzling interiors of **Farmleigh** mansion lying just beyond. Across the Liffey, the area west of the old city is dominated by the mammoth Guinness Brewery, whose wares are celebrated by the **Guinness Storehouse**. Further west lies the suburb of **Kilmainham**, home to the impressive **Irish Museum of Modern Art** and the forbidding **Kilmainham Gaol**, where the leaders of the 1916 Easter Rising were executed.

Phoenix Park

Europe's largest urban walled park, **Phoenix Park**'s undulating landscape sprawls across some 1750 acres. Originally intended as a deer park for Charles II (a small herd still ranges across its fields), the park takes its name from Phoenix House, the original residence of the British viceroys, whose title derived from the Irish *fionn uisce* ("clear water"). Much of the park is open space, sparsely dotted with trees, shrubs and wild flowers, though there are also areas of woodland and hawthorn. Overall it's an ideal place to escape the city's bustle, a popular venue for sports, and offers plenty of spots for a picnic.

By the park's Parkgate Street entrance lies the **People's Garden**, a pleasant area of formal flowerbeds and hedges. The nearby **Wellington Monument** took some 44 years to complete before it was finally unveiled in 1861. The obelisk – at some 60m – is the tallest of its kind in the British Isles – features bas-reliefs, using bronze from cannons captured at Waterloo, which depict scenes from the successful military campaigns of the "Iron Duke". West from here, alongside Military Road, is the derelict **Magazine Fort**, built on the site originally occupied by Phoenix House. It's an easy climb up the hill to take a trip around its walls and to take in some fine views.

Dublin Zoo

Phoenix Park • Mon–Sat 9.30am–6.30pm, Sun 10.30am–6pm; Oct–Feb closes at dusk; last admission one hour before closing • €16.50, children under 16 €11.80, children under 3 free • ⓦ dublinzoo.ie

Heading northwest from the People's Garden along Chesterfield Avenue will bring you to **Dublin Zoo**, spread over sixty acres, which focuses today on raising species threatened by extinction, such as Asian elephants, Amur tigers and waldrapp ibis. Its other attractions include the "African Plains", which has giraffes, rhinos and hippos, as well as aviaries, reptile houses, and enclosures for polar bears and gorillas. There is also a city farm for younger children.

Áras an Uachtaráin

Phoenix Park • Sat 10.30am–3.30pm • Free guided tours; tickets from Phoenix Park Visitor Centre only on the day

The impressive Palladian **Áras an Uachtaráin**, pronounced "arus an ucterawn", was the home of Britain's viceroys from the 1780s until Ireland's independence, and since 1938 it has been the official residence of the President of Ireland. Tours start from the Phoenix Park Visitor Centre (minibus transport provided) and whisk you through a section of the grandly decorated house, including the State Reception Rooms and the Presidential Office.

Phoenix Monument and Phoenix Park Visitor Centre

Phoenix Park Visitor Centre: April–Dec daily 10am–6pm; Jan–March daily 9.30am–5.30pm • Free

At the park's centre on Chesterfield Avenue rises the **Phoenix Monument**, dating from 1747, which more resembles an eagle or falcon than the phoenix it supposedly represents. To its southwest, by the US Ambassador's Residence, is the 30m-high stainless-steel **Papal Cross**, bearing testament to the spot where the late Pope John Paul II celebrated Mass in September 1979 before a congregation of around 1.25 million people.

Northwest of the Monument is the **Phoenix Park Visitor Centre**, which recounts the history of the park through the ages, focusing on its flora and fauna. Adjacent is **Ashtown Castle**, an early seventeenth-century tower house whose existence was only

1

uncovered when the former residence of the Papal Nuncio, which had been constructed around it, was demolished in 1978.

Farmleigh

Phoenix Park • Daily 10am–6pm • Free; hourly guided tours 10.15am–4.15pm • ⓦ farmleigh.ie

White's Gate on the park's northwestern fringe provides access to one of the most splendid buildings in the city, **Farmleigh**. Constructed in 1752 for the Trench family, the building was later purchased by Edward Cecil Guinness, the first Earl of Iveagh, as a rustic residence offering easy access to his brewery. Extensions were made in the 1880s, and the Guinness family remained in residence until 1992. Farmleigh was then purchased by the Irish government for use as a state guesthouse, and consequently tours may not be available if a visiting delegation is in residence. Tours commence in the dining room, whose unusual decorations include statues of Bacchus either side of the fireplace and a clock inlaid in its centre. The hall features Waterford-crystal chandeliers and a pair of debtors' chairs in which the paupers' legs would be trapped until they agreed to pay their debts, while the library contains four thousand items on loan from the Iveagh Collection, including a first edition of *Ulysses* and books dating back to the twelfth century. The Blue Room, which is dedicated to Ireland's Nobel Prize winners, has another strange fireplace – this one situated below a window. However, the real treat is the ballroom whose Irish oak floor was constructed of wood originally intended for Guinness barrels; the doors here, fringed with delicate linen portières, lead you out to a massive, plant-stocked conservatory. Behind the house there's a tearoom in the stable block and an extremely pleasant walled garden.

Farmleigh hosts a number of free **cultural events** from July to September, ranging from ballet and brass bands in the gardens to indoor concerts in the ballroom; tickets for concerts are strictly limited and only available via the house's website. There are also garden tours and a food market.

The Guinness Storehouse

St James's Gate • Daily: July & Aug 9.30am–7pm; Sept–June 9.30am–5pm • €18 • ⓦ guinness-storehouse.com

South of the Liffey, much of James Street, west of the old city, is centred around the colossal complex of the **Guinness Brewery**. Founded by Arthur Guinness in 1759, the Guinness Brewery initially manufactured ale, but in the 1770s started making porter, a drink so named because of its popularity with the porters of London's markets. Arthur's new brew, whose distinctive black colouring derived from the addition of roasted barley to the brewing process, found such favour that by 1796 it was being exported to London, and three years later ale production ceased altogether. From that point, Guinness and his successors never looked back and, at its peak in the middle of the twentieth century, their brewery produced some 2,500,000 pints of their now eponymous product a day.

The brewery is sadly not open to the public, but instead you can visit the seven-storey **Guinness Storehouse**, signposted from Crane Street, a high-tech temple to the black stuff. Its self-guided tour kicks off with the brewing process – a whirl of water (not from the Liffey, despite the myth) and a reek of barley, hops and malt – before progressing to the storage and transportation areas. A huge barrel dominates the section on the lost art of coopering, and nearby there's an engine from the brewery's old railway system. The remainder of the tour consists of an array of marketing memorabilia, supported by plenty of facts and figures about the Guinness empire, and there's a gallery on John Gilroy, an esteemed painter who designed many of the company's advertisements. Right at the top of the tower is the *Gravity Bar*, where you can savour your complimentary pint of perhaps the best Guinness in Dublin while absorbing the superb panorama of the city and the countryside beyond.

The Irish Museum of Modern Art

Military Rd, Kilmainham • Tues & Thurs–Sat 10am–5.30pm, Wed 10.30am–5.30pm, Sun & public hols noon–5.30pm; guided tours of the exhibitions Wed, Fri & Sun 2.30pm • Entry and tour free • ⓦ imma.ie

Based on Les Invalides in Paris, the **Royal Hospital** in Kilmainham was built between 1680 and 1684 to house war pensioners. Part of the building now houses the **Irish Museum of Modern Art** (IMMA), which has a justifiable reputation for its imaginative exhibitions, covering selections from both its own permanent collection of 3,500 works and loaned pieces. All shows are temporary and range from retrospectives of major international artists to new works by modern Irish painters and sculptors. Some of IMMA's most exciting exhibitions draw upon the museum's Outsider Art collection – works, largely paintings, by unschooled artists that explore the psyche – as well as the Madden Arnholz collection of Old Master prints, drawing upon the works of Goya, Rembrandt and Hogarth. The permanent "Old Man's House" exhibition recounts the history of the Royal Hospital site, from its days as an ancient burial ground and Viking settlement to the present day.

Kilmainham Gaol

Inchicore Rd • April–Sept daily 9.30am–6pm; Oct–March Mon–Sat 9.30am–5.30pm, Sun 10am–6pm; guided tours every 45min until 1hr 15min before closing • €6; Heritage Card

Beside **Bully's Acre**, one of the city's oldest cemeteries, lies **Kilmainham Gaol**, which holds an iconic position in the history of Ireland's struggle for independence and came to symbolize both Irish political martyrdom and British oppression. Opened in 1796, it became the place of incarceration for captured revolutionaries, including the leaders of the 1916 Easter Rising, who were also executed here. Even after the War of Independence, Republicans continued to be imprisoned here, though it closed in July 1924 after the release of its last inmate, Éamon de Valera – later to become Ireland's Taoiseach and president. **Tours** of the gaol provide a chilling impression of the prisoners' living conditions and spartan regime. Its single cells ensured that they were forced into solitary contemplation, and since the building was constructed on top of limestone, their health was often sorely affected by damp and severe cold in winter. Before embarking on the tour, it's well worth visiting the **exhibition galleries**. The ground-floor display includes a mock-up of a cell and an early mug-shot camera, and there is a small side gallery showing paintings by Civil War internees and a huge self-portrait of Constance Gore-Booth (see p.404), who was better known as the Countess Markiewicz, as the Good Shepherd. The upstairs gallery provides an enthralling account of the struggle for independence with numerous mementos, old cinematic footage of Michael Collins and the letter ordering the release of Charles Stewart Parnell.

The northern suburbs

You'll want fine weather for a trip north to the beautiful **Botanic Gardens** and the adjacent **Glasnevin Cemetery**, which has been the final resting place for major figures in Irish history since 1832. To the east lie **Croke Park**, a major sports arena and home to the innovative **GAA Museum**, the exquisite Georgian **Casino at Marino** and, at the end of the DART line, **Howth**, an attractive seaside village with a fine **cliff walk** (see box, p.86).

The National Botanic Gardens

Botanic Rd • Oct–Feb Mon–Fri 9am–4.30pm, Sat & Sun 10am–4.30pm; March–Oct Mon–Fri 9am–5pm, Sat & Sun 10am–6pm; guided tours Sun noon & 2.30pm • Entry and tour free • ☏ 01 857 0909, ⓦ botanicgardens.ie • From the centre, catch bus #13 from Merrion Square or O'Connell St, or #19 from South Great George's St or O'Connell St. The only entrance is on Glasnevin Hill, off Botanic Rd, where you'll find the visitor centre and café

The **National Botanic Gardens** on the south bank of the River Tolka in Glasnevin are a

1

THE HOWTH CLIFF WALK

Clinging to the slopes of a rocky peninsula and overlooking an animated fishing harbour, the village of **Howth** (rhymes with "both"), at the end of the DART line, is a good place to escape the rigours of the city centre when the weather is good, with some appealing quayside restaurants and pubs. By far the best way to appreciate the location is to do the **Cliff Walk** around the peninsula, taking in great views south over the city to the Wicklow Mountains and north to the Boyne Valley. The footpath runs for some 8km clockwise from the village round to the west-facing side of the peninsula, followed by a 3km walk by the sea along Strand Road and Greenfield Road to Sutton DART station; allow at least three hours in total. (Bus #31B, serving Sutton and Eden Quay in the city centre in one direction, Howth village or The Summit in the other, runs roughly parallel but well above the path for much of the way, along Carrickbrack Road, so you can bail out of the walk if you feel like it.)

You first head east out of Howth village along Balscadden Road to the **Nose of Howth**, before the path turns south, crossing the slopes above the cliffs, which are covered in colourful gorse and bell heather in season; for refreshment on this stretch, the area known as **The Summit**, just inland of the path, has a pub and a café. The southeast point is marked by the **Baily Lighthouse**, which, until March 1997, was the last manned lighthouse on Ireland's coastline. The path along the south-facing coast of the peninsula is the most spectacular part of the walk, providing close-up views of cliffs, secluded beaches and rocky islands.

---

great place to wander on a fine day, although their magnificent Victorian wrought-iron glasshouses offer diversion and shelter whatever the weather. Laid out between 1795 and 1825 with a grant from the Irish parliament, the gardens were, in 1844, the first in the world to germinate orchids from seed successfully, and, in August of the following year, the first to notice the potato blight that brought on the Great Famine. Nowadays, a total of around twenty thousand species and cultivated varieties flourish here, including an internationally important collection of cycads, primitive fern-like trees. Highlights include the rose garden, collections of heather and rhododendrons, the Chinese shrubbery and the arboretum.

Glasnevin Cemetery

Finglas Rd (with pedestrian entrance through the original Prospect Square Gate) • Museum Mon–Fri 10am–5pm, Sat & Sun 11am–5pm; guided tours 11.30am, 1pm & 2.30pm • Museum only €4, combined ticket with tour €8 • ☏ 01 830 1133, ⓦ glasnevintrust.ie • From the centre, take bus #40 or #40A/B/C from Parnell St

Founded as a burial place for Catholics by the nationalist political leader Daniel O'Connell in 1832, **Glasnevin Cemetery** is now the national cemetery, open to all denominations and groaning with Celtic crosses, harps and other patriotic emblems marking the graves of more than 1.5 million people. It's well worth timing your visit to coincide with one of the fascinating ninety-minute guided **tours**, which includes access to the renovated crypt of O'Connell. A small museum, which opened in 2010, has interactive exhibits telling the story of hundreds of the most famous people buried in the cemetery.

O'Connell himself is commemorated near the entrance by a 50m-high round tower, which managed to survive a Loyalist bomb in the 1970s. His corpse was interred in the tower's crypt in 1869, having been brought home from Genoa where he died (in fact, not all of his body is here: his heart was buried in Rome).

To the left of the round tower, O'Connell's political descendant, Charles Stewart Parnell, who asked to be buried in a mass grave among the people of Ireland, is commemorated by a huge granite boulder from his estate at Avondale, County Wicklow. Other notable figures among the dead at Glasnevin – most of them gathered around O'Connell's tower –include Countess Markiewicz (see p.404); Éamon de Valera, prime minister, president and architect of modern Ireland, and his old rival Michael Collins, the most charismatic leader of the successful independence struggle;

from the arts, there's Gerard Manley Hopkins's unmarked grave in the Jesuit plot (see p.67); W.B. Yeats's muse Maud Gonne MacBride; writer, drinker and Republican Brendan Behan; and Alfred Chester Beatty (see p.71). To the right of the tower is the Republican plot, with a memorial to hunger strikers, from Thomas Ashe who died in 1917 to Bobby Sands in 1981, while in front of the tower lie the recent graves of 18-year-old Kevin Barry and eight other Volunteers who were hung by the British during the War of Independence; originally buried in Mountjoy Prison, their bodies were moved here with the full honours of a state funeral in October 2001. For refreshment after your visit, exit via the pedestrian gate at Prospect Square beside *Kavanagh's (*aka *The Gravediggers*), a particularly atmospheric old pub (see p.104).

Croke Park and the GAA Museum

St Joseph's Avenue • **GAA Museum** May–Aug daily 9.30am–5pm; Sept–April Mon–Sat 9.30am–5pm, Sun & public hols 10.30am–5pm • €6 • ⓦ crokepark.ie/gaa-museum • **Stadium tour** 3–6 daily, see website for details or call ☎ 01 819 2323 to check availability and note there are no tours on match days • €12.50, including entry to the museum • **Skyline tour** hourly 10.30am–3.30pm • €20 including entrance to the museum • ☎ 01 819 2323, ⓦ skylinecrokepark.com

Home of the **Gaelic Athletic Association** (GAA), **Croke Park** is a magnificent, much redeveloped and now very modern stadium whose capacity of 82,000-plus puts it among the largest in Europe. Situated under the Cusack Stand is one of Dublin's finest museums, the **GAA Museum**, whose creatively designed exhibits provide an enthralling account of not only the sports of hurling and Gaelic football, but also lesser-known games such as camogie (the women's version of hurling) and handball. Historical and political contexts are explored in a thoroughly engaging manner – since its foundation in 1884 the GAA has always been irrevocably linked with Irish Nationalism. Thus the museum does not shirk from recounting key, politically sensitive events such as the first Bloody Sunday, when British troops fired on the crowd attending a match in 1920, killing twelve people in the process. On a lighter note, upstairs you can have a go at whacking a hurling ball or test your balance and reaction time via various simulations.

Taking the **stadium tour** is highly recommended, not just to view this remarkable arena at first hand, but to learn more about key events in its history – including, not least, the momentous decision in 2005 to suspend the GAA's constitution to allow professional Rugby Union and Association Football international matches to take place in the stadium while the Lansdowne Road stadium underwent redevelopment; previously only games of Irish origin, played by amateurs, could be staged here.

Visitors with no aversion to heights can take a skyline tour around a walkway 44m above the ground, for panoramic views of the city and its key landmarks.

The Casino at Marino

Cherrymount Crescent, off the Malahide Rd • Guided tours only: mid-March to late Oct daily 10am–5pm; last tour 45min before closing • €3; Heritage Card • ⓦ heritageireland.ie • To get here from the centre catch bus #20B or #27B from Eden Quay, or #27 from Talbot St, to the Malahide Rd, or take the DART to Clontarf, from which will leave a 15min walk

Sited in the suburb of Marino, the recently refurbished **Casino** is probably the finest piece of Neoclassical architecture in Ireland. The building was commissioned by **James Caulfield**, the first Earl of Charlemont, shortly after returning from eight years on the Grand Tour. Seeking to re-create an Italianate park with a *casino* ("little house" in Italian) as its focus, emphasizing the fine views of Dublin Bay that his estate then enjoyed, Charlemont turned to Sir William Chambers, the architect of Somerset House in London. Chambers also designed the earl's new town house at around the same time, which is now the **Dublin City Gallery – The Hugh Lane** (see p.79). Started in 1757, construction of the Casino lasted nearly twenty years and cost £20,000 sterling (equivalent to about €5 million today), depleting the estate to such a degree that the second earl was obliged to sell off his father's precious library and collection of art and antiquities.

The Casino's exterior is covered in exquisite and remarkably well-preserved carving in Portland stone, which reflects, notably in the ox skulls symbolizing animal sacrifice, the Enlightenment's preoccupation with pagan antiquity. To maintain the pristine Neoclassical appearance, Chambers disguised chimneypots as urns and used hollow Doric columns at the corners to act as drainpipes (with bronze chains inside to reduce the noise of the falling water). His most remarkable trick, however, was one of scale: from outside, the Casino appears to be a single-storey villa, but once inside you'll find three floors containing a total of sixteen rooms. To heighten the illusion, the main rooms have coffered ceilings, hidden doors and sky-blue domes to make them appear larger than they actually are. The standards of craftsmanship inside are as remarkable as on the exterior, with ornate plasterwork and beautiful wooden floors inlaid in geometric patterns. Nothing was allowed to mar the guests' views: the entrance doors convert into a window, and a series of tunnels was built under the surrounding land, including one that ran to the main house (now demolished) so that the servants wouldn't blot the landscape.

Malahide Castle and Gardens

Back Rd, Malahide • Daily 9.30am–4.30pm; last tour 1hr before closing • €12 • ☎ 01 890 5000, ⓦ malahidecastleandgardens.ie

Set on 250 acres of parkland in a pretty seaside town, **Malahide Castle** was home to the Talbot family for more than 800 years, until the last surviving member of the family died in 1973. The core building dates from 1185, making it one of the oldest castles in Ireland. Later additions such as the circular corner turrets, built after a fire in 1782, give it a fairy-tale appearance.

After extensive recent refurbishment, there's a new interactive exhibition on the fascinating history of the Talbot Family in the Great Hall, in addition to a new visitor centre in the courtyard. Guided tours take in the castle's extensive collection of eighteenth-century furniture and Irish artworks. The ornamental walled gardens, covering about 22 acres, are also worth exploring; they were largely created by the last Talbot to live in the castle, Lord Milo Talbot, an enthusiastic plant collector who is also believed to have been a Soviet spy.

South Dublin coast

A ride on a DART train south along the coast, as well as giving access to **Sandycove**'s James Joyce Museum and the charming historic neighbourhood of **Dalkey**, is a scenic attraction in itself, displaying the great sweep of Dublin Bay before dramatically skirting **Dalkey and Killiney hills** and arrowing off towards Bray and Greystones (see p.118).

The James Joyce Tower and Museum

Sandycove Point • Daily 10am–6pm; last admission one hour before closing • €7.50 • ☎ 01 280 9265, ⓦ jamesjoycetower.com • To get here, catch the DART to Sandycove & Glasthule station, from which it's a 10min walk down Islington Avenue then east along the seafront

The diverting **James Joyce Museum** in Sandycove is housed inside an impressive **Martello tower**, one of fifteen such towers erected along the coast between Dublin and Bray in 1804–06 against the threat of invasion by Napoleon. Built with 2.5m-thick, granite circular walls and an armoured door 4m off the ground as the only entrance, the towers never fired a shot. Joyce stayed here for just a week, in September 1904, a month before he left the country for Italy with Nora Barnacle. At the time, his host, the writer and wit Oliver St John Gogarty, was renting the tower from the War Office for £8 a year as digs during his medical studies. Joyce immortalized the tower as the setting for the opening chapter of his masterpiece, *Ulysses* – and Gogarty as "stately, plump Buck Mulligan" – and it's now the focus for readings and celebrations every year on June 16, Bloomsday (see box, p.80). Saved from closure by a group of locals in 2012, the museum is now run by volunteers from the local community.

Opened in 1962 by Sylvia Beach, who first published *Ulysses* in Paris in 1922, the museum displays Joyce's guitar, waistcoat and walking stick, as well as one of two official death masks (the other is in Zurich where he died in 1941). There are also copious letters, photos, and rare and first editions, notably one of *Ulysses* beautifully illustrated by Matisse. On the first floor, Gogarty's living quarters in the former guardroom have been re-created as Joyce described them, and you can climb up to the gun platform on the roof for panoramic views of Dublin Bay.

Dalkey

Around the coast from Sandycove, **Dalkey** (pronounced "Dawky") is a pretty seaside suburb set against the tree-clad slopes of Dalkey Hill. In medieval times, it prospered as a fortified settlement and the main port of Dublin, until the dredging of the River Liffey in the sixteenth century took away its business. Nowadays, with the building of the railway, Dalkey's characterful old houses and villas are much sought-after by well-to-do commuters, as well as celebrities seeking privacy.

Dalkey Castle and Heritage Centre

Castle St, Dalkey • Mon & Wed–Fri 10am–6pm, Sat, Sun & public holidays 11am–6pm; Living History theatre tours every 30min: Mon–Fri 10.15am–4.30pm; Sat, Sun & public holidays 11.15am–4.30pm • €8.50 • ☎ 01 285 8366, ⓦ dalkeycastle.com

Dalkey's main street boasts two fortified warehouses from the town's medieval heyday. Goat Castle – now known as **Dalkey Castle** – across the road from Archibold's Castle, serves as an attractive and well-designed **Heritage Centre**. The detailed exhibition, with panels written by playwright and local resident Hugh Leonard, covers the town's history, especially its transport systems and literary associations, the latter including an exhibit on Joyce, who set the second chapter of *Ulysses* in Dalkey. The castle interior is impressive in itself, and fine views are to be had from the battlements. The entry price includes Living History theatre tours in which suitably attired actors recount the lives and times of a selection of Dalkey's medieval residents.

DALKEY AND KILLINEY HILLS

A walk up adjoining **Dalkey and Killiney hills**, before descending to Killiney DART station, offers panoramic views of the city and its environs, and can all be done in an hour and a half from Dalkey DART station if you walk at a moderate pace. From Dalkey, head southeast on Sorrento Road, and then either take the easier route to the right up Knocknacree and Torca roads, or continue along cliffside Vico Road, from where steps and a path ascend steeply. On Torca Road, Shaw fans might want to track down privately owned **Torca Cottage**, where George Bernard Shaw lived for several years as a boy and where he occasionally returned to write in later years. On the way to Dalkey Hill's summit, with its crenellated former telegraph station and fine views over Dublin Bay, you'll pass Dalkey quarry, which provided the granite blocks for the massive piers of Dún Laoghaire harbour below.

From here, follow the partly wooded ridge up to Killiney Hill, where a stone obelisk, built to provide work during the severe winter of 1741, enjoys even more glorious views, north to Howth and south to Killiney Bay and the Wicklow Mountains. From the obelisk, you can quickly descend to the park gate on Killiney Hill Road; from here it's a fifteen-minute walk down Victoria Road and Vico Road through the leafy and exclusive borough of Killiney, to the DART station by the beach.

1

The Heritage Centre regularly organizes interesting guided historical walks in the town (June–Aug Wed & Fri at noon; €7), and can also arrange guided literary tours to settings in the work of James Joyce, George Bernard Shaw, Flann O'Brien, Hugh Leonard and Maeve Binchy , but only for groups of six or more (call for details). The Centre also participates in Bloomsday (see box, p.80), re-enacting the Dalkey schoolroom scene in *Ulysses* and staging a special Joycean evening of entertainment.

Dalkey Island

If you want to take a trip out to tiny **Dalkey Island**, some 300m offshore, then your best bet is to pay a visit to Coliemore Harbour, down Coliemore Road from the southern end of the town, and negotiate a trip with one of the local fishermen (high season only). Once a Viking base, the island features the ruins of a seventh-century church, a Martello tower and gun battery from Napoleonic times, a herd of semi-wild goats, and views of seals and a variety of seabird species.

ARRIVAL AND DEPARTURE — DUBLIN

Dublin's train and bus stations are centrally located while efficient local transport makes the city centre easily accessible from the airport and ferry terminals.

BY PLANE

Dublin Airport (☎ 01 874 1111, ⓦ dublinairport.com) is 11km north of the centre. The arrivals hall in both terminals (T1 and T2) has a tourist office (daily 8am–7pm in T1, daily 6am–7pm in T2), several ATMs and a number of car-rental outlets, while T1 also has a branch of the Bank of Ireland (Mon, Tues, Thurs & Fri 10am–4pm, Wed 10am–5pm), and a bureau de change (daily 5.30am–midnight).

Buses to the centre depart from outside the arrivals exit and the journey takes 30min–1hr depending upon the service and time of day.

By bus The most direct buses are the Airlink bus #747 (every 10–15min Mon–Sat 5.45am–11.30pm, every 15–20min Sun 7.15am–11.30pm; €6 single, €10 return), which runs via O'Connell St to Busáras, the central bus station; and #748 (every 30min Mon–Sat 6.50am–9.30pm, Sun 7am–10.05pm; same prices), which takes a similar route but continues to Heuston railway station. The slower but cheaper option (€2.35) is to take one of the regular Dublin Bus services such as the #16A to O'Connell St and College Green (every 10–35min Mon–Fri 6.50am–11.10pm, every 20–50min Sat 7.40am–10.20pm, every 25min–1hr Sun 8.30am–10.40pm) or #41 to Abbey St Lower, just off O'Connell St (every 15–30min Mon–Fri 6.20am–11.50pm, every 20–30min Sat 7am–11.45pm, every 30min–1hr Sun 7.15am–11.35pm). Additionally, the #746 (every 30min–1hr 15min Mon–Fri 9.15am–9.45pm, hourly Sat 9.45am–9.45pm & Sun 10am–7pm) runs to the centre and thence to Dún Laoghaire.

By coach Aircoach (ⓦ aircoach.ie) operates three services: from Dublin Airport to Stillorgan and Leopardstown via the city centre (every 15min daily 3.25am–midnight, every 30min midnight–3.25am); to Greystones via Ballsbridge (hourly); and to Dalkey via Sandymount and Dún Laoghaire (hourly). Tickets cost €6–15 single and €10–21 return, depending on how far you are going.

By taxi The taxi rank is also outside the arrivals exit; metered cab to the centre should cost around €250.

BY TRAIN

Information on train services and timetables is available on ☎ 01 836 6222, ⓦ irishrail.ie. Services listed are for Mon–Sat; extra services may run on Mon and/or Fri, but fewer on Sun.

Dublin Connolly Services from Belfast, Sligo and Rosslare terminate at Connolly Station, 15min walk east of O'Connell St and connected to the centre by regular buses and LUAS trams – it's also on the DART line.

Destinations Belfast (8 daily; 2hr 10min); Boyle (6–daily; 2hr 30min); Carrick-on-Shannon (6–8 daily; 2hr 10min); Drogheda (33 daily; 30min–1hr); Enniscorthy (3–5 daily; 2hr–2hr 15min); Newry (8 daily; 1hr 15min); Rosslare Harbour (Rosslare Europort; 3–6 daily; 3hr); Sligo (6–11 daily; 3hr 5min); Wexford (3–5 daily; 2hr 35min); Wicklow (4–6 daily; 1hr 10min).

Dublin Heuston Three kilometres west of the centre, Heuston Station serves trains from Cork, Galway, Kerry, Kilkenny, Limerick, Mayo and Waterford, and is connected to the centre by LUAS and buses #90 and #92. Left-luggage lockers are available on the concourse (€3 or €5).

Destinations Athlone (11 daily; 1hr 35min); Castlebar (6 daily; 3hr 10min–3hr 20min); Cork (12–15 daily; 2hr 50min); Galway (9–11 daily; 2hr 40min); Kildare (20–30 daily; 40min); Kilkenny (6 daily; 1hr 45min); Killarney (6 daily, most with a change at Mallow; 3hr 30min); Limerick (13–15 daily, most with a change at Limerick Junction; 2hr 15min–2hr 30min); Tralee (7 daily, most with a change at Mallow; 4hr); Waterford (6 daily; 2hr 25min); Westport (4 daily; 3hr 35min).

Tara Street and Pearse Two other southside stations, Tara Street and Pearse, serve DART and suburban railway

Note that some commuter trains from Co. Meath terminate at the Docklands Station, some 3km east of the centre.

BY BUS

Busáras Dublin's central bus station is on Store St behind the Custom House, some 10min walk east of O'Connell St. It serves Bus Éireann express coaches from all parts of Ireland (North and South) as well as the Airlink service and coaches from Britain. City buses run into the centre along Talbot St, a block to the north, while there are LUAS Red Line (see p.93) stops outside the bus station's northern exit or to the west on Abbey St Lower. Alternatively, a taxi can usually be hailed on Beresford Place just south of Busáras. There are left-luggage lockers in the station's basement (€6–10 depending on size).

Destinations Athlone (hourly; 2hr 5min); Belfast (20 daily; 2hr 30min–2hr 55min); Boyle (5–7 daily; 3hr–3hr 20min); Cahir (6 daily; 3hr 5min); Carrick-on-Shannon (5–7 daily; 2hr 45min–3hr); Carrick-on-Suir (6 daily; 3hr); Cashel (6 daily; 2hr 50min); Cavan (10–11 daily; 1hr 50min–2hr 10min); Cork (6 daily; 4hr 25min); Derry (11 daily; 4hr); Donegal town (11 daily; 3hr 45min); Drogheda (most services operate out of the Talbot St depot, but buses after 9pm leave from Busáras; hourly; 1hr 25min); Enniscorthy (hourly; 2hr 25min); Enniskillen (11 daily; 2hr 20min); Galway (15 daily; 3hr 30min); Kildare (mostly from Connolly LUAS stop; 13–15 daily; 1hr 30min); Kilkenny (7 daily; 2hr–2hr 30min); Killarney (5 daily, change at Limerick; 6hr 10min); Limerick (hourly; 3hr 40min); Letterkenny (9–10 daily; 4hr); Monaghan (20–21 daily; 1hr 55min); Newry (hourly; 1hr 35min); Omagh (19–21 daily; 2hr 55min); Rosslare Harbour (18 daily; 3hr 20min); Sligo (7 daily; 3hr 35min–4hr); Tralee (6 daily, change at Limerick; 6hr 10min); Waterford (13 daily; 3hr–3hr 30min); Westport (4 daily; 5hr–5hr 30min); Wexford (hourly; 2hr 50min); Wicklow (from Busáras or George's Quay; every 30min–1hr; 1hr–1hr 30min).

Private coaches from the north and west usually operate from and terminate at Parnell Square and O'Connell St, while those from the south and southwest tend to terminate at southside spots such as Nassau St – check with the service operator for details.

Note that most express services to Northern Ireland and Counties Donegal and Sligo also call at Dublin Airport. Additionally, the Wexford/Rosslare Harbour service now commences at the airport, picking up at Busáras en route.

BY FERRY

Dublin Port All services – except Stena Line's HSS (see below) – arrive at Dublin Port, 3km east of the centre. An unnumbered Dublin Bus service (4 daily; €3 single) meets arrivals and runs directly to Busáras and Heuston Station. The return service leaves Busáras daily at 7.15am, 1.15pm and 8pm. A free coach service to the city centre is available for Stena Line passengers arriving on the 1.50pm sailing from Holyhead; the return service departs from the Morton's Coaches stop on Westmoreland St at 7.15am.

Dún Laoghaire Stena Line HSS ferries arrive at Dún Laoghaire, 14km southeast of the city centre. The DART (see p.93) station is directly opposite the terminal and trains (€3.05) run every 20min to the centre (including the central Pearse, Tara St and Connolly stations). Alternatively, bus #46A (Mon–Sat every 5–15min, Sun every 15–40min; €2.35) runs from outside the Crofton Rd entrance to the station via Donnybrook to St Stephen's Green and O'Connell St. The Dún Laoghaire ferry terminal has a tourist office (Mon–Fri 9.30am–1.15pm & 2.30–5.30pm).

Ferry companies Irish Ferries ☎0818 300400, ⓦirishferries.com; Norfolkline ☎01 819 2999, ⓦnorfolkline.com; P & O ☎01 407 3434, ⓦpoferries.com; Stena Line ☎01 204 7799, ⓦstenaline.ie.

INFORMATION AND PASSES

Visit Dublin Centre The main Discover Ireland tourist office (Mon–Sat 9am–5.30pm, Sun & public holidays 10.30am–3pm; ⓦvisitdublin.com) is on Suffolk St, a short distance west of the Grafton St junction with Nassau St, and provides information and makes accommodation reservations (€5 per booking). There are also desks for currency exchange, the purchase of tickets for events and a branch of the Discover Northern Ireland tourist office. Outside is a touch-screen information console that accepts credit-card accommodation bookings. Discover Ireland's other offices are at the airport, Dún Laoghaire ferry terminal and 14 O'Connell St Upper (Mon–Sat 9am–5pm).

Listings information The national daily *Irish Times* and the local daily *Evening Herald* are useful sources of information, notably for cinema and theatre listings, and the former also produces a weekly Friday listings supplement, *The Ticket*. Free

listings magazines include *Totally Dublin* (ⓦtotallydublin.ie) and *Le Cool* (ⓦdublin.lecool.com), while listings websites *InDublin* (ⓦindublin.ie) and ⓦentertainment.ie are also useful. The O'Connell St Lower branch of Eason's stocks just about every magazine published in Ireland, along with all Irish and UK daily and Sunday newspapers.

Dublin Pass Available at any Discover Ireland Tourist Information Office or online at ⓦdublinpass.ie, the Dublin Pass provides free entry to over thirty of Dublin's top visitor attractions, as well as other special offers on theatre tickets, restaurants and shops. It also includes a one-way journey on the Aircoach service. It is available for one, two, three or six days, costing between €39 and €105 for an adult and between €21 and €54 for a child(5–15 years). It's well worth checking just how many attractions you'll be able to visit when judging whether this represents a good deal.

Heritage Card It can also be useful to acquire a Heritage

1

Card (€21) for free entry to attractions across the city – and the whole of the Republic (see p.43) – run by the Heritage Service (☎ 01 647 6592, ⓦ heritageireland.ie). Dublin attractions include: Áras an Uachtaráin, the Casino at Marino, Farmleigh, Kilmainham Gaol, Dublin Castle, National Botanic Gardens, Phoenix Park Visitor Centre, Royal Hospital Kilmainham, St Audoen's, St Stephen's Green and Croppy's Acre. Cards are available from Heritage Service sites or tourist offices.

Heritage Island The €6.99 Heritage Island brochur (☎ 01 236 6890, ⓦ heritageisland.com) offers a range o discounted admission prices, usually two visitors for the price of one or a percentage reduction, across the whole o Ireland (see p.43). Dublin attractions offering discount include Christ Church Cathedral, City Hall, Dalkey Castle Dublin Zoo, Dublinia, the GAA Museum, the Guinnes Storehouse, the Old Jameson Distillery and St Patrick' Cathedral.

TOURS

One of the easiest ways of seeing Dublin's attractions is a guided **city tour**, and there are plenty available – whether b open-top bus, on foot, along the river, or on a land and water tour. Adult prices are provided below, though most tou operators offer discounts for children, students and senior citizens.

OPEN-TOP BUS TOURS

If time is short a convenient way of seeing the sights is to take a ride on a hop-on-and-off open-top bus tour. Commentary is provided either by the driver (some of whom also readily break into fitting songs), an on-board guide or a pre-recorded tape. All tickets offer a range of discounts to the city's attractions.

All the tours follow roughly the same route, covering Parnell Square, Trinity College, St Stephen's Green, Dublin Castle, the cathedrals, the Guinness Storehouse, Kilmainham, Phoenix Park and Collins Barracks; some tours go to Glasnevin Cemetery. The full circular tour lasts around 1hr 30min, depending upon traffic congestion, and tickets are valid for 24hr from the time of first use.

Dublin Bus ☎ 01 873 4222, ⓦ dublinbus.ie. Dublin bus offers the daily Dublin City Tour, commencing from Cathal Brugha St, off O'Connell St Upper (daily every 10min 9.30am–3pm, every 15min 3–5pm). Tickets cost €19 (including a free walking tour) and can be purchased from the Dublin Bus office (see opposite) from the driver and from tourist information centres. The company also operates a Ghost Bus Tour (Mon–Thurs 8pm, Fri & Sat 7.30pm & 9.45pm; €28; not suitable for under-14s; 2hr 15min) visiting the city's spookier spots.

Irish City Tours ☎ 01 605 7705 or ☎ 01 458 0054, ⓦ loveireland.com. This company operates a City Sightseeing Tour (daily every 10–15min from 9am–7pm; €19). Tickets can be purchased from the driver and some hotels. Tours commence from outside 14 O'Connell St Upper.

LAND AND WATER TOUR

Viking Splash The award-winning Viking Splash tour (call ☎ 01 707 6000 for times, ⓦ vikingsplash.ie) provides a lively tour of the centre using reconditioned World War II amphibious vehicles known as Ducks and guides dressed in Norse costume. The tour culminates in a voyage from the Grand Canal Basin. Tours operate from St Stephen's Green North and tickets (€20) can be purchased at the departure points by telephone.

RIVER CRUISES

Dublin Discovered ☎ 01 473 4082, ⓦ liffeyrivercruise .com. A waterborne trip along the River Liffey. Sailing depart from Bachelors Walk (daily: March–Nov 11.30am 12.30pm, 2.15pm & 3.15pm, April–Oct 10.30am, 11.30am 12.30pm, 2.15pm, 3.15pm & 4.15pm). The 45min tou includes guided commentary and costs €14.

WALKING AND CYCLING TOURS

Several general and specialist walking tours are available covering all manner of subjects from the city's history and its physical and social fabric, to literature and music all led by informative and entertaining guides. If yo have an MP3 player, you can download one of a dozen o so free guided iWalks podcasts, providing a range o different walking tours with commentary from the notable local author and historian Pat Liddy (ⓦ visitdublin.com/Dublin).

The 1916 Rebellion tour ☎ 086 858 3847, ⓦ 1916risin .com. A tour that describes the events that lead up to the Easter Rising, the Rebellion itself and its aftermath Commences inside the International Bar, Wicklow S (March–Oct Mon–Sat 11.30am, Sun 1pm; 2hr; €12).

See Dublin by Bike ☎ 087 695 5976, ⓦ seedublinbybike .ie. Learn about Dublin's literary and rock-and-roll histor while pedalling between some of the city's most famou landmarks (2hr 30min, €20). The longer tour (3hr 30min €30) also takes in the fashionable southside residentia area, the fruit market, Grand Canal and the Docklands, an U2's recording studio, Windmill Lane. The tour departs from the Café Rothar bike shop (16 Fade St) at 10am daily.

Dublin Literary Pub Crawl ☎ 01 670 5602 ⓦ dublinpubcrawl.com. Starts upstairs at *The Duke* or Duke St and involves actors performing extracts from majo works in a number of pubs with literary connection (April–Oct Mon–Sat 7.30pm, Sun noon & 7.30pm; Nov– March Thurs–Sun 7.30pm; 2hr 15min; €12).

Fab Food Trails ☎ 01 497 1245, ⓦ fabfoodtrails.ie. Fo those keen to enjoy the local delicacies on offer, this guided saunter around the city's range of food outlets, with a decided leaning towards the artisan, will prove agreeably satiating (10am Sat all through the year and also Fri in summer; 2hr 30min; €55); starting points vary – call for details and to pre-book.

Hidden Dublin Walks ☎086 158 0949, ⓦhidden dublinwalks.com. Concentrating on the more salacious aspects of the city's history, this company offers a variety of tours (March–Sept daily; 1hr 30min–2hr; €13–25), including "Saints and Sinners" (focusing on the nation's moral foibles), a Northside Ghost Walk" and various other themed walks.

Historical Tours ☎087 688 9412 or ☎087 830 3523,

ⓦhistoricaltours.ie. A tour run by Trinity history graduates covering Dublin's development and major events, which starts from Trinity College's front gate (April & Oct daily 11am; May–Sept daily 11am & 3pm; Nov–March Fri–Sun 11am; 2hr; €12).

Traditional Irish Music Pub Crawl ☎01 475 3313, ⓦdiscoverdublin.ie/musicalpubcrawl.html. Two musicians guide you on a tour of half a dozen pubs, performing songs and music while recounting Ireland's musical history. Tours begin upstairs at *Oliver St John Gogarty's*, Fleet St (daily April–Oct 7.30pm; Nov–March Thurs–Sat 7.30pm; 2hr 30min; €12).

GETTING AROUND

The best way to get to know Dublin is on foot; however, to visit the city's outlying attractions you'll need to make use of the efficient and comprehensive **public transport** network.

BY BUS

Dublin Bus (ⓦdublinbus.ie) operates a network of 136 routes covering just about everywhere in the city and extending far beyond its boundaries into Dublin County, as well as Kildare, Meath and Wicklow.

Information Most of its bus stops display printed timetables and a basic route map, while many now have digital displays with real-time information on when the next bus is due to arrive. See ⓦdublinbus.ie for more ticket and route details, or download the excellent Dublin Bus app, which allows you to plan your route and search timetables by address. A free guide to the services, timetables and an excellent, free visitors' map are available from the company's offices at 59 O'Connell St Upper (Mon–Fri 9am–5.30pm, Sat 9am–2pm, Sun 9.30am–2pm).

Fares All bus fares are exact-change only and regular ticket prices range from €1.80 for a short ride to €3.05 for the longest journeys (child fares €0.90–1.30) within the suburban area, though there's a flat €0.70 shopper's fare for short-hop journeys within the city centre. If you do not have the exact fare and pay more than required, you will receive a refund voucher from the bus driver; this and your bus ticket should be presented at the Dublin Bus office (see above) to obtain a refund.

Timetables Most services operate around 6.30am–11.30pm on weekdays, starting later and finishing earlier on Sundays. Special Nitelink buses run in the small hours on a limited number of routes (Sat & Sun midnight–4am; every 30min–1hr; €6). These buses run from College St, D'Olier St and Westmoreland St; all routes carry the suffix "N" (e.g. 46N).

BY TRAM

LUAS (ⓦluas.ie) – the Irish for "speed" – currently operates two overground tramway routes (with a new route to connect both lines due to open in 2017), which are much quicker than buses and avoid traffic congestion. Trams run every 5–15min (Mon–Fri 5.30am–12.30am, Sat 6.30am–12.30am, Sun 7am–11.30pm).

Fares Singles cost €1.70–2.90 and returns €3.20–5.30 (children €0.90–1.10 and €1.70–2.10 respectively). Tickets can be bought from machines at the tramway stops.

The Green Line Commences at St Stephen's Green, then heads down Harcourt St before cruising along to the southeastern suburbs of Dundrum, Sandyford and Cherrywood.

The Red Line Runs from The Point in Docklands, joining a small branch from Connolly Station at Busáras, before heading along Abbey St to Collins Barracks and crossing the river at Heuston Station then heading southwest to the suburb of Tallaght.

BY TRAIN

The trains of the Dublin Area Rapid Transit system or DART (Mon–Sat 6.20am–midnight, Sun 9.20am–11.40pm; ⓦirishrail.ie) link Howth and Malahide to the north of the city with Bray and Greystones to the south via places such as Blackrock, Dún Laoghaire and Dalkey. It's certainly the quickest option for visiting some of the outlying attractions. Single fares range from €2.15–4.35, with returns at €3.85–8 (children's fares €1.15–1.75 and €1.90–3.05), though buying a Leap Card (see box, p.94) is a cheaper option. The suburban train services operated by Iarnród Éireann (ⓦirishrail.ie) utilize the same tracks as the DART, but stop at fewer stations (Connolly, Tara St and Pearse in the centre, the new Docklands station just east of the centre, Blackrock, Dún Laoghaire and Bray to the south and Howth Junction to the north). The Northern Commuter line from Pearse Station via Tara St and Connolly is the quickest means of making day-trips to Malahide and to Drogheda for Brú na Boinne.

BY TAXI

Dublin's taxis vary in shape and size from saloon cars to people carriers, though all are readily identifiable by an illuminated box on the roof displaying the driver's taxi licence number. Taxis can be hailed on the streat or at one of

1

TRAVEL PASSES

To save the hassle of buying individual tickets for each journey, the easiest solution is a pre-paid Leap Card. The three-day Leap Visitor Card (€19.50) is valid for travel on all Dublin Bus services (including Airlink but excluding Nitelink), LUAS and DART services within the short-hop zone (the entire DART network and suburban rail services as far as Balbriggan to the north, Maynooth and Celbridge to the west and Kilcoole to the south), and can be purchased in most newsagents. The electronic card must be validated at the beginning and end of your journey by touching it against the machines on board the bus or at LUAS and DART stations, until you hear the tone.

A bewildering range of **travel passes** is available from the Dublin Bus office (see p.93), newsagents and other shops displaying the Dublin Bus sign, and from DART and suburban railway stations. A three-day Freedom Ticket for tourists (adult €30, child €14) includes travel to and from the airport on the Airlink service (so is best bought at the airport's travel information desk), all Dublin bus services (except Nitelink) and the company's hop-on-and-off city tour (see p.92).

One-day passes for the LUAS service (see p.93) cost €6.40 and a seven-day pass is €23.50 when purchased from station machines. A combined one-day bus and LUAS pass is €10.

The price of most DART railway/suburban rail passes depends on the starting and finishing points of your journey. A one-day pass is €11.10 for adults or €18.90 for a family of two adults and two children.

---

the various ranks, such as at the northwest corner of St Stephen's Green, next to the Bank of Ireland on College Green, outside the *Westin Hotel* on Westmoreland St, in front of the *Gresham Hotel* on O'Connell St or on the western branch of Parnell St. The basic rate is currently €4.10 for a 1km journey for two people, rising to €8.10 for 5km and €13.40 for 10km, but prices are significantly higher between 8pm and 8am Mon–Sat and all day Sun and public holidays, and at any time when traffic congestion delays your journey. Taxis can use the city's bus lanes. Finding a taxi on the street in the city centre is much easier than it used to be. Smartphone users can download the excellent Hailo app (free), which allows you to order an approved taxi driver to collect you from your current location within minutes without any extra charge. City Cabs (☎01 872 7272), Satellite Taxis (Northside ☎01 836 5555, southside ☎01 454 3333) and Eurocabs (☎01 623 4100) are all reliable options. Most companies can supply a wheelchair-accessible taxi if booked one hour or more in advance.

BY CAR

Dublin's "rush-hour" covers the entire weekday periods from 7–10am and 4–7pm, and some areas, such as The Quays and Dame St, are best avoided at all times.

Car rental Rental companies include Atlas (airport ☎01 864 4859, ⓦatlascarhire.com); Avis (airport and 35–39 Old Kilmainham Rd ☎01 605 7500, ⓦavis.com); Budget (airport ☎01 844 5150 and 151 Drumcondra Rd ☎01 837 9611, ⓦbudget.ie); Hertz (airport ☎01 844 5466 and 151 South Circular Rd ☎01 709 3060, ⓦhertz.ie); Irish Car

Rentals (airport ☎01 814 4013 and 28 Parkgate St ☎01 648 5900, ⓦirishcarrentals.com).

Parking As for car parks, a good southside option is the Royal College of Surgeons multi-storey off the west side of St Stephen's Green (open 24hr, €4/hr or €10 overnight). On-street spaces are hard to find, but Merrion Square and Fitzwilliam Square are usually good bets.

BY BIKE

Following the likes of Paris and Vienna, Dublin introduced its own city-wide bike rental scheme, Dublinbikes (ⓦwww.dublinbikes.ie), in 2009. A three-day ticket costs €5 (credit/debit card required) and can be purchased from fourteen of the city's fifty bike stations, of which the most central are at St Stephen's Green East and West, Merrion Square West, Dame St, High St, the Custom House, Jervis St and Parnell Square North. You are provided with a personal ID number and a PIN of your own choosing and can then use your ticket to unlock a bike from the stands. The first 30min of any ride are free (as long as the bike is returned to a stand within that period); after that it's €0.50/1hr, rising to €6.50/4hr. Bikes come with automatic lights and a lock, but helmets are not provided. Note that €150 will be debited from your card if the bike is stolen or not returned within 24hr. Visitors can also rent a range of bikes by the day from Phoenix Park Bike Hire (just inside the Parkgate St entrance to Phoenix Park; ☎086 265 6258, ⓦphoenixparkbikehire.com; €10/day). Biking.ie (ⓦbiking.ie) rent good-quality mountain bikes (Ticknock; ☎083 414 7627; €40/day), as well as offering mountain-biking lessons and tours of Dublin and Wicklow (2hr 30min, €50).

ACCOMMODATION

The variety and standard of **accommodation** available in Dublin has improved a lot in the last decade, and room rates have come down considerably since the height of the boom in the mid-2000s. There is plenty to choose from for all budgets, with the northside and suburbs offering the best value. Hotels in the city centre tend to be expensive, though many offer discounts midweek or outside high season (especially via internet bookings), while B&Bs usually provide a very welcoming and comfortable alternative. If money is tight and you want to be near the action, hostels are the best option and almost all have private rooms. **Booking** in advance is always highly advisable, and is essential around major festivals such as St Patrick's Day, in July and August, and on weekends all year round, especially when major concerts or sporting events are taking place. There is one campsite on Dublin's outskirts.

HOTELS AND B&BS

Many of the city's top-range hotels are located around St Stephen's Green, though the northside also has some chic options. Temple Bar is the most central, but as the location of choice for hen and stag parties it can be very noisy at night. Dublin has a staggering number of B&Bs and you'll find economically priced options on the northside's Gardiner St or in the pleasant southside suburbs of Ballsbridge, Donnybrook and Rathmines, which are all within easy reach of the centre. All rooms listed provide en-suite bathrooms and wi-fi unless stated otherwise.

TEMPLE BAR

The Clarence 6–8 Wellington Quay ☎ 01 407 0800, ⓦ theclarence.ie; map p.69. Owned by U2, this former bolt hole for priests and lawyers up from the country has been transformed into an informal, luxury hotel. It contains the *Cleaver East* restaurant in the former ballroom and the swish *Octagon Bar*, as well as a two-storey penthouse suite (€1500/night) used by sundry rock stars. All 45 rooms come with a state-of-the-art multimedia system, and some have balconies overlooking the city. **€170**

Harding Hotel Copper Alley, Fishamble St ☎ 01 679 6500, ⓦ hardinghotel.ie; map p.69. Massively popular due to its budget-conscious high-season room rate and spacious twins, doubles, triples and family accommodation, the *Harding* also includes the atmospheric *Darkey Kelly's* bar taking its name from an eighteenth-century Copper Alley brothel-keeper), which supplies good food and a regular programme of live entertainment. **€109**

The Morgan 10 Fleet St ☎ 01 643 7000, ⓦ themorgan com; map. p.69. Sheer bliss in terms of the quality of its accommodation and with crisply designed rooms throughout, this establishment fully merits the term bijou. The hotel's rooms vary in size and facilities, but none is anything less than extremely comfortable. **€126**

Temple Bar Hotel 13–17 Fleet St ☎ 01 677 3333, ⓦ templebarhotel.com; map. p.69. From its bright and airy lobby to its attractive, modern en-suite bedrooms, the *Temple Bar* has a high reputation for service and good value, though some of its front-facing rooms can suffer from late-night street noise. The hotel's bar is a popular spot and there's reduced-rate secure car parking nearby. **€100**

THE INNER SOUTHSIDE

Brooks Hotel Drury St ☎ 01 670 4000, ⓦ brookshotel ie; map pp.60–61. Compact, four-star boutique hotel, on a quiet road that's handy for Temple Bar and Grafton St,

with bright and airy bedrooms, a small gym and sauna, and very friendly service. **€200**

Buswells Hotel 23–27 Molesworth St ☎ 01 614 6500, ⓦ buswells.ie; map. pp.60–61. Popular with politicians thanks to its proximity to Leinster House, *Buswells* offers pleasantly designed en-suite rooms in a converted Georgian town house. Ornate plasterwork and fireplaces testify to those origins and the hotel also has a splendid carvery/restaurant, its own bar and secure overnight parking. **€200**

Central Hotel 1–5 Exchequer St ☎ 01 679 7302, ⓦ centralhotel.ie; map pp.60–61. This centrally located place has been in business since 1887, making it, as its name suggests, one of the city's oldest hotels. Rooms are well equipped and reasonably well soundproofed, though some can feel a little cramped. The first-floor *Library Bar* is a popular spot for everything from morning coffee to pre-dinner drinks. **€129**

The Fitzwilliam Hotel St Stephen's Green ☎ 01 478 7000, ⓦ fitzwilliamhotel.com; map pp.60–61. With an expansive foyer and luxurious, colourful rooms designed by Sir Terence Conran, the *Fitzwilliam* offers deluxe accommodation in a marvellous central location. The double-room rate ranges considerably depending on size and facilities (though all include free internet access, a CD player and fresh flowers supplied daily), and there's also a beauty salon, roof garden, bars, secure parking and restaurant, and a penthouse suite (€3500/night) which includes its own private bar and grand piano. **€229**

Harrington Hall 70 Harcourt St ☎ 01 475 3497, ⓦ harringtonhall.com; map pp.60–61. Occupying elegant Georgian premises south of St Stephen's Green, this guesthouse has 28 thoughtfully furnished and generously sized rooms, complete with secondary glazing and ceiling fans. Substantial discounts available in low season. Free parking. **€159**

Jurys Inn Christchurch Christchurch Place ☎ 01 454 0000, ⓦ www.jurysinn.com; map pp.60–61. Bang opposite the cathedral (though don't compare the relative architectural merits), *Jurys* is a well-liked spot for families thanks to its low-cost room rate per night. Rooms are both restful and functional and the hotel offers a restaurant, café and bar. **€139**

★ **Kelly's Hotel** 36 Great George's St South ☎ 01 648 0010, ⓦ kellysdublin.com; map pp.60–61. This southside stalwart has been rejuvenated by the owners of *L'Gueuleton* (see p.101) downstairs, where a complimentary breakfast is served daily. Doubles are fashionably, but not uncomfortably, minimalist; the executive rooms offer more

1

space. The penthouse suite sleeps four people (€300). Doubles €129

Kilronan House 70 Adelaide Rd ☎01 475 5266, ⓦdublinn.com; map pp.60–61. It's hard to top the welcome at this fine Georgian town house which features elegant decoration, including Waterford crystal chandeliers, and orthopedic mattresses in all its rooms. Breakfast and free parking included. The economy rooms have shared bathrooms. €105

★**Merrion Hotel** Merrion St Upper ☎01 603 0600, ⓦmerrionhotel.com; map pp.60–61. The Duke of Wellington's dismissal of his Irish connections, "being born in a stable doesn't make one a horse", rings even hollower now that his birthplace at no. 24 Merrion St Upper is part of this very civilized luxury hotel. Four eighteenth-century town houses have been elegantly redecorated in Georgian style and hung with a superb collection of Irish art, overlooking a private landscaped garden. Facilities include the beautiful Tethra Spa and *Cellar Restaurant* (see p.100). €280

Mont Clare Hotel Merrion St Lower ☎01 607 3900, ⓦmontclarehotel.ie; map pp.60–61. Just off Merrion Square, this three-star hotel housed in a former bank has classically furnished rooms with a/c and plasma TVs, providing a high degree of comfort at excellent prices, as well as an attractive location. €140

The Portobello Hotel 33 Richmond St South ☎01 475 2715, ⓦportobellohotel.ie; map pp.56–57. Actually accessed by the canal-side Charlemont Mall and with reception on the first floor, this welcoming 24-room establishment has incredibly spacious and reasonably priced en-suite doubles. Most have views of the canal and to the Dublin Mountains beyond and all also have baths and showers. €189

Radisson Blu Royal Golden Lane ☎01 898 2900, ⓦradissonblue.ie; map pp.60–61. A spruce, modernist hotel tucked away off Aungier St with elegant and well-accoutred rooms and suites and its own brasserie, fitness club and secure parking. Doubles €209, suites €269

★**The Shelbourne** 27 St Stephen's Green ☎01 663 4500, ⓦmarriott.com; map pp.60–61. The grande dame of Dublin hotels has been gleamingly renovated and expanded by Marriott, under its "Renaissance" brand. A highlight of the new look is the gilded lobby, where the old lift has been removed to reveal the grand staircase. The *Horseshoe Bar* (see p.102) and the Lord Mayor's Lounge, where you can tuck into traditional afternoon tea, accompanied by views of the Green and the tinkling of a piano, have been refurbished but, mercifully, not reconstructed. There's a fitness room and a luxurious new spa and pool. €300

Stauntons on the Green 83 St Stephen's Green ☎01 478 2300, ⓦstauntonsonthegreen.ie; map pp.60–61. Set in an unbeatable location on the south side of the Green with its own private gardens, this luxurious guesthouse has thirty en-suite rooms, which offer both comfort and style befitting this Georgian building. All the rooms overlook either the Green or Iveagh Gardens. €149

Stephen's Green Hotel St Stephen's Green ☎01 607 3600, ⓦocallaghanhotels.com; map pp.60–61. Swish, classy, yet thoroughly modernist, this hotel occupies a spot overlooking the southwestern corner of the Green. As well as its lively bar and economically priced bistro, fitness centre and libraries, the hotel provides 68 spacious double rooms equipped with fridges and power showers and a number of even more luxurious suites. Doubles €230, suites €270

The Westbury Harry St, off Grafton St ☎01 679 1122, ⓦdoylecollection.com; map pp.60–61. The glossy lobby of this luxurious five-star hotel is an indicator of the treat that lie in store. Its bedrooms are not so much furnished as designed to pamper, and the range of facilities on offer includes a fitness centre, a svelte bar specializing in champagne cocktails, and underground parking. High season bargains without breakfast can be as low as €143 for a double. €290

The Westin Dublin Westmoreland St ☎01 645 1000, ⓦwestin.com/dublin; map pp.60–61. Hiding behind the façade of the old Allied Irish Bank building just north of Trinity College, the *Westin* is a marvellously luxurious establishment. Its 163 bedrooms feature a blend of mahogany furniture and sensitive colour design and are elegantly equipped, and some now include personal workout facilities. The bar is housed in the former bank's vaults, and the lounge has a stunning glass roof. Breakfast not included. €249

THE NORTHSIDE

Academy Plaza Hotel Findlater Place, Cathal Brugha St ☎01 878 0666, ⓦacademyplazahotel.ie; map p.76. Tucked away behind O'Connell St, this well-appointed Best Western hotel sports simply furnished en-suite rooms as well as a fine range of breakfasts and a friendly bar. Early internet bookings can be as low as €60/double, including breakfast. €135

Ashling Hotel Parkgate St ☎01 677 2324, ⓦashlinghotel.ie; map pp.56–57. Conveniently set near Heuston Station, this modern four-star hotel's luxuriously furnished rooms provide all essential amenities and plenty of space, as well as a pleasant bar and excellent breakfasts; secure parking is available. Rates exclude breakfast. €180

Belvedere Hotel Great Denmark St ☎01 873 7700, ⓦbelvederehoteldublin.com; map pp.56–57. The *Belvedere's* Georgian exterior encompasses a very amenable modern hotel. Rooms are attractively furnished, bright and airy, and most are wheelchair accessible. Big discounts available in off-season, with rates as low as €79. **€160**

Beresford Hotel IFSC Store St ☎01 813 4700, ⓦberesfordhotelifsc.com; map p.76. Though its setting opposite Busáras isn't exactly auspicious, the *Beresford's* attractive modern interior, friendly staff and one hundred well-accoutred bedrooms more than compensate. As well as a fitness room and a free shuttle to the airport, the hotel has an attached Italian restaurant and a cosmopolitan café-bar. Breakfast not included. **€179**

Clifden Guesthouse 32 Gardiner Place ☎01 874 6364, ⓦclifdenhouse.com; map pp.56–57. One of the northside's most reliable options, this comfortable Georgian house well maintained by very friendly hosts. Fifteen pleasant en-suite rooms include doubles as well as a triple and a family room. Off-street parking is available. **€140**

The Gresham Hotel 23 O'Connell St Upper ☎01 874 6881, ⓦgresham-hotels.com; map p.76. The *Gresham* isn't just a splendidly equipped four-star hotel, it is also one of Dublin's landmarks, a place where you don't have to be a guest to enjoy afternoon tea in the opulent surroundings of its lobby or sample the meals in its restaurant. Rooms are pleasantly furnished and spacious while the individually designed penthouse suites, including ones devoted to artist Marc Lamb, architect and designer of the Spire) Ian Ritchie, and actors Liz Taylor and Richard Burton, offer differing views of the city. Doubles **€180**, suites from **€300**

Jurys Inn Custom House Custom House Quay ☎01 607 5000, ⓦjurysinns.com; map pp.56–57. The riverside location really is hard to beat and the views of Dublin's developing docklands are staggering from rooms on the upper storeys. Facilities include a bar, café and restaurant. **€139**

Maldron Hotel Smithfield Village ☎01 485 0900, ⓦmaldronhotels.com; map pp.56–57. A great addition to the Smithfield area, this new-build hotel provides excellently equipped and furnished rooms, tastefully decorated using primary colours, and has a remarkably good-value restaurant. There's secure overnight parking nearby and it's handily placed for music sessions at *The Cobblestone* (see p.105). Excellent mid-week rates. **€180**

Maple Hotel 74 Gardiner St Lower ☎01 855 5442, ⓦmaplehotel.com; map p.76. A decent budget option on a busy street, this comfortable B&B provides en-suite rooms, all equipped with TV, telephone and tea/coffee-making facilities, as well as an excellent Irish breakfast. Limited parking is available. **€119**

Marian Guest House 21 Gardiner St Upper ☎01 874 4129, ⓦmarianguesthouse.ie; map pp.56–57. Immensely popular due to its budget prices and warm welcome, the *Marian* offers clean and comfortable en-suite and standard rooms, plus a filling breakfast. Most have

shared bathrooms but some en suites are available. There's off-street parking, and buses #16 and #41 stop around the corner on Dorset St Upper. **€60**

The Morrison Ormond Quay Lower ☎01 887 2400, ⓦmorrisonhotel.ie; map p.76. Following a €7 million refurbishment in 2013, shiny surfaces and clean lines dominate at this swish temple of minimalism. While natural tones prevail in the lobby and ultra-cool bar, the luxurious rooms are dazzlingly white with shocks of vibrant pinks and purples. The penthouse (from €1000) offering lush furnishings and all manner of creature comforts has spectacular riverside views. Doubles **€280**, suites **€360**

The Townhouse 47–48 Gardiner St Lower ☎01 878 8808, ⓦtownhouseofdublin.com; map p.76. This superbly converted Georgian house remains an oasis of calm in one of the city's busiest streets. Elegant twins, doubles, triples and a family room are thoughtfully decorated and include sizeable en-suite facilities (though the cheapest rooms have shared bathrooms). A buffet breakfast is served in an elegant dining room with a balcony, and there are secure off-street parking spaces. **€139**

★**Two Rooms in Dublin** 18 Summer St North ☎01 856 0013, ⓦtworoomsindublin.com; map pp.56–57. The two rooms in this beautifully decorated Georgian home, in a residential area a 10min walk from O'Connell St, are a delight, with Egyptian cotton sheets on Victorian cast-iron beds, and silk robes for lounging. The welcoming hosts cook up a gorgeous three-course breakfast, which changes daily, and also offer baked treats and coffee on arrival. Two-night minimum stay. **€100**

HOSTELS

Dublin has numerous hostels, the majority of which offer both dormitory accommodation (€12–25/person, depending on the season) and private rooms, usually sleeping between two and four people (€25–60/person). Most rooms are en suite and the standard of private rooms is often as good as at B&Bs. Several Dublin hostels belong to the IHH, though a few are members of the IHO (see p.33) – all those listed below are affiliated to IHH unless stated otherwise. Many hostels offer free breakfast and provide internet access.

THE SOUTHSIDE

Ashfield House 19–20 D'Olier St ☎01 679 7734, ⓦashfieldhouse.ie; map pp.60–61. One of the centre's most popular choices provides over 130 beds in a variety of bright and spacious rooms, all with en-suite facilities. Dorms come in a variety of sizes, from four to 18-bed, as well as comfortable doubles. Dorms **€11**, doubles **€55**

Avalon House 55 Aungier St ☎01 475 0001, ⓦavalon-house.ie; map pp.60–61. A 5min walk south of South Great George's St, *Avalon House* occupies a former medical school. It's a large hostel with 281 beds, kitchen facilites, a

1

TV and games room, and a café serving excellent coffee. Dorms €13, doubles €55

Barnacles Temple Bar House, 19 Temple Lane ☎ 01 671 6277, ⓦ barnacles.ie; map p.69. A modern and funky hostel right in the heart of Temple Bar, with brightly coloured en-suite rooms and comfortable common areas for lounging. Dorms €16, doubles €68

Kinlay House 2–12 Lord Edward St ☎ 01 679 6644, ⓦ kinlaydublin.ie; map pp.60–61. A very lively and busy hostel near Christ Church Cathedral, *Kinlay House* offers good-value private rooms as well as both small six-bed and much bigger 24-bed dorms. There's a large kitchen as well as a café, and computers for internet access. Dorms €15, doubles €50

Oliver St John Gogarty's 18–21 Anglesea St ☎ 01 671 1822, ⓦ gogartys.ie; map p.69. This well-equipped hostel above a popular tourist pub in the centre of Temple Bar has more than 130 beds in a range of accommodation, including standard and en-suite twins and up to eight- and ten-bed dorms. Kitchen and laundry facilities are available. Dorms €12, doubles €54

THE NORTHSIDE

Abbey Court 29 Bachelors Walk ☎ 01 878 0800, ⓦ abbey-court.com; map p.76. Right next to O'Connell Bridge, this upmarket, well-designed hostel provides en-suite twins/doubles and dorms ranging from four to twelve beds. Very security conscious, access is via keycards and there are lockers in every room. There is also a café, kitchen, two TV lounges, a conservatory and a barbecue area. Dorms €18, doubles €80

Abraham House 82–83 Gardiner St Lower ☎ 01 855 0600, ⓦ abraham-house.ie; map p.76. One of the larger northside hostels, *Abraham House* has both a friendly staff and atmosphere. En-suite rooms range in size from triples to four-, six-, eight-, ten- and twenty-bed dorms. There's a good kitchen and lockers. Dorms €10, doubles €72

Dublin International Youth Hostel Mountjoy St ☎ 01 830 1766, ⓦ anoige.ie; map pp.56–57. A gargantuan 293-bed establishment in a somewhat grim northside area, just west of the Black Church and Dorset St Upper, this An Óige flagship is housed in a former convent school. Much of the accommodation is in largish dorms, though there are some private and four-bed rooms. The former nun's chapel has been converted into a reasonably priced restaurant, while the old confessional box now houses a public telephone. Dorms €17, doubles €50

★ **Globetrotters** 46 Gardiner St Lower ☎ 01 873 5893, ⓦ globetrottersdublin.com; map p.76. Under the same excellent management as *The Townhouse*, this 94-bed hostel offers six- to twelve-bed dorms, equipped with some of the most comfortable bunks in Dublin. All are en-suite, there's a good kitchen, and a full Irish breakfast is included in the price, which can be eaten in the Japanese garden out back. Dorms €18

Isaacs Hostel 2–5 Frenchman's Lane ☎ 01 855 6125, ⓦ isaacs.ie; map p.76. Dublin's oldest independent hostel is still one of its best and consists of four- to sixteen-bed dorms and some cosy twin-bedded private rooms. Although none is en suite, the shared bathrooms are well equipped with hairdryers and straighteners. Efficiently run and very welcoming; facilities include a high-quality kitchen, a café, a sauna, a small garden hosting barbecues in summer, and internet access. Dorms €15, triples €85, twins €60

★ **Jacobs Inn** 21–28 Talbot Place ☎ 01 855 5660, ⓦ jacobsinn.com; map p.76. Dublin's largest hostel, which nevertheless remains one of the most convivial, with a ground-floor kitchen and dining room, a first-floor common room with pool table and large-screen TV, a rooftop terrace with great views and plenty of activities such as Irish dancing classes and a daily walking tour. Accommodation is en suite and well equipped, ranging from large private rooms with TVs to twelve-bed dorms. Dorms €16, doubles €72

Sky Backpackers 2–4 Litton Lane ☎ 01 872 8389, ⓦ irish-hostel.com; map p.76. Housed in a former recording studio in a quiet side-street off Bachelors Walk, this recently refurbished small hostel offers eight- and ten-bed en-suite dorms as well as comfortable private rooms. There's a sizeable kitchen, and they also run free daily walking tours. Dorms €17, doubles €88

CAMPING

Camac Valley Tourist Caravan & Camping Park Corkagh Regional Park, Naas Rd, Clondalkin ☎ 01 464 0644, ⓦ camacvalley.com. The only campsite with easy reach of the city centre lies 8km southwest of Dublin. This well-equipped, family-oriented site offers excellent facilities, including 24hr security, free internet and kitchen, as well as fine views of the surrounding countryside. Take bus #69 from Aston Quay, or it's a 5min drive from the Red Cow LUAS station. Camping/person tent €10

EATING

It's fair to say that no one comes to Dublin just for the cuisine, but the last twenty or so years have seen a remarkable growth in the variety of **places to eat**, from Lebanese to Nepalese. The downturn in the economy since 2008 has seen many of the overpriced places close down, making way for a plethora of vibrant new places offering excellent value. Many restaurants, however, offer lunch-time or early-bird (typically before 7pm) **set menus** of two or three courses, sometimes for as little as half the cost of their regular evening meals. Some cafés and restaurants, catering to a crowd who have spe

1

heir money carousing late into the previous night, also provide good-value **weekend brunch**. In addition, plenty of pubs (see p.102) dish up decent, reasonably priced, hearty food, with more ambitious menus available at gastropubs like *The xchequer* (see p.102) and *The Odeon* (see p.104).

AFÉS AND QUICK MEALS

ublin has long had a thriving café scene, but it is only ecently that Dubliners have got serious about coffee. A tring of artisan coffee shops has popped up all over the ty, where internationally acclaimed baristas take pride in elling you the perfect brew. While Irish breakfast tea is a erennial favourite, most cafés also offer a selection of erbal blends. As well as cafés, we've listed below other ood spots for a quick, tasty, inexpensive meal. For a plurge with a difference, "Art Tea" at the *Merrion Hotel* (see .96) is a lot of fun: delicious afternoon tea in the drawing ooms, with cakes that creatively reflect the surrounding aintings from the hotel's excellent collection of neteenth- and twentieth-century, mostly Irish, art (€36, cluding the catalogue of the collection).

HE SOUTHSIDE

★ **Avoca Café** 11 Suffolk St 📞 01 677 4215, 🌐 avoca.ie; ap pp.60–61. The bright, buzzy, modern Irish café on e top floor of this department store (see p.108) dishes up verything from fish platters (€19.95) to organic falafel 14.95) as well as an array of cakes, all beautifully esented and courteously served in a bright dining room ith vintage furniture. The foodhall and deli in the asement offers salads and sandwiches to take away (from .50). Mon–Sat 9.30am–4.30pm, Sun 11am–4.30pm.

ewley's 78 Grafton St 📞 01 672 7720; map pp.60–61. his genuinely iconic café (see p.58) spreads itself over several oors, including sought-after window tables overlooking the reet and six beautiful stained-glass windows by Harry Clarke the back of the ground floor. The menu features pizzas rom €11), pastas and excellent salads (€8), as well as more aditional Bewley's breakfasts and cream cakes. A light lunch served during short plays in the second-floor café theatre bewleyscafetheatre.com), which also hosts evening baret, jazz and comedy. Mon–Wed 8am–10pm, Thurs– at 8am–11pm, Sun 9am–10pm.

arluccio's 52 Dawson St 📞 01 633 3957 🌐 carluccios om; map pp.60–61. Spruce, authentic, Italian café- staurant and deli, part of the well-known UK-based ain, serving unfussy but well-judged food (mains from 4), including lots of antipasti, pastas, salads, panini and ood coffees. No bookings at lunch time. Mon–Sat 30am–10.30pm, Sun 9am–10pm.

ornucopia 19–21 Wicklow St 📞 01 677 7583; map .60–61. Friendly, vegetarian, buffet café serving an xcellent range of breakfasts, salads, soups and main urses, as well as cakes, breads, juices and organic wine. on & Tues 8.30am–9pm, Wed–Sat 8am–10.15pm, n noon–9pm.

★ **Dunne and Crescenzi** 14–16 South Frederick St 📞 01 677 3815, 🌐 dunneandcrescenzi.com; map pp.60–61. A cosy, popular Italian café-restaurant and wine bar, with croissants and spot-on coffee, all manner of Italian sandwiches and excellent plates of antipasti, as well as salads, pastas (from just €9.50) and daily special main courses. Bookings taken only for dinner. Mon–Sat 7.30am–10/11pm, Sun 9am–9pm.

★ **The Fumbally** Fumbally Lane 📞 01 5298732, 🌐 thefumbally.ie; map pp.60–61. One of the best brunch places in Dublin, serving excellent coffee, falafel wraps with purple slaw (€5), and gorgeous "green eggs" with avocado and fried chorizo (€6.50), in a cavernous empty retail space filled with mismatched vintage furniture. Mon–Fri 8am–5pm, Sat 10am–5pm.

Govinda's 4 Aungier St 📞 01 475 0309; & 83 Middle Abbey St 📞 01 661 5095; map pp.60–61. Excellent Hare Krishna-run vegetarian cafés, serving cheap and filling samosas, salads, curries and gratins. They also offer great juices and lassis, as well as cakes and desserts. Mon–Sat noon–9pm.

Honest to Goodness George's St Arcade 📞 01 623 7727, 🌐 honesttogoodness.ie; map pp.60–61. Tiny café that rustles up great sandwiches – from Irish ingredients where possible – on a wide variety of home-baked breads (from €4). Popular also for juices, smoothies, salads, soups and breakfast. Mon–Sat 9am–8pm, Sun 10am–4pm.

Irish Film Institute Café Bar 6 Eustace St 📞 01 679 5744, 🌐 ifi.ie; map p.69. Great for an inexpensive lunch or dinner, whether sitting in the smart bar or the echoing atrium. Simple meals range from lasagne (€8.65) and burgers to fish cakes and goat's cheese salad, with lots of vegetarian options. Daily 12.30–9pm.

Leo Burdock's 2 Werburgh St 📞 01 454 0306, 🌐 leoburdock.com; map pp.60–61. Dublin's most famous fish-and-chipper (takeaway only, but the garden of Christ Church Cathedral is just over the road) is all gleaming surfaces and friendly service. The multi-award-winning menu now stretches to lemon sole goujons (€6.99), but otherwise there are no surprises. Daily noon–midnight.

Queen of Tarts Cork Hill & Cow's Lane 📞 01 670 7499; map p.69. The former location is the cosy, original branch of this patisserie-cum-café, while the latter around the corner provides more elbow room and outdoor tables on the pedestrianized alley. Both offer veggie and meaty fry-ups (€9.75) and granola for breakfast; savoury tarts (€9.95) and a few other hot dishes, salads and all sorts of sandwiches (€7.50) for lunch; and yummy cakes baked fresh on the premises to keep you going between mealtimes. Mon–Fri 8am–7pm, Sat 9am–7pm, Sun 10am–6pm.

1

Roasted Brown Filmbase, Curved St ☎ 01 679 6716; map p.69. A friendly café in the first-floor atrium of a film-making centre, run by two baristas with a passion for every aspect of coffeemaking. The brew bar offers a selection of house blends, and beans from suppliers around the world. The Saturday brunch menu offers such delights as poached eggs with feta and pea crush (€8.50). Mon–Fri 10am–5.30pm, Sat 11am–4pm.

Silk Road Café Chester Beatty Library, Dublin Castle ⓦ silkroadkitchen.ie; map pp.60–61. Stylish and good-value museum café, spilling over into the library's sky-lit atrium. Mostly Middle Eastern food: Lebanese chicken (€11.95), falafel, spinach and feta filo pie and very good salads, as well as great coffee and titbits such as Turkish delight and baklava. Tues–Fri 10am–4.45pm, Sat 11am–4.45pm, Sun 1–4.45pm.

THE NORTHSIDE

Caffè Cagliostro Bloom Lane ☎ 01 888 0860; map p.76. A tiny Italian café serving excellent espresso and pastries (from €2.50), with newspapers for perusal and a sunny outdoor terrace. Mon–Fri 7am–6pm, Sat 8am–6pm, Sun 9am–6pm.

Cinnamon Coke Lane ⓦ cinnamoncafe.ie; map pp.56–57. Tucked away at the bottom of Smithfield, this cosy café, a popular spot with barristers coming from the Four Courts, offers a bright range of soups, snacks, sandwiches (from €4.85), wraps and salads as well as porridge with honey (€2.75) in colder months. Mon–Fri 6.45am–5.30pm, Sat 9am–3pm.

Cobalt Café and Gallery 16 North Great George's St; map pp.56–57. A relaxing haven in an area with a dearth of cafés, offering a range of coffees as well as light snacks (sandwiches from (€5.20), all of which can be enjoyed while admiring the original artworks displayed on the walls. Daily 10.30am–3.30pm.

Govinda's 84 Middle Abbey St ⓦ govindas.ie; map p.76. This inexpensive south Indian vegetarian restaurant has added some culinary variety to the northside, with soups, curries, stews and other veggie delights. A mixed plate costs €8.50 (small) or €11.95 (large). Mon–Sat noon–9pm, Sun noon–7pm.

The Gresham Hotel 23 O'Connell St Upper ☎ 01 874 6881; map p.76. Enjoy afternoon tea (€21/person, daily 2–6pm) in the opulent surroundings of this grand hotel's lobby. Booking essential. Daily 7.30am–10.30pm.

★ **The Woollen Mills** 42 Lower Ormond Quay ☎ 01 828 0835, ⓦ thewoollenmills.com; map p.76. One of the most exciting recent additions to the Dublin restaurant scene, this "eating house" in an old haberdashery sprawl over four floors, with huge windows and a roof terrace opening out over the Ha'penny Bridge. A sister restaurant to the *Winding Stair* (see p.101), the food is fresh, local and seasonal, and caters for all types of eaters at all times of the day: grab a good take-away coffee and a bun from their on-site bakery for breakfast, a salad box for lunch, or lounge over a supper feast of fresh mackerel with wasabi purple potato salad (€19) and a craft beer at night. Mon–Sat 8am–11pm.

Wuff 23 Benburb St ☎ 01 532 0347, ⓦ wuff.ie; map pp.56–57. A lively neighbourhood bistro in the heart of Smithfield, serving up the likes of veggie sausages and eggs (€8.50) for breakfast, pulled pork sandwiches (€8.50) and salads for lunch, and fancier dishes like confit duck with celeriac remoulade (€18) for dinner. Mon–Wed 7.30am–4pm, Thurs & Fri 7.30am–9.30pm, Sat 10am–9.30pm, Sun 10am–4pm.

RESTAURANTS

The majority of Dublin's restaurants are on the south side of the river in the city centre. An abundance of excellent new places to eat have opened up around the George's St/South William St area, stretching up Camden St as far as Portobello. Eating out in Temple Bar tends to be overpriced and underwhelming. It's worth booking ahead, especially in the evenings.

THE SOUTHSIDE

Camden Kitchen 3A Camden Market ☎ 01 476 0125 ⓦ camdenkitchen.ie; map pp.60–61. Housed in the historic Camden Market building on a residential Georgian street in Portobello, the top-class chefs combine a passion for local and wild Irish produce with inspiration from their travels abroad to create dishes such as organic Irish salmon with salt baked beets, orange fennel and razor clams (€20). The set lunch (three courses €19) and early bird (€24) offer the best value. Tues–Fri noon–2.30pm & 5.30–10pm, Sat & Sun 5.30–10pm.

Cellar Restaurant Merrion Hotel, Merrion St Upper ☎ 01 603 0600, ⓦ merrionhotel.com; map pp.60–61. Formal restaurant in an atmospheric cellar offering top-notch cuisine: try the superb sugar-cured salmon with hazelnut crème fraiche or the fish pie. Good value, too, at €27 for two courses on the set menu. Mon–Fri noon–2pm, & 5.30–10pm, Sat & Sun 5.30–10pm.

Chez Max 1 Palace St ☎ 01 633 7215, ⓦ chezmax.ie; map pp.60–61. Archetypal French bistro at the gate of Dublin Castle, offering a wide-ranging evening menu of classic dishes, supplemented by specialities from the owner's home

---

TOP 5 CHEAP EATS

Dunne & Crescenzi See p.99
The Fumbally See p.99
Green 19 See p.101
Jo Burger See p.101
Neon See p.101

---

egion in southwest France. Lunch consists of simpler main ourses, including a good-value *plat du jour* (€9.50) while cold eat and cheese platters are available all day long. It serves a mple French breakfast on weekdays and an early-bird menu efore 7pm daily (€19 for two courses). Mon–Fri 8am– idnight, Sat & Sun noon–midnight.

ly Wine Bar 22 Ely Place ☎ 01 676 8986, ⓦ elywinebar e; map pp.60–61. Popular, congenial and reasonably riced wine bar that offers wholesome snacks and meals, otably bangers and mash and beefburgers (€26), to ccompany around eighty wines by the glass. Carefully ourced, mostly organic Irish ingredients, including fresh eef and pork from their own farm in the Burren. Mon–Fri 0am–late, Sat & Sun 3pm–late.

allon and Byrne 11–17 Exchequer St ☎ 01 472 1000, ⓦ fallonandbyrne.com; map pp.60–61. Foodie heaven a converted telephone exchange: a smart grocery store nd deli (for lunch to sit in or take-away) on the ground oor; a seductive, Parisian-style brasserie upstairs, offering verything from burgers to superb smoked sea trout with range and fennel (€26); and a wine bar and shop in the asement, serving cheaper food. Sun–Thurs noon–3pm nd 6–9pm, Fri & Sat noon–3pm and 6–11pm.

★ Green 19 19 Camden St ☎ 478 9626, ⓦ green19.ie; ap pp.60–61. Simple yet top-quality dishes like slow-roast ork belly with a chorizo cassoulet, or corned beef with mash nd parsley sauce, all priced at €10, in a modern yet cosy ace. The cocktails (€9) are excellent, and the staff always iendly. Mon–Sat 10am–11pm, Sun noon–10pm.

★ Jo Burger 4/5 Castle Market ⓦ joburger.ie; map p.60–61. The gravity-defying burgers, with toppings anging from harrisa mint *aioli* (€11.50) to caramelized illi banana and bacon, are the best in Dublin, served up in funky space to a thumping soundtrack. Mon–Sat noon– 0/11pm, Sun noon–9pm.

★ L'Écrivain 109 Lower Baggot St ☎ 01 661 1919, ⓦ lecrivain.com; map pp.60–61. In two beautifully nverted Georgian coachhouses, inspired cooking of ulti-faceted but harmonious dishes such as venison loin ith pear fondant and celeriac purée, interwoven with rbets and other extras. There's an eight-course tasting enu (€75) and an early-bird deal (€50). Mon–Wed & Sat 30–10pm, Thurs & Fri 12.30–2pm & 6.30–10pm.

a Maison 15 Castlemarket ☎ 01 672 7258, ⓦ lamaisondublin.com; map pp.60–61. The outdoor bles at this quaint French restaurant on the edestrianized Castlemarket are the most in demand even winter when heaters and blankets keep diners warm hile they enjoy bowls of *moules frites* (€14.50). The giant oz *cote de beouf* for two people (€59) is especially commended. Daily 12.30–10pm.

e Larder 8 Parliament St ☎ 01 633 3581, ⓦ thelardercaferestaurant.ie; map p.69. Bare, attractively brick walls and wooden floors match uncomplicated main

courses such as duck breast and red cabbage (€18) at this multi-purpose café-restaurant, which also serves cheese and meat plates and, during the day, quiches, classy sandwiches and scrummy brownies. Early bird till 7.30pm (€15 for two courses). Daily noon–10pm.

L'Gueuleton 1 Fade St ⓦ lgueuleton.com; map pp.60– 61. Great French bistro food such as slow-roast pork belly with Jack McCarthy's black pudding and parsnip purée (€19) from an open kitchen at reasonable prices, accompanied by good-value French wine. No booking by phone; turn up in person to book for that evening. Daily 12.30–3.30pm & 5.30–10pm.

The Market Bar 14 Fade St ☎ 01 613 9094, ⓦ marketbar .ie; map pp.60–61. Housed in a huge converted abattoir, Dublin's first gastro-bar serves tapas (€4–12) with an Irish twist, such as haddock and coley stew, and smoked applewood cheddar croquettes. Daily noon–midnight.

Neon 17 Camden St ☎ 01 405 2222, ⓦ neon17.ie; map pp.60–61. This trendy Asian street-food restaurant is always buzzing, offering an array of fiery Thai curries (€11.50), Vietnamese soups (from €5) and stir-fries. Enjoy over a beer or glass of wine at the rustic communal tables, before pouring your own whipped ice-cream cone for dessert. Daily noon–11pm.

Trocadero 4 St Andrew's St ☎ 01 677 5545, ⓦ trocadero.ie; map pp.60–61. A welcoming haven, done out with plush booths, signed photos of showbiz visitors and yards of red velvet. Excellent though predictable food, whether à la carte or on the good-value pre-theatre set menu (vacate the table by 7.30pm; €27 for three courses). Mon–Sat 5–10pm.

Ukiyo 7–9 Exchequer St ☎ 01 633 4071, ⓦ ukiyobar.com; map pp.60–61. Chic Korean and Japanese bar-restaurant, serving bento boxes (€10) and wasabi tuna loin (€22), with a novel take on the Dublin snug: karaoke booths in the basement for €25/hr. Mon–Wed noon–midnight, Thurs, Fri & Sat noon–2.30am, Sun noon–1.30am.

THE NORTHSIDE

★ Chapter One 18–19 Parnell Square North ☎ 01 873 2266, ⓦ chapteronerestaurant.com; map pp.56–57. Housed in the cellars of the Dublin Writers Museum, this Michelin-starred culinary gem specializes in French-inspired modern Irish food, using an imaginative blend of herbs, spices and fruit to enhance a variety of fish and meat dishes such as Barbary duck breast in blood orange sauce and John Dory with fennel and Dublin Bay shrimps, plus a selection of desserts. The restaurant offers a pre-theatre menu (5.30–7pm, €36.50 for three courses), otherwise expect to pay around €70 plus wine. Tues–Fri 12.30–2pm & 5.30–10pm, Sat 5.30–10pm.

The Winding Stair 40 Ormond Quay Lower ☎ 01 872 7320, ⓦ winding-stair.com; map p.76. Set above the bookshop of the same name (see p.109), with its views

1

across the Liffey this is one of the most enjoyable northside spots for lunch (set three-course €23.95). Evenings feature a pre-theatre dinner (€29.95) or à la carte (around €45 for three courses) and all menus (which change daily) feature traditional Irish cooking with a modern twist using local and seasonal produce. Daily noon–10.30pm.

THE SUBURBS

★**Caviston's** 59 Glasthule Rd, Sandycove ☎ 01 280 9245, ⓦcavistons.com. Near Sandycove and Glasthul DART station, this restaurant works to a basic but huge successful formula – the day's freshest fish and seafoo cooked simply. Booking is essential and there are a fev outside tables in summer. Three lunch sittings: Tues to Sa noon, 1.30pm & 3pm, also Fri & Sat 6pm and 8.15pm. Thre courses will set you back around €40 plus wine, but th two-course early bird (5–7pm) is a steal at €19. Tues–We noon–3.20pm, Thurs–Sat noon–3.20pm & 6–9pm.

DRINKING

Dubliners boast that their city possesses the finest **pubs** in the world. They're probably right too, but with over seve hundred watering holes to choose from, forming the backbone of the capital's social life, there's no harm in checking ot their assertion. Along the way, you'll also be able to test out competing claims about the hometown drink, **Guinness**: th it tastes better here is not open to doubt, but locals argue about exactly which pub pours the best drop (is the travel-sh liquid better at *Ryan's*, just across the river from the brewery, than downstream at *Mulligan's*?). In general, the stout is be in the characterful and sociable historic pubs, many of which retain their cut-glass screens, ornate wood-carving and cos snugs, often with a private hatch to the bar.

Alongside the more traditional pubs – some are over 100 years old – a plethora of cosmopolitan **bars** has sprun up, be they cavernous microbreweries serving craft beers, studenty DJ bars or chic designer cocktail lounges. Pub operate strict trading hours, and most close at 11.30pm Sunday to Thursday and 12.30am on Friday & Saturday. Ba and nightclubs with late licences are noted in the reviews below. Traditional-music pubs (see p.105) are great for drink in their own right. Dublin also has a number of gay bars (see p.108) as well as some highly entertaining pub tou (see p.93).

TEMPLE BAR AND THE SOUTHSIDE

Anséo 18 Camden St ☎ 01 475 1321; map pp.60–61. Unpretentious, easy-going venue with plenty of velour banquettes to chill out on. DJs at weekends, comedy night on Wed and occasional live music. Mon–Thurs noon–11.30pm, Fri noon–12.30am, Sat 10–12.30am, Sun 10am–11pm.

★**The Bernard Shaw** 11–12 South Richmond St ⓦthebernardshaw.com; map pp.56–57. The walls of this ramshackle "bar, café and creative space" are covered in graffiti inside and the works of local artists inside. There's a colourful outdoor area with a pool table, nightly DJs playing everything from reggae to house, a Big Blue Bus serving excellent pizzas, and cheap mojitos (two for €10). On weekdays there's also a very good Italian café. Mon–Thurs 8.30am–midnight, Fri 8.30am–1am, Sat 1pm–1am, Sun 1pm–midnight.

Cassidy's 27 Westmoreland St ☎ 01 670 8604; map pp.60–61. With its graffitied walls, mismatched furniture and a spectacular array of craft beers on draught or by bottle, this refurbished hipster hangout is unrecognizable from its previous, more traditional incarnation. Mon–Thurs noon–11.30pm, Fri noon–12.30am, Sat 10am–12.30am, Sun 10am–11pm.

★**The Exchequer** 3 Exchequer St ☎ 01 670 6787, ⓦtheexchequer.ie; map pp.60–61. Sleek, modern gastropub where you can plonk yourself on a bar stool, a sofa or at a restaurant table. The cuisine is modern Irish, so

cockles and mussels and lots of black pudding, as well smoked haddock tartlet with sorrel salad and cheese ar meat platters; it's hard to go wrong with venison pie and pint of Guinness for €15. Mon–Wed noon–11.30pr Thurs noon–12.30am, Fri & Sat noon–1.30am, Su noon–11pm.

Grogan's Castle Lounge 15 South William St ☎ 01 67 9320, ⓦgroganspub.ie; map pp.60–61. Lively, eccentr traditional pub, popular with budding writers and artist with outdoor tables ideal for watching the world go by on sunny evening. Mon–Thurs 10.30am–11.30pm, Fri Sat 10.30am–12.30am, Sun 12.30–11pm.

The Horseshoe Bar Shelbourne Hotel, 27 Stephen's Green ☎ 01 663 4500; map pp.60–61. this renovated luxury hotel, the *Horseshoe*'s deep-re leather banquettes and white marble counter mainta a cosy pub feel. The recent cleaning of the cautiona satirical prints by Hogarth above the bar has n deterred the city's politicos and journos, who still gath here to swap tall tales and set the world to rights. Mon Sat 5pm–12.30am.

The International Bar 23 Wicklow St ☎ 01 677 925 map pp.60–61. Old-fashioned pub decorated with stain glass and ornate woodcarving that heaves congenially weekends. Nightly comedy shows including improv Mon, plus jazz on Thurs (usually) and poetry and music Mon. Mon–Wed 11am–11.30pm, Thurs–S 11am–12.30am, Sun 11am–11pm.

CLOCKWISE FROM TOP LEFT AVOCA (P.108); SHERIDANS CHEESEMONGERS (P.109); *O'DONOGHUE'S* (P.106); JO BURGER (P.101)

1

Kehoe's 9 South Anne St ☎ 01 677 8312; map pp.60–61. This meeting place used to double up as a grocery and is now a watering hole full of character, with cosy snugs and a low mahogany bar. Mon–Thurs 11.30am–11.30pm, Fri–Sat 11.30am–12.30am, Sun noon–11pm.

The Long Hall 51 South Great George's St ☎ 01 475 1590; map pp.60–61. Old-time classic, sporting ornate plasterwork, mirrors and dark-wood panelling, a suitably long bar, friendly staff and a good pint of Guinness. Mon–Wed 4–11pm, Thurs 1–11.30pm, Fri & Sat 1pm–12.30am, Sun 1–11pm.

Mulligan's 8 Poolbeg St ☎ 01 677 5582; map pp.60–61. A little off the beaten track, this large no-nonsense pub pours an excellent pint and remains a favoured watering hole for workers at the nearby *Irish Times*. Mon–Thurs 11am–11.30pm, Fri & Sat 11am–12.30am, Sun 12.30–11pm.

No Name Bar 3 Fade St ☎ 01 648 0010; map pp.60–61. With no formal name or a sign outside it can be easy to miss this place – it's on the first floor, entered to the left of *L'Gueuleton* (from whose kitchen weekend brunch is served). Lovely, big outdoor terrace, cool soundtrack and a loft feel, with bare floorboards, and modern art on the walls. Mon–Wed 1–11.30pm, Thurs & Sun 1pm–1am, Fri & Sat 1pm–2.30am.

The Odeon Old Harcourt St Station, Harcourt St ☎ 01 478 2088, ⓦ odeon.ie; map pp.60–61. Palatial and sophisticated bar sporting Art Deco fittings and plenty of outdoor tables under the portico of the old station. One of Dublin's few gastropubs, serving everything from tapas and sandwiches to risotto of the day and bouillabaisse. Mon–Wed noon–11.30pm, Thurs noon–12.30pm, Fri noon–2.30am, Sat 4pm–2.30am, Sun 4pm–1am.

★ **The Palace Bar** 21 Fleet St ☎ 01 671 7388; map pp.60–61. Relaxing, sociable, 200-year-old pub, former haunt of writers Behan, Kavanagh and Flann O'Brien, now famed both for the quality of its pint and for its handsome decor. Lunch-time soup and sandwiches. The overflow bar upstairs hosts sessions of traditional music on Wed, Thurs & Sun. Mon–Thurs 10.30am–11.30pm, Fri & Sat 10.30am–12.30am, Sun 12.30–11pm.

The Porterhouse 16 Parliament St ☎ 01 679 8847, ⓦ porterhousebrewco.com; map p.69. Rambling microbrewery-bar, where for €5 you can sample three different stouts, lagers or ales. Live music every night, including traditional sessions on Sun, and good food. Mon–Wed 11.30am–11.30pm, Thurs 11.30am–12.30am, Fri & Sat 10.30am–12.30am, Sun 12.30–11pm.

★ **The Stag's Head** 1 Dame Court ☎ 01 6793701; map p.69. Pretty Victorian bar, all dark woods and stuffed, tiled and stained-glass stags, that attracts a hugely varied crowd. Decent pub grub during the day (Mon–Sat) and a good live music session most Sundays from around 7–8pm. The upstairs bar hosts regular gigs, comedy and storytelling events. Mon–Thurs 10.30am–11.30pm, Fri & Sa 10.30am–12.30am, Sun 12.30–11pm.

THE NORTHSIDE

Dice Bar 78 Queen St ☎ 01 633 3936; map pp.56–57 Low-lit and compact, the *Dice Bar* is an ultra-cool, Nev York–style joint that remains atmospheric without eve feeling too cramped. DJs play nightly. Mon–Wed 4–11.30pm, Thurs 3pm–midnight, Sun 3–11pm.

Enoteca delle Langhe Bloom Lane ☎ 01 8880834 ⓦ wallacewinebars.ie; map p.76. A focal part of Dublin Italian quarter, the *Enoteca* brings all the flavours of a Umbrian bar to the city, serving up an astonishingly wid range of wines and a small but still intriguing menu c antipasti and other dishes. Tues–Sun 12.30pm–midnight.

The Flowing Tide 9 Abbey St Lower ☎ 01 874 4108 map p.76. Long connected with the Abbey Theatr opposite, this pub features tasteful stained-glass window a mural celebrating the theatre's history and a horseshoe shaped bar. Mon–Thurs 10.30am–11.30pm, Fri & Sa 10.30am–12.30am, Sun 12.30–11pm.

Frank Ryan & Son 5 Queen St ☎ 01 872 5204 ⓦ frankryans.com; map pp.56–57. Definitely a place fc respite from the city's hurly-burly, this sociable, old fashioned bar is cosiness incarnate. The friendly staff serv a grand pint of stout. Mon–Thurs 4–11.30pm, Fri & Sa 4pm–12.30am, Sun 6–11pm.

Hill 16 16 Gardiner St Middle ☎ 01 874 4239; ma pp.56–57. Named after Croke Park's most popula stand, the bar is a magnet for GAA devotees, particularl those who follow the fortunes of Dublin's Gaelic footbal team. Mon–Thurs 10.30am–11.30pm, Fri & Sa 10.30am–12.30am, Sun 12.30–11pm.

Kavanagh's (aka The Gravediggers) Prospect Square Glasnevin ☎ 01 830 7978; map pp.56–57. One of th city's finest old pubs, located just outside the old entrance t Glasnevin Cemetery, where it has consoled mourners (an changed little) since 1833. It's best reached from th present-day entrance by retracing your steps along Fingla Rd and taking the first small lane on the left along th cemetery walls. Mon–Thurs 10.30am–11.30pm, Fri & Sa 10.30am–12.30am, Sun 12.30–11pm.

The Lotts 9 Liffey St Lower ☎ 01 872 7669 ⓦ thelottscafebar.com; map p.76. Often standing room-only at this friendly corner bar, with a snug which lay claim to being the northside's smallest. It offers a tast selection of Mediterranean-inspired meals in its fashionabl café-bar next door. Mon–Thurs 10.30am–11.30pm, Fri & Sat 10.30am–12.30am, Sun 12.30–11pm.

★ **Ryan's** 28 Parkgate St ☎ 01 677 6097, ⓦ ryan .fxbuckley.ie; map pp.56–57. The longtime challenger t the reputation of *Mulligan's* (see above) for serving the bes pint of Guinness in the city, based on its proximity to th brewery just across the river, serves bar meals plus steaks an eafood in its upstairs restaurant. Mon–Thurs noon–11.30pm, Fri & Sat noon–12.30am, Sun noon–11pm.

Sin É 14–15 Ormond Quay Upper ☎01 555 4036; map p.76. This candlelit bar appeals to a lively cosmopolitan crowd because of its wide selection of brews and eclectic choice of nightly musical entertainment (sometimes live gigs, but mostly DJs). Mon–Wed 5pm–1am, Thurs–Sat 5pm–2.30am, Sun 5pm–12.30am.

LIVE MUSIC

Dublin's **music scene** is thriving but ever-changing, so it's always wise to check listings on ⓦindublin.ie, or in *The Ticket* (see p.91), or the fortnightly rock-and- style magazine *Hot Press*. Ticket prices are dependent on the venue's size and the performers' status, usually costing €8–30, although major gigs can be as much as €110. There are also a number of **open-air events** during the summer, including one-off gigs by major acts at places such as Croke Park and Marlay Park in Rathfarnham. **Traditional music** is flourishing in the city with a number of pubs offering sessions, usually commencing at around 9.30pm. Listings of these can be found at ⓦdublinsessions.ie, or ask for advice in Claddagh Records (see p.108).

LIVE MUSIC VENUES

3Arena Dame St ☎0818/719 300, ⓦ3arena.ie; map pp.56–57. Once a railway depot, the cavernous 3Arena, 1.5km east of O'Connell Bridge, is Ireland's largest dedicated music venue with a capacity of 13,000. Unsurprisingly, it hosts major international names with high prices to boot. The venue is served by the LUAS red line Docklands branch.

The Academy 57 Abbey St Middle ☎01 877 9999, ⓦtheacademydublin.com; map p.76. The latest occupant of these premises offers a variety of largely alt/indie gigs and club nights in its Main Room, Green Room and Academy 2 sections. Mon–Fri 11pm–2.30am, Sat 10.30pm–2.30am, Sun 11pm–1am (doors open earlier for gigs).

Button Factory Curved St ☎01 670 9202, ⓦbuttonfactory.ie; map p.69. A remarkably left-field venue with a more than eclectic booking policy covering everything from traditional music to alt/indie bands via modern jazz and tribute groups. The place transforms itself into a late club (until 3am Fri–Sun) at weekends – with a wide variety of differently themed events. Opening hours vary depending on event.

J.J. Smyth's 12 Aungier St ☎01 475 2565, ⓦjjsmyths.com; map pp.60–61. The best place on the southside to catch blues and jazz-fusion bands (to whom Sunday and often Thursday nights are devoted), this pub's intimate upstairs room rocks most nights to the sound of the city's finest 12-bar and "let's try that again in 7/4 time" merchants. Mon–Thurs 10.30am–11.30pm, Fri & Sat 10.30am–12.30am, Sun 12.30–11pm.

Olympia Theatre Dame St ☎01 679 3323, ⓦolympia.ie; map p.69. This old, intimate and much-esteemed venue continues to stage a variety of musical events, featuring major Irish names as well as international stars.

The Sugar Club 8 Leeson St Lower ☎01 678 7188, ⓦthesugarclub.com; map pp.60–61. A lush and plush southside venue, just off St Stephen's Green, *The Sugar Club* hosts a diverse and often far from mainstream variety of entertainment (bands, torch-singers, comedy, cabaret) – some divine, others dreadful, but the atmosphere is often very much on the button. Opening hours vary depending on event.

Vicar Street 58–59 Thomas St West ☎01 454 5533, ⓦvicarstreet.com; map pp.56–57. Arguably the city's premier small live music venue, this three-hundred-seater has an estimable programme that includes live music, comedy and other events, and features major names.

Whelan's 25 Wexford St ☎1890/200 078, ⓦwhelanslive.com; map pp.60–61. Featuring a popular front bar too, *Whelan's* has remained one of the city's most successful live venues over the last two decades, thanks to an extensive programme of the old and the new – a blend of traditional music, renowned folk acts, emerging talent and occasional one-off performances by major names. Mon–Wed 10.30am–1.30am, Thurs–Sat 10.30am–2.30am, Sun 2pm–1.30am.

TRADITIONAL-MUSIC PUBS

The Brazen Head 20 Bridge St Lower ☎01 677 9549, ⓦbrazenhead.com; map pp.56–57. Established in 1189 and laying claim to the title of Ireland's oldest pub, *The Brazen Head*'s many rooms feature all manner of music-related memorabilia on the walls and ramble round a large courtyard. Traditional musicians play every night (as well as Sun 1.30–4.30pm), though the quality of the sessions can be extremely variable. Mon–Thurs 10.30am–11.30pm, Fri & Sat 10.30am–12.30am, Sun 12.30–11pm.

★ **The Cobblestone** 77 King St North ☎01 872 1799; map pp.56–57. Arguably the best traditional-music venue in Dublin, this dark, cosy, wooden-floored bar is also a fine place to sample the hoppy products of the nearby Dublin Brewing Company. High-quality sessions take place nightly from around 9pm (from 7pm on Thurs), and on Sun afternoons, while the *Back Room* hosts a variety of gigs. Mon–Thurs 4–11.30pm, Fri & Sat 4pm–12.30am, Sun 1–11pm.

Hughes' Bar 19 Chancery St ☎01 872 6540; map pp.56–57. Tucked away behind the Four Courts, *Hughes' Bar* attracts the cream of the city's traditional musicians to

its nightly sessions (10pm until closing time). Fri can draw a large crowd, so arrive early to grab a seat. Mon–Thurs 7am–11.30pm, Fri & Sat 7am–12.30am, Sun 7–11pm.
O'Donoghue's 15 Merrion Row ☎ 01 676 2807; map pp.60–61. The centre of the folk and traditional-music revival that began in the late 1950s, forever associated with ground-breaking balladeers The Dubliners. Nightly sessions (from about 9.30pm) draw a considerable crowd of tourists, while the large heated courtyard is more of a draw for locals. Mon–Thurs 10am–11.30pm, Fri & Sat 10am–12.30am, Sun noon–11pm.

O'Shea's Merchant 12 Bridge St Lower ☎ 01 679 3797, map pp.56–57. Opposite the more famous *Brazen Head* the *Merchant* nurtures the atmosphere of a homely, good-natured country pub in the centre of the city, providing sanctuary for "culchies" from any county, but especially Kerrymen. Traditional sessions are hosted every night in high season from around 10pm, including set dancing on Mon & Wed, and it's a good place to watch a GAA game Mon–Thurs 10.30am–11.30am, Fri & Sat 10.30am–12.30am, Sun 12.30–11pm.

NIGHTLIFE

It is best to check the latest listings in the *Event Guide* or *Hot Press* (see p.105), as Dublin's **club scene** is volatile. Clubs can be found in most areas of the city centre and prices vary considerably, depending on the venue, night of the week and whether a "name" DJ is spinning the turntables – the venues listed below often have free entry, but can charge up to €20 on certain nights

Copper Face Jacks 29–30 Harcourt St ⓦ copperfacejacks.ie; map pp.60–61. The most popular of several similar late-night venues along Harcourt St, and notorious for its pop tunes and groups of single lads and lasses looking for a good time. Daily 9pm–2.30am.
Four Dame Lane 4 Dame Lane ☎ 01 679 0291, ⓦ 4damelane.ie; map p.69. Announced by burning braziers, this bar-club probably has the stylistic edge over its bare-brickwork-and-wood rivals. The tunes are good too, encompassing anything from techno to soul, with a DJ Thurs–Sun in the ground-floor bar, Fri & Sat in the upstairs room. Tues–Wed 5–11.30pm, Thurs–Sat 5pm–2.30am, Sun 5pm–1am.
The Grand Social 35 Lower Liffey St ☎ 01 873 4332, ⓦ thegrandsocial.ie; map p.76. On the northside of the Ha'penny Bridge, in-house and guest DJs spin funky disco, indie, classic rock and electro at the weekends. There's a popular jazz club every Mon night, and the indoor Ha'penny Flea Market on a Sat afternoon. Sun–Wed noon–12.30am, Thurs–Sat noon–2.30am.

Rí Rá 13 Dame Court ☎ 01 671 1220, ⓦ riraclub.ie; map p.60–61. Though nowadays more institution than innovator, there's still plenty to enjoy at one of Dublin's longest-running nightclubs, especially the "Vinyl Frontier" night on a Sat featuring everything from soul to funk and house. Mon–Sat 11pm–2.30am.
The Twisted Pepper 54 Abbey St Middle ☎ 01 873 4038, ⓦ bodytonic.com; map p.76. Decidedly funky café-bar with a penchant for driving bass rhythms in its basement club nights, including Saturday's much esteemed "Pogo" – a potpourri of electronic beats and live bands Café: daily 10.30am–7pm; Bar: Mon–Wed 6pm–1am Thurs–Sat 6pm–2.30am, Sun 6pm–1am.
Workman's Club 10 Wellington Quay ⓦ theworkmansclub.com; map p.69. A maze of interconnecting rooms in a red-brick building fronting the River Liffey house dance floors, venues for live music and poetry readings, themed bars and a rooftop terrace. The bar on the ground floor serves American-style barbecues (until 9pm), accompanied by craft beers and cocktails. Daily 5pm–3am.

ARTS AND CULTURE

Drama played a pivotal role in Ireland's twentieth-century cultural revival and Dublin's theatres continue to act as a crucible for innovation, alongside staging a range of Irish classics. Highlights include the **Dublin Theatre Festival** (late Sept to mid-Oct; ⓦ dublintheatrefestival.com) and the **Dublin Fringe Festival** (mid-Sept; ⓦ fringefest.com). Ticket prices vary, and you should expect to pay €10–20 per ticket for fringe shows, €20–40 for mainstream. Advance bookings can be made at the venues or through Ticketmaster (☎ 081 871 9300, ⓦ ticketmaster.ie). If you're budget-conscious, it's worth enquiring about low-cost previews and occasional cut-price Monday- and Tuesday-night shows, while students (with ID) and OAPs can sometimes find good concessionary rates.

All cinemas operate a policy of cheap seats daily before 5pm (6.30pm in some cases), during which time tickets cost around €5–7, after which time they cost €9–12. Student discounts are often available.

The Abbey Theatre Abbey St Lower ☎ 01 878 7222, ⓦ abbeytheatre.ie. The National Theatre of Ireland (see also p.77) tends to show international and Irish classics plus new offerings by contemporary playwrights.

Bord Gáis Energy Theatre Grand Canal Square ☎ 01 677 7999, ⓦ bordgaisenergytheatre.ie. Two-thousand-seater in the Docklands, mostly offering light entertainment and musicals.

Gaiety Theatre South King St ☎01 677 1717, Ⓦgaietytheatre.ie. The Gaiety hosts everything from opera and Irish classics to musicals, concerts and other family entertainment.

Gate Theatre 1 Cavendish Row, Parnell Square ☎01 874 4045 or ☎01 874 6042, Ⓦgate-theatre.ie. Founded in the 1920s in an eighteenth-century building leased from the Rotunda Hospital, the Gate has a reputation for staging adventurous experimental drama as well as established classics in its small, elegant auditorium, and gave an early boost to the acting careers of James Mason and Orson Welles.

Irish Film Institute 6 Eustace St ☎01 679 3477, Ⓦifi .ie. The focus for Irish cineastes provides a broad programme of international and new Irish films, as well as being the hub of the Jameson International Film Festival in Feb (Ⓦdubliniff.com) and the Look Out! gay and lesbian film festival in July (Ⓦdlgff/ie). There's an excellent film-related bookshop as well as a bar and café-restaurant (see p.99).

The Lambert Puppet Theatre 5 Clifton Lane, Monkstown ☎01 280 0974, Ⓦlambertpuppettheatre .com. Dublin's only puppet theatre produces shows of very high quality every Sat at 3.30pm throughout the year and daily (call for times) in May and June. To get here, take the DART from Connolly, Tara St or Pearse stations.

Light House Cinema Smithfield ☎01 879 7601, Ⓦlighthousecinema.ie. A little away from the centre, this four-screen cinema is acclaimed for its imaginative programming and hosts the Dublin Lesbian and Gay Film Festival (Ⓦgaze.ie) in late July/early August.

New Theatre 43 Essex St East ☎01 670 3361, Ⓦthenewtheatre.com. This theatre stages a variety of classic, rarely performed and new drama.

Project Arts Centre 39 Essex St East ☎01 881 9613, Ⓦprojectartscentre.ie. Renowned for its experimental and often controversial Irish and international theatre, this flagship of the contemporary art scene also hosts dance, film, music and performance art.

SPORTS

Dublin and its surrounds offer plenty of scope to exploit the national obsessions of football (Gaelic and regular), hurling, rugby and horse and greyhound racing. If they can't attend a match or a meet, Dubliners are always keen to indulge in a second national pastime, gambling.

Soccer The Republic's national team plays most of its home games at the Aviva Stadium (☎01 238 2300, Ⓦavivastadium .ie). The Aviva Stadium is on Lansdowne Rd, which is situated to the southeast of the centre, and is easily accessible via the adjacent DART station. The city currently has five teams playing in the professional League of Ireland: Bohemians (Ⓦbohemians.ie); St Patrick's Athletic (Ⓦstpatsfc.com); Shamrock Rovers (Ⓦshamrockrovers.ie); Shelbourne (Ⓦshelbournefc.ie); and UCD (Ⓦucdsoccer.com). Standards are about the equivalent of the English Football League's Second Division. Most games take place on Fri nights and tickets generally cost around €12–15.

Gaelic football and hurling Most of the season's major games are played at Croke Park (see p.87; ☎01 836 3222, Ⓦgaa.ie). In football, the All-Ireland Final occurs on the third or fourth Sun in Sept and has been won by Dublin on 24 occasions (a record beaten only by Kerry). The Dubs have a poor record at hurling, so the crowd at the All-Ireland Final on the first or second Sun in Sept mainly consists of out-of-towners. You'll be hard pushed to get tickets for either of the finals, but you're quite likely to get in for a semi-final at "Croker" – expect to pay around €35 to stand and sing, on the famous Hill 16, €50 to sit in the stands and less for earlier rounds.

Greyhound racing The city has two dog-racing venues: Harold's Cross (Mon, Tues & Fri), in the suburb of the same name, southwest of the centre; and Shelbourne Park (Wed, Thurs & Sat) in Ringsend, in Docklands, east of the centre. Entry to either is around €10 and details of events can be found at Ⓦigb.ie.

Horse racing Dublin's nearest large racecourse is Leopardstown (☎01 289 0500, Ⓦleopardstown.com), in the southern suburb of Foxrock (LUAS to Sandyford station then a 15min walk). Races are held at weekends at various points of the year and on Thurs evenings during June and July, but the main events are the four-day Christmas Festival starting on St Stephen's Day (Dec 26), and the Hennessy Cognac Gold Cup in Feb. The Irish Grand National is held on Easter Mon at Fairyhouse (☎01 825 6167, Ⓦfairyhouseracecourse.ie) in Ratoath, 24km northwest of Dublin, followed in April by the Irish National Hunt Festival at Punchestown (see box, p.131), 40km southwest of Dublin. Flat-racing classics are held at the Curragh, nearly 50km southwest of the capital (see box, p.131). Bus Éireann lays on race-day transport to Fairyhouse.

Rugby Ireland's home games are played at the Aviva Stadium (☎01 238 2300, Ⓦavivastadium.ie). The provincial rugby side Leinster (Ⓦleinsterrugby.ie) plays its own home games at the RDS in Ballsbridge, southeast of the centre.

GAY AND LESBIAN DUBLIN

As attitudes to homosexuality in Dublin have become increasingly liberal over the last two decades, so the capital's **gay** community has grown in confidence, and a small but vibrant scene has established a niche in the city's social life. The latest **information** on gay events and venues in Dublin is provided by *Outhouse*, 105 Capel St (☎01 873 4999, Ⓦouthouse.ie),

1

a gay and lesbian resource centre with a café (Mon–Fri 1–9.30pm, Sat 1–5.30pm) and a small library. The free magazine GCN (*Gay Community News* ⓦ gcn.ie) has detailed listings of upcoming events and can be found in the gay-friendly Books Upstairs, College Green, or in clubs and bars. Useful websites include ⓦ queerid.com for events and news and ⓦ gaire.com for information, message boards and online chat.

Dragon 64 South Great George's St ⓣ 01 478 1590; map pp.60–61. Expansive and extravagant gay bar in a former bank, decorated with botanical prints, Buddhas and dragons. As well as a dance floor, there are cosy booths and a large first-floor courtyard. Popular drag show on Mon, DJs at weekends. Mon & Thurs–Sat 8pm–2.30am.

The Front Lounge 33 Parliament St ⓣ 01 670 4112, ⓦ thefrontlounge.ie; map p.69. Sophisticated decor of polished wood floors and comfy red armchairs and contemporary art on the walls, plus a wide range of entertainment, including karaoke on Tues and DJs at the weekend. Mon–Thurs 10.30pm–midnight, Fri & Sat 10.30am–2am, Sun 11am–11.30pm.

The George 89 South Great George's St ⓣ 01 478 2983, ⓦ thegeorge.ie; map pp.60–61. Ireland's longest-established gay bar still draws huge crowds at weekends.

There are two distinct sections: a lushly decorated main venue on two floors, and a quieter, more traditional pub with an older clientele to the right. Entertainment includes karaoke, game shows, DJs and Sun-night jazz followed by bingo with drag queen Shirley Temple-Bar. Mon 2–11.30pm, Tues–Fri 2pm–2.30am, Sat noon–2.30am, Sun 12.30pm–1.30am.

Pantibar 7–8 Capel St ⓣ 01 874 0710, ⓦ pantibar .com; map p.76. Owned by Irish gay icon, drag queen Pandora "Panti" Bliss, this lush bar provides all manner of entertainment from Monday's "Make and Do with Panti" (an alternative take on domestic crafts and games) to various themed nights in the basement, including "Panticlub" (Thurs–Sat). Apartments are available to rent on the upper floors. Mon, Wed & Sun 5–11.30pm, Tues 5pm–2am, Thurs & Fri 5pm–2.30am.

SHOPPING

The southside is the most fruitful hunting ground for shoppers, offering Irish and global designer clothes around **Grafton St**, and more alternative boutiques in the George's St **Arcade** and **Temple Bar**. Also south of the river, you'll find an attractive and eclectic range of artisan products gathered from around the country, from cheeses and whiskey to ceramics. Despite a recent revamp, Dublin's most extensive shopping boulevard, **O'Connell St**, is likely to hold little of interest for the visiting consumer, though the raucous Moore St market, off Henry St, is always entertaining.

ARTS, CRAFTS AND FASHIONS

Avoca 11 Suffolk St ⓣ 01 677 4215, ⓦ avoca.ie. Highly successful, small department store, stocking its own clothing ranges for women and children, jewellery, beautiful rugs and throws woven at the original mill in Avoca, Co. Wicklow, plus deli goods. Mon–Wed & Sat 9.30am–6pm, Thurs & Fri 9.30am–7pm, Sun 11am–6pm.

Irish Design Shop 41 Drury St ⓣ 01 679 8871, ⓦ irishdesignshop.com. Tiny shop run by two Irish jewellers, selling a range of Irish woodcraft, textiles, prints and pottery. Mon–Wed, Fri & Sat 10am–6pm, Thurs 10am–7pm.

Kilkenny 6 Nassau St ⓣ 01 677 7066, ⓦ kilkennyshop .com. A varied collection of fine Irish crafts: Newbridge silver cutlery and jewellery; Jerpoint glassware; extensive ranges of ceramics; and women's clothes and accessories by contemporary designers. Mon–Wed, Fri & Sat 8.30am–7pm, Thurs 8.30am–9pm, Sun 10am–6pm.

Powerscourt Townhouse Centre South 59 William St ⓣ 01 6794144, ⓦ powerscourtcentre.ie. On the second floor of the building (see p.62), the Design Centre stocks established Irish designers of women's fashion, such as Philip Treacy and John Rocha, as well as diverse international names. The Loft Market opposite is a cutting-edge showcase for young local designers of clothes and

jewellery. Mon–Wed & Fri 10am–6pm, Thurs 10am–8pm, Sat 9am–6pm, Sun noon–6pm.

BOOKS AND MUSIC

Cathach Books 10 Duke St ⓣ 01 671 8676, ⓦ rarebooks.ie. Also known as Ulysses Rare Books, this is the place to come for first editions and other rare books by Irish writers, specializing in twentieth-century literature. Mon–Sat 9.30am–5.45pm.

Chapters Bookstore Ivy Exchange, Parnell St ⓣ 01 872 3297, ⓦ chapters.ie. Claiming to be Dublin's largest bookshop, its ground floor features a massive range of fiction and fact, including impressive sections on Irish literature and history. Upstairs is devoted to the secondhand section which also includes bargain-priced CDs and DVDs. Mon–Wed, Fri & Sat 9.30am–6.30pm, Thurs 9.30am–8pm, Sun noon–6pm.

Claddagh Records 2 Cecilia St, Temple Bar ⓣ 01 677 0262, ⓦ claddaghrecords.com. Unquestionably, the finest traditional and folk music emporium in Dublin with helpful and knowledgeable staff. Mon–Fri 10.30am–5.30pm, Sat noon–5.30pm.

Hodges Figgis 56–58 Dawson St ⓣ 01 677 4754. A Dublin institution since the eighteenth century, behind an ornate façade, including a huge range of books on and from reland on the ground floor. Mon–Wed & Fri 9am–7pm, Thurs 9am–7pm, Sat 9am–6pm, Sun noon–6pm.

Walton's 69 South Great George's St ☎01 475 0661, ⚙waltons.ie. Dublin's leading music shop sells traditional Irish instruments, as well as teaching aids, sheet music and recordings. The attached music school (☎01 478 1884, ⚙newschool.ie) offers 1hr or 2hr crash courses for beginners in the tin whistle and the *bodhrán*. Mon–Sat 9am–6pm, Sun noon–5pm.

The Winding Stair 40 Ormond Quay Lower ☎01 8726576, ⚙winding-stair.com. One of the city's oldest bookshops, stocking a selection of titles you might not find in larger stores. It has a small secondhand section, which is especially good on Irish literature and biography. Upstairs is one of the northside's finest restaurants (see p.101). Mon–Wed & Fri 10am–6pm, Thurs & Sat 10am–7pm, Sun noon–6pm.

DEPARTMENT STORES AND MARKETS

Brown Thomas 88–95 Grafton St ☎01 605 6666, ⚙brownthomas.com. The city's flagship department store is sophisticated and pricey, featuring a long roll call of Irish and international designer labels. Mon 9.30am–7pm, Tues 11am–8pm, Wed, Fri, & Sat 9.30am–8pm, Thurs 9.30am–9pm, Sun 11am–7pm.

Cow's Lane Market Off Essex St West. On a pedestrianized alley in Temple Bar stalls concentrate on contemporary women's clothes, bags and jewellery, generally sold by the designers themselves. Sat 10am–5pm; closed Jan & Feb.

George's Street Arcade Between South Great George's St and Drury St ⚙georgesstreetarcade.com.

DIRECTORY

Banks and exchange Fexco at the Dublin Tourism Centre, Suffolk St (Mon–Sat 9am–5pm). Many banks also provide exchange facilities.

Dentist For dental emergencies contact the Dublin Dental School and Hospital, Lincoln Place ☎01 612 7200, ⚙dentalschool.ie.

Embassies Australia, 7th floor, Fitzwilton House, Wilton Terrace ☎01 664 5300; Canada, 7–8 Wilton Terrace ☎01 234 4900; South Africa, Alexandra House, Earlsfort Centre, Earlsfort Terrace ☎01 661 5553; UK, 29 Merrion Rd ☎01 205 3700; US, 42 Elgin Rd ☎01 668 8777.

Hospitals Those with accident and emergency departments include: Beaumont Hospital, Beaumont Rd ☎01 809 3000; Mater Misericordiae, Eccles St ☎01 803 2000; St James's, James St ☎01 410 3000; and St Vincent's, Elm Park ☎01 221 4000. In emergencies dial ☎999 or ☎112 for an ambulance.

Laidback indoor market, which claims to be Europe's oldest, offering secondhand books and records, vintage and street clothing, jewellery, cafés and speciality foods. Mon–Wed, Fri & Sat 9am–6pm, Thurs 9am–8pm, Sun 11am–6pm.

Moore St Market Moore St. This lively street market is a long-standing Dublin institution and much reflects the city's changing ethnicity. The traditional butchers, fishmongers and greengrocers are still present, though you're bound to see price tags in Cantonese too, and there are also a number of Afro-Caribbean stalls and shops. Daily around 10am–dusk.

FOOD AND DRINK

Celtic Whiskey Shop 27–28 Dawson St ☎01 675 9744, ⚙celticwhiskeyshop.com. Probably the best selection of Irish whiskeys anywhere, including rare examples from distilleries that have now closed down. The well-informed staff always have bottles open to taste and will ship around the world. Mon–Sat 10.30am–8pm, Sun 12.30–7pm.

Sheridan's Cheesemongers 11 South Anne St ☎01 679 3143, ⚙sheridanscheesemongers.com. Fantastic, pungent array of cheeses, mostly by Irish artisan producers, plus cold meats and other deli goods, sold by knowledgeable staff. Mon–Wed & Fri 10am–6pm, Thurs 10.30am–6.30pm, Sat 9.30am–6pm, Sun noon–6pm.

Temple Bar Food Market Meeting House Square. A magnet for Dublin's foodies, but also one of your best bets to grab Sat lunch, with stalls selling crêpes, Mexican food, olives, sushi, breads, cakes, cheeses, and a West Clare oyster bar. Mon–Wed 10am–6pm, Thurs 10.30am–6.30pm, Fri 10am–6pm, Sat 9.30am–6pm, Sun noon–6pm.

Left luggage There are lockers at Busáras and Heuston railway station.

Lost property Dublin Bus ☎01 703 1321; Bus Éireann ☎01 836 6111; Connolly Station ☎01 703 2362; Heuston Station ☎01 703 2102; airport ☎01 814 5555.

Police The main police station (Garda Síochána) is on Harcourt Terrace (☎01 666 9500). The Irish Tourist Assistance Service (Mon–Fri ☎01 661 0652, Sat & Sun ☎01 666 8109, ⚙itas.ie) offers support to tourist victims of crime.

Post offices General Post Office, O'Connell St Lower (Mon–Sat 8.30am–6pm; ☎01 705 8333), or on St Andrew's St, Ormond Quay Upper or Merrion Row. For mail enquiries call ☎1850 575589. Many newsagents sell postage stamps.

Around Dublin: Wicklow, Kildare and Meath

LOUGH TAY, WICKLOW MOUNTAINS

Around Dublin: Wicklow, Kildare and Meath

The modern counties of **Wicklow**, **Kildare** and **Meath** equate roughly with the **Pale**, the fortified area around Dublin to which the English colonists retreated after 1300. The colonists coined the expression "beyond the pale" and implanted the language, customs and government of lowland England in these "obedient shires", leaving today's visitors a rich architectural legacy of castles, abbeys and, from a later period, stately homes. Wicklow, Kildare and Meath are much sought-after by modern-day settlers, too: unable to afford Dublin's property prices, thousands of the capital's workers have set up home in the hinterland in the last twenty years.

This chapter sweeps clockwise, starting from the Wicklow coast south of Dublin and pulling up just short of Drogheda in County Louth to the north. If you have your own transport, this would make a very satisfying loop around the capital through diverse terrains, from the expansive, sandy beaches and spectacular granite mountains of County Wicklow (Cill Mhantáin, ⓦ visitwicklow.ie), through the grassy, horse-rearing heath of the Curragh and the Bog of Allen in Kildare (Cill Dara; ⓦ kildare.ie), to the lush, undulating farmland of Meath (An Mhí; ⓦ meathtourism.ie). The **highlights** detailed opposite would form a sound basic itinerary. If you have more time to spare, in County Wicklow, add in Parnell's home **Avondale House**, designed by James Wyatt and surrounded by forested parkland; the Neoclassical marvels of **Russborough**; the atmospheric seat of the Celtic High Kings, the **Hill of Tara**; and the impressive, new **Battle of the Boyne Visitor Centre** in Meath.

It wouldn't be possible to cover this same arc by **public transport**, which tends to run radially in and out of Dublin. Most of the places described in this chapter, however, are accessible on a day-trip from the capital by bus or train, with organized **tours** also available in many cases (see box, p.116). If you are **driving**, you'll generally be travelling in the opposite direction from Dublin's rush-hour traffic jams, but be sure to avoid Friday afternoons coming out of the capital and Sunday or bank-holiday evenings returning, which are particularly bad.

The Wicklow coast

County Wicklow's main draw is without doubt the stunning scenery of the inland mountains, but the **coast** can offer some very attractive beaches, notably at **Brittas Bay**, south of Wicklow town, and is easily accessible from Dublin. The N11 runs the length of the county roughly parallel to the sea, while by **train**, the DART service runs as far as Bray and Greystones, and the scenic main line to Rathdrum, Enniscorthy, Wexford and Rosslare stops at Bray, Greystones and Wicklow town. Keen to maintain its independence from Dublin, **Bray** is a lively, sometimes rowdy, resort and commuter town, which offers an expansive beach and the finest walk along this coast, across Bray Head to the village of **Greystones**. Halfway down the county's seaboard, **Wicklow** town enjoys a fine setting and a good choice of upmarket places to stay – if you have your own transport, this would

TRIM CASTLE

Highlights

❶ Walking in the Wicklow Mountains Wild and desolate terrain, traversed by the Wicklow Way, within easy reach of Dublin. **See p.121**

❷ Powerscourt Beautiful ornamental gardens and the highest waterfall in Ireland. **See p.121**

❸ Glendalough Hidden deep in this remote valley lies one of the best-preserved and most charismatic monastic sites in the country. **See p.124**

❹ The National Stud, Kildare town Learn all about one of Ireland's major industries at the national horse-breeding centre and enjoy the quirky gardens. **See p.130**

❺ Castletown Just west of Dublin, a Palladian mansion of unrestrained extravagance. **See p.132**

❻ Trim A historic town boasting the largest Anglo-Norman castle in Ireland and other fine medieval remains. **See p.134**

❼ Loughcrew Cairns These Neolithic mounds are slightly less impressive than Brú na Bóinne, but more scenic and far less touristy. **See p.138**

❽ Brú na Bóinne Don't miss the extraordinary prehistoric passage graves of Newgrange and Knowth. **See p.141**

HIGHLIGHTS ARE MARKED ON THE MAP ON PP.114–115

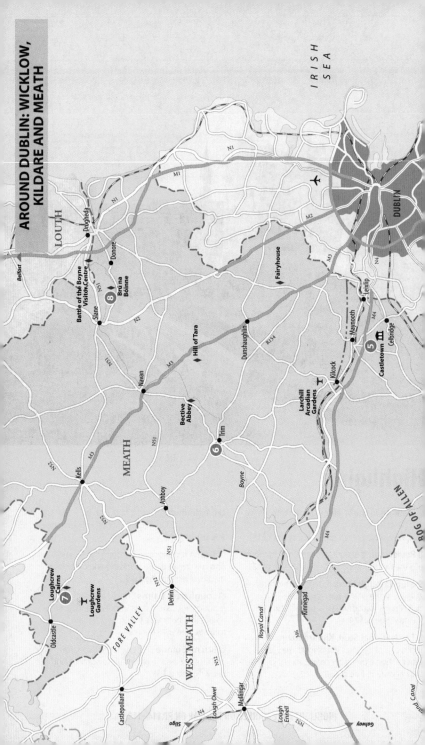

AROUND DUBLIN: WICKLOW, KILDARE AND MEATH

I R I S H

S E A

DUBLIN

LOUTH

Belfast

Drogheda

Donore

Battle of the Boyne Visitor Centre

Brú na Bóinne

⑧

Slane

Fairyhouse

Leixlip

Maynooth

Castletown

⑤

Celbridge

Hill of Tara

Dunshaughlin

Kilcock

Navan

Larchill Arcadian Gardens

Bective Abbey

Trim

⑥

MEATH

Kells

Athboy

Boyne

Loughcrew Cairns

⑦

Loughcrew Gardens

Oldcastle

Delvin

Kinnegad

BOG OF ALLEN

FORE VALLEY

WESTMEATH

Royal Canal

Castlepollard

Mullingar

Lough Owel

Lough Ennell

Sligo

Galway

N1

M1

N1

N51

N2

M3

R154

M3

N51

M3

N51

N52

N52

N51

M2

M3

N4

M4

M4

M6

N52

N4

Lough

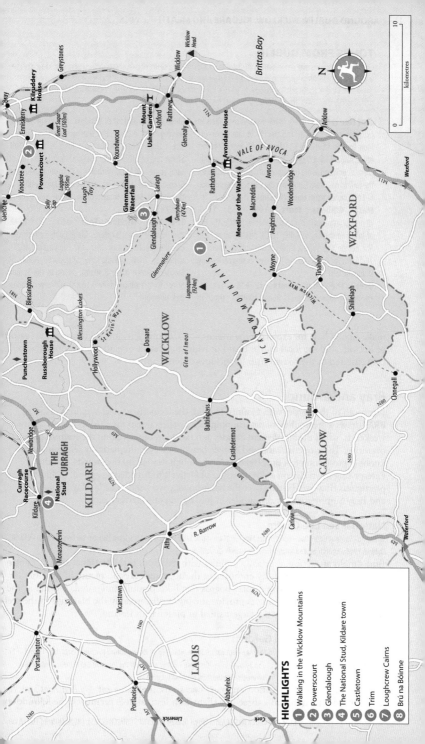

N

kilometres
0   10

WICKLOW MOUNTAINS

Wicklow Head
Brittas Bay
Greystones
Bray
Kilruddery House
Enniskerry
Powerscourt
Knockree
Glencree
Great Sugar Loaf (503m)
Mount Usher Gardens
Ashford
Rathnew
Wicklow
Roundwood
Glenealy
Avondale House
VALE OF AVOCA
Sally Gap
Lugala (595m)
Lough Tay
Glenmacnass Waterfall
Laragh
Glendalough
Derrybawn (474m)
Rathdrum
Meeting of the Waters
Avoca
Macreddin
Woodenbridge
Arklow
Wexford
Glenmalure
Lugnaquillia (924m)
Moyne
Aughrim
Tinahely
Wicklow Way
Shillelagh
WEXFORD
Blessington
Blessington Lakes
St Kevin's Way
WICKLOW MOUNTAINS
WICKLOW
Donard
Glen of Imaal
Hollywood
Russborough House
Punchestown
Clonegall
CARLOW
Baltinglass
Tullow
N80
Castledermot
N80
Newbridge
Curragh Racecourse
National Stud
THE CURRAGH
Kildare
Monasterevin
KILDARE
Athy
R. Barrow
Carlow
N80
Waterford
M9
Vicarstown
N80
Portarlington
N80
Portlaoise
LAOIS
Abbeyleix
Limerick
Cork

2

TOURS FROM DUBLIN

Organized tours are especially useful if you want to take in more than one sight in a day; those which include Newgrange (see p.142) guarantee a place on the guided tour of the passage grave. It's best to book in advance, either directly or through a tourist office or your hotel. All admission charges are usually included in the price, though not lunch.

Gray Line ☏ 01 898 0700, ⓦ loveireland.com. Runs an excursion to Newgrange and the Hill of Tara (April–Oct Mon, Tues, Fri & Sat 9am; €34) from the O'Connell St tourist office. Also a "Grand Wicklow Tour", including Russborough, Glendalough and Avoca (minimum of 6 people needed for the tour to run; from €28), from the City Sightseeing shop at 14 O'Connell Street Upper (9.45am).

Mary Gibbons Tours ☏ 086 355 1355, ⓦ newgrangetours.com. Takes in Newgrange, the Hill of Tara and the Boyne Valley (€35), picking up at *Pizza Hut* beside the Suffolk Street tourist office (Mon–Fri 10.15am, Sat & Sun 8.05am), as well as several leading Dublin hotels.

Over the Top Tours ☏ 1800 424252, ⓦ overthetoptours.com. Runs minibus trips to Glendalough and the Wicklow Mountains (€28), leaving from outside the *Gresham Hotel*, O'Connell Street Upper (daily 9.20am), calling at the Suffolk Street tourist office (daily 9.45am); and to the Hill of Tara, Slane and Monasterboice (€28) from outside the *Gresham Hotel* (Mon–Sat 9am, Sun 9.20am), calling at the Suffolk Street tourist office (Mon–Sat 9.20am, Sun 9.45am).

The Wild Wicklow Tour ☏ 01 280 1899, ⓦ wildwicklow.ie. Explores Glendalough and heads off the beaten track into the mountains (€28), departing from outside the *Shelbourne Hotel*, St Stephen's Green (daily 8.50am), calling at the Suffolk Street tourist office (daily 9.10am) and several other pick-up points.

---

make a good base for exploring the mountains. County Wicklow is known as the "garden of Ireland" and the local tourist board provides full details of gardens that can be visited, concentrated in the coastal strip (ⓦ wicklowgardens.com).

Bray and around

Just south of the border with County Dublin, the formerly genteel Victorian resort of **BRAY** draws a great influx of day-tripping city-dwellers down the DART line on summer weekends, when the amusement arcades and fast-food outlets along the seafront go into overdrive. The attractive sand and shingle beach, however, dramatically set against the knobbly promontory of **Bray Head**, is long enough to soak up the crowds, and the enterprising town lays on a diverse roster of **festivals** to broaden its appeal, including the prestigious Bray Jazz Festival over the bank-holiday weekend in early May (ⓦ brayjazz.com) and Bray Summerfest, an all-rounder in July (ⓦ braysummerfest.com).

National Sea Life Centre

Strand Rd • Summer daily 10am–6pm; winter Mon–Fri 11am–5pm, Sat & Sun 10am–6pm; last admission 1hr before closing • €12.50, children €9 (discounts if booked online); Heritage Island • ⓦ sealife.ie

Bray's main attraction, especially popular with children, is the **National Sea Life Centre** on the seafront. Run by fishy enthusiasts, the aquarium lays on plenty of activities for kids, as well as informative display boards that'll keep adults interested. Inevitably, the more exotic, far-flung creatures provide the big thrills, notably the blacktips in the reef shark tank and "probably the largest shoal of piranhas in Ireland".

Killruddery House and Gardens

Gardens April & Oct Sat & Sun 9.30am–6pm; May–Sept daily 9.30am–6pm • €6.50 **House** Guided tours July–Sept daily 1–4pm • €11 (includes gardens); Heritage Island • ☏ 01 286 3405, ⓦ killruddery.com • 20min walk from the southern end of the seafront or bus (Dublin Bus #84 or #184, or Finnegan's – ⓦ finnegan-bray.ie) from Bray DART station

Used as a film and TV location on many occasions, including for *My Left Foot* and *The Tudors* (and now home to a three-day silent-film festival in September), the **Killruddery**

2

estate on the southern edge of Bray is most notable for its **gardens**. Designed in the seventeenth century in early French formal style, and added to in the nineteenth, they're the oldest gardens in Ireland, featuring extensive walks flanked by hornbeam, beech and lime hedges, a café and an eighteenth-century "sylvan theatre" framed by a high bay hedge and terraced banks. The 200m-long twin ponds, once stocked with fish for the table, were designed as "water mirrors" in front of the main **house**. The latter, built in the 1820s in Tudor Revival style, is still home to the Brabazon family (the earls of Meath), and boasts some fine plasterwork ceilings. When the house is open, you can get into the **Orangery**, which was erected in the 1850s after the fashion of London's Crystal Palace and restored in 2000 – so styling itself "Ireland's Millennium Dome". Killruddery hosts an imaginative roster of **activities**, which might include foraging for wild food, gardening for kids and sheep shearing, as well as **Groove Festival**, a relaxed, family-friendly, boutique music festival over a July weekend (ⓦ groovefestival.ie).

ARRIVAL AND INFORMATION
BRAY AND AROUND

By train The suburban DART (see p.93) is a far preferable way to get here from Dublin than the bus.
Tourist office In the town council building in the Civic Centre on Main St, a 10min walk inland from the DART station (Mon–Fri 9.30am–4.30pm, Sat 10am–2pm; ⓣ 01 286 7128). The tourist office may at some point move back to its former home in the heritage centre, in the old courthouse on Lower Main St, which is currently closed pending refurbishment.

ACCOMMODATION AND EATING

The Porterhouse Strand Rd ⓣ 01 286 0668, ⓦ porterhousehotel-bray.com. On the seafront, this branch of the excellent *Temple Bar* microbrewery-pub serves its own great stouts, lagers and ales, as well as good, basic food such as pizzas, with a beer garden overlooking the esplanade. It's unlikely that you'll want to stay in Bray, but it might be worth knowing that *The Porterhouse* also offers chic, modern rooms, some with sea views. Mon–Thurs & Sun noon–midnight, Fri & Sat noon–2.30am. **€99**

Wicklow and around

WICKLOW, 27km south of Bray, is a modest, easy-going county town, though change is under way now that it's within the ever-expanding range of Dublin commuters, as evidenced by new boutiques and galleries, and the closure of several old pubs. Transport connections are less favourable for tourists than workers, however, as there are no buses from here into the heart of the Wicklow Mountains just to the west, but if you have a car, you could base yourself at one of several fine country hotels near the town for upland jaunts.

Built around a small port that busies itself with fishing, timber and yachts, the town is enlivened by its unusual setting: the Vartry River broadens into a lough here before

---

A WALK OVER BRAY HEAD TO GREYSTONES

There's an excellent two- to three-hour **walk** from Bray seafront south across Bray Head to **Greystones**, a small commuter town at the end of the DART line with several pubs serving food. You can follow the comparatively flat **cliff path** (ⓦ thecliffwalk.ie) that runs above the rail tracks for most of the way, giving close-up views of rocky coves and slate pinnacles, lashed by magnificent waves on windy days, as well as possible sightings of kestrels, peregrine falcons, dolphins, whales and basking sharks. Alternatively, if you have more time, take on the steep climb over the top of **Bray Head** for great views of Killiney Bay and the cone-shaped hills inland known as Little Sugar Loaf and Great Sugar Loaf, with a distant backdrop of the Wicklow Mountains. The latter route ascends rapidly from the end of Bray seafront through pine woods and over gorse slopes to a large cross, 200m above sea level, which was erected to mark the Holy Year of 1950; from here a track winds across the ridge below the 240m summit of Bray Head, before you turn sharp left down to join the cliff path which will bring you into Greystones.

flowing into the Irish Sea, cutting off a narrow strip of land, **the Murrough**, that's rich in bird life, notably wintering swans and geese. On a small rise above the harbour's south pier stand the meagre ruins of twelfth-century **Black Castle**, which affords fine views of the coast, north to the Sugarloaf Mountains and south to Wicklow Head.

Wicklow's Historic Gaol

Kilmantin Hill • **Gaol** Daily 10.30am–4.30pm • €7.30, children €4.50, family €19 **Ghost tours** daily every 15min, 7–8.30pm • €15 • ⓦ wicklowshistoricgaol.com

The town's major tourist attraction is **Wicklow's Historic Gaol**, dating from 1702, just up Kilmantin Hill from Market Square. The interactive tour builds up a lively and imaginative picture of life in the prison, focusing on the transportation of almost 50,000 Irish convicts to Australia and fleshed out by sections on the 1798 Rebellion and the Great Famine. On the last Friday evening of the month, the gaol also runs adults-only ghost tours.

Mount Usher Gardens

5km northwest of Wicklow, on the N11 just south of Ashford • Late Feb to Oct daily 10am–6pm, last admission 5.20pm • €7.50 • ⓦ mountushergardens.ie

Now owned by Avoca (see p.127), who run a very good café here, **Mount Usher Gardens** shelter a plethora of rare trees, shrubs and flowers, including dazzling rhododendrons, azaleas and maples, and the finest eucalyptus specimens in Europe, all growing in an informal style in the woodlands and meadows. The gardens straddle the Vartry River, which is broken up here by a remarkable series of nineteenth-century weirs, watercourses and miniature suspension bridges.

Silver Strand and Brittas Bay

Brittas Bay Any bus on the inland N11 to Arklow will put you off at Jack White's Crossroads, from where it's a 30min walk to the beach

Running south from Wicklow, off the R750 towards Arklow, is a series of fine, sandy beaches, beginning at **Silver Strand**, a lovely, sheltered spot just 5km from town. Backed by rolling dunes, **Brittas Bay**'s 3km strand, around 8km further on, is especially attractive and popular with weekending Dubliners, offering surfing and stand-up paddleboarding (ⓦ brittasbaysurfschool.com) and kiteboarding (ⓦ wicklowkiteboarding.com).

ARRIVAL AND INFORMATION

WICKLOW AND AROUND

By train The train station is a 15min walk northwest of the centre, off the Rathnew (Dublin) road.

Destinations Dublin Connolly (3–5 daily via Greystones, Bray, Tara St and Pearse; 1hr 10min); Rosslare Europort (3–4 daily via Rathdrum, Enniscorthy and Wexford; 1hr 45min).

By bus Buses stop either on Summer Hill, just east of Market Square, or on Marlton Rd behind the *Grand Hotel*, just west of the centre.

Destinations Avoca (1–2 daily via Glenealy, Meeting of the Waters and Rathdrum; 35min); Dublin (Airport, via several city-centre drop-off points; at least hourly; 1hr 50min); Enniscorthy (9 daily; 1hr 25min); Wexford (9 daily; 1hr 50min).

Tourist office The tourist office is on Fitzwilliam Square (Mon–Fri 9.20am–1.15pm & 2–5.15pm; dependent on staffing, may open Sat in summer – check times on ☎ 0404 69117), which is linked to Market Square to the east by Main St, and can provide details of the town's three-day arts festival in May (or go to ⓦ wicklowartsfestival.ie).

GETTING AROUND

By taxi Wicklow Cabs, Main St (☎ 0404 66888).

By bike Bespoke Cycles, South Quay (☎ 0404 32264, ⓦ bespokecycles.ie).

By car Sinnott Autos, Dublin Rd (☎ 0404 25200, ⓦ sinnottautos.ie)

ACCOMMODATION

★**Ballyknocken House** Glenealy, about 8km southwest of town just off the Rathdrum road ☎ 0404 44627, ⓦ ballyknocken.com. Charming, creeper-clad 1850s farmhouse furnished with antiques, which serves superb breakfasts, using home-grown fruit and homemade bread and cakes. Also on offer are a tennis court, cookery courses and walking programmes, plus plenty of hiking information including a specially commissioned book of local walks; excellent four-course set dinners, bringing to bear an Italian influence on local produce, are available at weekends if pre-arranged. **€110**

Captain Halpin's Bunkhouse Bachelor's Walk ☎0404 69126, ⓦwicklowtownhostel.ie. Homely hostel in a two-storey Georgian town house with spacious common areas, including a well-equipped kitchen and a back patio, on a leafy, central street overlooking the river. All dorms are en suite, while the two private rooms, with raised, loft double beds, share a bathroom. Bicycle and kayak rental available. Dorms **€14**, doubles **€44**

★**Hunter's Hotel** About 3km from Wicklow on the R761 north of Rathnew ☎0404 40106, ⓦhunters.ie. Sited on the old road from the southeast to Dublin, *Hunter's* is Ireland's oldest coaching inn, dating from the early eighteenth century. It's very comfortable yet unpretentious and welcoming, with an excellent restaurant and with most bedrooms overlooking the glorious two-acre gardens on the banks of the River Vartry, where afternoon tea is served in fine weather. Half-board packages available. **€130**

Tinakilly Just over 1km out of town on the Rathnew road ☎0404 69274, ⓦtinakilly.ie. Grand Victorian mansion, covered in creepers and set in huge, mature landscaped gardens that run down to the sea; some rooms have four-poster or half-tester beds. **€120**

EATING AND DRINKING

Bridge Tavern Bridge St ☎0404 64760. Founded in 1759 on the site of an earlier shebeen, the tavern has been given a new lease of life by its recent painstaking refurbishment. Seductive leather and dark wood now fill the spacious, well-lit bars, and there's a flower-strewn riverside courtyard. Mon–Thurs noon–11.30pm, Fri & Sat noon–12.30am, Sun noon–11pm.

Donelli's Market Square ☎0404 61333, ⓦdonellis.ie. With tables out on the square, *Donelli's* is a bustling, modern, daytime café-restaurant that also opens weekend evenings (2 courses with wine €29). On offer during the day are all manner of tasty sandwiches, soups, salads, cakes and a small range of main courses such as beef stroganoff, while dinner stretches to West Indian chicken curry and Moroccan-spiced lamb rump. Mon–Thurs 9am–4pm, Fri & Sat 9am–11.30pm.

Halpin's Bridge Café Bridge St ☎0404 32677. Friendly and well-kept café, where you can read their newspapers to a background of mellow jazz, while tucking into homemade chicken liver pâté (€7) or goat's cheese and roast red pepper quiche (€10). Also on offer are homemade soups, gourmet sandwiches, salads, cakes, and speciality teas and coffees. Mon–Fri 8.30am–6pm, Sat 9am–6pm, Sun 10am–4pm.

Phil Healy's Fitzwilliam Square ☎0404 67380. Congenial, wood-panelled pub with lots of craft beers in bottles and on tap, a creative food menu and traditional sessions on Wed. Mon–Thurs 4–11.30pm, Fri 4pm–12.30am, Sat 2pm–12.30am, Sun 2–11pm.

The Square Steakhouse Market Square ☎0404 66422, ⓦwww.steakhousewicklow.com. At this cosy, central restaurant, half of the menu's main courses feature steak in various incarnations – the speciality is Surf and Turf, fillet steak with prawns in garlic butter (€25) – but you'll also find fresh fish of the day (priced daily). Tues–Thurs 6–10pm, Fri & Sat 6–11pm.

The Wicklow Mountains

If your time in Ireland is limited, it's well worth considering a stay in Dublin, followed by a few days high up in the fresh air and magnificent scenery of the **Wicklow Mountains**. So close to the capital that they're often called the Dublin Mountains – by Dubliners, at any rate – they only rise to 924m at their highest point, Lugnaquillia, but form the largest area of continuous upland in Ireland. This granite mass is wild, desolate and sparsely populated at its centre, and, despite the influx of outdoorsy city-dwellers at weekends, never feels crowded. The range has been heavily glaciated to form attractive valleys, lakes and corries, while an extensive covering of peat supports purple heather and yellow gorse in abundance. To protect this huge natural playground on Dublin's doorstep, part of the massif has been designated as a national park, and walkers are signposted onto the **Wicklow Way**, a managed, long-distance trail that bisects the mountains from north to south. Wicklow Tourism's website (ⓦvisitwicklow.ie/category/walks-in-wicklow/) covers all manner of hiking across the county, with route maps and descriptions.

GETTING AROUND   THE WICKLOW MOUNTAINS

By public transport Dublin Bus will get you to Powerscourt's beautiful gardens and the neighbouring village of Enniskerry, and to the fine stately home of Russborough House on the western side of the

2

THE WICKLOW WAY

The Republic's oldest designated long-distance walk, opened in 1982, the **Wicklow Way** runs the length of the Wicklow Mountains from Dublin's southern suburbs, taking in wild uplands and picturesque valleys, as well as long, boring stretches of conifer plantation. The trail cuts across the Glencree valley, passes Lough Tay and continues to Glendalough, before entering Glenmalure and skirting Lugnaquillia, the highest Wicklow peak; the walk finishes after 130km at Clonegall on the Wexford–Carlow border. The whole route is waymarked with yellow signs and can be walked in five to six days, though some people take as many as ten.

The Way begins at Marlay Park in Dublin's southern suburbs – take the #16 bus from O'Connell Street to get there. Its highlight – if you lack the time or inclination to complete the whole Way – is probably the 29km section from **Knockree to Glendalough**, which passes the Powerscourt waterfall and can be covered in one very long day – or preferably two, with a short detour to overnight at Roundwood.

Finding **accommodation** is not usually a problem, and some B&Bs will collect you from, or deliver you to, parts of the route, or ferry your bags to your next resting place, if given prior notice; there's now also a dedicated and usually cheaper luggage transfer service (☎086 269 8659, ⓦwicklowwaybaggage.com), who also offer taxi transfers to the Way from Dublin Airport. Three An Óige hostels line the route – at Knockree (see p.123), Glendalough (see p.126) and Glenmalure (see p.126). Accommodation in Roundwood, Laragh/Glendalough and Glenmalure is detailed in the text. An excellent **website** (ⓦwicklowway.com) gives full details of other accommodation along the route, as well as trail descriptions, maps and other useful advice.

Ordnance Survey **maps** nos. 56 and 62 cover almost the whole route at 1:50,000, with nos. 50 and 61 picking up the extremities. EastWest Mapping (ⓦeastwestmapping.ie) also produce *The Wicklow Way Map Guide*, a booklet of 1:50,000 maps with accompanying text, as well as digital mapping of the region.

mountains. Further south, the dramatic monastic site of Glendalough and its service town Laragh, along with the lofty village of Roundwood, are all accessible from Dublin on the St Kevin's Bus service and make good bases from which to explore the mountains. Some Bus Éireann services on the Arklow route detour inland from Wicklow to Rathdrum and the intensely pretty Vale of Avoca, on the southern edge of the mountains. The nearest village to the former home and estate of Charles Stewart Parnell, Avondale House, Rathdrum also has a station on the Dublin–Wexford rail line and a minibus/ taxi service to Laragh, Glendalough and quiet, picturesque Glenmalure.

By guided tour Of course, you'll get the most out of the mountains and their many opportunities for walking if you have your own transport, but otherwise it's worth considering one of the many tours on offer. As well as the day-trips from Dublin detailed on p.116, there are guided walking tours in the mountains by outfits such as Irish Ways (see p.29), Hilltop Treks (☎087 784 9599, ⓦhilltoptreks.ie) and Footfalls (☎0404 45152, ⓦwalkinghikingireland.com).

Powerscourt

Enniskerry • **Gardens** Daily 9.30am–5.30pm; closes at dusk in winter • €8.50; Heritage Island **Waterfall** Daily: Jan, Feb, Nov & Dec 10.30am–4pm; March, April, Sept & Oct 10.30am–5.30pm; May–Aug 9.30am–7pm; closed 2 weeks prior to Christmas • €5.50 • ⓦpowerscourt.com

In the northeastern foothills of the Wicklow Mountains, 19km south of Dublin and less than 1km beyond the village of **Enniskerry**, lies the massive **Powerscourt Estate**, where, given fine weather, you could easily pass a whole day. Although the estate is now something of an all-round leisure complex, with a golf course, garden centre, craft shops and a luxury hotel, the central attraction remains the **formal gardens**, whose spectacular design matches their superb setting facing Great Sugar Loaf Mountain.

In the late twelfth century, a castle was built on this strategic site by the Anglo-Norman le Poer (Power) family, from whom it takes its name. However, what you see today dates from the early eighteenth century, when Richard Castle designed one of the largest Palladian mansions in Ireland here, flanked by terraced gardens that were further developed in the nineteenth century. The **house** remains impressive from a distance, but most of its interior was destroyed by a fire in 1974 (on the eve of a party to celebrate major refurbishment) and it now shelters an exhibition of dolls' houses and toys (ⓦ tarapalace.ie).

The gardens

The terraced **Italian Gardens** slope gracefully down from the back of the house. The uppermost terrace, with its winged figures of Fame and Victory flanking Apollo and Diana, was designed in 1843 by the gout-ridden Daniel Robertson, who used to be wheeled about the site in a barrow, cradling a bottle of sherry – the last of the sherry apparently meant the end of the day's work. A grand staircase leads down to a spirited pair of zinc winged horses guarding the **Triton Lake**, whose central statue of the sea god (based on Bernini's fountain in the Piazza Barberini in Rome) fires a jet of water 30m skywards.

On the east side of the terraces are the curious **Pepper Pot Tower** (accurately modelled on the pepper pot from the eighth Viscount Powerscourt's dinner set), surrounded by fine North American conifers, and a colourful **Japanese Garden** of maples, azaleas and fortune palms, laid out on reclaimed bogland. To the west of the Italian Gardens lies the **walled garden**, with its rose beds, herbaceous borders and fine ceremonial entrances: the Chorus Gate, decorated with beautiful golden trumpeters, and the Bamberg Gate, which originally belonged to Bamberg cathedral in Bavaria and features remarkable perspective arches as part of its gilded ironwork design.

The waterfall

The estate's final attraction, **Powerscourt Waterfall**, is Ireland's highest at 120m. The falls leap and bound diagonally down a rock face to replenish the waters of the River Dargle in the valley below. It's 6km further down the road from the main gate, but well signposted.

ARRIVAL AND DEPARTURE	**POWERSCOURT**
By bus Enniskerry is accessible from Dublin by taking the #44 bus from O'Connell St, D'Olier St or Merrion Square (hourly; 1hr), or the DART train to Bray followed by the	#185 bus (11–28 daily; 30min), which sometimes continues to the main gate of Powerscourt Estate.

ACCOMMODATION AND EATING

Avoca Terrace Café Powerscourt House. Excellent, self-service café, run by Avoca (see p.127), offering dishes such as lemon tart and smoked Wicklow trout salad, and a terrace that provides sumptuous views of the garden. Daily 9.30am–5pm.

Ferndale Enniskerry ☏ 01 286 3518, ⓦ ferndalehouse.com. You'll probably want to push on further into the mountains for somewhere to stay, but Enniskerry does have this good B&B on the village square, an attractive, all-en-suite place, furnished in period style, in an early Victorian house set in pretty gardens. **€70**

Glencree and around

To the west of Powerscourt, beyond Knockree, the village of **GLENCREE** lies at the head of its eponymous valley and on the old **military road** from Dublin south into the mountains. To flush out insurgents from the 1798 Rebellion, some of whom evaded capture in Wicklow until 1803, the authorities in Dublin were obliged to build this road right along the backbone of the range. In the village, there's a cemetery for German airmen who died in Ireland during the two world wars.

Glencree Centre for Peace & Reconciliation

Mon–Fri 9.30am–5pm, Sat & Sun 9.30am–5.30pm • ☏ 01 282 9711, ⓦ www.glencree.ie

A reconciliation centre set up for people affected by the conflict in the North, fittingly occupies a former British army barracks, built to guard the military road. It houses a café with an outdoor terrace and a visitor centre that displays diverse emporary exhibitions.

South into the mountains

South of Glencree, the military road climbs past the dramatic twin tarns of Lough Bray Lower and Upper (accessible by boggy paths opposite a car park) and then through ever wilder terrain towards one of the Wicklow Mountains' two main passes, the **Sally Gap**. From here the military road (R115) continues south through superb countryside, passing the beautiful **Glenmacnass Waterfall**, down to Laragh and Glendalough. If you fancy stretching your legs along the way, pull in at the car park 2.5km south of Sally Gap, cross the road and follow the rough, boggy path for 45 minutes or so to the prominent summit of **Luggala**, or Fancy Mountain; from here, you'll be rewarded with precipitous views straight down to Lough Tay and a panorama to the south and west of Lough Dan and the major Wicklow peaks.

Lough Tay

The R759 heading southeast of Sally Gap winds its way down to Sraghmore, 3km north of Roundwood, passing impressive **Lough Tay**, where scree slopes tumble headlong into the water from the summit of Luggala. You can walk from one of the car parks above Lough Tay north up the Wicklow Way for about fifteen minutes to the memorial to J.B. Malone (one of the pioneers of Irish hill-walking and of the Way itself) for the finest view of the ensemble, and on to the top of White Hill in another twenty minutes for further scenic delights.

ACCOMMODATION — **GLENCREE AND AROUND**

Knockree Youth Hostel 7km southwest of Enniskerry ⓣ01 276 7981, ⓦanoige.ie; several times a day the #185 from Bray DART station continues from Enniskerry to Shop River, about 3km, or a 40min walk, north of the hostel. Lying on the Wicklow Way, this ultra-modern "five-star" hostel is bright, colourful, well equipped and mostly en suite, with fine views of the lush valley of Glencree and Great Sugar Loaf. Breakfast available. Dorms €21, doubles €55

Roundwood

From Dublin, you can reach Glendalough on the old military road (R115), but the quicker route is along the N11 and R755 through **ROUNDWOOD**, which is accessible on the St Kevin's bus service (see p.125). This attractive village claims to be the highest in Ireland, at 220m above sea level, and enjoys a gentle setting on the eastern flank of the Wicklow range by the Vartry Reservoir – a good spot for an easy, flat, evening stroll. With a decent range of food and accommodation, Roundwood is a popular stop for hikers on the Wicklow Way, which is just 2.5km away. Wedged between the R759 and the R755 a little north of the village, **Ballinastoe Forest** is crisscrossed with mountain-biking trails, with bike rental, mountain-biking lessons and tours available (ⓣ083 434 6992, ⓦbiking.ie).

ACCOMMODATION AND EATING — **ROUNDWOOD**

Riverbank Dublin Rd, north of the village centre ⓣ01 281 8117, ⓔriverbank1@eircom.net. Family home with a lovely garden, bright, pine-floored and furnished en-suite bedrooms, and a drying room. Offers luggage transfer, transport to/from the trail for walkers, and packed lunches. Good rates for singles. March–Oct. €70

Roundwood Caravan & Camping Park At the north end of the village ⓣ01 281 8163, ⓦdublinwicklowcamping.com. Large, smart, well-equipped campsite with a shop, laundry service and campers' kitchen. May to late Sept. €26

★The Roundwood Inn Main St ⓣ01 281 8107. Roundwood's best place to drink is this cosy, seventeenth-century coaching inn. It also serves great bar meals, ranging from local seafood to delicious Irish stew, as well as dishes such as roast leg of Wicklow lamb in its more formal, weekend restaurant. Bar Mon–Thurs noon–11.30pm, Fri & Sat noon–12.30am, Sun noon–11pm; restaurant Fri & Sat dinner, Sun lunch.

Skylark's Rest (IHO) On the west side of the village ☎087 091 0342, ⓦskylarksrest.com. Budget accommodation aimed at walkers in a bright, modern house, with a well-equipped kitchen, lounge and drying room. Bike rental (free if you stay 2 nights). Light breakfast included. Dorms €22, doubles €50

Glendalough and Laragh

Visitor Centre and monastic site daily: mid-March to mid-Oct 9.30am–6pm; mid-Oct to mid-March 9.30am–5pm; last admission 45min before closing • Visitor Centre €3; monastic site free; Heritage Card • ⓦ heritageireland.ie

A deep glaciated valley in the heart of the Wicklow Mountains, **GLENDALOUGH** ("valley of the two lakes") provides a delightfully atmospheric location for some of the best-preserved monastic sites in Ireland. Despite the coach parties, enough of the valley's tranquillity remains for you to understand what drew monks and pilgrims here in the first place.

The Glendalough Visitor Centre, its adjacent car park and the main monastic site are on the eastern side of the **Lower Lake**, while further west up the valley is the larger and more impressive **Upper Lake**, with its wooded cliffs and dramatic waterfall as well as more ruins, the national park information point and another car park. On the main road in, about 2km east of the visitor centre, lies the small village of **LARAGH**, which has most of the area's amenities, notably accommodation (though no ATM – the nearest is in Roundwood or Rathdrum); the Green Road from the south end of Laragh will allow you to walk along the south bank of the river to the Glendalough Visitor Centre and beyond, away from the traffic on the main road.

Brief history

The monastery was established in the sixth century by **St Kevin** (Caoimhín), who retreated to Glendalough to pray in solitude. His piety attracted many followers to the site, especially after his death in 618, and the monastic community here came to rival Clonmacnois (see p.172) for its learning. It was raided by the Vikings at least four times between the eighth and eleventh centuries, then by the English in the fourteenth, and

---

WALKS AND ACTIVITIES AROUND GLENDALOUGH

The **Wicklow Mountains National Park Information Office** (May–Sept daily 10am–5.30pm; Feb–April & Oct Sat & Sun 10am–5.30pm; Jan, Nov & Dec Sat & Sun 10am–4pm; plus extra days during school holidays; ☎0404 45425, ⓦwicklowmountainsnationalpark.ie), at the eastern end of Glendalough's Upper Lake, has details of local walking routes and conditions and sells a series of leaflets on the national park, including *The Walking Trails of Glendalough* (also available from the visitor centre), which covers waymarked routes taking anything from 45 minutes to four hours. A map of the walking trails can be downloaded from the website, while a couple of good hikes in the area are also covered by Joss Lynam's *Easy Walks near Dublin*. The visitor centre contains an exhibition on the park's wildlife, which includes deer, red squirrels, hen harriers, red grouse and lots of birds of prey, and runs free guided nature walks, such as bat walks in summer and rut walks to observe deer in the autumn.

St Kevin's Way follows what was the main pilgrim path to Glendalough in medieval times. Waymarked with yellow pilgrim symbols, the 29km trail runs eastwards along country tracks and quiet roads from Hollywood, near the N81 south of Blessington, climbing to the **Wicklow Gap**, before following the descent of the Glendasan River for 7km to the Glendalough Visitor Centre. *St Kevin's Way*, a booklet by Peter Harbison and Joss Lynam, covers the route with comprehensive 1:50,000 maps and text.

The easiest to follow and most satisfying short hike is on the south side of Glendalough valley, where it's possible to climb 474m **Derrybawn** in around an hour, for spectacular views. Follow the Wicklow Way south from the national park information point past the Poulanass Waterfall, before eventually peeling left off the waymarked forest track up a narrow path, which climbs steeply to the edge of the forest and then straight up to Derrybawn's ridge and summit cairn.

For **horse riding**, try Glendalough House, about 3km north of Laragh in Annamoe (☎0404 45116, ⓦglendaloughhouse.ie).

was finally dissolved during the Reformation. Pilgrimages continued, however, as the pope declared that seven visits to Glendalough would earn the same indulgence as one to Rome, but the pilgrims' abstemious devotions on St Kevin's Day (June 3) were often followed by drink and debauchery, and in 1862 a local priest banned the gatherings.

The Lower Lake

The **visitor centre** features photographic displays and a film on Glendalough's place within Ireland's monastic heritage as well as a model of how the monastery is thought to have looked at the height of its activity.

Once you've entered the **monastic site**, through a double stone archway that was once surmounted by a tower, you'll come to its largest structure, the roofless but impressive **Cathedral of SS Peter and Paul**, begun in the early ninth century. Among the tombs outside stands **St Kevin's Cross**, one of the best remaining relics from the period, consisting of a granite monolith decorated with an eighth-century carving of a Celtic cross over a wheel; unusually, the quadrants of the cross have not been cut through, which suggests that it was left unfinished. Above the doorway of the nearby twelfth-century **Priests' House**, which may have been the site of Kevin's tomb-shrine, are faint carvings of figures believed to depict the saint and two (later) abbots. Downhill from here stands the two-storey, eleventh-century **St Kevin's Church**, whose steeply pitched roof and bell turret so resemble a chimney that the building is also known as "St Kevin's Kitchen", although it was almost certainly an oratory. Glendalough's **Round Tower** rises to over 30m, its conical roof having been restored in 1876. Such tapering stone towers are found only in Ireland and probably had multiple functions, as belfries, watchtowers, treasuries and places of refuge from danger – the entrance is usually well above ground level, accessible by a ladder that could be removed if necessary. To the south of St Kevin's Church, a footbridge crosses the river to the **Deerstone**, so called after a legend that claims that a tame doe squirted milk into the hollowed-out stone to feed the twin orphaned babies of one of Kevin's followers. In fact, it's a bullaun, one of many all over Ireland, a stone believed to have magical powers that was used for grinding medicines.

The Upper Lake

You can drive to the Upper Lake car park along the north side of the valley, but it's far preferable to walk from the Deerstone along the signposted **Green Road** (part of the Wicklow Way), a scenic track that skirts the south side of the Lower Lake. After twenty minutes or so, this will bring you to the Upper Lake and the tiny, ruined, late tenth-century, Romanesque **Reefert Church**, whose small cemetery is thought to contain the graves of local chieftains (its name means "royal burial ground" in Irish). From here a path runs up to **St Kevin's Cell**, a typically Celtic, corbel-roofed "beehive" hut on a promontory overlooking the lake. Further up the cliff, **St Kevin's Bed** is a small cave that may have been a Bronze Age tomb, into which the saint reputedly moved to avoid the allures of an admirer called Caitlín; he's supposed to have offered the final resistance to her advances by chucking the poor woman into the lake. On the opposite side of the lake, a trail runs along the north shore and on up the valley, passing nineteenth-century zinc and lead mines.

ARRIVAL AND DEPARTURE	GLENDALOUGH AND LARAGH
By bus St Kevin's bus service (☏ 01 281 8119, ⊕ glendaloughbus.com) runs daily from Dawson St in Dublin, via Bray (Town Hall, Main St) and Roundwood, to	Laragh and Glendalough Visitor Centre (11.30am and 6pm; 7pm on Sat & Sun from March to Sept; €13 single, €20 return). Minibuses from Rathdrum are detailed on p.127.

ACCOMMODATION AND EATING	
Derrymore Glendalough ☏ 0404 45493, ⊕ glendalough accommodation.com. Handily placed on the road between Laragh and Glendalough with views of the Lower Lake, this	B&B offers en-suite rooms furnished with antiques, good, varied breakfasts including home-baked soda bread and muffins, and a warm welcome. Packed lunches available for

2

walkers. Discounts for stays of 2 nights and more. **€80**

Glendalough Green Café Laragh ☎0404 45151. Attractive, welcoming deli-café with outdoor tables on the green, dishing up tasty homemade soups, home-baked breads and cakes, salads, speciality teas and coffees. Mon–Sat 8.30am–5pm, Sun 8.30am–6pm.

Glendalough Hermitage Centre St Kevin's Parish Church, just west of Laragh, on the north side of the road to Glendalough ☎087 935 6696, ⓦglendaloughhermitage.ie. This spiritual retreat run by the Sisters of Mercy offers pilgrims of all faiths comfortable, pine-furnished stone bungalows in a tranquil, gorse-strewn garden. Suggested donation **€70**

Glendalough Hotel Glendalough ☎0404 45135, ⓦglendaloughhotel.com. Recently extended, family-run Victorian hotel right by the visitor centre, offering great views from many of the colourful, en-suite bedrooms, some of which have balconies; good-value half-board deals available. Very good rates for singles. **€120**

Glendalough International Hostel Glendalough, on the road to the Upper Lake ☎0404 45342, ⓦanoige.ie. Large, comfortable, recently refurbished, all-en-suite hostel, offering breakfast and packed lunches, a

well-equipped kitchen, drying room and laundry facilities. Dorms **€16**, doubles **€48**

Lynham's Hotel Laragh ☎0404 45345 ⓦlynhamsoflaragh.ie. Airy, spacious, modern hotel overlooking the Glenmacnass River at the heart of the village, behind a popular bar with open fires in winter and outside tables by the river in summer; half-board deals offered. **€130**

Riversdale Wicklow Gap road, just over 1km northwest of the Glendalough Visitor Centre ☎0404 45858, ⓦglendalough.eu.com. Hospitable, well-run B&B in a tranquil location with great views. The en-suite rooms are simply and tastefully furnished, and breakfast is taken in the picturesque sun room overlooking the Glendasan River. Packed lunches available for walkers. Self-catering cottage available. **€80**

The Wicklow Heather Glendalough road, Laragh ☎0404 45157. Just off the green in Laragh, this is a cosy restaurant with a whiskey bar and attractive patio tables. It serves everything from breakfast and morning coffee to upmarket dinners featuring, for example, roast rump of local lamb (€22), as well as Wicklow trout, beef and venison. Daily 8.30am–9.30pm.

Glenmalure

Arrowing down from the northwest around the Avonbeg River, **Glenmalure** is the next valley south of Glendalough, overshadowed to the southwest by Wicklow's highest peak, wild and lonely **Lugnaquillia** (924m). Besides the river, this peaceful, enclosed glen has room only for a thin strip of emerald fields and a narrow, gorse-flanked road between its steep slopes of scree and forestry. For drivers and cyclists, the military road offers a scenic route there, branching off the R755 just south of Laragh and continuing southwest; walkers can follow the Wicklow Way out of Glendalough, skirting Derrybawn Mountain and 657m Mullacor before descending into the valley. At the point where the military road hits the glen stands a ruined barracks, used in the suppression of the 1798 Rebellion.

ARRIVAL AND DEPARTURE
GLENMALURE

By Bus Minibuses run from Rathdrum (see opposite).

ACCOMMODATION AND EATING

★**Glenmalure Lodge** ☎0404 46188, ⓦglenmalure lodge.ie. Quaint and welcoming, 200-year-old coaching inn in a beautiful spot on the Wicklow Way, near the military road, offering comfortable, en-suite B&B, decent food and a cosy bar with a turf fire and outdoor tables; its rooms are very popular at weekends with walkers, for whom luggage transfer and packed lunches can be arranged. **€70**

Glenmalure Youth Hostel ☎01 830 4555, ⓦanoige.ie. Northwest of *Glenmalure Lodge*, the valley road ends at a car park and footbridge over the river, where a track runs over and up to this hostel. It's very basic (no electricity or running water) but has a gas-powered kitchen and a log fire, and holds interest as the house formerly owned by playwright J.M. Synge and by W.B. Yeats's muse, Maud Gonne McBride. June–Aug daily, Sept–May Sat only. Dorms **€15**

Rathdrum and around

In the lush foothills at the southeastern edge of the Wicklow Mountains, the main settlement is peaceful **RATHDRUM**, its long main street and pretty village green perched high above the Avonmore River. A few kilometres downstream, the pretty village of

Avoca still trades on its role as the location for the now-defunct BBC-TV series *Ballykissangel*. Venturing further afield, you might well be tempted to stay or eat at the excellent *Brook Lodge and Wells Spa* (see p.128) to the west of Avoca at **Macreddin**, a village which had fallen into decline in the late nineteenth century but was beautifully redeveloped by the enterprising hoteliers.

Avondale House

April, May, Sept & Oct Tues–Sun 11am–4pm; June–Aug daily 11am–5pm • €5; open access to grounds, though parking on-site costs €5 (coins only); Heritage Island • ⓦ coillteoutdoors.ie

About 2km south of Rathdrum village stands **Avondale House**, birthplace and home of **Charles Stewart Parnell**, the nineteenth-century campaigner for home rule who was dubbed "the uncrowned king of Ireland". Completed in 1779 to a design by English architect James Wyatt, the small but nicely proportioned country house, which features an attractive basement café, is well worth a visit. Over the main door in the hall hangs a poignant banner, representing the arms of Ireland's four provinces in pastel colours; given to Parnell in the 1880s, when home rule seemed a racing certainty, it was vainly intended for display in the future Irish House of Commons. The beautiful, bright dining room nearby is adorned with delicate, foliate stuccowork in Wedgwood style by the Lafranchini brothers (who also decorated Dublin's Newman House). Upstairs, the highlight is the master bedroom where Parnell was born, with a bay of large windows overlooking the grounds. Stretching over five hundred acres, the **estate** is now owned by the Irish Forestry Board, Coillte, which has laid out several trails. These take between twenty minutes and three hours to cover, through the forested parkland, with its rare tree species and fine views of the Avonmore River.

Avoca

Set in the beautiful, thickly wooded **Vale of Avoca**, there's more to **AVOCA** than its picture-postcard looks used in Ballykissangel. Its most notable feature is its famous eighteenth-century **mill** – original home of the now-nationwide Avoca shops – where you can watch the weavers at work on a mill tour (daily: summer 9am–6pm; winter 9.30am–5.30pm; free; ⓦ avoca.ie). You can eat at the excellent **café** here and, of course, there's a shop selling the fruits of the looms as well as the other good-quality gifts the Avoca chain is known for.

ARRIVAL AND INFORMATION

RATHDRUM AND AROUND

By train The train station is located down by the river.

Destinations Dublin Connolly (3–5 daily via Wicklow, Greystones and Bray; 1hr 20min); Rosslare Europort (3–4 daily via Enniscorthy and Wexford; 1hr 30min).

By minibus Roughly connecting with services to and from Dublin, there's a minibus/taxi to Glendalough and Glenmalure, via Laragh, from the train station and the market square, which would allow you, for example, to walk the Wicklow Way from Glendalough to Glenmalure

(€7 single, based on 3 people travelling; advance booking required on ☎ 0404 29000 or ☎ 087 817 6630, ⓦ wicklowwaybus.com).

By bus Rathdrum (20min) and Avoca (35min) are served by one or two buses daily from Wicklow.

Tourist office There's a small tourist office in the market square, Rathdrum (Mon–Fri 9.30am–1pm & 2–5pm; ☎ 0404 46262), and another in the old courthouse, Avoca (Mon–Fri 9am–5pm; ☎ 0402 35022).

GETTING AROUND

By bike Cycle rental from McGrath's, Main St, Rathdrum (☎ 0404 46172).

ACCOMMODATION AND EATING

RATHDRUM

Bates 3 Market St ☎ 0404 29988, ⓦ batesrestaurant .com. In a cosy, grey-stone cottage just off the market square behind the Cartoon Inn, *Bates* is a top-quality, moderately priced restaurant with friendly service, serving dishes such as Wicklow venison loin with black pepper crust

and thyme jus. Set-price menu for Sun lunch €25. Tues–Sat 5.30/6–9/9.30pm, Sun 12.30–8pm.

Hidden Valley Holiday Park ☎ 086 727 2872, ⓦ irelandholidaypark.com. Down by the river, with its own lake, this camping and caravan park has a campers' kitchen and a laundry room, as well as various self-catering cabins

2

2

(minimum stays of at least two nights). Also on offer are kayak rental, swimming, a kids' fun park and lots of other activities. Mid-March to late Sept. Camping **€22**, cabin **€80**

Jacob's Well ☎ 0404 46282, ⊛ jacobswellrathdrum .com. Well-equipped, comfortable B&B (including power showers) on the main street, with cheery, pine-floored and furnished, en-suite bedrooms and a sitting room with a turf fire. It's in a separate building from the welcoming and popular pub, which offers well-prepared, hearty lunch and dinner, and good Guinness. **€70**

Old Presbytery (IHH) ☎ 0404 46930, ⊛ hostels-ireland .com. Overlooking the Fairgreen, this modern hostel offers comfortable five-to-twelve-person dorms (male, female and mixed), en-suite twins, large kitchen, dining and lounge areas, and laundry facilities. Dorms **€16**, doubles **€40**

AVOCA

Sheepwalk House ☎ 0402 35189, ⊛ sheepwalk .com. Tasteful, en-suite rooms in a welcoming early Georgian country house with cast-iron fireplaces, antiqu furniture and views of the sea, 3km away off the Arklov road; one bedroom boasts a four-poster. Attractiv self-catering cottages also available. Good rates fo singles. **€90**

MACREDDIN

★ **Brook Lodge and Wells Spa** Macreddin, 3km nort of Aughrim ☎ 0402 36444, ⊛ brooklodge.com. Locate in a secluded valley, this luxurious, modern country-house style hotel boasts a lovely spa, a swimming pool and tw restaurants: the excellent and innovative *Strawberry Tre* which uses only organic, free-range or wild ingredient and southern Italian *La Taverna Armento* – a pub with i own microbrewery, free bicycles and an equestrian centre From March to Oct, the first Sun of the month sees a bi organic food fair in the afternoon, with barbecues and jazz band, while Nov sees a wild food festival weeken (⊛ wildandslow.com). **€130**

Russborough House

Guided tours every hour, on the hour March–Sept daily 10am–5pm, but it's worth phoning to check both spring and winter hours • House **€10**; maze **€3**; Heritage Island • ☎ 045 865239, ⊛ russboroughhouse.ie

On the western edge of the Wicklow Mountains and 3km south of the village of **Blessington** stands **Russborough House**, a lavish Palladian country house designed by Richard Castle for Joseph Leeson, later Lord Russborough and the Earl of Milltown, whose family had made their money in the brewing trade. Castle died before the project was completed, leaving Francis Bindon to oversee the fulfilment of his grand design. Completed in 1751, the Wicklow-granite building's 200m frontage, with its curving colonnaded wings, is the longest of its kind in Ireland.

Russborough has gained widespread fame for its **art collections**, under both the Milltowns and latterly the Beits, who derived their fortune from the De Beers Diamond Mining Company and bought the house in 1952. Most of its artworks, however, have been donated to the National Gallery for safekeeping (see box, below), but with or without the paintings, the **interior** of the house is sumptuous, featuring Baroque plasterwork ceilings by the Lafranchini brothers, notably in the saloon, depicting the four seasons, and in the music room, where the ingenious geometrical design seems to add height to the room. Further beautiful stuccowork, representing hunting and garlands, adorns the cantilevered main staircase, which was ornately carved out of dark Cuban mahogany by Irish craftsmen in the eighteenth century.

PILFERED PAINTINGS AT RUSSBOROUGH

Renowned for its art collection, Russborough House has been **burgled** on no fewer than four occasions, though almost all of the stolen paintings have subsequently been recovered. The first burglary was in 1974, when nineteen paintings were stolen by Englishwoman Rose Dugdale in order to raise funds for the IRA. The house was again broken into in 1986, by "The General", aka Martin Cahill, one of Dublin's most notorious criminals (this episode featured prominently in John Boorman's 1998 film *The General*). Russborough was burgled again in 2001, possibly by an associate of Cahill's, when a Gainsborough portrait was stolen for the third time, along with a work by Bellotto. Both were recovered in September 2002, only days before a fourth break-in, which netted five pictures including two by Rubens.

Other highlights include the Italian-marble fireplace in the dining room depicting Bacchus and vines, and a series of French clocks dating back as far as the fifteenth century, which are still wound every Tuesday. The house has a pleasant **café**, as well as apartments in the West Wing that can be rented through the Irish Landmark Trust (Ⓦirishlandmark.com). In the **grounds** are a maze and about 4km of trails, which will take you past a walled garden.

ARRIVAL AND DEPARTURE   **RUSSBOROUGH HOUSE**

By bus Blessington is about 1hr 40min from central Dublin on the #65 bus from Poolbeg St or South Great George's St (10–14 daily). Some of these services (4–6 daily) continue southwest of Blessington, towards Ballymore Eustace, which will leave you much less of a walk to Russborough

House; otherwise you can walk to Russborough along the Blessington Greenway Walk, which runs through woodland along the shores of Blessington Lake from the Avon Rí Activity Centre at the south end of Blessington (Ⓦvisitwicklow.ie).

EATING

★Grangecon Kilbride Rd, just off Blessington's main street ☎045 857892, Ⓦgrangeconcafe blogspot.com. Excellent café-restaurant in the old schoolhouse, which sources the very best, mostly organic and seasonal ingredients from the top local

suppliers and makes everything in-house, from soda bread to lemon curd for their tarts. Great sandwiches (around €8) and shepherd's pie, and scrummy homemade lemonade. Tues–Sat 9am–4pm.

County Kildare

In contrast to the harsh landscape of the Wicklow Mountains to the east, **County Kildare** is prosperous farming country, which was gladly seized and fortified by the English as part of the medieval Pale. Rich pasture for cattle and horses in the north of the county gives way to fertile ploughland in the south, the **Bog of Allen** in the northwest providing the only unproductive blot on the landscape. The county's main attractions for visitors are neatly concentrated in two areas. Servicing the bloodstock farms on **the Curragh**'s lush heathland, **Kildare town** is generally a low-key affair, where you can explore the monastery and church founded by St Brigid in the fifth century, and see what all the equine fuss is about at the fascinating **National Stud**. To the north of town, you can trace the development of the Bog of Allen at the nature centre in **Lullymore**. Meanwhile, up on the county's northern edge lies one of Ireland's finest stately homes, **Castletown**.

Kildare town

In **KILDARE**'s quiet moments, of which there are many, you are keenly aware that the pre-eminent local business all takes place outside of town, for **the Curragh**, which stretches east from the town to the River Liffey, is Ireland's horse-racing centre. The underlying limestone of this huge plain, the largest area of semi-natural grassland in Europe, is good for a horse's bone formation, and the grass is said to be especially sweet. Consequently, the Curragh is home not only to a famous racecourse, but also to dozens of stud farms and stables, engaged in the multimillion-euro pursuit of breeding and training racehorses, one of the country's biggest sources of income – as vividly illustrated at the **National Stud**.

St Brigid's Cathedral

May–Sept Mon–Sat 10am–1pm & 2–5pm, Sun 2–5pm; tower closed in heavy rain • Cathedral free; tower €4

Kildare is arrayed around a triangular main square, which retains its central, nineteenth-century Market House and is overlooked by the huge Church of Ireland **Cathedral of St Brigid**. In the late fifth century, **St Brigid** is said to have founded a religious house here on a major pagan site, which became an important monastic centre of art, learning and culture – the *Book of Kildare*, for example, produced here in the seventh century but now lost, was,

2

THE GRAND AND ROYAL CANALS

County Kildare is traversed by the **Royal and Grand canals**, which run from Dublin to the River Shannon. Reminders of Ireland's mercantile confidence in the eighteenth century, before the disenfranchisement of the Act of Union, they were built to service the mills, distilleries and breweries of a minor industrial revolution. Passenger boats on both canals were soon eclipsed by the railways and stopped running around 1850, but freight services continued until as late as 1960.

Completed in stages between 1779 and 1805, the **Grand Canal** heads out from south Dublin to Robertstown in County Kildare, where it splits into two branches. The 50km southern branch (aka the Barrow Line), completed in 1791, meets the River Barrow at Athy in the south of the county, allowing passage as far south as Waterford; the main waterway runs west via Tullamore in County Offaly to Shannon Harbour, a total of 114km from Dublin.

The **Royal Canal**, a rival northern route opened between 1796 and 1816, was never quite as successful, though it managed to reach a peak tonnage of 112,000 in 1847. It runs along the northern border of County Kildare, before heading northwest to Mullingar and joining the Shannon, 144km from north Dublin, at Cloondara in County Longford.

The canals are flanked by a series of pleasantly undeveloped – and easy-to-follow – **trails**, the Royal Canal Way, the Grand Canal Way and the Barrow Way; go to W www.irishtrails.ie for full details and descriptions of the routes. It's also possible to **rent a narrowboat** from Royal Canal Cruisers in Dublin (T 01 820 5263, W royalcanalcruisers.com) or, for the Grand Canal and the Barrow, from Canalways, Rathangan, Co. Kildare (T 087 243 3879, W canalways.ie), or Barrowline Cruisers, Vicarstown, Co. Laois (T 05786 26060, W barrowline.ie).

according to twelfth-century scholar Giraldus Cambrensis, dictated by an angel and as magnificent as the *Book of Kells*. Brigid herself, who may well have originated as the Celtic goddess Brigantia, is Ireland's second most important saint after Patrick, with many holy wells that are thought to cure sterility dedicated to her. Known also for her healing, farming and negotiating skills, Brigid has seen a recent revival of interest as an icon of feminine spirituality and an alternative to the patriarchal institutions of the Church.

The present cathedral was originally constructed in the thirteenth century, but the north transept and choir were destroyed during the 1641 Rebellion, and the building was largely reconstructed in the nineteenth century. Its twelfth-century **round tower**, the second highest in Ireland at 33m, is surmounted by mid-eighteenth-century battlements that replaced the original roof, and affords a fine panorama from the top. On the north side of the church is the restored **fire temple** – Brigid had cannily preserved the pagan cult of fire, and a fire is still lit here every year on **St Brigid's Day** (Feb 1; W solasbhride.ie/feile-bride), formerly the pagan festival of spring, Imbolc. At this time, one of the few folkloric objects to persist into the modern era can be seen around Ireland: St Brigid's Cross, traditionally woven from rushes, but which can now be bought as a plastic replica in supermarkets, to be hung from your car windscreen for protection.

The National Stud

Based at Tully on the south side of Kildare, a well-signposted 2km from the town centre, across the M4 • Daily 9am–6pm; 35min guided tours noon, 2.30pm & 4pm • €12.50, children €7; tours free; Heritage Island • T 045 521617, W irishnationalstud.ie • Information about shuttle buses is given on p.132; ordinary buses to Kildare town and also daily buses all the way through to the National Stud, from Dublin's Connolly LUAS stop (Mon–Fri 9.30am, returning at 3.45pm; Sat at 9.30am & 1.30pm, returning at 11.20am & 3.50pm; Sun at 10am & noon, returning at 3.05pm & 5.35pm)

The **National Stud** shows the highly evolved business of horse breeding in action. Here, you can look round the stables themselves and stroll through two attractive on-site gardens (included in the admission price). You should try to time your visit to coincide with one of the entertaining **guided tours**.

The stud farm was established here, by the mineral-rich River Tully, in 1900 by Colonel William Hall Walker, of the famous Scotch whisky family. Hall Walker's methods were highly successful, though eccentric: each newborn foal's horoscope was read, and those on whom the stars didn't shine were immediately sold, regardless of their lineage or physical characteristics. In 1915, the colonel presented the farm to the British government – who

HORSE RACING IN KILDARE

Two of Ireland's major racecourses, where you're practically guaranteed a fun, boisterous day out, are just a short trot from Kildare. The major Irish flat-racing classics are held at the **Curragh Racecourse**, about 5km east of town (☎ 045 441205, ⓦ curragh.ie): the Irish 1000 Guineas and 2000 Guineas in May, the Irish Derby in late June or early July, the Irish Oaks in July and the Irish St Leger in September. You can take special **bus** services to get to the Curragh from Dublin on race days (ⓦ dublincoach.ie), and there are free shuttle buses to the course from Kildare village for passengers on Dublin Coach's other services (see below) and from Kildare **train station** (ⓦ irishrail.ie).

About 20km east, just south of the town of Naas, **Punchestown Racecourse** (☎ 045 897704, ⓦ punchestown.com) hosts the five-day Irish National Hunt Festival in April, a more rural affair that attracts a lot of farmers. Have a look at their website for details of special buses from Dublin and Naas (which is on the train line from Connolly Station) during the festival.

promptly made him Lord Wavertree – on condition that it became the British National Stud. It was finally transferred to the Irish government in 1944 at an agreed valuation. Within the attractive grounds, there are various yards, paddocks and stallion boxes, as well as a café. But the highlight of the tour has to be the horses themselves. They include Fallabellas from Argentina, the smallest horses in the world (above pony height), as well as top stallions who command up to €70,000 for what's quaintly called a live cover and who jet as far afield as Australia to mate with local mares. From February until July, you should be able to see mares and their young foals in the paddocks.

Japanese Garden

The beautiful and playful **Japanese Garden** was created by Colonel Hall Walker and two Japanese gardeners on a reclaimed bog between 1906 and 1910. A product of the Edwardian obsession with the Orient, it symbolizes the life of man from oblivion to eternity. Over miniature hills and waterfalls, past colourful flowers and trees, you follow from birth to death a delightful numbered trail, which yields a choice between bachelorhood and marriage, as well as a few false leads along the way.

St Fiachra's Garden

The recently created **St Fiachra's Garden** close by is perhaps a little less compelling. St Fiachra was an Irish monk from a noble family who established a much-revered hermitage near Kilkenny town in the early seventh century. The hermitage became too popular for its own good, however, and the saint was forced to move to France, where he eventually founded another retreat near Meaux, 40km northeast of Paris, before his death in about 670. Fiachra always encouraged his disciples to cultivate gardens, from which they could distribute produce to the poor, and thus became the patron saint of gardeners – as well as of French taxi-drivers (after the cabs, known as *fiacres*, which used to take pilgrims from Paris to his shrine at Meaux). The garden comes across as a stylishly enhanced arboretum, encompassing a lake in which has been placed a group of 5000-year-old bog-oak trunks, branchless and blackened, suggesting not only death but also longevity.

ARRIVAL AND INFORMATION   **KILDARE TOWN**

by bus As well as the Bus Éireann services detailed below, which stop on the main square, private buses include Dublin Coach (ⓦ dublincoach.ie) to Dublin, Dublin Airport, Limerick and Ennis; and J.J.Kavanagh (ⓦ jjkavanagh.ie) to Dublin, Dublin Airport, Limerick and Shannon Airport.
Destinations Dublin (mostly Custom House Quay, via O'Connell Bridge; Mon–Sat roughly hourly, Sun roughly every 2hr; 1hr 30min).

by train The train station is a 10min walk to the north of

the main square.
Destinations Dublin Heuston (20–30 daily; 40min).
Tourist office The tourist office (Mon–Sat 9.30am–1pm & 2–5pm; ☎ 045 530672) and its heritage centre (same hours; free; ⓦ kildare.ie/kildareheritage), which contains mildly interesting display boards and a short audiovisual on the history of Kildare and the Curragh, are in the eighteenth-century Market House in the centre of the main square.

GETTING AROUND

By bus Free shuttle buses, timed to connect with most Dublin trains (details on ⓦkildarevillage.com), link the train station, the main tourist office and Kildare Outlet Village, a shopping centre on the southwest side of town four or five a day also serve the National Stud.

ACCOMMODATION AND EATING

Harte's The Square ☎045 533557, ⓦhartesbar.ie. A nineteenth-century pub exterior with pretty hanging baskets conceals this lively gastropub, which presents some bold and successful menu choices such as confit of duck leg Wellington, using ducks from Skeaghanore in West Cork. For accompaniment, their "Bar Library" matches their craft beers with their main courses. A meal will set you back about €30/person. Mon–Thurs 4–9pm, Fri & Sat 4–10pm, Sun noon–9pm.

Lord Edward The Square ☎045 522232, ⓦlordedwardkildare.ie. Behind – and owned by – the *Silken Thomas* pub, with comfortable en-suite rooms in an eighteenth-century lodge that's been smartly converted using a lot of polished wood and earth tones. Breakfast is not included in the price, but is available at the pub; half-board packages also available. €71

★**Mahon's** Just off the square on Claregate St ☎045 521316. Smartly kept, old-time pub done out in cosy dark woods and green leather. Mon–Thurs 10.30am–11.30pm, Fri & Sat 10.30am–12.30am, Sun 12.30–11pm.

Silken Thomas The Square ☎045 522232, ⓦsilkenthomas.com. The town's major hospitality complex, with several bars, including an Irish theme pub, *Lil Flanagan's*, and a weekend nightclub. It offers tempting breakfasts, lunches and dinners (most dishes €10–15) in the main bar and has a smart, modern and popular evening restaurant, *Chapter 16*, where main courses such as duck leg confit cost €15–20. Mon–Thurs 8am–11.30pm, Fri & Sat 8am–12.30am, Sun 9am–11pm.

Singleton's 1 Dara Park, Station Rd ☎045 521964 ☎087 271 4164. Centrally placed B&B just north of the main square, offering three en-suite rooms and a guest living room in a modern, detached two-storey town house. Feb–Nov. €70

The Bog of Allen

To the north of Kildare town lies the great **Bog of Allen**, Ireland's most famous peatland. Actually a complex of bogs that once covered two thousand square kilometres between the rivers Liffey, Barrow, Shannon and Boyne, it's now much diminished by drainage and stripping.

Bog of Allen Nature Centre

Mon–Fri 10am–5pm, last admission 4pm, plus weekend openings for special events in summer • €5 donation requested • ☎045 860133, ⓦipcc

The best place to get a handle on the bog is in **LULLYMORE**, a tranquil parish and former monastic settlement on the road to nowhere 16km north of Kildare, which sits on an island of mineral soil, surrounded by peat. Here you'll find the **Bog of Allen Nature Centre**, run by the Irish Peatland Conservation Council, a charity whose aim is to ensure the conservation of a representative sample of Irish bogs. Informative exhibits at the centre, which is housed in the farm buildings of nineteenth-century Lullymore Lodge, trace the development of bogs, as well as their significance as habitats for rare animals and plants. The latter include species such as sundews, butterworts and pitcher plants, which have developed the capacity to eat insects, as the peat they grow on is deficient in nutrients; a greenhouse in the centre's back garden displays carnivorous plants from Ireland and around the world, and their various methods of drugging, gluing or otherwise catching the poor critters. Next to the centre, a 100m boardwalk has been built over Lodge Bog, a small raised bog that's home to around 150 species of plants, including carnivorous round-leaved sundews, as well as mountain hares, foxes and over seventy species of butterflies and moths.

Castletown

Celbridge, 18km west of Dublin • Hourly guided tours (1hr) mid-March to Oct Mon–Sat 10.15am–5pm, Sun 10am–5pm • €4.50; Heritage Card & Heritage Island • ⓦcastletown.ie • Dublin Bus #67, mostly from Connolly LUAS stop

The oldest and largest Palladian country house in Ireland, **Castletown** is also one of the ery finest. Its plain, grey but elegant façade, built in the style of a sixteenth-century talian town palace, conceals a wealth of beautiful and fascinating interior detail. The ouse, which has a café-restaurant in the west wing, is accessible by car direct from the 44 to the north (exit 6), or on foot through its extensive parkland, along a beautiful venue of lime trees that begins at the northern end of **CELBRIDGE**'s high street.

The house was built for William Conolly, son of a Donegal publican who, as legal adviser o William III, became the wealthiest man in Ireland from dealing in forfeited estates after he Battle of the Boyne. Though construction began in 1722, under first the Italian rchitect Alessandro Galilei and then his acquaintance, Edward Lovett Pearce, the interior vas still unfinished at the time of Conolly's death seven years later. A second phase of work egan in 1758, when great-nephew Tom Conolly married the 15-year-old Lady Louisa

2

BOGS

Bogs once covered around one-sixth of Ireland's surface, a higher proportion than any other European country apart from Finland. They began to form around 9000 years ago after the last Ice Age, when retreating glaciers and ice sheets left central Ireland covered by myriad shallow lakes. Gradually the partly decomposed remnants of mosses, pondweeds, water lilies and reeds built up on many of the lake beds as layers of peat, reducing the area of open water and eventually forming **fens**.

Between 7500 and 1500 years ago, further changes occurred to most of Ireland's fens. As the fen peat became so thick that it filled up the lakes, its surface was colonized by sphagnum moss which, able to hold twenty times its own weight in water, accelerated the accumulation of peat. Thus, huge, sponge-like domes of water were formed above the level of the surrounding land, known as **raised bogs**, which have an average peat depth of 9–12m. Around 4000 years ago, a different kind of bog began to develop in areas of very high rainfall, either along the west coast or in the mountains. These **blanket bogs** carpet the land surface with a layer of black peat, 2–6m thick.

It's not surprising that, as such a prominent part of the environment, bogs occupy a significant place in Irish **folk history**, as evidenced by the many songs, poems and stories associated with the annual harvesting of the turf. They are also **habitats** of great ecological value, sheltering many rare and protected species of plant and animal. And, as well as being important to biologists and climatologists, bogs have produced some of the most spectacular finds of Irish **archaeology**. The slow rate of organic decomposition that allowed the bogs to form in the first place has also preserved thousands of remarkable artefacts from the Neolithic period to the Middle Ages. These include ornaments and weapons, some of which were deliberately left in sacred bog pools as votive offerings during the Bronze Age; surprisingly intact human bodies, a few of which are now on display at Dublin's National Museum (see p.63); elaborate wooden roads from the Bronze and Iron Ages, such as the Corlea Trackway (see p.171); and indeed, whole settlements that were engulfed by peat, as at Céide Fields (see p.390).

The bogs of Ireland, however, are under grave threat. Man has **exploited** the peatlands on a small scale for many centuries. Marl, the chalky soil found beneath the peat, is a lime-rich fertilizer; the peat itself has always been cut and dried for use as fuel; and the overlying mat of vegetation on the bog surface was once used as roof insulation. However, in the twentieth century, exploitation dramatically accelerated. Bord na Móna (the Irish Turf Board) introduced large-scale, mechanized extraction schemes, especially from raised bogs, producing fuel for power stations and domestic use, as well as horticultural peat. There have been further losses to forestry programmes and agricultural intensification, to the extent that only twenty percent or so of the original peatlands, around one-thirtieth of Ireland's landmass, remains intact.

In the last few years, the vital role of peatlands regarding **climate change** has also been recognized: bogs are supremely efficient carbon sponges, locking away ten times more carbon per acre than any other system, including forests – about 1.2 billion tons of carbon in total across Ireland. Meanwhile, the West Offaly peat-fired power station at Shannonbridge attracted the country's first ever climate camp for a week in August 2009: peat generates three times more emissions per megawatt of electricity produced than even coal. Under pressure from the Irish Peatland Conservation Council, however, the Irish government has committed itself to acquiring 500 square kilometres of raised and blanket bog, around a quarter of what remains, for conservation. For more information on bogs, go to the Irish Peatland Conservation Council's excellent website at Ⓦ ipcc.ie.

Lennox, who set about altering and redecorating the house to restrained, Neoclassical designs by Sir William Chambers, the architect of the Casino at Marino, Dublin.

The engaging guided tour begins by the **Grand Staircase**, its cantilevered Portland-stone steps and solid brass banisters weighing at least ten tons. Rococo stuccowork by the Swiss-Italian Lafranchini brothers, depicting Tom Conolly in high relief and personifications of the four seasons, swirls extravagantly over the walls here, but in such a huge, white space manages to appear delicate and restrained. The ground-floor **Brown Study** is the only room to retain its original, rich pine panelling and narrow oak doors from the 1720s, and features a portrait of William III, donated to William Conolly by the king himself. On the same floor lies perhaps the most ostentatious display of wealth and fashion at Castletown: over six years, at huge cost and with painstaking effort, Lady Louisa had the walls of the **Print Room** papered with black-and-white prints from London and Paris, portraying everything from biblical scenes to famous actors of the day, complemented by decorative borders of swags, chains and masks; it must have looked fantastic in its original state, on a background of bright yellow paint.

The highlight upstairs is the **Long Gallery**, which was decorated by Lady Louisa with busts of Greek and Roman philosophers and murals of Classical scenes of love and tragedy, in the style of the recently rediscovered Pompeii. It must have been a bit of a blow, however, to Lady Louisa when the extravagant glass chandeliers arrived from Murano in Venice and were found to be the wrong shade of blue for her newly decorated living room. From the gallery's windows you can make out the **Conolly Folly** some 3km north, an arcane, 50m-high edifice consisting of an obelisk perched shakily on top of a cascade of arches. Attributed to Richard Castle, it was built in 1740 as a monument to Speaker Conolly by his widow, and as a Famine relief scheme.

County Meath

The rich limestone lowlands of **County Meath**, bisected by the River Boyne and supporting ample cattle pasturage, have always attracted settlers and invaders. The valley's Neolithic people somehow found the resources and manpower to construct the huge, ornately decorated passage graves of **Newgrange**, **Knowth** and **Dowth**, part of the extraordinary landscape of ritual sites known as **Brú na Bóinne**, which is today one of the country's most famous and best organized visitor attractions. In contrast, the **Loughcrew Cairns**, a similarly extensive grouping of burial mounds in the far northwest corner of the county beyond the small market town of Kells, have failed to garner present-day resources for excavation and tourist development, leaving you to explore this mysterious, hilltop landscape unaided and usually in solitude. The **Hill of Tara** started out as a Stone Age cemetery, too, but evolved into one of Ireland's most important symbolic sites, the seat of the High Kings of the early Christian period. Meath also caught the eye of the Anglo-Norman invaders, who heavily fortified and held several parliaments at **Trim**, where you can visit the mighty castle and several other well-preserved medieval remnants. Meath's other noteworthy sights are on either side of Brú na Bóinne in the northeast of the county: to the west, **Slane's** historic castle and monastery, which enjoy a picturesque setting on a steep, wooded hillside above the River Boyne; and to the east, the site of one of the most significant battles in Ireland's history, the **Battle of the Boyne**, now commemorated by a high-tech visitor centre.

Trim and around

Fifty kilometres northwest of Dublin, **TRIM** is one of the most attractive towns within striking distance of the capital. Its imposing Anglo-Norman castle overlooks the curving, tree-flanked River Boyne and some picturesque ruins across on the north bank, while green meadows run downriver to the extensive remains of two medieval

hurches and a fine bridge. Trim is also the easiest jumping-off point for the Cistercian
bbey of **Bective**, set in lush countryside to the northeast.

rim Castle

d-March to Oct daily 10am–6pm; Nov to mid-March Sat & Sun 9am–5pm; 45min guided tours of the keep every hour on the hour;
e to their popularity in summer, it's best to arrive as early in the day as possible; last admission and tour 1hr before closing • €4 for
mission to the castle grounds plus guided tour, €3 castle grounds only; Heritage Card • ⓦ heritageireland.ie

he town's outstanding centrepiece is **Trim Castle**, which is intact enough to have been
sed as a location for Mel Gibson's 1995 film *Braveheart*. In 1172, Henry II, fearing
at the adventurer Strongbow might try to establish his own Anglo-Norman kingdom
Ireland, granted the lordship of Meath to Hugh de Lacy, who along with his son
Valter gradually built the most impressive castle in Ireland, the "keystone of the Pale",
t this important ford over the Boyne. It's well worth taking one of the illuminating
uided **tours** of the keep, and leaving yourself enough time to poke around the
nclosure's assorted towers, ruined buildings and mighty curtain wall.

The cruciform floor plan of the **keep** was a unique experiment in military architecture
the design increased possible angles of attack and thus was not emulated elsewhere.
Iowever, with walls up to 5m thick and over 20m high, which have survived to this
ay, the keep was obviously stout enough. The tour inside reveals a chapel, the former
reat Hall, a bedroom with an early walk-in wardrobe and spectacular views of the
own from the battlements.

The fording of the Boyne was defended by the castle's strongest tower, the **Magdalen**
ower, at the northern tip of the curtain wall, but during a period of greater stability and
rosperity in the late thirteenth century, this was converted into private apartments, and
new **Great Hall** was built alongside. On the right-hand side of the hall, look out for a
assage cut through the bedrock from the river gate, which allowed stores brought by
oat from Drogheda on the coast to be delivered directly to the cellar.

The 450m **curtain wall**, with its ten D-shaped towers, is best appreciated from the
outh side of the keep. Low, marshy, easily defensible ground originally stood beyond
is part of the enclosure, to which was added a deep, wide moat that could be flooded
sing weirs on the River Boyne. This sector is punctuated by the **Barbican Gate**, whose
nusual but powerful design comprises a cylindrical tower linked by a heavily defended
ridge over the moat to a forward square tower. The future King Henry V was
nprisoned in this gate tower by Richard II, when his father, Henry of Bolingbroke,
unched his ultimately successful coup d'état in 1399.

albot's Castle

rossing the river by the footbridge under the castle walls, you can see the only
irviving remnant of the fourteenth-century outer walls, the arched **Sheep Gate**. Nearby
ands **Talbot's Castle** (privately owned), a beautiful tower house built in 1415 by Sir
hn Talbot, the Lord Lieutenant of Ireland. In the eighteenth century, Jonathan Swift
ee box, p.75), who was rector of nearby Laracor, bought the building and turned it
to a Latin school, whose most famous alumnus was Arthur Wellesley, later the Duke
f Wellington and MP for Trim. Over four days in early July, Trim holds a **Swift festival**
swiftsatirefestival.com), featuring debates, comedy and other entertainments. The
wer house had been constructed on the site of an Augustinian abbey, St Mary's, which
turn had been built over one of the first monasteries in Ireland, dating from the fifth
entury. All that remains of St Mary's is the **Yellow Steeple**, a huge, half-ruined belfry
at's so named because it glows in the evening sunlight.

ewtowntrim Cathedral

bout 1.5km east of the town centre on Lackanash Road, accessible off the Dublin road or
footpath along the north bank of the Boyne, the beautiful remains of thirteenth-century
ewtowntrim (SS Peter & Paul) Cathedral stand in riverside meadows. The priory of

Newtowntrim was founded here under the protective gaze of Trim Castle in 1202 by Simon de Rochfort, Bishop of Meath, and was soon elevated to become the seat of his diocese, with the construction of the largest and most sophisticated Gothic cathedral in Ireland. Substantial parts of the nave and chancel can still be seen, alongside a ruined refectory.

The priory and St Peter's Bridge

Just across the river is another fine ruin, the **Priory of St John the Baptist**, also founded by Simon de Rochfort in the early thirteenth century. It was used as a hospital and guesthouse (with its own brewery) by the *Fratres Cruciferi*, the Crutched (or Cross-bearing) Friars, Augustinian monks who had attended the Crusaders. Between the cathedral and the priory, the Boyne is spanned by the wonderful Norman **St Peter's Bridge**, which is reckoned to be the second-oldest bridge in the country.

Bective Abbey

In a beautiful setting by an old arched bridge on the west bank of the River Boyne, **Bective Abbey**, around 8km northeast of Trim, is a fine example of Cistercian architecture. To get here, take the Navan road from Trim, look out for a signposted right turn and then it's just over 1km on the left; continuing along these winding minor roads, you could move on to Tara, 5km due east.

Founded as a satellite of Mellifont (see p.153) in 1147, the abbey soon rose to prominence, its abbot holding a peer's seat in the Irish Parliament. The place was rebuilt in the thirteenth century, though only one wall of the nave remains from this phase. The majority of the extant building dates from the fifteenth century or later, remaining so remarkably intact because it was converted into a mansion house after Henry VIII's dissolution of the abbey in 1536. The sturdy and imposing fifteenth-century **tower** at the entrance is especially well preserved, and the south and west ranges of the **cloister** remain partly roofed – keep your eyes peeled for a carving of a monk near the southwest corner.

ARRIVAL AND INFORMATION   **TRIM**

By bus Buses stop by the Lidl superstore, on the ring road around the east of the compact town centre, though one or two also stop near the castle.
Destinations Drogheda (4–9 daily via Slane; 1hr 10min); Dublin (7–21 daily; 1hr).

Tourist office Next to the castle, the helpful tourist office (Mon–Fri 9.30am–5.30pm, Sat & Sun noon–5.30pm; ☎ 046 943 7227, ✉ trimvisitorcentre@eircom.net) houses an engaging audiovisual, *The Power and the Glory* (€3.20), on the medieval period in Trim and offers a genealogical service.

ACCOMMODATION AND EATING

Bridge House Hostel ☎ 046 943 1848, ⓦ bridgehousetouristhostel.com. Centrally placed hostel just off Bridge St, overlooking the River Boyne from its north side, with four-bed dorms, a large common room in the cellar, and kitchen and laundry facilities. Check-in 6–7pm or by arrangement. Dorms **€25**, doubles **€60**
Crannmór ☎ 046 943 1635, ⓦ crannmor.com. Welcoming B&B, popular with fishermen, in a creeper-clad Georgian country house set amid fine gardens and paddocks, 1.5km north of town on the Dunderry road. Very good rates for singles. March–Nov. **€75**
Franzini O'Brien's ☎ 046 943 1002, ⓦ franzinis.com. Solid all-rounder of a restaurant with a bright, informal air, set in a peerless location right opposite the castle entrance. The global menu includes nachos, Caribbean chicken curry and beef teriyaki noodles. Early-bird €20-for-2-courses deal available all evening midweek. Mon–Sat 5–10pm, Sun 1–9pm; closed Mon in winter.

James Griffin's Just across the river from the castle on High St ☎ 046 943 1295. *Griffin's* is a gnarly, hundred-year-old pub with bare stone walls, that offers a wide selection of Irish whiskies and craft beers, and hosts traditional-music sessions on Mon. Mon–Fri 3–11.30pm, Sat 1pm–12.30am, Sun 1–11pm.
Trim Castle Hotel ☎ 046 948 3000, ⓦ trimcastlehotel .com. Bright, spruce, four-star hotel right opposite the castle, sympathetically designed in a tasteful contemporary style. Lots of special offers on their website, including midweek room-only and weekend breaks with dinner. **€100**
The Welcome All Café Inside the tourist office. A popular, keenly priced, family-run café, offering home-baked scones with jam and cream (€2.30) and great combos such as leek and potato soup with a sandwich (€6) and lasagne with tea or coffee (€8.50). Mon–Fri 9.30am–5.30pm, Sat & Sun noon–5.30pm.

The Hill of Tara

Archaeological site open access **Visitor centre** mid-May to mid-Sept daily 10am–6pm, last admission 5pm • €3, including a guided tour of the site; Heritage Card • 🕸 heritageireland.ie

Perhaps more than anywhere else in Ireland, the **Hill of Tara** is loaded with both historical and mythical significance. It's best known as the seat of the High Kings of Ireland in the early centuries after Christ, but had been a major ritual site since the late Stone Age, giving it plenty of time to accrue prehistoric legends. The aura of this long, grass-covered hill, covered with mostly circular mounds and ditches, is unmistakable, and the views of the surrounding countryside are magnificent.

In the **visitor centre**, an impressive twenty-minute film provides the historical and mythological background and shows some stunning views of the hill from the air. The centre occupies a nineteenth-century church, adorned with beautiful painted windows showing the Pentecost and the Apostles. Executed by Evie Hone in 1935, they commemorate the 1500th anniversary of St Patrick's mission to bring Christianity to Ireland.

The site

Hard up against the wall of the church's graveyard, the first of the mounds you come to is the 83m-wide ring fort known as the **Rath of the Synods**, the reputed location of ecclesiastical synods in the sixth century. It's the untidiest of Tara's mounds: not only has it been partly destroyed by the church graveyard, but between 1899 and 1902 members of a cult, the British Israelites, dug up the rath, believing they would find the Ark of the Covenant. It's a particular shame that they kept no record of their efforts as this site went through many functions over the centuries: from early Bronze Age barrow, through palisaded ceremonial building, back to cemetery, and finally to ring fort. A Roman seal and lock have been found from this last phase, evidence of contact with the Roman world (probably Britain) in the fourth and fifth centuries AD.

The next tumulus to the south is the earliest on the site, the so-called **Mound of the Hostages**. It takes its name from the primitive medieval peacekeeping practice of exchanging hostages with neighbouring kingdoms, who were supposedly imprisoned within the mound by Cormac Mac Airt. Built around 3000 BC, it's actually a Neolithic tomb with a 4m-long passage that was reputed to have given entry to the other world. Access is no longer possible, but you can admire the typical concentric circles and zigzag patterns carved on one of the portal stones. No fewer than two hundred cremated late Neolithic burials were found here, to which were added around forty from the Bronze Age, some cremated, some inhumed, the latter including a high-ranking teenage boy wearing a necklace of jet, amber, bronze and exotic faïence beads.

A 1km-long circular bank, the **Royal Enclosure**, surrounds the Mound of the Hostages, and two larger, conjoined earthworks: the **Forrad**, a Bronze Age burial complex, and **Cormac's Residence**, an Iron Age ring fort to the east. In the centre of the Forrad is the **Stone of Destiny** (the *lia fail*), a phallic standing stone used in the coronation of the High Kings. Tradition states that the royal candidate had to drive his chariot wheel against the stone, and the gods, if they approved, would screech out his name. To the south of the Royal Enclosure lie the crescent-shaped remains of the **Enclosure of King Laoghaire** (see p.140), who is said to be buried here standing upright and dressed in his armour, facing his enemies, the Leinstermen.

To the north of the church, the so-called **Banqueting Hall** is actually two low banks of earth running parallel for over 200m. Though traditionally held to have been an enormous hall into which thousands of men from all over Ireland would have collected on ritual occasions, this was in fact probably Tara's ceremonial entrance avenue, aligned with the Mound of the Hostages and flanked by tombs and temples.

West of this avenue stands **Gráinne's Fort**, a burial mound surrounded by a circular ditch and bank. Like many ancient sites throughout Ireland, it has become associated with the tale of "The Pursuit of Diarmuid and Gráinne": the daughter of Cormac Mac Airt, Gráinne is betrothed to the king's elderly commander, Fionn Mac Cumhaill, but

2

TARA: HISTORY AND MYTH

It's likely that people started using the Hill of Tara in the Neolithic period (c.3500 BC) as a place for burials and for ritual gatherings, with no resident population. Around sixty monuments, mostly barrows, have been discovered on the hill, the latest probably dating to the late Iron Age (c.400 AD). So much for the archaeology, but mythology, literature and propaganda have imbued Tara with a far greater significance, as the ritual seat of kings – who did not have to be based here, but derived their authority from association with this revered place.

The earliest Irish sagas portray the hill as the home of the master-of-all-trades **Lug**, the greatest of the Celtic gods and the divine manifestation of Tara's kingship, and the goddess **Medb** (Maeve), who could also legitimize a king, sometimes by getting him drunk and sleeping with him – if she couldn't find a suitable candidate, Medb would rule herself. Of these legendary kings, the greatest were **Cormac Mac Airt** and **Conaire Mór**, semi-divine embodiments of peace, prosperity and righteousness. On somewhat firmer ground, seventh-century historical texts tell of recent struggles between the dynasties of Leinster, Northern Ireland and the **Uí Néills** (pronounced "Ee-nails"; based in the northwest and the midlands) for the kingship of Tara. The Uí Néills came out on top, but while the title *rí Temrach* (king of Tara) would have given them special status over the other kings, territorial control over the whole island was not a possibility until the ninth century, when the island became less politically fragmented. In the eleventh century, however, geopolitical reality bit, and Tara lost out to the big city, Dublin.

Tara's significance continues into modern times: during the **1798 Rebellion** some of the United Irishmen made a dramatic last stand on the hill, while in 1843 Daniel O'Connell harnessed the symbolic pull of the site to stage his biggest "monster meeting" here, attended by up to a million people, as part of his campaign to repeal the Union with England.

---

falls in love with one of his young warriors, Diarmuid, and elopes with him from Tara, with Fionn and his warriors in hot pursuit.

Beyond a line of trees to the west of Gráinne's Fort, two ring barrows known as the **Sloping Trenches** cling to the hill's steep western slope. To explain their unusual location, legend has it that the "trenches" were created when the palace of the bad king, Lugaid Mac Conn, collapsed, after his judgements were shown to be false by a young Cormac Mac Airt

ARRIVAL AND DEPARTURE   HILL OF TARA

By bus Dublin–Navan buses from Busáras will drop you at Tara Cross, about 1km from the site (every 30min; 1hr).

ACCOMMODATION AND EATING

Bellinter House ☎ 046 903 0900, ⊕ bellinterhouse.com. Just a few kilometres to the northwest of Tara off the M3, this Georgian manor house designed by Richard Castle, set in extensive grounds overlooking the River Boyne, has been converted to a chic hotel. A bolthole for the Dublin media crowd, it offers plenty of retro chic and quirky features in its redesign, an outdoor hot tub, seaweed baths and other spa treatments, as well as wellies to borrow. In the vaulted cellar there's an excellent restaurant, a branch of Dublin's *Eden*, that uses local, seasonal ingredients whenever possible. **€120**

Loughcrew Cairns and Oldcastle

Sited on a row of four hills at the far northwestern tip of County Meath, the **Loughcrew Cairns** consist of more than thirty chambered mounds and over a hundred curiously carved stones. Local folklore has bestowed on the hills a colourful name, **Sliabh Na Caillighe** (as now marked on Ordnance Survey maps, meaning "Mountain of the Sorceress"), and foundation legend: the said witch, believing she would become mistress of all Ireland if she leapt from hill to hill carrying an apron full of rocks, performed the mighty jumps, shedding handfuls of stones on each peak, but fell at the last, breaking her neck (a cairn at the bottom of the easternmost hill is traditionally known as the witch's grave). The true story of the cairns' construction is only slightly less amazing: archaeologists believe that between approximately 3500 and 3300 BC, Neolithic people travelled considerable distances to build these communal tombs, each of which may have taken anything from four to thirty years to complete. The alignment of the passage tombs and the elaborate carvings on their stone slabs display an association with sun worship, and it's obvious that this high-status ritual site was meant to be visible from far. In reverse, the cairns afford a magnificent panorama over quiet lakes and gently undulating farmland, encompassing up to sixteen counties on a clear day.

Though on a smaller scale, the Loughcrew Cairns are contemporary with the more famous burial sites at Brú na Bóinne, but, having never been comprehensively excavated, provide quite a different experience for the modern-day visitor. If you're going to visit both complexes, it makes sense to take the guided tours of the reconstructed mounds of Newgrange and Knowth first, before letting your imagination run wild on the unspoilt ritual landscape at Loughcrew. The cairns lie around 5km southeast of **OLDCASTLE**, a thriving village that sports several galleries and boutiques. While you're in this area, it's also well worth visiting the attractive **Loughcrew Gardens**.

2

Cairn T

late May to early Sept daily 10am–6pm, last admission 5.15pm; outside official opening hours, you can pick up the key and a torch from the café at Loughcrew Gardens (€50 or passport as deposit) • Free

The majority of the Loughcrew tombs are located on top of two hills, Carnbane East and Carnbane West, though unfortunately the latter is private land and currently inaccessible to visitors. To get to **Carnbane East**, turn off the N3 at the town of Kells and follow the Oldcastle road for about 15km, before forking left towards Loughcrew Gardens; after 3km a right turn leads to the car park beneath the summit of Carnbane East after about 1km. From the car park, it's a steep, ten-minute walk up to **Cairn T**, the focus of this summit and probably of the whole complex – most of the tombs on the other hills face towards it. The cairn's 113m circumference is reinforced by large kerbstones, behind which originally ran the thick layer of white quartz (as at Brú na Bóinne) that gave the hill its name: *carn bán* is Irish for "white cairn". On the north side is one of the largest kerbstones, known as the "Hag's Chair", where the witch of legend sat smoking her pipe (local lore adds that any wish you make while sitting here will come true). You can make out faint traces of carved Neolithic whorls on this stone, as well as a prominent cross, which strongly suggests that Masses (officially forbidden under the penal laws) were held in secret here during the eighteenth century.

The cairn's low, 5m-long **passage**, aligned with the rising sun on the equinox days in March and September (just south of east), leads into a roughly circular chamber with three side recesses. Once your eyes become accustomed to the gloom, you'll start seeing wonderful, mysterious carvings – chevrons, whorls, waves, petals – on the large stones all around you. These incisions are especially ornate in the back recess, where a prominent sun pattern may have been specifically designed to catch the first rays of the equinox sun along the passage.

Another six kerbstoned mounds cluster around the central cairn, including **Cairn U** just to the northeast, which features further enigmatic carvings on its passage and chamber stones, now open to the elements.

Loughcrew Gardens

mid-March to Oct Mon–Fri 9.30am–5.30pm, Sat & Sun 11am–5.30pm; Nov to mid-March Mon–Fri on request, Sat & Sun 11am–4pm • €5 • ⓦ loughcrew.com

Signposted on the southwestern side of Carnbane East, the **Loughcrew Gardens** are most famous for their impressive seventeenth-century avenue of grotesquely fluted yew trees. They also encompass nineteenth-century lawns, herbaceous borders, ponds and a grotto, as well as signposted woodland walks, a zipline and adventure course, a café and the family church of St Oliver Plunkett (see p.149), now roofless. The oldest part of the church was formerly a tower house, the seat of the Plunketts until the 1652 Act of Settlement, when Cromwell's surveyor, Sir William Petty, installed his brother-in-law, William Naper, at Loughcrew.

INFORMATION	LOUGHCREW CAIRNS AND OLDCASTLE

Tourist information *Kraft Kaffee*, a craft shop, café and official tourist information point on Millbrook Rd, Oldcastle (Tues–Sat 10am–5pm; ☏049 854 2645, ✉kraftkaffee @gmail.com).

ACCOMMODATION AND EATING

The Fincourt Oliver Plunkett St, Oldcastle ☏049 854 1153, ⓦfincourt.com. Places to stay and eat are now thin on the ground around Oldcastle (you might want to push on to Cavan, the Fore Valley or Mullingar), but this traditional inn can provide a warm welcome and five smart, comfortable and well-equipped en-suite rooms. The pub itself has bar food, an open fire and a quiet beer garden at the back. Self-catering also available. **€70**

Slane

Fifty kilometres north of Dublin, the village of **SLANE** enjoys a handsome setting on a south-facing slope above the leafy River Boyne, with the junction of the N2 and the N51 between Drogheda and Navan forming a prominent crossroads at the centre of the village.

Slane Castle

Guided tours late May to Aug Mon–Thurs & Sun noon–5pm, but sometimes closed for events, so check dates on the website • €7 • ⓦ slanecastle.ie

The village grew up around **Slane Castle**, whose estate extends westwards from the large Gothic gate by the bridge over the River Boyne. The main entrance for visitors, however, is now round the back of the house, about 1km west of the village crossroads. The era's finest architects – Gandon, Wyatt and Johnston – constructed the castle, with its mock battlements and turrets, from 1785 onwards, while Capability Brown designed the grounds. A devastating fire struck in 1991, however, and it took until 2001 for the castle to open again, with its interior redesigned in largely contemporary style as a venue for conferences and society weddings. Consequently, the guided tour smacks a little of *Hello* magazine, though there are one or two points of architectural interest remaining, notably the lofty ballroom, with its ornate fan vaulting and an original carved wooden chandelier, which was built by Thomas Hopper for George IV's 1821 visit to his mistress, Lady Conyngham. The present Conyngham, Henry, Lord Mountcharles, is a friend of rock band U2, who lived here while recording *The Unforgettable Fire* in 1984, and mounts huge concerts in the grounds most summers.

The Hill of Slane

From the main crossroads in the village, it's a fifteen-minute walk north and west up to the **Hill of Slane**, which affords views over rolling farmland to the Irish Sea at Drogheda and the Wicklow Mountains. Here, in 433, according to tradition, **St Patrick** lit the Paschal (Easter) Fire for the first time in Ireland, signalling the arrival of Christianity. In this he challenged the pagan *Bealtaine* fire on the Hill of Tara, 15km to the south, lit by the High King, Laoghaire, to celebrate the arrival of summer. Laoghaire was soon won over, however, and although the king did not take on the new religion himself, he allowed his subjects to be converted. These included St Earc, who became Patrick's great friend and follower, and established a **monastery** here on the hill, which eventually evolved into a Franciscan house. Today you can see the extensive remains of its sixteenth-century church and fine bell tower, along with an associated college built around an open quadrangle.

Francis Ledwidge Museum

Summer daily 10am–1pm & 2–5pm; phone for winter hours • €3 • ☏041 982 4544, ⓦ francisledwidge.com

Heading east from Slane's main crossroads on the N51 towards Drogheda, you'll find the **Francis Ledwidge Museum** after just over 1km. This simple farm labourer's cottage was the birthplace, in 1887, of the poet Francis Ledwidge, whose work derived inspiration from the beautiful landscape around his home here, as well as from the history and myth of County Meath. The small museum includes re-creations of the kitchen and the poet's bedroom, some fascinating display boards and a pretty, shady garden out the back.

Although a member of the Irish Volunteers, Ledwidge, like 150,000 other Irishmen, joined the British Army in World War I to protect the rights of small nations, to try to secure Home Rule after the end of the war and to fight "an enemy common to our civilization", as he put it. He survived the horrors of Gallipoli in 1915 – the year in which his only volume of poems, *Songs of the Fields*, was published – but was killed by a stray shell at the Third Battle of Ypres in 1917. Inscribed on a plaque by the cottage's front door are the lines written by Ledwidge about his poet friend, Thomas MacDonagh, who was executed by the British for his part in the 1916 Easter Rising:

2

He shall not hear the bittern cry
In the wild sky, where he is lain,
Nor voices of the sweeter birds
Above the wailing of the rain.

ARRIVAL AND DEPARTURE SLANE

By bus Drogheda (7–14 daily; 30min); Dublin (about 20 daily; 1hr); Monaghan (about 20 daily; 1hr); Trim (4–9 daily; 45min).

ACCOMMODATION AND EATING

Conyngham Arms Hotel ☎ 041 988 4444, ☺ conynghamarms.ie. Conveniently located just west of the main crossroads in the centre of the village, this recently refurbished eighteenth-century coaching inn has sixteen classically styled rooms with ornate beds, some four-poster, and nice touches such as blackout curtains and bathrobes, as well as a popular restaurant. **€130**

The Failte ☎ 041 982 4760, ☺ www.thefailtebandb.ie/rooms.htm. Colourful, modern, en-suite B&B, with very good rates for singles and reductions for stays of two nights or more, just off the N51 a short way west of the village crossroads. **€70**

George's Patisserie and Deli ☎ 041 982 4493. Lovely little bakery-café just north of the crossroads on the N2, serving sublime strawberry tarts and chocolate Sachertorte, as well as soup and sandwiches on homemade bread. Wed–Sat 9am–6pm.

Slane Farm Hostel ☎ 041 988 4985, ☺ slanefarmhostel .ie. Comfortable, attractive, en-suite budget accommodation can be found in the converted coach house and stables of this working farm, just over 2km west of the village beyond the castle; the hostel also offers a well-equipped kitchen, laundry facilities, camping and self-catering cottages. Dorms **€20**, doubles **€50**, camping **€20**

Brú na Bóinne

Visitor centre daily: Feb–April & Oct 9.30am–5.30pm; May & second half of Sept 9am–6.30pm; June to mid-Sept 9am–7pm; Nov–Jan 9am–5pm; last admission 45min before closing; Knowth closed mid-Oct to Easter • Visitor centre €3; combined ticket with Newgrange €6; combined ticket with Knowth €5; all three €11 • ☎ 041 988 0300, ☺ heritageireland.ie; Heritage Card • The last minibuses to Newgrange and to Knowth depart 1hr 45min before closing; for full transport details see p.142

To the east of Slane, between a U-bend in the River Boyne and the N51 to the north, **Brú na Bóinne** (the "palace of the Boyne") encompasses the spectacular 5000-year-old **passage graves** of **Newgrange**, **Knowth** and **Dowth**, high round tumuli raised over stone passages and burial chambers. Entry is funnelled through the impressive **visitor centre** on the south side of the river, which provides detailed information on the significance of the sites, their construction and artwork, and the Neolithic society that created them, as well as housing a **tourist information desk** and café. A footbridge crosses from the centre to the north side of the river, where the compulsory minibuses shuttle you to Newgrange and Knowth, which have both been comprehensively excavated and reconstructed, for **guided tours**. The passage tomb at Dowth, which has been badly damaged by road-builders and cack-handed nineteenth-century archaeologists, is closed to visitors.

Brú na Bóinne is one of Ireland's foremost attractions, and the **numbers** visiting each site daily are strictly limited. Booking by phone isn't possible, so it's advisable to arrive as early in the day as you can and book your places on the minibuses, which have timed departures. There's no point in arriving late in the day, as it takes at least three hours to see Newgrange, Knowth and the visitor centre.

2

Newgrange

Newgrange is unquestionably the most striking of the Brú na Bóinne mounds, not least because its façade of white quartz stones and round granite boulders has been reassembled. The quartz originally came from Wicklow, the granite from the Mourne and Carlingford areas, exemplifying the mind-boggling levels of resources and organization lavished on this project, by these farmers who used nothing but simple tools of wood and stone. It has been estimated that the tumulus, which is over 75m in diameter, weighs 200,000 tons in total and would have taken around forty years to build. It was the final resting place of a high-status family within the Neolithic community – the cremated remains and grave goods of at least five people were recovered from the burial chamber during excavation – but seems also to have had a wider purpose as a ritual site or gathering place.

The **entrance stone** is one of the finest examples of the art of the tomb-builders, who carved spectacular but enigmatic spirals, chevrons, lozenges and other geometric designs onto many of the large stones around the mound and up the 19m passage. The tomb's pivotal feature, however, is a **roof-box** above the entrance whose slit was perfectly positioned to receive the first rays of the rising sun on the day of the **winter solstice** (December 21); the light first peeps into the cruciform burial chamber itself before spreading its rays along the length of the passage. The engaging guided tour provides an electrically powered simulation in the burial chamber, while tickets for the real thing are decided by lottery each year. To prehistoric farmers, this solstice marked the start of a new year, promising rebirth for their crops and perhaps new life for the spirits of the dead.

It seems probable that by around 2000 BC, in the Late Neolithic or Early Bronze Age, the mound had collapsed and fallen into disuse, but it still provided a powerful focal point for ritual. During this era, a huge religious enclosure known as the **pit circle** was constructed here, consisting of a double circle of wooden posts, within which animals were cremated and buried in pits. To this was added a circle of around 35 **standing stones**, which may have had an astronomical function; about a dozen of them remain upright.

Knowth

It's well worth signing up for the lively guided tour of **Knowth** too, which provides some telling contrasts with the more famous Newgrange – not least in interpretation: the archaeologist in charge of this site, for example, thought the white quartz stones discovered around the main passage entrance were to reflect the sun, so left them as a shimmering carpet on the ground. The Knowth mound is pierced by two passages, each around twice the length of the Newgrange tunnel, aligned roughly with sunrise and sunset on the equinox days in March and September and leading to back-to-back burial chambers. Unfortunately, it's no longer possible to follow the passages themselves, but the tour takes you inside the mound to look along the eastern tunnel, and you can also climb on top of the mound for views of the Hill of Slane and the Wicklow Mountains.

Knowth is even richer in **Neolithic art** than Newgrange, with about 250 decorated stones discovered here – over half of all known Irish passage-tomb art. The mound is surrounded by over 120 huge kerbstones, one of which supports a carved pattern of crescents and lines that may represent the equinox; elsewhere, patterns of circular and serpentine incisions have been interpreted as local maps, showing the River Boyne and the burial mounds. Hard by the main mound, you can poke around eighteen smaller or **satellite mounds**, at least two of which were built before the main tomb. The Knowth mound attracted habitation in various eras right up until the sixteenth century AD, and your guide will show you several **souterrains**, underground tunnels that were dug in the early Christian period for hiding, escape and possibly food preservation.

ARRIVAL AND DEPARTURE   **BRÚ NA BÓINNE**

By bus Take Bus Éireann service #100 from Dublin to Drogheda (which is also served by trains from Pearse, Tara Street or Connolly stations), and then the #163 bus to the visitor centre, which connects with the #100 twice a day (Mon–Sat). Alternatively, a Newgrange shuttlebus (45min) operated by Over the Top Tours (see p.116; €17 turn) leaves the *Gresham Hotel*, O'Connell Street Upper (daily 8.45am & 11.15am), stopping outside Suffolk Street tourist office (daily 9am & 11.30pm), and returning from the visitor centre at 1.30pm & 4.30pm (return times may vary in peak season, and in winter the early departure may not run every day). Tickets can be purchased on board but it's better to book your seat in advance.

By car If you have your own transport, follow signs, either from the south side of the bridge in Slane or from the M1 motorway to the southwest of Drogheda, to the visitor centre, which is 2km west of Donore village.

CCOMMODATION

ewgrange Lodge ☎ 041 988 2478, ⓦ newgrangelodge om (An Óige & IHO). Just east of the Brú na Bóinne Visitor ntre in a substantially rebuilt farmhouse, *Newgrange Lodge* fers a wide range of attractive and comfortable en-suite udget accommodation with under-floor heating, and xtensive communal areas including a well-equipped kitchen d a barbecue area, as well as bike rental and camping. orms €18, doubles €53, camping €10

Rossnaree ☎ 041 982 0975, ⓦ rossnaree.ie. An Italianate Victorian country house about 2km west of the visitor centre on the Slane road, which offers four luxurious, individually styled rooms, as well as art courses and fly-fishing on the estate. Sumptuous breakfasts feature eggs from their own hens, seasonal vegetables from the walled garden, freshly squeezed orange juice and homemade muesli. €140

he Battle of the Boyne Visitor Centre

aily: March & April 9.30am–4.30pm; May–Sept 10am–5pm; Oct–Feb 9am–4pm • €4; Heritage Card • ☎ 041 980 9950,
battleoftheboyne.ie • Bus Éireann service #100 from Dublin to Drogheda (which is also served by trains from Pearse, Tara Street or nnolly stations), and then the #163 bus to the visitor centre, which connects with the #100 twice a day (Mon–Sat); can also be reached om Brú na Bóinne by car making for Donore, then heading north for 3km to the river, or from the Drogheda–Slane road (N51) by ossing the Obelisk Bridge

On July 1, 1690 (July 11, 1690 according to our modern, Gregorian calendar, though 's celebrated by Northern Protestants on July 12, after some convoluted mathematical interpretation following the eighteenth-century change to the Gregorian calendar), William III met his father-in-law, the deposed King James II, at the **Battle of the Boyne**, he largest ever set-piece battle on Irish or British soil. At stake were the English throne, ow held by the Protestant William with support from the pope and the Catholic king f Spain, and the dominance of Europe by the French, who backed the Catholic James. t the head of an army of 36,000 English, Dutch, Protestant Irish, French Huguenots nd Danes, William took up position on the north side of the river just west of Drogheda, while on the opposite bank, James commanded 24,000 men, mostly Irish regulars, but including seven thousand well-armed French soldiers. To counter William's flanking movement, upriver and around the Knowth mound, James was rawn into sending most of his force westward, which allowed the main Williamite rmy to cross the river to Oldbridge and put the Jacobite centre to flight. The Irish and rench regrouped to carry on fighting for another year, notably at Aughrim and imerick, but James kept running, via Dublin and Kinsale, to France, never to return. Oldbridge House, a fine 1740s limestone mansion on the south bank of the River oyne, has recently been turned into a **visitor centre**, commemorating the battle and e 1500 men who died. It houses an impressive exhibition, delicately worded but arshalling telling quotes from participants in the battle, and an audiovisual, which uts the blame on the French. Overlooking the walled garden, there's an attractive avilion café with outdoor tables. Admission is free to the surrounding parkland, which eatures display boards and five signposted battlefield walks of up to fifty minutes, and n summer Sundays and bank-holiday Mondays you can watch a musketeer and a avalryman giving hourly "living history" displays on the front lawn.

Louth, Monaghan and Cavan

THE LAKES OF CAVAN

Louth, Monaghan and Cavan

Louth, Monaghan and Cavan all share a border with Northern Ireland and, as throughout the North, still bear many signs of the Plantation in the form of grand country estates (known simply as "big houses") and planned towns. Louth is Ireland's smallest county and the most northerly in the Leinster province, and much of its activity is focused on the historic town of Drogheda, set on the banks of the Boyne whose fertile valley also boasts major religious sites at Monasterboice and Mellifont.

3

In Lough's northeast the **Cooley Peninsula** provides somewhat dramatic relief from the county's otherwise drab coastline and played an active role in the greatest of Irish mythological epics, the *Táin Bó Cúailnge* (Cattle Raid of Cooley; see box, p.155).

The topography of **Monaghan** and **Cavan**, both in the Northern Ireland province, is markedly different. Monaghan's landscape is characterized by eruptions of small hills, known as drumlins, and its sense of life is encapsulated in the writing of Patrick Kavanagh from **Inniskeen**. Monaghan's few towns offer little of interest, though the busy **county town** itself is attractively laid out and features a few buildings of note, plus one of the region's best festivals. To the southeast, the hilltop market town of **Clones** is a former ecclesiastical centre and also strongly associated with Irish lace-making. To Monaghan town's north lies **Glaslough**, an estate village set around the grandiose **Castle Leslie**.

In contrast, much of Cavan is defined by its waterways and small lakes, offering a multitude of choices for anglers. The **Shannon–Erne Waterway** offers the most readily navigable route through the lakes, for which **Belturbet** provides a good starting point. Away from the major roads that pierce both Monaghan and Cavan, the countryside has an unhurried charm, though it's easy to get lost when navigating its tangled grid of lanes without a map or compass. **Cavan** town itself is agreeable enough, but offers little to warrant more than a passing visit. The county's west provides some stark and rugged landscapes, ideally explored via the **Cavan Way**.

Most of the attractions in Louth (which has rail links to Dublin and Belfast) and Monaghan are easily accessible by **public transport**, but bus services in Cavan are somewhat less frequent.

Drogheda

DROGHEDA (pronounced "droch – as in loch – edda") was once two separate Viking settlements, huddled together on either side of the River Boyne. These developed into twin towns during the Anglo-Norman period, whose intermittent rivalry was quashed by a royal charter uniting the pair in 1412. The town incurred the most infamous onslaught of Cromwell's Irish campaign of 1649 when its defending garrison and many inhabitants were massacred by the Lord Protector's army.

Drogheda's attractions lie both sides of the **River Boyne**. The walled town, which developed in the late medieval period, became one of Ireland's most important religious and political centres – the parliament would occasionally convene in Drogheda – and a

Drogheda festivals p.152
Walks on the Cooley
  Peninsula p.154

Táin Bó Cúailnge (The Cattle Raid of
  Cooley) p.155
Clones lace p.158

CARLINGFORD

Highlights

❶ Drogheda One of Ireland's liveliest towns, rich in antiquities and with an array of atmospheric pubs. **See p.146**

❷ Monasterboice Ecclesiastical relics here include Ireland's tallest round tower and also two of the most splendid high crosses in the whole of the country. **See p.152**

❸ The Cooley Peninsula Closely associated with the Irish epic saga, the Táin Bó Cúailnge, Cooley's mountains offer tremendous views of

Carlingford Lough, while Carlingford itself has some terrific restaurants. **See p.153**

❹ Inniskeen The birthplace of one of the country's greatest poets, Patrick Kavanagh, celebrates its scion through an excellent and informative resource centre. **See p.158**

❺ The Lakes of Cavan Known collectively as Lough Oughter and linked by an extraordinary complex of atmospheric waterways, this is perfect walking territory. **See p.160**

HIGHLIGHTS ARE MARKED ON THE MAP ON P.148

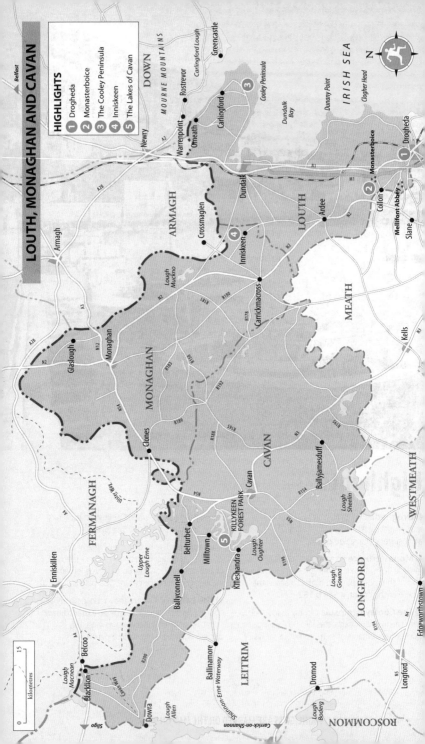

few remnants from this time are still visible. Later constructions by the town's Protestant middle classes, such as the **Tholsel** and **courthouse**, reflect a burgeoning confidence enhanced by Drogheda's growing importance as a manufacturing town, thriving on the export of linen, shoes and alcohol. Its old **docks**, which were once the focus for the numerous trades that developed here during the eighteenth and nineteenth centuries, are now being regenerated with vitality, not least in the shape of the huge **Scotch Hall shopping centre** on the south side of the river.

The northside

Start your exploration of **the northside** at the junction of West Street and Shop Street by the eighteenth-century **Tholsel**, the former town hall, a solid limestone building topped by a domed tower which features a four-faced clock; it now houses the tourist office (see p.151). A short distance east from here is **St Laurence Gate**, one of the few vestiges of the town's medieval walls. This imposing barbican, with its two tall rounded towers, once housed a portcullis protecting the tollgate just within; unfortunately, it's not open to visitors. Another dominant structure lies a little to the northwest of St Laurence Gate, in the shape of the two-storey **Magdalene Tower**, the erstwhile belfry and only remnant of a large Dominican friary founded here around 1224 by the Archbishop of Armagh, Lucas de Netterville.

The Highlanes Gallery

Laurence St • Mon–Sat 10.30am–5pm • Free, though suggested donation of €2 • ☎ 041 980 3311, ⓦ highlanes.ie

Housed in a former Franciscan church a few paces down from St Laurence Gate, the enlightening **Highlanes Gallery** features works from the municipal collection (dating from the seventeenth century) as well as a rolling programme of temporary exhibitions; these exhibitions are as varied as they are interesting, and you're just as likely to see sculpture, installations and children's art as you are conventional paintings. In an unusual aside, you'll also find here the sword and mace presented to Drogheda by William of Orange.

St Peter's Church (Church of Ireland) and Magdalene Tower

Uphill from the Tholsel, Magdalene Street Lower passes **St Peter's Church** (Church of Ireland), a graceful mid-eighteenth-century edifice whose porch and spire were added by the renowned Irish architect Francis Johnston in 1793. The church replaced the original thirteenth-century structure whose stone steeple was blown down by a violent storm in 1548 and subsequently refurbished with a wooden replacement. During the massacre that followed the 1649 siege of the town, many people sought sanctuary in the steeple but perished when Cromwell's troops set it ablaze.

St Peter's Church (Roman Catholic)

Along the main thoroughfare, West Street, stands the town's other **St Peter's Church** (Roman Catholic), a solidly neo-Gothic late nineteenth-century structure topped by an elegant spire and accessed via a sweeping stone stairway. Its interior is equally impressive, featuring stout granite pillars and walls of Bath stone, and just off its left-hand aisle is a small shrine devoted to **Oliver Plunkett**, Archbishop of Armagh and Primate of All Ireland from 1670. Towards the end of that decade, at a time of widespread anti-Catholic feeling in England, Titus Oates, a former Anglican clergyman and convicted perjurer who had earlier converted to Catholicism, hatched a fabricated claim (which became known as the Popish Plot) that the pope was preparing to invade the country and had installed Plunkett as one of the main organizers of the papal army. Plunkett was arrested and put on trial in Dundalk, but, when the jury failed to convict him, was moved first to Dublin and then to Newgate

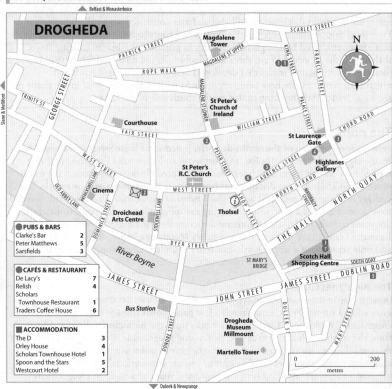

prison in London. Found guilty of treason on July 1, 1681, he was hanged, drawn and quartered, and his remains were thrown onto a fire, but his head and other parts of his body were rescued. The head finally arrived back in Ireland around 1722, following a circuitous route via Rome, and is now contained in a silver-ornamented box within the shrine. The other parts of Plunkett's body on view in the church did not return until after his canonization in 1975.

The southside

Cross the river to **the southside** and head for **Millmount Hill**, which rises above the Boyne's bank and is easily accessed via a stairway directly opposite **St Mary's Bridge**. The hill commands an unhindered view of the town, revealing its still largely extant, cramped medieval street pattern. Millmount features strongly in Irish mythology, supposedly being the burial place of the Celtic poet Amergin, while the hill's strategic value was quickly recognized by the Anglo-Normans who constructed a motte here in the late twelfth century. Subsequently, a castle was erected which stood until 1808 when the fortifications were demolished and replaced by the barracks and **Martello tower** which stand here today. The old castle provided the fiercest resistance to Cromwell during the 1649 siege, while the tower was severely damaged by shelling during the 1922 Civil War, though it has since been restored and can be visited by purchasing a ticket at the museum (see opposite). There's little to see inside, but a climb to the top does reveal a panoramic view of Drogheda and the surrounding area.

Drogheda Museum Millmount

Mon–Sat 10am–5.30pm, Sun & public holidays 2–5pm • Museum only €3.50, tower only €3, combined ticket €5.50 • ☎ 041 983 3097,
ⓦ droghedamuseum.ie

The barracks square houses the **Drogheda Museum Millmount**, featuring a rich assemblage of local artefacts. The best of the displays are contained within the **Industrial Room**, which focuses on Drogheda's manufacturing history – particularly the town's erstwhile role as a major producer of alcoholic beverages, when there were once no fewer than fourteen breweries and sixteen distilleries. Here too, you'll find a splendid collection of banners, many over two hundred years old and which represent the various crafts and trades that operated hereabouts in the late eighteenth and early nineteenth centuries, such as weavers, carpenters and fishermen. A **religious display**, meanwhile, concentrates on the life of Oliver Plunkett (see p.149).

ARRIVAL AND INFORMATION

DROGHEDA

By train The train station (☎ 041 983 8749) is on the southside, just off Dublin Road to the east of town.
Destinations Belfast (7 daily; 1hr 40min); Dublin (Mon–Sat every 20–30min, Sun hourly; 30min–1hr); Newry (7 daily; 40min).

By bus The bus station (☎ 041 983 5023) is on Donore Road, just south of the river. The local private bus company is Matthews (☎ 042 937 8188, ⓦ matthewscoach.ie).
Destinations with Bus Éireann Belfast (11 daily; 1hr 55min); Collon for Mellifont (Mon–Sat hourly; 15min); Donore for Newgrange (Mon–Sat 2 daily; 10min); Navan (Mon–Sat 8 daily, Sun 4; 30–55min); Newry (Mon–Sat 8 daily; 1hr 15min).

Destinations with Matthews Dublin (Mon–Sat hourly, Sun 10; 1hr).

Tourist office The tourist office is inside the Tholsel on West Street (Mon–Fri 9.30am–5.30pm, plus Sat April–Sept; ☎ 041 987 2843, ⓦ drogheda.ie).

Walking tours Guided tours of the town are organized through the Drogheda Museum Millmount, but must be booked in advance at the tourist office (May–Aug Tues–Sat 2.30pm daily; 1hr 30min; €3; ☎ 041 983 3097).

Bike rental Useful for getting to either Monasterboice or Mellifont Abbey, bikes can be rented from Quay Cycles at 11a North Quay (☎ 041 983 4526; €15 per day).

ACCOMMODATION

★**The D** Scotch Hall, Marsh Rd ☎ 041 987 7700, ⓦ thedhotel.com. Very style-conscious riverside establishment providing swish doubles, a great waterside bar and restaurant, and an utterly outré penthouse suite. Plenty of off-season and early-booking bargains on offer. **€110**

Orley House Bryanstown, Dublin Rd ☎ 041 983 6019, ⓦ orleyhouse.com. Completely unassuming bungalow in a quiet residential street just off the N1 near the train station, with sunny twin, double and triple en-suite rooms; there's also a comfy lounge and conservatory for guest use. **€75**

Scholars Townhouse Hotel King St ☎ 041 983 5410, ⓦ scholarshotel.com. The handsome red-brick frontage of this renovated former Christian Brothers residence conceals sixteen superior – albeit modestly sized – rooms; many of the original features have been retained, including

the oak panelling, stained-glass windows and high-coved ceilings. **€109**

Spoon and the Stars 13 St Mary's Terrace ☎ 086 405 8465, ⓦ spoonandthestars.com. Cheerful and relaxed independent hostel on the main N1 road with a range of small and large dorms, some with bathrooms. The chill-out space (a.k.a. "the Cave") is a basement lounge, complete with Sky TV. There's also a cute little terrace garden, a self-catering kitchen and laundry facilities. Bus #101 from Dublin stops right outside. Dorms **€20**, doubles **€54**

Westcourt Hotel West St ☎ 041 983 0965, ⓦ westcourt.ie. The most central of the town's hotels, this is a very welcoming and comfortable establishment with variously configured rooms furnished with attractive mahogany beds with deep mattresses and tastefully upholstered chairs. Great-value deals often available. **€99**

EATING AND DRINKING

★**Clarke's Bar** 19 Peter St ☎ 041 983 6724. Don't let the tatty exterior fool you: this former grocer's shop, all dark and woody with some very cosy snugs, is a fabulous boozer with bags of charm and plenty of chatter. Regular events too. Mon–Thurs 1–11.30pm, Fri & Sat noon–12.30am, Sun 12.30–11pm.

★**De Lacy's** Scotch Hall, Marsh Rd ☎ 041 987 7700, ⓦ delacys.ie. The *D* hotel's upmarket steak and seafood diner is the town's standout restaurant. You could do worse than start with the posh fish pie with monkfish, prawn, sea bass and scallops, while the four-course set menu (€29) is a steal. Thurs–Sun 5–10pm plus Sun 1–3pm.

3

DROGHEDA FESTIVALS

Drogheda offers a trio of excellent annual festivals, the first of which is the Arts Festival (ⓦdroghedaartsfestival.ie), which takes place over the May public holiday weekend; expect all forms of performance art including lots of vibrant street theatre. In June, it's the turn of the Irish Maritime Festival (ⓦmaritimefestival.ie), the highlight of which is a magnificent flotilla of Tall Ships sailing down the Boyne, and the Drogheda Samba Festival (ⓦdroghedasamba.com), a three-day celebration of Latin and African rhythms in the form of workshops, indoor and outdoor concerts and, of course, a carnival.

Peter Matthews 8/9 Laurence St ☎041 983 7371. Better known as *McPhail's Bar*, this has a similar vibe to *Clarke's*, with a traditional front bar lined with snugs, a back room hosting live music several nights a week and a beer garden. Daily 5pm–late.

Relish Highlanes Gallery, Laurence St ☎041 980 3295. Refreshingly bright, conservatory-style café-deli adjoining the Highlanes Gallery, offering a mouth-watering variety of gourmet sandwiches, charcuterie, meat and fish platters, homemade breads and pastries. The weekend brunches are very popular. Mon–Sat 9.30am–5.30pm, Sun 11.30am–5.30pm.

Sarsfields 28 Cord Rd ☎041 983 8032. Another inviting old bar, though a bit more low-key than the others in town. Still, some terrific evenings of music await, featuring anything from modern bluegrass to singer-songwriters.

Daily 11am–midnight.

Scholars Townhouse Restaurant King St ☎041 983 5410, ⓦscholarshotel.com. Little has changed, ambience-wise, in this hotel's (see p.151) high-class restaurant over the years, as the oak-panelled walls and antique-filled cabinets testify. The food, however, is a thoroughly modern affair, so expect the likes of saddle of lamb with feta and potato croquette and red pepper ragout. The three-course early-bird menu (5–7pm; €27) is great value. Mon–Sat 5–10pm, Sun noon–4pm.

Traders Coffee House 1 Laurence St ☎086 050 4571. This tiny little coffee house across from the Tholsel does the meanest caffeine shot in town; grab a newspaper and a bar stool, and savour a freshly roasted cuppa with a pastry. Mon–Sat 9am–5pm.

ENTERTAINMENT

Drogheda Road Bowls Club ☎087 225 1463, ⓦroadbowlingdrogheda.com. Drogheda is one of the last bastions of road bowling in the region (see box, p.555), so if you fancy spending a Sunday morning watching this entertaining activity (sport is perhaps overstretching it), matches take place each week at 11am along the Baltray

Road, which runs from Newtown Queensborough to the village of Baltray.

Droichead Arts Centre Stockwell Lane ☎041 983 3946, ⓦdroichead.com. All-purpose centre staging everything from visual art exhibitions and musical events to comedy, film and opera.

Monasterboice and Mellifont

Close to Drogheda to the north lie the remains of the monasteries of **Monasterboice** and **Mellifont**, two of Ireland's most significant ecclesiastical sites, the former including a superb high cross and the latter providing ample evidence of its erstwhile power and importance. Monasterboice is the more easily accessed, via the regular Drogheda–Dundalk bus – ask to be set down at the *Monasterboice Inn*, from which it's an easy fifteen-minute signposted walk. Getting to Mellifont is more problematic: the infrequent Drogheda–Collon bus will stop at Monleek Cross, from where it's a 3km walk.

Monasterboice

6km north of Drogheda • Dawn to dusk • Free

Monasterboice has an idyllic rural setting and the remains of its monastic settlement – founded in either the eighth or ninth century – include not only one of Ireland's finest high crosses, dating from the tenth century, but one of the best-preserved round towers in the country too. The two ruined **churches** within the enclosure, which date from the thirteenth century, probably had little connection with the, by then, defunct monastery.

The crosses

The stocky **St Muiredach's Cross**, just inside the churchyard, is the better preserved of the pair here. Its elaborate series of carved panels depict a variety of biblical events, loosely arranged in supposed chronological order. The base of its **east face** begins in the Garden of Eden, before moving upwards to the stories of Cain and Abel, David and Goliath, Moses bringing water to the Israelites and the Magi bearing gifts for the newborn Christ. Above these, the cross's carved wheel depicts the Last Judgement and the risen multitudes pleading for entry into Heaven. The **west face** depicts events during the later life of Christ, ranging from his arrest at Gethsemane to the Ascension, though the hub of the cross's wheel shows Moses with the Ten Commandments. Unusually, both flanks of the cross are also decorated and feature the Flight of the Israelites and saints Anthony and Paul.

The taller **West Cross**, unfortunately chipped at its top, features another array of biblical scenes, though erosion makes most of them indecipherable without the assistance of the adjacent display board. Certainly, its **east face** features David and the lion, and the **west** includes the Resurrection, but much of the remainder is difficult to discern.

Adjacent to the West Cross is what's reckoned to be the tallest **round tower** in Ireland, standing at some 30m high, though it has long since lost its conical cap and cannot be entered for safety reasons.

Mellifont Abbey

R168, 10km northwest of Drogheda • May–Sept daily 10am–6pm • €3; Heritage Card • ☎ 041 982 6459, ⓦ mellifontabbey.ie

Founded in 1142 by St Malachy, **Mellifont Abbey** was the first and subsequently most important Cistercian foundation in Ireland, eventually heading an affiliation of more than twenty monasteries. Set in a tranquil spot by the River Mattock, Mellifont must once have been a hugely impressive complex, though its scant ruins leave much to the imagination. After the Reformation the abbey passed into the hands of Edward Moore, who converted its buildings into a fortified residence. Here, in 1603, the great Irish chieftain **Hugh O'Neill** was besieged by Lord Mountjoy until starvation forced his surrender. During the Battle of the Boyne, William of Orange based himself at Mellifont, after which the property was abandoned and fell ultimately into dilapidation. It eventually passed into the hands of the Office of Public Works in the late twentieth century.

The site

Before touring the remains, take in the small exhibition in the **visitor centre** (same hours; free) by the entrance, which details the foundation's history and provides a scale model of the abbey's layout. Entrance to the site is via the church's **north transept** which features the remains of two stone *piscinae* – sinks for cleaning sacred serving vessels. As the church was built on sloping ground the broad nave has an uncommon feature, a crypt constructed to ensure it remained level. Next to the **south transept** stood the chapterhouse, whose floor features medieval glazed tiles, though some of these have been brought here from other parts of the abbey.

The tallest and finest remnant of the abbey stands in its expansive cloister garth, a remarkable, octagonal arched **lavabo**, with fountains and basins where the monks would wash. Behind the lavabo, the southern ruins included both the calefactory (or warming house), the only heated room in the entire complex, and the refectory. The remaining ruins rarely rise above knee height, and you'll need to consult the display-board map or buy the visitors' guide to interpret them.

The Cooley Peninsula

The **Cooley Peninsula** is Louth's most hyped tourist destination, and while it's true that the mountains and surrounding rich verdure offer great walking territory and many a stunning seascape, the countryside lacks the raw, rugged and often downright exhilarating feel of the Mournes (see p.544) over the other side of **Carlingford Lough**. That said, there's still plenty here to delight, even if **Carlingford** village itself has somewhat meretriciously cashed in on its waterside location.

If you start from Dundalk, look out for signs to the *Ballymascanlon Hotel*, a kilometre or so after the R173 turn-off from the N1. A footpath from the hotel's car park runs beside the golf course to the **Proleek Dolmen**, a regular photographic feature in tourist brochures. Perched on the points of three triangular stones, its massive capstone weighs a remarkable 46 tons and, having inspected the scene, you'll probably spend the rest of the day wondering about the ingenuity of prehistoric hoisting engineers.

Carlingford

Set a short distance back from the lough's southern shore, the trim and charming former fishing village of **CARLINGFORD** is by far the best base for exploring the peninsula. Its tight and tortuous streets reflect its medieval origins and house a host of places where you can eat, drink and sleep. However, this is not a place for the light of purse or pocket: prices here are significantly higher than elsewhere in the county or across the water in Down.

Carlingford's name is Old Norse in origin, deriving from "Kerlingfjörthr" (the fjord of the hag-shaped rock), and indicating that this was once a Viking settlement. Standing sentinel by the lough shore is the roofless ruin of **King John's Castle**, so-named after the English king who supposedly stopped in the village for two days in 1210 during the war with the Irish Knights. The village itself contains some impressive later buildings, not least the **Tholsel**, the sole surviving town gate from the fifteenth century, albeit heavily modified in the nineteenth century. Further along, and dating from the same period, stands the **Mint**, a fortified town house where coins were minted from the mid-fifteenth century onwards. Just beyond here you arrive in the market square (as central a point as any in the village) and the substantial ruins of **Taaffes Castle**, another superb medieval remnant, which was most likely a trading depot for the merchant classes.

The Heritage Centre

Mon–Fri 9.30am–5pm • €3 • ☎ 042 937 3454, ⓦ carlingfordheritagecentre.com

To learn more about Carlingford's history, visit the **Heritage Centre**, housed in the restored medieval Holy Trinity church, whose displays document the village's development from Norman times. The church also plays host to numerous **concerts** throughout the year, which are well worth looking out for.

ARRIVAL AND INFORMATION   CARLINGFORD

By bus Buses stop outside the old Station House on the waterfront.

Destinations Dundalk (Mon–Sat 5 daily; 40–50min); Newry (Mon–Sat 4 daily; 25–35min).

WALKS ON THE COOLEY PENINSULA

The varied terrain of the peninsula offers a range of opportunities for **walking**, whether in the hills, offering often sumptuous views across the lough to the Mournes, by the shore or along lush valleys. The longest waymarked walk is the 26km **Táin Trail**, which takes a circular route around Slieve Foye (587m), up to the west above Carlingford village, and includes much of the higher ground. Undertaking this requires proper walking equipment and clothing, and supplies of food and drink, as well as Ordnance Survey of Ireland Discovery map #36. However, there are plenty of less arduous walks, some of which, such as the **8km round-trip to Maeve's Gap**, are easily accessible from Carlingford village. For others you'll need to head northwest to Omeath or east to Greenore. The useful **Cooley Walks** pamphlet (€3.95 from the tourist office in Carlingford) outlines ten scenic walks in the area, ranging from one to four hours in duration.

TÁIN BÓ CÚAILNGE (THE CATTLE RAID OF COOLEY)

The location of many an Irish legend is still immediately identifiable thanks to a wealth of extant place names, and perhaps no more so than in the case of the **Táin Bó Cúailnge**. Set around 500 BC, many of the events in perhaps the greatest of the Celtic epics clearly take place in the mountains of the Cooley Peninsula. The villainess of the tale is **Medb**, the great Queen of Connacht, who so envies her husband Aillil's White Bull (Finnbenach) that she determines to capture the Brown Bull of Cooley (Donn Cúailnge). Drawing Aillil into her campaign, she begins a war against the east of Ireland, targeting Ulster in particular. All the Ulster men are rendered immobile by a curse except the tale's hero, **Cúchullain**, who is left to confront Medb's armies single-handedly. Much of the plot concerns his feats and victories, often achieved in bloodthirsty fashion, and the text is also brought to life by vivid topographical detail. The first known written version of the saga was included in the twelfth-century **Book of the Dun Cow**, and Thomas Kinsella's twentieth-century English translation encapsulates much of the vivacity of the Irish-language version (see p.620).

3

Tourist office The tourist office (daily 9.30am–5.30pm, Nov–March till 4.30pm; ☎ 042 937 3033, ⓦ carlingford.ie) is presently inside the Heritage Centre, though plans are afoot to move it back to the soon-to-be-restored station house on the waterfront.

Bike rental Bikes can be rented from On Yer Bike on Chapel Hill (☎ 042 937 3793, ⓦ onyerbike.ie; €20 per day).

Activities The Carlingford Adventure Centre on Tholsel Street (☎ 042 937 3100, ⓦ carlingfordadventure.com) offers a range of activities on both land and water, either on a daily basis or as part of a package including accommodation. They can also give you details about the new Skypark (ⓦ skypark.ie), located just outside the village and which features the country's highest zipwire – if nothing else, it's a novel way to see the mountains.

ACCOMMODATION

Belvedere House 3 Newry St ☎ 042 938 3848, ⓦ belvederehouse.ie. The *Belvedere*'s seven rooms offer a high level of comfort, each one vaguely themed on Celtic history. The colour combinations of grey, beige and mauve are tasteful enough, while the smart furnishings include sturdy wooden bedsteads and wood-framed mirrors. €90

★ **Ghan House** Just below the Heritage Centre ☎ 042 937 3682, ⓦ ghanhouse.com. Sitting pretty behind a high-walled garden, *Ghan House* is a beautifully kept eighteenth-century building with twelve exquisitely furnished rooms. It also has an exceptionally good restaurant (see below). €95

Mourneview Belmont, 2km south of Carlingford ☎ 042 937 3551, ⓦ mourneviewcarlingford.com. A welcome antidote to the hustle and bustle of the village itself, this charmingly run B&B sits in perfect rural isolation with delightful mountain views from its six neat rooms. €75

EATING AND DRINKING

Dan's Stonewall Café Market Square ☎ 042 938 3797. Buzzy street-corner café doling out steaming bowls of soup, fresh sandwiches and salads, and a decent selection of coffee, scones and cakes. Daily 9am–6pm.

★ **Ghan House** Just below the Heritage Centre ☎ 042 937 3682, ⓦ ghanhouse.com. The undoubted culinary star in Carlingford is *Ghan House*, which serves modern Irish cuisine over two fixed menus: a four-course restaurant menu (€45) and a six-course midweek tasting menu (Mon–Thurs; €33). Dishes might include pan-fried stone bass with saffron cream, or herb-crusted Cooley lamb in a bean and chorizo casserole, with ingredients from their own herb and vegetable gardens. Top class. Daily 6.30–9.30pm.

The Oystercatcher Bistro Market Square ☎ 042 937 3989. Black and white photos adorn the walls of this long-established family restaurant, whose dishes are occasionally given a Mediterranean/North African slant. On Sundays in the summer, you'll find the owners selling street food from a van outside. Daily 6–10pm, closed Mon & Tues Sept–June.

PJ O'Hares Tholsel St ☎ 042 937 3770. The liveliest of the village's many pubs, PJ's is a rambling, old-fashioned grocery-cum-pub with a warren of bars frequented by a good-natured crowd. Daily 11am–11pm.

★ **Ruby Ellens** Newry St ☎ 042 937 3385. An absolute gem of a teahouse, from the floral-patterned cushions and fresh flowers on the tables to an outstanding range of thirst-quenching brews, served in exquisite china teacups. Daily 9am–6pm.

Monaghan town

All the elements of post-Plantation urban planning are well to the fore in **MONAGHAN TOWN**, which derived its prosperity from the linen industry and was long the base of a British garrison. The hub of the town plan is the **Diamond**, in whose centre stands the Rossmore monument, a flamboyant nineteenth-century drinking fountain. A short distance west is **Church Square**, dominated by an impressive obelisk commemorating a garrison member who died at the Battle of Inkerman, and almost entirely surrounded by stately, early nineteenth-century buildings, including a Neoclassical courthouse, a very fetching Regency Gothic church and an appropriately sturdy bank. Just downhill from here on Market Street is the late eighteenth-century **Market House**, a charming, arched limestone edifice whose exterior is embellished with exquisite carvings of oak apples and leaves; now home to the tourist office, it also hosts occasional arts and literary events.

If you're in the region at the beginning of September, the rocking **Harvest Blues Festival** (wharvestblues.ie) is well worth checking out, as it does pull in some fine acts.

Monaghan County Museum

1–2 Hill St • Mon–Fri 11am–5pm, Sat noon–5pm • Free • ☏ 047 82928, w monaghan.ie/museum

To gain some understanding of the area's development, make tracks for the wonderful **Monaghan County Museum**, just behind the Market House. A hugely rich and varied collection begins with some superb archaeological finds, notably the remarkably well-preserved Lisdrumturk cauldron, made from beautifully riveted bronze sheets. The most exceptional exhibit, however, is the fourteenth-century **Cross of Clogher**, a glorious, finely worked oak cross encased in bronze and adorned with bosses and panels, the uppermost of which depicts the Crucifixion.

There's also comprehensive coverage of the county's various crafts and industries – many now sadly defunct – most notably **lace**, which was especially prominent in nearby Clones (see p.158). **Local heroes** are given due prominence too; in one cabinet you'll find the five shirts worn by rugby legend Tommy Bowe during Ireland's successful Six Nations triumph in 2009. Along the corridor, amid the otherwise sobering photos depicting life during the Troubles, is one of Barry McGuigan, standing triumphant on an open-top bus in Clones following his world title boxing victory in 1985.

ARRIVAL AND INFORMATION

MONAGHAN

By bus Monaghan's bus station (☏ 047 82377) is on North Road, a 5min walk north of Church Square.
Destinations with Bus Éireann Armagh (2–3 daily; 30min) Cavan (Mon–Fri 9 daily, Sat & Sun 5–6 daily; 1hr); Clones (Mon–Fri 4 daily, Sat 2; 30min); Letterkenny (8 daily; 1hr 50min); Omagh (10 daily; 45min).

Destinations with Ulsterbus Armagh (Mon–Sat 10 daily, Sun 4; 30–45min); Belfast (Mon–Sat 2 daily; 1hr 45min).
Tourist office The seasonal tourist office is located in the Market House on Market Street (June–Sept Mon–Fri 10am–1pm & 2–5pm, Sat 1–5pm; ☏ 047 81122 w monaghantourism.com).

ACCOMMODATION AND EATING

Andy's 12 Market St ☏ 047 82277, w andysmonaghan .com. If you like chicken, then this is the place to come: peppered chicken with red wine sauce, chilli chicken and salsa (€16.50), and so on, though there is more besides, including an excellent (homemade) burger menu. Tues–Fri 4–10pm, Sat noon–10pm, Sun 1.30–9.30pm.

Grove Lodge Old Armagh Rd ☏ 047 84677, w grovelodge-bnb.com. Large and modern family home a 10min walk southeast of the centre, with three pleasant en-suite rooms: two doubles and one family. €70

The Hillgrove Hotel Old Armagh Rd ☏ 047 81288, w hillgrovehotel.com. Fortunately, the gaudily designed reception area doesn't extend to the rooms which are far more tasteful, as well as being spacious and well furnished. There's an outstanding spa facility for guest use too. €89

Pinky & Perky's The Diamond ☏ 047 84562 w squealingpig.ie. For the best coffee in town, head to this happy little café where you'll more than likely end up sharing a table with one of the locals. In the same building the *Squealing Pig* operates as a bistro/bar. Café Mon–Fri 9am–5pm, Sat 10am–5pm; bar daily 10am–11pm.

County Monaghan

What few other sites Monaghan does have are dispersed around and about the county. In the north and west respectively, **Glaslough** and **Clones** both merit brief visits, while fans of Patrick Kavanagh can acquaint themselves with his work in **Inniskeen**, to the southeast.

Glaslough

Eleven kilometres northeast of Monaghan lies the somewhat otherworldly estate village of **GLASLOUGH**, dominated by a lengthy Famine wall (see p.587) which surrounds the estate of **Castle Leslie**. The Leslie family can reputedly trace back its origins to Attila the Hun and arrived in Ireland in 1633 in the shape of John Leslie who had been appointed Bishop of Raphoe. A colourful character, Leslie became known as the "fighting bishop", thanks to his victory as leader of an army over Cromwell at the Battle of Raphoe. When Charles II was restored to the throne, Leslie received £2000 as a reward for loyalty and used the sum to purchase Glaslough Castle and its demesne in 1665. His descendants have remained in occupation ever since and have included some equally intriguing figures. John Leslie's son Charles was charged with high treason for arguing a little too strenuously against the penal laws, but escaped and fled to France. Subsequently pardoned by George I, he returned to Glaslough where his children often entertained **Jonathan Swift**, who was not always complimentary about them in return:

Here I am In Castle Leslie
With Rows And Rows Of Books Upon The Shelves
Written By The Leslies
All About Themselves.

The current and very grand castle was built in the late nineteenth century and the family became connected by marriage to the Churchills – both Randolph and Winston stayed here. Later owners included Desmond Leslie who authored *Flying Saucers Have Landed*, a supposedly factual account of the first alien contact with humans. His daughter now runs the castle. Even if you're not staying here, you're free to wander around the estate, which has one of the finest **equestrian centres** in the country (€45 for a thirty-minute lesson); you can also fish and kayak on the lake.

ACCOMMODATION   GLASLOUGH

★**Castle Leslie** ☎047 88100, ⊛castleleslie.com. Often patronized by the rich and famous, *Castle Leslie* is an utterly majestic – though thoroughly unpretentious – place to stay. In the castle itself, accommodation consists of a range of sumptuously decorated and themed rooms, some defined by colour and others by historical reference (the Mediterranean room with its stone bed is brilliant), while *The Lodge*, which backs on to the stables, offers more contemporary rooms. *The Lodge* also accommodates the refined *Snaffles* restaurant, which offers an evening menu (€65 plus wine), and the somewhat more affordable *Conor's Lounge Bar*, where you can chomp on a burger (€14). You could also stop by for afternoon tea (€25). Lodge €150, castle €180

Clones

Near the border with Fermanagh, the town of **CLONES** (pronounced "clo-nez") lies 20km southwest of Monaghan town, overlooking drumlin country from its hilltop perch. Being right on the border, Clones was hit hard during the Troubles, and today feels a little neglected, though it does merit a brief stop if passing through. It's also the location for one of the country's best small **film festivals** (⊛clonesfilmfestival.com), held each October.

St Tiernach founded a monastery here in the sixth century and is supposedly buried in a reliquary stone coffin in a small graveyard off Ball Alley Lane, near which are the remains of a ninth-century **round tower** which was originally five storeys high. The

CLONES LACE

The area around Clones has a strong tradition of **lace-making**, a generally home-based industry which, at its peak in the 1850s, saw more than 1500 workers supplying markets as far afield as Paris, Rome and New York. Passed on from mother to daughter, the lace-making craft was introduced to Clones by the wife of the local Church of Ireland rector, Cassandra Hands, as a means of supplying income in the desperate post-Famine times. Rather than following the time-consuming Venetian needlework style, Clones women opted for a crochet hook as a means of expediency, and began producing work embellished by the flora of their local environs, often characterized by the multi-twirled **Clones knot**. Clones lace was embroidered into blouses and dresses, but its own elaborate style was gradually replaced by simpler designs. Nevertheless, it remains an important local tradition and, in 1989, a co-operative was established to reinvigorate the craft. There are still several lace-makers in the area and some of their work is on display at the **Ulster Canal Stores** (ⓦ clonelace.com; see below), where you can also purchase some of their wares.

monastic settlement was subsequently superseded by an Augustinian foundation and the sparse remains of the abbey are just a little way to the east, across MacCurtain Street. The town's other significant relic is a richly carved **high cross**, which stands in the Diamond, somewhat overshadowed by the sombre shape of **St Tiernach's Church** (Church of Ireland). The cross's front panels depict scriptural scenes, such as the Garden of Eden, while the reverse is devoted to scenes from Christ's life.

Neolithic Hill Fort

Just west of the town centre, above Cara Street, is the site of a **Neolithic hill fort**, which was used as the foundations for a short-lived twelfth-century Norman castle that was razed to the ground by local chieftains. Indeed, the English did not regain control of Clones until 1601 and much of the contemporary town owes its layout to that period.

Ulster Canal Stores

Cara St • Mon–Fri 9am–5pm • Free • ☎ 047 52125, ⓦ clonelace.com

Heading out of town on the road towards Cavan, you'll pass the **Ulster Canal Stores**, which once served as the distribution centre for wares arriving in Clones by water. Trade on the canal, which connected Belfast to Lough Erne, peaked in the 1890s, but competition from the railways led to the canal's demise, and it eventually closed in 1931. Nowadays it houses a lovely little **exhibition** on lace-making, as well as displaying works by local artists. There are tentative plans to reopen a section of the canal in the not-too-distant future.

ARRIVAL AND DEPARTURE

CLONES

By bus Bus Éireann: Cavan town (2–3 daily; 30min); Monaghan town (3–5 daily; 25min); Ulsterbus: Cavan (Mon–Sat 1 daily; 30min); Enniskillen (Mon–Sat 4–6 daily; 1hr); Monaghan town (Mon–Sat 1 daily; 30min).

ACCOMMODATION AND EATING

Creighton Hotel Fermanagh St ☎ 047 51055, ⓦ creightonhotel.ie. The only hotel in town is this spruce nineteenth-century building at the bottom of the street, with tip-top, though rather overpriced, rooms. **€100**

Cuil Darach Fermanagh St ☎ 047 52147, ⓦ cuildarach .com. Bed and breakfast above a pub/restaurant, with standard pine-furnished rooms; the restaurant itself is

practically the one decent place in town to eat, with a menu of attractively sauced chicken and steak dishes; it's more fun to eat in the bar, though. **€70**

The Paragon Fermanagh St ☎ 047 51566. The main street has a number of drinking dens, but this is the pick, by virtue of its traditional-music session on Saturdays. Daily 11am–11pm.

Inniskeen

Best accessed from Dundalk, a dozen kilometres east, the village of **INNISKEEN** was the irthplace of the influential poet and writer **Patrick Kavanagh**, born on a local farm in 904 (see p.612). The village itself is pretty enough, with plenty of reminders of its ncient past, such as the superb tenth-century round tower and twelfth-century Norman lookout post.

Patrick Kavanagh Rural and Literary Resource Centre

Tues–Fri 11am–4.30pm, plus June to Sept Sun 3–5.30pm • €5 • ☎ 042 937 8560, ⓦ patrickkavanaghcountry.com

At the heart of the village stands St Mary's Church, whose annexe houses the **Patrick Kavanagh Rural and Literary Resource Centre**, which has stacks of memorabilia related to the poet, including manuscripts and his death mask, as well as a specially commissioned series of twelve paintings based upon his epic and extraordinarily emotive poem *The Great Hunger*. The centre stages several weekends devoted to poetry and writing, plus an annual weekend in late September celebrating Kavanagh's life and work. His grave, along with that of his wife, can be found in the church cemetery.

ARRIVAL AND DEPARTURE **INNISKEEN**

By bus Iniskeen is served by the Dundalk–Carrickmacross bus service; Dundalk (Mon–Sat 5 daily; 20min).

ACCOMMODATION AND EATING

Gleneven House ☎ 042 937 8294, ⓦ gleneven.com. The only accommodation in the village is provided by this handsome Georgian house, located 100m or so towards Dundalk from the Resource Centre, which has a mix of comfy en-suite and standard rooms. **€70**

Poet's Rest Coffee Shop ☎ 087 136 7090. If you're in need of refreshment, try this sweet little café next to the church; enjoy a coffee with cake, or a light lunch, surrounded by books and bric-a-brac. Mon–Sat 10am–6pm, Sun 2–6pm.

Cavan town and around

Nowadays a busy market town, **CAVAN** was once the seat of the O'Reilly clan who built a Franciscan abbey here in 1300, although this succumbed to a fire in 1451. Later, the town itself was razed to the ground in 1576 by a female member of the clan and subsequently rebuilt. Much of what you see today dates from the nineteenth and twentieth centuries and all that remains of the reconstructed abbey is its eighteenth-century **bell tower**, on Abbey Street, standing next to the grave of Owen Roe O'Neill. In truth there's next to nothing to see in Cavan itself, but it does possess a clutch of decent places to sleep and eat, and makes an ideal base from which to explore the county's western reaches.

ARRIVAL AND INFORMATION **CAVAN TOWN AND AROUND**

By bus The bus station (☎ 049 433 1353) is at the southern end of Farnham Street.
Destinations with Bus Éireann Belturbet (7 daily; 20min); Clones (2–3 daily; 30min); Donegal town (7 daily; 2hr); Dublin (hourly; 2hr 10min); Enniskillen (8 daily; 45min–1hr 10min); Kells (hourly; 45min); Monaghan town (Mon–Fri hourly, Sat & Sun 3–4 daily; 55min); Navan (hourly; 1hr 5min).

Destinations with Ulsterbus Clones (Mon–Sat 1 daily; 30min); Monaghan town (Mon–Sat 1 daily; 55min).
Tourist office The tourist office (April–Sept Mon–Fri 9am–5pm; ☎ 049 433 1942, ⓦ cavantourism.com) is 300m northeast of the bus station in the Johnston Library and Farnham Centre. Bikes can be rented from here too; contact the council offices on the second floor (☎ 087 780 2049).

ACCOMMODATION AND EATING

Black Horse Inn 1 Main St ☎ 049 433 2140. A long moody bar with neon lighting and beer barrels for tables presages the inn's modern *Big Apple* restaurant, where you can sample hearty dishes like beef and Guinness casserole (€12.50). Food served noon–3pm & 6–10pm. Daily 11.30am–11.30pm, Fri & Sat till midnight.
Chapter 1 Main St ☎ 049 437 3488, ⓦ chapteronecafe.ie.

Old-school decor and a convivial atmosphere contrive to make this place a massive hit, but it's the freshly made New York-style bagels that really pull in the punters; live music on Thurs evenings too. Mon–Sat 8.30am–6pm, Sun 11am–5pm.
The Farnham Arms Hotel Main St ☎ 049 433 2577, ⓦ farnhamarmshotel.com. It could do with brightening up, but this hotel is smack-bang in the centre of town and

there's a bit of a buzz about the place. *Percy's*, the hotel bar, has a renowned traditional music session every Wed between 9pm and midnight. €99

Farnham Estate Hotel ☎ 049 437 7700, ⓦ farnhamestate.com. Set within the grounds of a vast country estate about 3km southeast on the Dublin road,

this super-luxurious spa hotel is as swish as you'd expect, with rooms in both the Great House itself and in a modern wing. If you fancy a bite to eat, eschew the restaurant and make a beeline for the terrific *Wine Goose Cellar Bar*. €130

Ballyjamesduff

BALLYJAMESDUFF is a pleasant, small crossroads town, 15km southeast of Cavan town along back lanes or a little further via the N3. James Duff himself, the Earl of Fife, was an early Plantation landlord of the area, and one of his descendants, Sir James Duff, commanded English troops during the suppression of the 1798 Rebellion – making the more sombre Irish version of his name, "Black Séamus", rather appropriate to local ears.

Cavan County Museum
Virginia Rd • Tues–Sat 10am–5pm; June–Sept also Sun 2–6pm • €3 • ☎ 049 854 4070, ⓦ cavanmuseum.ie

Housed in a former convent, the **Cavan County Museum** has an impressive collection covering all aspects of the county's history. Many of the post-eighteenth-century exhibits in the museum were donated by Mrs Phyllis Faris from her mammoth and eclectic "Pighouse Collection" of domestic artefacts and memorabilia in Killeshandra. Major items on display include the Killycluggin Stone, dating from 200 BC and decorated in classic Celtic La Tène artwork, and replicas of Celtic stone idols dating from the second century BC to the second century AD, as well as the impressive 1100-year-old Lough Errol **dugout boat**. One room explores the Great Famine, with some moving exhibits including shoes from a famine graveyard, as well as items removed from a famine workhouse near Enniskillen. On a lighter note, also represented here is the painter, poet and songwriter Percy French who worked in the county for a spell as an inspector of drains – one of his more famous comic songs is *Come Back Paddy Reilly to Ballyjamesduff*. A recent addition to the museum is the outdoor **Trench Experience**, an enormous 350m-long ditch designed to evoke conditions in the trenches during World War I. Complete with barbed wire and mock battlefield – and some clever sound and visual effects – it's impressively authentic. Some 659 men from Cavan perished in the Great War.

West Cavan

To the west of Cavan town lies the assortment of various-sized lakes that forms the system known as **Lough Oughter**, through which the River Erne contrives to manage a pathway to Upper Lough Erne (see p.577). Roads are few and landmarks limited to the occasional small hill, while the rush-fringed lakes lure many anglers. The land gradually assumes dominance over water west of the hillside town of **Belturbet**, beyond which the inhospitable and bleak strip doglegs between counties Fermanagh and Leitrim, becoming ever craggier as it rises through wild, boggy hills. At the county's northwestern tip, the **Cavan Way** terminates at the tiny border village of **Blacklion**.

Belturbet and around

One of the most pleasant bases for exploring the lough is **BELTURBET**, some 18km north of Cavan town, a hillside village rising steeply from the River Erne. Very popular with anglers, the village is also a base to explore the Shannon–Erne Waterway, though sadly there's nowhere that currently rents out boats.

Drumlane Church

Apart from the delights of lough-side walks, the major source of interest around the lakes is **Drumlane Church**, situated just south of Miltown on the R201 from Belturbet in a beautiful setting between two lakes. St Mogue, a pupil of Wales's patron St David, founded a monastery here in the sixth century, while the medieval church is part of an abbey founded here by monks from Kells in County Meath. Now ruined and roofless, the church's west doorway has carved heads of possibly ecclesiastical figures or monarchs, which probably date from the fifteenth century. Nearby, an eleventh-century **round tower** features now barely distinguishable carvings of birds, thought to be a cock and a hen and believed to bear some relevance to the Resurrection.

ARRIVAL AND DEPARTURE   BELTURBET

By bus Bus Éireann: Ballyconnell (3 daily; 10min); Cavan   town (8 daily; 15min).

ACCOMMODATION AND EATING

Church View 8 Church St ☏049 952 2358, ⓦ churchviewguesthouse.com. Located just behind the library, off the main road, this is a super-friendly B&B, popular with local fishermen; the seven en-suite rooms are complemented by a guest lounge with complimentary refreshments. €70

The Seven Horseshoes Main St ☏049 952 2166, ⓦ thesevenhorseshoes.com. One of the county's oldest hostelries holds a handful of functional rooms. Better is the warming, brick- and wood-panelled bar, easily the most appealing spot in the village for a bite to eat or a pint. Daily 10.30am–11.30pm, food served 12.30–4pm & 6–9pm. €80

The Cavan Way and Blacklion

The county's northwestern reaches provide superb walking terrain, best accessed via the signposted 25km **Cavan Way**, which runs through jagged landscapes from Dowra in County Leitrim (see p.413) to **Blacklion** where it joins the **Ulster Way**. The hills above Blacklion command dramatic views across Lough Macnean east to Fermanagh's lakelands and west to the mountains of Sligo and Leitrim. About halfway along the route is the **Shannon Pot**, the veritable source of Ireland's longest river but a mere trickle here.

Cavan Burren Park

Open access

Some 3km south of Blacklion, on the slopes of the Cuilcagh Mountain, is the **Cavan Burren Park**, a remarkable limestone plateau where megalithic tombs, cist graves and ancient stone huts comprise a fantastic trove of prehistoric treasures; many examples of rock art have also been identified here. Cavan Burren actually forms part of the Marble Arch Caves Geopark, which spills across the border into Fermanagh (see p.578), and which you can learn more about in the interpretive centre at the entrance to the park. Here, too, you can pick up information about several guided walks.

ARRIVAL AND DEPARTURE   BLACKLION

By bus Enniskillen (Mon–Sat 4 daily, Sun 2; 30min); Sligo   (Mon–Sat 4 daily, Sun 2; 1hr).

ACCOMMODATION AND EATING

Keepers Arms Bridge St, Bawnboy ☏049 952 3318, ⓦ keepersarms.com. Located in the village of Bawnboy, on the main road up towards Blacklion, this terrific little inn has eleven tidy rooms above a bar, which is otherwise a fun place to spend an evening chatting amongst the locals. €80

Macnean House Blacklion ☏071 985 3022, ⓦ macneanrestaurant.com. *Macnean House* is run by

one of Ireland's best-known chefs, Neven Maguire, whose modern Irish cooking is up there with the finest in the country. Expect scintillating combinations like stone bass with king crab and cassoulet beans, and buttermilk *panna cotta* with poached raspberries. Not cheap, but worth every penny; €72 for the set dinner menu and €39 for the Sunday lunch menu. Wed–Sat 6–9.30pm, Sun lunch sittings at 12.30pm & 3.30pm plus 7–8.30pm.

The Midlands: Westmeath, Longford, Offaly and Laois

BELVEDERE HOUSE

The Midlands: Westmeath, Longford, Offaly and Laois

Obeying the siren call of the west coast, most foreign tourists, and indeed Irish holiday-makers, put their foot down to motor through the Midlands as quickly as possible. It's true that you're unlikely to want to make a comprehensive tour of the area, but if you fancy a stopover off the main radial routes out of Dublin, there are some compelling sights, and a surprisingly varied landscape, to discover.

The dairy farms of **County Westmeath** (Iarmhí) are interspersed with large, glassy lakes, including Lough Ennell to the south of **Mullingar**, the county town, on whose shores **Belvedere House** is well worth a short detour off the N4. Among the county's more northerly lakes nestle the quirky gardens of **Tullynally Castle** and the pastoral charms of the **Fore Valley**, where you can poke around medieval monastic remains and be entertained by their wondrous legends. The N4 ploughs on through **County Longford** (An Longfort), mostly rich grasslands but blending into Northern Ireland's drumlin country in its northern third. In the south of the county, the **Corlea Trackway Visitor Centre** gives a fascinating glimpse of a prestigious but ill-fated Iron Age road-building project.

The **River Shannon** and its seasonal floodplain delineates most of the Midlands' western border, running down through **Athlone**, a major junction town whose **castle** has recently been give an excellent, high-tech redevelopment. Just south of here, the major ecclesiastical site of **Clonmacnois** enjoys a dreamy setting above the river's meanders and meadows. Elsewhere, **County Offaly** (Uíbh Fháilí) is known for its bogs, but the charming town of **Birr**, with its imposing castle and Georgian terraces, makes the best base in the Midlands. To its east rises the attractive bulge of **Slieve Bloom**, with a thick topping of blanket bog, beyond which **County Laois** (pronounced "leash") is mostly lush grazing and cereal land.

Brief history

These counties were mostly beyond the Pale, the enclave around Dublin that the Anglo-Normans retreated to in the fourteenth and fifteenth centuries, and indeed Offaly is named after the *Uí Failí* (O'Connor Faly), Irish chieftains who would attack the Pale and then retreat to their strongholds deep in the boglands. In the sixteenth century, however, this region was fairly comprehensively planted, when land was confiscated from native Irish owners and given to loyal English landlords. In 1541, Westmeath was split off from County Meath, and in 1556 Offaly and Laois were created as "King's County" and "Queen's County", respectively, with the latter's main town named Maryborough (now Portlaoise) after the current monarch. Bypassed by the Industrial Revolution, many of the planned estate-towns that were attached to these landholdings remain to this day, along with the vestiges of a slow, steady rural style of living.

GETTING AROUND

By bus and train Buses access all the main towns and villages, but as many of the attractions of this region are off the beaten track, you really need your own transport to get the best out of it. Only Athlone (on the line t Galway and Westport) and Mullingar (on the Sligo line are served by train.

Boat trips to Lough Ree and Clonmacnois p.172

Highlights

● **Belvedere House** A beautifully restored
Georgian hunting lodge, set in attractive
gardens, overlooking Lough Ennell. **See p.166**

● **The Fore Valley** Explore the rich
ecclesiastical history of this remote, green valley
or suspend your disbelief in appreciation of its
Seven Wonders. **See p.168**

● **Sean's Bar** Soak up the atmosphere at
this ancient and characterful pub in Athlone.
See p.172

❹ **Clonmacnois** The Midlands' pre-eminent
historical site, a prestigious complex of churches
and ornate high crosses overlooking the River
Shannon. **See p.172**

❺ **Birr Castle** Wander around the huge and
varied grounds and immerse yourself in the
scientific exploits of the talented Parsons family
at the Historic Science Centre. **See p.175**

HIGHLIGHTS ARE MARKED ON THE MAP ON P.166

Mullingar

Set in lush cattle-country, **MULLINGAR**, the county town of Westmeath, holds little of interest for visitors, except as a base for visiting **Belvedere House**, a Georgian mansion in a lovely setting on Lough Ennell.

Belvedere House

House daily: March–Oct 9.30am–5pm; Nov–Feb 9.30am–4pm; gardens daily: March & Oct 9.30am–6pm; April & Sept 9.30am–7pm; May–Aug 9.30am–8pm; Nov–Feb 9.30am–4.30pm; last admission 1hr before closing • €8; currently fifty percent discount with Athlone Castle (see p.170) ticket; Heritage Island • ☏ 044 934 9060, ⓦ belvedere-house.ie

Belvedere House stands in abundant gardens on the eastern shore of Lough Ennell, 5km south of Mullingar on the N52. The house was built in the 1740s by Richard Castle as a hunting lodge for Robert Rochfort, later the first Earl of Belvedere, the so-called "Wicked Earl", whose main pastime seems to have been making life hell for his wife and brothers.

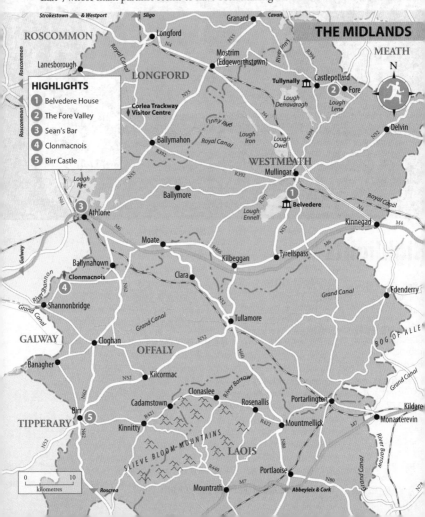

THE MIDLANDS

HIGHLIGHTS
1. Belvedere House
2. The Fore Valley
3. Sean's Bar
4. Clonmacnois
5. Birr Castle

n 1743 he falsely accused his wife Mary of having an affair with his brother Arthur and mprisoned her for the next 31 years at their nearby main residence, Gaulstown. It was nly when the Earl died that she was released by their son, whom she no longer ecognized. Meanwhile, the Earl had successfully pressed charges of adultery against Arthur, who, unable to pay the damages of £20,000, lived out his days in debtors' prison.

The **house** itself, which commands beautiful views of the lake, has been ainstakingly restored and authentically refurbished by Westmeath County Council. t holds some gorgeous fireplaces of carved Irish oak with Italian marble insets, but s most notable for the exquisite craftsmanship of its rococo ceilings, the work of a rench stuccodore, Barthelemij Cramillion. Look out especially for the vivid lepictions of the Four Winds, a fire-breathing dragon and a horn of plenty in the lining room, while the library, intended for night-time use, features sleeping herubs wrapped in a blanket of clouds, a crescent moon and stars, and on the ornice a swirl of flowers with their heads closed.

A feud between Robert Rochfort and his other brother George was behind one of the gardens' main sights, the **Jealous Wall**. When George commissioned Richard Castle in he 1750s to build Tudenham House, a much larger mansion than Belvedere, just 1km way, the Earl of Belvedere spent £10,000 building this huge Gothic folly, three storeys igh and nearly 60m long, just to block the view. Other features include a Victorian valled garden, enclosing an unusual collection of Himalayan plants, playgrounds for ids and a café in the old stable block by the entrance. Or you can just take a stroll round the extensive woodlands and lawns: the 45-minute Earl's Trail, for example, will ake you along the lakeshore and back, past a restored ice-house and follies known as he Octagonal Gazebo and the Gothic Arch.

See the website for details of the many concerts, festivals and other events hosted at 3elvedere throughout the year.

ARRIVAL AND INFORMATION

MULLINGAR

By train Trains on the Dublin–Sligo line stop at the station n the southwest side of the centre.

Destinations Dublin Connolly (6–9 daily; 1hr 15min); Sligo 6–7 daily; 1hr 50min).

By bus Most buses call at Castle St right in the heart of own, though some stop only at the train station.

Destinations Athlone (up to 4 daily; 1hr); Dublin (10–21 daily; 1hr 30min); Sligo (5–6 daily; 2hr 20min).

Tourist information Market House, just round the corner from the Castle St bus stop, on the main Pearse St (Mon–Fri 9.30am–5.10pm; ☎ 044 934 8650).

ACCOMMODATION

Greville Arms ☎ 044 934 8563, ⓦ grevillearms.com. 3ang in the centre of town, this welcoming and recently efurbished old coaching inn on Pearse St is mentioned in ames Joyce's *Ulysses*. Bedrooms are either contemporary nd colourful, or plush and traditional with swagged urtains, gilt mirrors and padded headboards on the beds. ood rates for singles. **€90**

ough Ennell Caravan Park ☎ 044 934 8101, ⓦ caravanparksireland.com. Quiet, sheltered and well-quipped, lakeside campsite, 5km south of town off the l52, just beyond Belvedere House, with a campers' kitchen,

laundry, games room, playground, restaurant and minimart. April–Sept. **€20**

Lough Owel Lodge ☎ 044 934 8714, ⓦ loughowellodge.com. The pick of the B&Bs around Mullingar, a friendly spot on an organic working farm 3km north of town off the N4 and a short stroll from the eponymous lake. The en-suite bedrooms (some with four-poster or half-tester beds) and lounges are large and attractive, with some pretty views, the breakfast is excellent, and there's tennis and table tennis. Family room; very good rates for singles. April–Oct. **€70**

EATING AND DRINKING

Dominik's 37 Dominick St, the westward continuation of Pearse St ☎ 044 939 6696, ⓦ dominiksrestaurant.ie. mart, contemporary restaurant with friendly service that ustles up crowd-pleasing main courses with a twist, such s duck breast with sweet potato purée and fruits of the

forest sauce. The à la carte menu is a little expensive but the early-bird menu (€23 for three courses) is available all evening Tues–Thurs & Sun, and until 7pm Fri & Sat, and there's a two-course Sun lunch menu for €13. Tues–Sat 5–10pm, Sun 1–9.30pm.

4

Ilia Café 28 Oliver Plunkett St, the westward continuation of Pearse St ☎ 044 934 0300. Tasty and relaxing daytime café, offering everything from soups, salads, bagels and simple main courses such as pork and leek sausages with mash and onion gravy (under €10), to cakes and pastries, alongside great coffees and freshly squeezed orange juice. Mon–Sat 9am–6pm.

Oscar's 21 Oliver Plunkett St ☎ 044 934 4909, ⓦ oscarsmullingar.com. Lively and unpretentious restaurant directly opposite *Ilia Café* that's well known locally for its reasonably priced pasta and pizza (around €15), as well as steaks, chicken and seafood (around €20–25). Mon–Thurs 6–9.30pm, Fri & Sat 6–10pm, Sun 12.30–2.15pm & 6–8.15pm.

Castlepollard and around

The far north of Westmeath shelters two compelling and whimsical attractions, the gardens of Tullynally Castle and the Seven Wonders of the Fore Valley, near **CASTLEPOLLARD**, a pretty eighteenth- and nineteenth-century village laid out around a large triangular green.

Tullynally Castle

Gardens and tea rooms Easter–Sept Thurs–Sun 11am–6pm • €6 • ☎ 044 966 1159, ⓦ tullynallycastle.com

A little over 1km northwest of Castlepollard on the Granard road, **Tullynally Castle** has been the seat of the Anglo-Irish Pakenhams, later Earls of Longford, since the seventeenth century. Remodelled as a rambling Gothic Revival castle to the designs of Francis Johnston in the early 1800s, it remains the family home, open only to prebooked group visits (minimum 20 people) and for occasional concerts. The extensive **gardens**, however, and tea rooms are open to casual visitors in the summer. Terraced lawns around the castle overlook parkland, laid out by the first Earl of Longford in 1760. From here winding paths lead through the woodland to lakes, a walled garden with a 200-year-old yew avenue and a limestone grotto, as well as a Chinese garden with a scarlet pagoda and a Tibetan garden of waterfalls and streams.

The Fore Valley

To the east of Castlepollard off the R195 Oldcastle road, the **Fore Valley** is a charming, bucolic spot, sheltered between two ranges of low, green hills and dotted with some impressive Christian ruins. Around 630, St Fechin founded a monastery here, which had grown into a community of three hundred monks by the time he died in 665. Over the centuries since, various sites in the valley have become associated with Fechin's miraculous powers, known as the **Seven Wonders of Fore**, though in truth they're far from jaw-dropping – it's unlikely that you'll be converted to this brand of folk religion, but the wonders add some fun and interest to an exploration of the locale. The historical and supernatural sites are all within walking distance of the village of **FORE** at the heart of the valley.

The Seven Wonders

To the west of the village, on the south side of the road, stands **St Fechin's Church**, now roofless, the oldest remaining building in the valley, dating probably from the tenth century. The first wonder lies over its main entrance, a massive lintel inscribed with a small cross-in-circle: the **stone raised by St Fechin's prayers**. Up the slope and across from the church, you'll find the **Anchorite's Cell**, a fifteenth-century tower to which the mausoleum chapel of the Greville-Nugent family was added in the nineteenth century (ask for the key behind the bar at the *Seven Wonders* pub in the village, which opens at around 12.30pm). Practising an extreme form of asceticism that was popular in the early and high Middle Ages, anchorites would stay in the tower, meditating and praying alone, with food brought to them by local people, until they died. Inside the chapel, an inscription commemorates the last hermit of Fore, and probably of all Ireland, Patrick Beglin, whose body is "hidden in this hollow heap of stones" – the second wonder, the **anchorite in a stone**. Like the other hermits, Beglin had vowed to remain in the cell until he died: in 1616, he fell trying to climb out, and broke his neck – thus enacting his promise.

Back down the slope and across the road you'll see the **water that will not boil**, a holy well known to cure headaches and toothaches, where in the nineteenth century rites were performed on St Fechin's Day (January 20). In the spring stands a dead ash tree, gaily festooned with sweet wrappers, stockings, knickers and coins (which caused the copper poisoning that killed the tree) – the fourth wonder, the **wood that will not burn**. Nearby, a stream that runs underground from Lough Lene to the south resurfaces at the ruined St Fechin's Mill – the **mill without a race**.

A couple of hundred metres across the marshy valley floor rise the substantial but compact remains of **Fore Priory** – the **monastery built on a bog**. It was erected in the early thirteenth century, one of very few in Ireland to follow the rule of St Benedict, the fifth-century Italian ascetic. Attached to the central cloister, of which several Gothic arches remain, you'll find the church to the north, the chapterhouse to the east, with the dormitory above, and the refectory to the south. A little away from the main buildings, up a small slope, there's a circular, thirteenth-century columbarium, where the monks kept doves, an efficient source of meat in the Middle Ages.

The seventh wonder is a little removed from the others to the south of the village – ask for directions at the coffee shop. A short woodland walk will bring you down to the attractive shore of Lough Lene, which is dotted with small, green islands. A stream flows out of the lake, apparently in the wrong direction, passing under an overgrown arched bridge, before disappearing into a sinkhole (to emerge at St Fechin's Mill) – the **water that flows uphill**.

ARRIVAL AND INFORMATION

By bus The daily bus service to Castlepollard and Granard from Dublin (1–2 daily; 2hr 20min) via Trim supplemented by a weekly Mullingar–Castlepollard bus on Thurs; 30min) might work out for a visit to Tullynally, but the Fore Valley is too long a walk from Castlepollard.

By car With your own transport, Castlepollard is easily approached from Mullingar on the R394, or from the

CASTLEPOLLARD AND AROUND

Loughcrew Cairns near Oldcastle, just across the border in County Meath (see p.138).

Tourist information The café in Fore (June–Sept daily noon–6pm; Oct–May Sat & Sun 11am–6pm; ☏ 044 966 1780, ✉ foreabbeycoffeeshop@gmail.com) hosts a 20min audiovisual on the monastery, sells literature, arranges guided tours and provides tourist information on the area.

ACCOMMODATION

Hounslow House Fore ☏ 044 966 1144, ☖ hounslowhouse.com. B&B in single, double, triple and family rooms is available at *Hounslow House*, a large,

200-year-old farmhouse set in extensive grounds with fine views of the valley, about 1km from the village and well signposted. April–Sept. **€70**

Athlone and around

Straddling the Shannon at its midpoint, **ATHLONE** is the bustling capital of the Midlands and an important road and rail junction on the Westmeath–Roscommon frontier. It probably derives its name from the *Táin Bó Cúailnge*, in which the remains of the white bull of Connacht, the Findbennach, after its defeat by Ulster's brown bull, are scattered throughout Ireland; its loins came to rest here at *Áth Luain*, the "Ford of the Loins". A bridge was first built over this ford in 1120 by Turlough O'Connor, king of Connacht, which the Anglo-Normans replaced with a stone bridge in 1210; they were also responsible for the mighty **castle**. Today, the town supports an important college, the Athlone Institute of Technology, as well as various civil-service offices and high-tech firms, but its main function for tourists is as a jumping-off point for the monastic site of **Clonmacnois** (see p.172). Fewer visitors know about the **Corlea Trackway Visitor Centre**, but the evocative, 2000-year old wooden road preserved here is also well worth a visit if you have your own transport. Over the bank holiday weekend at the beginning of June, the **Oliver Goldsmith International Literary Festival** is held in nearby Ballymahon and Abbeyshrule (ⓦgoldsmithfestival.ie).

Athlone Castle

Visitor Centre June–Aug Mon–Sat 10am–6pm, Sun noon–6pm; Sept & Oct Tues–Sat 11am–5pm, Sun noon–5pm; last admission 1hr before closing • €8; currently fifty percent discount with Belvedere House (see p.166) ticket, twenty-five percent discount with Viking Tour (see p.172) ticket; Heritage Island

Athlone Castle still casts a formidable shadow over the town, having weathered some bloody fighting during the Cromwellian Wars and the War of the Kings of the seventeenth century. The imposing, grey, thirteenth-century fortifications on the west side of the main bridge have been stylishly converted to house the lively and fascinating exhibitions of the **Athlone Castle Visitor Centre**. As well as some beautiful, early Christian, carved stone slabs, the centre houses impressive audiovisuals and interactive games, focusing on the vicious Sieges of Athlone during the War of the Kings. After the Battle of the Boyne, William III's army took control of eastern and southern Ireland, while the Jacobites attempted to defend the west along the line of the Shannon. In July 1690, Athlone Castle did its job, forcing the Williamites to retreat after a week; they returned with some serious artillery in June of 1691, however, and after building a pontoon over the river and reducing much of the castle to rubble, they took it from the Jacobites, who lost over 1200 men. Within two weeks of taking Athlone, William's men won the Battle of Aughrim, near Galway, and soon after the war was ended with the Treaty of Limerick.

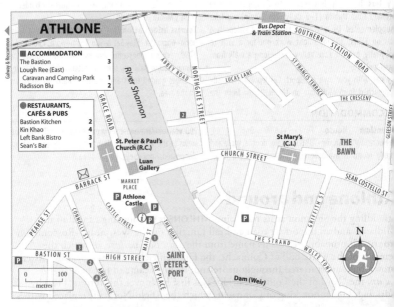

he Luan Gallery

:s–Sat 11am–5pm, Sun noon–5pm • Free • ☎ 090 644 2154, ⓦ athloneartsandtourism.ie

's well worth checking out the exhibitions, workshops and events at this lovely,
:w contemporary art gallery, on the west bank of the Shannon, opposite the
stle. The building was constructed in 1897 as Father Mathew [sic] Hall (named
ter the anti-alcohol campaigner), a temperance hall for entertainments to promote
briety among the employees of Athlone Woollen Mills. The addition of a
:autiful extension has created bright, airy exhibition spaces that afford great views
the river.

orlea Trackway Visitor Centre

ter–Sept daily 10am–6pm; guided tours every hour, on the hour, last tour 5pm • Free • ⓦ heritageireland.ie

's a little tricky to get to the fascinating **Corlea Trackway Visitor Centre**, which is
tually across the county border in Longford and signposted along a minor road
f the R392, 20km northeast of Athlone, but its isolation in the midst of a desolate
·g only adds to the appeal of the place. In 1984, Bord na Móna (the Peat Board)
scovered a buried *togher*, an early Iron Age trackway, while milling turf here in
·orlea raised bog. Dated to 148 BC, the trackway was made of split oak planks up
4m in length that were meant to float on the bog surface, one of the most
·bstantial and sophisticated of many such prehistoric roads found in Europe.
·owever, the builders knew more about woodworking than the properties of the
·g, because within ten years the heavy planks had sunk into the peat – which
·eserved them perfectly for the next two thousand years. The road connected dry
·nd to the east with an island in the bog to the west, but it's clear that such a
·estigious construction was intended for more than just the movement
animals by farmers: it may have been part of a ceremonial highway from the Hill
· Uisneach, the ritual "centre of Ireland" that marked the division of the five
·cient provinces, between Mullingar and Athlone, to the royal site of Rathcroghan
· Roscommon (see p.419), via the narrow crossing of the Shannon at
·nesborough.

·xcellent **guided tours** begin with the 18m of trackway that's been preserved
·der cover in the visitor centre (which also sports a tea room). Another 80m has
·en left outside under the turf, but the guides, as well as delving into the
·traordinary ecology of the bog, will take you to the wooden walkway built over it,
·hich gives a good idea of what the trackway would have looked like, undulating
·er the peaty tussocks.

4

RRIVAL AND INFORMATION

ATHLONE AND AROUND

train The train station is on the north side of the centre
Southern Station Rd.
·stinations Dublin Heuston (10–15 daily; 1hr 40min–2hr);
·lway (6–10 daily; 1hr 10min); Westport (4–5 daily; 2hr).
bus The Bus Éireann station is at the train station;
·ylink's most convenient stop is at AIT on Dublin Rd to the
·st of the centre.
·stinations Bus Éireann: Birr (2–3 daily; 50min); Dublin
·ost via the airport; hourly; 1hr 40min–2hr 20min);

Galway (roughly hourly; 1hr 30min); Kilkenny (1–2 daily;
2hr 50min); Limerick (2–3 daily; 2hr 10min); Mullingar (up
to 4 daily; 1hr); Waterford (1–2 daily; 4hr); Westport (2
daily; 2hr 45min–3hr). Citylink (ⓦ citylink.ie): Dublin &
Airport (7 daily; 2hr); Galway (7 daily; 1hr 40min).
Tourist office Inside the castle (mid-March to mid-May &
mid-Sept to Oct Mon–Fri 9.20am–5/6pm, closing for lunch
usually 1–1.30pm; mid-May to mid-Sept daily
9.20am–5/6pm; ☎ 090 649 4630).

·ETTING AROUND

·ycle rental** Buckley's, about 1km east of the river on
·blin Rd (☎ 090 647 8989, ⓦ buckleycycles.ie).

Car rental Europcar, about 5km west of the town centre
on the R362 (☎ 090 649 3999, ⓦ www.europcar.ie).

BOAT TRIPS TO LOUGH REE AND CLONMACNOIS

Viking Tours (☎086 262 1136, ⓦvikingtoursireland.ie; twenty-five percent discounts with Athlone Castle tickets) runs **trips on the Shannon** (roughly Easter–Oct), which involve sailing in a partly open, 20m wooden boat that's been made up to look like a longboat, with Viking costumes for kids to dress up in. Every day, the boat heads north around the islands of **Lough Ree** (1hr 15min; €10), which include Hare Island, site of a Viking encampment that has yielded considerable amounts of Viking treasure. Less often, it sails south on the scenic approach to **Clonmacnois** (see below; €16, including return by bus to Athlone; 1hr 30min), allowing you 1hr 30min to look around the site, before a bus (30min) takes you back to Athlone. Departures are from the west bank of the river below the castle, where the latest schedule of trips is always posted – or consult their website.

ACCOMMODATION

The Bastion 2 Bastion St ☎090 649 4954, ⓦthebastion.net. The pick of the town's B&Bs, a colourful, relaxing spot that serves healthy continental breakfasts (though prices are €10 cheaper without breakfast). The decor of polished wooden floors, white walls and crisp white linens is splashed with colour from modern artworks and Peruvian wall hangings; some bedrooms share bathrooms. **€65**

Lough Ree (East) Caravan and Camping Park 3km north of Athlone on the N55 in Ballykeeran ☎090 647 8561, ⓦathlonecampingandcaravan.com.

Peaceful, spacious and well-equipped, lakeside camps with a campers' kitchen, a recreation room and 500m stretch of the Breensford trout river. Mid-April Sept. **€20**

Radisson Blu Northgate St ☎090 644 26⬭ ⓦradissonblu.ie. This central hotel enjoys a peerl⬭ setting on the east bank of the Shannon overlooking ⬭ castle – have a sundowner at the heated riverside terra⬭ bar to make the most of it – and offers smart, we⬭ designed rooms with either an urban or soothing mar⬭ theme, a swimming pool and leisure club. **€84**

EATING AND DRINKING

Market Place by the castle hosts a lively **farmers' market** every Sat morning.

Bastion Kitchen Bastion St ☎087 972 1373. Small, popular and friendly health-food shop and café that serves great pitta sandwiches (€5), home-baked cakes and scones, and sausage baps with tomato and onion relish for breakfast. Mon–Fri 8am–6pm, Sat 10am–5pm, Sun noon–5pm.

★**Kin Khao** 1 Abbey Lane ☎090 649 8805, ⓦkinkhaothai.ie. Set in a cute yellow-and-red cottage, this is one of Ireland's best Thai restaurants. It offers tasty versions of all the classic Thai dishes, as well as delicious specialities such as *hor mok gai* (chicken curry soufflé; €18.50); wash it down with a craft beer and leave room for an authentic Thai dessert. Two-course lunch €10; early-bird deal (two courses for €20) until 7.30pm Mon–Thurs & Sun, 7pm Fri & Sat. Mon, Tues & Sat 5.30–11pm, Wed–Fri 12.30–2.30pm & 5.30– 11pm, Sun 1.30–11pm.

Left Bank Bistro Fry Place ☎090 649 4446. Styl⬭ restaurant offering plenty of seafood, some Asia⬭ influenced dishes and more classic fare like rump ⬭ Roscommon lamb with garlic confit and rosemary j⬭ Prices are high in the evenings, but you can ease the p⬭ by opting for the set menu (€20 for two courses; o⬭ available until 7pm Sat); lunch, which consists of var⬭ sandwiches, salads and a few select hot dishes, is cheap⬭ again. Tues–Sat 10.30am–9.30pm.

★**Sean's Bar** Main St, near the castle ☎090 649 23⬭ Another claimant to the title of Ireland's oldest pub. ⬭ certainly appealingly old-fashioned and sociable, w⬭ sawdust on the floor, live music most nights (includin⬭ traditional session Sat early evening) and a huge b⬭ garden at the back stretching down towards the ri⬭ Mon–Thurs 10.30am–11.30pm, Fri & S⬭ 10.30am–12.30am, Sun 12.30–11pm.

Clonmacnois

Daily: mid-March to May, Sept & Oct 10am–6pm; June–Aug 9am–6.30pm; Nov to mid-March 10am–5.30pm; last admission 45min before closing • €6; Heritage Card • ⓦheritageireland.ie • There are no buses to Clonmacnois from Athlone, 21km away, but the trip is perfectly manageable in a day by renting a bike or a car (see p.171) or by taking a boat tour down the Shannon (see above).

The substantial remains of **Clonmacnois**, pre-Norman Ireland's most important Christian site, enjoy an idyllic location on the grassy banks of the gently meandering Shannon. Here the river descends at a shallow gradient through flat land that floods extensively in winter, but in spring, the receding flow leaves beautiful, nutrient-rich water meadows, some of the last of their type in Europe. The **Shannon Callows**, as they are known, become the summer home of rare wildflowers, grazing cattle, lapwings, curlews, redshanks and rare corncrakes.

Brief history

The monastery was founded, as a satellite of St Enda's house on Inishmore (see p.361), in around 548 by **St Kieran (Ciarán)**, who with the help of Diarmuid of the Uí Néills, the first Christian High King of Ireland, erected a wooden church here. Kieran brought with him a dun cow, whose hide later became Clonmacnois' major relic – anyone who died lying on it would be spared the torments of Hell – and who was commemorated in the *Lebor na hUidre* (Book of the Dun Cow), the oldest surviving manuscript written wholly in Irish. Perfectly sited at the junction of the Slí Mhor, the main road from Dublin Bay to Galway Bay, and the major north–south artery, the Shannon, the monastery grew in influence as various provincial kings endowed it with churches and high crosses. With a large lay population, Clonmacnois resembled a small town, where craftsmen and scholars produced illuminated manuscripts, croziers and other remarkable artefacts, many of which can be seen in the National Museum in Dublin. However, between the eighth and twelfth centuries the site was plundered over forty times by Vikings, Anglo-Normans and Irish enemies, and church reforms in the thirteenth century greatly reduced its influence. In 1552, Athlone's English garrison reduced it to ruins, though, as the burial place of Kieran, it has persisted to this day as a place of pilgrimage, focused on the saint's day on September 9.

The visitor centre and high crosses

Visitor centre same hours

Clonmacnois' three magnificent high crosses have been moved into the excellent **visitor centre** (which also shelters a small café), to prevent further damage by the weather. Outside, the Office of Public Works has erected all-too-faithful replicas, complete with erosion – an attempt to re-create their appearance when first carved would have been far more constructive.) The finest is the **Cross of the Scriptures**, a pictorial sermon showing the Crucifixion, Christ in the Tomb and the Last Judgement. It was erected in the early tenth century by Abbot Colman and Flann, the High King of Ireland, who may be depicted together (with Flann holding a pole) in the bottom scene on the shaft's east face. Standing 4m high, the cross is carved from a single piece of sandstone and may originally have been coloured. The other two crosses are about a century older and much simpler, the **South Cross** featuring the Crucifixion surrounded by rich interlacing, spirals and bosses, while the **North Cross** is carved with abstract Celtic ornaments, humans and animals.

Elsewhere in the visitor centre there's a good audiovisual on Kieran's life and the history of Clonmacnois, and an interesting reconstruction of a *dairthech* (oak house), the type of small oratory that would have been built out of wood at this and other monasteries throughout Ireland before stone began to be used in the tenth century.

The site

Most of Clonmacnois' nine churches are structurally intact apart from their roofs, the largest being the **cathedral** straight in front of the visitor centre. It was built in 909 by Abbot Colman and King Flann, but its most beautiful feature now is the fifteenth-century north doorway, featuring decorative Gothic carving surmounted by SS Dominic, Patrick and Francis. The last High King of Ireland, Rory O'Connor, was buried by the altar here in 1198. Several smaller churches encircle the cathedral, notably **Temple Ciarán**, the burial place of St Kieran, dating from the early tenth century.

In the western corner of the compound rises a fine **round tower**, erected in 1124 by Abbot O'Malone and Turlough O'Connor of Connacht, High King of Ireland and father of Rory. There's another round tower attached to the nave of **Temple Finghin**, which is Romanesque in style and thought to date from 1160–70.

In a peaceful, leafy glade about 500m away from the main site and signposted from the east side of the compound, the **Nun's Church** is the place to escape to if a fleet of tour coaches descends. Founded by Queen Devorguilla, who retired here as a penitent in 1170, it boasts a fine Romanesque doorway and chancel arch carved with geometrical patterns.

The site's tranquillity is often broken by coach tours in summer so, if you can, time your visit for late afternoon, when you might be lucky enough to catch the birds singing as the sun sets over the river.

ACCOMMODATION AND EATING   CLONMACNOIS

Kajon House Under 2km southwest on the Shannonbridge road ☎ 090 967 4191, ⓦ kajonhouse .ie. If you want to stay near the site, head for *Kajon House*, a friendly, comfortable B&B with en-suite rooms, in a bright, modern, pine-furnished house. You'll be offered tea and homemade scones when you arrive, and there are pancakes for breakfast, and evening meals on offer. March–Oct. **€70**

4 Birr

Around 45km south of Athlone at the confluence of the Camcor and Little Brosna rivers, **BIRR** (ⓦ www.destinationbirr.ie) is the Midlands' most attractive town, planned around the estate of Birr Castle, the home of the Parsons family, later the Earls of Rosse. Around central Emmet Square – formerly Duke's Square, though the unpopular statue of the Duke of Cumberland, victor over the Jacobites at the Battle of Culloden in 1746, is long gone from the central pillar – you'll find several broad Georgian terraces, graced with fanlights and other fine architectural details, notably St John's Mall to the east and Oxmantown Mall to the north off Emmet Street. Running south from Emmet Square, O'Connell Street, which becomes Main Street, heads down to Market Square. Birr is not yet on the country's main tourist trail but supports some appealing places to stay and eat, making it an excellent base from which to explore the Shannon, Clonmacnois and Slieve Bloom. The town comes to life in early August during its **Vintage Week and Arts Festival** (ⓦ birrvintageweek.com), when shop assistants, bar staff and townspeople deck themselves out in historic regalia, and there's a varied programme of street theatre, music, and art exhibitions. In October, the five-day **Offline Film Festival** (ⓦ offlinefilmfestival.com) features screenings, workshops and a short-film competition.

Brief history

A monastery was first founded here in the sixth century, later becoming famous for the *Mac Regol Gospels* (now in the Bodleian Library, Oxford), an illuminated manuscript named after the early ninth-century abbot and bishop. Birr was settled by the Anglo-Normans, who built a castle here in 1208, later becoming the site of an O'Carroll stronghold between the fourteenth and seventeenth centuries. In the 1619 plantation of their territory (known as Ely O'Carroll), however, Sir Laurence Parsons was given Birr, which became known as Parsonstown. A descendant of his set about reconstructing the town in the 1740s in Neoclassical style, a development which continued in stages until as late as the 1830s.

Birr Castle

Grounds & Historic Science Centre daily: mid-March to Oct 9am–6pm; Nov to mid-March 10am–4pm; **castle** certain days in May, July & Aug only by advance booking through the website (no under-12s, no photography) • €9 • ⓦ birrcastle.com

Lying to the west of Emmet Square, the forbidding Gothic **castle** has restricted opening hours on a very expensive ticket, but there's plenty of interest in the **Historic Science Centre** in the coach houses, which also shelter a pleasant summertime café, and in the varied grounds. In the nineteenth century, the Parsons family gained an international reputation as scientists and inventors, partly it would seem because they were educated at home. The third Earl of Rosse, William Parsons, devoted himself to astronomy, and in 1845 built the huge **Rosse Telescope**, with a 72-inch reflector, which remained the largest in the world until 1917. It was fully reconstructed in the 1990s, along with the massive, elaborate housing of walls, cracks, pulleys and counterweights needed to manoeuvre it, and can be seen in the garden. The fourth Earl, Laurence, and his mother, Mary, a friend of Fox Talbot's, were eminent photographers, while Laurence's brother, Sir Charles Parsons, was carving himself a varied and colourful career, which included building a small flying machine and a helicopter in the 1890s and spending 25 years unsuccessfully trying to make artificial diamonds. He'll be best remembered, however, as the inventor of the steam turbine and for his exploits at the 1897 Spithead Naval Review, celebrating Queen Victoria's Diamond Jubilee when, frustrated at the Royal Navy's foot-dragging, he gatecrashed in the *Turbinia*, the first steam-turbine ship, racing through the fleet at the unheard-of speed of 34 knots. Within a few years the technology was adopted by navies and passenger liners around the world. All of this is set in historical and global context in the Science Centre, with plenty of astrolabes, cameras and other instruments, and some lively audiovisuals.

You could easily spend a couple of hours strolling around the beautiful **castle grounds**, especially if you buy the booklet on its fifty most significant trees or let your kids loose on the treehouse adventure area. Beyond the wildflower meadows, which are left to grow tall until July every year, lie a nineteenth-century lake, a fernery and fountain, and the oldest wrought-iron suspension bridge in Ireland, dating from 1820. The walled gardens feature the tallest box hedges in the world, which are over three hundred years old, as well as intricate parterres and paths canopied with hornbeams in the formal, seventeenth-century-style Millennium Garden.

ARRIVAL AND INFORMATION

BIRR

By bus Buses stop on Emmet Square.

Destinations Bus Éireann: Athlone (2–3 daily; 50min); Limerick (2–3 daily; 1hr 20min). Kearns Transport (ⓦ kearnstransport.com): Dublin (2–6 daily; 2hr); Galway via Portumna and Loughrea; Fri–Sun 1–2 daily; 2hr).

Tourist office Inside Jim Cashen's Auctioneers on Emmet Square (June–Sept Mon–Fri 10am–1pm & 2–5pm, Sat 10am–1pm; ☎ 057 912 3936).

Horse riding Birr Equestrian, Kingsborough House, about 3km east of Birr off the Kinnitty road (☎ 087 244 5545, ⓦ birrequestrian.ie), offers treks on Slieve Bloom by the half-day or day.

GETTING AROUND

By bike Bicycle rental from Velo, Roscrea Rd (☎ 057 912 0080, ⓦ velo.ie).

ACCOMMODATION

Dooly's Hotel Emmet Square ☎ 057 912 0032, ⓦ doolyshotel.com. The town's social hub, a welcoming Georgian coaching inn, with a chequered history; it was here in 1809 that the Galway Hunt partied a little too hard after a day in the field and managed to burn the hotel down, thus gaining a new name, the Galway

Blazers. The bedrooms, some of which are on the small side, don't quite match up to the period elegance of the public rooms. **€79**

The Maltings Castle St ☎ 057 912 1345, ⓦ themaltingsbirr.com. Off the west side of Market Square and overlooking the leafy river, this restored 1810

warehouse, which was used to store malt for Guinness, offers quiet, large rooms with en-suite bathrooms, and homemade bread and jams for breakfast. Very good rates for singles. €70

The Stables Oxmantown Mall ☏ 057 912 0263, ⓦ thestablesbirr.com. Fanlit nineteenth-century town house that's been fetchingly refurbished in a plush style, with chandeliers and gilt mirrors in the spacious bedrooms. There's an open fire in its cosy lounge, as well as a home-furnishings shop and tearooms with courtyard seating. €79

Townsend House Townsend St ☏ 057 912 1276, ⓦ townsendhouse-guesthouse.com. On a busy street to the north of Emmet Square, this central, welcoming guesthouse provides en-suite rooms and wonderful breakfasts, in an airy, high-ceilinged Georgian house that's tastefully furnished with antiques. Very good rates for singles. €80

EATING AND DRINKING

The Chestnut Green St, between Emmet Square and the castle ☏ 087 220 8524, ⓦ thechestnut.ie. Welcoming, nineteenth-century bar, stylishly outfitted with dark wood and leather seats, and backed by a large beer garden, which hosts live music – anything from traditional to rock – mostly at weekends, sometimes in the garden. Mon–Thurs 8am–11.30pm, Fri 5pm–12.30am, Sat 3pm–12.30am, Sun 3–11pm.

Craughwell's Castle St, off the west side of Market Square ☏ 057 912 1839. Very sociable and cosy pub, with a good pint of Guinness and traditional music at weekends. Mon–Thurs 7–11.30pm, Fri & Sat 7pm–12.30am, Sun 1–11pm.

★ **Emma's** 31 Main St ☏ 057 912 5678. Your best bet during the day, a mellow café with comfy banquettes, preparing delicious panini and soup, as well as speciality teas and coffees, and a tempting array of freshly baked cakes and scones. Mon–Sat 8.30am–6pm, Sun 10.30am–6pm.

The Emmet *Dooly's Hotel* (see p.175), Emmet Square. The hotel's main restaurant is a formal, luxurious affair, serving dishes such as grilled sea bass with lemon and caper cream (€18). Mon–Sat 6–9pm, Sun 12.30–3pm & 6–9pm.

The Thatch Crinkill, on Military Rd, which runs east off the N62, about 2km south of Birr ☏ 057 912 0682, ⓦ thethatchcrinkill.com. This quaint thatched white cottage conceals an equally appealing interior of exposed brick and stone, pine furniture, log fires and candlelight. The pub is most famous among locals for its food, such as rack of Kinnitty lamb with rosemary sauce (€22), while early birds can order warm smoked mackerel salad with lemon and chive crème fraiche, together with a pint of prosecco, for €18. Food served daily 4–8.30pm, plus Fri Sat & Sun 12.30–3pm.

ENTERTAINMENT

Birr Theatre and Arts Centre Oxmantown Mall ☏ 057 912 2911, ⓦ birrtheatre.com. Located on a fine Georgian street, the town's main creative hub hosts a varied programme of drama, music and artistic events throughout the year.

Slieve Bloom

To the east of Birr, straddling the Offaly–Laois border, rises **Slieve Bloom**, the "mountain of Bladhma", named for an ancient Connacht warrior who sought refuge here. Although it extends only for about 20km across and down, the massif provides welcome relief from the flatness of the Midlands and a refuge for wildlife including bog plants such as the insect-eating sundew, and birds including skylarks, kestrels and the rare peregrine falcon. The waymarked 77km **Slieve Bloom Way** describes a heavily indented circuit of most of the range, before passing underneath the highest point – Arderin (527m), which means, rather hopefully, the "height of Ireland". Six shorter, signposted loop walks are detailed on the very useful website, ⓦ slievebloom.ie, while the Ordnance Survey of Ireland **map** #54 covers the whole of Slieve Bloom. For something more organized, there are **walking festivals** over the bank-holiday weekend in early May and over a weekend in July, as well as **guided walks** at least every Sunday (€5 per person). Details are available on the website, which also has information about a four-day **storytelling festival** in October.

Kinnitty

The best base on the Offaly side of the mountains, within walking distance of the Slieve Bloom Way, is the charming village of **KINNITTY**, which huddles around a couple of pubs and a triangular green that's traversed by a tiny stream.

ACCOMMODATION   SLIEVE BLOOM

Ardmore House Kinnitty ☎057 913 7009, ⍵kinnitty com. This nineteenth-century stone house with a lovely garden and a fine view of the mountain offers attractive en-suite B&B, home-baking and turf fires, and is especially accommodating to walkers. Self-catering cottage also available. €80

Roundwood House Mountrath ☎057 873 2120, ⍵roundwoodhouse.com. On the Laois side of the range, about 20km southeast of Kinnitty on the R440, this handsome, three-storey Palladian villa set in extensive wooded gardens offers welcoming, traditional country-house accommodation, either in the spacious main house or the earlier, more compact Yellow House. Serves communal dinners. Self-catering also available. €130

4

Kilkenny, Carlow and Wexford

HOOK LIGHTHOUSE

5

Kilkenny, Carlow and Wexford

Ireland's southeast is largely flat and has the country's best climate. The geography helps explain why it's a hotbed of hurling, the more expansive of Ireland's traditional sports: Kilkenny, in particular, is mad about the game. The county's attractions centre on its namesake city, which offers many historical sites, fine pubs and restaurants. To the south lie the evocative monasteries and trim waterside villages of the verdant Nore valley. County Wexford has much allure around the genial county town itself, with its thriving music scene. Meanwhile, the county's southwestern corner features ruined abbeys and a sweeping arboretum, running between the bleak wonders of the Hook Peninsula and the historic river port of New Ross.

Thanks to its strategic position just across St George's Channel from south Wales, Ireland's southeast has borne the brunt of the country's colonization. The **Vikings** founded an early settlement here, which grew into Wexford town, while the **Anglo-Normans** quickly exploited the area's economic potential and greatly altered its physiognomy. They developed Kilkenny and Wexford towns and built castles across the two counties, while also transforming uncultivated areas into productive farmland. However, control was not always easily maintained. The MacMurrough-Kavanagh Irish dynasty, based in the north of County Wexford, continually frustrated English attempts to control the region, and full conquest only occurred when **Cromwell** arrived in the mid-1600s. Even after this, County Wexford witnessed some of the bitterest fighting during the 1798 Rebellion, before the insurgents were decisively defeated at Enniscorthy.

Kilkenny city and around

Unquestionably Ireland's most atmospheric medieval city, **KILKENNY** straddles the broad River Nore, doglegging past its imposing **castle**. Downhill from here lies a compact grid of narrow streets, dating back to the city's origins, though little of its former gated walls remains. The main street wends its way from the castle to Kilkenny's other main landmark, the well-preserved, medieval **St Canice's Cathedral** with its climbable round tower, en route passing **Rothe House**, architecturally impressive evidence of the city's Tudor wealth. North of the city the major attraction is the strange calcite formations of **Dunmore Cave**.

Brief history

The first known settlement at Kilkenny is believed to have been a sixth-century monastic community founded by St Canice (*Cill Chainnigh* means "the church of Canice"). After the arrival of the **Anglo-Normans**, Strongbow erected a motte and bailey fort overlooking the Nore, in 1172, which was later replaced with a stone structure by his son-in-law, William Marshall. The latter also built a city wall and

Kilkenny festivals p.185	Enniscorthy festivals p.197
Walks in southern Kilkenny p.189	Across the estuary to Waterford:
Wexford festivals p.193	Ballyhack p.199

KILKENNY CASTLE

Highlights

❶ Kilkenny city Vibrant and historic, Kilkenny preserves its medieval framework, centred upon its imposing castle, and has several exciting festivals to boot. **See p.180**

❷ Jerpoint Abbey Atmospheric twelfth-century ruins, featuring a wonderful colonnaded cloister and fascinating carvings. **See p.189**

❸ Inistioge Gorgeous riverside village overlooked by the rejuvenated Woodstock Estate. **See p.190**

❹ Wexford Lively town that retains much of its

medieval layout and is renowned for its opera festival. **See p.190**

❺ National 1798 Centre Enniscorthy's enthralling multimedia account of the 1798 Rebellion. **See p.197**

❻ Duncannon A charming seaside village flanked by a grand, sandy beach and a looming fort. **See p.199**

❼ Ros Tapestry Vibrant threads of local history, in an inspired community project in New Ross. **See p.201**

HIGHLIGHTS ARE MARKED ON THE MAP ON P.182

5

towers and forced the local population to live outside its boundaries in an area still known as "Irishtown" today. Subsequently, the city's ownership passed through variou: hands, before James Butler, the third Earl of Ormonde, purchased the demesne in 1391.

Following the 1641 Rebellion, Kilkenny became the focus for the **Catholic Confederation**, an unlikely alliance of royalists loyal to Charles I and Irish landowners dispossessed by the Plantation. This established a parliament in Kilkenny, aimed at attaining Irish self-government and, in the process, restoring the rights of Catholics. However, its powers were short-lived, and, after Cromwell's arrival in 1650, the city's prosperity began to wane.

Nonetheless, nowadays Kilkenny still possesses an undoubted grandeur, largely untarnished by inappropriate modern building developments and, thanks to its castle

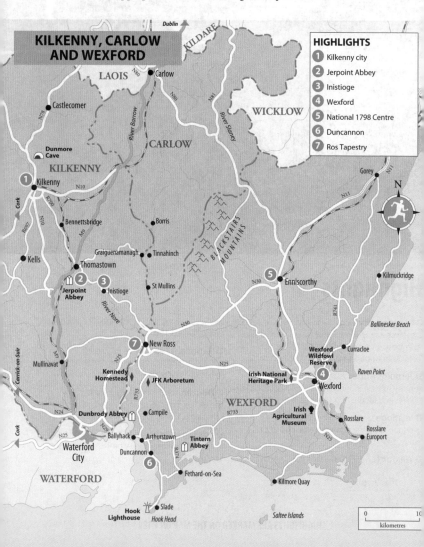

KILKENNY, CARLOW AND WEXFORD

HIGHLIGHTS

1. Kilkenny city
2. Jerpoint Abbey
3. Inistioge
4. Wexford
5. National 1798 Centre
6. Duncannon
7. Ros Tapestry

and numerous other sights, as well as a lively nightlife and cultural scene, has become an integral part of the Irish tourist trail.

Kilkenny Castle

Castle Daily: March 9.30am–5pm; April, May & Sept 9.30am–5.30pm; June–Aug 9am–5.30pm; Oct–Feb 9.30am–4.30pm; Nov–Jan admission by guided tour only • €6; Heritage Card • ⓦ kilkennycastle.ie **Butler Gallery** Daily: March 10am–1pm & 2–5pm; April 10am–1pm & 2–5.30pm; May–Sept 10am–5.30pm; Oct–Feb 10am–1pm & 2–4.30pm • Free • ⓦ butlergallery.com

Sitting strong above the Nore, Kilkenny's stately **castle** was built in the early thirteenth century by William Marshall, Earl of Pembroke, and purchased in 1391 by James Butler, third Earl of Ormonde. His family's wealth was founded upon huge areas of land acquired in Kilkenny and Tipperary, and his descendants, surviving siege by Cromwell in 1650, subsequently built the grand entrance gateway later that century and gradually developed the broad parklands that still extend to the southeast of the castle. Further work began around 1826, enhancing the castle's medieval exterior while adapting its interior in contemporary country-house style. The Butlers remained in residence until 1935, when a decline in the family's fortunes led to their departure and the auction of the castle's contents. The building fell into disrepair, until it was acquired by the Irish state in 1969, and has been much restored over subsequent decades.

Inside the castle, you'll be able to see the impressive hall, whose chequered floor is tiled with black **Kilkenny marble** (actually a polished limestone, but prevalent enough in the hills around Kilkenny to have given it the nickname "Marble City"), as well as a library, drawing room and nineteenth-century-style bedrooms. En route you'll pass a portrait of the first Duke of Ormonde which, for a period in its life, hung in the gents' toilet of a restaurant in New York – a far-flung result of the 1935 auction. The castle's crowning glory is its extraordinarily long gallery, which occupies almost the entire length of the River Wing, replete with twin fireplaces and marble carvings of key moments in the history of the Butler dynasty. Its 1825 hammer-beam roof, punctuated by curving columns bearing the heads of various mythical beasts, is decorated by whimsical Pre-Raphaelite daubs.

The former kitchens in the castle's basement house the prestigious **Butler Gallery**, devoted to temporary modern-art exhibitions (though at some stage the gallery is slated to move to the Evans Home on Barrack Lane).

Kilkenny Design Centre and National Craft Gallery

Kilkenny Design Centre April–Sept Mon–Sat 10am–7pm, Sun noon–6pm; Oct–March Mon–Sat 10am–6pm, Sun noon–6pm • ⓦ kilkennydesign.com **National Craft Gallery** Tues–Sat 10am–5.30pm, Sun 11am–5.30pm • Free • ⓣ 056 779 6147, ⓦ nationalcraftgallery.ie

Across the Parade from the castle, the converted eighteenth-century stables house the **Kilkenny Design Centre**, which retails a broad range of premium Irish crafts, and has a recommended upstairs café (see p.187). Behind the shop, you'll find the attractive, airy premises of the **National Craft Gallery**, which mounts a varied programme of exhibitions by Irish and international craftspeople, ranging from stained glass to quilts. Beyond the gallery, you can visit several small craft workshops in the courtyard and the beautiful walled gardens that back onto *Butler House*; if you're interested in further crafty exploration, pick up a "Craft Trail" leaflet from the gallery or the tourist office (or go to ⓦ madeinkilkenny.ie or ⓦ trailkilkenny.ie, which also has information on workshops and courses), detailing twenty or so other studios around the county.

High Street and Parliament Street

Heading down the Parade from the castle and across the junction to the High Street leads past the **Tholsel**, the city's erstwhile financial exchange and, subsequently, town

5

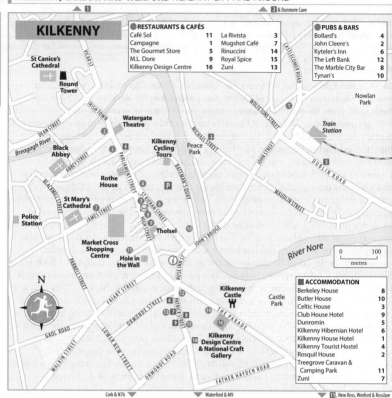

hall, constructed in 1761. The High Street blends seamlessly into Parliament Street, both replete with shops and cafés, intriguing alleys and offshoots.

Rothe House

Parliament St • April–Oct Mon–Sat 10.30am–5pm, Sun 3–5pm; Nov–March Mon–Sat 10.30am–4.30pm • €5 • ⓦ rothehouse.com

A complex of three dwellings linked by courtyards, **Rothe House** is the finest remnant of the city's Tudor prosperity. It was built for a wealthy Kilkenny merchant and his twelve children between 1594 and 1610, and is now, fittingly, home to the Kilkenny Archaeological Society and offers a genealogical service. A new interactive exhibition is planned to tell the history of the house, which is most interesting for its architecture, including two huge Kilkenny marble fireplaces on the first floor and the second floor's impressive king-post roof, made of Irish oak beams. Behind the house, two walled gardens – one for vegetables and herbs, the other a still immature orchard – have been restored to their early seventeenth-century state, stretching back to a rebuilt section of the city wall.

Black Abbey

Just before Parliament Street becomes Irishtown, on Abbey Street, stands the **Holy Trinity Church**, more commonly known as the **Black Abbey**, thanks to the colour of the habits of its founders, the Dominicans. Dating from 1225, the abbey was suppressed during the Reformation and fell into disrepair. Now fully restored, and again a

KILKENNY FESTIVALS

The major event in the city's packed cultural calendar is the ten-day **Kilkenny Arts Festival** (Ⓦ kilkennyarts.ie) in August, featuring all manner of music, as well as drama, film, various exhibitions and literary goings-on. **Kilkenny Tradfest** (Ⓦ kilkennytradfest.com) brings four days of traditional music, dance and workshops around St Patrick's Day in March, while the four-day **Rhythm and Roots Festival** (Ⓦ kilkennyroots.com), over the bank-holiday weekend at the start of May, spotlights American country and roots music. The bank-holiday weekend in early June, meanwhile, hosts the marvellous four-day comedy festival, **The Cat Laughs** (Ⓦ thecatlaughs.com), and the bank-holiday weekend in late October sees an imaginative four-day festival of food, **Savour Kilkenny** (Ⓦ savourkilkenny.com).

Dominican establishment, it houses some fine carvings and a glorious fifteen-panel rosary stained-glass window.

St Canice's Cathedral

Cathedral April, May & Sept Mon–Sat 10am–1pm & 2–5pm, Sun 2–5pm; June–Aug Mon–Sat 9am–6pm, Sun 1–6pm; Oct–March Mon–Sat 10am–1pm & 2–4pm, Sun 2–4pm • €4 **Tower** Access weather permitting (no under-12s) April, May & Sept Mon–Sat 10am–1pm & 2–5pm, Sun 2–5pm; June–Aug Mon–Sat 9am–6pm, Sun 1–6pm; Oct–March Mon–Sat noon & 3pm, Sun 3pm • €3, combined ticket with cathedral €6 • Ⓦ stcanicescathedral.com

Kilkenny's Church of Ireland cathedral, thirteenth-century **St Canice's**, looms above Irishtown. Though its spire collapsed in 1332, the rest of this grand Gothic structure remains true to its date of origin. The magnificently carved interior contains many splendid sixteenth- and seventeenth-century tombstones, often cut from black Kilkenny marble, including some remarkable effigies of the Butler family. In the churchyard stands a graceful ninth-century **Round Tower**, the only vestige of St Canice's monastic settlement, whose 30m summit affords a superb vista of the city spread out below.

Dunmore Cave

Mid-March to mid-June & mid-Sept to Oct daily from 9.30am, last tour 4pm; mid-June to mid-Sept daily from 9.30am, last tour 5pm; Nov to mid-March Wed–Sun from 9.30am, last tour 3pm • €3; Heritage Card • Ⓦ heritageireland.ie

Formed in a limestone outcrop of the Castlecomer plateau, 10km north of the city off the N78, **Dunmore Cave**'s series of chambers features numerous beautiful calcite creations – curtains and crystals, stalactites and stalagmites; the most remarkable of the last stands some 4.5m high. The cave is referenced in the *Annals of the Four Masters* (see box, p.429), which recounts that the Vikings massacred a thousand people here in 928, a tale partially substantiated in 1967 when excavations uncovered the skeletons of more than forty women and children, and a Viking coin.

ARRIVAL AND DEPARTURE   **KILKENNY CITY**

By train Kilkenny's MacDonagh Train Station is off Dublin Rd, a 10min walk along John St to the city centre.
Destinations Dublin (4–6 daily; 1hr 40min); Thomastown (4–7 daily; 10min); Waterford (4–7 daily; 35min).

By bus Bus Éireann services leave from the train station and most also stop on Ormonde Rd in the centre; J.J. Kavanagh's stop on Ormonde Rd; and Kilbride's New Ross buses stop on Ormonde Rd and the Parade, while their Graiguenamanagh buses stop at MacDonagh Junction, a shopping centre next to the train station, and the Parade.
Destinations Bus Éireann: Athlone (1–2 daily; 2hr 50min);

Cahir (Mon–Sat 1 daily; 1hr 35min); Carrick-on-Suir (6–7 daily; 45min); Cork (Mon–Sat 3 daily; 3hr); Dublin (9 daily; 2hr 10min); Inistioge (1 Thurs; 35min); New Ross (1 Thurs; 1hr 15min); Thomastown (1–2 daily; 25min); Waterford (3–5 daily; 1hr).
J.J. Kavanagh (Ⓦ jjkavanagh.ie): Dublin & Airport (6 daily; 2–3hr).
Kilbride (Ⓦ kilbridecoaches.com): Graiguenamanagh (Mon–Sat 2 daily; 55min); Inistioge (Mon–Sat 2 daily; 40min); New Ross (Mon–Sat 2 daily; 1hr); Thomastown (Mon–Sat 2 daily; 30min).

5

INFORMATION AND TOURS

Tourist office In the Shee Alms House, one of very few Tudor almshouses remaining in Ireland, on Rose Inn St (May, June & Sept Mon–Sat 9.30am–5.30pm; July & Aug Mon–Sat 9am–6pm, Sun 10.30am–4pm; Oct–April Mon–Sat 9am–5pm, sometimes closing for lunch; hours worth checking on ☎ 056 775 1500). Ask here about the Smithwick's Experience (ⓦ smithwicksexperience.com), a multimedia celebration of Kilkenny's 300-year-old ale on Parliament St (on the site of the old brewery), which was just about to open at the time of research.

Walking tours Pat Tynan's 70min walking tours of the medieval city (mid-March to Oct Mon–Sat 10.30am, 12.15pm & 3pm, Sun 11.15am & 12.30pm; €7; ☎ 087 265 1745, ⓦ www.kilkennywalkingtours.ie) depart from the tourist office.

Cycling tours Kilkenny Cycling Tours, Bateman's Quay (☎ 086 895 4961, ⓦ kilkennycyclingtours.com), provide tours of city and county, as well as rental.

Kayaking tours Go with the Flow (☎ 087 252 9700, ⓦ gowiththeflow.ie) offers guided and self-guided kayaking and canoeing trips on rivers Nore and Barrow.

ACCOMMODATION

Kilkenny has plenty of **accommodation**, but advance reservation is necessary – and prices often go up – at weekends throughout the summer and during festivals (see p.185).

HOTELS AND B&BS

Berkeley House 5 Patrick St ☎ 056 776 4848, ⓦ berkeleyhousekilkenny.com. Centrally located Georgian town house, offering very pleasant accommodation in airy, tastefully decorated en-suite rooms. Continental breakfasts served. **€100**

★ Butler House 16 Patrick St ☎ 056 772 2828, ⓦ butler.ie. This expansive former dower house of Kilkenny Castle was decorously refurbished in the 1970s by Kilkenny Design Centre (in whose café breakfast is served; see opposite). Its spacious rooms marry Georgian refinement and modern furnishings and facilities to stunning effect, and some overlook the beautiful garden and castle. **€135**

Celtic House 18 Michael St ☎ 056 776 2249. Welcoming, well-maintained, modern town house B&B, adorned with the artist owner's landscapes and set in a quiet, fairly central location. Rooms are colourful, airy and en suite. **€80**

Club House Hotel Patrick St ☎ 056 772 1994, ⓦ www .clubhousehotel.com. Kilkenny's oldest hotel, this well-run former coaching inn provides genteel traditional hospitality – think stags' heads and Rotary Club meetings – good breakfasts and comfortable, good-value bedrooms, many of them in the maze-like extension at the back, away from the main road. **€85**

Dunromin Dublin Rd ☎ 056 776 1387, ⓦ dunromin kilkenny.com. Welcoming, superbly maintained nineteenth-century family home, covered in creepers and flowers, on the main road near the train station, providing very comfortable en-suite B&B rooms and fine breakfasts. April–Oct. **€70**

Kilkenny Hibernian Hotel 1 Ormonde St ☎ 056 777 1888, ⓦ kilkennyhibernianhotel.com. Once a bank and later the HQ of a food company, this lovingly restored Victorian building features a variety of lavish accommodation furnished with red carpets and lots of polished wood, above two popular bars and a bar restaurant. Good-value half-board deals. **€90**

Kilkenny House Hotel Freshford Rd ☎ 056 777 0711, ⓦ kilkennyhousehotel.ie. A 15min walk from the centre, this modern, spacious, two-storey features large, bright, well-appointed rooms. A real bargain from Mon to Thur, and Sun, and a likely fallback at weekends, though prices almost triple on Sat. **€50**

★ Rosquil House Castlecomer Rd ☎ 056 772 1419, ⓦ rosquilhouse.com. An elegant and welcoming upmarket guesthouse, a 10min walk from the centre, with spacious, stylish and well-equipped rooms, an attractive sitting room and fine breakfasts. Self-catering mews also available. **€85**

Zuni 26 Patrick St ☎ 056 772 3999, ⓦ zuni.ie. Located above the restaurant of the same name in a converted century-old theatre, with 13 luxurious contemporary bedrooms featuring a minimalist decor of dark wood and white. Half-board deals available. **€90**

HOSTEL

Kilkenny Tourist Hostel 35 Parliament St (IHH) ☎ 056 776 3541, ⓦ www.kilkennyhostel.ie. Large and well-run hostel in a very central Georgian town house, featuring spacious dorms, a few private rooms, a well-equipped kitchen, a turf fire in the sitting room and laundry facilities. Front dorms can suffer from street noise at weekends. Dorms **€17**, doubles **€42**

CAMPSITE

Treegrove Caravan & Camping Park Danville House ☎ 056 777 0302, ⓦ treegrovecamping.com. Popular, well-equipped site 1.5km southeast on the R700 New Ross road (or a 25min walk or cycle ride down the tree-lined riverside path); campers' kitchen, laundry and bike rental. March to mid-Nov. **€17**

5

Kilkenny has more than a smattering of good **restaurants**, and there's an interesting farmers' market on Thurs mornings on The Parade, offering farmhouse cheeses, cakes and handmade chocolates. If you'd like to explore further, check out the food trail on ⓦtrailkilkenny.ie, which includes delicatessens, producers, cooking courses and restaurants. Plenty of attractive **bars**, generally untouched by the tasteless hands of refurbishment, serve decent snacks and meals, and some lay on great traditional **music** sessions. Weekends, however, can get a bit too rowdy for some tastes, as Kilkenny has become a popular venue for Irish stag and hen parties.

RESTAURANTS AND CAFÉS

Café Sol William St ☎056 776 4987, ⓦrestaurantskilkenny.com. Bright, warm and thus appropriately named, this fine café-restaurant offers great salads, sandwiches and various hot dishes at lunch, while the evening menu features an eclectic though mostly European array of meat, fish and vegetarian dishes with local ingredients well to the fore (currently €23 for 2 courses). Mon–Thurs 11.30am–9.30pm, Fri & Sat 11.30am–10pm, Sun noon–9pm.

Campagne 5 The Arches, Glasshouse Lane ☎056 777 2858, ⓦcampagne.ie. Recently awarded a Michelin star, *Campagne* offers elegant and confident modern French cooking using local produce, served in olive-green booths decorated with colourful paintings of country life. Keep your bank manager happy by coming for the lunch and early-bird set menu (€25 for 2 courses). Tues–Thurs 6–10pm, Fri & Sat 12.30–2.30pm & 5.30–10pm, Sun 12.30–3pm.

The Gourmet Store 56 High St ☎056 777 1727. Deli supplying wonderful multilayered sandwiches, salads and cakes to take away or eat in their small café, as well as stocking a vast assortment of culinary delights. Mon–Sat 9am–6pm.

★Kilkenny Design Centre The Parade. The centre's modern, daytime self-service café offers splendid salads, a variety of homemade soups, and more substantial meals, all at reasonable prices. On weekend evenings, the upstairs room turns into a classy restaurant, *Anocht* (meaning "Tonight"), serving dishes such as lemon and rosemary roasted sea bass (€22.50) on specially commissioned stoneware. Café daily 10am–6pm; restaurant Thurs–Sat 6pm–late.

La Rivista 22 Parliament St ☎056 777 1666. Hospitable Italian restaurant in a well-lit, high-ceilinged, modern space, dishing up moderately priced pizzas, tasty pasta and a varied selection of main courses, all in large portions. Good-value set menu, offering two courses for €20 (€23 on Sat, €17 at Sun lunch time). Mon–Sat 5–10pm, Sun 12.30–10pm.

M.L. Dore 65 High St ☎056 776 3374. Friendly, old-fashioned, self-service tearooms, styling itself the "nostalgia café", with a wide variety of cakes, snacks, soups, salads and meals on offer, served at tables out on St Kieran St and in a heated rooftop garden. Daily 8am–10pm.

Mugshot Café 25 James St ☎056 777 7798, ⓦwww .mugshotcafe.ie. Bright, welcoming café, using local ingredients from named sources wherever possible, with a pleasant, unobtrusive retro style. There's a wide choice for breakfasts, scones, waffles and delicious apple and almond crumble, and you can lunch on quiche and two salads for €9, or the hot special of the day. Mon–Sat 8.30am–5.30pm, Sun 11am–4pm.

Rinuccini 1 The Parade ☎056 776 1575, ⓦrinuccini .com. Authentic Italian-run restaurant where classily prepared traditional dishes such as *suprema di pollo ai funghi* (chicken with mushroom cream sauce; €22) are served with some élan; early-bird menu nightly. Mon–Fri noon–3pm & 5–10pm, Sat noon–3.30pm & 5–10pm, Sun noon–3.30pm & 5–9.30pm.

★Royal Spice 11 Patrick St ☎056 771 2646, ⓦroyalspice.ie. One of Ireland's best Indian restaurants, a stylish, modern affair that uses fresh local produce such as trout wherever possible. Less familiar dishes include a delicious lasuni prawn curry (€16.60) and there's a wide choice of vegetarian dishes, either as sides or mains. Three courses for €22 for early birds (5–7pm). Mon & Tues 5–10pm, Wed–Sat 5–11pm, Sun 12.30–10pm.

Zuni 26 Patrick St ☎056 772 3999, ⓦzuni.ie. Very fine and stylish modern-Irish dishes with Mediterranean and Asian influences, such as sesame-seed-coated tuna with avocado and wasabi purée, served in a contemporary café-restaurant that used to be a theatre. On the pricey side (most mains €20–25), but there are early-bird and tapas menus every evening and a cheaper, simpler lunch menu. Mon–Wed 8am–9.30pm, Thurs–Sat 8am–10pm, Sun 8am–9pm.

PUBS AND BARS

Bollard's St Kieran St. Friendly bar (and weekend wine bar) with craft beers on draught, fine meals (not Sun), pleasant tables on the alley and traditional music Fri, plus Tues & Thurs in summer. Mon–Thurs 10.30am–11.30pm, Fri & Sat 10.30am–12.30am, Sun 2–11pm.

John Cleere's 28 Parliament St ☎056 776 2573, ⓦcleeres.com. The city's longest-running traditional-music session is here on Mon, as well as an open session on Wed, and other music throughout the week in the bar's theatre, which also hosts comedy and drama. Mon–Thurs 11.30am–11.30pm, Fri & Sat 11.30am–12.30am, Sun 1–11pm.

Kyteler's Inn St Kieran St ⓦkytelersinn.com. This medieval inn's spooky reputation is linked to erstwhile resident Alice Kyteler who was tried for witchcraft in

5

1324. She fled to England, leaving her maid Petronella to take the rap – and her place on the burning woodpile. The bar has open fireplaces, solid oak beams and plenty of nooks and crannies, and offers traditional music at weekends in winter, twice nightly in summer – including give-it-a-go *bodhrán* lessons Mon & Tues at 6.30pm that are free and open to anyone. Mon–Thurs 11.30am–11.30pm, Fri & Sat 11.30am–2am, Sun 12.15–11.30pm.

The Left Bank The Parade ⓦ leftbank.ie. This hulking, granite, Neoclassical edifice on Kilkenny's main corner, a former Bank of Ireland branch, has been reborn as a popular good-time bar, with regular live bands and DJs on Sat. The interior has been fitted out with huge carved mirrors, leather armchairs and ornate fireplaces and screens, while smokers are pampered with a covered,

heated backyard with its own outdoor bar. Mon–Thurs noon–11.30pm, Fri & Sat noon–12.30am, Sun 12.30–11pm.

The Marble City Bar High St ⓦ langtons.ie/marble-city-bar. Central bar and tearooms serving delicious food and which have been revamped in a mostly Art Deco style and hung with black-and-white photos of movie stars with outdoor tables on St Kieran's St. Mon–Thurs 9am–11.30pm, Fri 9am–12.30am, Sat 9am–2am, Sun 9am–11pm.

Tynan's Bateman's Quay. You'll get a great pint of Guinness at this 300-year-old riverside pub, which is furnished with leather banquettes and a lovely carved wood horseshoe-shaped bar, topped with marble. Mon–Thurs 10.30/11am–11.30pm, Fri & Sat 10.30/11am–12.30am, Sun 11.30am/noon–11pm.

ENTERTAINMENT AND SPORT

Hole in the Wall Just off High St, behind Enable Ireland ☎ 087 807 5650, ⓦ holeinthewall.ie. Hard to categorize but impossible to ignore: Ireland's oldest-surviving town house, dating back to 1582, has been lovingly restored by a local cardiologist, who hosts regular musical evenings, including Singspiele, narrative shows on historical subjects enhanced with music, poetry and visuals. It's worth popping in to admire the architecture, even if it's just for a daytime coffee in the summer or an evening drink in the tiny tavern. Tavern Mon, Wed & Thurs 8pm–midnight, Fri 8pm–1am, Sat 2.30pm–1am.

Nowlan Park O'Loughlin Rd ☎ 056 776 5122 ⓦ kilkennygaa.ie. The main stadium in hurling-mad Kilkenny, with imminent plans to increase capacity to 40,000 – in a county whose population numbers only 95,000. Match tickets only cost around €15.

Watergate Theatre Parliament St ☎ 056 776 1674 ⓦ watergatetheatre.com. The leading venue in Kilkenny for the performing arts, the Watergate Theatre offers a varied programme of drama, classical and contemporary music, dance and comedy.

Southern Kilkenny

Some of the county's finest spots lie towards its southern extremity, countryside defined by the lush valleys of the rivers **Barrow** and **Nore**. Near the Nore are major ecclesiastical remains at **Kells** and **Jerpoint Abbey**, while above the beguiling village of **Inistioge** you can explore the extensive gardens and arboretum of the Woodstock Demesne.

Kells

Fourteen kilometres south of Kilkenny on the R697 lies the medieval village of **KELLS**, a petite and picturesque settlement straddling a tributary of the Nore, the King's River.

Kells Priory

Open access

A short stroll east from the village centre along the Stonyford road stands one of the country's most atmospheric ruins, **Kells Priory**, set by the river. This Augustinian foundation was established in 1193 and had a turbulent history, being sacked in both 1252 and 1327, before dissolution in the 1540s. Most of its remains date from the fourteenth and fifteenth centuries, and inside the still-standing curtain wall, with its gatehouse and towers (earning it the local nickname "Seven Castles"), are a church and chapel and several domestic buildings. All told, it's one of the largest and most outstanding Irish medieval sites, though the priory has no connection with the *Book of Kells* housed in Trinity College, Dublin, which is named after Kells in County Meath.

WALKS IN SOUTHERN KILKENNY

Several worthwhile waymarked **trails** cross southern Kilkenny. The **South Leinster Way** runs for 100km from Kildavin in County Carlow, via 800m Mount Leinster in the Blackstairs Mountains, to Carrick-on-Suir (see p.217) in Tipperary. The most attractive part is in southern Kilkenny, between Borris – where the path intersects the **Barrow Way** – and Mullinavat, especially the 16km from Graiguenamanagh to Inistioge. The southernmost section of the Barrow Way, a pretty 8km riverside path, is the most pleasant way to get from Graiguenamanagh to St Mullins, and there are new trails from **Kilkenny to Bennettsbridge** (12km) and from **Thomastown to Inistioge** (11km) along the Nore – for information on the latter and on the forthcoming Kilkenny–Inistioge path, as well as on other walking and cycling routes in the county, go to ⓦ trailkilkenny.ie, which features downloadable maps and apps.

Jerpoint Abbey

Daily: early March to Sept 9am–5.30pm; Oct 9am–5pm; Nov to early Dec 9.30am–4pm • €3; Heritage Card • ⓦ heritageireland.ie

The major tourist sight in the south of the county is **Jerpoint Abbey**, which lies on the N9, 20km south of Kilkenny city. Originally founded as a Benedictine house in 1158, the abbey was colonized by Cistercians some twenty years later. The oldest remains are the twelfth-century Romanesque church, but the rest, set around a beautifully colonnaded fifteenth-century cloister, follows the characteristic Cistercian design. The abbey features a number of thirteenth- to sixteenth-century tomb sculptures in the transept chapels and some intriguing carvings on the cloister arcade, including the "little man of Jerpoint" whose stomach-crossed hands and open-mouthed expression suggest either mirth or dyspepsia.

ACCOMMODATION   JERPOINT ABBEY

Abbey House ⓣ 056 772 4166, ⓦ abbeyhousejerpoint .com. Top-notch, all-en-suite B&B opposite the abbey, in a restored, creeper-clad eighteenth-century mill house on the River Arrigle, with freshly squeezed orange juice and local rainbow trout for breakfast. Very good rates for singles. €80

Thomastown

The jumping-off point for Jerpoint Abbey, **THOMASTOWN**, 2km to the northeast, is a pleasant riverside village on the Dublin–Waterford train line. A walled town of some note in medieval times, Thomastown now maintains scant sense of its own antiquity, other than its old **bridge** across the Nore and the ruined thirteenth-century church of St Mary's at the top of the main street, Market Street.

ARRIVAL AND DEPARTURE   THOMASTOWN

By train Destinations Dublin (4–6 daily; 1hr 55min); Kilkenny (4–7 daily; 10min); Waterford (4–7 daily; 30min).
By bus Destinations Bus Éireann to: Athlone (1–2 daily; 3hr 20min); Dublin (6 daily; 2hr 25min); Inistioge (1 Thurs; 10min); Kilkenny (1–2 daily; 25min); New Ross (1 Thurs; 50min); Waterford (10–11 daily; 30–40min).

J.J. Kavanagh (ⓦ jjkavanagh.ie): Dublin & Dublin Airport (7 daily; 2hr 10min–3hr); Waterford (6 daily; 45min).
Kilbride (ⓦ kilbridecoaches.com): Inistioge (Mon–Sat 2 daily; 10min); Kilkenny (Mon–Sat 2 daily; 30min); New Ross (Mon–Sat 2 daily; 30min).

EATING AND DRINKING

★**Blackberry** Market St ⓣ 086 775 5303, ⓦ theblackberrycafe.ie. Excellent, central, daytime café, which uses locally sourced ingredients where possible to rustle up keenly priced sandwiches, soups, quiches, salads and daily specials, as well as home-baked cakes and good coffees. Mon–Fri 9.30am–5.30pm, Sat 10am–5.30pm.

Sol Low St ⓣ 056 775 4945, ⓦ restaurantskilkenny .com. Around the corner from Market St, a cheery, modern, bistro-style restaurant, serving dishes such as roast chicken breast with chorizo and black pudding for dinner (currently €23 for 2 courses) and cheaper, simpler choices for lunch. Mon–Sat 11.30am–3pm & 5.30–9pm, Sun 11.30am–9pm.

5

Inistioge

Eight kilometres down the Nore from Thomastown is the quaint village of **INISTIOGE** (pronounced "Inisteeg"), set around a tree-lined green, an old church and a narrow-arched stone bridge over the river. Unsurprisingly, the attractive location, with its verdant hills rising above the village, has drawn film-makers, and both *Circle of Friends* and *Widows' Peak* were shot here in the 1990s.

Woodstock Demesne

Daily: April–Sept 9am–7.30pm; Oct–March 9am–4pm • Car €4, pedestrians free • ⓦ www.woodstock.ie

The steep lane rising from Inistioge's village green leads after 2km to the **Woodstock Demesne**. When its owners left Ireland during the War of Independence, the estate's Georgian mansion was taken over by the Black and Tans and, like many similarly tarnished dwellings, was burnt down after independence in 1922. However, since 1999 the county council have been restoring the Victorian **gardens**, and you can enjoy walks lined by firs and monkey puzzles, an arboretum, rose gardens, rockeries and breathtaking views of the Nore valley, as well as a summertime tea room in a cast-iron conservatory.

ARRIVAL AND DEPARTURE   INISTIOGE

By bus Destinations Kilbride (ⓦ kilbridecoaches.com): Kilkenny (Mon–Sat 2 daily; 40min); New Ross (Mon–Sat 2 daily; 20min); Thomastown (Mon–Sat 2 daily; 10min).

ACCOMMODATION AND EATING

Woodstock Arms ☏ 056 775 8440, ⓦ woodstockarms .com. The village's main provider of hospitality is the *Woodstock Arms*, a pleasant, family-run pub with tables out on the green, offering well-appointed en-suite rooms with good rates for singles. **€70**

Wexford town

WEXFORD is a happy-go-lucky kind of town with plenty of scope for enjoying music in its **pubs**, but it has its serious side too, not least in the shape of its internationally renowned **opera festival**. There are few sights to see in the town itself – more is on offer in the surrounding area (see p.194) – but the appeal of the place lies in its atmosphere and setting: its long, narrow medieval lanes huddle for shelter inland of the exposed quays, which line the southern shore of the wide Slaney estuary, with the railway line to Rosslare dividing the main road from the promenade and a busy little marina.

The town began life as a Viking base for incursions and trading, before becoming an early Anglo-Norman conquest in 1169. Wexford later housed an English garrison whose loyalty to the Crown resulted in vicious fighting against Cromwell's army in 1649. The town also played a significant role in the 1798 Rebellion, which was finally quelled at Enniscorthy (see p.196). Wexford's lengthy quays pay testimony to its re-emergence as a prosperous trading centre in the nineteenth century, though gradual silting of the harbour's entrance and the development of Rosslare Harbour led to its demise as a competitive port.

Westgate Tower and Selskar Abbey

Guided 45min tours (Tower and Abbey) March–Oct Mon–Sat 3pm • €3 • ⓦ wexfordwalkingtours.net

Wexford's walls once had five gates, but the only survivor is the **Westgate Tower**, completed in 1300. The adjacent **Selskar Abbey** was founded by Alexander de la Roche who left Ireland to fight in the Crusades, but returned to discover that his fiancée, incorrectly advised of his death, had become a nun. He also took holy orders, becoming an Augustinian, and established Selskar in the early twelfth century. After

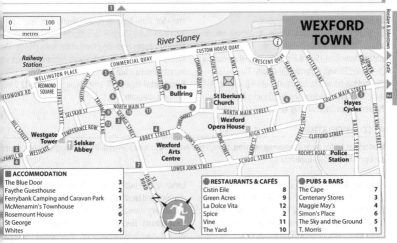

WEXFORD TOWN

ACCOMMODATION

The Blue Door	3
Faythe Guesthouse	2
Ferrybank Camping and Caravan Park	1
McMenamin's Townhouse	5
Rosemount House	6
St George	7
Whites	4

RESTAURANTS & CAFÉS

Cistin Eile	8
Green Acres	9
La Dolce Vita	12
Spice	2
Vine	11
The Yard	10

PUBS & BARS

The Cape	7
Centenary Stores	3
Maggie May's	4
Simon's Place	6
The Sky and the Ground	5
T. Morris	1

the murder of Thomas Becket in 1170, Henry II came to Selskar Abbey to do penance. The abbey must have survived Dissolution since Cromwell's troops took the trouble to destroy it when they captured the town. Alongside its remains stand a fourteenth-century tower house and a nineteenth-century church, while part of the old town wall can be seen running along one side of the graveyard.

The Bull Ring

Selskar Street leads to the town's narrow main drag, imaginatively entitled Main Street, albeit with South and North variations, which is lined with shops, bars and cafés. On North Main Street, the **Bull Ring** derives its name from the time when bull-baiting, a once popular form of entertainment, took place here – the bull's hide, apparently, was given to the mayor, the meat to the poor. It later became a rallying-point for politicians - Charles Parnell, James Connolly, Éamon de Valera and Michael Collins all addressed the crowd here. The bronze monument of a 1798 Pikeman that stands in the square was sculpted by Oliver Sheppard, also responsible for *The Death of Cúchulainn* housed in the GPO in Dublin. On Fridays and Saturdays, the Bull Ring now hosts an interesting **market**, peddling everything from artisan foods to antiques, and handmade clothes to soaps.

St Iberius's Church

The interior is best seen during one of the regular classical-music concerts hosted by the church • Ⓦ musicforwexford.ie

A little further along Main Street from the Bull Ring is Anglican **St Iberius's Church**, named after Ibar, the contemporary of St Patrick who Christianized Wexford. It dates back to the late seventeenth century but was much remodelled in 1760 and features a fine Georgian interior, possibly designed by John Roberts (see p.209). The church's unusual gallery was installed to accommodate troops stationed in the town, and its broader-than-long shape was an ingenious answer to the problem of the site's proximity to the city wall.

ARRIVAL AND INFORMATION | **WEXFORD TOWN**

By train O'Hanrahan Train Station, which has left-luggage facilities, is on Redmond Square at the north end of the quays.

Destinations Dublin (3–4 daily; 2hr 35min); Enniscorthy (3–4 daily; 25min); Rosslare (3–4 daily; 20min); Rosslare Europort (3–4 daily; 25min).

5

By bus Buses stop on Redmond Square.

Destinations Bus Éireann: Dublin & Airport (roughly hourly; 2hr–2hr 45min); Enniscorthy (roughly hourly; 20min); New Ross (5–8 daily; 40min); Rosslare Europort (5–7 daily; 30min); Waterford (5–8 daily; 1hr). Wexford Bus (ⓦwexfordbus.com): Dublin & Airport (9–12 daily; 2hr 30min); Enniscorthy (9–12 daily; 30min).

Tourist office Crescent Quay ☎053 912 3111 (July & Aug Mon–Sat 9am–6pm, perhaps opening Sun, too; Sept–June Mon–Sat 9.15am–5.15/5.30pm).

Walking tours Hour-long tours of the town (March–Oc Mon–Sat 11am; €5; ⓦwexfordwalkingtours.net) pick u from the tourist office.

Bike rental Hayes, 108 South Main St ☎053 912 2462 ⓦhayescycles.com.

ACCOMMODATION

Wexford has a good range of **accommodation**, though you should try to book a few months in advance for rooms durin the Opera Festival (see opposite).

The Blue Door 18 Lower George St ☎053 912 1047, ⓦbluedoor.ie. Welcoming, very central Georgian town house hung with pot plants, where the rooms are bright, attractive and comfortable and the breakfasts, served in the cheery front room, are tasty and generous. **€70**

Faythe Guesthouse The Faythe ☎053 912 2249, ⓦfaytheguesthouse.com. A fine Victorian house in a quiet part of town just southeast of the centre, whose pretty grounds include the remaining wall of an old castle, offering very agreeable rooms and a splendid lounge with an open fire. **€80**

Ferrybank Camping and Caravan Park ☎053 918 5256, ⓦwexfordswimmingpool.ie. Scenic, breezy seafront camping just across the bridge from the quays, with the public swimming pool, gym, sauna and steam room on site (discounted admission for campers), as well as a campers' kitchen, laundry, recreation room and playground. **€16.50**

★**McMenamin's Townhouse** 6 Glena Terrace, Spawell Rd ☎053 914 6442. An absolute gem, this late Victorian, red-brick town house features characterful rooms with antique bedsteads, very helpful owners with plenty of tips on enjoyin the town, and breakfasts – including homemade bread, jam and whiskey marmalades – to die for. **€90**

Rosemount House Spawell Rd ☎053 912 4609 ⓦwexfordbedandbreakfast.ie. This spruce Georgia town house offers plush, en-suite rooms furnished wit antiques and a fine array of breakfast goodies; very goo rates for singles. **€90**

St George George St ☎053 914 3474 ⓦstgeorgeguesthouse.com. Welcoming, remodelle Georgian town house set around a courtyard with brigh comfortable, en-suite rooms and plenty of local advice Reductions without breakfast or for stays of two nights o more; very good single rates. **€70**

Whites Abbey St ☎053 912 2311, ⓦwhitesofwexfor .ie. Wexford's most historic hotel, dating back to th eighteenth century, has been thoroughly redeveloped in lavish and airy contemporary style around a gran courtyard, with an attractive 20m swimming pool, a gyn and a spa. Their own website carries half-board and othe special offers. **€89**

EATING AND DRINKING

Wexford has plenty of good **cafés** and **restaurants** and numerous lively pubs, several of which serve bar meals an feature live **music**.

RESTAURANTS AND CAFÉS

★**Cistin Eile** 80 South Main St ☎053 912 1616. Far from being just "another kitchen" as its Irish name might suggest, this informal restaurant is an exceptional place, serving imaginative modern Irish food with a rustic bent, in dishes such as Wicklow venison salad, spiced apple, red wine and roseship. At lunch time, you can feast on the market fish dish of the day plus either a glass of wine or a dessert for a give-away €15. Mon & Tues noon–3pm, Wed–Sat noon–3pm & 6–9pm.

Green Acres Selskar St ☎053 912 2975, ⓦgreenacres .ie. A handsome red-brick house with a modern glass extension and attractive tables on a pedestrianized street. Inside you'll find a well-stocked deli and wine shop, a first-floor art gallery and a bistro serving creative fare such as Kilmore crab claws with grilled limes, ginger, sesame an soy glaze (€29.50). Mon–Sat 9.30am–10pm.

★**La Dolce Vita** 6–7 Trimmer's Lane ☎053 917 0806 Astonishingly good, authentic Italian food, served in delightful small café with outdoor seating on a broac pedestrianized street and at inexpensive prices too (pasta from €10). Mon–Thurs 9am–5.30pm, Fri & Sa 9am–9pm.

Spice Monck St, above the Crown Bar ☎053 912 2011 ⓦspicerestaurant.net. Upmarket Indian restaurant wit elegant modern decor, specializing in Keralan and othe South Indian dishes – try the tasty Goan fish curr (€18.50). Mon–Thurs 5.30–10.30pm, Fri–Sun 5–11pm

Vine 109 North Main St ☎053 912 2388 ⓦvinerestaurant.ie. Appealingly set in a lofty, ornatel orniced first-floor room, this largely authentic Thai restaurant covers all the standards (main courses around 20), including an especially wide range of appetizers, ustled up in an open kitchen by Thai chefs. Tues–Sun –10pm.

he Yard 3 Lower George St ☎053 914 4083, ☊theyard.ie. The varied setting – a tiny café on North Main St, leading to a bright, informal restaurant with olished wood floors and antique tables, which opens onto n attractive, leafy yard – matches the diverse global menu: everything from tasty sandwiches to duck salad with mango and crispy noodles. Early-bird dinner menu Mon–Wed 6–8pm, Thurs–Sat 6–7pm; €23 for 2 courses. Mon–Sat 9am–10pm.

PUBS AND BARS

★ **The Cape** The Bull Ring. The undertaking side of the usiness, as claimed by the sign, has long gone, and this opular meeting place is very much a place to catch up with local news and watch the world pass by, possibly from ne of the outdoor tables, while supping a good pint of uinness. Mon–Thurs 10.30am–11.30pm, Fri & Sat 0.30am–12.30am, Sun noon–11pm.

entenary Stores Charlotte St ☎053 912 4424. The tores are most famous among Wexford's youth as a weekend ightclub, but the original pub, at the heart of this ntertainment complex in two 1850s town houses, is still a ery congenial spot, with its dark wood floor and panelling, nd a pleasant, south-facing outdoor area. It has a diverse, nexpensive, daytime food menu and hosts a traditional ession Sun lunch time. Mon–Wed 10.30am–11.30pm,

Thurs–Sat 10.30am–2am, Sun 12.30pm–1am.

Maggie May's Monck St ☎053 914 5776. This long, narrow bar, with leather banquettes and chandeliers, a huge, covered beer garden with an open log fire and a good range of beers and cocktails, comes to life during its frequent music sessions, which include traditional/ballads on Sun and Mon. Mon–Thurs 10.30am–11.30pm, Fri & Sat 10.30am–12.30am, Sun 12.30–11pm.

Simon's Place South Main St ☎053 918 0041. Smart update of a traditional pub, boasting simple, fresh decor in dark brown and cream, with polished wood floors, chairs and tables, and a great selection of half-a-dozen craft beers on draught, including O'Hara's excellent stout from Carlow. Breakfast and lunch served Mon–Sat. Mon–Thurs 9.30am–11.30pm, Fri & Sat 9.30am–12.30am, Sun 6–11pm.

The Sky and the Ground 112 South Main St ☎053 912 1273. This dark and woody bar, with a large beer garden at the back, is an atmospheric place for a pint and some good food, staging regular live music, including Candlelight Sessions on Tues, which feature everything from acoustic soloists to roots/Americana bands. Mon–Thurs 2–11.30pm, Fri & Sat 2pm–12.30am, Sun 12.30–11pm.

T. Morris Monck St ☎086 842 0498. Friendly, gnarly old bar, fitted with bare wooden floors, old grocers' drawers and signs to give a relaxed, sprawling, anything-goes air. It has one of Ireland's cutest beer gardens, decorated with fairy lights, bamboo and roses, and hosts traditional music Wed, plus Mon and Tues in summer. Mon–Thurs 4–11.30pm, Fri 4pm–12.30am, Sat noon–12.30am, Sun 3–11pm.

ENTERTAINMENT

Wexford Arts Centre Cornmarket ☎053 912 3764, ☊wexfordartscentre.ie. Music, theatre, dance, comedy nd art exhibitions are just some of the offerings that are aid on by the Wexford Arts Centre, which is located in the ighteenth-century market house.

Wexford Opera House High St ☎053 912 2144, ☊wexfordoperahouse.ie. Wexford Opera Festival's home, which has undergone an impressive €30 million rebuilding programme, hosts drama, dance, comedy and music throughout the year and now offers a panoramic rooftop café and weekly guided tours.

WEXFORD FESTIVALS

The biggest event in Wexford's cultural calendar is undoubtedly the prestigious **Wexford Opera Festival** (☊wexfordopera.com) over two weeks in late October, which draws not only performers and companies from around the world, but international audiences too, attracted by its distinctive programme of rarely performed works – tickets (booking opens in May or June) and accommodation need to be reserved months in advance. The main performances are supplemented by a variety of concerts and talks; by a broad-based **fringe festival** (☊wexfordfringe.ie), featuring art exhibitions, drama, comedy and more music; and by an old-fashioned fairground and two **spiegeltents** on the Quays, which host cabaret, comedy and contemporary music (☊wexfordspiegeltent.com). There's a **food festival** over three days in late May (☊wexfordfoodfestival.ie), while late June's **Maritime Festival** (☊wexfordmaritimefestival .ie) involves special events at the county's maritime sights such as the Dunbrody Famine Ship, as well as boat races, music and lots of kids' activities in the town.

5

Around Wexford town

To Wexford's north lies Ireland's premier wildfowl sanctuary, **Wexford Wildfowl Reserve**, beyond which the coastline is punctuated by some lovely sandy beaches: 10km from town, past Curracloe, lies the powder-soft, dune-backed **Ballinesker Beach**, which deputized for Omaha Beach as the site of the D-Day landings in Steven Spielberg's World War II epic *Saving Private Ryan*; and further up the coast near Kilmuckridge is another broad beach popular with families, **Morriscastle**, known as "the golden mile".

To the west of Wexford is the impressive **Irish National Heritage Park**, while to the south runs rather bland countryside, though the ornate gardens of **Johnstown Castle** and the **Irish Agricultural Museum** are well worth visiting. The small seaside resort of **Rosslare** has a splendid beach, much enjoyed by families in summer, while **Rosslare Europort** is a major point of entry into Ireland. A little further out of the county town orbit, energetic **Enniscorthy** is best known for its associations with the 1798 Rebellion, which is commemorated in an excellent museum.

Wexford Wildfowl Reserve

Daily 9am–5pm • Free • ☎ 076 100 2660, ⓦ www.wexfordwildfowlreserve.ie

On the north side of the Slaney estuary, the **Wexford Wildfowl Reserve** will provide fascination for twitchers and laypeople alike. It occupies a charming patch of reclaimed land, 2m below sea level, known as the North Slobs (from Irish *slab*, meaning "mud, mire or a soft-fleshed person"), a maze of channels, reed beds, grazing lands and tillage. Between early October and mid-April, this peculiarly rich habitat is home to thousands of ducks, geese and swans, while in spring and autumn large numbers of birds on migration stop to feed here. Of particular importance in the former category are the ten thousand or so Greenland white-fronted geese, about a third of the world's population, which winter on the reserve after nesting in Greenland, as well as the two thousand pale-bellied brent geese, which arrive in mid-December after breeding in Canada. Year-round inhabitants include 42 wader species, mute swans and a healthy population of Irish hares.

To get to the reserve, head 3km up the R741 Gorey road, then turn right for 2km. As well as various hides, you'll find the well-run **visitor centre**, which houses an observation tower and an engaging little exhibition. It's not possible to walk by yourself in the protected environs of the reserve, but if you fancy stretching your legs at this stage, you could make for the nearby **Raven Nature Reserve**, an expanse of dunes and pine forest that runs down to Raven Point at the mouth of the estuary. To get there, retrace your steps to the R741, head north for 500m, then turn right; the reserve is 8km from the turn-off, via the village of Curracloe.

Irish National Heritage Park

Daily: May–Aug 9.30am–6.30pm, last admission 5pm; Sept–April 9.30am–5.30pm, last admission 3pm • €9 • ☎ 053 912 0733, ⓦ inhp.com

Four kilometres west of Wexford off the N11 Dublin road at **FERRYCARRIG**, the carefully researched **Irish National Heritage Park** will plug the gaps in your imagination with sixteen full-scale reconstructions of the sites and buildings that configure Ireland's known history, right through from Mesolithic times. A tour around the park, either with a costumed guide or by yourself with an audio guide, takes you past, and sometimes into, all manner of dwellings and ritual sites, while the undoubted centrepiece is an impressive facsimile of a twelfth-century castle (built over the ruins of a castle of that era).

FROM TOP HIGH STREET, KILKENNY CITY (P.183); KITESURFING, DUNCANNON (P.199); NATIONAL 1798 CENTRE (P.197)

5

Irish Agricultural Museum

Museum April–June, Sept & Oct Mon–Fri 9am–5pm, Sat & Sun 11am–5pm; July & Aug Mon–Fri 9am–5.30pm, Sat & Sun 11am–5.30pm; Nov–March Mon–Fri 9am–4pm, Sat & Sun noon–4pm • April–Oct €8 (includes admission to gardens); Nov–March €6
Gardens Daily: April–June, Sept & Oct 9am–5pm; July & Aug 9am–7pm; Nov–March 9am–4.30pm • April–Oct €3; Nov–March free •
🌐 irishagrimuseum.ie • The Wexford Bus services to Kilmore Quay and to Rosslare from Redmond Square both pass within walking distance of the agricultural museum (🌐 wexfordbus.com).

It's well worth taking a trip 6km south from Wexford town to **Johnstown Castle**. This nineteenth-century Gothic Revival mansion is not open to the public, but its extensive grounds feature an abundance of trees and plants, outdoors and in hothouses, as well as ornamental lakes, rich woodland, a sunken Italian garden and a ruined medieval tower house. The estate's old farm buildings are now home to the **Irish Agricultural Museum**, which explores rural history via displays, artefacts, a wealth of furniture and machinery, and re-created workshops and kitchens. As well as a café, there's also a specific display on the Famine, recounting its impact, the search for a cure for potato blight, and the massive changes in rural Ireland that ensued.

Rosslare and Rosslare Europort

Some 11km southeast of Wexford town, with a train station on the Rosslare Europort line, is **ROSSLARE** (aka Rosslare Strand), a single-street village with a massive and popular sandy beach and a superb **place to stay**, _Kelly's_ (see below). A little further southeast along the coast, **ROSSLARE EUROPORT** (🌐 rosslareeuroport .irishrail.ie) is a major ferry terminal surrounded by hotels and B&Bs, serving arrivals from Wales, France and Spain. Should you arrive by car, there's no reason to linger, and if you come on foot there are train and bus connections to various parts of Ireland.

ARRIVAL AND DEPARTURE   ROSSLARE AND ROSSLARE EUROPORT

By ferry The terminal hosts a bureau de change, a Budget car-rental outlet (☎ 053 913 3318, 🌐 www.budgetcarrental .ie) and offices of the ferry companies (see p.28): Irish Ferries (for Pembroke; ☎ 1890 313131) and Stena Line (for Fishguard; ☎ 053 916 1560).

By train There are stations both at the Europort and in Rosslare village.

Destinations Rosslare Europort to: Dublin (3–4 daily; 3hr); Enniscorthy (3–4 daily; 50min); Rosslare (3–4 daily; 5min);

Wexford (3–4 daily; 25min).
By bus Buses stop at the port and the village.
Destinations Rosslare Europort to: Dublin (Mon–Sat daily; 3hr 25min); Enniscorthy (Mon–Sat 1 daily; 1hr); New Ross (5–6 daily; 1hr); Waterford (5–6 daily; 1hr 25min); Wexford (5–7 daily; 30min).
Rosslare to: Rosslare Europort (5–6 daily; 5min); Waterford (5–6 daily; 1hr 20min); Wexford (Bus Éireann 5–6 daily; Wexford Bus 2–3 Mon–Sat; 20–40min).

ACCOMMODATION AND EATING

Hotel Rosslare ☎ 053 913 3110, 🌐 hotelrosslare.ie. Surveying the harbour from a cliff-top position, this hotel provides tastefully furnished, spacious rooms in an unobtrusive contemporary style, some with balconies with great views. Good deals on family rooms. **€79**

★ **Kelly's Resort** ☎ 053 913 2114, 🌐 kellys.ie. Nothing less than a national treasure, family-run _Kelly's_ sits in lovely Mediterranean gardens right by the 8km strand and continues to offer the highest standards of Irish service,

both attentive and relaxing. It offers an ESPA-designed spa with thermal, seawater and seaweed treatments, as well as a host of activities for adults and kids. Its walls – including those in its two excellent restaurants – are adorned with one of the finest private collections of modern Irish art. Both restaurants, the more formal and classical _Beaches_ and the more relaxed and innovative _La Marine Bistro and Bar_, use the finest of local produce. All manner of packages available. March–Nov. **€198**

Enniscorthy

Around 24km north of Wexford, the attractive old town of **ENNISCORTHY** straddles the River Slaney, its main streets, such as Castle Hill, rising steeply from the west bank towards Market Square.

ENNISCORTHY FESTIVALS

Dancing in the streets is the order of the day during the **Street Rhythms Festival** (ⓦenniscorthystreetfest.com) in June, while the **Strawberry Festival** (ⓦstrawberryfest.ie), over ten days at the end of June, includes lots of entertainments, a three-day literary festival and punnet-loads of Wexford's famous strawberries – which you'll see for sale at roadside stalls in and around the county at this time of year.

National 1798 Centre

arnell Rd (10min walk from Market Square, heading down Rafter St) • April–Sept Mon–Fri 9.30am–5pm, Sat & Sun noon–5pm; ct–March Mon–Fri 10am–4pm, Sat & Sun noon–5pm; last admission 1hr before closing • €7, €10 joint ticket with Enniscorthy Castle • ⓦ 1798centre.ie

he **National 1798 Centre** is a high-tech sound-and-vision fest, capturing the xcitement of events prior to the Rebellion, the rising itself and its aftermath, all ogently set within broader intellectual and political contexts that brought about American independence and the French Revolution. There's a marvellous display on he conflict between revolution and counter-revolution set out on a giant chessboard. Another highlight is an audiovisual featuring an enthralling debate between actors laying the roles of the Dublin-born Whig politician and philosopher Edmund Burke and Thomas Paine, the English radical and American revolutionary whose *Rights of Man* (1792) was a direct riposte to Burke's more conservative *Reflections on he Revolution in France* (1790). It was on the gorse-covered **Vinegar Hill**, opposite on he Slaney's eastern bank, that the rebels of 1798 met their demise at the hands of British forces.

Enniscorthy Castle

astle Hill • April–Sept Mon–Fri 9.30am–5pm, Sat & Sun noon–5pm; Oct–March Mon–Fri 10am–4pm, Sat & Sun noon–5pm • €4, €10 int ticket with 1798 Centre • ⓦ enniscorthycastle.ie

hough it's a proper castle in the heart of town, with turrets, round towers and renellations in the traditional style of Norman stone fortresses, **Enniscorthy Castle** as spent most of its 800-year existence as a private residence. Now completely enovated, it numbers among its exhibitions a first floor that's been re-created as it night have been when it was last inhabited, in the early twentieth century. Other ngaging and thoughtful displays cover the 1916 Easter Rising and pioneering modernist furniture designer, Eileen Gray, who was born at nearby Brownswood House. Staff will escort you to the crenellated roof for fantastic views of the town, he river, Vinegar Hill with its ruined windmill and, to the west, the Blackstairs Mountains.

St Aidan's Cathedral

ust west of Market Square along Main Street, **St Aidan's Cathedral** is an imposing Gothic Revival edifice, designed in the mid-nineteenth century by Augustus Pugin, whose other works include Killarney's cathedral and the interior of the Palace of Westminster. As well as impressively high pointed arches, the cathedral features an oak arved pulpit and beautiful stained-glass windows depicting saints and bishops.

ARRIVAL AND INFORMATION   ENNISCORTHY

y train The train station is on the east side of the river, st off Templeshannon, which leads north from niscorthy Bridge.

estinations Dublin (3–4 daily; 2hr 15min); Rosslare uroport (3–4 daily; 50min); Wexford (3–4 daily; 25min).

y bus Buses set down outside the Bus Stop Shop on the annon Quay on the eastern bank of the Slaney.

Destinations Dublin (roughly hourly; 2hr 25min); New Ross (4 daily; 40min); Rosslare Europort (Mon–Sat 1 daily; 1hr); Waterford (4 daily; 1hr 10min); Wexford (roughly hourly; 20min).

Tourist office Enniscorthy Castle is the official information point (☏ 053 923 4699).

5

ACCOMMODATION

Riverside Park ☎ 053 923 7800, ⚲ riversideparkhotel
.com. Top-notch hotel on the Promenade near the 1798 Centre,
with modern, attractive rooms, many of which overlook the
river, and its own indoor pool, gym and sauna. **€79**

Salville House ☎ 053 923 5252, ⚲ salvillehouse.com.
To the southeast of town, about 3km away off the N11

Wexford road, this attractive, creeper-clad, 1850s country
house in traditional style (no TVs in the bedrooms, lawn
tennis) enjoys fine views of the Slaney valley from its
hilltop perch; breakfasts and dinners (bring your own wine)
are excellent. Good rates for singles; self-catering also
available. **€100**

EATING AND DRINKING

Enniscorthy hosts a lively **farmers' market** every Sat morning on Abbey Square.

The Antique Tavern Slaney St, down towards the
quays from Market Square ☎ 053 923 3428. Great spot
for an atmospheric pint, a half-timbered, eighteenth-
century pub with a wealth of local photos and memorabilia
on its walls and a covered upstairs balcony for absorbing
views of the river and Vinegar Hill. Roughly Mon–Thurs
5–11.30pm, Fri & Sat 5pm–12.30am, Sun 5–11pm.

The Bailey On the quays near *Cottontree Café* ☎ 053
923 0353, ⚲ thebailey.ie. Converted into a café-bar from
a nineteenth-century malt warehouse and decorated in
plush Victorian style, *The Bailey* offers good food and
regular live gigs. Mon–Thurs 10.30am–11.30pm, Fri &
Sat 10.30am–12.30am, Sun 12.30–11pm.

Cottontree Café Slaney Place, on the west bank
opposite the old bridge ☎ 053 923 4641. Quirky café
with plenty of floral elements in its design, offering tasty
minestrone, gourmet sandwiches and mains such as goat's
cheese and tomato salad (€9). Mon–Sat 8.30am–5pm,
Sunday 11am–5pm.

Via Veneto 58 Weafer St ☎ 053 923 6921,
⚲ viaveneto.ie. A cosy, white-tablecloth restaurant
offering authentic Italian main courses, including plenty
of fresh fish, and much cheaper pizzas and pastas.
Three-course set menu €24.50, two-course early bird
(before 7pm, not Sat or Sun) €18.50. Mon & Wed–Sat
5.30–10pm, Sun 5–10pm.

Hook Peninsula and the Barrow estuary

The sightseeing highlight of Wexford's southwestern corner is the atmospheric ruin of
Tintern Abbey, at the neck of the blustery **Hook Peninsula**, which is punctuated with
sandy beaches and a fascinating medieval lighthouse. Circumnavigating Hook Head
brings you to the pleasant little resort of **Duncannon** and nearby **Ballyhack**, whence car
ferries cross the Barrow estuary to Passage East in County Waterford. This ferry service
is 20km south of the first road crossing of the Barrow, at the busy town of **New Ross**,
and is certainly worth taking if you're short of time, but that way you'd miss out on a
tight cluster of attractions on the east bank of the river, notably the glorious remains of
Dunbrody Abbey, the **John F. Kennedy Arboretum**, and the charming **Ros Tapestry** and
vivid **Dunbrody Famine Ship** at New Ross.

Tintern Abbey

Abbey Mid-May to late Sept daily 10am–5pm • €3; Heritage Card • ⚲ heritageireland.ie **Walled garden** Daily: May–Sept 10am–6pm;
Oct–April 10am–4pm • €3 • ⚲ www.colcloughwalledgarden.com

On the broad neck of the Hook Peninsula, 30km southwest of Wexford town off the
R374, lies the dramatic ruin of **Tintern Abbey**. This early thirteenth-century Cistercian
foundation was constructed by William Marshall, Earl of Pembroke, to give thanks for
being saved from drowning at sea, and was populated by monks from its better-known
namesake in Monmouthshire, Wales. After dissolution in 1536, the abbey was granted
to one of Henry VIII's officers, Anthony Colclough, who much modified the building
while subsequent additions, including the battlemented walls, were made by his
descendants, who lived here until the 1960s. Of the original cruciform church, the
tower, chancel, cloister walls and south transept chapels are extant. Beyond the abbey,
verdant woodland trails lead to the recently restored **Colclough Walled Garden**, which is
traversed by a stream crossed by five small bridges.

5

ACROSS THE ESTUARY TO WATERFORD: BALLYHACK

If you're heading for County Waterford, then the Passage East Car Ferry (☎051 382480, ⓦpassageferry.ie) from **Ballyhack**, 1km northwest of Arthurstown, is a boon, saving time and mileage with a five-minute crossing. Ferries operate a continuous service (April–Sept Mon–Sat 7am–10pm, Sun 9.30am–10pm; Oct–March Mon–Sat 7am–8pm, Sun 9.30am–8pm; car €8 single, €12 return; cyclist €2 single, €3 return). While waiting for the ferry, you might be tempted by a visit to **Ballyhack Castle**, a fifteenth-century tower house in the village built by the Knights Hospitallers of St John (June–Aug Mon–Wed, Sat & Sun 10.30am–5pm; free; ⓦheritageireland.ie).

Hook Head

Hook Head itself is entirely exposed to the elements, serene in good weather – though very dangerous for swimming – and excitingly wild in a storm. The rocky shoreline has a wealth of fossils and it's a popular location for birdwatchers, who visit to spot migrations, as well as whale- and dolphin-watchers.

Hook Lighthouse

Visitor centre Daily 9.30am–5/6pm; obligatory guided tours June–Aug every 30min, 10am–5.30pm; Sept–May hourly, 11am–5pm • €6 • ⓦ hookheritage.ie

The oldest operational lighthouse in the world, **Hook Lighthouse** was built by William Marshall (see opposite) in the early thirteenth century to guide ships safely into the Barrow estuary on their way to his thriving port of New Ross, replacing an earlier beacon. Apart from a short period during the 1600s, it has functioned ever since and became fully automated in 1996. Guided tours lead to the lighthouse's top, some 36m high, and recount its history, paying note to the monks who were the first light-keepers here; there's also a café and bakery. Check out their events roster on the website.

Duncannon and around

DUNCANNON is a small, friendly village with a lovely beach protected from the elements by a rocky coastline at its southern extremity. On the beach, you can take **kitesurfing** and **stand-up paddleboarding lessons** (☎087 675 5567, ⓦwww.hookedkitesurfing.ie), and in August there's a three-day **International Sand-Sculpting Festival**, in which a host of competitors produce astonishing, but sadly temporary, artworks, followed by a two-day **kitesurfing festival**.

Duncannon Fort

May–Sept daily 10am–5.30pm; Oct–April Mon–Fri 10am–4.30pm; optional guided tours on the hour, but worth checking on ☎051 389454 • €5 • ⓦ duncannonfort.com

Looming above the village from its lofty promontory is **Duncannon Fort**, constructed in 1586, on the site of a Celtic fort and a Norman castle, as a bulwark against Spanish invasion. Much remodelled since then, the fort was burnt down by the IRA in 1922. Though Ireland was officially neutral during World War II, the fort was rebuilt on its outbreak, becoming a base for the Irish Army until 1986. As well as art and crafts galleries and studios, and a café, the complex includes a small maritime museum, a dry moat with 10m-high walls, ramparts with great views of the Barrow estuary and down to Hook Head and, in a surviving older building, a fetid dungeon where the Croppy Boy, the subject of a well-known song of the 1798 Rebellion, was allegedly incarcerated.

ARRIVAL AND INFORMATION   DUNCANNON AND AROUND

By bus Destinations New Ross (Mon–Sat 3 daily; 35min); Waterford (Mon–Sat 3 daily; 1hr).

Tourist office Hook Tourism's office is by the post office (Mon–Fri 9.30am–5.30pm, plus May–Aug Sat 10am–2pm; ☎051 389530, ⓦ hooktourism.com).

5

ACCOMMODATION AND EATING

Dunbrody House Just before Arthurstown, 3km north of Duncannon ☎ 051 389600, ⓦ dunbrodyhouse.com. Sumptuous, traditional country-house accommodation in an 1830s mansion set in glorious parklands. As well as a luxurious spa, the hotel houses one of Ireland's foremost cookery schools so it's unsurprising that the restaurant here is exceedingly good; a simpler, cheaper menu is offered in the seafood bar afternoons and evenings, and there's a pub offering live music at weekends, and pizzas. Good-value half-board packages. **€198**

Glendine House On the east side of Arthurstown, 3km north of Duncannon ☎ 051 389500, ⓦ glendinehouse .com. With fine views of the estuary, this welcoming late Georgian country house in expansive grounds offers luxurious, upmarket B&B. Good rates for singles; self-catering also available. **€98**

The Moorings B&B By the fort and beach i Duncannon ☎ 087 992 9138, ⓦ mooringsbnbwexfor .com. Bright, modern, pine-floored and furnished hous with comfortable, well-kept en-suite rooms and a attractive garden. Very good rates for singles. Continent breakfast included. **€50**

★ **Roche's** By the beach in Duncannon ☎ 051 38918 ⓦ sqiglrestaurant.com. *Roche's* features a cosy, old fashioned front bar – home to traditional sessions on F – and larger spaces beyond, including a beer garden. Ba food includes their famous chowder and season Wexford strawberries, while the converted barn ne door houses *Sqigl*, their creative modern restaurant. Ba Mon–Thurs 11am–11.30pm, Fri & Sa 11am–12.30am, Sun 12.30–11pm; restauran summer Tues–Sat 6.30–9pm.

Dunbrody Abbey

Mid-May to mid-Sept daily 11am–6pm • Abbey €3; maze €6 (includes fee for pitch and putt course) • ⓦ dunbrodyabbey.com

A few kilometres up the R733 from Arthurstown lies ruined **Dunbrody Abbey**, a Cistercian monastery founded in 1170 by Hervé de Montmorency, on the instructions of his nephew, the Anglo-Norman invader, Strongbow. Overlooking th Barrow estuary, its magnificent remains centre on a 60m-long early Gothic church, whose most notable features are the elegant west doorway and east window. Following Dissolution, the abbey passed into the hands of the Etchingham family whose descendants added the tower and nearby buildings and own the land to this day. On site there's also a tea room, pitch and putt course, and a full-sized maze, which utilizes 1500 yew trees.

John F. Kennedy Arboretum and Kennedy Homestead

Arboretum Daily: April & Sept 10am–6.30pm; May–Aug 10am–8pm; Oct–March 10am–5pm; last admission 45min before closing • €3; Heritage Card • ⓦ heritageireland.ie **Homestead** Daily: April–Sept 9.30am–5.30pm; Oct–March 10am–5pm • €7.50 • ⓦ kennedyhomestead.ie

A few kilometres north of Dunbrody Abbey, on the east side of the R733, the horticultural connection continues at the **John F. Kennedy Arboretum**, funded by Irish-Americans in memory of the former US president, who returned to visit his ancestors' homeland in 1963. The arboretum houses an astonishing assortment of mo than 4500 trees and shrubs from the world's temperate regions, as well as a summertime tea room (May–Sept). Its grounds sweep upwards along the slopes of Slieve Coillte, whose 270m summit provides panoramic views of the surrounding countryside. JFK's great-grandfather, Patrick, was born a little to the northwest in Dunganstown, where the **Kennedy Homestead** describes his emigration to the US, fleeing the Famine in 1848, and traces the family's subsequent history.

New Ross

NEW ROSS squats beside the River Barrow, its quayside marred by poor redevelopment and heavy traffic, but there's still life in the old place, especially in the lanes behind the frontage. The river provided access to the upstream countryside of Wexford and Kilkenny, and the town's importance beyond being a local embarkation point is emphasized by the quayside presence of the **Dunbrody Famine Ship**. The **JFK Dunbrody**

Festival (@jfkdunbrodyfestival.org) takes place over three days towards the end of July and features a variety of musical and other events, as well as markets and street theatre.

Dunbrody Famine Ship

Daily: April–Sept 9am–6pm; Oct–March 9am–5pm • €8.50; Heritage Island • @ dunbrody.com

The **Dunbrody Famine Ship** tries to convey what life must have been like on a nineteenth-century "coffin ship". It's a faithful reconstruction, fully seaworthy, of the kind of three-masted barque that carried Irish emigrants to North America from ports such as New Ross, usually in appalling conditions – with death rates among the passengers commonly reaching twenty percent. Guided tours, complete with costumed actors playing passengers, take you around the ship. In the visitor centre, which houses a café, you can access a database of emigrants to the US between 1846 and 1851, the main Famine years when over a million people left Ireland.

Ros Tapestry

Mon–Sat 10am–5pm, plus Easter–Oct Sun 10am–5pm • €6; Heritage Island • @ rostapestry.com

Across the road from the Famine ship, it's well worth visiting the enchanting **Ros Tapestry**, a hugely ambitious and fruitful community project. Depicting scenes from the Norman history of New Ross and the locality, such as the founding of Tintern Abbey (see p.198), in 2m-wide panels, the tapestry has been hand-stitched by a hundred volunteers in various towns around Wexford and Kilkenny since 1999; there's a demonstration panel in the reception area that's often being worked on. Engaging guided tours show off the completed panels in their impressive exhibition area, explaining not only the historical detail but also the variety of pictorial styles in the vividly colourful work, which employs around four hundred shades of two-ply wool.

ARRIVAL AND INFORMATION

NEW ROSS

By bus Buses stop on the quayside.
Destinations Bus Éireann: Dublin (4 daily; 3hr 10min); Enniscorthy (4 daily; 30min); Kilkenny (1 Thurs; 1hr 15min); Rosslare Europort (5–6 daily; 1hr); Waterford (9–10 daily; 20–40min); Wexford (5–8 daily; 40min).

Kilbride (@ kilbridecoaches.com): Kilkenny (Mon–Sat 2 daily; 1hr).
Tourist office At the Dunbrody Famine Ship (same hours; @ 051 425239).

ACCOMMODATION AND EATING

New Ross hosts a **farmers' market** every Sat morning on The Quay.

Café Nutshell 8 South St @ 051 422777. Your best bet for eating out, parallel to and one block east of the quayside, an excellent daytime café and health-food deli serving everything from juices and smoothies to sandwiches around €7, meat, seafood and cheese platters, and daily-special hot dishes. Mon–Sat 9am–6pm.
The Galley North Quay @ 051 421723, @ rivercruises ie. If you fancy lunch, afternoon tea or dinner on the water, then book a table on *The Galley*, which plies between New

Ross and Inistioge on the Nore, up the Barrow towards St Mullins or down to Waterford, all dependent on the tide and numbers. April–Sept/Oct.
MacMurrough Farm Cottages @ 051 421383, @ macmurrough.com. On the northeast side of town, 3km or so out, this welcoming working farm rents out lovely, comfortable, well-equipped cottages with central heating and stoves, one with a piano, at very good rates by the night or week. **€50**

Waterford and Tipperary

CAHIR CASTLE AND THE RIVER SUIR

Waterford and Tipperary

The attractions of County Waterford (Port Láirge, or the Déise) are concentrated in its namesake city. Home to almost half the county's population, including a sizeable mob of students, Waterford City supports a lively nightlife and festival scene, and three fine museums displaying the Waterford Treasures. The county's coastline takes in several sandy beaches, not least at Dunmore East, as well as the blossoming harbour town of Dungarvan and the "holy city" of Ardmore, containing enthralling relics associated with St Declan. Waterford's northern fringe is dominated by the lonesome and boggy Comeragh and Knockmealdown mountains, the latter running down to the ancient ecclesiastical centre of Lismore, in the heart of the gorgeous Blackwater valley.

If you're driving or cycling between Waterford and Wexford, note that the most southerly road crossing of the River Barrow is up at New Ross, so it's worth considering the **ferry** between **Passage East**, 12km east of Waterford city, and Ballyhack (see p.199).

In contrast to squat, coastal Waterford, **Tipperary** (Tiobraid Árann) is the wealthiest of Ireland's inland counties, deriving its prosperity from the flat and fertile plain known as the **Golden Vale**, which provides rich pickings for dairy farmers and horse-breeders. It's also one of the largest counties, stretching over 100km from top to toe. Most of Tipp's attractions lie in its southern reaches, including the historic towns of **Carrick-on-Suir**, home to one of Ireland's most graceful mansions, and **Cahir**, with its imposing thirteenth-century castle and ornamental nineteenth-century baronial villa. But by far the county's most breathtaking lure is the **Rock of Cashel**, a magnificent isolated outcrop rising from the Golden Vale and crowned by impressive Christian buildings spanning various periods. This southern part of the county is traversed by the **Tipperary Heritage Way**, an easy 56km waymarked trail that runs down the Suir valley from Cashel to Cahir and Ardfinnan, finishing at The Vee, in the Knockmealdown Mountains near the Waterford border.

Waterford city

In many ways **WATERFORD** is Ireland's least discovered city, often bypassed by tourists heading from Rosslare for the more hyped destinations of Cork and Kerry further west. Even the hardiest defender of this dockland city's reputation would be hard-pressed to mount a campaign centred upon Waterford's immediate allures. Though neat wooded hillsides figure north of Rice Bridge, the vista mainly encompasses ugly industrial development, with cranes and a refinery dominating the skyline and the unappealing quays of the River Suir offering barely a hint of the vibrant city lying behind.

But Waterford is one of those places where scraping the surface reveals numerous delights. Behind those ugly quays lies a complex of narrow lanes, first formed in

Waterford festivals p.211   The rise of the Rock p.223

DUNGARVAN

Highlights

❶ **Waterford Treasures** A city's history brought evocatively to life in three museums of locally found discoveries from Viking and later times. **See p.206**

❷ **Dungarvan** Clustered around its broad bay, this attractive town has plenty to enthral, including some great places to eat. **See p.212**

❸ **Ardmore** A delightful village with potent reminders of Ireland's monastic past, as well as a grand beach and exhilarating cliff-top walks. **See p.213**

❹ **Cahir Castle** One of the country's best-preserved Anglo-Norman strongholds. **See p.218**

❺ **The Rock of Cashel** Stunning medieval religious site, set high above the surrounding countryside. **See p.220**

❻ **The Glen of Aherlow** River valley in a beautiful setting, dwarfed by the adjacent Galty Mountains. **See p.221**

HIGHLIGHTS ARE MARKED ON THE MAP ON P.206

medieval times, and many grand examples of Georgian town planning in the shape of sturdy town houses and elegant municipal and ecclesiastical buildings.

Waterford Treasures, the city corporation's historical collections dating right back to the Viking period, have recently been split across three museums: Reginald's Tower, the Medieval Museum and the Bishop's Palace. This has diluted their impact, though each of the sites has considerable architectural interest in its own right. Along with the **Waterford Crystal** shop and factory, the three museums form the core of what's been branded, somewhat strangely, the "Viking Triangle", a wedge between The Mall and the quays that shelters some other fine buildings, including **Christ Church Cathedral**, in a complex of tiny, sometimes tortuous, lanes. To the west of here, opposite the clock tower, Barronstrand Street leads south from the quays to the main shopping streets, passing **Holy Trinity Cathedral**, and thence, via a couple of name changes, to John Street, whose bars, pubs and clubs form the nightlife focus.

Brief history

Waterford's origins are integrally linked to the River Suir. The **Vikings** built a settlement here in the early tenth century to provide shelter for their longboats and to exploit the trading opportunities offered by the river, which along with the Barrow and the Nore provided easy access to the southeast's fertile farmland. The Viking settlement prospered and controlled much of this part of Ireland, exacting a tribute from the Celt called Airgead Sróine (Nose Money) since the punishment for welshers was to have their noses cut off.

Later, the course of both local and national history was much impacted by Strongbow's assault on the city in 1170, caused by **Dermot MacMurrough**'s attempts to gain sway over Ireland (see p.583). The success of the Anglo-Norman earl's bloody offensive not only led to his marriage to MacMurrough's daughter but brought his liege lord, **Henry II**, scurrying to Ireland the following year to assume control of the country's conquest. Henry granted a charter providing royal

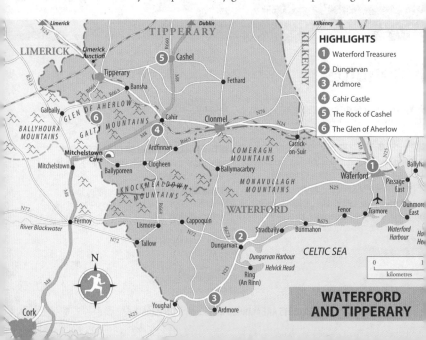

HIGHLIGHTS

1. Waterford Treasures
2. Dungarvan
3. Ardmore
4. Cahir Castle
5. The Rock of Cashel
6. The Glen of Aherlow

WATERFORD AND TIPPERARY

protection to the city, and his descendant, King John, increased its size by adding new walls and towers.

Though much affected by the Black Death and frequent incursions by both Irish and Anglo-Norman neighbours, Waterford continued to flourish as a **port**, reliant on trade in wool, hides and wine. Cromwell was repelled in 1649, but a year later Ireton's troops took control and expelled many of the Catholic merchants. Protestant domination of the city's trade was reinforced by William of Orange's accession. The eighteenth century witnessed major architectural developments, mostly designed by locally born John Roberts. Shipbuilding prospered during the nineteenth century, the city becoming second only to Belfast in terms of tonnage constructed, and many Waterford-built vessels transported the city's famous **crystal**, first manufactured here in 1783. However, Waterford suffered economically during the second half of the twentieth century and the beginning of this century, witnessing factory closures and the virtual end of shipbuilding here.

Reginald's Tower

Jan to mid-March Wed–Sun 9.30am–5pm; mid-March to Dec daily 9.30am–5.30pm • €3; Heritage Card • Ⓦ heritageireland.ie

Waterford's city walls were once punctuated by seventeen towers, of which six still survive. By far the most impressive of these is **Reginald's Tower**, which stands at the corner of The Mall and the quays on the site of a Viking wooden tower and was possibly named after Ragnall, the founder of the city in 914. Dating from the early thirteenth century, this circular, three-storey tower has 3m-thick walls. For a time it was a mint (the display on coinage here includes a tiny part of an Iraqi silver coin from 742 bearing a quotation from the Koran, "There is no god but Allah"), later becoming an arsenal before being used as a jail from around 1819. The tower now displays some of Waterford Treasures' Viking collection, including a meticulously carved bird-bone flute, a gaming board and a famously beautiful kite brooch.

Medieval Museum

June–Aug Mon–Fri 9.15am–6pm, Sat 9.30–6pm, Sun 11am–6pm; Sept–May closes 5pm • €7, or €10 with the Bishop's Palace; Heritage Island • Ⓦ waterfordtreasures.com

The second of the Waterford Treasures museums covers the medieval period, with impressive exhibits such as the Great Charter Roll of 1373, which includes a colourful image of the walled town of Waterford, and the Edward IV sword, a mighty piece of silver weaponry presented to the Mayor of Waterford in 1462. Wedged between the Christ Church Cathedral and the Theatre Royal, its lovely curving façade of honey-coloured limestone is thoroughly modern, but it cleverly incorporates two medieval structures: the Choristers' Hall, the lower chamber of the cathedral deanery dating from the 1270s; and the fifteenth-century Mayor's Wine Vault, given to the cathedral by James Rice, whose graphic tomb can still be seen in the church (see p.208).

The Bishop's Palace

June–Aug Mon–Fri 9.15am–6pm, Sat 9.30am–6pm, Sun 11am–6pm; Sept–May closes 5pm • €7, or €10 with the Medieval Museum; Heritage Island • Ⓦ waterfordtreasures.com

Next door to the Medieval Museum, it's hard to miss the **Bishop's Palace**, faced with forbidding, dark-grey Leinster limestone and fronted by the outdoor tables of its popular café. It was designed in the Palladian style in 1743 by Richard Castle, but completed after his death in 1750 by "Honest" **John Roberts**, designer of many of the city's finest Georgian buildings. The ground and first floors have been

6

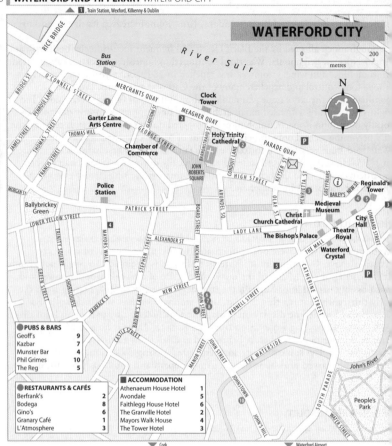

WATERFORD CITY

Train Station, Wexford, Kilkenny & Dublin

River Suir

Bus Station

Clock Tower

Garter Lane Arts Centre

Holy Trinity Cathedral

Chamber of Commerce

Police Station

Ballybrickey Green

Reginald's Tower

Medieval Museum

Christ Church Cathedral

The Bishop's Palace

City Hall

Theatre Royal

Waterford Crystal

John's River

People's Park

● PUBS & BARS	
Geoff's	9
Kazbar	7
Munster Bar	4
Phil Grimes	10
The Reg	5

● RESTAURANTS & CAFÉS	
Berfrank's	2
Bodega	8
Gino's	6
Granary Café	1
L'Atmosphere	3

■ ACCOMMODATION	
Athenaeum House Hotel	1
Avondale	5
Faithlegg House Hotel	6
The Granville Hotel	2
Mayors Walk House	4
The Tower Hotel	3

Cork

Waterford Airport

refurnished in Georgian style, though the exhibits here are perhaps less compelling than in the other two Waterford Treasures museums. The highlights are three Rococo gilt mirrors carved in Dublin in the eighteenth century with lively Chinese dragons, and the oldest surviving piece of Waterford crystal, a wide-lipped 1789 decanter.

Christ Church Cathedral

Mon–Fri noon–3pm, with extended hours and guided tours in summer • Donation requested • ⓦ christchurchwaterford.com

After completing the Bishop's Palace, John Roberts designed the adjacent Church of Ireland **Christ Church Cathedral**, which took almost a quarter of a century to complete once work began in 1773. This stately Neoclassical edifice, which sometimes hosts classical-music concerts, stands on the site of an eleventh-century Viking church, utilizing the base of the previous building. It features an ornate stuccowork ceiling and a fine "Arts and Crafts" window, added in the 1930s, by the stained-glass artist A.E. Child, as well as the somewhat grisly tomb of James Rice, a fifteenth-century mayor of Waterford, which graphically depicts his decaying corpse fed upon by worms and a toad. Just up from here on The Mall is another Roberts design, the squat **City Hall**.

Waterford Crystal

March Mon–Sat 9am–3.15pm, Sun 9.30am–3.15pm; April–Oct Mon–Sat 9am–4.15pm, Sun 9.30am–4.15pm; Nov–Feb Mon–Fri 9.30am–3.15pm • €13; Heritage Island • ⓦ waterfordvisitorcentre.com

Waterford Crystal was founded in 1783 but moved into this gleaming new shop and factory on The Mall in 2010. Tours of the factory, which now produces 45,000 pieces a year, will show you the making of the beech and pearwood moulds that only last a week, and crystal being cut with diamond-tipped wheels. However, the highlight has to be the heat and noise of the blowing room with its 1300°c furnace, where the red-hot molten crystal is shaped with supreme skill.

Holy Trinity Cathedral

John Roberts was the architect of the many-windowed **Chamber of Commerce** on George Street, but his prime ecclesiastical design is the Catholic **Holy Trinity Cathedral** (free) on Barronstrand Street. This dates from 1793, but was much revised in the following century, resulting in today's flamboyant building. Its heavily ornate interior features a Baroque oak pulpit dwarfed by a soaring baldachin, all set beneath an impressively high-vaulted ceiling and ten Waterford crystal chandeliers.

ARRIVAL AND DEPARTURE

WATERFORD CITY

By train Plunkett Train Station is just north of the river on Dock Rd.
Destinations Dublin (4–7 daily; 2hr–2hr 15min); Kilkenny (4–6 daily; 40min).

By bus Bus Éireann services use the bus station on Merchants Quay on the south bank, while J.J Kavanagh's (ⓦ jjkavanagh .ie) terminate by the Bank of Ireland on Parnell St.
Destinations Bus Éireann: Bansha (8 daily; 1hr 35min); Cahir (8 daily; 1hr 20min); Carrick-on-Suir (8–12 daily; 30min); Cork (hourly; 2hr 15min); Dublin & Airport (8–13 daily; 3hr–3hr 30min); Kilkenny (3–5 daily; 1hr); Killarney (hourly; 4hr

10min); Limerick (8 daily; 2hr 30min); New Ross (9–10 daily; 20–40min); Rosslare Europort (5–6 daily; 1hr 25min); Tralee (hourly; 4hr 45min); Wexford (5–8 daily; 1hr); Youghal (hourly; 1hr 25min).
J.J. Kavanagh's: Dublin & Airport (7 daily; 3–4hr).

By plane Flights from Birmingham and Manchester (ⓦ flybe.com) arrive at the airport (ⓦ flywaterford .com) in Killowen, 10km south of the city centre, which is not served by public transport; a taxi costs around €25, while car rental is available through Hertz (ⓦ hertz.ie).

INFORMATION AND TOURS

Tourist office 120 Parade Quay (July & Aug Mon–Sat 9am–6pm, plus some Sun 10am–4pm; gradually decreasing to 5 days/week in Jan & Feb, depending on staffing levels and budgets; ☎ 051 875823). Ask here about the city pass, which gives admission to the three Waterford Treasures museums and Waterford Crystal for €20.

Walking tours An entertaining and informative 1hr tour of the city convenes at the tourist office (daily 11.45am & 1.45pm; €7; ☎ 051 873711, ⓦ jackswalkingtours.com).
Cycling tours Tours of the city (2hr) are bookable at the Bishop's Palace (Sat 11am & 2pm, plus June Mon–Fri 7pm, July & Aug Mon–Fri 11am & 7pm; €15; ☎ 051 304500, ⓦ waterfordcyclingtours.ie).

ACCOMMODATION

Athenaeum House Hotel Christendom ☎ 051 833999, ⓦ athenaeumhousehotel.com. Set in parkland on the north bank of the Suir, 1.5km east of Rice Bridge, this spacious hotel offers richly coloured, contemporary bedrooms in a Georgian mansion with modern accoutrements such as CD players and wi-fi. Good-value room-only and half-board offers on their website. €81
Avondale 2 Parnell St ☎ 051 852267, ⓦ staywithus .net. Spruce accommodation in a sympathetically converted Georgian building, centrally located on the busy

continuation of The Mall and very handy for the main sights. Breakfast not included. €60
Faithlegg House Hotel 10km southeast of the centre, towards the mouth of the River Suir ☎ 051 382000, ⓦ faithlegg.com. Though it extends to a large modern annexe, this hotel has at its core an attractive late eighteenth-century mansion, where its best rooms come in traditional country-house style, with lofty ceilings, four-posters and huge sash windows. There's also a good restaurant, a spa, a large swimming pool with kids' pool, and a prominent golf course. €120

6

6

The Granville Hotel Meagher Quay ☎051 305555, ⓦgranville-hotel.ie. This smart riverfront establishment has housed many a famous guest over the years; Daniel O'Connell and Charles Parnell both stayed here. Thoughtfully designed throughout, with large, comfortable and well-equipped rooms and good service. €109

Mayors Walk House 12 Mayors Walk ☎051 855427, ⓦmayorswalk.com. A neatly kept nineteenth-century town house with high ceilings and a garden offering four bedrooms with washbasins, sharing two bathrooms. €50

The Tower Hotel The Mall ☎051 862300, ⓦtowerhotelwaterford.com. Big and block-like, a prominent landmark near the river, this well-equipped, 130-room hotel has generously proportioned bedrooms, a gym and a good-sized pool. Good single rates. €115

EATING AND DRINKING

Several of Waterford's cafés and **restaurants** have closed down in the last few years, but some of the **bars** serve good meals. As well as some characterful pubs, there's a clutch of lively DJ bars and clubs around the junction of Parnell and John streets; however, the city is not generally a good place to catch traditional music. Ask at the tourist office if Waterford's most characterful pub, 300-year-old Doolan's, has reopened yet.

RESTAURANTS, CAFÉS AND BISTROS

Berfrank's 86 The Quay ☎051 306032. Superior central café with outdoor tables on the quay, which rustles up zingy bruschettas with Knockdrina goat's cheese, pesto and sun-dried tomato (€9), as well as tasty apple and berry crumble. Mon–Fri 9am–5pm, Sat 10am–5pm.

Bodega 54 John St ☎051 844177, ⓦbodegawaterford .com. This bistro and wine bar is an attractive, informal setting for dishes such as slow-roasted organic pork belly with almond and crispy onion crumble (featuring on its "Home Grown" set menu, which is available all evening and costs €30 for 3 courses) and plenty of seafood. Early bird Mon–Fri 5–7pm 2 courses for €20; simpler lunch menus. Mon–Sat noon–10pm.

Gino's Apple Market, John St ☎051 879513. Bright, neat branch of the long-running Cork institution, a no-frills restaurant dishing up pizzas (around €10), salads, wine, beer and ice cream. Mon–Thurs 5–9.30pm, Fri 5–10pm, Sat 12.30–10pm, Sun 1.30–10pm.

Granary Café O'Connell St ☎051 854428, ⓦgranarycafe.ie. At the back of the airy eighteenth-century granary that used to host Waterford Treasures, this excellent self-service café offers a great selection of breakfasts, including espresso coffees, sandwiches from €4, quiches, pies and a daily special main course with two salads (€9.50). Mon–Sat 8am–5pm.

★**L'Atmosphere** 19 Henrietta St ☎051 858426, ⓦrestaurant-latmosphere.com. Authentic, informal bistro with a good reputation for its unfussy, classic French dishes such as cassoulet of duck confit and Toulouse sausage. Range of excellent-value set menus from €20. Mon–Fri 12.30–2.30pm & 5.30pm–late, Sat & Sun 5.30pm–late.

PUBS AND BARS

Geoff's 8–9 John St. Behind its striking façade of astroturf and electric blue window, there are lots of dark, cosy corners in this huge and characterful traditional bar, and an attractive beer garden outside. Also serves excellent food. Mon–Thurs 11.30am–11.30pm, Fri & Sat 11.30am–12.30am, Sun 1–11pm.

Kazbar 57 John St ☎051 843730, ⓦkazbar.ie. Louche, vaguely Egyptian decor, a roof terrace and several tables outside for watching the world pass by at this busy café-bar, which serves good cocktails and hosts DJs, live bands and a top-floor club at weekends, and traditional sessions on Mon, Wed and Thurs. Mon–Thurs 10.30am–11.30am, Fri & Sat 10.30am–2am, Sun 12.30pm–late.

Munster Bar Bailey's New St ☎051 874656, ⓦthemunsterbar.com. Down a narrow lane in the old quarter (also accessible from The Mall), this atmospheric 200-year-old pub is known particularly for its food, using local ingredients in dishes such as seafood pie, and hosts traditional sessions on Sun in summer. In good weather, enjoy the outdoor tables in the shadow of Greyfriars, a medieval Franciscan friary. Mon–Thurs 10.30am–11.30pm, Fri & Sat 10.30am–12.30am, Sun 12.30–11pm.

Phil Grimes 61 Johnstown ☎051 875759. Friendly, old-style bar with a small beer garden, live music in its upstairs venue and craft beers from the local Metalman and Dungarvan breweries. Mon–Thurs 4–11.30pm, Fri & Sat 4pm–12.30am, Sun 4–11pm.

★**The Reg** 2 The Mall ☎051 583000, ⓦthereg.ie. Great newcomer on the Waterford bar scene, right next to Reginald's Tower. The sprawling premises include a much-coveted, heated roof garden overlooking the tower and the river, and a whiskey bar with leather sofas. The service is very good, the excellent food comes in generous portions, accompanied by craft beers on draught, and there are traditional sessions nightly in summer. Mon & Wed 10am–11.30pm, Tues & Thurs 10am–1.30am, Fri & Sat 10am–2am, Sun 12.30pm–1.30am.

WATERFORD FESTIVALS

Festivals include **Spraoi** (ⓦspraoi.com) during the bank-holiday weekend in early August, which showcases street performances and world music. There's a **food festival** over a September weekend (ⓦwaterfordharvestfestival.ie), while over ten days in October, **Imagine** (ⓦimagineartsfestival.com) encompasses music, visual arts, dance, comedy, theatre and the John Dwyer Trad Weekend.

ENTERTAINMENT

Garter Lane Arts Centre O'Connell St ☎051 855038, ⓦgarterlane.ie. Set in an eighteenth-century building, the city's most interesting arts venue hosts performances of music, dance, comedy and theatre, as well as exhibiting artworks and showing independent films.

Waterford's coast

Waterford's coastline lacks the wildness of the shoreline further east, but there are still glorious, enticing beaches – especially at **Dunmore East**, **Stradbally** and **Ardmore** – and plenty of balmy cliff-top walks, not least at Ardmore, which is also a major ecclesiastical site. Among the larger towns here, it's best to give the kiss-me-quick resort of Tramore a wide berth, but **Dungarvan** enjoys a picturesque bayside setting and offers some fine places to stay, eat and listen to traditional music. A novel way to experience this coastline is on one of Sea Paddling's **sea-kayaking** courses and trips (☎051 393314, ⓦseapaddling.com), which explore the area's caves, islands and coves and are often blessed with sightings of whales and dolphins.

Dunmore East

DUNMORE EAST (ⓦdiscoverdunmore.com), 16km southeast of Waterford, is a picturesque getaway for the city's wealthier denizens. The village is actually split in two, with the sheltered eastern part set neatly around a small, sandy beach backed by sandstone cliffs, while the much busier western half is built above and around a marina, and one of Ireland's busiest fishing harbours. Down by the harbour, Dunmore East Adventure Centre (☎051 383783, ⓦdunmoreadventure.com) offers kayaking, canoeing, wind-surfing, stand-up paddleboarding, sailing and climbing (with indoor and outdoor climbing walls). There's a **food festival** over a weekend in late June, while in late August, the village comes to life for the four-day **Bluegrass Festival**.

ARRIVAL AND DEPARTURE   **DUNMORE EAST**

By bus The bus stop is located opposite the Bay Café. **Destinations** Suirway (ⓦsuirway.com): Waterford (Merchants Quay; summer 8–10 daily, winter 7 Mon–Sat; 30min).

ACCOMMODATION AND EATING

Bay Café ☎051 383900. Inexpensive daytime café with a few outside tables above the harbour. Stuffs plenty of seafood in its sandwiches – including its famous open crab sandwich – main courses and chowder. Daily 9am–5pm.

Beach Guest House ☎051 383316, ⓦdunmorebeach guesthouse.com. Excellently kept rooms, some with sea-facing balconies, at this very smart, modern house on the seafront in the east village, with fine views from its conservatory. Breakfast delights include smoked salmon and scrambled egg, and French toast. Good rates for singles. March–Oct. **€80**

Strand Inn ☎051 383174, ⓦthestrandinn.com. Life in the east village is focused around this popular eighteenth-century inn, where most bedrooms have balconies overlooking the sea, enjoying views out towards the Hook Head lighthouse; they have a fresh, modern style, with white bedding and splashes of colour, perhaps from pastel cushions or a sympathetic modern painting. Downstairs, the excellent restaurant (and the bar menu) specializes in fresh seafood, in dishes such as turbot with hollandaise sauce and devilled crab, with plentiful outdoor tables overlooking the beach. **€90**

6

Dungarvan

Attractive, bustling **DUNGARVAN** is splendidly situated on a large bay where the waters of the River Colligan broaden as they reach the sea, and where St Garvan founded a monastery in the seventh century. The handsome, early nineteenth-century streets of its town centre gather themselves around the main Grattan Square on the west side of the river. Unlike many of its fellow resorts, it remains largely unscathed by the blight of chain-store similitude. It plays host to the four-day **West Waterford Festival of Food** in April (⊛westwaterfordfestivaloffood.com) and a major **traditional-music festival** (⊛itsafeeling.com) over five days around the bank-holiday weekend in early June. Its fine restaurants and pubs are supplemented by a **farmers' market** of food and crafts every Thursday morning in Grattan Square.

Dungarvan Castle

Castle St · Guided tours late May to late Sept daily 10am–6pm · Free · ⊛ heritageireland.ie

The town's main attraction is **Dungarvan Castle**, squatting proudly at the eastern end of Davitt's Quay, also known as King John's Castle, as the king's constable, Thomas Fitz Anthony, lived here. Built in 1185 as an Anglo-Norman command base, it consists of a shell keep with a curtain wall. Inside are eighteenth-century barracks, occupied by the IRA during the Civil War and burnt down when they abandoned the site. Subsequently, these were restored to become the local Garda station and now contain displays and an audiovisual on the castle's history.

Waterford County Museum

St Augustine St · Mon–Fri 10am–5pm, plus some Sat in summer · Free · ⊛ waterfordcountymuseum.org

Five minutes' walk west along Main Street from the castle will bring you to the spruce **Waterford County Museum** in the old town hall, which is run by enthusiastic volunteers and houses well-organized exhibits and display boards on local history. From their website, you can download a town trail app, with an audio tour, map and lots of old photos.

ARRIVAL AND INFORMATION   DUNGARVAN

By bus Buses stop on Davitt's Quay near the bridge at the top of the bay.
Destinations Cork (hourly; 1hr 25min); Waterford (hourly; 50min); Youghal (hourly; 35min).
Tourist office In the old courthouse on Meagher St, around the corner from the bus stop, though it might be moving soon (early May to early Sept Mon–Fri

9.30am–5pm, Sat 10am–5pm; early Sept to early May Mon–Fri 9.30am–1pm & 2–5pm; ☎058 41741, ⊛ dungarvantourism.com).
Bike rental Tours and rental (delivered to your accommodation) by Lismore Cycling Holidays (☎087 935 6610, ⊛ cyclingholidays.ie).

ACCOMMODATION AND EATING

Cairbre House Strandside North, Abbeyside, 10min walk northeast of the centre ☎058 42338, ⊛ cairbrehouse.com. Creeper-clad Georgian B&B set in lovely gardens (which supply some of the produce for the very good breakfasts), with a deck and conservatory right on the east bank of the Colligan, an open fire in the lounge and airy, en-suite rooms with floral decor. Very good rates for singles. Mid-Jan to mid-Dec. **€80**

The Local 10 Grattan Square ☎058 41845, ⊛ thelocal .ie. A cosy bar run by a famous *uilleann* piper, with traditional music sessions at weekends, plus a winter concert series that has featured big names such as Liam Clancy and Liam O'Flynn. Mon–Thurs noon–11.30am, Fri & Sat noon–12.30am, Sun 12.30–11pm.

The Moorings Davitt's Quay ☎058 41461, ⊛ mooringsdungarvan.com. With waterfront tables on the quay and a large beer garden at the back, *The Moorings* is a lovely, old, nautical-themed pub serving good food. Upstairs are bright, high-ceilinged, en-suite bedrooms (very good rates for singles), some overlooking the harbour. Mon–Thurs noon–11.30pm, Fri & Sat noon–12.30am, Sun noon–11pm. **€90**

★ **Nude Food** 86 O'Connell St, near the southwest corner of Grattan Square ☎058 24594, ⊛ nudefood .ie. As well as global dishes such as slow-roasted pork belly with couscous, this reasonably priced, congenial deli, bakery and café rustles up great sandwiches (around €7), salads (in two sizes) and cakes, and there's a good kids' menu. Mon–Thurs 9.15am–6pm, Fri & Sat 9.15am–9.30pm.

★**The Tannery** 10 Quay St, near the castle ☎058 45420, ⓦtannery.ie. Excellent modern Irish restaurant in a stylishly converted leather warehouse, owned by TV chef Paul Flynn, who also offers cookery courses. Local, seasonal ingredients are used wherever possible in dishes such as crab *crème brûlée*, and the €30 evening set menu is a bargain (not available Sat). Tapas and

simple mains are available (Tues–Sat evenings) in the downstairs wine bar, and there are very smart and tasteful bedrooms (good rates for singles) in two nineteenth-century town houses around the corner, where continental breakfast is taken in your room and bicycles are freely available. Tues–Thurs 5.30–9pm, Fri 12.30–2.30pm & 5.30–9pm, Sat 5.30–9.30pm, Sun 12.30–4pm (longer hours in summer). **€110**

6

The Copper Coast

Best explored from Dungarvan to the west, the R675 towards Tramore traverses verdant countryside along the cliff-girt littoral that's been christened the **Copper Coast**, after the rich deposits that were extensively mined in the nineteenth century. Because of the area's geological heritage, it's recently been designated a UNESCO Geopark, with a **visitor centre** at **BUNMAHON**, 24km east of Dungarvan, in the deconsecrated, 200-year-old Monksland Church (Tues–Sun noon–6pm; ☎051 292828, ⓦcoppercoastgeopark.com; see the website for their varied menu of events). Detailed information on self-guided walks, including a short boardwalk trail over Fenor Bog, 12km east of Bunmahon, is available from the visitor centre or can be downloaded (some of the walks have podcasts) from the Geopark's excellent website. There are no buses along this stretch of coast, but a fun way to explore would be to rent a **bicycle** from Lismore Cycling Holidays in Dungarvan (see opposite).

Bunmahon's appealing **beach** supports a surf school (ⓦbunmahonsurfschool.com) and is backed by dunes and a caravan park, while scenic **STRADBALLY**, 8km west on a minor road off the R675, has several fabulous beaches nearby, the choicest being the sheltered, sandy **Stradbally Cove**, a little way west of the village. Seven kilometres further along the coast towards Dungarvan lies **Clonea Strand**, an expansive sandy beach, full of day-trippers in summer.

Ardmore

The seaside village of **ARDMORE**, 20km southwest of Dungarvan, is an enchanting place, rich in religious history and relics, mainly associated with St Declan who established a monastery here some thirty years before St Patrick came to Ireland. His saint's day is still celebrated in the village with a **pattern festival** of music, theatre, walks and street entertainment in late July (ⓦardmorepatternfestival.ie). There's a 1km-long sandy beach at the foot of the village, hemmed in by long, grassy headlands and flanked on its southern side by **St Declan's Stone**. According to legend, the saint's luggage was miraculously transported by this boulder when he travelled from Wales (and thus presumably avoided excess-baggage charges). Heading up the hill towards the southern headland leads past **St Declan's Well**, where the saint apparently conducted baptisms in the early fifth century, and where he later retired to a small cell for greater seclusion; on the site of the latter, a now-ruined church was built, probably in the twelfth century. From here there's an easy 4km **cliff walk**, with stunning views, around the headland, which will bring you back to the top of Main Street.

St Declan's Cathedral

Above the town (and near the end of the cliff walk), on the site of Declan's original monastery, stands a roofless but solid-looking twelfth-century Romanesque **cathedral** and a willowy, conically capped, 30m **round tower** of the same period. The cathedral contains two carved ogham stones, one of which is the longest in Ireland, while its west outer wall features an arcade from a previous building, embellished with remarkable carvings of biblical scenes: in the lower row, you can make out Adam and Eve, the Adoration of the Magi and the Judgement of Solomon; at the right end of the upper row, look out for the scales held by the Archangel Michael, in the Last Judgement. In a corner of the graveyard is **St Declan's Oratory**, which possibly dates from the eighth century. The pit in the floor, once covered with a flagstone, is where he was supposedly buried, but pilgrims have scooped out the earth from the grave as it's believed to protect against disease.

6

ARRIVAL AND ACTIVITIES   ARDMORE

By bus As well as the direct service between Ardmore and Cork below, there are hourly buses from Waterford and Dungarvan to Youghal and Cork that pass along the N25, about 5km from Ardmore.
Destinations Cork (1–3 daily; 1hr 35min); Youghal (1–3 daily; 20min).

Watersports From its shop at the south end of the beach, Ardmore Adventures (☎ 083 374 3889, ⓦ ardmoreadventures .ie) offers watersports such as kayaking, snorkelling and surfing, as well as rock-climbing.

ACCOMMODATION

★ **Cliff House** On the southern headland ☎ 024 87800, ⓦ thecliffhousehotel.com. Welcoming and hugely impressive hotel in an ingeniously striking but unobtrusive modern building, blending in homely touches and maritime features in a very Irish contemporary aesthetic. It makes the very most of its water's-edge location: all rooms have glorious views of the bay (many from their private balconies), as do the bar and restaurant (see below), the spa, the outdoor Jacuzzi and even the 15m indoor pool. €235

Cush On the R673 from Dunmore just before reaching the village ☎ 024 94474, ⓦ cushbandbardmorewaterford .com. Smart modern house overlooking the bay with a pretty garden to sit out in and bright en-suite and standard rooms, eggs freshly laid by the owner's hens for breakfast. April– Sept. €60

Round Tower College Rd ☎ 024 94494, ⓦ roundtowerhotel.ie. In sharp contrast to the Cliff House Hotel, this traditional family-run hotel offers just twelve restful en-suite rooms, a bar and restaurant in a century-old former convent, with an attractive garden which hosts live music on Sun evenings in summer. €85

EATING

The Ardmore Gallery and Tearoom Main St ☎ 024 94863, ⓦ ardmoregalleryandtearoom.ie. Cakes, soup and sandwiches either in the bright gallery, which displays works by local artists, or out in the garden. April–Sept daily 9.30am–6.30pm; Oct–March Sat & Sun 1–5pm.

The House *Cliff House Hotel* (see above). "McGrath's Black Angus Beef: Fillet, Grilled, Kilbeggan Whiskey, Beef Tea" . . . the menu entries at this superb Michelin-starred restaurant run on like a Joycean stream of consciousness. There's plenty of imagination, too, in the complex but supremely skilful combinations of unusual ingredients, and in their intricate, almost sculptural, platings. If you're not up to the Ulyssean epic of the tasting menu (€95), remember that the same

kitchen turns out fantastic dishes such as chicken with tarragon butter for the bar (lunch and dinner daily), which also shares the same broad deck and superb bay views. Tues–Sat 6.30–10pm; closed Tues in winter.

White Horses Restaurant Main St ☎ 024 94040. Homely café-restaurant with a back garden run by three sisters, serving everything from afternoon tea and cakes through lunches such as deep-fried plaice with tartare sauce, to interesting evening dishes such as crispy duckling with caramelized orange and kumquat sauce. May–Sept Tues–Sun 11am–late; Oct–Dec & mid-Feb to April Fri 6pm–late, Sat 11am–11pm, Sun noon–6pm.

Northern Waterford

The northern stretch of the county, along the border with Tipperary, is studded with two modest but pretty mountain ranges, the **Comeraghs** and the **Knockmealdowns**, neither of which rises higher than 800m. **Ballymacarbry**, 25km north of Dungarvan on the R671 towards Clonmel, is the best jumping-off point for the Comeraghs, while historic **Lismore**, 25km west of Dungarvan in the beautiful Blackwater valley, provides easy access to the Knockmealdowns.

The Comeragh Mountains

The best approach to the bleak moorland of the **Comeragh Mountains**, with its smattering of bogs, heather and upland lakes and its healthy ration of National Looped Walks (ⓦirishtrails.ie), is along the Nire valley. Now flanked by the signposted Comeragh Scenic Drive, the Nire descends westwards from beneath Knockaunapeebra (789m), the range's highest point, to waterside **BALLYMACARBRY**. There are three-day walking festivals in the Comeraghs in September (ⓦcomeraghswild.com) and October (ⓦnirevalley.com).

6

ACCOMMODATION AND EATING   COMERAGH MOUNTAINS

Ballymacarbry Hostel Right on the R671 ☎052 618 5483, ⓦballymacarbry.com. Large, en-suite dorms, as well as a gym, a sauna, a kitchen and dining room, are available in the village's spacious and handily located new community centre. **€20**

Glasha Farmhouse Just northwest of Ballymacarbry, signposted 1km westward off the R672 ☎052 613 6108, ⓦglashafarmhouse.com. Bright, tasteful rooms, some with Jacuzzi baths, an attractive garden and a

conservatory on a dairy farm, as well as excellent breakfasts and evening meals. Very good rates for singles. **€100**

★**Hanora's Cottage** About 5km from Ballymacarbry up the Comeragh Scenic Drive ☎052 613 6134, ⓦhanorascottage.com. This welcoming, adults-only guesthouse provides Jacuzzis in all the large, scenic rooms, a breakfast feast and splendid dinners in the restaurant; an ideal base for hiking in the mountains, *Hanora's* also offers a guided walking service, maps and packed lunches. **€110**

Lismore

Set amid verdant countryside on the south side of the River Blackwater lies the sleepy town of **LISMORE**, once a major religious centre. St Carthagh founded a thriving **monastery** here in 636 that became a great centre of learning and retained both religious and political importance for several centuries, despite periodic raids by the Vikings and later the Anglo-Normans. Over the bank-holiday weekend at the beginning of June, Lismore hosts a classical music festival (ⓦlismoremusicfestival.com), and in mid-June there's Immrama, a festival of travel writing that featured Paul Theroux in 2014 (ⓦlismoreimmrama.com).

St Carthagh's Cathedral

On the site of its medieval cathedral, wrecked by Edmund Fitzgibbon around 1600, stands the Church of Ireland **St Carthagh's Cathedral**, constructed some thirty years later – to get here head east up Main Street and turn left down North Mall. Much of its appearance derives from remodelling in the early 1800s, including the addition of its tower and spire, and it remains a charming building, set in a tree-lined cobblestone courtyard. Just inside the front door is a lovely stained-glass window by the Pre-Raphaelite Edward Burne-Jones, depicting two virtues: Justice and Humility. A Romanesque arch in the nave might possibly date from the original cathedral and leads to the imposing McGrath tomb which features carvings of the twelve Apostles, the Crucifixion and the martyr St Catherine. Stones set into the back wall, including a particularly stalwart bishop, date from the ninth to eleventh centuries.

Lismore Castle

Gardens Easter to mid-Oct daily 10.30am–5.30pm; last admission 4.30pm • €8 • ⓦlismorecastlegardens.com **Gallery** ☎058 54061, ⓦlismorecastlearts.ie

Despite the cathedral's attractions it is the extravagant and graceful **Lismore Castle**, its fairy-tale turrets magnificently set above the River Blackwater, that overshadows the town. The Irish home of the Dukes of Devonshire was designed by Joseph Paxton (also responsible for the Crystal Palace for London's Great Exhibition of 1851) in the mid-nineteenth century, taking as its starting point the remains of a castle built by Prince John in 1185. Though the bulk of the castle cannot be visited, its huge gardens, set within the seventeenth-century outer defensive walls, present numerous exterior views from different aspects. The gardens consist of woodlands and a host of magnolias, camellias and rhododendrons in season, as well as a yew-tree walk where Edmund Spenser is believed to have written *The Faerie Queen*. Modern sculptures dot the gardens, and the formerly derelict west wing of the castle has been transformed into a **gallery** that hosts some interesting exhibitions of contemporary art.

The Heritage Centre

The Old Courthouse, Main St • April–Oct Mon–Fri 9am–5.30pm, Sat 10am–5pm, Sun noon–5pm; Nov–March Mon–Fri 9am–5.30pm • €5; Heritage Island • ☎ 058 54975, ⓦ discoverlismore.com

Lismore's fascinating history comes to life at the **Heritage Centre**, whose galleries recount the stories of some of the town's famous figures, including the chemist Robert Boyle who was born in the castle in 1627; and there's a short and entertaining audiovisual, *The Lismore Experience*.

ARRIVAL AND INFORMATION
LISMORE

By bus Waterford (via Dungarvan; 1 on Sun; 1hr 40min).
Tourist office In the Heritage Centre (April–Oct Mon–Fri 9am–5.30pm, Sat 10am–5pm, Sun noon–5pm;

Nov–March Mon–Fri 9am–5.30pm; ☎ 058 54975). Walking tours of the town depart twice daily in summer (€5).

ACCOMMODATION

Ballyrafter Country House Hotel About 1km northeast of the centre, just off the N72 ☎ 058 54002, ⓦ waterfordhotel.com. Swish and spacious traditional country-house hotel set in broad, lawned grounds, built by the Duke of Devonshire in the early 1800s for his estate manager, with a snug bar, a restaurant with views of Lismore Castle and open fires; fishing is a speciality. €90

★ **Glenribbeen Lodge** About 2km northeast of town, just off the N72 ☎ 058 54499, ⓦ glenribbeen.com. Lovely, quirky, eco-conscious B&B, set in a rambling garden. Run by a musician and a painter, it offers attractive, well-designed rooms, a varied, mostly organic breakfast menu, and lots of activities including bicycles, canoes and a thatched meditation hut. Self-catering also available. €70

Pine Tree House Ballyanchor ☎ 058 53282, ⓔ pinetreehouse@eircom.net. A more conventional option than *Glenribbeen Lodge*, a modern house with en-suite double, twin and triple rooms, set in a large, attractive garden on Lismore's western outskirts, well signposted from the centre. €70

EATING AND DRINKING

The Classroom Bar Main St ☎ 058 53842. Friendly, old-fashioned bar, one of the few in Lismore to survive the recession. Serves a great pint of Guinness and hosts a long-running traditional music session every Thurs from about 10pm. Mon–Thurs 10.30am–11.30pm, Fri & Sat 10.30am–12.30am, Sun noon–11pm.

The Summerhouse Café Main St ☎ 058 54148, ⓦ thesummerhouse.ie. This café is tucked away at the back of a colourful gift and home decor shop, but is no afterthought: it has its own bakery, producing mouthwatering croissants, meringues and eclairs, and serves up tasty, simple lunches (Sun excepted), as well as great espresso coffees. Tues–Sun 10am–5.30pm.

The Knockmealdown Mountains

North from Lismore the R668 to Cahir undulates upwards through a lovely river valley, garnished with a mass of woody greenery, before heading into the mountains. To the east, after 10km, rises **Knockmealdown** itself (793m), whose name translates aptly as "bare brown mountain", while a little further up the road lies the spectacular viewpoint known as **The Vee**. At this popular beauty spot, famous for its magnificent display of rhododendrons in late May and early June, the valley sides offer a perfectly chevron-shaped scene of the fields of Tipperary laid out far below, a panoply of greens, browns and yellows. The **Tipperary Heritage Way** north to Cashel begins here at The Vee, while the 70km **East Munster Way** starts down at Clogheen (see p.220) and heads east from The Vee to Carrick-on-Suir, via the northern foothills of the Knockmealdowns and the Comeraghs.

The lower Suir valley

Rising in the Devilsbit Mountains in the north of Tipperary, the **River Suir**, Ireland's second-longest river after the Shannon, runs down the length of the county before abruptly turning east in the face of the Knockmealdown Mountains. Along the way it nourishes countless dairy cattle and three significant towns along the southern border with Waterford. While Clonmel holds little of interest for visitors, nearby **Cahir** is a compelling destination, with its mighty castle and the whimsical Swiss Cottage, and **Carrick-on-Suir** is the site of a rare and well-preserved Elizabethan manor house. Feeding into the Suir to the northwest of Cahir, the luscious **Glen of Aherlow** is one of the county's prettiest spots and a fine base for exploring the scenic Galty Mountains. Tucked away on the south side of the range are the fantastic stalactites and stalagmites of **Mitchelstown Cave**, while the attractive villages of **Clogheen** and **Ardfinnan** lie to the east of here in the lee of the Knockmealdowns.

6

Carrick-on-Suir

In the far southeastern corner of County Tipperary lies the market town of **CARRICK-ON-SUIR**, famous as the birthplace of the Clancy Brothers, who are celebrated in a four-day festival over the June bank-holiday weekend that features street entertainment, art exhibitions and of course music (ⓦclancybrothersfestival.org).

Ormond Castle

Guided tours early March to early Oct daily 10am–1.30pm & 2–6pm • Free • ⓦ heritageireland.ie

The town's main point of interest is multi-gabled **Ormond Castle**, Ireland's only surviving Elizabethan manor house, which is situated at the far eastern end of Castle Street, a continuation of Main Street. Erected in the 1560s by Thomas ("Black Tom") Butler, tenth Earl of Ormonde, for an (unrealized) visit by his cousin, Elizabeth I, the house contains numerous tributes to her, most notably in the elaborate series of panels in the long gallery. Also displayed is a fine collection of royal charters, including one of 1661 granting the title Duke of Ormonde to Tom's descendant James.

ARRIVAL AND INFORMATION

CARRICK-ON-SUIR

By train The train station is behind Greenside, the town park on the northeast side of the centre.
Destinations Cahir (2 Mon–Sat; 45min); Waterford (2 Mon–Sat; 25min).
By bus Buses stop at Greenside.
Destinations Cahir (8–10 daily; 50min); Cork (1 Mon–Sat;

2hr 15min); Dublin (5 daily; 3hr); Kilkenny (5–8 daily; 1hr); Limerick (8–10 daily; 2hr); Waterford (8–10 daily; 40min).
Tourist office The tourist office and small heritage centre are in a converted church just off the north side of Main St (Mon–Fri 10am–1pm & 2–5pm, Oct–May closes 4pm; ⓣ051 640200).

ACCOMMODATION AND EATING

The Carraig Main St ⓣ051 641455, ⓦcarraighotel .com. This smartly refurbished eighteenth-century hotel is the focal point of the town's hospitality, offering very reasonably priced rooms that have been tastefully updated in subdued colours, and fine meals in the bar and restaurant. Good-value half-board packages. **€89**

Cahir

With a name that means "fort", the dominant feature of **CAHIR** (ⓦvisitcahir.ie) is not surprisingly its castle, one of Ireland's largest and best preserved, surrounded by the waters of the River Suir at the western entrance to the town. The castle was a power base of the influential Butlers, the Earls of Ormonde, who were known as the Fitzwalters when they first came to Ireland with Prince John in 1185 and were granted a huge swathe of land in Munster. However, Theobald Fitzwalter was soon after made Chief Butler of Ireland, entitling him to a tenth of all incoming wine cargoes, and changed his family name to "Butler".

Cahir Castle

Daily: March to mid-June & Sept to mid-Oct 9.30am–5.30pm; mid-June to Aug 9am–6.30pm; mid-Oct to Feb 9.30am–4.30pm • €3; Heritage Card • ⓦ heritageireland.ie

The Butlers built their stronghold in the thirteenth century, though much, including the restored outer walls, dates from more recent times. It managed to survive a siege and bombardment by the Earl of Essex in 1599, as well as the invasions of Cromwell and William of Orange. However, after Cromwell's victory in 1650, the Butlers moved out and the castle fell slowly into disrepair, until it was given new life in the mid-nineteenth century by Richard Butler, the second Earl of Glengall, who impoverished himself in the process. The castle's entrance leads to the cramped middle ward, overshadowed by the thirteenth-century keep whose chambers feature various displays, including a model of the 1599 siege. To the left of here, a gateway, surmounted by defensive viewpoints on each side, leads to the more expansive outer ward. In the inner ward, parts of the larger of the two towers derive from the thirteenth and fifteenth centuries, though the banqueting hall was redesigned by William Tinsley in 1840 for use as the Butlers' private chapel.

The Swiss Cottage

Guided 40min tours early April to late Oct daily 10am–6pm, last admission 5.15pm (maximum 12 people, so you may have a wait during the busy summer months) • €3 • Heritage Card • ⓦ heritageireland.ie

Cahir's other major attraction is the **Swiss Cottage**, a thirty-minute riverside stroll through parkland south from the town or, if you're driving, off the Ardfinnan road. Designed by John Nash, architect of the Royal Pavilion at Brighton, this lavish, thatched *cottage orné* on the castle demesne was constructed in the early 1800s for Richard Butler, the first Earl of Glengall, though his precise reason remains unclear. A contemporary scurrilous theory held that it was to enjoy clandestine liaisons with his mistress, but there is evidence that it was used occasionally as a residence and for entertaining guests. It has now been thoroughly restored using appropriate timbers and period decor. Entertaining **guided tours** start from the basement kitchen and visit the elegant salon, whose interior is decorated with one of the first commercially manufactured Parisian wallpapers, and music room, and ascend via a spiral staircase to the grand master bedroom with its commanding views of the countryside.

ARRIVAL AND INFORMATION
CAHIR

By train Cahir's train station is off Church St, a 5min walk northeast of the castle.
Destinations Carrick-on-Suir (2 Mon–Sat; 45min); Waterford (2 Mon–Sat; 1hr 10min).
By bus Buses stop opposite the castle outside the tourist office.
Destinations Bansha (8–10 daily; 20min); Carrick-on-Suir

(8–10 daily; 40min); Cashel (6 daily; 20min); Cork (6 daily; 1hr 20min); Dublin & Airport (6 daily; 2hr 50min); Limerick (8–10 daily; 1hr 10min); Waterford (8–10 daily; 1hr 15min).
Tourist office In the castle car park (Easter to early Oct Tues–Sat 9.30am–1pm & 1.45–5.30pm; hours may be reduced from Sept; ☏ 052 744 1453).

ACCOMMODATION

Apple Farm Moorstown, 6km east of Cahir on the main N24 road towards Clonmel ☏ 052 744 1459, ⓦ theapplefarm.com. Eco-friendly campsite, appealingly

set among the orchards of Ireland's most famous fruit farm and well equipped: campers' kitchen in an apple barn, tennis court, playground and laundry facilities. May–Sept. **€14**

6

Cahir House Hotel The Square ☎052 744 3000, ⓦcahirhousehotel.ie. Built as a town house for the Butlers in 1770, this Georgian mansion has been thoroughly updated to provide comfy, colourful rooms and a small spa. Good room-only and single rates; packages include an excellent-value, midweek, half-board rate for singles. **€90**

Tinsley House The Square ☎052 744 1947, ⓦtinsleyhouse.com. Just uphill from the castle on the town's main square, this B&B in a nineteenth-century town house offers en-suite bedrooms attractively furnished with antiques and decorated in bright pastel colours. **€65**

EATING

Galileo Church St ☎052 744 5689, ⓦgalileocafe.com. Just off The Square, this café-restaurant is surrounded by crafts shops in an attractively converted granary and offers tasty, inexpensive pizza (from around €10), pasta and salads. Mon–Sat noon–10pm, Sun 1–9pm.

River House 1 Castle St ☎052 744 1951, ⓦriverhouse.ie.

Bright, modern, self-service café opposite the tourist office, with an outdoor terrace overlooking the castle and the river. Dishes up full breakfasts (€8), soups, all kinds of sandwiches, quiches and uncomplicated hot lunches, cakes, fresh juices and smoothies. Mon–Fri 8.30am–5pm, Sat & Sun 8.30am–6pm.

Ardfinnan and Clogheen

Two villages to the south of Cahir offer great places to stay and ready access to the east–west ridge of the Knockmealdown Mountains beyond (see p.216). Nine kilometres from Cahir on the banks of the Suir lies the pretty village of **ARDFINNAN**, which is traversed by the 56km Tipperary Heritage Way from Cashel, via Cahir, to the panoramic vantage point called The Vee. Nine kilometres southwest of Ardfinnan is **CLOGHEEN**, from where it's a short but steep trip up the R668 Lismore road to The Vee and into the mountains.

ARRIVAL AND INFORMATION   ARDFINNAN AND CLOGHEEN

By bus Carrick-on-Suir (2 Mon–Sat; 45min–1hr); Clonmel (1–3 daily; 15–30min); Cork (2–3 daily; 1hr

20min–1hr 35min); Kilkenny (2 Mon–Sat; 1hr 40min–1hr 55min).

ACCOMMODATION AND EATING

ARDFINNAN

★**Kilmaneen** 5km south of Ardfinnan on the Newcastle road (signposted from the Hill Bar in the village centre) ☎052 613 6231, ⓦkilmaneen.com. This staggeringly good B&B, set in a 200-year-old farmhouse and extensive gardens, not only serves delicious breakfasts and dinners (guests-only, advance reservation necessary), but provides the perfect starting point for walks in the surrounding countryside and offers courses in everything from cooking to beekeeping. Very good rates for singles; self-catering also available. **€80**

CLOGHEEN

Ballyboy House Just off the Ardfinnan road ☎052 746 5297, ⓦballyboy-house.com. Gorgeous seventeenth-century farmhouse, surrounded by lovely, diverse gardens

and extensive woodland that's accessible on trails. Four-posters and other antique furniture adorn the en-suite bedrooms, and breakfasts include home-baked bread; other meals can be provided by prior arrangement. Very good rates for singles; self-catering cottage available. **€70**

The Old Convent On the Vee road ☎052 746 5565, ⓦtheoldconvent.ie. An elegantly converted nunnery that styles itself a "gourmet hideaway", offering much-fêted, eight-course tasting menus in its restaurant (€65). Mid-May to mid-Sept Thurs, Fri, Sat & Sun; mid-Sept to early Jan & mid-Feb to mid-May weekends only; closed Christmas. **€170**

Parson's Green Just off the Ardfinnan road ☎052 746 5290, ⓦwww.clogheen.com. Spacious holiday park with campers' kitchens, laundry, café, pet farms and lots of other activities for kids. **€18**

Mitchelstown Cave

March–May, Sept & Oct daily 10am–5pm; June–Aug daily 10am–5.30pm; Nov–Feb Sat & Sun 10.30am–4pm • €9 • ⓦmitchelstowncave.com

At Ballyporeen, 7km west of Clogheen, follow the signs up the northern route from the central crossroads and you'll eventually arrive at **Mitchelstown Cave**; alternatively, it's easily accessed via the M8 west of Cahir. The convoluted system of grottoes, stretching

ome 3km underground, was discovered in 1833. Guided tours convey visitors through
only a small section of the cavities, but these reveal some stunning calcite formations,
uch as "The Pillars of Hercules" and the frankly weird 9m-high "Tower of Babel",
produced by the constant dripping of water on limestone over several eons.

The Glen of Aherlow

To Cahir's northwest lies the lush and resplendent **Glen of Aherlow**, spreading some 18km
from **Bansha** in the east to **Galbally** in the west, just across the border in County Limerick.
Lying beneath the northern façade of the Galty Mountains, the glen is a marvellous place
to drive or cycle around and the scenic circular route is well worth taking. The best vantage
point for spectacular views is by the entrance to the Glen of Aherlow Nature Park, 1.5km
north of the junction of the R663 and R664, which is the trailhead for five National
Looped Walks (wirishtrails.ie). From the wooded ridge of Slievenamuck, the glen lies
spread out below, light reflecting from the river, and the mountains looming beyond. The
signposted **Ballyhoura Way** runs through the Glen to Galbally, on its 80km journey from
the train station at Limerick Junction via the Ballyhoura Mountains to St John's Bridge in
north Cork. For information on walking (including leaflets with directions and maps,
which are also downloadable at waherlow.com) and the diverse festivals in the area, contact
the tourist information point (see below), while for details of local group walks throughout
the year, go to wgalteewalkingclub.ie.

6

INFORMATION

THE GLEN OF AHERLOW

Tourist information At the back of the *Coach Road*
Pub is a small tourist information point (Mon–Fri

9am–5pm, plus June–Sept Sat 10am–4pm; ☎062
56331, waherlow.com).

ACCOMMODATION

All of the establishments listed are near the R663/R664 junction.

Aherlow House Hotel ☎062 56153, waherlowhouse
ie. This former hunting lodge has bright, spacious rooms, its
own restaurant and a bar serving meals (including traditional
afternoon tea). Self-catering lodges also available. €69
Ballinacourty House ☎062 56000, wballinacourtyhse
com. These converted eighteenth-century stables house
pleasant en-suite rooms around a lovely cobbled courtyard
dotted with flowerbeds; there's also a popular, reasonably

priced restaurant here. Self-catering cottages also
available. Restaurant Wed–Sun evenings, plus Sun lunch
time. €70
Ballinacourty House Caravan and Camping Park
☎062 56559, wcamping.ie. Campsite in the
grounds of *Ballinacourty House*, with a campers'
kitchen, laundry, playground, tennis court and
minigolf. April–Oct. €23

Cashel

Though it has some other noteworthy sights, the town of **CASHEL** – the name derives
from the Irish *caiseal*, meaning "stone fort" – is utterly overshadowed by the stunning
Rock of Cashel, an outcrop that rears out of the surrounding fertile plain, the Golden
Vale. Surmounted by important ecclesiastical remains, the Rock is a hotspot on the
tourist trail, so is best visited in the early morning before the hordes arrive or in the late
afternoon when the coaches have departed. Cashel's annual **festival** (wcashelartsfest
com) offers a variety of cultural events over ten days in mid-November.

The Rock of Cashel

Daily: mid-March to early June & mid-Sept to mid-Oct 9am–5.30pm; early June to mid-Sept 9am–7pm; mid-Oct to mid-March
9am–4.30pm; last admission 45min before closing; free 45min guided tours, call ☎062 61437 for times • €6; Heritage Card •
w heritageireland.ie

Viewed from afar, the **Rock of Cashel** is a captivating sight, a freak and solitary lump of limestone, reflecting the light in diverse ways throughout the day and topped by a collection of walls, towers, turrets and crenellations of *Gormenghast* proportions. I might seem heretical to suggest so, but this vista is actually the best thing about the Rock, since, despite its staggering location and much-trumpeted billing, when you get there the site is actually far less atmospheric than other notable ecclesiastical complexes, not least Kells Priory (see p.188) and Quin Abbey (see p.322). Nonetheless, despite the swarms of coach-borne tourists, there's plenty to see and much to marvel at.

The Hall of the Vicars Choral

Once inside, the Rock's first sight is the fifteenth-century **Hall of the Vicars Choral**, which used to house the choir charged with singing at the cathedral's services. Its upper floor features a minstrels' gallery as well as a fine eighteenth-century Flemish tapestry showing Solomon receiving the Queen of Sheba, while the lower houses the original twelfth-century **St Patrick's Cross** (the one outside – on the cross's original spot – is a replica). Badly worn, it bears a carving of Christ on one side and the saint on the other, and is unusual in not having a ring around the cross head.

Cormac's Chapel

Currently accessible by guided tour only May–Sept

Directly opposite the Hall of the Vicars Choral is **Cormac's Chapel**, perhaps the most atmospheric of Ireland's Romanesque churches – though it's undergoing long-term conservation work. Its appealing south façade of brown sandstone, decorated with the typical blind arcades of the period, stands in warm contrast to the grey limestone used

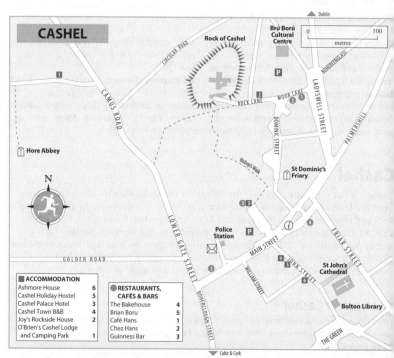

CASHEL

Rock of Cashel

Brú Ború Cultural Centre

Dublin

Circular Road

Camus Road

Hore Abbey

N

Rock Lane

Moor Lane

Dominic Street

Boherenaglass

Ladyswell Street

Palmershill

Bishop's Walk

St Dominic's Friary

Lower Gate Street

Police Station

Main Street

William Street

Golden Road

Boherclough Street

John Street

Friar Street

St John's Cathedral

Bolton Library

The Green

Cahir & Cork

■ ACCOMMODATION	
Ashmore House	6
Cashel Holiday Hostel	5
Cashel Palace Hotel	3
Cashel Town B&B	4
Joy's Rockside House	2
O'Brien's Cashel Lodge and Camping Park	1

● RESTAURANTS, CAFÉS & BARS	
The Bakehouse	4
Brian Boru	5
Café Hans	1
Chez Hans	2
Guinness Bar	3

THE RISE OF THE ROCK

According to legend, the **Rock of Cashel** (see opposite) first rose to political prominence in the fourth or fifth century AD, when a major fortress was established by the descendants of Eógan Mór who went on to found a dynasty of kings-cum-bishops reigning over this part of Munster. The Eóganacht were ousted from Cashel in 978 by the Dál Cais line from Killaloe in County Clare, Brian Boru becoming the overlord of Cashel, and subsequently achieving dominance over Ireland in 1002. His descendant, Murtagh, granted the Rock to the Church in 1101 and, some fifty years later, when the papacy established four archbishoprics in Ireland, one of which was at Cashel, an early medieval cathedral was built here. By then, however, the Eóganacht had regained control under Cormac Mac Cárthaigh, who built the adjoining Cormac's Chapel, finished in 1134. The whole site was sacked by Cromwell's forces in 1647, but was still used by the Church of Ireland until 1749 when cathedral status was granted to St John's Church on John Street.

elsewhere on the Rock and in most Irish churches. In the chancel you'll find some very rare surviving examples of medieval Irish paintwork. The most complete fragment, on the south wall, shows part of the baptism of Christ, while the ceiling features scenes relating to the Magi – though you wouldn't know it unless you were told. The elaborate chancel arch beyond, which is strangely off-centre to the nave, features vivid sculpted heads of people and animals. Although the adjacent cathedral obstructs the chapel's north door, formerly its main entrance, it's still possible to go out and have a look at a lively carving of a robust lion being hunted by a centaur, equipped with a bow and arrow and a Norman-type helmet.

The cathedral and round tower

Constructed on the site of the earlier establishment between 1230 and 1270, the huge Gothic **cathedral** is typically Anglo-Norman in form, with pointed arches and loftily set lancet windows. It also features some smaller quatrefoil casements, as well as a nave unusually shorter than the choir, caused by the construction of a **tower** on the west side, built for the archbishops' accommodation and refuge during the fifteenth or sixteenth century. Abutting the cathedral's north transept, the **Round Tower** is the Rock's earliest building, dating from the beginning of the twelfth century. It's nearly 30m high but cannot be climbed, so you'll have to make do with the fine views of the lush countryside around the Rock from ground level.

Brú Ború Cultural Centre

Sounds of History Mon–Fri 9am–5pm, last admission 4pm • €5 **Traditional music shows** (90min) late June to late Aug Tues–Sat 9pm, followed by a traditional session • €20 • ☎ 062 61122, ⦿ bruboru.ie

In the eastern shadow of the Rock, beyond the car park, is the **Brú Ború Cultural Centre**, which offers a genealogical service for South Tipperary. Its basement houses the entertaining **Sounds of History** multimedia exhibition, which races through the development of Irish cultural history, focusing particularly on St Patrick, Brian Boru, and traditional-music collectors such as Bunting and O'Neill. In summer the centre's theatre hosts shows of traditional music, song and dance staged by Comhaltas Ceoltóirí Éireann, the national organization for the promotion of Irish music.

Hore Abbey and the Bishop's Walk

Just downhill from the Rock's entrance, paths lead west and south. The former leads some of the way towards **Hore Abbey**, a thirteenth-century Cistercian monastery, probably built by those working on the Rock's cathedral. Set in open fields, the ruins themselves are impressive and afford an excellent unobstructed view of the Rock. The southerly path is the **Bishop's Walk**, a shortcut back to the town centre via the gardens of the **Palace Hotel**, which was designed in 1730 by Sir Edward Lovett Pearce, architect of Dublin's House of Parliament, for the wealthy Archbishop Theophilus Bolton, who also provided for the restoration of Cormac's Chapel.

6 Bolton Library and St John's Cathedral

John St • **Bolton Library** Go to the tourist office to hook up with the caretaker • Mon–Thurs 10am–2pm, Fri 10am–1pm • €2

Regarded as the leading contemporary ecclesiastical lawyer, Archbishop Bolton of Cashel (1729–44) was also an avid collector of books and manuscripts, bequeathing the fruits of his labours to the diocese. The collection forms part of the **Bolton Library**, although the bulk of its rare maps, manuscripts and books, some dating back to the twelfth century, was acquired from Bolton's mentor, William King, Archbishop of Dublin from 1702 to 1729. The library stands in the grounds of the elegant Palladian **St John's Cathedral**, the successor to the cathedral on the Rock.

The Heritage Centre

In the market house, Main St • Mid-March to mid-Oct Mon–Fri 9.30am–5.30pm, Sat 9.30am–5.30pm; mid-Oct to mid-March Mon–Fri 9.30am–5.30pm • Free • ☎ 062 61333, 🖳 cashel.ie

Also in the town centre, look in on the **Heritage Centre** attached to the tourist office (see below), which is home to a scale model of Cashel as it looked in 1640 (accompanied by an audio commentary on the history of the town), as well as the original charters granted to the town in the seventeenth century by Charles II and James II.

ARRIVAL AND INFORMATION CASHEL

By bus Buses stop near the market house on Main St. Listed services are run by Bus Éireann.
Destinations Cahir (6 daily; 20min); Cork (6 daily; 1hr 40min); Dublin & Airport (6 daily; 2hr 30min).

Tourist office In the market house, Main St (Mon–Fri 9.30am–5.30pm, plus mid-March to Mid-Oct Sat 9.30am–5.30pm; ☎ 062 61333, 🖳 cashel.ie). A town audioguide is downloadable from the website.

ACCOMMODATION

Despite the Rock's popularity you should have no problems finding **accommodation**, with plenty of B&B options in town and many more in the surrounding countryside, especially on the Dualla road.

Ashmore House John St ☎ 062 61286, 🖳 ashmorehouse.com. Centrally positioned between Main St and the Bolton Library and run by friendly owners, this homely, comfortably furnished Georgian town house offers en-suite rooms and a private car park. **€70**

Cashel Holiday Hostel 6 John St (IHH An Óige) ☎ 062 62330, 🖳 cashelhostel.com. Appealing, central hostel in a Georgian town house, with a well-equipped kitchen and sociable dining area, a cosy sitting room, laundry facilities and a barbecue area. Dorms **€16**, doubles **€45**

★**Cashel Palace Hotel** Main St ☎ 062 62707, 🖳 cashel-palace.ie. Housed in the Georgian former archbishop's palace with its spacious and elegant sitting rooms, and set within extensive, peaceful gardens, this hotel offers top-notch accommodation, the cheapest in the

adjoining coach house, and first-class service. Good rate for singles. **€134**

Cashel Town B&B 5 John St ☎ 062 62330, 🖳 cashelbandb.com. Under the same management as Cashel Holiday Hostel next door, with a wide variety of cheery, colourful standard and en-suite bedrooms, and homemade bread for breakfast, which is not included in the rates. Self-catering apartments available. **€55**

Joy's Rockside House Rock Villas ☎ 062 63813, 🖳 joyrockside.com. At the foot of the Rock is this welcoming en-suite B&B with bright, pastel-coloured chintzy rooms, some with views up to the ruins. Mid-Feb to Oct. **€80**

O'Brien's Cashel Lodge and Camping Park Dundrum Road, about 1km from the main tourist office on the northwest side of town near Hore Abbey ☏ 062 61003, ⓦ cashel-lodge.com. In a bucolic setting looking up towards the Rock, this well-run en-suite B&B with a self-catering kitchen is situated in an attractively renovated 200-year-old outhouse on a working farm. Camping available. Good single and family rates. Doubles €80, camping €20

EATING AND DRINKING

The Bakehouse Main St, opposite the tourist office. A bakery with pavement tables and an upstairs self-service coffee shop serving cakes, pies, salads and sandwiches, such as tuna melt panini (€6). Daily 9am–5.30pm.

Brian Boru Main St ☏ 062 63381, ⓦ brianborubar.ie. Vast, stylish but unpretentious bar, which offers good food and hosts DJs and/or bands at weekends, a nightclub on Sat and a traditional session on Thurs. Mon–Thurs 10am–11.30pm, Fri & Sat 10am–2.15am, Sun 10am–11.30pm.

Café Hans Moor Lane ☏ 062 63660. A slimmed-down, more informal and more economically priced version of its adjacent sibling, serving salads, sandwiches and dishes such as Toulouse sausage with tarragon and onion gravy (€12), as well as great desserts. No bookings. Tues–Sat noon–5.30pm.

★ **Chez Hans** Moor Lane ☏ 062 61177, ⓦ chezhans .net. Cashel's finest restaurant, in a beautiful nineteenth-century building that was once a church lecture hall. The food is exceptional, employing locally sourced meat and wild Irish fish, and prices are more manageable if you come for the weekday menu (Tues–Thurs 6–10pm, Fri 6–7pm: €27 for two courses). Tues–Sat 6–10pm.

Guinness Bar *Cashel Palace Hotel* (see opposite). In the atmospheric cellar of the old archbishop's palace, with tasty and good-value salads, sandwiches and meals such as sausages with onion gravy and mash (€10.50). Mon–Thurs 11am–11.30pm, Fri & Sat 11am–12.30am, Sun noon–11pm; kitchen noon until around 9pm.

6

Cork

KINSALE

Cork

Cork is far and away Ireland's largest county, though nearly all visitors simply ignore its massive hinterland of dairy farms, dotted with low mountains and evergreen plantations. The coast's the thing, and in an east–west spread of over 170km it unfurls an astonishing diversity. Based around an island near the mouth of the River Lee, Cork city, the capital of the self-styled "rebel county", is renowned for its independent spirit, and packs a good cultural and social punch in its compact, vibrant centre. With its excellent restaurants, cafés and specialist food market, the city also sets a high culinary tone, which much of the rest of the county keeps up.

7

Further reminders of a prosperous seafaring past can be seen around Cork city in the ports of **Cobh**, **Youghal** and especially **Kinsale**, each of which has reinvented itself in its own singular way as a low-key, pleasurable resort. To the west of the city as far as **Skibbereen**, the coastline, though it meanders wildly through inlets and hidden coves, remains largely gentle and green, with a good smattering of sandy beaches and a balminess that has attracted incomers and holiday-homers from the rest of Ireland and Europe. Facing each other across the shelter of Roaring Water Bay, the good-time ports of **Baltimore** and Schull are popular with a cosmopolitan, watersports crowd, but the offshore islands of **Sherkin** and **Clear** presage wild country ahead. **Mizen Head** is the first of Cork's and Kerry's five highly irregular, southwesterly fingers of folded rock, which afford spectacular views of each other and the Atlantic horizon. The next, narrow **Sheep's Head**, is perhaps the most charming, where – especially if you slow down to walking pace – you'll feel as if you're getting to know every square kilometre of gorse, granite and pasture and just about every inhabitant. Shared between Cork and Kerry, the **Beara Peninsula** is especially dramatic, epitomized by mild, verdant **Glengarriff**'s backdrop of dark, bare rock and lonely mountain passes.

GETTING AROUND
CORK

By bus Buses will get you around most of the county. Bus Éireann is augmented in the far west by a couple of private minibus services, as well as by West Cork Rural Transport (Ⓦ ruraltransport.ie), though you'll need to check its timetables carefully as services tend to be weekly or monthly rather than daily.

By bike/on foot The elaborate landscape of west Cork is great country for walking or cycling, both of which pursuits are served by waymarked routes on the Sheep's Head and the Beara. Bikes can be rented in the main towns.

Cork city

The Republic's second city, **CORK** (Corcaigh, "marshy place") is strongly characterized by its geography. The centre sits tight on a kilometre-wide island, much of which was reclaimed from marshes, in the middle of the River Lee, while the enclosing hills seem to turn this traditionally self-sufficient city in on itself. Given this layout and its history

THE SHEEP'S HEAD WAY

Highlights

Kinsale A pretty harbour, impressive forts and ome of the best restaurants in Ireland. **See p.246**

Drombeg One of the country's finest Bronze ge stone circles, in a bucolic setting with views f the sea. **See p.251**

Lough Hyne A unique and scientifically mportant marine lake, in a beautiful setting. ee **p.255**

Clear Island Hop on the ferry for varied irdwatching and pleasant walking. **See p.258**

The Sheep's Head Way The shortest and asiest major walking route in southwestern

Ireland, around a wild and lonely peninsula. See **p.261**

6 Bantry House and Gardens Sumptuous art treasures in a beautiful spot overlooking Bantry Bay. **See p.262**

7 Garinish Island Take a magical boat trip from Glengarriff to this elaborate horticultural folly. **See p.265**

8 Allihies Stupendous views, a fascinating copper-mining museum and walking trails, in the back of beyond. **See p.267**

HIGHLIGHTS ARE MARKED ON THE MAP ON P.230

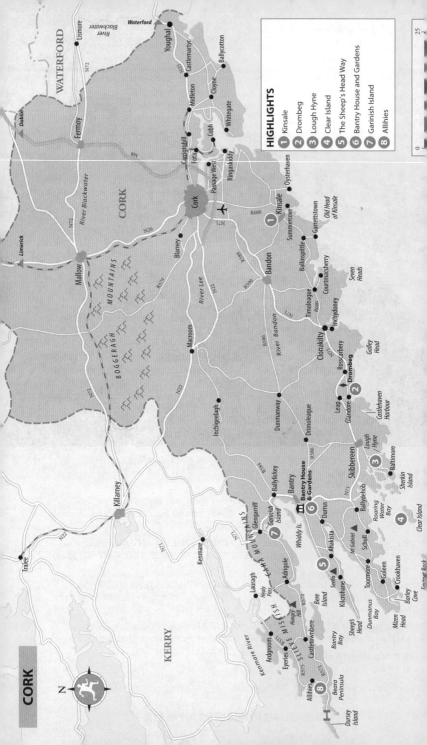

CORK

N

HIGHLIGHTS

1. Kinsale
2. Drombeg
3. Lough Hyne
4. Clear Island
5. The Sheep's Head Way
6. Bantry House and Gardens
7. Garinish Island
8. Allihies

0 ———— 25

t comes as no surprise that Corkonians have a reputation in Ireland for independence of spirit, not to say chippiness. Indeed, in many ways, Cork sees itself not in second place but as a rival to Dublin. It produces its own national newspaper, *The Irish Examiner*, brews Murphy's and Beamish, its own versions of the national drink, stout (though now under the aegis of the Dutch brewer, Heineken), and supports a vigorous artistic, intellectual and cultural life of its own. Even its social divisions match Dublin's: here too the south side of the river is generally more affluent, while the north side has more public housing and a stronger working-class identification.

In colonial times, Cork also maintained its own strong links with London, through its role as a major **port**, proof of which can still be seen all around town. The main drag, curving St Patrick's Street, was originally a waterway lined with quays, while you can still spot eighteenth-century moorings on Grand Parade. Though contemporary Cork doesn't make the most of its long riverfront, much of which is now lined by major roads, the channels of the Lee, spanned by more than twenty bridges, break up the cityscape and pleasantly disorientate. The harbour area has Ireland's largest concentration of chemical factories, fortunately downstream of the centre, while the city's other main modern industry, computers, is linked to the prestigious university, to the west of the centre. All of this has spawned a widespread commuter belt, but the compact island is still the place for the many excellent restaurants, lively pubs and artistic venues.

The best of the city's sightseeing options are the **Crawford Art Gallery**, with its fine collection of eighteenth- to twentieth-century art, **Cork City Gaol**, which vividly evokes life in a nineteenth-century prison, and the hi-tech cosmological displays of **Blackrock Castle Observatory**. In truth, however, none of Cork's sights are absolute must-sees, though it's a pleasant place to stroll around on a fine day. The city centre is essentially the eastern part of the island, with its quaysides, bridges, old warehouses and the narrow alleys of the medieval heart, plus a segment to the north of the River Lee that has MacCurtain Street as its central thoroughfare.

Brief history

In the seventh century, **St Finbarr** established a monastery at Cork, on the site of today's cathedral, to the southwest of the modern centre. Three centuries later, the Vikings

BLARNEY

Blarney, Blarney, what he says he does not mean. It is the usual Blarney.

So spoke Queen Elizabeth I, and a legend and its accompanying tourist phenomenon were born. Though supposedly loyal to the queen, the **Lord of Blarney**, Cormac MacCarthy, had been stalling her emissary, Sir George Carew, who had been sent to restore English control of Munster, sidetracking him with wine, women and words. MacCarthy, it was said, could talk "the noose off his head", and over the centuries blarney came to mean "flattering, untrustworthy or loquacious talk associated with…Irish people" (*The Encyclopedia of Ireland*). This story of the word's origin, however, may itself be blarney…

At some stage in the nineteenth century, with the beginnings of mass tourism to the southwest of Ireland, it became popular to kiss the **Blarney Stone**, part of the machicolations of **Blarney Castle**, a fine fifteenth-century tower house, set in attractive grounds, in the village of the same name, 8km northwest of Cork. The stone stands over a 26m drop, and planting a smacker on it is meant to grant "the gift of the gab". If you're really feeling that tongue-tied, buses run to Blarney from Parnell Place bus station (Mon–Sat every 30min, Sun hourly; 20–30min), and the castle is open year-round (May & Sept Mon–Sat 9am–6.30pm, Sun 9am–5.30pm; June–Aug Mon–Sat 9am–7pm, Sun 9am–5.30pm; Oct–April daily 9am–5.30pm or sunset, whichever is earlier; last admission 30min before closing; €12; Heritage Island; ⓦ blarneycastle.ie). Legions of the verbally challenged queue up in summer, when it's best to turn up early in the morning or late in the afternoon.

CORK CITY

■ ACCOMMODATION

An Brú	7
Auburn House	5
Blarney Caravan and Camping Park	1
The Blarney Stone	11
Clarion Hotel	9
Cork International Hostel	13
Garnish House	12
Hayfield Manor	16
Isaac's	8
Jurys Inn	6
Kent House	4
Kinlay House	2
River Lee Hotel	14
Shandon Bells	15
Sheila's of Cork	3
Victoria Lodge	10

● PUBS & BARS

An Spailpín Fánach	23
Bodega	6
Chambers	16
Charlie's	22
The Corner House	15
Crane Lane Theatre	2
Franciscan Well	4
The Long Valley	10
Mayne's	14
The Poor Relation	11
The Porterhouse	12
Sin É	1

● RESTAURANTS & CAFÉS

Café Paradiso	18
The Crawford Art Gallery Café	5
The Electric	24
The Farm Gate Café	13
Gino's	7
Isaac's	3
Ivory Tower	19
Market Lane	9
Nash 19	20
Orso	17
The Quay	25
Wagamama	8
Wild Ways	21

■ CLUB

Savoy	1

● SHOPPING

English Market	1
Liam Ruiséal	2
Mother Jones Flea Market	3

M8 to Dublin, N25 to Youghal & Waterford

Blackrock Castle Observatory

LWR GLANMIRE ROAD

Train Station

St Patrick's

PENROSE QUAY

Channel

VICTORIA QUAY

ALBERT STREET

SOUTH CITY LINK ROAD

CLONTARF BRIDGE

City Hall

Police Station

ANGLESEA STREET

PARNELL BRIDGE

Bus Station

OLIVER PLUNKETT STREET

PLACE

PARNELL PLACE

Southern

UNION QUAY

SOUTH TERRACE

MORRISON'S QUAY

Lee

MERCHANT'S QUAY

ST PATRICK'S QUAY

WELLINGTON ROAD

MACCURTAIN STREET

Everyman

Great Island Car Rental

ST PATRICK'S HILL

Limerick & Blarney

ST PATRICK'S BRIDGE

Merchants Quay Shopping Centre

MAYLOR STREET

MERCHANT STREET

BRIDGE ST

LEITRIM STREET

CARROLL'S QUAY

CAMDEN QUAY

CORURG STREET

JOHN REDMOND STREET

DOMINICK STREET

O'CONNELL SQUARE

St Anne's Shandon

Butter Museum

River

Opera House

LAVITTS QUAY

EMMET PL

PAUL ST

Crawford Art Gallery

ACADEMY ST

FRENCH CHURCH ST

CAREY'S LN

Savoy

WINTHROP ST

ST PATRICK'S STREET

COOK STREET

PEMBROKE STREET

PHOENIX ST

SOUTH MALL

Holy Trinity Church

FATHER MATHEW QUAY

GEORGE'S QUAY

DUNBAR STREET

MARY STREET

DOUGLAS STREET

English Market

Church of St Peter & St Paul

Triskel Arts Centre

MARKET LANE

PRINCES STREET

Bishop Lucey Park

TUCKEY ST

GRAND PARADE

SULLIVAN'S QUAY

PROBY'S QUAY

POPE'S QUAY

COAL QUAY

CORNMARKET ST

CASTLE ST

SOUTH MAIN STREET

NORTH MAIN STREET

AUGUSTINE ST

LITTLE HANOVER ST

TOBIN ST

SHANDON STREET

Cork City Gaol

SUNDAY'S WELL RD

NORTH MALL

BATCHELOR'S QUAY

GRATTAN STREET

WASHINGTON STREET

SHEARE STREET

MARDYKE WALK

WESTERN ROAD

Killarney & N22

University, Fitzgerald Park & Cork Public Museum

St Finbarre's Cathedral

DEAN STREET

SHARMAN CRAWFORD STREET

BARRACK STREET

N

metres

0   200

created a separate settlement, an island in the River Lee's marshes, which was taken over in the twelfth century by the Anglo-Normans. They strengthened the defences of the central part of the island with the construction of vast city walls, leaving the west and east ends to the swamp and later developing suburbs on the slopes to the north and south. The fortifications were largely destroyed, however, in the successful **Williamite siege** of 1690, and became redundant when the marshes were reclaimed soon after. The next century witnessed great wealth, through the trade in butter and pickled meat and the development of the port for provisioning westbound sailing ships. Brewing and distilling plants were established, which persist to this day, along with glass, silver and lace industries, but the Act of Union and the introduction of steamships brought stagnation in the nineteenth century. At the start of the last century, Cork took an active part in the **War of Independence** and the **Civil War**, and suffered as a consequence. In 1920, the Royal Irish Constabulary murdered the Lord Mayor, Tomás MacCurtain, and as a reprisal for an ambush, the Black and Tans burnt much of the city centre to the ground in 1921. MacCurtain's successor as mayor, Terence MacSwiney, was incarcerated and went on hunger strike, which after 74 days led to his death on October 24, 1920.

7

The centre

Three roughly east–west arteries define Cork's commercial centre, bracketed to the west by the wide boulevard of **Grand Parade**: the crescent of **St Patrick's Street** (aka Patrick Street), bustling with major chainstores; **Oliver Plunkett Street**, home to more traditional shops and pubs; and the city's grand financial and legal hub, **South Mall**. On the north side of Patrick Street, restaurants line the pedestrianized alleys of the old French quarter around **Paul Street**, though the main culinary venue is the covered **English Market** (see p.240), a joy for the senses that's well worth wandering through.

The Crawford Art Gallery

Emmet Place • Mon–Wed, Fri & Sat 10am–5pm, Thurs 10am–8pm • Free • ☎ 021 490 7855, ⓦ crawfordartgallery.ie

The city's major set-piece sight is the **Crawford Art Gallery**. Its main focus is its interesting temporary exhibitions of Irish and international art in a striking modern extension, but it also has an excellent café (see p.238) and a permanent collection of Irish and British art from the eighteenth century onwards that's worth a quick mosey. The lion's share of the collection is housed on the first floor, where you'll have to wade through some sentimentally cloying nineteenth- and twentieth-century works. Look out, however, for a fascinating *View of Cork*, painted in about 1740 by John

---

NEO-GOTHIC CORK

For those with a taste for it – and with shoe leather to spare – there's plenty of **neo-Gothic church architecture** to see in Cork, mostly along the river banks. The highlight is William Burges's **St Finbarre's Cathedral** on Proby's Quay (Mon–Sat 9.30am–5.30pm, plus April–Nov Sun 12.30–5pm; €5; ⓦ www.cathedral.cork.anglican.org), consecrated in 1870, whose three soaring, French Gothic spires are visible all over the city. The well-lit interior, which is elaborately decorated with red Cork marble, stained glass and Italianate mosaics, also impresses with its lofty proportions. Leading nineteenth-century practitioners Augustus Pugin and George Pain also worked in Cork. The **Church of SS Peter and Paul**, just off St Patrick's Street in the centre, was designed by Pugin and sports some fine woodcarving. Pain was the architect of **Holy Trinity Church** on Father Mathew Quay, with its handsome lantern spire, which was built in the 1830s and 1840s by booze-busting Father Theobald Mathew, who persuaded three million people to take the "total abstinence pledge", as well as of **St Patrick's Church** out to the northeast on Lower Glanmire Road.

Butts: you can pick out the waterway that is now Patrick Street, the 1724 Custom House (with a Union Jack in the courtyard), which is now the gallery you're visiting, and the Dutch-style houses on the quays, evidence of Cork's role in expanding Anglo-Dutch trading influence in the North Atlantic. There are also some fine representative works by Limerick-born Seán Keating (1889–1977), many of whose academic realist paintings have achieved iconic status. Though obviously posed in a studio, his *Men of the South* (1924) achieves the restrained grandeur of a classical frieze, depicting a grim-faced IRA column waiting to ambush British soldiers. Keep an eye out also for a piercing portrait of actor Fiona Shaw by Victoria Russell on the staircase to the first floor.

West of the centre

The west end of the island narrows around a residential area, which is home to hospitals and university buildings as well as a couple of interesting small museums.

Glucksman Gallery

University College Cork • Tues–Sat 10am–5pm, Sun 2–5pm • Free • ☎ 021 490 1844, ⓦ glucksman.org

In the northeast corner of the university's main campus, just over 1km from Grand Parade off the south side of Western Road, it's worth checking out the **Glucksman Gallery**. This striking building of wood, glass, limestone and steel, which was shortlisted for the 2005 RIBA prize, hosts rotating exhibitions of contemporary art, as well as free guided tours, talks, concerts and a restaurant.

Fitzgerald Park and Cork Public Museum

Cork Public Museum Mon–Fri 11am–1pm & 2.15–5pm, Sat 11am–1pm & 2.15–4pm, plus April–Sept Sun 3–5pm • Free • ☎ 021 427 0679, ⓦ corkcity.ie

Five minutes' walk from the Glucksman Gallery off the north side of Western Road, facing the leafy north channel of the River Lee, sits **Fitzgerald Park**, where you'll find the **Cork Public Museum**, a celebration of Cork and Corkonians – including sports personalities Sonia O'Sullivan and Roy Keane, both of whom have donated shirts. The museum traces the city's history through interesting documents and memorabilia, with a particular concentration on the period from the Great Famine to The Emergency, as World War II was known in Ireland. Some beautiful examples of Cork silver- and glassware are on display, alongside archaeological finds from the Neolithic era onwards and engaging temporary exhibitions on subjects such as prehistoric gold. From here it's a fifteen-minute walk across the river and up to Cork City Gaol (see opposite), signposted over the nearby footbridge.

Shandon

To the north of the island, **Shandon**'s narrow residential streets and alleys tumble down the slope towards the River Lee. At the centre of this area stands cobbled O'Connell Square, home to the round and tubby former **butter market**.

Butter Museum

O'Connell Square • March–June, Sept & Oct daily 10am–5pm; July & Aug daily 10am–6pm; Nov–Feb Sat & Sun 10am–3.30pm • €4 • ☎ 021 430 0600, ⓦ corkbutter.museum

The fascinating story of the dairy trade and its major impact on the development of the city is told in the **Butter Museum**, opposite the old butter market. The museum begins with dairy culture in early Ireland, as illustrated by a keg of bog butter: on remote grazing lands, milk was churned into butter on the spot and preserved in the bogs for later use; to this day, such kegs are often turned over by peat-cutters, who'll swear the butter is still edible. In the eighteenth century, thanks to its fertile hinterland and its site on the largest natural harbour in the northern hemisphere, Cork became the main provisioning port in the Atlantic for both the British Navy and trade convoys, with most Cork butter ending up in the West Indies. In the following century, the city managed to ride out the agricultural collapse caused by the Napoleonic Wars and the Famine, by gearing the butter trade to the English market through rigorous controls – the butter-market building you see outside was where barrels were washed and weighed, to avoid underhand practices by farmers. The story is brought up to date with a film on the successful development of the Kerrygold brand by tycoon and museum sponsor, Tony (now Sir Antony) O'Reilly.

St Anne's Shandon

March–May & Oct Mon–Sat 10am–4pm, Sun 11.30am–3.30pm; June–Sept Mon–Sat 10am–5pm, Sun 11.30am–4.30pm; Nov–Feb Mon–Sat 11am–3pm, Sun 11.30am–3pm • €5 • Ⓦ shandonbells.ie

Just up the slope from here, **St Anne's Shandon** is a graceful, early eighteenth-century Anglican church, built partly of white limestone, partly of puce sandstone – a combination that is said to have inspired the red-and-white "rebel" flag of County Cork. Its steeple, the city's most famous landmark, is flanked by four huge, notoriously unreliable clocks – earning the nickname "the four-faced liar" – and topped by a giant golden salmon as a weather vane. It's possible to climb the tower for matchless views of the city and to ring the bells.

Cork City Gaol and Radio Museum

Convent Ave, Sunday's Well • Daily: March–Oct 9.30am–5pm; Nov–Feb 10am–4pm; guided 1hr tours of the gaol Thurs 6pm • Cork City Gaol €8; Radio Museum €2; guided gaol tours €10 (book at least 24hr in advance on the website) • Ⓦ corkcitygaol.com

Away to the west of Shandon, in the posh suburb of Sunday's Well, is the forbidding red sandstone of **Cork City Gaol**. Walking, it's about thirty minutes from the centre, fifteen from the Public Museum; the Cork City Tour bus (see p.236) stops here.

Skilfully designed for its punishing purpose in 1818 by the Pain brothers, George and James, the gaol operated until 1923 when Republican prisoners – among them Countess Markiewicz (see p.85) and short-story writer Frank O'Connor – were released after the Civil War. A lively and informative audio tour (€3) guides you round the well-preserved cells, where the individual stories of real-life prisoners are recounted. An audiovisual courtroom drama finishes the tour evocatively, projected onto the walls of one of the gaol's imposing drum galleries.

From the late 1920s until the early 1950s, the gaol was home to the studios of Radio Éireann (now RTÉ), which have now been replaced by the **Radio Museum**. There's lots of interesting material on the pioneers of radio here, a re-creation of the old studio, a large collection of early radios, and a "juke box" of archival recordings.

Blackrock Castle Observatory

2km east of centre on south bank of River Lee • Mon–Fri 10am–5pm, Sat & Sun 11am–5pm, last admission 4pm; tower and dungeon tours Mon–Fri on application, Sat & Sun 1.30pm & 3.30pm • €6.50; children €4.50; family €18 • ☎ 021 435 7917, Ⓦ bco.ie • City bus #202 towards Mahon from bus station (Mon–Fri every 15min, Sat & Sun every 20–30min) will put you off at the pier in Blackrock village, leaving an easy 10min walk to the castle

Originally built in the sixteenth century, 2km east of the centre on the south bank of the River Lee, **Blackrock Castle Observatory** is now home to a dynamic and imaginative exhibition for both adults and children, **Cosmos at the Castle**, as well as a good café-restaurant. Beautifully produced, large-screen audiovisuals contain up to three hours of material that you can explore interactively in as much depth as you choose, not just on cosmology, but on life, the universe and everything. There's also a twenty-minute video game, Comet Chaser, in which you try to save the Earth from a comet, and tours of the castle's towers and dungeon.

ARRIVAL AND DEPARTURE

By train Cork Kent Station is 1km northeast of the city centre on the Lower Glanmire Rd.

Destinations Cobh (Mon–Sat at least hourly, 12 on Sun; 25min); Dublin Heuston (hourly; 2hr 40min); Fota (Mon–Sat at least hourly, 12 on Sun; 15min); Killarney (6–9 daily, often with a change at Mallow; 1hr 30min–2hr); Midleton (Mon–Sat at least hourly, 9 on Sun; 25min); Tralee (6–9 daily, often with a change at Mallow; 2hr–2hr 30min).

By bus The Bus Éireann station is on Parnell Place alongside Merchant's Quay. Harrington's and O'Donoghue's private buses to Castletownbere (see p.266) stop nearby on Parnell Place, while Aircoach and Citylink buses use St Patrick's Quay on the north side of the river, the latter starting from Cork Airport 30min earlier. Most city buses stop on the central St Patrick's Street.

Destinations Bus Éireann: Adrigole (8 weekly; 3hr); Baltimore (Mon–Sat 2 daily, change at Skibbereen; 2hr 30min); Bantry (4–6 daily; 1hr 50min); Cahir (6 daily; 1hr 20min); Carrick-on-Suir (1 Mon–Sat; 2hr 15min); Cashel (6 daily; 1hr 40min); Castletownbere (8 weekly; 3hr); Clonakilty (7–8 daily; 1hr); Dublin & Airport (6 daily; 3hr 45min–4hr 10min); Ennis (hourly; 3hr); Galway (hourly; 4hr 20min); Glengarriff (2–3 daily; 2hr 30min); Goleen (1 daily; 2hr 45min); Kenmare (via Cork Airport, Kinsale, Clonakilty, Rosscarbery, Skibbereen, Bantry and Glengarriff, with a good connection on to Killarney; 1 daily late June to late Aug; 4hr); Kilkenny (Mon–Sat 3 daily; 3hr); Killarney

(hourly; 1hr 30min); Kinsale (from Kent Train Station, via the bus station and the airport; hourly; 1hr); Limerick (hourly; 1hr 45min); Midleton (6–10 daily; 30min); Schul (1–2 daily; 2hr 20min); Shannon Airport (hourly; 2hr 30min); Skibbereen (5–7 daily; 1hr 45min); Tralee (hourly 2hr 15min); Waterford (hourly; 2hr 15min); Yougha (hourly; 50min).

Aircoach (ⓦaircoach.ie): Dublin & Airport (hourly 3hr–3hr 20min).

Citylink (ⓦcitylink.ie): Galway (5 daily; 3hr); Limerick (5 daily; 1hr 30min).

By plane Travelling by plane, you'll arrive at Cork Airpor (ⓦcorkairport.com), which lies 7km south of the centre of the Kinsale road and has ATMs and a bureau de change From here, Bus Éireann's #226/226A bus runs, in one direction, to the bus station on Parnell Place and Kent Train Station (Mon–Sat every 30min, Sun hourly; 30min) and, in the other direction, to Kinsale (hourly; 30min). In summer, Bus Éireann lays on a service from the airport along the West Cork coast to Kenmare, with a connection to Killarney (see p.273). If you want a quick getaway, Citylink (see above) operates through-coaches from Cork Airport to Limerick and Galway.

By car If you're arriving by car, note that parking on the street requires a disc, which can be picked up from the tourist office or newsagents. There's a useful multistorey car park on Coal Quay beside the Opera House.

GETTING AROUND

Bike rental Cycle Scene, 396 Blarney St (☏021 430 1183, ⓦcyclescene.ie).

Car rental Most of the big multinationals such as Budget (☏021 431 4000, ⓦbudget.ie) are represented at Cork Airport. There are few local outfits, but they include friendly

and amenable Great Island Car Rentals, who are centrally placed at 47 MacCurtain St (☏021 481 1609, ⓦgreatislandcarrentals.com) and can deliver to the airport

Taxis There are ranks on Patrick St. Companies include Cork Taxi Co-op (☏021 427 2222, ⓦcorktaxi.ie).

INFORMATION AND TOURS

Tourist office Grand Parade (Mon–Sat 9am–5pm; from roughly June to mid-Sept till 6pm, and most Suns in July and Aug; ☏021 425 5100, ⓦdiscoverireland.ie/cork). City walking tour podcasts can be downloaded on website. Beware several look-alike, green-liveried, "TOURIST INFORMATION" offices around town, which are actually shops selling tours.

Walking tours Tours of the city pick up at the tourist office (April–Sept Mon–Sat 11.15am; 1hr 30min; €8; ☏087 700 4981, ⓦcorkcitywalktours.com).

Bus tours Cronin's operates a hop-on, hop-off tour in an

open-top double-decker (March & Nov 5 daily; April, May Sept & Oct every 45min; June–Aug every 30min; 1hr 15min; buy tickets on board or at the tourist office; €14, valid for 2 consecutive days; ☏021 430 9090 ⓦcorkcitytour.com), departing from opposite the tourist office and passing the train station, the public museum and the Glucksman Gallery, St Anne's Shandon and Cork City Gaol.

Boat tours Atlantic Sea Kayaking runs kayaking trips (from €45 per person; see p.254) around the city by river or out into the harbour.

ACCOMMODATION

Hotels in Cork range from no-frills to luxurious, and there are scores of **B&Bs** and more upmarket **guesthouses** which are mostly concentrated near the university along Western Road (city bus #208 from St Patrick's Street or #205 from Kent Train Station and St Patrick's Street), and at the opposite end of town on the busy Lower Glanmire Road, near the train station. A variety of **hostels** can be found mostly on the north bank of the River Lee; for summer accommodation in halls try ⓦstudentvillage.ie. Beds are in short supply during the city's many festivals (see p.240), when early booking is advisable.

HOTELS

Clarion Hotel Lapp's Quay ☎021 422 4900, ⓦclarionhotelcorkcity.com. Set in a quiet, central location overlooking the south channel of the river and built around a striking, full-height atrium, this luxury hotel sports a fresh, contemporary style, as well as a spa with a long menu of treatments, swimming pool and fitness centre. €170

★**Hayfield Manor** Perrott Ave, College Rd ☎021 484 5900, ⓦhayfieldmanor.ie. Giving a taste of the countryside among the terraces of the southwestern suburbs, 500m west of St Finbarr's Cathedral, this five-star 1920s manor house has been decorated in a fresh, modern, rural style and much extended. Service is attentive and congenial, while facilities include an imposing pool, an outdoor Jacuzzi in the pretty garden, a spa, a conservatory bistro and an excellent modern Irish restaurant, Orchids. €179

Isaac's 48 MacCurtain St ☎021 450 0011, ⓦisaacscork .com. Good-value, well-run hotel in a former furniture warehouse with an attractive courtyard and waterfall behind its grand, Victorian, red-brick façade, and smart, colourful, well-equipped bedrooms. Serviced apartments also available. €78

Jurys Inn Anderson's Quay ☎021 494 3000, ⓦjurysinns.com. Bright, smart accommodation in a large, efficiently run, welcoming hotel. Central but in a slightly quieter location towards the east end of the island. €89

River Lee Hotel Western Rd ☎021 425 2700, ⓦdoylecollection.com. Pleasing modern hotel decorated with pale stone and grainy wood, a 10min walk from the centre overlooking the leafy university campus. The rooms are large and well designed with comfortable beds and their own music system. The bistro and bar feature broad terraces on the river, and there's an attached leisure club with pool, gym and spa. €181

GUESTHOUSES AND B&BS

Auburn House 3 Garfield Terrace, Wellington Rd ☎021 450 8555, ⓦauburnguesthouse.com. Well-maintained, en-suite B&B in a central but peaceful spot north of the river, with fine breakfasts, including vegetarian, and parking facilities. Good rates for singles. €80

The Blarney Stone 1 Carriglee Terrace, Western Rd ☎021 427 0083, ⓦblarneystoneguesthouse.ie. Gleaming white nineteenth-century guesthouse opposite the university, lavishly refurbished with Waterford Crystal chandeliers, antique fireplaces and swag curtains, offering a diverse breakfast menu that caters for various dietary requirements, and off-street parking. €99

Garnish House Western Rd ☎021 427 5111, ⓦgarnish.ie. Victorian guesthouse of a high standard opposite the university, where you'll get a warm welcome and a delicious breakfast from a diverse menu that stretches to eggs Benedict with smoked salmon; some rooms have a Jacuzzi. Self-catering is also available, as is off-street parking. €99

Kent House 47 Lower Glanmire Rd ☎021 450 4260, ⓦkenthousecork.eu. Comfortable, well-equipped B&B in an end-of-terrace Victorian town house near the train station, offering a wide range of en-suite rooms and homemade bread for breakfast. Very good rates for singles. €84

Shandon Bells Western Rd ☎021 427 6242, ⓦshandonbells.com. Very helpful and informative B&B 15min from the centre, overlooking the southern channel of the river near the university. Offers bright, colourful, en-suite rooms, a varied breakfast menu and a waterside patio for fair weather. Off-street parking available. €70

HOSTELS AND STUDENT HALLS

★**An Brú** 57 MacCurtain St (IHH & IHO) ☎021 455 9667, ⓦbruhostel.com. The city's most central hostel, a welcoming, rambling former hotel above a sociable backpackers' bar, which hosts DJs, live bands and a free Sun-night BBQ. The clean, basic, high-ceilinged rooms (private rooms and four- or six-bed dorms) all have private bathrooms, and there's a kitchen, dining and TV room (lots of DVDs to borrow) and laundry facilities. Prices include a simple breakfast. Ten percent discount for Aussies and Kiwis. Dorms €15, doubles €36

Cork International Hostel 1 Redclyffe, Western Rd ☎021 454 3289, ⓦanoige.ie. Well-appointed and organized 96-bed hostel opposite the university in a grand red-brick building with a garden. The place has been refurbished to An Óige four-star standards, with en-suite bathrooms throughout. Dorms €14, doubles €40

Kinlay House Bob and Joan's Walk, Shandon (IHH) ☎021 450 8966, ⓦkinlayhousecork.ie. Large, well-run, partly en-suite hostel, on a quiet lane next to St Anne's Church, with laundry facilities, kitchen and single rooms. Price includes a light breakfast. Dorms €15, doubles €46

Sheila's of Cork 4 Belgrave Place, Wellington Rd (IHH & IHO) ☎021 450 5562, ⓦsheilashostel.ie. Cork's biggest hostel, efficiently run and welcoming, with a good kitchen, laundry facilities, a cinema room and a sauna. Dorms €15, doubles €44

Victoria Lodge Victoria Cross ☎021 494 1200, ⓦucccampusaccommodation.com. About a 30min walk west of the centre beyond the university, one of several student halls that rent out good-value, self-catering single rooms and apartments of varying sizes to the public by the night or week, during the summer. Singles €32, 3-bed apartment (for 4 people) €90

7

CAMPSITE

Blarney Caravan and Camping Park Stoneview, 3km north of Blarney ☏ 021 451 6519, ⓦblarneycaravanpark.com. The nearest campsite, about 10km northwest of the city centre, with campers' kitchen, laundry and an 18-hole pitch'n'putt. April to late Oct. €22

EATING

Eating out is one of the great pleasures of Cork. The city's chefs place a high premium on sourcing the best of local, artisanal ingredients, which they creatively put to good use. And with plenty of competition and an increasingly discriminating public to keep happy, **cafés** and **restaurants** are generally good value, certainly compared with Dublin. The best place to get a feel for Cork's culinary enthusiasm is the **English Market** (see p.240).

RESTAURANTS

THE ISLAND

Café Paradiso 16 Lancaster Quay, Western Rd ☏ 021 427 7939, ⓦcafeparadiso.ie. Popular, unpretentious restaurant serving excellent and innovative Mediterranean-influenced vegetarian and vegan cuisine. Dinner costs from €33 for two courses, but there are cheaper early-bird (till 6.45pm) and lunch menus. Stylish accommodation also available for diners. Mon–Fri 5.30–10pm, Sat noon–2.30pm & 5.30–10pm.

The Electric 41 South Mall ☏ 021 422 2990, ⓦelectriccork.com. Behind the Art Deco exterior of a former bank, this innovative bar-restaurant shelters a lovely light-filled bistro upstairs, as well as a white-tiled fish bar (no reservations) with an industrial finish overlooking the river, which rustles up dishes such as *cioppino*, a delicious Italian fish stew (€8.50). The downstairs bar has tempting tables on a riverside boardwalk. Bistro daily noon–9pm; fish bar Wed–Sat 5–10pm; bar Mon–Thurs 10am–11.30pm, Fri & Sat 10am–12.30am, Sun noon–11pm.

Gino's Winthrop St ☏ 021 427 4485. The epitome of cheap'n'cheerful, a bright, no-frills Italian restaurant dishing up pizza (around €10), salads, wine, beer and a wide range of homemade ice cream. Mon–Thurs noon–8pm, Fri & Sat noon–9pm, Sun 1.30–8pm.

Ivory Tower Princes St ☏ 021 427 4665, ⓦivorytower .ie. Small, eccentric, first-floor restaurant that draws its culinary inspirations from Japan, Mexico and all over the world to produce imaginative, off-the-wall combinations, such as venison, chocolate and chipotle chimichanga – the effects can be hit-and-miss but are never boring. €50 for a five-course set menu including soup and sorbet; there's also a Japanese tasting menu and, in summer, an Irish tasting menu. Thurs–Sat 7pm–late.

Market Lane 5 Oliver Plunkett St ☏ 021 427 4710, ⓦmarketlane.ie. Crisp bistro decor featuring lots of polished wood, an open kitchen and a long bar in a bright corner location provides the setting for bargain €10 lunches of soup, a half-sandwich, a chocolate pot and coffee (Mon–Fri). Later in the day you can tuck into tasty fare such as lamb and stout puff pastry pie, perhaps taking advantage of their early bird (Mon–Thurs 5–7pm, Sun 1–7pm; €22.50 for 3 courses). Mon–Sat noon–late, Sun 1–9pm.

Nash 19 19 Princes St ☏ 021 427 0880, ⓦnash19.com. Bright, efficient daytime buffet restaurant serving delicious, high-quality cuisine – including a fish dish (around €15), a pasta dish and a warm salad of the day, sandwiches, and hot and cold breakfasts – at reasonable prices; various dietary requirements catered for. Mon–Fri 7.30am–6pm, Sat 8.30am–4pm.

Wagamama 4–5 South Main St ☏ 021 427 8874, ⓦwagamama.ie. Branch of the reliable chain of Japanese noodle bars, offering tasty fried and soup noodles (€10–15), rice dishes, dumplings and invigorating juices. Mon–Sat noon–10pm, Sun 1–10pm.

OFF-ISLAND

★**Isaac's** 48 MacCurtain St ☏ 021 450 3805, ⓦisaacsrestaurant.ie. Popular, informal and welcoming restaurant in an eighteenth-century warehouse with bare stone walls, candles and a buzzy atmosphere. The short, global menu, supplemented by daily specials, ranges from Indian lamb curry to chicken with herb stuffing and spiced cranberry sauce (€18.50). There's plenty of choice for veggies and some great comfort desserts like apple and raspberry crumble. Set menu €22 for two courses Mon & Tues all evening, Wed–Sat 6–7pm. Mon–Sat 12.30–2.30pm & 6–10pm, Sun 6–9pm.

CAFÉS

THE ISLAND

The Crawford Art Gallery Café Emmet Place ☏ 021 427 4415. Classy and affordable café-restaurant in a gorgeous ground-floor room of the gallery (see p.233). You can lunch on their famous fish cake with homemade tartare sauce (€11) and, after a short spin round the gallery, you might well find yourself tempted back for tea and cake. Mon–Fri 8.30am–4pm, Thurs 8.30am–4pm & 4.30–8pm, Sat 9am–4pm.

★**The Farm Gate Café** English Market, Princes St ☏ 021 427 8134, ⓦfarmgate.ie. Superb café-restaurant overlooking the market's bustling stalls from its skylit balconies, where localism is everything and the fishmonger in the market below advises each morning on what'll be best for their "catch of the day" dish. Cooked breakfasts, great cakes and desserts and excellent lunches, which feature salads and savoury tarts, as well as many traditional Irish dishes. One balcony has table service (mains around €10; worth booking if you want to come around 1pm), the other is self-service (with a cheaper menu that includes sandwiches). Mon–Sat 8.30am–5pm; breakfast 8.30–11am; lunch noon–4pm.

Orso 8 Pembroke St ☎021 243 8000, ☻orso.ie. Head for this small, mellow café for great breakfasts, superb espressos and mostly Middle Eastern mains at lunch, such as feta, spinach and raisin pie with salad (€9.50). Dinners are more complex and the cakes – like their popcorn, chocolate and malteser bar – serious. No bookings. Mon 8.30am–6pm, Tues–Sat 8.30am–10/10.30pm.

Wild Ways 21 Princes St ☎021 427 2199, ☻wildways .net. Friendly organic self-service café, offering good breakfasts, smoothies and coffees, and delicious sandwiches, salads and soups for lunch. Mon–Fri 7.45am–5pm, Sat 8.30am–4pm.

OFF-ISLAND

The Quay Co-op 24 Sullivan's Quay ☎021 431 7026, ☻quaycoop.com. Self-service, partly organic workers' cooperative café above a health-food store and bakery, serving tasty, substantial and cheap vegetarian and vegan meals (and catering for many other dietary requirements), great salads, soups, cakes, puddings, breakfasts, teas and coffees. Mon–Sat 9am–9pm, Sun noon–9pm.

NIGHTLIFE

The city boasts dozens of great **bars**, specializing in characterful and unreconstructed old **pubs**. These would generally be worth seeking out for their atmosphere alone, but a high proportion of them also host **music**, traditional or otherwise. Look out for the forthcoming Rising Sons microbrewery and bar on Cornmarket Street opposite Bodega (see below), where craft beers such as Mi Daza stout and Sunbeam pils will be produced. For general **information** on the arts, nightlife and entertainment, consult the free monthly leaflet, *Whazon* (☻whazon.com), which can be picked up in cafés and arts venues. Plugd Records (☎021 427 6300, ☻plugdrecords.com), a well-stocked music shop in the Triskel Arts Centre on Tobin St (see p.240), is a good place for info on the gig and club scenes, and organizes some interesting club nights and gigs itself, often at *Gulpd Café* in the arts centre.

PUBS AND BARS
THE ISLAND

An Spailpín Fánach 28 South Main St ☎021 427 7949. Rambling, rustic and unpretentious, the "Migrant Worker" was established opposite the recently closed Beamish and Crawford Brewery in the eighteenth century, and hosts traditional music most nights. Mon–Thurs noon–11.30pm, Fri & Sat noon–12.30am, Sun 12.30–11pm.

Bodega Cornmarket St ☎021 427 3756, ☻bodegacork .ie. Barn-like all-rounder in a former covered food market (the Irish Market, a cheaper version of the English Market), which has been redecorated in theatrical fashion, with a lofty bar, chandeliers, arched colonnades and acres of red velour. The food's especially good here, including meat and cheese plates and brunches. Late on Fri & Sat nights, it turns into one of Cork's most popular clubs. Mon–Thurs 10am–11.30pm, Fri & Sat 10am–2am, Sun 11am–11pm.

Crane Lane Theatre Phoenix St ☎021 427 8487, ☻cranelanetheatre.ie. Cosy, vibrant theatre bar, offering a wide range of craft beers, though much of the action happens under the hanging plants in the big, heated courtyard out front. Live bands – anything from folk and blues to Henry Rollins – and/or DJs every night. Mon–Fri 2pm–2am, Sat & Sun noon–2pm.

The Long Valley 10 Winthrop St ☎021 427 2144, ☻thelongvalleybar.com. Fine traditional bar, sporting a large snug at the front and decorated with plants, old views of Cork and a mishmash of wooden furniture, some of it rescued from a cruise-liner. Famous for its tasty doorstep sandwiches at lunch time. Poetry, stories and acoustic music on Mon nights (☻obheal.ie) and live traditional, folk and bluegrass on Thurs. Mon–Thurs 11am/noon–11.30pm, Fri & Sat 11am/noon–12.30am, Sun roughly noon–11pm.

Mayne's Pembroke St ☎021 427 9449. Atmospheric, not to say creepy, conversion of an ancient pharmacy with dozens of old apothecary items left on the shelves, beyond which cellar-like cubicles connect with the Crane Lane Theatre bar. If you can peel your eyes away from the decor for a minute, you'll find an excellent menu of well-kept wines by the glass, as well as meat and cheese plates, sandwiches and even breakfasts. Mon–Thurs 10am–1.30am, Sun noon–1.30am.

The Poor Relation Parnell Place ☎021 494 9049. This friendly new branch of Sin É (see p.240) has more of a contemporary feel than its older, more prosperous relative, though it also offers craft beers, lots of nooks and crannies, and candles in bottles. Traditional sessions 11pm Fri and Sat. Mon–Thurs 9.30am–11.30pm, Fri & Sat 9.30am–12.30am, Sun noon–11pm.

The Porterhouse Sheare St ☎021 427 3000. Small, dimly lit new branch of the excellent Dublin microbrewery-pub, with lots of leather sofas, a popular bar menu and lots of other craft beers beside their own fine brews. Mon–Thurs 5–11.30pm, Fri & Sat 5pm–12.30am, Sun 5–11pm.

OFF-ISLAND

Charlie's Union Quay ☎021 431 8342, ☻charliesbarcork.com. Dimly lit, grungy pub with an early licence and frequent live music, mostly blues but including traditional session on Sun afternoon. Mon–Sat 7am–late, Sun 12.30pm–late.

★**The Corner House** 7 Coburg St ☎021 450 0655.

7

Welcoming pub, similar in feel to *Sin É* next door, though more spacious and airy. Bluegrass every Sun and Mon, traditional music Tues and Wed, blues Thurs. Mon–Thurs 3.30–11.30pm, Fri & Sat 3.30pm–midnight, Sun 3.30–11pm.

Franciscan Well 12A North Mall ☎021 421 0130, ⓦfranciscanwellbrewery.com. On the site of a medieval monastery whose well was known for its curative properties, this microbrewery-bar knocks out great stout, lager, ale and wheat beer, which can be enjoyed out the back in the sunny/heated beer-yard. Also offers pizzas from a wood-fired oven (Mon–Fri eves) and brewery tours (Mon–Fri 6.30pm), while diverse events include a Wed-night storyteller. Mon–Thurs 3–11.30pm, Fri & Sat 3pm–12.30am, Sun 3–11pm; in summer Mon–Sat opens 1pm.

Sin É 8 Coburg St ☎021 450 2266. Cosy, candlelit pub, hung with all sorts of bric-a-brac and memorabilia and offering a wide range of beers. Frequent, varied live music, including traditional Tues, early evenings Fri and Sat, and all day Sun. The name means "That's It" because there used to be a funeral parlour next door. Mon–Thurs 12.30–11.30pm, Fri & Sat 12.30pm–12.30am, Sun 12.30–11pm.

CLUB

Bodega (see p.239) turns into a popular club on weekends.

Chambers Washington St ☎021 465 8100, ⓦfacebook .com/chamberscork. The city's main gay bar and club, with DJs every night and regular events; €5 admission Fri & Sat after 11pm. Wed & Fri–Sun 8.30pm–2am.

ENTERTAINMENT

Cork Opera House Emmet Place ☎021 427 0022, ⓦcorkoperahouse.ie. The city's main performance venue, hosting high-quality drama, dance, opera, comedy and concerts of all hues, with more eclectic shows in the attached Half Moon Theatre.

Everyman MacCurtain St ☎021 450 1673, ⓦeverymancork.com. Cork's oldest traditional theatre, dating back to the late nineteenth century, offers a varied menu of drama, dance, opera, music and comedy.

Triskel Christchurch Bishop Lucey Park and Tobin St ☎021 427 2022, ⓦtriskelartscentre.ie. The main contemporary arts centre splits itself between Christchurch, a fine, early Georgian Protestant church, deconsecrated and beautifully renovated, where arthouse films, interesting gigs and art exhibitions are put on; and its original home on Tobin St, which includes an art gallery and a café, *Gulpd*. Hour-long guided tours of the church Tues at noon and Thurs at 2pm (€3).

SHOPPING

English Market Accessed either from Princes St or Grand Parade ⓦenglishmarket.ie. A Victorian covered market with the city's best fishmongers, greengrocers and butchers – stocking the local delicacies of tripe and *drisheen*, a type of black pudding – and all manner of pungent specialist stalls where you could build a great picnic (perhaps for eating in the small Bishop Lucey Park, on the other side of Grand Parade): cheeses, cold meats and smoked fish, olives, salads and deli goods, bread, cakes, and even wine and chocolates. Mon–Sat 8am–6pm.

Liam Ruiseal 49 Oliver Plunkett St ☎021 427 0981. The best local bookshop, including a good range of books on and from Cork and Ireland. Mon–Sat 9am–5.30pm.

Mother Jones Flea market York St, near the corner of MacCurtain St ☎085 175 1554. Purveys vintage clothes, antiques and books. Fri–Sun 11am–6/7pm.

DIRECTORY

Exchange The main banks are on and around St Patrick's St, and there are bureaux de change at the big hotels and at *Cork International Hostel*.

Gaelic football and hurling Cork is one of the few counties that's strong on both Gaelic games, and Páirc Uí Chaoimh, 2km east of the centre off Centre Park Rd, is one of the country's major stadiums; for fixtures, consult ⓦgaacork.ie or the *Irish Examiner*.

Pharmacy Phelan's Late Night Pharmacy, 9 Patrick St ☎021 427 2511.

Police The main police station is on Anglesea St ☎021 452 2000.

CORK FESTIVALS

Cork hosts plenty of lively festivals, of which the largest and most prestigious are the **midsummer festival**, a wide-ranging celebration of the arts in late June (ⓦcorkmidsummer .com), the **jazz festival** in October (ⓦguinnessjazzfestival.com) and the **film festival** in October or November, with a particular focus on short films (ⓦcorkfilmfest.org). There's also an international **choral festival** in late April or early May (ⓦcorkchoral.ie), the gay pride festival in July/August (ⓦcorkpride.com) and **an early-music festival** in October, shared between the city and East Cork (ⓦeastcorkearlymusic.ie).

East Cork

East Cork occupies a blind spot in the eyes of many visitors, their focus set on the more spectacular coastline to the west, but several interesting places are worth considering, all of them served by public transport. A suburban train service makes possible an excellent, varied day-trip across the Lee estuary to **Fota Island**, with its sensitively restored Neoclassical hunting lodge and wildlife park, and on to the attractive harbour town of **Cobh** on Great Island. Further east lies **Midleton**, the traditional home of Jameson whiskey and a culinary hub. In an expansive setting at the mouth of the River Blackwater, the historic, easy-going resort of **Youghal**, some 40km east of Cork, marks the border with County Waterford.

Fota House

April–Sept Mon–Sat 10am–5pm, Sun 11am–4pm; guided tours (bookable by phone) from 11am, with the last tour at 3.30pm • €8, car parking €3 • ☎ 021 481 5543, Ⓦ fotahouse.com

If you travel from the mainland by road, you're hardly aware that **Fota** is an island in Cork Harbour. Its main attraction is **Fota House**, built in the 1740s as a hunting lodge for the Barry family, whose main seat had by then moved from nearby Barryscourt Castle to Castlelyons near Fermoy. In the early nineteenth century, the house was substantially redeveloped and extended in elegant Neoclassical style, and now lies a ten-minute walk from Fota train station. Excellent guided tours reveal plenty of telling details, with the highlights being the **entrance hall**, a beautifully symmetrical space divided by striking ochre columns of *scagliola* (imitation marble), and the ceiling of the **drawing room**, with its plasterwork doves, musical instruments, hunting implements and delicately painted cherubs and floral motifs. The tour also goes below stairs to the **servants' quarters**, which include an impressive octagonal game-larder and such features as gaps at the top of the windows of the butler's servery – added so that food smells would tantalize the poor servants rather than the house guests. For visitors, there's now a nice little café in the long gallery and billiard room. Much of the estate's formal gardens and its internationally significant **arboretum**, laid out in the mid-nineteenth century, are under the care of the Office of Public Works, with free access. At its best in April and May, the arboretum hosts a wide range of exotic trees and shrubs, with many rare examples, including some magnificent Lebanese cedars, a Victorian fernery and a lush, almost tropical, lake.

Fota Wildlife Park

Mon–Sat 10am–6pm, Sun 10.30am–6pm; last admission 5pm • €14.50, children €9.50, family ticket from €44, car parking €3 • ☎ 021 481 2678, Ⓦ fotawildlife.ie

In the former estate of Fota House, **Fota Wildlife Park** is renowned for its success in breeding cheetahs, which, along with monkeys, giraffes, bison and many other species, wander about in seventy acres of open countryside. There's also a new tropical house, featuring snakes, lizards and turtles, while events include the daily cheetah run and other animal feeding times, as well as weekend wildlife talks.

Cobh

On the southern coast of Great Island, with extensive views of Cork Harbour, **COBH** (pronounced "cove") makes a great escape from the city on a fine day. This historic and unpretentious resort, clinging onto a steep, south-facing slope, sports a stony beach, a promenade with a bandstand and gaily painted rows of Victorian hotels and houses. Much of the tourist traffic comes now from the dozens of huge cruise-liners that dock here every year, continuing a long tradition for this fine natural harbour: Cobh was a port of call for the *Sirius*, the first steamship to cross the Atlantic, in 1838, and for the *Titanic* on her disastrous maiden voyage in 1912, while many of the victims of the sinking of the *Lusitania* in 1915 (see p.247) were buried in the Old Church Cemetery, 2km north of Cobh. The port was also a major supply depot during the American and Napoleonic wars, and became Ireland's main point of emigration after the Great Famine.

Cobh Heritage Centre: the Queenstown Story

May–Oct Mon–Sat 9.30am–5.30pm, Sun 11am–5.30pm; Nov–April Mon–Sat 9.30am–4.30pm, Sun 11am–4.30pm; genealogical service available • €9; Heritage Island • ⓦ cobhheritage.com

Cobh's long and often tragic seafaring history is vividly detailed at the **Queenstown Story**, a multimedia heritage centre with a pleasant café in the former Victorian train station on the seafront (the town was renamed Queenstown after a visit by Queen Victoria in 1849, but its old name was restored after Independence).

The Titanic Experience

Daily: summer 9am–6pm; winter 10am–5.30pm; last tour about 1hr before closing • €9.50 • ⓦ titanicexperiencecobh.ie

Cobh was the last port of call for the *Titanic*, with the final 123 passengers boarding here on April 11, 1912. The White Star Line ticket office where they assembled, backed by its now-ruinous wooden pier, has been turned into a visitor experience, a short way east of the tourist office along the seafront. Amid re-creations of third- and first-class cabins, it's revealed that while first had a heated swimming pool, the 700 third-class passengers had to share two baths. There are some interesting audiovisuals, including footage of the wreck, discovered in 1985, as well as games and interactive quizzes.

Cobh Museum

Scots Church, High Rd • March/April–Oct Mon–Sat 11am–1pm & 2–5/5.30pm, Sun 2.30–5.30pm • €2.50 • ⓦ cobhmuseum.com

If your appetite for salty tales and memorabilia still hasn't been sated, get along to the **Cobh Museum**, housed in a nineteenth-century Presbyterian church on the west side of the town centre, opposite the railway station.

ARRIVAL AND INFORMATION COBH

By train The station is towards the western end of the seafront.

Destinations Cork (Mon–Sat at least hourly, 12 on Sun; 25min).

By ferry Cork Harbour Ferry runs between Glenbrook near Passage West, on the mainland southeast of Cork city, and Carrigaloe, a few kilometres north of Cobh on Great Island (daily 7am–10pm, every 10min or so; 4min; car €5 single, €7.50 return; adults €1 single, €1.50 return; bikes carried free; ☎ 021 481 1485).

Tourist office Right on the waterfront, Cobh's helpful tourist office (Mon–Fri 9/9.30am–5/5.30pm, Sat & Sun 10.30am–5pm; ☎ 021 481 3301, ⓦ cobhharbourchamber .ie) shares the old yacht club with the Sirius Arts Centre (ⓦ siriusartscentre.ie), home to some interesting art exhibitions and concerts.

COBH TOURS AND WATERSPORTS

Ireland's – and possibly the world's – first **yacht club** was founded in Cobh in 1720 (the Royal Cork Yacht Club, now moved across the harbour to Crosshaven), and messing about in **boats** is still a strong feature of life in the town. Sail Cork, which is based 5km out at East Ferry Marina at the eastern end of Great Island (☎ 021 481 1237, ⓦ sailcork.com), runs **sailing and kayaking courses**, and there's a people's regatta in August. In summer you can take a thrice-daily **cruise** from Kennedy Pier (1hr 10min; €15; ☎ 086 416 9662, ⓦ corkwaterbus.com) around Cork Harbour, which is said to be the second-largest natural harbour in the world (by navigable area) after Sydney. The engaging and enterprising Michael Martin (☎ 021 481 5211, ⓦ titanic.ie) organizes hour-long walking tours, starting from the *Commodore Hotel* opposite the tourist office, both *Titanic*-themed (daily 11am & 2pm; €9.50–12.50; Oct–March pre-booking essential) and *Lusitania*-themed (summer Wed & Sun 12.30pm; €9.50). He also offers a tour of Spike Island in the bay, with its imposing star-shaped fortress and prison (June–Aug daily 2pm; €13.50 including boat trip).

GETTING AROUND

Car rental Great Island (see p.236) has a car rental base at Rushbrooke, just north of Cobh, and meets disembarking passengers at the cruise-ship terminal.

ACCOMMODATION

Ardeen 3 Harbour Hill ☎087 664 5021. Good, central, all-en-suite choice in a recently refurbished 200-year-old town house loftily located just beneath the cathedral, with great views from some of the rooms and an open fire in the sitting room. €76

Gilbert's 11 Pearse Square ☎021 481 1300, ⓦgilbertsincobh.com. Above a restaurant on one of two pleasant squares that sit next to each other on the harbourfront, with spacious, stylish and bright contemporary bedrooms and well-equipped bathrooms with black and white tiles and big-head showers. Very good rates for singles. €70

Waters Edge Yacht Club Quay ☎021 481 5566, ⓦwatersedgehotel.ie. Between the heritage centre and the tourist office stands this tastefully decorated hotel, where many of the bright, spacious bedrooms – as well as the fine restaurant – have seafront verandas. €79

EATING AND DRINKING

Gilbert's 11 Pearse Square ☎021 481 1300, ⓦgilbertsincobh.com. With leather banquettes and bent-wood chairs inside and a few tables out on the square, this chic café-restaurant prepares tasty sandwiches, soups and simple mains for lunch, and bistro dishes such as Mediterranean seafood pie (€18) in the evenings, when there's a two-course set menu for €21 (not available after 6.30pm on Fri & Sat). Tues–Thurs 9am–8.30pm, Fri & Sat 9am–9.30pm; winter closed Tues.

The Quays Bar 17 Westbourne Place ☎021 481 3539, ⓦthequays.ie. A modern pub next to the tourist office that serves tasty lunch and dinner, specializing in seafood, with tapas and barbecues in summer, but its main draw is its lovely big patio right on the harbourside. Mon–Thurs 10.30am–11.30pm, Fri & Sat 10.30am–1.30am, Sun 10.30am–11pm.

Rob Roy Pearse Square ☎021 481 1055. This friendly, attractively renovated black-and-white pub with tables out on the square offers craft beers and a clever sampler tray of three stouts (Guinness up against the local Murphy's and Beamish). There are traditional sessions on Thurs and early evening Sun, and live music, usually traditional or blues, on Sat. Opens around noon or later, sometimes 10am if there's a cruise liner in; closes 11.30pm Mon–Thurs, 12.30am Fri & Sat, 11pm Sun.

Midleton

The busy market town of **MIDLETON**, burgeoning with Cork commuters especially now that the local train line has reopened, is creating a strong culinary reputation for itself and in early September hosts a **food festival** (ⓦmidletonfoodfestival.ie). It's arrayed round a broad, lively main street, which is bypassed to the south by the N25, so makes a pleasant stopover, just 18km east of Cork.

The Jameson Experience

Daily: April–Oct 10am–4.30pm (start of last tour); Nov–March tours at 11.30am, 1.15pm, 2.30pm & 4pm • €14 (€12.60 online); Heritage Island • ⓦjamesonwhiskey.com • April–Sept shuttle bus daily 10am & 2pm from St Patrick's Quay, Cork

The town's main visitor activity is **The Jameson Experience**, at the **Old Distillery** off the south end of the main street. Whiskey is no longer made in this partly eighteenth-century distillery, but you'll be shown around the carefully restored machinery – including the largest pot still in the world, with a capacity of 32,000 gallons – in the atmospheric old buildings, and you'll get a taste of the "water of life" (*uisce*) at the end.

INFORMATION   MIDLETON

Tourist office At the distillery entrance (summer only, irregular hours, but usually Mon–Fri 10am–1pm & 2–5pm; ☎021 461 3702).

ACCOMMODATION

An Stór Drury's Lane (IHH) ☎021 463 3106, ⓦanstor .ie. In a converted wool store off the east side of Main St, this comfortable, welcoming, all-en-suite hostel has a women's 6-bed and a mixed 8-bed dorm, twin, double and

7

family private rooms, a kitchen/dining room and plenty of local information at hand. Dorms €20, doubles €60

★**Ballymaloe House** Around 10km southeast of Midleton, off the R629 Cloyne–Ballycotton road ☎021 465 2531, ⓦballymaloe.ie. Attached to the famous restaurant (see below), accommodation in this delightful, vine-covered, originally fifteenth-century manor house and adjacent courtyard mixes country-house style with contemporary art. There's a summertime outdoor pool, five-hole golf course, croquet and a tennis court, plus bicycles for guests' use and walks around the extensive grounds, farm and the garden of Ballymaloe's nearby cookery school. Attached to the house is a seventeenth-century grainstore that's been converted into a venue for music, theatre and events such as a festival of books and food in May. Various packages available; very good single rates. €240

Castlemartyr Resort 10km east of Midleton on the N25 ☎021 421 9000, ⓦcastlemartyrresort.ie. Opulent hotel – think electronic curtains and traditional afternoon teas – in an eighteenth-century manor house, flanked by a striking modern extension and the ruins of the original medieval castle that was once owned by Sir Walter Raleigh. There's a luxurious ESPA spa and an excellent modern Irish restaurant, The Bell Tower, using the best of local, seasonal ingredients, and bikes are available for guests to explore the 200-acre estate, which was landscaped by Capability Brown but now encompasses an eighteen-hole golf course. €156

Glenview House 4km north of Midleton off the R626 Fermoy road ☎021 463 1680, ⓦglenviewmidleton .com. Upmarket B&B in an eighteenth-century country house run by friendly and solicitous owners. As well as beautiful gardens, the house has large, comfortable bedrooms and many fine Georgian architectural features, which were rescued from Fitzwilliam St, Dublin, when the electricity board knocked down a row of houses there in the 1960s (see p.66). March–Sept; self-catering cottages available year-round. €70

EATING AND DRINKING

★**Ballymaloe House** Around 10km southeast of Midleton, off the R629 Cloyne–Ballycotton road ☎021 465 2531, ⓦballymaloe.ie. Ireland's most famous restaurant, serving exceptional modern Irish cuisine using local ingredients, such as poached wild salmon with samphire in tomato and basil sauce, with some nice traditional touches – you'll be asked if you want second helpings and you choose your dessert from a groaning trolley. Five-course set dinner menu €70. Lunch daily at 1pm, dinner Mon–Sat 7–9.30pm, Sun (buffet) 7.30–8.30pm.

★**The Farm Gate** Coolbawn, off the west side of Main St ☎021 463 2771, ⓦfarmgate.ie. Big sister to The Farm Gate Café (see p.238) in Cork, a bustling café-restaurant where they prepare local ingredients carefully and simply, at reasonable prices. For lunch (noon–3.30pm) most main dishes are €10–15; for dinner, a little more expensive. Their own bakery and deli out front sells fresh artisanal produce. Tues & Wed 9am–5pm, Thurs–Sat 9am–5pm & 6.30–9.30pm (last orders).

Finín's 75 Main St ☎021 463 1878, ⓦfinins.ie. Don't be fooled by the traditional pub frontage here – it's more restaurant than bar, decorated with colourful modern paintings, where you can choose between light dishes such as delicious chicken-liver pâté with salad (€8.50) and fancier meals like fillet steak in wine, cream and mushroom sauce (€28). Simple three-course menu €25. Mon–Sat 10.30am–10pm.

McDaid's 55 Main St ☎021 463 1559. This traditional pub occupies two neo-Gothic houses designed by Augustus Pugin in 1851 on the east side of Main Street, and holds regular gigs at its folk club upstairs. Mon–Thurs 10.30am–11.30pm, Fri & Sat 10.30am–2am, Sun 12.30pm–1.30am.

O'Donovan's Opposite the distillery on Main St ☎021 463 1255. Formal white-tablecloth restaurant offering excellent dishes such as duck confit with chorizo and black-eyed peas, a warm welcome and a good-value early-bird menu (three courses for €27.50). Tues–Fri 5–9pm, Sat 6–9pm.

Wallis' 74 Main St ☎021 463 3185. Next door to Finín's and also known as The Town Hall Bar, Wallis' hosts a traditional session on Tues, an open-mike night Wed, plus plenty of other live music. Mon–Thurs 9am–midnight, Fri 9am–1am, Sat 10am–1am, Sun 12.30–11.30pm.

SHOPPING

Farmers' Market Midleton Green, off the east side of Main St ⓦmidletonfarmersmarket.com. Midleton hosts one of the country's best farmers' markets, offering everything from cheese, smoked fish and meats to breads, cakes and chocolate. Sat 9.30am–1pm.

Youghal

YOUGHAL (pronounced "yawl") enjoys a lush, picturesque setting on the west bank of the River Blackwater's estuary, the border with County Waterford. It was one of Ireland's leading ports in the medieval era, with a scattering of ancient buildings to show for it – as well as a historical festival in late September (ⓦyoughalcelebrateshistory.com), when field trips, concerts and other entertainments accompany an international historical conference. It later became a centre for the carpet industry, but today is popular with holidaying Irish families, who take their leisure on the long sandy beach to the southwest.

Main Street

Youghal's long, gently curving **Main Street** is lined with tall, colourfully painted nineteenth-century buildings, interspersed with a few more historic structures. Bridging the south end of the street, the most obvious of these is the Georgian **clock tower**, which stands on the site of a medieval gate. It's a huge but well-proportioned sandstone affair that once served as a prison and may reopen for public visits in the future.

Further north on Main Street, you'll find the **Red House**, a typically steep-roofed Dutch-style home built around 1710, and, opposite, a restored tower house, **Tynte's Castle**, from the fifteenth century.

Collegiate Church of St Mary's

Church St • Summer Mon–Sat 10am–4.30pm, Sun 12.30–4pm; winter Mon–Sat 10.30am–4pm, Sun 12.30–4pm

Turning left off Main Street, at the seventeenth-century almshouses near the Red House, onto Church Street will shortly bring you to Youghal's main historic site, the Anglican **Collegiate Church of St Mary's**. On the site of the fifth-century monastic settlement of St Declan of Ardmore, it's one of the oldest functioning churches in Ireland, built in about 1250. On its north side stands an unusual fortified bell tower, dating probably from the fifteenth century, while inside, the squat Gothic nave boasts impressive oak roof trusses. Look out also for an elaborate, painted sword-rest, which was used for the mayor's sword in the seventeenth century, and a beautifully carved eighteenth-century oak pulpit. Almost bursting out of the south transept, an extravagant, multicoloured monument commemorates Richard Boyle, the seventeenth-century Earl of Cork who did much to develop Youghal, along with his two wives and children, including the chemist Robert. Beyond the church lie the pretty gardens of St Mary's College and the well-preserved thirteenth-century town walls, which provide great views of the bay.

ARRIVAL AND DEPARTURE   YOUGHAL

By bus Buses stop at the north end of Main St.

INFORMATION AND TOURS

Tourist information The tourist office and the attached heritage centre, which recounts the port's history since the ninth century, are on Market Square, between Main St and the harbour near the clock tower (summer daily 9am–5pm; winter Mon–Fri 10am–3pm; heritage centre free; ☎024 20170, ⓦyoughal.ie).

Boat tours In summer, Blackwater Cruises (☎087 988 9076, ⓦblackwatercruises.com) runs 90min trips up the beautiful Blackwater River, lined with castles, country houses and ruined abbeys, from the jetty near the tourist office.

Walking tours Interesting tours of the town depart from the tourist office (July & Aug Mon–Fri 11am & 3pm; at other times, book through the tourist office; 1hr 30min; €7). Meanwhile, the "Youghal App", available free from the App Store or Google Play, covers four tours of Youghal and the surrounding area.

ACCOMMODATION

As well as the **accommodation** below, there are also dozens of B&Bs, many of them out on the Cork road near the beach.

★**Aherne's** 163 North Main St ☎024 92424, ⓦahernes.net. Superb small hotel in the centre of town, with spacious luxury bedrooms around a courtyard; the rooms are tastefully decorated with antique furniture, and breakfasts are great. Half-board packages and self-catering apartments also available. Good rates for singles. €120

Avonmore House South Abbey ☎024 92617, ⓦavonmoreyoughal.com. Bright, colourful, en-suite rooms in an elegant, centrally located Georgian mansion, a short way south of the tourist office, with home-baked soda bread and kippers or pancakes for breakfast. Very good rates for singles. **€70**

Clonvilla Clonpriest, around 7km southwest of town near the beach, on the R633 towards Ballymacoda about 4km off the N25 ☏024 98288, ✉clonvilla@ hotmail.com. This caravan and camping park offers a campers' kitchen, laundry facilities and a playground, as well as inexpensive B&B. March–Oct. **€20**

Roseville New Catherine St ☏024 92571, ⊕rosevillebb.com. Located right in the town centre, north from the tourist office, this is an attractive, detached, period house with a large garden and good breakfasts. Mid-Jan to mid-Dec. **€72**

EATING AND DRINKING

★**Aherne's** 163 North Main St ☏024 92424, ⊕ahernes.net. The excellent restaurant here (2 courses for €24) uses local, seasonal ingredients, such as beef and lamb, wherever possible but is known especially for its fresh seafood – and a mean chocolate pudding – or you can choose from the all-day menu, including sandwiches, by the open fire in the very congenial bar. Restaurant daily 6–9pm.

The Nook (Treacy's) 20 North Main St, by the turn-off for St Mary's Church ☏024 92225. Relaxing and cosy, traditional, hundred-year-old pub with a spruce black-and-white café at the front and a beer garden at the back, which is very popular for its varied lunches (Mon–Fri). Traditional music Wed, Thurs & Fri in summer. Mon–Thurs 10.30am–11.30pm, Fri & Sat 10.30am–12.30am, Sun noon–1pm.

Paddy Linehan's Bar Market Square, opposite the tourist office ☏024 92756. One for movie buffs: for the filming of *Moby Dick* with Gregory Peck in 1954, John Huston transformed Youghal's waterfront into New Bedford, Massachusetts, and the pub where he planned each day's filming is now hung with signed photos of the shoot. Mon–Thurs 10.30am–11.30pm, Fri & Sat 10.30am–12.30am, Sun noon–11pm.

★**Sage** North Main St, just north of the clock tower ☏024 85844. Superb café-restaurant where everything is homemade and locally sourced whenever possible. Sit in the crisp, contemporary interior or at the sun-trap tables on the back patio and tuck into delicate plaice, freshly landed at Youghal, with chive *beurre blanc* (€14). There are soups, salads, sandwiches and quiches if you're less peckish, or you could round things off with a fantastic rhubarb tart, among a mouthwatering display of cakes and desserts. Mon–Sat 10am–6pm.

ENTERTAINMENT

Comhaltas Brú na Sí, Blackwater Heights, on the west side of town ☏087 793 4504, ⊕comhaltas.ie. In summer, the local branch of this non-profit organization for the promotion of Irish traditional music puts on a stage show of song, dance and storytelling. July & Aug Mon & Thurs evenings.

Kinsale

KINSALE, 25km south of Cork city, enjoys a glorious setting at the head of a sheltered harbour around the mouth of the Bandon River. Two imposing forts and a fine tower-house remain as evidence of its former importance as a trading port, and Kinsale has built on its cosmopolitan links to become the culinary capital of the southwest. Add in plenty of opportunities for watersports on the fine local beaches and a number of congenial pubs, and you have a very appealing, upscale resort town.

Brief history

St Multose founded a monastery at Kinsale in the sixth century, and by the tenth the Vikings had established a trading post. After the Anglo-Normans walled the town in the thirteenth century, it really began to take off, flourishing on trade, fishing and shipbuilding in its excellent deep harbour, which became an important rendezvous and provisioning point for the British Navy. The **Battle of Kinsale** in 1601 was a major turning point in Irish history, leading to the "Flight of the Earls" to the Continent six years later which saw the end of the old Gaelic aristocracy: Philip III of Spain had sent forces to Kinsale to support the Irish chieftains, but communications were poor and Chief Hugh O'Neill, more accustomed to guerrilla warfare, was defeated by Elizabeth I's army in a pitched battle.

In 1689 **James II** landed here in his attempt to claim back the throne, only to flee ignominiously from this same port a year later, after defeat at the Battle of the Boyne. His supporters fought on, however, burning the town and holing up in James Fort and Charles Fort. After a series of decisive attacks by the Duke of Marlborough, they surrendered on favourable terms and were allowed to go to Limerick for the final battle under Patrick Sarsfield (see p.312).

During World War I, in May 1915, a German submarine torpedoed the passenger liner *Lusitania* off the Old Head of Kinsale, as it was sailing from New York to England. Twelve hundred of the passengers and crew were lost, and the sinking was a major factor in the USA's eventual entry into the war.

Kinsale Regional Museum

Market Place • Wed–Sat 10.30am–1.30pm • Free

The **Kinsale Regional Museum** is immediately recognizable in the warren of lanes behind the tourist office by its Dutch-style triple gables, which were added in 1706 to the market house of 1600. Upstairs, the courtroom where the inquest into the loss of the *Lusitania* took place has been left partly as it was, augmented, poignantly, by an almost pristine deckchair from the wreck, as well as a medal produced in Germany to celebrate the sinking. Otherwise, the museum is a dusty collection of tools, maps and any old rope, dotted with a few curiosities such as the shoes of the eight-foot three-inch Kinsale Giant, who made a fortune on the English stage in the eighteenth century as a novelty act.

Desmond Castle

Cork St • Easter–Sept daily 10am–6pm, last admission 5pm • €3; Heritage Card • ⓦ heritageireland.ie

A fine example of an urban tower-house, **Desmond Castle** was built around 1500 as a town residence and customs house by the Earl of Desmond, who had recently been given control of the wine trade from France, Spain and Portugal to Bristol by King Henry VII. The architectural highlight is the façade, pierced by ogival windows,

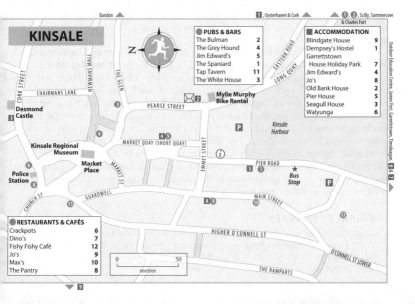

including unusual corner pairs on the first floor, and stamped with the Desmond coat of arms surmounted by Henry VII's royal standard. Interesting displays inside trace the building's chequered, often grim history – including stints as a jail and workhouse – as well as local connections with the global wine trade. Many of the "Wild Geese", Irishmen who fled the country in the sixteenth to eighteenth centuries, especially after the Battle of Kinsale and the Battle of the Boyne, went on to have successful second careers in viticulture, notably Richard Hennessy of Cork who settled in Cognac in the 1740s, and the Lynches of Galway, producers of the famous claret, Château Lynch-Bages.

James Fort

On the west side of the harbour, Kinsale spreads south for a couple of kilometres to the broad mouth of the Bandon River. On a long spit of land between the river and the outer harbour, **James Fort** is a great place for a picnic, with fine views that stretch from the town around to the open sea. Built in 1602–4 on the site of a walled fortification that was easily captured by the English from the Spanish forces at the Battle of Kinsale, it's a five-sided fort whose walls are now fetchingly overgrown with ferns and brambles. The new fort, however, proved equally vulnerable when, in 1649, a well-placed gun on the higher ground to the west led to its surrender to the Cromwellians, and in the 1680s, the building of Charles Fort finally rendered James Fort obsolete. On the southeast-facing side of the narrow peninsula, there's a small and pleasant sandy **beach** (signposted).

Charles Fort

Jan & Feb Tues–Sun 10am–5pm; early March, Nov & Dec daily 10am–5pm (closed for a week over Christmas); mid-March to Oct daily 10am–6pm; last admission 1hr before closing • €4; Heritage Card • Ⓦ heritageireland.ie

Kinsale's most compelling sight, the formidable **Charles Fort**, lies on the east side of the harbour, 3km southeast of town beyond the village of Summercove. On a fine day, the best way to get there is to **walk**, skirting round Scilly village and then following the lower, shoreline road, with refreshment available at *The Spaniard* and *The Bulman* (see p.250). It's also possible to extend the walk along the scrub-covered slopes out to the point at the end of the outer harbour (2hr return from the fort at an easy pace).

Begun in 1678, Charles Fort stands on the site of Anglo-Norman Ringcurran Castle, which had been destroyed on Cromwell's orders in 1656. **Sir William Robinson**, architect of the Royal Hospital, Kilmainham (see p.85), adapted the classic, star-shaped design of the great French military engineer Vauban, but his advice to build extra fortifications at the top of the hill was not followed – though the fort was almost impregnable from the sea, the Duke of Marlborough was easily able to unseat the Jacobites by attacking on land in 1690. Most of the buildings on the twelve-acre site were damaged during the Irish Civil War in 1922, but the eerie roofless shells are substantial enough to give a ready impression of what life in the fort must have been like for its garrison of four hundred, and you can flesh out the picture by sampling the fascinating displays and audiovisuals in the rebuilt Barracks Stores. The former ordnance sheds opposite now house a café.

KINSALE FESTIVALS

Kinsale hosts a varied and prestigious ten-day arts festival in September (Ⓦ kinsaleartsfestival .com); a weekend **gourmet festival** in early October (Ⓦ kinsalerestaurants.com); and a fringe jazz festival to coincide with the main jazz festival in Cork over the bank-holiday weekend in late October.

ARRIVAL AND INFORMATION   KINSALE

By bus Buses stop on Pier Rd, right at the heart of Kinsale.

Tourist information The friendly, well-informed tourist office, which has plenty of useful free literature on the town, is on Pier Rd (June–Oct Mon–Sat 9.15am–5pm, closing for lunch some days, perhaps opening Sun in July & Aug; Nov–May Tues–Sat 9.15am–5pm, closing for lunch; ☎ 021 477 2234, ⊛ kinsale.ie).

TOURS AND ACTIVITIES

Bike rental Mylie Murphy, 8 Pearse St (☎ 021 477 2703).

Cruises The tourist office has the times of cruises past the two forts to the outer harbour and the Bandon River on the *Spirit of Kinsale* (roughly March–Oct; €12.50; ☎ 086 250 5456, ⊛ kinsaleharbourcruises.com).

Horse riding For horse riding, contact Kinsale Equestrian Centre, 2km northwest of the centre off the Bandon road (☎ 086 853 0894, ⊛ kinsale-equestrian.com).

Walking tours From the tourist office, Dermot Ryan (1–2 daily; 1hr; €5; ☎ 086 826 7656, ⊛ kinsaleheritage.com) and Don and Barry (1–2 daily; 1hr; €6; ☎ 021 477 2873, ⊛ historicstrollkinsale.com) run engaging historical walking tours, while evening ghost tours meet at the *Tap*

Tavern on Guardwell (roughly May–Sept Sun–Fri 9pm; 1hr; €10; ☎ 087 948 0910).

Watersports Both the Outdoor Education Centre (☎ 021 477 2896, ⊛ kinsaleoutdoors.com), on the harbour near the town centre, and Oysterhaven Activity Centre (☎ 021 477 0738, ⊛ oysterhaven.com), 5km east of Kinsale on Oysterhaven Bay, have sailing, windsurfing and kayaking. At long, sandy Garrettstown Beach, 12km southwest of town, H2O does sea-kayaking trips and courses (☎ 087 393 1633, ⊛ h2oseakayaking. com), while Kinsale Surf Adventures offers surfing and stand-up paddleboarding (☎ 083 107 5757, ⊛ surfkinsale.com). Ocean Addicts (☎ 087 790 3211, ⊛ oceanaddicts.ie) does diving and snorkelling.

ACCOMMODATION

There are dozens of **B&Bs** and a particularly good selection of upmarket **guesthouses** in Kinsale, as well as a **hostel**. Booking is advisable in high summer and during festivals.

Blindgate House Blindgate ☎ 021 477 7858, ⊛ blindgatehouse.com. Bright, stylish and welcoming guesthouse a 5min walk west of the town centre up the hill. Decorated with natural fabrics and contemporary furniture, and offering great breakfasts and a quiet garden to relax in. **€99**

Dempsey's Hostel Eastern Rd ☎ 021 477 2124, ⊖ dandempseykinsale@gmail.com (IHH). Basic hostel with a pleasant conservatory and garden on the main Cork road, about 1km from the centre; basic camping facilities. Dorms **€15**, doubles **€40**

Garrettstown House Holiday Park 10km southwest of Kinsale, beyond Ballinspittle ☎ 021 477 8156, ⊛ garrettstownhouse.com. Campsite on the extensive grounds of the ruined eighteenth-century *Garrettstown House*, 1km from the beach, with a shop, laundry and playground, and lots of activities such as tennis and children's discos. May to mid-Sept. **€20**

Jim Edward's Market Quay ☎ 021 477 2541, ⊛ jimedwardskinsale.com. Above a very fine pub and restaurant, smart, comfortable, good-sized, en-suite rooms and excellent breakfasts, right in the heart of things. **€70**

Jo's 55 Main St ☎ 087 948 1026, ⊛ joskinsale.com. Wake up to the smell of fresh baking at this friendly guesthouse above *Jo's* café (see p.250), where rooms are basic, comfortable and cheery, most with en-suite bathrooms, and prices are a bargain. April–Oct. **€45**

Old Bank House 11 Pearse St ☎ 021 477 4075, ⊛ oldbankhousekinsale.com. Very comfortable and luxurious Georgian town house in a central location, with its own bakery-café and deli. Many of the well-equipped rooms overlook the harbour, and there's plenty of choice for an excellent breakfast. Very good single rates. **€130**

★**Pier House** Pier Rd ☎ 021 477 4169, ⊛ pierhousekinsale.com. A charming haven in a pretty garden right in the centre of town, with a bright, contemporary-rustic look enlivened with modern art. Most of the well-equipped rooms have sleigh beds and terraces or balconies, some with views of the harbour, and breakfast includes such delights as crêpes with fresh fruit. **€100**

Seagull House Cork St ☎ 021 477 2240, ⊖ marytap @iol.ie. Next to Desmond Castle in the centre, basic but cosy and very welcoming B&B under the same ownership as the *Tap Tavern* (see p.250), with en-suite doubles and good single rates. Mid-March to Oct. **€70**

Walyunga Sandycove, 3km from town off the R600 Timoleague road ☎ 021 477 4126, ⊛ walyunga.com. Spacious, very welcoming and mostly en-suite bungalow, with landscaped gardens and outstanding sea and valley views, in a quiet location. Excellent breakfasts served on the panoramic patio in good weather. March to late Oct. **€60**

EATING AND DRINKING

Kinsale is a magnet for foodies, its many **cafés** and **restaurants** making the most of local seafood and land-based ingredients, often with a French influence. There's a great **farmers' market** on Wed mornings on Market Quay (Short Quay), with cheeses, olives, salads, breads, crafts and live acoustic music. The town boasts a wide array of genial **pubs** too, many of which also serve good food. Pick up a copy of the free *Kinsale Advertiser* (ⓦ kinsalenews.com) at the tourist office, or go to their website to check out what's on around town each week.

RESTAURANTS AND CAFÉS

Crackpots 3 Cork St ☎ 021 477 2847, ⓦ crackpots.ie. Informal restaurant/wine bar/patisserie with an outdoor terrace and an excellent, diverse menu that might include lemongrass-infused salmon (€22). All dishes are served on artistic crockery (also for sale) and there's a good-value early bird (until 7pm). Mon–Sat 6–9pm, Sun 1–3pm, shorter hours in the depths of winter, longer hours at the height of summer.

Dino's Pier Rd ☎ 021 477 4561. Waterfront chippy of good repute, whose menu stretches to chowder, fish cakes, wine and craft beers, with plenty of comfy tables inside and a few outside if you want to sit down and eat; fish and chips with tartare sauce is €10.95 to eat in, much cheaper to take away. Daily 9am–10pm.

★**Fishy Fishy Café** Pier Rd ☎ 021 470 0415, ⓦ fishyfishy.ie. Superb seafood restaurant with very attractive tables on a quiet, leafy terrace in the summer, dishing up excellent daily specials such as scallops with chorizo and semi-sundried tomatoes (€19), as well as the trusty "Fishy Fish Pie". Reservations for dinner only. Daily noon–9pm; shorter, changeable hours in winter.

Jo's 55 Main St ☎ 087 948 1026, ⓦ joskinsale.com. Cute little farmhouse-style café, baking its own great cakes such as strawberry and mascarpone tart, as well as preparing good coffees, hot chocolate, breakfasts, soups, salads and sandwiches. Summer Mon–Fri 8am–6pm, Sat 9am–6pm, Sun 10am–6pm; winter Mon, Thurs & Fri 8am–5pm, Sat 9am–5pm, Sun 10am–5pm.

Max's Main St ☎ 021 477 2443, ⓦ maxs.ie. Cosy, upmarket, "Irish-French" spot with a small conservatory, specializing in seafood in summer, game in winter on a constantly changing menu that's posted on their website. Good-value early-bird two-course menu for €24.70 (until 7.30pm, Sat 7pm). Feb to mid-Dec daily 6–9.30pm; hours may be shorter in the shoulder season.

The Pantry Guardwell ☎ 021 477 4453, ⓦ www .thepantrykinsale.com. With lovely tables out front, this café is run by an ex-chef at *Fishy Fishy Café* (see above), who dishes up good chowder, tasty quiches (€3) and lemon- and fennel-infused fish and chips (€11.50), as well as great cakes and desserts. Tues–Sat 9am–6pm.

The Quay Food Company Market Quay (Short Quay) ☎ 021 477 4000, ⓦ quayfood.com. Serving delicious pâtés, cheeses and olives, this is a great deli and sandwich bar for putting together a picnic, perhaps to be enjoyed at James Fort (see p.248). Mon–Sat 9.30am–5.30pm.

PUBS AND BARS

The Bulman Summercove, 2km out towards Charles Fort on the east side of the harbour ☎ 021 477 2131. This attractive bar, adorned with nauticalia and warmed by open fires, dishes up good food such as smoked chicken salad with pine nuts and blue cheese (€10.50), while the upstairs restaurant, *Toddies*, which enjoys great views of the harbour, serves more sophisticated fare. Bar Mon–Thurs noon–11.30pm, Fri & Sat noon–12.30am, Sun noon–11pm; restaurant Tues–Sun evenings.

The Grey Hound Just off Market Square ☎ 021 477 2889. Popular, cosy, seventeenth-century pub with quaint wooden partitions and seats outside on the pedestrianized alley. Mon–Thurs roughly 1/2–11.30pm, Fri & Sat 1/2pm–12.30am, Sun 1/2–11pm.

★**Jim Edward's** Market Quay ☎ 021 477 2541, ⓦ jimedwardskinsale.com. Cosy, welcoming, central pub with a pleasant evening-time restaurant; the same menu of excellent, simple, fresh seafood, sourced from named local suppliers, is served in both. You can't go wrong with the grilled black sole or lobster from their own tank, or there are cheaper "gastropub" dishes such as fish with (great) chips (€16.50), which are available on a set dinner menu of €20 for two courses. Daily noon–10pm.

The Spaniard 1km from the centre around the east side of the harbour, in the suburb of Scilly ☎ 021 477 2436. Named after the plucky leader of the Spanish at the Battle of Kinsale, a cosy flagstoned pub that offers good food, either at the bar or in the restaurant, and regular traditional music, usually Wed. Mon–Thurs 10.30am–11.30pm, Fri & Sat 10.30am–12.30am, Sun 12.30–11pm.

Tap Tavern Guardwell ☎ 021 477 3231. Simple, sociable inn hung with bric-a-brac, good for a quiet pint most nights, with a nice beer garden. Mon–Thurs 5–11.30pm, Fri & Sat 5pm–12.30am, Sun 5–11pm.

The White House The Glen ☎ 021 477 2125. Reasonably priced, good-quality bar food, with dishes such as seafood pancakes and a catch of the day, plus frequent live music, usually traditional or ballads. Mon–Thurs 8am–11.30pm, Fri & Sat 8am–12.30am, Sun 8am–11pm; food served till 10pm.

7

Clonakilty and around

CLONAKILTY is an appealing if undramatic service town, whose main draw is the **beach**, 4km to the south, on **Inchydoney Island**, which is now locked to the mainland by two causeway roads that enclose reclaimed pasturage. This gorgeous expanse of pristine white sand is split in two by Virgin Mary's Point, where the road ends, and flanked by headlands of rolling green fields. Clonakilty also offers plenty of traditional music in the pubs, but is most famous as the home of award-winning **black puddings** – especially from Twomey's the butcher on the main street – and as the birthplace of Republican leader **Michael Collins**. In September, De Barra's pub (see p.254) organizes a weekend **guitar festival** (Ⓦ clonguitarfest.com) that includes workshops and live music on the streets.

West Cork Model Railway Village

On the southeast edge of town off the Inchydoney road · **Railway Village** Daily: July & Aug 10am–6pm; Sept–June 11am–5pm · €7, children €4, family ticket €20 **Road train** Usually June–Sept daily; Oct–May Sat & Sun · €10, children €6, family ticket €30, all including entry to model village · Ⓣ 023 883 3224, Ⓦ modelvillage.ie

Kids in particular will enjoy the **West Cork Model Railway Village**, which replicates the 1940s West Cork Railway and the towns it served in great detail at 1:24 scale. There's also a quirky cafeteria serving tea and cakes, housed in a full-size 1940s train carriage outside. Departing from here, a "road train" makes a tour of Clonakilty several times daily.

West Cork Regional Museum

The west end of Clonakilty's main street (here Western Road) · Summer Tues–Sat 11am–4pm; staffed by volunteers, so hours liable to change · Donation requested

If poor weather rules out any outdoor exploration, you could do worse than holing up in the **West Cork Regional Museum**, which covers the area's contribution to the War of Independence and Clonakilty's once-prosperous linen industry, and displays a host of agricultural implements.

Michael Collins Centre

Roughly mid-June to mid-Sept Mon–Fri 10.30am–5pm, Sat 11am–2pm · €5 donation requested · Ⓣ 023 884 6107, Ⓦ michaelcollinscentre.com

Four kilometres east of Clonakilty, off the R600 towards Timoleague, is the eclectic but highly recommended **Michael Collins Centre**. Engaging guided tours full of anecdotes, particularly about his distant relative Michael Collins, are led by Mr Crowley; features include photos, memorabilia and an audiovisual on Collins, and the Ambush Trail, a reconstruction of Collins' fatal ambush in 1921 at Beal na Bláth. If you want to explore further, you can book Mr Crowley for tours (usually in your own car) of nearby sites associated with Collins and the War of Independence, taking in the actual Beal na Bláth and what is left of Collins' birthplace, incinerated in 1921 by the Black and Tans.

Drombeg

Accessible via the R597 Rosscarbery–Glandore road, signposted after 5km

About 17km west of Clonakilty lies one of the area's few compelling historical sites, the Bronze Age **Drombeg stone circle** (which unfortunately is not served by any buses). Looking out over pretty cattle pastures with the Atlantic in the distance, these seventeen well-preserved stones are associated with the winter solstice, when the sun sets on the southwest horizon at a point aligned with the lowest, axial, stone (known as the "Druid's Altar") and the two tallest portal stones. Close by in the same field sits one of the best examples of a *fulacht fiadh*, a ritual cooking site (literally "deer roast"), in Ireland. It consists of a 1.5m-long stone-lined trough for water, into which red-hot stones from the adjacent hearth would have been rolled. Experiments have shown that this would have successfully boiled the water, and that meat wrapped in straw and plunged into the trough would have cooked in the same time it takes to do your turkey at Christmas, twenty minutes per pound, plus an extra twenty minutes for the pot.

Glandore

A popular yachting haven 20km west of Clonakilty, **GLANDORE** enjoys a particularly beautiful elevated position, overlooking the turquoise waters of a deep inlet and the village of Union Hall opposite, and surrounded by lush, tree-carpeted slopes.

ARRIVAL AND INFORMATION

By bus Buses stop either on Pearse St – part of the town's long, one-way (westward) high street, which to the east becomes Ashe St and then Wolfe Tone St, to the west Western Rd – or on the short bypass, just south of Wolfe Tone St.

Tourist information The helpful tourist office at 25 Ashe St (Tues–Sat 9/9.15am–1pm & 1.30/1.45–5pm; ☎023 883

CLONAKILTY AND AROUND

3226, ⓦclonakilty.ie) stocks a free *What's On* guide, which includes local road-bowling fixtures (see box on p.555).

Bike rental MTM Cycles, 33 Ashe St, near the tourist office (☎023 883 3584).

Surfing Inchydoney Surf School (☎086 869 5396, ⓦinchydoneysurfschool.com).

ACCOMMODATION

An Súgán 41 Wolfe Tone St ☎023 883 3719, ⓦansugan.com. Guesthouse in a tasteful contemporary style with comfortable beds and great breakfasts that use local produce wherever possible, in a quiet Georgian town house behind the seafood bar and restaurant (see below). Very good rates for singles. **€90**

Bay View Old Timoleague Rd ☎023 883 3539, ⓦbayviewclonakilty.com. Flower-bedecked, brightly decorated and welcoming en-suite B&B on the east side of town, with good breakfasts, a lovely garden and fine views of Clonakilty Bay; rooms include a garden suite with private sun lounge. **€80**

Bay View Glandore, in the centre of the village ☎028 33115, ⓔtphilbhamilton@gmail.com. Your best bet for B&B accommodation, a bright and comfortable, all-en-suite, waterside house in the centre of the village with great views. **€80**

Desert House On a dairy farm 500m from the centre of Clonakilty ☎023 883 3331, ⓔdeserthouse@eircom .net. Campsite with campers' kitchen, laundry facilities and a playground, with great views of Clonakilty Bay; head east out of town, turn right at the roundabout and follow the

signs. May–Oct. **€20**

★**Inchydoney Island Lodge and Spa** Mid-point of Inchydoney Beach ☎023 883 3143, ⓦinchydoney island.com. Beautifully sited luxury retreat, decorated in plush but cheery contemporary style, with extravagant touches such as espresso-makers in the rooms, which all have sea views and a balcony or terrace. Attached are a bistro-pub, a fine-dining restaurant and a well-equipped spa, offering a wide range of seawater and other treatments, as well as a large indoor heated seawater pool. **€198**

Meadow On the R597, about 1km east of Glandore ☎028 33280, ⓔmeadowcamping@eircom.net. Trim and peaceful campsite with a campers' kitchen and laundry facilities. Easter & May to mid-Sept; at other times by prior arrangement. **€20**

O'Donovan's Hotel Pearse St ☎023 883 3250, ⓦodonovanshotel.com. Parnell and Marconi stayed at this lively traditional meeting place on the main street, and it's still run by the welcoming O'Donovan family, retaining some of its period charm after recent refurbishment. Very good rates for singles. **€90**

EATING AND DRINKING

RESTAURANTS AND CAFÉS

An Súgán 41 Wolfe Tone St ☎023 883 3719, ⓦansugan .com. Good, fresh fish and shellfish, ranging from chowder and oysters to lobster and seafood pie (€17), in this plush, cosy bar-restaurant with a pretty courtyard. Mon–Fri 5–7pm €20 for two courses. Food daily noon–9.30pm.

Hart's 8 Ashe St ☎023 883 5583. This small, attractive café, which can be found on the main street in the centre of town, serves tasty ciabattas, hot meals and all-day breakfasts, as well as scrummy cakes and good coffees Mon–Sat 10am–5.30pm.

Malt House Granary 30–31 Ashe St ☎023 883 4355,

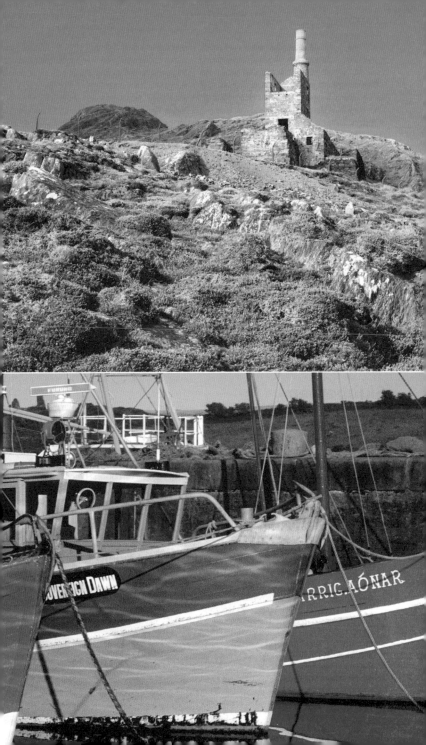

Ⓦmalthousegranary.ie. Local artisan produce and organic vegetables are used wherever possible at this relaxing, informal restaurant, to create dishes such as chicken stuffed with Gubbeen sausage with whiskey and mustard sauce, and some devilish desserts. Two-course early bird €19.50 (until 7pm). June–Oct daily 5–10pm; Nov–May Tues–Sat 5–10pm.

★**Richy's** Wolfe Tone St, next to the tourist office Ⓣ023 882 1852, Ⓦrichysbarandbistro.com. With an impressive menu that lists their local suppliers and what's currently in season, this attractive, informal evening restaurant might offer delicious tandoori monkfish and prawn brochettes (€12) to start, followed by excellent beef Wellington with rosemary jus (€27). Until 5pm, *Richy's* operates as a café serving cakes, sandwiches and a wide range of simpler, cheaper mains. Three-course early bird €27.50 (5–7pm). Daily 9am–10pm.

PUBS AND BARS

★**De Barra's** 55 Pearse St Ⓣ023 883 3381,

Ⓦwww.debarra.ie. The pick of Clon's old-time pubs, with great live music most evenings, including a popular traditional session on Mon and an acoustic session on Tues. Mon–Thurs roughly 10am–11.30pm, Fri & Sat 10am–12.30am, Sun noon–11pm.

Hayes Bar Glandore Ⓣ028 33214. You can tuck into some chowder, a salad or a sandwich here, sitting either on a sofa or armchair inside, or at one of the gorgeous tables outside, overlooking the village's beautiful community garden and harbour. Summer Mon–Thurs 11am–11.30pm, Fri & Sat 11am–12.30am, Sun noon–11pm.

Shanley's Piano Bar Connolly St, running south from Pearse St Ⓣ023 883 3790. Plush, welcoming, well-tended bar with a pretty, flower-filled beer garden, hosting an acoustic session on Thurs, easy listening/jazz/American folk at weekends. Mon–Thurs roughly 3–11.30pm, Fri 3pm–12.30am, Sat noon/1.30pm–12.30am, Sun noon/1.30pm–11pm.

ENTERTAINMENT

An Teach Beag *O'Donovan's Hotel* (see p.252), Pearse St Ⓣ023 883 3250, Ⓦodonovanshotel.com. This storehouse, which has been reconstructed as a traditional cottage *("the little house")* at the back of the hotel, hosts Irish music (sometimes augmented by set dancing and storytelling), and there's more trad on Tues in the hotel itself. July & Aug daily 9.30pm–midnight; Sept–June Fri 9.30pm–midnight, plus a song night the last Sun of the month from 9pm.

Skibbereen

SKIBBEREEN (often shortened to "Skibb"), the lively administrative centre for this part of west Cork, is a good spot to take a break and recharge your batteries, with plenty of restaurants and accommodation options and an excellent heritage centre. To the south, it gives access to a rich coastal landscape where green pastures begin to alternate with the scrubby, rocky slopes so typical of more westerly parts. If you have your own wheels, you shouldn't miss the uniquely beautiful lagoon of **Lough Hyne**. Bypassed by the main N71 to the north, the town's **layout** is easy once you've got the hang of it, though sometimes clogged with traffic: beneath a slow bend in the Ilen River, the two narrow main streets form a V shape, North Street pointing to the northeast, and Main Street (which becomes Bridge Street) pointing northwestwards. The town's two big

WHALE WATCHING AND KAYAKING AROUND SKIBBEREEN

The seas off Skibb, rich feeding grounds for herring and sprat, are earning a reputation as one of Europe's premier **whale-watching** sites, with minke (roughly from April), fin (from June or July), more rarely, humpback (from September) and occasional killer whales, as well as scores of dolphins and porpoises, coming remarkably close to shore; September to November is the peak time. For further information, consult the website of the Irish Whale and Dolphin Group, Ⓦiwdg.ie. Two companies run daily four-hour boat trips, costing €50 per adult: Cork Whale Watch (Ⓣ086 327 3226, Ⓦcorkwhalewatch.com) from Reen Pier, well to the southeast of Skibb on Castlehaven Harbour; and Whale Watch West Cork (Ⓣ086 120 0027, Ⓦwhalewatchwestcork.com) from Baltimore. Along the coast here, there are also **sea-kayaking** trips, ranging from half-day to two-day expeditions, run by Atlantic Sea Kayaking based in Skibbereen (Ⓣ028 21058, Ⓦatlanticseakayaking.com); they also offer starlight outings in Castlehaven Harbour or Lough Hyne, accompanied, at certain times of year, by an astonishing bioluminescence emitted by marine life.

estivals are the arts festival at the end of July, featuring music, poetry, dance, drama nd art (Ⓦskibbereenartsfestival.com), and the ten-day **food festival** in September Ⓦatasteofwestcork.com), with farm tours, markets and workshops.

The heritage centre

pper Bridge St • Mid-March to mid-May & mid-Sept to Oct Tues–Sat 10am–6pm; mid-May to mid-Sept Mon–Sat 10am–6pm; winter pening by appointment "or just try the door"; genealogy service by appointment • €6; Heritage Island • ☎028 40900, Ⓦ skibbheritage.com

The first-rate **heritage centre**, set in an attractively restored gasworks, is the home of wo contrasting exhibitions. Introduced by actor and local resident Jeremy Irons, *The Great Famine Commemorative Exhibition* film provides a sensitive and vivid ommentary on the Famine of the 1840s. The Skibbereen area was especially badly hit, vith nearly a third of its population of a hundred thousand losing their lives and a urther eight thousand being forced to emigrate – even though the Famine's effects on he town were widely publicized by the famous stark drawings of James Mahony for he *Illustrated London News*. The ninety-minute **Skibbereen Trail**, marked by bronze laques and detailed in a leaflet available from the heritage centre, takes in some of the amine sites, including **Abbeystrewery Cemetery** on the N71 on the western edge of own, where between eight and ten thousand victims were buried in pits. The other xhibition introduces the amazing diversity of nearby **Lough Hyne** (see below), with an udiovisual and abundant pictures of its flora and fauna.

West Cork Arts Centre

orth St • ☎028 22090, Ⓦ westcorkartscentre.com

The lively **West Cork Arts Centre**, which hosts temporary exhibitions, especially of ontemporary visual art, as well as drama, films and all sorts of other events, is well vorth a look (in the long term, the centre plans to move to a new site off Bridge Street, n the south side of town).

Lough Hyne

f you head out of Skibb on the Baltimore road and take a left turn after about 3km, ou'll come upon **Lough Hyne** (Lough Ine) after a further 3km or so. Ireland's first narine nature reserve, this tidal lake is joined to the sea only by a narrow channel, nown as the rapids, but reaches depths of 45m in places. A combination of warm vaters from the Gulf Stream and diverse habitats – sea caves, whirlpools, shallow and eep areas – supports an astonishingly rich variety of saltwater species here, over a housand in less than a square kilometre. Many are rare species that are generally only ound in the deep ocean or the Mediterranean, such as the triggerfish and the ed-mouthed goby. Sheltered by varied slopes of gorse, woods and bare rock, the placid vaters are also popular among swimmers and kayakers (see box, opposite). To make the nost of a visit, see the exhibit at the Skibbereen heritage centre first (see above), where ou can also pick up a brochure for the **Knockomagh Wood Nature Trail**. Beginning vhere the road from Skibb meets Lough Hyne, at its northwestern corner, this 2km trail igzags upwards and westwards past fine viewpoints of the lake, ancient sessile oaks and luebell meadows, to the 197m summit of Knockomagh Hill, which affords a panorama f the coastline stretching from Galley Head in the east to Mount Gabriel above Schull.

ARRIVAL AND INFORMATION · SKIBBEREEN

y bus Buses drop off and pick up from *Cahalane's* bar on ridge St.

ourist office North St (late May to roughly Oct Mon–Sat m–5pm, sometimes closing 1–2pm; plus Sun noon–4pm in roughly July & Aug; ☎028 21766, Ⓦ skibbereen.ie).

Bike rental and tours Cycle West Cork, 11 Market St (☎087 392 1894, Ⓦ cyclewestcork.com).

ACCOMMODATION

Bridge House Bridge St ☎ 028 21273, ⓦ bridgehouses kibbereen.com. Very centrally located on the busy main street, this is the standout among the town's handful of B&Bs, an eccentric, Victorian-styled place stuffed with antiques, swags and china dolls. **€70**

Russagh Mill Hostel and Adventure Centre 1km southeast on the R596 Castletownshend road (IHO) ☎ 028 22451, ⓦ www.russaghmillhostel.com. A fine hostel encompassing two kitchens, a BBQ area and several common rooms in a lovingly restored, 200-year-old mill;

camping available. Simple breakfast included. March–Oct Dorms **€15**, doubles **€40**

West Cork Hotel Ilen St ☎ 028 21277 ⓦ westcorkhotel.com. A traditional hotel and hub o local social life, which has recently been renovated t make the most of its riverside setting, includin spacious, colourful and well-equipped bedrooms, an tables out on the old railway bridge over the Ilen. Egg Benedict and other breakfasts served until noon. **€79**

EATING AND DRINKING

There's a great **farmers' market** on Sat mornings on Fair Field, behind Bridge St, where you'll also find crafts an antiques.

Baby Hannah's Bridge St ☎ 028 22783. A lively spot with a lovely big beer garden and lots of craft beers in bottles, which hosts traditional music on Tues year-round and early Sun evenings in summer. Mon–Thurs 5–11.30pm, Fri & Sat 4pm–12.30am, Sun 4–11pm.

Corner Bar Bridge St, opposite *Baby Hannah's* ☎ 028 21522. Sessions are held here on Sat throughout the year and on Mon in July and Aug, with a singers' club on the first Fri of the month. Mon–Thurs 4/5–11.30pm, Fri & Sat 4/5pm–12.30am, Sun 4/5–11pm.

Island Cottage Heir Island ☎ 028 38102, ⓦ islandcottage.com. For a meal with a touch of adventure thrown in, make a reservation at this excellent, charming island restaurant that uses local and organic or wild ingredients whenever possible. To get here you'll need to drive or cycle west along the N71 towards

Ballydehob for 5km, then follow the signs down th small peninsula for about another 5km to Cunnamore from where a small boat will ferry you across to the islan in 5min. Set menu €40. Mid-June to mid-Sept Wed–Sa 8.10–11.45pm.

Kalbo's North St ☎ 028 21515. Small, justifiably popula café that uses local, seasonal produce wherever possible, i dishes such as a delicious open Castletownbere cra mayonnaise sandwich (€5/€10) and the house chilli on ric (€5). Mon–Thurs 9am–6pm, Fri & Sat 9am–9pm.

Riverside North St ☎ 028 40090, ⓦ riverside ibbereen.ie. Airy, modern café-restaurant with a prett riverside terrace and a menu that ranges from homemad fish cakes (€10.75) to rack of West Cork lamb (€25) fo dinner. Mon–Thurs 10am–5pm, Fri & Sat 10am–9pm Sun 11am–3pm.

Baltimore

Though isolated at the end of a stubby peninsula to the southwest of Skibbereen, **BALTIMORE** comes as a lively surprise, bustling with fishing and pleasure boats, and ferries to Sherkin and Clear islands. In fine weather, there are few more pleasant spots in Cork than the small, sun-trap square above the harbour, filled with café an bar tables. Basking in the shelter of large inshore islands, the port is particularly busy during the **regatta** held in early August, but there's also a fiddle **festival** in earl May (ⓦ fiddlefair.com) and a combined food and sailing festival during the last weekend in May (ⓦ baltimorewoodenboatfestival.com).

Dún na Séad

April–Sept daily 11am–6pm • €4 • ⓦ baltimorecastle.ie

Overlooking the square stands **Dún na Séad**, a thirteenth-century tower house that was the chief residence of the infamous pirates, the O'Driscolls, but fell into ruins from the end of the seventeenth century until its painstaking recent restoration as a private home. It's worth a visit in summer to see the imposing great hall on the first floor and to take in the commanding views of the harbour and Roaringwater Bay from the battlements.

BALTIMORE: MESSING ABOUT IN BOATS

In summer, **boat tours** from Baltimore include trips via Cape Clear to the famous hundred-year-old lighthouse out in the open sea on Fastnet Rock (W fastnettour.com), known as "Ireland's Teardrop" because it was the last part of Ireland seen by thousands of emigrants to North America. In addition, Baltimore Sea Safari offers a variety of trips in a smaller, speedier RIB (T 028 20753, W baltimoreseasafari.ie). You can take a **diving** course or trip at Aquaventures (T 028 20511, W aquaventures.ie), who also run half-day **snorkelling** trips, while Glenans offers **sailing** courses (T 028 20630).

Sherkin Island

Ferries 5–12 daily; 10min • €10 return • T 087 244 7828, W sherkinferry.com

Guarding the west side of Baltimore Harbour, **Sherkin** (Inis Arcáin, "Island of the Porpoise"; W sherkinisland.ie) is a tranquil, pretty island that shares the mixed scrub and pastoral landscape of the mainland hereabouts. On a half-day stroll around the boot-shaped island, you could take in the highest point, Slievemore, to the southwest on the toe of the boot, and the best beaches, Trá Bawn, Trá Eoghan Mhór and Silver Strand, to the north of Slievemore. **Ferries** from Baltimore land at the easterly pier, behind which stands a plain fifteenth-century Franciscan **abbey**, with its 15m tower intact; you can still see the outline of its cloister and the walls of a curious seventeenth-century fish "palace", where pilchards were salted and barrelled for export to Spain.

INFORMATION

BALTIMORE

Tourist information As well as selling some beautiful pottery and knitwear made on Sherkin and Clear islands, Island Crafts, in a hut down by the quay, provides tourist information on Baltimore and the islands in summer (Easter–Sept daily 10am–6.30pm; T 028 20347 or T 028 20022, W islandscrafts.com).

ACCOMMODATION AND EATING

The village specializes in hospitality all-rounders, where you can **sleep**, **eat** and **drink** under the same roof. Standards are generally very high, and you'll find a surprisingly diverse range of food for somewhere so small and remote. Booking accommodation in advance is highly recommended in July and Aug, over bank-holiday weekends and during festivals (see opposite).

Baltimore Townhouse Near the village centre T 028 20197, W caseysofbaltimore.com. Owned by *Casey's Hotel*, this gleaming house encompasses four stylish and well-equipped suites. Breakfast is either continental, including freshly baked bread, or full Irish, taken at *Casey's*, which is also where you check in. **€110**

Bushe's Bar On the main square T 028 20125, W bushesbar.com. With the best view of the harbour from its seats outside on the main square, this popular pub serves excellent cheap chowder and seafood sandwiches and platters during the day. Upstairs are basic but comfortable bedrooms, with TVs and en-suite bathrooms; you'll pay more for a harbour view. Self-service continental breakfast is taken in your room. Bar Mon–Thurs 9/10am–11.30pm, Fri & Sat 9/10am–12.30am, Sun 12.30–11pm. **€60**

★ **Casey's Hotel** On the main Skibbereen road, 1km from the harbour T 028 20197, W caseysofbaltimore.com. Charming, family-run hotel with large and very comfortable en-suite bedrooms, very good food in the bar and restaurant, and glorious views over the peaceful inlet to Ringarogy Island, especially from the beer garden. Traditional music Sat year-round, more frequently in high summer. All sorts of packages on offer, as well as self-catering apartments. **€110**

La Jolie Brise Café On the main square, part of the *Waterfront Hotel* (see p.258). Serving everything from breakfast to late suppers, with tables outside overlooking the harbour. On offer are simple main courses such as pizza, salmon and steak, as well as cheap local oysters and mussels (€13.50 for moules marinière). Daily: summer 8.30am–11pm; winter 5–10pm.

★ **Rolf's** Left turn off the main road into the village, a 10min walk from the harbour T 028 20289, W rolfscountryhouse.com. Civilized, tranquil and friendly spot in beautiful subtropical gardens with fine sea views. The good-value pine-furnished rooms are bright and spruce, with a continental buffet breakfast included, and well-equipped self-catering cottages are also available. The relaxing restaurant uses as much home-grown, organic and local produce as possible in generously proportioned dishes such as succulent cod with potato and herb crust. Very good rates for singles. Restaurant Wed–Sun 6–9pm, plus 12.30–2.30pm in summer. **€90**

Waterfront Hotel On the main square ☎028 20600, ⓦwaterfrontbaltimore.ie. Bright, pleasant, spacious en-suite rooms; the best are done out in nautical blue and cream in a new extension, and have either great views of the harbour or a patio-style garden. Good rates for singles. **€100**

Clear Island (Oileán Chléire)

Ireland's most southerly inhabited point, **Clear Island** (Oileán Chléire, also known as **Cape Clear**; ⓦcapeclearisland.ie) is an isolated outpost of the **Gaeltacht**, which welcomes teenagers from all over the country to learn Irish during the summer, and generally reaches out to visitors, with plenty of facilities and information available. The island also holds a traditional story-telling **festival**, with concerts, workshops, walks and music, over the first weekend of September.

Clear describes a very rough figure-of-eight, just 6km square, with **North Harbour**, where ferries dock, and cliff-girt **South Harbour** almost meeting in the middle; the westerly part of the figure-of-eight is home to a fifteenth-century castle, **Dún an Óir** ("Fort of Gold"), a ruined O'Driscoll stronghold on an isolated rocky outcrop near North Harbour. The island's landscape of steep, rolling hills of heather and pasture is crossed by narrow, hedge-lined roads and paths, affording fine views of Roaringwater Bay and of Fastnet Rock to the west in the open sea, where whales, dolphins and sharks can sometimes be spotted. Clear Island is most famous as one of the best places to watch seabird migration in Europe, as well as supporting breeding colonies of black guillemots, choughs and rock doves; twitchers can take field courses and stay at the **bird observatory** at North Harbour (ⓦbirdwatchireland.ie).

Up the steep bank to the east of North Harbour, visitors are welcome at **Cleire Goat Farm** (☎028 39126, ⓦemara.com/goats) which offers goat husbandry courses, starting from as little as two hours in duration, and produces ice cream, cheese and sausages. A short walk further along the same road from the goat farm, by the church, the tiny **heritage centre** (summer daily roughly noon–4pm; €3; ☎028 39119 or ☎028 39190, ⓦcapeclearmuseum.ie) hosts some detailed and interesting displays, especially on maritime history and archaeology.

St Ciarán's Church

The island is reputed to have been the sixth-century birthplace of **St Ciarán of Saighir** (not to be confused with Ciarán of Clonmacnois), who is (spuriously) claimed to have brought Christianity to Ireland thirty years before St Patrick. According to legend, he ended his days in Cornwall, where he was known as St Piran and credited with the discovery of tin. His twelfth-century church, graveyard and holy well lie on the west side of North Harbour.

ARRIVAL AND INFORMATION

By ferry The *Cailín Óir* sails from Baltimore (2–4 daily; 45min; €8; ☎028 39159 or ☎086 346 5110, ⓦcailinoir .com), and there are summertime boats from Schull (see opposite; Baltimore–Clear return tickets are accepted on the Clear–Schull ferry. A minibus meets all ferries and charges €2/person to anywhere on the island.

Tourist information The crafts shop at North Harbour dispenses tourist information (June & Sept Mon–Sa 11.15am–12.30pm & 3.30–4.30pm, Sun 11.45am–1pm & 4–5/6pm; July & Aug daily 11am–1pm & 2–6pm; ☎02 39100). There's no ATM on the island – the nearest is in th supermarket in Baltimore.

ACCOMMODATION AND EATING

As the island can get busy in high summer, it's best to book **accommodation** before you come.

An Siopa Beag North Harbour ☎028 39099, ⓦsiopabeag .ie. The island's grocery store at North Harbour offers internet access and wi-fi, as well as a café serving sandwiches, salads seafood and, on Fri & Sat evenings in summer, handmad pizzas. Upstairs is the island's social club, *Club Cléire*, which hosts traditional music on summer weekends. Shop open year-round, hours depending on boat times; closed Sun in winter; *Club Cléire* no fixed hours.

Ard na Gaoithe Up behind the youth hostel along a steep lane above South Harbour ☎ 028 39160, ⓦ ardnagaoithe .ie. This welcoming en-suite B&B, in a renovated nineteenth-century house on a working farm, offers organic eggs and pancakes on a varied breakfast menu. €70

Cape Clear Hostel By the pebbly beach at South Harbour ☎ 028 41968, ⓦ anoige.ie. This basic hostel occupies the old coastguard station. As well as 4- to 10-bed dorms, it offers a cosy lounge with an open fire, a large kitchen and dining room, laundry facilities and table tennis. Jan–April & Oct–Dec pre-booking only. €18

Chléire Haven South Harbour ☎ 086 197 1956, ⓦ yurt-holidays-ireland.com. The island campsite at South Harbour has expanded its horizons to offer yurts with wooden beds, stoves, gas cookers and cool boxes (for a family of up to 6 people), and teepees with self-inflating mattresses. Those bringing their own tents have to pre-book. Camping €20, yurts for 2 nights in summer from €240, teepees per person €20

Ciaran Danny Mike's On the road between the two harbours ☎ 028 39153, ⓦ capeclearisland.eu. This spacious pub with a pool table and outdoor seating is popular for lunch and dinner and often hosts traditional music. (It also has self-catering cottages and a guesthouse.) Open all year; check the blackboard at the gate for the latest opening times.

The Mizen Head Peninsula

Mizen Head is a wild and beautiful peninsula, projecting southwestwards around the substantial mass of copper-rich **Mount Gabriel**. The whole of its empty northern coast presents sheer cliffs and stupendous views. The south coast is more populous, sheltering safe harbours, the large village and resort of **Schull** and the remote sandy beaches of **Barley Cove** and **Galley Cove**, while the only tourist attraction of any note is the signal station at the very tip, the **Mizen Head Visitor Centre**.

Schull

The peninsula's main settlement, **SCHULL** (ⓦ schull.ie), is a congenial harbour town that's not only popular with yachties but also has an artistic bent, with crafts shops, galleries and a weekly food and crafts market (Sun morning Easter–Sept; ⓦ schullmarket.com). It shelters in the lee of 407m **Mount Gabriel**, to the north, topped by an aircraft-tracking station and blessed with fine views. The walk up there (about 8km there and back) is detailed, along with four other local walks, in a very useful annual booklet, *Discover Schull*, that's available around the town; since the mountain was actively mined for centuries, take care on the way that you avoid uncovered mine shafts.

Schull also boasts a **planetarium**, developed by a local German resident in the village's community college on Colla Road, which runs south off Main Street. It's generally open only in the summer (June to late Aug), with a detailed programme of starshows €5, children €3.50, family ticket €15; ☎ 028 28315). Schull's annual events include a five-day **short-film festival** in late May (ⓦ fastnetshortfilmfestival.com) and **Calves Week** sailing regatta in early August (ⓦ shsc.ie).

INFORMATION AND ACTIVITIES · SCHULL

Tourist information The community office for information and the short-film festival is on Main St near the start of the pier road (summer daily roughly 10am–6pm; winter hours variable, perhaps 3 days/week; ☎ 028 28600).

Activities Fastnet Marine and Outdoor Education Centre offers sailing courses (☎ 028 28515, ⓦ schullsailing.ie), while diving is organized by Divecology (☎ 086 837 2065, ⓦ divecology.com).

GETTING AROUND

By ferry In summer, a ferry runs from Schull to Clear Island (June–Sept 1–6 days/week; 45min; €16 return; ☎ 087 389 9711, ⓦ schullferry.com); on the days when this is running, you could hook up with the Fastnet Rock tours from Baltimore (see p.257). Schull–Clear return tickets are accepted on the Clear–Baltimore ferry.

7

ACCOMMODATION AND EATING

Ellen's Towards the east end of Main St ☎ 028 27613. Bright, well-run and sociable traditional café that's popular with locals, serving dishes such as cottage pie and chips (€10). Mon–Sat 8.30am–5pm.

Grove House Colla Rd ☎ 028 28067, ⓦ grovehouseschull.com. Overlooking the harbour, this creeper-clad mansion has been quirkily and stylishly redecorated with antiques and modern paintings, with bedrooms named after famous former guests such as George Bernard Shaw. Outdoor seating, a conservatory and open fires cover all the seasons, while the restaurant uses home-grown and local produce wherever possible. Good single rates. €90

★ **Hackett's** Main St ☎ 028 28625. Great old bar with stone floors, bench seating and a vaguely alternative feel, helped along by a good soundtrack, regular live music and bottles of craft beer. Tasty bar lunches include beef in Guinness stew (€8.50). Mon–Thurs noon–11.30pm, Fri &

Sat noon–12.30am, Sun noon–11pm.

L'Escale Harbourside ☎ 028 28599. Your best bet for dinner is this high-class chipper (fish and chips €9.80) which has lots of outdoor tables, some of them covered for enjoying the harbour views. It also offers seafood platters, pancakes and wine. June–Aug daily 10am–10pm.

Newman's West Main St ☎ 028 27776, ⓦ tjnewmans .com. Wine bar and café serving tasty hummus with pitta (€4.90), pizzas, seafood pie and pancakes, with a sun deck upstairs. Daily 9/10am–11pm.

Stanley House About 1km southwest of the centre of Colla Rd ☎ 028 28425, ⓦ stanley-house.net. En-suite B&B in a large, immaculately kept modern house with a pleasant garden, fine views across the bay, especially from its conservatory, and home baking and free-range eggs for breakfast. Good single rates; self-catering accommodation also available. March–Oct. €76

Goleen, Crookhaven, Brow Head and Mizen Head

Infrequent buses run 15km southwest down the peninsula from Schull as far as the quiet village of **GOLEEN**. The southernmost tip of the Mizen Head Peninsula, **Brow Head**, which is also the southernmost point of mainland Ireland, rather surprisingly shelters a golden sandy beach in **Barley Cove**, punctured by a stream and backed by dunes, which are thought to have been thrown up by the tsunami that followed an earthquake off Portugal in 1755. A wild spit of land pushes east of here, past another beautiful sandy beach, **Galley Cove**, to the village of **CROOKHAVEN**, which would feel like the end of the world were it not for the pleasure boats anchored in the long, fjord-like inlet.

Mizen Head Signal Station

Mid-March to May, Sept & Oct daily 10.30am–5pm; June–Aug daily 10am–6pm; Nov to mid-March Sat & Sun 11am–4pm • €6; Heritage Island • ⓦ mizenhead.ie

To the west of Barley Cove, the narrow road heads upwards and outwards to **Mizen Head** itself. The **visitor centre** here, which comprises a café and the famous, hundred-year-old signal station (now automatic), isn't up to much, but it's worth paying the entrance fee to walk out to the head, which turns out to be an island, accessed by a slender, arched bridge: with the 50m Fastnet lighthouse and the tip of the Beara Peninsula to either side and the whole of Ireland behind you, you're left to plot the folds of the jagged cliffs, the movements of the clouds and the churning contours of the ocean.

ACCOMMODATION AND EATING

GOLEEN, CROOKHAVEN AND MIZEN HEAD

The Crookhaven Inn Crookhaven ☎ 028 35309. Cosy pub-restaurant in the village itself, with an open stove and outside tables overlooking the inlet, serving excellent food including home-cured gravadlax. April to mid-Oct daily 11am–8/9pm.

Fortview House 9km northeast of Goleen on the R591 towards Durrus ☎ 028 35324, ⓦ fortviewhouse.ie. Lovely farmstay, where guests are welcome to walk the estate and help with the milking. Smart en-suite rooms

feature large brass and iron beds, and top-notch breakfast include homemade pancakes, freshly laid eggs and local farmhouse cheeses. Self-catering cottages available year round. Very good rates for singles. April–Oct. €100

Galley Cove Just west of Crookhaven ☎ 028 35137, ⓦ galleycovehouse.com. Welcoming en-suite B&B in a spruce, modern, pine-floored bungalow with fine views of the sea and Fastnet lighthouse. Good rates for singles. €75

The Sheep's Head

The **Sheep's Head** (ⓦ livingthesheepsheadway.com), a precarious sliver of land between Dunmanus and Bantry bays, is the quietest and smallest of the major southwestern peninsulas. Gorse and heather sprout from its long granite spine, leaving room for narrow pockets of green pasture on its north and especially its south coast. With magnificent views of the larger peninsulas on either side, it can be best appreciated by pedalling the easy-to-follow 90km **Sheep's Head Cycle Route**, or by walking the 88km **Sheep's Head Way** (ⓦ thesheepsheadway.ie), both of which are waymarked circuits from Bantry; the latter is relatively easy walking, avoiding the round-peninsula road for most of the way, and is covered by OS Discovery Series map number 88. It can be done in four days, with two nights in Kilcrohane after two long days' walking and a night in Durrus; the last day is missable, so you might want to catch a bus back to Bantry from Durrus.

Durrus

At the head of Dunmanus Bay, **DURRUS** is a relatively busy junction village between the Mizen Head and Sheep's Head peninsulas, supporting several pubs and a fine restaurant.

ACCOMMODATION AND EATING · DURRUS

Blairscove House & Restaurant About 2km southwest down the R591 towards Crookhaven ☎ 027 61127, ⓦ blairscove.ie. In beautiful grounds overlooking Dunmanus Bay, *Blairs Cove House* combines spacious luxury apartments with an excellent restaurant, renowned for its buffet-style starters and grilled meats and fish. Good rates for singles. Restaurant Tues–Sat 6–9.30pm. Mid-March to late Oct. €220

Good Things Café On the Ahakista road ☎ 027 61426, ⓦ thegoodthingscafe.com. A bright, modern, seasonal restaurant (and cookery school) that makes creative use of local land and sea ingredients, in dishes such as pork loin baked in bay and brandy (€24). Hours variable but usually open for the Easter period, July & Aug, plus bank holidays throughout the year.

Kilcrohane and beyond

KILCROHANE, 15km southwest of Durrus, supports a couple of **bars** serving food and a combined shop, petrol station and post office. A new complex on the road in from Durrus shelters the Sheep's Head Producers Shop, where local artisans sell everything from jams to jewellery (including Sheep's Head Way maps), as well as a café and a proposed bike rental shop.

From Kilcrohane, a road loops along the quieter north coast of the peninsula, reaching its highest point at a spectacular pass 2km north of the village; for even better views, it's possible to walk to the top of **Seefin**, Sheep's Head's highest hill (344m), in about twenty minutes from the pass.

West of Kilcrohane, the Sheep's Head is dotted with small lakes and becomes more jagged and hummocky as it narrows to a lighthouse at the tip. The tarmac runs out at the Sheep's Head Café (see p.262), from where it's a half-hour walk down to the lighthouse.

ACCOMMODATION AND EATING · KILCROHANE AND BEYOND

Bridge View House By the church ☎ 027 67086, ⓦ bridgeviewhouse.com. This attractive house provides friendly en-suite B&B, a large garden and excellent home cooking. Self-catering available. Good rates for singles. €60

Sea Mount Farmhouse Glenlough, 10km from Kilcrohane towards Bantry ☎ 027 61226, ⓦ seamountfarm.com. Outstanding B&B less than 1km off the Sheep's Head Way. The welcoming all-en-suite farmhouse provides magnificent views of Bantry Bay, fine home baking, walking tours and plenty of useful information about exploring the area. €62

Sheep's Head Café 11km west of Kilcrohane ☎ 086 877 8604, ⓔ bernietobin7@eircom.net. In a wild, end-of-the-road setting, this cosy café nourishes travellers with hearty soups, sandwiches and homemade cakes, and offers walking information. Mid-March to Oct daily 11.30am–6/7pm.

Bantry

BANTRY enjoys a glorious location, ringed first by lush wooded slopes and then by wild bare mountains, at the head of 35km-long **Bantry Bay**, one of the finest natural harbours in Ireland. The prime viewpoint is naturally occupied by **Bantry House**, which with its sumptuous interior and garden is one of West Cork's few unmissable historic sites. At the junction of several important roads, Bantry is also a substantial market (Fridays) and service town, with plenty of amenities for visitors.

Wolfe Tone Square

Bantry gathers itself around the expansive, bayside **Wolfe Tone Square**, which features a statue of the eponymous United Irishman pointedly holding a telescope behind his back. In December 1796, Tone persuaded the French to send a fleet carrying some thirteen thousand seasoned soldiers to invade Ireland in support of a Republican Revolution. Contrary winds prevented them from landing in Bantry Bay – though they were "close enough to toss a biscuit on shore" according to Tone – and the fleet was forced to return to Brest. Had they landed, it's likely that they would have overwhelmed the inexperienced forces in Ireland at the time.

Bantry House

Easter–Oct Tues–Sun 10am–5pm; guided tour Tues 2pm • House and garden €11, garden €5; guided tour €15 • ⓦ bantryhouse.com

On the southern approach to town, **Bantry House** is one of Ireland's most compelling country houses, both for its lavish artworks and for its magnificent setting, among formal gardens overlooking the bay. Built in the early eighteenth century and extended a hundred years later, it was spared destruction during the Irish Civil War, when it acted as a hospital for the wounded of both sides. Many of its beautiful furnishings were gathered by the Second Earl of Bantry on his nineteenth-century grand tour and boast name-dropping provenances, such as the gorgeous Aubusson tapestries made for Marie Antoinette on her marriage to the future Louis XVI. The highlight is the dining room, which resembles an extravagant stage set: rich Chartres-blue walls, a marble colonnade and vast seventeenth-century sideboards carved with cherubs and classical scenes. There's a very attractive **café**, with tables under the house's west balcony, which serves teas and simple lunches.

ARRIVAL AND INFORMATION   BANTRY

By bus Buses stop on the central Wolfe Tone Square.
Tourist office At the east end of Wolfe Tone Square (May to late Sept daily 10am–6pm; ☎ 027 50229). Free guided

historical walks (June–Aug Tues & Thurs 11am).
Bike rental Nigel's, a short way out on the Glengarriff road (☎ 027 52657).

ACCOMMODATION

There's a decent range of **accommodation** in Bantry, with dozens of B&Bs lining the Glengarriff road on the north side of town, but it's advisable to book ahead in July and Aug, especially during the town's festivals.

★ **Bantry House** On the N71 at the southern entrance to town ☎ 027 50047, ⓦ bantryhouse.com. Luxurious digs

with great views in one of the country's finest mansions, which is still the home of the White family, former Earls of Bantry. The

---

BANTRY FESTIVALS

Bantry hosts the prestigious nine-day **West Cork Chamber Music Festival** (ⓦ westcorkmusic.ie), generally at the beginning of July, followed immediately by the seven-day **West Cork Literary Festival** (ⓦ westcorkliteraryfestival.ie). August sees a five-day **traditional-music festival**, "Masters of Tradition" (ⓦ westcorkmusic.ie).

huge, chandeliered library, with its coffered ceiling, and the billiards room are now guest lounges. Easter–Oct. **€169**

Eagle Point Caravan and Camping Park Ballylickey, 6km from Bantry along the Glengarriff road ☎027 50630, ⓦeaglepointcamping.com. This large, well-organized campsite sits on its own headland in Bantry Bay, with a laundry, a small playground, a tennis court and pebbly beaches for swimming. Easter to late Sept. **€29**

The Maritime Just off Wolfe Tone Square on the main road to Skibbereen ☎027 54700, ⓦthemaritime.ie. This smart contemporary hotel is plush and thoughtfully equipped, with very helpful reception staff and a leisure centre that features a 19m pool, gym, jacuzzi and sauna. **€99**

The Mill Newtown, 1km along the Glengarriff road ☎027 50278, ⓦthe-mill.net. Excellent B&B in a large bungalow, roomy, comfortable and decorated in pastel colours; all the bedrooms are en suite, and there's a conservatory, landscaped gardens and great breakfasts. March–Nov. **€70**

EATING AND DRINKING

The Anchor Tavern New St, off the southeast corner of the square ☎027 50012. A popular haunt for visiting musicians, this sociable 150-year-old traditional pub is adorned with nautical memorabilia, plain stone floors and communal pews around the walls. Mon–Thurs roughly noon–11.30pm, Fri & Sat noon–12.30am, Sun noon–11pm.

The Brick Oven Wolfe Tone Square, southwest corner ☎027 52500. Accomplished all-rounder serving good baguettes and salads (warm smoked chicken €15.90), plus pizzas from a wood-burning oven and tasty bistro dishes. Daily noon–10pm.

★**Ma Murphy's** New St, off the southeast corner of the square ☎027 50242. Cosy bar-grocery with a cool soundtrack and a very pleasant cobbled back yard; also on offer are good pies, soup and pizza, and plenty of whiskeys and bottles of craft beer. Open mike Thurs, live music at weekends. Mon–Thurs roughly noon–11.30pm, Fri & Sat noon–12.30am, Sun noon–11pm.

★**O'Connor's** Wolfe Tone Square ☎027 55664, ⓦoconnorsbantry.com. Elegant, top-quality restaurant specializing in seafood (including oysters from its own seawater tank) and local lamb, pork and steaks, in ample portions. Try the Bantry Bay scallops with honey-roast ham hock and pea risotto (€26.50), and leave room for excellent desserts such as rhubarb crumble. Early bird €22.50 for two courses (until 6.30pm). The simpler menu at lunch time includes baguette of the day. Mon–Fri & Sun 12.30–3pm & 5.30–9.30pm, Sat 5.30–9.30pm; winter closed Tues & Wed.

Organico 100m off the square at the start of the Glengarriff road ☎027 55905, ⓦorganico.ie. Popular, easy-going vegetarian and organic café, bakery and health-food store, dishing up tasty hummus salads (€7.50), sandwiches and soups. Mon–Sat 10am–5pm.

Stuffed Olive 2a Bridge St, the continuation of New St off the square's southeast corner ☎027 55883. Excellent deli-café and bakery serving creative sandwiches and salads such as smoked duck (€5.50), cakes, good coffees and juices. Mon–Sat 9am–6pm.

The Beara Peninsula

The largest and most remote of Cork's peninsulas, the **Beara** (ⓦbearatourism.com) careers southwestwards for 50km between Bantry Bay and the Kenmare River. Patterns in the landscape are hard to distinguish here, and contrasts are frequent. Indeed, the peninsula's most popular tourist spot, **Glengarriff**, has built an industry on the stunning contrast between its lush subtropical setting and the irregular barren rocks of the Caha Mountains behind. The mountainous spine is often augmented by ribs, and particularly in the awesome Slieve Miskish Mountains at the Beara's tip, the coast road is forced to climb through whatever passes can be found. Round on the north coast, half of which belongs to County Kerry (see p.290), the only settlements occupy occasional cups of green farmland beneath the stony ridges. This diverse scenery is linked together by two routes: the **Beara Way**, a 200km waymarked walk (9–11 days), following mostly tracks and minor roads from Glengarriff west (via Adrigole, Castletownbere and a ferry to Bere Island, which can easily be missed out) to Dursey Island, then along the north coast of the peninsula (via Allihies, Eyeries, Ardgroom and Lauragh) to Kenmare and back to Glengarriff; and the 138km **Beara Way Cycle Route**, which mostly follows the quiet main road around the peninsula. Route guides are available locally, there's a downloadable map guide of the walking route at ⓦbearatourism.com, and the Ordnance Survey 1:50,000 Discovery map 84 covers nearly the whole peninsula.

Glengarriff

The founders of **GLENGARRIFF** (⟨w⟩glengarriff.ie) were perhaps having an off-day when they named it *An Gleann Garbh*, the "rugged glen" – or, to be charitable, maybe the climate has changed since then. It's true that above and behind stands the magnificent backdrop of the wild, bare Caha Mountains, but the village itself sits in a sheltered oasis of balmy greenery. This picturesque juxtaposition, warmed by the Atlantic Gulf Stream, has attracted tourists since the eighteenth century, when the *Eccles Hotel* was built. The village now straggles east–west for several kilometres from the *Eccles*, with most of its amenities towards the western end around the N71–R572 junction. The landscape – and the gift shops – still pull in the coach parties, but Glengarriff's popularity also means there's a decent range of places to stay, making it a good base for exploring some of Cork's most beautiful countryside or for just hopping over to see the horticultural delights of **Garinish Island**. Over a weekend in late June, Glengarriff hosts a vibrant **uilleann pipes festival**, with concerts, workshops and sessions of traditional music (⟨w⟩jimdowlingfestival.com).

Bamboo Park

Daily 9am–7pm • €6 • ⟨w⟩bamboo-park.com

Glengarriff's microclimate is mild enough to support the **Bamboo Park**, a beautiful thirteen-acre private garden with a tearoom towards the east end of the village, planted with thirty different species of bamboo, as well as various palms, ferns and eucalyptus. The maze of paths here would be great for kids, who get in free, to have a very long game of hide-and-seek, while the seashore frontage, with private beach and picnic area, reveals idyllic views of tufted green islets in the bay.

Glengarriff Woods Nature Reserve

⟨w⟩www.glengarriffnaturereserve.ie

As well as the Beara Way and Cycle Route, there are plenty of opportunities in the immediate vicinity of Glengarriff for exploration on foot or by bike (or a combination of both). About a kilometre up the N71 Kenmare road is **Glengarriff Woods Nature Reserve**, a forest park of ancient sessile oaks, birch and holly, that shelters Mediterranean species such as strawberry trees. It's crossed by waymarked nature trails (about 3hr walking in total), including the short climb up to **Lady Bantry's Lookout**, which is rewarded with panoramic views of Glengarriff, Bantry Bay and the Sheep's Head.

Barley Lake and Zetland Pier

Further up the N71 from the nature reserve, about 10km from Glengarriff, lies **Barley Lake**, a beautiful armchair or corrie lake. Zetland Pier, about 10km west off the R572, hosts a sandy **beach**.

INFORMATION   GLENGARRIFF

Tourist information There's no longer an official tourist office in Glengarriff, but a souvenir shop next to the Blue Pool ferry service and the bus stop has a few local brochures. Note that there are no banks in Glengarriff, though the Spar supermarket and post office can change foreign cash.

Bike rental The Black Cat Internet Café (O'Shea's; ☎027 63756), opposite Casey's Hotel (see below).

ACCOMMODATION AND EATING

Casey's Hotel Main St ☎027 63010, ⟨w⟩caseyshotel glengarriff.ie. Friendly, family-run nineteenth-century hotel, with crisply refurbished rooms, a patio and garden. Very good food such as beef and Guinness pie, and plenty of seafood in the bar or smart evening restaurant. Good rates for singles. **€90**

Glengarriff Caravan and Camping Park (Dowling's) About 2km out on the R572 Castletownbere road ☎027 63154, ✉glengarriffccp@gmail.com. You can camp in some comfort at this woodland site, which has laundry facilities, a playground and traditional music in its on-site bar. April–Oct. **€25**

Glengarriff Park Hotel Main St ☎027 63000, ⟨w⟩glengarriffpark.com. Tasteful, modern "standard" rooms, some with baths, plus slightly more expensive "luxury" rooms with more space, more elaborate decor and armchairs. Downstairs are a bistro and *MacCarthy's*, a pleasant, well-run bar serving tasty food. **€110**

The Maple Leaf Main St ☎ 027 63021. Located among a tight concentration of pubs at the main junction, this friendly spot offers live music every night in summer, at weekends in winter. Mon–Thurs noon–11.30pm, Fri & Sat noon–12.30am, Sun noon–11pm.

Perrin Inn (Cottage Bar and Restaurant) Main St ☎ 027 63226, ⓦ theperrininn.ie. Basic en-suite B&B rooms at the back and cheap traditional food such as smoked mackerel salad or lasagne in the streetside bar-restaurant. Value-for-money half-board deals and self-catering also available. Bar-restaurant daily 9am–9pm. **€60**

Garinish Island (Ilnacullin)

April, May & Sept Mon–Sat 10am–6.30pm, Sun noon/1–6.30pm; June, July & Aug Mon–Sat 9.30/10am–6.30pm, Sun 11am–6.30pm; Oct Mon–Sat 10am–4pm, Sun 1–5pm • €4; Heritage Card • ⓦ heritageireland.ie • Boat €12 return with *Harbour Queen* Ferries (☎ 027 63116, ⓦ harbourqueenferry.com) from opposite the *Eccles Hotel* at the east end of Glengarriff; or €10 either with *Blue Pool* Ferry (☎ 027 63333, ⓦ bluepoolferry.com) in the centre of Glengarriff, or with the *Lady Ellen*, from Ellen's Rock, about 2km west of the village off the Castletownbere road (☎ 027 63110).

In 1910, the MP Annan Bryce bought **Garinish** (aka Ilnacullin) from the British War Office and, after shipping in all the topsoil, gradually turned the rocky inshore island into an exotic garden oasis. Having passed into public ownership in 1953, the island is now a delightful and accessible escape from the mainland, especially in summer, when colourful plants from around the world set the island alight against a backdrop of the sparse, jagged mountains just across the water. The island's centrepiece is a formal Italianate garden, surrounded by a walled garden and wilder areas, a Grecian temple with magnificent views of the Caha Mountains, and a Martello tower. There's a coffee shop and a self-guided trail around the gardens, and serious horticulturalists should pick up the Heritage Service's guidebook, which includes detailed plant lists. The ten-minute **boat trip** (see above) to the island takes you past the lush islets of Glengarriff Harbour, where you may see basking seals.

Castletownbere

Over 100km west of Cork city at the end of the peninsula, the bustle of **CASTLETOWNBERE** (sometimes referred to as Castletown Berehaven or just Castletown; ⓦ castletownbere.ie) comes as quite a surprise. Benefiting from the country's second-largest natural harbour, it's Ireland's biggest white-fish port, and especially during strong winter gales, Atlantic trawlers of many nationalities put in here. Not surprisingly, there's a good range of amenities for visitors, with the fairly compact area around the main square offering cafés, restaurants, banks and some boisterous pubs.

Puxley Mansion and Dunboy Castle

Just off the R572 Dursey road • Open access

To the west of town, there's a pleasant 3km walk to **Puxley Mansion**, the poignant skeleton of a neo-Gothic pile. It was constructed in the nineteenth century by the Puxleys – made famous by Daphne du Maurier in her novel *Hungry Hill* – who built up a vast fortune from copper-mining around Allihies in the nineteenth century (see p.267) but were burnt out by the IRA in 1921. Further on through the grounds, the overgrown seafront ruins of **Dunboy Castle** afford dramatic views back along the Beara Peninsula. Built in the fourteenth century, the castle was besieged by the English in 1602 after the Battle of Kinsale. Facing an army of 4000, its garrison of 143 men held out for eleven days, but in the end were all slaughtered and the castle blown up. Their chieftain, **Donal Cam O'Sullivan Bere**, then embarked on his famous long **march** up to County Leitrim in the winter of 1602–03 with a thousand men, women and children. Harassed by the English and the Irish, he arrived two weeks later with just 35 followers left. The march is now commemorated by the **Beara-Breifne Way** (ⓦ bbgreenway.com), a 500km walking route from Dursey Island to Blacklion on the borders of Leitrim, Cavan and Fermanagh, where it links with the Ulster Way.

ARRIVAL AND INFORMATION

CASTLETOWNBERE

By bus Buses stop on the main square, except Harrington's which pick up from the Supervalu supermarket just to the east.

Destinations Bus Éireann: Cork (8 weekly; 3hr); Kenmare, via Eyeries, Lauragh and the north side of the Beara (July & Aug Mon–Sat 2 daily; 1hr 20min).

Harrington's Buses (☎027 74003, ⓦwestcorkcoaches .com): Cork (Mulligan's Bar, opposite the bus station on Parnell Place; Mon–Wed & Fri–Sun 1 daily; 2hr).

O'Donoghue's Buses (☎027 70007): Bantry (Mon 2 daily, Tues, Fri & Sat 1 daily; 1hr 10min); Cork (Mulligan's Bar opposite the bus station on Parnell Place; 1 on Thurs; 2hr 45min).

Tourist office Just west of the square along the main street (usually Mon–Fri 9am–5pm, but might be worth checking on ☎027 70054); they have details of short signposted loop walks on the peninsula.

Bike rental Bike'n'Beara, Great Gas petrol station, 2km east of the centre on the Glengarriff road (☎086 128 0307, ⓦbikenbeara.ie).

ACCOMMODATION

Berehaven Golf Club 5km east on the Glengarriff road at Filane ☎027 70700, ⓦberehavengolf.com. You can camp on the shores of Bantry Bay at the golf club, shower in the clubhouse and drink in the daytime bar in the summer. Laundry room and reduced green fees for campers. €18

Garranes Hostel 8km west of town on the Dursey road ☎027 73032, ⓦdzogchenbeara.org. Segregated dorms and a family room open to all-comers at a Tibetan Buddhist retreat centre in a traditional farmhouse cottage. It offers a fully equipped kitchen, a sitting room and plenty of tranquillity; there's a café on site too. Dorms €15, family room €40

Rodeen 2km east of town ☎027 70158 ⓦrodeencountryhouse.com. Charming retreat set in beautiful subtropical gardens overlooking the bay, with stylish en-suite rooms, and home-baked scones for breakfast. Very good rates for singles. €70

EATING AND DRINKING

Issie's To the east of the square opposite Supervalu ☎086 215 5804. Simple café serving delicious handmade chocolates, homemade ice cream (€2/scoop) and espressos. March–Oct Mon–Thurs 11am–6pm, Fri & Sat 11am–7pm, Sun noon–6pm.

★ **MacCarthy's** On the main square ☎027 70014. This grocery-bar does soups and fresh crab and smoked salmon sandwiches for lunch, and is the best place to drink, with tables on the street and regular traditional sessions. Mon–Thurs 10.30am–11.30pm, Fri & Sat 10.30am–12.30am, Sun 12.30–11pm.

Murphy's East of the square on the main street ☎027 70244. Unprepossessing restaurant, famous for its fresh, simple fish and seafood (lemon sole with chips and salad €10). Daily 9am–9pm.

Olde Bakery About 500m west of the square on the main street ☎027 70869. Retaining the bakery's original stone walls, this upmarket but informal spot specializes in white fish from the port in dishes such as monkfish and tiger prawn kebab with a sweet chilli cream. Early bird until 7pm; €18.95 for two courses. Summer Mon–Sat 5.30–10pm, Sun noon–5pm & 5.30–10pm; winter Mon–Sat 6–9pm, Sun noon–5pm & 6–9pm.

Twomey's On the main street west of the square ☎027 70114. Spruce bar with a sunny yard running down to the harbour, which runs set dancing on summer Fri and live music on Sat. Mon–Thurs 12.30–11.30pm, Fri & Sat 12.30pm–12.30am, Sun 12.30–11pm.

Garnish Bay and Dursey Island

Cable car: mid-June to Sept daily 9am–7.30pm; 7pm or earlier, depending on visitor numbers, for returning passengers only; Oct to mid-June Mon–Sat 9–10.30am, 2.30–4.30pm &, for returning passengers only, 7–7.30pm, Sun 9–10am, 1–2pm &, for returning passengers only, 7–7.30pm • €8 return • ⓦdurseyisland.ie

Beyond Castletownbere, you can skirt round through a few tiny, remote but dramatically set villages to the north side of the peninsula and on towards Kerry. Three kilometres before the tip of the peninsula, the R572 passes beautiful, north-facing **Garnish Bay**, which boasts one of the Beara's few sandy beaches and crystal-clear water.

The Beara lays on a bit of excitement at its very end, in the form of Ireland's only **cable car**, which teeters across the roaring sound to the bird sanctuary of **Dursey Island** and sometimes attracts long queues in summer. There are no facilities on the island (wild camping is legal), but you can walk its circular 11km stretch of the Beara Way for seemingly endless views across the Atlantic, beyond Calf, Cow and Bull islands.

Windy Point House ☎ 027 73017, ⓦ windypointhouse .com. The cable-car operator and his wife run a pleasant en-suite B&B, nearby on the mainland on their farm overlooking Dursey Sound, with stupendous views from all the bright, pine-furnished bedrooms, the dining room, the conservatory and the large garden terrace. Dinners and packed lunches available to guests if pre-booked. Good single rates. April–Nov. **€70**

Allihies

Looping round an especially harsh and rocky part of the peninsula on the R575, you'll come upon **ALLIHIES**, its brightly coloured houses dramatically huddled together against the leathery creases of Slieve Miskish's western flank and blessed with superb sunset views.

Allihies Copper Mine Museum

Daily: April–Oct 9.30am–5pm; Nov–March generally 10am–4pm, but worth calling to check • €5 • ☎ 027 73218, ⓦ new.acmm.ie

In 1812, the Industrial Revolution descended on remote Allihies with a vengeance, bringing state-of-the-art engineering and Cornish mining techniques to work the copper ore in the mountains above the village. At any one time, up to 1500 people, including women and children, worked for the mines here in desperate conditions, until their closure in the 1880s, when many of the miners emigrated to the huge copper lode in Butte, Montana. The story is now engagingly told at the excellent **Allihies Copper Mine Museum**, set up by a group of dedicated local enthusiasts, in a renovated Methodist church that was built for the immigrant Cornish miners. Highlights of the thoughtful displays include video recollections of local men who worked in the mines when they briefly reopened in the 1950s, bits of ore that you can handle and a small-scale reconstruction of a steam pump. There's also a very attractive **café** (see below) and an upstairs exhibition area for local artists. In addition, a network of **signposted trails** has been laid out in the surrounding countryside, allowing you to take in ruined mine buildings and spectacular views.

Ballydonegan Strand

One of the trails from the copper mine museum leads down to **Ballydonegan Strand** and its simple campsite (☎ 027 73002), 1km to the southwest. This sandy beach is actually composed of crushed quartz produced in the copper extraction process, but you'll need to beware the currents when swimming.

Allihies Hostel In the centre of the village ☎ 027 73107, ⓦ allihieshostel.net (IHH). This bright, appealing hostel offers smart dorms, twins, doubles and family rooms (plus singles in the off-season), laundry facilities, a large sitting room, a kitchen and outdoor barbecue, as well as plenty of local information. Dorms **€16**, doubles **€45**

The Copper Café Allihies Copper Mine Museum (see above) ☎ 027 73218, ⓦ new.acmm.ie. The café in the copper mine museum near the southern entrance to town serves good coffee, homemade cakes, chowder and lunch dishes such as West Cork mussels. April–Oct daily 9.30am–5pm.

O'Neill's Bar Next to *Allihies Hostel* ☎ 027 73008, ⓦ oneillsbeara.ie. Boasting an unmissable crimson façade, this pub-restaurant serves lunch and dinner in summer, and is also your best bet for traditional music (weekends year-round, more often in summer). Choose between tables out front on the street with great views, or the log fire inside, depending on the weather. Mon–Thurs noon–11.30pm, Fri & Sat noon–12.30am, Sun noon–11pm.

Sea View On the main street in the village centre ☎ 027 73004, ⓦ seaviewallihies.com. In a twostorey terrace house, *Sea View* offers ten comfortable en-suite bedrooms in pastel and earth tones and good breakfasts, as well as self-catering accommodation. **€80**

7

Kerry

TO THE SKELLIGS SCULPTURE, CAHERSIVEEN

Kerry

Kerry has been making visitors' romantic dreams of Ireland come true since the eighteenth century, when the grandeur of the lakes and mountains around Killarney first came to widespread attention. Encompassing the highest range in the country, Macgillycuddy's Reeks, the landscape here is, of course, still magnificent today, and the Killarney area shelters some fine, underrated architectural sights too, while the town itself has plenty of amenities and entertainment, though little soul. Most of the one million tourists who come to Kerry every year, however, stick rigidly to Killarney and the Ring of Kerry, the scenic drive around the neighbouring Iveragh Peninsula, so it's pretty easy to avoid the crowds.

The Iveragh itself measures around sixty by thirty kilometres, with plenty of tracks across its vast, rugged hinterland and coastal branch roads such as the **Ring of Skellig** to explore by car, bike or on foot. The small-scale but intriguing attractions of **Valentia Island** and **Caherdaniel**, perched on a scenic hillside above a great beach, should be enough to tempt you off the Ring of Kerry to spend at least a night out here. The island of **Skellig Michael** off the end of the peninsula, one of the most remarkable hermitages in the world and now a UNESCO World Heritage Site, remains the ultimate place to get away from it all. At the southeastern corner of the peninsula, **Kenmare** contrasts well with Killarney, providing some excellent accommodation, restaurants and nightlife in a trim, picturesque setting, as well as access to further scenic delights on Kerry's part of the **Beara Peninsula**.

Kerry's other peninsula, **Dingle**, experienced its own minor visitor boom on the release of David Lean's film, *Ryan's Daughter*, in 1970, which pumped as much as £3 million into the local economy during a long and troubled location shoot here (including the near-drowning of star Robert Mitchum off Dunquin and the building of an entirely new village, Kirrary, on the remote slopes above). It's still nothing like as touristed as the Ring, and offers a jagged landscape of stark mountains and spectacular beaches, an especially rich heritage of early Christian sites, and a fine, all-round base in the main settlement, **Dingle town**.

Despite the centuries of tourist traffic, Kerry has maintained a strong sense of independence, though perhaps doesn't shout about it as much as its neighbour, Cork. It's one of the least urbanized counties in Ireland, with a sweet, country lilt to the accent. Distinctive H-shaped goalposts are everywhere, not just on village GAA fields but on most farms, evidence of the county's obsession with **Gaelic football**. The self-styled "Brazil" of the sport, the county team have won the All-Ireland Championship far more than anyone else – 37 times and counting – and produced the finest team ever between 1975 and 1986, winning the championship eight times in those eleven years. The Dingle Peninsula, one of Ireland's strongest Gaeltacht areas, has

GALLARUS ORATORY

Highlights

❶ Killarney National Park Beautiful – and popular – landscape of mountains and lakes, which can be explored by boat, bike and on foot. **See p.273**

❷ The Kerry Way A 213km walking route through the wild, awe-inspiring scenery of the Iveragh Peninsula. **See p.276**

❸ The Puck Fair Bacchanalian festival in August, when Killorglin comes under the reign of a wild goat. **See p.277**

❹ The Skelligs Spectacular, inhospitable islands, haunt of seabirds and the ghosts of early medieval hermits. **See p.285**

❺ Kenmare An agreeable base with a great selection of places to eat, sleep and drink. **See p.288**

❻ Dingle town Traditional music, great pubs and seafood – what more could you want? **See p.293**

❼ The Blaskets Lonely islands off the scenic Dingle Peninsula, with an astonishing literary heritage that's imaginatively documented in the visitor centre. **See p.298**

❽ Gallarus Oratory A unique, early Christian remnant and a graceful, evocative piece of architecture. **See p.300**

HIGHLIGHTS ARE MARKED ON THE MAP ON P.272

nurtured not only great footballers, but also a fine community of musicians and the extraordinary **writers** of the wild **Blasket Islands**, who put their rich oral tradition of Irish-language storytelling to paper in the early twentieth century. The county's other most obvious concentration of literary talent has been in the flatlands of **North Kerry**, as celebrated in the genial market town of **Listowel**.

GETTING AROUND   KERRY

By bus In this deeply rural county, public buses are few and often far between. Bus Éireann is augmented by Kerry Community Transport (ⓦ kerrytransport.ie), whose minibus network may be of use to visitors, though its complex weekly timetable is mostly designed to get people from rural areas into the big towns for the day.

KERRY

HIGHLIGHTS

1. Killarney National Park
2. The Kerry Way
3. The Puck Fair
4. The Skelligs
5. Kenmare
6. Dingle town
7. The Blaskets
8. Gallarus Oratory

Killarney and around

KILLARNEY was developed as a resort on the doorstep of Ireland's finest lakeland scenery in the eighteenth and nineteenth centuries, and has steadily grown as a tourist town since, busy, lively and easily accessible, with hundreds of places to stay in all price ranges. Backpackers are particularly well catered for, with an appealing selection of hostels and all manner of land- and water-borne tours available for those without their own transport. The town's kiss-me-quick hedonism and souvenir shops are not to everyone's taste, but the attraction of the place is still the same as three hundred years ago: beginning in the very heart of town, **Killarney National Park** encompasses three beautiful lakes, beyond which rise the splendid **Macgillycuddy's Reeks**, the country's highest mountain range, known in Irish as Na Cruacha Dubha, the "Black Stacks". The only building of architectural interest in the town is Pugin's elegant **cathedral**, but the national park shelters three diverse and very well preserved monuments, **Ross Castle**, **Muckross Friary** and **Muckross House**.

St Mary's Cathedral

On the west side of the town centre • Hours variable • Free

Seat of the Bishop of Kerry, **St Mary's Cathedral** is Ireland's finest neo-Gothic church, built in stages between 1842 and 1912 to a design by Augustus Pugin. Set in spacious gardens by the entrance to the national park, its exterior, with a lofty steeple over the transept, is strikingly elegant. Inside, the rough grey stonework is colourfully lit by dozens of stained-glass windows, which depict in their upper range the life of Christ, in the lower the lives of the Irish saints, notably Patrick and Brendan the Navigator, patron saint of the diocese. The huge redwood tree outside the west door marks a mass children's grave from the time of the Famine: work on the church was suspended in the late 1840s, when the partly roofed building was used as a hospital and shelter.

8

Killarney National Park

Visitor centre Muckross House • Mid-March to Sept daily 9am–5.30pm **Information point** Killarney House gate lodge • June to mid-Sept daily 9.30am–5.30pm • ⓦ heritageireland.ie

Killarney National Park now protects the glaciated limestone valleys around the three lakes, Leane (or Lower), Muckross (or Middle) and Upper (see p.276). The lakeshores are covered with virgin forest that features oak, yew and such Mediterranean plants as the arbutus, or strawberry tree – so termed because of its red, but inedible, fruit. Among the park's notable mammals are Ireland's only wild herd of red deer, otter, pine marten, red squirrels and Irish hare, while its 140 bird species include the white-tailed sea eagle

---

KILLARNEY FESTIVALS AND EVENTS

Killarney lays on a long menu of seasonal **festivals and events**, with music and sport featuring strongly. There's a five-day festival of traditional music in late February (ⓦ thegathering.ie), while Spraoí Chiarraí is a series of free concerts of traditional music, dancing and storytelling in the summer (ⓦ timosheaandfriends.com).

In May, July and August, Killarney's **racecourse** (ⓦ killarneyraces.ie), in a scenic spot on Ross Road, hosts boisterous, well-supported racing. The first weekend in May, when the Rally of the Lakes (ⓦ rallyofthelakes.com) pulls crowds of motoring fans to the area, is not a good time to experience the serenity of the mountains.

Killarney is a good place to sample the Kerry fervour for **Gaelic football**: major matches are held at Fitzgerald Park on Lewis Road (ⓦ kerrygaa.ie), which is named after Dick Fitzgerald, greatest player of the early twentieth century and author of the first training manual on the game, and enjoys a magnificent mountain backdrop from its north terraces. The local side, Dr Croke's, All-Ireland club champions in 1992, have their stadium across the road.

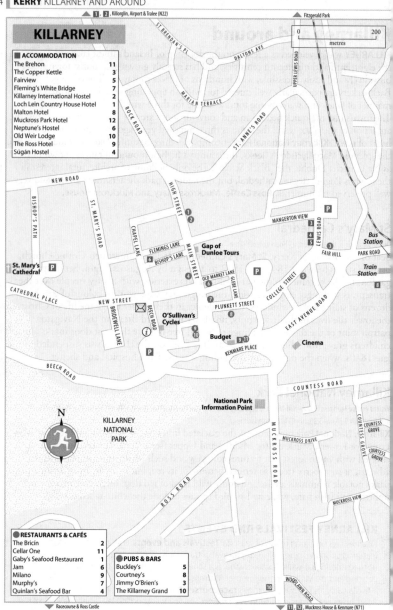

KILLARNEY

ACCOMMODATION

The Brehon	11
The Copper Kettle	3
Fairview	5
Fleming's White Bridge	7
Killarney International Hostel	2
Loch Lein Country House Hotel	1
Malton Hotel	8
Muckross Park Hotel	12
Neptune's Hostel	6
Old Weir Lodge	10
The Ross Hotel	9
Súgán Hostel	4

RESTAURANTS & CAFÉS

The Bricín	2
Cellar One	11
Gaby's Seafood Restaurant	1
Jam	6
Milano	9
Murphy's	7
Quinlan's Seafood Bar	4

PUBS & BARS

Buckley's	5
Courtney's	8
Jimmy O'Brien's	3
The Killarney Grand	10

(reintroduced from Norway in 2007), the peregrine falcon and the hen harrier. Running roughly parallel to, but just outside the park's western border is the dramatic glacial breach known as the **Gap of Dunloe** (see p.277). The **National Park Visitor Centre** at Muckross House provides information about all aspects of the park, including a twenty-minute audiovisual on the landscape, flora and fauna. A useful free **map** of the park is available both here and at the **National Park Information Point** in the gate lodge of Killarney House,

KILLARNEY NATIONAL PARK TOURS AND ACTIVITIES

GUIDED WALKS

Two-hour **guided walks** through the park set off from opposite St Mary's Cathedral every morning at 11am (Nov–April advance booking required; €9; ☎087 639 4362, ⓦ killarneyguidedwalks.com).

PONY TRAPS

Jaunting cars (pony traps) tout for business at several locations, including Kenmare Place in town, Muckross House and Kate Kearney's Cottage (see p.278; for the Gap of Dunloe). On the east side of the Kenmare Place roundabout, a sign in front of the Celtic cross war memorial and the *Killarney Avenue Hotel* gives a map of their routes and a detailed price list, though you might still have to haggle with the "jarveys" – as the drivers are known. A one-hour trip, for example, through the national park and along the lakeside to Ross Castle should cost €40 for up to three passengers (add €12 for each extra passenger). Reputable jarveys include Paul and Michael Tangney, usually to be found at Kenmare Place (☎064 663 3358 or ☎087 253 2770, ⓦ killarneyjauntingcars.ie).

HORSE RIDING

Killarney Riding Stables, 1km west of town on the Killorglin road (☎064 663 1686, ⓦ killarney-riding-stables.com), offer **horse riding** in the national park on day-trips, as well as on the two- or five-day Reeks Trail.

KAYAKING

Kayaking on the lakes is offered by Outdoors Ireland (☎086 860 4563, ⓦ outdoorsireland .com) and Cappanalea Outdoor Education Centre (☎066 976 9244, ⓦ cappanalea.ie).

ORGANIZED TOURS OF THE PARK

Several tour operators, including O'Donoghue Brothers, *Old Weir Lodge*, Muckross Road (☎064 663 1068, ⓦ killarneydaytour.com), and Gap of Dunloe Tours, with a base at *O'Connors Pub*, 7 High St, in the summer (☎064 663 0200 or ☎087 267 2821, ⓦ gapofdunloetours.com), offer full-day **combination tours**, which take you by bus to the starting point of Kate Kearney's Cottage (see p.278), from where you walk or ride a jaunting car or pony through the Gap; then after a lunch stop at Lord Brandon's Cottage you take a boat ride through the three lakes to Ross Castle, and finally a bus brings you back into town (€30 per person, €50 with jaunting car, €60 with pony-trekking). Simpler **bike-on-boat tours** (you cycle through the Gap of Dunloe and sling your bike on a boat between Lord Brandon's Cottage and Ross Castle) can be arranged through the hostels, or O'Donoghue Brothers (as above) or Gap of Dunloe Tours. Or you can put this together yourself: from roughly early March to late October, the boats leave Ross Castle at 11am, returning from Lord Brandon's at 2pm (€15), and bikes can be rented from O'Sullivan's (see p.278).

ORGANIZED TOURS OF LOUGH LEANE

From the pier at Ross Castle, **tours of Lough Leane** are operated by two large waterbuses, which in summer each run up to five one-hour trips a day (€10): the *Lily of Killarney* (contact O'Donoghue Brothers, as above); and the *Pride of the Lakes* (☎064 663 2638, ⓦ killarneylaketours .ie), which offers a connecting shuttle bus from town. In summer, O'Donoghue Brothers also operates small motorboats to heavily wooded **Inisfallen**, the largest of Lough Leane's islets (€7.50), or you could rent a boat at Ross Castle to row yourself there.

HOP-ON HOP-OFF BUSES

Killarney currently supports no fewer than three **hop-on hop-off bus** services (all €10/day, or €15 for 2/3 days). Two of them are open-top double-deckers, which depart from East Avenue Road three times a day and run south to Ross Castle, Muckross House and Torc Waterfall, as well as west to Aghadoe: Killarney Heritage Trail (☎087 342 8259, ⓦ killarneyheritagetrail.com) and Big Red Killarney Bus Tour (☎087 765 4555, ⓦ killarneytour.com), which reduces its service to once daily in winter. Killarney Shuttle Bus (☎087 138 4384, ⓦ killarneyshuttlebus.com) starts at the tourist office, offers single tickets (from €3) as well as day passes, and covers two routes: west to the Gap of Dunloe (3 daily) and south to Muckross House and Torc Waterfall (9 daily).

just inside the "Golden Gates" (actually black) on Muckross Road in the centre of town, while the Ordnance Survey of Ireland produces a more detailed (1:25,000) map.

There's all manner of tours and transport available (many of which can be booked at the tourist office), including boats at Ross Castle (see below) and Muckross House (see opposite), and rented bikes (see p.278).

Ross Castle

Guided tours (40min) mid-March to late Oct daily 9.30am–5.45pm, last admission 5pm; maximum 15 people per tour, so you may have a wait at busy times • €4; Heritage Card • Ⓦ heritageireland.ie

The gates of Knockreer Estate opposite the cathedral and the "Golden Gates" by the National Park Information Point on Muckross Road give immediate access from the town centre to the national park. Paths through the grounds, which blaze in spring with rhododendrons, azaleas and magnolias, lead south after less than half an hour to **Ross Castle**. Alternatively, a more roundabout route from the cathedral to the castle runs along the shore of Lough Leane, affording magnificent views of the lake's thirty-odd islands and the mountains to the southwest; or you can drive there via a turning off the N71.

Engaging and informative **tours** focus on the history, architecture and day-to-day life of the castle. It's an impressive example of a medieval tower house, probably built in the late fifteenth century by one of the O'Donoghue Ross chieftains, who had undisputed hold over the Killarney area at the time. They clearly had something to fear, however: the austere stronghold features murder holes and stumble steps – of irregular dimensions, designed to trip unwary attackers – while the cross-planked and spiked oak doors are further protected by raised thresholds and pointed arches. The flagstoned rooms, which include a Great Hall with its own pantry and minstrels' gallery and a tiny cubbyhole for around fifteen servants to sleep in, have been decked out with authentic fifteenth- to seventeenth-century furniture and tapestries.

Lough Leane

For boat trips, see box p.275

The monastery established on Inisfallen by St Fionán the Leper in the early seventh century became a major centre of learning, numbering among its tenth-century alumni Ireland's most famous king, Brian Boru. The *Annals of Inisfallen*, written by the monks between the eleventh and thirteenth centuries and now housed in the Bodleian Library in

---

THE KERRY WAY AND CARRAUNTOOHIL

The 213km-long **Kerry Way** is a spectacular, circular, waymarked footpath that starts in Killarney, takes in the Muckross Estate, Torc Waterfall, the Upper Lake and the Black Valley before crossing to Glencar, then goes right around the Iveragh Peninsula anticlockwise, with short offshoots to Glenbeigh, Cahersiveen, Waterville and Caherdaniel, finally passing through Sneem and Kenmare. Mostly following a network of green roads, many of which are old "butter roads", the route provides magnificent views both of the Iveragh's mountains and of the neighbouring peninsulas, Dingle and Beara. OS 1:50,000 **map** numbers 78 and 83 are essential, and Cork Kerry Tourism produces a useful *Kerry Way Map Guide*. The whole thing can be done in nine or ten days, or, with careful study of bus timetables, you could do day-walks along the Way beyond Glenbeigh in summer, or on the section between Glenbeigh and Waterville in winter.

An excellent **website**, Ⓦ kerryway.net, provides trail descriptions, maps and full details of hostels and other walker-friendly accommodation, offering services such as luggage transfer, evening meals and packed lunches, along the route.

Experienced walkers may well be tempted off the Kerry Way to tackle Ireland's highest peak, **Carrauntoohil** (1038m). Two of the finest approaches are described in *Best Irish Walks* by Josh Lynam: the Coomloughra Horseshoe, a seven-hour, occasionally vertiginous circuit, starting from the bridge at Breanlee on the Beaufort–Glencar road, which also takes in the second- and third-highest peaks, Beenkeragh and Caher; and a tough, nine-hour Macgillicuddy's Reeks ridge walk, beginning at *Kate Kearney's Cottage*, bagging six peaks and ending at the Breanlee bridge.

THE PUCK FAIR

For three mad days in the middle of August, the **Puck Fair** (🌐 puckfair.ie) draws in crowds of up to thirty thousand to the small, otherwise missable town of Killorglin, 19km west of Killarney. Granted its charter by James I in 1613, the fair begins when a wild goat is stalked in the mountains, then caged and crowned as king of the town, which raises the curtain on a Dionysian festival of wine and song, accompanied by a traditional horse fair. The event has pagan roots in the Celtic harvest festival of Lughnasa, though these particular ceremonies are meant to commemorate the herd of goats that ran down into Killorglin, to warn the townsfolk that Cromwell's army was on its way. For further information, contact Killorglin's Mid-Kerry Tourism office (☎ 066 976 1451, ✉ midkerrytourism@eircom.net).

Oxford, are the main source for the history of Munster of the period. The original churches and dwellings are long gone, but you can see the picturesquely weathered ruins of a thirteenth-century oratory and a mostly thirteenth-century Augustinian priory.

Muckross Estate

The huge section of the national park known as **Muckross Estate** begins about 3km south of Killarney off the N71, where a gate and a gaggle of jaunting cars signal the short walk through the woods to **Muckross Friary** (free access). Founded in the fifteenth century, this strict Franciscan friary originally enshrined a miraculous statue of the Virgin Mary. It's in a remarkable state of preservation, with an intact two-storey cloister shaded by a gnarled yew tree at its centre.

Muckross House

House Guided tours daily: July & Aug 9am–7pm; Sept–June 9am–5.30pm; last tour 1hr before closing; closed one week at Christmas • €7.50; Heritage Card • **Farms** March, April & Oct Sat, Sun & public hols 1–6pm; May & Sept daily 1–6pm; June–Aug daily 10am–6pm; last admission 5pm • €7.50, joint ticket including the house €12.50; Heritage Card not accepted • 🌐 muckross-house.ie

From Muckross Friary, you can continue through the estate on foot or by bike, but car drivers will have to continue down the main road for 1km to **Muckross House**. Guided tours lead visitors around the rich Victorian interiors of this fine nineteenth-century neo-Elizabethan stately home. On the other side of the car park are the three traditional **working farms** where you can chat to actors playing out the roles of farmers and their wives. In fine weather, you can sit outside at the splendid **café-restaurant** in the crafts centre, overlooking the pretty **gardens**, which are noted for their rhododendrons and azaleas.

Muckross Lake

Boat trips can be organized at the nearby Dundag Boathouse (☎ 087 278 9335 or ☎ 087 120 0420)

Starting from Muckross House (where you can pick up a walks leaflet), there's a delightful 10km trail around **Muckross Lake**, mostly on paved paths, but with a short section on the main Kenmare road. Passing through gnarled, mossy, ancient woods with a thick undergrowth of heather and ferns, you'll reach Brickeen Bridge where lakes Muckross and Leane meet, and shortly after the Meeting of the Waters, where the outflow from the Upper Lake runs into Muckross Lake. Just above this second meeting is an irresistibly photogenic, tree-shaded pool with the arches of the ruined Old Weir Bridge as a backdrop. Also much photographed is a nearby eighteenth-century hunting lodge, **Dinis Cottage**, which serves refreshments in summer. On your way back, you can take in 20m **Torc Waterfall** on a short detour, or take on the steep climb up to the summit of **Torc Mountain** (535m) for magnificent views of the lakes and the Reeks.

The Upper Lake

Further down the main N71, 16km from Killarney, is **Ladies' View**, which apparently was chosen by the ladies-in-waiting of Queen Victoria on her visit in 1861 as the finest view in the land – with some justification. From the car park here, you look directly down on the **Upper Lake**, with its many channels running down to lakes Muckross and Leane on one side, and the Carrauntoohil massif rising on the other. Just before reaching Ladies' View on the main road, there's a signposted path, part of the Kerry Way, through Derrycunihy Woods to Lord Brandon's Cottage (see below); beyond Ladies' View, spectacular vistas continue at least as far as **Moll's Gap**, where the Avoca craft shop and its good café mark the parting of the Kenmare road and the R568 to Sneem.

The Gap of Dunloe

The **Gap of Dunloe**, a glacial defile which cuts off Tomies and Purple mountains from Macgillycuddy's Reeks, is justifiably one of the area's most popular attractions. Try, if you can, to come here late in the day, when the light is at its best and the road at its quietest.

The usual approach is from the north, where **Kate Kearney's Cottage**, a pub and restaurant 4km from Beaufort, stands at the foot of the Gap. Beyond here the narrow road is not designed to handle motor traffic at busy times, and should be left free for walkers, cyclists, pony trekkers and jaunting cars; at quiet times, you should be OK to drive it if you need to. It's a starkly beautiful 7km climb to the Head of the Gap, walled in by a steep patchwork of grass and bare purple rock, with tumbling waterfalls after rain, past reedy lakes and one or two sheep. Then from the Head, you can make a glorious descent into the broad **Black Valley**, hemmed in by 784m Broaghnabinnia at its western end and so named because all its inhabitants died during the Famine. It now supports a few sheep farms, a primary school and a basic An Óige hostel, on the Kerry Way 3km from the Head of the Gap. About 2km further down the road, in a delightful spot at the head of the Upper Lake, is **Lord Brandon's Cottage**, a nineteenth-century hunting lodge, now summertime café, where the boats from Ross Castle terminate (see p.275).

ARRIVAL AND INFORMATION
KILLARNEY AND AROUND

By plane Kerry's airport (☏ 066 976 4644, ⌨ kerryairport .ie) is 15km from Killarney on the N23, 2km northeast of the village of Farranfore, which is on the Tralee–Killarney train line. Buses between Limerick and Killarney (plus a few Tralee–Killarney services) call at the airport roughly every 2hr; a taxi into town costs about €30 (contact, for example, Euro Taxis on ☏ 064 663 7676, ⌨ eurotaxiskillarney.com, if you want to book one).

By train Killarney's train station is very centrally placed, off East Avenue Rd.

Destinations Cork (6–9 daily, often with a change at Mallow; 1hr 30min–2hr); Dublin (6–9 daily, most with a change at Mallow; 3hr–3hr 30min); Farranfore (7–8 daily; 20min); Tralee (7–8 daily; 40min).

By bus The Bus Éireann station is on Park Rd, while Citylink buses use East Avenue Rd.

Destinations Bus Éireann: Caherdaniel (July & Aug 1 daily; 2hr 15min); Cahersiveen (July & Aug 1–3 daily, rest

of year Mon–Sat 2 daily; 1hr 30min); Cork (hourly; 1hr 30min); Dingle, changing at Tralee (2–5 daily; 2–3hr); Dingle, via Inch and Anascaul (July & Aug Mon–Sat 2 daily; 1hr 20min); Kenmare (via Kilgarvan; July & Aug 2–3 daily, rest of year Mon–Fri 2 daily; 50min); Kerry Airport (Farranfore; 6–7 daily; 20min); Killorglin (4–6 daily; 30min); Limerick (5–6 daily; 2hr); Ring of Kerry (July & Aug 1 daily; 5hr 15min, with a break in Sneem); Tralee (10–16 daily; 40min); Waterford (hourly; 4hr 10min); Waterville (July & Aug 1–2 daily, rest of year Mon–Sat 1 daily; 1hr 55min).

Citylink (⌨ citylink.ie): Galway (2 daily; 2hr 45min).

Tourist office The excellent tourist office is on Beech Rd (June–Sept Mon–Sat 9am–6pm, Sun 9am–1pm; Oct–May Mon–Sat 9am–5pm; ☏ 064 663 1633). It's not to be confused with a look-alike, green-liveried "TOURIST INFORMATION" office on Main St, which is actually a shop selling tours.

GETTING AROUND

Bike rental O'Sullivan's, Beech Rd opposite the tourist office (☏ 064 662 2389), as well as from several of the hostels.

Car rental Budget (⌨ budget.ie) has car-rental outlets

both at the airport (☏ 066 976 3199) and in town (☏ 064 663 4341), in the *International Hotel* on Kenmare Place.

Taxis There's a taxi rank on College St or call, for example, Euro Taxis (☏ 064 663 7676).

CCOMMODATION

s certainly worth booking **accommodation** in Killarney in advance, but there are scores of B&Bs, upmarket guesthouses nd hotels in town – if none of the listings below can fit you in, the friendly tourist office should be able to help. Prices are steep high summer, during festivals and bank holidays, and on Sat nights, but you can get big discounts outside of these times.

HOTELS

he Brehon 1km south of town on the N71 ☎064 663 700, ⓦthebrehon.com. Imposing and stylish contemporary otel with 125 spacious and well-equipped rooms, a fine staurant, *Danú*, and an excellent spa. All guests have free ccess to the spa's vitality suite, and to the comprehensive isure centre at the adjacent *Gleneagles Hotel*. **€169**

och Lein Country House Hotel Fossa, 5km west of wn just off the N72 ☎064 663 1260, ⓦlochlein.com. good-value choice if you'd prefer to stay away from the wn's bustle, this peaceful, welcoming and well-run small otel has views of Lough Leane and the mountains, acious, tastefully decorated rooms and a restaurant that ecializes in local produce. **€140**

alton Hotel East Avenue Rd ☎064 663 8000, ⓦthemalton.com. Ivy-clad Victorian railway hotel, rmerly the *Great Southern*, where the huge lobby sports andeliers and marble floors, the breakfast room an ornate, lded ceiling, and where rooms, especially in the original uilding, are very attractive. Extensive gardens with two nnis courts, spa and swimming pool to relax in too. **€140**

uckross Park Hotel N71, about 5km south of town ☎064 662 3400, ⓦmuckrosspark.com. Dating from 1795, nd much extended since, this opulent hotel is right opposite e entrance to Muckross Friary, giving immediate access to e national park trails (bicycles available free of charge). ome rooms have four-posters and views of the Blue Pool ver, there's a fine spa and the excellent Yew Tree restaurant rings a creative touch and local ingredients to classic French uisine. **€200**

he Ross Hotel East Avenue Rd ☎064 663 1855, ⓦtheross.ie. Luxurious boutique hotel right at the heart of e action, with bright and breezy contemporary bedrooms, reat breakfasts and excellent service. Guests are free to use e 20m indoor swimming pool, gym, sauna, Jacuzzi and utdoor hot tub at sister hotel, *The Park*, across the road. **€170**

GUESTHOUSES AND B&BS

he Copper Kettle Lewis Rd ☎064 663 4164, ⓦcopperkettlekillarney.com. Pleasant B&B on the north de of the town centre with a variety of tasteful, en-suite ooms, all with cable TV, some with Jacuzzis and king-size eds. **€90**

airview Michael Collins Place, off College St ☎064

663 4164, ⓦfairviewkillarney.com. Attractive and welcoming central guesthouse (with parking), where the tasteful, comfortable rooms all have en-suite bathroom and cable TV; great breakfasts, too. **€110**

Old Weir Lodge Muckross Rd, a 10min walk from the centre ☎064 663 5593, ⓦoldweirlodge.com. Thirty-room, mock-Tudor guesthouse that feels like a hotel, with spacious, well-equipped and comfortable rooms. It retains the personal touch, with a warm welcome and plenty of local information. **€120**

HOSTELS

Killarney International Hostel 5km west of town just off the Killorglin road ☎064 663 1240, ⓦanoige .ie. Well-run, eco-conscious hostel in a renovated eighteenth-century country house in spacious grounds, with open fires in the large common rooms and over 130 beds, including single rooms and four- to ten-bed dorms; laundry facilities available. Catch the Bus Éireann service towards Killorglin to Fossa Cross, then it's a 5min walk up the Dingle road. March–Oct. Dorms **€17**, doubles **€44**

★**Neptune's Hostel** Bishop's Lane, off New St ☎064 663 5255, ⓦneptuneshostel.com (IHH). Excellent, eco-friendly, central hostel, huge but welcoming, with plenty of local information on offer. Three- to eight-bed dorms, twins, doubles and singles, some en suite, are available, as well as laundry facilities and free luggage storage. Simple breakfast included. Dorms **€16**, doubles **€44**

Súgán Hostel Lewis Rd ☎064 663 3104, ⓦsuganhostelkillarney.com. Central, cosy hostel, in a colourful eighteenth-century house, with welcoming if cramped dorms and bike rental. Staff are friendly and the hostel is a good source of local information. Simple breakfast included. Dorms **€12**, doubles **€38**

CAMPSITE

Fleming's White Bridge 1km east of town, signposted off the N22 Cork road ☎064 663 1590, ⓦkillarneycamping.com. Among several campsites around Killarney, this quiet spot on the banks of the River Flesk has a summertime shop, two laundries, a campers' kitchen, a games room, a TV lounge and bike rental. Mid-March to Oct. **€25**

8

EATING AND DRINKING

ating out in Killarney is generally a pricey undertaking, though several places offer good value for money. In a tourist town hat's constantly reinventing itself, it's perhaps inevitable that there are few characterful old **pubs** left. Entertainment's the ame of the game, and most bars provide regular live music, of wildly varying quality.

KILLARNEY NATIONAL PARK AND THE IVERAGH PENINSULA

Tralee

Cork

Lough Guitane

Kilgarvan

Killarney

Ross Castle

Muckross Friary

Muckross House

Fossa

Inisfallen

Lough Leane

Torc Mountain

Mangerton Mountain

Bonane Heritage Park

KILLARNEY NATIONAL PARK

Tomies Mt

Muckross Lake

Purple Mt

Upper Lake

Ladies View

Kerry Way

Castlemaine

Beaufort

Kate Kearney's Cottage

Gap of Dunloe

Lord Brandon's Cottage

Kenmare

Glengarriff

N72

Black Valley

M A C G I L L Y C U D D Y ' S R E E K S

Moll's Gap

N71

Carrauntoohil (1038m)

Killorglin

Templenoe

Gleninchaquin Park

Castlemaine

Breanlee

Glencar

Caragh Lake

Blackwater Bridge

R571

Laragh

R574

CORK

C A H A M O U N T A I N S

Derreen Gardens

Tahilla

N70

Rossbeigh Strand

Glenbeigh

Seefin

RING OF KERRY

Mullaghanattin

I v e r a g h P e n i n s u l a

Sneem

Ardmroom

Ballaghisheen

Knockmoyle

Teermoyle Mt

River Inny

Kerry Way

Kenmare River

Staigue Fort

Castle Cove

Dingle Bay

Kells

N70

Mastergeehy

Lough Currane

Coomakista Pass

Caherdaniel

Derrynane Bay

Knocknadobar

Kerry Way

N70

Abbey Island

Cahersiveen

Reenard Point

N70

Waterville

Ballinskelligs Bay

Deenish Island

Scariff Island

Doulus Head

Knightstown

Geokaun

Chapeltown

Portmagee

Ballinskelligs

St Finan's Bay

Bolus Head

Valentia Island

Bray Head

RING OF SKELLIG

Puffin Island

Little Skellig

Skellig Michael (Great Skellig)

N↑

0   5
kilometres

8

RESTAURANTS AND CAFÉS

The Bricín 26 High St ☎ 064 663 4902, ⓦ bricin.com. Homely restaurant that serves traditional Irish food, notably filled boxties (potato pancakes), as well as more eclectic dishes such as prawns in a Calvados cream sauce. Early-bird (€25, before 6.45pm) and set 3-course menus from €27) available. Tues–Sat 6–9pm.

Cellar One The Ross Hotel (see p.279), East Avenue Rd ☎ 064 663 1855, ⓦ theross.ie. Cool cellar restaurant where the wine store has become part of the decor, enhanced by a dramatic, glass curving staircase. Seasonal produce from local, named suppliers is used wherever possible in excellent dishes such as confit of Skeaghanore duck leg with sweet potato mash; leave room for the Amaretto crème brûlée for dessert. €25 for two courses and a cocktail until 7pm (not Sat). Mon–Sat 6–9.30pm, Sun 6–9pm; closed Mon–Thurs in winter.

Gaby's Seafood Restaurant 27 High St ☎ 064 663 2519. Killarney's finest and most expensive seafood restaurant, formal but not at all stuffy, serving great platters of seafood (€30) and lobster from the tanks in the front window. Mon–Sat 6–10pm.

Jam Old Market Lane, off Main St ☎ 064 663 7716, ⓦ jam.ie. Branch of Kenmare's thoroughly modern bakery-café, serving great cakes, scones and coffee, as well as delicious sandwiches, quiches (€9 with 2 salads) and soups. Mon–Sat 8am–5.30pm, Sun 10am–5.30pm.

Milano 16 Main St ☎ 064 662 0620, ⓦ milano.ie. Typically fresh, contemporary setting for the Irish version of Britain's *Pizza Express*, offering a huge range of top-notch pizzas (from €11) plus salads and simple pastas. Mon–Thurs & Sun noon–10pm, Fri & Sat noon–11pm.

Murphy's 37 Main St ☎ 087 052 3145, ⓦ murphysicecream. ie. Branch of Dingle's excellent ice-cream shop (eat in or take away) with deckchairs out on the street in summer. Also serves great cakes and coffees. Daily noon–10pm.

Quinlan's Seafood Bar Main St ☎ 064 662 0666. Branch of Tralee's superior fish'n'chip shop – take away or tuck into dishes such as deep-fried squid (€14) in the informal seafood restaurant. Daily noon–10pm.

PUBS AND BARS

Buckley's Arbutus Hotel, College St ☎ 064 663 1037. Smartly refurbished traditional bar with long, sociable bench seats and traditional sessions Fri & Sat, plus Sun lunch time and evening. Mon–Sat 10.30am–2.30am, Sun 12.30pm–2.30am.

Courtney's Plunkett St ☎ 064 663 2689, ⓦ courtneysbar.com. Appealingly plain, bare-wood and stone-floored pub, popular among a twenty-something crowd, with a great range of whiskeys and beers. In the summer it hosts traditional and folk music Mon–Thurs, live bands on Fri and DJ sessions on Sat. Mon–Thurs 2–11.30pm, Fri & Sat 2pm–12.30am, Sun 2–11pm.

Jimmy O'Brien's Fair Hill ☎ 064 663 1786. The yellow and green façade gives the game away – this traditional lounge bar is a veritable museum of Kerry Gaelic football, hung with dozens of photos and clippings (plus material on the notably lively dance music and *sean-nós* singing of Sliabh Lucra, the mountains to the east of Killarney). Decent pint of Guinness, too. Mon–Thurs 1–11.30pm, Fri 1pm–12.30am, Sat noon–12.30am, Sun noon–11pm.

The Killarney Grand (aka Sheehan's) Main St ☎ 064 663 1159, ⓦ killarneygrand.com. A large but often crowded bar, popular with locals and tourists, with nightly live entertainment: ballads or traditional music 9–11pm, with a cover charge for bands and a club after 11pm (after 10pm on Sat), and for the set dancing on Wed evenings (9pm). Mon–Sat 7.30pm–2.30am, Sun 7.30pm–1.30am.

The Iveragh Peninsula: the Ring of Kerry

The **Ring of Kerry** is often used as a substitute name for the **Iveragh Peninsula**, but more properly it refers to the 175km road that encircles this vast, scenic leg of land. Tourists have been coming to the peninsula in ever-increasing numbers over the past century, but most of them do the Ring by bus or car in a day from Killarney. If you stay in one of the Iveragh's few small towns or venture off the main route, for example onto the **Ring of Skellig** at the very tip, you'll have to yourself this giant's landscape of mountains, lakes and long ocean views, which is at its most spectacular when illuminated by a sudden shaft of light through the clouds like a flash bulb.

GETTING AROUND · THE IVERAGH PENINSULA: THE RING OF KERRY

By bus Bus Éireann circles the whole Ring only in July and Aug, at other times venturing out of Killarney only as far as Waterville via the north coast.

On foot You can walk around the peninsula on the Kerry Way (see box p.276).

By bike Cycling, often up steep gradients and against strong

winds, is a shorter – three days at the least – but perhaps just as physically demanding option. The waymarked 215km Ring of Kerry Cycle Route (map guide available from local tourist offices) of necessity follows the main road for around a third of its journey, but includes a long, scenic loop through Ballinskelligs, Portmagee and Valentia Island, and covers the

8

north coast of the peninsula and the area around Killarney almost entirely on minor roads. Coach tours from Killarney, which ply the Ring of Kerry in flotillas in summer, are required to travel anticlockwise: you can weigh up the

disadvantages of getting stuck in a convoy – plenty of time to admire the views – against meeting the buses on the many blind corners. In the account on below, we've covered the Ring anticlockwise.

Cahersiveen

CAHERSIVEEN (sometimes spelt Caherciveen or Cahirsiveen, but always pronounced with the stress on the last syllable) is the main service town for the west end of the peninsula. Functional rather than attractive, its one long, narrow street is at various points named East End, Church Street, Main Street and New Street. Cahersiveen holds a lively **music and arts festival** (ⓦcelticmusicfestival.com) over the bank-holiday weekend at the beginning of August, which has attracted big names such as Sinead O'Connor and the Hothouse Flowers. By the side of the N70 as it enters the town from the east is a striking local landmark, Éamonn O'Doherty's *To the Skelligs*. Installed in 1995, the sculpture depicts Brendan the Navigator (see p.322) and fellow monks making their way to the islands.

O'Connell Memorial Church
Main St • Hours variable • Free

The town's most famous son was Daniel O'Connell (see p.586), to whom the **O'Connell Memorial Church** on the main street was dedicated – a remarkable tribute for a politician. Built between 1888 and 1902, largely with money from the US and Australia, it's a huge, lumbering edifice made of concrete, faced with Irish granite.

The Old Barracks
ⓦ oldbarrackscahersiveen.com

The heritage centre in the fearsome, castle-like **Barracks** is currently undergoing major restoration work, with plans to refocus its exhibits on the life of Daniel O'Connell. The construction of these heavily fortified quarters for the Royal Irish Constabulary was prompted by the Fenian uprising of 1867, when local Republicans tried to cut the transatlantic cable at Valentia.

ARRIVAL AND INFORMATION   CAHERSIVEEN

By bus Buses stop on the main street, opposite the O'Connell Church.

Tourist office The tourist office has been residing in the old library next to the church on the main street (June–Sept Mon–Fri 9.30am–1pm & 2–5pm, Sat 10am–4pm; Oct–May Mon–Fri 9am–1pm & 2–5pm; ☏ 066 947 1300) but may move back into the Old Barracks. They can give you details of the Beentee (8km) and Laharn (12km) loop walks

and of several attractive spots on the nearby Doulus Head peninsula that are accessible on foot or by bike, including a ruined fifteenth-century tower house, a couple of well-preserved ring forts and White Strand, a fine, curving sandy beach. Go to ⓦoldbarrackscahersiveen.com for information on events in town.

Bike rental Casey's, New St (☏ 066 947 2474, ⓦbikehirekerry.com).

ACCOMMODATION

The Final Furlong 1.5km from the town on the road to Killorglin ☏ 066 947 3300, ⓦthefinalfurlong.com. Pleasant, seafront, en-suite B&B accommodation on a working farm; they also offer horse riding. Very good rates for singles. Discounts for longer stays. May–Sept (April & Oct available by advance booking). **€60**

Mannix Point Camping and Caravan Park West side of town ☏ 066 947 2806, ⓦcampinginkerry.com. Welcoming and very well-equipped waterfront campsite; a

spot with impromptu music sessions and a turf fire in the evening. Mid-March to mid-Oct. **€23**

★**QC's** 3 Main St ☏ 066 947 2244, ⓦqcbar.com. Beautifully designed, wood-panelled rooms with separate street door behind the restaurant, large and bright with comfy beds, iPod docks, espresso machines and power showers. There's also a lovely, spacious sitting room and a sun deck. Generous continental breakfasts are taken in your room. **€110**

Sive 15 East End ☎ 066 947 2717, ⓦ sivehostel.ie (IHH). Friendly, smartly refurbished hostel on the main street, a small terraced house with en-suite and standard private rooms and dorms, a kitchen, sitting room and laundry facilities. Simple breakfast included. Dorms €17, doubles €44

EATING AND DRINKING

An Bonnán Buí (McCarthy's) Main St, a few doors west of QC's ☎ 066 948 1731. Good, varied pub grub can be had at this welcoming spot, which has a pleasant beer garden and is a likely spot for traditional music in summer. Mon–Thurs noon–11.30pm, Fri & Sat noon–12.30am, Sun noon–11pm.

Petit Delice Main St, a few doors east of QC's ☎ 087 890 3572. Small but authentic French patisserie and café, serving very tasty quiches, filled baguettes and croissants, as well as good lemon tarts and artisan breads. Mon–Sat 8.30/9am–5/6pm.

The Point Bar (O'Neill's) 5km west at Reenard Point ☎ 066 947 2165. Located at the terminus of the Valentia Island ferry (see below), this pub-restaurant is very popular for its high-quality food, especially seafood (lobster €26/round). Mon–Thurs roughly 12.30–11.30pm, Fri & Sat 12.30pm–12.30am, Sun 12.30–11pm; closed for two (variable) months in winter, then open only on weekend evenings in the shoulder season.

★ **QC's** 3 Main St ☎ 066 947 2244, ⓦ qcbar.com. One of the best places to eat on the Ring of Kerry, a stylish, nautical-themed bar-restaurant with a lovely, covered back patio. As the owners' family have their own boats and fish-processing factory, seafood is, unsurprisingly, the speciality, in delicious dishes such as hake fillet on a broth of smoked haddock, mussels, prawns and fennel (€24). Cheaper lunch menu and an early bird until 6.45pm (€21 for 2 courses), plus a great tapas menu. Easter–Sept Mon–Sat noon–3pm & 5.30–9.30pm (with simpler dishes served 3–5.30pm), Sun 5.30–9.30pm; Oct–Easter Thurs & Sun 5.30–9.30pm, Fri & Sat noon–3pm & 5.30–9.30pm, with longer hours during holidays.

Portmagee

8

The attractive harbour village of **PORTMAGEE** is the jumping-off point by road for Valentia, situated beside the long bridge to the island.

The Skellig Experience

Visitor centre March, April, Oct & Nov 10am–5pm 5 days/week – phone for details; May, June & Sept daily 10am–6pm; July & Aug daily 10am–7pm; last admission 45min before closing • €5 **Cruises** Standard cruises 2hr (subject to demand – contact the centre in the morning); in worse weather, 45min mini-cruises around Valentia channel occasionally laid on • Standard €30, including admission to the visitor centre; mini-cruise €22, including admission to the visitor centre • ☎ 066 947 6306, ⓦ skelligexperience.com

Portmagee's **Skellig Experience**, which is actually just across the bridge from the village, gives some fascinating background on seabirds and other marine life, lighthouses and early monastic life, with an impressive short film about Skellig Michael. The centre also has a café with fine views of Portmagee, and runs **cruises** around, but not onto, Skellig Michael, which are useful for those who can't manage the 650 steps to the island's summit and which may be running on some days when the weather isn't quite good enough for boats to land on the island.

ACCOMMODATION AND EATING — PORTMAGEE

★ **The Moorings** ☎ 066 947 7108, ⓦ moorings.ie. Tastefully decorated and well-equipped accommodation is available – it's worth paying extra for a room overlooking the harbour – at this well-run, eco-conscious inn, which offers various half-board deals and activities packages. Good food is served here too, either in the restaurant or the lively, friendly Bridge Bar, and there's traditional music on Fri (with set dancing) and most Sun nights, a night of music, dancing and storytelling on Tues in July and Aug, and a festival of music and set dancing over the May Holiday weekend (among various themed activities weekends). Good rates for singles. Bar/restaurant Mon–Thurs & Sun 8.30am–11.30pm, Fri & Sat 8.30am–1am. €100

Valentia Island

Separated from the mainland by a long, narrow channel that's now bridged, **VALENTIA** barely feels like an island. For such a small, remote spot, it boasts a surprising number of claims to fame: as well as being known from the radio shipping forecasts and for Valentia slate, which was used for the Houses of Parliament in London and the Paris Opera House, it was from here that the first transatlantic telegraph cable was laid in 1866. To add to the island's repute, the oldest fossilized footprints in the northern hemisphere, the so-called Tetrapod Trackway, were discovered here in 1992 by a Swiss geology student. Most of the island's amenities are in or around **Knightstown** at the northeastern tip, which provides dramatic views of the Iveragh Mountains, as well as a seasonal **ferry** link to the mainland (see below).

At the western edge of the village, the **Valentia Heritage Centre** (April–Sept daily 10am–5pm, though hours sometimes irregular; €3.50; ☎066 947 6411) houses a tidy display on the island's history in the old primary school.

Glanleam House

Gardens April–Oct daily 10am–7pm • €6

Walking up School House Road from the heritage centre, then forking right, will bring you after about 1km to **Glanleam House**, which was formerly the seat of the Knight of Kerry. Developed in the 1850s, the beautiful subtropical **gardens** here encompass lily-of-the-valley trees, ferns and other exotic specimens from South America, Australasia and China, which thrive in this mild, sheltered location.

Tetrapod Trackway

About 5km from Knightstown near the island's northernmost tip, it's possible to see for yourself the **Tetrapod Trackway**, though you might have to show some perseverance as it's not very well signposted (basically, head up School House Road from the heritage centre and take the second right). From a car park by the island's radio station, a short path leads down to a precarious shelf of black rock by the Atlantic, on which the small foot- and tail-prints of the creature – a metre-long, crocodile-like amphibian with a large, paddle-shaped tail, that lived some 385 million years ago – are quite clearly visible. What can feel like the end of the world on a stormy day is a suitably awesome location to come toe-to-toe with our first landborne ancestors.

Valentia Island Farmhouse Dairy

1km southwest of Knightstown on the main island road, the R565 • May–Sept daily 11am–7pm • ⓦ valentiaisland.ie/food-and-drink/valentia-island-farmhouse-dairy/

This traditional **dairy farm** makes its own delicious ice cream, which it sells at its farm and craft shop. It also offers sightseeing tours of the island from Knightstown in a horse-and-carriage (€9/person; booking recommended on ☎087 349 7385).

Geokaun Mountain and Bray Head

Geokaun Mountain car parking €5; pedestrians and cyclists €2 • ⓦ geokaun.com

Near the middle of the north coast, the spectacular **Fogher Cliffs** and **Geokaun Mountain**, the island's highest point, have been turned into a viewing area, with the installation of fifty information panels and a 1500m loop walk. Further exciting views are provided by the ruined lookout tower on **Bray Head**, at the southwestern end of the island.

ARRIVAL AND INFORMATION
VALENTIA ISLAND

By ferry From Reenard Point, 5km west of Cahersiveen (see above), a ferry operates a continuous shuttle service across to Knightstown on Valentia Island (mid-March to June & Sept to mid-Oct Mon–Sat 7.45am–9.30pm, Sun 9am–9.30pm; July & Aug Mon–Sat 7.45am–10pm, Sun 9am–10pm; cars single €6, return €9; cyclists single €2,

return €3; ☎087 241 8973).

Tourist office On the waterfront in Knightstown, almost opposite the clock tower (April–Sept Tues–Sun 10am–4.30pm; ☎066 947 6985, ⓦvalentiaisland.ie). In front of the office, kayaking, sailing and other watersports are available in summer (☎086 871 7846).

ACCOMMODATION

Atlantic Villa Behind the Y-junction at the church in Knightstown ☎066 947 6839, ⓦanirishexperience

.com. Overlooking the sea in the nineteenth-century former cable-master's house, this B&B offers six pleasant

-suite bedrooms, fresh produce from their organic arden for breakfast, open fires, a sauna, bike rental and vening meals. Self-catering cottage also available. Very ood single rates. **€70**

★ **Glanleam House** About 2km west of Knightstown 066 947 6176, ⊛hiddenireland.com/glanleam-ouse-kerry. This elegant eighteenth- and nineteenth-entury house set in beautiful subtropical gardens offers elightful accommodation in spacious, comfortable ooms, with especially attractive bathrooms and fine views of Valentia Harbour. Dinner available if booked the previous day. Good rates for singles; self-catering cottages also available. Mid-March to early Nov. **€160**

Spring Acre On the waterfront in Knightstown 066 947 6141, ⊛springacrebb.com. A spruce, en-suite bungalow with two double rooms and two family rooms, a lovely lawn, home-baked brown soda bread for breakfast and great views. Very good single rates; self-catering also available. March–Oct. **€75**

ATING AND DRINKING

od By the church in Knightstown 066 947 6995. heery pancake café and gift shop with outdoor tables, erving imaginative savoury galettes (€8 for smoked salmon, ream cheese and chives), sweet crêpes and espresso coffees. ummer daily 10/10.30am–5pm, but they'll stay open if hey have customers, sometimes till midnight.

he Royal Pier Knightstown 066 947 6144. The town's landmark 200-year-old inn enjoys glorious views of the harbour and the mainland mountains from its seafront lawn, serves dishes such as chicken in tarragon and white wine sauce (€15) for lunch and dinner (not Jan & Feb) and often hosts traditional music. Mon–Thurs 10.30am–11.30pm, Fri & Sat 10.30am–12.30am, Sun noon–11pm.

The Skellig Islands

n incredible, impossible, mad place…I tell you the thing does not belong to any world that you and I have lived nd worked in: it is part of our dream world…

George Bernard Shaw

8

A voyage to the **Skelligs** (Na Scealga, "the crags"), islands of durable Old Red Sandstone hat rise sharply from the sea 12km off the tip of the Iveragh Peninsula, is one of the most xciting and inspiring trips you can make in Ireland. On top of the larger of these two nhospitable, shark's-tooth islands, **Skellig Michael** (or Great Skellig), a monastery was omehow constructed in the late seventh or early eighth century, in imitation of the desert ommunities of the early Church fathers, and dedicated to St Michael, the patron saint of igh places. The exposed, often choppy boat-ride out, followed by Manx shearwaters, torm petrels and puffins from Puffin Island, a nature reserve at the edge of St Finan's Bay, nly adds to the sense of wild isolation. **Little Skellig** is a nature reserve too, crawling with ver fifty thousand gannets; landing is forbidden here, but the boatmen will come in close o you can watch the gannets diving for fish and hear their awesome din.

Skellig Michael

f you come in spring or early summer, you'll have thousands of cute breeding puffins o keep you company on the 200m ascent from Skellig Michael's quay. The compact, emarkably well-preserved **monastery** in the lee of the summit is a miracle of ingenuity nd devotion. It was built entirely on artificial terraces, facing south–southeast for naximum sunlight, with sturdy outer walls to deflect the winds and to protect the egetable patch made of bird droppings; channels crisscross the settlement to funnel ainwater into cisterns. You can walk into the **dry-stone beehive huts**, **chapels** and **efectory**, which would have sheltered a total of twelve to fifteen monks at any one ime and have withstood the worst the Atlantic can throw at them for 1300 years. The igh cross beside the large oratory probably marks the burial of the founder, reputed to ave been St Fionán, or an early saint.

At least three Viking raids in the ninth century were not enough to dislodge the monks, ut during the climatic change of the twelfth and thirteenth centuries, the seas became ougher and more inhospitable. Around the same time, pressure was brought to bear on he old independent monasteries to conform, and the monks adopted the Augustinian rule and moved to Ballinskelligs on the mainland. Pilgrimages to Skellig Michael, however, continued until the eighteenth century, even after the Dissolution of the Monasteries.

A **visit to the island** is only for those with good mobility, as there's a vertical ladder up onto the quay, and then 650 steep, uneven steps with unprotected edges – slippery when wet – to the windy summit (the alternative is a cruise around the islands – see below). Bring walking shoes, warm waterproof clothes, water and food (but take all litter away with you), as there are no facilities on Skellig Michael (toilets are on the boats).

ARRIVAL AND INFORMATION
SKELLIG ISLANDS

BY BOAT

Only a dozen operators are allowed to land on Skellig Michael (May–Sept, sometimes with extra departures April & Oct, dependent on the weather); they need to be booked the day before your trip at the latest. However, there's sometimes a delay of several days before the boats will sail because of bad weather – the captains make a decision on the weather early each morning. The boats operate mostly from Portmagee (departing 10–11am; 45min–1hr to reach Skellig Michael; allow at least 2hr on the island; around €50/person).

OPERATORS

Eoin Walsh is a knowledgeable skipper (☎066 947 6327 or ☎087 283 3522, ⓦskelligboattrips.ie), and if you sail with him you'll get free entry to the Skellig Experience (see p.283). Sean Feehan sails across from Ballinskelligs, a slightly shorter route (€50–70; ☎086 417 6612, ⓦskelligboats.com), and also offers diving off the islands; John O'Shea departs from Caherdaniel (☎087 689 8431). A complete list of operators is available from local tourist offices and on ⓦskelligexperience.com, but most accommodation owners in the area will offer to do the booking for you, which is the easiest way to arrange your trip.

CRUISES

Cruises around the islands are offered by the Skellig Heritage Centre (see p.283) and Skellig Michael Cruises (☎087 617 8114, ⓦskelligmichaelcruises.com).

The Ring of Skellig

To the south of Portmagee runs the **Ring of Skellig**, a quiet, scenic though often very steep route around the most westerly promontory of the Iveragh Peninsula, via wild and exposed **St Finan's Bay** – which is the unlikely home of the high-quality Skelligs Chocolate Factory (visitors welcome to taste and buy; Feb–Easter & mid-Sept to mid-Dec Mon–Fri 10am–4.30pm; Easter to mid-Sept Mon–Fri 10am–5pm, Sat & Sun 11am/noon–5/5.15pm; ⓦskelligschocolate.com) and its seasonal coffee shop (Easter to mid-Sept). From the highest point of the road between Portmagee and St Finan's Bay, you can climb the hill on the seaward side of the saddle in twenty minutes or so for the most magnificent views out to the Skellig Islands, across to the Dingle Peninsula and the Blaskets, and inland to the Iveragh Mountains.

Ballinskelligs (Baile an Sceilg)

On the far shore of the promontory lies **BALLINSKELLIGS** (Baile an Sceilg; ⓦvisitballinskelligs.ie), behind a lovely, curving, sheltered beach with great views of Waterville and the mountains, where Skelligs Watersports (☎087 917 8808, ⓦskelligsurf.co.m) offers **surfing**, **wind-surfing**, **kayaking** and **stand-up paddleboarding**. The monks of Skellig Michael retreated here in the twelfth century, constructing a new **abbey** which in turn was largely rebuilt in the fifteenth century. By walking south along the shoreline for five minutes, beyond a badly ruined tower house, you can still see its delicate purple-grey sandstone church and traces of its cloister. The small but sprawling village of Ballinskelligs is part of a Gaeltacht (Irish-speaking) enclave, Uíbh Ráthach, and draws hosts of teenagers to Irish college in the summer.

The striking thatched roundhouse at the north end of the village is an **art gallery** (mid-May to Sept daily 11am–6pm; Oct to mid-May by appointment Thurs–Sun 11am–5pm; ☎066 947 9277, ⓦcillrialaigartscentre.org) and café-restaurant. Attached to the Cill Rialaig retreat for artists, writers and composers, it hosts art workshops for children and adults in July and August.

EATING

Caife Cois Tra ☎066 947 9323, ⊛facebook.com/cafecoistra. In a beachside wooden chalet with plenty of outside tables on the grass, this café serves soup, sandwiches and home-baked cakes. It also houses a crafts shop specializing in historical photographs. On Sun (11am–4pm) from June to Aug, it hosts a country market with live music. Summer daily 10am–6pm.

Waterville

On the east side of Ballinskelligs Bay, **WATERVILLE** (An Coireán, "the little whirlpool") is an incongruously genteel resort in this distant wilderness. Its exposed, pebbly beach is backed by a long, grassy promenade – now sporting a statue of Charlie Chaplin, who spent several holidays here – and large, neat houses with well-tended lawns, many of them built for workers on the transatlantic telegraph cable, which was extended from Valentia to Waterville in the 1880s. August sees a five-day **festival of classic and contemporary films**, with attendant street entertainment and music (⊛chaplinfilmfestival.com). There's no bank in Waterville but the post office behind the prominent *Butler Arms Hotel* on the seafront changes money.

ACCOMMODATION AND EATING

Old Cable House Seaview Terrace ☎066 947 4233, ⊛oldcablehouse.com. Set back from the seafront in part of the nineteenth-century cable station, this attractive and congenial establishment in a pleasant garden offers good-value, en-suite accommodation and excellent dinners. Breakfast not included. **€55**

Peter's Place At the southern entrance to the village ☎087 995 0199, ✉petersplacecafe@hotmail.com. Basic, compact hostel, where one double room at the back and two triples with good views at the front share a bathroom. Downstairs are a kitchen and a small sitting room with a turf fire, as well as a cosy café, which has outdoor tables in a fantastic position on a raised seafront lawn with views of the Skelligs. Here you can tuck into soups, sandwiches and home-baked cakes, breads, croissants and fruit pies. Mid-March to Oct. Dorms **€15**

Smugglers' Inn 1km north of the centre on the beach ☎066 947 4330, ⊛the-smugglers-inn.com. Comfortable upmarket rooms are provided by this well-run and welcoming inn in a restored nineteenth-century farmhouse, which has the best views of Ballinskelligs Bay from its isolated spot. Noted for its fresh fish and seafood, it's your best bet for eating in Waterville, whether in the bar, the conservatory restaurant or the beer garden. Food served daily noon–3pm & 6–8.30/9.30pm. Early April to late Oct. **€110**

Derrynane Bay and around

Beyond Waterville, the Ring of Kerry climbs steeply to the **Coomakista Pass**, where a viewing point affords glorious views of Deenish and Scariff islands in the foreground at the mouth of the Kenmare River, and Bull, Cow and tiny Calf islands off the end of the Beara Peninsula.

Hidden away beneath, at the southernmost point of the Iveragh Peninsula about 10km south of Waterville, is **Derrynane Bay** (pronounced "Derrynaan", meaning the "oak wood of St Fionán"). From the wide, sandy beach with 3km of dunes and good swimming, you can stroll across to atmospheric Abbey Island, which shelters a graveyard and ruined abbey, founded by St Fionán in around 700. At the inlet on the western side of the island causeway, Derrynane Sea Sports (☎087 908 1208, ⊛derrynaneseasports.com) offers canoeing, sailing, wind-surfing and other **waterborne activities** in the summer. From here you can pick your way west for over 1km along a beautiful Mass Path – which formerly led worshippers to the secret Mass Rock at Derrynane House – to Béaltrá Pier; follow the lane uphill from the pier and turn onto the Kerry Way heading east back towards Derrynane House for a very satisfying circular **walk** of a couple of hours or so. Above the bay, attractively sited on its steep eastern flank, the sprawling village of **CAHERDANIEL** is one of the nicest bases on the Ring of Kerry.

Derrynane House

April, Oct & most of Nov Wed–Sun plus bank holidays 10am–5pm; May–Sept daily 10.30am–6pm; last admission 45min before closing • €3; Heritage Card • ⓦ heritageireland.ie

On the north side of the bay, **Derrynane House** was once the home of, and is now a shrine to, Daniel O'Connell, the hugely popular, nonviolent campaigner who in 1829 achieved partial Catholic emancipation (see p.586). The plain, elegant house, which was largely rebuilt by the "Liberator" himself when he inherited it in 1825, contains all manner of memorabilia, as well as a tearoom and a lively, 25-minute audiovisual that's well worth catching. The most striking relic is a chariot presented by Dubliners to O'Connell on his release from prison in 1844: modelled on a Roman triumphal car, with gold and purple silk, mouldings and armchairs, it carried him at the head of a crowd of 200,000 to his home in Merrion Square, Dublin.

The pretty gardens and wooded parklands around the house, accessible on signposted trails, have been declared a national historic park, and give onto the beach in Derrynane Bay.

Staigue Fort

Visitor centre summer daily 10am–9pm • €2.50

Around 7km east of Caherdaniel on the N70, a sign points left to **Staigue Fort**, near the village of Castlecove; there's a small visitor centre near the junction, attached to a café and friendly bar with outdoor tables. After 4km up a narrow road, you'll come to a sophisticated ring fort, at least 2000 years old, with 5m-high dry-stone walls surrounded by a bank and ditch; it's in an excellent state of preservation. Beyond Castlecove at Sneem, there's a fork in the main road eastward: a mountain road (the R568) heads up to **Moll's Gap** (see p.278) and from there to Killarney, while the less scenic N70 continues along the seashore to Kenmare.

ACCOMMODATION AND EATING DERRYNANE BAY AND AROUND

The Blind Piper Caherdaniel ⓣ 066 947 5126. Lovely old stone-built pub decorated with colourful flowers, with outdoor tables on a large lawn by the stream. You can eat well in either the bar or, in the summer, the restaurant, and you can often catch live music (Thurs & Sat in summer). Mon–Thurs 11am–11.30pm, Fri & Sat 11am–12.30am, Sun 12.30–11pm.

Iskeroon Down the lane by the Scarriff Inn, 4km west of Caherdaniel on the N70 ⓣ 066 947 5119, ⓦ iskeroon.com. Set in a beautiful location, these tasteful suites boast small kitchens, DVD libraries and iPod docks, all set in extensive, semi-tropical gardens running down to the sea, where you can take out a kayak to explore the harbour. Minimum stay 3 nights; self-catering apartment also available. **€100**

Sugarshack Cakery Caherdaniel ⓣ 087 261 7522 ⓦ sugarshackcakery.ie. Old-fashioned tea rooms that specializes in home-baked cakes, as well as serving soups, sandwiches, tarts, Valentia Dairy ice cream and, until 8pm Thurs–Sun mid-July to mid-Aug, takeaway pizzas (from €11). Daily: Easter–June 11am–4pm; July & Aug 10am–6pm.

Traveller's Rest On the main road in the centre of Caherdaniel ⓣ 066 947 5175, ⓦ hostelcaherdaniel.com (IHO). Very good hostel in an attractive cottage, with small dorms (up to five-person), a well-equipped kitchen and a dining area with open fire. Mid-Feb to Oct. Dorms **€18**, doubles **€42**

Kenmare

Sitting at the head of the Kenmare River – actually a narrow, 40km-long sea inlet – **KENMARE** is an excellent base for exploring not only the Ring of Kerry but also the **Beara Peninsula**, part of which, including the contrasting scenic beauties of **Gleninchaquin** valley and **Derreen Gardens**, lies in County Kerry. The cosmopolitan town is neat and attractive in itself, with a fine array of restaurants and accommodation and a lively, sociable nightlife. Kenmare's major streets are Henry St (one-way, south–north) and Main St (one-way, north–south), which meet at Fair Green and are linked at their southern ends by Shelbourne St.

Brief history

Kenmare was established after the 1652 Act of Settlement, which followed Cromwell's brutal campaign in Ireland and forced Irish landowners to give up their estates to English settlers. Sir William Petty, who mapped and allocated these forfeited lands, managed to get hold of a quarter of Kerry for himself, and in 1670 established **Nedeen** (or An Neidín, "the little nest") here, a colony of English and Welsh Protestants to work in his lead mines, pilchard fisheries and ironworks. His descendant, the first Marquis of Lansdowne, rebuilt the town on its current X-shape in 1775, with the pretty, tree-shaded **Fair Green** (which still belongs to the Lansdownes) at its fulcrum, and rechristened it **Kenmare** – mistranslating *Neidín* as "nest of thieves", he adapted an earlier Irish name, *Ceann Mara* ("head of the sea inlet"), with which he was also able to honour his good friend, Lord Kenmare. The town's colourful history is carefully detailed in the **heritage centre** at the back of the tourist office (same hours – see below; free).

Stone circle

min walk from the Green (signposted) on the riverbank

Apart from the heritage centre, Kenmare's only other sight as such is a Bronze Age **stone circle**. Around 17m in diameter, it's the largest of its kind in Kerry and may be orientated on the setting sun. At its centre stands a burial dolmen, three standing stones supporting a large capstone.

ARRIVAL AND INFORMATION

KENMARE

By bus Buses stop at the top of Main St.

Destinations Castletownbere via Lauragh and Eyeries (July & Aug Mon–Sat 2 daily; 1hr 20min); Cork (via Glengarriff, Bantry, Skibbereen, Clonakilty, Kinsale and Cork Airport July & Aug 1 daily; 4hr); Killarney (via Kilgarvan; July & Aug 2–3 daily, rest of year Mon–Fri 2 daily; 50min).

Tourist information The helpful tourist office, which is on Fair Green (Easter–June, Sept & Oct 5 days/week 9.30am–5.15pm, sometimes closing 30min for lunch; July & Aug daily 9.30am–5.15pm; ☎ 064 664 1233), has information on local walks, including the 3km of trails in lovely Reenagross Woodland Park, which lies between the *Park Hotel* (see p.290) and the Kenmare River.

Bike rental Finnegan's, at the top of Henry St (☎ 064 664 1083, ⓦ kenmare.com/finnegan).

TOURS AND ACTIVITIES

Tours In summer Finnegan's (☎ 064 664 1491 or ☎ 087 748 0800, ⓦ kenmarecoachandcab.com) runs scheduled minibus tours of the Ring of Kerry (Mon, Wed & Fri), Beara Peninsula (Tues) and Glengarriff and Garinish Island (Thurs); book at the tourist office or the Kenmare Lace Centre upstairs, or call number quoted.

Cruises Seafari run cruises (roughly April–Oct; 2–3hr; €25; ☎ 064 664 2059, ⓦ seafari.ie) from the pier, taking in the islands of the Kenmare River, a colony of a hundred seals and prolific birdlife.

Activities Based at Dauros, 6km away on the north shore of the Beara, Star Sailing and Adventure Centre (☎ 064 664 1222, ⓦ staroutdoors.ie) lays on a range of activities including sailing, kayaking and boat trips on the Kenmare River (1hr; €15). Diving trips and courses are on offer either from further along the Beara, at Kilmakilloge Harbour near Lauragh, or from Sneem (☎ 087 699 3793, ⓦ kenmarebaydiving.com).

ACCOMMODATION

Kenmare has an excellent choice of **accommodation**, including a good hostel and one of Ireland's finest hotels.

Fáilte Corner of Shelbourne and Henry streets ☎ 064 664 2333, ⓦ kenmarehostel.com (IHH & IHO). Spacious, well-kept hostel in the town centre, with spick-and-span dorms and en-suite and standard private rooms, a cosy sitting room and a well-equipped kitchen. Mid-May to mid-Oct. Dorms €18, doubles €44

Hawthorn House Shelbourne St ☎ 064 664 1035, ⓦ hawthornhousekenmare.com. Highly recommended spot in the centre of town: great hospitality, attractive, well-appointed, en-suite rooms, plenty of local information and fine breakfasts. Self-catering apartments also available. €80

O'Donnabhain's Henry St ☎ 064 664 2106, ⓦ odonnabhain-kenmare.com. The large, bright, modern rooms, decorated in earth tones, at this friendly B&B are spread over several floors of a long, zigzagging building, so all are well away from the pub downstairs.

8

Self-catering also available. Mid-Jan to mid-Dec. **€79**

★**Park Hotel** Shelbourne St ☎ 064 664 1200, ⓦ parkkenmare.com. Dating from the late nineteenth century, this elegant luxury hotel stands in splendid grounds above the Kenmare River. Service is charming, and a stunning modern spa has been carefully blended into its leafy setting. There's an excellent restaurant, and plenty of free activities such as guided walks and croquet. Early March to late Oct and Christmas and New Year. **€410**

Sallyport House On the southern edge of town ☎ 064 664 2066, ⓦ sallyporthouse.com. Spacious, upmarket guesthouse on the shore of the Kenmare River. Rooms are furnished with antiques and boast large bathrooms and fine views of the gardens or the harbour. **€110**

Silver Trees Killowen Rd ☎ 064 664 1008, ⓦ silvertreeskenmare.com. A friendly, efficient and rather plush B&B, 5min walk from the centre, opposite the golf course on the road towards Kilgarvan, with spacious, comfortable en-suite rooms. Good rates for singles. March–Oct. **€70**

★**Virginia's Guesthouse** 36 Henry St ☎ 086 372 0625, ⓦ virginias-kenmare.com. Centrally located above *Mulcahy's* (see below), this charming, compact home-from-home has comfortable thoughtfully equipped, en-suite rooms and excellent, varied breakfasts. Good rates for singles. **€90**

EATING AND DRINKING

Kenmare is fast acquiring a good reputation for **eating out**, and now claims to be the only town in Ireland with more restaurants than pubs. Henry St and Main St shelter about a dozen **pubs**, so finding somewhere congenial to drink is very straightforward, and many of them host traditional music once or twice a week.

Crowley's Henry St ☎ 064 664 1472. Atmospheric old-time bar with a snug and communal seating around the walls, and traditional sessions on Mon, Tues & Wed in summer, Sun in winter. Mon–Thurs roughly 5.30–11.30pm, Fri & Sat 4pm–12.30am, Sun 4–11pm.

Jam Henry St ☎ 064 664 1591, ⓦ jam.ie. Very successful update of a traditional, self-service bakery-café. Good cakes, scones and coffee, as well as delicious sandwiches, quiches and lasagne (€10). Mon–Sat 8am–5.30pm, Sun 9am–5.30pm.

McCarthy's Main St ☎ 064 664 1516, ⓦ pfskenmare .com. Lively, sociable spot that pulls in the thirty-somethings with a popular food menu and early traditional sessions on Fri & Sun. Mon–Thurs noon–11.30pm, Fri & Sat noon–12.30am, Sun noon–11pm.

★**Mulcahy's** 16 Henry St ☎ 064 664 2383. Crisp, modern decor and pricey but excellent creative cuisine with global influences, such as halibut with a mussel, bacon and clam cream sauce (€26). Summer Mon & Wed–Sun 5–10pm, shorter hours in winter.

O'Donnabhain's Henry St ☎ 064 664 2106, ⓦ odonnabhain-kenmare.com. This cosy pub with outdoor tables on the street and a heated patio at the back serves tasty food (until 9pm) using local ingredients whenever possible, including a good seafood chowder (€6.45). Mon–Thurs noon–11.30pm, Fri & Sat noon–12.30am, Sun noon–11pm.

Packies Henry St ☎ 064 664 1508. Homely, upmarket restaurant with a good reputation, under the same management as *The Purple Heather*), cooking up plenty of seafood as well as dishes such as rack of lamb with rosemary and redcurrant jus (€26). Mon–Sat 6–10pm.

The Purple Heather Henry St ☎ 064 664 1016. A relaxing daytime bistro-bar, serving light meals such as homemade chicken-liver pâté with Cumberland sauce (€10.20). Mon–Sat 10.45am–5.45pm.

South of Kenmare: the Beara Peninsula

To the south of Kenmare lies the **Beara Peninsula**, most of which is in County Cork (see p.263). At first the countryside here is green and thickly wooded, but head west on the R571 towards the end of the peninsula (served by buses from Kenmare in July and August), or uphill on the scenic N71 towards Glengarriff (also served by Kenmare buses in July and August), and the terrain soon becomes more windswept and lonely. The other main route across the peninsula is the R574, which heads south from Lauragh towards Adrigole, climbing to the county border at the narrow and dramatic **Healy Pass** and providing magnificent views.

Bonane Heritage Park

Open access but €4 entry fee • ⓦ bonaneheritagepark.com

Signposted off the N71, 8km from Kenmare, is **Bonane Heritage Park**. Here, a large, grassed-over ringfort, a stone circle and other ancient remains have been linked by a circular 2km gravel trail, with fine views of the lush Sheen valley and the bare, wrinkly Caha Mountains behind.

Gleninchaquin

Around 13km from Kenmare along the R571, it's well worth turning onto the dramatic minor road up **Gleninchaquin**, a narrow coomb valley which bowls out at its head around the eponymous lake. After 3km, you'll come upon **Uragh Stone Circle** in a truly magical setting: hemmed in by glaciated hills, on a slender rise between lakes Inchaquin and Uragh, with views down the valley and across to Macgillycuddy's Reeks. To the south runs **Uragh Wood**, one of Ireland's few remaining stands of sessile oak, where numerous birds of prey, red squirrels and stoats reside.

Gleninchaquin Park

Daily dawn–dusk · €6 · ⓦ gleninchaquin.com

Five kilometres further up the valley road from Uragh Stone Circle, you'll reach **Gleninchaquin Park**, where easy-to-follow walks have been laid out around the head of the beautiful valley. It's not the wild, man-against-nature experience of the Beara Way, but it seems to be a neat solution to the problems between walkers and farmers that have been occurring in some parts of the country – and it's hard to get lost. The main, two-hour, circular trail takes you up via a corrie lake to the top of the waterfall, which affords the most spectacular views of the valley. If you fancy an easier outing, there's a river and water garden walk (30min), a farm walk (1hr) and a heritage trail (90min), or you can opt for longer trails (4hr or 7hr) taking in further lakes above the waterfall.

Derreen Gardens

25km southwest of Kenmare · Daily 10am–6pm · €7

On the northwest side of **Lauragh**, the extensive, subtropical **Derreen Gardens** run down to the sea. Still owned by the descendants of Sir William Petty, they're planted with mature exotic species such as giant Australian ferns, Chilean myrtles, acacias, bamboo and mighty eucalyptus trees and are known especially for their rhododendrons. There are plenty of marked trails to keep you going for anything from thirty minutes to two hours, including paths along Kilmakilloge Harbour where a belvedere affords fine views across to the Iveragh Peninsula. Further opportunities for walking, and for cycling, are provided by the nearby Pedals and Boots café (see below).

ACCOMMODATION AND EATING · THE BEARA PENINSULA

Beara Camping On the R571, almost opposite the turn-off for Gleninchaquin ☎064 668 4287, ⓦ bearacamping.com. *Beara Camping* provides camping, dorm accommodation in cabins and mobile homes (price quoted for 2 people), cooking and laundry facilities and a café-restaurant. Camping **€18**, dorms **€15**, mobile homes **€40**

Pedals and Boots At the post office on the R571 in Lauragh (west of the turn-off for Derreen Gardens) ☎064 668 3101, ⓦ pedalsandboots.ie. This café rustles up home-baked cakes, scones and biscuits, soups and sandwiches, as well as renting out bikes, with lots of info and maps for cycling and for walking in the vicinity. June–Aug daily 10am–6pm; Sept–May Fri & Sat 11am–4pm.

The Dingle Peninsula

One wonders, in this place, why anyone is left in Dublin, or London, or Paris, when it would be better one would think, to live in a tent, or a hut, with this magnificent sea and sky, and to breathe this wonderful air, which is like wine in one's teeth.

J.M. Synge, In West Kerry

THE DINGLE PENINSULA

N

8

Listowel ▲   Killarney ▲   Killarney ▲

Tralee
Blennerville
Castlemaine
Milltown
Ballyheigue
Ardfert
Killorglin
Banna Strand
Fenit
SLIEVE MISH MOUNTAINS
Castlemaine Harbour
Tralee Bay
Camp
Dingle Way
Inch
Maharees Peninsula
Scraggane Bay
Sandy Bay
Castlegregory
Fahamore
Stradbally
Beenoskee (826m) ▲
Anascaul
Dingle Bay
Brandon Bay
CONOR PASS
Lispole
Brandon
Cloghane
Mount Brandon (950m) ▲
Ballynavenooragh
Dingle
Dingle Harbour
Brandon Creek
Feohanagh
Glaise Bheag
Kilmalkedar
Gallarus Oratory
Milltown
Ballydavid Head
Ballydavid
Murreagh
Riasc
Ventry
Dún Beag
Smerwick Harbour
Ballyferriter
Mount Eagle (514m) ▲
Dunquin
Sybil Head
Clogher Head
Slea Head
Blasket Islands
Inishtooskert
Great Blasket Island
Inishnabro
Inishvickillane

0 5
kilometres

The last of southwestern Ireland's five great peninsulas, **Dingle** is perhaps the most distinctive of them all. Arrowing westwards for over 50km, its heavily glaciated topography is especially irregular, with an L-shaped ridge of mountains that peaks at its north end at **Mount Brandon**, the highest summit in Ireland outside of Macgillycuddy's Reeks. Five-hundred-metre **Mount Eagle** at the very tip of the peninsula sets up a truly spectacular drive, cycle or walk around **Slea Head.** On the coasts, the long, exposed sandbars at **Castlegregory** and **Inch** draw surfers and wind-surfers, while the deeply recessed sandy beaches at **Ventry** and **Smerwick Harbour** encourage gentle swimming.

Dingle has an unusually rich heritage, including over five hundred Celtic *locháns* (corbelled, dry-stone beehive huts) and the early Christian **Gallarus Oratory**, with its stunningly simple dry-stone construction. The peninsula is also one of the strongest **Irish-speaking** districts in the country, known as **Corca Dhuibhne** (meaning "the followers of Davinia", a Celtic goddess). As the main settlement at the heart of this thriving Gaeltacht (which officially begins just west of Anascaul and Castlegregory), **Dingle town** (An Daingean) feels like a capital. It supports some top-notch restaurants and places to stay, complemented by a vibrant traditional-music scene, and is perfectly located for varied day-trips. One of the best of these is the boat trip to the abandoned **Blasket Islands** just off Slea Head, which were responsible for an astonishing body of Irish-language writing in the early twentieth century.

The south coast

If you're heading towards Dingle town from Killarney or the Ring of Kerry, a direct, often narrow road, served by summertime buses from Killarney, will bring you along the peninsula's south coast, with fine views of Dingle Bay and the Iveragh Peninsula. At **Inch**, a dune-covered sandbar with a beautiful 5km-long beach on its western side thrusts out into the bay, mirrored by Rossbeigh Strand over on the Iveragh. In the summer, Kingdom Waves offer **surfing** lessons, board and wetsuit rental (☎087 744 7958, ⦿kingdomwaves.com).

EATING AND DRINKING   **THE SOUTH COAST**

★**The South Pole Inn** Anascaul, 7km west of Inch ☎066 915 7388. Founded by local man, Tom Crean, unsung hero of Shackleton's and Scott's Antarctic expeditions, this pub is an atmospheric and very congenial spot in a pretty riverside location. Hung with polar memorabilia and photos, it offers traditional music on Sat (plus Sun in summer) and good food. Mon–Thurs noon–11.30pm, Fri & Sat noon–12.30am, Sun noon–11pm.

Dingle town (An Daingean)

Sheltered from the ravages of the Atlantic by its impressive natural harbour, **DINGLE** is an excellent base, not only for exploring the western end of the peninsula ("back west" as it's known locally), but also for a variety of water-borne activities. Even if the weather gets the better of you, there are plenty of welcoming cafés, restaurants and pubs, which host some

DINGLE FESTIVALS

The principal events on Dingle's busy calendar are a four-day **film festival** in March (⦿dinglefilmfestival.com); **Feile na Bealtaine** (⦿feilenabealtaine.ie), a week-long multidisciplinary festival of arts and politics in early May; a well-received series of **folk and traditional concerts** in summer (roughly May–Oct) at the pretty St James's Church in Main Street (☎087 284 9656); the riotous **Dingle Races** at Ballintaggart Racecourse on the east side of town over three days in early August (⦿dingleraces.ie); the **Dingle Regatta** for traditional *currachs* later in the month; a four-day **festival of traditional music** in September (⦿dingletradfest.com); and a diverse **food festival** over a weekend in early October (⦿dinglefood.com).

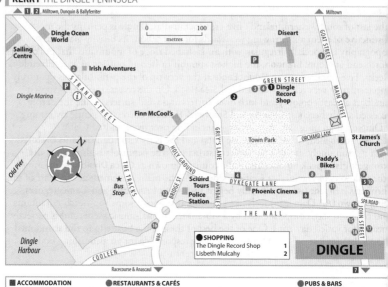

■ ACCOMMODATION		● RESTAURANTS & CAFÉS				● PUBS & BARS	
Ashe's	5	An Café Liteártha	11	Murphy's Ice Cream	7	Adam's	6
Benners Hotel	3	Ashe's	10	Novecento	14	An Droichead Beag	13
Captain's House	6	The Chart House	16	Out of the Blue	2	The Blue Zone	4
Castlewood House	1	Cúl Gairdín	9	Wren's Nest	8	Dick Mack's	3
Hideout Hostel	4	Goat Street Bistro	1			John Benny's	5
Pax House	7	Half Door	17			O'Flaherty's	12
Rainbow Hostel	2	Idás	18			O'Sullivan's Courthouse	15

excellent traditional music, to retreat to. Tourism is far from the only industry here: in medieval times, Dingle was Kerry's leading port, protected by town walls, and it's still a major fishing harbour. From the extensive quays, narrow streets of stone houses, colourfully painted and appealingly substantial, run up the slope to the bustling main street.

Fungie the Dolphin

Swimming Bookable at Brosnan's B&B on Cooleen, a street on the east side of the harbour • €45, including wetsuit • ☎ 066 915 1146
Dingle Boatmen's Association Bookable at any time of day • €16 • ☎ 066 915 2626, ⓦ dingledolphin.com **Dingle Bay Charters** In the same building as the tourist office • Boat trips bookable at any time of day; cruises summer twice daily, includes 15min with Fungie • Boat trips €16; cruises €10 • ☎ 066 915 1344, ⓦ dinglebaycharters.com

Dingle's most famous resident is undoubtedly **Fungie**, a playful 300kg bottlenose dolphin who has made the harbour his home since 1983. If you want to go for an early-morning swim with him, you'll need to book in advance. Otherwise there are hour-long boat trips or cruises, or just walk along Cooleen, which turns into a footpath along the shoreline to the narrow mouth of the harbour, and watch him from there.

Dingle Oceanworld

Daily: July & Aug 10am–7pm; Sept–June 10am–5pm; last admission 1hr before closing • €13, child €7.50, family from €32 • ⓦ dingle-oceanworld.ie

If nautical pursuits have whetted your curiosity, head for **Dingle Oceanworld** (Mara Beo) on the waterfront. As well as a centre for marine conservation, Oceanworld is a richly detailed aquarium, where you can stick your hands in the touch pool, observe sharks, stingrays, piranhas, turtles and their newest arrivals, penguins (feeding at 2pm), at close quarters and walk underneath a variety of fish from around the Irish coast in the tunnel tank.

Díseart

nstitute Summer Mon–Fri 9am–5pm, Sat 10am–4pm • €3 **Workshops** June–Aug Tues & Thurs 4pm • €10; booking essential on ☎ 087 685 2428 • ⓦ diseart.ie

At **Díseart Institute of Irish Culture and Spirituality**, a former convent of the enclosed order of Presentation Sisters on Green Street, you can admire twelve **stained-glass windows** by Harry Clarke, one of the foremost artists in the medium in the last century; commissioned in 1922, they depict scenes from the life of Christ in opulent detail. Díseart also hosts Irish-language workshops for visitors.

ARRIVAL AND INFORMATION   DINGLE TOWN

By car If you're driving, you'll need to get used to Dingle's fierce, roughly anticlockwise one-way system. Holy Ground and its continuation, Dykegate Lane, are up only (south–north), Main St is up only (east–west), while Green St, which leads back down towards the harbour, is down only. There's a useful free car park on Green St near Díseart.

By bus Buses stop in the car park behind the Supervalu store, down near the harbour.

Destinations Ballyferriter (Mon & Thurs 2 daily; 20min); Dunquin (Mon & Thurs 2 daily; 30min); Gallarus (Tues & Fri 1 daily; 10min); Killarney, via Inch (July & Aug Mon–Sat 2 daily; 1hr 20min); Tralee (via the N86; 3–5 daily; 1hr 20min).

Tourist office Strand St by the harbour (June–Sept daily 9.15am–5pm; Oct–May Mon–Sat 9.15am–5pm; ☎ 066 915 1188).

TOURS AND ACTIVITIES

Tours Fascinating archaeological tours of the peninsula by minibus are run in the summer by Sciúird Tours, Avondale St (2 daily; 2hr 30min; from €20/person; ☎ 066 915 1606, ⓔ archeo@eircom.net).

Activities As well as boat trips in the harbour (see opposite) and to Great Blasket (see p.298), Dingle offers plenty of other activities.

Bike rental Paddy's, Dykegate Lane (☎ 066 915 2311, ⓦ paddysbikeshop.com).

Kayaking and mountain biking Irish Adventures, off Strand St, behind *Out of the Blue* restaurant (☎ 087 419 0318, ⓦ irishadventures.net).

Sailing Dingle Sailing Centre at the marina (☎ 087 718 7557, ⓦ dinglesailingclub.com) offers sailing courses in July and Aug.

Surfing Finn McCool's Surf Shop, Green St (☎ 066 915 0833, ⓦ finnmccools.ie), for equipment rental and lessons.

ACCOMMODATION

Dingle has a good range of **accommodation**, particularly of guesthouses. **Camping** is possible at *Rainbow Hostel* (see below).

Ashe's Main St ☎ 066 915 0989, ⓦ ashesbar.ie. Attractive, bright and central rooms with smart, en-suite bathrooms, in a whitewashed nineteenth-century building above a pub. Breakfast not served. **€80**

Benners Hotel Main St ☎ 066 915 1638, ⓦ dinglebenners.com. Characterful and welcoming town house hotel and social hub that's been skilfully refurbished: bedrooms are brightly furnished with pine and floral prints, while the dark-wood lobby and bar are warm and cosy. **€189**

Captain's House The Mall ☎ 066 915 1531, ⓦ homepage.eircom.net/~captigh/. Hospitable, central, en-suite B&B, quirkily furnished with items collected on the eponymous captain's voyages. Great breakfasts, including homemade bread, scones and jam, are served in the conservatory, which overlooks the picturesque garden and stream. Self-catering also available. April–Nov. **€90**

★**Castlewood House** 1km from the tourist office along the continuation of Strand St ☎ 066 915 2788, ⓦ castlewooddingle.com. Quiet, welcoming guesthouse with large and very thoughtfully and lavishly designed rooms, which stretch to DVD players and whirlpool baths, and nearly all have fine views of the bay. Excellent, varied breakfasts and plenty of local information. **€138**

Hideout Hostel Dykegate Lane ☎ 066 915 0559, ⓦ thehideouthostel.com (IHO). Friendly, laidback and all-en-suite hostel in a livid green and red, modern terrace house, with a well-equipped kitchen, a sitting room with an open fire and laundry facilities; light breakfast included. Dorms **€18**, doubles **€50**

Pax House Upper John St, 1km east of the town centre ☎ 066 915 1518, ⓦ pax-house.com. Peaceful, upmarket B&B, tastefully decorated with colourful paintings in contemporary style, with spectacular views of the bay from seven of the rooms and the large patio, and great breakfasts and afternoon teas. **€120**

Rainbow Hostel 2km west of the centre in Milltown ☎ 066 915 1044, ⓦ rainbowhosteldingle.com (IHO). Sociable, family-run hostel, with landscaped gardens, large kitchen, bike rental and laundry facilities. Free lifts from the bus stop in town. Dorms **€16**, doubles **€36**

8

EATING AND DRINKING

Although it doesn't shout about being a foodie town, Dingle has several first-rate **restaurants**. Seafood, naturally, features strongly on their menus, and also in the town's **bar food**, while several homely **cafés** are great for whiling away rainy afternoons. On Fri mornings, there's a very good farmers' market in the car park on Holy Ground. Dingle is a hotbed of **traditional music**, with some locally based, nationally known performers turning up in the town's **pubs**. *West Kerry Live* (ⓦwestkerrylive.ie), a free fortnightly magazine available from the tourist office, details sessions and gigs in town and across the peninsula.

RESTAURANTS

Ashe's Main St ☎066 915 0989, ⓦashesbar.ie. Easy-going spot, more restaurant than pub, which specializes in seafood, but also offers some cheaper dishes such as a very good Irish lamb stew. Early-bird two courses for €23 till 6.45pm. Daily noon–3pm & 5.30–9.30pm.

The Chart House By the roundabout at the bottom of The Mall ☎066 915 2255, ⓦthecharthousedingle.com. Relaxing restaurant in a stone cottage with posh-rustic decor, preparing dishes such as cod with orange, fennel and chorizo risotto (€25.70). Value menu two courses for €25. Wed–Sun 6–9.30pm, plus Tues (same hours) in summer.

Goat Street Bistro Goat St ☎066 915 2770, ⓦgoatstreetbistro.com. Civilized and sociable café, hung with paintings and photos by local artists, rustling up imaginative, tasty salads, soups and dishes such as seafood tagliatelle in a pesto and herb cream (€13) during the day, and offering the likes of hake in a chilli, ginger and coconut broth (€19) on summer evenings. Summer Mon–Wed 10am–4pm, Thurs–Sat 10am–4pm & 6–9pm; winter Mon–Sat 10am–4pm.

★**Half Door** John St ☎066 915 1600. Relaxing, white-tablecloth restaurant with excellent cooking – mostly seafood – a good wine list, delicious desserts such as apple and pear crumble, and friendly, efficient service. It's pricey, but there are various set menus on offer (including €27 for two courses at lunch time and €29.50 for three early evening). Summer Mon–Sat 12.30–2.30pm & 5–10pm; winter hours depend on trade, but at least weekends, though closed 2 weeks in Jan.

Idás John St ☎066 915 0885. Stylish new restaurant with a great soundtrack, polished wood floors and bare stone and white walls. Their John Dory and lemon sole fillets on a chorizo and white bean casserole (€18) is a winning combination, nicely executed, or you can splash out a bit more (€25–30) for more complex dishes using more expensive cuts. Tues–Sun 5.30–roughly 9.30pm; may close end Oct for the winter.

Out of the Blue Opposite the tourist office on Strand St ☎066 915 0811, ⓦoutoftheblue.ie. Unpretentious seafood restaurant, serving up whatever fish and shellfish are fresh from the pier opposite, in excellent dishes such as Blasket Islands scallops with Calvados flambé (€29). March–Oct Mon–Sat 5/5.30–9.30pm, Sun 12.30–3pm & 5/5.30–9.30pm.

CAFÉS AND SNACKS

An Café Liteártha Dykegate Lane ☎066 915 2204. Daytime bookshop-café that offers cheap, unpretentious food: soup, scones, cakes, sandwiches and warm brie with raspberry jam, salad and bread (€7.50). Mon–Sat 11am–3pm.

Cúl Gairdín Main St ☎066 915 0993. Quirky little vegetarian café (with vegan options) serving crêpes with herbs and cheese (€8.50), salads, soups, cakes, smoothies and power drinks. There's art for sale on the walls and a big back garden with a lawn and a covered patio. Mon–Sat 10.30am–4.30pm, plus some early evenings in summer.

Murphy's Ice Cream Strand St ☎087 133 0610, ⓦmurphysicecream.ie. Delicious homemade ice cream to eat in or take away, as well as other great desserts, and excellent coffee. Daily: summer 11am–9.30pm; winter 11am–5/6pm.

Novecento Main St ☎066 915 0663, ⓦnovecento.ie. Great pizzas, either whole (starting at €8) or by the slice, to take away in the evenings. Mon–Thurs & Sun 4–10pm, Fri & Sat 4–11pm.

Wren's Nest Dykegate Lane ☎086 177 3119. Laidback café in a simple stone cottage with a lovely, secluded garden at the back. Tuck into tasty quiche and salad (€6.50), omelettes, baked potatoes, cakes and homemade blueberry ice cream. Open-mike night Thurs. March–Nov daily 11am–5pm.

PUBS AND BARS

Adam's Main St ☎066 915 2133. This likeable pub offers reasonable and tasty homemade lunches – including lemon chicken and walnut salad (€8) and Irish stew – and traditional music at weekends. Mon–Thurs 10.30am–11.30pm, Fri & Sat 10.30am–12.30am, Sun 10.30am–11pm.

★**An Droichead Beag** At the bottom of Main St ☎066 915 1723. A cosy, popular spot, "The Small Bridge" has great sessions just about every night at 9/9.30pm, usually followed by a DJ. Mon–Thurs 3pm–late, Fri–Sun noon–late.

The Blue Zone Above the Dingle Record Shop (see opposite) on Green St ☎066 915 0303. For something completely different, head for this late-night wine bar which offers jazz (Thurs & Fri in winter, most nights, though not Sat, in summer) and tasty pizzas. Daily 5.30pm–late.

Dick Mack's Green St ☎066 915 1787. Crusty, beery former cobblers' shop, with attractive tables in a quiet courtyard at the back and stars on the pavement outside to ommemorate such diverse former customers as Robert Mitchum and Julia Roberts. Mon–Thurs roughly 11am–11.30pm, Fri & Sat 11am–12.30am, Sun 11am–11pm.

John Benny's Strand St ☎066 915 1215, ⓦjohnbennyspub.com. Cosy, refurbished pub that's popular for its microbrewed beers and reasonably priced bar food, such as Irish stew (€15), bacon and cabbage, Glenbeigh oysters, salads and sandwiches, with vegetarian options. John and his wife are noted musicians who host traditional music every night in summer (and often enough in winter). Mon–Thurs 10.30am–11.30pm, Fri & Sat 10.30am–12.30am, Sun 10.30am–11pm.

O'Flaherty's Bridge St, down by the roundabout ☎066 915 1983. Spartan but sociable pub, with a flagstone floor and an old stove, its walls hung with interesting memorabilia. Owned by a family of musicians, it hosts sessions most nights. Mon–Thurs roughly 11/11.30am–11.30pm, Fri&Sat 11/11.30am–12.30am, Sun 11/11.30am–11pm.

O'Sullivan's Courthouse The Mall ☎066 915 2853, ⓦosullivanscourthousepub.com. Another Dingle pub owned by a musician: "no TV, no juke box, no pool table", just bare wood, white paint and an old stove – with a cute beer garden – as the setting for great nightly sessions, washed down with craft beers. Mon–Thurs 3–11.30pm, Fri 3pm–12.30am, Sat 2pm–12.30am, Sun 2–11pm.

SHOPPING

Green Street shelters all manner of crafts shops, art galleries, delicatessens and bookshops. See ⓦoriginalkerry.com for information about the county's craft makers, most of whom are in Dingle.

The Dingle Record Shop Green St ☎087 298 4550, ⓦdinglerecordshop.com. This tiny shop with a big welcome has a great selection of traditional CDs, especially by local musicians, at keen prices and is a good source of information about sessions, as well as selling tickets for the St James's church concerts (see p.293). Roughly Mon–Sat 11am–5pm.

Lisbeth Mulcahy Green St ☎066 915 1688, ⓦlisbethmulcahy.com. Gorgeous scarves, jumpers and other wool items, as well as pottery by Lisbeth's husband, Louis (see p.300). Summer Mon–Fri 9.30am–7pm, Sat 10am–6pm, Sun noon–5pm; winter Mon–Sat 10am–5pm.

The Slea Head Loop

The vast, spectacular mountain- and seascapes which stretch out to the tip of the peninsula, **Slea Head**, are the undoubted highlights here, followed by the **Blasket Islands heritage centre** at Dunquin – or even a **boat trip to the islands** themselves – and the elegant, dry-stone **Gallarus Oratory**.

Ventry (Ceann Trá)

VENTRY, the first bay to the west of Dingle, is just as impressive, sheltering a crescent of fine, sandy, gently sloping beach and low dunes in the lee of 514m Mount Eagle. The strand here was the suitably epic location for the legendary single combat between Fionn Mac Cumhaill and Daire Donn, the King of the World, to save Ireland from invasion by Daire's armies.

Celtic and Prehistoric Museum

March–Nov daily 10am–5.30pm • €5

On the west side of Ventry Bay, it's well worth calling in to the small but fascinating **Celtic and Prehistoric Museum**. Here you can gawp at a fossilized nest of dinosaur eggs, a baby dinosaur skeleton and the complete skull and tusks of a woolly mammoth, of the type that would have been roaming Ireland over twenty thousand years ago. From the Stone Age come jewellery, statuettes and tools – when the engaging owner is around, he'll show you how they were used. There are also some lovely Bronze Age spiral ornaments and Celtic amulets, money and burial offerings.

Dún Beag

Entry fee includes a 10min audiovisual in the *Stonehouse* restaurant opposite • €3 • ⓦdunbegfort.com

It's a fine drive or cycle out to **Slea Head** (Ceann Sléibhe), as the road narrows beyond Ventry and the slopes of Mount Eagle steepen towards the end of the peninsula. This

> ## BOAT TRIPS TO THE BLASKETS
>
> In the summer, **boats** to Great Blasket leave the pier on the south side of **Dunquin** in good weather every hour or so (15–30min; €25 return; ☎066 915 6422, ⓦblasketisland.com). There are also three types of tour from **Ventry** (booking essential on ☎086 335 3805, ⓦmarinetours .ie): a 2hr 30min trip in the morning, landing on Great Blasket (€25); a 4hr guided cruise around the Blasket Islands in the afternoon (€40), taking in the spectacular Cathedral Rocks on Inishnabro, puffins (in spring and early summer, depending on the weather) and grey seals and red deer on Inishvickillane, and possibly basking sharks, whales and dolphins; and a 7hr trip that combines the guided cruise with landing on Great Blasket (€50). In addition, from **Dingle town** Dingle Bay Charters (see p.294) run ferries to Great Blasket once a day (50min, leaving you 3hr 30min on the island; €35 return), and guided cruises around the islands that include 1hr on Great Blasket (6hr; €50).

landscape is dotted with several Iron Age dry-stone forts, known as the **Fahan Group**, of which the most interesting is the first, around 1km beyond the Celtic Museum. In a spectacular setting above the boiling sea overlooking the Iveragh Peninsula, **Dún Beag** has four lines of defensive banks and five corresponding ditches, traversed by a 16m souterrain or underground escape route. Within the 3m-high walls stand the remains of beehive huts or *clocháns*. Dún Beag used to be even more spectacular, but in January 2014 winter storms eroded the cliff and caused a large section of the site to fall into the Atlantic.

The Blasket Islands (Na Blascaodaí) and Dunquin (Dún Chaoin)

Ionad an Bhlascaoid Mhóir April–Oct daily 10am–6pm; last admission 5.15pm • €4; Heritage Card • ⓦheritageireland.ie

Just off Slea Head lie the **Blaskets**, dramatic island mountains with steep, gashed sides. Despite their inhospitableness, the largest island, Great Blasket (An Blascaod Mór), was inhabited by up to two hundred people for at least three centuries until 1953, when, with no school, shop, priest or doctor, it was finally abandoned. Because of their isolation, however, the islanders maintained a rich oral tradition in the Irish language, which in the early twentieth century, encouraged by visiting scholars, evolved into a remarkable body of written **literature**. Works such as *An tOileánach* (*The Islandman*) by Tomás Ó Criomhthain, *Fiche Blian ag Fás* (*Twenty Years A-Growing*) by Muiris Ó Súilleabháin and *Peig* by Peig Sayers (an oral account written down by her son) give a vivid insight into the hardships of island life.

The island's story is told with great imagination at the Great Blasket heritage centre, **Ionad an Bhlascaoid Mhóir**, on the mainland opposite, at the north end of Dunquin. Though the building doesn't look like much as you approach, inside is a beautiful museum space. There are excerpts from the island writers, and a moving section on Great Blasket's abandonment in 1953 and the migration of many islanders to Springfield, Massachusetts – where they still receive the *Kerryman* newspaper from Tralee every week. Every October, the centre hosts a commemorative festival, featuring lectures, stage productions and other events (ⓦceiliuradh.com).

If you take a boat trip (see box, above) to **Great Blasket**, you can wander the white-sand beach, Trá Bán, at its eastern end and the grassy footpaths that cross its 6km length, passing the ghosts of the old village. Accompanied by seals, puffins, storm petrels and shearwaters, you can contemplate the 3000km that separates you, here on Europe's most westerly islands, from North America where most of the islanders ended up, and the treacherous 2km of Blasket Sound which made living on the island untenable.

Ballyferriter (Baile an Fheirtearaigh) and around

BALLYFERRITER, 8km on from Dunquin, is a byword for remoteness in Ireland, but actually ticks a surprising number of boxes when it comes to amenities. There's a lovely beach, **Wine**

Strand, just to the north on sheltered **Smerwick Harbour**, and some pleasant walking to the northwest where the peaks of **Sybil Head** and the **Three Sisters** rise like a row of waves to meet the sea. In late February, the village hosts a five-day **traditional-music school**, Scoil Cheoil an Earraigh (⊛ scoilcheoil.com), featuring classes, concerts, lectures and other events.

Músaem Chorca Dhuibhne

June–Aug daily 10am–5.30pm; off-season by appointment • ☎ 066 915 6100, ⊛ westkerrymuseum.com • €2.50

The old village school has been converted into the **Músaem Chorca Dhuibhne**, which houses a small but tidy display on the archaeology and history of the peninsula since Mesolithic times, its geology and its more recent role as a location for movies such as *Ryan's Daughter*. There's a café that does home baking at the museum, where you can also find out about looped walks around the village and about the wealth of ancient ruins in the area, such as Riasc, a sixth-century monastic site, and the ring fort at Ballynavenooragh.

Louis Mulcahy Pottery

4km west of Ballyferriter on the R559 (about 4km from Dunquin) • Summer Mon–Fri 9am–7pm, Sat & Sun 10am–7pm; winter Mon–Fri 9am–5.30/6pm, Sat & Sun 10am–5.30/6pm • ☎ 066 915 6229, ⊛ louismulcahy.com

One of Ireland's leading potters, Louis Mulcahy, has his **pottery**, shop and café near the tip of the Dingle Peninsula. There's an open room where you can watch a potter at work on the wheel and you can have a go at throwing a pot yourself (pre-booking recommended).

Gallarus Oratory

Access to state-administered oratory free, so no need at all to pay at the privately run visitor centre, sitting between the most obvious car park and the church; instead, continue a short way along the hedgerowed and fuchsia-lined one-track paved road to a small car park with space for half a dozen vehicles, which gives direct access to the oratory

Five kilometres east of Ballyferriter, off the R559 towards **Murreagh** (An Mhuiríoch), the beautiful **Gallarus Oratory** is Dingle's most compelling historic monument, dating from somewhere between the seventh and twelfth centuries. Built entirely of dry gritstone in the shape of an upturned boat, the church sits proudly in its field at the very western edge of Europe like a Platonic ideal of architectural purity, still quite intact and unadorned. Its stones, carefully selected and smoothed off inside and out, and gracefully corbelled to form the roof, are now weathered to soft tones of green, brown, purple and orange. It's lit by a single window opposite the doorway, while the only features inside are two large, pierced stones above the lintel which probably served for the attachment of a flap-like door.

Kilmalkedar

Open access

At the crossroads at Murreagh, the R559 turns right, passing after 2km **Kilmalkedar**, an attractive, mid-twelfth-century church in the Irish Romanesque style. Dedicated to local saint, Maolcéadair, who died in 636, it offers fine views west to the sea. Look out for a strange, carved animal head inside, above the doorway, and, in the surrounding graveyard, an early sundial, a high cross and an ogham stone, whose inscription is probably asking for a prayer for the soul of one Maile Inbir.

GETTING AROUND   **THE SLEA HEAD LOOP**

By bike/car You can make an immensely satisfying day-trip from Dingle by driving or cycling the R559 on its meandering, circular route, or by taking a tour (see p.295). Coaches are required to follow the narrow winding road in a clockwise direction and it's best to follow suit, than risk meeting them head-on.

By bus The bus schedules would allow you half-day trips to Dunquin or Ballyferriter on Mon or Thurs and to Gallarus on Tues or Fri.

On foot An 18km waymarked path, Cosán na Naomh (The Saint's Road), crosses this area mostly on minor roads and lanes, from Ventry Strand via Gallarus and Kilmalkedar to the foot of Mount Brandon, with an associated map-guide (⊛ heritagecouncil.ie).

ACCOMMODATION AND EATING

VENTRY

Páidí Ó Sé's By the church ☎ 066 915 9011, ⓦ paidiose .com. Congenial pub offering food, a few outdoor tables and good traditional sessions at weekends; formerly owned by the eponymous late great Kerry Gaelic footballer and manager, it's hung with sporting memorabilia. Mon–Thurs roughly 11am–11.30pm, Fri & Sat 11am–12.30am, Sun noon–11pm.

DÚN BEAG

The Stonehouse Opposite the fort ☎ 066 915 9970, ⓦ stonehouseventry.com. Built in a *clochán* style with stone walls and roof, this café-restaurant offers main courses such as crab salad (€16), soup, sandwiches, homemade scones and good views of the Skelligs from its outdoor tables. Daily: high season 10.30am–9pm; low season 11am–5.30pm (closed Dec to mid-Feb).

DUNQUIN

An Portán In the middle of the village ☎ 066 915 6212, ⓦ anportan.ie. En-suite B&B in a one-storey quadrangle of large, bright rooms around a lawn, with a dining room for guests and a daytime café. Very good rates for singles. April–Sept. €70

Dún Chaoin Youth Hostel Near the heritage centre ☎ 066 915 6121, ⓦ anoige.ie. An Óige hostel on the Dingle Way, with great views over the Blaskets, four- to ten-bed dorms, en-suite twins, a kitchen and laundry facilities and a drying room for walkers. Note that there are no shops for 8km (Ballyferriter), so you'll need to

bring supplies with you. March–Oct. Dorms €16.50, doubles €42

BALLYFERRITER AND AROUND

★**Gorman's Clifftop House and Restaurant** Glaise Bheag, north of Murreagh towards Feohanagh (An Fheothanach) ☎ 066 915 5162, ⓦ gormans-clifftophouse .com. The lovely, large, bright rooms at this welcoming and well-informed guesthouse are very comfortable and thoughtfully equipped, with great views of either the Three Sisters or Mount Brandon. There's bike rental for guests and you can feast on dishes such as Dingle Bay prawns and crab claws at their very good restaurant (reservations essential). Discounts for longer stays. Restaurant Mon–Sat dinner served 7–8pm, Sun for residents only at 7pm. Mid-March to mid-Oct. €130

Tig Áine Just west of Louis Mulcahy's pottery on the R559 ☎ 066 915 6214, ⓦ tigaine.com. Boasting fine views of Sybil Head from its picture windows and outside terrace (with binoculars and telescopes for spotting birds and marine life), *Tig Áine* encompasses an art gallery and a café-restaurant, rustling up tasty dishes such as seafood pie (€13). May–Sept daily noon–6pm, plus July & Aug Tues–Sun 6–9pm.

Tigh an tSaorsaigh (Sears) On the R559 in the village ☎ 066 915 6344, ⓦ searspub.com. Pleasant, en-suite B&B is available at this genial 150-year-old flagstoned pub that's done out in striking green and red. With its piano and open stove, the bar offers simple pub grub. €60

The Conor Pass and the north coast of the peninsula

To the northeast of Dingle town rises a great L-shaped ridge of mountains, running south from the highest, **Mount Brandon** (Cnoc Bréanainn; 950m), and across to Beenoskee (826m). The steep and narrow **Conor Pass** road, which cuts across the ridge to the peninsula's north coast, ascends to a car park at over 500m giving spectacular views of stark uplands, corrie lakes and the huge sweep of **Brandon Bay** to the north, and back over Dingle harbour to the Iveragh Peninsula and the Skelligs.

Cloghane

Signposted archaeological and walking trails, including the Dingle Way, crisscross the area around **CLOGHANE** (An Clochán), a tiny village fringed by lovely beaches on the eastern flank of Mount Brandon. Experienced walkers could take on the classic, six-hour there-and-back ascent of Mount Brandon, roughly marked by yellow painted arrows, from Faha, 2km northwest of Cloghane. Cloghane comes to life over the last weekend in July for the **Feile Lughnasa**, celebrating the Celtic harvest festival with guided walks, poetry and music.

ACCOMMODATION CLOGHANE

Mount Brandon Hostel ☎ 086 136 3454, ⓦ mountbrandonhostel.com (IHO). All-en-suite, eco-conscious hostel with spruce wooden floors and furniture, a well-equipped kitchen, a cosy lounge and a patio

overlooking the bay. The hostel hosts an evening of music, poetry and storytelling every Mon throughout the year. Luggage transfer can be arranged for walkers. Light breakfast included. Dorms €17, doubles €45

Castlegregory

Separating Brandon Bay from Tralee Bay, the **Maharees Peninsula** is an exposed, beach-girt spit of land to the north of the village of **CASTLEGREGORY**. What's reckoned to be some of the best **wind-surfing** in the world is possible here – it's good in all wind directions, with a variety of west-, north- and east-facing spots suitable for all levels of ability; there's a good break for **surfers**, too (see box, below). If all that sounds too energetic, just flop out on the nearest beach to Castlegregory, east-facing **Sandy Bay**.

ACCOMMODATION AND EATING — CASTLEGREGORY

Anchor About 5km east of the village on the R560 ⓣ066 713 9157, ⓦanchorcaravanpark.com. This well-signposted campsite gives onto kilometres of quiet, sandy beach, and has a campers' kitchen, a children's play area, laundry facilities and a rinsing area for wetsuits. April–Sept. €18

Fitzgerald's Euro-Hostel Strand St ⓣ066 713 9951, ⓦeurohostelireland.com. If you're not on a package with Waterworld (see box, below), you might want to crash at this hostel back in town, which has basic dorms, single, twin and double rooms and a large kitchen above a shop café and bar. Dorms €15, doubles €30

Spillane's Bar and Restaurant About halfway along the Maharees Peninsula ⓣ066 713 9125 ⓦspillanesbar.com. Your best bet for something to eat in the area, specializing in steaks (€22.50 for Irish sirloin) and seafood, with the day's catch – maybe local mussels, crab claws and prawns – listed on a blackboard. Self-catering accommodation available. Spring and autumn daily 5–9pm, summer daily 1–9pm.

8

North Kerry

North Kerry, flat, rich farming land that runs as far as the Shannon estuary, feels quite different from the rest of the county – and they've even been known to play hurling rather than Gaelic football up here. Instead of the remote, spectacularly set coastal villages of the peninsulas, you'll find – or avoid – the traditional kiss-me-quick resorts of Ballyheigue and Ballybunion, while the county town of **Tralee** seems quite anodyne if you've just come up from Dingle, for example. It is worth making time, however, for **Listowel**, a characterful small town that's a hotbed of literary activity. North again from here, the useful **Shannon ferry** cuts down travelling time to County Clare from **Tarbert**.

Tralee and around

Although **TRALEE** has a long history as a market town, originally built around an Anglo-Norman castle and priory, its attractions today are modern and rather functional. It's currently trying to broaden its appeal to families by offering combination tickets for the County Museum, the Wetlands Centre and Blennerville Windmill for just €33 (up to two adults and three children).

Kerry County Museum

Ashe Memorial Hall, Denny St • June–Aug daily 9.30am–5.30pm; Sept–May Tues–Sat 9.30am–5pm • €5 • ⓦkerrymuseum.ie

Chief among Tralee's sights is the **Kerry County Museum** in the centre of town, which incorporates a comprehensive run-through of the history of Ireland and

WATERSPORTS ON THE MAHARAEES PENINSULA

Based about halfway along the peninsula, Jamie Knox offers wind-surfing and surfing tuition and rental, and **stand-up paddleboard** rental (ⓣ066 713 9411). **Diving** trips, courses and accommodation packages are run by Waterworld, a PADI Five-Star IDC Centre, from their base, Harbour House, at Scraggane Bay at the end of the Maharees (ⓣ066 713 9292, ⓦwaterworld.ie); they also offer surf lessons and rentals, as well as canoeing and other watersports.

THE DINGLE WAY

Probably the best way to soak up the Dingle Peninsula's dramatic, shifting landscapes is to walk all or part of the waymarked, 180km **Dingle Way**, which begins in Tralee, heads west to Camp, then loops round the rest of the peninsula, via long, sandy beaches, the steep north face of Mount Brandon and most of Dingle's major sites and villages. The whole thing can be done in seven or eight days, catching a bus out towards Camp on the first day to avoid repeating the stretch between there and Tralee. An excellent **website**, Ⓦ dingleway.com, provides trail descriptions, maps and full details of walker-friendly accommodation, offering services such as luggage transfer, evening meals and packed lunches, along the route. On this remote peninsula, you'll need to check carefully that you'll be able to get dinner after each day's walking, especially outside of July and August. OS 1:50,000 **map** no. 70 covers most of the route, with the eastern end of the peninsula on no. 71.

Kerry since the Stone Age, with plenty of activities for kids, as well as the Medieval Experience, a series of re-created scenes of mid-fifteenth-century Tralee complete with artificial smells.

Tralee Bay Wetlands Centre

Ballyard Rd, on the southwest side of the centre, just off the Dingle road • Daily: July & Aug 10am–7pm; Sept–June 10am–5pm • €6 • Ⓦ traleebaywetlands.org

Dug out from the marshland where three rivers meet Tralee Bay, this new attraction offers fascinating, guided, nature-watching tours in silent electric boats around one of the largest beds of eelgrass in Europe. Gliding through the rustling reeds here, you're likely to see herons, warblers, curlews, frogs, dragonflies and, in winter, thousands of Brent geese and the rare Whooper swans. There are also hides, a short boardwalk and a 20m observation tower with views of Slieve Mish on the Dingle Peninsula, a pleasant café and a leisure lake with pedalos and rowing boats.

Blennerville Windmill

April, May, Sept & Oct daily 9.30am–5.30pm; June–Aug daily 9am–6pm • €5

About 3km southwest of the centre on the Dingle road is the largest working windmill in Ireland and Britain, the **Blennerville Windmill**, which has its own visitor and crafts centre and where the millers will give you a guided tour of the flour-making process.

Ardfert

May–Sept daily 10am–6pm, last admission 5.15pm • €3; Heritage Card • Ⓦ heritageireland.ie • The bus schedules between Tralee and Ardfert only allow a return trip to the cathedral July & Aug afternoons

Probably the most interesting visit you can make in the Tralee area is to the ruined cathedral at **ARDFERT**, 9km to the northwest, on the site of a monastery that was established by St Brendan the Navigator in the sixth century near his birthplace. The slender tenth-to-thirteenth-century cathedral is the largest pre-Gothic church in Ireland and features fine lancet windows behind the altar. Look out especially for some beautiful Romanesque sandstone carving, in geometric and floral designs, on the west doorway and around the window of the small twelfth-century church nearby.

ARRIVAL AND INFORMATION

TRALEE AND AROUND

By train The train station, which has left-luggage facilities, is just a few minutes' walk northeast of the centre of town.

Destinations Cork (6–9 daily, often with a change at Mallow; 2hr–2hr 30min); Dublin (6–9 daily, most with a change at Mallow; 4hr); Farranfore (7–8 daily; 20min); Killarney (7–8 daily; 40min).

By bus Buses stop at the train station.

Destinations Adare (6–7 daily; 1hr 40min); Ardfert (July & Aug 2 daily, rest of year Mon–Fri 1 daily; 15min);

Castlegregory (2 on Fri; 40min); Cloghane (2 on Fri; 1hr 10min); Cork (hourly; 2hr 15min); Dingle (via the N86; 3–5 daily; 1hr 20min); Killarney (10–16 daily; 40min); Limerick (6–7 daily; 2hr 5min); Listowel (6–8 daily; 30min); Ring of Kerry (July & Aug 1 daily; 6hr 35min, with a break in Sneem).
Tourist office The friendly and helpful tourist office (Mon–Sat 9am–5pm, plus July & Aug Sun 10am–5pm, Ⓣ 066 712 1288), in the Ashe Memorial Hall underneath the Kerry County Museum, has maps of town and details of local traditional sessions.
Bike rental Tralee Gas Supplies, High St, on the west side of town (Ⓣ 066 712 2018).

ACCOMMODATION AND EATING

Denny Street, part of the town centre's roughly clockwise one-way system leading down to the museum and tourist office, shelters a couple of good **accommodation** options among its lovely Georgian buildings that were built from the stones of the old castle.

Finnegan's Denny St Ⓣ 066 712 7610, Ⓦ finnegans.hostel.com (IHO). Well-appointed hostel, with en-suite dorms, doubles and twins, a bar-restaurant in the cellar, a large kitchen, a TV room with an open fire and laundry facilities. Dorms €17, doubles €50

The Grand Denny St Ⓣ 066 712 1499, Ⓦ grandhoteltralee.com. Traditional county-town hotel with lots of dark wood panelling and leather banquettes in its bar and restaurant, though its rooms, most of which are set back from the busy street, have had a colourful, modern makeover. €120

Quinlan's The Mall Ⓣ 066 662 0666. Your best bet for somewhere to eat is this superior chipper and fishmonger, which serves beer-battered fish from their own boats out of Valentia (from €10), seafood chowder and deep-fried squid with homemade sweet chilli jam. Eat in or take away to the nearby town park (down Denny St by the tourist office). Daily noon–10pm.

Seán Og's Bridge St Ⓣ 066 712 8822, Ⓦ sean-ogs.com. Friendly, dimly lit and cosy pub just off The Mall, with two big open fires, bare stone walls and regular traditional music. Mon–Thurs 11am–11.30pm, Fri & Sat 11am–12.30am, Sun noon–11pm.

ENTERTAINMENT

Siamsa Tíre (National Folk Theatre of Ireland) Next to the tourist office Ⓣ 066 712 3055, Ⓦ siamsatire.com. Excellent Irish shows in the summer, as well as a varied international programme of drama, music, dance and art, and literary events during the rest of the year.

Listowel

Up the N69, 27km northeast of Tralee, **LISTOWEL** is a congenial market town in a leafy setting on the north bank of the River Feale. It's best known for its literary associations (see box, opposite). Listowel's most celebrated literary figure is probably the late **John B. Keane**, author of plays such as *The Field*, a dramatization of a shocking murder that took place in this region in the 1950s.

Seanchaí – The Kerry Writers' Museum

March–May & Sept–Nov Mon–Fri 10am–4pm; June–Aug Mon–Sat 9.30am–5.30pm • €5 • Ⓣ 068 22212, Ⓦ kerrywritersmuseum.com

In a Georgian house in the imposing town square stands **Seanchaí**, the **Kerry Writers' Museum**. As well as hosting literary workshops and readings and a good, cheap café, the museum provides tourist information about the area. Its rooms are devoted to local writers such as Keane, Bryan MacMahon and Brendan Kennelly, and have been imaginatively designed, with recorded extracts, to reflect the personality of each. There are some interesting audiovisuals, including Kerryman Eamon Kelly, Ireland's most famous storyteller (or *seanchaí*, pronounced "shanakee").

Listowel Castle

Guided tours late May to Aug Wed–Sun 9.30am–5.30pm; last tour 4.45pm • Free • ⓦ heritageireland.ie

From Seanchaí's reception, informative and entertaining tours depart for formidable **Listowel Castle** next door. When the castle was built in the early or mid-fifteenth century for the Fitzmaurices, the Lords of Kerry, the adjacent River Feale would have been navigable and was probably forded at this point, but from the eighteenth century onwards, in more peaceful times, the building fell into disrepair and was quarried for stone. Nevertheless, two of the four original towers remain, rising to a height of 15m.

The Lartigue Monorail and Museum

Early May to mid-Sept daily 1–4.30pm • €6 • ⓦ lartiguemonorail.com

On the north side of town off John B. Keane Drive, you can take a highly unusual train ride at the **Lartigue Monorail and Museum**. Between 1888 and 1924, this low-cost railway system covered the 15km between Listowel and Ballybunion on the coast, and its steam locomotive and a 500m section of the track have recently been restored for short jaunts.

ACCOMMODATION AND EATING   LISTOWEL

★**Allo's** 41 Church St ☏068 22880, ⓦallosbarbistro-townhouse.com. The pick of Listowel's accommodation, off the northeast corner of the town square, offering three lovely rooms furnished with antiques, including one with a four-poster and a huge bathroom, above an appealing, antique-furnished bar and bistro. Here you can dine on dishes such as pork rack cutlet with sun-dried tomato tapenade (€23), or simpler, cheaper fare at lunch time. Breakfast not served. Bistro Tues & Wed noon–7pm, Thurs–Sat noon–9pm. €70

★**The John B. Keane** William St ☏068 21127. At this cosy, truly characterful pub off the northeast corner of the town square, John B's son Billy keeps the literary flame burning, with poetry readings, history talks, music sessions and informal pub theatre. Mon 7–11.30pm, Tues–Thurs 1–11.30pm, Fri & Sat 1pm–12.30am, Sun 6.30–11pm.

Listowel Arms The Square ☏068 21500, ⓦlistowelarms.com. Charming traditional hotel in a creeper-covered, Georgian mansion, where some of the rooms, which are attractively furnished with antiques, boast views of the river. Good-value three-night packages available. €120

8

Limerick and Clare

QUIN ABBEY

9

Limerick and Clare

Although Limerick lives somewhat in the shadow of its neighbours Kerry and Clare, the county is ideal for activities such as cycling, walking and golf. Some of Ireland's most impressive archaeological sites are to be found here too, alongside cathedrals, priories and abbeys. There is a distinctly pastoral feel to much of Limerick as it sweeps from the rolling farmland of the Golden Vale over to the Shannon estuary. Limerick city, meanwhile, has gone through a sea change in recent years, reinventing itself with a vibrant cultural life.

The superb **Hunt Museum** houses the Republic's richest art and antiquities collection outside Dublin, while outside the city, the enigmatic Neolithic sites of **Lough Gur** and the historic village of **Adare** are reasons to branch out. You'll need your own transport for the former but the city is well served by trains – from Galway and points east and south via Limerick Junction – and by buses from just about anywhere.

Across the broad River Shannon, **County Clare** has a wealth of scenic attractions and is renowned worldwide for its vibrant musical traditions. Its coastline all the way from **Kilkee** to **Fanore** is dotted with golden beaches. Near the village of **Doolin**, famed for its year-long, tourist-driven diet of traditional music, stand the awesome **Cliffs of Moher**, while the county's northern interior is characterized by the craggy, mysterious landscape of **the Burren**, home to numerous prehistoric sites. Its county town, **Ennis**, is an animated place with excellent music pubs and some atmospheric religious remains, further examples of which are dotted around the countryside, such as at **Quin Abbey**, **Dysert O'Dea** and the settlement on **Scattery Island**. The castles and tower houses of Clare's erstwhile dynasties, the O'Briens and MacNamaras, inform the landscape too, notably at **Bunratty** and **Leamaneh**. At Clare's eastern extremity lies the expansive **Lough Derg**, whose waters are best explored by renting your own boat or taking a cruise. Shannon International Airport, in Clare's southeast, lies within easy reach of Ennis, which itself is the county's transport hub. Clare is reasonably well covered by buses in summertime, though the county's north is best accessed from Galway.

Limerick city and around

All manner of routes – road, rail and air – lead to **LIMERICK**, the Republic's third city and a place that has been revitalized in recent years. An imaginative urban improvement project alongside the river, the renovation of **King John's Castle** and the gloriously restored **Milk Market** in the newly designated Market Quarter have all contributed to a feel-good atmosphere. As well as substantial renovation of the Shannon **quays**, regeneration efforts have included the extensive campus at **Plassey**, 3km southeast, which is also the site of the **National Technological Park**. The three colleges here (the university, Institute of Technology and College of Education) certainly help to enliven the city's cultural pulse and nightlife. More than anything, though, Limerick is synonymous with sport – in particular with rugby – and the expansion of Thomond Park Stadium has helped boost the city's status.

The limerick p.314	Musical Tulla and Feakle p.327
Limerick festivals p.315	The West Clare Railway p.330
Ennis festivals and traditional music p.325	The coast to Ballyvaughan p.334

THE CLIFFS OF MOHER

Highlights

❶ **Hunt Museum** This diverse, personal collection of beautiful art and antiquities is Limerick's finest attraction. **See p.313**

❷ **Lough Gur** Atmospheric rural lake surrounded by fine Neolithic remains. **See p.318**

❸ **Quin Abbey** Evocative monastic settlement in an idyllic setting. **See p.322**

❹ **Ennis** The county town offers numerous opportunities to experience Clare's lively traditional music scene. **See p.322**

❺ **Scattery Island** Deserted for more than thirty years, this tranquil island in the middle of the Shannon estuary was once a major ecclesiastical settlement. **See p.329**

❻ **The Cliffs of Moher** Massive sea-battered cliffs, providing exhilarating views of the Atlantic Ocean. **See p.333**

❼ **The Burren** A desolate rock-scape peppered with numerous Neolithic and Iron Age remains. See p.334

HIGHLIGHTS ARE MARKED ON THE MAP ON PP.310–311

9

Brief history

The **Vikings** sailed up the Shannon in about 922 and established a settlement here on a river island, formed by a narrow branch off the main flow that is today called the Abbey River. This port at the lowest fording point of the river was coveted by the **Anglo-Normans** who, in 1197, seized and set about fortifying the town. This involved building high city walls around what became Englishtown, to keep out the

HIGHLIGHTS

1. Hunt Museum
2. Lough Gur
3. Quin Abbey
4. Ennis
5. Scattery Island
6. The Cliffs of Moher
7. The Burren

local Irish, who retreated to a ghetto to the southeast across the Abbey River – Irishtown.

The seventeenth century
In the late seventeenth century, the final bloody scenes of the War of the Kings were played out here. After their defeat at the Boyne in 1690, the Jacobite forces in

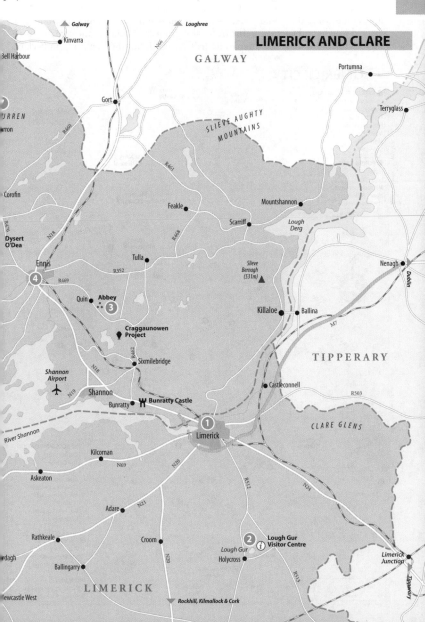

LIMERICK AND CLARE

9

Limerick castle, under the Earl of Tyrconnell and local hero **Patrick Sarsfield**, refused to surrender. Though beset by a vastly superior force, Sarsfield managed to raise the siege by creeping out at night with five hundred men and destroying the Williamite supply train. When William's army came back in 1691, however, the medieval walls of the castle were unable to withstand the artillery bombardment. Tyrconnell having died of a stroke, Sarsfield surrendered on October 3, 1691, on supposedly honourable terms, according to the **Treaty of Limerick**. The Jacobites – some twelve thousand in all, later known as the "Wild Geese" – were permitted to go to France, in whose cause Sarsfield fought and later died. The treaty also promised Catholics the comparative religious toleration they had enjoyed under Charles II, but the English went back on

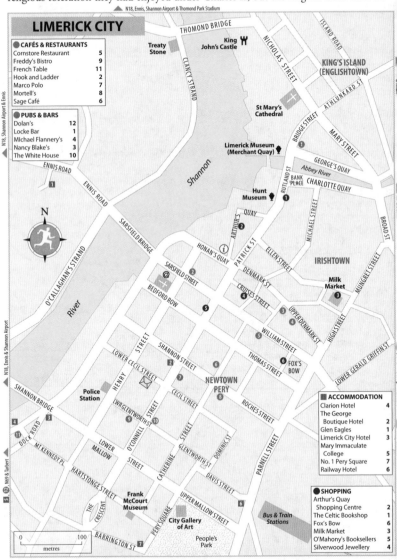

▲ N18, Ennis, Shannon Airport & Thomond Park Stadium

LIMERICK CITY

● CAFÉS & RESTAURANTS
Cornstore Restaurant	5
Freddy's Bistro	9
French Table	11
Hook and Ladder	2
Marco Polo	7
Mortell's	8
Sage Café	6

● PUBS & BARS
Dolan's	12
Locke Bar	1
Michael Flannery's	4
Nancy Blake's	3
The White House	10

■ ACCOMMODATION
Clarion Hotel	4
The George Boutique Hotel	2
Glen Eagles	1
Limerick City Hotel	3
Mary Immaculate College	5
No. 1 Pery Square	7
Railway Hotel	6

● SHOPPING
Arthur's Quay Shopping Centre	2
The Celtic Bookshop	1
Fox's Bow	6
Milk Market	3
O'Mahony's Booksellers	5
Silverwood Jewellery	4

THOMOND BRIDGE
ISLAND ROAD
Treaty Stone
King John's Castle
NICHOLAS STREET
KING'S ISLAND (ENGLISHTOWN)
CLANCY STRAND
ATHLUNKARD ST
St Mary's Cathedral
BRIDGE STREET
MARY STREET
Limerick Museum (Merchant Quay)
GEORGE'S QUAY
Abbey River
BANK PLACE
CHARLOTTE QUAY
RUTLAND ST
ENNIS ROAD
Shannon
Hunt Museum
SARSFIELD BRIDGE
QUAY
MICHAEL STREET
BROAD ST
O'CALLAGHAN'S STRAND
ARTHUR'S
PATRICK ST
ELLEN STREET
IRISHTOWN
HONAN'S QUAY
DENMARK ST
Milk Market
MUNGRET STREET
SARSFIELD STREET
CRUISES STREET
UPPER DENMARK ST
HIGH STREET
LOWER GERALD GRIFFIN ST
BEDFORD ROW
WILLIAM STREET
River
SHANNON STREET
THOMAS STREET
FOX'S BOW
LOWER CECIL STREET
NEWTOWN PERY
CECIL STREET
ROCHES STREET
SHANNON BRIDGE
Police Station
HENRY STREET
LWR GLENTWORTH ST
O'CONNELL STREET
GLENTWORTH ST
DOMINIC ST
PARNELL STREET
DOCK ROAD
MT KENNEDY PL
LOWER MALLOW STREET
CATHERINE STREET
DAVIS STREET
HARTSTONGE STREET
Frank McCourt Museum
UPPER MALLOW STREET
City Gallery of Art
Bus & Train Stations
THE CRESCENT
PERY SQUARE
BARRINGTON ST
People's Park

N

N18, Shannon Airport & Ennis
N18, Ennis & Shannon Airport
N69 & Tarbert

0   100
metres

the deal, and between 1692 and 1704 the Irish Parliament passed the harshly anti-Catholic penal laws.

The eighteenth century onwards

The eighteenth century proved to be far more prosperous for Limerick, which in the 1750s received a grant of £17,000 from the Irish Parliament towards a major redevelopment. Completed in 1840 and named after the local MP, **Newtown Pery** comprised a grid of broad Georgian terraced streets, built well to the south of the cramped, fetid medieval city. In the early **twentieth century**, however, Limerick suffered greatly during the Nationalist struggles, which, in 1919, gave rise to a radical movement that's unique in Irish history: in protest against British military action during the War of Independence, the local Trades Council called a general strike and proclaimed the **Limerick Soviet**. With help from the IRA, they took over the city, controlling food distribution, setting up a citizens' police force and even printing their own money. It lasted only a few weeks, however, collapsing under pressure from the Catholic bishop. In 1921, both Limerick's mayor, George Clancy, and the former mayor, Mícheál O'Callaghan, were murdered by the Royal Irish Constabulary. One of the effects of the Troubles was that the rich were persuaded to move out of the city: many of their Georgian houses in Newtown Pery became tenements and some remain dilapidated to this day. The traditional distinctions between Englishtown – focused on the castle and now signposted as King's Island – Irishtown and Newtown Pery no longer matter very much, as there's little of the medieval city left in the first two areas, while Newtown Pery's grid is scattered with modern developments.

Hunt Museum

The Custom House, Rutland Street • Mon–Sat 10am–5pm, Sun 2–5pm • €5 • ☎ 061 312833, ⓦ huntmuseum.com

The fascinating displays in the **Hunt Museum**, dating from the Stone Age to modern times, are the best place to start a tour of the city. Over the course of the twentieth century, John and Gertrude Hunt gathered together this diverse collection of art and antiquities, especially known for its religious works, and bequeathed it to the people of Ireland. You'll get the best idea of the spirit of the place in the **Epilogue Room**, which juxtaposes pieces of wildly different origins, such as an eighteenth-century Chinese porcelain cockerel and an English stone rabbit from the fifteenth century.

There are regular guided tours every day (phone for details) and a light-filled basement café. Particular pieces to look out for include the beautiful, early ninth-century **Antrim Cross**, one of the finest examples of early Christian metalwork from Ireland. Made of bronze decorated with enamel in geometric and animal designs, it was discovered by chance in the River Bann in the nineteenth century. Keep an eye out also for the **Beverley Crozier**, a piece of walrus ivory intricately carved with miracles of healing, dating from the eleventh century. Other highlights include works by Irish artists William Orpen, Jack B. Yeats and Roderic O'Connor, and a room devoted to depictions of the Crucifixion.

St Mary's Cathedral

Bridge Street • Summer Mon–Sat 9am–4.30pm, except during services; winter Mon–Fri 9am–4.30pm, Sat 9am–1pm, except during services • Suggested donation €3 • ⓦ cathedral.limerick.anglican.org

Just across the river from the Hunt Museum, the Church of Ireland **St Mary's Cathedral** boasts a fine, almost homely interior of rough stone walls, brightly coloured stained glass and beautiful barrel-vaulted ceilings. It was founded on the site of the Viking *thingmote* or meeting place in 1168 – from which time dates the Romanesque west doorway, carved with monstrous heads, stylized flowers and chevrons – but has gained so many accretions over the centuries that it's now as broad as it is long, with an intriguingly confused layout.

9

The cathedral's highlight is its set of dark-oak **misericords** in the Jebb Chapel, the only example left in Ireland. Dating from the late fifteenth century, they're ornately carved with symbols of good and evil, including a delicate, sinuous swan, cockatrices, griffins and all sorts of other mythical monsters. Look out also for the limestone **reredos** behind the main altar, which was carved in Celtic Revival style by Michael Pearse, father of the Irish patriot, Pádraig, and the nearby tomb of the cathedral's founder, King Donal Mór O'Brien of Munster, decorated with three heraldic lions and a Celtic cross. The cathedral stages lunch-time **music recitals** every Wednesday (1.10pm) during the summer.

Limerick Museum

Istabraq Hall, Civic Buildings, Merchant's Quay • Mon–Fri 10am–1pm & 2–5pm • Free • ☎ 061 417826, ⓦ limerick.ie

On the quayside, the **Limerick Museum** (also known as the **Jim Kemmy Municipal Museum**, after a former Mayor and proud Limerick man) is nothing if not varied, stuffed with grandfather clocks, medals and an old-fashioned diving suit, as well as examples of Limerick silver and lace, prehistoric finds and relics of the Limerick Soviet (see p.313), including currency notes and *The Bottom Dog*, a Labour news-sheet of the time. If you want to see the infamous **treaty stone** on which the surrender terms of the 1691 siege were signed (see p.312), cross Thomond Bridge to the west bank, where the stone was put on a 2m-high pedestal facing the castle in 1865.

King John's Castle

King's Island • Daily 9.30am–5.30pm; last admission 1hr 30min before closing • €10; Heritage Island • ☎ 061 370500, ⓦ shannonheritage.com

The dramatically sited Anglo-Norman **King John's Castle** is the city's most eye-catching building – especially when viewed from the banks of the Shannon. An imposing five-sided fortification inaugurated by the king himself in 1210, it had no keep and no tower at its southeast corner facing Englishtown, until a rectangular artillery bastion was added at the beginning of the troubled seventeenth century. In 2013 a new €5m **visitor centre** facilitated the castle's twenty-first-century rebirth, bringing fresh life into the building with dazzling new displays. Audiovisuals focus on early Gaelic society; the Normans, whose arrival in 1169 made Limerick a Royal city; the change and conflict during the sixteenth-century Reformation; the three horrendous sieges the castle suffered in 1642, 1651 and 1690–91; and the history of the castle's excavation. The sights, smells and sounds of the times are graphically captured in the galleries.

Frank McCourt Museum

Hartstonge Street • Mon–Fri 11am–4.30pm, Sat & Sun 2–4pm • €3 • ☎ 061 319710, ⓦ frankmccourtmuseum.com

The remarkable life of the Pulitzer Prize-winning author **Frank McCourt** is on display in his old school at Leamy House. Although born in Brooklyn, McCourt was educated in

---

THE LIMERICK

Limericks became common in Britain in the nineteenth century, popularized by Edward Lear, but their origin is shrouded in the mists of time. In Limerick city you'll find one on the walls of the city's oldest pub, the *White House* (see p.317):

The limerick is furtive and mean;
You must keep her in close quarantine,
Or she sneaks up to the slums
And promptly becomes
Disorderly, drunk and obscene.

Limerick and wrote the bestselling *Angela's Ashes* about his childhood there. The museum includes a mock-up of his schoolroom, complete with maps, blackboard and inkwells, and an upstairs re-creation of the McCourt family's flat. After your visit you might join one of the **walking tours** (arranged through the tourist office or via ⓦlimerickwalkingtours.com) that take in places from the book, including the post office where he worked as a telegraph boy, *South's* bar where he had his first pint, and the beautiful Pery Square, Limerick's finest example of late Georgian architecture.

Limerick City Gallery of Art

Carnegie Building, Pery Square • Mon, Wed & Fri 10am–5.30pm, Tues 11am–5.30pm, Thurs 10am–8.30pm, Sat 10am–5pm, Sun noon–5pm • Free • ☏ 061 310633, ⓦ gallery.limerick.ie

By the entrance to the People's Park stands the **Limerick City Gallery of Art**. Remodelled in 2012 with renovated galleries, the building is a hybrid of the old and new. Displayed on a rotating basis, the permanent collection of eighteenth- to twenty-first-century paintings and drawings by artists such as Sean Keating, Paul Henry and Jack Butler Yeats will appeal to aficionados of Irish art, but best of all is the gallery's exciting programme of **contemporary exhibitions** by Irish and international artists. A sculpture, *The Siege of Limerick*, by the renowned New York-based artist Brian O'Doherty, was installed to mark the reopening.

Thomond Park Stadium and Museum

Old Cratloe Road • Mon–Fri 10am–5pm; stadium and museum tours 11am, 2pm, 3.30pm • €10 • ☏ 061 421100, ⓦ thomondpark.ie

A couple of kilometres northwest of the city centre, **Thomond Park Stadium** is home to the Munster rugby team – a huge presence in this part of the world – and also stages rock concerts following a redevelopment which doubled its capacity to 26,500. **Tours** promise an intimate account of the Munster players' experience on match day, taking in the dressing room, dugouts and the pitch itself. Also included is a short film recounting the team's history and a visit to the **museum**, which features club memorabilia as well as footage from the "match of all matches" when Munster beat the mighty All Blacks 12-0 in 1978.

ARRIVAL AND DEPARTURE | LIMERICK CITY

By plane Limerick is the nearest city to Shannon International Airport (☏ 061 712000, ⓦ shannonairport.com), which serves direct flights from North America, the UK and several other European countries, as well as Irish internal services. The airport has good bus links with Limerick and Ennis, as well as with Cork, Dublin, Galway and Killarney. For timetables consult Bus Éireann (☏ 061 313333 or ☏ 065 682 4177, ⓦ buseireann.ie). A taxi to either Limerick or Ennis will cost around €35; there's a taxi desk (daily 6am–midnight, ☏ 061 471538) in the arrivals

---

LIMERICK FESTIVALS

The city lays on a compelling menu of **festivals** throughout the year. One highlight is **EVA** (ⓦ eva.ie), Ireland's pre-eminent biennial exhibition of contemporary art. From mid-March to late May, works by Irish and foreign artists, as selected by a leading international curator, are installed at galleries and around the cityscape. In late May, the **Limerick International Music Festival** (☏ 061 202620, ⓦ irishchamberorchestra.com) is a four-day showcase for the Irish Chamber Orchestra and prestigious guest artists. Also in May, **Riverfest** is one of Ireland's biggest festivals, with fireworks, fashion shows and street performances. In June and early July, **Blas** (ⓦ blas.ie), a highly regarded two-week summer school of traditional music and dance, takes place at the Irish World of Academy of Music and Dance, Limerick University, with associated concerts and sessions around the city. An international poetry festival, **Cuisle** (☏ 061 407421, ⓦ limerick.ie), encompassing readings, open-mike sessions and workshops, takes place in mid-October.

9

hall. Also here is a tourist office (daily 7am–5.30pm, ☎ 061 712000; accommodation booking €5), a bank (Mon 10am–5pm, Tues, Thurs & Fri 10am–4pm, Wed 10.30am–4pm), a bureau de change (daily 6am–10pm), ATMs and several car-rental outlets.

By train The train station (☎ 061 315555) is on Parnell Street.

Destinations Athenry (4–5 daily; 1hr 40min); Cork (7–12 daily, with a change at Limerick Junction; 2hr); Dublin Heuston (hourly, often with a change at Limerick Junction; 2hr 20min–2hr 40min); Ennis (8–10 daily; 40min); Waterford (Mon–Sat 3 daily, with a change at Limerick Junction; 2hr 25min–3hr 10min).

By bus The bus station (☎ 061 315555) is on Parnell Street, adjacent to the train station.

Destinations Adare (hourly; 20min); Athlone (2–4 daily 2hr 10min); Birr (2–4 daily; 1hr 15min); Bunratty (hourly 20min); Cliffs of Moher (2–3 daily; 1hr 50min); Cork (hourly; 1hr 50min); Doolin (2–3 daily; 2hr 15min); Dublin (hourly; 3hr 40min); Ennis (hourly; 1hr); Galway (hourly 2hr 20min); Killaloe (Mon–Sat 4–5 daily; 40–55min) Killarney (6 daily; 2hr); Lisdoonvarna (2–3 daily; 2hr) Listowel (8–9 daily; 1hr 25min); Shannon Airport (Mon–Sat frequent service, Sun at least hourly; 30–55min); Tralee (8–9 daily; 2hr); Tulla (Wed 1 at 5.30pm; 55min); Waterford (6–8 daily; 2hr 30min).

INFORMATION AND TOURS

Tourist information Arthur's Quay (July & Aug Mon–Sat 9am–5.30pm, Sun noon–5pm; Sept–June Mon–Sat 9am–5pm; ☎ 061 317522, ⓦ discoverireland.ie). Dispenses a useful guide-map of the city and county.

Tours A hop-on-hop-off city bus tour with nine pick-up locations is run by Red Viking Tours (April–Oct 7 daily; €12; ☎ 061 394033, ⓦ redvikingtours.com), operating from

Arthur's Quay Park. Barratt Tours (☎ 061 333100 ⓦ www.4tours.biz) run coaches daily to the Burren and Cliffs of Moher (€27) as well as to further-flung destinations such as Cork and Blarney at weekends. Railtours (☎ 01 856 0045, ⓦ railtoursireland.com) take in the Cliffs of Moher and Bunratty Castle Mon–Sat.

ACCOMMODATION

Clarion Hotel Steamboat Quay ☎ 061 444100, ⓦ clarionhotellimerick.com. A striking addition to the Limerick cityscape, this oval hotel, the tallest in Ireland, juts out over the river with spectacular views. Expect stylish, contemporary rooms, a health and leisure club with swimming pool overlooking the river, and good food, either European in the restaurant or Thai and Malaysian in the bar. **€120**

The George Boutique Hotel O'Connell St ☎ 061 460400, ⓦ thegeorgeboutiquehotel.com. Boutique hotel on the upper floors above the main street, offering well-equipped rooms in a dark wood and red or green contemporary style. Free overnight parking. **€159**

Glen Eagles 12 Vereker Gardens ☎ 061 455521, ⓔ gleneaglesbandb@eircom.net. The closest B&B to the city centre on a peaceful cul-de-sac off the N18 Ennis road. All rooms are en suite with TVs. Closed Christmas and New Year. **€60**

Limerick City Hotel Lower Mallow St ☎ 061 207000, ⓦ limerickcityhotel.ie. No-frills hotel with over 140

comfortable rooms. Very handy for the centre, but right or one of Limerick's busiest junctions, so unless you're eager for a view of the river, ask for a room at the back. **€75**

Mary Immaculate College Courtbrack, Tarbert Rd ☎ 061 302500, ⓦ courtbrackaccom.com. During summer the university's Mary Immaculate College opens up its student accommodation to visitors. A light breakfast is included in the room price. May–Aug. Singles **€26**, twins **€52**

★**No 1 Pery Square** 1 Pery Square ☎ 061 402402 ⓦ oneperysquare.com. Beautifully designed boutique hotel occupying a restored Georgian town house next to People's Park. Some rooms reflect the building's period origins, featuring sash windows and individually designed beds, while others have a spruce contemporary finesse There's a spa too and a restaurant offering everything from brunch to gourmet tasting nights. **€165**

Railway Hotel Parnell St ☎ 061 413653 ⓦ railwayhotel.ie. A brightly painted, traditional hotel opposite the train station, offering standard and en-suite accommodation with a family-run atmosphere. **€65**

EATING AND DRINKING

CAFÉS AND RESTAURANTS

Cornstore Restaurant Thomas St ☎ 061 609000, ⓦ cornstorerrelimerick.com. Covering three floors and incorporating a wine and cocktail bar, the lively *Cornstore* specializes in seafood and dry-aged steaks with ingredients from organic and artisan suppliers. Set-price lunch and dinner menus (€14.95/€28.95) and Sunday brunch (€19.95 for two courses). Lunch daily noon–4pm; dinner

Mon–Wed 5–9.30pm, Thurs 5–10pm, Fri & Sat 5–10.30pm, Sun 5–9pm.

★**Freddy's Bistro** Theatre Lane ☎ 061 418749 ⓦ freddysbistro.com. A cosy hideaway with a rustic feel natural stone walls and a cosmopolitan menu, with dishes such as braised lamb shank, pan-fried hake and pork belly The early evening menu offers two courses for €20. Tues–Sat 6–10pm.

French Table Steamboat Quay ☎061 609274, ⓦfrenchtable.ie. Wonderful French food featuring Languedoc- and Dordogne-style classics such as escargots, garlic or Toulouse sausage with an imaginative Irish twist. Duck, lamb, hake and sirloin are menu standards. Expect to pay at least €30 for two courses. Lunch Tues–Fri noon–4pm; dinner Tues–Sun 6–10pm.

Hook and Ladder 7 Sarsfield St ☎061 413778, ⓦhookandladder.ie. This family-run newcomer, housed in a former bank, is open for breakfast, lunch and early evening meals. Sandwiches, bagels and wraps as well as Mediterranean salads, chowder and quiche are all available. You can also indulge in home-baked cakes, pastries and breads, speciality teas, premium coffees and a wide wine selection. The average main course price is €11. Mon–Sat 8am–7pm, Sun 9am–6pm.

Marco Polo O'Connell St ☎061 412888, ⓦmarcopolo.ie. This buzzy restaurant's two-course lunch is excellent value at €9.95 and runs until 5pm. For dinner, four courses start from around €25 and may include goat's cheese crostini, duck confit or trio of seafood. Mon–Wed & Sun 12.30–9pm, Thurs–Sat 12.30–10pm.

Mortell's 49 Roches St ☎061 415457, ⓦmortellcatering.com. Established in the 1950s, this appealing, family-run business – an informal combination of seafood restaurant and deli – is a Limerick institution. Irish fish fresh off the boats is cooked to order by your chosen method with main courses averaging €12. Mon–Sat 8.30am–4pm.

Sage Café 67 Catherine St ☎061 409458, ⓦthesagecafe.com. Along the coffee-shop-jammed shopping artery of Catherine Street, this seductive and bright café, decorated in off-whites and light woods, stands out for its revitalizing lunches: Caesar salads, soups, delicious sandwiches on homemade brown bread and gluten-free choices are all on offer. Mon–Sat 9am–5pm.

PUBS

Dolan's Dock Rd ☎061 314483, ⓦdolans.ie. Top dog for live music, Dolan's features traditional tunes in the bar every night, and everything from jazz and singer-songwriters to indie and tribute bands – plus comedy nights – in its two gig venues, The Warehouse and Upstairs. Snow Patrol, Franz Ferdinand and Sharon Shannon have all performed here. Mon–Thurs 5–11.30pm, Fri 5pm–1.30am, Sat 9am–1.30am, Sun 10am–11pm.

Locke Bar 3 George's Quay ☎061 413733, ⓦlockebar.com. Large, congenial gastropub offering traditional music every night. With tables out the front overlooking the Abbey River, it's a great spot on a sunny day. Mon–Wed 10am–11.30pm, Thurs 10am–midnight, Fri 10am–12.30am, Sat noon–1am, Sun 11am–11pm.

Michael Flannery's 17 Upper Denmark St ☎061 436677, ⓦflannerysbar.ie. Whiskey connoisseurs love this authentic pub with a pedigree stretching back to 1898. It claims to have over one hundred different types of Irish whiskey and once bottled its own Jameson: a "Whiskey Bible" complete with tasting notes lists them all. If you're feeling peckish, ask for a farmhouse bread sandwich to help soak up the *uisce beatha* (water of life). Mon–Wed 10am–11.30pm, Thurs–Sat 10am–1am, Sun noon–11.30pm.

Nancy Blake's 19 Upper Denmark St ☎061 416443. Welcoming, time-burnished watering hole with bare wooden floors covered in sawdust, home to traditional music Sun–Wed. Through the back, a large, covered and heated courtyard and a modern bar hosts a DJ on Fri. Mon & Tues 10.30am–11.30pm, Wed–Sun 10.30am–2.30am.

★**The White House** 52 O'Connell St ☎061 412377, ⓦwhitehousebarlimerick.com. Established in 1812 and furnished in dark wood, this is Limerick's finest old pub, with traditional music on Sun featuring acoustic singers and a well-attended poetry session on Wed. The Irish president himself, Michael D. Higgins, a Limerick man and published poet, has recited his poetry here. Mon–Wed 10am–11.30pm, Thurs 10am–midnight, Fri 10am–12.30am, Sat noon–1am, Sun noon–11.30pm.

ENTERTAINMENT

For details of all arts events, pick up a copy of the *Limerick Events Guide* (*LEG*), a free **monthly listings magazine** available at the tourist office and in cafés and bars. Although many poetry, music and comedy performances take place in pubs, Limerick has its share of quality theatre and concert venues.

Lime Tree Theatre Mary Immaculate College, Courtbrack Ave ☎061 774774, ⓦlimetreetheatre.ie. This 500-seater hosts drama, music and children's shows. Two excellent theatrical touring companies – the Abbey from Dublin and the Druid from Galway – stage shows here. The box office is open Tues–Sat 1–5pm, and 1–8pm on performance days.

University Concert Hall Foundation Building, University of Limerick, Castletroy ☎061 331549, ⓦuch.ie. Audiences have enjoyed large-scale operas including *Aida*, *Carmen* and *Madame Butterfly* at the UCH. Sir James Galway, Christy Moore and Billy Connolly have all performed here, and the Irish Chamber Orchestra holds an annual programme of events.

9

SHOPPING

Limerick's deep-rooted connections with the past are reflected in the many **traditional shop fronts** and you will stumble across victuallers, saddlers and barbers. Don't miss **Fox's Bow**, a funky alleyway of craft, jewellery and gift shops between Thomas and William streets. For pharmacies, branches of **O'Sullivan's** are on O'Connell St (Mon–Fri 9am–6pm; ☎ 061 405509, ⓦ osullivanspharmacy.com) and round the corner on Sarsfield St (Mon–Fri 9am–11pm).

Arthur's Quay Shopping Centre Patrick St ☎ 061 412462, ⓦ arthursquay-shopping.com. A bright mall with plenty of Irish and British chain stores and designer names. Mon–Sat 8am–10pm, Sun 10am–8pm.

The Celtic Bookshop 2 Rutland St ☎ 061 401155. A place to lose yourself for an hour or so on a quest for rare or out-of-print Irish classics. Mon–Sat 11am–4.30pm.

Milk Market Cornmarket Row ☎ 061 214782, ⓦ milkmarketlimerick.ie. Saturday morning is the best time to enjoy this bustling food market, held in a stone building that was once a corn market and featuring fresh farm produce from all over Munster. Under its new canopy you'll find a superb selection of stalls offering farmhouse cheeses, organic sausages, spelt breads, fruit and vegetables, chutneys, jams and artisan chocolates.

You can also snack on soup, crunchy salads, inventive sandwiches, wraps and crepes, and freshly brewed tea and coffee. Fri & Sun 11am–3pm, Sat 8am–3pm.

O'Mahony's Booksellers 120 O'Connell St ☎ 061 418155, ⓦ omahonys.ie. Long-established independent bookshop, particularly strong on Irish fiction and non-fiction, plus local heritage and maps. Mon–Sat 9am–6pm, Sun 1–5.30pm.

Silverwood Jewellery 32 Cruises St ☎ 061 312348 ⓦ silverwoodjewellery.com. Artfully crafted bespoke jewellery, ranging from Celtic to abstract pieces, are on sale in this eye-catching store. Brooches, necklaces, pendants and rings sit alongside gold and silver, freshwater pearls and semi-precious stones. Most pieces come with an Irish hallmarked silver stamp of quality. Mon–Sat 9.30am–5.30pm.

Lough Gur

Lough Gur Heritage Centre, Lough Gur, Bruff • March–Sept Mon–Fri 10am–5pm, Sat & Sun noon–6pm; Oct–Feb Mon–Fri 10am–4pm, Sat & Sun noon–5pm; last admission 30min before closing • €5 • ☎ 061 385386, ⓦ loughgur.com • The only bus from Limerick to Lough Gur is the 10.30am (Mon–Sat) Kilmallock service – ask for Holycross – with returns at 12.30pm and 4.50pm; a taxi from Limerick will cost €20 one-way

Set in a serenely peaceful valley surrounded by hills, 20km south of Limerick city on the R512 towards Kilmallock, stands one of Ireland's most astonishing and atmospheric places. A cluster of grassy limestone hills springs unexpectedly from the plain, sheltering in their midst **Lough Gur**, the site of dozens of largely prehistoric monuments. Their importance lies in the fact that many of them are not ceremonial sites but stone dwelling places, dating from around 3000 BC onwards, which have furnished archaeologists with most of their knowledge of the way of life in Neolithic Ireland. That's not to say that this curious landscape did not have a ritual aspect, as it was also revered as the territory of the sun goddess, Áine, and accrued a powerful mythical reputation, for example as the location of some of Fionn Mac Cumhaill's adventures in the *Ulster Cycle*. Before it was partly drained in the nineteenth century, the lake (now C-shaped) formed an approximate square, with a 9km shoreline around a large triangular island, **Knockadoon**. The drainage, which left a marsh on the eastern side of the island and lowered the lake's level by 3m, revealed hoards of prehistoric items, including gold and bronze spearheads, a bronze shield, swords and stone and bronze axes.

Heritage Centre

Tours (2hr 30min; €50 for a minimum of two people, with admission to site included) must be booked one day in advance

Following an extensive makeover in 2013, the **Heritage Centre** features new exhibits and a multimedia exhibition that bring alive 6000 years of history through touch screens, listening posts and audiovisual presentations. For children there is a dressing-up corner, an interactive archaeological dig model and a Neolithic reconstruction. The centre also provides a pamphlet detailing trails around Lough Gur (also downloadable from the website) – you can explore on your own or join a guided tour.

The stone circle

The first site you'll come to, on the R512 to the west of the lake at Holycross, is the largest and finest **stone circle** in Ireland. Now set in a grassy glade surrounded by majestic trees, it consists of 113 large stones propped upright in sockets, around an artificial floor of gravelly earth 70cm above the original ground level. Built around 2100 BC, the circle is associated with **Crom Dubh**, the harvest god. The entrance to the northeast is aligned towards sunrise around May 21 before the summer solstice and, correspondingly, around July 22 as the sun travels southwards on the horizon after the summer solstice. Archaeologists believe that while such dates cannot now be interpreted in a calendrical sense, it is probable that people convened in large numbers inside and around the circle on these and other dates throughout the year.

Gallery grave

About 1km south of the stone circle, the access road to Lough Gur heads east off the R512 around the south shore. Just over 1km in, on the south side of the road, you'll see the so-called Giant's Grave, a wedge-shaped **gallery grave** dating from about 2600 BC, where the remains of eight adults and four children were discovered. It's yet another ancient Irish site where Diarmuid and Gráinne are meant to have lain together on their flight from Fionn Mac Cumhaill, though it has added significance as Gráinne is the alter ego of Áine, the sun goddess.

Knockadoon

Causeways lead across from near the visitor centre and the Giant's Grave to the island of **Knockadoon**, which is fun to explore though parts are covered in dense woodland. Visible from the visitor centre at the northeast corner of the island is **Bourchier's Castle**, a privately owned, fifteenth-century tower house, while the overgrown remains of the thirteenth-century **Black Castle** face the Giant's Grave from the southern shore. Working west from here, you'll see traces of huts and ring forts on the grassy slopes, and around on the northwest-facing shore of the island, a limestone seat on a small, grassy mound known as the **Housekeeper's Chair**. This was held to be the birth-chair of Áine, from which she turned green corn to gold, for Crom Dubh to carry off at harvest time. A little further on, near the northernmost point of the island, is a **cave** said to be the entrance to Tír na nÓg, the land of eternal youth.

Adare

With its broad main street lined with thatched cottages and colourful doors, **ADARE** has long been a much-admired stopping place for tourists and draws in coach parties from far afield. Its chocolate-box quaintness can be too sickly for some, however, and, sited some 15km southwest of Limerick on the N21 towards Kerry, it is also marred by its location on a major national road. As the **Heritage Centre** reveals, it was made picturesque by design: the earls of Dunraven, landlords of Adare Manor, beautified their estate village (according to the contemporary fashion for pastoral romanticism) with ornamental thatched cottages in the early nineteenth century, and with Arts and Crafts-style houses in the early twentieth century. Set beside a prim town **park** on the south bank of the River Maigue, Adare's appeal is enhanced by some impressive remnants, mostly ecclesiastical, of its medieval heyday.

Heritage Centre and castle

Main St • April–Sept daily 9am–6pm; Oct–March daily 10am–5pm • Free; Heritage Island • ☏ 061 396425, ⓦ adareheritagecentre.ie • **tours** June–Sept daily • €6 • **Walking tours of village** June–Sept daily • €4

The best place to start is the **Heritage Centre**, centrally located opposite the park on Main Street, which houses the tourist information office (see p.316) and sells castle admission tickets. The centre also houses a free exhibition and there's a craft and gift

9

shop too, plus a restaurant with outdoor terrace seating. From June to September, the restored, early thirteenth-century **Desmond Castle**, on the north side of the Maigue River bridge, can be visited on hour-long guided tours which set off by bus from the centre (departure times vary so check with the reception desk). During this period there are also daily guided walking tours of the village.

The Trinitarian Abbey and Augustinian Friary

The Catholic parish church next door to the Heritage Centre, a trim, multi-aisled affair with an imposing, oak-beamed roof, was part of the **Trinitarian Abbey** until the mid-nineteenth century. Founded around 1230 with an attached hospital, it was the only house of the Order of the Holy Trinity in Ireland. Down an alley to one side is a circular stone tower with a conical roof, where the monks kept pigeons – not as a hobby, but for the refectory table. Five minutes' walk away, on the south side of the Maigue bridge, stands the **Augustinian Friary**, which is now an Anglican parish church and school. Founded in 1315, it has an attractive, fifteenth-century cloister, carefully restored by the Dunravens in the nineteenth century then spoiled by the insertion of their brutal family mausoleum.

ARRIVAL AND INFORMATION

By bus Limerick to Adare (hourly; 20min)
Tourist information Main St (April–Sept daily 9am–6pm; Oct–March daily 10am–5pm; ☏ 061 396425,

ⓦ adare.heritagecentre.ie). Based in the Heritage Centre the office supplies a variety of maps and literature covering Limerick county and city.

ACCOMMODATION

Adare Camping and Caravan Park 4km south of Adare off the R519 Ballingarry road ☏ 061 395376, ⓦ adarecamping.com. This well-equipped site is handy for exploration of the village and countryside. Mid-March to Sept. Tent pitch **€20**

Adare Manor Hotel ☏ 061 605200, ⓦ adaremanor .com. The Dunravens' many-turreted Gothic pile of 1832, set in huge grounds on the east side of the main street, is now a luxurious hotel with a chandeliered drawing room that looks out over a golf course; there's also a swimming pool and spa. Substantial savings with internet booking. **€500**

Berkeley Lodge Station Rd ☏ 061 396857, ⓦ adare .org. There are dozens of B&Bs in and around Adare, including this neat and homely pick. It is a comfy and quiet base, and after a high-quality breakfast you can walk it off

with a short stroll into the town centre. **€85**

Clonunion House Limerick Rd ☏ 061 396657 ⓦ clonunionhouse.com. A 200-year-old farmhouse with large, antique-furnished rooms, set in spacious grounds which include a horse cemetery. April–Oct. **€80**

★**Fitzgerald's Woodlands House Hotel & Spa** ☏ 061 605100, ⓦ woodlands-hotel.ie. A gym, pool and spa are part of the deal at this comfortable and welcoming family-owned hotel, 2km from the centre in a secluded setting off the Limerick road. Many of the sizeable rooms are furnished with comfy settees, and the bistro, *Timmy Macs*, has a delightful vintage feel with Victorian-style Shannonbridge pottery. The guaranteed Irish menu features beef from the owners' very own cattle herd. Good value midweek breaks are available. **€105**

EATING AND DRINKING

1826 Adare Main St ☏ 061 396004 ⓦ 1826adare.ie. The focus of this chic new restaurant, set in a delightful row of thatched cottages, is on keenly priced casual dining. Their signature dish is the free-range pork tasting plate of loin belly cheek and black pudding, but you may also find blackboard specials such as sole and braised meats. Wed–Fri 5.30–9.30pm, Sat 6–10pm, Sun 3–10pm.

Aunty Lena's Irish Pub Main St ☏ 061 396114, ⓦ auntylenas.com. The extensive bar menu (daily noon–9pm) offers salads, sandwiches, wraps and panini, plus more substantial grub such as bangers and mash and burgers (mains around €12). In summer, traditional music is played on Fri and audience participation is encouraged.

Daily noon–11.30pm.

The Good Room Café Main St ☏ 061 396218. A calming bistro café with outdoor seating, serving breakfast, lunches and early evening meals. Has a large selection of teas including detox and caffeine-free varieties, plus juices smoothies and healthy options. Mon–Wed 8.30am–5.30pm, Thurs–Sat 8.30am–7.30pm, Sun 10am–5.30pm.

★**The Mustard Seed** Ballingarry, 8km south of Adare on the R519 ☏ 069 68508, ⓦ mustardseed.ie. Set in *Echo Lodge*, a country residence, this is one of the country's foremost restaurants, the kitchen's inspired modern Irish cuisine drawing from the produce of its own organic garden. The four-course "classic" dinner is €60; main courses include rib-eye of beef, monkfish and guinea fowl. A cheaper dining option is the twilight menu (Mon–Fri & Sun 6.45–7.45pm) at €45, featuring fish, lamb or organic shitake mushrooms. Dinner daily 7.15–9.30pm; closed first two weeks of Feb.

Wild Geese Restaurant Rose Cottage, Main St ☎061 396451, ⓦthewild-geese.com. Picture-postcard cottage where the owners serve well-judged, French-influenced cuisine such as salmon on a bed of mangetout and asparagus with deep-fried aubergine, all in a relaxed setting. Quality doesn't come cheap – the early bird is €30 for two courses, €37 for three. Tues–Sat 6.30–9.30pm, Sun 12.30–3pm.

Kilmallock

To escape the crowds and tour coaches of Adare, head south along the N20 and then east on the R515 to **KILMALLOCK**. On the face of it a workaday market town, Kilmallock's position at the centre of Ireland's political development for five centuries has made it something of a heritage hub. Wander around and you'll encounter many vestiges of its medieval history, including the town walls, early church sites, a priory and castle standing foursquare, and the formidable **Blossom Gate**, the only one surviving of five sixteenth-century town gates. Kilmallock makes a superb base from which to explore the Ballyhoura Mountains, noted for mountain biking, cycle loops and walking trails, and you can also sample part of the **Ballyhoura Way**, a waymarked trail running through southeast Limerick and on to Tipperary.

ARRIVAL AND INFORMATION

KILMALLOCK

By bus Limerick to Kilmallock (3 daily; 40min).

Tourist information County Council Office on Millmount off Lord Edward St (daily 9am–1pm; ☎063 98019, ⓦkilmallock.ie and ⓦvisitballyhoura.com). Pick up a town map which will take you on a self-guided tour of the main historic sites. Information is also available on mountain-biking trails and looped cycle routes of the area and the Ballyhoura Way.

ACCOMMODATION AND EATING

Deebert House Hotel ☎063 31200, ⓦdeeberthouse hotel.com. This delightful family-run hotel on the site of an historic mill at the edge of town is a good base for exploring the built heritage and surrounding countryside. The 20 en-suite rooms are spacious and comfortable and the *Cloister* restaurant is open daily for lunch and dinner with locally sourced produce such as sausages, steak and chicken. Traditional music nights are held on Tues in summer and special packages are available for cyclists and walkers. **€75**

Southeast Clare

Heading north from Limerick to Galway along the busy N18, it's easy to miss some of the attractions of the county's nether region. Consisting largely of flat farmland, its lanes, ideal for cycling, lead to several sites of historic interest. The most southerly is the impressive **Bunratty Castle**, while a short hop further north lies the imaginative **Craggaunowen Project**, with its re-creations of dwellings from bygone times, and idyllically set monastic site of **Quin Abbey**.

Bunratty Castle and folk park

Daily 9.30am–5.30pm; June–Aug Sat & Sun open till 6pm; last admission to castle 4pm and to folk park 4.15pm • €15; Heritage Island • ☎061 711200, ⓦshannonheritage.com • Buses: Ennis (hourly; 35min); Limerick (hourly; 20min) • **Banquets** daily subject to demand 5.30pm & 8.45pm • €50

Some 12km west of Limerick, bypassed by the main N18 Ennis road, lies the village of Bunratty whose **castle** and **folk park** form one of Ireland's most popular attractions. A castle was first built here in 1277 during the Anglo-Normans' brief occupation of southeast Clare, though the present version dates back to the mid-fifteenth century and was constructed for the MacNamaras, a branch of the O'Brien clan. Majestically

9

restored in the 1950s, its keep contains an impressive array of artwork and furniture, mostly dating from the fifteenth and sixteenth centuries. In the evenings, **"medieval" banquets** are staged here, their entertainment consisting of a somewhat twee form of traditional dance, music and song. The expansive castle grounds host the **folk park**, a re-creation of a nineteenth-century village, replete with post office, shops, a church and a pub, all populated by actors in contemporary dress.

ACCOMMODATION AND EATING

BUNRATT

Bunratty Castle Hotel ☎ 061 478700, ⓦ bunrattycastlehotel.com. In the village centre, this Georgian hotel has elegant accommodation in period-furnished rooms, as well as fine meals and its own spa. Special package rates are available for two nights' accommodation and dinner at the "Bunratty Earl's Banquet" in the castle. **€124**

Bunratty Villa ☎ 061 369241, ⓦ bunrattyvilla.com. A comfortable modern house a short stroll from the castle. The buffet breakfasts of full Irish or pancakes with maple syrup will sustain you for most of the day. March–Nov. **€7**

Durty Nelly's Low Rd ☎ 061 364861, ⓦ durtynellys.ie A choice of dining is available here at one of Ireland's best known pubs. The relatively expensive *Loft* restaurant offers an early-bird (5.30–7.30pm) and an evening menu which might include sea bass, duck or spiced chicken breast (mains around €18–€27). The pub features a calendar of events, including traditional sessions geared to more popular tastes. Mon–Thurs & Sun 10.30am–11.30pm, Fri & Sat 10.30am–12.30am.

The Craggaunowen Project

April to early Sept daily 9.30am–5pm; last admission 4pm • €9; Heritage Island • ☎ 061 367178, ⓦ shannonheritage.com

Around 7km northeast of Bunratty, just past Sixmilebridge, a turning leads east off the R462 to the **Craggaunowen Project**, which features reconstructions of dwellings, hunting sites and other aspects of life during prehistoric and early Christian times. Hour-long self-guided tours begin with a sixteenth-century tower house whose displays of medieval art and artefacts include some notable European wood-carvings, before moving on to re-creations of a *crannóg*, ring fort and souterrain, as well as **The Togher**, a real Iron Age wooden roadway which was moved here from County Longford (see p.171). Proof that replicas can sometimes match the real McCoy comes in the form of **The Brendan**, a *currag* whose hull consists of leather hides stretched over an ash frame, in which Tim Severin and his four-man crew crossed the Atlantic in 1976. A ninth-century manuscript describes how St Brendan the Navigator became the first European to reach the Americas in the sixth century in such a boat – and, though impossible to prove that Brendan did so, Severin certainly demonstrated that the technology described was sufficient for the task.

Quin Abbey

April–Oct Tues–Sun 10am–4.30pm, Sat & Sun 9.30am–3.30pm • Free

Some 7km northwest of Craggaunowen, and 10km southeast of Ennis, on the R469, the ruined **Quin Abbey** occupies a glorious pastoral setting. Unusually, the original building incorporated parts of a castle, built by Thomas de Clare in the late thirteenth century, which was subsequently attacked by the Irish, leaving it "a hideous, blackened cave" according to one contemporary observer. In the 1430s the MacNamaras brought Franciscans to Quin to found the friary and used the ruins of the old castle as a base, constructing a remarkable edifice in the process, including a striking colonnaded cloister and a tall, trim tower. The friary was dissolved in 1541.

Ennis and around

With a population of around twenty-five thousand, **ENNIS** is far and away Clare's largest town. It began its life in the thirteenth century as a small settlement grouped

9

around a long-disappeared O'Brien castle. Nowadays it's a buzzing town set on both sides of the River Fergus, and still largely based around its medieval street pattern and the central, often traffic-clogged O'Connell Street. Though there's little to see here apart from the ruins of a medieval **friary**, to the north of O'Connell Street, the town has decent restaurants, a joyous range of bookshops and independent boutiques and, above all, a thriving **traditional music** session scene. Glór, on Causeway Link (☎065 684 3103, ⓦglor.ie), is a purpose-built **concert hall** with traditional music concerts, tribute nights and festival summer schools. A **farmers' market** takes place every Friday (8am–2pm) in the car park on Upper Market Street.

The friary

April, May & mid-Sept to Oct Tues–Sun 10am–5pm; June to mid-Sept daily 10am–6pm • €3; Heritage Card

Ennis's only real building of note is its thirteenth-century Franciscan **friary**, founded by the O'Briens, and considered, at one time, to be one of Ireland's major educational institutions. While other such establishments did not survive the Reformation, this one did thanks to Murchadh O'Brien's acknowledgement of the rule of the Tudors – he become the first Earl of Thomond in the process, though the friars were finally expelled in the 1570s. Subsequently, the buildings were used as assizes and a jail, as well as providing rooms for visiting dignitaries. In the late seventeenth century the friary became a parish church of the Church of Ireland, before finally being abandoned in 1871. In a niche one on the fifteenth-century tower's piers is a **carved relief** of St Francis, complete with a habit whose girdle bears the three characteristic knots of the Franciscans, representing chastity, poverty and obedience. In the chancel is the **Creagh Tomb**, which dates from 1843 and

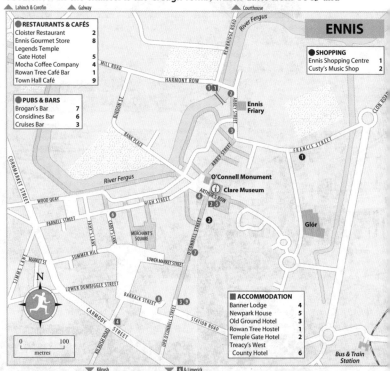

ENNIS

● **RESTAURANTS & CAFÉS**
Cloister Restaurant	2
Ennis Gourmet Store	8
Legends Temple Gate Hotel	5
Mocha Coffee Company	4
Rowan Tree Café Bar	1
Town Hall Café	9

● **PUBS & BARS**
Brogan's Bar	7
Considines Bar	6
Cruises Bar	3

● **SHOPPING**
Ennis Shopping Centre	1
Custy's Music Shop	2

■ **ACCOMMODATION**
Banner Lodge	4
Newpark House	5
Old Ground Hotel	3
Rowan Tree Hostel	1
Temple Gate Hotel	2
Treacy's West County Hotel	6

ncorporates sculptured panels from an earlier fifteenth-century tomb, decorated with astonishingly detailed scenes of Christ's suffering.

O'Connell Square and around

Away from the friary are several monuments devoted to Ennis's later political significance. O'Connell Square is dominated by a tall obelisk celebrating **Daniel O'Connell**, elected as Clare's MP in 1828. As a Catholic he could not take his seat, but his large majority was a factor in Westminster's subsequent implementation of the Catholic Emancipation Act and he was able to attend the Commons when re-elected in 1830. The former Taoiseach **Éamon de Valera**, who represented East Clare (including Ennis) at the Dáil for more than thirty years, is commemorated by a monument outside the Courthouse on Gort Road.

For a fuller picture of Clare's history, the **museum**, which shares the same building as the tourist office on Arthur's Row, covers everything from local archaeological finds to the West Clare Railway (see box, p.330), taking in a re-creation of a Viking longboat, port, music and dance on the way. A permanent exhibition, "The Riches of Clare", tells the story of the people, places and treasures of the county.

ARRIVAL AND DEPARTURE

ENNIS

By plane Buses and taxis run into town from Shannon Airport (see p.315).

By bus The bus station (☎065 682 4177) on Station Rd is a 5min walk from the town centre.

Destinations Bunratty (hourly; 35min); Cliffs of Moher (2–3 daily; 50min); Cork (hourly; 3hr); Corofin (Mon–Sat 1 daily; 20min); Doolin (2–3 daily; 1hr 15min); Ennistymon (3 daily; 35–50min); Feakle (Thurs 1; 55min); Galway (hourly; 1hr 20min); Kilkee (3–4 daily; 1hr 10min); Kilfenora (Tues–Thurs & Sat 1 daily; 40min); Kilrush (3–4

daily; 55min); Lahinch (3 daily; 40min–1hr); Limerick (hourly; 1hr); Liscannor (2–3 daily; 45min); Lisdoonvarna (2–3 daily; 1hr 10min); Miltown Malbay (Mon–Sat 1 daily; 1hr 20min); Shannon Airport (hourly; 30min); Tulla (Thurs 1; 35min).

By train The train station (☎065 684 0444) is on Station Rd, adjacent to the bus station.

Destinations Athenry (4–5 daily; 1hr); Galway (4–5 daily; 1hr 20min); Gort (4–5 daily; 30min); Limerick (9–11 daily; 40min).

INFORMATION AND TOURS

Tourist information Arthur's Row (July & Aug Mon–Sat 9.30am–5.30pm; Sept–June Tues–Sat 9.30am–5.30pm; ☎065 682 8366, Ⓦdiscoverireland.ie/clare). For information on events around the county visit Ⓦclarefocus.ie.

Tours Walking tours set off May–Oct from outside the

tourist office (Mon, Tues & Thurs–Sat 11am; 1hr 30min; €8; ☎087 648 3714, Ⓦenniswalkingtours.com). For a coach tour of Clare's major sites, Barratt Tours run summer trips (Mon–Thurs, Sat & Sun; €27; ☎061 348700, Ⓦwww.4tours.biz) to the Cliffs of Moher and the Burren.

ACCOMMODATION

Ennis has a broad range of **accommodation**, though can get busy during July and August and at **festival** times (see box, above), when it's worth booking ahead.

Banner Lodge Market St ☎065 682 4224, Ⓦbannerlodge.com. This town-centre guesthouse has eight peaceful and sizeable en-suite rooms, all maintained to a high standard. **€50**

Newpark House Tulla Rd ☎065 682 1233, Ⓦnewparkhouse.com. A couple of kilometres east of Ennis off the R352 Scarriff road in a woodland setting, this splendid house dates from 1650 and provides stylish period

9

rooms, some including canopy beds. April–Oct. €100

Old Ground Hotel O'Connell St ☎065 682 8127, ⊛flynnhotels.com. The town's finest hotel is set in an ivy-clad, eighteenth-century building with its own relaxing gardens. The rooms are spacious, elegantly designed and furnished, and include a number of suites. There's a library too, plus a fine restaurant and popular bar, as well as the stylish *Town Hall Café* (see below). €150

★**Rowan Tree Hostel** Harmony Row ☎065 686 8687, ⊛rowantreehostel.ie. One of Ireland's finest hostels – formerly a gentlemen's club – with rooms ranging from doubles to fourteen-bed dorms. Well equipped and thoughtfully furnished, accommodation is mostly en suite, and there's an excellent café-bar on site

(see below). Double dorms €18

★**Temple Gate Hotel** The Square ☎065 682 3300, ⊛templegatehotel.com. A soothing blend of old and new, this hotel's swish design incorporates a nineteenth century former convent that still retains its exquisite stained glass. Bedrooms are modishly decorated, especially the classy suites, which feature king-sized beds and tapestry wall coverings. *Preachers'* pub serves a wide choice of excellent meals from 10am–9.30pm. €129

Treacy's West County Hotel Clare Rd ☎065 682 3000, ⊛treacyswestcounty.com. A modern hotel, 1km south of town, with a leisure centre featuring swimming pools, gym, a hot tub and sauna. It also runs its own programme of children's entertainment, based around its play centre. €99

EATING AND DRINKING

Brogan's Bar O'Connell Street. Local musicians feature here every night in summer with exhilarating performances and a chance to join in a sing-along. Mon–Wed 10am–11.30pm, Thurs–Sat 10am–12.30am, Sun noon–11pm.

★**Cloister Restaurant** Abbey St ☎065 686 8198, ⊛cloister.ie. Once part of the Abbey complex (where the kitchens were based), this atmospheric upstairs restaurant overlooking the River Fergus retains the original features from its historical culinary link. The food is top-notch, with main courses priced around €20 which might include baked lemon sole, medallions of pork fillet or duo of salmon and scallops. Bar Tues–Sun noon–11.30pm; restaurant Fri & Sat 7–9.30pm.

Considines Bar Parnell St. Locally known as *Faffa's*, this welcoming pub is highly regarded for its music and holds weekly sessions each Thurs evening, as well as some other nights. Mon–Thurs 11.30am–11.30pm, Fri & Sat 11.30am–12.30pm, Sun noon–11pm.

Cruises Bar Abbey St. Dating from 1658 and named after John Cruise, an English settler and an original merchant of Ennis, this building was one of the "houses of hospitality" attached to the Abbey and converted to a pub in 1993. It is still renowned for its hospitality and for links to traditional Irish music. Daily 11am–11.30pm.

Ennis Gourmet Store Barrack St ☎065 684 3314. *The* place to pick up premium ingredients for a picnic, and also a source of terrific lunch-time sandwiches, salads, tapas and mini quiches – not to mention the

town's finest coffee. You can enjoy it – or perhaps a craft beer – out on the terrace. Mon–Sat 10am–9pm, Sun noon–8pm.

Legends Temple Gate Hotel The Square ☎065 682 3300. Broadly modern European food (monkfish, Mediterranean vegetable and Clare goat's cheese tart served in splendid surroundings. At dinner (daily 6.30–9.00pm), main courses run from €18.50, while Sunday lunches (12.30–3pm) are especially popular and good value. Bar daily 11am–11.30pm.

Mocha Coffee Company Arthur's Row ☎065 682 1326. A dazzling range of coffees and teas (think everything from soya-milk lattes to wild-berry infusions) to wash down bagels, panini, Greek salads and low-carb wraps and pittas. Wine is also available and you can choose from indoor and outdoor seating. Daily 9am–5.30pm.

★**Rowan Tree Café Bar** Harmony Row ☎065 682 8669, ⊛rowantreecafebar.ie. Fine café at the eponymous hostel (see above), offering a tasty blend of tapas, pizzas and pasta at reasonable prices. Vegetarian and vegans are also well catered for. Daily 10.30am–11pm.

Town Hall Café *Old Ground Hotel*, O'Connell St ☎065 682 8127. Occupying, as the name suggests, Ennis's former municipal centre, this splendidly spacious room is the venue for everything from coffee to filling lunches, tea and scones, and an imaginative evening menu. Mains from €13. Daily 11am–11.30pm.

O'Dea Castle and Dysert O'Dea

Corofin • May–Sept daily 10am–6pm • €5 • ☎065 683 7401, ⊛dysertcastle.com

Well signposted off the R476, 12km north of Ennis, **O'Dea Castle** was the stronghold of the O'Dea branch of the O'Brien clan until 1691. Nowadays it houses an archaeological centre and is the best starting point for a history trail leading across fields to the **Dysert O'Dea** site, where St Tola founded a **monastery** in the eighth century. Several later religious remains can be found here, including a twelfth-century Romanesque **church**, extensively rebuilt in the seventeenth. This features a finely carved doorway and gargoyle-like carvings of human faces and animal heads. Nearby stands a **round tower**, badly damaged by Cromwell's guns, and the twelfth-century **White Cross of Tola**, which bears elaborate patterning and several impressive carvings.

Corofin

On the R476, **COROFIN** is a sturdy, well-defined village that makes a fine base for visiting the Burren. It is noteworthy as the birthplace of one of Ireland's foremost traditional musicians, the accordionist Sharon Shannon. The displays at the **Clare Heritage Centre** on Church Street (May–Oct daily 10am–6pm; €4; ☎ 065 683 7955, ⓦ clareroots.com) provide a fascinating glimpse of bygone living conditions and focus on the Famine and emigration.

ARRIVAL AND DEPARTURE   COROFIN

By bus Ennis (Mon–Sat 1 daily; 25min); Ennistymon (Mon–Sat 1 daily; 35min); Kilfenora (Tues–Thurs & Sat 1 daily; 15min); Lahinch (Mon–Sat 1 daily; 35min); Miltown Malbay (Mon–Sat 1 daily; 50min).

ACCOMMODATION

Corofin Camping & Hostel Main St ☎ 065 683 7683, ⓦ corofincamping.com. This family-run hostel offers comfortable budget accommodation and camping. The Burren Way starts outside its door and the owners supply maps to help you find your way. April–Sept. Tent pitch **€20**, doubles **€40**

Corofin Country House Station Rd ☎ 065 683 7791, ⓔ corofincountryhouse@eircom.net. Comfortable en-suite rooms and a handy base for touring the southern Burren region and (if you feel up to it) climbing Mullaghmore mountain. Feb–Dec. **€65**

Lakefield Lodge Ennis Rd ☎ 065 683 7675, ⓦ lakefieldlodgebandb.com. Pleasant accommodation on the edge of the Burren. The owners will set up a glorious breakfast and help you plan hiking, cycling or fishing trips. April–Oct. **€70**

East Clare

Less visited than other parts of the county, East Clare still has plenty of attractions, with most focused upon small towns and villages, of which **Killaloe**, sitting by the edge of **Lough Derg**, is the highlight. Offering numerous angling opportunities, the lake itself constitutes the county's eastern boundary and is popular with the more upmarket set, with its villages reminiscent of the English Cotswolds. Away from the lough the countryside has a vastly different character from the remainder of Clare – it's a mass of hills and a warren of tiny lanes, with interest focused upon two of the county's greatest traditional music centres, **Tulla** and **Feakle**.

MUSICAL TULLA AND FEAKLE

The villages of Tulla and Feakle are renowned for their musical pedigree. The **Tulla Céilí Band** is famed throughout the land – although you're more likely to catch them at a festival somewhere else than in Tulla. Feakle, meanwhile, 20km east of Ennis, proudly hosts a weeklong **International Traditional Music Festival** (ⓦ feaklefestival.ie) in early August, featuring major singers and musicians. You'll hear some majestic performers such as the searing voice of Sean Tyrrell from the Burren, the trad superstar Martin Hayes and the celebrated accordion player Donal Murphy. If you're attending the festival, village **accommodation** consists of a well-equipped hostel in the centre, *Loughnane's* (IHO; ☎ 061 924200, ⓦ eastclarehostels.com; dorms €20, private rooms €25), and a friendly farmhouse B&B in *Laccaroe House* (☎ 061 924150; doubles €70). Impromptu sessions are often held in the two major music pubs in Feakle: *Shortt's* and *Pepper's*. Both villages have sporadic bus links with Ennis (see p.325) and each other (Thurs 1 daily; 20min), while a once-weekly bus also runs from Limerick to Tulla (see p.316).

9

Killaloe

Hillside **KILLALOE** commands a strategic position above the point where the Shannon leaves Lough Derg. It was here that Brian Ború, the eleventh-century High King of Tara and founder of the O'Brien clan, built his palace, Kincora, a massive fort that was the centre of power in Ireland until Brian's death at the Battle of Clontarf in 1014 (see p.583). This stood on the summit of the hill in the spot now occupied by the Catholic church, though no trace of the building remains. About 1km to the north of the town, off the Scarriff road, is the Bronze Age ring fort **Béal Ború**, perhaps occupied by Brian Ború before Kincora's construction.

The local **festival**, Féile Brian Ború, is held over the first weekend of July with street entertainment and a mass Shannon swim.

St Flannan's Cathedral

Just down Royal Parade from the bridge • Open access 9.30am–5pm

Killaloe later became a religious centre, based around thirteenth-century **St Flannan's Cathedral**, featuring an impressive Romanesque doorway, taken from an earlier church that occupied the site, as well as a low, square bell tower. Just beside the doorway is the massive **Thorgrim Stone**, unusually bearing both runic and ogham inscription.

Brian Ború Heritage Centre

Lough House, The Bridge • May to mid-Sept daily 10am–5pm; last admission 4.30pm • €3.35 • ☏ 061 376866, ⓦ shannonheritage.com

In 2014 a series of events for the one thousandth anniversary of his death led to a revival of interest in Brian Ború (see above). The **Brian Ború Heritage Centre** occupies a building on the delightful thirteen-arch stone bridge which leads to Killaloe's "twin-town", Ballina. The story of his life, his triumphs and death at Clontarf is told through a ten-minute audiovisual display.

ARRIVAL, INFORMATION AND TOURS   KILLALOE

By bus Limerick (Mon–Sat 5 daily; 55min).
Tourist information Beside the bridge in the Brian Ború Heritage Centre (May–Sept daily 10am–5pm; ☏ 061 376866).

Boat tours Lough cruises on *The Spirit of Killaloe* (May to mid-Sept daily 1pm; €12.50; ⓦ spiritofkillaloe.com) leave from across the bridge in Ballina.

ACCOMMODATION AND EATING

The best options for accommodation and eating are over the bridge in Ballina, around 1.5km away.

★**Cherry Tree Restaurant** Ballina ☏ 061 375688, ⓦ cherrytreerestaurant.ie. Locally sourced food such as Tipperary beef or Atlantic halibut in an elegant lough-side setting. The five-course dinner costs €35 and the early-bird three course is €26 (Tues–Thurs 6–9pm, Fri & Sat 6–7.30pm). Tues–Sat 6–10pm.
Gooser's Limerick Rd, Ballina ☏ 061 376791, ⓦ goosers .ie. A rustic country pub feel with an adjacent busy evening restaurant. Its wide-ranging menu features a local favourite: bacon and cabbage (€12.95) or a choice of steaks, fish, chicken or duck. Mon–Sat noon–10pm, Sun

12.30–9.30pm.
Kincora House B&B Church St, Killaloe ☏ 061 376149 ⓦ kincorahouse.com. An attractive town house with four well-appointed rooms in a building whose pedigree stretches back 350 years. April–Sept. **€80**
Lakeside Hotel Ballina ☏ 061 376122, ⓦ lakeside hotel.ie. Across the bridge in Ballina in an unbeatable waterside location with its own private jetty. Some rooms overlook the river but you'll pay an extra €20 per night for the privilege. Food served Mon–Sat noon–10pm, Sun 12.30–9.30pm. **€98**

Southwest Clare

It's a relatively long haul from Ennis to Clare's southwest, but well worth the effort for the attractions offered by two popular holiday spots and the chance to explore the glorious scenery of the **Loop Head peninsula**. Of the resorts, **Kilkee** is the livelier, with a sweeping beach and access to Loop Head; **Kilrush** is more stolid, but still attractive in its own way and is a base for dolphin watching and the ferry to **Scattery Island**, a major monastic site.

Kilrush and around

Some 40km from Ennis, **KILRUSH** is a graceful planned town whose broad main drag, Frances Street, leads down to a bustling marina where you can catch a ferry to **Scattery Island**. At the town's core stands the **Maid of Éireann** statue, honouring the Manchester Martyrs, three Fenians who were executed in the English city in 1867 for a daring attempted rescue of some of their comrades arrested during a failed uprising.

Vandeleur Walled Garden

Mon–Fri 10am–5pm, plus April–Sept Sat & Sun noon–5pm • €5; Heritage Island • ☎ 065 905 1760, ⓦ vandeleurwalledgarden.ie

In the early nineteenth century, wealthy landlord John Ormsby Vandeleur built Kilrush House, which stood in an estate 800m east of town by the Killimer road (N67). The building was demolished in 1973, but the restored **Vandeleur Walled Garden** is an attractive spot featuring an abundance of subtropical plants.

Scattery Island

June–Sept daily 10am–6pm • €12 payable at the ticket office at Kilrush marina, includes return ferry and Island Centre admission • ☎ 065 905 1327, ⓦ discoverdolphins.ie

In high season some three or four daily ferries run from Kilrush's marina to **Scattery Island**, 2.5km offshore. A monastery was established here by St Senan in the sixth century, and the island retained ecclesiastical importance until its exposed position attracted Viking raiders in 870, who occupied it until defeated by Brian Ború in the late tenth century. Medieval church building is evident in the form of several ruins, and there is a reasonably well-preserved, 35m-high **round tower** which is most impressive when the sun seems to reflect off its yellowy, lichen-covered stone. Derelict since the last inhabitants left in 1978, Scattery has a timeless air. It's well worth making a trip to the island's southern point – where a **lighthouse** and gun battery remain from the time of the Napoleonic wars – for the sense of peaceful isolation and spectacular views. By the pier the **Scattery Island Centre** houses an exhibition on the island's history.

ARRIVAL AND INFORMATION KILRUSH

By bus Ennis (2–3 daily; 55min); Kilkee (2–3 daily; 15min).

Tourist information Ask at *Crotty's Pub* (see below) for information about the Loop Head peninsula's towns and villages.

ACCOMMODATION AND EATING

★**Crotty's Pub & B&B** Market Square ☎ 065 905 2470, ⓦ crottyspubkilrush.com. Occupying a prime corner position with charmingly furnished standard rooms and good-value bar food, this is the pick of places to stay. The bar retains its original Victorian mirrors, shelves and walls filled with historical memorabilia. Lunch and evening meals are available and there are traditional sessions in summer on Tues and Wed, and live music every other weekend all year. €75

The Haven Arms Henry St ☎ 065 905 1267. Bar food is available during the day, with seafood a speciality, but you'll also find burgers and chicken curry on the menu along with other lunch specials. Mon–Thurs 10.30am–11.30pm, Fri & Sat 10.30am–12.30am, Sun 12.30pm–11.30pm.

Katie O'Connor's Hostel Frances St ☎ 065 905 1133, ⓔ katieoconnors@eircom.net. Close to the main town square, this is a well-run place with a fully equipped kitchen. Open turf fires in the living room are a big attraction. Ten-, six- and four-bed dorms are available, as well as private rooms. Mid-March to Sept. Dorms €18, private rooms €22

THE WEST CLARE RAILWAY

A few kilometres north of Kilrush at Moyasta is the only extant section of the **West Clare Railway** (April–Sept Mon–Sat 10am–5pm, Sun noon–5pm; €6; ☎065 905 1284, ⓦwestclarerailway.ie), which opened in August 1892 and linked Ennis – via a roundabout route through Corofin – to southwest Clare until its closure in 1961. Much of the track was then sold to a Kenyan railway company, but the Moyasta station house and a 2km stretch of the line have been restored and it's possible to take a trip back and forth. The railway was immortalized by the singer **Percy French** who, in 1902, along with his troupe of music-hall entertainers, was due to play an engagement in Kilkee. Unfortunately, the train broke down in Miltown Malbay and French arrived late to discover that most of his audience had already left. He sued the railroad for damages, winning the princely sum of £10, and wrote the song *Are Ye Right There Michael* as an account of his experiences, the Michael in question being Michael Talty, who was the guard on the train when the incident occurred.

Kelly's Steak and Seafood House 26 Henry St ☎065 905 1811. A variety of steaks and fish dishes such as baked salmon, crab cakes or squid make up the menu in this informal and relaxing restaurant. Food served daily 6–10pm with main-course prices starting at around €10. Tues–Sun 11am–11.30pm, Mon 11am–3pm.

Kilkee and around

Thirteen kilometres northwest of Kilrush, **KILKEE** is a jaunty holiday resort, long popular with Limerick city folk, whose main attraction is a gorgeous, sandy, crescent-shaped **beach** that offers breathtaking cliff-top walks at both its ends. If the sun's hiding, alternative activities include the indoor 60m slide at **Waterworld** (11am–5.45pm: June Sat & Sun; July & Aug daily; €6; ☎065 905 6855, ⓦkilkeewaterworld.ie).

Loop Head peninsula

A tapering, elongated stretch of land, the **Loop Head peninsula** reaches southwest from Kilkee for some 25km. Though mostly low-lying, there are some staggeringly beautiful cliff-top walks; alternatively, it's possible to encompass virtually the whole peninsula by taking the scenic signposted drive from Kilkee or from just west of Moyasta. From the harbour at the village of **Carrigaholt**, which also houses the ruins of a fifteenth-century castle, Dolphinwatch (April–Oct daily 8am–6pm; €25; ☎065 905 8156, ⓦdolphinwatch .ie; advance booking essential) run excellent two-hour summer trips to see and hear (through a hydrophone) the Shannon **dolphins**. The village also holds an oyster and traditional music **festival** in early May. To the north are the so-called **Bridges of Ross** at Ross Bay – natural arches formed by the ocean's erosion of the cliffs – though in fact there's now only one of the original pair.

ARRIVAL AND INFORMATION   KILKEE AND AROUND

By bus Ennis (2–3 daily; 1hr 10min); Kilrush (2–3 daily; 15min).
Tourist information Ask at Any Occasion Gift Shop on

Circular Rd (Mon–Sat 11am–6pm; ☎065 905 6880, ⓔanyoccasion@outlook.com).

ACCOMMODATION AND EATING

Green Acres Campsite Doonaha ☎065 905 7011. A well-equipped site near the sea and handy for an exploration of Loop Head. It's also in an ideal location for a cycle tour of a section of the Wild Atlantic Way. Tent pitch €18

Kilkee Thalassotherapy Centre Grattan St, Kilkee ☎065 905 6742, ⓦkilkeethalasso.com. A family-run health spa which also provides thalassotherapy in the form of

seaweed baths and other related relaxations (not included in the accommodation price). Five en-suite rooms are available one triple, one twin, two doubles and one single. €72

The Lighthouse Inn Kilbaha ☎065 905 8358. This bar in a quiet fishing village near the peninsula's tip serves both a decent pint and meals (breakfast, lunch, and dinner till 9.00pm). Mid-week céili nights are held and there's generally music at weekends. You can also stock up on provisions at the grocery shop end of the business. Daily 9am–11.30pm.

★**The Long Dock** Main St, Carrigaholt ☎ 065 905 8106, ⓦ thelongdock.com. This renowned traditional music pub (summer sessions Wed & Fri–Sun) also offers such delights as fish pie, fried fish or chowder. The outdoor tables make for a memorable dining experience. An early bird menu is served Mon–Fri 5.30–7pm. Mon–Thurs & Sun 11am–11.30pm, Fri & Sat 11am–12.30am.

Murphy Blacks Restaurant The Square, Kilkee ☎ 065 905 6854. An excellent seafood option: try their fabulous signature dish of zarzuela, a Spanish stew of mussels, clams, prawns, white fish and tomato sauce. Main courses from €12. April–Sept Mon–Sat 6–9pm; Oct–March Sat & Sun 6–9pm.

Naughton's O'Curry St, Kilkee ☎ 065 905 6597, ⓦ naughtonsbar.com. Fishy dishes such as sea bass, hake, sole, turbot and halibut along with the ever popular fish and chips. Main courses from €10. Daily 6–9pm.

O'Mara's O'Curry St, Kilkee ☎ 065 906 0967. A decent old-fashioned bar where the music happens spontaneously when walk-in musicians arrive at short notice armed with their instruments. Daily 1.30pm–midnight.

★**Strand Guest House** Strand Line, Kilkee ☎ 065 905 6177, ⓦ thestrandkilkee.com. Enjoying panoramic views of the ocean, this guesthouse features modern, well-presented rooms, often with special offers available. The business also supports a café (11am–4.30pm) and the *Strand Seafood Bistro* whose signature dish is oven-roasted fillet hake; fresh fish is delivered six days a week straight off the fishing boats at Carrigaholt. **€72**

West Clare

More than any other area of Clare, the county's west is associated with **traditional music** – there's many a vibrant session in village pubs all along the coast and **Miltown Malbay** hosts one of Ireland's major music festivals. There are also sandy **beaches**, notably at the attractive resort of **Lahinch**, while, further north, you'll come to the towering **Cliffs of Moher**, close to the traditional music magnet of **Doolin** and, inland, the old-fashioned town of **Ennistymon**.

Miltown Malbay

Though set back some distance from the sea, **MILTOWN MALBAY**, 30km northeast of Kilkee, originated as a Victorian holiday resort. Today a thriving small town with an appealing mix of modern cafés, restaurants and pubs and traditional, family-run shops, it makes an excellent base to explore sections of the Wild Atlantic Way or to soak up some traditional music. The town hosts the week-long **Willie Clancy Summer School** (ⓦ scoilsamhraidhwillieclancy.com), beginning on the first Saturday in July and named after the *uilleann* piper, singer and raconteur who died in 1973. More than a thousand people turn up for the music and dance classes, with seats at a premium.

ARRIVAL AND DEPARTURE   **MILTOWN MALBAY**

By bus Ennis (Mon–Sat 1 daily; 40min–1hr 20min); Ennistymon (Mon–Sat 1 daily; 30min); Lahinch (Mon–Sat 1 daily; 20min).

ACCOMMODATION AND EATING

An Gleann Ennis Rd ☎ 065 708 4281, ⓦ angleann.net. A friendly two-storey house 1km from town with four en-suite rooms. Breakfasts are generous and vegetarians are catered for. **€60**

Berry Lodge Spanish Point, 3km west of Miltown Malbay ☎ 065 708 7022, ⓦ berrylodge.com. This Victorian family home is in an idyllic location near the beach at Spanish Point. Breakfasts include celiac pancakes with berries and pumpkin seeds. The owner also runs one-day cookery courses, after which you eat what you cooked. **€80**

Lahinch

The seaside resort of **LAHINCH**, 12km north of Miltown Malbay, is renowned for its glorious sandy strand. If the Atlantic is too cold then right by the beach is **Seaworld** (April–Sept Mon–Wed 7am–9.30pm, Thurs & Fri 9am–9pm, weekends 10am–8pm; €7; ☎ 065 708 1900, ⓦ lahinchseaworld.com) with a 25m swimming pool, leisure centre and gym.

9

By bus Cliffs of Moher (2–3 daily; 10min); Corofin (Mon–Sat 1 daily; 25min); Doolin (2–3 daily; 45min); Ennis (2–3 daily; 45min–1hr); Ennistymon (2–3 daily; 5–15min); Liscannor (2–3 daily; 5min); Lisdoonvarna (2–3 daily; 25min); Miltown Malbay (Mon–Sat 1 daily; 20min).

ACCOMMODATION AND EATING

Atlantic Hotel Main St ☏065 708 1049, ⓦatlantichotel.ie. Flickering log fires greet guests at this intimate, family-run hotel. Its fine selection of en-suite rooms comes with crisp cotton duvets, and special offers include discounts for staying a second or third night. **€140**

★**Barrtrá Seafood Restaurant** 5km south of Lahinch on the N67 ☏065 708 1280, ⓦbarrtra.com. For a more upmarket marine dinner or Sunday lunch option, the owners of this whitewashed cottage provide top-class seafood such as hot buttered lobster with gratin potatoes, a seafood "symphony" consisting of the fresh fish of the day, and a surprise seafood menu for €30. Daily noon–2.30pm & 6–10pm.

Lahinch Hostel Church St ☏065 708 1040, ⓦlahinchhostel.ie. A well-appointed hostel which also rents bikes, offers laundry facilities and can arrange group tours to the Cliffs of Moher and the Burren. Four-, six- and eight-bed dorms. **€17**

O'Looney's Bar & Restaurant The Promenade ☏065 708 1414, ⓦolooneys.ie. The menu in this split-level bar-restaurant has a bias towards the fruits of the sea with Atlantic seafood chowder, surf 'n' Caesar salad, pan-fried salmon and fillet of plaice. Main dinner courses average €14.50. Afterwards (from 10.30pm) you can party till the small hours at *O'Looney's Surf Bar and Nightclub*. Daily noon–2.30am.

Ennistymon

Straddling the River Cullenagh, the relaxed town of **ENNISTYMON**, 4km east of Lahinch, promotes itself as "the town of old shop fronts", to which its long main street bears ample testimony. The **Cascades Walk**, signposted on Main Street, leads along the river bank past the falls, whose waters tumble over rocks by an old arched bridge. Ennistymon's most famous son was the poet **Brian Merriman**, born here in 1747, who wrote the epic and juicily salacious 1200-line poem, *The Midnight Court*. There aren't many ATMs in West Clare, but you'll find one on Parliament Street in Ennistymon.

Byrne's Main St ☏065 707 1080, ⓦbyrnes-ennistymon.ie. Pleasant rooms – some looking out over the cascading Cullenagh River – in a nineteenth-century Edwardian town house. The high-ceilinged restaurant, noted for its fresh seafood, might include the likes of pan-fried plaice or fresh cod in *beurre blanc*. **€70**

Falls Hotel Lahinch Rd ☏065 707 1004, ⓦfallshotel.ie. A Georgian-style hotel set in woodlands by the water, with pleasant and spacious accommodation. Activities include an aqua and fitness centre. **€130**

Doolin and around

In the 1960s the then tiny village of **DOOLIN**, 7km north of the Cliffs of Moher, developed a reputation for its **traditional music**, largely thanks to the reputation of a bachelor farmer Micho Russell, a singer, flute and whistle player who enjoyed an international touring career. Attracted by his music, a trickle of enthusiasts began to visit Doolin's pubs to hear the playing of Micho and his two brothers Packie and Gussie, all sadly departed. Today, Doolin is awash with visitors virtually throughout the year, with **pubs** such as *O'Connor's* (in Fisher Street on the way to the harbour), *Fitzpatrick's Bar* in the *Hotel Doolin* (see opposite) and *McGann's* and *McDermott's* at the northern end frequently packed with tourists. Unfortunately, most of the music churned out nightly is not the "pure drop", but either neatly adjusted to suit popular tastes or amplified garbage, and in truth there are many other and better places to hear Clare's often fabulous traditional music. Non-musical highlights include **Doolin Cave** (mid-Feb to mid-March & Nov Fri–Sun noon–5pm; mid-March to June daily 11am–5pm; July–Sept daily 10am–6pm; Oct daily noon–5pm; tours at 10am, 11am and every 30min from 11.30am; €15; ⓦdoolincave.ie), where a 7m silver-gleaming stalactite hangs from the ceiling of the dome-like central cavern; and **boat-trips** from Doolin pier to the Aran Islands (see p.359) and to view the Cliffs of Moher.

The Cliffs of Moher

Visitor centre March & Oct Mon–Fri 9am–6pm; April Mon–Fri 9am–6.30pm; May & Sept Mon–Fri 9am–7pm; June daily 9am–7.30pm; July & Aug daily 9am–9.00pm; Nov–Feb daily 9.15am–5pm • €6 includes car parking; Heritage Island • ☎ 065 708 6141, ⓦ cliffsofmoher .ie • **O'Brien's Tower** Open daily but hours vary so check with staff • €2

Some 10km south of Doolin are the **Cliffs of Moher**, stretching downwards to the Atlantic for almost 200m. The cliffs take their name from an old promontory fort, Mothar, and extend some 8km from Hag's Head, west of Liscannor, to a little beyond O'Brien's Tower, which was constructed by a local altruist in 1835 at their highest point. Hidden within the hillside, the visitor centre is an impressive architectural feat with a first-floor **restaurant** that offers panoramic seascapes and a reasonable choice of meals. The centre houses the Atlantic Edge exhibition whose interactive touch screens, computer games and 3-D film do in part provide lucid explanations of the cliffs' evolution and wildlife, but overall form a ludicrous electronic counterpoint to the actual glories outside. The best bet is to head straight past the centre and to the steps which curve upwards towards the cliff-top. Then you can opt for turning south towards Hag's Head or in the opposite direction to O'Brien's Tower where a **viewing platform** offers the best sight of the wave-battered cliffs below, enhanced by the resonant roar of the Atlantic waves pummelling the rocks at shore level. Alternatively, you can gain a different perspective of their prodigious stature from one of the regular **boat-trips** that run from the pier at Doolin.

ARRIVAL AND TOURS

DOOLIN AND AROUND

By bus Ballyvaughan (1 daily; 40min–1hr); Cliffs of Moher (2–3 daily; 30min); Ennis (2–3 daily; 1hr 30min); Ennistymon (2–3 daily; 50min); Fanore (1 daily; 40min); Galway (Mon–Sat 2 daily, Sun 1; 1hr 35min–2hr 10min); Lahinch (2–3 daily; 45min); Limerick (2–3 daily; 2hr 15min); Lisdoonvarna (3–5 daily; 15min).

By boat From March to Nov, Doolin2Aran Ferries (☎ 065 707 5949, ⓦ doolin2aranferries.com) runs to Inishmore

and Inishmaan (10am and 1pm) and to Inisheer (10am, 11am and 1pm). They also offer a Cliffs of Moher cruise (noon, 3pm and 5.15pm; €20). Doolin Ferry (☎ 065 707 4455, ⓦ doolinferry.com) runs to Inisheer (March–Nov 2–3 daily; 30min), Inishmaan (April–Oct 1 daily; 45min), Inishmore (March–Nov 1 daily; 1hr 15min) and Cliffs of Moher (March–Nov 3–6 daily; €15).

ACCOMMODATION AND EATING

Aille River Hostel (IHH) At the crossroads on the R479, 2km from *Doolin Holiday Cottages* ☎ 065 707 4260, ⓦ ailleriverhosteldoolin.ie. Centrally situated cottage-style hostel offering a variety of dorms, a big kitchen and wood-burning stove. Camping facilities are well sheltered in a flat garden behind a stone wall. Dorms €15.50, tent pitch €20

Aran View Country House Hotel Coast Rd ☎ 065 707 4061, ⓦ aranview.com. Dramatically sited above the village, this is a fine country-house hotel offering tremendous views from its attractive rooms and tasty seafood such as sea bass in its bistro (7–8.30pm). €100

★ **Cullinan's Guesthouse** On the R479, 2km from *Doolin Holiday Cottages* ☎ 065 707 4183, ⓦ cullinansdoolin.com. Excellent B&B run by welcoming hosts, adjacent to the T-junction in the village centre. Well-appointed en-suite rooms and a splendid restaurant (Easter–Oct Mon, Tues & Thurs–Sat 6–9pm) – try the crab meat and scallops. Mid-Feb to Dec. €90

Hotel Doolin On the R479, 2km from *Doolin Holiday Cottages* ☎ 065 707 4111, ⓦ hoteldoolin.ie. Doolin's

plushest hotel also features a restaurant (Wed–Sun 6–9.30pm), pizzeria (6–11pm), café (11am–4pm) and *Fitz's Bar and Eatery*, where "The Trawler", a platter towering with fresh seafood, is best washed down with a glass of their own smooth red "Dooliner" ale. The annual Doolin craft beer festival is based here at the end of Aug each year. €140

Rainbow Hostel (IHH) Roadford, Doolin ☎ 065 707 4415, ⓦ rainbowhostel.net Unquestionably the cosiest Doolin hostel, by *McDermott's* pub in the north of the village. It is well equipped and offers bike rental. Dorms €16, private rooms €35

Roadford House Restaurant and B&B Roadford, Doolin ☎ 065 707 5050, ⓦ roadfordrestaurant.com. A "melody" of seafood (a combination of shellfish and white fish) is the signature offering at this delightful combination of restaurant (Mon–Wed & Fri–Sun 6–8.30pm) and guesthouse. Rooms range from a queen-size double, to family or standard rooms and a two-bedroom self-catering apartment that sleeps four for a minimum three-night stay. April–Oct. €90

9

The Burren

The Burren's name derives from the Irish word *boireann*, meaning "stony place" – an apt description for this desolate plateau that occupies the county's northwest. Its northern and western edges hug the coast road from Doolin up to Ballyvaughan, while, to the south and east, the rocks gently slope towards lush green fields. Formed mainly of fissured limestone pavement, pitted by occasional valleys hidden beneath ominous-looking cliffs, the Burren is a thoroughly otherworldly place with barely a sign of life. The starkness of the landscape, crisp white in sunlight, deep grey-brown in rainfall, has a primeval allure and remains utterly fascinating. Few now live within its bounds, but many endured this harsh environment in the past, leaving relics of their inhabitation. Ancient burial practices are reflected in the abundance of **Stone Age monuments**, while later, Iron Age people built ring forts and circular stone dwellings, many of which remain well preserved. The area's coastal outskirts include attractive resorts such as lively **Ballyvaughan** and tiny **Fanore**, while inland lie the spa town of **Lisdoonvarna**, famous for its matchmaking festival, and the renowned traditional music village **Kilfenora**; all make fine bases.

INFORMATION AND ACTIVITIES   THE BURREN

Tourist information For detailed online information about the Burren see ⓦburrenbeo.com. Tim Robinson's exceptionally detailed maps covering different areas are widely available.

Walking tours Excellent themed walks and treks are organized by Burren Hill Walks of Corkscrew Hill, Ballyvaughan (☎065 707 7168, ⓦhomepage.eircom .net/~burrenhillwalks); Burren Guided Walks of Fanore (☎065 707 6100, ⓦburrenguidedwalks.com); and Heart

of Burren Walks with the knowledgeable local author Tony Kirby (☎065 682 7707, ⓦheartofburrenwalks.com).

Horse riding The Burren Riding Centre (☎065 707 6140, ⓔjjq@eircom.net) in Fanore offers horse riding, including trails along the "green roads", trekking in the Burren and beach hacks.

Surfing If you fancy learning to surf, then the Aloha Surf School at Fanore beach (☎087 213 3996, ⓦsurfschool.tv) provides all necessary equipment.

Lisdoonvarna and around

LISDOONVARNA, 8km east of Doolin, is a small town with a long street that developed in the nineteenth century around its old spa, whose sulphated waters were believed to have curative properties. Reinvigoration aside, Lisdoonvarna's calendar is focused upon its **matchmaking festival** (ⓦmatchmakerireland.com), an annual September rally for the lovelorn, which runs for almost a month. The festival dates back to the times when dealers at street fairs acted as matchmakers, arranging marriages for bachelor farmers too land-tied to seek their own nuptial bliss.

Burren Smokehouse

May–Sept daily 9am–6pm; Oct–Dec, March & April Mon–Fri 9am–5pm, Sat & Sun 10am–4pm; Jan & Feb Mon–Fri 9am–5pm, Sat 10am–4pm • Free • ☎065 707 4432, ⓦburrensmokehouse.ie

You may be tempted by the **Burren Smokehouse**, just west of the central crossroads,

---

THE COAST TO BALLYVAUGHAN

One of the most dramatic routes around the Burren is the R477 – now part of the Wild Atlantic Way driving route (see box, p.31) – which traces the shoreline from just northwest of Lisdoonvarna to **Ballyvaughan**. Inland, and inaccessible by car, is a crisscross pattern of the old "green roads", offering upland walking and majestic panoramic views. Just 5km northwest of Lisdoonvarna, near the junction with the R479 Doolin road, you'll spot **Ballynalackan Castle**, a fifteenth-century tower house, perched high above the road. The coast road north of Ballynalackan is dramatic and sometimes shrouded in the mornings by the haze of a sea fret. The road rounds Black Head where you can climb up to **Caheerdoonfergus** ring fort and gaze across Galway Bay before heading on to Ballyvaughan.

which specializes in smoked salmon and sells a tantalizing range of local artisan gourmet foods. The visitor centre includes a video about the smoking process.

ARRIVAL AND DEPARTURE

By bus Ballyvaughan (Mon–Sat 2 daily, Sun 1; 25–45min); Cliffs of Moher (2–3 daily; 15–25min); Doolin (2–3 daily; 10min); Ennis (2–3 daily; 1hr 10min); Ennistymon (2–3

LISDOONVARNA AND AROUND

daily; 30min); Galway (Mon–Sat 2 daily, Sun 1; 1hr 20min); Lahinch (2–3 daily; 25min); Limerick (2–3 daily; 2hr).

ACCOMMODATION AND EATING

LISDOONVARNA

Burren Sleepzone Hostel Kincora Rd ☎ 065 707 4036, ⓦ sleepzone.ie. An excellently equipped An Óige-affiliated hostel set in the landscaped grounds of a former hotel. Double dorms €15

★**Rathbaun Hotel** Main St ☎ 065 707 4009, ⓦ rathbaunhotel.com. A well-maintained hotel with 10 en-suite rooms. In the summer, music is guaranteed every night since the hotel has a pool of eight live-in musicians, ranging from banjo players to *uilleann* pipers who perform in the bar. May to mid-Oct. €70

Roadside Tavern Kincora Rd ☎ 065 707 4084, ⓦ roadsidetavern.ie. Sunday roasts are the main feast here, while the owner, Peter Curtin, runs a microbrewery producing craft beers such as the Burren Black. He can also explain the link between J. R. R. Tolkien and the Burren. Mon–Thurs 10.30am–11.30pm, Fri & Sat till 12.30am, Sun noon–11pm.

Royal Spa Hotel Main St ☎ 065 707 4288, ⓦ royalspahotel.com. Dating from 1832, this hotel features tastefully decorated en-suite bedrooms, but ask to see a few as some are on the small side. Nightly sessions in summer and tasty pizzas in the bar Tues–Sun 6–10pm. Bar daily 6–11.30pm. €70

★**Sheedy's Country House Hotel** ☎ 065 707 4026, ⓦ sheedys.com. The oldest building in the village, with rooms decorated in traditional country-house style,

featuring floral patterns and mahogany furniture. Local produce is used for everything from bread and jam to ice cream. The rack of Burren lamb is highly recommended in the restaurant (6.30–8.45pm) and evening bar meals are also available. Easter to Sept. €135

Wild Honey Inn Kincora Rd ☎ 065 707 4300, ⓦ wildhoneyinn.com. A stylish gastro bar/bistro that serves much-talked-about food and offers accommodation in fourteen amenable rooms, many with original features. All ground-floor rooms have doors that open on to the garden, each with its own terrace. The dinner signature dish is braised pork cheek, and the menu also showcases farmed chicken, lamb or *tarte flambée* with prices averaging €16. Mid-Feb to Dec Mon 5–9pm, Wed–Sun 1–3.30pm & 5–9pm. €64

FANORE

Annaly House B&B ☎ 065 707 6154, ⓦ macsatlanticcottage.com. Idyllically situated on a working farm that runs down to the seashore, where you can potter around on the limestone pavement. Breakfast choice is the full Irish, pancakes or a healthy fruit and yoghurt option. May–Sept. €60

Rocky View Farmhouse ☎ 065 707 6103 ⓦ rockyviewfarmhouse.com. Tremendous views, relaxing en-suite rooms and a great base for touring the coastline and the enigmatic Burren landscape. April–Oct. €70

Kilfenora

Nine kilometres southeast of Lisdoonvarna, the village of **KILFENORA** is one of Clare's most celebrated **traditional music** centres. Its fame is intrinsically linked to the Kilfenora Ceili Band, Ireland's oldest and most illustrious, and on Wednesday nights in summer the KCB plays in *Linnane's* pub. *Vaughan's* pub, meanwhile, has set dancing in its barn (Thurs & Sun) as well as a session in the pub itself (Tues).

Burren Centre

Daily: mid-March to May, Sept & Oct 10am–5pm; June–Aug 9.30am–5.30pm • €6; Heritage Island • ☎ 065 708 8030, ⓦ theburrencentre.ie

The **Burren Centre** provides an entertaining account of the area's history, with its "In a Walk through Time" exhibition featuring imaginative and sometimes interactive displays and models that explain its geology and antiquities. Don't miss the permanent exhibition on traditional music ("The Kilfenora Ceili, Band Parlour"), which traces the one-hundred-year history of Ireland's oldest and most illustrious ceili band, which sometimes performs live here. There's also a café and a shop selling crafts and books.

9

Kilfenora Cathedral

Hard by the Burren Centre stands the ruined twelfth-century **Kilfenora Cathedral**, site of the county's largest concentration of high crosses. The twelfth-century Doorty Cross in the chancel is especially impressive; its faces depict various ecclesiasts and a scene from the Crucifixion.

ARRIVAL AND DEPARTURE   KILFENORA

By bus Corofin (Tues–Thurs & Sat 1 daily; 15min); Ennis (Tues–Thurs & Sat 1 daily; 40min); Ennistymon (Tues–Thurs & Sat 1 daily; 15min); Lahinch (Tues–Thurs & Sat 1 daily; 20min); Miltown Malbay (Tues–Thurs & Sat 1 daily; 40min).

ACCOMMODATION

★ **Ballinalacken Castle** 5km north of Lisdoon on the R477 coast road ☎ 065 707 4025, ⊚ ballinalackencastle .com. Converted Victorian mansion, now a country-house hotel, where some of the bedrooms enjoy fantastic views of the Aran Islands. Its restaurant serves sumptuous dinners (closed Tues) using local produce such as scallops and lamb. Mid-April to Oct. **€160**

Kilfenora Hostel (IHO) ☎ 065 708 8908, ⊚ kilfenorahostel.com. Spacious, well-equipped hostel on the site of an old sheep fair. The owners also run *Vaughan's Pub* next door (forever to be known as the "Father Ted Pub", since one episode of the Channel 4 comedy classic series featured scenes in the bar) so they have their finger on the village's musical pulse. **€20**

Ballyvaughan and around

Built in 1829 to assist the fishing industry, **BALLYVAUGHAN**'s harbour saw the village develop as a major trading centre and, not long afterwards, steamers began to ply between here and Galway, bringing visitors and establishing the tourist trade. It's an eye-catching village, especially when the sun gleams on its predominantly white and cream houses, and is an ideal base for exploring the Burren. Roads south from Ballyvaughan lead to a wealth of **ancient** and some **medieval sites**. The first of these, a kilometre or so down the R480 and off to the west, is **Newtown Castle** (May–Sept Mon–Fri 10am–4pm; free; ☎ 065 707 7200, ⊚ burrencollege.ie). This restored sixteenth-century tower house with walls almost 4m thick, complete with murder holes and gun loops, is now part of the grounds of the Burren College of Art.

Aillwee Cave

Ballyallaban Rd • Daily 10am–5.30pm; July & Aug until 6.30pm; flying displays noon and 3pm daily (additional times May–Aug) • €18; Heritage Island • ☎ 065 707 7036, ⊚ aillweecave.ie

A little way south of Newtown Castle, **Aillwee Cave** is reckoned to be two million years old. Guided tours visit caverns and bridged chasms, allowing you to marvel at weird rock formations, numerous stalagmites and stalactites, and the hibernation chambers of a long-extinct species of brown bear. The ticket price also includes entry to the **Burren Bird of Prey Centre** (same hours), which stages flying displays of various avian predators and also offers the opportunity to "take a hawk for a walk".

Gleninsheen Wedge Tomb

About 3km south of Aillwee Cave, and just off the eastern side of the R480, is the **Gleninsheen Wedge Tomb**, the best preserved of its kind in the area. In 1930 a remarkable, finely worked gold collar was discovered here by a boy hunting rabbits and is now held by Dublin's National Museum (see p.63). Just a kilometre south from here is the **Poulnabrone dolmen**, the best known and most photographed of the Burren's seventy or so megalithic tombs. When excavated in 1986, the remains of some thirty people were uncovered, along with tools, utensils and jewellery, providing evidence that the tomb dated from around 2500 BC.

Caherconnell Stone Fort

Daily March–Oct 10am–5.30pm; July & Aug until 6.30pm • €7 • ☎ 065 708 9999, ⓦ burrenforts.ie

A kilometre south of the Poulnabrone dolmen is **Caherconnell Stone Fort**, the most substantial of the Burren's many ancient remains. Such circular homesteads, with their dry-stone walling, were built from around the fifth century onwards; this one is 40m in diameter with nearly 4m-thick walls. Displays recount how the daily life of its residents might have been spent, as well as describing the building's design and other Burren monuments.

Leamaneh Castle

No public access

South of the fort, by the junction with the R476, is another O'Brien fortress, **Leamaneh Castle**, which, though long abandoned, is still in reasonable shape. Its tower dates from around 1480 and the adjoining four-storey house with its segmented windows was added in 1640 by Conor O'Brien.

ARRIVAL AND DEPARTURE

By bus Cliffs of Moher (1 daily; 55min); Doolin (Mon–Sat 2 daily, Sun 1; 40min); Galway (Mon–Sat 2 daily, Sun 1; 1hr 10min); Kinvara (Mon–Sat 2 daily, Sun 1; 30min); Lisdoonvarna (Mon–Sat 2 daily, Sun 1; 25min).

BALLYVAUGHAN AND AROUND

ACCOMMODATION AND EATING

An Fulacht Fia Coast Rd, 2km west of Ballyvaughan ☎ 065 707 7300, ⓦ anfulachtfia.ie. Spectacularly sited at the base of Cappanwalla Mountain and with coastal views, this is a dreamy location to enjoy modern Irish cuisine with a European twist. Main courses start around €15. Thurs–Sat 5.30–9pm, Sun 1–4pm.

An Fear Gorta Pier Rd ☎ 065 707 7023, ⓦ tearoomsballyvaughan.com. A daytime café with a delightful conservatory for lunches and snacks, noted for its delectable cakes. Steven Spielberg is a fan – he has visited the café on several occasions while passing through this part of the west. May–Sept daily 10am–6pm; Oct Thurs–Sun 11am–5pm; Nov & Dec Fri–Sun 11am–5pm.

Dolmen Lodge Tonarussa ☎ 065 707 7202, ⓦ dolmenlodge.com. A modern farmhouse 800m east of the village in a rural setting, perfect for immersing yourself in the mystery of the Burren. April to mid-Oct. **€80**

★ Gregans Castle Hotel 5km south of Ballyvaughan on the N67 ☎ 065 707 7005, ⓦ gregans.ie. A luxurious eighteenth-century building with astonishing evening dining-room views of the ever-changing colours of the limestone landscape. Setting and food combine to create the perfect ambience. Mid-Feb to Nov. **€250**

Hyland's Burren Hotel ☎ 065 707 7037, ⓦ hylandsburren.com. In central Ballyvaughan beside the T-junction, with a welcoming fire and pleasant modern facilities. Bar meals such as Irish stew, fish and chips and chicken dishes are served noon–9pm. Ask for an upper-floor room for Burren views. May–Sept. **€110**

Logues Lodge Main St ☎ 065 707 7003, ⓦ logueslodge .ie. First-class accommodation with a bar and adjoining restaurant where Burren lamb reigns supreme on the menu. **€90**

★ Ó Loclainn's Bar Pier Rd ☎ 065 707 7006, ⓦ irishwhiskeybar.com. As good for local lore as it is for drinks – Margaret, who runs the bar with her husband, dispenses tourist information and drams from their dazzling array of whiskies in equal measure. Daily 8.30–11.30pm, open on Sun after Mass from around 2.30pm.

Galway and Mayo

INISHEER

Galway and Mayo

Sweeping strokes of geology have carved up the landscape of Galway and Mayo, forming a many-pronged block between Galway and Donegal bays that's almost cut off from the mainland by a string of lakes. In the south, the 40km stretch of Lough Corrib neatly bisects County Galway, the second-largest county in Ireland after Cork. On one side, the largely flat, gentle grasslands of east Galway stretch across to the Shannon, sheltering a fascinating diversity of historic castles, cathedrals, monasteries and country estates. Between Corrib and the sea, however, stands the violent jumble of Connemara, a much-romanticized land, but with plenty to get sentimental about.

10

Interest here is provided in abundance by the ever-changing scenery of beaches, bogs, lakes and wild mountains, though if you're looking for specific tourist attractions, there's a diverting cluster around the lakeside village of **Oughterard**. Connemara's main base, however, is **Clifden**, which boasts a fine range of facilities at the heart of the mountains. On the narrow neck of land between these eastern and western halves sits **Galway city**, an animated, historical town with an enjoyable social, musical and artistic life. The city gives a whiff of the Gaelic culture that's far more noticeable out on the **Arans**, starkly beautiful islands that used to form a barrier across the entrance to Galway Bay. As well as sheltering some breathtaking prehistoric and early Christian sites, the islands are part of the country's largest Irish-speaking area, which also comprises the eastern section of Connemara.

Though ranking just behind Galway in terms of size, **County Mayo** has only half its population and is far less developed for tourism. An exception is the eighteenth-century planned town of **Westport**, a comfortable, elegant base from which to tackle the pilgrims' path to the top of **Croagh Patrick**, and to visit the diverse inhabited **islands** at the mouth of Clew Bay. In the north of the county, the intriguing Neolithic agricultural remains at **Céide Fields** provide a compelling focus, surrounded by kilometre after unexplored kilometre of desolate bogland and rugged seascapes.

Galway city

Known for its festivals, music and bars, **GALWAY** (Gaillimh; ⓦdiscoverireland.ie) is a vibrant, fun-loving place and, though it has few sights to visit, many people end up staying longer than they'd intended. Conveniently, history and leisure combine here: the **pubs**, many of which retain their original, huge fireplaces and other

Highlights

❶ Galway festivals and pubs It's hard not to have a good time in the vibrant, youthful capital of the west. **See p.344 & p.351**

❷ Islands Choose between the wild beauty of the Arans, the grandiose scenery of accessible Achill, and Inishbofin's small-scale charms. **See p.359, p.387 & p.374**

❸ Dun Aengus, Inishmore The most exciting of the many ancient forts on the Aran Islands, spectacularly sited on a 90m cliff face. See p.362

❹ Walking in Connemara The best way to

appreciate the dramatic mountains, bogs and lakes. **See p.369**

❺ Croagh Patrick A tough climb, enriched by historical and religious associations, and outstanding views. **See p.382**

❻ National Museum of Country Life, Castlebar A fascinating peek at the realities of traditional life in rural Ireland, debunking the nostalgic myths. **See p.386**

❼ Céide Fields A 5000-year-old farming community preserved under the bog. See p.390

HIGHLIGHTS ARE MARKED ON THE MAP ON PP.342–343

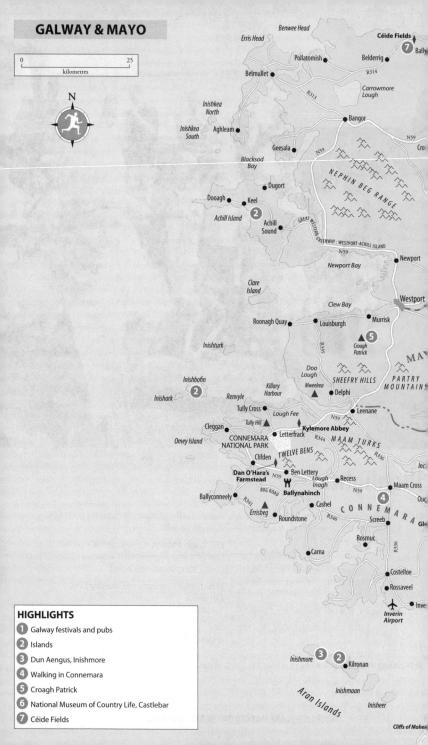

GALWAY & MAYO

0   25
kilometres

N

Benwee Head
Erris Head
Céide Fields
Céide Fields 7 Bally
Pollatomish
Belderrig
R314
Belmullet
R313
Carrowmore
Lough
Inishkea North
Bangor
N59
Cro
Inishkea South
Aghleam
Geesala
N59
Blacksod Bay
NEPHIN BEG RANGE
Dugort
Dooagh Keel
2
Achill Island
Achill Sound
GREAT WESTERN GREENWAY : WESTPORT–ACHILL ISLAND
N59
Newport Bay
Newport
Clare Island
Clew Bay
Westport
Roonagh Quay
Louisburgh
Murrisk
5
Croagh Patrick
MAY
Inishturk
R335
Doo Lough
SHEEFRY HILLS
PARTRY MOUNTAINS
Inishbofin
2
Killary Harbour
Mweelrea
Delphi
Inishshark
Renvyle
Lough Fee
Leenane
N59
Tully Cross
Tully Hill
Cleggan
CONNEMARA NATIONAL PARK
Letterfrack
Kylemore Abbey
MAAM TURKS
R344
R336
Omey Island
Clifden
TWELVE BENS
N59
Ben Lettery
Dan O'Hara's Farmstead
Lough Inagh
Recess
Maam Cross
Inc
Ballynahinch
BOG ROAD
4
Ballyconneely
R341
Cashel
R340
C O N N E M A R A
Oug
Glo
Errisbeg
Roundstone
Screeb
Carna
Rosmuc
R336
Costelloe
Rossaveel
Inve
Inverin Airport
Inishmore
3 2
Kilronan
Inishmaan
Aran Islands
Inisheer
Cliffs of Moher

HIGHLIGHTS

1. Galway festivals and pubs
2. Islands
3. Dun Aengus, Inishmore
4. Walking in Connemara
5. Croagh Patrick
6. National Museum of Country Life, Castlebar
7. Céide Fields

10

Gothic features, are the best places to get a feel for the medieval city. As the **capital** of the Gaelic West – it's the only city in the country where you might possibly hear Irish spoken on the streets – Galway draws young people to study at the National University of Ireland at Galway and the Institute of Technology. In the summer holidays, however, its bohemian diversity becomes more overt, as hundreds of English-language students renew the city's traditional maritime links with the Continent, while dozens of buskers from all over the world sing for their supper. This cosmopolitan atmosphere is reinforced by the setting: Galway is the only coastal city in Ireland that really seems to open up to the sea, and its docks sit cheek by jowl with the compact city centre, as you're constantly reminded by salty breezes and seagulls. The jewel in the city's crown, the long, pedestrianized main drag of **William**, **Shop**, **High** and **Quay streets**, becomes a boisterous, Mediterranean-style promenade during summer, lined with pub and restaurant tables. At its lower, western end, the street narrows to its original medieval dimensions, then flows into Galway Bay along with the thundering **River Corrib**, providing faraway views of the Burren hills of County Clare.

Brief history

Strategically located in the narrow gap between Lough Corrib and the sea, Galway was little more than the site of a twelfth-century fort when it was captured from the Gaelic O'Flaherty clan in 1232 by the Anglo-Norman **Richard de Burgo**, who built a castle by the river. From the fifteenth century, the town was controlled by an oligarchy of mostly Anglo-Norman families, by the names of Athy, Blake, Bodkin, Browne, Darcy, Deane, Ffrench, Ffront, Joyce, Kirwan, Lynch, Martin, Morris and Skerrett. Cromwell later dubbed them the "**Tribes of Galway**", an epithet which they adopted as a badge of honour – to this day, Galwegians nickname themselves the Tribesmen. Under this oligarchy, Galway grew wealthy as a largely independent **city-state**, far removed from the centres of power in Dublin and London but trading extensively with Europe, especially Spain and France.

The town remained proudly loyal to the English Crown, but this only elicited harsh treatment when Cromwell's forces arrived in 1652. Thereafter, Galway went into decline, exacerbated by the **Williamite War** later in the century, and fluctuating with the development of adjacent Salthill as a seaside resort in the early nineteenth century, the arrival of the railways and the building of navigable waterways to Lough Corrib in the 1840s and 1850s, alongside the depredations of the Great Famine. Growth returned in the **late 1960s** with industrial and tourism development, and Galway is now the fourth-largest city in the Republic.

GALWAY'S FESTIVALS

The city's biggest shindig is the two-week **Galway Arts Festival** in July (Ⓦgalwayartsfestival .com), a volatile mix of drama, music, poetry, dance and the visual arts, with a headlining parade by flamboyant local street-theatre company Macnas. Hard on its heels, in late July or early August, comes the even headier brew of the **Galway Races** at Ballybrit, about 5km east of town (Ⓦgalwayraces.com), when farmers and politicians rub shoulders to party and bet. The diverse festival calendar also includes part of the **Father Ted** jamboree (see box, p.363); **Cúirt**, an international festival of literature in late April (Ⓦgalwaycuirt.ie); the **Galway Early Music Festival** in late May (Ⓦgalwayearlymusic.com); the **Galway Sessions** of Irish and Scottish music in June (Ⓦgalwaysessions.com); and a prestigious, week-long cinema festival in early July, the **Film Fleadh** (Ⓦgalwayfilmfleadh.com). There's a weekend **jazz festival** in mid-September (Ⓦgalwayjazzfestival.com), while at the end of September the riotous, four-day **Galway Oyster Festival** (Ⓦgalwayoysterfest.com) includes the world oyster-shucking championships. Towards the end of the year, **Baboró** is an international arts festival for children in October (Ⓦbaboro.ie), while November's **TULCA** is a festival of contemporary visual art (Ⓦtulca.ie).

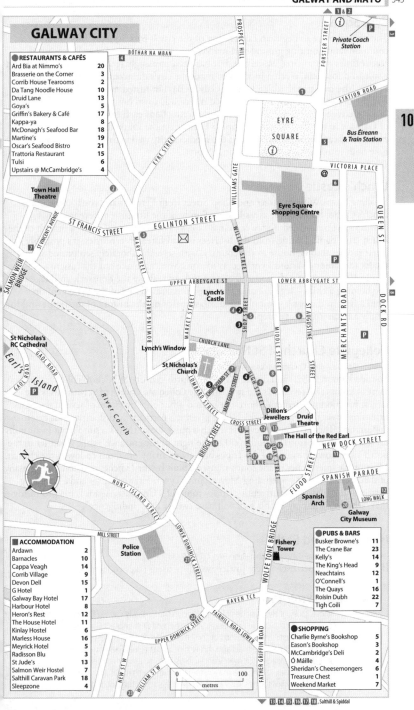

GALWAY CITY

RESTAURANTS & CAFÉS
Ard Bia at Nimmo's	20
Brasserie on the Corner	3
Corrib House Tearooms	2
Da Tang Noodle House	10
Druid Lane	13
Goya's	5
Griffin's Bakery & Café	17
Kappa-ya	8
McDonagh's Seafood Bar	18
Martine's	19
Oscar's Seafood Bistro	21
Trattoria Restaurant	15
Tulsi	6
Upstairs @ McCambridge's	4

ACCOMMODATION
Ardawn	2
Barnacles	10
Cappa Veagh	14
Corrib Village	9
Devon Dell	15
G Hotel	1
Galway Bay Hotel	17
Harbour Hotel	8
Heron's Rest	12
The House Hotel	11
Kinlay Hostel	6
Marless House	16
Meyrick Hotel	5
Radisson Blu	3
St Jude's	13
Salmon Weir Hostel	7
Salthill Caravan Park	18
Sleepzone	4

PUBS & BARS
Busker Browne's	11
The Crane Bar	23
Kelly's	14
The King's Head	9
Neachtains	12
O'Connell's	1
The Quays	16
Roisin Dubh	22
Tigh Coili	7

SHOPPING
Charlie Byrne's Bookshop	5
Eason's Bookshop	3
McCambridge's Deli	2
Ó Máille	4
Sheridan's Cheesemongers	6
Treasure Chest	1
Weekend Market	7

Eyre Square

The natural place to begin an exploration of the city is **Eyre Square**. This former common land, jousting ground and market square outside the city walls was until recent times a municipal wasteland, but has been pleasingly renovated. Here you'll find a splendid **fountain**, erected in 1984 to mark the city's quincentenary, which evokes a hooker (the traditional sailing boat of Galway Bay) in rusted metal and rushing water; and the **Browne doorway**, a finely carved mercantile town house entrance forlornly set in a concrete wall. The square's fourteen fluttering **flags** each represent one of the Tribes of Galway. In the Eyre Square Shopping Centre, on the southwest side, stands an extensive, heavily restored section of the medieval **city wall** with a couple of towers, now built into the back wall of Dunnes Stores.

10

Lynch's Castle

Strolling down William Street and Shop Street from Eyre Square, you'll come upon **Lynch's Castle**, home of the city's leading family of the fifteenth to seventeenth centuries, who provided no fewer than 84 mayors of Galway – it's now a branch of the Allied Irish Bank. Dating from the fourteenth and fifteenth centuries, it's probably the finest medieval town house in the country, with several elaborately sculptured slabs on the façade: among various Lynch coats of arms, you can make out the insignia of King Henry VII, featuring a dragon and greyhound, and, above the doorway, an image of an ape holding a child – legend has it that the animal saved one of the Lynch children from a fire. In the bank vestibule are display boards on the history of the house and the family and an impressive fireplace.

Collegiate Church of St Nicholas

Market St • Daily 9am–6pm • €2 suggested donation • ☎ 091 564648, ⓦ stnicholas.ie

Founded around 1320 and dedicated to the fourth-century St Nicholas of Myra, patron saint of sailors and revered as Santa Claus, the **Collegiate Church of St Nicholas** is the largest functioning medieval church in Ireland – but only by virtue of several slate-grey extensions over the centuries which have given it a particularly disharmonious external appearance. The interior, however, is worth a quick look. There's a simple but beautifully carved font dating from around 1600 to the right of the entrance, while a banner in the north aisle shows the arms of the Tribes of Galway, many of whom endowed the church. Most of the interest lies in the south transept, built by the Lynches and containing many of their ornate **tombs** – including Mayor James Lynch Fitzstephens – and a curiously personal thirteenth- or fourteenth-century tomb of a Crusader, Adam Bure, promising that "whoever will pray for his soul will have twenty days' indulgence".

Hall of the Red Earl

Druid Lane • Mon–Fri 9.30am–4.45pm, Sat 10am–3pm • Free • ☎ 091 564646

If you want to experience where justice was dispensed, taxes collected and banquets

---

A GALWAY LYNCHING

The most famous story of the Lynches is embodied in the ornately carved **Lynch's Window**, around the corner from the castle on Market Street, behind St Nicholas's Church. In the 1490s young Walter Lynch Fitzstephens, jealous of the attentions a Spanish guest was giving his girlfriend Ann Blake, stabbed the man and threw him into the sea. The boy was duly sentenced to death, but the town pleaded for mercy and the usual executioner refused to do his duty. It was left to the boy's father, James, the mayor, to hang him from this jail window, which is now carved with a skull and crossbones. Galwegians claim this to be the origin of the term "lynching".

held in Galway's early days, make your way to the stunning **Hall of the Red Earl**. The ruins, protected by glass panelling with a raised viewing walkway, were opened in 2010 and are the oldest surviving settlement within Galway's ancient walls. There are interpretive panels explaining the significance of the site, plus display cabinets holding clay pipes, a gold cuff link and a human skull.

Claddagh museum

Quay Lane • Mon–Sat 10am–5pm • Free • ☎ 091 534494, ⓦ claddaghjewellery.com

A small, informal museum at the back of Dillon's Jewellers traces the engaging cultural history of the **Claddagh ring**. Designed by a late seventeenth-century Galwegian who had been captured by pirates and enslaved to a Moorish goldsmith, this style of ring has been worn by the likes of Queen Victoria and John Wayne. It features a pair of hands, symbolizing friendship, a heart, for love, and a mitred crown, traditionally for loyalty, and is often given as a love token. The museum also displays old photos of **the Claddagh** (An Cladach; "a flat, stony shore"), a former fishing village on the south bank of the river.

Galway city Museum

Spanish Parade • Tues–Sat 10am–5pm • Free • ☎ 091 532460, ⓦ galwaycitymuseum.ie

Down by the river, near the sixteenth-century **Spanish Arch**, stands the recently rebuilt, glass-fronted **Galway city Museum**, which hosts some interesting temporary exhibitions. Its permanent collection has relatively few artefacts, but traces the city's history in vivid fashion, dealing with the Claddagh on the second floor, the medieval town on the first, and bringing matters up to date on the ground floor. The highlights are a 9m hooker boat, suspended in all its glory in the atrium, which was specially commissioned for the museum; and a statue of Galway-born **Pádraic Ó Conaire** (see p.613), the first modernist fiction writer in Irish.

Fishery Tower

Wolfe Tone Bridge • Mon–Sat 10am–3pm • Free • ☎ 091 564646

One of Galway's most delightful landmark buildings, the unique **Fishery Tower** was built in 1852 as a draught netting station. It was used as a lookout point to monitor fish stocks coming up the Corrib River and to spot any illegal fishing. Visitors can look out over the river to the Claddagh and, via a live link, see salmon spawning.

Salthill and Silver Strand

Galway Atlantaquaria The Promenade • Mon–Fri 10am–5pm, Sat & Sun 10am–6pm; Oct–Feb closed Mon and Tues; feedings at 1pm, 3pm & 4pm; free talks and tours on weekends and during school holidays • €11.50, children €7.50 • ☎ 091 585100, ⓦ nationalaquarium.ie

About 1km southwest of Wolfe Tone Bridge begins the resort suburb of **Salthill**, Galway's summer playground. The long promenade is lined with high-rise apartment blocks, hotels and amusement arcades, as well as safe beaches with fine views across the bay to the Burren. It's a Sunday afternoon tradition to walk its length and kick the wall at the end by the diving platform (for good luck, of course) before turning back.

On the front, the National Aquarium of Ireland, **Galway Atlantaquaria,** is a big hit with kids, entertainingly showcasing Ireland's sea, river and canal life. Beyond Salthill and just 5km west of the centre, **Silver Strand** is the nicest beach in the vicinity of the city, a small, sandy affair with a Blue Flag and a gentle shelf, beneath a grassy headland. It's accessible on buses towards Spiddal.

ARRIVAL AND DEPARTURE

BY TRAIN

Céannt Station (☎ 091 537582) is on Station Road, on the southeast side of Eyre Square.

Destinations Athenry (11–13 daily; 15min); Athlone (7–9 daily; 1hr); Dublin (6–8 daily; 2hr 30min–3hr); Ennis (4–5 daily; 1hr 20min); Gort (4–5 daily; 50min); Kildare (2–4 daily; 2hr); Limerick (4–5 daily; 2hr).

BY BUS

The city's Bus Éireann station is beside the train station, while private companies mostly use the new coach station behind the tourist office on Forster Street. Of the latter, Citylink (☎ 091 564164, ⓦ citylink.ie) and Gobus (☎ 091 564600, ⓦ gobus.ie) each run frequent coaches between Galway city and Dublin city centre and airport, with some buses running via Loughrea and Athlone. Citylink also runs several coaches a day to Gort and Shannon Airport; to Gort, Limerick, Killarney, Cork city centre and Cork airport; and to Oughterard, Clifden, Cleggan and Letterfrack. Feda O'Donnell Coaches (☎ 091 761656, ⓦ fedaodonnell.com) operates daily services between Galway city (departing from the Catholic cathedral) and Knock, Sligo, Bundoran, Donegal, Letterkenny and Gweedore.

Destinations by local bus Achill (Fri & Sun 1 daily; 3hr 20min–4hr); Athenry (Mon–Sat 3–4 daily; 35min); Athlone (hourly; 1hr 30min); Ballina (4–7 daily; 2hr 15min); Castlebar (5–6 daily; 1hr 45min); Clarenbridge (hourly; 20min); Clifden (summer Mon–Sat 4–5 daily, Sun 2 daily; winter Mon–Sat 3 daily, Sun 1 daily; 1hr 45min–2hr 15min); Cliffs of Moher (summer 2–4 daily; winter 1 daily; 2hr); Cong (2–3 daily; 45min–1hr); Cork (hourly; 4hr 15min); Derry (3–5 daily; 5hr 15min); Doolin (summer 2–5 daily; winter 1–2 daily; 1hr 30min); Dublin (hourly; 3hr 45min); Ennis (hourly; 1hr 15min); Gort (hourly; 45min); Ireland West Airport (5–7 daily; 2hr); Kilcolgan (hourly; 30min); Kinvarra (1–6 daily; 30min–1hr); Kylemore (summer Mon–Sat 1 daily; winter 1 weekly; 1hr 45min–3hr); Leenane (summer Mon–Sat 1 daily; winter 1 weekly; 1hr 20min–3hr); Letterfrack (winter 1 weekly, summer Mon–Sat 1 daily; 1hr 50min–3hr); Letterkenny (3–5 daily; 4hr 40min); Limerick (hourly; 2hr 15min); Loughrea (hourly; 35min); Oranmore (at least hourly; 10min); Oughterard (Mon–Sat 4–7 daily, Sun 2–3; 40min); Rosmuc (Mon & Fri 1; 1hr 15min); Roundstone (winter 3 weekly, summer 1–2 daily; 1hr 30min); Shannon Airport (hourly; 1hr 45min); Sligo (5–6 daily; 2hr 30min); Spiddal (Mon–Sat 5–9 daily, Sun 2; 40min); Westport (2–4 daily; 2hr).

INFORMATION

For local listings, pick up a copy of the *Connacht Tribune* at Eason's Bookshop (see p.352).

Tourist office Forster Street (summer daily 9am–5.45pm; winter Mon–Sat 9am–5.45pm; ☎ 091 537700, ⓦ discoverireland.ie). There's also an information kiosk on Eyre Square (summer daily 9.30am–1.30pm & 2.30–5.30pm; winter Mon–Sat 9.30am–1.30pm & 2.30–5.30pm). In winter, either the main office or the kiosk will generally remain open on Sundays from 9am until 12.45pm.

GETTING AROUND

By bus Bus Éireann (☎ 091 562000) city and suburban services leave Eyre Square for many parts of the city including Salthill (#401; every 20min 9am–7pm; every 40min (7–11.40pm) and College Rd (#40; every 15min 9am–7pm) for B&Bs (see opposite). An all-day, unlimited pass costs €4.10 (€1.70 per single journey). A weekly pass costs €20.20.

By taxi Galway Taxis at 57 Lower Dominick St (☎ 091 561111). There are taxi ranks at Eyre Square.

By car Pay and display on the street; there's a car park next to the tourist office off Forster St and multistoreys on Dock Rd and Merchants Rd.

By bike West Ireland Cycling on Earls Island St (☎ 091 588830, ⓦ westirelandcycling.com).

TOURS AND ACTIVITIES

Walking tours In the summer themed walking tours of the city depart from either the tourist office or the City Museum (see p.347), generally lasting 1hr 30min–2hr (€10; book at the tourist office).

Bus tours Hop-on, hop-off, open-top bus tours of Galway and Salthill operate in the summer from the tourist office (1hr; €10), where you can also sign up for longer-distance tours. Tours to Connemara, the Burren and the Cliffs of Moher run from the private coach station with the Galway Tour Company (☎ 091 566566, ⓦ galwaytourcompany .com; €15).

River tours In summer, 90min *Corrib Princess* cruises (May, June & Sept 2 daily; July & Aug 3 daily; €16; ☎ 091 592447, ⓦ corribprincess.ie) depart from Woodquay (beyond Salmon Weir Bridge and behind the Town Hall Theatre). Cruises head 8km up the river, passing a couple of ruined castles, before entering Lough Corrib. Buy tickets at the tourist office.

Watersports Windsurfing rental and tuition available at Rusheen Bay, at the west end of Salthill (☎ 087 260 5702, ⓦ www.rusheenbay.com). Various kayaking trips on offer with Kayakmór (☎ 087 756 5578, ⓦ kayakmor.ie).

ACCOMMODATION

At festival time (see box, p.344), especially during the Galway Races, rooms are at a premium – often in both senses of the word. The city centre boasts a high standard of **hotels**, while the scores of **B&Bs** are nearly all on the outskirts, including large clusters on College Road (the continuation of Forster Street) and Dublin Road, and in Salthill (see below).

HOTELS

★**Galway Bay Hotel** The Promenade, Salthill ☎091 530530, ⓦgalwaybayhotel.net. Stylish hotel with attractive rooms and a terrace overlooking the bay. The pool and leisure centre offer added value and there's a range of special offers. €170

G Hotel Wellpark, Dublin Rd, 2km from the centre on the N6 ☎091 865200, ⓦtheghotel.ie. Designed by local lad, the milliner Philip Treacy, this hotel is a bold fashion statement in an inauspicious location next to a shopping centre. The public rooms, featuring mirror-ball lamps, veer towards high camp, but the spacious bedrooms are beautifully designed and equipped, and there's an elegant, black-marble, Japanese-themed ESPA and fitness centre. €160

Harbour Hotel The Harbour ☎091 894800, ⓦharbour .ie. This crisp, modern hotel offers bright, well-equipped rooms, decorated in strong colours and blonde wood, as well as a gym. €149

The House Hotel Lower Merchants Rd ☎091 538900, ⓦthehousehotel.ie. A luxurious boutique hotel converted from a warehouse, featuring well-equipped rooms with sound-proofed windows and colourful, contemporary public rooms. €149

★**Meyrick Hotel** Eyre Square ☎091 564041, ⓦhotelmeyrick.ie. This imposing Victorian railway hotel, formerly the *Great Southern*, has been renovated and brought into the same stable as the *G Hotel*. The bedrooms attractively mix traditional and modern decor, and there's a top-floor spa with outdoor hot tub and gym. Various offers available. €199

Radisson Blu Lough Atalia Rd ☎091 538300, ⓦradissonhotelgalway.com. A modern, Scandinavian-run luxury hotel overlooking Galway Bay from a fine position on the northeast side of the train station. A long list of leisure facilities includes an extensive spa, swimming pool, gym, outdoor hot tub and sauna. Colour schemes in the bedrooms are dominated by purple and beige, set off with elegant furnishings and soft lighting. €200

B&BS

Ardawn 31 College Rd ☎091 568833, ⓦardawnhouse .com. Welcoming, upmarket B&B a 10min walk from the centre in a red-brick, modern house. Smart, comfortable rooms, plenty of local information, free wi-fi and lavish breakfasts. €100

Cappa Veagh 76 Dalysfort Rd, Salthill ☎091 526518, ⓦcappaveagh.com. This comfortable and clean, modern en-suite house is close to the seafront and on the #401 bus route, with knowledgeable hosts. March–Nov. €90

Corrib Village Newcastle Rd, 3km north of the centre ☎091 527112, ⓦcampusaccommodation.ie. In summer (June–Aug), this large complex on the campus of Galway University offers a variety of standard and en-suite B&B accommodation or apartment rentals, all with wi-fi access. Sited on the banks of the River Corrib, the "village" includes a café, mini-market, kids' club, tennis courts, laundry facilities and a complimentary shuttle bus to Eyre Square (10am–7pm), and guests have reduced-rate access to the university's wide-ranging sports facilities. €50

Devon Dell 47 Devon Park, Lower Salthill ☎091 528306, ⓦdevondell.com. Helpful and well-run B&B in a quiet cul-de-sac near the seafront. The attractive, en-suite rooms and the varied breakfasts are delicious and range from pancakes and waffles to smoked salmon and goat's cheese. Mar–Oct. €90

★**Heron's Rest** 16 Long Walk ☎091 539574, ⓦtheheronsrest.com. Hospitable B&B in a peerless location, steps from the city centre but overlooking the quiet river and Galway Bay. Attractive rooms, with extras such as bathrobes, decanters of port and binoculars. Gourmet breakfasts include crab cakes and seared scallops. Easter–Oct. €130

Marless House Threadneedle Rd, Salthill ☎091 523931, ⓦmarlesshouse.com. Comfortable, mock-Georgian modern home, 3km from the centre by the beach, with bright, colourful, en-suite rooms; there's free wi-fi and a varied breakfast menu. €80

St Jude's 110 Lower Salthill ☎091 521619, ⓦst-judes .com. Grand, manorial 1920s family home with elegant, en-suite bedrooms and good breakfasts, a 10min walk from the centre. Dinner, cookery courses and good single rates available. €90

HOSTELS

Barnacles 10 Quay St (IHH) ☎091 568644, ⓦbarnacles.ie. Large and efficiently run hostel right in the hub of Galway's nightlife. All rooms are en suite, and a light breakfast is included. There are laundry and kitchen facilities, free internet and wi-fi. Double dorms €66

Kinlay Hostel Merchants Rd (IHH) ☎091 565244, ⓦkinlaygalway.ie. Modern hostel that's friendly and well run, with laundry, a kitchen, free wi-fi, and some en-suite rooms. Prices include a simple continental breakfast. Double dorms €58

Salmon Weir Hostel St Vincent's Ave (IHO) ☎091 561133, ⓦsalmonweirhostel.com. Small and simple, with some en-suite rooms, this comfortable hostel has a kitchen, laundry facilities, wi-fi and friendly atmosphere. Breakfast not included. Double dorms €64

10

Sleepzone Bóthar na mBan ☎091 566999, ⓦsleepzone .ie. Modern, well-maintained, 200-bed hostel affiliated to An Óige, a 5min walk north of Eyre Square. All rooms are en suite, with singles, twins and doubles available, as well as free internet and wi-fi, kitchen, laundry facilities and a bureau de change. Double dorms €58

CAMPING

Salthill Caravan Park Knocknacarra ☎091 523972, ⓦsalthillcaravanpark.com. Beside the seashore with superb views of Galway Bay and access to an excellent beach. The campsite has room for 30 tents. Mid-May to Aug. Tent pitch €20

EATING

10

★**Ard Bia at Nimmo's** Spanish Arch Long Walk ☎091 561114, ⓦardbia.com. Set in a stone-built medieval customs house by the river, with rustic-chic decor, and modern art on the walls. The top-notch modern Irish food focuses on expertly prepared local, seasonal ingredients, with a few Middle Eastern touches (the mezze plate is especially good). Lunch includes power salad, potato hot pot or pulled pork with prices averaging €8. Main dinner courses start from around €12. Daily 10am–3.30pm & 6pm–midnight (kitchen closes 10pm).

Brasserie on the Corner Eglinton St ☎091 530333, ⓦbrasseriegalway.com. Galway is shellfish central and many come here to sample "Marty's Meaty Mussels", rope-cultivated specimens from Killary Harbour, served with zingy sauces. Delicious brown soda to mop up. Main courses run from €12–17. Daily noon–10pm.

★**Corrib House Tearooms** 3 Waterside, Woodquay ☎091 446753, ⓦcorribhouse.com. This delightfully situated café in a Georgian-style mansion has a range of lunch-time dishes such as grilled chicken, lamb burgers, quiches, salads and soups. Grab a window seat to look out on the salmon weir and the Corrib. Mains average €9. Mon–Fri 9.30am–5pm, Sat 10am–5pm.

Da Tang Noodle House Middle St ☎091 561443, ⓦdatangnoodlehouse.com. Hung with art exhibitions, this reasonably priced spot provides good, mostly northern Chinese noodles – either in soup, sauce or pan-fried – as well as sizzling dishes, hotpots and summertime salads. Main courses run from €12–17. Daily noon–10pm, closed Sun lunch.

Druid Lane 9 Quay St ☎091 563015. Relaxed, informal restaurant, with helpful staff and excellent bistro food, such as duck breast with apricot stuffing; or you can perch at the bar for a glass of wine and snacks. Early-bird menu until 7pm. Daily 1–10.30pm.

Goya's Kirwan's Lane ☎091 567010, ⓦgoyas.ie. Elegant café with tables on the alley, serving home-baked cakes and pastries that are little short of perfection. Lunch-time goodies include soups, salads, quiches and pies. Main dishes €7–10. Mon–Sat 9am–6pm.

Griffin's Bakery & Café 21 Shop St ☎091 563683, ⓦgriffinsbakery.com. It's part of the sensory experience of Galway to walk into this family-owned artisan bakery (in business since 1876 and now in its fifth generation) for their unbeatable breads including

bracks, rye, soda, gluten-free and sourdough – and even one with an Irish whiskey kick. Lunches consist of soups, sandwiches and light snacks as well as cakes and muffins in a traditional tea room at the back, where the turf fire offers a welcoming glow on chilly days. Prices start from €5 for light lunches. Mon–Sat 8.30am–7pm, Sun 10am–7pm.

Kappa-ya 4 Middle St ☎091 865930. Small, relaxing café-restaurant serving carefully prepared and reasonably priced Celtic-Japanese food – the chicken teriyaki sushi rolls are especially good, and leave room for some wasabi and pistachio ice cream. On Sat evenings (by reservation), you can sample more elaborate dishes such as nigiri sushi. Prices for mains range from €9–15. Mon–Sat noon–4pm, Tues–Sat also 7–9.30pm.

McDonagh's Seafood Bar 22 Quay St ☎091 565001, ⓦmcdonaghs.net. This Galway institution features nautical paraphernalia and a menu that casts its net wide: pan-fried mackerel, baked monkfish, trout, scampi, grilled ray, wild Clarinbridge mussels, crabs and scallops are all on offer. The two-course set menu with a glass of wine is €19.95, while battered cod or haddock are popular from the takeaway section. Mon–Sat noon–10pm.

Martine's Quay St ☎091 565662, ⓦwinebar.ie. Friendly, wood-panelled bistro with tables outside. The fairly conservative evening menu (think rack of lamb, chicken, duck or lasagne) is enlivened by a more adventurous list of daily specials, notably seafood. The €20 early-bird set menu is served all evening. Daily 1–3pm & 5–10.30pm.

★**Oscar's Seafood Bistro** Dominick St ☎091 582180, ⓦoscarbistro.ie. Savvy locals like this bistro just a few minutes' walk from the crowds of Quay St. And it's worth the short hike for some of the freshest local seafood, such as Clare Island salmon or spicy popcorn shrimp. The prix fixe menu at €15 for two courses is served Mon–Thurs evening and till 7pm on Fri. Mon–Sat 5.30–10pm.

Trattoria Restaurant 12 Quay St ☎091 563910, ⓦtrattoriarestaurant.ie. Cheery Italian place decorated with nostalgic murals of Rome, dishing up lots of good, homemade pastas, risottos, huge pizzas and a few meat and fish mains with prices from €12. Good-value set menus. Mon–Thurs 5–10pm, Fri 5–10.30pm, Sat & Sun noon–10pm.

Tulsi Buttermilk Walk, Middle St ☎091 564831, ⓦtulsigalway.com. Galway's best Indian restaurant rustles up very good vegetarian and meaty food and even tries its hand at Indo-Galwegian fusion dishes such as tandoori mackerel for an appetizer. Main courses average €10. Early-bird offer Mon–Thurs till 7.30pm. Daily 5.30–10pm.

★**Upstairs @ McCambridge's** Shop St ☎091 562259, ⓦmccambridges.com. A wonderful addition to the Galwegian culinary scene, above a deli that has been in business since 1925. The lunch or early evening dinner all-day menu showcases cold platters of cheese, meat or seafood, salads, frittatas, and hot dishes such as lamb kebabs or roasted prawns. Prices average €10–13. Daily 9am–8pm.

DRINKING AND NIGHTLIFE

10

A slow crawl through the **pubs** of Shop, High and Quay streets is a must, soaking up the atmosphere of their historic interiors in winter, and the buzzy street life at their outdoor tables in summer. You're bound to find a traditional session here, although the best pub for music is *The Crane Bar*, just over the bridge (see below).

Busker Browne's Cross St ☎091 563377, ⓦbuskerbrownes.com. This popular bar in a former Dominican convent offers medieval fireplaces, a lofty, Gothic hall, and floor upon floor of alcoves and armchairs in a complementary modern design. Food is served – try the seafood chowder – and there are DJs at weekends, plus jazz Sun lunch times. Daily 10.30am–1.30am.

★**The Crane Bar** Sea Rd ☎091 587419, ⓦthecranebar.com. Atmospheric pub with an upstairs venue, this is the top spot for traditional music, with sessions every night which can involve up to twelve musicians, plus all manner of other folk music, blues and singer-songwriters. Occasional entry charge. Daily 3pm–midnight.

Kelly's Bridge St ☎091 563804, ⓦkellysbar.ie. A loving re-creation of a mid-twentieth-century Irish pub, with wooden benches, two snugs, scones on the bar and leather banquettes. Fortunately, the food has been updated and is especially popular at weekends for brunch. The upstairs venue hosts DJ nights Thurs–Sat and live acts. Daily 10.30am–11.30pm, Fri & Sat till 2am.

The King's Head High St ☎091 566630, ⓦthekingshead.ie. Busy three-storey pub in a medieval building with flagstone floors, stone walls and an early seventeenth-century marriage stone above the fireplace. The bar's name comes from the fact that the man who requisitioned this building, Colonel Peter Stubbers, was widely rumoured to have been Charles I's executioner. Popular for its food and live bands nightly (traditional on Wed), plus DJs on Sat. Mon–Thurs & Sun 10.30am–11pm/midnight, Fri & Sat till 2am.

★**Neachtains** 17 Cross St ☎091 568820, ⓦtighneachtain.com. Galway's finest traditional pub, serving a wide choice of craft beers and whiskies in what was once the town house of Humanity Dick (see p.372). In winter, the homely warren of small rooms, bars, bench seats and snugs draws a diverse crowd, who migrate to the plentiful tables on the busy corner of Cross and Quay streets in summer. Daily 10.30am–midnight.

O'Connell's Eyre Square ☎091 563634. At this 150-year-old pub, choose between the traditional, sociable front bar with its bench seats (a good spot to catch TV sport), the quirky parlour rooms behind, and the two beer gardens and outdoor bar. Local craft and international beers and good Guinness all available on tap. Daily 11am–11.30pm, Fri & Sat till 2.30am.

The Quays Quay St ☎091 568347. Regular two-storey façade conceals an eccentric, warren-like pub, decorated with mullioned and stained-glass windows, carved beams and Gothic wooden arches. Traditional sessions Mon, Tues and early evening Sun, plus a balconied venue with a large stage for live cover bands and DJs. Late bar every night. Mon–Sat 10.30am–2am, Sun 12.30pm–1am.

Roísín Dubh Lower Dominick St ☎091 586540, ⓦroisindubh.net. This pub is Galway's best general live venue, hosting gigs of every style from rock and reggae to folk and funk, with a late bar every night and a pleasant terrace overlooking the river. Comedy club Wed night. Daily 11am–1am.

★**Tigh Coili** Mainguard St ☎091 586540. Welcoming, central and sociable traditional family-run pub with daily sessions in old-fashioned surroundings: Mon–Sat around 6pm & 9.30pm, Sun 2pm & 7pm. Getting a seat in here on a busy night is difficult, so on a sunny evening you can enjoy your drink outside. Daily 10.30am–11.30pm, Fri & Sat to 12.30am.

ENTERTAINMENT

Town Hall Theatre Courthouse Square, Woodquay ☎091 569777, ⓦtownhalltheatregalway.com. Built in the 1820s, the Town Hall Theatre is the city's main performance venue, putting on drama, dance, music and opera by visiting companies throughout the year.

Druid Druid Lane ☎091 568660, ⓦdruidtheatre.com. Local theatre company whose highly acclaimed productions have included the complete cycle of six plays by John Millington Synge. They generally open their new shows at their theatre on Druid Lane before touring.

SHOPPING

★Charlie Byrne's Bookshop Cornstore Mall Middle St ☎091 561 766, ⓦcharliebyrne.com. Huge range of new, secondhand and discounted books with an extensive Irish section; the ideal place to dip into some of Tim Robinson's magisterial trilogy on the topography of Connemara. Mon–Wed & Sat 9am–6pm, Thurs & Fri 9am–8pm, Sun noon–6pm.

Eason's Bookshop 33 Shop St ☎091 562284, ⓦeason .com. A large general bookshop that sells a wide variety of magazines and newspapers: everything from the *Connacht Tribune* (for local listings) to *Le Monde*. Mon–Wed & Sat 9am–6.15pm, Thurs & Fri 9am–9pm, Sun noon–6pm.

McCambridge's Deli Shop St ☎091 562259, ⓦmccambridges.com. A dazzling array of chutneys, preserves, herbs and spices alongside Butlers Irish chocolates, truffles, toffee, the unique Hadji Bey's Irish Turkish delight and Murphy's ice cream. On-site café too. Mon–Wed 8am–7pm, Thurs–Sat 8am–9pm, Sun 10.30am–6pm.

Ó Máille 16 High St ☎091 562696, ⓦomaille.com. If you're after woollen garments such as scarves, hats, throws, rugs or Aran sweaters, this is the best place. Their proud boast is that the shop supplied many of the tailored costumes for *The Quiet Man* (see p.378), filmed in Galway and Mayo in 1951. Mon–Sat 10am–7pm, Sun noon–6pm.

★Sheridan's Cheesemongers 14–16 Churchyard St ☎091 564829, ⓦsheridancheesemongers.com. Outstanding Irish, Swiss and French cheeses and other speciality foods, including the local Ardrahan honey (used for boosting the immune system and beating hay fever). A wine bar upstairs offers carefully sourced cheese, meat and smoked-fish plates. A mixed board is €10. Tues 5–10pm, Wed & Thurs 1–10pm, Fri & Sat 3pm–midnight, Sun 3–10pm.

Treasure Chest 31–33 William St ☎091 563862, ⓦtreasurechest.ie. An elegant gift, craft and fashion shop on a large corner site showcasing many of Ireland's leading brand names. You will find Waterford and Galway crystal, Belleek china, Claddagh rings, Irish linen and knitwear. Mon–Sat 9.30am–6pm, Sun 1–5pm.

Weekend Market Churchyard St ⓦgalwaymarket.net. The lively Saturday market transforms the area around St Nicholas's Church (there's a smaller version on Sunday) and hosts craftspeople, market gardeners and foodstalls. You could make up a picnic of cheese, bratwurst, homemade bread, smoked salmon, hummus, olives and doughnuts. Sat 8am–6pm, Sun (Fri in July & Aug) noon–6pm.

East Galway

East Galway (ⓦgalwayeast.com) is a vast tract of flat, fertile land bordered by the Shannon and its tributary the River Suck, the southern half of which shelters some compelling places to visit. The west's first designated "heritage town", **Athenry**, is a fascinating stop, while **Kinvarra** is a justly popular honeypot down on the shores of Galway Bay. Several historic attractions ring the town of **Gort** just inland, notably **Coole Park**, Lady Gregory's idyllic woodland estate, W.B. Yeats's tower house, Thoor Ballylee (closed to visitors due to flooding) and the monastic ruins and round tower at **Kilmacduagh**. Out on a limb on the shores of Lough Derg, **Portumna** is an easy-going boating resort, with a fine castle and forest park, which gives access to **Clonfert Cathedral**, one of the country's finest Romanesque churches.

Southeast of Galway city, the N18 runs around the shores of **Galway Bay**, which are lined with native European Flat Oyster beds. The oysters are celebrated at the long-running **Clarenbridge Oyster Festival** (ⓦclarenbridge.com), held over three days in early September. This kicks off the season which lasts until April. Beyond Kilcolgan, the N18 heads inland towards Gort, Ennis and Limerick, while the N67 towards the Burren hugs the coast via the village of Kinvarra following the route of the Wild Atlantic Way (see box, p.31).

Kinvarra and around

Tucked away at the head of its own inlet in the southeastern corner of the bay, pretty **KINVARRA** (ⓦkinvara.com) is a popular getaway for Galwegians, with several attractive pubs and cafés. The village lays on a music **festival**, the *Fleadh na gCuach* (the Cuckoo Fleadh), usually over the bank holiday weekend at the start of May, and the *Cruinniú na mBád* (the Meeting of the Boats), over a weekend in August (depending on the tides). The latter features the racing of Galway Bay's traditional, wooden, red-sailed boats – known as **hookers** – which can often be seen docked in the harbour.

Dunguaire Castle

May–Sept daily 10am–5pm • €6 • ☎ 091 637108, ⊛ shannonheritage.com

The name of **Dunguaire Castle**, an intact, four-storey tower house built in 1520, comes from Guaire – the seventh-century king of Connacht who was so renowned for his generosity that his right arm was said to have grown longer than his left – and *dún* (fort), which may refer to the ancient earthwork on the headland to the east.

10

Doorus Peninsula

On the west side of Kinvarra Bay, the tranquil **Doorus Peninsula**, which was an island until the eighteenth century, shelters on its north shore the Blue Flag **Traught beach** (6km from Kinvarra), and provides ample opportunity for scenic walks or cycle rides – *Kinvarra: A Ramblers' Map and Guide* can be picked up from Murphy Store (☎ 091 637760), a crafts and coffee shop in a renovated grain store at Kinvarra quay.

ARRIVAL AND GETTING AROUND   KINVARRA AND AROUND

By bus There is a regular (6–7 daily) Bus Éireann service to Clarenbridge and Kilcolgan along the N18 between Galway and Limerick, but a limited service (two buses in high season) that turns off the main road, the N67 to Kinvarra, Ballyvaughan, Doolin and the Cliffs of Moher. Buses stop outside *Keogh's* pub on the main street.

ACCOMMODATION AND EATING

Breacan Cottage Parkmore Pier ☎ 091 638266, ⊛ breacan.com. Out near the northeastern corner of the Doorus peninsula, this rustic, tastefully designed B&B at the water's edge is named after a holy well in a nearby field. Excellent breakfasts, including fresh fruit salad or cheese and chive omelette with mushrooms, accompany stunning views across Galway Bay. **€70**

Connolly's The Quay, Kinvarra ☎ 091 637131, ⊛ connollyskinvara.com. This flower-bedecked pub with attractive outdoor tables has been in the same spot since 1898 and sells Kinvarra (made in Offaly) on draught. Traditional musicians flock here in the summer every night (except Thurs) and on Sun afternoon at 5pm. Daily noon–midnight.

Greens Main St, Kinvarra ☎ 091 637110. Part of the fabric of Kinvarra for many generations, this is an old-fashioned spot where the shelves heave with a variety of beers and whiskies. They hold frequent impromptu sessions, so it's best to call in advance if you want to hear some trad. Daily 5–11.30pm, Fri & Sat till 12.30am.

Keogh's Bar and Restaurant Main St, Kinvarra ☎ 091 637145. Reasonably priced snacks and full meals, including local smoked salmon and oysters in season, with prices from €10 (the seafood platter for two is €24.95) – plus an open fire to keep things cosy. Music in bar Thurs–Sun in high

season. Daily noon–10pm, Sat till 10.30pm.

Merriman Main St, Kinvarra ☎ 091 638222, ⊛ merrimanhotel.com. Most people visit Kinvarra for the day from Galway, but the village has a good-value hotel named after the eighteenth-century satirical Irish-language poet (see p.332) from nearby Ennistymon in Clare. Boasting one of Ireland's largest thatched roofs, the hotel is tastefully decorated with well-appointed rooms. Dinner is available in the restaurant, while the *Thatch Bar* has cheaper options. **€110**

Moran's Oyster Cottage The Weir, Kilcolgan ☎ 091 796113, ⊛ moransoystercottage.com. A bar and restaurant set by the bay and famed for native oysters (from their own beds) accompanied by brown bread and a creamy pint of stout. Seafood platters, crab claws, mussels or Aran Islands prawns are all available. Mains from €9. Mon–Thurs noon–11.30pm, Fri & Sat noon–midnight, Sun noon–11pm.

Paddy Burke's Main St, Clarenbridge ☎ 091 796226, ⊛ paddyburkesgalway.com. A renowned pub which has fed and watered royalty and celebrities for many years. Shellfish dominates but the menu also offers cod, trout and plaice, and alternatives such as deep fried camembert, duck, pasta or beef. Main courses from around €12. Daily 10am–11.30pm.

Gort and around

About 12km southeast of Kinvarra and 19km south of Kilcolgan, **GORT** is a traffic-laden workaday town of multicoloured houses on the busy N18 Galway–Limerick road, with some relief provided by the large, triangular market square in the centre.

Kinvarra and Galway would be more congenial bases for exploring the surrounding **historic sites** (for which you'll need your own transport).

Coole Park

3km north of Gort on the N18 • Visitor centre open daily: April & May 10am–5pm; June–Aug 10am–6pm; park open daily: summer 8.30am–7.30pm; winter 8am–6pm; café daily: April, May & Sept 10.30am–5pm; June & Aug 10.30am–6pm • Free • 𝟎 091 631804, 𝗪 coolepark.ie

Coole Park is the former estate of **Lady Augusta Gregory** (1852–1932), dramatist, folklorist and co-founder of the Abbey Theatre in Dublin (see p.77), the world's first national theatre. At the beginning of the last century, Coole was the centre of the Irish Literary Revival, visited by Synge, Shaw, O'Casey and, most of all, Yeats, who spent over twenty summers here or at Thoor Ballylee. After Lady Gregory's death, however, the estate passed into the hands of the Department of Agriculture and Lands, who left the house to fall into disrepair and demolished it in 1941. The demesne is now a beautiful **woodland park**, home to pine martens, red deer and red squirrels, and laid out with two signposted nature trails (6km in total), which will bring you down to a seasonal lake and its many swans. In the walled garden stands the **autograph tree**, a beautiful, swooping copper beech on which all the great writers and painters who stayed here carved graffiti.

The **visitor centre** features a highly engaging exhibition based on the memoirs of Lady Gregory's granddaughter, who was born and brought up at Coole, including computer re-creations of the house, and film footage and sound recordings of Yeats.

Kilmacduagh

5km southwest of Gort, off the R460 to Corofin • Open access • Free

The extensive monastic ruins of **Kilmacduagh** stand in an unspoilt setting with magnificent views of the Burren's limestone terraces to the west. The monastery was founded by Saint Colman Mac Duagh, a member of one of the local royal families, around 632, but the buildings you can see today date mostly from around five hundred years later. They're impressive by virtue of their scale and quantity – a **cathedral**, four churches, the "Glebe House" (possibly the abbot's house) and a 35m-high, leaning round tower – rather than any architectural finery, but look out for the grim-faced bishop carved over the cathedral's south doorway.

ARRIVAL AND DEPARTURE
GORT

By bus During the day (Mon–Fri), Bus Éireann services run hourly to Gort from Galway, a 45min journey. Pick up/drop off point is outside the Allied Irish Bank in the Square.

By train Gort is served on the Galway–Limerick line (Mon–Sat 6 daily, Sun 4 daily).

EATING

Fredericks Gallery Café The Square 𝟎 091 630630. Formerly a spinning house, and retaining its original whitewashed stone walls, this stylish café is a popular spot. Dishes on offer include mezze, pizzas and hearty salads (some with St Tola goat's cheese from nearby Inagh). Wash it down with a Ballycross apple juice or Johnny Jump Up, an organic cider made in Gort. Wed & Sat 11am–9pm, Thurs

& Fri 11am–10pm, Sun 11am–7pm.
O'Grady's Bar The Square 𝟎 091 631096 𝗪 ogradysgort.net. At lunch time, expect buffet-style carvery roasts plus burgers and lasagne priced from €8–12 dinner (from 4pm) includes grills and fish such as scampi o Corrib salmon – average main course €16. Daily 11am–11.30pm.

Portumna and around

PORTUMNA (𝗪 portumna.net), 47km east of Gort through the pine-clad Slieve Aughty mountains, is a compact market town surrounded by forests and open land that run down to the meeting of the River Shannon with Lough Derg.

CLOCKWISE FROM TOP ARAN ISLANDS (P.359); CROAGH PATRICK PILGRIMAGE (P.382); NATIONAL MUSEUM OF COUNTRY LIFE (P.386) >

10

Portumna Castle

April–Sept daily 9.30am–6pm; Oct Fri, Sat & Sun 9.30am–5pm; last admission 45min before closing • €4; Heritage Card • ☎ 090 974 1658, ⓦ heritageireland.ie

On the southwest side of the town centre stands the early seventeenth-century fortified mansion **Portumna Castle**, which was gutted by fire in 1826 and is currently being renovated. Restoration work is under way (and will continue for several years) to open up the first floor, but currently you're confined to the ground floor, which is arrayed with display boards on the de Burgo family who lived here, the house and its conservation. In front of the house, the elegant, geometric Renaissance **garden**, one of the first in Ireland, has been re-created, as has the walled kitchen garden to one side.

Portumna Friary and Forest Park

Open access

Beyond the castle gatehouse, about 400m down the road towards the lake, lie the extensive remains of **Portumna Friary** in a leafy setting. Originally a Cistercian chapel, it was rebuilt by the Dominicans in the early fifteenth century, with ornate, traceried windows in the east wall and south transept of the church, and a small, pretty cloister, now heavily restored. Part of Portumna Castle's former estate – still home to a sizeable herd of fallow deer – constitutes the **Portumna Forest Park**, where you can stroll along marked trails through the woodland to the lake shore.

Clonfert Cathedral

25km northeast of Portumna • May–Oct daily 9.15am–6pm

Infrequently used by the Church of Ireland, **Clonfert Cathedral** was founded in the sixth century by St Brendan, who was later buried here, and the present building has been in continuous service from around the tenth century. Regarded as the high point of Irish Romanesque, its rounded, golden-brown, sandstone **doorway**, topped by a triangular gable, may have been added for a synod held at Clonfert by St Laurence O'Toole, Archbishop of Dublin, in 1179. It's carved with a remarkable diversity of inventive motifs, some of which have been traced to Scandinavia and western France, including human and animal heads, interlace and other geometrical devices. Dating from around 1600, the adjacent **bishop's palace** later became home to the English fascist, Oswald Mosley, but has rapidly rotted since it was accidentally burned down in 1954.

Irish Workhouse Centre

St Brigid's Rd • Daily: April–Sept 9.30am–6pm; Feb, Mar & Oct 9.30am–5pm; last admission 1hr before closing • €6 • ☎ 090 975 9200, ⓦ irishworkhouse.centre.ie

Buildings in the former Portumna Workhouse (a poorhouse for the destitute opened in 1852) have been converted into the **Irish Workhouse Centre**. You can visit the waiting hall, boardroom, schoolroom and women's quarters. Interpretive panels tell the history of the Workhouse which at one time was described as the most feared and hated institution ever established in Ireland.

ARRIVAL AND INFORMATION PORTUMNA AND AROUND

By bus Kearns Transport (☎ 057 912 0124, ⓦ kearnstransport .com) runs daily services between Portumna and Dublin, via Birr, and at weekends between Birr and Galway city (Merchant's Rd) via Portumna and Loughrea.

Tourist office St Brigid's Rd (Feb–Nov daily 9.30am–5pm; ☎ 090 975 9200). Located in the Irish Workhouse Centre

(see above), the tourist office provides maps and brochures on East Galway as well as offering internet access and wi-fi

Boat hire If you're so tempted by the water that you want to live on it for a week or two, contact Emerald Star (☎ 07˙ 962 7633, ⓦ emeraldstar.ie), who rent out self-drive cruisers from the marina at the east end of town.

ACCOMMODATION AND EATING

The Beehive St Patrick's St ☎ 090 974 1830. A basic café-restaurant serving salads, sandwiches, simple pastas

and other main courses and cakes, plus tasty, popula pizzas in the evenings. Mains average €10. Tues–Sa

9am–5pm, Thurs–Sun 6–9.30pm.

Horan's Pub Brendan St ☎ 090 97 41007. One of the best spots for an impromptu session on any night and a good spot to meet the locals. Daily 6–11.30pm.

Le Bouchon St Patrick's St ☎ 090 974 1780. A chic upstairs restaurant that rustles up a mix of high-quality European and Irish dishes. Main courses (average around €18) include the likes of beef bourguignon, slow-cooked

duck and grilled sea bass. The two-course early bird priced at €20.95 is served 5.30–7pm. Wed & Thurs 6–9.30pm, Fri–Sun 12.30–2.30pm & 6–9.30pm.

Oak Lodge B&B St Brendan's Rd ☎ 090 974 1549, ⓦ oaklodgeportumna.ie. A conveniently located guesthouse with four en-suite rooms. The common room is a focal point for visitors, featuring a wood-burning stove and local interest books. Open all year. **€60**

Loughrea and around

LOUGHREA, 32km northwest of Portumna, is a small market town on the lake of the same name. It's unlikely that you'll want to stay here, but it's well worth detouring off the N6 bypass to visit the late nineteenth-century **St Brendan's Cathedral**.

St Brendan's Cathedral

Barrack St • Mon–Fri 10am–1pm & 2–5.30pm • ☎ 091 841212, ⓦ loughreacathedral.ie • 30min audio-tour available from adjacent presbytery at weekends

St Brendan's Cathedral is a shining product of the Arts and Crafts movement – which in its Irish manifestation is often referred to as the Celtic Revival. The interior is decorated with rich marble, playfully carved Irish-oak pews and Mediterranean-style column capitals in the nave telling the story of St Brendan. Its most notable feature, however, is the stained glass, which was mostly produced by **An Túr Gloine** ("The Shining Tower"), a cooperative Arts and Crafts studio based in Dublin from 1903 to 1944. Look out especially for the 1930s works by the Dublin-born artist **Michael Healy**, who was heavily influenced by the Renaissance art he'd studied in Florence. His *St Joseph* in the right-hand aisle is sombrely emotive, but in *The Queen of Heaven*, further down the same aisle, he deals only in brilliant colours and composition, to convey Mary's regal splendour. Healy's masterpieces, however, are *The Ascension* and *The Last Judgement* in the west transept, sparkling tapestries of colour inlaid with the dramatic heads of his characters.

Clonfert Diocesan Museum

Adjoining the cathedral • Open on request Mon–Fri 9.30am–6pm • Donation requested • ☎ 091 841212

The **Clonfert Diocesan Museum** houses tapestries designed by Jack B. Yeats and made by the **Dun Emer Guild**, the weaving and printing arm of the Irish Arts and Crafts movement, founded in 1902 and named after the needleworking wife of the mythical hero, Cúchulainn. There's also a primitive, polychrome carving of the Virgin and Child dating from the late twelfth or early thirteenth century, the oldest surviving wooden statue in Ireland.

EATING   LOUGHREA AND AROUND

Maggie Mays Bride St ☎ 091 847880, ⓦ maggiemaysloughrea.com. A bustling bar and restaurant whose menu brims with locally sourced produce. Typical offerings might include glazed pork fillet, duck, chicken goujons, duo of salmon and lemon sole, and vegetarian dishes. Main course prices average €16. Daily noon–11.30pm.

Taste Matters Millennium House, Westbridge St ☎ 091 880010. Among the town's best places to eat with a menu that might include haddock with risotto, grilled marinated chicken, or braised pork belly and pork schnitzel. Main courses from €11 for lunch, rising to an average €18 for dinner. Tues–Sun 1–9.30pm.

Athenry

ATHENRY's name in Irish, Baile Átha an Rí, "town of the ford of the king", reveals its ancient significance as a crossing point of the River Clarin, 20km due east of Galway city on what is still the main road-and-rail route to Dublin. Many of its historic sites are well preserved, including nearly all its fourteenth-century town **walls**, plus the North Gate, five towers, and castle. In the market square stands the only **market cross** *in situ* in the country, though it's a badly damaged stump; dating from the fifteenth century, it's carved with scenes of the Crucifixion and the Virgin and Child. East from here, just across the river, the extensive remains of the thirteenth- to fifteenth-century Dominican **Priory of SS Peter and Paul** (open access) include a fine collection of carved grave slabs from medieval times onwards.

10

Athenry Castle

Easter–Sept daily 9.30am–6pm; Oct Mon–Thurs 10am–6pm; last admission 5.15pm • €4; Heritage Card • ☎ 091 844797, ⊛ heritageireland.ie

Standing at the northeast corner of the walls, guarding the ford, the **castle** dates back to the thirteenth century. It is a forbidding, almost windowless, three-storey hall with a keep that features some fine Romano-Gothic floral carvings.

Athenry Heritage Centre

Opposite the castle • March–May, Sept & Oct 11am–4pm, June–Aug daily 10am–5pm • €4 (45min guided tour included in price); Medieval Experience €7.50 • ☎ 091 844661, ⊛ athenryheritagecentre.com

The lively **Athenry Heritage Centre** occupies a nineteenth-century church built within the ruins of a medieval predecessor. The big attraction for kids is the "Medieval Experience", which comes complete with stocks, a re-created dungeon, summertime archery and lots of objects to handle – and everyone, big or small, gets to wear a medieval costume.

ARRIVAL AND DEPARTURE   ATHENRY

By train The station is on Church St. Destinations Athlone (10 daily; 1hr); Galway (18 daily; 45min); Limerick (5 daily; 1hr 45min).

ACCOMMODATION AND EATING

★ Caheroyan House Monivea Rd ☎ 091 844858, ⊛ caheroyanhouseathenry.com. Athenry's outstanding B&B choice is a 5min walk from the North Gate. Set in a pretty garden, this tastefully refurbished eighteenth-century manor house offers spacious bedrooms and fine breakfasts that feature home-grown grapes and homemade jam. Guests are free to explore the expansive organic farmland and woodland. Self-catering one- and three-bedroom cottages also available. **€90**

La Rustica North Gate St ☎ 091 845301. A casual evening diner that serves pizzas, panini, basic pastas, kebabs and fish 'n' chips. The courgette, bacon and mushroom carbonara (€12) is a big hit. Daily 4–9pm (Fri & Sat till 10pm).

The Old Barracks Cross St ☎ 091 877406, ⊛ oldbarracks.ie. Set in a former RIC police barracks the place combines pantry, bakery and a restaurant offering lunch and dinner. Mains (averaging €13) include steak, burgers, chicken and vegetable fajitas; be sure to finish off with the delicious Linnalla artisan ice cream made in the Burren. Summer Wed–Sat noon–9pm, Sun, Mon & Tues noon–7pm; rest of year noon–6pm.

THE FIELDS OF ATHENRY

Athenry is probably most famous for the song **The Fields of Athenry**, penned by singer-songwriter Pete St John in the 1970s as an adaptation of a poignant 1880s ballad about the abominations of the Famine. It's an emotive, catchy number, popular in pubs and at football and rugby matches, and you may well find yourself joining in, at least with the chorus:

Low lie the fields of Athenry
Where once we watched the small, free birds fly
Our love was on the wing
We had dreams and songs to sing,
It's so lonely round the fields of Athenry

The Aran Islands

Once part of a land barrier across the south side of Galway Bay, the **Aran Islands** (Oileáin Árann; 🌐visitaranislands.com) – **Inishmore**, **Inishmaan** and **Inisheer** – have proved alluring to travellers for centuries. Until recently, their isolation allowed the continuation of an ancient Gaelic culture, traces of which remain, while Irish is still the main language of the islands. Fishing and farming are to this day the principal activities on Inishmaan, with tourism the major earner on Inishmore and Inisheer.

As well as the islands' heritage, their dramatic landscapes, continuing the limestone pavement of the Burren in County Clare into the sea, are a major draw. This bleak geology manages to sustain over four hundred varieties of wild flower, including the rare Alpine Spring gentian, as well as a healthy population of butterflies and endangered bird species such as the chough and the little tern. Here too is one of the richest concentrations of pre-Christian and early Christian archaeological sites in Europe, including seven massive **stone forts**, some of which are survivals from the Bronze Age (1100 BC). The pick of these is **Dun Aengus**, a spectacular prehistoric ring fort on the edge of Inishmore's sea cliffs.

Brief history

From the fifth or sixth century onwards, the islands were a centre of **monastic learning**, their wildness and remoteness drawing students from far and wide. St Enda's monastery on Inishmore, the first of Ireland's dozens of island monasteries, was also one of the most influential of the age, training monks who went on to found important houses of their own, such as Brendan of Clonfert, Ciarán of Clonmacnois and Colmcille of Iona.

The monasteries of the Arans had gone into decline by the early thirteenth century, at which time Galway city began to take off as a trading port under the Anglo-Normans. For controlling piracy – and their own piratical instincts – in Galway Bay, the Gaelic lords of Aran, the **O'Briens** of County Clare, received an annual payment from the city. In the sixteenth century, however, the O'Briens fell into dispute with the O'Flahertys of west Galway over the islands – to their mutual detriment. The argument was eventually resolved by Queen Elizabeth I who, seeing the Arans as strategically

---

THE ARAN ISLANDS AND THE GAELIC REVIVAL

In the late nineteenth century, the Arans became a living museum for anthropologists, antiquarians and linguists, seeking out the unbroken heritage of Irish language, beliefs and customs here, which in turn provided fuel for the **Gaelic Revival** and the Nationalist movement. Written and spoken Irish was a particular focus of interest, as even by this time the islands were one of the few areas of the country where the native language was in daily use. Patrick Pearse came specifically to learn Irish on Inishmaan, which was also visited by writers Yeats, Lady Gregory and, most notably, J.M. Synge – George Russell later joked that Synge's knack was to discover that if you translated Irish literally into English, you achieved poetry.

The Arans themselves have nurtured several excellent writers, notably **Liam O'Flaherty** (see p.611) and poet **Máirtín Ó Direáin** (see p.613), both from Inishmore. In 1934 the documentary-maker **Robert Flaherty** released his classic *Man of Aran* in which he sought to record the islands' vanishing way of life – some of it had already disappeared, but he wasn't averse to re-creating scenes that were no longer witnessed. A few of the traditions captured in the film still exist – you'll still see people collecting seaweed for fertilizer, building dry-stone walls and fishing from **currachs** (traditional pointed skiffs), though these are no longer covered with animal skins. In more recent years, *The Cripple of Inishmaan*, Martin McDonagh's black comedy starring Daniel Radcliffe, has been performed to packed houses on stages in Broadway and the West End, and has captured the imagination of the critics. The storyline – about a crippled teenager who tries to get a role in the *Man of Aran* – focuses on a Hollywood director visiting the island.

10

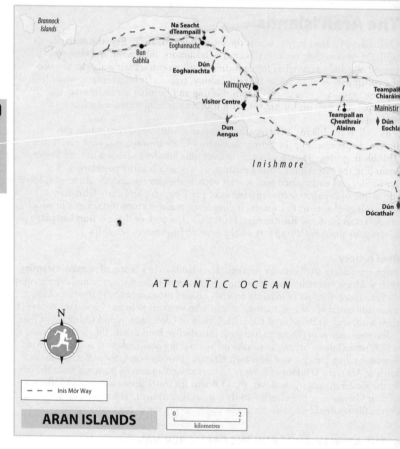

Brannock Islands

Na Seacht dTeampaill

Eoghannacht

Bun Gabhla

Dún Eoghanachta

Kilmúrvey

Visitor Centre

Dun Aengus

Teampall Chiaráin

Mainistir

Teampall an Cheathrair Alainn

Dún Eochla

Inishmore

Dún Dúcathair

ATLANTIC OCEAN

N

--- Inis Mór Way

ARAN ISLANDS

0   2
kilometres

important against the Spanish and French, annexed the islands to the Crown. In 1588, the Arans were sold to the **Lynch** family of Galway, who were required to keep a garrison of soldiers there. The family, however, remained loyal to the king during the English Civil War of the 1640s, and the victorious Cromwell declared Sir Robert Lynch a traitor and his lands forfeit.

Thereafter, the islands passed through a succession of landowners, whose main interest was the income from ever-increasing rents. The islands escaped the worst effects of the Famine of the 1840s, as the availability of **food from the sea** and the shore helped to compensate for the failure of the potato crop. It wasn't until 1922 that the absentee landlords sold their interests and the islands' farmers finally came to own their land.

ARRIVAL AND DEPARTURE   THE ARAN ISLANDS

There are coach connections (€4–5) from Galway to Rossaveel (25min) and Inverin airport (45min from Galway city) for most flights and boat departures.

By boat Ferries sail from Rossaveel (Rós an Mhíl) and from Doolin in County Clare (see p.333) to the Aran Islands. Aran Island Ferries has branches on Forster St and on Merchants Rd in Galway city (☎091 568903, evenings ☎091 572273,

ⓦ aranislandferries.com). All destinations cost €25 return or €13 single; packages are available with the *Kilronan* hostel (see p.364) and cost €37 for one night's B&B and return ferry. Destinations Inishmore (2–3 daily with extra sailings in summer; 35min); Inisheer (2 daily; 1hr); the Inisheer boat calls at Inishmaan (50min from Rossaveel) on both outward and return journeys.

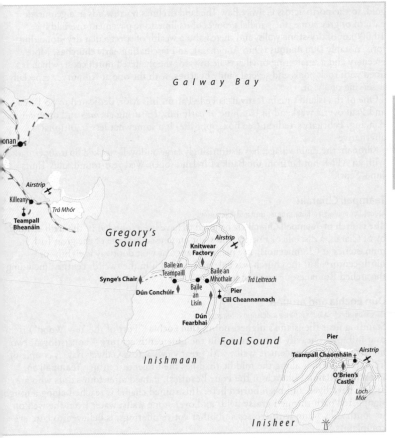

By plane Flights operate from Connemara Regional Airport at Inverin (Indreabhán), around 30km west of Galway city. Aer Árann Inverin (☏091 593034, ⓦaerarannislands.ie) flies to all three islands (up to 8 daily to Inishmore in high season, 2 daily to Inishmaan and Inisheer). Flights cost €25 single, €49 return, and must be booked in advance.

INFORMATION

Maps and guides The Ordnance Survey cover the Arans on a single 1:25,000 map, while *The Aran Islands: A World of Stone* is an excellent introductory book, published by O'Brien Press. Tim Robinson has produced a comprehensive map and guidebook of the islands, which is knowledgeable on archaeology, local lore and the derivation of Irish place names, while his books, *The Aran Islands: Pilgrimage* and *Labyrinth*, provide even more detailed and fascinating analysis.

Inishmore

One of the great attractions of **Inishmore** (Inis Mór, "Big Island", but often referred to simply as Árainn) is its topography, which is stark, simple and easily appreciated. Sheer cliffs, lashed at their base by the relentless Atlantic, run the 14km length of its south coast, their tops offering an ethereal panorama, from the echoing wall of the Cliffs of Moher in the southeast to the Connemara Mountains, tinged with green, purple and

10

gold, to the north across Galway Bay. The land declines northwards in a geometric pattern of grey stone, the parallel grooves of its limestone pavement overlaid by 10,000km of **dry-stone walls**, and there's also a wealth of spectacular dry-stone ring forts, notably **Dun Aengus** (Dún Aonghasa), and fascinating **early churches**. More greenery and a smattering of villages lie towards the sheltered north coast, which is lined with rock pools and several sandy **beaches**, with the one at Kilmurvey especially deserving of a visit.

One of the island's main **festivals** is Féile Patrún Inis Mór, dedicated to SS Peter and Paul over a weekend in late June or early July, featuring *currach* and open-air set dancing. February's Tedfest (see box, opposite) is a somewhat less traditional alternative.

Kilronan, the main village, has a surprisingly large and well-stocked Spar supermarket, with an ATM, not far from the Bank of Ireland (open Wed year-round, plus Thurs June–Sept).

Teampall Chiaráin

About 1.5km northwest of Kilronan on the coast road • Open access

The church of **Teampall Chiaráin** is believed to have been founded in the sixth century by St Ciarán, a disciple of Enda's, who went on to establish one of the great Irish monasteries at Clonmacnois. The plain, rectangular west doorway is eighth- or ninth-century, but the church was enlarged around it in the twelfth century, including the arched Romanesque east window.

Dún Eochla and around

Three kilometres from Kilronan off the middle road • Open access

Standing near the island's highest point, **Dún Eochla** ("Fort of the Yew Wood") is an oval hill fort – heavily reconstructed in the nineteenth century – consisting of two massive, roughly concentric walls, with great views across Galway Bay. A couple of kilometres further along the middle road lies the fifteenth-century **Teampall an Cheathrair Alainn** (Church of the Four Beauties), named after four saints who are said to have lived and been buried here. This ruined chapel is reached along a rough, signposted path through grassy fields and over stone walls; water from the well on its south side, hung with crosses and other votive offerings, is believed to cure eye complaints.

The middle and coast roads meet at the horseshoe beach of **Kilmurvey** (Cill Mhuirbhigh), a gently sloping, Blue Flag stretch of fine sand, with magnificent views across to Connemara.

Dun Aengus (Dún Aonghasa)

Signposted to the south of Kilmurvey • Daily: April–Oct 10am–6pm; Nov–March 10am–4pm • €4; Heritage Card • ☏ 099 61008, ⓦ heritageireland.ie • Access to the site is via a visitor centre and café, from where it's an uphill walk of nearly 1km to the fort

By far the Aran Islands' most compelling ancient site, **Dun Aengus** is a semicircular fort of three concentric enclosures, hard up against the edge of sheer, 90m cliffs.

HY BRASIL

From Dun Aengus, you might be lucky enough to see the famous mirage known as **Hy Brasil** (after which the South American country was supposedly named), which appears in the sea to the west as a mountainous island. Local folklore represents this mythical land variously as the island of the blessed, the Garden of Eden, Tír na nÓg (the land of eternal youth), the Isle of Truth, of Joy, of Fair Women and of Apples. In the early twentieth century, islanders believed it appeared once every seven years, but up until the mid-nineteenth century it was actually shown on some sea charts of the Atlantic. On the unforgiving, sea-battered Arans, it's easy to understand how this fantasy of a prosperous paradise grew up.

TEDFEST

On the **last weekend in February**, a friendly invasion of visitors – amounting to nearly half the island's population – arrives en masse for a madcap festival on Inishmore. Since 2006 they have been coming in their hundreds to celebrate cult classic **Father Ted**, the TV comedy whose setting, the fictitious Craggy Island, was inspired by the Arans. Based in Kilronan in *Ti Joe Watty's* bar (see p.365), the weekend is a party place for "Ted Heads". Entertainment includes comedy shows, sketches, a "lovely girls" competition and a raft of other shenanigans. Musical parameters are wide, stretching from traditional Irish, country and folk to bluegrass and rock 'n roll, featuring up to 20 bands from Ireland and the UK. Tickets are limited to 420 so book early and organize your accommodation well in advance. It all kicks off at noon on the Thursday, continuing unabated until the small hours of Monday morning. Go to ⓦtedfest.org for information and tickets.

From here, on a clear day, you can see Kerry Head, northwest of Tralee, and occasionally Mount Brandon on the Dingle Peninsula – if you're truly blessed, you might spot the island of Hy Brasil to the west. The fort is named after Aengus of the **Fir Bolg**, a legendary ancient race, said to have been of Greek origin and to have ruled Ireland for 37 years, before being conquered by the equally mythical Tuatha Dé Danann.

The **inner citadel** comprises a wall, 6m high and 4m wide, of massive blocks of limestone that were quarried on site and put together without mortar. In the site's heyday, the inhabitants would have lived here and in the middle enclosure, with livestock in the outermost enclosure. Some time after 500 BC, Dun Aengus contracted, and a still-imposing *cheval de frise* was constructed between the middle and outer walls, a 10m-wide field planted with razor-sharp standing stones up to 1.8m high, designed to slow down attackers.

Dún Eoghanachta
just under 2km northwest of Kilmurvey

Look out for signposts pointing south along a dwindling trail for the twenty-minute walk up to the impressive **Dún Eoghanachta**. Probably built between 650 and 800 AD, it's the smallest of the Aran forts, a perfect circle of rectilinear, almost brick-like, light-grey, limestone blocks.

The Seven Churches
to the north of Eoghanacht village

The monastic complex of **Na Seacht dTeampaill**, or the **Seven Churches**, actually consists of the substantial ruins of two churches and five domestic buildings. It was founded by St Brecan, who arrived on the island in the fifth or early sixth century, succeeded Enda as the abbot of the main monastery at Killeany, and was famous for his piety and severity. Occupying land with some of the deepest soil on the island, the site is still used as a graveyard. The older of the churches, Teampall Bhreacáin, dates from the eighth century but was gradually enlarged with some fine arches. Teampall A'Phoill ("Church of the Hollow"), which goes back only as far as the fifteenth century, was used as a parish church until relatively recently.

Dún Dúchathair (Black Fort)
to the south of Kilronan

Enjoying a spectacular location on a promontory, **Dún Dúchathair** ("Black Fort") is guarded by cliffs on three sides, and a *cheval de frise* on the fourth. The fort consists of a single massive wall, 60m long, that slices across the neck of the headland. Once through the narrow entrance at the eastern end (the main gate here collapsed into the sea in the early nineteenth century) you'll find the remains of four oval *clocháns*.

Teampall Bheanáin

Just south of and above the village of Killeany

The eleventh-century **Teampall Bheanáin** stands in a magnificent hilltop location that's especially enchanting at sunset. Built of huge stone slabs, it's notable for its north–south alignment, its unusually steep gables and its size – at just 5m long, some claim it to be the smallest church in Europe. It was probably part of St Enda's early monastic site (*Cill Einne*, "Church of Enda"), formed around 490, which was torn down by Cromwell's soldiers to strengthen Arkin Castle in the village in 1652.

10

ARRIVAL AND INFORMATION   INISHMORE

By boat Ferries (see p.360) dock at the main village Kilronan (Cill Rónáin) from either Rosaveel in Connemara or Doolin in Clare, usually arriving around 11am.

By plane Flights from Inverin on the nine-seat Islander planes arrive during the day into the airstrip at An Trá Mhór. A minibus will pick you up and drop you at your

accommodation or chosen destination.

Tourist office The office opposite the pier (Daily: Nov–June 10am–5pm; July–Sept 10am–6pm; ☎ 099 61263) has maps and walking route leaflets for all of the islands, information on accommodation and details of sailing and flight timings.

GETTING AROUND

By minibus Minibuses operate all over Inishmore with a basic shared journey costing €10 per person. Drivers also offer set tours that take up to 3hr, including 1hr 30min at Dun Aengus and 15min at the Seven Churches.

By bike Aran Bicycle Hire by the pier in Kilronan (☎ 099 61132, ⓦ aranislandsbikehire.com). It's easier if you follow a circuit going out on the coast road and coming back by the

hillier middle road, with the prevailing west wind at your back.

On foot The most scenic way to get around is to follow looped walks of 3–5 hours; route leaflets are available at the tourist office. Make sure you have stout walking boots. For more information, go to ⓦ discoverireland.ie/walking.

By pony buggy Tours of the island cost €40–60 for a group of up to four adults, with a choice of three set routes.

ACCOMMODATION

Aran Islands Hotel Lower Kilronan ☎ 099 61104, ⓦ aranislandshotel.com. Smart, modern hotel, tastefully fitted with pine floors and bare stone walls; the best rooms have king-size beds and panoramic balconies. From the hotel's restaurant (try the fresh deepwater prawns) there are spectacular views of Kileaney Bay. €118

Kilmurvey House Kilmurvey ☎ 099 61218, ⓦ kilmurveyhouse.com. Near the Dun Aengus visitor centre, but quiet at night, this B&B occupies an impressive and welcoming eighteenth-century country house with a ruined church in its extensive garden. April to mid-Oct. €85

Kilronan Hostel (IHO) Kilronan ☎ 099 61255, ⓦ kilronanhostel.com. Beside *Tigh Jo Mac*'s pub, this hostel has small, 4- to 6-bed, en-suite dorms, with a kitchen and TV room. Free wi-fi. Breakfast included. €18

Mainistir House Hostel (IHO) Mainistir ☎ 099 61169, ⓦ mainistirhousearan.com. Attractive private rooms and a wide variety of dorms, about 2km northwest of Kilronan on the road to Kilmurvey. Laundry facilities, internet access and good, mostly vegetarian, buffet dinners. Breakfast

included. Dorms €20, doubles €50

★ **Man of Aran Cottage** Kilmurvey ☎ 099 61301, ⓦ manofarancottage.com. Film buffs will relish staying at this thatched and whitewashed place, set in a colourful garden on the west side of the beach, which Robert Flaherty built in the local style as a set for his film *Man of Aran*. Bedrooms have fine views of Connemara and there are delicious dinners, using the garden's herbs and vegetables. Main-course prices are €19. March–Oct. €90

Pier House Kilronan ☎ 099 61417, ⓦ pierhousearan .com. Richly decorated guesthouse with attractive, pine-furnished rooms, occupying a peerless spot by the jetty with panoramic views. Self-catering apartments available. €90

Seacrest Kilronan ☎ 099 61292, ⓦ aranaccommodation .com. Out of a dozen or so B&Bs in and around the main village, this bungalow is a good bet in the centre, with smart, en-suite rooms, a spacious living room and hearty breakfasts. They also run three-hour horse-and-carriage tours of the island for €25. €76

EATING AND DRINKING

No one comes to Inishmore just for the food, though the **restaurants** offer plenty of fresh seafood such as local lobster if you have the cash.

The Bar ☎ 099 61130, ⓦ inismorbar.com. Formerly called the *American Bar*, this convenient bar serves food

from lunch time till 9pm and holds spontaneous traditional music sessions. Daily noon–11.30pm.

Lios Aengus Café By the Spar supermarket ☎087 643 5279. Come here for fine breakfasts and lunches of sandwiches and soups, as well as cakes and great coffee (closed Mon in winter). Daily 10am–5.30pm.

Man of Aran Café ☎085 710 5254. This is the place to come to watch the *Man of Aran* film (see box, p.359), which they show daily for €5. The café also sells crafts, guidebooks and maps, and offers a left luggage facility, charging €1 per bag. April–Sept daily 10am–5pm.

The Pier House ☎099 61811, ⓦaranrestaurant .com. This is the ideal spot for food on a sunny day overlooking the waterfront. It serves tasty lunches with dishes such as grilled potato fish cakes, smoked chicken salad or fresh Aran seafood platter. For dinner, expect brill, lobster or oysters. Main courses from €15. Daily noon–11.30pm.

Ti Joe Watty's ☎086 049 4509, ⓦjoewattys.com A tree-shaded beer garden at a crossroads with all sorts of live music (summer: nightly & 2–4pm Fri–Sun; weekends only from Oct). It's popular for varied lunches and dinners such as crab claws, steamed mussels, fish and chips or Irish stew. Daily noon–11.30pm.

Inishmaan

Approaching from the west or east, **Inishmaan** (Inis Meáin, "Middle Island") looks like a rising wave about to break over Galway Bay to the north. From the grey limestone pavement at its northern end, tiny pastures, separated by a maze of dry-stone walls, rise to the main east–west ridge, along which lies a ribbon of villages. The so-called "back of the island" slopes off more gradually to the south. This is the most unspoilt of the Arans, and the most thoroughly Irish-speaking (though English is understood), where people are still largely engaged in farming and fishing, with wild salmon caught from black, pointed *currachs*. On Sundays, meanwhile, older women wear traditional multicoloured shawls to go with their thick woollen skirts. The island's historic sites are on a smaller scale than Inishmore's – though the imposing ring fort of **Dún Conchúir** is worth singling out – and there are far fewer amenities, but for some people this tranquil, low-key place will be the perfect getaway.

The **Bank of Ireland** operates on the second Tuesday of every month, while Baile an Mhothair, the Inis Meáin Knitting Company (☎099 73009, ⓦinismeain.ie), on the north side of the island, produces beautiful **knitwear** based on traditional Aran patterns, usually for exclusive export markets, but available here from the factory at discounted prices.

Cill Cheanannach and around

East side of the island, immediately southwest of the pier

A tiny, roofless church with steeply pitched gables, **Cill Cheanannach** was built some time before 1200. Just to the north, in the graveyard, lies a curious, roughly triangular slab of limestone: the end-stone of a tomb-shrine, it is pierced with a hole through which pilgrims could touch the bones of the saint inside (possibly the shadowy Cheanainn). On the slope above the church perches the overgrown **Dún Fearbhaí**, a small, rectilinear ring fort, probably dating from the ninth century AD or later.

Baile an Teampaill

From the pier, the island – and the main road – rises in rough steps through the adjoining hamlets of Baile an Mhothair and Baile an Lisín to **Baile an Teampaill** at its midpoint. It's well worth calling in to the village **church** here to see the gorgeous stained-glass windows executed by Harry Clarke in 1939. Made up of glass pieces of varying thicknesses, the

---

INISHMAAN AND J.M. SYNGE

Inishmaan's most famous visitor was **J.M. Synge**, who, on the advice of W.B. Yeats, spent long periods of time on the island between 1898 and 1902, living on mackerel and eggs. He found artistic liberation here, as well as plenty of plot ideas in the stories told him by the islanders, writing his first play, *When the Moon has Set*, in 1901. His book *The Aran Islands* is a moving account of the way of life he encountered.

richly coloured images swim before your eyes – look out especially for Cavan (Caomhán), the patron saint of Inisheer, with a man rowing a *currach* behind his feet.

Teach Synge

June–Sept noon–2pm & 2.30–4.30pm; by appointment at other times • €3 • ☎ 099 73036, ⓦ discoverireland.ie

Further along from the church stands **Teach Synge**, a former post office where Synge stayed, as well as Lady Gregory, W.B. Yeats and Patrick Pearse before him. It's a charming 300-year-old cottage, thatched and whitewashed, with typically small windows (rents on the islands were often calculated on the basis of the size and number of windows). A dresser, a butter churn and most of the other furniture from Synge's time are still inside, as well as fascinating photos taken by the playwright, on the first camera to be brought to the island.

Dún Conchúir

Signposted up a lane from Teach Synge

Near Inishmaan's highest point, **Dún Conchúir** is one of the Arans' most imposing forts, with fine views of Connemara and down Ireland's west coast. Its ramparted, dry-stone walls are 5m thick and 6m high, with a walled gateway defending the main entrance at the northeastern corner. According to legend, Conchúir was the younger brother of Aengus, who is commemorated with his own fort on Inishmore, backing up the theory that there was a prehistoric confederation of the islands, with its capital at Dun Aengus. The last inhabitant of the fort was a nineteenth-century Connemara man called Malley, who, having accidentally killed his father, hid out here for several months, before escaping to America – a tale used as inspiration by Synge for the plot of *Playboy of the Western World*.

Synge's Chair

About 20min walk west of Baile an Teampaill

The playwright's favourite contemplative spot, **Synge's Chair**, is a semicircle of stones he gathered himself, on the site of an old lookout facing Gregory's Sound. From here, you can take a two- to three-hour west-coast hike along towering cliffs to the blowholes at the southwest corner, before cutting up the middle of the island to the village.

ARRIVAL AND DEPARTURE
INISHMAAN

By plane Flights operate from Connemara Regional Airport at Inverin (Indreabhán). Aer Árann (☎ 091 593034, ⓦ aerarannislands.ie; €25 single, €49 return; book in advance) flies twice daily to Inishmaan and Inisheer.

By boat Ferries sail twice daily from Rossaveel (Rós an Mhíl) and from Doolin in County Clare (see p.360) to both Inishmaan and Inisheer.

ACCOMMODATION AND EATING

An Dún Dún Conchúir ☎ 099 73047, ⓦ inismeainaccommodation.ie. An attractive, well-designed guesthouse with five en-suite rooms and a sauna. The restaurant menu (7–9pm) showcases home-grown organic vegetables, including the delectable Inishmaan floury potatoes that are fertilized in seaweed; in summer there's a daytime café. March–Nov. €90

Ard Alainn ☎ 087 285 6778, ⓔ ardalainn_inismeain@ eircom.net. A hospitable guesthouse in a lofty position between Dún Conchúir and Synge's Chair, offering a fine panorama of Galway Bay. Modern standard and en-suite rooms and self-catering also available. Phone for free pick-up from the pier. €70

Inis Meáin Suites & Restaurant North side of island ☎ 086 826 6026, ⓦ inismeain.com. The family that owns the knitwear factory (see p.365) also runs this place, whose contemporary style blends in beautifully with the landscape. Each suite has a huge picture window to make the most of the views of Galway Bay, plus an outdoor sitting area. Expect breakfasts of free-range eggs, fresh fish and treacle bread, while shellfish, lobster and scallops dominate the dinner menu (dinner available to residents Mon–Sat and to non-residents Wed–Sat by advance booking; four-course menu €65). Prices include breakfast, a hotpot lunch and bicycle use. April–Sept. €209

Inisheer

Lying just 10km off the Clare coast, **Inisheer** (Inis Oírr, "East Island") is the smallest and least dramatic Aran. Its historic sites aren't quite as appealing as Inishmaan's, and it's much more of a lively pleasure ground, attracting crowds of teenagers from the local Irish college and day-trippers from Doolin in summer. There's a lovely, partly sheltered, sandy **beach** east of the pier on the north coast, along which nearly all of the habitation on this 3km-wide island spreads. The 10km, waymarked **Inis Oírr Way** traces a circular route round the northern half of the island, taking in O'Brien's Castle and Teampall Chaomháin, and you could easily branch off between the latter and Loch Mór to add on a walk down the road to the **lighthouse** at the southeastern tip of the island, which affords fantastic views of the Cliffs of Moher. There are no ATMs on the island, but the Bank of Ireland visits on the fourth Tuesday of the month.

O'Brien's Castle

Above and behind the beach, **O'Brien's Castle** (Caisleán Uí Bhriain) is attractively sited above low, ivy-covered cliffs, a short, green valley and a network of dry-stone walls. It's well worth walking up to the castle for views of the harbour and the north half of the island, if nothing else. Covered in brown lichen, it's extant up to two storeys, with some crenellations and one roofed room remaining.

Teampall Chaomháin

Climb the sand dune, topped with modern gravestones and wild flowers, on the southeast side of the beach and you're in for a surprise: sunk into the dune's summit lies **Teampall Chaomháin**, a roofless church dedicated to St Cavan (still a common boy's name on the island), who is thought to have been the brother of St Kevin of Glendalough. Retaining walls now help to protect the ruin from the shifting sand, but it still has to be shovelled out every year on June 14, the saint's feast day. The primitive lintelled doorway of the original tenth-century oratory here was retained as the main west entrance of this larger late-medieval church, while an ornately carved slab just to the northeast marks Cavan's grave.

Áras Éanna

A 15min walk south from the West village in the north of the island • ☎ 099 75150, ⓦ araseanna.ie

A multipurpose arts centre, **Áras Éanna** has a gallery showing temporary art exhibitions, runs demonstrations of traditional basket-making and weaving in the summer and hosts music, films and plays in its theatre.

INFORMATION AND GETTING AROUND INISHEER

Inisheer Island Co-operative Situated beyond the east end of the beach, this business (☎ 099 75008, ✉ ccteo@eircom.net) can provide information as well as internet access.

By bike Bikes can be rented from the helpful office (☎ 099 75049) in front of the pier, where you can also charter a pony and trap for a tour of the island.

ACCOMMODATION AND EATING

Brú Radharc na Mara hostel ☎ 099 75024, ⓦ bruhostelaran.com; IHH. Sited hard by the pier, this hostel offers laundry facilities, a kitchen, dining room and common room with open fire, as well as smarter en-suite accommodation in the attached B&B. Mid-March to Oct. Double dorms €55, B&B €70

INISHEER FESTIVALS

Musicians flock here at the end of June when the island hosts a five-day **bodhrán festival** (ⓦ craiceann.com), while mid-September sees enthusiasts of **stone walls** (and there are more than you'd think) arrive for a weekend of events and activities that include tuition on the art of stone wall building and carving.

10

Island Co-operative Campsite ☏099 75008. The only place to camp is this site by the beach, which is open all year round and has toilets and hot showers. Tent pitch **€10**

Radharc an Chláir ☏099 75019, ✉bridpoil@eircom .net. A dormer bungalow near the castle, with a conservatory and fine views. Breakfasts cover the spectrum from the full Irish to porridge or kippers. Easter to mid-Sept. **€64**

South Aran House ☏087 340 5687, ⓦsoutharan.com. At the west end of the village, this place has bright, tasteful en-suite rooms with underfloor heating and free wi-fi. Open all year; minimum stay two nights from Oct. **€80**

South Aran Restaurant ☏086 340 5687, ⓦsoutharan.com. This attractive restaurant decorated in marine colours is attached to *South Aran House*. The dinner menu includes crab linguini, fish pie and vegetarian dishes. with prices for main courses around €12. Daily 6.30–9pm.

Tigh Ned's West village ☏099 75004. A cosy pub by the *Brú Radharc na Mara* hostel with a pleasant garden overlooking the harbour, and food and traditional sessions in summer. Lunch (no dinner) served till 4pm. Daily noon–11.30pm.

Connemara

Comprising all of Galway to the west of the city, **Connemara** (ⓦconnemara.ie) is a ravishingly diverse tract of land. Cut off from the rest of the county by the sweep of **Lough Corrib**, the lie of the land at first looks simple, with two statuesque mountain ranges, the **Maam Turks** (Mám Tuirc, the "boar pass") and the **Twelve Bens** (or sometimes Twelve Pins; Na Beanna Beola, the "Peaks of Beola", a mythical giant), bordered by the deep fjord of **Killary Harbour** to the north. The coast, however, is full of jinks and tricks, a maze of little islands, winding roads, bogs and hills, where it can be hard to tell small loughs from sea inlets. All around the littoral are quiet white-sand **beaches** that are great for swimming. It's hard to miss out **Clifden** on your travels, the likeable and lively main town, poised dramatically between steep hills and the harbour. Other likely bases are the pretty fishing village of **Roundstone**, and **Oughterard**, an angler's delight, not far out of Galway city on the lush banks of Lough Corrib. Oughterard has a good selection of visitor attractions, but the only really compelling historic sight in west Connemara is **Kylemore Abbey and Gardens**. Just off shore near here, you can sample easy-going island life on **Inishbofin**.

GETTING AROUND CONNEMARA

By bus Bus Éireann's main services from Galway run along the coast via Spiddal to Carraroe, and along the N59 via Oughterard to Clifden, sometimes branching off to Roundstone. A few of their services to Clifden branch off at Maam Cross and detour via Leenane, Kylemore and Letterfrack, and in summer they operate a daily (Mon–Sat) bus from Clifden to Westport, via Letterfrack, Kylemore and Leenane. Citylink buses (☏091 564164, ⓦcitylink.ie) from

Galway serve Oughterard, Clifden, Cleggan and Letterfrack three or four times a day.

By car The major route through the area is the N59 from Galway, which cuts across to Clifden before skirting the Twelve Bens en route to Westport, but there are plenty of scenic side-roads through the mountains and around the frilly coastline.

Oughterard and around

Around 28km from Galway on the N59, **OUGHTERARD** is a busy little town, at the start of the Western Way (see box, opposite), with plenty of varied attractions in the

CONNEMARA AND THE IRISH LANGUAGE

Connemara's harsh land has always been thinly populated and isolated, and this has ensured the persistence of rural traditions and of the **Irish language**. It contains the country's largest Gaeltacht, stretching as far west as Roundstone, with Raidió na Gaeltachta and TG4, the Irish-speaking radio and TV stations, both broadcast from here. Four-week **Irish-language courses** for adults, supplemented by cultural activities and singing and dancing classes, are held each summer by NUI Galway at Árus Mháirtín Uí Chadhain (ⓦnuigalway.ie/iss) in An Cheathrú Rua (Carraroe)

WALKING IN CONNEMARA

Connemara offers a stunning variety of **walking**, including mountains over 700m – though be aware that the nearest rescue team is in Galway. A good **map** and guidebook for serious walkers is *The Mountains of Connemara*, available from local bookshops and tourist offices, with a 1:50,000-scale map derived from aerial photography and fieldwork by Tim Robinson, and an excellent guide to eighteen walks of varying length and difficulty by Joss Lynam. The Ordnance Survey has produced their own maps at 1:50,000.

A good introduction to the Maam Turks, with breathtaking views of the Twelve Bens across Lough Inagh, would be the ascent of **Cnoc na hUilleann** and **Binn Bhriocáin** from the **Inagh Valley** back road north of Recess, on a three- to four-hour circuit described in *The Mountains of Connemara*. Also described are the classic Twelve Bens walk, the seven-hour **Gleann Chóchan Horseshoe**, starting from the *Ben Lettery* youth hostel (see p.374) and bagging six of the peaks; and the tough, high-level **Maam Turks Walk**, which traverses the range from north of Maam Cross to Leenane – it can be done in one very long day, but most people will want to do it in two.

The Mountains of Connemara also covers the waymarked **Western Way**, which runs for 50km from Oughterard to Leenane. This varied, low-level trail starts as a pleasant, sometimes boggy, walk beside Lough Corrib, before crossing over from the village of Maam into the dramatic Inagh Valley, which runs between the Bens and the Turks. The walk can be done in two long days, with an overnight near Maam.

Worthy **short walks** include the ascent of Errisbeg and other routes near Roundstone (see p.371), the sky road from Clifden (p.373), a circuit of Inishbofin (p.374), the excellent trails at Connemara National Park (p.376) and the climb up Tully Hill (p.377).

Walking tours are organized from Clifden by Connemara Safari on the sky road (☎095 21071, ⊛www.walkingconnemara.com), which runs five-day walking and island-hopping trips.

10

surrounding area to keep you occupied. Its main asset, however, is not immediately obvious from the long main street: behind the trees to the north of town lies the great expanse of **Lough Corrib**, a paradise for angling or for just messing about in boats, studded with hundreds of tree-clad islets (365 of them, one for each day of the year, if you believe the locals). May is the busiest time for fishing, when the mayflies hatch from the lake bed, while the annual agricultural and horticultural show at the end of August also attracts crowds (⊛oughterardshow.com).

Inchagoill island

If taking a boat tour (see p.370), you'll likely stop off at **Inchagoill island**. Little is known of this uninhabited island's history beyond the meaning of its name, "Isle of the Foreigners". It was, however, the site of an early monastery, featuring the Romanesque Saints' Church, which was restored by Sir Benjamin Guinness in the nineteenth century and is most notable for its attractively carved west doorway.

Aughnanure Castle

Signposted 3km from the centre of Oughterard, about 1.5km off the N59 • April–late Oct daily 9.30am–6pm • €3; Heritage Card • ☎091 552214, ⊛heritageireland.ie

Just east of Oughterard stands a particularly impressive and well-preserved early sixteenth-century tower house, **Aughnanure Castle**, which rises to six storeys and still retains its outer defensive walls; it occupies what is virtually a rocky island near the banks of Lough Corrib. The strongest bastion of the O'Flahertys, who were masters of Connemara from the thirteenth to the sixteenth century, Aughnanure boasts a frightening array of defensive features, including arrow slits aimed at the main staircase, secret prison chambers and a trap door in the hall above a subterranean river, through which were thrown guests who had outstayed their welcome.

Brigit's Garden

Pollagh, Roscahill; look for signs pointing off the N59, 4km southeast of the turn-off for Aughnanure Castle • Daily 10am–5.30pm • €7.50, children €4.50, family ticket €22 (discounts off season) • ☎ 091 550905, ⓦ brigitsgarden.ie

The delightful **Brigit's Garden** is named after the saint (see p.129) whose feast day, February 1, and symbol, the snowdrop, mark the start of spring. This beautifully designed 10-acre garden includes an area devoted to the four Celtic seasons, featuring sculptures, standing stones, symbolic plantings and a thatched roundhouse. Beyond this, you'll find a stand of ancient woodland, a herb garden, wild-flower meadows, a small lake, a ring fort and Ireland's largest sundial, with nature discovery trails laid on for adults and kids (who also get to cavort in the willow play area). There's an excellent **garden café**, a gift shop and various talks and events.

Glengowla Mine

3km west of Oughterard on the N59 • March–Oct daily 10am–6pm • €11 • ☎ 091 552360

For a fascinating change from all the glorious scenery hereabouts, head underground into the restored **Glengowla Mine**. This silver and lead mine was worked between 1850 and 1865 and reluctantly yielded from the area's tough marble around three hundred tons of the ore galena. Entertaining guided tours (45min) bring to life the hardships of drilling by hand and blasting the rock by candlelight, often in deep pools of water.

ARRIVAL AND INFORMATION

OUGHTERARD

By bus Bus Éireann services (Mon–Sat 5 daily; Sun 2 daily) from Galway to Clifden stop in Oughterard.

Tourist office Oughterard's tourist office is based in a community centre on the main street (daily Mon–Fri 9am–5.30pm; ☎ 091 552092).

Boat tours From June to August you can take a day cruise (☎ 087 283 0799, ⓦ corribcruises.com) across to Cong in County Mayo from the pier 2km north of the main street along Pier Road. The tour takes in Inchagoill island and the gardens of Ashford Castle (see p.379), and costs €28.

ACCOMMODATION AND EATING

The Boat Inn The Square ☎ 091 552196, ⓦ theboatinnconnemara.com. A pleasant and affordable restaurant where wild mushroom ravioli, fillet of hake or Connemara mountain lamb are typical offerings on the dinner menu. Prices are around €14 for mains. Daily 12.30–9.30pm.

Breathnachs Bar Camp St ☎ 091 552818, ⓦ breathnachs.com. A family-run bar by the central junction offering breakfast, lunch and dinner – and music at weekends. You can choose from sandwiches, salads, chowder, shellfish tagliatelle, Irish stew or grilled Atlantic salmon. Main courses from €10. Daily 10am–11.30pm, Fri and Sat till 12.30am.

Camillaun Eighterard ☎ 091 552678, ⓦ camillaun .com. A tastefully decorated, modern guesthouse, with a tennis court, hot tub and snooker table, set in gardens on the banks of the Owenriff River (rowing and motor boats for rent). €70

★**Currarevagh House** Glann Rd ☎ 091 552312, ⓦ currarevagh.com. Six kilometres northwest of town, this charming, traditional country house was built in the 1840s on the lakeshore. It has its own boats and ghillies, and there's fine walking on the wooded 100-acre estate and immaculate gardens with fine views of the lake. The unpretentious dinners are based on local produce and there's complimentary afternoon tea for residents. Mid-March to Oct. €150

Outgherard Hostel Station Rd ☎ 087 248 8964, ⓦ oughterardhostel.com. Good hostel in a large, modern house with an extensive lawn, signposted off the west end of the main street, less than 1km from the tourist office. Rooms are all en suite, and fishing tuition and guided trips are available. Feb–Oct. Double dorms €46

Waterfall Lodge Clifden Rd ☎ 091 552168, ⓦ waterfalllodge.net. A little out of town, northwest on the Clifden road, this handsome Victorian house is furnished with antiques and set in wooded gardens by a stream. Fine breakfasts include the likes of smoked salmon and scrambled eggs. Private game fishing. €80

Spiddal (An Spidéal)

The R336 coast road arrows west out of Galway through a gently sloping landscape of shrubs, ferns and boulders, offering fine views of the slate-grey Burren across the water but marred by a monotonous ribbon development of white bungalows. Relief comes after 18km with the lofty trees and church of **SPIDDAL** (An Spidéal, "the hospital"), the effective capital of the Gaeltacht, which is known for its traditional-music sessions. The main daytime draw here is the **Spiddal Craft Village** (Ceardlann an Spidéil; ☎091 897847, ⓦspiddalcrafts.com), a group of studios – with an on-site bistro-café – making and selling fine pottery, weaving, jewellery, woodwork, leather goods, sculpture and musical instruments. In open country 5km north of the central crossroads, **Cnoc Suain** ("restful hill"; ☎091 555703, ⓦcnocsuain.com) is a "cultural hill-village" of restored thatched and slate-tiled stone cottages that hosts residential programmes in Irish music, language and natural history.

10

ACCOMMODATION AND EATING
SPIDDAL (AN SPIDÉAL)

An Crúiscín Lán Main St ☎091 553148, ⓦancruiscinlanhotel.ie. An upmarket option with large, bright rooms – two with sea-view balconies – and a smart evening restaurant. Closed Jan. **€100**

★Builín Blasta 16 An Ceardlan ☎091 558559, ⓦspiddalcrafts.ie. Tucked away at the back of the Craft Village is this top-notch café, whose name translates as "The Tasty Loaf". Lunch includes salads (€7.50), chowder with breads (€6.50), inventive pizzas (€9), or go for Connemara High Tea: scones with mixed berry compote (€5). Mon–Sat 9.30am–5.30pm.

Cloch na Scíth 2km east of town ☎091 553364, ⓦthatchcottage.com. An en-suite B&B in a traditional thatched cottage, with pine furniture and brass beds, where your hostess demonstrates how to cook bread in a pot over the peat fire. Self-catering thatched cottage also available. **€70**

Páirc Saoire an Spidéil ☎091 553372, ⓦspiddal mobilehomes.ie. Campers should head for this well-equipped site, 1.5km inland from the centre of the village. Tent pitch **€18**

Tigh Giblin Main St ☎091 504787, ⓦtighgiblin .com. The best bar in the area with music Tues–Sun, starting around 9.30pm. Fresh local food, especially fish dishes, dominates the menu. Daily noon–9pm.

Teach an Phiarsaigh

Near Rosmuc, at the end of a small peninsula off the R340 • Easter period Thurs–Mon 10am–5pm; late May–Aug daily 10am–6pm; first half of Sept Sat & Sun 10am–6pm; last admission 45min before closing • €3; Heritage Card • ⓦheritageireland.ie

A thatched and whitewashed traditional cottage, **Teach an Phiarsaigh** was the summer residence of the revolutionary and writer, Patrick Pearse (see p.590). Here Pearse ran summer schools for his pupils from St Enda's in Rathfarnham, Dublin, and wrote his famous eulogy for the nationalist Jeremiah O'Donovan Rossa on his death in 1915. Inside are mementos and an exhibition on Pearse, but the cottage is more noteworthy for its atmosphere and setting, with dramatic views of the sea and mountains. At the time of writing, a visitor centre was planned for completion in 2016.

Roundstone and around

On the R341 coast road, which eventually loops round into Clifden, **ROUNDSTONE** (ⓦroundstone.ie) is a delightful fishing village set in some of Connemara's finest scenery. The stone harbour looks out on the many islands of Bertraghboy Bay and across to the peaks of the Twelve Bens and the Maam Turks, while behind looms a lone mountain, the 300m-high Errisbeg. There are some beautiful woodland **walks** along lake shore and river bank in the estate of **Ballynahinch Castle** (see p.372), which are described in a leaflet available from the hotel reception. Three kilometres southwest of the village, the beautiful sandy beaches of **Gurteen Bay** and **Dog's Bay** are separated by a narrow, dune-covered isthmus.

The village is well known for its **crafts shops**, including Malachy Kearns' famous *bodhrán* workshop in a former Franciscan monastery in Killeen Park at the south end of the village (☎095 35875, ⓦbodhran.com). Here you can watch the drums being made, test them out in a sound room or have one painted in the Celtic motif of your choice while you wait. Ferron's Supermarket on the main street contains a post office and ATM.

The highlight of the year for many is the Roundstone Hooker Regatta, a **boating festival** held over the third weekend of July. It includes *currach* racing, hooker sailing events, guided maritime heritage walks and live music gigs.

10

Erissbeg and the Roundstone bog

From the centre of the village, you can take a short but very satisfying **walk** to the summit of **Errisbeg**, which offers majestic views in all directions. Take the paved lane beside *O'Dowd's* bar (see below) and follow the rough track that it turns into; you'll have to pick your way over often boggy ground and boulders towards the top, which, despite appearances from below, turns out to be a ridge of three summits. On three sides runs a coastline of white-sand beaches, where peninsulas are barely distinguishable from islands; to the north, set against one of the finest prospects of the Bens and the Turks, lies huge, sparse **Roundstone Bog**, one of the finest blanket bogs in the country, covered with a glittering crazy-paving of tiny lakes and crossed by a single narrow road.

ARRIVAL AND DEPARTURE   **ROUNDSTONE**

By bus Bus Éireann (☎091 562000) runs daily services to Roundstone from Clifden.

ACCOMMODATION AND EATING

★**Angler's Return** Toombeola, 10min north of Roundstone ☎095 31091, ⓦanglersreturn.com. A no-children policy leads to a deep sense of adult calm in this stylish 1820s sporting lodge set in pretty gardens, favoured not just by fisher folk but also cyclists and walkers. Homemade breads, jams and honey adorn the breakfast table. Debit or credit cards not accepted. **€106**

Ballynahinch Castle ☎095 31006, ⓦballynahinch-castle.com. Set on its own fishing river and lake towards the N59, this eighteenth-century castle was once the home of Richard Martin – aka Humanity Dick – the animal-rights campaigner and co-founder of the RSPCA in 1824, and later of cricketing maharaja, Ranjitsinhji. It's now a romantic luxury hotel in a glorious estate setting, with an excellent restaurant and a wood-panelled fishermen's bar where food is also available; activities include tennis, cycling, fly-fishing tutorials, and guided walks. **€260**

Cashel House Hotel ☎095 31001, ⓦcashelhouse.ie. About a 20min drive east from Roundstone, this elegant country house is in beautiful gardens. Rooms are well

appointed and the dinner choice includes early bird, à la carte or fixed menu options; bar meals are served during the day. Feb–Dec. **€170**

Gurteen Bay Caravan Site ☎095 35882, ⓦrgurteenbay.com. West of Roundstone, this idyllic site is right by the beach of the same name and also offers self-catering apartments. Tent pitch **€20**

★**O'Dowd's Seafood Bar & Restaurant** Main Street ☎095 35809, ⓦodowdsbar.com. A sociable spot that is the nerve centre of the village. Daytime bar food includes a huge variety of shellfish as well as meat and chicken dishes (mains average €13). Attached to the pub is an evening restaurant, while *O'Dowd's Café* a few doors down offers coffee, salads and pizzas. Daily: bar noon–11.30pm; restaurant 5–10pm; café 9am–6pm.

St Joseph's Main Street ☎095 35865, ⓦroundstonebandb.com. A welcoming en-suite place with great breakfasts in the heart of the village. The owner holds evening demonstrations on making chowder and guests are welcome to participate – and tuck in. Dinner is served at 7.30pm. **€70**

Clifden and around

CLIFDEN, the English-speaking capital of Connemara, is a popular, animated service town, enhanced by a spectacular setting: it perches on a steep, verdant hillside, where the lofty grey spires of the Catholic and Anglican churches compete for attention, while on its western side the land plunges abruptly down to the deeply indented harbour. Several stately town houses sprinkle the three major streets – **Main Street**, the continuation of the Galway road culminating in Market Square, with **Bridge Street** and **Market Street** branching off it at either end and meeting to form a rough triangle. By basing yourself here, you'll be able to explore the varied attractions of coast and mountain hereabouts, and sample the often lively nightlife.

There's not much to do on a rainy day in the town itself, although you may find some diversion at the **Station House Museum** near the tourist office on the Galway road (May–Oct Mon–Sat 10am–5pm; ☎095 21494; €2), which has displays on local history and on the history, breeding and racing of Connemara ponies. These rugged, passive workhorses have their day in mid-August, when they're judged at the **Connemara Pony Show** (ⓦcpbs.ie). The other highlight of Clifden's calendar is the prestigious and lively **arts festival** (ⓦclifdenartsweek.ie) at the end of September.

Cleggan Beach Equestrian Centre (ⓣ095 44746, ⓦclegganridingcentre.com), 10km to the northwest, offers **horse riding**, often on one of the area's fine beaches.

The sky road and bog road

A fine diversion is to walk or cycle the spectacular **sky road**, signposted from the west side of the town, which loops scenically round the narrow peninsula on the north side of Clifden Bay (13km in total). It ends up by the long, thin inlet of Streamstown Bay, passing a quarry for the streaky, green Connemara marble, before hitting the Westport road just north of Clifden.

Alternatively, you can complete an excellent, scenic bicycle ride from Clifden by turning left off the R341, 4km north of Roundstone, on to the **bog road**, which undulates westward across the stark peatland back to town.

About 5km south of Clifden on the R341, on the right-hand side, you'll pass a 3m limestone sculpture of an aeroplane wing commemorating the first transatlantic flight, by **Alcock and Brown** in June 1919. The intrepid aviators circled Clifden twice in celebration, but then nosedived into the bog here, wrecking their plans to continue their triumphal flight to London. On the opposite side of the Ballyconneely road is the site of a telegraph station, where **Marconi** sent the first commercial wireless transmission across the Atlantic in 1907; the station was burnt out by Republicans during the Civil War in 1922 and abandoned, with around a thousand local people losing their livelihoods. About 5km off the R341, southwest of Ballyconneely at Bunowen Pier, you can watch the process of preparing smoked salmon and taste some of the finished product at the **Connemara Smokehouse** (Mon–Fri 9am–5pm; guided tours Wed 3pm, €5; booking advisable on ⓣ095 23739; ⓦsmokehouse.ie).

Dan O'Hara's Homestead and the Connemara Heritage and History Centre

Lettershea, 7km east of Clifden on the N59 • April–Oct daily 10am–6pm; last admission 5pm • €8 • Heritage Island • ⓣ095 21246, ⓦconnemaraheritage.com

The area's main set-piece tourist attraction is **Dan O'Hara's Homestead and the Connemara Heritage and History Centre**, which sounds rather kitsch but is quite engaging. Fascinating displays by local archaeologist Michael Gibbons and a short video introduce you to the history of Clifden and Connemara, and to Dan O'Hara himself. A tenant farmer whose house was famous for its ceilis, O'Hara was evicted in 1845 and eventually found his way to New York, where, having little English, he sold matches and inspired the famous eponymous song. Outside, you can view reconstructions of an oratory, a dolmen tomb, a wooden ring fort and a *crannóg*, a thatched dwelling set in a small lake. If there are enough people around, you can take a **guided tour** in a tractor-borne bus up to Dan O'Hara's refurbished cottage for great views south over the bogs and lakes to Roundstone and Errisbeg, and for demonstrations that might include sheep-shearing, thatching and turf-cutting. There's also a craft shop and daytime tea room for snacks such as soup and sandwiches.

ARRIVAL AND INFORMATION	CLIFDEN AND AROUND
By bus Bus Éireann services (Mon–Sat 3 daily, Sun 2 daily; 1hr) run from Galway to Clifden. The drop-off/pick-up point is outside the library on Market St. Citylink also operates 5 daily services (1hr 30min) from Galway to Clifden. Other destinations include Westport via Letterfrack (Mon–Sat 2 daily).	**Tourist information** Galway Road, near the Station House (Mon–Sat: mid-March to May & most of Sept 10am–5pm; June–Aug 10am–5.45pm; ⓣ095 21163). Provides information on the town and Connemara. **Bike rental** John Mannion's, Bridge Street (ⓣ095 21160).

ACCOMMODATION

Ardagh 2km south of town on the Ballyconneely road ☎ 095 21384, ⓦ ardaghhotel.com. Relaxing and comfortable, family-run hotel with views of the bay, pleasant staff, wi-fi and an excellent restaurant. Various special offers available. Sea-view rooms €10 extra per night. Easter–Oct. €145

Ben Lettery Hostel (An Óige) 13km east of Clifden on the N59 ☎ 086 849 3712, ⓦ anoige.ie. Right at the foot of Ben Lettery, one of the Twelve Bens, with fine views, this is a cosy and welcoming forty-bed hostel, geared towards walking in the mountains (it has drying rooms, for instance). June–Sept. €36

Ben View House Bridge St ☎ 095 21256, ⓦ benviewhouse.com. Very central, flower-bedecked nineteenth-century house, offering friendly and comfortable B&B. Plenty of local information available from owners on cultural activities in the area. €70

Buttermilk Lodge 400m out on the Westport road ☎ 095 21951, ⓦ buttermilklodge.com. A well-appointed modern guesthouse set in a large garden, with spacious en-suite bedrooms, wi-fi and internet access. €90

Clifden Town Hostel (IHH) Market St ☎ 095 21076, ⓦ clifdentownhostel.com. Attractive hostel in a central, terraced house, with family rooms, two well-equipped kitchens and a comfy sitting room. Feb–Nov. Dorms €16, doubles €38

Dolphin Beach Country House 5km west on Lower Sky Rd ☎ 095 21204, ⓦ dolphinbeachhouse.com. Skilfully converted farmhouse by the seashore with its own sandy cove and spectacular views. Thirteen elegantly simple bedrooms, spacious, open-fired sitting rooms and local meat, seafood and organic veg for dinner (book in advance; not open to non-residents). €100

★**The Quay House** ☎ 095 21369, ⓦ thequayhouse .com. Down at the harbour and set in an early nineteenth-century harbourmaster's house, which later became a convent, this is an outstanding guesthouse with a sociable, house-party atmosphere. Rooms are elegantly decorated with antiques and paintings; most overlook the water, and some have working fireplaces, four-posters or balconies. Breakfasts are served in the large conservatory. Mid-March to early Nov. €125

Sea Mist House near Market Square ☎ 095 21441, ⓦ seamisthouse.com. Relaxing and central, this 200-year-old stone cottage in a lush garden offers four stylish en-suite rooms, wi-fi, great breakfasts and plentiful local knowledge. €80

Shan Shanaheever Campsite 2km out of town off the Westport road ☎ 095 22150, ⓦ clifdencamping.com. A quiet and efficiently run site in peaceful surroundings. Handy for the town but also a wonderful place to drink in the ever-changing light of the Twelve Bens. Mid-April to Sept. Tent pitch €20

EATING AND DRINKING

Cullen's Café Market St ☎ 095 21983. Basic, economical and easy-going place serving unpretentious dishes for lunch and dinner such as poached Connemara salmon, BLTs, and rhubarb crumble dessert. Main courses from €10. Daily noon–9pm.

Guy's Bar & Restaurant Main St ☎ 095 21130. A tremendous range of seafood such as tempura prawns, steamed mussels, crab salad and calamari, plus Thai red chicken curry, are on the menu here. Main courses for lunch and dinner range from €10–15. Daily 10.30am–11.30pm.

Mannion's pub Market St ☎ 095 21780. One of the best spots for pub grub, serving soup, sandwiches, fish cakes,

Killary mussels, and Irish stew with local lamb, all in hearty portions; prices around €13. Also good for traditional music. Daily noon–11pm.

Mitchell's Seafood Restaurant Market St ☎ 095 21867. Clifden's best restaurant, providing well-judged and beautifully presented cuisine, heavily weighted towards fresh fish and seafood platters. Cheaper, simpler dishes are available at lunch time. Mid-March to Oct daily 12.30–3pm & 5.30–10pm.

Walsh's Bakery & Coffee Shop Market St ☎ 095 21283. Traditional daytime café serving delicious cakes, a varied menu of sandwiches and hot and cold plates at lunch time. Daily 8am–6.30pm.

Inishbofin

With just two hundred inhabitants, **INISHBOFIN** (ⓦ inishbofin.com) continues the diversity of the Connemara landscape into the sea, though in a gentler, miniature format. A mere 5km wide, the island – which rises to just 90m at its highest point, **Cnoc Mór** – encompasses cliffs and the rocky outcrops known as **the Stags** on its western side; tranquil, reedy **Lough Boffin**, the haunt of swans, at its centre; and several sandy beaches – the one in the southeast corner provides the best swimming, while beautiful **Trá Ghael**, beneath Cnoc Mór in the west, is also worth visiting, though its currents are too dangerous for a dip. A combined **heritage museum** and gift shop

> **INISHBOFIN ACTIVITIES**
>
> Contact Aidan Day (☎095 45974) to arrange **angling trips**, while **scuba diving** is available with Islands West (☎087 222 7098, ⓦislandswest.ie). For **horse riding** get in touch with Inishbofin Equestrian Centre (daily 9am–6pm; ☎087 950 1545, ⓦinishbofinequestriancentre.com).

(☎087 969 6732) opens during the summer months a short way east of the pier, and over a weekend in May – or sometimes early September (check with the tourist office) – there's a lively, three-day arts festival. Year round you're assured plenty of traditional music, featuring the island's own renowned ceili band. Note that the only shop (and post office) near the pier is pricey, so bring as much stuff over with you as you can.

The first historical reference to Inishbofin comes from the seventh century: after the Irish and Roman Churches fell out at the Synod of Whitby in 664, St Colman left Lindisfarne and journeyed here via Iona. Though the monastery he established was destroyed in 1334, you can still see the atmospheric shell of a fourteenth-century **chapel** on the site, to the east of the pier, beyond a small, lily-strewn lake. In the island cemetery surrounding the chapel, two stone crosses and a couple of **holy wells** are said to date from Colman's foundation. The island's other historic site is visible on the right as you enter the excellent natural harbour, a forbidding, mottled-black **castle**, built in the sixteenth century and strengthened by Cromwell, which is accessible at low tide.

ARRIVAL AND DEPARTURE   INISHBOFIN

By bus and ferry The MV *Island Discovery* (☎095 45819 or 44878, ⓦinishbofinislanddiscovery.com; €20 return) crosses the 11km to Inishbofin from Cleggan, 10km northwest of Clifden. Sailings (30min) are thrice daily from Easter to August, and two or three times a day for the rest of the year. Citylink buses run from Galway, via Clifden, to Cleggan (3 daily).

INFORMATION AND GETTING AROUND

Tourist information You can get information at the island community centre above the pier (Mon–Fri 9am–10pm; ☎095 45895). Maps of the island are available on the boat or at the tourist office/community centre.

Bike rental If there's no sign of Paddy Joe King and his bikes, head to his house 700m east of the pier near the hostel or call ☎095 45833.

ACCOMMODATION AND EATING

Day's Inishbofin House Just east of the pier ☎095 45809, ⓦinishbofinhouse.com. The pick of the accommodation on Inishbofin, this chic, modern hotel offers rooms that mostly have balconies overlooking the harbour. There's also a spa and a sophisticated evening restaurant specializing in seafood, plus bar food. **€140**

Dolphin Hotel 700m east of the pier ☎095 45991, ⓦdolphinhotel.ie. This small hotel offers large, bright, well-equipped en-suite rooms, some with outdoor terraces. Its restaurant menu includes the likes of rump of roast lamb and plenty of fish and shellfish (depending on what's fresh). Mid-March to Oct. **€90**

Elliott's 500m east of the pier ☎095 45853, ✉joanne@inishbofin.com. The island's best self-catering option, renting out an elegant, secluded room with its own entrance and a panoramic conservatory. **€70**

★ **Inishbofin Island Hostel** (IHH & IHO) 700m east of the pier ☎095 45855, ⓦinishbofin-hostel.ie. Well-maintained hostel in a converted farmhouse with a conservatory and garden, laundry facilities and camping space. They'll pick up your luggage at the pier, and offer reduced prices if you stay a second night. April–Oct. Tent pitch **€20**, doubles **€45**

Letterfrack and around

The tiny, nineteenth-century Quaker village of **LETTERFRACK**, around 15km northeast of Clifden, is the unlikely site of the Galway Mayo Institute of Technology, and plays host to two notable, long-standing festivals (ⓦceecc.org), both featuring plenty of traditional music: **Bog Week**, celebrating the landscape with walking events at the end of May; and **Sea Week**, with a conference on marine heritage in late October.

Connemara National Park & Visitor Centre

Entrance on the west side of Letterfrack · March–Oct 9.30am–5.30pm; grounds open all year round · Free · ☎ 095 41054, ⓦ connemaranationalpark.ie

The **Connemara National Park** covers a thin slice of the northwest sector of the Twelve Bens, stretching east as far as Benbrack, Bencullagh, Muckanaght and Benbaun. It includes an excellent walkway to the top of **Diamond Hill** (445m; about 2hr 30min return), which affords fantastic views of the mountains, bays and islands all around. There are three shorter **nature trails** across the lower slopes, through some natural woodland and over bogland, with free guided walks on Wednesday and Friday mornings in July and August. The park's **visitor centre** contains a fascinating exhibition on the wildlife and geology of Connemara and a café. There's also a children's playground. A trail map is available to download from the website.

ARRIVAL AND DEPARTURE LETTERFRACK

By bus Bus Éireann services (Mon–Sat 1–2 daily) from Clifden.

ACCOMMODATION AND EATING

Bard's Den By the central junction ☎ 095 41042, ⓦ bardsden.com. This pub offers en-suite rooms and lays on a wide variety of food including fish and lamb stew. Main courses average €7–13; food served noon–9pm. €60

Letterfrack Lodge and Walking Centre (IHH) North side of central junction ☎ 095 41222, ⓦ letterfracklodge.com. This partly en-suite hostel in a modern, stone-clad and pine-floored house offers plenty of local information, laundry facilities and three kitchens. Late May to mid-Sept.

Double dorms €60

★ **Rosleague Manor** 1.5km west of village ☎ 095 41101, ⓦ rosleague.com. An elegant, early nineteenth-century hotel with a relaxed country-house atmosphere. The sitting rooms are charming, and extensive gardens and woodlands stretch down to the sea. The restaurant (open 7–9.30pm) offers lamb, steak and fresh seafood. Half-board and other value packages are available. Mid-March to Oct. €150

Kylemore Abbey

5km east of Letterfrack on the N59 · Easter–Oct 9am–6pm; Nov–March 10am–4.30pm; 20min history talk daily at 11.30am, 1pm and 3pm; 30min garden tour 2.30pm daily May–Sept; shuttle bus every 15min · €13; Heritage Island · ☎ 095 52001, ⓦ kylemoreabbeytourism.ie; fishing ☎ 095 41178, ⓦ kylemoreabbeyfishery.net

Grey, castellated **Kylemore Abbey** sits behind a glassy lake against the rugged green backdrop of Dúchruach hill. Built with Manchester cotton money in the 1860s, it's now a small Benedictine convent, but you can visit three of the reception rooms and the main hall, and learn about the place's history from the display boards and audiovisual presentation. There's an extensive crafts shop and restaurant too, and **fishing** on the lake and Kylemore River can be arranged. Also on the lake shore is a beautiful neo-Gothic **church**, which incorporates elements copied from the great English cathedrals of the late twelfth and early thirteenth centuries.

From the abbey, you can walk (20min) or catch a shuttle bus to the restored **walled garden**. Laid out in the 1860s with no fewer than 21 glasshouses, the huge garden deteriorated after the estate was sold in 1903, but an ambitious project has returned it more or less to its former state, using only original Victorian plant specimens. Beyond the beautifully tended ornamental flower garden lie stream and fern walks and beds of herbs and vegetables, with everything from dill to parsnips (all labelled), divided by a long herbaceous border. The head gardener's house and his workers' far more basic bothy have been refurbished, but the most striking remnants are the very fine, original cabbage trees.

Renvyle Peninsula

North of Letterfrack, it's well worth exploring the minor roads that crisscross the **Renvyle Peninsula**, eventually looping around by the gentle waters of Lough Fee to meet the N59 near Killary Harbour. On the south side of the peninsula, 3km from Letterfrack overlooking Ballynakill Harbour, you'll come to the **Ocean and Country Visitor Centre** (March–Nov daily 10am–6pm; ☎095 43473 or ☎086 199 1988; €5, €20 with a cruise), which features exhibits of sea life and local maritime history, lots of children's activities and hour-long wildlife cruises in a glass-bottomed boat four times a day until the end of October (if there are enough takers), to view deserted islands and, hopefully, seals and dolphins. From the museum quay, a walk up **Tully Hill** is highly recommended (about 3hr return), whose 355m summit affords a matchless panorama, with the towering mountains of Connemara arrayed to the east.

10

In summer, the **Renvyle Teach Ceoil** centre (☎095 41047), whose name means "music cottage", hosts a weekly show of Irish music, song, dance and storytelling (Tues 8.30–11pm). **Scuba Dive West** in Glassillaun (☎095 43922, ✆scubadivewest.com) is a PADI 5-star resort offering courses and diving off the coast and nearby islands.

ACCOMMODATION AND EATING   **RENVYLE PENINSULA**

The peninsula's main settlements are the adjacent hamlets of **Tully Cross** and **Tully**, 4km north of Letterfrack.

Connemara Camp Site ☎095 43406, 5km east of Tullycross. This popular campsite is situated near Lettergesh Beach, a concave stretch of fine sand with views of the offshore islands. Tent pitch **€18**

Paddy Coyne's Tullycross ☎095 43499. A 200-year-old pub noted for its food and traditional music. The menus showcase Killary mussels, wild salmon and pollock; the signature dish of Renvyle scallops with black pudding costs €18. In the summer there's music on Thurs and Sat night, while in the winter it's Mon. Feb–Dec daily noon–3pm & 5–9pm.

Renvyle Beach 2km west of Tully Cross towards end of peninsula ☎095 43462, ✆renvylebeachcaravanpark .com. A good campsite with direct access to a fine beach and ideally placed for exploration of the villages and countryside. Easter–Oct. Tent pitch **€20**

Renvyle House Renvyle ☎095 43511, ✆renvyle.com. In a dreamy location seemingly on the edge of the world, this relaxing luxury hotel occupies the former home of the surgeon, writer and wit Oliver St John Gogarty (see p.80). It is set amid pretty gardens, woodland and a lake, and comes with a long menu of facilities such as golf, tennis, boating, Ayurvedic treatments and a heated outdoor swimming pool. The perfect place to de-stress. Feb–Dec. **€190**

Killary Harbour

Killary Harbour is one of Ireland's very few fjords, a truly dramatic oddity with Connacht's highest mountain, Mweelrea (817m), plunging sheer into the dark water on its north bank. This glacial gouge runs for 16km between the uplands of Galway and Mayo, and with a typical depth of 15m is perfect for salmon and mussel farms, and for enjoying a relaxing boat cruise or indulging in some adventure sports. The only waterside settlement, **Leenane** (✆leenanevillage.com), enjoys a snug, scenic location near the head of the fjord.

Sheep and Wool Centre

Leenane • Mid-March–Oct daily 9.30am–6pm • €5, €3 children, €13 family ticket • ☎095 42323, ✆sheepandwoolcentre.com

The **Sheep and Wool Centre** may not sound too promising, but makes for a fascinating visit. Accompanied by an enthusiastic guide, you'll get to see demonstrations of spinning and weaving; the centre also has a good, inexpensive café-restaurant.

ARRIVAL AND DEPARTURE   **KILLARY HARBOUR**

By bus A Bus Éireann service (Mon–Sat 1–2 daily) runs from Clifden.

TOURS AND ACTIVITIES

Boat tours Killary Fjord Boat Tours (☎091 566736, ✆killaryfjord.com), based at Nancy's Point, 2km west of Leenane, offer 90min fjord cruises (April–Oct daily 2–4pm; €21, children under 10 are free).

Activities Killary Adventure Centre (☎095 43411, ✆killaryadventure.com) about 5km west of Leenane on the N59, offers all manner of activities and courses, from rock climbing and kayaking to bungee jumping and paintballing.

ACCOMMODATION AND EATING

Blackberry Café Letterfrack Rd, Leenane ☎095 42240. An attractive, welcoming café-restaurant, offering reasonably priced dishes (mains around €13–15), such as wild salmon with dill sauce, hake, duck and steak. Easter–Sept, noon–9pm.

Connemara Hostel (IHO) Leenane ☎095 42929, ⓦsleepzone.ie. A superb variety of en-suite hostel accommodation, plus free wi-fi, tennis court and camping. Daily bus service in summer from Westport to Galway. Reductions for online bookings. **€49**

Leenane Hotel Leenane ☎095 42249, ⓦleenanehotel .com. A traditional coaching inn with a delightful garden and fountain right on the water's edge. An ideal location from which to launch yourself into a hike over the Maumturk Mountains. Restaurant open daily 6.30–9pm. **€90**

Portfinn Lodge Leenane ☎095 42265, ⓦportfinn .com. Bright, attractive, en-suite rooms with free wi-fi and an evening restaurant, in a large modern bungalow. It's a magical location offering stunning views of the fjord and the mountains. **€80**

County Mayo

Far from pulling up at the county border, the wonderful mountain scenery found in Connemara marches on into the south of **County Mayo** (Maigh Eo; ⓦvisitmayo.com), in the substantial shape of Mweelrea, the Sheefry Hills and the Partry Mountains. These ranges culminate in the conical peak of Ireland's holy mountain, **Croagh Patrick**, beyond which change is announced by the trough of **Clew Bay**, the extension of a geological fault that runs all the way to the Scottish Highlands. Unless you're beetling direct to Westport on the N59, two possible routes out of Connemara into south Mayo present themselves. You can detour east to the abbey town of **Cong**, right on the county border and sharing many similarities with Oughterard, to which it is linked by boat trips across Lough Corrib. Or you can forge through the heart of the mountains from Leenane to **Louisburgh**, which gives access to the islands of **Inishturk** and **Clare** at the mouth of Clew Bay. Either way, you're almost certain to end up in **Westport**, a refined, lively, Georgian base, terminus of the railway line from Dublin and hub for local buses. The county's other main tourist centre is **Achill** at the northwest corner of Clew Bay, Ireland's largest island and a popular resort. Beyond this, there's kilometre after kilometre of wild, dramatic landscape, but only a few specific attractions: the stunning discovery of a Neolithic farm system at **Céide Fields** justifies a journey to the north coast if you have the time, while a short way east of Westport is the impressive **National Museum of Country Life** at Castlebar.

ARRIVAL AND GETTING AROUND
COUNTY MAYO

By plane Some 40km east of Castlebar and 8km south of Charlestown, Ireland West Airport (☎094 936 8100, ⓦirelandwestairport.com) is a useful, often cheap, way into the county. It is still generally known by its former name of Knock Airport. The airport is served by the Bus

Éireann Galway–Derry express service and a local service to Westport (see p.382). Car-rental is available at the airport from Avis (☎094 936 7707, ⓦavis.ie) and Casey's (☎094 906 0500, ⓦcaseycar.com), among others.

Cong

The pretty village of **CONG** sits right on the county border, between the green plains of south Mayo and Galway's Connemara Mountains, on the neck of land separating loughs Corrib and Mask. Its main claim to fame these days is that the film *The Quiet Man*, a famed if sentimental emigrants' portrayal of Ireland that starred John Wayne and Maureen O'Hara (who was herself born in Dublin), was filmed here in 1951.

Quiet Man Museum

April–Oct daily 10am–5pm; closed 30min for lunch • €5 • ☎094 954 6089, ⓦwww.quietman-cong.com/cong-museum

If you're happy to get into the kitschiness of it all, head for the **Quiet Man Museum** just around the corner from the tourist office, a painstaking replica of the cottage built for the making of the film; the only "real" thing in it is a horse's harness used in the film.

Cong Abbey and the Cross of Cong

The village does boast a site of genuine historical interest, **Cong Abbey**, which was originally founded in the seventh century and rebuilt in the twelfth and thirteenth centuries by Turlough, Rory and Cathal O'Connor, kings of Connacht and the last high kings of Ireland. The ruined Augustinian abbey's sculpture-work suggests links with western France, particularly the very fine geometrical and foliate carvings on the doorways to the chapterhouse from the cloister. Inside, the elaborate **Cross of Cong**, which was created for Turlough O'Connor in 1123, reflects the place's former wealth.

At one time the abbey housed a population of three thousand, and the logistics of feeding such a crowd are hinted at in the **fishing house** over the River Cong, whence a line ran to a bell in the refectory to let cook know when fish had been caught. From the **bridge** over the river by the abbey, you can stroll through the woods to Lough Corrib, passing through *Ashford Castle Hotel*'s grounds (see below), though in summer be aware that it charges €5 for the privilege.

10

ARRIVAL AND INFORMATION   CONG

By bus Bus Éireann run a Galway–Ballina service (Mon–Fri 2 daily) that stops at Cong each weekday, and a summer service via Lennana to Clifden.

Tourist information Abbey St (March–Oct Mon–Thurs & Sun daily 9.15am–5.15pm, closes 1–1.45pm for lunch; ☏ 094 954 6542). Has plenty of detailed literature about the area's sights.

Boat tours Corrib Cruises (☏ 087 994 6380, ⓦ corribcruises.com) operates a number of boat trips around and across Lough Corrib. A history cruise (daily 11am; 1hr; €20) runs from Lisloughrey pier (near the hostel) and there's also a cruise from here to Inchagoill Island (see p.369; June–Sept daily 3pm; 2hr 15min; €20), which includes 45min on the island.

ACCOMMODATION AND EATING

Ashford Castle Hotel ☏ 094 954 6003, ⓦ ashford .com. Standing at the point where the Cong River runs into Lough Corrib, this hotel – one of Ireland's most prestigious – was built by Sir Arthur Guinness in the nineteenth century. The hotel's grounds are far larger than the adjoining village, and rooms range from comfortable doubles to fashionably chic suites. Expect fine views and a long list of amenities that includes a health spa, horse riding and falconry. **€475**

Cong Hostel (An Oige, IHH & IHO) 2km from the centre of the village off the Headford road in Lisloughry ☏ 094 954 6089, ⓦ quietman-cong.com. This well-run, comfortable hostel screens *The Quiet Man* every night, rents out fishing rods and rowing boats, and has a campsite, a playground and a bureau de change. Tent pitch **€20**, doubles **€25**

★ Cullen's at the Cottage ☏ 094 954 5332, ⓦ ashford .com. Housed in a traditional thatched cottage with outdoor seating in the grounds of *Ashford Castle Hotel*, this seasonal bistro serves everything from soups, salads and sandwiches to fresh lobster from the tank and the signature dish of fish curry. Average dinner mains cost €20. April–Dec daily 1–9.30pm.

Danagher's Abbey St ☏ 094 954 6028. Reasonably priced bar meals, such as the ever-popular bacon and cabbage or Irish stew, plus salads and sandwiches. Dinner menu main courses from around €15. Daily noon–4pm & 6–10pm.

Hungry Monk Café Abbey St ☏ 094 954 5842. A smart little café near the tourist office which rustles up wholesome meals, snacks, salads or sandwiches (€10 for mains), as well as great coffee. March–Oct Tues–Sun 10am–5pm.

★ Michaeleen's Manor ☏ 094 954 6089, ⓦ quietman-cong.com. A smart, en-suite, *Quiet Man*-themed B&B (named after the film's drunken matchmaker), with each room bearing the name of a character in the film. There's a tennis court, a DVD player in every room, tourist information and discount vouchers for local cafés, restaurant and bike rental. **€65**

Delphi

The obvious road north from Connemara into Mayo is the N59 from Leenane to Westport, but the seemingly impenetrable mountains on the north side of Killary Harbour conceal a far more scenic route. Winding between the Mweelrea massif and the Sheefry Hills, the R335 brings you first to the noted fishing lake at **DELPHI**, so named by the second Marquis of Sligo in the early nineteenth century: after swimming the Hellespont with Byron, the Marquis arrived at Delphi in the mountains of central Greece, where he was overcome with homesickness as it reminded him so much of his fishery back here in Mayo.

10

The Famine Memorial

Beyond Delphi, the road skirts the black water of Doo Lough, past an interesting **memorial**. In March 1849, hundreds of men, women and children marched the 16km from the small crossroads town of Louisburgh through this bleak, exposed valley to Delphi Lodge, where the Famine Commissioners were staying. When they arrived, the commissioners were eating a hearty lunch and would not be disturbed, then refused any help, leaving the starving people to struggle back through the snow to Louisburgh, a journey on which many of them died. Every year towards the end of May, a Famine Walk commemorates the event, as well as more recent famines.

ACCOMMODATION DELPHI

Delphi Lodge ☎095 42222, ⓦdelphilodge.ie. In a glorious setting by the lake facing the lower slopes of Mweelrea, this luxury hotel offers half-board packages and 5 self-catering cottages. Imaginative dinners (guests only) are taken communally around one large table, with the angler who has caught the biggest fish that day at the head. The menu might feature leg of Connemara lamb, poached salmon, or other locally sourced dishes. Open for B&B and dinner March–Sept; self-catering all year. €230

Delphi Mountain Resort & Spa ☎095 42208, ⓦdelphiadventure.com. A luxury spa and adventure resort running activities and courses in surfing, canoeing, mountaineering and more, for both adults and children. You can choose from seven different types of accommodation, ranging from luxury suites to simple doubles – but all come with stunning views. Feb–Dec. €98

Louisburgh and around

With a range of cafés and accommodation choices, little **LOUISBURGH** is an excellent base for exploration of the area. The **Granuaile Centre** in the library (June–Sept Mon–Fri 10am–5pm; rest of the year Mon–Fri 11am–4pm; ☎098 66341; €5) focuses on seafaring in Ireland in the sixteenth century, in particular **Grace O'Malley** (Gráinne Ní Mháille, often corrupted to Granuaile; c. 1530–1603), the formidable sea captain and pirate queen of Clare Island, who ruled the sea from Galway Bay to Donegal Bay. Over the bank holiday weekend at the start of May, Louisburgh hosts a lively **festival** of traditional music, Féile Chois Cuain (ⓦfeilechoiscuain.com), featuring concerts, classes and plenty of impromptu sessions.

The sparsely inhabited coastline southwest of Louisburgh is lined with sandy **beaches**, notably White Strand, a long, west-facing stretch around the mouth of a stream about 15km away, and Silver Strand, a great desert of a beach at the mouth of Clew Bay, a couple of kilometres on from the end of the road to the north of the town, that is flanked by rocks and low dunes in the shadow of bulky Mweelrea. About 4km west of town at Carrownisky Strand, Surf Mayo (☎087 621 2508, ⓦsurfmayo.com) offers **surfing** instruction and equipment hire all year round.

ARRIVAL AND DEPARTURE LOUISBURGH

By bus Bus Éireann services (Mon–Sat 3–4 daily) from Westport.

Clare Island

Measuring just 8km by 5km, **Clare Island** (ⓦclareisland.info) features two hills – Knockmore (462m) and its little brother Knocknaveen (223m) to the east – behind which the mighty sea cliffs along the northwest shore are home to important breeding colonies of seabirds, notably fulmars. Other rare birds include peregrines, choughs and barnacle geese, while petalwort, a species of liverwort, figures among the notable plants. The harbour, which shelters a Blue Flag **beach** with fine views of the mainland mountains, is guarded by a well-preserved sixteenth-century **tower house** ruin, which was the stronghold of Grace O'Malley (see above). The main island **festivity** is a currach and yawl regatta in July.

CLARE ISLAND ACTIVITIES

A leaflet available on the boats details five **walks** on the island, including a complete circuit which takes about six hours, while **scuba diving** is available May to October with Islands West (☎087 222 7098, ⓦislandswest.ie), and a variety of activities, including snorkelling, orienteering, rock-climbing and abseiling, is offered by **Clare Island Adventures** (☎087 346 7713, ⓦclareislandadventures.ie). Ballytoughey Loom & Craft Shop (Mon–Sat 11am–5pm, Sun noon–4pm; ☎098 25800, ⓦclareislandhandweaver.com) offers courses in **weaving** and **spinning** (May–Sept) and has wool, linen and silk for sale.

10

The abbey

In the middle of the island's south shore, a mid-thirteenth-century Cistercian **abbey** (ask for the key at the nearby O'Malley's foodstore and post office) bears an ornate Gothic tomb in which Grace O'Malley – or more likely a relative of hers – is said to be buried. More notable from an artistic point of view are the **frescoes** in the chancel, among the finest extant medieval paintings in Ireland.

ARRIVAL AND GETTING AROUND CLARE ISLAND

By boat Ferries run from Roonagh Quay at Clew Bay, 6km west of Louisburgh (May–Sept 5 boats a day; in winter at least 2 a day; 15min; €15 return). Contact O'Malley's (☎098 25045, ⓦomalleyferries.com) or Clare Island Ferry (☎098 23737, ⓦclareislandferry.com).

By bike and taxi You can rent bikes or hire a minibus taxi from the pier (☎098 25640).

ACCOMMODATION

Cois Abhainn About 3km from the harbour at the island's southwest tip ☎098 26216. Pitch your tent in the field behind the beach, with toilets, showers and a laundry available in the community centre. The owner will even pick you up and make evening meals. Feb–Nov. Tent pitch **€10**, doubles **€70**

Macalla Farm & Yoga Retreat Centre Ballytoughey, in the north of the island ☎087 250 4845, ⓦyogaretreats.ie. This centre offers courses in yoga, meditation, mindfulness and natural horsemanship.

Residential courses and occasional self-catering are also available. Accommodation is in refurbished traditional cottages which use natural materials such as wood, hemp and terracotta. **€80**

Seabreeze Capnagower, above the harbour ☎098 26746. This pleasant guesthouse, with both en-suite and standard accommodation, is an ideal base from which to roam around the island. Evening meals are available if requested in advance. **€70**

Inishturk

To the south of Clare Island lies the even smaller and less developed island of **Inishturk** (ⓦinishturkisland.com), a tranquil, 200m-high lump of rock and grass that survives on farming and lobster fishing. From the tiny harbour, the island's paved road branches north and south: to the north, there's a particularly fine **walk**, veering west off the road around a small lake, before climbing to a ruined watchtower in around 45 minutes. The south road rises to the **community centre** after about fifteen minutes, opposite which a narrow gate points down through the fields to the island's finest sandy **beach**, a sheltered strand with clear blue water and views of the mainland.

ARRIVAL AND DEPARTURE INISHTURK

By boat The Clare Island Ferry runs boats over from Roonagh Quay (May–Sept 3 daily Mon, Wed and Fri–Sun, 2 daily Tues, 1 daily Thurs; Oct–April 1–2 daily; 50min; €20 return) though may be affected by weather.

ACCOMMODATION

Tránaun Beach House ☎098 45641, ⓦtranuanhouse .com. A 5min walk up the south road at the post office, with en-suite rooms, pick-ups from the harbour and day-trips to other islands organized by the owners. You get complimentary tea and fresh scones on arrival, and lovely grilled mackerel at breakfast, while the community centre next door doubles as the island pub in the evenings, with regular music sessions and ceilis, and serves evening meals. **€70**

10

Croagh Patrick

Rising to 764m to the east of Louisburgh, the cone of **Croagh** (pronounced "croak") **Patrick** dominates Clew Bay and the Westport area. It was the pagan home of the mother goddess, now converted into the holiest mountain in Christian Ireland, and on a fine day offers an awesome panorama, stretching from the Twelve Bens in the south to Slieve League in the north. During his long missionary tour of the island, **St Patrick** is supposed to have passed the forty days of Lent in 441 alone on the mountain, finding time to hurl all of Ireland's snakes to their deaths over the precipice of Lugnanarrib just to the south of the summit. This association with the saint has made Croagh Patrick the focus of major **pilgrimages**, which take place three times a year, on March 17 (St Patrick's Day), August 15 (Assumption Day) and – the main event – on the last Sunday in July, Reek Day (which coincides with the pagan harvest festival of Lughnasa). On this day, tens of thousands of pilgrims still make the climb to attend Mass on the summit, some fasting and barefoot.

The starting point for the ascent of Croagh Patrick is the excellent **visitor centre** (daily: mid-March to Oct 10am–5pm; July & Aug 9am–6pm; ☎098 64114, ⓦcroagh-patrick.com) on the R335 on the north side of the peak, about halfway between Westport and Louisburgh. Here you'll find lockers, showers, advice about the climb and the weather, an excellent **café** and a DVD on the **history** of the mountain. The **climb** itself, taking on average three and a half hours return, is easy to follow though steep in places – you'll need good walking shoes and a stick, available from the visitor centre. At the summit you'll find a small **chapel** that took twelve men six months to construct in 1905.

The Famine Monument

In a small park opposite the visitor centre stands the national **monument** to *an nGórta Mór* (the Great Famine), commissioned in 1997 for the 150th anniversary. The bronze sculpture of a coffin ship, with skeletons floating around its masts and prow, looks more eerie and shocking now that it's been weathered green by the rain.

Murrisk Abbey

On the shoreline behind the Famine Monument, well-preserved **Murrisk Abbey**, which features some unusual battlements on the south wall of the church, was established by the O'Malley family in 1457. An Augustinian foundation dedicated to St Patrick, in former times it housed famous relics such as the Shrine of St Patrick's Tooth and his Black Bell, both now in Dublin's National Museum. From the abbey there are fine views of the islands of **Clew Bay**, which are actually half-submerged drumlins (see p.626); there are said to be enough of them for a year and a day – 366.

ARRIVAL AND DEPARTURE   CROAGH PATRICK

By bus If you're relying on public transport for a day-trip to Croagh Patrick, the best day to attempt the climb is Thurs (the main shopping day in Westport), with three or four buses in each direction between the town and Louisburgh; Tues and Sat are also possible.

ACCOMMODATION AND EATING

Béal-an-t-Sáile ☎098 64012, ⓦbealantsaile.com. Overlooking the sea less than 1km east of the visitor centre at Murrisk, with great breakfasts that include Clew Bay mackerel. Rooms are well appointed, though some are on the small side. **€60**

The Tavern Bar & Restaurant Murrisk ☎098 64060, ⓦtavernmurrisk.com. With Clew Bay on its doorstep it's no surprise local lobster (served with sea lettuce) and Achill sea trout are menu staples. You can choose from pub grub (mains average €14) or dine in the evening restaurant where prices rise to around €20. There's also a beer garden and outdoor tables. Daily 11am–11.30pm.

Westport

Set on the shores of Clew Bay, **WESTPORT** (ⓦwestporttourism.com) is an agreeable, easy-going town that matches its location with some fine architecture. Its main visitor attraction is **Westport House**, a graceful Georgian mansion now surrounded by a country park of rides and amusements, which separates the town centre from Westport Harbour. The centre itself was laid out in classical style in 1780 for the Browne family of Westport House by James Wyatt, who built a striking octagonal square and canalized the Carrowbeg River, flanking it with the tree-lined Mall. More recently, the town has developed an artsy, cosmopolitan feel, attracting many visitors and residents from other parts of Ireland and Europe. During the summer, the place is abuzz, especially for the prestigious ten-day **Arts**

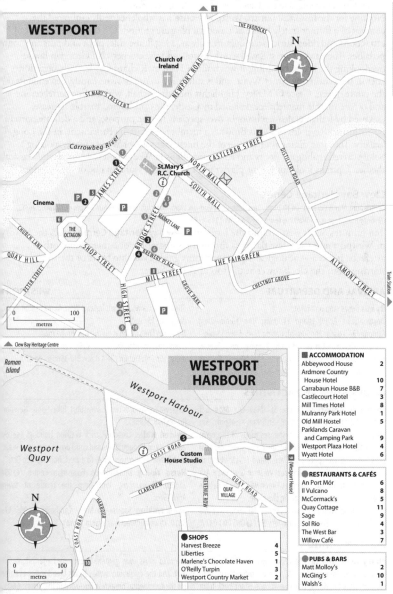

WESTPORT

THE PADDOCKS

Church of Ireland

ST. MARY'S CRESCENT

NEWPORT ROAD

Carrowbeg River

CASTLEBAR STREET

DISTILLERY ROAD

St. Mary's R.C. Church

JAMES STREET

NORTH MALL

SOUTH MALL

Cinema

P

THE OCTAGON

SHOP STREET

CHURCH LANE

QUAY HILL

PETER STREET

BRIDGE STREET

MARKET LANE

BREWERY PLACE

P

THE FAIRGREEN

ALTAMONT STREET

MILL STREET

HIGH STREET

GROVE PARK

CHESTNUT GROVE

Train Station

P

0   100
metres

Clew Bay Heritage Centre

Roman Island

WESTPORT HARBOUR

Westport Harbour

Westport Quay

COAST ROAD

Custom House Studio

Westport House

QUAY ROAD

CLAREVIEW

REVENUE ROW

QUAY VILLAGE

COAST ROAD

HARBOUR

0   100
metres

ACCOMMODATION	
Abbeywood House	2
Ardmore Country House Hotel	10
Carrabaun House B&B	7
Castlecourt Hotel	3
Mill Times Hotel	8
Mulranny Park Hotel	1
Old Mill Hostel	5
Parklands Caravan and Camping Park	9
Westport Plaza Hotel	4
Wyatt Hotel	6

RESTAURANTS & CAFÉS	
An Port Mór	6
Il Vulcano	8
McCormack's	5
Quay Cottage	11
Sage	9
Sol Rio	4
The West Bar	3
Willow Café	7

SHOPS	
Harvest Breeze	4
Liberties	5
Marlene's Chocolate Haven	1
O'Reilly Turpin	3
Westport Country Market	2

PUBS & BARS	
Matt Molloy's	2
McGing's	10
Walsh's	1

Festival in early October (⊛westportartsfestival.com). Another big attraction is the newly established Great Western Greenway (⊛greenway.ie), a 42km cycling and walking route on traffic-free roads along a former railway track running from Westport to Achill Island.

Westport House

Entered from Westport Harbour • **House and gardens** 11.30am–5.30pm: April–Sept daily; March & Oct Sat & Sun • €12.50, children €6.50 • **Attractions** Easter week & June–Aug daily, May Sun plus Bank Holiday Mon • All attractions, plus house and gardens €21, children €16.50, one-day family ticket €75; Heritage Island • ☎ 098 27766, ⊛ westporthouse.ie

Not one for the historical purists, **Westport House** has wholeheartedly embraced the concept of a former stately home as a modern pleasure ground. On the estate is a host of **attractions and rides**, such as a miniature railway, a log flume ride, pitch and putt and swan pedaloes. The gardens are still well worth a stroll, and the creeper-clad Georgian house overlooking the lake is beautiful. It was built in 1730 by Richard Castle, with alterations later in the century by James Wyatt, and is still home to the Browne family, descendants of the pirate queen, Grace O'Malley. Highlights include the hall, with its fine barrel ceiling and ornate marble mantelpiece designed by Castle, the cantilevered marble staircase, executed by Italian craftsmen brought over specially for the purpose, and a delicate portrait by Sir Joshua Reynolds of Denis Browne, a member of Grattan's Parliament, in the Long Gallery. The large dining room is one of the finest examples of Wyatt's work, sporting boldly carved mahogany doors and relief medallions in Wedgwood style on playful classical themes. Upstairs look out for the playwright J.M. Synge's violin in one of the corridors.

Clew Bay Heritage Centre

Centre April, May & Oct Mon–Fri 10.30am–2pm; June–Sept Mon–Fri 10am–5pm; July & Aug also Sun 3–5pm • €3 • ☎ 098 26852, ⊛ westportheritage.com • **Walking tours** July & Aug Wed 11am • €6

Ten minutes' walk west around the harbour, **Clew Bay Heritage Centre** traces the history of Westport and the Clew Bay area through photographs, documents and other artefacts; it has a genealogical service and runs guided **walking tours** of the town, starting from the clock tower at the top of Bridge Street.

ARRIVAL AND DEPARTURE
WESTPORT

By bus Buses stop on Mill St.
Destinations Achill Island (1 daily; 1hr 10min–2hr); Athlone (2–3 daily; 2hr 50min); Ballina (2–5 daily; 55min–1hr 25min); Castlebar (8–14 daily; 20min); Cong (Tues & Thurs 1 daily; 1hr); Dublin (3 daily; 4–5hr 40min); Galway (2–4 daily; 2hr); Louisburgh (Mon–Sat 2–4 daily; 35min); Sligo (2–3 daily; 2–3hr); Ireland West Airport (Mon–Sat 2 daily; 1hr 15min).

By train The station is on the Ballinrobe road.
Destinations Athlone (3–4 daily; 2hr); Castlebar (3–4 daily; 15min); Dublin (3–4 daily; 3hr 35min–4hr).

INFORMATION AND ACTIVITIES

Tourist information Bridge St (May–Oct Mon–Sat 9am–5.45pm; Nov–April Mon–Fri 9am–4.45pm, Sat 10am–1pm; ☎ 098 25711). Dispenses maps of the town and leaflets on the Clew Bay Trail linking 21 archaeological sites between Westport and Clare Island (⊛ clewbaytrail.com), looped walks, and the Great Western Greenway. Ask for a brochure on the Gourmet Greenway, which details local artisan food suppliers along the route.

Bike rental Westport Cycle Centre, James St (☎ 098 25471); Clew Bay Bike Hire, Distillery Rd (☎ 085 703 0177, ⊛ clewbayoutdoors.com); Westport Bike Shop, Newport Rd (☎ 098 24966).

Guided walks Croagh Patrick Walking Holidays (☎ 098 26090, ⊛ walkingguideireland.com) organize guided walks in the area lasting from a day to a week from April to Oct.

Horse riding Drummindoo Equestrian Centre (☎ 098 25616), Knockranny, 1km from the centre of town April–Sept.

Sea-kayaking Saoirse na Mara, Caraholly (☎ 086 173 3610, ⊛ irelandwestseakayaking.com).

ACCOMMODATION

Abbeywood House Newport Rd ☎ 098 25496, ⊛ abbeywoodhouse.com. A former monastery with stained-glass windows, this guesthouse is set back from the road in its own garden. Rooms are large, bright and airy, and the engaging owner bakes bread every evening for the continental breakfast (included in the price). **€60**

Ardmore Country House Hotel The Quay ☏ 098 25994, ⓦ ardmorecountryhouse.com. Overlooking Clew Bay, this small, fashionable hotel has rooms decorated and equipped in stunning style, a superb breakfast menu that includes eggs Benedict and Achill kippers, and a tempting restaurant serving locally sourced products. Mid-March to Oct. **€140**

Carrabaun House B&B On the road to Leenane ☏ 098 26196. Highly recommended B&B, with a wide range of breakfast options and fine views, in a spacious, en-suite, period-style modern house with tastefully decorated rooms. **€70**

Castlecourt Hotel Castlebar St ☏ 098 55088, ⓦ castlecourthotel.ie. Together with the adjacent, co-owned *Westport Plaza*, this family-orientated hotel offers a swimming pool, gym, a wide choice of restaurants, a kids' club in school holidays, and all manner of themed breaks, half-board offers and other packages. **€110**

★**Mill Times Hotel** Mill St ☏ 098 29200, ⓦ milltimeshotel.ie. A conveniently located hotel with an informal and friendly atmosphere just a few minutes' walk to the town centre. Traditional rooms range from superior suites to doubles with queen-size beds. Good midweek deals available off season. **€98**

Mulranny Park Hotel Mulranny ☏ 098 36000, ⓦ mulrannyparkhotel.ie. In a stunning location looking out over Clew Bay, this contemporary hotel, with hot tub and pool, is ideally sited to explore the area, particularly as the Greenway trail runs behind it. Rooms are stylish and comfy; if you want extra space, opt for the sea-view apartments. **€170**

Old Mill Hostel (IHH & IHO) Barrack Yard, James St ☏ 098 27045, ⓦ oldmillhostel.com. Accessed through an archway, this former mill and brewery is now a comfortable hostel, with a light breakfast and laundry facilities included in the price. Closed Christmas & New Year. Dorms **€22.50**

Parklands Caravan and Camping Park ☏ 098 27766, ⓦ westporthouse.ie. Campers should head for this park in the delightful grounds of Westport House estate – a perfect location from which to explore the town and countryside. Late March to mid-Sept. Tent pitch **€30**

Westport Plaza Hotel Castlebar St ☏ 098 51166, ⓦ westportplazahotel.ie. Welcoming, elegant, chic and contemporary hotel, offering spacious and well-equipped rooms with king-sized beds, Italian marble bathrooms and hot tubs. Shares facilities with *Castlecourt Hotel*. **€118**

Wyatt Hotel The Octagon ☏ 098 25027, ⓦ wyatthotel .com. Congenial small hotel decorated in bare wood and bold colours, in an unbeatable central location. Ask about its various special deals. **€110**

EATING

An Port Mór Brewery Place, Bridge St ☏ 098 26730, ⓦ anportmor.com. Broad mix of modern Irish cuisine, especially fish and shellfish, artfully cooked and tastefully presented; expect to pay around €34 for three courses. Daily 5–9.30pm.

Il Vulcano High St ☏ 098 24888. Bustling, authentic Italian restaurant with an open kitchen, just up from the clock tower, which provides pasta, risotto, pizza, and some meat and seafood main courses. Daily 5.30–10pm.

McCormack's Bridge St ☏ 098 25619, ⓦ katemccormack andsons.ie. Brightly painted, inviting café and art gallery above a butcher's, which serves coffee, salads, homemade soup and fine sandwiches. Mon, Tues & Thurs–Sat 9am–6pm.

★**Quay Cottage** The Harbour ☏ 098 50692, ⓦ quaycottage.ie. In a pretty, atmospheric stone cottage by the gates to Westport House, this restaurant has a good, long-standing reputation locally, especially for its seafood dishes. They have also introduced a Wild Atlantic Way (see box, p.31) menu based on food sourced along the coastline. The early bird menu is €20.50. 6–9.30pm: July & Aug daily; winter Wed–Sat.

Sage High St ☏ 098 56700, ⓦ sagewestport.ie. Italian-influenced restaurant, serving delicious pasta dishes and a wide range of tasty meat and fish specials, with plenty of vegetarian options. Expect to pay around €32 for a three-course dinner or €21.50 for the early bird, two-course option. 5.30–10pm: July & Aug daily; winter Mon, Tues & Thurs–Sun.

Sol Rio Bridge St ☏ 098 28944, ⓦ solrio.ie. Colourful and informal, if somewhat pricey, upstairs restaurant, with a Portuguese influence, that efficiently covers all the bases: salads, pasta, pizza and more expensive fish and meat dishes, augmented by sandwiches at lunch time. Daily noon–3pm & 6–10pm.

The West Bar Bridge St ☏ 098 25886, ⓦ thewest.ie. A gastropub that is noted for its award-winning chowder. The bar menu (noon–9pm) includes platters of fish, cold meat and cheese, as well as surf'n'turf, pasta, pork belly, chicken and burgers. Main courses from €13. Good range of cocktails too. Daily 11am–11.30pm.

★**Willow Café** High St ☏ 087 707 4500, ⓦ thewillowcafe.com. An elegant tea room with outdoor tables beside the clock tower, strategically sited to view the bustling town centre. They offer an exquisite selection of organic and herbal leaf teas as well as Chinese flowering teas, homemade cupcakes, scones and gluten-free food at lunch time. Daily 9am–5.30pm.

DRINKING AND NIGHTLIFE

★**Matt Molloy's** Bridge St ☏ 098 26655, ⓦ mattmolloy.com. The town's most famous pub, owned by the eponymous Chieftains' flute player, is an affable time-burnished place that fills up for its nightly traditional music sessions. A wide selection of Mayo craft beers is available. Daily 11am–11.30pm.

10

McGing's High St ☎098 26870. Congenial and traditional bar that boasts the best pint of Guinness in Mayo and is enlivened on Sun and Mon by a guitarist. The bright blue-and-yellow exterior means you'll have no trouble spotting it. Daily 11am–11.30pm.

Walsh's James St. Also known as *Blouser's*, this is a popular spot with a 30-something crowd, who come for the weekend DJ nights, and the live music and salsa nights during the week. Daily 11am–11.30pm.

SHOPPING

Harvest Breeze Bridge St ☎098 56339. A celebration of lavender products and a sensory experience as you browse the shelves and tables. Mon–Sat 10am–6pm, also Sun 11am–5pm in summer.

Liberties The Quay ☎098 50273, ⓦliberties.ie. Large selection of fashion brands, accessories, gifts, art, jewellery, furnishings and homeware. Mon–Sat 10.30am–5.30pm, Sun noon–5pm.

Marlene's Chocolate Haven Limecourt James St ☎098 24564. A mouth-watering selection of homemade chocolates (including some sugarless ones), ranging from truffles and nut pralines to luscious ganaches. Daily 10am–6pm.

O'Reilly Turpin Bridge St ☎098 28151, ⓦoreillyturpin.ie. Long-established gift shop selling Irish silver and gold handcrafted jewellery, art and prints as well as ceramic, wood, glass and metal products. Mon–Sat 10am–6pm.

Westport Country Market James St car park ☎098 25645. An appetizing array of local farm produce and home baking sold from stalls that draw crowds of both locals and visitors. Thurs 8.30am–1pm.

Castlebar and around

CASTLEBAR, the county town of Mayo, has a lot less going for it than Westport, just 18km away to the west. It's a busy workaday town with many long-established, family-run businesses. The oldest building, **Christ Church**, on the corner of the Mall, dates from 1769 and has survived rebellions, risings and the threat of demolition, but the main attraction hereabouts is the **National Museum of Country Life** at nearby **Turlough**.

National Museum of Country Life

Turlough Park, 8km east of Castlebar off the N5 • Tues–Sat 10am–5pm, Sun 2–5pm • Free • ☎094 903 1755, ⓦmuseum.ie • A bus serves Turlough from Westport (Mon–Sat 12.15pm, returning at 5.10pm); taxis are available in Castlebar on ☎094 903 4700

The sleek, modern **National Museum of Country Life** digs beneath the dewy-eyed nostalgia that besets popular images of rural Ireland to reveal the harsh realities of country life from 1850 to 1950. The exhibition is on three levels: **Level -1** includes a brief but worthwhile history of the period from an ordinary person's point of view, with examples of the ingenious use of twisted straw rope for baskets, hens' nests, mattresses, stools and horse collars. **Level -2** chronicles the unremitting work of farming and fishing, of housewives, craftsmen and tradesmen, including a recording of a poignant letter home from an emigrant to America, and footage of men making a coracle on the River Boyne. Probably the most interesting section here deals with the seasons and festivals: churning butter on May Day to ward off evil, leaving food and drink out for dead relatives on Halloween, and grainy footage of **Wren Boys**, who would knock on doors on St Stephen's Day (December 26) with the corpse of a wren, asking for money to bury it while singing songs and telling jokes – the money, of course, would be spent on a party. **Level -3** presents personal reminiscences of the changes in rural life. You can also look inside the adjacent "Big House" of the landowners, the nineteenth-century Gothic Revival **Turlough Park House**, designed by Thomas Newenham Deane, architect of the National Museum in Dublin. There's also a café and gift shop if you have the time to browse.

ARRIVAL AND DEPARTURE   CASTLEBAR

By bus Buses run to Ballina (Mon–Sat 6–8 daily, Sun 2 daily; 30min–1hr), Dublin (3–5 daily; 4hr 50min) and Westport (9–13 daily; 20min).

Achill Island

The grandeur of **ACHILL ISLAND**'s scenery, with its towering sea-cliffs and bare mountains that rise above 650m, can seem forbidding in poor weather, but on a sunny day the Atlantic glitters as though stolen from the Aegean Sea. It's the largest of the Irish islands and, connected to the mainland by a road bridge, among the most developed, with plenty of accommodation and a ribbon of white-painted holiday homes on the south coast. Drawn by sweeping **sandy beaches** (five of which have earned a Blue Flag) and fairground rides, fun-seekers descend in droves on August weekends, when the place can get a bit rowdy. Germans are also attracted to Achill by associations with novelist and Nobel Laureate Heinrich Böll, who lived at Dugort in the 1950s. One of the best times to come is during **Scoil Acla** (ⓦscoilacla.com), a week of cultural programmes with plenty of traditional music at the end of July. There's also a walking festival over the St Patrick's bank holiday weekend in March, the Heinrich Böll literary festival in May and a seafood festival in mid-July.

The road bridge crosses the narrow, winding strait to the island at **ACHILL SOUND** (Gob an Choire), which is not the best base for exploration though has some useful facilities. On the island side of the bridge, there's an ATM at the side of *Sweeney's* restaurant and supermarket. The lively village of **KEEL** is the nerve centre for much of the island, boasting a lovely 3km Blue Flag sandy **beach**, backed by a large lake.

The south end of the island

The "Atlantic Drive", now part of the Wild Atlantic Way (see box, p.31), around the south end of the island from Achill Sound brings you after 6km to the ruined eighteenth-century **church** and holy well of Damhnait (Davnet or Dympna), a

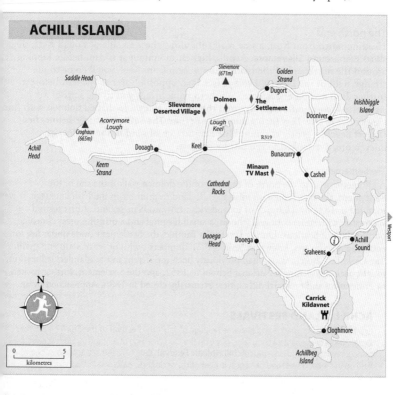

seventh-century saint who sought refuge and built a church (*cill*) here. Just beyond, its pink stone set attractively on the shoreline, rises the redoubtable outline of **Carrick Kildavnet**, an almost perfectly preserved, fifteenth-century, O'Malley tower house. Fantastic views of the Atlantic open up as you round the nearby headland, continuing as far as the village and Blue Flag beach of **Dooega**. Above the settlement looms **Minaun**, Achill's third-highest mountain; a left turn will bring you up to the TV mast near its summit for one of the island's most spectacular panoramas.

10

Dooagh and the west of the island

West along the road from Keel is the small village of **DOOAGH**, overlooking its own sandy beach. At its base here, the enterprising **Achill Field School** (☎098 43564, ⓦachill-fieldschool.com) lays on a raft of activities, including weekly lectures from June to August. The field school also runs one- to eight-week archaeology courses, featuring the dig and summer open days at the **Deserted Village** (see box, opposite).

Beyond Dooagh, the main road rises and descends very steeply to Blue Flag **Keem Bay**, a gorgeous strip of white sand hemmed in by steep, green slopes – on a sunny day, you'll feel as if you're looking down on a Mediterranean cove, with basking sharks often visible in the limpid waters. A turning off the up-slope towards Keem Bay will bring you to **Acorrymore Lough**, a black corrie lake, now reservoir, cradled by grassy scree slopes. From here you can set out on the steep ascent of **Croghaun**, the island's second-highest mountain (665m), which boasts spectacularly high cliffs on its seaward side. An easier walk, with only slightly less dramatic views, begins at the Keem Bay car park, heading up to the cliff-tops and west along the humped back of **Achill Head**.

The north end

Heading north from Keel, a side road runs along the west side of Lough Keel, then skirts east around **Slievemore**, Achill's highest mountain at 671m, before looping around the north end of the island. About 2km from Keel, you'll come to the strange sight of the **Deserted Village** (see box, opposite) over to the left, before a further 2km east on Slievemore's southern flank brings you to the start of a signposted ten-minute walk up from the road to a keyhole-shaped **dolmen** with fine views of Keel Bay. Less than a kilometre beyond **The Settlement** (see below) lies **Dugort Beach**, a gently curving, Blue Flag stretch of sand in the shadow of Slievemore, overlooked to the east by Dugort.

The Settlement

A kilometre or so to the north of the start of the dolmen walk is the site of **the Settlement**, the first Protestant mission in Ireland to minister in the Irish language. It was founded in 1834 by a Church of Ireland vicar, Edward Nangle, and at first proved successful, with stone cottages, schools, a small hospital and a printing press churning out regular publications. During the 1840s Famine, the Settlement came under fire for encouraging converts, known as "soupers" or "jumpers", with offers of soup and grain. The Catholic Church, which had previously been indifferent to the islanders' education, fought back by opening a National School in 1852, and the Settlement, further rocked by emigration and financial difficulties, eventually closed in 1886. Approached by an

---

> ### ACHILL ISLAND FESTIVALS
>
> Celebrating the rich marine and maritime heritage of Achill, the **Festival of the Sea** (*Féile Na Mara*; ☎098 20400, ⓦfeilenamara.com) takes place on the third weekend of July and includes seaweed tasting, yawl racing and boat trips. **Achill Holistic Festival** (☎087 278 9912, ⓦachillholistic.com), held on the second weekend of August in Keel, offers workshops, walks and individual therapies.

AN AMATEURISH SET FOR A GHOST FILM

A couple of kilometres north of Keel, at Slievemore, lies a settlement of almost a hundred crumbling stone dwellings – but what led to its **abandonment** is still unknown. Its most recent period of habitation ended in the early twentieth century, when locals used it as a **booley**: during the summer, they would occupy the cottages while grazing their cattle on the mountainside, returning to their homes in Dooagh for the winter months. This is one of the last places in Europe to have practised *booley*-ing, or transhumance, and the village is being excavated by the Achill Field School (see p.388) every summer, in the hope that it will give up its secrets. German novelist Heinrich Böll (see p.387) described the deserted village as looking like "an amateurish set for a ghost film."

10

avenue of trees on the east side of the road, the mission's **church** of 1855 is still standing, containing a prominent memorial to Nangle.

ARRIVAL AND INFORMATION

ACHILL ISLAND

By bus Bus Éireann run services from Westport (2 daily; 1hr) to Achill Sound (1hr) and Dooagh (1hr 20min).

Tourist office Achill Sound (Mon–Fri 9am–5pm, Sat 10am–3pm in summer; ☎098 47353, ⓦachilltourism .com). Sells detailed maps of the island and a guide to circular walks.

ACCOMMODATION

ACHILL SOUND

Óstán Oileán Acla ☎098 45138, ⓦachillislandhotel .com. Immediately before you cross the bridge at Achill Sound stands this comfortable hotel with fine views of the island. It's a local social hub too, with food served all day till 8.30pm in the summer (8pm rest of year); burgers, fish 'n' chips, chicken and steak are all available. **€80**

Railway Hostel (IHO) ☎098 45187, ⓦrailwayhostel .ie/achill. By the bridge beside Blacksod Bay and based in an old station, this hostel is handy for bus pick-ups and drop-offs. Big log fires create a welcoming atmosphere, some of the rooms are en suite and camping is possible. Tent pitch **€10**, doubles **€36**

DOOAGH

Teach Cruachan ☎098 43301, ⓔteachcruachan @eircom.net. On the west side of Dooagh, this comfy guesthouse has en-suite rooms and good breakfasts, as well as laying on guided tours of the island. **€75**

West Coast House School Rd ☎098 43317, ⓦgachillwestcoasthousebandb.com. Set on an elevated site in the shadow of the majestic Croaghaun mountain, this well-run bungalow offers superb sea views. **€60**

DUGORT

Gray's ☎098 43244. Occupying several houses of the former settlement, this is a relaxing guesthouse with a garden and croquet lawn. An old-fashioned atmosphere prevails but rooms are nonetheless comfortable and there's an appealing friendliness about the house. Dinner is available. **€80**

★**Lavelle's Campsite** ☎086 231 4596, ⓦlavelles caravanpar.com. Beside the pristine Blue Flag Golden Strand beach with good facilities, this site boasts an idyllic and serene location. April–Oct. Tent pitch **€18**

Valley House Hostel ☎098 47204, ⓦvalley-house .com. A fine, mid-nineteenth-century house, formerly the Earl of Cavan's hunting lodge, with a sociable courtyard bar and camping. Rooms are basic but functional – the house steals the show. Double dorms **€22**

KEEL

★**Achill Cliff House** ☎098 43400, ⓦachillcliff.com. One of the island's best places to stay, this hotel in the centre of the village offers bright and spacious rooms, sea views, a sauna and a seafood restaurant for residents. **€80**

★**Bervie Guest House** ☎098 43114, ⓦbervieachill .com. In a former coastguard station right by the beach, this place enjoys a dream location and is unquestionably Achill's premier accommodation. Summery ground-floor rooms lead out to a pretty garden which brings you, via a small gate, right out on to the beach. Dinner is served each evening. April–Oct. **€100**

Ferndale Crumpaun ☎098 43908, ⓦferndale-achill .com. Some 200m up the lane by the *Annexe* pub, this place has six lavishly furnished rooms and also serves an ambitious range of world cuisine in the evening, such as the sensational Mongolian barbecue. Non-residents should reserve dinner (served 6.30–8.30pm) a day in advance. **€85**

Joyce's Marian Villa ☎098 43134, ⓦjoycesachilll .com. First-class accommodation in a large seaside villa with 15 bedrooms. The sunroom looks out to the beach and the cliffs of Minaun. Breakfasts include local jams and preserves. **€90**

Keel Sandybanks Caravan & Camping Park ☎098 43211, ⓦachillcamping.com. A swanky caravan park beside the beach, handy for the shops and cafés. April to early-Sept. Tent pitch **€15**

ISLAND ACTIVITIES

Achill Cycle Hub Trails range in distance from 12–44km, with **bikes** available to rent from Achill Bike Hire in Dooagh (☎ 098 43301). North of Keel, on the lower slopes of Slievemore, Calvey's (☎ 087 988 1093, ⓦ calveysofachill.com) offers **horse-riding** treks and tuition. **Scuba diving** can be arranged with Achill Dive Centre (☎ 087 234 9884, ⓦ achilldivecentre.com), and you can organize **surfing** through Blackfield (☎ 098 43590, ⓦ blackfield.com).

10 EATING AND DRINKING

The island's best eating is in Keel, not least at *Ferndale*'s restaurant (see p.389). *Óstán Oileán Acla* at Achill Sound (see p.389) is also worth a look.

Bayside Bistro Keel ☎ 098 43798, ⓦ baysidebistro.ie. Classic bistro-style cooking with dishes such as almond-crusted salmon, as well as mussels *marinières* with handcut chips. Main courses from €12. Daily noon–10pm.

★ **The Beehive** Keel ☎ 098 43134. An informal daytime self-service café-restaurant and craft shop with outdoor tables on a terrace overlooking Keel beach. The menu promotes wholesome local produce, especially seafood such as organic Clare Island salmon and Clew Bay mussels or smoked mackerel. Main-course lunches from €10. Feb–Nov daily 9.30am–6pm.

Calvey's Keel ☎ 098 43158, ⓦ calveysofachill.com. A smart restaurant with comfy banquettes and great views, conveniently next to its own butcher's shop for dishes such as the famed Achill mountain lamb. Main courses average €25. Easter–Sept daily 5–10pm.

★ **Gielty's** Dooagh ☎ 098 43119, ⓦ gieltys.com. Large modern pub, restaurant and café at the west end of Dooagh village that claims to be Ireland's most westerly pub. Lunches and dinners served. Outdoor tables and live music, including regular traditional sessions. Daily 10am–11.30pm.

Céide Fields and around

8km west of Ballycastle • April–Oct daily 10am–5pm (till 6pm June–Sept) • €4; Heritage Card • ☎ 096 43325, ⓦ heritageireland.ie

Isolated on Mayo's dramatic, cliff-girt north coast, the prehistoric site of **Céide** (pronounced "cage-a") **Fields** is difficult to get to, but repays the effort. Here, archaeologists have discovered a unique, 5000-year-old agricultural landscape, miraculously preserved under a thick layer of peat and undisturbed by later farming. A highly organized system of dry-stone field walls, dotted with individual houses and gardens in what were apparently peaceful times, covers an area of thirteen square kilometres, making Céide Fields the largest Stone Age monument in the world. Rough contemporaries of the tomb-builders of Newgrange (see p.142), these farmers cleared the area's forest to make fields for their cattle, sheep, wheat and barley, and built **wooden houses**, of which trenches and postholes are now the only traces. However, after only five hundred years, the climate deteriorated, causing the bog gradually to rise up over their farms. What's remarkable about the site is its very ordinariness and similarity to much of the Irish countryside today, as Seamus Heaney noted in *Belderg*:

A landscape fossilized, its stone wall patternings
Repeated before our eyes in the stone walls of Mayo.

There's an impressive, well-designed **visitor centre**, which features exhibitions and audiovisuals on the history and geology of the area and the formation of the bog, as well as a viewing platform and a fine café. Regular fifty-minute guided tours take visitors outside to see excavated walls, animal and house enclosures and to learn about the ecology of the bog that swallowed them up. From the adjacent cliff-top viewpoint you can see Donegal's Slieve League on a clear day, and in the near distance the sea stack of Downpatrick Head, neatly layered and tufted with grass: according to legend, this is the severed head of the last snake that St Patrick chased from Ireland.

Ballycastle

The nearest town to Céide Fields is **BALLYCASTLE** (ⓦballycastle.ie), which comes as a pleasant surprise among the barren, grossly proportioned mountains of North Mayo. Set in the broad Ballinglen valley, it's surrounded by green fields, trees and cattle, with a fine sandy beach at the river mouth. Changing exhibitions of works by internationally known artists attached to the local **Ballinglen Arts Foundation** are held at the gallery opposite *Polke's* pub. For further exploration of the coast, the **North Mayo Sculpture Trail** (ⓦmayoireland.ie/tirsaile.htm), marked by brown *Tír Sáile* ("Land of the Salty Wind") signposts, is a striking series of modern outdoor sculptures, celebrating the wild beauty and cultural heritage of the area. It starts just west of the town.

10

ARRIVAL AND INFORMATION

BALLYCASTLE

By bus There's no public transport to Céide Fields but Ballycastle is linked by bus to Ballina, 28km to the southeast, which in turn has regular services to and from Galway (see p.340), Westport (see p.382) and Castlebar (see p.386).

Tourist information Information on the local attractions and the Wild Atlantic Way is available at the Ballycastle Resource Centre (Mon–Fri 10am–5pm; ☏096 43407) on Main St, which also houses a craft shop and displays the work of local artists.

ACCOMMODATION AND EATING

Healy's Bar Main St ☏096 43019. A family-run bar where occasional music sessions are held on Fridays. The beer garden and decking area is popular with party-goers and, during the August bank holiday (first weekend in Aug) they hold the Healy Fest, which attracts musicians from all over Ireland and further afield. Daily 4–11.30pm, Sun from noon.

Keadyville B&B Carrowcubic ☏096 43288, ⓦkeadyvillehouse.com. A modern and friendly five-room guesthouse, convenient for a tour of North Mayo with views of Bunatrahir Bay. If you don't have transport the owners will take you out to the Céide Fields or Downpatrick Head. **€70**

Stella Maris Hotel ☏096 43322, ⓦstellamarisireland .com. Positioned on the Wild Atlantic Way, this elegantly refurbished former coastguard station and convent offers fine ocean views. The 11 luxurious rooms are individually furnished with their own antiques, and you can immerse yourself in the beauty of the Mayo landscape from the large conservatory. Dinner is served 7–9pm, with lamb's kidneys the most popular choice. Easter–Oct. **€150**

Mary's Cottage Kitchen Main St ☏096 43361. Breakfasts and lunches are served at this homely café and bakery. Easter to Oct daily 10am–6pm.

Sligo, Leitrim and Roscommon

SCULPTURE OF RED HUGH O'DONNELL, BOYLE

Sligo, Leitrim and Roscommon

Sligo, Leitrim and Roscommon are blessed with majestic scenery, mighty castles and a countryside littered with antiquities. The area is also renowned for the flamboyance of its traditional music: known as the North Connacht style, it is characterized by flutes and fiddles. The principal hub, lively Sligo town has the best facilities for visitors, with the possibility of day-trips to the vibrant seaside resort of Strandhill and, set atop Knocknarea Mountain, the megalithic sites of Carrowmore Cemetery and Medb's Cairn.

11

Lough Gill, its celebrated island **Innisfree** and a number of other sites in the north of Sligo are inextricably linked with W. B. Yeats, an appreciation of whose writing is enhanced by a visit to **Drumcliffe**, the place of his burial, set below Benbulben Mountain. The cultural highlight of Sligo, however, is the stunning **Lissadell House**, which has been extensively renovated and showcases some of Ireland's most precious treasures. Yeats's brother, the painter Jack B., was also inspired by the county's dramatic land- and seascapes, which continue to its northern tip with fine beaches such as at **Mullaghmore**.

Ireland's least populated county by some stretch, **Leitrim** crams a dizzying diversity into its landscape, though lacks any really notable sights. Bordering no fewer than six counties, Leitrim extends some 80km from its southeastern border with Longford to a narrow strip of Atlantic shoreline in the northwest, with the expansive **Lough Allen** at its core. Two of its most attractive assets – **loughs Gill and Glencar** – lie to the west, spanning the border with Sligo. In the south, the River Shannon is the principal feature, not least in the attractive boating town, **Carrick-on-Shannon**, while rolling countryside to the river's east, especially between **Keshcarrigan** and **Ballinamore**, is sprinkled with tiny lakes and drumlins.

County Roscommon may not feature prominently on tourists' itineraries but, in its far north, the **Arigna Mountains** provide a wild and vivid contrast to the flat landscape that defines most of Roscommon, and can be explored from the historic town of **Boyle**. Further south, sites around **Tulsk**, including the newly rebranded **Rathcroghan Centre**, are intrinsically associated with major events in Celtic mythology. The planned town of **Strokestown**, meanwhile, features a memorable Georgian mansion with an impressive museum devoted to the Great Famine.

Sligo town

Bustling **SLIGO** town rose to prominence following the Anglo-Norman invasion of Connacht in 1235, its strategic importance linked to its location at the point where the River Garavogue enters the sea. A Dominican friary was founded here in 1252, but the town's shape was largely developed following the building of a castle by Richard de Burgo in 1310. This edifice lasted but five years, however, before it was destroyed by the O'Donnell clan which retained control of the burgeoning

CARROWKEEL CEMETERY

Highlights

❶ The Model Renowned for its exhibitions of experimental art and its Jack B. Yeats collection See **p.399**

❷ Lough Gill Utterly tranquil and unspoilt and the inspiration, alongside its island, Innisfree, for much of the poetry of Yeats. See **p.403**

❸ Lissadell House The ancestral home of the Gore-Booth family was the holiday retreat of W. B. Yeats and is a treasure trove of eclectic delights. See **p.405**

❹ Carrowkeel Cemetery The remains of a Bronze Age village, offering a stunning panorama of County Sligo from its hilltop position. See **p.407**

❺ Arigna Mining Experience Devoted to the vicissitudes of life for the miners who once literally scraped a living in the mountains here – completely gripping. See **p.417**

❻ Strokestown Park House Arguably the most eye-catching Plantation mansion in all Ireland, whose former stables house the enthralling National Irish Famine Museum. See **p.418**

HIGHLIGHTS ARE MARKED ON THE MAP ON PP.396–397

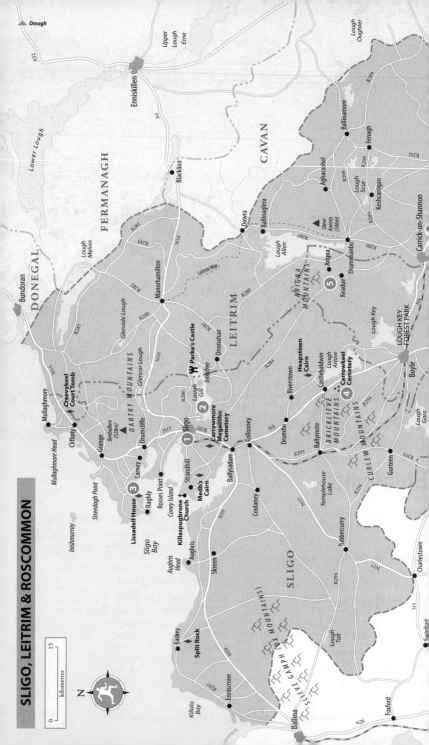

WESTMEATH

LONGFORD

OFFALY

ROSCOMMON

GALWAY

Dromod

Rooskey

Longford

N4

N55

Athlone

N62

Lough
Ree

River Shannon

N5

Strokestown

6

Tulsk

N61

Rathcroghan

N5

Roscommon

N60

N63

Ballinasloe

R355

N6

Castlerea

N60

Ballymoe

River Suck

N63

N83

Ballyhaunis

Claremorris

N60

N17

N17

N84

Knock

N84

Lough
Cara

Ballinrobe

Cross

Bright's Garden

Lough
Corrib

N59

Galway

Athenry

N6

N17

N63

River Shannon

N61

N63

settlement over the next few centuries. After the terrible times of the Great Famine of the 1840s, Sligo re-emerged as a busy port and mercantile centre in the late nineteenth century and nowadays is a thoroughly absorbing place. The town has long been renowned for its **traditional music**, but is also firmly on the tourist trail thanks to its numerous associations with the poet **W. B. Yeats**, a lively arts scene, which spawns several **festivals** (see box, opposite), and its location as a base for exploring the county's numerous attractions.

West of the **friary**, at the bottom of Market Street, the **Lady of Erin** statue commemorates the 1798 uprisings. The statue presides over the newly designated **Erin Quarter**, comprising long-established family business along Grattan, Market and Castle streets and set up to provide friendly rivalry with the Italian Quarter, a riverside area bustling with Italian restaurants and cafés.

Yeats Memorial Building

Douglas Hyde Bridge • Mon–Fri 10am–5pm • €2 • ☎ 071 914 2693, ⓦ yeats-sligo.com

The attractions of Sligo town can easily be enjoyed within a day and, considering all his associations with it, probably the best place to begin is the **Yeats Memorial Building** on Douglas Hyde Bridge. This houses the Yeats Society, serves as the venue for the

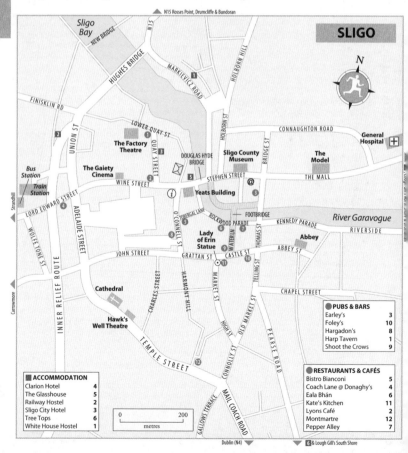

SLIGO

PUBS & BARS
Earley's	3
Foley's	10
Hargadon's	8
Harp Tavern	1
Shoot the Crows	9

RESTAURANTS & CAFÉS
Bistro Bianconi	5
Coach Lane @ Donaghy's	4
Eala Bhán	6
Kate's Kitchen	11
Lyons Café	2
Montmartre	12
Pepper Alley	7

ACCOMMODATION
Clarion Hotel	4
The Glasshouse	5
Railway Hostel	2
Sligo City Hotel	3
Tree Tops	6
White House Hostel	1

SLIGO FESTIVALS
Sligo Sea Shanty Festival Rosses Point ☎085 1204 781, ⓦrossespointshanty.com. A rip-roaring line-up share their sea-dog songs in village bars and hotels in mid-June.
So Sligo Food & Culture Festival ⓦsosligo.ie. Held annually in mid-June.
Tread Softly Sligo town ☎ 071 917 1905, ⓦtreadsoftly.ie. Held in July and exploring the relationship between the Yeats brothers.
Yeats International Summer School Hyde Bridge ☎071 914 2693, ⓦyeats-sligo.com. Runs from the end of July to early August, attracting literary luminaries.
Sligo Live Music Festival ⓦsligolive.ie. An October festival of traditional music sessions, as well as a variety of major acts.

International Summer School commemorating the poet each August, and includes displays on his life and works with photographs and copies of drafts of poems.

Sligo County Museum

Stephen St • Tues–Sat 9.30am–12.30pm, also May–Sept 2–4.45pm • Free • ☎ 071 911 1850

Beside the library, **Sligo County Museum** holds drawings by Jack B. Yeats (as well as a portrait of him by Estella Solomons) and a fiddle once owned by Michael Coleman (see box, p.410). You will also find the apron worn by Countess Markiewicz (see p.405) while imprisoned in England, and a remarkable painting by Kathleen Fox of her arrest in 1916 outside the College of Surgeons in Dublin. West of the museum on Holborn Street, a **plaque** on the wall of no. 5 commemorates the house where Leo Milligan, the father of Spike, the late comedian and writer, was born – references to the town are included in Spike's comic masterpiece **Puckoon**.

The Model

The Mall • Tues–Sat 10am–5.30pm, Thurs till 8pm, Sun noon–5pm • Free; guided tours Sat 3pm €3 • ☎071 914 1405, ⓦthemodel.ie

A couple of hundred metres east of the museum stands one of Ireland's finest art galleries, **The Model**. Behind a drab Victorian façade, the spacious and airy modern extension houses a range of temporary, experimental exhibitions, as well as selections from the Niland Collection, including works by Jack B. Yeats and Paul Henry.

The Abbey

Abbey St • April to mid-Oct daily 10am–6pm • €4; Heritage Card • ☎071 914 6406

The Dominican friary, more commonly known as **the Abbey**, was founded around 1252 by Maurice Fitzgerald. Accidentally burnt down in 1412, it was rebuilt shortly afterwards and, unusually, continued to be occupied after the Reformation on condition that the friars became secular clergy. Damaged during a siege of the nearby castle (of which no trace remains) in 1595, the friary, along with most of the town, was sacked in 1641 by Sir Frederick Hamilton and his Puritan army, and its friars massacred. However, the friary's remains are in remarkably good condition and include a delicately decorated **high altar**, gracefully carved tombs and sculptures, and well-preserved **cloisters**. Seek out the love knot found in the Cloister East Ambulatory, said to represent the bond between earthly and spiritual love and, according to local custom, a wishing stone.

ARRIVAL AND INFORMATION   SLIGO TOWN

By bus The bus station (☎071 916 0066) is on Lord Edward St.

Destinations Ballymote (Mon–Wed 1 daily, Sat 2; 35–45min); Ballyshannon (8–9 daily; 40min–1hr); Boyle (5–6 daily; 40min); Bundoran (8–11 daily; 35–55min); Carrick-on-Shannon (5–7 daily; 1hr); Derry (6–8 daily; 2hr 30min); Donegal town (6–8 daily; 1hr 5min); Drumcliffe (9am–12 daily; 15min); Dublin (5–7 daily; 3hr 15min–3hr

50min); Easkey (Mon–Sat 3–5 daily, Sun 1; 55min); Enniscrone (Mon–Sat 3–5 daily, Sun 1; 1hr 15min); Enniskillen (2–3 daily; 1hr 25min); Galway (5–7 daily; 2hr 45min); Gurteen (Sat 2; 1hr); Keadue (Fri 1; 50min); Lissadell (1 Mon–Fri during school terms, Sat 2 all year; 20min); Riverstown (Thurs & Fri 1 daily; 40min); Rosses Point (4–7 daily; 20min); Skreen (Mon–Sat 2–3 daily, Sun 1; 30min); Strandhill (3–7 daily; 20min); Strokestown (Mon–Sat 1 daily; 1hr); Tubbercurry (6–7 daily; 35min); Westport (2–3 daily; 1hr 55min).

By private bus. The arrival point for Feda O'Donnell (ⓦ fedaodonnell.com) buses is opposite the Ulster Bank on Stephen St while departure point is Connolly's pub on Markievicz Rd.

Destinations Donegal (Mon–Thurs & Sat 2 daily, Fri 4; 50min); Galway (Mon–Thurs & Sat 2 daily, Fri & Sun 3 daily; 2hr 10min).

By train The train station (ⓣ 071 916 9888), just off the Inner Relief Route, is close to the town centre. All services operate Mon–Sat 7–8 times daily, Sun 6.

Destinations Ballymote (20min); Boyle (35min); Carrick-on-Shannon (45min); Dublin (3hr 5min); Mullingar (1hr 55min).

Tourist information Old Bank Building, O'Connell St (May–Sept Mon–Fri 9am–5.15pm, Sat 10am–3pm; Oct–April Mon–Fri 9am–5pm; ⓣ 071 916 1201; ⓦ discoverireland.ie). For info on events check one of the two weekly newspapers, *The Sligo Champion* or *Sligo Weekender*.

ACCOMMODATION

There are numerous **hotel** options dotted around, plus plenty of **B&B**s along the main roads leading out of the town. For **camping**, your best bets are in Strandhill and Rosses Point (see p.402 & p.404).

Clarion Hotel Clarion Rd, Ballinode ⓣ 071 911 9000, ⓦ clarionhotelsligo.com. Swish and modern establishment, 1km out of town off the N16 Enniskillen road, with sparklingly clean rooms and fresh fruit on the table. **€99**

★**The Glasshouse** Swan Point ⓣ 071 919 4300, ⓦ theglasshouse.ie. This literally dazzling (when the sun shines) place by Hyde Bridge is a dramatic glassy counterpoint to the adjacent waters of the Garavogue. Its chic rooms offer floor-to-ceiling windows and a high degree of comfort. **€90**

Railway Hostel (IHO) 1 Union Place ⓣ 071 914 4530, ⓦ therailway.ie. Small, welcoming, family-run hostel handy for the train and bus stations. Most beds are singles, not bunks; all bathrooms are shared. Free internet access. **€20**

Sligo City Hotel Quay St ⓣ 071 914 4000, ⓦ sligocityhotel.com. Plush hotel providing elegant accommodation, extremely efficient service and good deals, all just a 5min walk from the bus or train stations. Stay two nights and get a third one free. **€99**

Tree Tops Cleveragh Rd ⓣ 071 916 2301 ⓦ sligobandb .com. A comfortable and well-appointed guesthouse with a pleasant garden, just off Pearse Rd. The best thing about staying here is the breakfast: choose from a dazzling assortment of cereals, fruit and yoghurt as well as pancakes, waffles, croissants, rice or cakes and brown bread. **€74**

White House Hostel (IHH) Markievicz Rd ⓣ 071 914 5160, ⓔ whitehousehostel@gmail.com. Handily placed in the town centre, this small and convivial if somewhat basic hostel provides mostly dorm accommodation with some family rooms. Good location also for bus connections to Galway and Donegal. April–Oct. **€15**

EATING AND DRINKING

There's no shortage of stylish restaurants and decent bars serving food, all contributing to making Sligo the cuisine capital of the northwest. The town boasts a plethora of old-fashioned **pubs**; many serve reasonably priced bar lunches and evening meals and offer lively **traditional music** sessions.

CAFÉS AND RESTAURANTS

★**Bistro Bianconi** Tobergal Lane ⓣ 071 914 1744, ⓦ bistrobianconi.ie. Convivial Italian restaurant in the flourishing Italian Quarter serving excellent pasta and pizza. Early-bird (5–7pm) pizzas from €9. Daily 5–10pm.

Coach Lane @ Donaghy's 1–2 Lord Edward St ⓣ 071 916 2417, ⓦ coachlane.ie. The upstairs restaurant features a diverse mix, with highlights including Cajun chicken, *patatas bravas* and bouillabaisse. Eat downstairs for cheaper bar meals such as fish pie and Italian meatballs served at red-check tablecloths. Daily noon–11.30pm.

Eala Bhán Rockwood Parade ⓣ 071 914 5823, ⓦ ealabhan.ie. Modern Irish food with a French twist. The three-course early bird (daily 5–6.30pm) is great value at €19.95. Lunch Tues–Sat noon–3pm, dinner daily 5–9.30pm.

★**Kate's Kitchen** Castle St ⓣ 071 914 3022, ⓦ kateskitchen.ie. Call in for a coffee and sample some of the gourmet artisan products on the heaving shelves: handcrafted farmhouse cheese, elderflower cordial, Aine's handmade chocolates and delicious homemade tea brack are a selection of the offerings. Mon–Sat 9am–5.30pm.

Lyons Café Quay St ☎071 914 2969, ⓦgarystafford.com. Upstairs in one of Sligo's old family-run clothing stores, this time-burnished café (breakfasts, soups, cakes) has been a popular meeting place since it opened in 1923 – some of the original lights, tables and chairs are still in place. Lunches from €10. Mon–Sat 9am–5pm.

Montmartre 1 Market Yard ☎071 916 9901, ⓦmontmartrerestautant.ie. The town's most upmarket restaurant is French-run and offers a varied menu including rabbit in mustard crust and fresh Lissadell mussels. For a four-course meal expect to pay around €36 plus wine; two-course set menu €21.50. Tues–Sat 5–11pm, Sun on bank holiday weekends.

Pepper Alley Rockwood Parade ☎071 917 0720, ⓦpepperalley.ie. A bright riverside café (with an outstanding deli) serving a mix of breakfasts, lunches and snacks. Particularly recommended are the nori wraps, eggs benedict and sweet treats such as chocolate cake, fudge brownies and banoffee pie. Mon–Sat 9.30am–5.30pm.

PUBS

Earley's Bridge St ☎071 914 2171. This cosy old bar features a great Thurs night session and other music on Sat and Sun. Beamish is one of the top-selling beers and much cheaper than some of their dark rivals. Mon–Thurs 10.30am–11.30pm, Fri & Sat till 12.30am, Sun 12.30–11pm.

Foley's Castle St ☎071 916 8900. Traditional bar with a superb range of whiskeys, and sessions year-round on Thurs & Sat, plus Wed from June to Sept. Mon–Thurs & Sun 11.30am–11.30pm, Fri & Sat till 12.30am.

★**Hargadon's** O'Connell St ☎071 915 3709. No visit to Sligo is complete without enjoying a drink or light meal in this early nineteenth-century pub with snugs, snob screens and marble-top counter to boot. Lunch (Mon–Sat noon–3.30pm) and evening menus (Mon–Sat 4–9pm) feature shellfish, seafood and tapas. Mon–Thurs 11.30am–11.30pm, Fri & Sat till 12.30am, Sun 6–11pm.

Harp Tavern Quay St ☎071 914 2473. Noted for traditional music on Fri nights, with live bands performing on Sat & Sun nights 6–9pm. Mon–Thurs & Sun 11.30am–11.30pm, Fri & Sat till 12.30am.

Shoot the Crows Grattan St. A long, narrow, slightly dishevelled bar across from the Lady of Erin statue, and a lively place to meet the locals. It has retained its original features including the timber wainscoting. Musicians frequently occupy a corner in the small bar at the front. Mon–Thurs 11.30am–11.30pm, Fri & Sat till 12.30am, Sun 11.30am–11.30pm.

ENTERTAINMENT AND SPORT

Sligo Rovers FC play at The Showgrounds on Knappagh Rd (☎071 917 1212, ⓦsligorovers.com). If you fancy a flutter, head for the **Sligo Races** at Cleveragh Rd (☎071 918 3342, ⓦcountysligoraces.com) from May to Oct.

The Factory Theatre Lower Quay St ☎071 917 0431, ⓦblueraincoat.com. Hosts the innovative Blue Raincoat Theatre Company.

Gaiety Cinema Wine St ☎071 916 2651, ⓦgaietysligo.ie. A modern 12-screen cinema with a Kids' Club at 2pm at weekends.

Hawk's Well Theatre Temple St ☎071 916 1518, ⓦhawkswell.com. Presents a range of dramatic productions and a variety of musical events.

Around Sligo town

West of Sligo town lies the famous surfing beach at **Strandhill**, a grand base for exhilarating coastal walks, while inland is one of Europe's most significant collections of passage graves at **Carrowmore Megalithic Cemetery**. Both the resort and the graveyard are overlooked by the numinous Knocknarea Mountain, on whose summit sits the mystical **Medb's Cairn**.

Strandhill

Eight kilometres west of Sligo town and set against the backdrop of Knocknarea Mountain, seaside **STRANDHILL** boasts a gorgeous situation. It is just the way a seaside resort should be, too: traditional cafés and tea rooms, amusements, ice-cream parlours, beach stores and stunning sunsets. In recent years it has upped its game with a selection of trendy restaurants and bars, while the creative community has come together to hold a funky **Peoples' Market** on Sunday mornings, selling local crafts, artisan foods, and fresh fruit and vegetables.

Dolly's Cottage

June Sat & Sun 2–6pm; July & Aug daily 2–6pm • Free

On the way into the village look out for **Dolly's Cottage**, a tiny thatched dwelling named after its last occupant, Dolly Higgins, who died in 1970. Maintained as it was, with a turf fire and a pouch bed, the cottage sells handicrafts as well as homemade jams and preserves.

The beach

Strandhill's **beach** is its most renowned feature, a wild stretch pounded by huge Atlantic breakers. Because of rip currents it is absolutely unsafe for swimming but is massively popular with **surfers** and regularly witnesses the Sligo Open Championship over the first weekend in August. Right by the beach, the Perfect Day Surf School (�📻perfectdaysurfing.com) offers a range of classes. Adjacent on the front you can luxuriate in the curative and pleasantly soporific waters of the **Voya Spa Seaweed Baths** (daily 10am–8pm; �📻voyaseaweedbaths.com; €25 single, two adults sharing €35), which also offers reflexology and massage treatments.

11

Killaspugbrone Church

The beach offers bracing walks, especially a few kilometres north towards **Killaspugbrone Church**, whose ruins largely date from the twelfth and thirteenth centuries, though its tower is a later addition. Visiting the church some centuries earlier, St Patrick somehow contrived to stumble and dislodge a tooth in the process, which he promptly donated to the sacristan, Bishop Bronus. This relic was kept and passed down, and, in the fourteenth century, an exquisite **casket**, the Fiacal Pádraig, was created to house it – the tooth subsequently disappeared, but its container is on view in the National Museum in Dublin (see p.63).

ARRIVAL AND TOURS   STRANDHILL

By bus Sligo (4–7 daily; 20min).

Tours Seatrails (☎087 240 5071, �📻seatrails.ie) offer first-rate guided tours of Strandhill and the surrounding coastal areas, run by maritime archaeologist Auriel Robinson. The Streedagh beach tour gives intriguing insights into the Spanish Armada landings of 1588. Prices from €15.

ACCOMMODATION

Ocean Wave Lodge Top Rd ☎071 916 8115, �📻oceanwavelodge.com. An attractive guesthouse located on what is known locally as the "top road" in Strandhill, a 10min stroll from the seafront. The twelve rooms range from twins or doubles to family rooms, and there's also a reading room and well-equipped kitchen. **€60**

Strandhill Caravan and Camping Park Strandhill beach ☎071 916 8111, �📻sligocaravanandcamping.ie. Campers can choose from a large area of grass with a sandy base which is mud-free even on wet days. Ideally placed for exploration, and for activities ranging from swimming and surfing to horse riding and golf. April to Sept. Tent pitch **€20**

★**Strandhill Lodge and Suites** Top Rd ☎071 912 2122, �📻strandhilllodgeandsuites.ie. A sleekly designed boutique hotel overlooking Strandhill Bay. The modern bedrooms, in calming cream and beige decor, are finished to a high standard; some are deluxe and come with a patio opening on to a courtyard. **€99**

Strandhill Lodge Hostel and Surf School Shore Rd ☎071 916 8313, �📻surfnstay.ie. A well-equipped accommodation near the beach. Rooms are small but well presented and good value. An unbeatable location as well as being handy for the bus connection to Sligo – the stop is just 100m away. Double dorms **€40**

EATING AND DRINKING

Mammy Johnston's Ice Cream Parlour Shore Rd ☎087 288 6915. Catch the right evening and MJs is the best place from which to view the western sunset and Atlantic breakers while you agonize over a delectable choice of ice creams and crêpes. They've been making ice cream since 1938, and the walls, adorned with pictures of old Strandhill, reflect the historic link. April–Sept daily 9am–9pm.

★**Shells Café** Shore Rd ☎071 912 2938, �📻shellscafe .com. This delightful combination of fish restaurant and bakery is a west of Ireland gem, with mismatched wooden chairs and an innovative menu that includes everything from veggie burgers, battered haddock and sardines on toast, to berries and wild garlic foraged from the beach.

Mon–Thurs 9.30am–7pm, Fri 9.30am–8pm, Sat 9am–8pm, Sun 9am–7pm.

Strand Bar Shore Rd ☏ 071 916 8140, ⓦ thestrandbar .ie. At the bottom of Shore Road with a turf fire, cosy snugs and wholesome pub meals (average price €10), this is a place where surfers meet the locals. Mon–Sat 10.30am–11.30pm, Sun 12.30–11pm.

The Venue Bar & Restaurant Top Rd ☏ 071 916 8167, ⓦ venuestrandhill.ie. The conservatory of this convenient restaurant looks out on the golf course and ocean and offers a wide selection of seafood, fajitas, steaks, meats and grills. Main courses are from around €12. Mon–Thurs 12.30pm–11.30pm, Fri & Sat till 12.30am, Sun till 11pm.

Carrowmore Megalithic Cemetery

April to mid-Oct daily 10am–6pm; last admission 5pm • €4; Heritage Card

Four kilometres southwest of Sligo town, **Carrowmore Megalithic Cemetery** presents a remarkable array of some thirty megalithic passage tombs – easily the biggest prehistoric graveyard in Europe. The oval-shaped cluster of monuments spreads out within a 1km-by-600m field and ranges from the most basic, a small circle of stones surrounding a central roofed chamber, through to the largest, known as **Listoghill**, covered by an impressive rounded cairn. Excavations have uncovered cremated human remains as well as jewellery carved from bones and antlers.

Medb's Cairn

To get here from Carrowmore head west for 1km, take a right turn at the junction with the R292, then left at the first crossroads – after another 1km a lane leads right towards the car park at the base of the mountain, from where it's a steep 4km hike to the summit

Carrowmore is made all the more atmospheric for being set below one of Ireland's most significant burial places, the massive **Medb's Cairn** on the summit of Knocknarea Mountain – 55m wide and 10m high, and surrounded by a 3m-high earthen bank. Whether Medb, the legendary queen of Connacht and one of the protagonists of the **Táin Bó Cúailnge**, is actually buried here is unknown, since the site has not been excavated, but it's well worth making the trek, not only for views of the cairn itself, but for spectacular outlooks north to Donegal and west to Mayo. On your way up to the top, pick up a stone and leave it on the cairn, making a wish as you do so and, as local legend has it, the force of Queen Medb may be with you.

Lough Gill

To the east of Sligo town lies one of Ireland's most entrancing lakes, **Lough Gill**, set beneath wooded slopes which provide the backdrop to almost all its 40km shoreline. The best route around the lough, and one easily navigable in less than a day's cycling, is to follow the shore clockwise by following the R286 from Sligo town, and taking in the plantation **Parke's Castle**, just inside County Leitrim, from where you can board a cruise boat and catch a sight of idyllic **Innisfree**.

Parke's Castle

April–Sept daily 10am–6pm • €4; Heritage Card; free on first Wed of every month • ☏ 071 916 4149

Some 11km northeast of Sligo, towards the lake's eastern extremity, **Parke's Castle** is a plantation fort erected by Captain Robert Parke in the 1620s and elegantly restored in the late twentieth century by the Office of Public Works. A moated tower house once stood here, home of the Irish chieftain Brian O'Rourke, who in 1588 was charged with high treason after sheltering Francesco de Cuellar, one of the few survivors of the Armada ships wrecked off the Sligo coast. O'Rourke was hanged at Tyburn in 1591 and his lands confiscated, later being distributed to the Leitrim planters, whose number included Parke. You can wander around the battlements, admire expansive views of the lough and take in an **exhibition** on the remodelling of the castle with displays on other notable vernacular buildings.

11

Innisfree

Waterbus Easter–Oct daily 12.30 & 3.30pm; call ☎ 071 916 4266 to check sailings, Ⓦ roseofinnisfree.com; €15 • Bike rental from Chain Driven Cycles (Ⓦ chaindrivencycles.com) on High St, Sligo

From the pier beside Parke's Castle the "Rose of Innisfree" waterbus operates a tour of Lough Gill, taking in views of Yeats's beloved isle of **Innisfree**, and featuring recitals of the poet's works by the skipper, almost certainly including the poet's **Lake Isle of Innisfree**:

I will arise and go now, and go to Innisfree,
And a small cabin build there, of clay and wattles made:
Nine bean-rows will I have there, a hive for the honey-bee,
And live alone in the bee-loud glade.

Alternatively, head a few kilometres southwards through Dromahair and pick up the R287. About 4km along this road a signposted lane leads down to the water where there's a fabulous view of the lough and Innisfree in all its serene beauty. If you fancy exploring the area on two wheels then the Lough Gill cycle loop is a 40km flat route that takes you through peaceful scenery and along quiet roads. Note that there's no access onto the island itself.

North Sligo

The majority of **North Sligo**'s attractions are easily accessible from the county town. Much of the landscape is irrevocably associated with W. B. Yeats, particularly Benbulben Mountain, under whose green-tinged slopes and surmounting tableland the poet is buried at **Drumcliffe**. To the mountain's south lie the magical waters of **Glencar Lake** with its exhilarating waterfall, while to its west is **Lissadell House**, home to Yeats's friends Eva Gore-Booth and Constance Markiewicz and a place filled with paintings, books and the lore of Irish cultural history. The coastline is less stimulating, though it includes a fine beach at **Mullaghmore**, a harbour village not far from one of Ireland's major funerary monuments, **Creevykeel Court Tomb**.

Rosses Point

Eight kilometres northwest of Sligo town, off the N15, **ROSSES POINT** is a seaside resort which has not moved with the times and is all the better for its lapse. There's a grand **beach**, ideal for swimming, and splendid views across the bay, both of which provided inspiration for Jack B. Yeats, the poet's artist brother. From here, fine, often blustery, walks lead around the headland.

ARRIVAL AND DEPARTURE   ROSSES POINT

By bus Sligo (Mon–Fri 7, Sat 5; 20min).

ACCOMMODATION AND EATING

Austie's Bar & Restaurant ☎ 071 917 7111. A convivial bar where retired sea captains hold court alongside local musicians. The wooden snugs and table which the musicians gather round on weekend nights are made from shipwrecked timber, and maritime memorabilia lines the walls. For food, main courses average €14. Mon–Thurs & Sun 11.30am–11.30pm, Fri & Sat till 12.30am.

Greenlands Caravan and Camping Park ☎ 071 917 7113, Ⓦ greenlandscaravanpark.com. An efficiently run site close to two sandy beaches with good swimming and sailing facilities. April to mid-Sept. Tent pitch __€20__

Yeats Country Hotel & Spa Leisure Club ☎ 071 917 7211, Ⓦ yeatscountryhotel.com. A sleekly designed boutique hotel looking out over Strandhill Bay, with bedrooms spread over three floors. The rooms come in beige and terracotta colour schemes and complement the overall style of the hotel. Their murder mystery weekends are a big hit. __€99__

Drumcliffe and Glencar Lake

Buses drop off/pick up on the main street in Drumcliffe, serving Ballyshannon (8–10 daily; 35–50min) and Sligo (7–11 daily; 15min)

Eight kilometres due north of Sligo along the N15, the tiny seaside village of DRUMCLIFFE is the site of a **monastery** established in 574 by St Colmcille, though only a round tower and an eleventh-century high cross, set on opposite sides of the main road, remain today. The graveyard of the adjacent and somewhat stark nineteenth-century church is where the poet **W. B. Yeats** is buried and, as a consequence, is very much on the tourist trail. Yeats died in 1939 in Roquebrune, France, but before doing so requested that his body be interred locally for "a year or so" before being returned to Sligo. His wishes were granted in 1948 when his remains were transferred from France to Drumcliffe, where his great-grandfather had been rector, and buried, as one of his last poems stated, "Under bare Ben Bulben's head". His headstone, which also marks the resting place of his wife George, bears the last three lines of that poem, *Under Ben Bulben*:

Cast a cold Eye
On Life, on Death.
Horseman, pass by!

Next to Drumcliffe church is a good **café** and craft shop situated in the former visitor centre.

Heading east from Drumcliffe along minor roads, you'll come to **Glencar Lake** after some 8km, gorgeously set amid tree-lined slopes. Near the eastern extremity of its northern shore a signposted footpath leads up to an impressive 15m-high **waterfall**, cascading down into a deep pool from the rocky mountainside above, which provided the inspiration for part of Yeats's poem *The Stolen Child*:

Where the wandering water gushes
From the hills above Glencar,
In pools above the rushes that
Scarce could bathe a star.

Lissadell House

A few kilometres northwest of Drumcliffe • April to mid-Sept daily 10.30am–6pm • €12 • ⓦ lissadellhouse.com

Lissadell House, the lavishly restored ancestral home of the Gore-Booth family, whose members Eva and Constance were close friends of W. B. Yeats, is a must-see attraction. The house, an austere but classical residence built in 1834, reopened to the public in summer 2014 after a prolonged legal dispute over public rights of way. It was the holiday retreat of **W. B. Yeats** and the childhood home of Constance Gore-Booth, who later became Countess Markievicz and fought in the 1916 Easter Rising in Dublin. She was the first woman to be elected to the House of Commons (although she did not take her seat) and later became the first female member of the Dáil, the Irish Parliament. The house is now owned by two barristers, Constance Cassidy and Edward Walsh, who spent €9 million renovating the dilapidated estate. The building is a storehouse of **family archives** and other cultural treasures: one room is crammed with the exhibits of Henry Gore-Booth's expedition to the Arctic in search of a friend. The surrounding **gardens** also make for a pleasant stroll.

Creevykeel Court Tomb

Twenty-two kilometres north of Sligo town, and just north of the village of Cliffony, lies **Creevykeel Court Tomb**, probably the best example of its kind in Ireland. A cairn-covered, trapeze-shaped barrow constructed between 3500 and 3000 BC, though now lacking many of its stones, the tomb features two central burial chambers, faced by an oval-shaped court in which rituals were conducted. Excavations in 1935 uncovered cremated remains, alongside Neolithic pottery, arrowheads, axes and artefacts, all now held by Dublin's National Museum (see p.63).

Just before Creevykeel a lane leads northwards for 4km to **MULLAGHMORE**, an enticing village set around a secluded, walled harbour with a glorious expanse of sandy beach just to its south, offering fabulous views north to the mountains of Donegal and back towards Benbulben.

ACCOMMODATION AND EATING   **CLIFFONY AND MULLAGHMORE HEAD**

Beach Hotel and Leisure Club The Harbour, Mullaghmore ☎071 916 6103, ⓦbeachhotelmullagh more.com. Ideally situated at the waterfront with leisure facilities and activity breaks. The 28 rooms are decorated in tranquil pastels, and many have sea views and window boxes. Weekends only Nov–mid-March. **€99**

Eithna's By the Sea The Harbour, Mullaghmore ☎086 851 5607, ⓦbythesea.ie. Serves deliciously fresh seafood: starters may include lobster and seafood bisque; for mains

(average €20), expect shellfish platters, baked hake or Mullaghmore crab claws. On sunny summer evenings, tables are placed outside for al-fresco dining. Thurs–Sun 6–9.30pm.

Seacrest B&B The Harbour, Mullaghmore ☎071 916 6468, ⓦseacrestguesthouse.com. A beautifully appointed guesthouse set in a stunning location beside the beach. The rooms look out over Benbulben Mountain and across Donegal Bay. The owners offer a packed lunch service costing €7 and will order the food for a beach BBQ for guests. **€70**

West Sligo

The shoreline of **West Sligo**, stretching from near Sligo town almost as far as Mayo's Ballina, is probably the least visited in the county. Yet set against the looming southern backdrop of the Ox Mountains, it offers plenty of diversions including bracing seascapes at **Aughris**, exhilarating surfing at **Easkey** and a dazzling beach at **Enniscrone**. A little way inland, the memorable funerary sepulchres at **Skreen** are well worth a detour en route.

Skreen and Aughris

Twenty-five kilometres west of Sligo town along the N59, the tiny village of **SKREEN** is worth visiting for the astonishing collection of 23 **box tombs** situated in its Church of Ireland's graveyard and created by a local family of stonemasons, the Diamonds, between 1774 and 1886. Named after one Andrew Black, who had the tomb erected in memory of his father in 1825, the most remarkable of these is the Black Monument, which carries an ornate carving of a ploughman, atypically dressed Fred Astaire-style in top hat and tails.

Back on the N59 and just west of the village, a signpost points towards the secluded hamlet of **AUGHRIS**. From the pier here you can follow a 5km cliff walk, which takes in splendid views, sights of numerous seabirds and, from June to August, basking dolphins.

Easkey

Buses run to Enniscrone (Mon–Sat 3–5 daily, Sun 1; 20min) and Sligo (Mon–Sat 3–5 daily, Sun 1; 50min)

The village of **EASKEY**, 15km west of Aughris, began life as a monastic community, much later becoming the base for the MacDonnells, originally gallowglasses who served the ruling O'Dowd clan and built seaside **Roslee Castle** (now ruined) in the fifteenth century. Thanks to the constancy of its waves, Easkey is a popular **surfing** centre and houses the headquarters of the Irish Surfing Association (☎096 49428, ⓦisasurf.ie).

Enniscrone

Bath House June–Sept daily 10am–8pm; Oct–May Mon–Fri noon–8pm, Sat & Sun 10am–8pm • Bath and steam €25, or €32 for two sharing • ⓦkilcullenseaweedbaths.com • Buses run from Enniscrone to Easkey (Mon–Sat 3–5 daily, Sun 1; 20min) and Sligo (Mon–Sat 3–5 daily, Sun 1; 1hr 15min)

Some 14km southwest along the coast from Easkey, **ENNISCRONE** is blessed with a gorgeous 5km arc of golden **strand**. Its other main draw is **Kilcullen's Bath House**, where you can wallow in a bath full of seaweed – the iodine-rich water is not only sheer relaxation but is also reckoned to offer relief for rheumatism and arthritis – before enjoying a hot steam in a cedarwood cabinet.

ACCOMMODATION AND EATING   WEST SLIGO

Atlantic and Riverside On the R297, Easkey ☎096 49001, ⓦeaskeybandb.com. Beside the Easkey River with comfortable en-suite rooms, convenient to shops and pubs, and an ideal stopover while touring the coastline. **€70**

Atlantic Caravan Park Enniscrone ☎096 36132. Camp by the golf course beside natural sand dunes in a pleasant park

looking across Killala Bay. March–Sept. Tent pitch **€18**

★**The Beach Bar** Aughris ☎071 917 6465, ⓦthebeachbarsligo.com. A thatched pub serving such delights as creamy seafood chowder, freshly steamed mussels or Irish stew. It also provides amenable en-suite B&B in the adjacent bungalow. Daily noon–11.30pm. **€60**

South Sligo

South Sligo's attractions are spread over a wide area, ranging from the glorious **Lough Arrow** in the east, via megalithic sites, such as **Heapstown Cairn** and the atmospheric **Carrowkeel Cemetery**, set in the Bricklieve Mountains, to creeper-clad castles and **Lough Talt** in the west. Above all, however, the area is renowned for its **traditional music**, especially within the triangle of **Ballymote**, **Gurteen** and **Tubbercurry**.

Riverstown and Sligo Folk Park

Folk Park May–Sept Mon–Sat 10am–5.30pm, Sun 12.30–6pm; Oct–April Mon–Fri 10am–5pm • €6 • ⓦ sligofolkpark.com • Buses run from Riverstown to Boyle (Thurs & Fri 1 daily; 35min) and Sligo (Thurs & Fri 1 daily; 40min)

The tranquil village of **RIVERSTOWN**, some 20km southeast of Sligo, is home to the **Sligo Folk Park**, a well-designed collection of buildings that includes a museum devoted to rural history and farm implements, re-created craft workshops with occasional craft demonstrations, a nature trail along the banks of the Unshin, plus a crafts shop and café.

During the August bank-holiday weekend Riverstown is taken over by the **James Morrison Traditional Music Festival**, celebrating the music of the famous fiddler, born in nearby Drumfin in 1893. He emigrated to the US in 1915 and became famous playing with his bands in the dancehalls of New York.

Heapstown Cairn and Lough Arrow

Five kilometres south of Riverstown, by the road to Ballindoon, stands the impressive **Heapstown Cairn**, which, at 60m in diameter, is Ireland's largest megalithic passage tomb outside the Boyne Valley. From the cairn it's a short jaunt to the eastern shore of **Lough Arrow**, whose limpid waters are peppered with tiny islands.

Castlebaldwin and Carrowkeel Cemetery

At **CASTLEBALDWIN**, 6km south of Riverstown on the N4, minor roads of diminishing width and reliability lead towards the Bronze Age **Carrowkeel Cemetery**. The last kilometre or so has to be negotiated on foot, but your efforts will be rewarded by a spellbinding panoramic view of the surrounding countryside. Here on the uplands of the Bricklieve Mountains is a remarkable collection of fourteen cairns, plus an assortment of other stonework. Excavation in 1911 produced a wealth of jewellery and relics, and several of the cairns, consisting of roofed, cruciform **passage graves**, can be entered. The most striking is cairn K, which, in complete contrast to County Meath's Newgrange (see p.142), is illuminated by the sun's rays during the summer solstice (June 21).

Ballymote and around

The largest place in southern Sligo is **BALLYMOTE**, 20km from the county town. Richard de Burgo built a **castle** here in 1300 which, switching ownership numerous times during its history, proved to be a veritable straw in the wind of Irish politics. In 1317 it fell to the O'Connors and remained in Irish hands until captured by Bingham, the governor of Connacht, in 1584. It was soon afterwards reclaimed by the McDonaghs who then sold it to Red Hugh O'Donnell (see p.450) for £400 and 300 cows – he marched from here to catastrophic defeat at Kinsale in 1601. Later taken by Cromwell's army, it fell yet again to the O'Connors in 1690, before they in turn surrendered the castle to Williamite troops who determined to put an end to the whole farrago by tearing down much of the building and filling in the moat. The ruins lie just west of the town centre, and the stripped interior can be visited by acquiring a key from the Enterprise Centre (Mon–Fri 9am–5pm) on Emmet Street. Towards the end of the fourteenth century, the **Book of Ballymote** was assembled here, significant not just for the vast deal of information on Irish lore and history it contains, but also because it unlocks the secrets of the carved ogham letters that appear on numerous Neolithic standing stones. The book is held by the Royal Irish Academy in Dublin.

The **Paddy Killoran Traditional Music Festival** is held in Ballymote on the third weekend in June (@comhaltas.ie/events/detail/paddy_killoran_traditional_festival).

ARRIVAL AND DEPARTURE

By bus Boyle (Mon–Wed & Sat 1 daily; 30min); Gurteen (Sat 1; 20min); Sligo (Mon–Wed 1 daily, Sat 2; 40min); Tubbercurry (Wed 2; 30min).

BALLYMOTE AND AROUND

By train The train station, on the Sligo–Dublin route, is opposite the castle ruins, off the Tubbercurry road.

ACCOMMODATION AND EATING

Hayden's Lord Edward St ☎071 918 3188. An old-style welcoming bar that boasts 350 years of history and was the former home of the Sheriff of Sligo. Irish traditional music is played on Sun nights in the summer months. Mon–Thurs 3–11.30pm, Fri & Sat till 12.30am, Sun 12.30–11.30pm.

Millhouse Keenaghan, on the southern outskirts of Ballymote ☎071 918 3449, ✉millhousebb @eircom.net. An agreeable, modern guesthouse with comfortable if slightly small bedrooms. Delicious breakfasts are served and it is handy for an exploration of the area. **€70**

Stonepark Teeling St. A central restaurant and café offering reasonably priced meals with main courses running €9–14. The menu features burgers, chicken, pork, steak and fish. Daily 9am–9pm.

★**Temple House** 5km northwest of town ☎071 918 3329, @templehouse.ie. The area's most exclusive accommodation, offered in a lakeside setting. Dating originally from the late seventeenth century, this majestic country house offers six of its hundred rooms as en-suite guest accommodation, and residents can sample a fine modern European three-course dinner for around €49 (plus wine). April–Nov. **€170**

Gurteen

South of Ballymote the R293 runs parallel to the Dublin railway line before drifting away through fertile farmland and reaching the crossroads village of **GURTEEN** after 11km. Gurteen sits at the heart of South Sligo's **traditional music** scene, and its greatest son was the fiddler Michael Coleman (see box, p.410). Gurteen hosts the **Coleman Traditional Festival** over the last weekend in August.

Coleman Irish Music Centre

Mon–Sat 10am–5pm; shows (€10) July & Aug Wed & Sat 9pm • Exhibition €4 • @ colemanirishmusic.com

Right by the crossroads stands the **Coleman Irish Music Centre**, which stages traditional music and dance shows, has an interactive exhibition area and a shop selling a range of books and CDs, including several collections of recordings from its own archives.

MICHAEL COLEMAN

Arguably the greatest of Irish fiddlers, **Michael Coleman** was born in 1891 in Killavil, just north of Gurteen, and grew up in a household noted for its strong musical tradition. Taking up the fiddle in early childhood, he developed rapidly under the tuition of his elder brother James and acquired a phenomenally extensive repertoire. Coleman moved to New York in 1914, where he found a living playing first on the vaudeville circuit and later in the city's Irish dancehalls and bars. With a ready-made Irish market for the nascent US recording industry, Coleman made his first 78s in 1921 and over the next fifteen years released numerous others on a variety of labels, while frequently broadcasting on the radio. He made his last commercial recording in 1936.

The impact of these recordings, the embodiment of the fluid **Sligo style** of music – characterized by its sweet tone and sometimes flamboyant ornamentation – was enormous not just in the US but also back home, and the approach taken by Coleman and his fellow Sligo émigrés, Paddy Killoran and James Morrison (see p.407), came to dominate Ireland's traditional music. Coleman died in 1945, but you'll still encounter many a traditional session throughout Ireland where the sequence of tunes exactly replicates one of his 78rpm recordings.

11

ARRIVAL AND DEPARTURE · GURTEEN

By bus Ballymote (Sat 1; 20min); Boyle (Thurs 2; 25min); Sligo (Sat 2; 55min–1hr 5min); Tubbercurry (Sat 1; 25min).

ACCOMMODATION

Church View B&B Main St ☎071 918 2935, ⓦ thechurchview.com. A modern town house, centrally placed, with attractive en-suite rooms. Each room is decorated in a different colour scheme and comes with tea- and coffee-making facilities. **€70**

Tubbercurry and around

Some 30km southwest of Sligo, **TUBBERCURRY** is a rather docile small town but traditional music thrives here, focused on the week-long **South Sligo Summer School** (ⓦ sssschool.org) in mid-July, with classes, pub sessions and concerts. Tubbercurry's origins date back to the late fourteenth century, but it remained a sleepy little settlement until becoming a stop on one of Bianconi's coaching routes in 1853. The burgeoning town was all but destroyed by fire during a zealous Black and Tan reprisal in 1920, and little remains from earlier times.

Some 15km to Tubbercurry's west, along a lonely road that passes through flat land before rising into the Ox Mountains, lies **Lough Talt**. Trout-rich, the lake attracts plenty of anglers as well as walkers keen to enjoy the 6.5km path circumnavigating its waters.

ARRIVAL AND DEPARTURE · TUBBERCURRY AND AROUND

By bus Ballymote (Wed 2; 30min); Galway (6–8 daily; 1hr 55min); Gurteen (Sat 1; 25min); Sligo (6–8 daily; 35min); Westport (1–2 daily; 1hr 20min).

ACCOMMODATION AND EATING

Cawley's Emmet St ☎071 918 5025, ⓦ cawleysguesthouse.ie. A comfortable guesthouse with 14 rooms. The restaurant is open to non-residents and serves a mix of French-inspired and Irish cuisine. **€75**

Killoran's Teeling St ☎071 918 5679. A traditional restaurant supplying filling breakfasts and lunches with an adjacent bar. Main courses might include steak, chicken, haddock or oysters, and average €10. Daily 9am–9pm.

Murphy's Hotel Teeling St ☎071 918 5598, ⓦ murphyshotel.ie. Well-equipped en-suite rooms and a range of meals in both its restaurant and bar. Music sessions are held in the bar most weekends. **€80**

Carrick-on-Shannon and around

CARRICK-ON-SHANNON, Leitrim's county town, grew up around a strategic crossing point on the River Shannon, the importance of which was recognized by the English who began building a planned settlement that was incorporated as a borough in 1613. Modern Carrick developed after the 1840s when the Shannon navigation scheme reached the town; its stone bridge and quays date from this period.

At the tourist office you can pick up a booklet, *A Walk through Carrick-on-Shannon* (€2), detailing a signposted **trail** of the historic buildings. But Carrick's main draw is its proximity to the river, its busy **marina** often jam-packed with barges and cruisers.

The Dock Arts Centre and Leitrim Design House

St George's Terrace • Mon–Sat 10am–5.30pm • ☎ 071 965 0828, Ⓦ thedock.ie

Just above the river, off the top of Bridge Street, stands the former courthouse, built in 1821 and known as **The Dock**. The arts centre within includes a one-hundred-seater performance space staging theatre, comedy and music events, as well as a café. The building also houses the **Leitrim Design House**, showcasing contemporary works by local artists and craft workers, and hosts regular exhibitions.

St George's Heritage Centre

St Mary's Close • Daily 11am–4.30pm • €7 (includes admission to Workhouse) • ☎ 071 962 1757, Ⓦ carrickheritage.com

The **Heritage Centre**, adjacent to St George's Church (1827), tells the story of Leitrim, its landscape and people through an engaging audiovisual. The church is also worth visiting to see the magnificent altarpiece, *The Adoration of the Shepherds*, restored and hanging in a gilt frame.

Carrick Workhouse

Gallows Hill • Daily 11am–4.30pm • €7 (includes admission to St George's Visitor Centre) • ☎ 071 962 1757, Ⓦ carrickheritage.com

Carrick Workhouse opened in 1842 to accommodate 800 people but it was besieged during the Great Famine of 1845–47. With its long rectangular rooms, bare floorboards and whitewashed walls, it looks much as it did in the 1840s and is an atmospheric place to linger. The significance of the Workhouse has been interpreted by the Wexford artist Alanna O'Kelly through a permanent multimedia installation, *No Colouring Can Deepen the Darkness of Truth*.

Costello Memorial Chapel

Bridge St • Daily 11am–4pm; or contact the tourist office for a key • Free

The restored **Costello Memorial Chapel** – one of the smallest churches in Ireland – was erected in 1879 by Carrick businessman Edward Costello in memory of his wife, Mary Josephine. The interior is lined with yellow Bath stone and its tiny dimensions measure a mere 5m long, 4m wide and 6m high.

James Gralton wall plaque

As you walk along the main street admiring the handsome shop fronts you come to the site

---

GETTING OUT ON THE WATER IN CARRICK-ON-SHANNON

Moon River (☎ 071 962 1777, Ⓦ moonriver.ie) runs €12 **river trips** with commentary from the bridge. If you want to go it alone, Emerald Star (☎ 071 962 7633, Ⓦ emeraldstar.ie) offers Shannon **cruisers** for weekly rental; expect to pay around €650–3000, depending on the size of the boat and season. Carrick Craft (☎ 01 278 1666, Ⓦ cruise-ireland.com) rents two to twelve-berth cruisers. Inland Waterways Association of Ireland (Ⓦ iwai.ie) supplies more **information** on the Shannon–Erne waterway and sells guides and navigation charts.

CARRICK-ON-SHANNON FESTIVALS AND EVENTS

Water Music Festival ⓦ carrickwatermusic.com. Held over the second weekend in July, featuring concerts ranging from traditional to classical music.

Carrick Rowing Club Regatta ⓦ carrickrowingclub.com. At the beginning of August a lively regatta, run by the oldest rowing club in Ireland, is the high point of the boating season and attracts large crowds.

Coarse Fishing Festival ☎ 071 962 0313. In mid-September anglers come from many countries for a week-long festival devoted to coarse fishing.

---

of the Allied Irish Bank, formerly a shop where **James Gralton** (1888–1945) worked in the early 1900s. Gralton was a left-wing political activist who joined the Revolutionary Workers Group, but following a political witch-hunt he became the only Irishman ever to be deported from his native land. His fascinating story is told in a 2014 Ken Loach film *Jimmy's Hall*.

11

ARRIVAL AND INFORMATION
CARRICK-ON-SHANNON

By bus Buses arrive either beside or opposite *Coffey's Pastry Case*, by the Shannon bridge (☎ 071 916 0066).
Destinations Boyle (5–7 daily; 15min); Drumshanbo (Sat 1; 25min); Dublin (5–7 daily; 2hr 30min–3hr); Sligo (5–7 daily; 1hr).
By train The train station (☎ 071 962 0036) is a short distance off the Elphin road on the southern side of the river. All services operate Mon–Sat 7–8 times daily, with 6 on Sun.
Destinations Boyle (15min); Dublin (2hr 20min); Mullingar (1hr 10min); Sligo (45min).
Tourist office In the Old Barrel Store, under the bridge (mid-May to mid-Sept Mon–Sat 9.30am–5pm; ☎ 071 962 0170, ⓦ leitrimtourism.com).

ACCOMMODATION

Bush Hotel Main St ☎ 071 967 1000, ⓦ bushhotel .com. The rooms at this traditional-style hotel range in size, though they are all well equipped and extremely comfortable. A fascinating mini-museum of local photographic history lines the walls of the main corridor. **€139**
Ciúin House Hartley, on the outskirts of town ☎ 071 967 1488, ⓦ ciuinhouse.ie. Excellent guesthouse with elegant furnishings and a range of rooms, two of which include a hot tub. A good base too for exploring south Leitrim and the surrounding area. **€100**
★**The Landmark Hotel** Dublin Rd ☎ 071 962 2222, ⓦ thelandmarkhotel.com. A modern hotel with sprucely furnished rooms and views of the Shannon. Great cocktail bar and *Boardwalk* café too, for views of the riverfront with free newspapers. **€129**

EATING AND DRINKING

Anderson's Thatched Pub 5km south of Carrick on the R368 Elphin road ☎ 087 228 3288, ⓦ andersonspub .com. An inviting bar with a pedigree stretching back to 1734. Superb sessions are held nightly from June to August, and on Wednesday and Saturday the rest of the year. Mon–Thurs & Sun 8–11.30pm, Fri & Sat 8pm–12.30am.
Art of Coffee Mercantile Plaza ⓦ artofcoffee.ie. A hip, relaxing coffee roastery with papers and books to peruse while enjoying the barista's choice and a slice of decadent cake. Mon–Sat 9am–6pm.
Coffey's Pastry Case Bridge St ☎ 071 962 0929. A buzzy daytime café in a central location for coffee, muffins, scones, vegetarian pizza, salads and light bites; the seating upstairs is ideal for river gazing. Daily 8am–7pm.
The Cottage Restaurant Jamestown ☎ 071 962 5933, ⓦ cottagerestaurant.ie. Three kilometres outside Carrick in Jamestown, and right beside the river, this is one of the classiest restaurants in the area. The two-course early-bird menu on Wed and Thurs is €25, while mains, which might include duck breast, loin of lamb or glazed chicken, average €20. Wed–Sat 5.30–10pm, Sun lunch noon–4pm, dinner 5.30–9pm.
★**The Oarsman** Bridge St ☎ 071 962 1733, ⓦ theoarsman.com. Imaginative, modern Irish cuisine such as farmhouse pork, Thornhill duck or sea trout for half the price you'd pay in Dublin (around €35 for three courses plus wine). Try some of their local craft beers including Sunburnt Red, Howling Gale Ale or Knock me down Porter. Mon–Thurs 11.30am–11.30pm, Fri & Sat till 12.30am.
Victoria Hall Quay Rd ☎ 071 962 0320, ⓦ victoriahall .ie. In delightful surroundings and offering a mix of Thai and modern Irish food; a three-course meal here will set you back around €24. Daily 12.30–10pm.
Vittos Market Yard, Main St ☎ 071 962 7000, ⓦ vittosrestaurant.com. Serves a dazzling selection of pizzas, pasta, salads and grills. Mains average €12.95. Mon–Fri 5.30–10pm, Sat & Sun 1–5pm.

Drumshanbo and Lough Allen

Some 12km north of Carrick, **DRUMSHANBO** is a lively village with a strong musical tradition at the tip of **Lough Allen**'s southern shore. In the third week of July, the seven-day Joe Mooney Summer School (@joemooneysummerschool.com) is held here, offering **traditional music** classes and concerts. At the beginning of June the village also hosts the **An Tostal Festival** (@antostalfestival.ie) with a variety of music.

From Drumshanbo roads lead north along both eastern and western shores of **Lough Allen**. The western route crosses into Roscommon and skirts the Arigna Mountains (see p.416) while its alternative to the east heads up through bleak flatlands below Slieve Anierin. The waymarked 48km **Leitrim Way** (map available from local tourist offices) follows Lough Allen's shoreline before taking in higher ground on its way to the remote village of **Dowra**, the starting point for the **Cavan Way** (see p.161).

At **Ballinaglera**, 13km north of Drumshanbo, the **Lough Allen Adventure Centre** (@loughallenadventure.com) offers a variety of activities, such as wind-surfing, kayaking and hill-walking.

Sliabh an Iarainn Visitors Centre

Acres Lake on the Carrick-on-Shannon road, on the outskirts of Drumshanbo but within the limits of the town • May to Oct Mon–Fri 9am–5pm • @leitrimtourism.com

The newly renovated **Sliabh an Iarainn Visitors Centre** is an excellent introduction to the area. Exhibitions feature topography and geology as well as musical heritage and scenic attractions. Audiovisuals take you on a local-history journey, focusing on transport and industry. A **Musicians' Corner** showcases the flautist John McKenna and other renowned Leitrim musicians; you can listen to tracks featuring the different styles of the area's music.

ARRIVAL AND GETTING AROUND
DRUMSHANBO

By bus Ballinamore (Fri & Sat 1 daily; 25min); Carrick-on-Shannon (Sat 1; 25min); Dowra (Sat 1; 25min); Keadue (Fri 1; 15min); Sligo (Fri 1, Sat 2; 1hr 15min–1hr 40min).

By bike Bike rental is available at Moran's on Convent Avenue (@moransmotorcycles.com).

ACCOMMODATION AND EATING

Fraoch Ban ☎071 964 1260, @fraochban.com. Comfortable modern bungalow surveying the lake, 1km up the Dowra road. An ideal location for walking, cycling or driving around the serene north Leitrim countryside. April–Oct. €70

Henry's Haven Convent Ave ☎071 964 1805. The best place in the area for good-value bar meals starting from around €9.50 for main courses. Food served daily to 9pm. Mon–Thurs 10.30am–11.30pm, Fri & Sat till 12.30am, Sun noon–11.30pm.

Lough Allen Hotel & Spa ☎071 964 0100, @loughallenhotel.com. Don't be put off by the approach road; the setting is a stunning location beside Lough Allen. Elegantly furnished bedrooms and spectacular suites await the visitor, as well as a spa, fitness centre and pool. €99

Sweet Geranium Café High St. Serves a range of light bites and snacks as well as more substantial lunches, featuring chicken, fish or steak. Main-course prices start from €8. Mon–Sat 9.30am–5.30pm.

East from Drumshanbo

Take the R208 **east from Drumshanbo** and then head along the R210 and join the R209 to a jumble of little lakes surrounded by low hills. **KESHCARRIGAN**, about 8km east of Drumshanbo on the Shannon–Erne Waterway, is worth a stop (even though the village has been blighted by inappropriate modern housing developments) for its amiable bars. Six kilometres east, **FENAGH** was once an important ecclesiastical centre, founded by St Caillin in the sixth century. The area's history is recounted in the **Heritage Centre** (Mon–Fri 10am–5.30pm; free; ☎071 964 5590, @fenagh.com), which also includes a café and an indoor soft play area. **BALLINAMORE**, 5km northeast of Fenagh, is a focus for **cruising** on the Shannon–Erne Waterway, with barges available from Riversdale Barge Holidays (☎071 964 4122, @riversdalebargeholidays.com; €650–1540 per week).

ACCOMMODATION AND EATING

KESHCARRIGAN AND BALLINAMORE

The Canal Stop Main St, Keshcarrigan ☎ 071 964 2252. Beside Ballyconnell canal and known locally as *Gerties*, this is an ideal place to tuck into hearty meals at reasonable prices. The menu includes steak, chicken and lasagne; main courses from €11. Food served Fri & Sat 6–9pm, Sun 1–8pm; bar Mon–Thurs 11am–11.30pm, Fri & Sat till 12.30am, Sun noon–11pm.

The Commercial and Tourist Hotel High St, Ballinamore ☎ 071 964 4675, ⊛ hotelcommerical.com. A perfect base to explore the Erne–Shannon Waterway and surrounding countryside. Spacious rooms. **€75**

Hamill's B&B Ballinamore ☎ 071 964 4311, ⊛ hamillsbedandbreakfast.com. Centrally sited just off High St, there are no fancy frills here but the 13 en-suite rooms are agreeable enough and the location is pleasant. **€70**

★**The Old Rectory** Fenagh Glebe, Ballinamore ☎ 071 964 4089, ⊛ theoldrectoryireland.com. A child-friendly Georgian house on a working farm offering well-kept en-suite rooms, brilliant breakfasts, canoes and bikes for rent, and views of Fenagh Lough from the grounds. **€75**

Boyle and around

Rising gently above its own namesake river, engaging **BOYLE** is a relaxed town with congenial bars, a couple of sites of noteworthy historical interest and a lively arts festival. It also makes an ideal base for exploring not only Roscommon's northern attractions, such as **Lough Key Forest Park**, but neighbouring Leitrim and South Sligo too. The town hosts several summer **festivals**, of which the biggest is the Boyle Arts Festival (⊛ boylearts.com) at the end of July with a broad-ranging programme of drama, concerts, exhibitions and lectures. Some 3km north of Boyle, overlooking the N4 Sligo–Dublin road where it skirts the Curlew Mountains, stands an intriguing metal **sculpture** representing Gaelic chieftain Red Hugh O'Donnell. Known locally as "the ass in the pass", artist Maurice Harron's work marks the site of the Battle of the Curleius between Irish and English forces in 1599.

Brief history

Boyle's origins lie in the establishment of a **Cistercian monastery** in 1161, but as it was situated on an important trading route, the abbey became embroiled in numerous internecine and Irish–English skirmishes and was sacked on a number of occasions. It lingered on for several decades after the Dissolution – its last abbot was executed in 1584 for refusing to disavow allegiance to Rome – and from 1599 until the end of the eighteenth century it was used as a barracks by the English and known as Boyle Castle. In 1603 the building passed into the hands of Sir John King and remained in the family's possession until 1892. It was Staffordshire-born King who transformed Boyle, constructing a grand **mansion** to the west of the abbey and an avenue (now the town's main street) leading up to it. At the same time he began to amass thousands of acres of land, which would eventually become the largest estate in County Roscommon, **Rockingham**.

Boyle Abbey

Easter to mid-Sept daily 10am–6pm • €3; Heritage Card

It's easy to find your way around Boyle, and the town's two major attractions are well signposted from the centre. The first of these is **Boyle Abbey**, consecrated in 1218, whose alluring remains abut the river on the eastern side of town. Despite various onslaughts during the course of its history, it remains perhaps the finest surviving Cistercian church in Ireland and its sixty-year building process bears traces of both the Romanesque and the then newly arrived Gothic styles of architecture. The abbey's ruins are entered via its gatehouse, which contains an **exhibition** on the foundation's history and a model of how it once might have looked. Inside the nave the transition from Romanesque to Gothic is neatly contrasted by windows and arches, circular facing pointed. Some of the capitals bear ntriguing secular decorations – one features little figures standing between trees and clutching the branches somewhat stiffly – while high on the western wall is a carving of a Sheila-na-Gig (see p.627).

King House

April–Sept Tues–Sat 11am–4pm • €5; Heritage Island • ⓦ kinghouse.ie • 1hr weekday guided tours available

The original seat of the King family was destroyed by fire, but its replacement, **King House**, is well worth visiting. This impressive stone mansion was built around 1730 and sold to the War Office when the Kings moved to Rockingham, becoming the barracks for the Connaught Rangers from 1788 until 1922. The Irish Army then occupied the building until the 1940s, after which it passed into private hands, becoming at one time a store for feed and fuel, before falling into dereliction. Thoroughly restored, its ground floor now houses Boyle's **Civic Art Gallery**, largely displaying works by local painters, while upper storeys employ interactive high-tech gadgetry to retell the story of the house and the family who built it, with child-oriented exhibits. The story of Henry's son Edward, who built Rockingham, is wittily recounted in one exhibit, "How to become an earl in six easy stages", describing how he rose to become Earl of Kingston in 1768. One section of the house is devoted to the Connaught Rangers and recalls their role in various military campaigns.

King House runs a programme of classical music **events** as well as drama and comedy shows in the spring and summer.

11

ARRIVAL AND INFORMATION	BOYLE

By train Boyle's train station (ⓣ071 966 2027) is 200m south of the centre just off Elphin St.
Destinations Ballymote (15min); Carrick-on-Shannon (15min); Dublin (2hr 35min); Mullingar (1hr 25min); Sligo (35min). All services operate Mon–Sat 7 times daily, Sun 6.
By bus Buses set down on Carrick Rd.
Destinations Ballymote (Mon, Wed & Sat 1 daily; 30min);

Carrick-on-Shannon (5–6 daily; 15min); Dublin (5–6 daily; 3hr); Gurteen (Thurs 2; 25min); Riverstown (Thurs & Fri 1 daily; 35min); Sligo (5–7 daily; 40min); Strokestown (Mon–Sat 1 daily; 40min).
Tourist office The Una Bhán tourist office (daily 9am–6pm; ⓣ071 966 3033, ⓦvisitroscommon.ie) is just by the entrance to King House and stocks maps and other information on the area.

ACCOMMODATION AND EATING

Abbey House ⓣ071 966 2385, ⓦabbeyhouse.net. In the abbey's shadow is this delightful Victorian structure, with five spacious and well-furnished en-suite rooms. Visitors are greeted on arrival with tea or coffee and home-baked cakes, and the mature gardens are pleasant for a stroll. March–Oct. **€70**
Aunty Bee's Tea Rooms & Restaurant ⓦkinghouse .ie. Set within the grounds of King House, this café serves wholesome snacks and lunches for an average of €7. Main meals may include quiche, vegetarian or meat salad plates; calorie counters (and those on a budget) can get half portions of the hot lunch special for €5.50. Daily 10am–5pm.
Cesh Corran Abbey Terrace, opposite the abbey on the main road ⓣ071 966 2265, ⓦmarycooney.com. Hospitable Edwardian house with stained-glass windows, fresh flowers and simply but tastefully furnished rooms. At breakfast the owners serve up every conceivable combination of eggs and fried accompaniments alongside

gluten-free breads and homemade preserves. Packed lunches are also available. **€70**
Kate Lavin's Patrick St. All dark oak panelling and wooden benches, this old-style bar is a great place to meet the locals. Its strength is its simplicity: no television or pool table, but a glow from the turf fire and friendly welcome from the owners. The Guinness has a "short run" because it comes from underneath the stairs. Daily 6–11.30pm.
★ **Lough Key House** 5km from Boyle ⓣ071 966 2161, ⓦloughkeyhouse.com. An exquisite Georgian house set in beautiful grounds adjacent to the main entrance to Lough Key Forest Park. Sumptuous breakfasts are served by the affable owners and bedrooms with period features are tastefully decorated. **€89**
Moylurg Inn The Crescent. A welcoming bar with a variety of music, including ballad singing, at weekends. Mon–Thurs 11.30am–11.30pm, Fri & Sat till 12.30am, Sun noon–11pm.

Lough Key Forest and Activity Park

Just off the N4, 3km east of Boyle, lies **Lough Key Forest and Activity Park**, an area once the focal point of the Kings' Rockingham estate. However, the demesne was abandoned by the family in 1957 after their mansion, designed by the English architect John Nash, was destroyed by fire – all that now remains of the grandiose 365-windowed creation are two still-accessible subterranean servants' tunnels through which the Kings' menials scurried to fulfil their duties.

If you don't wish to embark on any of the paid-for activities, you can still enjoy the circular 5km **walk** (free) around the waters of the lough, which encompasses various megalithic and medieval ruins. There are other signposted trails – ranging from easy to strenuous – around the estate, too, and you can take a **boat trip** out on the lake or rent a rowing boat during the summer months (☎086 084 6849, ⓦloughkeyboats.com). Rowing boats cost €20 while the boat trip is €12.

Lough Key Experience

March–June, Sept & Oct daily 10am–6pm; July & Aug Mon–Thurs 10am–6pm, Fri–Sun 10am–9pm; Nov–Feb Wed–Sun noon–4pm; last admission 1hr 30min before closing • €7.50; car €4, though parking free if spending €20 or more on activities or in the restaurant; Heritage Island • ⓦloughkey.ie

Though almost all the park's woodland and trails remain unsullied, a massive commercial revamp has restricted access to certain areas, focal to which is the **Visitor Centre** at the end of a driveway 2km from the park's Gothic gateway on the N4. It's here that you can buy tickets to the **Lough Key Experience** and pick up the headset that provides a guided commentary to a walking trail around a segment of the park. Apart from recounting the park's history and describing its wildlife and flora, the trail takes you through the aforementioned tunnels as well as to the top of the five-storey **Moylurg viewing tower** which commands splendid vistas of the lake and its numerous islands, including **Trinity Island**, which was once the site of a Cistercian foundation and a medieval castle. The island holds a special place in Irish mythology as the last resting place of Una Bhán MacDermott, who died of grief after being forbidden to marry her lover Thomas Costello – the song *Una Bhán*, recounting the tale, is one of the greats of the *sean-nós* tradition (see p.603). The trail concludes with the 300m-long **Tree Canopy Walk** whose timber-and-steel construction rises steadily to a 9m-high view of the park from the treetops.

Adventure Play Kingdom, Boda Borg and other activities

Adventure Play Kingdom Last admission 1hr before closing • €5 • **Boda Borg** Last admission 2hr before closing; minimum of three participants • €15; free parking if you spend €20 or more within the visitor centre

Near the visitor centre there's the children's outdoor **Adventure Play Kingdom** and **Boda Borg**, a Swedish-designed two-storey puzzle-house which relies upon teamwork to solve various, instruction-less problems. Other attractions include the Zipit Forest Adventure in which you hurtle down a zipwire, electric bike trails and woodland segways which include tours of the Rockingham estate and thirty-minute lawn glides.

The Arigna Mountains

The far north of County Roscommon stretches up to Lough Allen where gentle farmland ascends to the moors and lakes of the **Arigna Mountains**. Albeit small-scale, this was once one of the few areas of Ireland to play a role in the Industrial Revolution, based first on **iron** extraction for a fifty-year period after 1788 – the local ironworks forged pikes in preparation for the 1798 Rebellion – and, subsequently, **coal**, which was worked here until 1990. The **Arigna Miners Way** is a waymarked 120km walking trail through the area, linking up with both the Leitrim Way and a historical trail taking in Boyle and parts of Sligo.

Keadue

KEADUE, 12km northeast of Boyle, is an attractive village of traditional cottages, stone walls and well-kept gardens. It is associated with the blind harper Turlough O'Carolan (see p.600), whose grave lies by the ruins of Kilronan Abbey, just out on the Sligo road. The musician is commemorated at the **O'Carolan Heritage Park**, a well-kept public park in the heart of the village with, as its centrepiece, a bronze replica of one of his harps. Keadue also hosts two musical events in July/August: first a traditional-music summer school, which is followed by a harp and traditional music festival (ⓦocarolanharpfestival.ie).

ARRIVAL AND DEPARTURE   KEADUE

By bus Drumshanbo (Fri 1; 20min); Sligo (Fri 1; 50min).

ACCOMMODATION AND EATING

Harp & Shamrock B&B Main St ☎071964 7288, ⓦharpandshamrock.net. A delightful combination of bar, beer garden, grocery shop and accommodation all rolled into one friendly service. None of the seven rooms is en-suite but there are three separate bathrooms along the corridor. **€60**

Kilronan Castle Hotel ☎071 961 8000, ⓦkilronancastle.ie. A couple of kilometres down the Ballyfarnon road, this is a luxury hotel set in tranquil parkland estate. It features a fine spa and the *Douglas Hyde* restaurant where mains might include fillet of dry-aged beef, rack of Irish lamb or roast monkfish. **€139**

Arigna Mining Experience

Jan to mid-March Mon–Fri 10am–5pm; mid-March to Dec daily 10am–5pm • €10; Heritage Island • ⓦarignaminingexperience.ie

From the dusty village of **Arigna** itself, a little further north, a winding lane leads a couple of kilometres upwards, past a smokeless fuel plant, to the **Arigna Mining Experience**. Perched high on a hilltop and commanding stunning views of Lough Allen, this brilliantly designed and enthralling museum is based around one of the last working pits in the area. The history of local coal mining is documented in the reception area, but, once equipped with hard hat, it's the forty-minute **tours** of the mine that are most informative and thought-provoking. Led by ex-miners, these are rich in anecdote and thoroughly explore both the nature of the industry and the atrocious and exploitative working conditions the miners endured – the tunnels are dark and foreboding, and the sound of dripping water and footsteps is amplified by the acoustics. Especially astonishing was the ability of the miners to squeeze themselves into the tightest of seams in the quest for coal.

Strokestown and around

The impressively planned settlement of **STROKESTOWN**, with its wide, tree-lined mall, embodies Ireland's troubled history in microcosm. It is the ideal base from which to delve into the historic riches of this part of south Roscommon, an area of rolling agricultural land. At the western end of Strokestown's mall sits an octagonal church, now housing the **County Roscommon Heritage and Genealogy Company** (Mon–Fri 2.30–4.30pm; ☎071 963 3380, ⓦroscommonroots.com), which conducts research for anyone seeking to trace their Roscommon roots; the eastern end of the mall terminates in a three-arched gateway, marking the entrance to Mahon's (see p.418) massive estate.

Strokestown holds a major **poetry festival** (ⓦstrokestownpoetry.org) over the May public holiday weekend and a **traditional music festival**, Féile Frank McGann (ⓦfeilefrankmcgann.com), in early October.

Brief history

The land on which Strokestown lies, and the surrounding area, known as **Corca Achlann**, belonged for more than a thousand years to the MacBranan clan, underlords of the powerful O'Connor kings who ruled Connacht, until dispossessed by Cromwell in the 1650s. Subsequently, part of their territory was granted by Charles II to Nicholas Mahon, whose kin later amassed more than thirty thousand acres for their huge estate, second only in size to Rockingham (see p.414) in Roscommon, becoming one of the great landed families of Ireland in the process. In the early nineteenth century, his descendant Lieutenant-General Thomas Mahon, Second Lord Hartland, requiring a grandiose symbol reflecting the extent of his property, determined to have constructed a **central avenue** wider than Vienna's Ringstrasse.

Strokestown Park House

Mid-March to Oct daily 10.30am–5.30pm; house tours April–Oct daily at noon, 2.30pm & 4pm, Nov–March at 2.30pm only • House, Famine museum and gardens €9 each, €13.50 for all three; Heritage Island • ⓦ strokestownpark.ie

The magnificent Georgian **Strokestown Park House** was the seat of the Mahon family from its completion in 1696 for almost three hundred years. This huge Palladian mansion originally consisted of a two-storey central block and basement until the 1740s when Thomas Mahon, MP for Roscommon, hired the architect Richard Castle to construct a third storey and two extra wings. Mahon's son, Maurice (who became the First Lord Hartland in 1800), made subsequent additions including the library and many decorative features, such as cornices and chimneypieces, while the Second Lord Hartland added the porch and its huge pilasters. The house remained in Mahon ownership until 1979 when it was sold, along with its contents, to a local garage owner who undertook restoration work and opened it to the public in 1987.

Few Irish "big houses" retain their original owners' property (in this case ranging from furniture to children's toys), which is a vital factor in making the **guided tours** so entertaining. The main hall features early eighteenth-century wood panelling, while the spacious dining room, decorated in rich rose-pink damask wallpaper, is equipped with furniture from the early 1800s and a mammoth turf-bucket. The library was originally a ballroom – hence the bowed space at one end, which housed musicians – and has glorious Chippendale bookcases, while the smoking room was converted into a laboratory and photographic darkroom by Henry Pakenham-Mahon in the 1890s. The north wing includes a superb kitchen, replete with spits and ovens, and a balustraded gallery, the only surviving example in Ireland of a kind favoured by Castle, from which the housekeeper could keep an eagle eye on business down below and, according to Strokestown legend, drop menus for the week's meals down to the cook.

National Irish Famine Museum

Among the property passed on by the Mahons were numerous documents and letters relating to the family's role in relation to the Great Famine of 1845–51. The house's former stables – marvellously vaulted buildings in their own right – house an often chilling and stimulating **museum** detailing the Famine's effects upon the Mahons' tenants and its wider impact across Ireland. The intricate, informative displays and films focus on the concatenation of factors in Ireland – the growth of the rural population, the conacre system of agricultural tenancy, the reliance on the potato crop and the spread of the potato blight – that combined with Britain's economic policy of non-interference to have such a devastating effect on human life. Exhibits also highlight the role in local events of **Major Denis Mahon**, who had inherited the Strokestown estate after the death of the third and last Lord Hartland in 1845. The malevolent major not only evicted the majority of his tenants, but contracted dangerously unseaworthy vessels (the infamous coffin ships) to transport some of them in atrocious conditions to North America. The displays document contemporary newspaper reports condemning his actions and, in 1847, his assassination by vengeful ex-tenants. The museum was redesigned in 2013 and the restored **gardens** include a fernery, fruit and vegetable patch and lily point representing horticultural practices and garden architecture from the 1740s onwards.

ARRIVAL AND DEPARTURE   STROKESTOWN

By bus Boyle (1 daily; 40min); Dublin (6 daily; 2hr 25min); Frenchpark (7–8 daily; 25min); Sligo (Mon–Sat 1 daily; 1hr); Tulsk (6–7 daily; 15min).

ACCOMMODATION AND EATING

Manly's Bridge St. A venerable institution with quiet conversation and a great place to soak up some stories from the locals. It hosts traditional music sessions on the first Thursday of each month. Daily 5–11.30pm.

Percy French Hotel Bridge St ☎ 071 963 3300, ⓦ percyfrenchhotel.com. The town's centre of life, with 18 pleasant en-suite rooms and a decent bar. Meals are available in the bar – carvery roasts are popular – throughout the day up to 9pm. **€80**

Douglas Hyde Interpretive Centre

Frenchpark • Open by appointment May–Sept • Free • ☎ 087 782 3751

Five kilometres from Strokestown lies the village of **Frenchpark**, where the former Church of Ireland parish church is home to the **Douglas Hyde Interpretive Centre**. The centre recounts the life of **Douglas Hyde** (1860–1949), one of the key figures in the Irish cultural revival, with informative displays and an entertaining video. Note that it is essential to phone in advance to gain admission to the centre.

Tulsk

Located around the village of **TULSK**, 15km southeast of Frenchpark, is **Rathcrogan**, a rich array of earthworks, ring forts, standing stones and caves betokening one of Ireland's major mythological areas. According to *The Annals of the Four Masters* (see p.429) it was here that Medb, the warrior queen and earth goddess who features heavily in the *Táin Bó Cúailnge* (see p.155), sited her palace Cruachan, the location of the epic's opening and gory conclusion.

Rathcroghan Visitor Centre

May–Sept Mon–Sat 9am–5pm, Sun noon–4pm; tours 12.30pm, 2.30pm • €7 combined tour price • ⓦ rathcroghan.ie

Before visiting the monuments, it's wise to head for the newly designed **Rathcroghan Visitor Centre** just west of the crossroads in Tulsk. Audiovisuals bring the history of the site to life; you'll see a reconstruction of the **Oweynagat** ("the cave of the cats"), which supposedly provided the entrance to the otherworld. A highlight is the collection of ten black-and-white facsimile illustrations of the *Táin*, drawn by the Irish artist Louis le Brocquy, who died in 2012.

DOUGLAS HYDE

Born in Castlerea, 13km south of Frenchpark, to Anglo-Irish Ascendancy stock, **Douglas Hyde** learnt Irish at an early age and developed a lifelong interest in the nation's rich vernacular tradition and folklore. After attending Trinity College, he became professor of Modern Irish Language and Literature at the National University of Ireland and produced numerous articles, essays and reviews in Irish, as well as collaborating on a number of Irish-language plays with Lady Gregory (see p.354). Hyde travelled the country widely, gathering material, much of which was transcribed in collections such as the highly influential *Love Songs of Connaught*. In 1893, he was a co-founder of the Gaelic League, which aimed to enhance Irish culture via a revival of musical and linguistic traditions, though Hyde later became concerned by the League's increasing links with the Independence movement and resigned as its president in 1915. Elected to the Irish Senate in 1925, he retired from public life in 1932 until he was appointed the country's first president in 1938. He died in 1949.

Donegal

THE COAST NORTH OF DERRYBEG, GWEEDORE

Donegal

Second in size only to County Cork, County Donegal has unquestionably the richest scenery in the whole of Ireland, featuring a spectacular 300km coastline – an intoxicating run of headlands, promontories and peninsulas rising to the highest sea-cliffs in Europe. Perhaps the most satisfying landscape is that of northern Donegal, not least the Rosguill and Inishowen peninsulas, while the interior region around Errigal Mountain, Lough Beagh and Lough Gartan merits an extended visit. Elsewhere, Donegal manifests a wonderful, and often wonderfully bleak, terrain of glens, rivers and bogland hills.

Donegal's original name was *Tír Chonaill*, which translates as "the land of Conal"; Chonaill was one of the twelve sons of Niall of the Nine Hostages, reputed to have ruled Ireland in the fifth century. After the Flight of the Earls in 1607 (see p.584), the English changed the name to that of their main garrison *Dún na nGall* ("fort of the foreigners"), which has a certain irony, because Donegal always eluded the grip of English power thanks to its wild and infertile terrain. Donegal is the most northerly part of Ireland, which confuses some into believing that it is part of Northern Ireland. It never actually has been, since in 1922, at the time of Partition, the Unionists believed that Donegal's Catholic population would threaten the stability of the new statelet by voting the county and the whole of the North back into the Republic.

Aside from the aforementioned places, Donegal's best-known destinations are the Glencolmcille Peninsula and around Ardara and Glenties in the southern part of the county, while other noteworthy areas are the Rosses and Gweedore, which are reminiscent of the more barren stretches of Connemara and make up the strongest Irish-speaking districts in the county.

12

GETTING AROUND

DONEGA

By bus The county has an extensive network of public and private bus services, with the sporadically interesting towns of Letterkenny and Donegal serving as its major transport hubs. However, there are limited services to some areas, especially outside high season.

By car You'll need your own transport to reach som outlying attractions, such as Glenveagh and parts of th Rosguill, Fanad and Inishowen peninsulas.

South Donegal

Entered via the N15 from Sligo (which now largely bypasses the most scenic spots), South Donegal might lack the wildness characteristic of much of Donegal's coastline, but the area still has some marvellous beaches, especially at **Bundoran** and **Rossnowlagh**, both popular surfing spots, while **Ballyshannon** is an attractive hillside town situated at the mouth of the River Erne. Further north, **Donegal town** has a pleasant bayside setting and remains of a notable castle, while to its north and southeast respectively lie graceful **Lough Eske** and **Lough Derg**, a major site for Catholic pilgrimage.

Ballyshannon festivals p.427
The Annals of the Four Masters p.429
Walks around Slieve League p.434
John Doherty p.439

Paddy "the Cope" Gallagher p.440
The Tory Island artists p.443
Walking in Glenveagh p.445

TORY ISLAND

Highlights

❶ **Slieve League** No visit to Donegal would be complete without a walk along the top of this mountain's awesome sea-cliffs. **See p.434**

❷ **Húdaí Beag's pub** Unquestionably one of the best traditional-music sessions in Ireland takes place here on Monday nights. **See p.442**

❸ **Tory Island** Bleak, barren, wet and windy – why would anyone choose to live here? Take a trip and discover a thriving local culture and a world quite different from the mainland. **See p.443**

❹ **Glebe House** Home of the late artist Derek Hill, Glebe House contains some of the most remarkable modern art in Ireland. **See p.446**

❺ **The Grianán Ailigh** This restored, circular stone fort commands unbeatable panoramic views of Donegal from its hilltop setting. **See p.455**

❻ **Malin Head** Ireland's most northerly point offers dramatic seascapes and, thanks to a lack of visitors, wonderfully unspoilt landscapes too. **See p.458**

HIGHLIGHTS ARE MARKED ON THE MAP ON PP.424–425

DONEGAL

0 ——— 20
kilometres

N

*ATLANTIC
OCEAN*

Tory Island
3
West Town East Town

Tory Sound

Inishbofin

Horn Head

Marble

*Bloody
Foreland*

Magheroarty

Falcarragh

N56

Dunfanac

Gortahork

*Muckish
Mountain*

Cre

Gola Island

Derrybeg

**Donegal
Airport** ✈

Bunbeg

GWEEDORE

Rannafast

Meenaleck

Crolly

*Errigal
Mountain
(752m)*

R351

Lough

**Glenve
Cast**

Rosses Bay

Annagry

Lough Nacung

Torneady Point

*Upper
Rosses*

Money Beg

*Poisoned
Glen*

Arranmore Island

Leabgarrow

Burtonport

*DERRYVEAGH
MOUNTAINS*

Lough Garte

Rutland Island

*Lower
Rosses*

Inishfree Upper

Dungloe

*Slieve Snaght
(683m)*

Crohy Head

N56

R254

Ulster Way

Doocharry

DONEG

*Gweebarra
Bay*

Fintown

Portnoo

Narin

Lettermacaward

Lough Finn

Kilclooney

♦ **Kilclooney Dolmen**

R253

Rosbeg

Dawros Head

Glenties

**Assarancagh
Waterfall**

Maghera

Ardara

N56

*BLUE STACK
MOUNTAINS*

Port

R261

N56

Glen Head

*Glengesh
Pass*

R262

Glen Bay

Glencolmcille

N56

Lough Eske

Malin Bay

Malinmore

Malinbeg

*SLIEVE
LEAGUE*

1

Carrick

Teelin

*Bunglass
Cliffs*

Kilcar

Killybegs

Dunkineely

Donegal

*Lo
D*

Carrigan Head

Muckros Head

*Inver
Bay*

St. John's Point

Rossnowlagh

Donegal Bay

Creevy

Ballyshannon

Mullaghmore Head

Bundoran

N15

Belleek

N15

Malin Head
6

Rossan

sguill insula

ings

Fanad Head

Dunaff Head

Pollan Bay

Daagh Isle

Malin

Culdaff Bay

Culdaff

Kinnagoe Bay

Clonmany

Ballyliffin

● Carrigart

Dunree Head

Portsalon

Mamore Gap

R244

Carndonagh

R238

Inishowen Head

Glen

Inishowen

Greencastle

Magilligan Point

▲ Slieve Snaght
(615m)

Moville

Ferry

● Kilmacrennan

Rathmullan

Buncrana

Gráinne's Gap

R238

R245

R247

Inch Island

Fahan

Lough Swilly

Lough Foyle

A2

Ramelton

Burnfoot

Burt

N56

Grianán Ailigh
(Stone Fort)
5

Derry

Letterkenny

N13

A6

N14

N13

Raphoe

Cavanacor House

Beltany Stone Circle

Lifford

N56

Strabane

A5

N15

A505

A5

Omagh

A32

A35

A5

Bundoran

Once described by an Irish newspaper as like "the back streets of Las Vegas only with cheaper hookers", **BUNDORAN** isn't quite that bad, but it's hard to avoid disappointment if the town is your first sight of Donegal. Lying at the county's southern extreme, this popular, though intermittently tacky, seaside resort offers little indication of the pleasures that lie beyond. It's 5km of Blue Flag beaches are among the finest in the country, and are a real pull for surfers of all abilities.

The tiny River Doran separates the more genteel **West End** from the **East End**, with its down-at-heel Main Street and a headland dominated by a **golf course**. Bundoran's chief attraction is the lovely golden-sanded **Tullan Strand**, a bracing stroll along the coastal promenade from the northern end of the town beach. The walk takes in rock formations known as the **Fairy Bridge** and the **Puffing Hole**, with the Atlantic thundering below and appetizing views across to the much more rewarding Glencolmcille Peninsula.

ARRIVAL AND DEPARTURE   BUNDORAN

By bus Buses stop at various points along Main Street. Destinations Ballyshannon (Mon–Sat 10 daily; 10min); Donegal Town (6–7 daily; 30min); Sligo (Mon–Sat 10 daily 35–50min).

INFORMATION AND ACTIVITIES

Tourist office The tourist office is by the bridge on Main Street (daily 9am–5pm; ☎ 071 984 1350).

Bike rental The Bike Stop, East End (Mon–Sat 8.30am–6pm, Sun noon–4pm; ☎ 085 248 8317; €15/day); also do repairs.

Surfing Tullan Strand and Rossnowlagh beach (see above) are exciting surfing spots, and tuition is available from Bundoran Surf Co., Main Street (☎ 071 984 1968, ⓦ bundoransurfco .com), Surfworld, Main Street (☎ 071 984 1223, ⓦ surfworld .ie), and Donegal Adventure Centre, Bayview Avenue (☎ 07 984 2418, ⓦ donegaladventurecentre.net); the latter also offe kayaking and canoeing.

ACCOMMODATION AND EATING

Great Northern Hotel On the headland east of town ☎ 071 984 1204, ⓦ greatnorthernhotel.com. Prominently sited, this huge hotel adjoining the fabulous Bundoran golf course has glorious views from just about eve ry room; facilities include spa and gym. **€120**

Homefield Rock Hostel Bayview Avenue, West End ☎ 071 982 9573, ⓦ homefieldrockhostel.com. Easy-going, music-themed hostel with a range of mixed and single-sex dorms plus private en-suite rooms, plus a large self-catering kitchen and a couple of lounge areas covered wall-to-wall with gig posters. Dorms **€18**, doubles **€50**

La Sabbia Bayview Avenue ☎ 071 984 2253, ⓦ lasabbiarestaurant.com. Next to *Homefield Roc Hostel*, this easy-going, evening-only restaurant is know principally for its gourmet burgers and pizzas, but the seafood, for example cod pasta and trout timbale, is no les appetizing. Daily 6–10pm.

Maddens Bridge Bar West End ☎ 071 984 2050 ⓦ maddensbridgebar.com. Wonderful, woody ba cluttered with hanging pots, jars, boots and suchlike Heading upstairs to the restaurant, grab a window seat an soak up the sparkling ocean views while tucking int meaty dishes like Lough Erne lamb shank, and beef an Guinness casserole (€10.95). Daily 11am–11pm.

Ballyshannon

The lively town of **BALLYSHANNON**, 6km north of Bundoran, was the site of a major battle in 1591 when Hugh Roe O'Donnell saw off the besieging English army, but nowadays its hilly streets become most animated during several upbeat festivals (see box, opposite).

St Anne's Church

Ballyshannon's main arteries form a wishbone leading up the town's steep northern slope, and signposted near the top of the left-hand branch is **St Anne's Church** and graveyard, built on the site of the ancient palace of Mullaghanshee. A simple marble slab, inscribed with the word "poet", lies left of the church, marking the burial place of locally born **William Allingham** (1824–89). His first volume, *Poems* (1850), includes his best-known work, *The Fairies* ("Up the airy mountain/Down the rushy glen/We daren't go a-hunting/

BALLYSHANNON FESTIVALS

The town's main event is the **Folk Festival** (ⓦ ballyshannonfolkfestival.com) over the first weekend in August, featuring major Irish and international musicians. Sticking with the musical theme, the **Rory Gallagher International Festival** (ⓦ rorygallagherfestival.com) on the last weekend of May pays homage to the local guitar legend, with concerts on several stages throughout town. Lastly, in November, the **Allingham Festival** (ⓦ allinghamfestival .com) brings to life the works of the native poet, through storytelling, screenings and workshops.

For fear of little men…"). Such verse attracted him to the Pre-Raphaelites – another work, *Day and Night Songs*, was illustrated by Rossetti and Millais – before Allingham moved on to the more serious poetic subject of his homeland. His posthumously published *Diary* recounts his friendships with literary contemporaries, most notably Tennyson.

Ballyshannon Museum

Slevins Department Store, Market Yard • Mon–Sat 10am–6pm • Free • ☎ 087 193 7166

To gain further insight into the history of the town – it lays claim to being Ireland's oldest – pop your head into the **Ballyshannon Museum**, peculiarly located on the top floor of the local department store (it's on the top floor, past the beds). In truth, it's a curiously mixed bag, with exhibits ranging from a cannonball from the Battle of Ballyshannon and wreckage retrieved from one of the three ships from the Spanish Armada sunk in the waters hereabouts, to some personal effects belonging to local notables William Allingham (first editions, writing box and ink well) and rock star Rory Gallagher, who died in 1995 (see above).

12

ARRIVAL AND DEPARTURE

BALLYSHANNON

By bus Buses drop off on, and depart from, the bottom of Main Street, near the bridge.

Destinations Belleek (9 daily; 10min); Bundoran (Mon–Sat 10 daily; 10min); Donegal town (6–7 daily; 25min); Sligo (Mon–Sat 10 daily; 45min–1hr).

ACCOMMODATION AND EATING

Dorrian's Imperial Hotel Main Street ☎ 071 985 1147, ⓦ dorriansimperialhotel.com. Handsome eighteenth-century building with warm and comfortable, if agreeably old-fashioned, rooms and public spaces, plus a decent bar and restaurant; it's fairly pricey, mind. **€120**

Elmbrook East Port ☎ 071 985 2615 ⊖ elmbrookbandb @eircom.net. Across the river and over the roundabout, this friendly B&B offers four tidily furnished en-suite rooms, and a comfy lounge for guests to enjoy, and you'll get a home-baked treat or two as well. March–Oct. **€65**

Lakeside Caravan and Camping Off the R230 Belleek Road ☎ 071 985 2822, ⓦ lakesidecaravanandcamping .com. Superb lakeside campsite with a full complement of facilities including modern shower blocks, laundry, games room plus a kids' playground. Canoe rental available too. Easter–Oct. **£20**

Nirvana The Mall ☎ 071 982 2369, ⓦ nirvana restaurant.ie. Sharp-looking restaurant-cum-wine-bar, serving comfort-food lunches and more extravagant evening meals like honey-glazed duckling with apricot stuffing and sweet plum sauce (€19.50). Also holds popular Tapas and Italian evenings. Tues–Fri 12.30–3pm & 5.30–9.30pm, Sat 5.30–9.30pm, Sun noon–9.30pm.

★ **The Thatch** Bishop Street ☎ 071 985 1147. An old fisherman's haunt, this diminutive little pub manifests a sweet cottage-kitchen interior with white-painted walls and red-painted doors – it's known for its legendary traditional music sessions, which could be any night the pub happens to be open. Wed, Fri & Sat 7pm–late.

ENTERTAINMENT

The Abbey Centre Market Street ☎ 071 985 2928, ⓦ abbeycentre.ie. Dynamic arts centre hosting a range of musical, cinematic and theatrical events, plus a regular, rotating programme of exhibitions. It's also one of the main venues for the town's several festivals (see above).

12

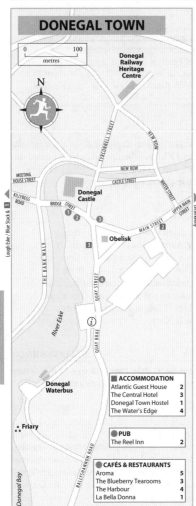

DONEGAL TOWN

0 ——— 100
metres

N

Donegal Railway Heritage Centre

TYRCONNELL STREET

NEW ROW

MEETING HOUSE STREET

NEW ROW

CASTLE STREET

WATER STREET

KILLYBEGS ROAD

BRIDGE STREET

Donegal Castle

THE BANK WALK

River Eske

MAIN STREET

UPPER MAIN STREET

Obelisk

QUAY STREET

QUAY BRAE

Letterkenny

Lough Eske / Blue Stack &

Donegal Waterbus

Friary

BALLYSHANNON ROAD

Donegal Bay

■ **ACCOMMODATION**
Atlantic Guest House ... 2
The Central Hotel ... 3
Donegal Town Hostel ... 1
The Water's Edge ... 4

● **PUB**
The Reel Inn ... 2

● **CAFÉS & RESTAURANTS**
Aroma ... 5
The Blueberry Tearooms ... 3
The Harbour ... 4
La Bella Donna ... 1

▼ 4 , 5 , Ballyshannon, Sligo & Donegal Craft Village

Donegal town and around

DONEGAL town is not the most exciting of places, but it's a pleasant enough spot to pass a few hours, rating one or two attractions and a fair sprinkling of hotels and restaurants clustered around its triangular and central **Diamond**, the old market place.

Many tourists head for the town in the mistaken belief that they'll find themselves in the midst of the county's famously wild terrain, and then discover its rather more sedate setting. However, southeast of the town, the landscape is replete with little lakes well stocked for fishing; the largest of these, and a place of pilgrimage, is **Lough Derg**. Less than 8km upriver from Donegal town is another spot of gentle natural beauty, **Lough Eske**, from where you can walk into the wilds of the **Blue Stack Mountains**, which rise to the north.

Donegal Castle

Tirconnell St • Easter to mid-Sept daily 10am–6pm; mid-Sept to Easter Mon & Thurs–Sun 9.30am–4.30pm • €4; Heritage Card • ☎ 074 972 2405

Donegal's original "fort of the foreigners" was thought to have been built on the banks of the River Eske by invading Vikings. Later, the first Red Hugh O'Donnell, king of Tír Chonaill, had a Norman-style tower house, known as **O'Donnell's Castle**, constructed on its site in the fifteenth century. When the English defeated the second Red Hugh in 1603, Sir Basil Brooke was given command of the town and it was he who rebuilt and extended the old castle, retaining the lower parts of the original tower, which had been razed to the ground by Red Hugh to prevent its capture. This well-restored example of Jacobean architecture is a fine marriage of strong defence and domestic grace, featuring mullioned windows, arches, ten gables and no fewer than fourteen fireplaces, over the grandest of which are carved the escutcheons of Brooke and his wife's family, the Leicesters. Brooke topped the tower with a Barbizon turret and added the mansion on the left, with the kitchens and bakery on the ground floor and living quarters on the floor above. Brooke was highly prolific in Donegal and was responsible for the overall design of the town.

Donegal Railway Heritage Centre

Tirconnell St • March–Dec Mon–Fri 10am–5pm; also July & Aug Sat & Sun 2–5pm • €3 • ☎ 074 972 2655, ⊛ donegalrailway.com

Railway fans will enjoy a visit to the **Donegal Railway Heritage Centre**, which occupies the Old Station House, standing just as it did when the County Donegal Railway, which ran from Derry to Ballyshannon, closed in 1959. Inside you'll find a model of the old railway alongside nostalgic memorabilia and some of the original station signs. Outside,

---

THE ANNALS OF THE FOUR MASTERS

In Donegal town's Diamond stands an obelisk commemorating the compilers of the famed **Annals of the Four Masters**. The Annals were begun in the town's **Franciscan friary**, whose ruined remains stand on the left bank of the River Eske, and were a systematic attempt to collect all known Irish documents into a history of the land beginning in 2958 BC, including mythical invasions by Firbolgs and Milesians, and ending in 1616 AD. The friary itself was built in 1474 by the first Red Hugh and his wife Nuala O'Brien of Munster. It was occupied by the English in 1601 and seriously damaged by the besieging O'Donnell army, being finally abandoned after the Flight of the Earls (see p.584). The Annals were completed by friars who had moved to a site by the River Drowse, near Kinlough, Country Leitrim. Manuscript copies of the Annals are occasionally on display at **Trinity College library** in Dublin.

---

you can enter a restored nineteenth-century coach and railcar, and while there's nothing inside, save for a DVD on the history of the railway, you may be lucky enough to catch one of the model railway exhibitions that are often held here. There's also a seven-and-a-quarter-inch-gauge train that shuttles passengers back and forth – it won't set the pulse racing, but it's good fun all the same. The old signal box now functions as a toilet.

Donegal Craft Village

Just outside town, down the Sligo road • Mon–Sat 9.30am–5.30pm • ☎ 074 972 5928, ⊛ donegalcraftvillage.com

The **Donegal Craft Village** comprises half a dozen or so workshops showcasing a range of local crafts, including glassware, textiles, painting and ceramics, jewellery and wood sculpture. Many of the items are available to buy, and there's a fabulous little café here too (see p.430).

Lough Eske and the Blue Stacks

The soft beauty of **Lough Eske** is easily accessible from Donegal town. To get here take the minor road that runs north of the river, signposted "Lough Eske Drive", 500m out on the Killybegs road. This leads to a forgotten forested estate, once belonging to the Brooke family but now owned by the Forestry Commission. The lough is no longer a particularly great fishing spot, though it is known as a place to catch char, a tasty 20cm-long species of the salmon family, which lurk in the depths at the centre of the lake, moving out to the shallower edges around late October, where they can easily be fished using worms. The sandy banks of the River Eske are also known for freshwater oysters – some of which are reputed to contain pearls – but they're a protected species so it's illegal to take them. The ruins of an **O'Donnell tower**, once a prison, stand on one of the small islands on the lake.

Carrying on along the western shore of Lough Eske, you'll reach the spot where the river flows in at the lough's northern tip. A dirt road here runs off to the left into the **Blue Stack Mountains**. At the top of the pathway that leads on from the track there are superb views over the lough. From here you can join the waymarked **Bluestack Way**, which passes Lough Belshade, guarded in legend by a huge black cat. If you're intending to tramp around the mountain range, it's best to keep to the skirts of the hills as there are many marshy patches on lower ground – and be prepared for misty pockets during bad weather.

Lough Derg and Station Island

Retreats May to mid-Aug • €30–55 • ☎ 071 986 1518, ⊛ loughderg.org • Buses from Ballyshannon or Enniskillen drop you in Pettigo village, though some continue to Lough Derg in the summer

In the middle of **Lough Derg**, 25km east of Donegal town, is a rocky islet known as **Station Island** or, more popularly, St Patrick's Purgatory, a retreat for Catholics needing rigour and solitude to recharge their faith. A national shrine of pilgrimage since the fifth century, it was described by Girardus Cambrensis in *Topography of Ireland* (1186) as "an island, one part of which is frequented by good spirits, the other by evil spirits". Contemporary scholars have argued that, as St Patrick never referred to Lough Derg in his writings, he probably never visited the island, but nevertheless it still thrives today as a strong centre for **pilgrimage**.

Participants in the three-day retreats abjure sleep and food (apart from black tea and toast) and walk barefoot over rocks, praying at Stations of the Cross around the island. *Station Island*, a collection by Seamus Heaney, contains a number of poems dealing with the mystique surrounding this ritual, while the late Pete McCarthy graphically recounted his experience of a retreat in *McCarthy's Bar* (see p.622). The island is approached via the R233 from **Pettigo**, 9km south. Pettigo also has a remarkable number of pubs for such a small village, suggesting an importance placed on spiritual nourishment of a rather different kind.

ARRIVAL AND DEPARTURE

DONEGAL TOWN

By bus Buses stop outside the *Abbey Hotel* on The Diamond. Destinations Ardara (Mon–Fri 3 daily, Sat & Sun 1 daily; 45min–1hr 10min); Ballyshannon (every 1hr–1hr 30min; 20–30min); Bundoran (7–9 daily; 30min); Derry (6–7 daily; 1hr 25min); Dungloe (Mon–Sat 3 daily, Sun 1; 1hr 30min); Enniskillen (8 daily; 1hr 10min); Glencolmcille (2–4 daily; 1hr 15min–1hr 30min); Glenties (Mon–Sat 3 daily, Sun 1; 35min–1hr 20min); Killybegs (Mon–Sat 8 daily, Sun 1; 30–45min); Letterkenny (7–9 daily; 50min); Sligo (7–8 daily; 1hr 5min).

INFORMATION AND ACTIVITIES

Tourist office The tourist office is located in a waterside building in The Quay car park (July & Aug Mon–Sat 9am–5pm, Sun 10am–3pm; Sept–June Mon–Sat 9am–5pm; ☎074 972 1148).
Boat tours Down at the quay, a Waterbus (€20; ☎074 972 3666, ⓦ donegalbaywaterbus.com; 1hr 10min) offers trips around Donegal Bay.
Bike rental Ted's, out on the Killybegs Road (around €20/day; ☎074 974 0774, ⓦ tedsbikeshop.ie), and The Bike Shop, Waterloo Place (around €20/day; ☎074 972 2515).

ACCOMMODATION

Atlantic Guest House Main St ☎074 972 1187, ⓦ atlanticguesthouse.ie. The best-value, and certainly the most hospitable, place in town, offering brightly coloured, if modestly sized, rooms, most with bathrooms but some just with sinks. **€80**
The Central Hotel The Diamond ☎074 972 1027, ⓦ centralhoteldonegal.com. Prominently positioned on the main town square, this refurbished hotel has bright and airy rooms (some overlooking the bay), and its own leisure centre with pool; although it's not cheap, they do offer some good deals. **€120**
Donegal Town Independent Hostel 800m out on the Killybegs road ☎074 972 2805, ⓦ donegaltownhostel .com. One of the county's best hostels, this welcoming and efficiently run place has two- to six-bed rooms (some with bathrooms), self-catering kitchen and lounge areas. Dorms **€17**, doubles **€44**
★**Harvey's Point Country Hotel** Towards the southern end of Lough Eske ☎074 972 2208, ⓦ harveyspoint.com. The rooms – essentially mini-suites – here offer nothing less than unbridled luxury, from the magnificently upholstered furnishings to the sumptuous, marble-tiled bathrooms and imperious lake views. The restaurant, with its theatrical open kitchen, is no less impressive; €49 for dinner. Nov–March closed Sun eve and all day Mon & Tues. **€200**
Solis Lough Eske Castle South of the Lough (and best approached from Donegal town via the N15 Lifford road) ☎074 972 5100, ⓦ solishotels.com/ lougheskecastle. This glorious five-star hotel and spa is set within a renovated Victorian castle in perfectly maintained grounds. Accommodation here ranges from swish doubles to lavish suites. **€220**
The Water's Edge Glebe, a few hundred metres up the Sligo road ☎074 972 1523, ⓦ thewatersedge.ws Beautifully kept house on the shores of the bay, offering comfortable en-suite rooms, some of which overlook the adjacent abbey. **€70**

EATING AND DRINKING

Aroma Donegal Craft Village, just outside town, down the Sligo road (see p.429) ☎074 972 3222. Exceptionally good coffee shop and home bakery serving a range of salads and savouries, including some spicy Mexican specials, plus lush cakes fresh from the oven. Mon–Sat 9.30am–5.30pm.
The Blueberry Tearooms Castle St ☎074 972 2933. A friendly place with a pretty, fairy-lit interior, serving excellent soups, sandwiches and lunches, but for a real treat, try one of the desserts, perhaps the steamed

chocolate pudding or a slice of homemade blueberry pie. Mon–Sat 9am–7pm.

The Harbour Quay St ☎074 972 1702, ☯theharbour .ie. Long-standing, local institution offering a wide-ranging, if slightly curious, mix of menus comprising seafood and steaks alongside stone-baked pizzas and a handful of Mexican dishes. Mon–Sat 5–10pm, Sun 3–9pm.

La Bella Donna Bridge St ☎074 972 5789, ☯labelladonnarestaurant.com. This sleek Italian establishment just about shades it as the pick of the town's restaurants, offering up some interesting variations on traditional dishes, such as Italian sausage and wild mushroom tagliatelle (€13.95). Tues–Sun 5–10pm.

The Reel Inn Bridge St ☎087 11 9994. The place to come in town for traditional music, and it's no exaggeration to say that there's something on here every night of the week, every day of the year. Music aside, this is a real boozer's pub with oodles of character, and characters. Daily 10.30am–midnight.

Southwest Donegal

The most appealing route out of Donegal town heads west along the shore of Donegal Bay all the way to Glencolmcille, some 50km away. Highlights along this coast include the tapering peninsula leading to **St John's Point** and extraordinarily dramatic coastal scenery, which reaches an apogee in the mammoth sea-cliffs of **Slieve League**. The **Glencolmcille Peninsula** is a Gaeltacht (Irish-speaking area) and its attractive villages are rich in traditional folklore and music.

St John's Point

Just west of the single-street village of **Dunkineely**, 17km west of Donegal town, a deviation left from the main road brings you down to *Castle Murray House Hotel* (see below). In the small car park opposite stands a sandstone rock **memorial** to some forty fishermen (it may have been more) who lost their lives in Bruckless Bay during a great storm on February 11, 1813; what is undisputed is that more than two hundred curraghs (wooden-framed boats covered in animal hides) were lost at sea that night. Though little documented, it constitutes one of Ireland's worst ever fishing tragedies.

From here, continue down a long, narrow promontory to **St John's Point**, where a crumbling castle stands at the tip and there are great **views** over Donegal Bay, especially back towards the narrow entry of Killybegs Bay, with **Rotten Island** at its mouth. This is one of the finest spots in all of Europe for scuba diving.

ACCOMMODATION AND EATING   **ST JOHN'S POINT**

Castle Murray House Hotel St John's Point ☎074 973 7022, ☯castlemurray.com. Although well regarded for its comfortable accommodation – not least the magnificent views – it's the French-inspired gourmet meals that people flock to this place for – for example, pan-fried turbot with white balsamic beurre blanc and shrimp foam; set dinner €48, Sun lunch €33. Booking recommended. Wed–Sat 12.30–3.30pm & 6.30–9.30pm, Sun 1.30–3.30pm & 6.30–8.30pm. **€130**

Killybegs

Sticking to the coast road west of Bruckless, you'll round Killybegs Bay and arrive in what was once the most successful fishing port in Ireland: **KILLYBEGS**, the halfway point between Donegal town and Glencolmcille.

After years of decline, this atmospheric little town appears to be on the up again, partly due to the ongoing development of the marina, though no less important has been the introduction of Killybegs as a destination for major cruise liners, this being one of very few deep sea ports in the country. Moreover, there are some excellent places to stay and eat at in and around town.

Around 8km west of town, en route to Kilcar, the road divides: for the scenic route, take the left-hand fork, a narrow switchback ride along the coastline with stupendous

12

views over the ocean, especially from **Muckross Head**, and the looming presence of the hills and mountains to your right.

Killybegs Maritime and Heritage Centre

Fintra Rd • Mon–Fri 9.30am–5.30pm • €5 • ☎ 074 974 1944, ⓦ visitkillybegs.com

Ever since Alexander Morton began producing hand-knotted carpets here in Donegal in 1898, the county has been one of the world's foremost carpet manufacturers, producing bespoke pieces for Buckingham Palace, the White House and the Vatican, among others. At the **Killybegs Maritime and Heritage Centre**, housed within the magnificent stone-and-timber framed barn that is the Killybegs carpet factory, you can witness first hand some of these beautiful pieces, many of which were produced on the factory's colossal 13m-long loom, the largest of its kind in the world. In its heyday, there were thirty looms rattling away here, but today there are just six, operated by a similar number of women. As well as watching a demonstration of the weaving process, visitors are encouraged to have a go themselves.

The second part of the centre focuses on the local fishing and maritime industry, with various displays, though the obvious attraction here is the Bridge Simulator, whereby you can attempt to navigate a vessel safely into dock.

ARRIVAL AND INFORMATION
KILLYBEGS

By bus Buses generally stop off and pick up in front of the Tara Hotel.

Destinations Ardara (Mon–Sat 4 daily, Sun 2; 20min); Carrick (2–4 daily; 30min); Donegal town (Mon–Sat 4 daily, Sun 2; 30–45min); Glencolmcille (2–4 daily; 45min); Glenties (Mon–Sat 4 daily, Sun 2; 45min); Kilcar (2–4 daily; 20min).

Tourist office The tourist office is located in a cabin on Shore Rd (June–Aug Mon–Sat 9.30am–5pm; Sept–May Mon–Fri 9.30am–5pm; ☎ 074 973 2346, ⓦ killybegs .ie); they can book accommodation here, and there are a couple of terminals for internet access. Note that there are no ATMs beyond Killybegs in the direction of Slieve.

ACCOMMODATION AND EATING

★**Bay View Hotel** Main St ☎ 074 973 1950, ⓦ bayviewhotel.ie. Handsome harbour-facing building which mixes classic and contemporary styles to dazzling effect, from the cool, crisp all-white rooms to the glittering elegance of the restaurant, which is where breakfast is taken. Pool and sauna too. **€89**

Kitty Kelly's Largy, on a bend in the road some 5km west of Killybegs ☎ 074 973 1925, ⓦ kittykellys.com. This sensitively restored farmhouse looks terrific and the food is divine; seafood is king here, so expect the likes of pan-roasted hake with crab hollandaise sauce and a cardamom and peach chutney (€22). They even offer a shuttle service from Killybegs for €2.50 per person. June–Sept daily 1–4.30pm & 5–9.30pm.

Mrs B's Main St ☎ 074 973 2656. Perky, cheerily staffed

coffee shop knocking up freshly prepared seafood chowder, sandwiches and quiches – including gluten-free options – but best of all, an enticing selection of homemade treats; takeaway coffee too. Mon–Sat 9am–5pm.

Ritz Hostel Fintra Rd, parallel to Main St ☎ 074 973 1309, ⓦ theritz-killybegs.com. As the name suggests, this was a former cinema, but it now operates as a top-of-the-range hostel with twins and doubles alongside four- and six-bed dorms, all with TVs; the self-catering facilities plus lounge and dining areas give it a real home-from-home feel. Dorms **€16**, doubles **€50**

Tara Hotel Main St ☎ 074 974 1700, ⓦ tarahotel.ie. A few paces from the Bay View Hotel, the Tara is a little more discreet, with sunny, if unspectacular, rooms facing either the harbour or, less attractively, the street behind. **€89**

Kilcar

The roads meet again at **KILCAR**, a pleasant village and a centre for the Donegal **tweed industry**: there are a couple of small factories open to visitors; try Studio Donegal (☎ 074 973 8194, ⓦ studiodonegal.ie) at the Glebe Mill in the centre of the village, where you can watch the spinners and weavers at work. The village hosts a three-day folk, blues and bluegrass **festival** on the May bank holiday weekend, plus a raucous street festival over the first weekend in August and a week-long traditional music festival during the same month. There are traditional music **concerts** in the Community Hall on Saturday evenings in summer.

ARRIVAL AND DEPARTURE

By bus Buses drop off and depart from the main street. Destinations Carrick (2–4 daily; 10min); Donegal town (1–3 daily; 50min–1hr 5min); Glencolmcille (2–4 daily; 25min); Killybegs (1–3 daily; 20min).

ACCOMMODATION

Derrylahan Hostel 3km west on the coast road towards Carrick ☎074 973 8079, ⊚homepage.eircom .net/~derrylahan. This place, set on a working farm, is one of the friendliest hostels in the country, with a mix of small dorms, a kitchen, common room with turf fire, and laundry; camping is also available, with its own washing and kitchen facilities. Dorms €18, doubles €50, camping €8

Mocklers Tearoom Main St ☎074 973 8870. Engaging brick-walled tearoom – all dinky wooden tables, cushioned seating and the odd little corner sofa – offering the classic combination of freshly brewed tea and freshly baked pastries; more substantial meals are rustled up on weekend evenings. Mon–Thurs & Sun 10am–6pm, Fri & Sat till 8pm.

Ocean Spray On the road towards Muckross Head ☎074 973 8438, ⊚oceanspray.littleireland.ie. A welcoming seaside B&B with three pine-heavy en-suite rooms, though only one has ocean views. €60

Carrick and Teelin

Derrylahan Hostel (see above) is an ideal base for exploring the beautiful countryside around **CARRICK**, especially Teelin Bay and the awesome Slieve League cliffs to the west. The southern road from Carrick to **TEELIN** follows the west bank of the River Owenee, whose rapids and pools are good for **fishing**. The village is Irish-speaking and rich in storytelling, with many stories having been recorded by the late Seán Ó'hEochaidh, Donegal's great folklorist.

12

ARRIVAL AND INFORMATION

By bus Buses drop off on, and depart from, Main Street. Destinations Donegal town (1–3 daily; 1hr–1hr 15min); Glencolmcille (2–4 daily; 15min); Kilcar (1–3 daily; 10min); Killybegs (1–3 daily; 30min).

Fishing and boat trips Licences are available from Teelin Sea Angling Club (☎074 973 9079). Sea-angling and sightseeing boat trips to the Slieve League cliffs are provided by Paddy Byrne, based down at the pier in Teelin (March–Oct; €20–25; ☎074 973 9365, ⊚sliabhleagueboattrips.com).

ACCOMMODATION AND EATING

Rusty Bar Teelin ☎074 973 9101. Teelin has a long musical tradition, and the best place to hear some local sounds is this cosy village pub, which has a dynamic Sat session, plus occasional music on other evenings too. Daily 11am–11pm.

Slieve League Lodge Carrick, in the centre of the village ☎074 973 9973, ⊚slieveleaguelodge.com. This jolly pub keeps twelve hostel-type rooms, all en suite and sleeping between two and four, plus a self-catering kitchen. The pub itself is Carrick's social hub, and has traditional music sessions most weekends. Set to one side of the pub is the Cook's Pantry, a self-sufficient café where you can pick up light lunches, cakes and coffee. Pub and café daily 11am–11pm. €50

Glencolmcille and around

As the road from Carrick approaches **GLENCOLMCILLE**, it traverses desolate moorland that's dominated by oily-black turf banks amid patches of heather and grass. After this, the rich beauty of the Glen, as it's known, comes as a welcome surprise. Settlement in the area dates back to the Stone Age, as testified by the enormous number of **megalithic remains** scattered around the countryside, especially court cairns and standing stones. There's evidence, too, of the Celtic era, in the form of earthworks and stone works. According to tradition, **St Columba** founded a monastery here in the sixth century, and some of the **standing stones**, known as the Turas Cholmcille, were adapted for Christian usage by the inscription of a cross. Every Columba's Day (June 9) at midnight, the locals commence a barefoot circuit of the fifteen Turas, including Columba's Chapel, chair, bed, wishing stone and Holy Well, finishing up with Mass at 3am in the village church. (Columba and Columbcille/

Colmcille are the same person – the latter is the name by which he was known after his conversion, and means "the dove of the church".)

Widespread emigration post-Famine and in the early twentieth century left the Glencolmcille area a typical example of rural decay. In 1951, however, a new and energetic curate, Father James McDyer, instigated efforts to revitalize the community, while retaining and strengthening its culture. Electricity arrived and road improvements reduced its isolation and allowed new collective enterprises in kntting and agriculture to thrive, and encouraged the development of local tourism.

Folk Village Museum and Heritage Centre

Doonalt • Easter–Sept Mon–Sat 10am–6pm, Sun noon–6pm • €4.50 • ☏ 074 973 0017, ⓦ glenfolkvillage.com

Just a stone throw's from the beach stands the wonderful **Folk Village Museum and Heritage Centre**, a cluster of replica thatched cottages, each equipped with the furniture and artefacts of the era it represents. Founded in 1967, the museum was the initiative of Father James McDyer (see above), whose life is celebrated in the first of the six buildings as you enter. The older cottages are notable for their bog oak and straw roofs and uneven flooring, which contrast markedly with those from the mid-nineteenth century, which manifest smoother, neater lines.

One building introduces you to the area's history and cultural heritage, including a door from a cupboard reputedly used by Charles Stuart (Bonnie Prince Charlie), who sought refuge here following the Battle of Culloden in 1746. The **Dooey School House** replica has a display of informative photographs and research projects, and a section on the American painter Rockwell Kent, who painted marvellous treatments of the area's landscapes during his time here in 1926. Close by is a wonderful example of an

WALKS AROUND SLIEVE LEAGUE

There are two routes up to the ridge of **Slieve League**. The less-used back one, known as Old Man's Track, follows the signpost pointing to the mountain just before Teelin and looks up continually to the ridge, while the frontal approach follows the signs out of Teelin to **BUNGLASS**, swinging you spectacularly round sharp bends and up incredibly steep inclines to one of the most thrilling cliff scenes in the world, the **Amharc Mór**. The sea moves so far below their peak that the waves appear silent, and the 600m face glows with mineral deposits in tones of amber, white and red. They say that on a clear day it is possible to see one-third of the whole of Ireland from the summit. **Sightsèeing tours** of the cliffs from the waters below are organized from Teelin, weather permitting (see p.433).

If you want to make a full day of it, you can climb up to the cliffs from the Bunglass car park and follow the path along the top of the ridge, which eventually meets Old Man's Track. From here One Man's Pass, a narrow path with steep slopes on each side, leads up to the summit of Slieve League. Bear in mind that the route can often be muddy and very windy – it is certainly not advisable in misty weather or if you suffer from vertigo. From the top of Slieve League, you can either retrace your steps to Teelin or continue west over the crest of the mountain and down the heather-tufted western slope towards the verdant headland village of **MALINBEG**, where there's a sublime, crescent-shaped golden strand enclosed by a tight rocky inlet. Malinbeg itself is a village of white bungalows, with the land around ordered into long narrow strips. On the cliff edge a ruined Martello tower faces **Rathlin O'Beirne Island**, 5km offshore, a place with many folklore associations. There are occasional boats across (enquire in Teelin – see p.433), but nothing to see aside from some early Christian stone relics and a ruined coastguard station.

Beyond Malinbeg, it's relatively easy to extend your walk through **MALINMORE** and on to Glencolmcille. The whole distance from Teelin to Malinmore can be comfortably completed in six hours.

ACCOMMODATION

The Malinbeg Hostel Malinbeg ☏ 074 973 0006, ⓦ malinbeghostel.com. Just a 5min walk from the beach, this well-equipped hostel offers exhilarating views from most of its rooms. Dorms €25, doubles €38

old-style **Pub-Grocers**, few of which exist today, but sweetest of all is the tiny **Fisherman's cottage**, which relays the history of the local fishing industry.

Glen Head, Port and Glenlough

From behind the hostel (see below), **cliff walks** steer off around the south side of the bay above a series of jagged drops. Rising from the opposite side of the valley mouth, the promontory of **Glen Head** is surmounted by a Martello tower. On the way out you pass the ruins of **St Colmcille's Church**, with its "resting slab" where St Columba would have lain down exhausted from prayer. North across this headland you can climb and then descend to the forgotten little cove of **Port** a few kilometres away, a village deserted since the 1940s. Absolutely nothing happens here – although Dylan Thomas once stayed in the next valley at **Glenlough**, renting a cottage for several weeks in a doomed attempt to "dry out" in an area replete with poteen stills.

The Glengesh Pass and Maghera

Heading northeast from Glencolmcille, the minor road to Ardara runs through the heart of the peninsula, travelling via the dramatic **Glengesh Pass** before spiralling down into wild but fertile valley land. Just before reaching Ardara, a road to the left runs along the southern edge of **Loughros Beg Bay** for 9km to **MAGHERA**, passing the transfixing **Assarancagh Waterfall**, from where you can embark on a hardy 10km waymarked walk uphill to the Glengesh Pass.

Maghera itself is an enchantingly remote place, dwarfed by the backdrop of hills and glens and fronted by an expansive and deserted strand that extends westwards to a rocky promontory riddled with **caves**. One of the largest is said to have concealed a hundred people fleeing Cromwell's troops; their light was spotted from across the strand and all were massacred except a lucky individual who hid on a high shelf. Most of the caves are accessible only at low tide and a torch is essential. Beware of the **tides**, however, as even experienced divers have been swept away by the powerful currents. Behind the village, a tiny road, unsuitable for large vehicles, runs up to the **Granny Pass**, an alternative and very scenic route to Glencolmcille.

12

ARRIVAL AND DEPARTURE

GLENCOLMCILLE AND AROUND

By bus Buses drop off on, and depart from, the centre of the village. Services to the Glencolmcille peninsula are much reduced outside July and Aug.

Destinations Carrick (1–3 daily; 15min); Donegal town (1–3 daily; 1hr 15min–1hr 30min); Kilcar (1–3 daily; 25min); Killybegs (1–3 daily; 45min).

ACCOMMODATION AND EATING

Dooey Hostel Glencolmcille ☎074 973 0130, ⓦglencolmcille.ie/dooey.htm. Positioned high above the fine shingle strand at the mouth of the valley, this offbeat hostel offers sensational views from each of its eight-bed rooms, as well as the communal areas, which means you'll hardly ever want to leave. To get here on foot, keep on the village road as far as the Folk Village, and then take a path up to the left; in wet weather the longer route by road may be easier (fork left 800m before the Folk

Village). Dorms €16; camping €10

Folk Village Tearoom Folk Village Museum, Glencolmcille (see opposite) ☎074 973 0017. After visiting the Folk Village Museum (and even if you don't), the teahouse at the Folk Village makes for a welcome pit stop with its warming comfort food like minestrone soup and fresh brown bread, and apple pie with cream, all of which is freshly made/baked on the premises. Mon–Sat 10am–6pm, Sun noon–6pm.

Central Donegal

The area around the bustling town of **Ardara** contains some of the most contrasting landscapes in Donegal. Rugged mountains lie to the southwest, traversed by the steeply sinuous **Glengesh Pass** and fringed by the unspoiled expanse of **Maghera** strand. Inland to the northeast sits the stately village of **Glenties**, while to the north the coastline forms peninsulas punctuated by the **Gweebarra** River, which, in turn, leads inland to the tranquil villages of Doocharry and Fintown, virtually surrounded by mountain scenery of an almost lunar quality.

Ardara

Sixteen kilometres north of Killybegs on the N56 lies lively **ARDARA**. Traditionally a weaving and knitwear centre, this is an excellent place to buy cheap **Aran sweaters**. Molloy's, 1km south of town, is the biggest outlet, but Kennedy's, uphill from The Diamond, the main square, is handier (its owner is also a mine of local tourist information); both stores are well stocked with hand-loomed knitwear and tweeds.

The Catholic **church** west of Ardara's Diamond has a striking stained-glass window, *Christ among the Doctors*, by the Modernist-inspired **Evie Hone**, one of the most influential Irish artists of the twentieth century. The authors of the Gospels are depicted symbolically with the infant Christ at the centre and David and Moses above and below. Traditional music is big business in this part of Donegal, and Ardara stages a plethora of festivals, the best of which are the **Cup of Tae** traditional music festival (ⓦcupoftaefestival.com) over the first weekend of May and the **Johnny Doherty** Music and Dancing Festival (ⓦjohnnydohertyfestival.com) at the end of September.

ARRIVAL AND INFORMATION ARDARA

By bus Buses drop off on, and depart from, The Diamond. **Destinations** Donegal town (2 daily; 30min–1hr 30min); Dungloe (Mon–Sat 3 daily; 40min); Glenties (Mon–Fri 3 daily, Sat & Sun 1 daily; 10–20min); Killybegs (Mon–Sat 1–2 daily; 20min).

Tourist office The tourist office is located inside the Heritage Centre on The Diamond (June–Aug Mon–Fri 10am–6pm, Sat 11am–4pm; Sept–May Mon–Fri 10am–6pm; ☎074 954 1704, ⓦardara.ie).

Bike rental is available from Don Byrne, just west of the Catholic church on West End (Tues–Sat 10am–6pm; ☎074 954 1658).

ACCOMMODATION AND EATING

Brae House Front Street ☎074 954 1296, ⓔbraehouse@eircom.net. Spruce, mint-coloured town house with five pleasing rooms spread over two floors, generally painted in gentle mauve and magenta tones – and a super-friendly welcome is guaranteed too. **€70**

Corner House Bar The Diamond ☎074 954 1736. A lovely, warming pub with a little log fire, that really cranks into gear at weekends when the traditional music sessions get going, though during the summer, there's a good chance of catching something most nights of the week. Daily 10.30am–midnight.

★**Nancy's** Front Street ☎074 954 1187. Run by the same family throughout its two-hundred-year-old history, the warren of small, cosy rooms spreading out from a central front bar are utterly delightful. The food is first rate too, with mussels in white wine and garlic (€12) typical of a largely seafood oriented menu. March–Oct Mon–Sat noon–11.30pm, Sun 12.30–11pm; Nov–Feb Mon–Sat 4–11.30pm, Sun 4–11pm.

Nesbitt Arms Hotel The Diamond ☎074 954 1103, ⓦnesbittarms.com. Named after George Nesbitt, a prominent eighteenth-century landowner in these parts, this similarly aged hotel is a decent, if somewhat pricey, option. **€99**

Woodhill House 1km east of town ☎074 954 1112, ⓦwoodhillhouse.com. This stylish seventeenth-century manor house is set in its own extensive grounds with rooms in both the main house and converted outbuildings. Its restaurant offers classic French-Irish-influenced cuisine (grilled sea bass on a Julienne of leek with a Chablis reduction) and is well worth the €38 per head for the three-course dinner. Restaurant daily 6.30–10pm. **€95**

Glenties

Set at the foot of two glens 10km east of Ardara, **GLENTIES** is a tidy village, with a beautiful modern **church**, at the Ardara end of town, designed by the Derry architect

Liam McCormack; its vast sloping roof reaches down to 2m from the ground, and rainwater drips off the thousand or so tiles into picturesque pools of water. In October, the town is overrun, thanks to the enormously popular **Fiddlers Festival**, when the town's pubs heave with fiddlers from across the world.

St Conall's Museum and Heritage Centre

Opposite the church • May–Oct Mon–Sat 10am–1pm & 2–4.30pm • €2.50

This is one of the best small-town museums in the country and displays much material of local interest, focusing on wildlife, Donegal's railways, antiquities, and the effects of the Great Famine. There's a special display on local music, featuring the travelling Doherty family (see opposite) and an old 1885 Edison phonograph. Upstairs is devoted to the playwright **Brian Friel**, whose mother hailed from here – his film, *Dancing at Lughnasa*, bears a dedication to "The Glenties Ladies" and was partly filmed in the neighbourhood – and the town's most famous son, author **Patrick MacGill**, whose semi-autobiographical *Children of the Dead End* brilliantly recounts the wayward lives of migrant navvies: a summer school is held in his honour in late July, attracting hundreds of people to its exhibitions, seminars and literary debates (ⓦmacgillsummerschool.com).

By bus Buses drop off on, and depart from, Main St. Destinations Ardara (2–3 daily; 10–20min); Donegal town (2–3 daily; 45min–1hr 30min); Dungloe (Mon–Sat 2–3 daily; 30min).

ACCOMMODATION AND EATING

Glen Inn 5km out on the Ballybofey road. A bar-cum-grocery beautifully situated by the river at the foot of the Blue Stack Mountains. There are sessions here most Fri and Sat nights, often featuring one of the Campbell brothers, well-known fiddlers in these parts and beyond. Open daily.

Highlands Hotel Main Street ☎074 955 1111, ⓦhighlandshotel.ie. Long-standing village hotel with comfortable, if occasionally dated, rooms. A plaque commemorates the room where actress Meryl Streep stayed for the local premiere of *Dancing at Lughnasa*. The Sun-night music sessions here are worth looking in for. **€90**

Kennedy's Main Street ☎074 955 1050, ⓦkennedysbarandrestaurant.com. Modern restaurant set over two floors serving big portions of steaming comfort food like battered cod with chips (€12.50), though it's just as much fun to take a stool at the long bar and kick back with a pint. June–Sept daily noon–midnight; Oct–May Thurs–Sat noon–midnight.

Lisnadar B&B Mill Rd ☎074 955 1800, ⓦlisdanar .com. Just a 5min walk from the centre of the village, this is by far the most appealing of Glenties' several guesthouses. Set within extensive gardens, the house has four big rooms, with a guest lounge and breakfast conservatory attached – the hospitality is second to none. **€59**

The Dawros Head Peninsula and around

To the immediate north of Ardara, the **Dawros Head Peninsula** is much tamer than Glencolmcille, with many tiny lakes dotting a quilt of low hills. The terrain of purple heather, fields, streams and short glens makes a varied package for the enthusiastic walker. The first turning off the R261 Narin road leads to **ROSBEG**, an isolated village, straggling beside a series of rock-strewn coves, which nevertheless has a campsite (see p.440).

If you're heading directly from Ardara towards Narin and Portnoo, in **KILCLOONEY** look out for the **Kilclooney dolmen**, just before the pastel-shaded church on the right. These are probably the best-preserved portal stones in the country, with the capstone measuring over 4m long and the structure reckoned to date from around 3500 BC.

Doon Fort

Turn left at the "Rosbeg/Tramore Beach" signpost 1km or so before Narin, then head right up the lane just after a school; a few hundred metres later you'll see a sign for boat rental leading down to a farmhouse, where you can rent a rowing boat inexpensively to take you across to the island

Continuing onwards towards Narin, the most worthwhile sight on the peninsula is **Doon Fort**, which occupies an entire oval-shaped islet in the middle of **Lough Doon**. The idyllic setting, rarely disturbed by visitors, makes the hassle of getting there worth it: although its walls are crumbling, the fort has been untouched for over two thousand years. The walls stand 5m high and 4m thick; their inner passages were used in the 1950s for storing poteen.

Narin and Iniskeel Island

In **NARIN** the spearheaded, 4km-long **strand** is a wonderful beach, safe for bathing. At low tide you can walk out to **Iniskeel Island**, where St Conal founded a monastery in the sixth century. This has long since disappeared, but there are the ruins of two twelfth-century churches with some cross-inscribed slabs.

Doocharry

East of Narin the N56 hugs the shoreline, twisting and turning until it crosses the Gweebarra and enters Lettermacaward. From here a minor road follows the river 8km inland to tiny **DOOCHARRY**, with just a pub and a grocery, which acts as the gateway to some of the most dramatic scenery in the county. From here, you can head further upstream northeast along a narrow and tortuous lane past **Slieve Snaght**, through the **Glendowan Mountains** and skirting the southern edge of the **Glenveagh National Park** to **Lough Gartan** (see p.446). The desolate though beautiful countryside bears little sign of human impact and you'll be lucky to see any life beyond the odd sheep or fluttering bird.

Fintown

A more major road heads 9km southeast from Doocharry through rugged, rock-strewn moorland to **FINTOWN**, a simple roadside village set at the foot of towering mountains in the Finn Valley where the river broadens to form an elongated strip of lake.

Narrow-gauge railway

Fintown (signposted) • 40min journeys on the hour: June & Sept Mon–Wed 11am–4pm, Sun 1–5pm; July & Aug Mon–Sat 11am–4pm, Sun 1–5pm • €8 • ☎ 074 954 6280, ☻ antraen.com

You can take a waterside trip along a restored section of the old County Donegal narrow-gauge **railway**. In its late nineteenth-and early twentieth-century heyday, the railway extended for some 200km, before the gradual increase in the use of road traffic to shift freight forced the line's closure in 1959.

JOHN DOHERTY

Fintown's cemetery is the resting place of Donegal's **greatest traditional fiddler**, **John Doherty** (c.1895–1980), whose dynamic yet intricate style remains a major influence on the region's fiddle players, over thirty years after his death. Many of the tunes you'll hear played in Donegal today owe their origins to his repertoire and that of his brothers, Mickey and Simon, and several excellent CDs of his work are still available.

Lake House Hotel Clooney, 1.5km east of Narin ☏074 954 5123, ⓦlakehousehotel.ie. This lovely country residence dates from 1847 and provides high-quality accommodation, including self-catering cottages with open-hearth fires, and a fine restaurant with an eclectic menu; three courses €27.95. Restaurant Mon–Sat 6–9pm, Sun 1–9pm. **€100**

Tramore Beach Rosebeg ☏074 955 1491 ⓦtramorebeach-rosbeg.com. Wonderful little camping spot among the dunes, with some two dozen pitches and decent facilities including shower/toilet block and shop. Easter–Sept. **€15**

The Rosses

The **Rosses**, a vast expanse of rock-strewn land and stony soil, is a strong Gaeltacht area. Dotted with over 120 tiny lakes, the crumpled terrain stretches from **Dungloe** in the south to **Crolly** in the north, but the forbidding nature of much of the landscape meant most settlements could only survive near the sea, so following the shoreline route around the Rosses is far more rewarding than the more direct road north.

Dungloe

An Clochán Liath is the name you'll see on signposts approaching **DUNGLOE**, referring to the grey-coloured stepping stones that were once used to cross the river here. The modern Anglicized version comes from Dún gCloiche, the name of a stone fort situated on a rock a few kilometres offshore. When the fair that was held at the fort moved in the eighteenth century to the village of An Clochán Liath, which had grown up around the stepping stones, the fort's name stuck, though Irish-speakers still refer to the town by its original name. For fans of Daniel O'Donnell aside, there's little to detain you here, but at the end of July, the **Mary From Dungloe festival** (ⓦmaryfromdungloe.com), centred around a rather wholesome beauty pageant, provides a good pretext for general festivities, plenty of music and street entertainment. There's no antiquity behind the festival's origins or name – it dates from 1968 and the title comes from an Irish hit single by the Emmet Spiceland band.

Daniel O'Donnell Visitor Centre

Main St • April–Oct Mon–Sat 10am–6pm, Sun noon–6pm • €5 • ☏074 952 2334, ⓦdanielodonnellvisitorcentre.com

Attracting fans from far and wide, the **Daniel O'Donnell Visitor Centre** pays homage, literally, to the local pop star crooner, who was born in the town and still lives in the area. Among the wealth of exhibits are old schoolbooks, the jumper that he wore for his first concert, and a stack of gold and platinum discs – O'Donnell was the first artist to have an album in the British charts for twenty-five consecutive years. Inevitably, the exhibition is not short on tack, with one glittering cabinet stuffed with wedding paraphernalia, including his and his wife's wedding outfits; you don't have to be a fan to enjoy this, but it helps.

By bus Buses drop off on, and depart from, Main Street. Destinations Ardara (2 daily; 45min); Donegal town (2 daily; 1hr 15min–1hr 30min); Glenties (2 daily; 30min). **Tourist office** The tourist office is on Chapel Rd, in the old

---

PADDY "THE COPE" GALLAGHER

Dungloe is synonymous with the rejuvenating work of **Paddy "the Cope" Gallagher** (1871–1966), who envisaged the salvation of the Rosses' then poor communities through cooperative ventures, in particular by reducing their dependency on moneylenders. Oddly enough, the enterprise's practical origins lay in Paddy's discovery that the price of manure was reduced when purchased by societies. As a result, he founded the Templecrone Co-operative Agricultural Society (the "Cope") in 1906, and its central branch still stands proudly on Dungloe's main street, with others elsewhere in the Rosses.

church just off the top of Main Street (June & Sept Mon–Fri 10am–1pm & 2–5.30pm; July & Aug Mon–Fri 10am–1pm & 2–5.30pm, Sat 10.30am–1pm & 2–4pm; ☎074 952 1297). In the same building, the library offers internet facilities.

ACCOMMODATION AND EATING

Doherty's 16 Main Street ☎074 952 1654. A no-fuss all-rounder serving breakfasts, lunches and dinners, plus takeaways. Coffees and pastries too. Mon–Fri 9am–8.30pm, Sat 9am–10pm.

Patrick Johnny Sally's Bar Main Street ☎074 952 1479. At the top of the street, this chunky grey-stone building is a genuine old-timers' pub, with a terrace offering fabulous views of the ocean. No TVs or music, just a good old-fashioned drinking den. Mon–Sat 10.30am–11.30pm, Sun noon–11pm.

Radharc an Oileain Quay Road ☎074 952 1093, ✉gbmccauley@eircom.net/dungloebedabdbreakfast .com. Located a few minutes' walk from Main St, this modern, family-run bungalow has three terrific en-suite rooms, with wet rooms, all of which overlook the bay. **€70**

Burtonport

Seven kilometres northeast of Dungloe, **BURTONPORT** is the embarkation point for **Arranmore Island** and, if you can find a boatman at the harbour to take you out, for other smaller islands. In the late eighteenth century, the village's founder, William Burton, attempted to establish **Rutland Island**, just offshore, as a major trading centre, and consequently this area became the first English-speaking district in the whole of Donegal. During the 1798 Rebellion **James Napper Tandy** landed on the island with French troops, but became somewhat inebriated on hearing of Wolfe Tone's capture and was carried back on board (see p.586). Apart from busy activity at the harbour, Burtonport has little to say for itself.

12

Arranmore Island

Arranmore's permanent population of around eight hundred people is almost entirely concentrated along the eastern and southern coastlines – the island's main village, **LEABGARROW**, is on the eastern side. The high centre-ground of bogland and lakes reaches a greater altitude than anywhere else in the Rosses, and it's well worth hiking a few hundred metres upland for great views back across the water to Burtonport.

A circuit of the whole island, with cliff-top views of the Atlantic, takes around six hours, and the terrain isn't especially taxing though it can be blustery. Many ships have foundered in the choppy seas hereabouts, but in 1983 the lone American yachtsman Wayne Dickenson landed on the island's west coast after 142 days at sea in the smallest boat ever to cross the Atlantic. In the cliffs below St Crone's Church on the southern shore is **Uaimh an Áir** (the "cave of slaughter"), where seventy hiding islanders were massacred in the seventeenth century by a certain Captain Conyngham, in an action that lay somewhat outside his remit from Charles I to rid the Rosses of "rogues and rapparees". Two islanders later took revenge by killing the captain in Dunfanaghy. Uninhabited **Green Island**, at the southwestern tip, is now a **bird sanctuary** and rare species have been spotted hereabouts, including the snowy owl in 1993. The most dramatic of the several **beaches** is at the northwestern end of the island, on the way to the lighthouse and approached by a set of steps down the side of a perpetually crumbling cliff.

ARRIVAL AND DEPARTURE   ARRANMORE

By boat Arranmore Ferry runs a car ferry (6–9 sailings daily; 15min; €15 return; ☎074 952 0532, ⓦarranmoreferry.com), as does Arranmore Car and Passenger Ferries (5–7 sailings daily; 15min; €15 return; ☎087 317 1810, ⓦarranmorefastferry.com).

ACCOMMODATION AND EATING

Facilities on the island are limited, but there are a number of places to sleep, and several pubs – none particularly stands out, but they suffice for a pint and some local banter.

Glen Hotel Leabgarrow ☎074 952 0505, ⓦtheglenhotel.weebly.com. Nineteenth-century hotel in pleasant grounds just a 5min walk from the ferry pier; the rooms won't set the pulse racing, but they're clean and decently priced. The restaurant here is the best place to eat on the island. Restaurant daily 12.30–9pm. **€70**

Gweedore and Tory Island

Like its southern neighbour, the Rosses, the interior of the **Gweedore** district is largely desolate and forbidding country, and settlements again cling to the shoreline. To the southwest lie the villages of **Bunbeg** and **Derrybeg**, their cottages sprinkled across a blanket of gorse and mountain grasses. The ruggedness intensifies as it continues up the coast and round the Bloody Foreland to Gortahork in the Cloghaneely district, yet surprisingly, there has been significant house-building here and the area is quite densely populated. Some distance offshore lies Ireland's most literally isolated community, Irish-speaking **Tory Island**, a place rich in folkloric and musical traditions.

Bunbeg

The main appeal of the roadside village of **BUNBEG** is its gorgeous little harbour, 1.5km from the village along an enchanting rollicking road. Packed with smallish trawlers, it's also the departure point for year-round **ferries** to Tory Island (see opposite), as well as boat trips to uninhabited **Gola Island** in summer (☎087 660 7003; €10).

12

ACCOMMODATION AND EATING   BUNBEG

Bunbeg House Down by the harbour ☎074 953 1305, ⓦbunbeghouse.com. Pleasant B&B in a fantastic spot, with sparky little rooms offering waterside views. It's almost worth staying here just to enjoy breakfast on the outdoor terrace. March–Oct. **€75**

★**Leo's Tavern** Meenaleck, 5km south of Bunbeg ☎074 954 8143, ⓦleostavern.com. This famous pub is run by a member of the Brennan family. Parents, Leo and Baba, were both well known on the dance-band circuit in the 1950s and 1960s, though other family members have achieved greater fame. Three of their children (Máire, Pól and Ciarán) were members of the group Clannad, and another is the celebrated singer/musician Enya – the pub's

walls are decorated with a variety of awards and mementos. As you might expect, the music sessions, including open-mic nights, are superb. Mon–Fri 4pm–midnight, Sat & Sun noon–midnight.

★**Teach Húdaí Beag** By the harbour crossroads ☎074 953 1016. Fantastic pub, which hosts a famous Mon-night traditional session, sometimes involving as many as twenty musicians, as well as a smaller Fri-night one too. Best of all, though, is the riotous Cabaret Craiceáilte on the last Sat of the month, where all manner of genres (roots, reggae, contemporary) are performed in Gaelic. Like Leo's, it pulls in some stellar names. Opening times often at whim of owner, but typically daily 4pm–midnight.

Glassagh

At **GLASSAGH**, about 7km north of Derrybeg, the road climbs abruptly to Knockfola, loosely translated as the **Bloody Foreland**, a grim, stony, almost barren zone, crisscrossed by stone walls, and so-called because of the red hue acquired by its heather from the light of the setting sun. From Knockfola, the road turns eastwards hugging the side of the mountain, with the bogland and its hard-worked turf banks stretching below towards the Atlantic. You should be able to spot the distinctive shape of **Tory Island** far out to sea and, at **MAGHEROARTY**, 8km east of Derrybeg, a road runs down to the pier, where you can pick up a ferry to the island (see, opposite) and possibly arrange a trip to largely deserted **INISHBOFIN**, just offshore.

ACCOMMODATION   GLASSAGH

Teac Jack Glasslagh ☎074 953 1173, ⓦteacjack.com. If you fancy lingering a while, the best place to stay is this prominent roadside hotel, with bunks in some rooms, at level

just beyond budget. The hotel's enormous horseshoe-shaped bar, meanwhile, is a great venue for the regular programme of music and dancing, typically Tues, Thurs and Sat nights. **€70**

THE TORY ISLAND ARTISTS

Tory islanders are famed for their **painting**, a development that originated in a chance encounter between the English painter Derek Hill and one of the island's fishermen, **James Dixon**, in 1968, both now deceased. Dixon had never lifted a brush before the day he told Hill that he could do a better job of painting the Tory scenery, but he went on to become the most renowned of the island's school of **primitive painters** – Glebe House has a remarkable painting by him (see p.446). You can view the islanders' work and, more than likely, meet the artists, at the **James Dixon Gallery**, the originator's former home, a little way to the east of the harbour.

Tory Island

With its ruggedly indented shores pounded by the ocean, **TORY ISLAND**, though only 12km north of the mainland, is notoriously inaccessible. Only 4km long and less than 1.5km wide, its vulnerability to the elements means little can grow here. Yet despite the island's barren landscape and the ferocity of the elements, the Tory islanders are thriving, a situation no one could have predicted thirty years ago. Back then, conditions on the island were very poor, lacking essential amenities such as a water supply, proper sanitation, reliable electricity and a ferry service. The arrival of a new priest, **Father Diarmuid Ó Péicín**, in the early 1980s stimulated a transformation. Rallying the islanders, the pastor began to lobby every possible target, securing backing from such disparate characters as the US senator Tip O'Neill (who had Donegal ancestry) and the late Ian Paisley. The campaign attracted media attention and conditions gradually began to improve. Nowadays, around 160 people live permanently on the island and 25 children attend the local junior school, a happy sign of the island's revival (older children spend term times in Falcarragh).

According to local mythology, Tory was the stronghold of the **Fomorians**, who raided the mainland from their island base and whose most notable figure was the cyclops **Balor of the Evil Eye**, the Celtic god of darkness. Intriguingly, the local legend places his eye at the back of his head. There's also said to be a crater in the very heart of the island that none of the locals will approach after dark, for fear of incurring the god's wrath. In the sixth century, **St Colmcille** landed on Tory with the help of a member of the Duggan family. In return, the saint made him king of the island; the line has been unbroken ever since, and you're more than likely to meet the present king, **Patsy Dan Rodgers**, who regularly greets arrivals at the harbour.

Some monastic relics from St Columba's time remain on Tory, the most unusual of which – now the island's emblem – is the **Tau Cross**. Its T-shape is of Egyptian origin, and is one of only two such monuments in the whole of Ireland. It has now been relocated and set in concrete on Camusmore Pier in West Town, one of the island's two villages. There are other mutilated stone crosses and some carved stones lying around, several by the remains of the **round tower** in West Town, which is thought to date from the tenth century and is uniquely constructed from round beach stones. A local superstition focuses on the **wishing stone** in the centre of the island, three circuits of which will supposedly lead to your desires being granted.

12

ARRIVAL AND DEPARTURE   TORY ISLAND

By boat Turasmara (☎ 074 953 1320, ⊛ toryislandferry .com) operate two year-round, daily services to Tory island (from Bunbeg Mon & Fri 7.45am, Tues–Thurs, Sat & Sun 8.45am; from Magheroarty daily 11.30am & then either 3pm, 4pm or 5pm depending upon the month, with extra sailings 1.30pm & 7pm in July & Aug; return trip from either departure point €22). Departure times for both services are often affected by the tides and the weather, so always call ahead to check.

ACCOMMODATION AND EATING

Óstán Thoraigh By the landing stage ☎ 074 913 5920, ⓦ hoteltory.com. The *"Harbour View"* Hotel provides comfortable accommodation in twelve rooms, plus one of only two bars on the island, and a fine seafood restaurant.

The owners here also organize a range of summer events, including traditional music and song, painting and birdwatching weekends, as well as running the Dive Tory centre for aquatic fans. **€70**

The Derryveagh Mountains and Glenveagh

Inland from Gweedore lies some of the most dramatic scenery in Donegal, an area dominated by mountains such as **Errigal** and **Slieve Snaght**, and loughs of startling beauty. This is popular hill-walking country, especially along the Poisoned Glen, part of the much-visited **Glenveagh National Park**. Further on, towards Letterkenny, the countryside becomes gentler and increasingly verdant, especially in the environs of **Lough Gartan**, an area rich in associations with St Columba.

The loughs and Mount Errigal

Heading east on the N56 from Gweedore, the imposing and starkly beautiful mass of **Mount Errigal** becomes increasingly prominent. From a distance the mountain appears to be snow-covered, but skirting the northern shore of **Lough Nacung**, it becomes apparent that the white coloration has geological, rather than meteorological, causes.

Quite often the area around Errigal is shrouded in mist, but on a clear day the beauty of the mountain is unsurpassable, its silvery slopes resembling the Japanese artist Hokusai's images of Mount Fuji. The hour-long hike up to the top is a must, and there's a waymarked trail from the road, 2km past the Poisoned Glen turn-off, up the southeast ridge. The climb to the summit is well worth it for the stupendous **views**: virtually all of Donegal, and most of Northern Ireland, is visible, and you could easily spend several hours just sitting and absorbing the contrasts provided by coastline, loughs and mountains.

Dunlewey Lakeside Centre

April–Oct daily 10.30am–5pm • Tour of cottage, farm and outbuildings €5.95; boat trip €5.95; combined tour and boat ticket €10; pony rides €3; treks €20–25 • ☎ 074 953 1699, ⓦ dunleweycentre.com

Back down in Money Beg, a lane runs south to the narrow strip of land which divides Lough Nacung from Dunlewey Lough. On the way there's the **Dunlewey Lakeside Centre**, an impressive visitor centre by the shore. The key attractions here are a tour around the cottage of the notable local weaver, Manus Ferry, where you'll get to see demonstrations of spinning and weaving, and a **boat trip** around Dunlewy Lough, which is a lovely thirty-minute excursion. This extremely child-friendly centre extends to a small farmyard "zoo", adventure playground (included in tour price) and pony rides; the trekking centre here also offers a range of cross-country treks. And once you're done with that little lot, there's an excellent **restaurant** and a crafts shop.

Dunlewey is also an important centre for traditional music, and between June and August, there are concerts (€8) in the centre every Tuesday at 8.30pm; during the rest of the year, there are occasional concerts (free) on Sundays at 1.30pm.

ACCOMMODATION

THE LOUGHS AND MOUNT ERRIGAL

An Chúirt Hotel On the N56, 5km east of Bunbeg ☎ 074 953 2900, ⓦ gweedorecourthotel.com. You can stay very comfortably at the rather grand *"Gweedore Court"* Hotel, which, although largely catering to wedding parties, makes for a good base if spending some time in the loughs. **€90**

Errigal Hostel Dunlewey ☎ 074 953 1180, ⓦ anoige.ie.

Situated in the shadow of Mount Errigal, this is a stunning purpose-built place, entirely in keeping with the area. It features private en-suite doubles, plus four-bed rooms and innovative split-level six-bed dorms, internet room, laundry and self-catering kitchen, plus bike rental (€20 per day). March–Oct. Dorms **€19**, doubles **€50**

WALKING IN GLENVEAGH

To reach the **Poisoned Glen**, head a little way further east of Money Beg on the R251 and take the signposted lane leading downhill to the right. Just below the ruined church at the eastern end of Lough Nacung turn off to the left and follow the track over the old bridge. The path dwindles away and you should follow the left bank of the river deep into the gorge until it turns sharply left. Walk through the water here, usually just a trickle in summer, to the opposite bank and climb up towards a granite crest. From here, walk beside the small stream through a gully and finally you'll emerge on a ridge. It's not an easy tramp, for a lot of the ground is marshy, but the views are fantastic, with the River Glenveagh flowing into Lough Beagh down below.

You're now in the **Glenveagh National Park** and may well see deer hereabouts. If you don't want to retrace your tracks and are prepared for a longer hike, you have a number of options. However, it's vital to follow all the basic rules of hill-walking and essential to keep to the designated roads and paths during the winter deer-culling season (Sept–Feb), or you run the risk of being shot. Experienced hill-walkers will probably be tempted by the sight of **Slieve Snaght**, the highest point in the park, off to the southwest. Alternatively, if you head downhill to the southeast, the Glendowan road at the bottom leads eastwards to **Lough Gartan** (see p.446) and westwards to **Doocharry** (see p.439). If you take the road east towards Gartan for a short distance, an old disused vehicle track to the left will lead you down the barrel of the glen alongside the river to Lough Glenveagh.

Glenveagh National Park

According to legend, the **Poisoned Glen**, east of Dunlewey Lough, is where the cyclops Balor of the Evil Eye (see p.443) was slain by Lugh, poisoning the ground on which his single eyeball fell. There are many other explanations for the origins of its name, from the darkly conspiratorial (the glen's waters were polluted to kill English soldiers) to the purely botanical (poisonous Irish spurge used to grow here).

National Park Visitor Centre and Glenveagh Castle

Visitor Centre Daily: March–Oct 9.30am–6pm; Nov–Feb 9am–5pm; restaurant Easter–Sept 10.30am–5pm • Free •
ⓦ www.glenveaghnationalpark.ie **Castle** Obligatory guided tours daily 10am–5pm; tearooms Easter–Sept 10.30am–5pm • €5
• Minibuses (€3 return) from visitor centre (no cars beyond here), otherwise a 40min walk

Located at the northernmost end of Lough Veagh, the **Glenveagh National Park Visitor Centre** has detailed and interactive displays on the area's ecology and geology. More interesting is the exhibition on the park's wildlife, and in particular its eagles, whose population died out here in the early 1900s; in 2000, a programme to reintroduce golden eagles was established, and it is estimated that there are currently seven pairs in this corner of County Donegal. There's also a reasonably priced restaurant here, though it's not as enjoyable as the Castle tearooms.

From the visitor centre, minibuses shuttle back and forth to **Glenveagh Castle**, built on a small promontory for wealthy landowner George Adair between 1870 and 1873. Adair was the creator of the estate that now forms much of the park, but while you might admire the end product, it's impossible to condone the means by which it was achieved. Though some land was obtained through purchase, during what is now known as the **Derryveagh Evictions**, Adair evicted 244 tenants during the bitterly cold April of 1861, forcing many into the workhouse and others to emigrate to Australia. The rhododendron-filled gardens surrounding the castle were very much the work of Adair's wife, Cornelia, who also introduced herds of red deer to the estate. The steep ascent to the viewpoint behind the gardens is more than worthwhile for the wonderful views down to the castle and along the lough deep into the glen. Guided tours of the castle focus on the furniture and artwork collected by the millionaire Irish–American, Henry McIlhenny, the last owner of Glenveagh, who in 1983 bequeathed the castle and its contents to the nation.

12

Lough Gartan and around

The environs of **Lough Gartan** are one of the supreme beauties of Ireland. **St Colmcille** was born into a royal family here in 521; his father was from the house of Niall of the Nine Hostages and his mother belonged to the House of Leinster. If you walk over from Glenveagh you'll pass Colmcille's **birthplace** – take the first road right at the first house you see at the end of the mountain track, and you'll come to a colossal **cross** marking the spot; the site is also signposted from the road running along the lough's southern shore. Close by is a slab known as the **Flagstone of Loneliness**, on which Colmcille used to sleep, thereby endowing the stone with the miraculous power to cure the sorrows of those who also lie upon it, though nowadays it's bestrewn with coins. During times of mass emigration, people used to come here on the eve of departure in the hope of ridding themselves of homesickness. Archaeologically, it's actually part of a Bronze Age gallery tomb and has over fifty cup marks cut into its surface.

Going back to the track leading downhill will bring you to the lakeside road, where a left turn leads to the remains of a church known as the **Little Oratory of St Colmcille**. It's an enchanting ruin, no larger than a modern living room, with a floor of old stone slabs with grass growing up through the cracks. A holy well is here too and nearby the Natal Stone, where the baby Colmcille first opened his eyes; to this day pregnant women visit the slab to pray for a safe delivery.

Glebe House

Obligatory guided tours Easter week daily 11am–6.30pm; June–Sept Mon–Thurs, Fri & Sat 11am–6.30pm • €3 • ☎ 074 913 7071

Glebe House is a gorgeous Regency building set in beautiful gardens on the northwest shore of Lough Gartan. Richly decorated both inside and out, it owes its fame to the time of its tenure by the English artist Derek Hill (1916–2000), though it's now run as a **gallery** by the Heritage Service. The converted stables are used for visiting exhibitions, while the rooms of the house itself display a rich collection of paintings, sketches and numerous other items once owned by Hill, including works by Kokoschka, Yeats, Renoir and Picasso. The study is decked out in original William Morris wallpaper and there are Chinese tapestries in the morning room. The kitchen has various paintings by the Tory Island group of primitive painters (see p.443), most remarkably James Dixon's impression of Tory from the sea.

Colmcille Heritage Centre

Easter week & May–Sept Mon–Sat 10.30am–5pm, Sun 1.30–5pm • €3 • ☎ 074 913 7306, ⓦ colmcilleheritagecentre.ie

Moving on round the northeast of the lake, in the direction of Church Hill, a right turn immediately after crossing the bridge will take you down to the modern **Colmcille Heritage Centre**, on the opposite shore from Glebe. The exhibition space is devoted to St Colmcille's life and the spread of the Celtic Church throughout Europe. If you have no interest in ecclesiastical history, there are other intriguing items, including very beautiful stained-glass windows of biblical scenes by Ciarán O'Conner and Ditty Kummer, and a step-by-step illustration of vellum illumination and calligraphy.

Doon and Kilmacrennan

Lying a few kilometres northeast of Lough Gartan, **the Rock of Doon** and **Doon Well** are signposted off the R255 shortly after the village of **Termon** on the way to Kilmacrennan. Following the directions leads to a rural cul-de-sac right next to the well. A path from here ascends to a large bushy outcrop that is the Rock of Doon. From 1200 to 1603 this was the spot where the O'Donnell kings were crowned, standing above a huge gathering of their followers. The inauguration stone on the summit is said to bear the imprint of the first Tír Chonaill king, a mark into which every successor had to place his foot as his final confirmation. Doon, an ancient pagan healing **well**, is still a place of pilgrimage, marked out by a bush weighed down with personal effects left behind by the sick, hoping for a cure. You're meant to take off your shoes as you approach and be well intentioned before taking the water.

KILMACRENNAN is a crossroads village on the road southeast to Letterkenny. Four hundred metres towards Ramelton is yet another site with Colmcille connections, **Cill Mhic n-Eanain**, where Columba was fostered and educated by Cruithnechan in around 528. A monastery stood here from the sixth century to 1129, and it was also the site of the O'Donnells' religious inauguration following the rites at Doon. The ruins on the left are of a sixteenth-century Franciscan **friary**, while the Church of Ireland building to the right dates from 1622 and fell into disuse around 1845.

The north Donegal coast

Running from the Cloghaneely district, which adjoins Gweedore, the **north Donegal coast** holds some of the most spectacular scenery in the whole country, where the battle between the elements is often startlingly apparent. Overshadowed at first by the bleak beauty of **Muckish Mountain** to the south, the main road from **Gortahork** to Milford passes through verdant countryside as it meanders around the deep bays and inlets and alongside the glorious and often deserted beaches which punctuate the shoreline. On the way, the Plantation town of **Dunfanaghy** provides a good base for exploring one of the coastline's two breathtaking peninsulas: **Horn Head**, with its rugged, sea-battered cliffs; and, further to the east, **Rosguill**, almost circumscribed by the marvellous Atlantic Drive.

12

Gortahork to Falcarragh

The first place you'll encounter in **Cloghaneely**, east of the Bloody Foreland, is **GORTAHORK**, an Irish-speaking village with a strong cultural history, albeit with little in the way of sights.

Three kilometres east of Gortahork, **FALCARRAGH** is livelier and better supplied with shops. A short distance east of the central crossroads is **An tSean Bhearic** (Falcarragh Visitor Centre; Mon–Fri 10am–5pm, Sat 11am–5pm; free; ❶074 918 0655, ⓦfalcarraghvisitorcentre.com), housed in the old police barracks. This has a craft shop and café, as well as displays on the town and its policing history, and regularly hosts temporary exhibitions and cultural events. Falcarragh **beach** is reached by heading north at the village crossroads and turning right about 1.5km further on, then continuing east for 3km. This is one of the more beautiful strands on this northwest coast, but a strong undercurrent makes it **unsafe for swimming**.

Muckish Mountain

The road south from Falcarragh to Glenveagh passes through **Muckish Gap**. The slate-grey mass of **Muckish Mountain** dominates the view, its sides pitted with old workings where quartzite sand was extracted for the manufacture of optical glass. It's a relatively easy climb from the roadside shrine at the Gap up a grassy ridge to the **summit** and, on a clear day, the entire coastline from the Bloody Foreland to Malin Head is splendidly visible from here.

Dunfanaghy

The small Plantation town of **DUNFANAGHY**, 10km east of Falcarragh, is the gateway to the **Horn Head Peninsula**, and whil there's little to get excited about in the town itself, it is a good little base, and there are a couple of fabulous places to eat.

Workhouse Heritage Centre

Mon–Sat 10am–4pm • €4.50 • ☎ 074 913 6540, ⓦ dunfanaghyworkhouse.ie

On its western outskirts is the **Workhouse Heritage Centre**, sympathetically restored as a local history and community resource. Built in 1845 on the eve of the Great Famine, at first it had only five inmates, but by 1847, as the Famine intensified, over six hundred people were crowded inside. The Famine story is recounted upstairs through the tale of one local inmate, Hannah Herrity, who lived until 1926 – though the narrative method (a distinctly dull and disappointing series of tableaux) undermines the power of her story. The centre also displays work by local artists, and it has a coffee shop, and, somewhat surprisingly, a screen for film viewings, which usually take place on the last weekend of each month.

ACCOMMODATION AND EATING　　　　　　　　　　　　　　　　　　　DUNFANAGHY

Arnold's Main St ☎ 074 913 6208, ⓦ arnoldshotel.com. The rooms here are nothing beyond the ordinary, but as it's the town's sole hotel, the prices are rather inflated; much better is the food, served in both its bar and restaurant. They also have riding stables and organize a variety of activities (including writing, photography and cycling). Nov–March weekends only. **€130**

The Mill By the lake on the western edge of town ☎ 074 913 6985, ⓦ themillrestaurant.com. This family-run restaurant serves scrumptious evening meals (€41); its seafood is especially well regarded, for example spiced Greencastle Monkfish and grilled Killybegs turbot. It also has superbly furnished en-suite rooms, all with lake views. Restaurant mid-March to June & Sept–Dec Wed–Sun 7–9.30pm; July & Aug Tues–Sun 7–9.30pm. **€95**

Muck'n'Muffins The Square ☎ 074 913 6780, ⓦ mucknmuffins.com. This once derelict grey-stone building is now a super little pottery studio-cum-café; watch the ceramicists at work downstairs before heading upstairs to the warm café for coffee and a pastry. Mon–Sat 9.30am–5pm, Sun 10.30am–5pm.

Horn Head

Horn Head is magnificent, an almost 200m rock face scored by ledges on which perch countless guillemots and gulls, and small numbers of puffins. The best view of the cliffs, sea stacks and caves is from the water, but the cliff road is vertiginous enough in places to give you a good look down the sheer sides.

To get here, take the slip road at the western end of Dunfanaghy village; it descends to skirt the side of a beautiful inlet before rising steeply to go round the east side of the head. A spectacular vista of headlands opens up to the east – Rosguill, Fanad and Inishowen – but none can match the drama of Horn Head's **cliffs**, their tops clad in a thin cover of purplish heather. Alternatively, you can walk from Horn Head Bridge, 800m from Dunfanaghy on the Horn Head road, and head west across the dunes to **Tramore Beach**. Then follow the sheep track north, passing two small blowholes called the **Two Pistols** and then a much larger one, **McSwyney's Gun**, so-called because of the power of the sonic boom produced by the explosion of compressed air from the cavern. Erosion has occurred over the years, however, and you'll be lucky to hear anything these days. Continuing onwards, you'll come to **Pollaguill Bay** and beach. The next wondrous site is the more than 20m-high **Marble Arch**, cut by the sea through the base of Trawbreaga Head. Horn Head itself soon becomes visible as you ascend the next headland.

The **walk** as far as here takes around three hours from Dunfanaghy, and you can either complete the whole circuit of the peninsula or head back by road.

Marble Hill and Ards Forest Park

Ard Forest Park Daily: April–Sept 8am–9pm; Oct–March 8am–4.30pm • Free, cars €4

East of Dunfanaghy, the road follows the edge of **Sheephaven Bay**, and, shortly after passing through Portnablagh, a signposted turn-off leads to **Marble Hill Strand**, a vast, glorious sweep of sand. Overlooking the strand, Marble Hill House was once owned by **Hugh Law**, MP for Donegal from 1902 to 1918 and TD for the county from 1927 to 1932, who entertained all manner of celebrities here, including W.B. and Jack Yeats. Nearby, **Ards Forest Park** occupies the former demesne of the Capuchin friary of Ard Mhuire; a 1.5km-long avenue alongside Lough Lilly takes you into its centre, where there are fine walks through the woodland as well as along the shore of Sheephaven Bay.

Creeslough and around

The sleepy village of **CREESLOUGH** occupies a slope commanding gorgeous views across the head of Sheephaven Bay. Partway down its main street is a **church** designed by Liam McCormack, its whitewashed whorl and back-sloping table roof reflecting the thickly set Muckish Mountain nearby. **Lackagh Bridge**, about 6km east of Creeslough, offers a tremendous viewpoint of Sheephaven Bay, the curving silted shoreline lying downstream and a ginger-brown picture of rushes and heather reaching deep into the hills. Immediately after the bridge there's a turn-off running for 3km to **GLEN**, well worth taking for the opportunity to drop in at the *Olde Glen bar* (see below). A minor road south from Glen leads up through gorgeously lonely landscapes and past a tremendous viewpoint overlooking Lough Salt before descending to Termon (see p.446).

EATING AND DRINKING   CREESLOUGH AND AROUND

Olde Glen Glen ☏ 083 158 5777, ⊕ oldeglenbar restaurant.com. Great-looking red-and-white-painted pub with an atmospheric, low-ceilinged interior and wonky stone flooring. People come from miles around to try the crab linguine or roasted duckling in the modern restaurant, but it's equally fab just for a pint of ale and some chatter in the front bar. Tues–Sun 11am–11pm.

The Rosguill Peninsula

The route onto the extremely beautiful and very manageable **Rosguill Peninsula** starts by the side of the church in **Carrigart**, 13km northeast of Creeslough, and passes rabbit-infested dunes at the back of a tremendous and usually deserted **beach**. At the top of the strand is **DOWNINGS**, a sprightly holiday centre patronized mainly by Northern Irish tourists, with caravan sites hogging the rear end of the beach and holiday chalets creeping up the hillside behind the village.

Downings' main street heads northwards to become the panoramic **Atlantic Drive**, which runs around the headland and also makes for a stupendous 13km walk. The range of views encompasses the essence of Donegal – rugged landscapes in constant tussle with the Atlantic Ocean – though, sadly, this is becoming increasingly blighted by large numbers of new-build houses and caravan sites. About halfway along, a turning leads to **Melmore Head**, where you'll find the rather fine **Trá na Rosann** beach. A quicker way to get here is to take the right-hand fork on the way into Downings from Carrigart.

ACCOMMODATION AND EATING   THE ROSGUILL PENINSULA

Harbour Bar Uphill at the far end of the village ☏ 074 915 5920. This is one of the most enjoyable pubs along this stretch of coast; along with glorious views of the bay, there's a toasty fire, lots of *craic* and music at weekends. Daily 10.30am–midnight.

Rosapenna Hotel Downings ☏ 074 915 5301, ⊕ rosapenna.ie. Two of the north coast's finest golf courses straddle this upmarket hotel whose rooms are as plush as you might expect and, naturally, have stunning ocean views. April–Oct. **€160**

Trá na Rosann Hostel Downings ☏ 074 915 5374. Designed by Edwin Lutyens, this erstwhile hunting lodge – a listed building – is now a superb alpine-style hostel with a mix of dorms and a self-catering kitchen. June–Aug. Dorms **€17**

12

The Fanad Peninsula

The least tempting of Donegal's peninsulas is **Fanad**, circumnavigated by the well-signposted **Fanad Drive**. The western shoreline has little to offer scenically, and the whole peninsula is best approached from Kilmacrennan through the pleasant towns of **Ramelton** and **Rathmullan**, the latter with some very swish accommodation, before heading on to **Fanad Head** itself.

Rathmullan and around

Heading east out of Kilmacrennan, it's worth a quick stroll through **Ramelton**, a quaint and sedate little town sitting attractively on the eastern bank of the broad black flow of the salmon-rich River Leannan. Beyond here, **RATHMULLAN** is no less pretty, with its long row of multicoloured houses facing Lough Swilly; like Ramelton, though, the town has suffered badly in recent years, and many places have closed down, as has the ferry across to Buncrana in Inishowen. In 1587 the rebellious **Red Hugh O'Donnell** was lured onto a British merchant ship here on the pretext of a merry drink, and ended up in Dublin gaol for six years; and in 1607 Rathmullan was a departure point for the **Flight of the Earls**, the event that marked the end of the Gaelic nation. In October 1798 the French frigate *Hoche*, with Wolfe Tone on board, was intercepted in the lough nearby and Tone was captured and taken to Dublin for trial.

ACCOMMODATION AND EATING   **RATHMULLAN AND AROUND**

★ **Rathmullan House** By Lough Swilly ☎ 074 915 8188, ⓦ rathmullanhouse.com. Gracious country house set amid lush landscaped gardens. Most of the magnificent, classically furnished rooms have water views, while some have their own patio. Meanwhile, log fires burn away in sumptuously furnished lounges, but if you fancy more vigorous activity, you can avail yourself of the stunning indoor pool. **€160**

The Taproom Rathmullan House, by Lough Swilly ☎ 074 915 8874. The original kitchens in *Rathmullan House* have been converted into this brilliant cellar bar offering a simple but cracking combination of wood-fired pizzas and craft beers, the latter from the neighbouring Kinnegar Brewery. June–Sept daily 1–9pm; Oct–May Thurs–Sun 1–9pm.

Portsalon and Fanad Head

North of Rathmullan the R247 climbs to give great views across to **Dunree Head** and the **Urris** range of mountains on the Inishowen Peninsula to the east. Taking the first right turn will lead you along a minor road hugging the coastline, as it twists and turns up to the cliff-top approach to **Saldanha Head**. Here you'll witness the most spectacular views on the entire peninsula, looking across to Inishowen and down onto the 5km stretch of golden sand at Ballymastocker Bay.

Most of the 8km route north from Portsalon to **Fanad Head** is through humpy and barren land, with clusters of granite pushing through marshy ground. Before reaching the Head, there is one curiosity worth taking in, just 2km north of Portsalon: the rock formation known as the **Seven Arches**, created by the constant erosive battering of the waters. To get here, follow the signpost on the right of the road, then take the path down to the new house, and finally cross the fields to the rocky strand. From here the main road leads straight on to **Fanad Head**, where it reaches a dramatically placed cliff-edge **lighthouse**.

Letterkenny

Whatever your means of transport, if you're travelling through northern Donegal, you're almost certain to pass through **LETTERKENNY**, the county's largest town. There's very little by way of actuals sights in the town itself, which has undergone massive

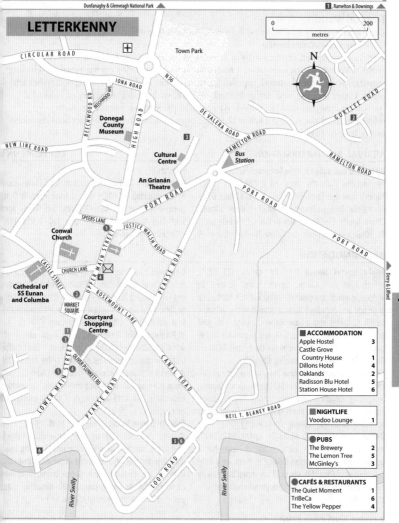

LETTERKENNY

CIRCULAR ROAD

Town Park

IONA ROAD

N56

BEECHWOOD RD

BEECHWOOD AVE

HIGH ROAD

DE VALERA ROAD

RAMELTON ROAD

NEW LINE ROAD

Donegal
County
Museum

3

Cultural
Centre

Bus
Station

PORT ROAD

RAMELTON ROAD

An Grianán
Theatre

PORT ROAD

PORT ROAD

SPEERS LANE

1

JUSTICE WALSH ROAD

Conwal
Church

UPPER MAIN STREET

PEARSE ROAD

CASTLE STREET

CHURCH LANE

4

Cathedral
of SS Eunan
and Columba

2

ROSEMOUNT LANE

MARKET
SQUARE

Courtyard
Shopping
Centre

CANAL ROAD

1
3

OLIVER PLUNKETT RD

5   4

LOWER MAIN STREET

PEARSE ROAD

NEIL T. BLANEY ROAD

6

3 6

River Swilly

LOOP ROAD

River Swilly

Derry & Lifford ▶

12

■ ACCOMMODATION	
Apple Hostel	3
Castle Grove Country House	1
Dillons Hotel	4
Oaklands	2
Radisson Blu Hotel	5
Station House Hotel	6

■ NIGHTLIFE	
Voodoo Lounge	1

● PUBS	
The Brewery	2
The Lemon Tree	5
McGinley's	3

● CAFÉS & RESTAURANTS	
The Quiet Moment	1
TriBeCa	6
The Yellow Pepper	4

redevelopment in recent years, though it does retain a lively arts scene and some thriving nightlife. Its most notable visual element is the huge nineteenth-century **Cathedral of Saints Eunan and Columba** at the top of Church lane, with its intricate stone-roped ceiling, flying buttresses and Gaelicized Stations of the Cross.

Donegal County Museum

gh Rd • Mon–Fri 10am–12.30pm & 1–4.30pm, Sat 1–4.30pm • Free • ☎ 074 912 4613

The main point of interest in town is the **Donegal County Museum**, housed in part of the old Letterkenny workhouse. Temporary exhibitions occupy the downstairs area while upstairs is a typical display of artefacts from megalithic to more recent times, including the keys and lock of the old Lifford jail, and an account of the Donegal County Railway, which ran to and from Letterkenny.

Tropical World

Alcorns Garden Centre, Loughnagin, 3km north of town on the R245 to Ramelton • April–Sept Mon–Fri 10am–5.30pm, Sun 1–5.30pm • €7.50 • ☎ 074 912 1541, ⓦ tropicalworld.ie

The Alcorns garden centre north of town is the unlikely setting for the sweet little **Tropical World**, which comprises a **mini-zoo**, housing sections on mammals (including lemurs, raccoons and otters), reptiles (snakes, geckos and lizards), creepy crawlies and birds. Here, too, is a wonderful **Butterfly House**, with a fabulous array of colourful specimens from around the world. Afterwards, parents can partake in some refreshment in the tearoom while the little ones fool around in the excellent monkey swing indoor play area.

ARRIVAL AND INFORMATION   LETTERKENNY

By bus The bus station is at the bottom of Port Road.
Destinations Ballyliffin (Mon–Fri 4 daily, Sat 1; 1hr 10min); Buncrana (Mon–Fri 4 daily, Sat 1; 45min); Derry (7–9 daily; 35min); Donegal town (7–9 daily; 50min); Lifford (hourly; 25–50min); Moville (Mon–Fri 3 daily, Sat 1; 1hr 30min); Raphoe (Mon–Sat 7 daily; 20–35min); Sligo (6

daily; 2hr).
Tourist office The tourist office is on Neil T. Blaney Road by the roundabout 800m out of town towards Derry (June–Aug Mon–Fri 9am–5.30pm, Sat 10am–4pm; Sept–May Mon–Fri 9.15am–5pm; ☎ 074 912 1160; ⓦ letterkennytourism.ie).

ACCOMMODATION

Apple Hostel House Port Rd ☎ 074 911 3291, ⓦ letterkennyhostel.com. Smart hostel located in secluded grounds up behind the cultural centre, with a mix of private and dormitory accommodation in two adjacent buildings; there's also a large kitchen, lounge with pool table, and laundry facilities. Camping is possible in the grounds and campers are free to use the hostel's facilities. Dorms €16, doubles €36, camping €8

Castle Grove Country House Ballymaleel, 3km out on the Ramelton road ☎ 074 915 1118, ⓦ castlegrove .com. This elegant seventeenth-century house, pitched among stately grounds overlooking Lough Swilly, offers splendidly furnished, Georgian-era rooms. €130

Dillons Hotel 29–45 Main St ☎ 074 912 2977, ⓦ dillons-hotel.ie. This most central of hotels has a decent stock of rooms, even if some of them are a little careworn in places; still, the staff are incredibly friendly and it's fairly priced. Moreover, a major refurbishment is in the pipeline. €89

Oaklands 8 Oaklands Park, Gortlee Rd ☎ 074 912 5529, ⓦ letterkennybandb.com. A 10min walk from the centre, this tidy B&B is a little tricky to find – it's at the end of a residential cul-de-sac – but the six rooms are immaculately kept and the hospitality is genuinely warm. €70

★ **Radisson Blu Hotel** The Loop Road ☎ 074 91 4444, ⓦ radissonblu.ie/hotel-letterkenny. The location on a main road opposite a retail park, is rather dull, but the discreet high-rise is as plush as you'd expect from this hotel chain; the rooms are supremely comfortable, the service impeccable, and there are a couple of superb eating areas (see opposite). €120

Station House Hotel Lower Main St ☎ 074 912 3100, ⓦ stationhouseletterkenny.com. You wouldn't think so to look at it, but this is the old station house building, hence the name and the occasional nod to the old railway that used to run through these parts; bright, light-filled corridors lead to perky rooms with gleaming glass-panelled bathrooms. Breakfast is extra. €69

EATING AND DRINKING

Letterkenny has a trio of excellent **restaurants**, beyond which you'll find a cluster of places strung along Main Street. The town has enough **bars** to defeat the hardiest pub-crawler, and many have live music or DJs at weekends; again, the majority of these are along Main Street.

The Brewery Market Square ☎ 074 912 7330, ⓦ thebrewerybar.com. Popular, always lively, bar-cum-restaurant with a striking all wood and brass interior. An exciting line-up of more than twenty craft beers complements fine menus in both the bar and restaurant. Live music Tues–Sat. Daily 11am–11pm; bar food noon–10pm; restaurant 6–10pm.

The Lemon Tree Lower Main St ☎ 074 912 5788, ⓦ thelemontreerestaurant.com. Delicious modern

Irish cuisine with a discernible French influence manifest in dishes like baked duck breast with caramelized pear soy and honey sauce (€21.95); the restaurant, with its subtle pastel colours and candle-topped tables, looks fantastic. Mon–Sat 5–10pm, Sun 1–2.30pm & 5–10pm.

McGinley's Lower Main St ☎ 086 784 0783. Of all the street's many hostelries, McGinley's is by far the most agreeable – and most frequented – thanks to its dark yet cosy bar, and pretty much nightly music sessions, the most popular which takes place on Wed. Daily 10.30am–midnight.

The Quiet Moment Upper Main St ☏ 074 912 8382. Letterkenny's most enticing café captures the ambience of the old Dublin *Bewley's* (see p.99) with some success, thanks to its thick, oak-panelled walls and deep green leather armchairs; great coffee, snacks, lunches and all-day breakfasts. Mon–Sat 8am–6pm, Sun 10am–4pm.

★ **TriBeCa** Radisson Blu Hotel ☏ 074 919 4444. Tip-top dining in the *Radisson's* dazzling restaurant, featuring wonderful seafood like Atlantic salmon, and grilled fillet of hake with crab claws (€21.95). For something more casual, and a little cheaper, head across the corridor to the Port Bar & Grill, where you can indulge in stone-baked pizzas and steak sandwiches. Restaurant daily 6–9.30pm; bar daily 11am–9pm.

Voodoo Lounge 36 Lower Main St ☏ 074 910 9815, ⓦ voodoovenueletterkenny.com. Good-time, state-of-the-art multi-roomed club-cum-live-venue with top-name DJs at weekends and occasional live bands; they also offer food. Opening times vary.

★ **The Yellow Pepper** 36 Lower Main St ☏ 074 912 4133, ⓦ yellowpepperrestaurant.com. The cast-iron pillars and thick stone walls are reminders of what was once an old shirt factory; these days, however, this is a cheery, family-run restaurant where you can tuck into dry-aged sirloin and seafood platters along with one of the many bottles of wine stacked up high behind the bar. Exemplary service too. Daily noon–10pm.

ENTERTAINMENT

An Grianán Port Rd ☏ 074 912 0777, ⓦ angrianan.com. Top-notch local theatre offering an impressive drama programme. It's also one of Ireland's best music venues, from traditional to classical. There's a super little café here too. Café Mon–Fri 9.30am–3pm.

Regional Cultural Centre 46 Port Rd ☏ 074 912 9186, ⓦ regionalculturalcentre.com. Just behind An Grianán, the regional cultural centre mounts a variety of exhibitions and a regular programme of concerts, covering jazz to traditional music. It's also the principal venue for the two-week Ethe Earagail Arts Festival in mid-July (ⓦ eaf.ie). Tues–Fri 11am–5pm, Sat 1–5pm.

Raphoe

Thirteen kilometres southeast of Letterkenny, **RAPHOE** is set trimly around one of the largest Diamonds in the county. Once a see in its own right, its ecclesiastical importance is still indicated today by its inclusion in the Church of Ireland bishopric of Derry and Raphoe. The town's **cathedral**, dedicated to St Eunan (the biographer of St Columba), was founded in the ninth century, but the present plain Gothic-cathedral version dates merely from 1702. Transfixed in the inner wall is a stone block with some peculiar, indecipherable carvings, and there's a very impressive and resonant wooden baptismal chapel.

Beltany Stone Circle

Three kilometres south of Raphoe is the **Beltany Stone Circle**, one of the best-preserved circles in the country. Consisting of approximately sixty stones, varying in height between 30cm and over 1m, it provides an atmospheric vantage point for a marvellous panoramic view of the local valleys and distant mountains. To get here, follow the signs from the south of The Diamond in Raphoe and you'll arrive at the entrance to a farm. The circle is 400m up the bridle path to the right, over a stile and across a field full of sheep.

ARRIVAL AND DEPARTURE   RAPHOE

By bus Buses stop in the centre of the village.
Destinations Letterkenny (Mon–Sat 6 daily; 20–35min); Lifford (Mon–Sat 3 daily; 15min).

Lifford

Courthouse The Diamond · Mon–Fri 9.30am–3.30pm · €6; mugshot €3 · ☏ 074 914 1733, ⓦ liffordoldcourthouse.com

Six kilometres southeast of Raphoe, **LIFFORD** was formerly Donegal's legal centre and the County Council is still based here. The graceful **Old Courthouse**, dating from 1746, houses a **visitor centre**, which tells the story of the O'Donnell clan and Napper Tandy (see p.441), as well as notable events in Donegal's history. In the basement cells there's a pretty gruesome re-creation of the prison conditions and you can have your mugshot taken behind the bars. And once you've done that, take a coffee in the Courthouse Bistro (same hours).

Cavanacor House

Tues–Sat noon–6pm • Free • ☎ 085 164 2525, ⓦ cavanacorgallery.ie

A few kilometres northwest of Lifford, off the N14, **Cavanacor House** is a fine seventeenth-century mansion where **James II** dined in 1689, and which was also the ancestral home of **James Knox Polk**, US president from 1845 to 1849. The real treat is its **art gallery**, displaying a changing array of work by contemporary Irish and international painters and sculptors.

ARRIVAL AND DEPARTURE		LIFFORD
By bus Buses stop in the centre of the village. Destinations Letterkenny (hourly; 25–45min); Raphoe	(Mon–Sat 5 daily; 15min).	

The Inishowen Peninsula

The **Inishowen Peninsula** in the northeast of County Donegal is perhaps the great overlooked treasure of the Irish landscape (and certainly has the longest signposted scenic drive – the "Inishowen 100"), offering a diverse and visually exciting terrain, where the views usually encompass the waters of the loughs or the Atlantic waves. Virtually every aspect of the landscape is superb – the beaches (especially Kinnego Bay, Culdaff, Tullagh and Pollan), the towering headland bluffs (Malin, Inishowen, Dunaff and Dunree) and the central mountain range, with towering **Slieve Snaght** at the middle of it all.

The peninsula derives its name from **Eoghán**, who was made First Lord of the island by his father Niall, High King of Ireland. Phases of the peninsula's history before and after Eoghán have left a legacy of fine antiquities, from the **Grianán Ailigh** fort to a host of beautiful early **Christian crosses** (Cloncha, Mura, Carrowmore and Cooley).

GETTING AROUND	THE INISHOWEN PENINSULA
By bus Services on the peninsula are extremely limited and, though you can reach places such as Buncrana and	Ballyliffin fairly easily, you'll certainly need your own transport to explore Malin Head.

Burt Church

The approach to the most stimulating of all Inishowen's sights, the ancient fort known as the Grianán Ailigh, passes the Liam McCormack–designed **Burt Church**, near Bridgend on the N13 Letterkenny–Derry road, the most beautiful twentieth-century church in all Ireland – like other McCormack designs in Donegal (see p.438 & p.449), its structure is evocative of the mystical landmark nearby. The seating is set concentrically, under a whitewashed ceiling that sweeps up into a vortex to allow sunlight to beam down directly upon the altar; the allusions in every detail to Neolithic sepulchral architecture (especially Newgrange – see p.142) are fascinating and very atmospheric. In a survey of Irish architects the church was voted Ireland's building of the twentieth century.

To learn more about the church and its legends, head to the *An Grianan Hotel*, just down the road in the village of **Burt**, which incorporates the somewhat confusingly named **Old Church Visitor Centre** (Mon–Fri 10.30am–5pm, Sat & Sun 11am–5.30pm; €3; ☎ 074 936 8900, ⓦ oldchurchvisitorcentre.com), which concentrates on both Burt Church and the area's myths and legends.

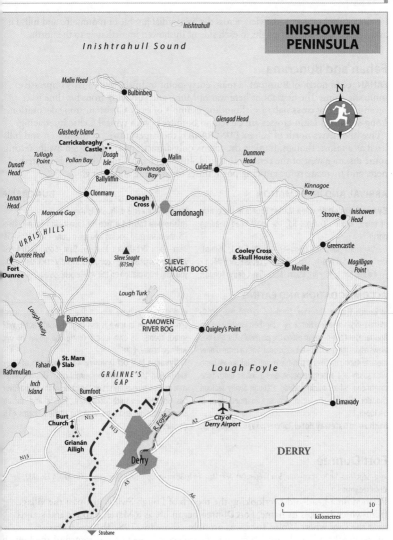

Grianán Ailigh

Open access

The origins of the **Grianán Ailigh**, 3km up the hill from Burt Church, date from 1700 BC, and it's thought to be linked to the Tuátha Dé Danann, pre-Celtic invaders. It was sufficiently significant to be included by Ptolemy, the Alexandrian geographer, in his second-century AD map of the world, and was the base of various northern Irish chieftains. Here, in 450, St Patrick is said to have baptized Eoghán, the founder of the O'Neill clan that ruled the kingdom of Ailigh for more than five hundred years. In the twelfth century, the fort was sacked by Murtagh O'Brian, King of Thomond, in retribution for a raid on Clare, and a large amount of its stone was carried away. Today's impressive building was largely reconstructed in the 1870s by Walter Bernard from Derry and is the only remaining terraced fort in Ireland. It's enclosed by three earthen banks, but its most stunning asset is the view across the primordial jumble of mountains and hills far away to the west and the loughs to each side of Inishowen immediately to the north.

Fahan and Buncrana

FAHAN, 6km north of **Burnfoot**, a main entry-point to Inishowen, boasts impressive monastic ruins. The first abbot here was St Mura, and surviving from his time is a seventh-century **cross slab**, a spellbinding example of early Christian stone decoration. Long-stemmed Latin crosses are carved on both faces with typical Celtic interlacing.

Five kilometres north of Fahan, **BUNCRANA** is the largest town on Inishowen and bills itself as a resort, though, frankly, the town's only attractions are its Lough Swilly setting some distance west of the centre. That said, Inishowen's sole tourist office is located here, and there are some enticing possibilities for sleeping and eating.

ARRIVAL AND INFORMATION   BUNCRANA

By bus Buses set down on Market Square in the centre of town, and on Corkhill Rd, the main road heading north.
Destinations Ballyliffin (Mon–Fri 4 daily, Sat 1; 25min); Derry (Mon–Sat hourly, Sun 2; 35min); Letterkenny (Mon–Fri 4 daily, Sat 1; 45min); Malin (Mon–Sat 1 daily; 40min);

Moville (Mon–Fri 3 daily, Sat 1; 1hr).
Inishowen tourist office The tourist office is on Railway Rd, the main road leading into town (June–Sept Mon–Sat 9am–5pm; Oct–March Mon–Fri 9am–5pm; ☎074 936 2602, ⍇visitinishowen.com). Its friendly staff can supply you with information on the whole peninsula.

ACCOMMODATION AND EATING

★**Beach House** The Pier, Swill Rd ☎074 936 1050, ⍇thebeachhouse.ie. Not only the best restaurant in Buncrana, but one of the finest on the peninsula; the glorious views aside, the food here is exceptional, with a main dinner menu featuring the likes of pan-fried rump of Inishowen lamb with salsify and aubergine purée, and a lighter lunch-time café menu, which might include a Lough Swilly seafood chowder. Wed–Fri 5–10pm, Sat & Sun noon–4pm & 5–10pm.
Inishowen Gateway Hotel Railway Rd ☎074 936 1144,

⍇inishowengateway.com. The most prominent accommodation in town is this large roadside hotel, with spruce rooms, its own leisure centre and pool, spa and wellness centre. **€80**
Tullyvaran Mill Off Drumree Rd, 2km north of town ☎074 936 1613, ⍇tullyarvanmill.com. This renovated corn mill, picturesquely set on the banks of the Crana River, has spotless en-suite dormitory, family and private accommodation, and a self-catering kitchen. Dorms **€15**, doubles **€40**

Fort Dunree

June–Sept Mon–Sat 10.30am–6pm, Sun 1–6pm; Oct–May Mon–Fri 10.30am–4.30pm, Sat & Sun 1–6pm • €6 • ☎074 936 1817, ⍇dunree.pro.ie

Perched on a headland overlooking the mouth of Lough Swilly, just past the village from which it takes its name, **Fort Dunree** began life as a Martello tower and stands near the spot where Wolfe Tone was brought ashore in 1798. The tower was subsequently enlarged into a fortress to guard against the possible return of the French and was further developed in the late nineteenth century. It now has a **museum** of predictable military memorabilia, with interactive displays providing an insight into the fort's former use; more interesting is a Siemens searchlight dating from 1899, which is still put to use on special occasions. The fort's upper reaches, meanwhile, keep two impressive breach-loading guns dating from 1911; otherwise, the views are quite wonderful.

Marmore Gap and Ballyliffin

North out of Dunree village the road climbs steeply past a scattering of weather-beaten thatched cottages before crossing a small bridge close to the **MAMORE GAP**, which seems like a chunk bitten out of the Urris Hills. From the top of the Gap the road spirals steeply downwards, each bend providing an ever wider and more spectacular view of the flat foreground to **Dunaff Head**. The gorgeous, 1.5km-long **Tullagh Strand** to the east of Dunaff Head is a safe bathing beach.

The route from here insinuates itself inland between the mountains to **Clonmany**, a neat village of predominantly cream-coloured houses, quiet for most of the year but hyperactive during its week-long **festival** in early August (ⓦclonmanyfestival .com). Two kilometres beyond is the more upmarket **BALLYLIFFIN**, home to the Ballyliffin **golf** club – comprising two championship links courses. Golfing aside, there is some excellent accommodation here, plus one or two enjoyable places to eat and drink.

ARRIVAL AND DEPARTURE BALLYLIFFIN

By bus Buses drop off on, and depart from, the centre of the village.
Destinations Buncrana (Mon–Fri 4 daily, Sat 1; 25min);
Letterkenny (Mon–Fri 4 daily, Sat 1; 1hr 15min); Moville (Mon–Fri 3 daily, Sat 1; 35min).

ACCOMMODATION AND EATING

Ballyliffin Hotel Main St ☎074 937 6106, ⓦballyliffin.com. It's a toss-up between the four hotels in the village, but the Ballyliffin is as accomplished as any of them; warm, maroon-coloured rooms and a very creditable restaurant. **€110**

Nancy's Barn Main St ☎086 843 28977. Handsome stone barn with a warming cottagey interior, serving great coffee, delicious home-baked treats and desserts, and more substantial fare like warming soups and toasted sandwiches. Daily 9am–6.30pm.

The Rusty Nail Crossconnell, Clonmany ☎074 937 6116. Cheery roadside pub offering good-value bar food, but better known for its gut-busting Sun lunches, plus there's live music at weekends. Daily noon–11pm.

12

Carrickabraghy Castle and Doagh Isle

North of Ballyliffin is the entrancing **Pollan Strand**, at whose furthest tip stands the ruin of **Carrickabraghy Castle**, a sixteenth-century O'Doherty fortification. Much weathered by spray and sea salt, the castle's stones are streaked with colours ranging from the darkest hues to golden yellows. The strand itself has wonderfully wild breakers, which unfortunately make swimming dangerous. The castle sits on the western side of **DOAGH ISLE**, now linked to the mainland through centuries of silt accumulation, on whose eastern edge lies **Trawbreaga Bay**, an exquisite piece of coastline. The mouth of the bay is bewitching: strolling onto the beach here you'll discover rocks fashioned into extraordinary shapes and colours by the sea.

Doagh Famine Village

Mid-March to Oct Mon–Fri 10am–5.30pm • €7.50 • ☎086 846 4749, ⓦdoaghfaminevillage.com

One sight not to be missed in this part of the peninsula is the outdoor **Doagh Famine Village**, which, for the most part, recalls the struggles of those who lived through the Famine of the 1840s. That aside, the museum manifests an enlightening, if slightly peculiar, coterie of attractions, including a Wake House, a Republican Safe House and, somewhat bizarrely, a haunted house. Visitors are free to nosey around by themselves, but you'll get much more out of the visit if you partake in one of the hugely entertaining guided tours (included in the price) – and once you're done, you'll be invited inside the teahouse for a cup of tea and some wheaten bread with jam, which is also included.

Culdaff

CULDAFF is a cosy village whose nearby **beach** forms a stunning natural crescent. There's a major **sea-angling festival** here at the end of July and, in early October, a cultural weekend commemorates the eighteenth-century actor, **Charles Macklin**. Otherwise, its main point of interest is the superb village hotel/pub.

ARRIVAL AND DEPARTURE
CULDAFF

By bus Buses drop off on, and depart from, Main St. Destinations Ballyliffin (Mon–Fri 2 daily, Sat 1; 25min); Buncrana (Mon–Fri 2 daily, Sat 1; 55min); Letterkenny (Mon–Fri 2 daily, Sat 1; 1hr 40min); Malin town (Mon–Fri 2 daily, Sat 1; 5min).

ACCOMMODATION AND EATING

McGrory's Main St ☎ 074 937 9104, ⓦ mcgrorys.ie. This fabulous all-rounder offers classy rooms, many having retained their original exposed brickwork, and an equally fine bar, offering cracking meals including locally caught shellfish. Entertainment-wise, its *Backroom* is one of the best venues in Ireland for live music, regularly pulling in some big names, while the Front Bar hosts traditional sessions, typically on Tues and Fri. Bar daily 11.30am–midnight. **€99**

Malin and Malin Head

Seven kilometres west of Culdaff is the planter settlement of **MALIN**, tucked picturesquely into the side of Trawbreaga Bay, with a charming grassy Diamond at its centre. A little way north of Malin, a signpost points to **Five Fingers Strand**, across the bay from Doagh Isle – it's worth the diversion to experience the ferocity of the breakers on the beach and the long walks on its sands, though the strand has undergone recent severe coastal erosion.

Sixteen kilometres north of Malin village, **Malin Head**, the northernmost extremity of Ireland, might not be as stupendous as other Donegal headlands but is nevertheless excellent for blustery, winding coastal walks – and for ornithologists: choughs, with their glossy black plumage, red legs and bill, inhabit the cliffs, and the rasping cry of the rare corncrake can be heard in the fields. The tip of the headland is marked by **Bamba's Crown**, a ruined Napoleonic signal tower, and the western path from here heads out to **Hell's Hole**, a 75m chasm in the cliffs, which roars with the onrushing tide.

ARRIVAL AND DEPARTURE
MALIN AND MALIN HEAD

By bus Buses drop off on and depart from the Diamond. Destinations Buncrana (Mon–Fri 2 daily, Sat 1; 40min); Culdaff (Mon–Sat 1 daily; 5min); Derry (Mon–Sat 2 daily; 1hr).

ACCOMMODATION AND EATING

Malin Hotel The Diamond ☎ 074 937 0606, ⓦ malinhotel.ie. Boutiquey accommodation in the centre of the village, whose rooms manifest a distinct French feel. The hotel also hosts a variety of entertainment and has a very good restaurant. **€90**

Sandrock Holiday Hostel Port Ronan Pier ☎ 074 937 0289, ⓦ sandrockhostel.com. In a fantastic location just above the beach, this bungalow-like building has two simple dorms, each sleeping ten, and both with wonderful sea views. Self-catering kitchen, lounge with library, and bikes for rent (€10/day). Dorms **€13.50**

Seaview Tavern Malin Head ☎ 074 937 0117, ⓦ seaviewtavern.biz. Attached to a tiny public-bar-cum-shop, this rather ordinary-looking restaurant is actually very good, though you'll not want to venture far from the ocean-facing terrace in warmer weather; fish straight off the boat, including unbeatable Atlantic wild lobster. Daily 11am–9.30pm.

★ **Whitestrand B&B** Malin Head ☎ 074 937 0335, ⓦ whitestrand.net. Delightful three-room guesthouse just a short stroll from the beach, whose proprietor couldn't be more welcoming – you'll get home-baked goodies upon arrival and a sumptuous breakfast to see you on your way. **€65**

Greencastle

The harbour village of **GREENCASTLE** on the eastern side of Inishowen has a pleasant view across to Magilligan Strand on the opposite side of Lough Foyle, and there's a

ferry from here to Magilligan Point in Derry. By the road to Stroove are the ruins of the fourteenth-century Anglo-Norman **castle** from which the village gets its name, built on a rocky knoll to guard the narrowest part of the lough.

Maritime Museum and Planetarium

Easter–Oct Mon–Sat 9.30am–5.30pm, Sun noon–5.30pm; Nov–Easter Mon–Fri 9.15am–5.30pm • Museum €5, museum and planetarium €10 • ☎ 074 938 1363, ⓦ inishowenmaritime.com

By the harbour, in the old coastguard station, is the **Maritime Museum and Planetarium**, which recalls maritime travel from bygone times through a range of Irish boats from 2m to 20m in length. Among the maritime memorabilia, pride of place goes to a nineteenth-century rocket cart used to fire flares to aid survivors of wrecked ships. The state-of-the-art planetarium takes you on exhilarating trips through the universe, while regular laser light shows feature a traditional-music soundtrack; there are also custom shows (minimum ten people) where you can choose your own musical backing.

ARRIVAL AND DEPARTURE · GREENCASTLE

By bus Buses drop off on, and depart from Main St. Destinations Derry (3 daily; 1hr 10min); Moville (3 daily; 25min).

By boat Magilligan Point (daily on the hour: March–June, Sept & Oct 9am–7pm; July & Aug 9am–8.15pm; Nov–Feb 9am–5pm; pedestrians €3 single, €4 return; cars €14 single, €20 return; ☎ 074 938 1901, ⓦ loughfoyleferry .com).

EATING AND DRINKING

★ **Kealy's** The Harbour ☎ 074 938 1010, ⓦ kealys seafoodbar.ie. Unsurprisingly, Greencastle is a great spot for seafood, but the one place to aim for is *Kealy's* seafood bar, reckoned to be one of the best in Donegal, and here's why: lobster thermidor, pan-fried medallions of monkfish, whole Dover sole on the bone with capers, plus loads more. Thurs–Sun 12.30–11.30pm.

12

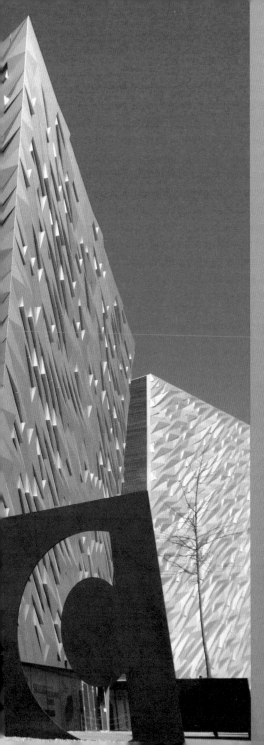

Belfast

TITANIC BELFAST

13 Belfast

Bustling and vibrant Belfast is a city reborn. Not only has Northern Ireland's capital successfully shaken off the "war-torn" label it earned during the Troubles – it's fair to say the city has undergone a full-blown renaissance. In the aftermath of the peace process, instigated by the 1998 Good Friday Agreement, investment has poured in, resulting in a thriving restaurant scene and a buzzing café culture, while new hotels – running the gamut from five-star glitz to funky and boutique – have sprung up in response to dramatically increasing tourist numbers. In keeping with its long tradition of supplying a stream of musicians, poets, artists and writers to the world stage, Belfast has also welcomed several new arts and music festivals: the Belfast Festival at Queens still takes place every autumn, but Open House, Belsonic, Festival of Fools and the Cathedral Quarter Arts Festival (CQAF) are also established fixtures in the city's calendar.

At first glance, Belfast has much in common with the large industrial ports found elsewhere in the UK, with its docklands and business districts. But then you encounter the people, a set of inhabitants whose pride and sense of humour remained undimmed even as the world's media camped on their doorstep, broadcasting their woes and turmoil around the globe. It is they, together with the near-miraculous revival in their city's fortunes over the past decade, that really set the place apart. You can easily – and richly – fill at least a few days here, although the geography of the North makes Belfast a good base for exploring virtually anywhere else in the Province.

Though the **city centre** is still characterized by numerous elegant Victorian buildings, there's been an enormous transformation, not least in the greater prosperity of the shopping streets. Big brands that once shunned Belfast because of its escalating insurance costs now occupy large units in the main commercial drags leading off from **Donegall Square North** (home to the iconic City Hall with its distinctive copper dome) and in the newly developed upmarket shopping complex, Victoria Square.

The rejuvenated area of refurbished warehouses and shop fronts from Ann Street to Donegall Street is now known as the **Cathedral Quarter** and plays host to a lively arts scene and a fantastic choice of bars and restaurants. A short walk northeast across the River Lagan brings you to the newly developed **Titanic Quarter** with its multimillion-pound Titanic Visitor's Centre (Titanic Belfast), charting the design, build, launch and sinking of the world's most famous ocean liner, RMS *Titanic*. This area is set to become the city's media hub with plans in motion for new film studios and broadcast facilities – the globally successful HBO fantasy series, *Games of Thrones*, is already filmed here in the Paint Hall Studios. To the south of the city centre proper lie **Queen's University** and the extensive collections of the newly refurbished **Ulster Museum**, set in the grounds of the **Botanic Gardens**.

CAVE HILL

Highlights

❶ The Titanic Quarter The city's redeveloped docklands are home to the multimillion-pound interactive museum, Titanic Belfast, which tells the story of the ill-fated RMS Titanic. **See p.469**

❷ Ulster Museum A multitude of fascinating exhibits dating back to prehistoric times, as well as one of Ireland's major art collections and a superb children's zone. **See p.472**

❸ Stormont The seat of government in Northern Ireland, set in glorious parkland to the east of the city. **See p.474**

❹ Cave Hill The best spot for a panoramic view of the city, with Belfast Lough spread out below. **See p.475**

❺ West Belfast An essential part of any visit to the city: the murals, Peace Line, cemeteries and fortified bars put everyday life into stark political context. **See p.475**

❻ The Cathedral Quarter Belfast's cultural hub, with a plethora of great restaurants, cafés, pubs, arts centres, music venues and its very own Cathedral Quarter Arts Festival (CQAF). **See p.486**

HIGHLIGHTS ARE MARKED ON THE MAPS ON P.464 AND P.471

13

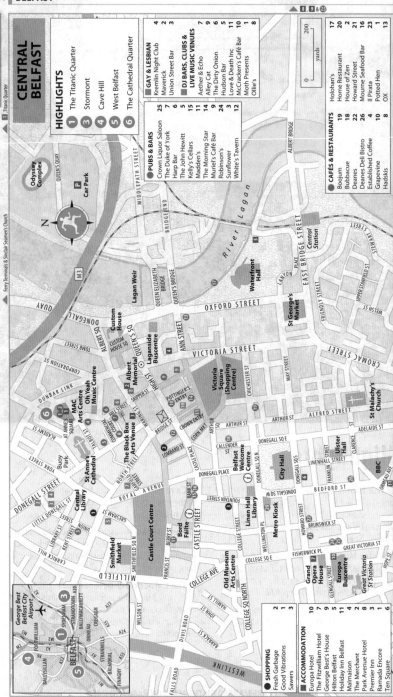

CENTRAL BELFAST

HIGHLIGHTS

1. The Titanic Quarter
2. Stormont
3. Cave Hill
4. West Belfast
5. The Cathedral Quarter

GAY & LESBIAN

Kremlin Night Club	4
Maverick	2
Union Street Bar	3

DJ BARS, CLUBS & LIVE MUSIC VENUES

Aether & Echo	7
Alley Cat	9
The Dirty Onion	6
Hudson Bar	5
Love & Death Inc	11
McCracken's Café Bar	10
Moth Presents	1
Ollie's	8

PUBS & BARS

Crown Liquor Saloon	25
The Duke of York	7
Harp Bar	6
The John Hewitt	15
Kelly's Cellars	15
Madden's	11
The Morning Star	14
Muriel's Café Bar	9
Robinson's	24
Sunflower	3
White's Tavern	12

CAFÉS & RESTAURANTS

Boojum	19
Bubbacue	18
Deanes	22
Deanes Deli Bistro	26
Established Coffee	4
Grapevine	10
Hadskis	8
Holohan's	17
Home Restaurant	20
House of Zen	21
Howard Street	21
Mourne Seafood Bar	16
Il Pirata	23
Potted Hen	1
OX	13

SHOPPING

Fresh Garbage	2
Good Vibrations	1
Sawers	3

ACCOMMODATION

Europa Hotel	10
The Fitzwilliam Hotel	7
George Best's House	9
Hilton Belfast	11
Holiday Inn Belfast	5
Malmaison	4
The Merchant	2
Park Avenue Hotel	8
Premier Inn	1
Ramada Encore	6
Ten Square	3

0   200
0   yards

Further out, a couple of miles to the north, a climb up **Cave Hill** rewards with marvellous views of the city, spread out around the curve of its natural harbour, **Belfast Lough**. The city's once-formidable security presence and fortifications are now virtually invisible, but the iron blockade known as the **Peace Line** still bisects the Catholic and Protestant communities of **West Belfast**, a grim physical reminder of sectarian divisions. A short bus ride to the east of the city delivers visitors to the **Stormont Estate**, home to the Northern Ireland Assembly. On a sunny day, the grounds surrounding the instantly recognizable "white house on the hill", as locals refer to it, provide the ideal picnic spot with woodland walks.

Brief history

Belfast began life as a cluster of forts built to guard a ford across the **River Farset**, which nowadays runs underground beneath the High Street. An **Anglo-Norman castle** was built here in 1177, but its influence was limited, and within a hundred years or so control over the Lagan Valley had reverted firmly to the Irish, under the O'Neills of Clandeboye. In 1604, **Sir Arthur Chichester**, whose son was to be the First Earl of Donegall, was "planted" in the area by James I, and shortly afterwards the tiny settlement was granted a charter creating a corporate borough. It was not until the end of the seventeenth century, though, that Belfast began to grow significantly, when French Huguenots fleeing persecution brought skills which rapidly improved the fortunes of the local **linen industry** – which, in turn, attracted new workers and wealth.

The eighteenth and nineteenth centuries

Through the eighteenth century, the cloth trade and **shipbuilding** expanded tremendously, and the population increased tenfold in a hundred years. With economic prosperity, Belfast became a city noted for its **liberalism**: in 1791, three Presbyterian Ulstermen formed the **Society of United Irishmen**, a gathering embracing Catholics and Protestants on the basis of common Irish nationality, from which sprang the **1798 Rebellion**. However, the rebellion in the North was quickly and ruthlessly stamped out by the English, and within two generations most Protestants had abandoned the Nationalist cause. Presbyterian ministers began openly to attack the Catholic Church, resulting in a **sectarian divide** that as time drew on became wider and increasingly violent. At the same time, the nineteenth century saw vigorous commercial and industrial expansion, and by the time Queen Victoria granted Belfast **city status** in 1888, its population had risen to 208,000, soon exceeding that of Dublin.

The twentieth century to the present day

With **Partition** came the creation of Northern Ireland with Belfast as its capital and Stormont as its seat of government. Inevitably, this boosted the city's status but also ensured that it would ultimately become the focus for much of the Troubles. The economic status of the Catholic population was deliberately maintained at a low level by a **Stormont government** that largely consisted of Protestant landowners and businessmen and saw no reason to challenge existing sectarian employment, housing and policing policies – all fuel to the fire which was to follow.

For 25 years from 1969, Belfast witnessed the worst of the **Troubles** (see p.593 and box on p.475), and by the time the IRA declared a **ceasefire** in 1994, much of the city resembled a battle site. There then followed a sea change in the city's fortunes as Britain and the EU funded a **revitalization** programme costing billions of pounds. Major shopping centres were built, swish hotels, bars and restaurants seemed to spring up almost overnight, and buildings such as the Waterfront Hall and Odyssey complex fundamentally altered the city's skyline. In the past decade, a crop of new entrepreneurs returned home, many having cut their teeth in businesses, restaurants and bars overseas, and set about effecting a new round of changes. Derelict buildings have been

13

successfully restored and reopened in various guises, serving as everything from restaurants to accommodation options for all budgets. At times, sectarianism still raises its ugly head – but on the whole, vibrant new areas such as the Cathedral and Titanic quarters keep Belfast looking to the future.

The city centre

The core of Belfast is stately **Donegall Square**, home to the copper-domed City Hall and its pristine gardens, where locals and visitors congregate for lunch-time picnics in fine weather. Buses and taxis depart for every part of the city from the sides of the square, ensuring that it's always busy with both pedestrians and traffic. The city's main shopping area once lay a stone's throw to the north until upstaged by the Victoria Square complex, with its raft of upmarket retailers, just to the east. Entertainment and accommodation options proliferate immediately south and north of the square, although the rejuvenation of St Anne's Square has helped to establish the **Cathedral Quarter** as Belfast's coolest night-time hub. Most of the grand old Victorian buildings that characterize the city are to the north and east, towards the river, including St Malachy's church which underwent a £3.5 million restoration in 2008–09.

The **River Lagan** flows towards Belfast Lough along the eastern side of the city centre, offering excellent riverside walks. It is also the focus for the first of the city's radical new developments in peace times, the **Laganside**, focused on the Waterfront Hall and the Odyssey Complex across the water. Beyond the Odyssey stands the city's latest success story, **Titanic Belfast**, a fully interactive museum built at a cost of £77 million to commemorate the centenary of the ill-fated RMS *Titanic* in the heart of the **Titanic Quarter**.

City Hall

Donegall Square North • Tours (45min) Mon–Fri 11am, 2pm & 3pm, Sat 2pm & 3pm • Free • ⓦ belfastcity.gov.uk/cityhall • Access for tours is via the front entrance on the north side of the square, though on Sat it's the back door on the south side

The vast Neoclassical bulk of **City Hall** dominates Donegall Square and the entire centre of Belfast. Completed in 1906 and made of bright white Portland stone, its turrets, saucer domes, scrolls and pinnacle pots are all representative of styles absorbed by the British Empire. In front stands an imposing statue of Queen Victoria, the apotheosis of imperialism, while at her feet, sculpted in bronze, proud figures show the city fathers' world-view: a young scholar; his mother with spinning spool; and his father with mallet and boat, the three representing "learning, linen and liners", the alliterative bedrock of Belfast's heritage.

Inside, arching 160ft above you, is the **main dome** with its (inaccessible) whispering gallery; modelled on St Paul's Cathedral in London, it is adorned around its rim with zodiac signs, both painted and in stained glass. The palatial marbled **entrance hall** features staircase pillars, colonnades and bronze and marble statues. Two of the statues portray Frederick Robert Chichester, Earl of Belfast (1827–53): the first, upright and stern, stands on the principal landing, while the other, showing Frederick embraced by his mother on his deathbed, stands in the octagonal entrance porch. Also on the principal landing is a **mural**, executed in 1951 by John Luke, celebrating Belfast's now mostly defunct traditional industries – rope-making, shipbuilding, weaving and spinning. The building's highlight is the oak-decorated **council chamber**, with its hand-carved wainscoting and councillors' pews as well as a visitors' gallery. As part of the building's £11 million refurbishment programme in 2007–09, the ground floor is now home to a coffee shop, *The Bobbin*, with two permanent audiovisual and photographic exhibitions: "Waking the Giant" and "No Mean City".

Linen Hall Library

17 Donegall Square North (entrance at 52 Fountain St) • Mon–Fri 9.30am–5.30pm, Sat 9.30am–4pm • ⓦ linenhall.com

At the northwest corner of Donegall Square stands Belfast's oldest library, the substantially revamped **Linen Hall Library**, established in 1788. Its main feature is the Political Collection, a unique accumulation of over 100,000 publications reflecting every aspect of Northern Irish political life since 1966; also here are prison letters smuggled out of Long Kesh, which, in its more widely used name of the Maze, was the scene of the 1981 hunger strike (see p.594). The library also boasts excellent facilities for tracing family trees, a café, and stocks all the daily newspapers. Regular literary events take place throughout the year, including specialist workshops.

The Entries and around

A little way northeast of Donegall Square, a handful of narrow alleyways known as the **Entries** links Ann Street and the High Street. You'll stumble across some great old saloon bars down here, such as *The Morning Star* in Pottingers Entry, with its large frosted windows and Parisian-café-like counter (see p.484), and *White's Tavern* in Winecellar Entry, which dates from the seventeenth century (see p.484). Crown Entry was where the Society of United Irishmen (see p.586) was born, led by the Protestant triumvirate of Wolfe Tone, Henry Joy McCracken and Samuel Nielson. Nielson also printed his own newspaper in this area, the *Northern Star*; heavily influenced by the French revolutionary ideals of liberty, equality and fraternity, the newspaper's inflammatory material led to his being hounded out of town.

   Just to the north, no. 2 Waring Street was originally built as a market house in 1769, but is more renowned as the venue for the **1792 Belfast Harp Festival:** by the end of the eighteenth century, the old Gaelic harping tradition had reached almost terminal decline and the convention was a deliberate attempt by its organizers, the United Irish Society, to record some of the harpers' airs for posterity. The transcriber, Edmund Bunting, was stimulated to tour Ireland collecting further airs, 77 of which were published in his illustrious collection of 1809.

Cathedral Quarter

The area north of Waring Street has experienced more than two decades of regeneration, a process kick-started when chef Nick Price gambled on the then mainly derelict area by opening his *Nick's Warehouse* restaurant in 1989. With Price's recent retirement, that Hill Street venue, which proved a huge success, is now *The Harp Bar* (see p.484). His punt, meanwhile, is looking a sure thing, with an ever-increasing number of restaurants and bars and a fresh title, the **Cathedral Quarter** (ⓦthecathedralquarter.com), for this once-scruffy patch. Testament to the changes is that the city's only five-star hotel, *The Merchant* (see p.481) – whose owner, Bill Wolsey, has converted building after building in the Quarter – is located here.

   The University of Ulster's Belfast Campus sits across from the newly opened **MAC** (Metropolitan Arts Centre; see p.487) on the edge of **St Anne's Square**, a foodie honeypot with some of Belfast's finest restaurants in residence around its fringes, *Potted Hen* (see p.483) and *House of Zen* (see p.487) among them. Arts and music venues such as the Black Box (see p.483) and Oh Yeah Music Centre (see p.487) and live music pubs throng the cobbled streets, while the Quarter's cultural hub status is cemented by its hosting of a number of Belfast's more bohemian **events**, from the Cathedral Quarter Arts Festival (CQAF; see p.486) to the Open House music festival (see p.486).

13

LORD EDWARD CARSON

Lord Edward Carson is a name that Northern Ireland has never forgotten. A Dubliner of Scots-Presbyterian background, he took the decision in 1910 to accept the leadership of the opposition to Home Rule, which in effect inextricably allied him to the Ulster Unionist resistance movement. Yet, though this association is about the only thing for which he is remembered, his personality and integrity went far deeper than this. He abhorred religious intolerance, and behind the exterior of a zealous crusader was a man who sincerely believed that Ireland couldn't prosper without Britain and only wished that a federalist answer could have involved a united Ireland. Nonetheless, this was the same man who, as a brilliant orator at the bar, and in the role he loved the most, brought about the humiliating destruction of Oscar Wilde at the writer's trial in 1895.

St Anne's Cathedral

Donegall Street · Mon–Sat 9am–5pm, Sun 1–3pm; between services only · Free · ⓦ belfastcathedral.org

A couple of hundred yards up Donegall Street from where it meets Waring Street you'll find the most monolithic of all the city's grand buildings, the Protestant **St Anne's Cathedral**, a neo-Romanesque basilica started in 1899, but not fully completed until 1981. Entrance is via the huge west door, immediately to the right of which is the baptistery, with an intricately designed representation of the Creation on its ceiling consisting of 150,000 tiny pieces of glass. Most significant, however, is the cathedral's only tomb, marked by a simple slab on the floor of the south aisle, which contains the body of **Lord Edward Henry Carson** (1854–1935; see box, above). The symbol of Partition, he's seen either as the province's saviour or as the villain who sabotaged Ireland's independence as a 32-county state (see box, above). The cathedral attracts a lot of media attention in the run-up to Christmas each year as the incumbent Dean undertakes a "sit-out" on Donegall Street to collect donations for the poor and charitable causes, a tradition started by Dean Sammy Crooks in 1976. Dressed in the black Anglican clerical cloak, he is referred to as "Black Santa".

Great Victoria Street

The strip of Belfast running south along **Great Victoria Street** to Shaftesbury Square and thence to the university area and beyond was once known as the "Golden Mile". It is rarely called that these days, but Great Victoria Street itself is worth checking out, not least for the grandiose Victorian **Grand Opera House** (see p.487), which sits at its northern end. Although locals complained about the modern extension added to the theatre in 2006, it is now accepted as part and parcel of the city skyline. A few paces south lies the **Europa Hotel**; once renowned for being Europe's most bombed, it now stands as one of Belfast's finest after a complete refurbishment. Almost opposite the Europa stands one of the greatest of Victorian gin palaces, the **Crown Liquor Saloon** (see p.484), now owned by the National Trust. The saloon has a glittering tiled exterior resembling a spa baths more than a serious drinking institution, while inside, the scrolled ceiling, patterned floor and the golden-yellow and rosy-red hues led John Betjeman to describe it as his "many-coloured cavern".

The Laganside

The beginning of the **Laganside** area is marked at the High Street's eastern end by the **Prince Albert Memorial Clock Tower**. Built in 1867–69 and tilting slightly off the perpendicular as a result of its construction upon gradually sinking wooden piles, it's a strange memorial – especially as Prince Albert never had anything to do with Belfast – but it's a handy landmark enabling visitors to the area to find their bearings.

North of the Albert Clock, along Dunbar Link, you'll come across a series of grand buildings inspired by the same civic vanity as that behind the design of the City Hall. The restored **Custom House** on Donegall Quay is a Corinthian-style, E-shaped edifice designed between 1854 and 1857 by Charles Lanyon, who was responsible for several of the city's finest buildings. Unfortunately, it's not open to the public, leaving you unable to verify rumours of fantastic art masterpieces stored in its basements – though it is known that Anthony Trollope, the nineteenth-century novelist (and inventor of the pillar box), once worked here as a surveyor's clerk.

Just beyond the Custom House on Donegall Quay is the ambitious **Laganside** development project, the first component of which to be completed was the **Lagan Weir**, designed to protect the city against flooding. Millions of pounds have been pumped into dredging the river to maintain water levels and revive the much depleted fish population – successfully it seems: there was salmon fishing on the weir's inauguration day in 1994. Look across the river to the **Harland & Wolff** shipyard (see below) and you'll spot its landmark yellow cranes ("Samson" and "Goliath").

Further south along Oxford Street, on Lanyon Place, stands a 60ft-high metal **statue** depicting a girl holding aloft a ring of thanksgiving (for the peace process). Erected in 2007, *Beacon of Hope* (or "Nuala with the Hula", as locals affectionately call her) has fast become a city icon. Nearby sits the glittering 2000-seater **Waterfront Hall** concert hall, which is embarking on a substantial £29.5 million extension programme that is set for completion in spring 2016.

The Titanic Quarter

It takes 10min on foot from Donegall Square to the Titanic Quarter. Alternatively, take Metro bus #26 from Donegall Square West or the train from Belfast Central or Great Victoria Street, disembarking at the Titanic Quarter stop

Across the river on Queen's Quay, the massive **Odyssey** leisure complex (see p.487) marks the beginning of the **Titanic Quarter** (ⓦtitanic-quarter.com), an area of the city that has seen huge financial investment in recent years. Luxury apartments now line the water's edge behind the Odyssey Complex, overlooking the area's eye-catching figurehead, **Titanic Belfast**. The Quarter is gaining a reputation as a media hub, with Paint Hall studios the setting for several big-budget Hollywood movies and the HBO series, *Game of Thrones*, and a further two studios recently announcing plans to move in to the area. To the rear of the Odyssey building is the **Whowhatwherewhenwhy** scientific discovery centre (ⓦw5online.co.uk), known as **W5**, with more than 150 interactive exhibits, aimed primarily at children. For more grown-up insights, it's worth taking a tour of the area (see p.480).

THE DOCKS AND THE RMS TITANIC

Much of Belfast's waterside heritage is associated with English engineer Edward James Harland (1831–95) who, together with his German-born assistant Gustav Wilhelm Wolff (1834–1913), founded the **Harland & Wolff** shipbuilding company here in 1861. Starting from a small shipyard on Queen's Island, the company grew rapidly and over the following decades had gained a reputation for innovations such as iron (rather than wooden) decks and flatter, squarer hulls designed to maximize capacity. The firm continued to flourish after Harland's death and Wolff's retirement, most notably when it constructed three steamships for the White Star Line – the *Olympic*, the *Britannic* and, most famously, the **Titanic**. Completed in 1912, the RMS *Titanic*, then the world's largest passenger-carrying steamship, sank on April 14 of the same year, just four days into her maiden voyage from Southampton to New York, having collided with an iceberg in the North Atlantic. More than 1500 of the 2200-plus passengers and crew drowned, a tragedy that continues to hold a macabre fascination today. Belfast is still proud of its role in creating the world's most famous ship ("She was fine when she left here" goes the saying, along with "Built by Irishmen, driven by an Englishman"), and the centenary of her launch was marked by numerous events focused upon the Laganside and the new Titanic Quarter.

13

Titanic Belfast

1 Olympic Way, Queens Rd • Daily: April & June–Aug 9am–7pm; May & Sept 9am–6pm; Oct–March 10am–5pm • ⓦ titanicbelfast.com

The city's newest landmark, the £77 million **Titanic Belfast**, opened its doors on the ship's centenary in April 2012 to great aplomb, with a concert staged on the slipway where the liner was first launched. Designed by CivicArts with Todd Architects as the lead architect, the prow-like structure is the same height as the ship's hull (38m) and glistens in the sunlight courtesy of some 3000 silver-anodized aluminium shards.

Inside, an interactive **museum** takes visitors on a journey from the RMS *Titanic*'s conception and its build in the nearby Harland & Wolff dry dock to its disastrous maiden journey and the incident enquiry. The attraction has exceeded all expectations of visitor numbers, with over 800,000 passing through the doors in its first year, nearly twice as many as anticipated, while the slipway has hosted everything from a World Title boxing match to the BBC Proms.

South Belfast

Towards the old Golden Mile's southern extremity lies the **university area**, the focal point for South Belfast's attractions (ⓦ southbelfast.org) with plenty of eating places, pubs and a range of budget accommodation options. Near Queen's University are the lush **Botanic Gardens**, within which sits the vast **Ulster Museum**, displaying everything from dinosaur bones and an Egyptian mummy to contemporary art. Heading south from here along Stranmillis Road it's a relatively short step east to the river-skirting **Lagan Towpath**, which runs several kilometres southwest to Lisburn, while a detour along the way leads to the Neolithic earthwork known as the **Giant's Ring**.

The University Quarter

Just south of Shaftesbury Square stand three churches – Moravian, Crescent and Methodist – whose distinctive steeples frame the entrance to the **University Quarter**. From here, leading up to the university buildings, the roads are lined with early Victorian terraces that represent the final flowering of Georgian architecture in Belfast. The **Upper Crescent** is a magnificent curved Neoclassical terrace, built around 1845 but sadly neglected since; it is now used mainly for office space. The **Lower Crescent**, perversely, is straight.

Queen's University

Queen's Welcome Centre Mon–Fri 9.30am–4.30pm, Sun 10am–1pm • Group tours (1hr) £3.50; self-guided tours free • ⓦ qub.ac.uk/vcentre

Queen's University is the architectural centrepiece of the area, flanked by the most satisfying example of a Georgian terrace in Belfast, **University Square**, where the red brickwork mostly remains intact, with the exception of a few bay windows added in the Victorian era. The university building itself was constructed in 1849 as a mock-Tudor remodelling of Magdalen College, Oxford, to a design by Charles Lanyon, and houses a visitor centre which provides information about the university and runs guided tours.

The Italianate **Union Theological College**, nearby on College Park, also by Lanyon, was temporarily the site of the Northern Ireland Parliament until 1932 when Stormont was built.

The Botanic Gardens

College Park, Botanic Ave • Daily 7.30am–sunset; Palm House and Tropical Ravine Mon–Fri 10am–noon & 1–5pm, Sat & Sun 2–5pm; Oct–March same hours but closes 4pm Mon–Fri • Free • Buses #8A, #8B and #8C from Donegall Square East

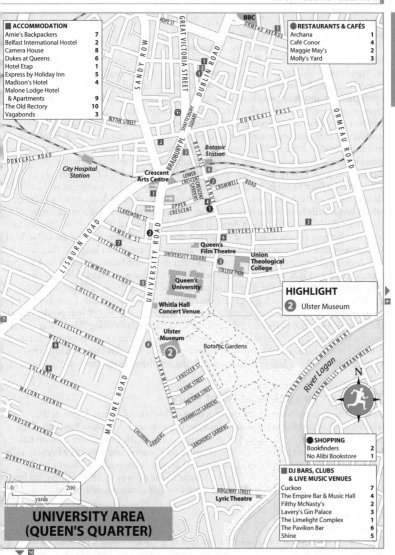

ACCOMMODATION

Arnie's Backpackers	7
Belfast International Hostel	2
Camera House	8
Dukes at Queens	6
Hotel Etap	1
Express by Holiday Inn	5
Madison's Hotel	4
Malone Lodge Hotel & Apartments	9
The Old Rectory	10
Vagabonds	3

RESTAURANTS & CAFÉS

Archana	1
Café Conor	4
Maggie May's	2
Molly's Yard	3

HIGHLIGHT

2 Ulster Museum

SHOPPING

Bookfinders	2
No Alibi Bookstore	1

DJ BARS, CLUBS & LIVE MUSIC VENUES

Cuckoo	7
The Empire Bar & Music Hall	4
Filthy McNasty's	2
Lavery's Gin Palace	3
The Limelight Complex	1
The Pavilion Bar	6
Shine	5

UNIVERSITY AREA (QUEEN'S QUARTER)

ust below the university are the popular **Botanic Gardens**, first opened in 1827 and
well protected by trees from the noise of the surrounding traffic. Within the gardens is
the **Palm House**, a hothouse predating the famous one at Kew Gardens in London, but
very similar in style, with a white-painted framework of curvilinear ironwork and glass.
It was the first of its kind in the world, another success for Lanyon, who worked in
tandem on this project with the Dublin iron-founder Richard Turner. The nearby
Tropical Ravine is a classic example of Victorian light entertainment – a hundred-year-
old sunken glen chock-full of "vegetable wonders" extracted from far-flung jungles and
replanted for the delight of the visiting Belfast public. It's currently being restored so
plants are being stored in the Palm House on a temporary basis.

13

Ulster Museum

Tues–Sat and Bank Holiday Mon 10am–5pm • Free • ⓦ nmni.com/um

The Botanic Gardens also house the **Ulster Museum**, which reopened in 2009 after a long redevelopment programme. Retaining its original eighty-year-old shell, the museum now incorporates a bold modernist design and sheds light both literally and figuratively on subjects ranging from the North's troubled history to Ireland's geological past. The grand open-plan **ground floor**, which also features a much-improved café, includes everything from an impressive dinosaur skeleton to contemporary haute couture. From here, the curators recommend heading up to the **third floor** to explore the art exhibits. The undoubted highlights here are the modern art collection (featuring Francis Bacon's macabre *Head II*, Bridget Riley's unnerving *Cataract IV* and Stanley Spencer's thought-provoking *The Betrayal*), and the stunning landscapes and rural scenes by painters such as Belfast's Sir John Lavery, plus Turner's highly symbolic *Dawn of Christianity*.

The **second floor** features the "Nature Zone", depicting the Earth's origins and Ireland's development up to the Ice Age. Far more engrossing are the **first floor**'s history galleries, which begin with Neolithic remains and Bronze Age finds (including a remarkable decorated shield), before taking a detailed look at the medieval period – two exhibits to look out for here are the somewhat skewwhiff stone inauguration chair of the O'Neills of Clandeboye and the silver gilt arm-reliquary supposedly created to house St Patrick's hand. The Armada gallery includes plenty of relics from the ill-fated *Girona*, which sank off the Antrim coast in 1588, while the Ascendancy section includes a remarkable rag-bound tally-stick, used to record the number of prayers said during the then illegal outdoor Catholic service, as well as highlighting the effects of the Great Famine. From here the exhibits quicken up a pace, especially when focusing upon the War of Independence and the North's resistance to Dublin rule, before looking at Belfast during World War II and concluding with a space devoted to the Troubles. The museum's most popular exhibit however is Takabuti, a 2500-year-old Egyptian mummy that was first revealed to museum visitors in 1835. After 180 years in residence, she still draws in the crowds.

The Lagan Towpath and Giant's Ring

Beyond the university area lie the glades of middle-class suburbia. A gate at the southern tip of the Botanic Gardens leads to the river and the **Lagan Towpath**. This tarmacked trail can be tramped for about eight miles south to Lisburn, passing old locks and lock houses, woodland and marshes on the way. The waterway became fully navigable in the late 1790s, ready to carry the newly discovered coal from Lough Neagh, but its utility declined with the advent of the railway in 1839. Today, it's been harnessed as part of the Ulster Way, for rambling and canoeing enthusiasts.

Giant's Ring

Free access dawn to dusk

If you leave the towpath at Shaw's Bridge (the ring-road crossing), it's a one-mile signposted walk along country lanes to the **Giant's Ring**, a colossal, 600ft-wide earthwork thought to have served as a burial ground or meeting place. You wouldn't be far wrong in thinking that its inwardly sloping wall would make an excellent speed-track circuit, for in the eighteenth century it was used for horse racing: six circuits made a two-mile race, with the punters jostling for position on the top of the rampart. Most captivating of all is the huge **dolmen** at the central hub of this cartwheel structure. As a single megalithic remain, it is immediately more impressive than even the great structures of the Irish High Kings at Tara, though here there's little information concerning its origins and usage. The setting chosen for the site, high above the surrounding lowlands (probably once marshy lake), is impressive – there's a powerful feeling that the great dramas and decision-making of the ancient northeast must have been played out here.

East Belfast

From Donegall Square West, the Metro bus #4A runs every 8min to East Belfast. Alternatively, from Belfast Central train station, a 25min walk straight down the Alberbridge Road leads to the Holywood Arches

East Belfast's (ⓦeastbelfastpartnership.org) skyline is dominated by the cranes – named "Samson" and "Goliath" – which tower above the **Harland & Wolff shipyard** (see box, p.469). The shipyard is the city's proudest international asset – though the company's work is nowadays centred on offshore wind farm installations – and is said to possess the largest dry dock in the world: over 2000ft long and 300ft wide. The surrounding area is now home to one of Europe's biggest redevelopment projects, the Titanic Quarter (see p.469), and increased financial investment is being channelled towards housing developments and retail outlets as well as community and cultural projects.

The area's pride in the famous figures it has given to the literary, sporting and music worlds remains undimmed; the theologian and author of the *Chronicles of Narnia*, **C.S. Lewis**, was born in Dundela Villas, and there's a plaque commemorating him at Dundela Flats. Fans of the *Chronicles* should also pay a visit to the Holywood Arches, where they will find a magnificent bronze statue depicting one of the Narnia characters, Digory Kirke, peering into the famous wardrobe. Another plaque on Burren Way in the Cregagh Estate marks the childhood home of the late footballer **George Best** (see box, below), whom many herald as being the greatest footballer of all time. **Van Morrison** (see box, p.474) fans, meanwhile, might want to seek out his birthplace, a private house (with no public access) at 125 Hyndford Street, off Beersbridge Road, and the many streets that feature in his songs (Cyprus Avenue, Castlereagh Road and others). The Connswater Community Greenway (ⓦcommunitygreenway.co.uk/trails) group has recently launched a series of **trails** for all three East Belfast sons, each leading you through the streets where the men grew up and the places that influenced and inspired them. They are free and downloadable from the website.

GEORGE BEST

Maradona good, Pele better, George Best (popular Belfast sporting adage).

Born in East Belfast in 1946, **George Best** became (and remains to this day) Northern Ireland's most celebrated footballer, signed by Manchester United after being rejected by local clubs. Making his debut aged 17, Best starred in the 1964–65 and 1966–67 Championship-winning teams, cementing his reputation as a dazzling, jinking and goal-scoring winger. His good looks, long hair, gift of the gab and love of the high life also led to his acquisition of the sobriquet "the fifth Beatle". Further fame was assured when United beat Benfica 4–1 in the 1967 European Cup Final, Best scoring one of the goals and running the Portuguese team's defence so ragged before a vast televised audience that his award of European Footballer of the Year was a foregone conclusion.

The latter half of the 1960s saw Best's celebrity lifestyle (by then he owned nightclubs and boutiques and had dated at least one Miss World) consumed by gambling, **alcoholism** and chasing women. He walked out of United in 1974, and after that his footballing career declined rapidly, taking in spells in the US and Australia. Alcohol addiction led to a stint in prison in 1984, after which Best was found guilty of drunk driving and assaulting a police officer. By 2002 his health was so poor that he underwent a liver transplant, but continued to drink after its success and eventually succumbed to multiple organ failure in November 2005.

Some 100,000 mourners lined the streets of Belfast as Best's coffin travelled to his **funeral** service at Stormont. Belfast City Airport was subsequently renamed in his honour and, in 2006, the Ulster Bank issued one million £5 notes bearing his picture – the entire issue was rapidly snapped up for keepsakes. The great sadness of Best's football career was that, despite 37 caps for Northern Ireland, he never appeared in a major international competition such as the World Cup, but he inspired a host of young footballers and, indeed, numerous jokes, not least his own oft-quoted remark: "I spent a lot of my money on booze, birds and fast cars. The rest I just squandered." Avid fans can now book to stay overnight in the Best family home on the Cregagh Estate (see p.482).

13

VAN MORRISON

Belfast boasts an impressive roster of musical talent, from singer Ruby Murray (the Madonna of the 1950s, in terms of chart success), flautist James Galway and pianist Barry Douglas, to rock guitarists Eric Bell and Gary Moore, both of whom played with Thin Lizzy. Without doubt, however, Belfast's most renowned musical son – and the one who most vocally celebrates his Belfast beginnings – is **Van Morrison**. Emerging from the city's early 1960s' blues scene with the group Them, it was Morrison's first solo single *Brown Eyed Girl* that brought him international success. He followed this up with *Astral Weeks* in 1968, an impressionistic song cycle drawing on his experiences growing up in Belfast, which remains his masterpiece. Throughout his subsequent career he has embraced jazz, folk and blues, producing a body of work that, for sheer quality and diversity, is rivalled only by Dylan.

Whatever the style of music, Morrison frequently harks back to his East Belfast childhood: he often name-checks specific streets and places, including Hyndford Street where he was born, and the nearby Cypress Avenue; and his collaboration with traditional Irish musicians The Chieftains in 1988 on their Irish Heartbeat album included *I'll tell Me Ma*, a traditional Belfast children's rhyme. In 2013 he was granted the freedom of the city, and in 2014 he played three ecstatically received concerts in his old school in Orangefield. The **Van Morrison Trail** is a 3.two-mile self-guided walk taking in eight places that were important to Morrison and inspirational to his music.

Stormont

4-miles east of the centre, off the Newtownards Road • Mon–Fri 9am–4pm; guided tours 11am & 2pm, except July, Aug, Easter & Halloween when tours leave at 10am & 3pm • Free • Buses #20A and #23 from Donegall Square West

The home of the Northern Ireland Parliament until the introduction of direct rule in 1972, **Stormont** now houses the Assembly created by the 1998 Good Friday Agreement. It's a magnificent sight, a great, white Neoclassical mansion crowning a rise in the middle of a park at the end of a long, straight drive. You can wander freely in the grounds, and free public tours have recently been introduced. There's also a wonderful children's playground, named in honour of the late Mo Mowlam, previous Northern Ireland Secretary of State. Also here, though not open to the public, is **Stormont Castle**, the office of the British Secretary of State for Northern Ireland.

North Belfast

North Belfast boasts baronial **Belfast Castle**, the impressive wildlife collection of **Belfast Zoo** and superb panoramic city views from **Cave Hill**. The castle and the city's zoo, both out on the Antrim Road, sit conveniently alongside one another on the slopes of Cave Hill, served by bus #1 from Donegall Square West.

Belfast Castle

Antrim Rd • Tues–Sat 9am–10pm, Sun & Mon 9am–5.30pm • Free • ⓦ belfastcastle.co.uk

Built in 1870 to the designs of Lanyon and surrounded by a wooden estate, the sandstone **Belfast Castle**'s exterior is in Scottish Baronial style, inspired in part by the reconstruction of Balmoral Castle in Aberdeenshire in 1853. It features a six-storey tower, a series of crow-stepped gables and conically peak-capped turrets, but the most striking feature of all is the serpentine Italianate stairway that leads down from the principal reception room to the garden terrace below. Restored and refurbished in 1990, the interior is, however, virtually empty of Victorian period accoutrements. Upstairs, the revamped **visitor centre** traces the locality's history from prehistoric cave-dwellers to the castle's construction.

Belfast Zoo

Antrim Rd • Daily: April–Sept 10am–7pm; Oct–March 10am–4pm • Adults £11, children 4–17 £5.50, under 4 free • ⓦ belfastzoo.co.uk

Adjoining the castle is the well-landscaped parkland of **Belfast Zoo** which stretches up towards Cave Hill. A fifteen-year renovation programme and an investment of £10 million has improved its layout immeasurably. Within, you'll find primates and big cats, elephants, penguins and sea lions, and a free-flight aviary, where rare species have room to breed. There's also an impressive annual programme of family-friendly events.

Cave Hill

Castle and zoo aside, it's **Cave Hill** itself that should be your main port of call in North Belfast. Several paths lead up from the castle estate to the hill's summit – a rocky outcrop known as "Napoleon's Nose" (believed to have been an inspiration for Jonathan Swift's novel, *Gulliver's Travels*) – which affords an unsurpassable overview of the whole city and lough. From here you can't help but appreciate the accuracy of the poet Craig Raine's aerial description of the city in his *Flying to Belfast* as "a radio set with its back ripped off". Cave Hill was once awash with Iron Age forts, for there was flint (for weapon making) in the chalk under the basalt hill-coverings. In 1795, Wolfe Tone, Henry Joy McCracken and other leaders of the United Irishmen stood on the top of Cave Hill and pledged "never to desist in our efforts until we have subverted the authority of England over our country and asserted our Independence".

West Belfast

Metro bus #11A/B/C/D runs down the Fall from Chichester St; for the Shankill, take Metro bus #10A/B/C/D/E/F/G/H from Queen St

Though the nexus of the Troubles for 25 years, today **West Belfast** (ⓦvisitwestbelfast .com) is as safe as anywhere else in the city to visit. There is, however, little of architectural note among the mainly residential streets, and most of the "sights" are

THE TROUBLES IN WEST BELFAST

The **Troubles in West Belfast** have their origins in the nineteenth century, when the city's population expanded dramatically as people flocked from the countryside to work in the booming new flax and linen industries. Many of these migrants were crammed into jerry-built housing in the grids of streets which still today define this part of the city. Conditions were deplorable and did nothing to ease tensions between Catholic and Protestant residents. There were numerous **sectarian riots** – the worst was in 1886, during the reading of the Home Rule Bill, when 32 people died and over 370 were injured – leading to the almost inevitable definition of two separate neighbourhoods, as Protestant and Catholic families alike began to migrate to more secure surroundings.

In 1968 and 1969, this division was pushed to its limit when, across the city, sectarian mobs and gunmen evicted over eight thousand families from their homes, mainly in Catholic West Belfast. The Royal Ulster Constabulary, or RUC, called for government assistance, and **British troops** arrived on the streets on August 15, 1969. A month later the makeshift barrier dividing the Catholic Falls from the Protestant Shankill had become a full-scale reinforced "peace line". British intervention may have averted a civil war, but it failed to prevent an escalation in sectarian conflict. Indeed, the army soon came to be viewed as an occupying force and a legitimate target for a reviving IRA, though local sympathies for its aims were much diminished by the 1972 Bloody Friday bombings (see p.594). In return, Loyalist paramilitaries sought to avenge Republican violence, often through indiscriminate killings. A cycle of tit-for-tat attacks ensued, finally reaching its nadir with the **Shankill Road bombing**, a botched attempt to blow up Loyalist paramilitary leaders supposedly meeting above a fish shop on the Shankill Road in 1993, which instead killed customers and the shop's owner.

13

associated with the area's troubled past. Much of the old terraced housing has been replaced in recent years by rows of modern estates, but it's impossible to miss examples of the partisan **mural paintings** that decorate walls and gable ends in both Catholic and Protestant areas (see box, opposite). Tourist information about the area is available from the West Belfast Tourist Information Point located inside the Culturlann Arts & Culture Centre (see p.487). You might also consider taking a Black Taxi Tour (⒲niblacktaxitours.com) covering both sides of the Peace Line – a divide longer than the Berlin Wall.

The Falls Road

From the city centre, Divis Street, a westward continuation of Castle Street, leads to the **Falls Road**, which heads on for a further 3km west past Milltown Cemetery and into Andersonstown. The first part of the Falls Road is known as the **Lower Falls** where, these days, most of the land to the left (south) consists of modern red-brick terraced housing. The right-hand side of the road features some of the main local landmarks, including the bright blue and pink leisure centre and the last remaining of the three Carnegie Libraries built in Belfast, this one dating from 1908. Turn right off the Falls Road at the leisure centre on to North Howard Street and Cupar Way and you'll encounter the infamous **Peace Line** – a wall of concrete and iron separating the area from the Protestant working-class district of Shankill.

Conway Mill
5–7 Conway St • Mon–Fri 9am–5pm • ⒲ conwaymill.org

Down Conway Street stands the old **Conway Mill**, revitalized by a concerted community effort. Inside you can investigate the wares of the numerous small businesses and local artists who operate from here, as well as an art gallery and a small exhibition depicting the mill's history.

Cultúrlann MacAdam Ó Fiaich
216 Falls Rd • Mon–Thurs 9am–9pm, Fri & Sat 9am–6pm, Sun 11am–4pm • ⒲ culturlann.ie

Housed in a disused Presbyterian church, the **Cultúrlann MacAdam Ó Fiaich** is a cultural centre for Irish-speakers, housing an extensive bookshop (that also sells traditional-music CDs), an excellent café and a thriving theatre, often host to musical events. Although you're unlikely to hear it spoken on the streets or in most pubs, the Irish language is flourishing in Catholic areas of Belfast and throughout the North.

The Shankill Road and around

The Protestant population of West Belfast lives in the area abutting the Falls to the north, between the **Shankill Road** and the Crumlin Road, with a Peace Line running along Alliance Avenue. As an interface between the Protestant and Catholic communities, the Crumlin Road area was the scene of many violent sectarian incidents during the Troubles – and despite regeneration and new housing developments it remains a potential flashpoint, particularly during the July marching season. As with the Falls, the main draw for visitors to the area is the **murals**.

Crumlin Road Gaol
53–55 Crumlin Rd • Daily: first tour 10am, last tour 4.30pm (1hr 15min) • £8.50, aged 5–15 £6.50, under 5s free • ⒲ crumlinroadgaol.com

From the Westlink you'll pass between the **courthouse** and the notorious **Crumlin Road Gaol**, the two connected by an underground tunnel; former inmates include Éamon de Valera, Gerry Adams and Ian Paisley before it closed in 1996. The gaol has now been successfully refurbished and offers fascinating and entertaining guided tours as well as occasional cultural events.

BELFAST'S MURALS

The politically inspired **murals** of Northern Ireland are among the most startling sights not just in Belfast, but in the whole country. This ephemeral art form, which recycles the images and slogans of the Troubles, characterizes the violent struggles of the last few decades. Though many have been in place now for over a decade, some of the slogans and murals mentioned here may have vanished by the time of your visit: new murals are painted over old ones or the houses they adorn are demolished. One of the consequences in the immediate aftermath of the Good Friday Agreement (see p.596) was that many of the sectarian Loyalist murals were replaced by murals celebrating local history, including the *Titanic* – yet when trouble flares or discontent rises, the old-style murals frequently reappear. A detailed archive of Northern Ireland's murals is maintained by the University of Ulster at ⓦcain.ulst.ac.uk/mccormick.

LOYALIST MURALS

For most of the twentieth century, mural painting in Northern Ireland was a predominantly **Loyalist** activity. The first mural appeared in East Belfast in 1908 and, like many of its successors, celebrated William of Orange's (King Billy) victory at the **Battle of the Boyne**. Loyalist murals have tended to use imagery symbolic of power, such as the clenched scarlet fist, known as the **Red Hand of Ulster**, or flags, shields and other heraldic icons. However, the Loyalist response to the Troubles translated into what is now the most common form of painting, the militaristic mural. The greatest concentration of Loyalist murals is to be found on and around the Shankill Road, especially the Shankill Estate, to the north, and Dover Place, off Dover Street, to the south. Other areas are Sandy Row and Donegall Pass in South Belfast, and Newtownards Road, Martin Street and Severn Street in East Belfast.

REPUBLICAN MURALS

Republican murals were at first limited to simple sloganeering or demarcation of territory, the best-known example being the long-standing "You are now entering Free Derry" in that city's Bogside district (see p.517). As with much else in Republican politics, however, the 1981 hunger strikes had a significant influence. Murals in support of the ten hunger strikers abounded and the (usually smiling) face of **Bobby Sands** – the IRA commander in the Maze prison who led the strike – remains an enduring image. Murals soon became a fundamental part of the Republican propaganda campaign: prominent **themes** have been resistance to British rule, the call for the withdrawal of troops and questioning the validity of the police. More recently, however, Republican muralists have turned increasingly to Irish legends and history as their sources of inspiration, and the only militaristic murals tend to be found in flashpoints such as the Ardoyne area of North Belfast. Equally, artists have paid tribute to other international liberation movements, as in a striking series of murals on Divis Street just before the beginning of the Falls Road. Further Republican murals can be found nearby on Beechmount Avenue, further west on Lenadoon Avenue in Andersonstown, and on New Lodge Road in North Belfast.

ARRIVAL AND DEPARTURE   BELFAST

Belfast's two **airports** are well connected to the city centre by public transport, while a limited Metro bus service operates between the city centre and the **ferry terminals** Mon–Fri. The city also has an efficient bus network. Visit the excellent journey planner at ⓦtranslink.co.uk (or get the associated app) to fine-tune your rail and bus journey to and from Belfast.

BY PLANE

Belfast International Airport ☎02894 484848, ⓦbelfastairport.com. The larger of the city's two airports is located 19 miles west of the city in Aldergrove; from here, the 24hr Airport Express 300 bus drops passengers at the city's Europa Buscentre (30-40min; £7.50 single, £10.50 return). A taxi to the city centre costs £31 (for a meet-and-greet service try ☎07730 782798, ⓦbelfastairporttaxis.com). The airport's arrivals hall has an ATM, a bureau de

change, car-rental outlets and a tourist information desk (Mon–Fri 7.30am–7pm, Sat 7.30am–5pm, Sun 8am–11am).

George Best Belfast City Airport ☎02890 939093, ⓦbelfastcityairport.com. Many domestic flights from Britain use this airport, just 3 miles northeast of the centre, from which the Airport Express 600 bus runs to the Europa Buscentre (Mon–Fri every 20–35min 6am–10.05pm, Sat every 20–40min 6am–9.50pm, Sun every 40–50min

13

7.30am–9.45pm; £2.60 single, £3.60 return). Alternatively, take the free shuttle bus to Sydenham train station and hop on a train to Belfast Central or Great Victoria Street stations (Mon–Fri every 20–30min 6.20am–10.50pm, Sat every 30min 6.35am–10.50pm, Sun hourly 9.20am–10.20pm; £1.80). A taxi from City Airport to the city centre costs £10 (📞 02890 809080, 🌐 valuecabs.co.uk). The terminal's ground floor has ATMs, a bureau de change, car-rental outlets and a tourist information desk (Mon–Fri 7.30am–7pm, Sat 7.30am–4.30pm, Sun 11am–6pm).

BY BOAT

West Bank Road terminals Stena ferries (📞 0844 770 7070, 🌐 stenaline.co.uk) from Cairnryan and Norfolkline ferries (📞 0844 499 0007, 🌐 norfolkline.com) from Liverpool dock here, a 30min walk from Donegall Square. A taxi costs £9 (📞 02890 333333, 🌐 fonacab.com). Metro Bus 96 runs to Upper Queen Street (Mon–Fri; £1.60).

Larne P&O ferries (📞 0871 664 4999, 🌐 poirishsea.com) from Cairnryan and Troon and Stena ferries from Fleetwood dock at the town of Larne (see p.496), 20 miles to the north, which is connected by Ulsterbus to the Europa Buscentre and by train to Great Victoria Street and Central stations.

BY TRAIN

Most trains call at the central Great Victoria Street Station, except trains from Dublin and some from Larne, which terminate at Central Station near the Waterfront Hall on East Bridge Street, a little way east of the centre.

Getting into town Various Metro buses stop outside Central Station en route to Donegall Square – travel is free to holders of railway tickets. From Central Station you can also hop on a connecting train for the 10min journey to Great Victoria Street Station, which stops en route at Botanic and City Hospital stations, both of which are useful if you're staying in the University Quarter. Alternatively, a 10min journey in the opposite direction will take passengers to the Titanic Quarter.

Destinations from Belfast (Central) Bangor (Mon–Sat every 15–30min, Sun hourly; 20–30min); Carrickfergus (Mon–Sat every 30min, Sun 9; 25min); Cultra for the Ulster Folk and Transport Museum (Mon–Sat every 20–30min, Sun hourly; 15min); Derry (Mon–Sat 8–9 daily, Sun 5; 2hr); Drogheda (5–7 daily; 1hr 35min); Dublin (5–8 daily;

2hr–2hr 15min); Larne harbour (Mon–Sat hourly, Sun 10; 55min); Larne town (Mon–Sat hourly, Sun 10; 50min); Newry (5–7 daily; 55min).

Destinations from Belfast (Great Victoria St) Bangor (Mon–Sat every 15–30min, Sun hourly; 25–40min); Cultra for the Ulster Folk and Transport Museum (Mon–Sat every 20–30min, Sun hourly; 20min); Derry (Mon–Sat 8–9 daily, Sun 5; 2hr 15min); Larne harbour (Mon–Sat hourly, Sun 10; 1hr 5min); Larne town (Mon–Sat hourly, Sun 10; 1hr).

BY BUS

Express buses arrive at one of Belfast's two stations. The Europa Buscentre, accessed via the Great Northern shopping mall on Great Victoria Street, handles services to the Republic and the airports. It also serves all parts of Northern Ireland except North Down and the Ards Peninsula which utilize the Laganside Buscentre in Queen's Square (near the Albert Clock), though on weekday evenings and Sundays even these use the Europa. Aircoach (🌐 aircoach.ie) services from Dublin Airport arrive at Glengall Street.

Destinations from Belfast (Europa) Armagh (Mon–Fri 13–14 daily, Sat 6, Sun 4; 1hr 5min–1hr 25min); Cavan (Mon–Sat 1 daily; 2hr 45min); Derry (Mon–Fri every 30min, Sat 20, Sun 11; 1hr 40min); Downpatrick (Mon–Sat 15–18 daily, Sun 6; 50min–1hr); Drogheda (14 daily; 1hr 40min–1hr 55min); Dublin (24 daily; 2hr 40min–2hr 55min); Dublin Airport (24 daily; 2hr 10min–2hr 35min); Dungiven (Mon–Fri every 30min, Sat 20, Sun 11; 1hr 5min); Enniskillen (Mon–Fri hourly, Sat 7, Sun 2; 1hr 50min–2hr 15min); Hillsborough (Mon–Sat hourly, Sun 8; 25min); Larne (Mon–Fri 19 daily, Sat 9, Sun 2; 55min–1hr 15min); Magherafelt (Mon–Fri & Sun 2 daily, Sat 5; 1hr 10min); Moneymore (Mon–Fri & Sun 2 daily, Sat 5; 1hr 25min); Newcastle (Mon–Sat 18–20 daily, Sun 8; 1hr 10min); Newry (Mon–Fri every 30min, Sat hourly, Sun 8; 1hr 10min); Omagh (Mon–Fri hourly, Sat 11, Sun 6; 1hr 30min–1hr 50min).

Destinations from Belfast (Laganside) Bangor (Mon–Sat every 30min, Sun 8; 45min); Cultra for the Ulster Folk and Transport Museum (Mon–Sat every 30min, Sun 8; 30min); Newtownards (Mon–Sat very frequent, Sun 10; 35min); Portaferry (Mon–Fri 10 daily, Sat 9, Sun 2; 1hr 15min–1hr 45min).

INFORMATION

Tourist information The recently relocated Visit Belfast Welcome Centre is at 8–9 Donegall Square North, opposite the City Hall (Jan–May & Oct–Dec Mon–Sat 9am–5.30pm, June–Sept till 7pm, year-round Sun 11am–4pm; 📞 028 9024 6609, 🌐 visit-belfast .com). Stocks a vast range of information on the city and the rest of the North, provides an accommodation

booking service (Ireland and UK-wide), has interactive tourist information touch-screen terminals and sells tickets for events. It also has free customer wi-fi, a bureau de change and the only left-luggage facilities in the city (£3 per item for up to 4 hours, £4.50 per item for longer). The West Belfast Tourist Information Point is in the Culturlaan arts centre (see p.487).

13

Listings Consult the monthly listings freesheet *The Big List* (Ⓦthebiglist.co.uk) or the free bimonthlies *What About, Belfast in Your Pocket* (Ⓦinyourpocket.com) or *Go Belfast*, all available at the Welcome Centre and from pubs, clubs and record shops. A more recent addition to the scene is *Love Belfast* (Ⓦlovebelfast.co.uk), providing listings and blogs on local events for visitors to the city. The *Belfast Telegraph* newspaper (Ⓦbelfasttelegraph.co.uk) also has daily listings.

TOURS

The **Titanic Quarter** and docklands can be enjoyed via a boat tour (Ⓦlaganboatcompany.com), which relates Belfast's rich maritime history, or the rather more quirky Segway Titanic Tour (Ⓦsegwayni.co.uk). Visit Ⓦcycleni.com for information on **cycling** tours.

WALKING TOURS

There's a wealth of walking tours available. The "A History of Terror in Belfast" tour (☎07716 949460, Ⓦdeadcentretours.com; £15), led by a conflict resolution specialist, lasts 2hr and covers over 2 miles of the city, visiting places significant to the Troubles. There are also various political walking tours of West Belfast, delivered by former political prisoners (call for times and to book; £8; ☎02890 200770, Ⓦwww.coiste.ie), which depart from the Divis Tower at the city end of the Falls Road; advance booking is essential. "The Hidden Belfast Walking Tour" (daily July and Aug), meeting at the front gates of Belfast City Hall at 10am, 12.15pm and 2pm; £5) lasts an hour and aims to uncover the city's less well-known gems, both historical and recent. As the name suggests, "Ghost Walk Belfast" (Wed, Fri & Sun; 1hr 15min; £8; ☎07961 717992, Ⓦghostwalkbelfast.com) offers a spooky journey through the dark entries and alleyways of "haunted" Belfast. There are also walking tours (Ⓦtitanicwalk.com) around the docks, taking in the Titanic Drawing Office and Pump House, and a pub crawl that hits the city's finest watering holes (Fri & Sat 7.30pm, meeting at the Albert Clock; £8; ☎07712 603764, Ⓦbelfastcrawl.com). Tickets for all of these except the political and Titanic Quarter tours can be purchased at the Visit Belfast Welcome Centre (see p.478), which also publishes a range of leaflets describing other walks in the city.

BUS TOURS

Several companies operate hop-on hop-off open-top bus tours, with most taking in the Laganside, city centre, Titanic, Cathedral and University quarters and West Belfast: City Sightseeing (daily 10am–4pm; ☎02890 321321, Ⓦbelfastcitysightseeing.com; £7.50, valid 48hr), running from Chichester Street; Belfast City Tour (daily 10am–4pm; ☎02890 770990, Ⓦbelfastcitytour.com; £10, valid 48hr), also from Chichester Street; and Allen's Tours (daily 10.15am–4.15pm; ☎02890 915613, Ⓦallenstours.co.uk; £9, valid 72hr), departing from High Street.

TAXI TOURS

West Belfast is one of the features of several guided taxi tours, including the recommended Paddy Campbell's "Famous Black Cab Tours" (☎07990 955227, Ⓦbelfastblackcabtours.co.uk), World Famous Belfast Black Taxi Tours (☎02890 642264, Ⓦbelfasttours.com), Harpers Taxi Tours (☎02890 742711, Ⓦharperstaxitours.com) and Belfast Taxi Tours (☎02890 315777, Ⓦtaxitrax.com). Each tour lasts around 1hr 30min, exploring the Falls and Shankill roads (including the murals and the Peace Line), plus Milltown Cemetery, the docks and the university. Tours operate daily, must be pre-booked and usually cost a minimum of £30.

GETTING AROUND

Although you can easily **walk** around the city centre, distances to some of the outlying attractions are considerable, and a number of **places to stay** are also a little way out.

BY BUS

Network and times The excellent Metro service provides frequent buses to almost every conceivable destination within the city, while the blue-and-white, long-distance services of Ulsterbus (which principally covers the rest of the North beyond Belfast's boundaries) connect to some of the sights on the city's fringes, such as the Giant's Ring. Almost all Metro buses set off from Donegall Square or the streets immediately around it, while Ulsterbus uses the Europa Buscentre on Great Victoria Street. You can pick up a network map from the Visit Belfast Welcome Centre or the Metro kiosk in Donegall Square West (Mon–Fri 8am–6pm, Sat 8.30am–5.30pm; bus information on ☎02890 666630, Ⓦtranslink.co.uk). In general buses operate 6am till 11pm Monday to Saturday and 9am till 11pm on Sunday.

Tickets and fares Metro fares are determined by a zonal system within 12 geographical corridors. An unlimited Metro Day Travel ticket that is valid network-wide costs £3.50 (5 days £15, 10s day £30). Alternatively, there are Smartlink Multi-Journey Cards, available in 5, 10, 20, 30 and 40 journey options, costing from £4.75 to £36 depending on how many journeys. Cards can be purchased from the Metro kiosk on Donegall Square West, the two central bus stations and any Smartlink agent (including many newsagents).

BY TAXI

Metered black taxis, based at the main rank in Donegall Square East and other points throughout the city, charge a minimum £3, which rapidly starts to increase if you're going any distance at a rate of £1.67 per additional mile). Alternatively, you can phone a minicab (try Citi Cabs ☎02890 665566, fonaCAB ☎02890 333333 or Value Cabs ☎02890 809080); these too are metered, charge similar rates to the black cabs and are a good idea late at night as passing taxis are hard to grab.

BY BIKE

Full Cycle (☎02890 741569, ⓦfullcyclebikeshop.com) at 387 Antrim Rd offer road bikes for £30 per day, or £50 for a full weekend. Mountain bikes and hybrids also available. Cycle NI (ⓦcycleni.com) also provides useful additional information on cycle routes, bike rental and cycling tours.

ACCOMMODATION

Belfast has a broad range of **accommodation**, especially at the top end of the market, while the recent tourist boom has seen a number of well-known **budget hotels** open up across the city. The main concentration of hotels can be found on Great Victoria Street, around the University area and in the Cathedral Quarter.

CITY CENTRE

★**Europa Hotel** Great Victoria St ☎02890 271066, ⓦhastingshotels.com; map p.464. Belfast's Grand Old Dame, looking resplendent after a multimillion-pound refurbishment, offers views across the city with modern, spacious and luxurious bedrooms and suites. **£180**

The Fitzwilliam Hotel 1–3 Great Victoria St ☎02890 442080, ⓦfitzwilliamhotelbelfast.com; map p.464. One of the latest additions at the city's luxury end of the market features astonishingly well-equipped and thoughtfully accoutred rooms, with king-size beds sheeted in Egyptian cotton, mini hi-fi systems and flatscreen TVs. **£145**

Hilton Belfast 4 Lanyon Place ☎02890 277000, ⓦhilton.co.uk/belfast; map p.464. Huge and extravagant dockland addition to the Belfast skyline with staggering views across the city and a range of lavish rooms and suites. **£114**

Holiday Inn Belfast 22–26 Ormeau Ave ☎0871 942 9005, ⓦholidayinn.com/belfast; map p.464. Vast modern edifice opposite the BBC's Broadcasting House, offering well-equipped bedrooms and a health and leisure centre. **£89**

Ten Square 10 Donegall Square South ☎02890 241001, ⓦtensquare.co.uk; map p.464. A gem of a hotel in a much-refurbished, former linen house bang opposite City Hall, featuring just 23 individually designed rooms, with an utterly opulent feel that draws its influences from colonial Shanghai. **£155**

CATHEDRAL QUARTER

★**Malmaison** 34–38 Victoria St ☎02890 220200, ⓦmalmaison-belfast.com; map p.464. Installed in an elegantly converted warehouse on the periphery of the city's cultural hub, *Malmaison* features chic doubles, sumptuous suites named after the Samson and Goliath cranes (see p.464), and an attractive bar and restaurant. **£119**

The Merchant 16 Skipper St ☎02890 234888, ⓦthemerchanthotel.com; map p.464. Once the HQ of the Ulster Bank, this Victorian sandstone edifice has been converted into a wonderful hotel, complete with many of the original Italianate fittings and its own art gallery and spa. Rooms are spacious and luxuriously furnished in either Victorian or Art Deco style and its suites are impeccably elegant. **£220**

Premier Inn 2–6 Waring St ☎0871 5278070, ⓦpremierinn.com; map p.464. A more affordable option for the budget conscious, situated right in the heart of the Cathedral Quarter. Rooms are basic but modern and clean. **£90**

Ramada Encore 20 Talbot St ☎02890 261800, ⓦencorebelfast.co.uk; map p.464. Sitting on the edge of St Anne's Square and surrounded by some of the area's finest restaurants, the reasonable room rates here mean more money for eating out. The 165 rooms are bright and contemporary, all with en-suite wet rooms. **£102**

UNIVERSITY AREA (QUEEN'S QUARTER) AND AROUND

Arnie's Backpackers 63 Fitzwilliam St ☎02890 242867, ⓦarniesbackpackers.co.uk; map p.471. Convivial IHH- & IHO-affiliated hostel with 22 beds in five dorms, plus laundry and cooking facilities and a pair of Jack Russells. **£15.60**

Belfast International Hostel 22–32 Donegall Rd ☎02890 324733, ⓦhini.org.uk; map p.471. Large HINI hostel with twins and a couple of en-suite doubles, but mainly four- and six-bed dorms. There's also a café, self-catering kitchen and laundry, and tours of Belfast and to the Giant's Causeway are offered. Dorms **£14.50**, doubles **£21**

Camera House 44 Wellington Park ☎02890 660026, ⓦcameraguesthouse.com; map p.471. An elegantly decorated town house offering en-suite and standard accommodation, complete with open fire and library. The guesthouse is family run with free wi-fi and cooked Irish breakfasts. **£71**

Dukes at Queens 65–67 University St ☎02890 236666, ⓦdukesatqueens.com; map p.471. Smart,

13

modern, four-star redevelopment of a fine Victorian building, a few minutes' walk from the University, featuring luxurious bedrooms and a fashionable bar. **£76**

Hotel Etap 35 Dublin Rd ☎02890 328126, ⓦaccorhotels.com; map p.471. Modern, minimalist, clean and budget pretty much sums this place up. Ideal if you're not bothered about the absence of frills. **£85**

Express by Holiday Inn 106 University St ☎02890 311909, ⓦhiexpressbelfast.com; map p.471. The smaller sister to the Ormeau Ave branch (see p.481) might lack its sibling's amenities, but the recently refurbished rooms here still provide very restful accommodation at a fair price. **£116**

Madison's Hotel 59–63 Botanic Ave ☎02890 509800, ⓦmadisonshotel.com; map p.471. A small hotel with only 35 modern, spacious and reasonably priced rooms. The hotel's bar and nightclub are a popular weekend haunt with the city's 30-somethings. **£80**

Malone Lodge Hotel & Apartments 60 Eglantine Ave ☎02890 388060, ⓦmalonelodgehotelbelfast.com; map p.471. Welcoming and well-equipped hotel near Queen's, with off-street parking, pleasantly decorated rooms and a notable restaurant, *The Knife & Fork Grill & Deli*. **£99**

The Old Rectory 148 Malone Rd ☎02890 667882, ⓦanoldrectory.co.uk; map p.471. This beautifully converted former clergyman's house (Church of Ireland),

about 1 mile south of the university, offers both standard and en-suite rooms, and high-quality breakfasts. **£80**

★**Vagabonds** 9 University Rd ☎02890 233017, ⓦvagabondsbelfast.com; map p.471. A modern and funky hostel in the Queen's Quarter, designed and run by seasoned travellers, Tara and Curt. Close to bars, restaurants, Botanic Gardens and the Ulster Museum. Dorms **£13**, doubles **£40**

EAST BELFAST

George Best House 16 Burren Way, Cregagh Estate ☎07595 710916, ⓦgeorgebesthouse.com; map p.464. An opportunity to spend the night in George Best's old bedroom in his family home. Landmark East purchased the house in 2011 and have lovingly restored it to the way it would have looked before George left to join Man Utd in 1963. It's jam-packed with memorabilia and there are three bedrooms to choose from. Self-catering only. **£60**

Park Avenue Hotel 158 Holywood Rd ☎02890 65 6520, ⓦwww.parkavenuehotel.co.uk; map p.464. Well-designed modern hotel a few miles from the centre, next to the vibrant Belmont Road, offering very commodious doubles and spacious suites; plenty of off-street parking spaces too. **£100**

EATING AND DRINKING

There are plenty of options for food during the day in the city centre and around the University area, ranging from **cafés** many of which in the city centre stay open until 8.30pm on Thurs nights, to **traditional pubs**, which generally only serve lunch but in some cases continue to provide food until 9pm. Most of the city's well-established **restaurants** are around Donegall Square, although the Cathedral Quarter has fast become a dining-out hub. Restaurants are often fully booked on Friday and Saturday evenings, so **reserving** is essential unless you are prepared to eat early. There is a great range of cuisine, from modern Irish and European, with French and Italian especially popular, to a smattering of Indian and East Asian restaurants and some new chicken and barbecue joints.

Pubs Whether you're after raucous dancing, **traditional music** or simply a quiet pint of the black stuff, you're going to be spoilt for choice. First-time visitors tend to be drawn to the older pubs on **Great Victoria Street**, while the city's trendier residents and students frequent the **University Quarter** and the **Lisburn Road**. For a more eclectic mix of pubs in a smaller area (making for a great pub crawl), head to the **Cathedral Quarter**. If you're short of time, you could always join the guided **Belfast Pub Crawl** (see p.480), covering four well-known bars, complete with free drinks and some live music. A good resource for pub reviews is ⓦwww.belfastbar.co.uk.

CAFÉS

Café Conor 11A Stranmillis Rd ☎02890 663266, ⓦcafeconor.com; map p.471. Opposite the Ulster Museum in the former studio of artist William Conor, this café has an affordable Mediterranean menu. Good for brunch. Daily 9am–10pm.

Deanes Deli Bistro 44 Bedford St ☎02890 248800, ⓦmichaeldeane.co.uk; map p.464. Offshoot of Michael Deane's restaurants (see p.464), serving splendid sandwiches and more substantial meals. Mon–Sat noon–3pm & 5.30–10pm.

★**Established Coffee** 54 Hill St ☎02890 319416 map p.464. Award-winning barista Mark and his partner Bridget offer arguably the city's finest coffee here in th Cathedral Quarter, using filter, Chemex and Aeropress Expect simple industrial decor (and beards) and a warm and welcoming atmosphere. Mon–Fri 7am–6pm, Sat 8am–6pm, Sun 9am–6pm.

★**Grapevine** 5 Pottingers Entry ☎07794 653259; map p.464. Tucked away but worth seeking out for soul-warming soups, stews and gumbo plus homemade sandwiches (gluten-free options too). Mon–Fri 8am–5pm, Sat 9am–5pm.

RESTAURANTS

Archana 53 Dublin Rd ☎02890 323713, 🖰archana
.co.uk; map p.471. Belfast's best bet for spicy, good-value
curries and balti dishes with plenty of veggie options. "The
Usual" section on the menu features some of the
restaurant's regulars' favourite dishes – worth trying.
Mains run £10–15. Mon–Sat noon–2pm & 5–11pm, Sun
5–11pm.

Boojum Chichester St ☎02890 230600, 🖰boojummex
.com; map p.464. Minimalist interior with a canteen feel
but serving the best burritos in Belfast. Mid-week lunch
queues often extend down the street. Mon–Fri
11.30am–9pm, Sat noon–9pm, Sun 1–6pm.

Bubbacue 12 Callender St ☎02890 278220,
🖰bubbacue.com; map p.464. Deep South barbecue
cooked to perfection for twelve hours in a traditional
smoker. Pulled pork and beef brisket are the house
specialities with a choice of homemade barbecue sauces.
Tues–Sat noon–8pm, Sun 1–7pm.

Deanes 28–40 Howard St ☎02890 331134,
🖰michaeldeane.co.uk; map p.464. An elegant venue for
stunning modern Irish cuisine with a strong French
influence. Standing shoulder to shoulder are a dedicated
fish restaurant, the so-called "meat locker" and the
intriguing, Friday-only EIPIC (serving five-, six- and seven-
course set menus, each with a story). From £35 plus wine.
Loves Fish Mon–Sat noon–10pm, Sun 1–6pm; Meat
Locker Mon–Sat noon–3pm & 5.30–10pm; EIPIC Wed–
Sat 5.30–10pm plus Fri noon–3pm.

Hadskis 33 Donegal St ☎02890 325444, 🖰hadskis
.co.uk; map p.464. A new kid on the block in the über-cool
Cathedral Quarter, offering game, seafood and pasta dishes
made with locally sourced produce, often served with a
twist. Bank on around £30 plus wine. Mon–Fri noon–
11pm, Sat 11am–11pm.

★**Holohan's** 1 Lanyon Quay ☎02890 235973,
🖰belfastbarge.com/holohans; map p.464. The
Belfast Barge, moored on the River Lagan next to the
Waterfront Hall, is a fine setting for Holohan's hearty
dishes of traditional Irish cuisine with a twist,
some based on the chef's own family recipes. The
boxty alone is worth a special visit. Expect to pay around
£18 plus wine. Mon–Wed 10am–4pm, Thurs–Sat
10am–midnight.

Home Restaurant 22 Wellington Place ☎02890
34946, 🖰homebelfast.co.uk; map p.464. Originally a
pop-up restaurant, Home's simple, hearty offerings proved
to be such a success that it's now moved to permanent
premises and continues to be a huge hit with local foodies.
Gluten free, "Skinny" and children's menus available for
lunch and dinner. Around £20 plus wine. Mon noon–4pm,
Tues–Thurs noon–9.30pm, Fri & Sat noon–4pm &
5–10pm, Sun 1–9pm.

House of Zen 3 St Anne's Square ☎02890 278688,

🖰houseofzen.co.uk; map p.464. Fine Asian cuisine
(you'll pay around £20 plus wine) served in the beautiful
setting of St Anne's Square. Mon–Fri noon–3pm &
5–11.30pm, Sat 1–3pm & 5–11.30pm, Sun
1.30–10.30pm.

Howard Street 56 Howard St ☎02890 248362,
🖰howardstbelfast.com; map p.464. A relatively new
addition to the Belfast scene but already one of its finest
restaurants, offering wholesome dishes ranging from beer-
battered fish to dry-aged steaks. Excellent vegetarian
menu available. Around £30 plus wine. Tues–Sat noon–
2pm & 5–9.30pm.

Il Pirata 281 Upper Newtownards Rd ☎02890
673421, 🖰ilpiratabelfast.com; map p.464. Rustic
Italian dishes served in quirky surroundings outside of
the city centre. Choose a selection of small plates, from
goat's cheese polenta fritters to the incredibly tasty duck
ragu. Vegetarian and gluten-free options available.
Expect to pay £20 for a selection of plates and dessert.
Mon–Thurs & Sun noon–10pm, Fri & Sat
noon–11pm.

Maggie May's 50 Botanic Ave ☎02890 322662,
🖰maggiemaysbelfastcafe.co.uk; map p.471. Huge
and reasonably priced portions of wholesome Irish
cooking (try the hearty Ulster fry at breakfast) with lots
of veggie choices. Be prepared to queue and bring your
own wine in the evenings. Mon–Sat 8am–11pm, Sun
9am–11pm.

Molly's Yard 1 College Green Mews ☎02890 322600,
🖰mollysyard.co.uk; map p.471. Belfast's only
microbrewery-cum-restaurant is a two-floor affair with a
bistro serving keenly priced dishes such as seafood
chowder and Irish stew below a more exotic upstairs
restaurant offering the likes of roast rump of lamb or pan-
fried trout (around £25 for two courses). Mon–Thurs
noon–9pm, Fri & Sat noon–9.30pm.

Mourne Seafood Bar 34–36 Bank St ☎02890 248544;
map p.464. Cracking place for all piscivores, serving
everything from shellfish and oysters to exotic dishes
incorporating hake or monkfish. Reasonably priced too,
and there's even an on-site fishmonger's if you fancy
cooking your own. Expect to pay £25 plus wine. Mon–
Thurs noon–9.30pm, Fri & Sat noon–4pm &
5–10.30pm, Sun 1–6pm.

★**OX** 1 Oxford St ☎02890 314121, 🖰oxbelfast.com;
map p.464. Attracting culinary praise from foodies far and
wide for its creative use of local produce, OX is worth a visit
if you're keen to sample the city's finest. Booking essential.
Expect to pay £35 plus wine. Tues–Fri noon–2.45pm &
5.45–10pm, Sat 1–2.45pm & 5.45–10pm.

★**Potted Hen** St Anne's Square ☎02890 234554,
🖰thepottedhen.co.uk; map p.464. This place's urban-
chic decor of dark-grey slate floors and cream walls lets the
food shine: expect imaginatively prepared, contemporary

13

dishes that make the most of Northern Ireland's finest produce. Bank on £25 plus wine. Mon–Thurs noon–3pm & 5–9.30pm, Fri & Sat noon–3pm & 5–10pm, Sun noon–9pm.

PUBS AND BARS

The Crown Liquor Saloon 46 Great Victoria St ☎02890 243187, ⓦnicholsonpubs.co.uk/thecrownliquorsaloon belfast; map p.464. Owned by the National Trust, Belfast's most famous and spectacular pub is an old Victorian gin palace with an ornate ceiling, painted mirrors and frieze-decorated oak panelling. Once armed with drinks, try to grab one of the snugs, where you press a button to receive service. If the snugs are busy, it's still a great experience to linger at the bar, with its carved-timber dividing screens. There's a good repertoire of Northern Ireland food on offer too, along with pints of Strangford oysters, when Oyster season descends in Sept. Mon–Wed 11.30am–11pm, Thurs–Sat 11.30am–midnight, Sun 12.30–10pm.

★**The Duke of York** 11 Commercial Court, off Donegall St ☎02890 241062, ⓦdukeofyorkbelfast.com; map p.464. Nestled on a cobbled alleyway in the Half Bap area in the heart of the Cathedral Quarter. The decor takes you back to bygone times, its walls strewn with memorabilia and antiquities. Regular traditional music sessions and outdoor benches for balmy summer evenings. Mon 11.30am–11pm, Tues–Fri 11.30am–1am, Sat 11.30am–2am, Sun 2–8pm.

The Harp Bar 35 Hill St ☎02890 329923, ⓦharpbarbelfast.com; map p.464. The more refined big brother of the Duke of York, housed in the former head office of the Old Bushmills whiskey distillery. Plush, red-velvet fabrics and antique furnishings recall Victorian Belfast, and there's an impressive range of whiskies and independent draught beers. Regular music nights upstairs. Mon–Sat 11.30am–1.30am, Sun 11.30am–11.30pm.

The John Hewitt 53 Donegall St ☎02890 233768, ⓦthejohnhewitt.com; map p.464. Light and airy pub run by the Belfast Unemployed Resource Centre, with newspapers, paintings by local artists on sale, plus an excellent traditional session (Sat 6pm), traditional jazz on Fri (8.30pm), singer-songwriters on Mon (9pm) and various other events during the week. Also serves healthy, reasonably priced meals. A great place to while away a few hours sampling local craft beers and ciders. Mon–Sat 11.30am–1am, Sun noon–11pm.

Kelly's Cellars 30 Bank St ☎02890 246058; map p.464. Belfast's oldest-surviving, continuously run pub was opened in the sixteenth century. According to legend, it was a frequent meeting place for the United Irishmen

behind the doomed 1798 Rebellion (Henry Joy McCracken is said to have hidden under the bar counter from British soldiers). Good lunches, including thumping portions of homemade Irish stew and steak pie, a turf fire and traditional music several nights a week. Mon–Sat 11.30am–1am, Sun 1pm–midnight.

Madden's 74 Berry St ☎02890 244114; map p.464. This wonderful, unpretentious and atmospheric pub is off the beaten path but well worth seeking out. Its two large rooms (one upstairs, one downstairs) are filled with locals, there's cheap stew and soup, and also excellent traditional sessions (Mon, Fri & Sat 9.30pm) and set dancing (Wed). Mon–Sat 11.30am–1am, Sun noon–midnight.

The Morning Star 17 Pottingers Entry ☎02890 235986, ⓦthemorningstarbar.com; map p.464. This fine old-fashioned bar is something of a living museum, retaining many of its original fittings and fixtures including the original mahogany counter. It tends to be busy by day and quiet at night, and serves a wonderfully good-value buffet lunch for £4.50 (Mon–Sat noon–4pm), daily seafood specials and a whopping 24oz steak. Mon–Thurs 11.30am–11pm, Fri & Sat 11.30am–midnight, Sun 12.30–11pm.

Muriel's Café Bar 12–14 Church Lane ☎02890 332445; map p.464. Named after a Belfast Madam who, rumour has it, sold hats by day and ran a brothel by night, the ground floor here is themed on a 1920s millinery shop while the upstairs lounge area is all "Parisian boudoir", with its opulent furnishings and candlelight. The food is top-notch, with a full bistro menu and deli-style platters on offer. Mon–Sat 11.30am–1am, Sun noon–midnight.

★**Sunflower** 65 Union St ☎02890 232474, ⓦsunflowerbelfast.com; map p.464. This former working man's drinking den has had a revamp, turning it into quite a cool pub, with an interior that offers more than a passing nod to the 70s and 80s. Regular live music upstairs and impromptu traditional sessions downstairs make it a popular haunt for the city's music lovers. Also holds comedy nights. Mon–Sat noon–1am, Sun noon–11pm.

White's Tavern 2–4 Winecellar Entry, High St ☎02890 243080; map p.464. Founded in 1630, White's is an atmospheric old Entries bar, with stone floors and an open fire, serving excellent lunches and hosting traditional sessions downstairs (Thurs) and DJs upstairs (Fri and Sat). Children are welcome before 6pm, with a kids' menu available. Mon–Wed noon–10pm, Thurs–Sat noon–1am, Sun noon–midnight.

NIGHTLIFE

Like most UK cities, Belfast's "superclubs" have long gone, replaced though with numerous smaller **clubs**, usually housed in an upstairs room above a popular city bar and catering for all tastes. **Admission** may be free early in the week (and a some places all week) and as low as £2 or £3 up to Thurs, while weekend prices are usually around £5 to £15. Many places stay open until 1am Mon to Thurs and till 2am on Fri and Sat. For the latest **listings**, the monthly listings freesheet *The Big List* is essential (online version at ⓦ thebiglist.co.uk), or check out the Clubs section of ⓦ viewbelfast.co.uk. As well as the traditional **music** on offer in pubs (see p.484), Belfast also benefits from a thriving, grass-roots indie and rock scene, while the number of visiting international performers has increased dramatically since the arrival of the Waterfront Hall and Odyssey Complex (see p.487).

CLUBS AND VENUES

Aether & Echo 11 Lower Garfield St ☏ 02890 239163, ⓦ aetherandecho.com; map p.464. A wonderful Victorian bar (formerly known as the *Deer's Head*) whose refurbishment has retained its original charm while seeing it become one of the city centre's hottest venues, with a wide range of club nights taking place upstairs. Check website for programme. Fri & Sat 10pm till late.

★**Alley Cat** Church Lane ☏ 02890 233282, ⓦ alleycatbelfast.com; map p.464. This cool bar specializes in cocktails and mouth-watering handmade burgers and hot dogs, served until 11pm every night of the week. Also live music on Thurs and Sun nights and DJs on Fri and Sat (no reservations and no cover charge). Daily noon–1am.

Cuckoo 149 Lisburn Rd ☏ 02890 667776; map p.471. The trendy folk of the Lisburn Road flock to Cuckoo for craft beers, ping pong and dancing. Club nights include "forgotten anthems" on Thurs, indie on Fri, and bass, hip-hop, dub and house on Sat. DJs from 9pm till late.

★**Hudson Bar** 10–12 Gresham St ☏ 02890 232322, ⓦ hudsonbelfast.com; map p.464. This relatively new addition to Belfast's bar scene bears a sign reading "Purveyors of the finest Whiskeys, Ales and Disco" – and it manages to wear several different hats quite successfully, with live music nights midweek and DJs at weekends, when things tend to get busy. Thurs–Sat 11.30am–2am.

Lavery's Gin Palace 12–18 Bradbury Place ☏ 02890 871106, ⓦ laverysbelfast.com; map p.471. A Belfast institution, particularly popular with students, with "Retro Disco" and "Rip It Up" (soul, funk and indie) nights currently alternating on Sat in the Back Bar, and "Beat Connection" (funk, soul, hip-hop and house) in the Ballroom. On Sun night in the Ballroom it's DJ request night, with punters racking up their next game of pool to a soundtrack of favourites. Sat 11.30am–1am, Sun 12.30pm–midnight.

Love & Death Inc 10a Ann St ☏ 02890 247222, ⓦ loveanddeathinc.com/club; map p.464. This nightclub, cocktail bar and restaurant is a popular Sat haunt for its regular "Love Party" club night, featuring house, disco and dance anthems from the 80s and 90s. Cover £5–7. Sat 10pm–3am.

McCracken's Café Bar 4 Joys Entry ☏ 02890 326711, ⓦ mccrackenscafebar.co.uk; map p.464. A classy gastropub that sees live music from 7pm on Fri, then a live DJ set come 10pm with pop classics, funk, soul and r'n'b (no cover charge). On Sat, outside in the beer garden, there's a live acoustic set, while r'n'b night Club ON (cover charge from free to £10) takes over from 10pm. Fri & Sat till late.

Moth Presents T13 at the Titanic Quarter ⓦ t13.tv or ⓦ mothevents.com; map p.464. The city's only warehouse night is a relative newcomer to Belfast's club scene. Events aren't held regularly, but when they do happen, they are huge, attracting headline DJs and drawing in clubbers from far and wide. There are usually early-bird specials available for tickets, so keep an eye out for dates via the website.

Ollie's 16 Skipper St ☏ 02890 234888, ⓦ olliesbelfast .com; map p.464. Part of the 5-star *Merchant* hotel, *Ollie's* delivers all that you might expect that to entail, with a decadent, velvet-and-mahogany bedecked club area alongside a private members' bar. Regular club nights take place on Mon (£5), Thurs (£5), Fri (£7) and Sat (£10). Open 8pm till late.

Shine Queen's University Student Union ☏ 02890 243418, ⓦ shine.net; map p.464. *Shine* has a UK-wide reputation, spanning almost twenty years, for attracting the biggest DJs to Northern Irish shores, from Felix Da Housecat and David Guetta to Deadmau5 and Dave Clarke. Keep an eye out on the website for what's coming up.

LIVE MUSIC

The Dirty Onion 3 Hill St ☏ 02890 243712, ⓦ thedirtyonion.com; map p.464. This live-music pub, a recent conversion of one of the city's oldest buildings, offers something different every night – from *bodhrán* lessons to bluegrass sessions. On-site chicken rotisserie restaurant too. Daily noon–1am.

The Empire Bar & Music Hall 42 Botanic Ave ☏ 02890 308112, ⓦ thebelfastempire.com; map p.464. Cellar bar in a former church just up from the station, with a boisterous beer-hall atmosphere. Good-value food and bands most nights of the week with DJs and bigger-name bands upstairs. Mon–Sat 11.30am–1am, Sun 12.30pm–1am.

Filthy McNasty's 45 Dublin Rd ☏ 02890 246823, ⓦ thefilthyquarter.com/filthymcnastys; map p.471. With a secret garden, a club room (the "gypsy lounge") and

13

a backdrop of quirky furnishings, local Belfast musicians can be heard doing their thing from 10pm most nights, with an open mic session on Sun. Mon–Wed & Sun 11am–11pm, Thurs 11am–midnight, Fri & Sat 11am–1am.

★**The Limelight Complex** 17 Ormeau Ave ☎02890 327007, ⓦlimelightbelfast.com; map p.471. Recently refurbished, this Belfast institution – one of the North's leading live-music venues – is now home to two music venues, a bar and the open-air "Rock Garden". Expect an eclectic mix of singers and bands, plus DJs and club nights. Daily noon–1am with extended opening hours until 2am on club nights.

The Pavilion Bar 296 Ormeau Rd ☎02890 283283, ⓦpavilionbelfast.com; map p.471. Possibly "the" place to catch up-and-coming young indie bands as they take to the stage to pedal their tunes. Mon–Sat 11.30am–1am, Sun 12.30pm–midnight.

FESTIVALS IN BELFAST

Belfast has numerous festivals: below is a selection of the highlights; visit ⓦwww.visit-belfast .com/whats-on/festivals for a full calendar. One year-round programme is **Open House** (ⓦopenhousefestival.com), which sees rock, folk and traditional music held at various venues around the Cathedral Quarter at various dates throughout the year.

FEBRUARY, MARCH & APRIL

Guinness Belfast Nashville Songwriters Festival ⓦwww.belfastnashville.com. The North's love of country is reflected by this citywide weeklong event in late Feb, featuring local talent and major US names (Nanci Griffith is a favourite headliner).

St Patrick's Day ⓦbelfastcity.gov.uk/events. Carnival parade on March 17, followed by a major open-air concert in Custom House Square.

Belfast Film Festival ☎02890 246609, ⓦbelfastfilmfestival.org. The second half of April sees a host of left-field films and related events with screenings in cinemas, pubs, clubs and other venues.

MAY & JUNE

Festival of Fools ⓦfoolsfestival.com. Five-day international street-theatre festival, held over the first weekend in May, with events around the city centre.

Cathedral Quarter Arts Festival ⓦcqaf.com. Lively arts festival, featuring Irish and international acts, spread over ten days in early May.

Belfast City Blues Festival ⓦbelfastcityblues.com. Three days of 12-bar honky-tonk and foot-stomping riffs at the end of June.

JULY & AUGUST

Orange Order Parades Orange Order Lodges throughout Belfast commemorate the Battle of the Boyne with parades on July 12.

Féile An Phobail ⓦfeilebelfast.com. Week-long music and dance festival at the beginning of Aug, based in West Belfast.

Belsonic ⓦbelsonic.com. A week during mid-Aug of A-list music acts giving open-air performances at Custom House Square. Previous headliners include Biffy Clyro, Fleet Foxes, Nile Rodgers, Example and Queens of the Stone Age.

Belfast Mela ⓦartsekta.org.uk/festivals. The region's largest multicultural festival, celebrating South Asian culture through live music, dance, food, arts and crafts in the city's Botanic Gardens (see p.470) at the end of Aug.

SEPTEMBER & OCTOBER

Belfast Festival at Queen's ⓦbelfastfestival.com. Fortnight-long event held in late Oct which claims to be Britain's second-biggest arts festival after Edinburgh.

Culture Night Belfast ⓦculturenightbelfast.com. For one Friday night in Sept, buildings across Belfast open their doors to host free live performances by musicians, dancers and entertainers: expect everything from carnival parades to BMX displays.

Belfast Comedy Festival ⓦbellylaughsbelfast.com. For a fortnight at the end of Sept or beginning of Oct, comedians from near and far flock to Belfast to tread the boards at venues across the city.

ENTERTAINMENT

CONCERT VENUES AND THEATRES

Grand Opera House Great Victoria St ☎02890 241919, ⍵goh.co.uk. Belfast's most prestigious venue, featuring regular operatic performances as well as many of London's West End productions.

Lyric Theatre 55 Ridgeway St, off Stranmillis Rd ☎02890 381081, ⍵lyrictheatre.co.uk. The Lyric's new theatre opened in 2011 and stages serious contemporary drama along with family performances.

Odyssey Arena 2 Queen's Quay ☎02890 739074, ⍵odysseyarena.com. Where the biggest rock and pop singers and bands perform when they come to town.

Oh Yeah Music Centre 15–21 Gordon St ☎02890 310845, ⍵ohyeahbelfast.com. A music venue in the heart of the Cathedral Quarter that aims to showcase local music and educate the ears of the good people of Belfast. A hidden gem worth seeking out for live gigs and DJ sets.

Ulster Hall Bedford St ☎02890 334455, ⍵ulsterhall .co.uk. Most of the city's classical music performances are given by the Ulster Orchestra (⍵ulsterorchestra.com); the hall is also used for big rock and pop concerts.

Waterfront Hall Lanyon Place, Laganside ☎02890 334455, ⍵waterfront.co.uk. Hosts classical music and ballet, mainstream jazz and occasional big names from the world of middle-of-the-road pop and rock.

Whitla Hall Queen's University ☎02890 273075. Stages some professional and amateur classical concerts.

ARTS CENTRES AND CINEMA

Black Box 18–22 Hill St ☎02890 244400, ⍵blackboxbelfast.com. An arts and performance space in the Cathedral Quarter with an eclectic programme of live events and exhibitions including art, dance and music.

Crescent Arts Centre 2–4 University Rd ☎02890 242338, ⍵crescentarts.org. A focus for much of Belfast's left-field arts and performance activities.

Culturlaan 216 Falls Rd ☎02890 964180, ⍵culturlann .ie. An arts centre with an exciting and vibrant programme that promotes the Irish language and culture. Also houses the West Belfast Tourist Information Point.

The MAC Saint Anne's Square ☎02890 235053, ⍵themaclive.com. The Museum Arts Centre (MAC) occupies a brand-new six-storey building in the Cathedral Quarter with a programme that focuses on experimental and fringe productions, while also hosting major art exhibitions.

Queen's Film Theatre (QFT) 20 University Square ☎02890 971097, ⍵queensfilmtheatre.com. Two-screen independent cinema, showing art-house movies at exceptionally good prices.

GAY AND LESBIAN BELFAST

The number of gay **bars** and **venues** in Belfast has increased substantially over the last few years and the majority are geared towards men (check ⍵gaybelfast.net/scene.htm for comprehensive listings). The area around **Union Street** is affectionately known as "Queer Quarter" or the "Gay Village" by the city's gay community. **Gay Pride** (⍵belfastpride.com) week begins on the last Sat in July.

RESOURCES

The main resource for Belfast's gay scene is Queerspace (⍵queerspace.org.uk) at 9–13 Waring Street. It is part of Cara-Friend, a collective that aims to serve the needs of and raise the profile of the LGBT community of Belfast and Northern Ireland. It holds collective meetings on the afternoons of the first and third Sat of the month (2.30pm), followed by drop-in sessions at their InSpace Coffee Lounge (3.30pm). Alternatively, there's ⍵gaybelfast.net, which provides plenty of information on entertainment and nightlife. Helplines include Cara-Friend (☎02890 322023; Mon–Wed 7.30–10pm) and Lesbian Line (☎02890 238668; Thurs 7.30–10pm).

VENUES

Kremlin 96 Donegall St ☎02890 316060, ⍵kremlin -belfast.com; map p.464. Ireland's biggest gay venue,

featuring three bars and various themed nights of music, fun and games, including the hugely popular "Revolution" on Sat. Tues, Thurs & Sun 10.30pm–2.30am, Fri–Sat 9pm–3am.

Maverick 1 Union St ☎02890 246925, ⍵maverick belfast.com; map p.464. The newest gay bar in town bills itself as a "Den, Lounge & Disco". It offers plenty of kitsch decor and an eclectic mix of theme nights. Mon–Wed 2pm–1am, Thurs–Sat 2pm–2am, Sun 2pm–1am.

Union Street Bar 14 Union St ☎02890 316060, ⍵unionstreetpub.com; map p.464. This trendy daytime gastropub has been a firm favourite in Belfast's gay scene since first opening its doors in 2003, offering a variety of themed nights for men seven days a week, ranging from karaoke to bingo, via deck-thumping DJs. Mon–Sat noon–1am, Sun 1.30pm–1am.

13

SPORT

The Northern Irish are very passionate about their sport, with a reputation for producing excellent **individual players**, such as George Best (football), Mary Peters (athletics), Dennis Taylor and Alex Higgins (snooker), Joey Dunlop (motorcycling) and Rory McIlroy (golf).

Football (soccer) Northern Ireland's team has enjoyed little success on the international stage over the last twenty years but still attracts a loyal following at home games at Windsor Park (the home ground of the Linfield club) near the Lisburn Road. If there are no international matches being played during your visit, you may still be able to get tickets for an Irish League Premiership game with four teams – Cliftonville, Glentoran, Linfield and Crusaders – all based in Belfast.

Gaelic football (GAA) and hurling Although both are immensely popular nationwide, neither sport has a huge following in Belfast city. However, you can still see both sports being played most weekends at Roger Casement Park, on Andersonstown Road.

Rugby union The provincial team, Ulster Rugby, has an ever-growing fan base that has resulted in a significant extension at the club's Kingspan Stadium (85 Ravenhill Park), still referred to by many as simply "Ravenhill". It can now hold over 18,000 spectators, yet many home games are sold out. Cup and league successes have seen the team go from strength to strength in recent years, regularly supplying the national squad (Ireland) with players, along with the British & Irish Lions.

Ice hockey The Belfast Giants – champions of the UK's Elite Ice Hockey League in 2011/2012 and 2013/2014 – regularly play at the Odyssey Complex in front of over 4000 fans.

SHOPPING

With post-ceasefire insurance premiums more affordable, **shopping** in Belfast has vastly improved in recent years with the arrival of many High Street names. Victoria Square is home to over fifty different stores, including a multi-floored House of Fraser, while the top two floors feature a multiscreen Odeon cinema and a number of well-known restaurants that had previously ignored Belfast, such as Wagamama and Prezzo. The mall is open daily, with late-night shopping until 9.30pm from Wed to Fri. Take the lift to the Viewing Dome for spectacular vistas across the city and beyond.

Bookfinders 47 University Rd; map p.471. A dark and dingy second-hand bookshop filled with out-of-print and hard-to-find editions (the rarest are behind glass, under lock and key). The shop also has a café area where bookworms can while away an hour or two buried in a good read. Mon–Sat 10am–5.30pm.

Fresh Garbage 24 Rosemary St; map p.464. This Belfast institution first opened in 1969 and is awash with band memorabilia, tour T-shirts, jewellery and funky accessories. Locals often refer to it simply as "Fresh". Mon–Wed 10am–5.30pm, Thurs 10am–9pm, Fri & Sat 10am–5.30pm, Sun 1–5pm.

Good Vibrations 89–93 North St; map p.464. An independent record shop run by the legendary Godfather of Punk, Mr Terri Hooley (his life story, *Good Vibrations*, hit

the big screen in 2012). Terri is heralded as having discovered The Undertones, and if you're lucky you'll make a rare find yourself, while listening to tales from the good man himself. Opening hours vary.

No Alibi Bookstore 83 Botanic Ave; map p.471. A specialist crime fiction store with friendly, passionate staff, immortalized in local author Colin Bateman's *Mystery Man* series. Regularly plays host to readings and literary events. Mon–Sat 9am–5pm.

Sawers Fountain Centre, College St ⓦ sawersbelfast .com; map p.464. This Aladdin's cave of tasty local delicacies and exotic delights from far-flung shores was first established in 1897 and once had outlets in Glasgow, Birmingham and Dublin; the Belfast store is the only one that remains. Mon–Sat 9am–5.30pm.

ST GEORGE'S MARKET

Belfast is immensely proud of **St George's Market** (East Bridge St), which oozes Victorian charm and is home to speciality markets (Fri 6am–2pm, Sat 9am–3pm, Sun 10am–4pm). It first opened as a covered market in the 1890s and underwent a £4.5 million facelift in 1999. The Friday food and variety market is by far the most popular, with about two hundred traders taking part, while Saturday focuses on organic produce and gardens. The Sunday market operates at a more leisurely pace, with live music and takeaway food on offer. It was voted the Nation's Favourite Heritage Project in the 2014 National Lottery Awards.

13

DIRECTORY

Hospital Royal Victoria Hospital, Grosvenor Rd ☎ 02890 240503.

Internet access Visit Belfast Welcome Centre, 8–9 Donegall Square North; *Browsers Café*, 77 Dublin Rd; *Revelations*, 27 Shaftesbury Square.

Laundry Globe, 37–39 Botanic Ave ☎ 02890 243956.

Left luggage Visit Belfast Welcome Centre (see p.478), 8–9 Donegall Square North.

Lost property Musgrave Street police station, off Ann St ☎ 02890 650222.

Pharmacy Boots, 35–47 Donegall Place.

Police In an emergency, call ☎ 999 or ☎ 112. The main city-centre police station is in North Queen St.

Post offices 16 Howard St; 16–22 Bedford St; 1–5 Botanic Ave; and 12–16 Bridge St (Mon–Sat 9am–5.30pm).

Antrim and Derry

WHITE ROCKS, PORTRUSH

14

Antrim and Derry

Much of the coastline of County Antrim is as spectacular as anything you'll find across the whole of Ireland – consequently, unlike other parts of the North, it has always attracted an abundance of tourists. North from the ferry port of Larne, the A2 coast road takes in attractive villages and small towns, such as Carnlough, Cushendall and the port of Ballycastle, all set against or within the verdant Antrim Glens. A short boat trip from Ballycastle, meanwhile, is rugged Rathlin Island, while further along the coast to the west, blustery cliff-top walks lead to the strange basalt formations of the Giant's Causeway. With an attractive backdrop, Portrush and, just over the county border in Derry, Portstewart are popular seaside holiday resorts.

County Derry's coastline is also blessed with wonderful strands, overlooked by **Mount Binevenagh** and the eccentric **Mussenden Temple**. **Derry city** itself is a lively place, set on the banks of the Foyle, with its hilltop core still enclosed by some of the best-preserved city walls in Europe. The county's hinterland is more dramatic than Antrim's, especially where it skirts the Sperrin Mountains. The flatter territory towards Lough Neagh features some noteworthy Plantation settlements at **Magherafelt** and **Moneymore**.

North from Belfast

The coastal strip heading **north from Belfast** to Larne is largely uninspiring farmland, although there are a few spots to detain you as you head towards the more enticing Antrim Glens further north.

Carrickfergus

Heading out of Belfast's northern suburbs, the A2 skirts the edge of Belfast Lough before reaching **CARRICKFERGUS**, an unremarkable town whose seafront is dominated by its only real point of interest, well-preserved **Carrickfergus Castle**.

Carrickfergus Castle

Daily: Easter–Sept 10am–6pm; Oct–March 10am–4pm • £5 • ☎ 028 9355 1273, ⓦ discovernorthernireland.com

One of the earliest and largest Irish castles, built on a rocky promontory above the harbour around 1180 by the Anglo-Norman invader John de Courcy (and garrisoned until 1928), **Carrickfergus Castle** reflects the defensive history of this entire region. In 1315, the castle endured a year's siege before falling to the combined forces of Robert and Edward Bruce, after which the English retook it. The castle has been restored, and there's an informative **exhibition** on its history.

THE GIANT'S CAUSEWAY

Highlights

❶ The Antrim Coast Road The route from Larne to Portrush, skirting the Glens of Antrim, is one of Ireland's most scenic, with magical seascapes, staggering cliff-top walks and some of the North's prettiest villages. **See p.496**

❷ McCollam's Bar, Cushendall One of Ireland's best pubs for traditional-music sessions – not to be missed. **See p.498**

❸ Rathlin Island Northern Ireland's only inhabited offshore island, Rathlin offers exhilarating walks and views, top-class birdwatching opportunities and insights into a thriving local culture. **See p.501**

❹ The Giant's Causeway Get there early to beat the crowds and marvel at one of the strangest geological formations in Europe. **See p.503**

❺ Portstewart Strand The north coast's top beach where you can swim, surf, sunbathe or walk the dunes before ending your visit with dinner at the rustic *Harry's Shack*. **See p.507**

❻ Walls of Derry A circuit of these seventeenth-century defences is an essential part of any visit to the "Maiden City". **See p.515**

HIGHLIGHTS ARE MARKED ON THE MAP ON PP.494–495

ANTRIM & DERRY

HIGHLIGHTS

1. The Antrim Coast Road
2. McCollam's Bar, Cushendall
3. Rathlin Island
4. The Giant's Causeway
5. Portstewart Strand
6. Walls of Derry

Greencastle
Magilligan Point
Lough Foyle Ferry
Ramore Head
Portrush
Portb
Dunlu
Cast
5 Portstewart
Mussenden Temple
Castlerock
Downhill
Hezlett House
Coleraine
A2
A29
A54

DONEGAL

Lough Foyle
Bellarena
Mount Binevenagh
B201
A2
A37
A29

Letterkenny
N13

Limavady
Roe Valley Country Park

6 Derry
A2

DERRY

River Foyle

Strabane

A6
Dungiven
Banagher Old Church

A6
Maghera

S P E R R I N M O U N T A I N S

A5

A29

TYRONE

Draperstown

Magherafelt
Slieve Gallion
A20
A31

A505

Moneymore
Spri

Cookstown

Omagh

A29

A5

Dungannon

A4

0   10
miles

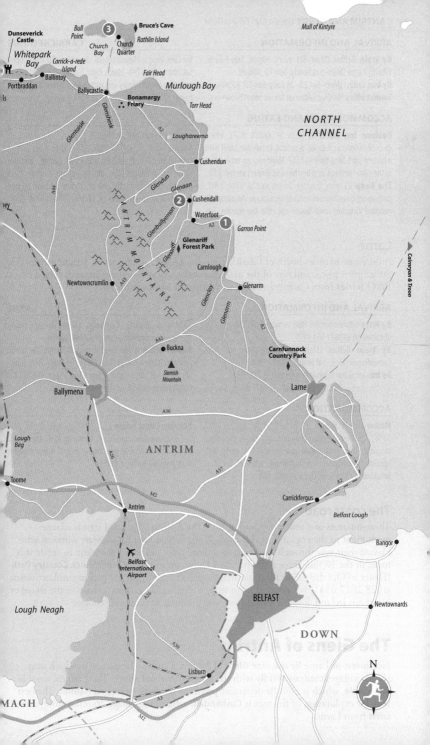

14

By train Belfast (Mon–Sat every 30min, Sun hourly; 30min); Larne (Mon–Sat hourly, Sun 10; 30min).

By bus Belfast (Mon–Sat 22–26 daily, Sun 10; 40min).

Tourist office The Civic Centre on Antrim Street houses both the Carrickfergus Museum (April–Sept Mon–Fri 10am–6pm, Sat 10am–4pm; Oct–March daily 10am–5pm; free), which traces the town's history and archaeological remains, and the tourist office (same hours; ☎ 028 9335 8049).

ACCOMMODATION AND EATING

Dobbins Inn Hotel 6 High St ☎ 028 9335 1905, ⊕ dobbinsinnhotel.co.uk. A central, family-run hotel with a history stretching back to 1567. Handy for an exploration of the castle or town, and lunches and dinners served. **£70**

The Keep 93 Irish Quarter South ☎ 028 9336 7007, ⊕ thekeepguesthousecarrickfergus.co.uk. An elegantly restored Victorian town house opposite the marina. The owners also run a grill in West St. **£55**

Sozo 2 North St ☎ 028 9332 6060, ⊕ eatsozo.com. A café-bistro serving modern European cuisine, and, for those on a budget. The dining options include steak burgers, bacon chop, lasagne or chicken chapatti on rice. Average main course prices are £7. Mon–Thurs 8am–5pm, Fri & Sat 8am–9pm.

Larne

A dozen or so miles north of Carrickfergus lies **LARNE**, an important freight centre, if a rather grim town, and one of the main ports of entry to Northern Ireland, served by P&O **ferries** from Cairnryan (all year) and Troon (summer only).

By ferry Information for P&O services from Larne can be obtained on ☎ 0871 664 4999.

By train Belfast (Mon–Sat hourly, Sun 10; 1hr); Carrickfergus (Mon–Sat hourly, Sun 10; 30min).

By bus Local bus information on ☎ 028 2827 2345.

Destinations Belfast (Mon–Sat 12–21 daily, Sun 2; 55min–1hr 35min); Carnlough (Mon–Sat 6–8 daily; 35min); Glenarm (Mon–Sat 6–8 daily; 30min).

Tourist office If you need to stay in Larne, the tourist office on Narrow Gauge Road (Mon–Fri 9am–5pm; June–Sept also Sat 10am–4pm & Sun 11am–3pm; ☎ 028 2826 0088) will book B&B accommodation for you.

ACCOMMODATION

Manor Guest House 23 Olderfleet Rd ☎ 028 2827 3305, ⊕ themanorguesthouse.com. Near the ferry terminal, this comfortable guesthouse has eight well appointed bedrooms. The homemade wheaten bread at breakfast is a big draw. Open all year. **£60**

Seaview Guest House 154–156 Curran Rd ☎ 028 2827 2438, ⊕ seaviewlarne.co.uk. Living up to its eponymous name, this amenable guesthouse is just a few minutes' walk from the harbour. **£60**

The coast road

Three-quarters of a mile north of Larne on the Antrim coast road stands a large **monument** to the engineer of this road, William Bald, and his stalwart workers, who blasted their way through, over and round the cliffs and rocky shoreline to create this route in the 1830s. Three miles north of Larne, meanwhile, **Carnfunnock Country Park** (Easter to Oct daily 9am till dusk; free though charges apply for parking and activities; ☎ 028 2827 0541) is a good place to stop, with a walled garden, a maze in the shape of Northern Ireland, a miniature railway, and a nine-hole mini-golf course.

The Glens of Antrim

Northwest of Larne lie the nine **Glens of Antrim**, a curious landscape in which neat seaside villages contrast vividly with the rough moorland above. Their largest town is **Ballycastle**, which is also the departure point for the ferry to rugged **Rathlin**. The best base for exploration of the area is **Cushendall**, a charming village 26 miles along the coast from Larne.

Glenarm

The southernmost of the Glens, **Glenarm**, is headed by a village of the same name, which grew up around a hunting lodge built by Randal MacDonnell after Dunluce Castle, further up the coast, was abandoned (see p.505). **Glenarm Castle** (Easter to Sept Mon–Sat 10am–5pm, Sun 11am–5pm; £5; ☎028 2884 1203, ⊚glenarmcastle.com), which became the major seat of the Earls of Antrim, is worth seeing for its conflicting architectural styles and walled garden.

14

Carnlough

Rounding the next bay from Glenarm, you'll arrive at **CARNLOUGH**, standing at the head of **Glencloy**. Until the 1960s, Carnlough's way of life was linked to its limestone quarries, and the village's most striking feature today remains its sturdy limestone buildings, dating mainly from the mid-nineteenth century. Right in the village centre, running over the main road, there's a solid **stone bridge** that once carried a railway bringing material down to the **harbour**, which itself has an impressive breakwater, clock tower and limestone courthouse.

ARRIVAL AND DEPARTURE   CARNLOUGH

By bus Cushendall (Mon–Fri 3 daily; 25min); Glenarm (Mon–Sat 5–8 daily; 10min); Larne (Mon–Sat 5–8 daily; 10min).

ACCOMMODATION AND EATING

Bridge Inn 2 Bridge St ☎028 2888 5669. There are five guestrooms above the bar, open all year. Live bands appear regularly on Fri night and there's sometimes music on Sat and Sun evenings. __£60__

Londonderry Arms Hotel ☎028 2888 5255, ⊚glensofantrim.com. On the seafront, this solid, comfortable hotel was originally a coaching inn and once briefly owned by Winston Churchill. You can sample Glenarm smoked salmon in the restaurant or just enjoy a drink and admire the bizarre collection of mementos of 1960s champion steeplechaser Arkle. __£90__

Waterfoot and Glenariff

From Carnlough the road skirts round a gaunt shoulder of land and on to **WATERFOOT**, a short strip of houses with a couple of bars that come to life in the evenings. It's **Glenariff**, though, that is the real attraction here, a wide, lush and flat-bottomed valley that is abruptly cut off by the sea. A few miles up the glen from Waterfoot is the **Glenariff Forest Park** (daily 9am–dusk; car £4.50, pedestrians free), which has a **campsite** (☎028 2955 6000; contact the head forester in advance) and four scenic waymarked trails. Opt for the Waterfall Trail to see a spectacular series of **cascades**, skirted by a timber walkway.

ACCOMMODATION   WATERFOOT AND GLENARIFF

Dieskirt Farm 104 Glen Rd ☎028 2177 1308, ⊚dieskirtfarm.co.uk. A welcoming farmhouse whose three en-suite rooms offer tremendous views of the surrounding countryside. It's a working farm so comes complete with sheep, cattle and friendly donkeys. April–Nov. __£70__

Cushendall and around

CUSHENDALL, which lies at the head of three of the nine Glens, is a delightfully understated village, its charming colour-washed buildings grouped together on a spectacular shore. The red-sandstone **tower** at the central crossroads was built in 1817 by Francis Turnley, an official of the East India Company, as "a place of confinement for idlers and rioters", and the village makes a fine base for exploring the countryside and catching a traditional music session. If possible, time your visit to coincide with the **Heart of the Glens** festival (⊚glensfestival.com) in the middle of August, one of the area's oldest events, replete with music, sporting events and much merriment, culminating in a huge street ceili on the Sunday.

ARRIVAL AND INFORMATION
CUSHENDALL

By bus Ballycastle (Mon–Fri 1 daily; 40min); Carnlough (Mon–Fri 2 daily; 25min); Cushendun (Mon–Sat 3–6 daily; 10min); Glenariff (Mon–Sat 3–6 daily; 10min); Waterfoot (Mon–Sat 3–6 daily; 5min).

Tourist information The office (Mon–Fri 10am–1pm & 2–5.30pm, also June–Sept Sat 10am–4pm; ☎ 028 2177 1180) is on Mill Street, west of the central crossroads.

ACCOMMODATION

Cullentra House 16 Cloughs Rd ☎ 028 2177 1762, ⓦ cullentrahouse.com. A mile northwest of the village, this guesthouse is set amid superb countryside. Breakfasts have a kick, thanks to walnut and Guinness wheaten bread and homemade Bushmills whiskey marmalade. **£56**

Cushendall Caravan Park 62 Coast Rd ☎ 028 2177 1699, ⓦ glenscoastcaravanparks.com. Next to Cushendall Boat Club, three-quarters of a mile towards Waterfoot. Camping pods available. April–Sept. **£25**

Glens Hotel 6 Coast Rd ☎ 028 2177 1223, ⓦ theglenshotel.com. The most comfortable option right in the centre, this one-hundred-year-old hotel has a regular programme of live entertainment. An excellent base for touring the area. **£75**

The Meadows 81 Coast Rd ☎ 028 2177 2020. A friendly B&B option with six spacious rooms on the outskirts of town about three-quarters of a mile towards Waterfoot. Also offers disabled access and free wi-fi. **£60**

★**The Village B&B** Mill St ☎ 028 2177 2366, ⓦ thevillagebandb.com. One of the most central B&B options, with generously sized en-suite rooms. The owner dispenses maps, logistical and practical walking information, and will enrich your stay with local cultural history. March–Oct. **£60**

EATING AND DRINKING

★**Harry's** 10 Mill St ☎ 028 2177 2022. Exceptionally good-value meals in the downstairs bar, including huge roast dinners and fresh fish; more refined modern Irish fare served upstairs. Main dinner courses average £14. Daily noon–9pm.

★**McCollam's** 23 Mill St ☎ 028 2177 2849. A cottage-style pub known to all as *Johnny Joe's*, which hosts traditional music sessions on Fridays. There's also music on Tues, Sat and Sun in high season. Mon–Sat 4–11.30pm, Sun noon–11pm.

The Skerry Inn 12 Old Cushendun Rd, Newtowncrumlin ☎ 028 2175 8669. Eight miles southwest on a quiet road, but undoubtedly worth the detour for some great traditional singing as well as sessions every Wed and Sat evening. Mon–Sat 10am–11.30pm, Sun 7–11.30pm.

Upstairs at Joe's 23 Mill St ☎ 028 2177 2849. The first-floor rooms above *McCollam's* pub serve as a top-notch restaurant offering a wide range of meat and seafood. Potted shellfish, scallops and lobster are on the menu along with lamb stew and steaks. Mains average £13. Daily: March–June & Sept 5.30–9pm, July & Aug noon–9pm.

Cushendun and around

The once-fashionable resort of **CUSHENDUN**, some five miles northwest of Cushendall, is an architectural oddity almost entirely designed by Clough Williams-Ellis, the innovative architect of Portmeirion in Wales, and constructed between 1912 and 1925. Built to a commission from Ronald McNeill, the first (and last) Baron Cushendun, and his Cornish wife, Maud, Cushendun's houses are of rugged, rough-cast whitewash with slate roofs – a Cornish style that clearly weathers the sea storms as efficiently here as in Cornwall. Much of Cushendun is National Trust property, and it shows: it's a tiny and well-tended place.

The main road from Cushendun northwest to Ballycastle runs inland, traversing some impressively rough moorland, and passes **Loughareema**, the "vanishing lake", so termed because of its tendency to drain away completely in hot weather. The narrow, winding **coastal road** is a better bet, however; edged with fuchsia and honeysuckle, it switches back violently above the sea to **Torr Head**, the closest point on the Irish mainland to the Mull of Kintyre in Scotland.

ARRIVAL AND DEPARTURE
CUSHENDUN

By bus Ballycastle (Mon–Fri 1 daily; 30min); Cushendall (Mon–Sat 3–6 daily; 10min).

ACCOMMODATION AND EATING

Mary McBride's 2 Main St ☎ 028 2176 1511. This excellent bar-restaurant offers substantial fish lunches and dinners such as steak and Guinness pie or crispy chilli chicken. Main courses average £15. March–Oct Mon–Thurs 10.30am–11pm, Fri & Sat till 1pm, Sun noon–10.30pm; Nov–Feb Mon–Thurs 3–11pm, Fri & Sat till

1pm, Sun noon–10.30pm.
Sleepy Hollow 107 Knocknacarry Rd ☎ 028 2176 1513. Set on a quiet road, this small but perfectly formed B&B comes with king-size beds and sweeping views of the countryside; an ideal location for exploration of the coast and glens. **£55**

14

Murlough Bay and Fair Head

Murlough Bay is the most spectacular of all the bays along the northern coast. From the rugged cliff-tops, the hillside curves down to the sea in a series of wildflower meadows that soften an otherwise harsh landscape. The last headland before Ballycastle is **Fair Head**, whose massive 200m cliffs offer stunning views across the North Channel to Scotland – the Mull of Kintyre and further to Islay and the Paps of Jura – a proximity that sheds light on the confusion of land ownership between Ireland and Scotland. A prime example is Rathlin Island (see p.501), which was hotly contested up until the seventeenth century. **Lough na Cranagh**, one of three lakes in the hinterland behind the cliffs, houses a *crannóg*, encircled by a parapet wall. A walk from the Fair Head car park to Murlough Bay takes 45 minutes, but muddy paths and changeable weather make walking boots and a waterproof essential.

Ballycastle

The lively market town and port of **BALLYCASTLE** sits at the mouth of the two northernmost Antrim Glens, **Glenshesk** and **Glentaisie**, and makes a pleasant base for exploring the Causeway Coast or the Glens themselves. The best time to visit Ballycastle is for the **Ould Lammas Fair**, Ireland's oldest fair, dating from 1606. Held on the last Monday and Tuesday in August, it features sheep and pony sales, while stallholders do a roaring trade in dulse, an edible seaweed, and yellowman, a tooth-breaking yellow toffee that's so hard it needs a hammer to break it up. These delicacies feature in a sentimental song that originates locally:

Did you treat your Mary Ann
To dulse and yellowman
At the Ould Lammas Fair in Ballycastle–O?

Ballycastle has a prosperous feel about it that derived originally from the efforts of an enlightened mid-eighteenth-century landowner, Colonel Hugh Boyd, who developed the town as an industrial centre, providing coal and iron ore mines, a tannery, a brewery and soap, bleach, salt and glass works, all now defunct. It was from its **coal mines** particularly that the town garnered most of its wealth; lignite was mined at Ballintoy on the coast a few miles further west, an enterprise which came to an abrupt end when the entire deposit caught fire and burned for several years.

At the seafront there's a memorial to **Guglielmo Marconi**, the inventor of wireless telegraphy, who in 1898 made his first successful radio transmission between Ballycastle and Rathlin. From here, Quay Road leads gradually uphill past houses and shops to **The Diamond**, the town's focus, and thence up the steeper Castle Street.

Ballycastle museum

Castle Street • July & Aug Mon–Sat noon–6pm • Free

The town's tiny **museum** occupies the old eighteenth-century courthouse. Temporary exhibitions are hosted upstairs, while the former cells downstairs hold a collection of

14

artefacts produced by the pre-World War I Irish Home Industries Shop. Pride of place goes to the Glentaisie banner for the first *Feis na nGleann* ("festival of the Glens") in 1904.

ARRIVAL AND INFORMATION

By bus Ballintoy (Mon–Fri 8–9 daily; Sat & Sun 2–3 daily; 15min); Bushmills (Mon–Fri 7 daily, Sat 2; 35min); Cushendall (Mon–Fri 1 daily; 40min); Cushendun (Mon–Fri 1 daily; 30min); Giant's Causeway (Mon–Fri 8 daily, Sat & Sun 2–3 daily; 30min).

Tourist information Portnagree House, 14 Bayview

BALLYCASTLE

Rd (July & Aug Mon–Fri 9.30am–7pm, Sat 10am–6pm, Sun 2–6pm; Sept–June Mon–Fri 9.30am–5pm; ☎028 2076 2024, ⓦheartofthecausewaycoastandglens.com). A good place to ask about accommodation, stock up on literature for the region, or find out about tours and special events.

ACCOMMODATION

Kenmara House 45 North St ☎028 2076 2600. An historic house uphill from the front with stunning seascape views. Opt for the bedroom with the elegant bathroom from where Marconi conducted his very first tests. **£80**

★**Marine Hotel** 1–3 North St ☎028 2076 2222, ⓦmarinehotelballycastle.com. This hospitable and well-run hotel with 31 comfortable bedrooms is handy for

the ferries to Rathlin Island (or simply gazing across to it). The on-site bar and bistro (daily noon–9pm, till 9.30pm at weekends) offers a range of fish and meat dishes. **£120**

Watertop Open Farm 188 Cushendall Rd ☎028 2076 2576, ⓦwatertopfarm.co.uk. Camping is available at this working farm (July & Aug 11am–5.30pm), which can arrange pony trekking and fishing. Easter–Oct. Tent pitch **£15**

EATING AND DRINKING

Anzac Bistro 5 Market St ☎028 2076 2445. Has a deserved reputation for its splendid cooking with steaks and fish dominating. Dover sole, teriyaki salmon, and surf 'n' turf are popular. The seafood comes fresh each day from the acclaimed Morton's fishmonger at Ballycastle harbour. Average mains £13. Mon–Fri 5–10pm, Sat & Sun 12.30–9pm.

★**Cellar** The Diamond ☎028 2076 3037. Ballycastle's best restaurant is hidden down steps in an atmospheric setting. Specials might include whole lobster, red mullet or tiger prawns from the cold Atlantic waters. Mains are around £14 and there's a good-value early bird (Mon–Fri 5–7pm) with two courses for £9.95.

Central 12 Ann St ☎028 2076 3877, ⓦcentralwinebar .com. A lively atmosphere greets you at this bustling combination of bar, restaurant and cocktail lounge. The

dinner menu might offer up Asian-style seafood hotpot (£14.95), rope-grown mussels (£11.95) or curry-roasted sea bass (£15.95).

Diamond Bar The Diamond ☎028 2076 2142. A keenly priced bar and bistro with dishes such as Clonakilty chicken with black pudding and mash (£12) or a seafood platter with mussels, prawns and crab claws (£18) Average mains are £11. Mon–Thurs 11.30am–11.30pm, Fri & Sat 11.30am–12.30am, Sun noon–11pm.

The House of McDonnell Castle St ☎077 1166 8797. Also known as *Tom's*, this bar has been in the same family for an astonishing fourteen generations, stretching back to 1766, and is just the place to channel the "spirit" of an older age via Irish, American or Scotch whiskies galore. Friday is music night, attracting youngish locals. Fri & Sat 2.30–11.30pm.

Bonamargy Friary

Free access

Just out of town, on the Cushendall road, are the ruins of **Bonamargy Friary**, founded by the dominant MacQuillan family around 1500. One family member, Julia, insisted on being buried in the main walkway, so that she might be humbled for eternity by the stepping feet of others. A number of the rival MacDonnell family are also buried here, including the hero of Dunluce Castle, Sorley Boy MacDonnell, and his son Randal, first Earl of Antrim (see p.505). An indication of the erstwhile strength of the Irish language in these parts is that the tomb of the second earl, who died in 1682, is inscribed in Irish as well as the usual English and Latin; the Irish translation reads, "Every seventh year a calamity befalls the Irish" and "Now that the Marquis has departed, it will occur every year". The **River Margy**, on which the Friary stands, is associated with one of the tragic stories of Irish legend, that of the Children of Lir, whose jealous stepmother turned them into swans and forced them to spend three hundred years on the Sea of Moyle (the narrow channel between Ireland and the Scottish coast).

Rathlin Island

Rathlin Island lies five miles north of Ballycastle and just twelve miles west of the Mull of Kintyre in Scotland. Shaped like a truncated figure seven, Rathlin is an impressive, craggy place, with a coastline consisting almost entirely of cliffs, and a lighthouse at each tip. The sea dominates the landscape and its salty winds discourage the growth of vegetation – wind turbines harness this energy source for electricity generation.

The presence of dry-stone walls and numerous ruined cottages points to a time when the population was far larger than the 120 or so current inhabitants concentrated in **Church Quarter**. Halfway towards the western lighthouse is the site of a **Stone Age** axe-making site, and, to its north, earthworks known as **Doonmore**. In the early Christian period, the island was a haven for monks, who left evidence of their presence in the form of a sweathouse (a kind of primitive sauna) at **Knockans**, back towards Church Bay. You can discover more about the island's history and culture in the Boathouse, down by Church Quarter's harbour, which has been converted to a **visitor centre**.

Rathlin's two major events are the week-long **festival** in mid-July, with everything from ceilis to model-yacht racing, and the regatta on the last weekend in August.

Brief history

In 795 AD Rathlin was the first place in Ireland to be raided by the **Vikings**. Later raids saw two bloody massacres, first by the English and then by the Scots. In 1575, the mainland MacDonnells sent their women, children and old people to Rathlin for safety from the English, but that didn't stop the invading fleet, under the Earl of Essex (whose soldiers included **Sir Francis Drake**), from slaughtering the entire population. In 1642, a later generation of MacDonnells was then butchered by their Scottish enemies, the Campbells, causing Rathlin to be deserted for many years afterwards.

Bruce's Cave

The foot of the cliff is punctured by caves, many of them accessible by boat only in the calmest of weather. **Bruce's Cave**, on the northeast point of the island, below the lighthouse, is a cavern in the black basalt where, in 1306, so the story goes, the despondent Robert the Bruce retreated after being defeated by the English at Perth. Seeing a spider determinedly trying to spin a web gave him the resolve to "try, try and try again", so he returned to Scotland and defeated the English at Bannockburn.

ARRIVAL AND INFORMATION   RATHLIN ISLAND

By ferry Ferries (❶028 2076 9299, ⓦrathlinballycastleferry .com) make the 20–45min trip from Ballycastle harbour to Rathlin ten times daily April–Sept; a return ticket costs £12. Outside these months services are much reduced.

Tourist information Visitor centre at Church Quarter harbour (May–Aug daily 10.30am–4pm; ❶077 0886 9605).

ACCOMMODATION AND EATING

Bruce's Kitchen Church Quarter ❶028 2076 0011. Offers lunches and early evening meals such as burgers,

goujons, sandwiches and panini. The adjacent *McCuaig's* pub is open all year for drinks (winter from 4pm) as well as

---

BIRDS AND WILDFLOWERS ON RATHLIN ISLAND

The island's cliffs are superb for **birdwatching**, particularly Bull Point, on the western tip, part of a large RSPB nature reserve. The viewpoint at the western lighthouse provides wonderful views of Northern Ireland's largest colony of seabirds that includes puffins, guillemots and razorbills. If you are here in the spring you may also see a rare **wildflower**, the sky-blue pyramidal bugle, which is widespread from near the West Lighthouse to the north of Church Bay – the only recorded sighting of it in Northern Ireland. A minibus plies between the west lighthouse and Church Bay in summer.

14

social activity, including occasional music, and island gossip. Summer daily 10am–8pm.

Emma's Chip Ahoy Church Quarter ☎ 077 9528 2881. It may be a basic takeaway (a shed with some benches) but the food, including fish such as crab claws, is fresh as can be. Be warned: eating here is weather dependent. May–Sept daily noon–10pm.

Manor House ☎ 028 2076 3964, ⊛ rathlinmanorhouse .co.uk. A restored late Georgian home dating from around 1760 on the site of weavers' cottages, now run by the National Trust as a guesthouse. The TV-free bedrooms have harbour views, or you can choose to steal away and hide yourself in the walled garden. Easter–Oct. **£74**

Soerneog View Hostel ☎ 028 2076 3954, ⊛ rathlin -island.co.uk. Overlooking Mill Bay, a 10min walk to the south from Church Bay where the boats dock, is this tiny hostel with three rooms. Also rents out bikes. April– Sept. **£30**

The north Antrim coast

The north coast of County Antrim, west of Ballycastle, is dominated, from a tourist perspective, by Northern Ireland's most famous tourist attraction, the bizarre formation of basalt columns at the **Giant's Causeway**, a UNESCO World Heritage site. On the way, near the town of **Ballintoy**, there are several pleasant diversions, not least the precarious rope bridge to **Carrick-a-rede Island**. West of the Causeway, you can sample some whiskey at **Bushmills** and visit the imposing and well-preserved remains of **Dunluce Castle**, the stronghold of the local MacDonnell clan. The coastline west of Dunluce is another major holiday spot, with **Portrush** filled with tourists in summer and students the rest of the year.

GETTING AROUND   THE NORTH ANTRIM COAST

BY BUS
Public transport along the coast, particularly to and from the Causeway, is well organized with regular bus services. All services are operated by Translink unless stated otherwise (⊛ translink.co.uk)

The Antrim Coaster (Goldline Express Service #252) operates from Belfast all the way around the Antrim coast to Portrush (via Larne, the Glens, Ballycastle and the Giant's Causeway) and Portstewart, terminating at Coleraine. The service operates all year (Mon–Sat), leaving Belfast Europa Buscentre at 9.05am and reaching Coleraine at 1pm. A second bus departs from Larne at 4.25pm, arriving in Coleraine at 7.50pm. The respective returns leave Coleraine at 9.35am (to Larne only) and 3.40pm (all the way to Belfast). From July to late Sept the timetable includes Sun, operating at the same times from both directions (£9).

The North Coast Open Topper (☎ 028 7032 5400)

runs from Coleraine through Portrush and Bushmills to the Giant's Causeway, weather permitting, four times daily during July and Aug; an all-day hop-on, hop-off fare is £6.

The Causeway Rambler runs from Bushmills to Carrick-a-rede four times daily, via the Giant's Causeway, Dunseverick Castle and Ballintoy from early June to early Oct; an all-day ticket is £6.

BY TRAIN
Regular services operate from Belfast or Derry to Coleraine; transfer to a bus to reach the Causeway. A restored narrow-gauge railway runs from Bushmills to the Causeway (7 trains daily on the hour 11am–5pm, returning 30min later from the Causeway: June, Sept & Oct Sat & Sun; July & Aug daily; 20min; ☎ 028 2073 2844, ⊛ freewebs.com/giantscausewayrailway; single £5.25, return £6.75).

Carrick-a-rede Island

Rope bridge Daily, weather permitting: late Feb to late May, Sept & Oct 9.30am–6pm; late May to Aug 10am–7pm; Nov & Dec 10.30am–3.30pm • £5.60 • ☎ 028 2076 9839, ⊛ nationaltrust.org.uk

As you draw level with **Carrick-a-rede Island**, not far before Ballintoy on the coast road west from Ballycastle, you'll see the island's **rope bridge**. Strung almost 25m above the sea, the rope-connected planks lead to a commercial salmon fishery on the southeast side of Carrick-a-rede (the name means "rock in the road": the island stands in the path of migrating salmon) – but its main function seems to be to scare tourists, something it does very successfully.

Ballintoy and around

BALLINTOY has a dramatic harbour, much loved by artists, with a dark, rock-strewn strand contrasting oddly with the neat, pale-stone breakwater. It's lively with boats in the summer, but bleak and exposed in winter. At the top of the harbour road stands a little white **church**, which replaced an earlier one in which local Protestants took refuge from Catholics in 1641 before being rescued by the Earl of Antrim.

Portbraddan

The coastal path from Ballintoy leads west to **PORTBRADDAN**, a tiny hamlet of multicoloured houses, where St Gobban's, a slate-roofed little church, just 12 feet by 6, is supposedly the smallest church in Ireland. Needless to say, there are other contenders: the ruins of an even smaller one, St Lasseragh's, stand on the cliff above.

14

Dunseverick Castle

From Portbraddan the coast path leads round a headland, through a spectacular hole in the rock and then, by degrees, up to the cliffs of **Benbane Head**. The road and path almost converge at the ruins of a sixteenth-century gatehouse, all that's left of **Dunseverick Castle**. This was once the capital of the old kingdom of Dalriada, which spread over north Antrim and Scotland, and the terminus of one of the five great roads that led from Tara, the ancient capital of Ireland.

ARRIVAL AND DEPARTURE   BALLINTOY

By bus The Antrim Coaster (Goldline Express Service #252) stops in Ballintoy (2 daily) from Coleraine. Between April and early Oct, the Causeway Rambler (Service #402) runs a regular service (4 daily) from Coleraine that terminates in Ballintoy.

ACCOMMODATION AND EATING

Fullerton Arms 22 Main St ☎028 2076 9613, ⊚fullerton-arms.com. A comfortable, family-run guesthouse with 12 rooms, well placed for an exploration of the surrounding area. Meals are served. Ask about special deals. **£80**

HINI Hostel ☎028 2073 1745, ⊚hini.org.uk. At the foot of Knocksoghey Brae and beside Whitepark Bay, a delightful, mile-long sweep of white sand, this hostel organizes all manner of events and activities. April–Oct. **£42**

Sheep Island View Hostel (IHH) 42A Main St ☎028 2076 9391, ⊚sheepislandview.com. Well-equipped hostel accommodation, plus a camping barn. Open all year. Tent pitch **£20**, dorms **£35**

The Giant's Causeway

Ever since 1693, when the Royal Society first publicized it as one of the great wonders of the natural world, the **Giant's Causeway** has been a major tourist attraction. The highly romanticized pictures of the polygonal basalt rock formations by the Dubliner Susanna Drury, which circulated throughout Europe in the eighteenth century, did much to popularize the Causeway; two of them are on show in the Ulster Museum in Belfast (see p.472). Not everyone was impressed, though. A disappointed William Thackeray commented, "I've travelled a hundred and fifty miles to see *that*?", and especially disliked the tourist promotion of the Causeway, claiming in 1842 that "The traveller no sooner issues from the inn by a back door which he is informed will lead him straight to the causeway, than the guides pounce upon him." Although the tourist hype is today less overtly mercenary, the Causeway (now managed by the National Trust) still attracts hundreds of thousands of visitors annually.

For sheer otherworldliness, the Causeway can't be beaten. Made up of an estimated 37,000 **black basalt columns**, each a polygon (hexagons are by far the most common, with pentagons second, though sometimes the columns have as many as ten sides), the sight is the result of a subterranean explosion, some sixty million years ago, that

14

FIONN MAC CUMHAILL: THE GIANT OF THE CAUSEWAY

According to mythology, the Giant of the Causeway was Ulster warrior **Fionn Mac Cumhaill** (also known as Finn McCool), and two legends of Fionn's exploits provide an entertaining alternative to geologists' explanations of the Causeway's origins. In one, Fionn became besotted with a woman giant who resided on the Scottish island of Staffa (where the Causeway's fault-line resurfaces) and constructed a **highway across the sea** by which he could travel to woo her. An alternative version of the story suggests that Fionn built the Causeway in order to head over to Scotland to give another giant a good kicking, but, when confronted by his enemy's superior size, fled back to Ireland and hid in an extra-large cot which he'd persuaded his wife to construct. When the pursuing Scots giant arrived, he took just a glance at the sheer size of Fionn's supposed "baby" and fled back to Scotland.

stretched from the Causeway to Rathlin and beyond to Islay, Staffa (where it was responsible for the formation of Fingal's Cave) and Mull in Scotland. A huge mass of molten basalt was spewed out on to the surface, which, on cooling, solidified into what are, essentially, crystals.

Giant's Causeway Visitor Experience

Feb–March & Oct 9am–6pm; April–June & Sept 9am–7pm; July & Aug 9am–9pm; Nov–Jan 9am–5pm; last admission to centre 1hr before closing • £8.50 (£7 if using the park and ride in Bushmills) • ☎ 028 2073 1855, ⓦ nationaltrust.org.uk/giantscauseway

After many years of wrangling, the newly built **Giant's Causeway Visitor Experience** opened in 2012 at a cost of £18.5 million. Sunken into the ground and made from locally quarried basalt, the centre blends into the landscape with indigenous grasses on the roof providing a habitat for wildlife. Exhibition panels along with **3-D displays** provide absorbing detail on the geological and scientific nature of the area. After meeting the McCool family through some fun animation, children can enjoy devising their own Finn McCool story and make a rubbing of the site.

The stones

On foot 20min (downhill); alternatively, get a leaflet from the visitor centre or nearby tourist information office detailing four colour-coded, waymarked trails • **Minibus** Every 15min June & Sept 10am–6pm; July & Aug 10am–7pm; Oct–May 10am–4.30pm • £1 single, £2 return • **Guided tours** Leave hourly from 10am from the visitor centre (included in admission charge); audioguides also available

The first of the distinctive stone columns once you reach the pavement are the 12m-high **Organ Pipes**. Many of the other formations have names ("the Camel", "the Wishing Chair" and "the Granny") invented for them by the guides who so plagued Thackeray and his contemporaries. At least one, **Chimney Point**, further north, has an appearance so bizarre that in September 1588 it persuaded the crew of the *Girona*, a ship of the Spanish Armada, to think it was Dunluce Castle (see opposite), where they thought they might get help from the MacDonnells. Instead, their vessel was wrecked on the rocky shore at Port-na-Spánaigh, just before Chimney Point. Its treasure was recovered by divers in 1968, and some of the items are on show in the Ulster Museum in Belfast (see p.472) and in Derry's Tower Museum (see p.515).

ARRIVAL AND INFORMATION   THE GIANT'S CAUSEWAY

The Causeway is served by a number of buses.

By car The roads around the Causeway are congested, particularly on weekends, so it's best to use the park-and-ride bus in Bushmills and buy a Green Travel Admission Ticket, thereby saving £1.50 on the standard adult admission price.

Tourist information The tourist office (daily 10am–5pm;

☎ 028 2073 1855) is located just across from the main visitor centre (next door to the *Causeway Hotel*) and stocks a supply of maps and information on coastal walking, cycling and driving routes, as well as activities and events during the north coast's summer season. Pre-booking tickets is a good idea, especially in summer. You can do this online at ⓦ giantscausewaytickets.com.

ACCOMMODATION

Carnside Guesthouse 23 Causeway Rd ☎ 028 2073 1337, ⓦ carnsideguesthouse.co.uk. A well-equipped farmhouse close to the Causeway with superb views; its

eleven rooms are filled with antiques and mismatched chairs. March–Oct. **£60**

Bushmills

Distillery 2 Distillery Rd • Tours March–Oct Mon–Sat 9.15am–5pm, also Sun noon–5pm; Nov–Feb Mon–Fri 10am–3.30pm, Sat & Sun 12.30–3.30pm • £7.50 • ☎ 028 2073 3218, ⓦ bushmills.com

The foremost attraction in **BUSHMILLS** is the **Old Bushmills Distillery** on the outskirts of town. Whiskey has been distilled here legally since 1608, making it the oldest licit distillery in the world, and it is well worth taking the **tour**. Bushmills whiskey is distilled three times, once more than Scotch, but perhaps the biggest surprise is just how little subtlety is involved in the industrial manufacture of alcohol, despite all the lore that surrounds it. The distillery is a massive factory where an extraordinary range of (mostly unpleasant) smells assails your nostrils, making it difficult to imagine that the end product really does delight the tastebuds.

ARRIVAL AND INFORMATION   BUSHMILLS

By bus Coleraine (Mon–Fri 10 daily; 15min) Ballycastle (Mon–Fri 10 daily; 20min). The Causeway Rambler (402) (Mon–Fri 7 daily) operates from mid-April to the end of Sept between Portrush (Dunluce Ave) and Ballintoy, and stops in Bushmills at the Distillery, Ballyness Caravan Park

and at the war memorial in the centre of town.
Tourist office 44 Main St (March, April & Oct Sat & Sun 10am–4pm; May & June daily 10am–5pm; July & Aug till 6pm; ☎ 028 2073 0390, ⓦ heartofthecauseway coastandglens.com).

ACCOMMODATION AND EATING

★**Bushmills Inn** 9 Dunluce Rd ☎ 028 2073 3000, ⓦ bushmillsinn.com. A former coaching inn with a cottage-style interior (inglenook turf fires, hayloft snugs) and a restaurant featuring traditional dishes such as the Botchan (local soup) or Dalriada cullen skink (smoked haddock fillet). There's music in the *Gas Bar* on Sat night with local band Scad the Beggars. **£158**

The French Rooms 45 Main St ☎ 028 2073 0033, ⓦ thefrenchrooms.com. The fragrant smell of lavender draws you into this elegant restaurant, café and gift shop

all rolled into one. Lunches and dinners may include tomato ravioli, sea trout, hake or guinea fowl with main courses averaging £12. Wed, Thurs & Sun 10am–3pm, Fri & Sat 10am–9pm.

Tartine at the Distillers Arms 140 Main St ☎ 028 2073 1044, ⓦ distillersarms.com. The £16 early-bird menu (5–6.30pm) here is great value; choose from dishes like beef bourguignon or seafood thermidor. Mon–Sat 5–9pm, Sun 12.30– 3pm.

Dunluce Castle

Daily: Easter–Sept 10am–6pm; Oct–Easter 10am–4pm • £5 • ☎ 028 2073 1938, ⓦ discovernorthernireland.com

The most impressive ruin of this entire coastline is the dramatically sited sixteenth-century **Dunluce Castle**. Perched on a fine headland, high above a cave, it looks as if it only needs a roof to be perfectly habitable once again. Its history is inextricably linked to that of its original owner, **Sorley Boy MacDonnell**, whose clan, the so-called "Lords of the Isles", ruled northeastern Ulster from this base. English incursions into the area culminated in 1584 with Sir John Perrott laying siege to Dunluce, forcing Sorley Boy ("Yellow Charles" in Irish) to leave the castle. But as soon as Perrott departed, leaving a garrison in charge, Sorley Boy hauled his men up the cliff in baskets and recaptured the castle, later repairing the damage with the proceeds of the salvaged wreckage of the *Girona* (see opposite) and arming the fort with three of its cannons. Having made his point, Sorley Boy agreed a peace with the English, and his son, Randal, was created Viscount Dunluce and Earl of Antrim by James I. In 1639, Dunluce Castle paid the penalty for its precarious, if impregnable, position when the kitchen fell off the cliff during a storm, complete

14

with cooks and dinner. Shortly afterwards, the MacDonnells moved to more comfortable lodgings at Glenarm, and Dunluce was left empty.

The castle remains an extraordinary place. The MacDonnells' Scottish connections – Randal continued to own land in Kintyre – are evident in the **gatehouse**'s turrets and crow-step gables, and in the tapering chimneys of the seventeenth-century **Great Hall**. There's a strange touch of luxury in the **loggia**, though it oddly faces away from the sun. A steep path takes you down to the **cave** below the castle that pierces right through the promontory, with an opening directly under the gatehouse.

Portrush

The town of **PORTRUSH** has everything you'd expect from a seaside resort, from sandy **beaches** backed by dunes, which run both east and west, to summertime theatrical productions in the town hall. There's plenty of entertainment for children, including the long-established **Barry's Amusements** (☎028 7082 2340, ⓦbarrysamusements.com) just behind the seafront. Many students from the University of Ulster at Coleraine live here and make it a considerably livelier place than you might expect, even out of season. The huge popularity of the local **dance scene** draws clubbers from all over the North, meaning the town can have a distinctly raucous feel at weekends, and there are numerous opportunities to watch or take part in sport and other activities. The long, sandy beach towards Dunluce ends at the **White Rocks**, where the weather has carved the soft limestone cliffs into strange shapes, most famously the so-called **"Cathedral Cave"**, nearly 60m from end to end.

ARRIVAL AND INFORMATION

By train The train station is a short hop south of the town centre on Eglinton Street.
Destinations Coleraine (Mon–Sat 16–21 daily, Sun 11; 15min) for connections to Belfast (Mon–Sat 9–10 daily, Sun 5; 1hr 30min).
By bus Portstewart (Mon–Sat every 30min, Sun hourly;

15min).
Tourist office Town Hall, 1 Mark St (March & Oct Sat & Sun noon–5pm; April–June & Sept Mon–Fri 9.30am–5pm, Sat & Sun noon–5pm; July and Aug Mon–Fri 9.30am–6pm, Sat & Sun 11–5pm; ☎028 7082 3333).

ACCOMMODATION

Note that **accommodation** fills up quickly in high season, especially in July for the major golf championships, and in May during the North West 200 motorbike road races.

Beulah Guesthouse 16 Causeway St ☎028 7082 2413, ⓦbeulahguesthouse.com. Nine well-presented rooms await guests at this convenient B&B that provides splendid breakfasts covering everything from the full fry-up to gluten-free and vegetarian dishes. A big bonus at congested traffic times is a private car park. **£70**
Maddybenny Farmhouse Loguestown Rd ☎028 7082 3394, ⓦmaddybenny.com. Offers splendidly equipped

rooms, a feast of a breakfast, plus a snooker table and a games room. **£70**
Ramada Portrush 73 Main St ☎028 7082 6100, ⓦramadaportrush.com. The 69 rooms in this centrally located hotel feature contemporary elegant design, some with sea views. Off-season special deals are available from Oct–March. **£179**

EATING, DRINKING AND NIGHTLIFE

Arcadia Café West Strand Ave ☎028 7082 3924. Once known as the Ladies Bathing Place, this was a popular venue for dance bands in the 1950s and 60s. Now it's a lunch spot (wraps and melts etc.), with ice cream and shakes adding to the seaside vibe. Dine outside and gaze across to the Skerries or watch the waves break on the beach. Easter–Sept 10am–dusk.
Coast The Harbour ☎028 7082 3311, ⓦramore

restaurant.com. Specializes in stone-baked pizza, pasta dishes and burgers, with main courses averaging £5. April–Sept Mon–Fri 5–9.30pm, Sat 4.30–10.30pm, Sun 3–9pm. Closed Mon & Tues in winter.
Harbour Bar The Harbour ☎028 7082 2430. The most convivial bar in town: great for meeting the locals and admiring the maritime memorabilia and fine sea views. An adjacent bistro opens Wed–Sun from 4.45pm. Mon–Sat

noon–1am, Sun till 11.30pm.

Kiwi's Brew Bar 47 Main St ☎ 028 7082 2402. A good place to sample a range of Irish craft beers from Cork, Armagh and Donegal as well as Italian ciders. Every Friday they host live music and guest beers from 5pm; on Sundays in summer there's a popular "Brews and Blues" session from 4.30–7.30pm. Mon–Fri 5.30–11.30pm, Sat 5.30–1am, Sun 5.30pm–midnight.

Lush at Kelly's Hotel Bushmills Rd ☎ 028 7082 6611, ⓦ kellysportrush.co.uk. Saturday night's Lush at one of the North's biggest clubs attracts major DJs and clubbers from far and wide.

★ **Neptune & Prawn** 54 Kerr St ☎ 028 7082 2448. An über-cool setting with its white wood panelling and bare brick walls, and picture windows showing off the harbour. Perfect for light lunch nibbles – the wood-burning oven turns out flatbreads with tomato, cheese, garlic and mozzarella, or you can enjoy mini lobster burgers or Spanish cured meats from £3–6. The dinner menu showcases the likes of fajitas, hot dogs and burgers. Mon–Thurs 5–9pm, Fri–Sun 5–1am, plus Sat & Sun 1–3pm.

Ramore Wine Bar Above Coast ☎ 028 7082 4313. Serves a range of meat and fish dishes with a few veggie lunch and dinner options. Choices include hake, sea bream, meat kebabs or marinated chilli chicken (average main course £12). Mon–Fri 12.15–2.15pm & 5–9.30pm, Sat 12.15–2.30pm & 4.45–10.30pm, Sun 12.30–3pm & 5–9pm.

Springhill Bar 15 Causeway St ☎ 028 7082 3361. There's a regular traditional session at this lively bar every Thursday from 9pm. Saturday night features local DJs from 10pm till late. Mon–Sat 12.30pm–12.30am, Sun till 11.30pm.

SPORT AND ACTIVITIES

The biggest event in the sporting calendar, attracting tens of thousands, is the annual **North West 200 motorbike race** (ⓦ northwest200.org), held in the second week of May when roads close for the weekend. The annual **raft race** (ⓦ portrushraftrace.co.uk) at the end of May sees participants race each other across the harbour on homemade rafts. In Sept, the **Northern Ireland Air Show** (ⓦ airwavesportrush.co.uk) is a spectacular event based around the East Strand.

Surfing This is surfing country par excellence and there is rewarding surfing off the West Strand and White Rocks. You can rent boards and gear, and take lessons, at Troggs Surf Shop at 88 Main St (☎ 028 7082 5476, ⓦ troggssurfshop .co.uk), who'll also advise on the condition of the waves.

Golf Royal Portrush Golf Club (☎ 028 7082 2311, ⓦ royalportrushgolfclub.com) is the North's premier club, boasting two eighteen-hole courses, and in 2012, it hosted the Irish Open. Demand is high in the summer, especially in good weather, and it's wise to book ahead.

Northern County Derry

West of Portrush the A2 continues to hug the coastline as it traverses the northern part of County Derry, taking in marvellous beaches all the way from **Portstewart**, near which it crosses the River Bann, to **Magilligan Point**. On the way there are impressive seascapes visible from the cliff-top **Mussenden Temple** and stunning views from the land around **Mount Binevenagh**. The land becomes drabber as the road nears the small manufacturing town of **Limavady**, which retains a few remnants of Georgian times. A **train line** runs along the coast to Derry, with stations at Castlerock and Coleraine.

Portstewart

Derry's largest coastal resort, **PORTSTEWART**, like its near neighbour Portrush (see opposite), is full of Victorian boarding houses. Of the two, Portstewart is decidedly more sedate and has always had more airs and graces: the train station is said to have been built a mile out of town to stop hoi polloi from coming. In terms of sheer location, though, Portstewart wins hands down.

Portstewart Strand

Cars March–June & Sept £4.50, July & Aug £5

Just west of the town is **Portstewart Strand**, a long sand beach firm enough to drive on – which the locals delight in doing – with some of the best **surfing** in the country. It's a grand place, too, if you hit fine weather and feel like getting out your bucket and spade. The best way to take the sea air is the bracing **cliff-side walk**, which runs between

14

the beach and the town, passing battlements and an imposing Gothic mansion, now a Dominican college. For advice on local surfing and equipment visit Ocean Warriors, 80 The Promenade (☎028 7083 6500, ⊛oceanwarriors.co.uk)

ARRIVAL AND INFORMATION

PORTSTEWART

By bus Portrush (Mon–Sat every 30min, Sun hourly; 15min).

Tourist information The tourist desk in the library on

The Crescent (July & Aug Mon–Sat 10am–1pm & 2–4.30pm; ☎028 7083 2286) can help with accommodation bookings.

ACCOMMODATION

Cul-Erg House 9 Hillside ☎028 7083 6610, ⊛culerg .co.uk. Stay here if you want to be near the strand; it's a large Victorian guesthouse with 11 en-suite rooms and private kitchen for guests. **£75**

Juniper Hill Caravan Park 70 Ballyreagh Rd ☎028 7083 2023. Space for caravans and camping about a mile

down the A2 towards Portrush. April–Oct. Tent pitch **£20**

Rick's Causeway Coast (IHH) 4 Victoria Terrace ☎028 7083 3789, ⊕rick@causewaycoasthostel.fsnet.co.uk. A well-run hostel, handy for cafés, bars, restaurants and walking the seafront. Price includes breakfast and free tea/coffee. **£40**

EATING AND DRINKING

Amici Ristorante Portmore Rd ☎028 7083 4444, ⊛amiciportstewart.com. Transformed from an old golf clubhouse, this is one of the most scenically sited of all the north-coast restaurants. Neapolitan pizzas (£9) with homemade dough, plus meat, poultry and fish cooked in a charcoal oven (mains average £11). Daily noon–3pm & 5.30–9.30pm.

Anchor Bar 86–87 The Promenade ☎028 7083 2003, ⊛theanchorbar.co.uk. Part of the fabric of the town since 1898, you can choose from bar or bistro food (noon–9pm) with mains averaging £11. Mon–Sat 11.30am–1am, Sun till 11pm.

The Burger Club 81 The Promenade ☎028 7083 3959, ⊛burgerclubni.com. Burgers every which way: beef, turkey, lamb, chicken, cheese or vegetarian, all priced at £6.95. Daily noon–10pm.

★**Harry's Shack** The Strand ☎028 7083 1783. With its raw wood tables, this place is all about elegant simplicity.

Starters might be smoked mackerel fish cakes or shoreline mussels (£6) along with Guinness wheaten bread. Hake or plaice, fresh from Greencastle in Donegal, are main-course favourites, as are meaty options such as steak and pork belly; mains average £13. You may also bring your own wine. Daily: brunch 10.30am–4pm, lunch 12.30–4pm, dinner 5–9pm.

Morelli's 53–56 The Promenade ☎028 7083 2150, ⊛morellisportstewart.co.uk. Famous for over 100 years for its ice cream and monster sundaes such as "Morelli's Madness" – seven scoops of ice cream for £9.95. Also serves snacks and pastries. Daily: Easter–Oct 9am–10pm; rest of year 9am–5.30pm.

Sizzlin Sausage 12 The Diamond ☎028 7055 7100. Typical mains here include bubble-and-squeak chicken, porterhouse steak and bangers and mash – all around £9. Breakfasts are served all day with free tea till 11am. Daily, summer 8am–10pm; winter 9am–7pm.

Hezlett House

April to mid-Sept daily 10am–5pm; mid-Sept to March Sat & Sun 10am–5pm • £4.70, includes Mussenden Temple (see opposite) • ⊛nationaltrust.org.uk

Some seven miles west of Coleraine along the A2, at the Castlerock crossroads, is **Hezlett House**, built in 1690. The house is a fine example of cruck-truss construction, an early method of prefabricated building using wooden frames filled with clay and rubble that was common in England but is enough of a rarity here to warrant preservation by the National Trust. The last owner of the house is buried in the graveyard at Downhill (see opposite), where his gravestone quaintly bears both his own version of the spelling of his name and that of his father, a Mr Hazlett.

Downhill Palace

Daily dawn–dusk • Free

Ornate gates alongside the A2 mark the main entrance to the ruins of **Downhill Palace**, built in the 1780s by **Frederick Augustus Hervey**, Anglican Bishop of Derry and fourth Earl of Bristol. Hervey was an enthusiastic grand traveller (all the many Hotel Bristols throughout Europe are named after him), and was also an art collector and sportsman, once organizing a preprandial race between Anglican and Presbyterian clergy along the local strand. His palace, accessed through pleasant **gardens**, was last occupied by US troops, billeted here during World War II, and was dismantled on their departure.

Mussenden Temple

Call ☎ 028 7084 8728 for opening times • £4.70, includes Hezlett House (see opposite)

Across fields at the back of Downhill Palace is the diminutive **Mussenden Temple**, which clings precariously to the eroding cliff-edge and offers stunning sea views. Its classic domed **rotunda** was apparently modelled on the Temple of Vesta in Rome and was built by Hervey in honour of his cousin Mrs Frideswide Mussenden, who died aged 22 before it was completed, after which it was used as a summer library. Later, with characteristic generosity and a fairly startling lack of prejudice, Hervey allowed a weekly Mass to be celebrated in the temple, as there was no local Catholic church. The inscription on the temple **frieze** translates rather smugly as: "It is agreeable to watch, from land, someone else involved in a great struggle while winds whip up the waves out at sea."

Downhill

West along the A2 the road curves steeply downwards to reach the appositely named **DOWNHILL** on the edge of an enormously long **beach**. Overlooked by Mussenden Temple on the cliff-edge above, the beach is accessible by car, though with no shops in Downhill, stock up on provisions in advance if you intend to stay. From here it's possible to take the Bishop's Road (constructed at Hervey's bidding) southwards to reach **Mount Binevenagh** and its fabulous viewpoints.

ACCOMMODATION   DOWNHILL

Downhill Beach House 12 Mussenden Rd ☎ 028 7084 9077, ⓦ downhillbeachhouse.com. A spacious hostel close to many attractions and handy for the ferry to Donegal. March–Dec. Double dorms **£46**

Magilligan Point

From Downhill the A2 huddles between a vertiginous cliff and the railway line before reaching **Magilligan**. Two miles further along the main road a turning leads to **Magilligan Point**, running across the dunes past a prison (once an army base and later an internment camp) before reaching the tip of the peninsula. Here, at the narrow entrance to Lough Foyle, stands a **Martello tower** (free access), with walls more than 3m thick.

ARRIVAL AND DEPARTURE   MAGILLIGAN

By ferry A daily ferry service (15min) across Lough Foyle to Greencastle in County Donegal is operated by Lough Foyle Ferry company (pedestrians £2.50 single, £3.50 return; cars £12 single, £17 return; ☎ 00353 7493 81901, ⓦ loughfoyleferry.com). From Magilligan sailings are at a quarter past the hour from 9.15am–7.15pm (8.15pm in summer). From Greencastle sailings are every hour on the hour from 9am–7pm.

ACCOMMODATION AND EATING

Benone Tourist Complex Benone Ave, off Seacoast Rd ☎ 028 7775 0555, ⓦ benoneni.com. Includes a caravan site, tennis courts, putting green and swimming pool (weekends in summer) and camping. April–Sept. Tent pitch **£20**

Point Bar Magilligan Point ☎ 028 7775 0440. An excellent place to refuel, especially for ferry passengers with time to kill. Food served noon–9pm (try the lemon sole and seafood chowder); mains average £10. Daily 11.30am–11.30pm.

14

> **DANNY BOY**
>
> The lyrics for the quintessential "Oirish" ballad **Danny Boy** were actually composed by an English lawyer, Fred E. Weatherley, in 1912 and, a year later, fitted to *The Londonderry Air*, a tune collected by Jane Ross, a resident of 51 Main Street, Limavady, from a travelling fiddler in 1851. The song achieved renown in Ireland when recorded in the 1930s by Margaret Burke-Sheridan and has since seen many other tear-jerking renditions (Sinéad O'Connor recorded an idiosyncratically spine-tingling version); it still remains endearingly popular with dewy-eyed expats and Irish-Americans. Limavady holds the annual **Danny Boy festival** in mid-May (Ⓦ www.dannyboyfestival.com), featuring a variety of music.

Limavady and around

LIMAVADY was once a major settlement, its old site lying two miles further south down the valley of the River Roe. The town was refounded as Newtown Limavady in the early seventeenth century by Thomas Phillips, speaker of the Irish House of Commons. The town possesses a few features of its illustrious past: the six-arch **bridge** spanning the river was built in 1700, and Main Street, which runs down from it, is still recognizably Georgian. The town hosts an excellent jazz and blues **festival** in the second week of June (Ⓦ limavadyjazzandblues.com), as well as the Roe Valley Folk Festival in late October (Ⓦ roevalleyarts.com).

Roe Valley Country Park

Visitor centre Daily: April–Sept 9am–6pm; Oct–March 9am–5pm • Free • **Museum** July & Aug daily 1–5pm; May, June & Sept Mon, Tues & Thurs–Sun 1–5pm • Free

The **Roe Valley Country Park**, a couple of miles south of Limavady, preserves Northern Ireland's first hydroelectric power station, opened in 1896, with much of the original equipment intact and viewable, as well as a visitor centre and the **Green Lane Museum**. This focuses on the area's history, including its erstwhile importance in linen production, and features craft displays on Saturdays (2–4pm).

ARRIVAL AND INFORMATION
LIMAVADY

By bus Castlerock (Mon–Sat 6–10 daily; 45min); Derry (Mon–Sat 8–14 daily, Sun 4; 40–55min); Dungiven (Mon–Fri 5 daily; 35min).

Tourist information Roe Valley Arts Centre, 24 Main St (Mon–Fri 9am–5pm; ☏028 7776 0650, Ⓦ roevalleyarts .com).

ACCOMMODATION AND EATING

Roe Park Resort 40 Drumrane Rd ☏028 7772 2222, Ⓦ roepark.com. This luxurious hotel comes with a golf course, leisure centre and spa facilities. There's a range of dining on offer too, and *O'Cahan's* bar, with a splendid cocktail list and live music on Fri and Sat nights from 9.30pm. **£105**

Derry city

DERRY, which lies at the foot of Lough Foyle, is a crossroads city in more ways than one: roads from all cardinal points arrive here, but it was also a major point of emigration from the eighteenth century onwards, an exodus that reached tumultuous proportions during the Great Famine. Derry is the fourth-largest city in Ireland and the second biggest in the North, but it has a markedly different atmosphere from Belfast, being two-thirds **Catholic**. While roads into the city are signposted in Irish welcoming visitors to Derry, the city still appears as "**Londonderry**" on many road maps and signs, a preference adhered to by the British government, Unionists and television news bulletins. It is referred to by the press and broadcast media as "Derry-Londonderry", a tactful placating of both Nationalist and Unionist.

Approached from the east in winter twilight or under a strong summer sun, the city presents a beguiling picture, with the vista of the **River Foyle** and the rise of the city's two hillsides, terraced with pastel-shaded houses and topped by the hueless stone spires of the ever-present religious denominations. With its rich history, Derry has several worthwhile attractions, mostly enclosed within the seventeenth-century **walls**, themselves the most significant reminder of the city's past.

Brief history

Though **St Columba** established a monastery here in 546 AD, the development of Derry (originally called Doire Calgaigh, "oakwood of Calgach", after a legendary warrior) only really began in medieval times, when in the fourteenth century it was granted to the Anglo-Norman de Burgos. By 1500, the power of the O'Dohertys had spread from Inishowen and they constructed a tower house, which was later absorbed into the seventeenth-century walls.

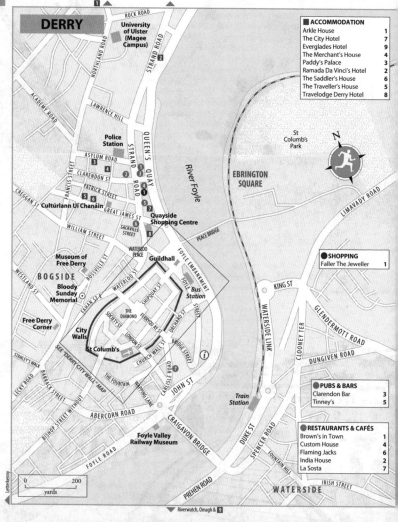

DERRY

■ ACCOMMODATION	
Arkle House	1
The City Hotel	7
Everglades Hotel	9
The Merchant's House	4
Paddy's Palace	3
Ramada Da Vinci's Hotel	2
The Saddler's House	6
The Traveller's House	5
Travelodge Derry Hotel	8

● SHOPPING	
Faller The Jeweller	1

● PUBS & BARS	
Clarendon Bar	3
Tinney's	5

● RESTAURANTS & CAFÉS	
Brown's in Town	1
Custom House	4
Flaming Jacks	6
India House	2
La Sosta	7

THE SIEGE OF DERRY

Derry's walls underwent – and withstood – siege on a number of occasions during the seventeenth century. The last of these, in **1688–89**, played a key part in the Williamite army's victory over the Catholic James II at the **Battle of the Boyne** (see p.585), when the Derrymen's obduracy crucially delayed the plans of James and his ally Louis XIV to maintain Catholic ascendancy over the kingdom.

The suffering and heroism of the fifteen-week siege, the longest in British history, still have the immediacy of recent history in the minds of Derry Protestants. James's accession in 1685 had seen the introduction of a policy of replacing Protestants with Catholics in leading positions in the Irish administration and army. In December 1688, a new garrison attempted to enter the city, but was prevented when a group of young apprentices seized the keys and locked the city's gates. Eventually, after negotiation, an **all-Protestant garrison** under Governor Robert Lundy was admitted. Over the following few months the city's resident population of two thousand swelled to thirty thousand as people from the surrounding area took refuge from Jacobite forces advancing into Ulster. Fearing that resistance against the Jacobite army was futile, Lundy departed; his effigy is still burnt each December by Protestants. Around seven thousand Protestants died during the siege that followed, the survivors being reduced to eating dogs, cats and rats. Today, the siege is commemorated with a skeleton on the city **coat of arms**, and the lyrical tag "maiden city", a somewhat sexist reference to the city's unbreached walls.

14

Towards the end of the sixteenth century the uprising of Hugh O'Neill, Earl of Tyrone, provoked an English invasion. Doire's strategic position on the River Foyle was quickly appreciated, though it took some years for it finally to be captured. In 1600, the English commander **Sir Henry Docwra** began fortifying the remains of the medieval town as a base for incursions against the Irish, but in 1608 Sir Cahir O'Doherty rebelled against Docwra's successor, Pawlett, and burnt Doire, by now anglicized as Derry, to the ground. This destruction made the city ripe for the plantation of English and Scottish settlers, and the financial assistance of the wealthy businessmen of the City of London was obtained to achieve this. A new walled city was constructed and renamed **Londonderry** in 1613 in honour of its backers, the Twelve Companies of the Corporation of London.

The seventeenth century was the most dramatic phase of Derry's evolution, culminating in the **siege** of 1688–89 (see box, above). Following this, many Derry people emigrated to America to avoid harsh English laws, and some of their descendants, such as the pioneer frontiersman Daniel Boone, achieved fame there. Derry's heyday as a **seaport** came in the nineteenth century, a period when industries such as shirt-making began to flourish – by the beginning of the twentieth century the city was the largest shirt-manufacturer in the UK. However, after **Partition**, the North–South dividing line lay just a couple of miles from Derry's back door, and the consequent tariffs reduced much of its traditional trade. The shirt industry began its long decline, finally being phased out in the face of much cheaper imports from Asia.

Though Derry remained relatively peaceful after Partition, its politics were among the North's most blatantly discriminatory, with the substantial Catholic majority denied its civil rights by gerrymandering geared towards ensuring the Protestant minority's control of local institutions. In October 1968 Derry witnessed a two-thousand-strong **civil rights march**. Confronted by the batons of the Protestant police force and the notorious B Specials, rioting spilled over into the Catholic Bogside district and over eighty people were injured. The clash is seen by many as the catalyst for the modern phase of the Troubles: faith in the impartiality of the Royal Ulster Constabulary was destroyed once and for all, and the IRA was reborn a year or so later. The following year's Protestant **Apprentice Boys' march** (see box, above) was another significant step, and, on January 30, 1972, came **Bloody Sunday** (see box, p.517).

14

DERRY
CITY WALLS

River Foyle

GUILDHALL SQUARE ROUNDABOUT
FOYLE EMBANKMENT

Coward's Bastion
Magazine Gate
Guildhall
Bus Station
GUILDHALL SQUARE
Shipquay Gate
Water Bastion
UNION HALL STREET
BANK PLACE
WATERLOO PLACE
Tower Museum
Hangman's Bastion
SHIPQUAY STREET
FOYLE STREET
Millennium Forum
HIGH ST
MAGAZINE ST
Castle Gate
CASTLE STREET
NEWMARKET STREET
ORCHARD STREET
Foyleside Shopping Centre
THE BOGSIDE
WATERLOO ST
Nerve Centre
Gunner's Bastion
LINEN HALL ST
Richmond Shopping Centre
Newgate Bastion
BRIDGE STREET
Butcher's Gate
BUTCHER ST
THE DIAMOND
FERRYQUAY STREET
FAHAN STREET
MAGAZINE STREET
Apprentice Boys' Memorial Hall
BISHOP STREET WITHIN
PUMP STREET
MARKET STREET
Ferryquay Gate
CARLISLE RD
SOCIETY STREET
LONDON STREET
ARTILLERY ST
The Playhouse
Ferry Bastion
HAWKIN STREET
PALACE STREET
St Augustine's Church
Royal Bastion
GRAND PARADE
Verbal Arts Centre
New Gate
St Columb's Cathedral
Courthouse
Church Bastion
Bishop's Gate
Double Bastion
BISHOP STREET WITHOUT
THE FOUNTAIN
THE FOUNTAIN

0   50   yards

● RESTAURANTS & CAFÉS
Café del Mondo   3
The Exchange   4
Java   5

● PUBS & BARS
Badgers   7
The Gweedore Bar   2
Peadar O'Donnell's   1
Sandino's Café Bar   6

● SHOPPING
Austin's Department Store   2
Bedlam Market   3
Craft Village   1
Thomas the Goldsmith   4

■ ACCOMMODATION
Maldron Hotel   1

The city has undergone dramatic changes in recent times, renovating and repackaging its built heritage. The major public buildings have been given a recent facelift and the legacy of the peace process has led to the opening of the spectacular **Peace Bridge**.

The medieval walls

Derry's centre, focused on its **medieval walls**, is remarkably compact, and it's easy to combine all the main attractions in one circuit. The walls are one of the best-preserved defences in Europe. A mile in length and as high as a two-storey house in places, they are reinforced by bulwarks and bastions and a parapeted earth rampart as wide as any thoroughfare. Within their circuit, the original medieval street-pattern has remained, with four **gateways** surviving from the original construction, albeit in slightly revised form.

14

The Guildhall

Guildhall Square • Mon–Fri 9am–5pm • Free • ☎ 028 7137 6510, ⓦ derrycity.gov.uk

The best approach to the walls is from the Guildhall Square, once the old quay, east of Shipquay Gate. The neo-Gothic ecclesiastical appearance of the **Guildhall** belies its function as the place where the political parties hold their monthly meetings. Inside, the city's history is depicted in a series of newly restored stained-glass windows. A **permanent exhibition** installed as part of a £10m conservation programme tells with flair and imagination the story of the Plantation of Ulster and the building of the walls. Touchscreens give insights into outstanding features such as the elaborate ceilings, baronial wood panelling and magnificent organ. The terrace at the *Guild Café* offers fine views of the Peace Bridge.

Peace Bridge

Forming a graceful arc across the River Foyle, the **Peace Bridge**, which opened in 2011, represents a symbolic, curvilinear-shaped handshake between the city's east and west banks. Popular with walkers, joggers and cyclists, the bridge links the city centre with **Ebrington Square**, a redeveloped military parade ground that is now a cultural hub, providing the venue for open-air concerts and hosting the Turner Prize in 2013. A new city landmark, the bridge has helped rebalance the communities, meaning that the Foyle is no longer seen as a religious divide.

Tower Museum

Union Hall Place • Jan–June & Sept–Dec Tues–Sat 10am–5pm; July & Aug Mon–Sat 10am–5pm, Sun noon–4pm • £4 • ☎ 028 7137 2411, ⓦ derrycity.gov.uk/museums

A reconstruction of the medieval O'Doherty Tower here houses the **Tower Museum**, whose showpieces are a series of stimulating displays and galleries recounting the city's history. A splendid **exhibition**, spread over four storeys, focuses on Spanish Armada Treasures, which features gold artefacts and finely worked jewellery from *La Trinidad Valencera*, which sank in Kinnegoe Bay (off Inishowen) in 1588.

St Columb's Cathedral

Mon–Sat 9am–5pm • £2 suggested donation • ☎ 028 7126 7313, ⓦ stcolumbscathedral.org

Occupying the southwestern corner of the walled city, the Church of Ireland **St Columb's Cathedral** was built in 1633 in a style later called Planters' Gothic and was the first post-Reformation cathedral in the British Isles. Displayed in the entrance porch is a cannon shell catapulted into the church during the 1688–89 blockade by the besieging army – their terms of surrender were attached. The cathedral was used as a battery during the siege, its **tower** serving as a lookout post; today it provides the best view of the old city. The present **spire** dates from the late Georgian period, its

14

lead-covered wooden predecessor having been stripped to fashion bullets and cannon shot during the siege.

Inside, an open-timbered **roof** rests on sixteen stone corbels carved with figures of past bishops. Other things to look out for are the finely sculpted stone reredos behind the altar, the eighteenth-century bishop's throne and the window panels showing scenes as diverse as the relief of the city on August 12, 1689, and St Columba's mission to Britain. In the **chapterhouse museum** are more relics of the siege, including the padlocks and keys used to lock the city gates, plus the grand kidney-shaped desk of the eighteenth-century philosopher George Berkeley, erstwhile dean of the cathedral (who only visited Derry once), and mementos of Cecil Frances (1818–95), wife of Bishop Alexander and composer of the famous hymns *Once in Royal David's City* and *There is a Green Hill Far Away*.

The courthouse and The Fountain

Close to Bishop's Gate stands the **courthouse**, built of white sandstone from Dungiven in crude Greek-Revival style. The gate itself was remodelled for the first centenary of the siege and reopened in 1789. Immediately outside the walls here is **The Fountain** area, named after the freshwater source that once supplied the city, though few remnants of any antiquity remain apart from a tower of the old Derry jail, jammed up against the grim modern houses. The Fountain is a tiny enclave, the only remaining Protestant area on the west bank, and is of interest solely for its Union Jack kerb paintings and huge **murals**, which read as direct responses to the more famous Catholic "Free Derry" mural in the next valley.

The Double Bastion and Verbal Arts Centre

Centre ☎ 028 7126 6946, Ⓦ verbalartscentre.co.uk • **Café** Mon–Sat 8.30am–4pm

North from Bishop's Gate, you reach the **Double Bastion**, where the "Roaring Meg" cannon sits. During the siege, it was said that "the noise of the discharge was more terrifying than were the contents of the charge dangerous to the enemy". Just by here is the **Verbal Arts Centre**, a unique project aimed at sustaining and promoting forms of communication and entertainment once central to Irish culture: legend, folklore, *sean-nós* – an unaccompanied narrative form of singing (see p.603) – and storytelling performed by a *seanachie* (storyteller). The centre, incorporating designs by Louis le Brocquy, commissions works from writers, and hosts poetry readings and storytelling events. *Bloom's* **café** serves scones, soups and stews.

Royal Bastion and The Nerve Centre

The Nerve Centre Mon–Fri 9am–9pm, Sat 9am–5pm • ☎ 028 7126 0562, Ⓦ nerve-centre.org.uk

Constructed between 1826 and 1828, the **Royal Bastion** used to be topped by a 3m-high statue of Reverend George Walker, the defender of Derry "against an arbitrary and bigoted monarch" (to quote the still-legible inscription). The statue was blown up in 1973 and the surrounding area is a flashpoint every August 12 when the Apprentice Boys march in their predecessors', and Walker's, memory (see box, p.513). The view from here across the Bogside district is expansive.

A little further downhill, on the south side of Magazine Street, is the main focus of Derry's dynamic cultural world, **The Nerve Centre**, which contains sound, film and video studios and editing suites, an art-house cinema, two music venues, a bar and a café.

Foyle Valley Railway Museum

Foyle Rd • Mon–Fri 10am–4.30pm • Free • ☎ 028 7126 5234, Ⓦ derrycity.gov.uk/museums

Just outside the city centre and near to the Craigavon Bridge is the **Foyle Valley Railway Museum** where visitors can learn about the city's rail history – at one time it was served by four different railway systems. Displays include a re-created railway platform, a small steam engine and carriages.

The Bogside

In the valley below the northern city walls is the Catholic **Bogside** district where, at the start of the Troubles, ferocious rioting took place following the Apprentice Boys' march, with the army and police responding to bricks and petrol bombs with tear gas, rubber bullets and careering Saracen armoured cars. The area at the foot of the escarpment used to be full of streets of compact terraced housing, but was redeveloped in the 1960s in the form of a dual carriageway, an estate of tenement flats and empty concrete precincts. Clinging to the opposite hillside, and in stark contrast, are early twentieth-century terraces of stucco façades, blue tile roofs and red chimney stacks.

Most eye-catching in this panorama is a gable-end **mural** showing the former Independent Republican MP and one of the organizers of the People's Democracy movement, Bernadette Devlin, megaphone in hand, in front of the old "You are now entering Free Derry" mural. Another mural, the "Death of Innocence", commemorates a 14-year-old girl, Annette McGavigan, who died in 1971, caught in crossfire between the British Army and IRA. There are also striking murals featuring a gas-mask-clad petrol bomber and a British soldier smashing down a door with a sledgehammer during Operation Motorman (see box, below). These and the nearby 1968 civil rights march mural were painted by the Bogside artists Kevin Hasson, Tom Kelly and William Kelly, who have published an illustrated book on their work. Another mural, on Westland Street, depicts those killed on Bloody Sunday.

The Museum of Free Derry

55 Glenfada Park, off Rossville St • Mon–Fri 9.30am–4.30pm, plus April–June Sat 1–4pm, July–Sept Sat & Sun 1– 4pm • £3 • ☎ 028 7136 0880, ⓦ museumoffreederry.org

During 2015 the **Museum of Free Derry**, which explores the city's troubled history, is undergoing a £2.2m renovation and will move with its exhibits to temporary premises near Glenfada Park. The museum focuses especially on the decade following the origin

---

BLOODY SUNDAY

For the first two years of the Troubles, the part of the Catholic Bogside area beyond the original "Free Derry" mural was a notorious no-go area, the undisputed preserve of the IRA, its boundary marked by a gravestone-like monument declaring: "You are now entering free Derry". This autonomy lasted until 1972, when the British army launched **Operation Motorman**; the IRA men who had been in the area were tipped off, though, and got across the border before the invasion took place.

To the right of the "Bernadette Devlin" mural in the Bogside stands a **memorial pillar** to the thirteen Catholic civilians killed by British paratroopers (a fourteenth died later of his wounds) on "**Bloody Sunday**", January 30, 1972, in the aftermath of a civil-rights demonstration. The soldiers immediately claimed they had been fired upon, an assertion later disproved, though some witnesses came forward to report seeing IRA men there with their guns. The bitter memory of the subsequent Widgery Commission's failure to declare anyone responsible for the deaths festered in Catholic Derry, and pressure was maintained on successive governments to reopen investigations. In 1999, after years of mounting demands for a full examination, the British government established the **Saville Inquiry**, which conducted its proceedings in Derry's Guildhall before moving to Westminster in 2002. It finally reported in June 2010, concluding that the British Army's actions were "unjustified and unjustifiable", that all those killed or wounded were innocent victims and that some soldiers had committed perjury in giving their evidence.

of the civil rights movement; it features a wealth of intriguing displays, photographs and posters related to that period.

Riverwatch Aquarium and Visitor Centre

22 Victoria Rd • Mon–Fri 10am–4pm; July & Aug also Sat 10am–4pm • Free • ☎ 028 7134 2100, ⓦ loughs-agency.org

Across the river, opposite the *Everglades Hotel* (see opposite), is the Loughs Agency's **Riverwatch** visitor centre which focuses on the Foyle waterway and its environment. The centre features five **aquaria**, home to a range of local fresh and saltwater fish and crustaceans (feeding time is Mon, Wed, & Sat 3pm), as well as interactive displays.

14

ARRIVAL AND INFORMATION

By plane The tiny City of Derry Airport (☎ 028 7181 0784, ⓦ cityofderryairport.com) is seven miles northeast of town on the A2 road. It's connected by Ulsterbus services #143 and #234 to the train station and Foyle Street bus station.

By taxi From the airport to the city centre costs around £13.

By train Derry's train station (☎ 028 7134 2228) is in the Waterside across the River Foyle and a 15min walk to the town centre across the Peace Bridge, or a free shuttle bus service drops you in Foyle St.

Destinations Belfast (Mon–Sat 8–9 daily, Sun 5; 2hr 10min); Castlerock (Mon–Sat 8–9 daily, Sun 5; 40min).

By bus The central bus station on Foyle St is served by Ulsterbus (☎ 028 7126 2261) for all the main Northern Ireland destinations and Bus Éireann (information from Ulsterbus), which operates buses to Dublin, Donegal town, Galway and Sligo. In addition, North West Busways (☎ 074 938 2619) run services across the border into Donegal; the former operates from the bus station and the latter from Patrick St. McGonagle Bus and Coach Hire operate an hourly service (Mon–Fri 8am–6pm) between Buncrana (Main St) and Derry (Whittaker St).

Destinations Belfast (Mon–Sat every 30min, Sun 10; 1hr 45min); Buncrana (North West Busways: Mon–Sat 4 daily; 35min); Carndonagh (North West Busways: Mon–Sat 4 daily; 45min); Culdaff (North West Busways: Mon–Sat 2 daily; 1hr 5min); Donegal town (Bus Éireann: 5–6 daily; 1hr 20min); Dublin (Bus Éireann: 11 daily; 4hr); Dungiven (Mon–Sat every 30min, Sun 10; 30min); Galway (Bus Éireann: 2–3 daily; 5hr 30min); Greencastle (North West Busways: Mon–Sat 4 daily; 1hr); Letterkenny (Bus Éireann: 5–6 daily; 35min); Limavady (Mon–Sat 8–12 daily, Sun 4; 45min); Monaghan (Bus Éireann: 11 daily; 1hr 50min); Moville (North West Busways: Mon–Sat 5 daily; 40min); Omagh (Mon–Sat 12 daily, Sun 5; 1hr 5min); Raphoe (Bus Éireann: Mon–Sat 3 daily; 45min); Sligo (Bus Éireann: 5–6 daily; 2hr 30min).

Tourist office 44 Foyle St (July–Sept Mon–Fri 9am–7pm, Sat 10am–6pm, Sun 10am–5pm; Oct–June Mon–Fri 9am–5pm, Sat 10am–5pm; ☎ 028 7126 7284, ⓦ derryvisitor.com). Books accommodation, has a bureau de change, provides a mass of information about both the North and the Republic, and offers bicycle lockers. Ask for a free *Visitor Guide* for up-to-date information about the city's attractions and facilities. The Nationalist *Derry Journal* newspaper (Tues & Fri; ⓦ derryjournal.com) is good for entertainment listings.

GETTING AROUND AND TOURS

By taxi Taxis wait on Foyle St and William St, or call Delta Cabs (☎ 028 7127 9999) or the Derry Taxi Association (☎ 028 7126 0247).

By bike Bee's Cycles, 2 Waterloo St (☎ 028 7137 2155).

Tours Martin McCrossan leads insightful and entertaining walking tours of the historic city centre, leaving from the tourist office (April–Oct Mon–Sat 10am, noon, 2pm &

4pm; £4; ☎ 028 7127 1996). A "Free Derry" walking tour (daily 10am & 2pm; £5; ☎ 028 7126 2812) takes in the Bogside, politics and murals, and leaves from the Museum of Free Derry (see p.517). Open-top bus tours (April–Sept daily & hourly 10am–5pm; Oct–March call for times; £12.50; ☎ 077 9116 4431) depart from near the tourist office and also pick up by the Guildhall.

ACCOMMODATION

Although Derry has plenty of upper-end **accommodation**, finding a more economically priced room in the centre can be difficult, especially in high season and at weekends. It's worth **booking in advance** or calling in at the tourist office when you arrive.

Arkle House 2 Coshquin Rd ☎ 028 7127 1156, ⓦ derry hotel.co.uk. A late nineteenth-century "gentleman's residence" about 2km from the city centre. The five rooms

are well appointed with some original fittings. **£65**

★The City Hotel 14–18 Queens Quay ☎ 028 7136 5800, ⓦ cityhotelderry.com. One of Derry's most fashionable hotels, offering spacious rooms furnished in a warm, contemporary style, some offering views of the Foyle, and all the leisure facilities imaginable. **£124**

Everglades Hotel 41–53 Prehen Rd ☎ 028 7132 1066, ⓦ hastingshotels.com. Looking somewhat like the top half of a Mississippi paddle-steamer, this top-notch hotel (complete with super-comfy "cloud beds") is set on the southern banks of the Foyle in a quiet location a few kilometres southwest of the centre. **£150**

Maldron Hotel 7–17 Butcher St ☎ 028 7137 1000, ⓦ maldronhotelderry.com. A modern 90-room establishment providing bright rooms, all equipped with cable TV, just inside the city walls, with a bistro and excellent café-bar. Strategically sited for the shops, cafés and pubs. **£99**

Paddy's Palace 1 Woodleigh Terrace, Asylum Rd ☎ 028 7130 9051, ⓦ paddyspalace.com. A modern hostel with four- and six-bed dorms and some private en-suite rooms.

Includes breakfast. **£40**

Ramada Da Vinci's Hotel 15 Culmore Rd ☎ 028 7127 9111, ⓦ davincishotel.com. Impressively modish hotel offering a range of 65 crisply furnished comfortable rooms. **£134**

★ **The Saddler's House** 36 Great James St ☎ 028 7126 9691, ⓦ thesaddlershouse.com. Stylish, period-furnished Victorian town house B&B very near the city centre, off Strand Road. **£65**

The Traveller's House 12 Princes St ☎ 028 7128 0542, ⓦ derry-hostel.co.uk. Welcoming and cosy hostel offering a mix of private rooms and small dorms; prices include breakfast, internet access, tea and coffee. **£40**

Travelodge Derry Hotel 22 Strand Rd ☎ 028 7127 1271, ⓦ travelodge.ie. Modern if somewhat functional rooms from the well-known hotel chain, in a prime city-centre location. **£49**

14

EATING

Derry's options for **eating out** are varied and prices are reasonable compared with other parts of Ireland. You can choose from pub grub or bistros and brasseries to restaurants in the larger hotels.

Brown's in Town 23 Strand Rd ☎ 028 7136 2889, ⓦ brownsrestaurant.com. A sleek candlelit city-centre restaurant that showcases Greencastle monkfish and hake as well as lamb, beef, pork and duck. The three-course early bird is excellent value at £19.95. Mon–Sat noon–3pm & 5.30–9.30pm, Sun 5–8.30pm.

Café Del Mondo Craft Village ☎ 028 7136 6877, ⓦ cafedelmondo.org. A daytime café that turns into an evening restaurant in the heart of the lovingly restored Craft Village. Dinner offerings range from fillet steak to chicken, fish and pork; two courses for £15. Café Mon–Sat 8.30am–6pm, Sun 10am–noon; restaurant Tues–Sat 6–10.30pm, Sun noon–6pm.

★ **Custom House** Custom House St, Queen's Quay ☎ 028 7137 3366, ⓦ customhouserestaurant.com. Based in a building dating from 1876 where taxes were collected from ships, the first floor of this classy restaurant has been transformed into a buzzy dining room. Main courses (around £15 at dinner; £8 at lunch) include crispy pork belly or salt-and-chilli squid. Look out for the stunning Italian-made chandelier with thousands of octagonal glass crystals. Mon–Sat noon–9.30pm, Sun noon–9pm.

The Exchange Exchange House, Queen's Quay ☎ 028 7127 3990, ⓦ exchangerestaurant.com. A varied menu

with plenty of daily specials and a riverside setting. Dishes include the likes of grilled sea bass (£15.95), "Louisana" chicken (£15.75) and steak fajitas (£14.95). Mon–Sat noon–2.30pm & 5.30–10pm, Sun 4–9pm.

★ **Flaming Jacks** 31–35 Strand Rd ☎ 028 7126 6400. A bistro-style place serving dishes inspired by all four corners of the planet at economical prices: steaks, seafood and poultry dishes with some vegetarian options from around £9. Booking ahead is essential and prices are reduced most nights of the week before 8pm. Daily 1pm–midnight, except Wed open from 3pm.

India House 2A Clarendon St ☎ 028 7126 0532, ⓦ saffron.com. The city's longest-established Indian restaurant is still the best, offering a reasonably priced menu (two courses around £15) with tandoori dishes and Punjabi cuisine a speciality. Daily 4.30–11pm.

Java 33 Ferryquay St ☎ 028 7136 2100. A family-owned café with possibly Derry's finest coffee, plus a wide choice of juices and smoothies and plenty of tasty soups and snacks. Mon–Sat 8.30am–6pm, Sun 11am–5pm.

La Sosta 45A Carlisle Rd ☎ 028 7137 4817, ⓦ lasostarestaurant.co.uk. Intimate, cozy family-run establishment serving authentic, modern Italian cuisine. The meat-filled cannelloni is recommened(£13.20). Tues–Sat 6–11pm.

DRINKING AND NIGHTLIFE

Derry has some of the liveliest and most sociable **pubs** in Ireland, and plenty provide musical entertainment too.

Badgers 16–18 Orchard St ☎ 028 7136 3306. A convivial spot for a drink either before or after a visit to the Millennium Forum. Food is served Mon–Thurs noon–7pm,

Fri & Sat noon–9pm, Sun noon–4pm. Daily 11am–11.30pm.

Clarendon Bar 44 Strand Rd ☎ 028 7126 3705. A

14

central, local's favourite with a relaxed atmosphere and late opening hours. The main focus is drinking, but lunch is also served Mon–Fri noon–3pm. Mon–Fri 11.30am–1.30am, Sat 11.30am–2.30am, Sun 1pm–midnight.

Peadar O'Donnell's 59 Waterloo St ☎028 7126 7295. In the same family since 1847, *Peadar's* and the attached *Gweedore Bar* are at the social and musical centre of the city – there's traditional music most nights in the former while its neighbour is more DJ-centric. Mon–Sat 11.30am–1am, Sun noon–midnight.

★**Sandino's Café Bar** Water St ☎028 7130 9297, wsandinos.com. Derry's hippest hangout features a variety of live music in its back bar and club room. Mon–Sat 11.30am–1am, Sun 1pm–midnight.

Tinney's 3–4 Patrick St ☎028 7136 2091. One of the best places for traditional music with a regular Tues night session. You can also get the lowdown here on "the bars", which is how local news and gossip is referred to in Derry. Mon–Thurs 11.30am–12.30am, Fri & Sat 11.30am–1am, Sun 12.30pm–11.30pm.

ENTERTAINMENT

Film buffs are catered for by the **Omniplex** cinema in the Quayside Centre, Strand Road (womniplex.ie), and **The Nerve Centre** (see p.516), which stages regular screenings of left-field films.

Cultúrlann Uí Chanáin 37 Great James St ☎028 7131 4132, wculturlann-doire.ie. Dedicated to the promotion of the Irish language, arts and culture and hosts occasional events, such as traditional music concerts.

Millennium Forum Newmarket St ☎028 7126 4455, wmillenniumforum.co.uk. This huge theatre offers a broad if somewhat middle-of-the-road programme, including well-known ballets and opera.

The Playhouse Artillery St ☎028 7126 8027, wderryplayhouse.co.uk. A more innovative range of theatre and dance is on the bill at The Playhouse.

Waterside Theatre Glendermott Rd ☎028 7131 4000, wwatersidetheatre.com. Across the river and dishing up a mixed bag of a programme, ranging from classic drama to local versions of TV game shows.

SHOPPING

The top brands are found in the three major **shopping centres** of Foyleside, Richmond and Quayside, but for a flavour of the town, it's worth seeking out and supporting the local businesses.

Austin's Department Store The Diamond ☎028 7126 1817, waustinsstore.com. Austin's claims to be the world's oldest department store and represents the shopping essence of Derry, offering fashions, linens and homeware. The rooftop restaurant offers panoramic views. Mon–Thurs & Sat 9.30am–5.30pm, Fri 9.30am–7pm, Sun 1–5pm.

Bedlam Market Pump St. Up to fifteen traders operate at this former hotel and convent in an eclectic maze of rooms brimful of vintage clothes, holistic treatments, antiques and everything retro imaginable. Mon–Sat 10am–5pm.

Craft Village Shipquay St ☎028 7136 8276. A wonderful array of craft and artisan producers come together in this collective that has re-created life between

the sixteenth and nineteenth centuries. You'll find tweeds and knitwear, exquisite jewellery and glass, soaps and candles and secondhand books. Mon–Sat 9.30am–5.30pm.

Faller The Jeweller 12 Strand Rd ☎028 7136 2710, wfaller.com. Look out for the golden teapot that hangs outside the shop and discharges a plume of environmentally friendly smoke from its spout. Inside you can buy a selection of brooches and charms from their "Drop of Derry" range, which reflects the city's culture. Mon–Sat 9.15am–5.30pm.

Thomas The Goldsmith 7 Pump St ☎028 7137 4549, wthomasgoldsmiths.com. Exquisite handcrafted and individually designed jewellery which includes the "Peace Bridge Collection". Mon–Sat 9.30am–5.30pm.

DIRECTORY

Hospital Accident and emergency department, Altnagelvin Hospital, Glenshane Rd (☎ 028 7134 5171); call this number also for dental emergencies after working hours or at weekends.

Police The main police station is located on Strand Rd

(☎ 028 7136 7337).

Post Office Custom House St (Mon & Wed–Fri 9am–5.30pm, Tues 9.30am–5.30pm, Sat 9am–12.30pm; ☎ 0845 722 3344) and 3 Bishop St (Mon–Fri 9am–5.30pm, Sat 9am–12.30pm).

Southern County Derry

14

The Derry–Antrim A6 road follows a river valley through fertile farmland then ascends to the Glenshane Pass on the northeastern fringe of the **Sperrin Mountains**. Southeast from here are Magherafelt and Moneymore, two attractive and entirely **planned towns**, the latter adjacent to the grand Plantation manor house of **Springhill**. The huge expanse of Ireland's biggest lake, **Lough Neagh**, laps against the county's southeastern corner and here too is one of the must-see sights of the entire North: **Bellaghy Bawn** castle.

The plantation towns and around

Southeast of Dungiven and over the Glenshane Pass on the way to the northern tip of Lough Neagh, it is worth making a detour to see some examples of town planning – the **plantation towns** of the London companies, most of them characteristically focused around a central Diamond. One example is **Magherafelt**, granted to the Salters' Company by James I, which has a wide, sloping main street and makes a reasonable base for exploring the lough and the Bellaghy area. **Moneymore**, about five miles further south, was originally constructed by the Drapers in the early seventeenth century (and restored by them in 1817), and was the first town in the North to have piped water – amazingly enough, as early as 1615.

Springhill

20 Springhill Rd, Moneymore • Noon–5pm: Feb–early April & Sept Sat & Sun; May Fri–Sun; June Thurs–Sun; July & Aug daily • £3.50 • ☎ 028 8674 8210, ⓦ nationaltrust.org.uk

A mile outside Moneymore off the B18, **Springhill** is a grand Plantation manor house built between 1680 and 1700 by William "Good Will" Conyngham in order to fulfil a marriage contract with the father of his bride-to-be, Anne Upton. Elegant both without and within, its sober whitewashed architecture houses fine rooms, equipped with original period furniture and paintings belonging to William and his descendants, who occupied the house until 1959. Upstairs, the **Blue Room** is said to be haunted by the ghost of Olivia Lenox-Conyngham, whose husband George was found shot here in 1816. Outside, the stables house a **costume collection**, which adopts a specific theme each year, drawing upon three thousand items collected from the mid-seventeenth century to the 1970s. There are delightful **gardens**, a tower dating from the 1730s, which was probably originally part of a windmill, and a pleasant walk through beech and yew trees.

ARRIVAL AND INFORMATION

By bus Magherafelt to: Bellaghy (Mon–Sat 5–8 daily; 15min); Moneymore (Mon–Fri 10 daily, Sat 3; 15min). Moneymore to: Magherafelt (Mon–Sat 6 daily; 15min).

THE PLANTATION TOWNS

Tourist information The Bridewell, 6 Church St (Mon & Thurs 10am–8pm; Tues, Wed, Fri & Sat 10am–5pm; ☎ 028 7963 1510).

ACCOMMODATION AND EATING

District 45 7 Garden St, Magherafelt ☎ 028 7930 0333, ⓦ district45.co.uk. A new bistro catering for a range of

tastes with a menu of sea bass, lamb, duck breast and burgers. Their beat-the-clock deal (5–7pm) offers certain

14

dishes for £7.95 while main courses in the evening average £12.95. Wed–Sun 5–9pm, Fri & Sat till 10pm, also Sun lunch time.

Laurel Villa 60 Church St, Magherafelt ☏028 7930 1459, ⓦlaurel-villa.com. An ivy-clad Victorian town house with elegantly furnished, personality-packed rooms (one, named after the poet Seamus Heaney, features framed versions of his best-known work). The owners describe this as Ireland's only poetry guesthouse and organize poetry readings, tours of Heaney country and an annual festival in Sept (see box, opposite). **£80**

Mary's 10 Market St, Magherafelt ☏028 7930 2616, ⓦmarys-bar.com. Modernized in recent years but retaining its original name, this is one of the best pubs for both food and live music. Lunch (noon–3.30pm) features soup and lighter meals, while the evening menu (5–9pm, Sun 3.30–8pm) offers steak, burgers, chicken and pork. There's live music Thurs, Fri and Sun nights and a DJ on Sat. Mon–Thurs 11.30am–11.30pm, Fri & Sat 11.30am–12.30am, Sun noon–11pm.

Lough Neagh

East of Magherafelt and Moneymore are the fish-filled waters of the biggest lake in Ireland, **Lough Neagh**. Tributaries flow from every point of the compass: the Lower Bann, which drains the lake and runs north to **Lough Beg** (finally reaching the sea north of Coleraine), contains some huge trout, including the dollaghan, unique to these waters. Similar to salmon (which are also common), dollaghan grow by three pounds every year and can be caught by spinning, worming and fly-fishing: the Ballinderry Black and the Bann Olive are famous flies derived from this region. The best fishing is from mid-July to October, but you will need a Fisheries Conservation Board Rod **licence**, available from tourist offices. Information on day-tickets for fishing and specialist boat-trips, respectively issued and run by the Lough Neagh Angling Association, can also be obtained from the tourist office in Bellaghy (see below).

Bellaghy

Like many of the plantation settlements in the area, **BELLAGHY**, just west of Lough Beg, has a history that reflects the divisions between communities. Indeed, two of the ten 1981 hunger strikers (see p.594) – cousins Francis Hughes and Thomas McElwee – came from the village, and Orange parades have been a regular flashpoint.

Bellaghy Bawn

Easter–Sept Wed–Sun 10am–5pm; Oct–Easter Wed 10am–4pm, Sun noon–4pm • Free • ☏ 028 7938 6812

Bellaghy is neatly laid out around a T-junction, and wandering south past the whitewashed terraces on Castle Street leads to one of the best surviving examples of a Plantation castle, **Bellaghy Bawn**, built in 1618 by the Vintners' Company. Most of its fortifications were lost in 1641, but it still retains a striking circular flanker tower which has been well restored. Inside you'll find fascinating interpretive **displays** explaining the 7000-year-old history of the settlements in this area, the construction of the village – today's houses still occupy the same original allocated plots of land – and the diverse ecology of the Lough Beg wetland area. The real treasure here, however, is the dedication of much of the Bawn's space to **Seamus Heaney**, the poet who was born and raised nearby (see box, opposite). Heaney is the star of a unique and atmospheric film showing in the Bawn, *A Sense of Place*, in which he reflects on the influence of his upbringing, local character and landmarks on his poetry. His father rented grazing rights on the strand at Lough Beg; in his poem *Ancestral Photograph*, Heaney recalls helping to herd the cattle that grazed there down Castle Street on their way to market.

Lough Beg and Church Island

You can see the shimmering Lough Beg from the windows of the Bawn's flanker tower, and a stroll down to the lake is well worthwhile. In summer, its waters recede and **Church Island** becomes accessible from the shore. Besides a walled graveyard, you'll find the ruins of a medieval church here, said to have been founded centuries before by the

SEAMUS HEANEY (1939–2013)

It's impossible to conceive of a contemporary poet, Irish or otherwise, whose works are more evocative of time and place than **Seamus Heaney** who, at the time of his death aged 74 on August 30, 2013, was arguably the best-known poet in the world. Heaney was born, the eldest of nine children, on the family farm of Mossbawn (itself the title of two poems in his fourth collection, *North*), in the townland of Tamniarn, near Castledawson, on April 13, 1939. Heaney's family background, his Catholic upbringing and his study of Irish at school imbued him with a strong sense of being Irish in a state that considered itself British, a paradox that would form a major motif in his work during the 1970s. While at Queen's University, Belfast, he was further influenced by the literature he discovered in Belfast's **Linen Hall library** (see p.467), especially the works of John Hewitt, the Antrim-born "Poet of the Glens", and the English "naturalist" poet Ted Hughes, in whose work he found an "association of sounds in print that connected with the world below".

Heaney's first poem, *Tractors*, was published in the *Belfast Evening Telegraph* in 1962. His first significant collection, *Death of a Naturalist*, followed in 1966 and was immediately recognized for its earthiness and command of diverse metrical forms. In the 1960s, while lecturing at Queen's, Heaney's career expanded into journalism and television and he became increasingly involved in the **civil-rights movement**. His response to the Troubles saw him seeking for "images and symbols adequate to our predicament" and he began to see poetry as a mode of resistance. Eventually, though, the violence so disturbed him that he moved with his family to County Wicklow, prompting Ian Paisley's *Protestant Telegraph* to bid farewell to "the well-known papist propagandist" on his departure to his "spiritual home in the popish republic". While his 1970s collections *North* and *Field Work* had mixed receptions – some saw the strong influence of Robert Lowell on the former – Heaney found himself turning increasingly to his **Irish heritage** as a source of inspiration, particularly the long medieval poem *Buile Suibhne* (*The Madness of Sweeney*), and published his own *Sweeney Astray* collection in 1983. The following year's *Station Island* drew on his experiences as a participant in St Patrick's Purgatory (see p.429).

The hunger strikes of the early 1980s brought a new urgency to Northern politics and a revival of Heaney's polemicism. Prompted by the staging in Derry in 1980 of Brian Friel's play *Translations*, which showed English surveyors travelling through eighteenth-century Ireland anglicizing all the place names, Heaney cofounded the **Field Day Theatre Company** with Friel, his old friend and fellow academic Séamus Deane, the actor Stephen Rea and others. While the group's theatrical activities were themselves controversial, it was their publications that engendered the most antipathy. Their pamphlets were criticized as attempts to over-intellectualize the Troubles, and the 1991 *Field Day Anthology of Irish Writing* was decried for its under-representation of work by women writers, though a subsequent volume entirely devoted to them has since been published.

In 1995, Heaney's body of work was more widely recognized by the award of the **Nobel Prize for Literature**. His later works included a translation of the Anglo-Saxon epic poem *Beowulf*, his dramatic retelling of this tale of monster- and dragon-slaying managing to breathe new life into a work that was long considered too dense and metaphorical for a modern readership; his collection, *District and Circle*, which won the prestigious T.S. Eliot Prize for Poetry in 2006; and his twelfth and final collection, *Human Chain* (2010), which is overshadowed by ageing and mortality.

The **annual festival** celebrating Heaney's life and work, "On Home Ground" (Ⓦ laurel-villa .com) is held in mid-September and reflects the inspiration and influence of the area on his Derry childhood.

ubiquitous St Patrick, with a tower and spire added in 1788 by the eccentric Frederick Augustus Hervey (see p.508) to improve his view from Ballyscullion House on the mainland nearby. He commissioned Charles Lanyon to build a huge replacement for the original house which stood here with, apparently, 365 windows, but died abroad before ever moving in, and the building subsequently fell into ruin.

ARRIVAL AND DEPARTURE   BELLAGHY

By bus Magherafelt (Mon–Sat 5–9 daily; 15min).

Down and Armagh

THE MOURNE MOUNTAINS

Down and Armagh

Counties Down and Armagh occupy the southeastern corner of Northern Ireland, between Belfast and the border, and contain some of the region's most attractive countryside, especially around the coast. You're also never far away from places associated with St Patrick, who sailed into Strangford Lough to make his final Irish landfall in County Down, founded his first bishopric at Armagh and is buried at either Downpatrick or Armagh, depending on whose claim you prefer.

15

Heading south from Belfast, the glowering **Mourne Mountains** increasingly dominate the panorama, and it's in this direction that most of the attractions lie. If you simply take the main roads in and out of Belfast – the A1 for Newry and the border, or the M1 motorway west – you'll come across very little to stop for: it's in the rural areas, the mountains and coast, that the charm of this region lies. One of the best options is to head east from Belfast around the Down shore – past the **Ulster Folk and Transport Museum**, one of the best in the North, and the blowsy suburban resort of **Bangor** into the **Ards Peninsula** or along the banks of **Strangford Lough**. Near the Lough's southern tip, **Downpatrick** is closely associated with the arrival of St Patrick. There are plenty of little beaches, early Christian sites, defensive tower houses and fine mansions to visit on the way towards **Newcastle**, the best base for excursions on foot into the Mourne Mountains. Beyond the Mournes a fine coast road curves around to **Carlingford Lough** and the border. Inland, **Hillsborough**, resembling an English Cotswolds-style village, is closely linked to the political development of the North.

Below **Lough Neagh**, the north of County Armagh is dominated by the developed industrial strip known as **Craigavon** which contains the towns of **Lurgan** and **Portadown**, and has little to attract you. Away from the towns, however, there are two stately homes of interest, **Ardress** and the **Argory**, and some excellent cycling country north of **Loughgall**. The villages of **South Armagh** – a predominantly Catholic area – were the heartland of violent Republicanism, and often referred to as "Bandit Country" or "The Killing Fields", even by locals. **Armagh city**, however, is well worth visiting for its ancient associations, cathedrals and fine Georgian streets, while South Armagh has some startlingly attractive country, especially around the peak of **Slieve Gullion**.

GETTING AROUND   DOWN AND ARMAGH

By public transport Getting around by public transport is relatively easy, though you'll need to rent a bike or walk to enjoy the best of Strangford Lough's western shore.

Hillsborough

The historic village of **HILLSBOROUGH**, just a mile off the main A1 road and twelve miles southwest of Belfast, merits a quick detour. Its main street has a chintzy,

ST PATRICK'S ROMAN CATHOLIC CATHEDRAL, ARMAGH CITY

Highlights

❶ The Ulster Folk and Transport Museum
Possibly the best museum in Northern Ireland
– it consummately encapsulates much of the
North's cultural and industrial history. **See p.531**

❷ Portaferry A superb waterside location,
tremendous sunsets and the best base for
exploring Strangford Lough and the Ards
Peninsula. **See p.535**

❸ The Mourne Mountains Brooding and
dominating South Down, the Mournes offer
magnificent walking, intoxicating views and a
total escape from the contemporary world.
See p.544

❹ Armagh city Probably the most graceful city
in the North, with two cathedrals and a
captivating Mall. **See p.551**

❺ The Argory A magnificent nineteenth-
century mansion, set in gorgeous grounds and
featuring one of the most illuminating guided
tours in Ireland. **See p.559**

❻ Slieve Gullion Drive or hike to the top of this
mountain and enjoy the panorama of the
unmissable South Armagh countryside laid out
below. **See p.549**

HIGHLIGHTS ARE MARKED ON THE MAP ON PP.528–529

Middle English ambience, reinforced by a sprinkling of tearooms and antique shops. You get the best of Hillsborough by following a route that starts from the **war memorial** and heads up the magnificent approach to the eighteenth-century Gothic **parish church**. Bear right here for the main entrance to Hillsborough's elegant but ruined **fort** (April–Sept Mon–Sat 10am–6pm, Sun 11am–6pm; Oct–March Mon–Sat 10am–4pm, Sun 11am–4pm; free), constructed by Colonel Arthur Hill

DOWN & ARMAGH

DERRY

ANTRIM

TYRONE

Lough Neagh

Dungannon

Oxford Island

M1

Lurgan

Hillsb

🏛 **The Argory**
⑤

🏛 **Ardress House**

Benburb

Loughgall

Portadown

DOWN

Armagh
④

Navan Fort

Banbridge

River Bann

Legan Do

GOSFORD FOREST PARK

Markethill

ARMAGH

Monaghan

A29

Bessbrook

Hilltown

MONAGHAN

Camlough

Newry

M O

Killeavy Churches

Slieve Gullion (1879ft) ▲ ⑥

Warrenpoint
Rostrevor

Creggan

Mullaghbawn

Carlingford Lough

Kilfea Do

Crossmaglen

Forkhill

Ulster Way

Carlingford

Green

LOUTH

Dundalk

Cooley Peninsula

HIGHLIGHTS

① The Ulster Folk and Transport Museum
② Portaferry
③ The Mourne Mountains
④ Armagh city
⑤ The Argory
⑥ Slieve Gullion

(after whom the village is named) in 1650 and remodelled in the eighteenth century as a venue for family feasts and entertainment. Beyond this, a deciduous **forest** (dawn–dusk; free) opens up, curving around a **lake** stocked with brown and rainbow trout. Footpaths meander through the trees in all directions – a circuit of the lake takes around thirty minutes.

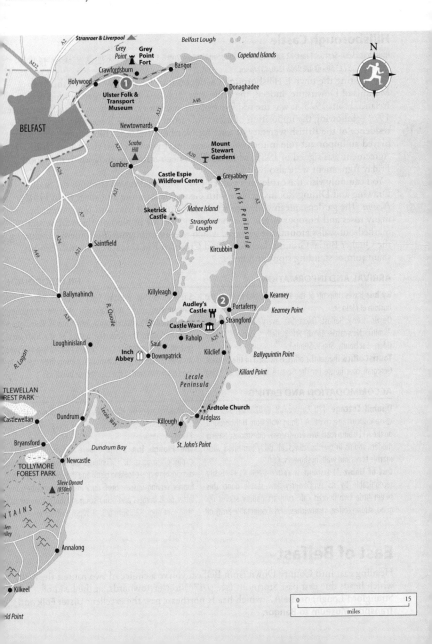

15

OYSTER FESTIVAL

During the first week of September, Hillsborough is taken over by the wonderful **Oyster Festival** (ⓦ hillsboroughoysterfestival.com), which, as its centrepiece, hosts the World International Oyster Eating Championships. Oysters aside, there's plenty more going on, including concerts, fairs, a motor show and a wacky soapbox derby.

Hillsborough Castle

House tours April–Sept Sat 11am, 12.30pm, 2pm & 3.30pm; Sun 12.30pm, 2pm & 3.30pm; gardens 10am–sunset • Castle and gardens £7, gardens only £3.50 • ☎ 028 9268 1300, ⓦ hrp.org

Dominating the town is **Hillsborough Castle**, built in 1770 by Wills Hill, the first Marquis of Downshire; indeed, the Hills were, at one stage, the largest landowners in Ireland. From 1925, it was the residence of the governor of Northern Ireland, but since 1973 – following the imposition of direct rule from London – it has been the official residence of the British secretary of state for Northern Ireland. Hillsborough has also played an important role in the peace process, for it was here that the Anglo-Irish Agreement was signed in 1985, while informal negotiations leading up to the Good Friday Agreement were also held here.

You can only visit the castle on a guided tour, which takes you through the State Drawing and Dining Rooms, replete with Georgian furniture and silver from HMS *Nelson*. The gardens, meanwhile, are lovely, particularly in May and June when the many roses and Europe's largest rhododendron bush are in bloom. There are several marked-out walks around the gardens, which take in numerous monuments, including the Quaker Burial Ground, Ice House and Cromlyn Ruin, a late eighteenth-century sham ruin of standing stone and lintel.

ARRIVAL AND INFORMATION
HILLSBOROUGH

By bus Buses drop off at the War Memorial towards the bottom of Main St.
Destinations Belfast (Mon–Sat every 30min, Sun 8; 25min); Newcastle (Mon–Fri 3 daily; 55min); Newry (Mon–Sat hourly, Sun 9; 50min).
Tourist office The tourist office is housed in the elegant Georgian courthouse on The Square at the top of Main

Street (Mon–Sat 9.30am–5.30pm; ☎ 028 9268 9717, ⓦ visitlisburn.com). You can visit the old courtroom, located behind the tourist office, which has an illuminating little exhibition (free) on the history of the Irish legal system; the courthouse itself ceased functioning in 1986. Also, on the last Sat of each month, a lovely little crafts and food market is held in the courthouse building.

ACCOMMODATION AND EATING

Dunhill Cottage 47b Carnreagh ☎ 028 9268 3024, ⓦ dunhillcottage.co.uk. A 10min walk from Hillsborough on the A1 Lisburn road, this eco-friendly guesthouse has six modern rooms in two buildings, all tidily furnished with marble tiling and walk-in showers. **£80**
Out of Habit 21 Lisburn St ☎ 028 9268 8191. Easily recognizable by its sunflower-yellow stable door, this sweet little two-floored café-cum-art gallery serves up good, strong coffee, sandwiches, and a delectable array of

traybakes; there's live music every other Fri, plus occasional themed food evenings. Mon–Sat 9.30am–5pm, Sun 11am–4.30pm.
The Plough Inn 3 The Square ☎ 028 9268 2985, ⓦ ploughgroup.com. Centuries-old coaching inn comprising a great-looking bistro and the cool Bar Retro, the former serving upscale beef, duck and salmon dishes, the latter posh burgers and other scrummy lunch-time treats. Mon–Sat noon–2.30pm & 5–9.30pm, Sun noon–8pm.

East of Belfast

Heading east into County Down from Belfast, you've a choice of two routes: the A20, which heads due east past Stormont (see p.474) to **Newtownards**, at the head of Strangford Lough; or the A2, which heads northeast past the excellent **Ulster Folk and Transport Museum** to **Bangor**.

Scrabo Tower and around

Easter week, April–June & Sept daily 1–5pm; July & Aug daily 10am–5pm; Oct Sun noon–4pm • Free

Following the A20, the single interesting sight as you near Newtownards is **Scrabo Tower**, whose looming presence dominates the surrounding area. The tower protrudes from the top of a rocky, gorse-strewn hump of a hill (a long-extinct volcano) – follow the signs to **Scrabo Country Park** and you'll arrive in the car park just below. The hill itself is pitted with quarries used to extract Scrabo stone, employed for all manner of local buildings. Built in 1857 as a memorial to the third Marquess of Londonderry, in recognition of his efforts for his tenants during the Great Famine, the tower looks like a monstrous rocket in its launcher, hewn out of rough black volcanic rock. The spot was originally a Bronze Age burial cairn, probably the resting place of one of the grand chieftains of the area, and there's evidence of a huge hill fort here, too. It's well worth ascending the 122 steps to the tower's top for the wonderful **views** across Strangford Lough and the healthy, blustery weather that often curls around the side of the hill.

Newtownards and around

Scrabo Tower looks down on **NEWTOWNARDS**, a place strong on manufacture but unexciting for the traveller. Despite its name, it's an old town, founded in 1244, though there's little evidence of this beyond the ruined Dominican priory just off Castle Street. The Scrabo-stone **Market House** (1765), now the town hall and arts centre, lords it over a large square filled on Saturdays by market activity. A better reason to visit is for the **Ards International Guitar Festival** (ⓦardsguitarfestival.co.uk) in early October, which attracts a high-calibre roster of international artists, with the principal venues being the Ards Arts Centre and the Queen's Hall.

Somme Heritage Centre

Obligatory tours hourly April–June & Sept Mon–Thurs 10am–4pm, Sat 11am–4pm; July & Aug Mon–Sat 10am–5pm; Oct–March Mon–Thurs 10am–4pm & first Sat of each month 11am–4pm • £5 • ☏ 028 9182 3202, ⓦ irishsoldier.org

Two miles north of Newtownards on the A21 Bangor road, you'll find the **Somme Heritage Centre** with re-created front-line trenches staffed by guides in battledress who provide a sobering and moving account of the role of the Irish and Ulster divisions in the futile World War I battle that took place in July 1916 – 5500 men of the 36th (Ulster) Division alone were reported dead, wounded or missing in only the first two days. The Battle of the Somme itself is brought to life courtesy of an unusually informative audiovisual presentation.

ARRIVAL AND INFORMATION   NEWTOWNARDS AND AROUND

By bus The bus station is in the centre of town on Regent St. Destinations Bangor (Mon–Sat every 30min, Sun 7; 20min); Belfast (Mon–Sat every 10–20min, Sun every 30min–1hr; 15min); Portaferry (Mon–Sat every 1hr–1hr 15min, Sun 5; 50min–1hr 15min).

Tourist office Next to the bus station at 31 Regent St (Mon–Fri 9am–5.15pm, Sat 9.15am–5.30pm; ☏ 028 9182 6846, ⓦ ards-council.gov.uk).

The Ulster Folk and Transport Museum

March–Sept Tues–Sun 10am–5pm; Oct–Feb Tues–Fri 10am–4pm, Sat & Sun 11am–4pm • Museums £9 each, combined ticket £11 • ☏ 028 9042 8428, ⓦ nmni.com/uftm • Train from Belfast Central to Cultra or bus #1 or #2 from Belfast's Laganside Buscentre

Seven miles east of Belfast, the **Ulster Folk and Transport Museum** is one of the most fascinating museums in all of Ireland. The main site is an open-air **museum village** where about thirty typical buildings from all over the North, some dating from the eighteenth century, have been taken from their original sites and rebuilt complete with authentic furnishings, including an entire street from Dromore and Belfast terraces. Conceptually, you can walk from one part of Northern Ireland to another, amid appropriate scenes. Traditional **farms** have also been created and assorted livestock

15

roam between the buildings. The starting point is a gallery on Ulster's social history and an introduction to the buildings themselves. From here you walk around the grounds, visiting the various buildings, including a small village street with church and rectory, two schools, various typical farm dwellings, a forge and other buildings used in light manufacture. Each of these is "inhabited" by a member of staff, garbed in period costume and informative about the building and its origins. Such historical realism is impressive, though sometimes a little disquieting: the Kilmore Church graveyard contains real tombstones donated by family members.

Outside the transport galleries there's a miniature railway that runs on summer Saturdays, and back in the main section there's a decent **restaurant**, located in the Education Centre. The museum also regularly stages temporary exhibitions and occasional cultural events.

Transport Galleries

On the far side of the main road, across a bridge, are the **transport galleries**, where the exhibits include every conceivable form of transport, from horse-drawn carts to lifeboats and a vertical take-off plane, but especially veteran cars, motorcycles and trams; among this remarkable collection of vehicles is a Belfast Telegraph van from 1952 and, from the late nineteenth century, a wonderfully old-fashioned ice-cream van and a Giant's Causeway tram, the first tram system in the world to be operated by hydro-electricity. You'll also meet **Old Maeve**, the largest locomotive ever built in Ireland, and a DeLorean sports car from the infamously defunct factory. The **Titanic** exhibit documents the origins and fate of the Belfast-constructed liner, while "The Flight Experience" examines the history of aviation through films, models and interactive displays.

Crawfordsburn Country Park

Daily April, May, Sept & Oct 9am–7pm; June–Aug 9am–9pm; Nov–Feb 9am–4.30pm; Visitor Centre daily 10am–5pm • Free

The short stretch of coast east from Helen's Bay is part of the **Crawfordsburn Country Park**, an estate handed down from the Scottish Presbyterian Crawford family, then acquired by Lord Dufferin (whose mother Helen gave her name to the bay) and which is now in public hands. Its glens and dells are replete with beeches, cypresses, exotic conifers, cedars, the usual burst of rhododendrons and also a Californian giant redwood, but the park's best features are the wild-flower meadow and the woodland planted with native species.

Grey Point Fort

April to mid-Sept daily 10am–5pm; mid-Sept to March Sat & Sun noon–4pm • Free

One of the most scenic of the waymarked trails is the path to **Grey Point Fort**, which leads through the best of the woodland, under a fine nineteenth-century railway viaduct and up to a waterfall at the head of the glen and thence to the bay. Positioned to command the mouth of Belfast Lough, along with its sister fort at Kilroot on the other side, Grey Point has an impressive battery of gun emplacements, ready to challenge the shipping that entered the lough during the two world wars. In the event, the two six-inch breech-loading guns were never fired except in practice (local residents had to be warned to open their windows and doors to prevent blast damage), apart from one occasion in World War II, when a merchant ship failed to respond to the signal "heave to or be sunk" and received a warning shot across its bows. The guns were sold for scrap in 1957 when the Coast Artillery was disbanded. After the fort was opened to the public in 1987, an identical six-inch gun was relocated here from the prison on Spike Island in Cork harbour. There's also a selection of photos showing the original guns and their positions; but it's really as a viewpoint that the fort is worth a visit for nowadays.

Bangor

With a curving bay set between a pair of symmetrical headlands, **BANGOR**'s sheltered position made it ideal for exploitation as a holiday resort. The town has been hugely popular with Belfast people since the railway came in the 1860s, but today it's as much a suburb of Belfast as a holiday spot. Still, it's well worth a visit for its recently renovated waterfront, which includes a 500-berth **marina** and a surprisingly tasteful funpark, while inland, the superb little museum and walled garden – inside the old castle grounds – make for a most enjoyable hour or two.

North Down Museum

July & Aug Mon–Sat 10am–4.30pm, Sun noon–4.30pm; Sept–June Tues–Sat 10am–4.30pm, Sun noon–4.30pm • Free •
☏ 028 9127 1200, **ⓦ** northdownmuseum.com

Bangor's period of greatest historical significance was almost entirely associated with its **abbey**, which was founded by St Comgall in 586 AD, and from which missionaries set forth to convert pagan Europe. Though the abbey remained powerful for eight hundred years, there's not a trace of the building left. The only vestige of its fame is the Antiphonarium Benchorense, one of the oldest-known ecclesiastical manuscripts, consisting of collects, anthems and some religious poems; the original now lies in the Ambrosian Library in Milan, but you can view a facsimile of it in the **North Down Museum**, tucked away in the old stables of Bangor Castle. Other displays trace the rise of the Ward family (see p.541), who were largely responsible for the town's development and who built the castle.

15

   Best of all are the archaeological discoveries, notably the Ballycroghan swords, three superb bronze weapons dating from 500 AD, and the ninth-century Bangor Bell, a splendid one-piece casting which was retrieved from a local graveyard in 1780. On a more recent note, there's a lovely little exhibition on the history of local cinematography and, more specifically, the once beautiful Art Deco Toni cinema, which stood on Hamilton Road; once the hub of Bangor's social scene – it also functioned as a ballroom – the cinema's last screening was in 1983 before it burnt down in 1992.

Bangor Castle Walled Garden

April, Sept & Oct daily 10am–5.30pm; May–Sept Mon–Thurs 10am–8pm, Fri–Sun 10am–6pm • Free

A short walk from the museum, through the tree-laden Ward Park, you'll come to the delightful **Bangor Castle Walled Garden**. Originally the site of a Victorian walled garden, which supplied the castle kitchen with vegetable, fruits and herbs, the garden fell into disrepair after World War I, before its quite spectacular renovation just a few years ago. Hidden beyond a 4m-high red-brick wall, the garden is divided into quadrants, namely, the flower garden, the herb and topiary garden, kitchen garden and damp garden; separating these are neatly gravelled avenues with fragrant, rose-covered arches, while a beautifully sculpted fountain stands as the garden's central feature. On a warm summer's day, it's a wonderful spot to rest up, and there's a café on-site too.

ARRIVAL AND DEPARTURE

BANGOR

By train The train station is at the top of Main St, which itself leads down to the waterfront.
Destinations Belfast (Mon–Sat every 15–30min, Sun hourly; 30min).

By bus The bus station is adjacent to the train station.
Destinations Belfast (Mon–Sat every 20–30min, Sun 8; 50min); Newtownards (Mon–Sat every 30min, Sun 7; 20min).

INFORMATION AND ACTIVITIES

Tourist office Down by the marina in the Tower House at 34 Quay Street (Mon, Tues, Thurs & Fri 9.15am–5pm, Wed & Sat 10am–5pm, plus May–Aug Sun 1–5pm; **☏** 028 9127

0069, **ⓦ** northdowntourism.com).
Fishing and boat trips Bangor Boats (**☏** 07510 006 000, **ⓦ** bangorboat.com) runs family-friendly, deep-sea

fishing trips from the harbour (July & Aug daily 9.15am & 6.30pm; June, Sept & Oct call for times; £17), and short boat trips (July & Aug 2pm; £5) around the bay from the Pickie Fun Park.

ACCOMMODATION

★**Cairn Bay Lodge** 278 Seacliff Rd ☎028 9146 7636, ⓦcairnbaylodge.com. Charming, family-run guesthouse with eight beautifully finished rooms, all quite distinct from one another, and some of which have stunning bay views. In any case, the gourmet breakfast is reason alone to pitch up here: smoked salmon omelette with rocket and lemon crème fraiche, or crab with scrambled eggs and chilli jam are just two of the possibilities; even if you're not staying here, you can book in to have breakfast. **£80**

Salty Dog 10–12 Seacliff Rd ☎028 9127 0696, ⓦsaltydogbangor.com. By far the most attractive of an otherwise unappealing cluster of hotels down by the marina, this smallish hotel has a range of differently configured rooms decked out in fetching cream and mauve; try and bag a sea-facing room if you can, for which there is no extra charge. **£85**

EATING AND DRINKING

Blu BBQ 52 High St ☎028 9147 0698. Authentic wood-smoked barbecued meats from the grill, like spiced lamb ribs, and peppered burger with sautéed mushrooms and black peppercorn sauce, make this a tempting possibility for dinner; the decor is muted and the atmosphere pleasingly informal. Mon–Sat 10am–10pm, Sun 11am–8pm.

The Boat House 1A Seacliff Rd ☎028 9146 9253, ⓦtheboathouseni.co.uk. The cool, brick-vaulted cellar of the old Harbour Master's Office – an inconspicuous grey stone building by the marina – is now home to a distinguished restaurant, whose Dutch chef specializes in concocting breathtakingly original dishes like charred salmon with chocolate mayonnaise, pickled red cabbage and sour dough croute; three-course evening menu £32.50.

Wed–Sat noon–2.30pm & 5.30–10pm, Sun 1–8.45pm.

Jamaica Inn 188 Seacliff Rd ☎028 9147 1610, ⓦthejamaicainn.co.uk. In a fantastic location overlooking the bay, this warm and lively inn is by far the best spot in Bangor for a good night out, with live music several nights a week and a rollickingly good pub quiz on Tues. Daily 11.30am–midnight.

Salty Dog 10–12 Seacliff Rd ☎028 9127 0696, ⓦsaltydogbangor.com. The classy bistro in the hotel of the same name (see above) offers both classic pub fare and an à la carte menu, the latter featuring a short but exquisite selection of dishes like pan-seared Atlantic cod with brioche and black pudding crust (£17), and a sloe gin crème brûlée with almond cream. Mon–Thurs & Sun noon–9pm, Fri & Sat noon–10pm.

Strangford Lough

Ancient annals record that **Strangford Lough** was formed around 1650 BC by the sea sweeping in over the lands of Brena. This created a beautiful, calm inlet, the archipelago-like pieces of land along its inner arm fringed with brown and yellow bladderwrack and tangleweed, and tenanted by a rich gathering of bird life during the warmer months and vast flocks of geese and waders in the winter. It's an attractive haven for small boats and yachts, and several picturesque halts for the land-bound make the road along the lough's western shore the most interesting route leading south from Belfast.

The eastern shore

The eastern edge of Strangford Lough is not as indented as its opposite shore but betters it in having a major road (the continuation of the A20) that runs close to the water virtually all the way down. Also the scenery is delightful, and there's an engrossing place to stop off en route to Portaferry – the **Mount Stewart** house and gardens – as well as a splendid restaurant in **Kircubbin**.

Mount Stewart House and Garden

Gardens daily: March–Oct 10am–5pm; Nov–Feb 10am–4pm; House April–Oct daily 10am–5pm; Nov–March Sat & Sun noon–3pm; Temple of the Winds March–Oct Sun 2–5 pm • £5.80 • ☎028 4278 8387, ⓦnationaltrust.org.uk/mount-stewart • Bus #9 and #10 from Belfast's Laganside Buscentre

Five miles southeast of Newtownards is **Mount Stewart House and Gardens**, the ancestral home of the Londonderry family. The undoubted highlight of the estate is the 98 acres of **gardens**, laid out by Lady Londonderry, wife of the seventh marquess, in the 1920s – and a thorough job she made of it: among others, there are Spanish and Italian gardens, a Space Garden and the Shamrock Garden (with a topiary harp and an appropriately leaved Red Hand of Ulster). The trees and shrubs here are no more than seventy to eighty years old, but they've grown at such a remarkable rate that they look twice that. The principal reason for this is the unusually warm and humid microclimate: the gardens catch the east-coast sun, causing a heavy overnight dew, and the Gulf Stream washes the shores only a stone's throw away. Despite the northerly latitude, conditions here rival those of Cornwall and Devon.

Although the gardens are the highlight, the **house** is also worth viewing, especially following a recent, massive renovation. The family was a leading member of the Protestant Ascendancy and its members included Lord Castlereagh, who was Foreign Secretary under Pitt the Younger and is best remembered for guiding the Act of Union into operation. Among the splendid (and occasionally eccentric) furniture inside is a set of 22 Empire chairs used by the delegates to the Congress of Vienna in 1815, who included the Duke of Wellington and Talleyrand; the chairs were a gift to Castlereagh's brother Lord Stewart, another high-ranking diplomat of the time. The Continental connection is flaunted further in bedrooms named after various historically important cities: Rome, St Petersburg, Madrid, Moscow and Sebastopol (from the time of the Crimean War). The house contains a number of paintings, particularly portraits of Castlereagh's political contemporaries, but the most notable and largest is **Hambletonian** (1799) by George Stubbs, showing the celebrated thoroughbred being rubbed down after a victory at Newmarket.

ACCOMMODATION AND EATING   THE EASTERN SHORE

★**Paul Arthur's** Main Street, Kircubbin ☏ 028 4273 8192, ⓦ arthurskircubbin.com. Around five miles south of Mount Stewart, it comes as some surprise to find the quiet loughshore village of Kircubbin home to one of the county's finest restaurants. Though there's usually a fish of the day on the menu, meat and poultry dishes are the speciality here, with such delights as pan-fried pigeon fillets with truffle mash, and honey roast Barbary duck fillet with balsamic glaze (£16.50). You can stay here too in one of the very comfortable and well-decorated bedrooms. Restaurant Tues–Sun noon–2.30pm & 5–9pm. **£80**

Portaferry

Portaferry, at the mouth of the lough, is petty enough, though this small town's main attraction is the marvellous **sunset** looking across the "Narrows" to Strangford, a view enhanced by a ten-minute climb to the stump of the old windmill just behind the town. In any case, it's quite likely that you'll wind up here, as it is the departure point for ferries across to Strangford and the Lescale Peninsula.

Located in these waters are three **turbines**, the largest of their kind in the UK, and the third largest in the world; these powerful tidal electricity generators harness the exceptionally strong tidal flow in the loch to power up to a thousand homes, while keeping the environmental impact down to a minimum.

Exploris Aquarium

Castle St · April–Aug Mon–Fri 10am–6pm, Sat 11am–6pm, Sun noon–6pm; Sept–March Mon–Fri 10am–5pm, Sat 11am–5pm, Sun 1–5pm · £7.50 · ☏ 028 4272 8062, ⓦ www.exploris.org.uk

Portaferry's star attraction is the **Exploris** aquarium, featuring the north's only seal sanctuary where they've been rescuing and rehabilitating common and grey seal pups for more than 25 years. The aquarium also has a touch-tank for the brave to stroke a stingray, an open-sea tank where you can view the odd roaming shark, and a discovery pool for plenty of hands-on fun. Look out for the various special events.

15

By bus Buses depart from the main square. Destinations Belfast (Mon–Sat 8 daily, Sun 4; 1hr 25min–1hr 45min); Newtownards (Mon–Sat every 30min–1hr, Sun 5; 50min–1hr 15min).

By ferry Regular ferries make the 5min ride across the lips of the lough to Strangford (every 30min, Mon–Fri 7.45am–10.45pm, Sat 8.15am–11.15pm, Sun 9.45am–10.45pm; ☎028 4488 1637; £1 single, £2 return; car £5.80 single, £10 return).

Tourist office In The Stables, Castle Street (Easter–Aug Mon–Sat 10am–5pm, Sun 2–6pm; ☎028 4272 9882), next to the ruined tower house.

ACCOMMODATION AND EATING

Annie's 16–17 The Square ☎028 4272 9796, ✉anniesbnb@yahoo.co.uk. Wonderfully quirky B&B with an elegant spiral staircase leading up to three light-filled rooms with original fireplaces, wicker bedsteads and colourfully patterned textiles. Annie's also doubles up as a shabby-chic tearoom – all polka-dot formica and distressed wood – which extends to a marvellous rooftop terrace with views across the Lough. Tearoom daily 9am–6pm. **£55**

Fiddlers Green 10–14 Church St ☎028 4272 8383, ⓦfiddlersgreenportaferry.com. You can't miss the turquoise-green painted exterior of this erstwhile grocery store, now a convivial hostelry, which has singalong folk sessions and traditional music most nights, plus quiz night on Thurs. Daily 11am–11pm.

Portaferry Hotel 10 The Strand ☎028 4272 8231, ⓦportaferryhotel.com. This distinctive salmon-pink building right by the ferry harbours decent, high-ceilinged rooms with a subtle maritime theme; there's a £10 supplement for Lough-facing rooms. The restaurant has a good reputation, particularly for its fish dishes. **£90**

Ballyquintin Point and Kearney

The coast road south of Portaferry leads to **Ballyquintin Point** and, on the way, passes the entrance lane to **St Cowey's Wells**, where the faithful optimist is spoilt for choice: there's a drinking well, a wishing well and a well for bathing sore eyes. Look out for the rock nearby – the indentations are supposed to mark the places where the saint's hands and feet rested as he prayed. Northeast from here **KEARNEY** is a charming seaside village, consisting almost entirely of whitewashed cottages and now mostly owned by the National Trust. You can walk from here to **Kearney Point**, an often blustery ten-minute stroll with panoramic views across the Irish Sea.

The western shore

Leaving Scrabo Tower just east of Belfast on the A22, you'll pass through **COMBER** – famous for its potatoes – before reaching a turning east to **Castle Espie Wildfowl and Wetland Centre**. From Castle Espie, you can wind along the very edge of the lough on a series of minor roads. Travelling this scenic route is enjoyable in itself, but there are a couple of spots worth making for, the first of which is **Mahee Island**. From here, back on the road along the lough, follow the signs to Ardmillan, Killinchy and then Whiterock to reach **Sketrick Island**. The tiny coves and inlets at the feet of little drumlins continue as far as Killyleagh, almost any of them worth exploring.

Castle Espie Wildfowl and Wetland Centre

Daily: March–Oct 10am–5.30pm; Nov–Feb 10am–4.30pm • £7.05 • ☎028 9187 4146, ⓦwwt.org.uk/wetland-centres/castle-espie

At the **Castle Espie Wildfowl and Wetland Centre**, admission earnings are ploughed back into conserving the wetlands area for the seven thousand birds that visit it as well as the resident population of waterfowl, including the largest gathering of ducks, geese and swans in Ireland; the outdoor duckery is not to be missed, particularly in summer when the new hatchlings arrive. Part of the wetlands site was formerly a brick and lime works, and the old kiln here has been superbly converted into the Limekiln Observatory, now the centre's principal birdwatching spot. The centre also has a coffee shop and art gallery and hosts numerous events throughout the year, related both to ornithology and arts and crafts, as well as plenty of activities for children, including a climbing wall in the Limestone Pavilion nearby.

Mahee Island

Visitor Centre Easter–Sept daily 10am–6pm; Oct–Easter Sun noon–4pm • Free

Mahee Island, named after St Mochaoi, supposedly the first abbot of the island, is reached via a twisting lane and several causeways. Heading past the crumbling remains of sixteenth-century Mahee Castle at the entrance to the island, and over the final causeway, you come to the Celtic **Nendrum Monastic Site**, a few hundred yards further on. It's a marvellously isolated spot, surrounded on three sides by water. Annals and excavations indicate that a sizeable community lived here from the seventh century onwards, but the remaining ruins probably date from the twelfth century at the very earliest. It was clearly a substantial establishment, with church, round tower, school and living quarters all housed in a cashel of three concentric wards. Today, the inner wall shelters the ruined church, and a reconstructed sundial uses some of the original remnants. There's an illuminating reconstruction map at the site and a helpful visitor centre.

The Lecale region

Jutting into the southern reach of Strangford Lough, the **Lecale Peninsula** is above all **St Patrick** country. Ireland's patron saint was a Roman Briton, first carried off as a youth from somewhere near Carlisle in northern England by Irish raiders. He spent six years in slavery in Ireland before escaping home again and, at the age of 30, decided to return to Ireland as a bishop, to spread Christianity. Christianity had already reached Ireland a while earlier, probably through traders and other slaves, and, indeed, St Patrick was not in fact the first bishop of Ireland, but he remains easily the most famous. He arrived in Ireland this second time, according to his biographer Muirchú (also his erstwhile captor, converted), on the shores of the Lecale region, and his first Irish sermon was preached at **Saul** in 432. Today the region commemorates the association with sites at Struell Wells and Saul, as well as at **Downpatrick**.

The **Lecale Way** is an almost forty-mile waymarked walking tour of the peninsula starting in Raholp and running to Strangford and thence around the coast to Clough and onwards to Newcastle (maps available from the Downpatrick tourist office – see p.540).

Downpatrick

DOWNPATRICK, 23 miles south of Belfast, is a pleasant enough place of little more than ten thousand people, and its compact size and the proximity of some rich and well-preserved historical sites make for an easy and worthwhile day's visit.

The **Hill of Down**, at the north of the town, was once a rise of great strategic worth, fought over long before the arrival of St Patrick made it famous. A **Celtic fort** of mammoth proportions was built here and was called first Arús Cealtchair, then later Dún Cealtchair. Celtchar was one of the Red Branch Knights, a friend of the then King of Ulster, Conor MacNessa, and, according to the Book of the Dun Cow, "an angry terrific hideous man with a long nose, huge ears, apple eyes, and coarse dark-grey hair". The Dún part of the fort's name went on to become the name of the county, as well as the town.

By the time the Norman knight **John de Courcy** made his mark here in the late twelfth century, a settlement was well established. Pushing north out of Leinster, and defeating Rory MacDonlevy, King of Ulster, de Courcy dispossessed the Augustinian canons who occupied the Hill of Down to establish his own **Benedictine abbey**. He flaunted as much pomp as he could to mark the occasion, and one of his festive tricks was to import what were supposedly the disinterred bodies of St Brigid and St Columba to join St Patrick, who was (allegedly) buried here. One of the earliest accounts of Patrick's life asserts that he's buried in a church near the sea; and since a later account admits that "where his bones are, no man knows", Downpatrick's claim seems as good as any.

St Patrick Centre

St Patrick's Square • Daily 9am–5pm, plus July & Aug Sun 1–5pm • £5.50 • ☎ 028 4461 9111, Ⓦ saintpatrickcentre.com

Just off the main drag Market Street, the large glass-and-brick-built **St Patrick Centre** aims to recount the life of the saint and his influence in extensive detail. Its hagiographic, multimedia approach is pretty arid, however, and by the time you've been round its maze of interactive displays and sat through the five-screen 180-degree virtual helicopter ride through Christian history, you might even wish you'd never heard of him.

Down Cathedral

Mon–Sat 9.30am–4pm, Sun 2–4pm • Free • ☎ 028 4461 4922, Ⓦ downcathedral.org

Uphill from the St Patrick Centre, you'll reach the elegant, spacious Mall, at the end of which stands **Down Cathedral**. Built by John de Courcy, the cathedral was destroyed in 1316 during Edward Bruce's invasion, and a new abbey erected in the early sixteenth century was even more short-lived. Today's cathedral dates basically from the early 1800s, though it incorporates many aspects of earlier incarnations. Its unique feature is the private box-pews, characteristic of the Regency period and the only ones remaining in use in Ireland.

The site of the three graves of Columba, Patrick and Brigid is meant to be just to the left of the tower entrance and is marked today by a rough granite boulder, put there around 1900 to cover a huge hole created by earlier pilgrims searching for the saints' bones.

Down County Museum

The Mall • Mon–Fri 10am–5pm, Sat & Sun 1–5pm • Free • ☎ 028 4461 5218, Ⓦ downcountymuseum.com

Where the Mall segues into English Street, both streets crowded with handsome Georgian buildings, you come to the eighteenth-century jail, now home to the **Down County Museum**. The three-storey Georgian **Governor's House** in the centre of the walled courtyard houses a local-history gallery entitled "Down through Time"; the displays are both varied and enlightening, ranging from some superb pre-history artefacts – notably Bronze Age tools and Norman grave covers – to photos of local worthies, including the town's most famous musical export, the indie band, Ash. Not to be missed either are a couple of beautifully embroidered quilts: the Ballybranagh Quilt, dating from 1849, depicts biblical scenes, as well as important events that have taken place in Down, while the Killyleagh Quilt is a dazzling velvet and silk patchwork made by local girl Martha Geddis in 1894.

The cell block at the back of the enclosure once held the United Irishman Thomas Russell, who had already survived the 1798 Rebellion but was found guilty of complicity in Robert Emmet's uprising and was duly hanged in 1803 from a sill outside the main gate of the jail; the restored cells remain, while the main room here is used to host temporary exhibitions, which are often excellent.

Mound of Down

Between the jail and the barricaded courthouse and inauspiciously tucked behind a secondary school, you'll find the **Mound of Down**, a smaller prominence than the Hill of Down and half-submerged in undergrowth. It's in fact 60ft high and inside its outer

ON THE TRAIL OF ST PATRICK

About four miles west of Inch Abbey (take the B2 to Annacloy and then the first turning on the left), **Loughinisland** is probably the most worthwhile of all the sites in the area associated with St Patrick, and indeed one of the most idyllic spots in County Down. It comprises a reed-fringed lake contained by ten or so little drumlin hills, one of which forms an island in the lake. Here, across a short causeway, are the ruins of three small churches, set next door to each other. The smallest one, **MacCartan's Chapel** (1636), has an entrance door no taller than four or five feet. The larger northern church was used by both Catholics and Protestants until they quarrelled on a wet Sunday around 1720 over which camp should remain outside during the service. The Protestants left and built their church at Seaforde instead.

The next St Patrick landmark is at **Saul**, a couple of miles northeast of Downpatrick off the Strangford road. St Patrick is said to have landed nearby, sailing up the tiny River Slaney, and it was here that he first preached, immediately converting Dichu, the lord of this territory. Dichu gave Patrick a barn as his first base and the saint frequently returned here to rest from his travelling missions – legend has it that he died here in 461. Today a **memorial chapel** and round tower in the Celtic Revival style, built of pristine silver-grey granite in 1932 to commemorate the 1500th anniversary of the saint's arrival, is open to visitors (daily 9am–5pm; free). Two cross-carved stones from between the eighth and twelfth centuries still stand in the graveyard, though there's not a trace of the medieval monastery built here by St Malachy in the twelfth century.

A short distance further south, between Saul and Raholp, **St Patrick's Shrine** sits atop Slieve Patrick, a tract of hillside much like a slalom ski-slope, with the Stations of the Cross marking a pathway up. This huge Mourne-granite statue, clad at the base with bronze panels depicting Patrick's life, was erected in the same year as Saul church. The summit is no more than a twenty-minute climb and offers a commanding view of the county, a vista of the endless little bumps of this drumlin-filled territory.

At **Raholp** is the ruined church of **St Tassach**, named after the bishop from whom the dying Patrick received the sacrament. Patrick gave Raholp to Tassach as a reward for crafting a case for Christ's crozier, the Bachall Isú, one of Ireland's chief relics until its destruction in 1538. The ruins here were mainly restored in 1915 from the rubble that lay around, but their material is thought to date from the eleventh century. If you're eager for the complete St Patrick experience, it's a mile from the car park of the Slaney Inn in Raholp to the spot on the lough shore where he is believed to have first landed: head towards Strangford, then left down Myra Road; cross the main Strangford road and turn left at the first fork; at the bottom of the hill, take the track on the right to the shore.

The easiest way to find the last St Patrick site, **Struell Wells**, is to return to Downpatrick. Take the Ardglass road southeast, turn left just past the hospital, then right down a narrow track into a secluded rock-faced valley and you'll come to the wells. The waters here, believed to be the wells referred to in early accounts of Patrick's mission, have been attributed with healing powers for centuries. In 1744 Walter Harris described the scene: "Vast throngs of rich and poor resort on Midsummer Eve and the Friday before Lammas, some in the hopes of obtaining health, and others to perform penance." The site contains a couple of wells, one for drinking and another known as the eye well whose waters are supposed to have curative powers, and men's and women's bathhouses. Mass is still said here on midsummer night, and people bring containers to carry the water home with them.

15

ditch is a horseshoe-shaped central mound of rich grass. Once a rath, or round hill fort, it was considerably altered and enlarged to create a Norman motte-and-bailey fortification, with a **bretasche** (a wooden archery tower) at the centre. Its view of the Hill of Down clearly displays the attractions the hill had for its earliest settlers; it's believed by some to be the site of the palace of the kings of Ulster.

Downpatrick and County Down Railway

Mid-June to mid-Sept Sat & Sun 2–5pm, plus bank holidays and special event days · £6 return · ⓦ downrail.co.uk

At the rear of the market car park on Market Street is the enthusiast-run **Downpatrick and County Down Railway**, which operates short steam-train trips along a restored section of the Belfast–Newcastle main line to Inch Abbey. The station has a small photographic exhibition (same times; free) on railways in County Down, as well as several steam and diesel locomotives on show.

ARRIVAL AND INFORMATION   DOWNPATRICK

By bus The bus station (☎ 028 4461 2384) is on Market Street, a hundred yards south of the St Patrick Centre. Destinations Ardglass (Mon–Fri 11 daily, Sat 8, Sun 3; 25min); Ballyhornan (2–4 daily; 30–40min); Belfast (Mon–Sat every 30min–1hr, Sun 8; 1hr); Castlewellan (Mon–Fri 10 daily, Sat 4, Sun 3; 30min); Killough (Mon–Fri 9 daily, Sat 6, Sun 3; 15min); Newcastle (Mon–Sat every 30min–1hr, Sun 5; 25–35min); Newry (4–6 daily; 1hr 15min); Raholp (Mon–Sat 5–9 daily; 15min); Strangford (Mon–Fri 8 daily, Sat 5; 30min).

Tourist office Inside the St Patrick Centre (July & Aug Mon–Sat 9am–5pm, Sun 1–5pm; Sept–June Mon–Sat 9am–5pm; ☎ 028 4461 2233); offers an accommodation booking service.

ACCOMMODATION

Denvir's 16 English St ☎ 028 4461 2012, ⓦ www .denvirshotel.com. One of Ireland's oldest coaching inns, with six en-suite rooms that are surprisingly simple, furnished throughout in dark, heavy wood, but cosy all the same. **£70**
Dunleath House 33 St Patrick's Drive ☎ 028 4461 3221, ⓔ dunleathbb@btinternetcom. Tucked away in a residential area very close to the centre of town, this welcoming family home has four good-sized, ground-level rooms with French doors leading off to a patio area; cracking breakfast as well. **£70**
The Mill Drumcullen Rd, Ballydugan ☎ 028 4661 3654, ⓦ ballyduganmill.com. This converted flour mill, dating from 1792, retains eleven rustically styled rooms on the building's upper two floors, each with exposed beams and rough-hewn stone walls. The Mill also has its own café and restaurant. **£90**

EATING AND DRINKING

★**The Daily Grind** 20a St Patrick's Avenue ☎ 028 4461 7173. The permanently packed tables will tell you how popular this place is; pop in for late morning coffee or one of the utterly scrumptious fruit salads, perhaps topped with a honey mustard vinaigrette (£5). Mon–Sat 10am–4pm.
Denvir's 16 English St ☎ 028 4461 2012, ⓦ denvirshotel.com. Chunky oak beams, flagstoned floors and a fine inglenook fireplace comprise the restaurant, lounge and snug bars of this hotel (see above), and provide the setting for superb lunches (including a Tex-Mex lunch, and two courses for £10) and evening meals. Daily 11am–11pm.
The Quoile Tavern 6 Scotch Str ☎ 028 4461 7777. The most appealing of Downpatrick's numerous pubs, by virtue of its live music sessions, which usually take place on Sun evenings. Daily 11.30am–midnight.

ENTERTAINMENT

Down Arts Centre 2–6 Irish St ☎ 028 4461 0747, ⓦ www.downartscentre.com. The excellent Down Arts Centre has an extensive programme of events, and you'll find all genres of art and performance here, from poetry and painting to music and comedy. Mon–Sat 10am–4.30pm.

Inch Abbey

Open access

A mile northwest of Downpatrick, on the other side of the Quoile Marsh, lie the remains of the Cistercian **Inch Abbey**. The exquisite setting is visible from the town, but the river's intervention means that the only access is a mile out along the Belfast road, taking the left turn down Inch Abbey Road just before the defunct Abbey Lodge Hotel, followed by another signposted left turn shortly afterwards – alternatively, you can take a train ride from Downpatrick (see p.539). The site was once an island, and an earlier nearby foundation was destroyed by John de Courcy in 1177 because it was fortified against him. In atonement he built a replacement here and, in 1180, invited Cistercian monks from Furness Abbey in Lancashire over to populate the building, with the intention of establishing a strong centre of English influence. Little of it is now left standing – it was burnt in 1404 and monastic life was completely over by the mid-sixteenth century. Still, its setting, among small glacial drumlins and woodland, is picturesque, and strolling up the valley sides is a pleasant way to pass half-an-hour or so.

Strangford

If you're following the A2 round the coast of the Ards Peninsula, your arrival on Lecale will be at tiny **STRANGFORD** village, directly opposite Portaferry and linked by a regular ferry service (see below). The earlier name of this inlet was Lough Cuan (cuan being Irish for "harbour" or "haven"), but it was renamed Strangfiord by the Vikings over a thousand years ago because of the strong-knot current in the narrows, which has enabled the recent introduction of underwater turbines (see p.535). The centre of the village is a neatly manicured green framed by pastel-coloured stone tenements, while its small harbour makes a pleasant setting for watching the to and fro of the ferry boats.

ARRIVAL AND DEPARTURE   STRANGFORD

By bus Buses stop by the main square just up from the ferry landing stage.
Destinations Downpatrick (Mon–Fri 9 daily, Sat 5; 30min); Raholp (Mon–Fri 9 daily, Sat 5; 10min).

By ferry Regular ferries make the 5min trip across to Portaferry (every 30min, Mon–Fri 7.30am–10.30pm, Sat 8am–11pm, Sun 9.30am–10.30pm; ☏ 028 4488 1637; £1 single, £2 return; car £5.80 single, £10 return).

ACCOMMODATION AND EATING

The Cuan On the village green ☏ 028 4488 1222, ⓦ thecuan.com. This long-established inn offers nine elegantly furnished, fragrant-smelling rooms with splashes of artwork. In addition, there's a splendid, though not cheap, restaurant with plenty of fish dishes on offer; and if you fancy a quiet pint, make for the sociable bar. **£90**

Lobster Pot On the village green ☏ 028 4488 1288. If fresh lobster straight off the boat takes your fancy, then look no further than this smart, but easy-going, restaurant; prawn and mussel linguine (£11.95) and pan-fried scallops

with black pudding and pea purée are typically mouthwatering, but very affordable, dishes. Daily noon–9.30pm.

★**Strangford Cottage** A short walk up from the village green ☏ 028 4488 1208, ⓦ strangfordcottage .com. This handsome, flower-fronted Georgian terraced house accommodates three sublime rooms, variously furnished with brass beds, roll-top baths and bits of local arts and crafts: the Lough Suite is the most lavish of the three, though both the coral and yellow rooms look fantastic. April–Oct. **£115**

Castle Ward

House Daily mid-March to Oct 11am–5pm; grounds daily: April–Sept 10am–8pm; Oct–March 10am–4pm; Strangford Lough Wildlife Centre daily mid-March to Oct 11am–5pm • £7.30 • ☏ 028 4488 1204, ⓦ nationaltrust.org.uk/castle-ward

The most worthwhile place in the immediate surrounds of Strangford is **Castle Ward**, the eighteenth-century residence of Bernard and Anne Ward, later Lord and Lady Bangor, but now owned by the National Trust. It's a positively schizophrenic building, thanks to the opposing tastes of its creators (they later split up): Bernard's half is in the Classical Palladian style, Anne's neo-Gothic, a split carried through into the design and decor of the rooms inside. Outside there are pleasant **gardens** and preserved farm buildings. There's also a sixteenth-century tower house (Old Castle Ward) inside the grounds; the fifteenth-century **Audley's Castle** just outside on the lough shore, with a superb view across the lough (though there's a better example of a tower house just south of Strangford at Kilclief; see p.542); and the **Strangford Lough Wildlife Centre**, housed in a restored barn.

Cloghy Rocks

A signposted turning one mile south of Strangford directs you to the **Cloghy Rocks** observation point. The rocks themselves are 60ft or so out in the lough and for most of the day look decidedly inconsequential, but this is the best place to spot basking **seals**, both common and grey seals. They're well camouflaged against the seaweed, so a pair of binoculars would be handy. Here, too, you can see herons, redshank and oystercatchers, and you may even be lucky enough to spot an otter or two.

Kilclief Castle and St Patrick's Well

Kilclief Castle July & Aug daily 1–5pm • Free

Continuing down the southern shore, you'll soon arrive at the hamlet of Kilclief, which consists of little more than **Kilclief Castle**, one of Ireland's earliest tower houses, a well-preserved fifteenth-century example that was originally the home of John Cely, Bishop of Down – until he was defrocked and thrown out of the Church for living with someone else's wife.

Beyond Kilclief is **St Patrick's Well**, set on a wonderful rocky shore between Ballyhornan and Chapeltown. You can get to within a few hundred yards of the well by road, but the best approach is to start from Ballyhornan – where you'll see a narrow strip of water separating the village from Guns Island, accessible at low tide and still used for grazing – and follow the foreshore path for about a mile. The well is easily spotted: it looks rather like a sheep dip with concrete walls, but with a crucifix at its head. Its holy water has turned into something closer to stagnant consommé than an ever-youthful source of new life.

Ardtole Church

The ruin of fifteenth-century **Ardtole Church** is well signposted just a few hundred yards east of the road. It's set on the spur of a hill, which gives it a fine perspective out to sea and back across the undulating flat of Lecale. Once dedicated to St Nicholas, patron saint of sailors, the church was used by English fishermen until a quarrel broke out with the Irish around 1650. The story goes that the fishermen tied a sleeping Irish chief to the ground by his long hair so that he couldn't get up when he awoke. Tradition has it that Swift derived the similar episode in *Gulliver's Travels* from this tale, and certainly the Ardtole region runs amok with tiny drumlins – very much like the description of the Lilliputian mountains.

Ardglass

ARDGLASS is set on the side of a lovely natural inlet. Its domestic buildings, rising steeply from the harbour, are interspersed with seven fortified mansions, towers and turrets, dating from a vigorous English revival in the sixteenth century, when a trading company first arrived to found a colony here. In the nineteenth century, Ardglass was the most thriving **fishing** port in the North; and even today, aside from the prawns, herrings and whitefish brought in by the fishing fleet, there's very good rod-fishing to be had off the end of the pier for codling, pollack and coalfish. It's often sometimes possible to buy direct from fishing boats or from the cannery on the quay.

The castles

The best preserved of the fortifications, though it's no longer open for visits on safety grounds, is **Jordan's Castle**, next door to the Anchor pub on the Low Road, the most elegant and highly developed of all the Down tower houses. The tall, crenellated building with white-plaster trimming up on the hill was once **King's Castle**; its nineteenth-century renovation is obvious, as is modern work to turn it into a nursing home. The lone ornamental-looking turret on the hilltop is **Isabella's Tower**, a nineteenth-century folly created by Aubrey de Vere Beauclerc as a gazebo for his disabled daughter.

ARRIVAL AND DEPARTURE

By bus Buses stop on the main road just above the harbour. Destinations Ballyhornan (Mon–Fri 6 daily, Sat & Sun 3; 10min); Downpatrick (Mon–Fri 12 daily, Sat 7, Sun 3; 20–25min); Killough (Mon–Fri 10 daily, Sat 6, Sun 3; 5min).

ACCOMMODATION AND EATING

Aldo's 7 Castle Place ⊕ 028 4484 1315, ⓦ aldosardglass.com. Well-regarded restaurant that's been in the hands of the same Italian family for more than forty years; fresh fish off the boat and pasta made on the premises make for an outstanding combination. Thurs–Sat 5–9.30pm, Sun noon–9.30pm.

Burford Lodge 30 Quay St ⊕ 028 4484 1141, ⓔ burfordlodge30@gmail.com. Home-from-home hospitality in this super-value Georgian guesthouse opposite the harbour offering six rooms with big bay windows inviting fantastic sea views. £55

Killough

KILLOUGH, a few miles west of Ardglass, is a tranquil village stretching around a harbour that is much larger than its neighbour's but is now silted up. Killough's main street is a fine French-style avenue of sycamores with a string of picturesque cottage terraces at its southern end, making an unlikely major thoroughfare. The Wards, of Castle Ward, built the harbour in the eighteenth century, and there's still a road running inland, virtually in a straight line, from Killough to their castle. Untouched by tourism, there is no accommodation in the village and only bar meals in a couple of pubs.

St John's Point

From the southern end of Killough you can head out to **St John's Point** – much favoured by birdwatchers – on which lie the ruins of one of the North's best examples of a **pre-Romanesque church**; it's an enjoyable two-and-a-half-mile walk. The tiny west door of the tenth-century church has the distinctive sloping sides, narrowing as the doorway rises, that were a common feature of these early churches. Also still apparent are the **antae**, enclosures created by the extension of the west and east walls to give extra support to the roof. Excavations in 1977 showed up graves that extended under these walls, indicating that an even earlier church existed in the early Christian period, probably made of wood.

ARRIVAL AND DEPARTURE

By bus Buses stop in the centre of the village. Destinations Ardglass (Mon–Fri 10 daily, Sat 7, Sun 3; 5min); Downpatrick (Mon–Fri 10 daily, Sat 6, Sun 3; 15min).

Newcastle

NEWCASTLE, with its lovely stretch of sandy beach, is the biggest seaside resort in County Down – packed with trippers from Belfast on bank holidays and summer weekends – and, with Slieve Donard rising behind the town, it's by far the best base if you want to do any serious walking or climbing in the **Mourne Mountains**. The resort isn't exactly exciting – there's next to nothing by way of sights, and the main strip is interspersed with tacky amusement arcades and souvenir shops – but it does have some appealing accommodation and dining possibilities, and is also well equipped for a range of outdoor activities, including **walking** in the Mourne Mountains southwest of town, **pony trekking** and **fishing** on the river.

The town has a few literary connections too: **Seamus Heaney** was a waiter in the 1950s at the long-gone Savoy Café; Brook Cottage, on Bryansford Road, was home to the dramatist and dialect-poet Richard Valentine Williams, better known as Richard Rowley; and a fountain on The Promenade commemorates the popular Irish songwriter Percy French, composer of "The Mountains of Mourne" and numerous comic songs.

15

ARRIVAL AND DEPARTURE

By bus The bus station (028 4372 2296) is on Railway St at the eastern end of Main St. The Mourne Rambler (May–Aug Tues–Sun 5 daily, 9.05am–5.35pm; all-day ticket £6.50; 028 9066 6630) is a circular service starting in Newcastle with numerous stops including Tollymore and the Silent Valley.

Destinations Belfast (Mon–Sat hourly, Sun 8; 1hr 20min 1hr 45min); Bryansford (Mon–Fri 4 daily; 10min Castlewellan (Mon–Sat every 30min–1hr, Sun 6; 10min Downpatrick (Mon–Sat every 30min–1hr, Sun 25–35min); Hillsborough (Mon–Fri 3 daily; 55min); New (4–6 daily; 55min).

INFORMATION AND ACTIVITIES

Tourist office The tourist office is at 10–14 Central Promenade (April–June & Sept Mon–Sat 9.30am–5pm, Sun 2–6pm; July & Aug Mon–Sat 9.30am–7pm, Sun 1–7pm; Oct–March Mon–Sat 9.30am–5pm, Sun 2–5pm; 028 4372 2222, visitmournemountains .co.uk).

Royal County Down golf course Newcastle's prestigious championship golf course (028 4372 3314,

royalcountydown.org) has a reputation as one of th most challenging links in the world.

Soak 5 South Promenade (July & Aug dail 11.30am–8pm; Sept–June Mon & Thurs–Su 11.30am–8pm; €25; 028 4372 600; soakseaweedbaths.co.uk). Reinvigorating seawee baths, as well as a variety of health and holisti treatments.

ACCOMMODATION

Beach House 22 Downs Rd 028 4372 2345, beachhouse-newcastle.co.uk. The chief appeal of this refurbished Victorian dwelling is the sea view from each of the three, mostly all-white, rooms (two doubles and a twin). Feb–Oct. **£100**

Hutt Hostel 30 Downs Rd 028 4372 2133, hutthostel.com. Occupying a fine seafront town house, this buzzy, well-appointed hostel has a variety of three- to eight-bed dorms, plus "The Padd", an apartment-like

annexe sleeping five. There's also a cool lounge and a larg self-catering kitchen for use, though breakfast is included Dorms **£22**, annexe per person **£25**

Slieve Donard Downs Rd 028 4372 106 hastingshotels.com. This ostentatious red-brick pile positioned on the beachfront and next to the Royal Count Down golf course, is Newcastle's premier hotel, a mega luxurious establishment with grand rooms – most with sea view – and its own spa. **£110**

EATING AND DRINKING

Anchor Bar 9 Bryansford Avenue 028 4372 3344. Owned by the team running the *Hutt Hostel* (see above), this fun pub is similarly funky, fitted out with nautical and railway paraphernalia. Popular with ramblers and climbers, there's decent bar food, plus pool tables and live music at weekends. Daily 11am–11pm.

Café Crème 139–141 Main St 028 4372 6589. There are dozens of cafés along Main St, but this is the best by a country mile, serving up all-day breakfasts, sandwiches, panini and scrumptious traybakes, not to mention the freshest, tastiest coffee in town. Mon–Fri 8.45am–5pm, Sat & Sun 8.45am–6pm.

Sea Salt Bistro 51 Central Promenade 028 4372 5027. Head to this small bistro for seafood treats. The place operates as a café in the mornings, then serves

appetizing lunches, including tapas, and substantia dinners (Fri & Sat only) at reasonable prices, thoug you'll need to bring your own wine. Mon–Thurs & Su 9am–6pm, Fri & Sat 9am–8.30pm.

Vanilla 67 Main St 028 4372 2268 vanillarestaurant.co.uk. The pick of severa restaurants along the town's main thoroughfare, stylis *Vanilla* features two uniform rows of polished woode tables underneath wall-length mirrors; the food i equally accomplished, with the likes of duck and choriz scotched hen's eggs, and grilled flat-iron steak wit mushrooms and crushed walnuts; two courses £15.95 Mon–Thurs & Sun 11am–3.30pm & 5–9pm, Fri & Sa 6–9.30pm.

The Mourne Mountains

The **Mourne Mountains** are a relatively youthful set of granite mountains, which explains why their comparatively unweathered peaks and flanks are so rugged, forming steep sides, moraines and occasional sheer cliffs. Closer up, these give sharp, jagged outlines; but from a distance they appear much gentler, like a sleeping herd of buffalo. The wilder topography lies mostly in the east, below Newcastle, although the fine cliff of **Eagle Mountain** (636m), to the southwest, is wonderful if you can afford the time and effort to get there, and the tamer land above Rostrevor has views down into **Carlingford Lough** that rival any in Ireland.

In summer at least (winters can be surprisingly harsh), there are plenty of straightforward hikes in the Mournes that require no special equipment, with obvious tracks to many of the more scenic parts. There are also, of course, more serious climbs and **climbing courses** in the Mournes are run by the Tollymore National Outdoor Centre in Bryansford (⊛tollymore.com), but they must be booked well in advance.

The Legananny dolmen

The **Legananny dolmen** is worth a considerable detour, which it will be, wherever you are, due to its remoteness; it's signposted at the village of Leitrim, three miles north of Castlewellan. Approaching the site, you'll find yourself on narrow humped lanes, gradually ascending the southern edge of the Slieve Croob range, and feeling increasingly distant from modern realities. You may also experience a sense of déjà vu when you arrive at the site, for the dolmen is a popular choice of guidebook and tourist-board photographers. There's no doubting the impressiveness of the structure, looking for all the world like a giant stone tripod.

15

Silent Valley

Valley and visitor centre daily: May–Sept 10am–6.30pm; Oct–April 10am–4pm; café June–Aug daily 11am–6.30pm • Pedestrians £1.60, car £4.50 • Sandy Lough shuttle bus May, June & Sept Sat & Sun; July & Aug daily (£1.50 return)

The A2 south along the coast from Newcastle is a beautiful road, trailing the shore around the edge of the mountains. It takes you past the chasm known as **Maggie's Leap**, after a local woman who jumped to avoid the attentions of an unwanted suitor, and over the **Bloody Bridge**, reputedly so-called because of a nearby massacre during the 1641 Rebellion. Inland, a mile or so from the fishing village of Annalong (seven miles south of Newcastle) and serviced by the summer-only Mourne Rambler bus (see opposite), signposts point to the aptly named **Silent Valley**, where you'll find Belfast and County Down's **reservoir**, a huge thirty-year engineering project that was completed in 1933. There's a car park by the lower reservoir, bounded by the Mourne Wall, a sturdy 22-mile-long granite boundary to the catchment area that links the summits of fifteen mountains along its route. The views out to Slieve Binnian and Ben Crom, behind it to the west, are worth the effort of the three-mile circular **Viewpoint Walk** (starts at the car park). Less energetic, but still superb, is the half-mile Sally Lough stroll up to the dam at Ben Crom; again the views are spectacular. Halfway between the car park and the dam there's a small café and a **visitor centre** exhibiting displays on the reservoir's development.

Rostrevor

On the western edge of the Mournes, fifteen miles further on from Annalong, along the A2 a signpost points to the **Kilfeaghan dolmen**, a mile inland then a short walk through a couple of fields and kissing gates. Its capstone is enormous and could only have arrived here during the retreat of the glacial drift.

Further up the lough, the village of **ROSTREVOR** lies at the point where the bay waters dramatically begin to narrow towards Newry – and where the population and political climate turn more in favour of the Nationalist communities of County Armagh and those across the ever-nearing border. Rostrevor is a charming and sleepy village of Victorian terraces and friendly pubs, meandering up the lower slopes of **Slieve Martin**.

WALKS IN THE MOURNES

While there's little to see in Newcastle itself, the **Mourne Mountains** offer some beautiful walks close to town, as well as plenty of more serious hiking routes throughout the range, including the **Newcastle Challenge Trail**, a 44km waymarked hike, split into five sections, starting and finishing in the town. There's also an annual **walking festival** (@mournewalking.co.uk) over three days at the end of June, featuring a variety of lowland and mountain walks, rambles and hikes.

SLIEVE DONARD

The climb up **Slieve Donard**, just south of Newcastle, is the obvious first choice. Although at 850m it's the highest peak in Northern Ireland, the ascent is a relatively easy one on a well-marked trail that starts three miles out of town on the Annalong road at Bloody Bridge (see p.545) and ends at the massive hermit cell on the summit; from here the views across the whole mountain landscape are quite spectacular.

For gentler local walking, there are several pleasant parks created from the estates of old houses in the vicinity. The nearest is **Donard Park** (free access) on the slopes of Slieve Donard. There's a good meander along the River Glen from Newcastle town centre to the park, and if you keep following this path uphill you'll emerge on the other side and eventually come to the Saddle, a col between the two mountains of Slieve Donard and Slieve Commedagh. If you want to carry on further into the mountains from here, a good route is via **Trassey Burn** towards the **Hare's Gap**, where minerals have seeped through the rock to form precious and semiprecious stones – topaz, beryl, smoky quartz and emerald – in the cavities of the **Diamond rocks** (hidden behind an obvious boulder stone on the mountainside). Around this point in spring, you might hear the song of the ring ouzel, a bird that migrates from Africa to breed in these upland areas.

TOLLYMORE FOREST PARK

Two miles inland from Newcastle, along the Bryansford road, **Tollymore Forest Park** (daily 10am–dusk; cars £4.50; @nidirect.gov.uk) is considerably bigger and better equipped than Donard, and has a **campsite** (see opposite). The park creeps up the northern side of the Mournes, and its four picturesque trails (ranging from just half a mile to five miles in length) wind through woodland and beside the river. You enter the park by one of two ornate Gothic folly gates – there are more follies in Bryansford nearby – and there's an information kiosk in the car park.

CASTLEWELLAN FOREST PARK

Castlewellan Forest Park (same hours and prices) is also inland about five miles further north, outside the elegant market town of Castlewellan. The estate lies in the foothills of the

A good time to be here is the last week of July for the Fiddler's Green Festival (@fiddlersgreenfestival.co.uk), a major event attracting folk and traditional musicians from across Europe.

ARRIVAL AND DEPARTURE   ROSTREVOR

By bus Buses drop off on, and depart from, Warrenpoint Road, the main through road.
Destinations Newry (Mon–Sat every 30min–1hr, Sun

25min); Warrenpoint (Mon–Sat every 30min–1hr, Sun 8; 10min).

ACCOMMODATION AND EATING

Kilbroney Caravan Park Shore Rd @028 4173 8134. Camping is available at this park where you can hike up the hill to the thirty-ton Cloughmore ("big stone") for views across the lough to the Cooley Mountains over the border. April–Sept. **£18**

The Old School House 39 Church St @028 4173 8211. The erstwhile school house might look quite ordinary, but the food here is anything but; beyond light lunches, you can sit down to more substantial evening fare later in the

week with the likes of Carnhill duck breast with grilled polenta cake and parsnip purée (£15.95). Mon–Wed 9am–5pm, Thurs–Sun 9am–9pm.

The Sands 4 Victoria Square @028 4173 8151, @thesandsbandbrostrevor.co.uk. Fabulously located B&B on a spruce Victorian square out on the road towards Newcastle, offering two double rooms and a sweet little single, each with a clear sea view. **£70**

Mournes, and a two-and-a-half mile trail from the entrance leads to the highest point in the forest, **Slievenaslat**, providing panoramic views over the mountain range. A wonderful **arboretum**, dating originally from 1740 but much expanded since, is the forest park's outstanding feature: the sheltered south-facing slopes of its hills, between the Mournes and the Slieve Croob range, allow exotic species to flourish. There's trout **fishing** in its main lake and coarse fishing in the smaller lakes (enquire at the Newcastle tourist office for details of this and other local fisheries).

There's a pleasant campsite in the park here, too (see below), as well as the Life One Great Adventure centre (☎028 4377 0714, ⓦonegreatadventure.com), which offers various activities, including canoeing, kayaking and trail biking; bike rental costs £12.50 per day. Nearby **riding schools** offering trekking through the forest parks include Mount Pleasant Riding and Trekking Centre, 15 Bannanstown Rd, Castlewellan (☎028 4377 8651, ⓦmountpleasantcentre .com), and Mourne Trail Riding Centre, 96 Castlewellan Rd, a couple of miles out of Newcastle on the A50 (☎028 372 9107, ⓦmournetrailridingcentre.co.uk). In Castlewellan itself, the lively Celtic Fusion Festival (ⓦcelticfusion.co.uk) in mid-July includes concerts by major folk and traditional musicians.

LONGER HIKES

If you're planning on more serious hiking in the Mournes, heights worth chasing include **Slieve Binnian**, beyond the Hare's Gap, reached through the Brandy Pad passes by the Blue Lough and Lough Binnian; **Slieve Commedagh**, with its Inca-like pillars of granite; and **Slieve Bearnagh**, up to the right of the Hare's Gap. Also, try and cross the ridge from **Slieve Meelmore** to **Slieve Muck**, the "pig mountain", descending to the shores of Lough Shannagh, where there's a beach at either end – useful for a dip, though the water's freezing. In the panorama beyond the Hare's Gap, the places not to miss are the eastern slopes of the **Cove Mountain** and **Slieve Lamagan**. If you're sticking to the roads, all you can really do is circle the outside of the range, though there is one road through the middle, from Hilltown to Kilkeel.

CAMPING IN THE MOURNE MOUNTAINS

Tollymore Caravan and Camping Tollymore Forest Park (signposted) ☎028 4372 2428. Year-round site with decent facilities including showers, compost loos and electric hook-ups. **£16.50**

Castlewellan Camping Castlewellan Forest Park (signposted) ☎028 4377 8664. This campsite has almost identical facilities to the site in Tollymore, but is only seasonal. Easter–Sept. **£16.50**

Warrenpoint

Warrenpoint is as picturesque as Rostrevor, with a colourful esplanade of seafront housing and a spacious central square. It's a much more traditional seaside resort than its neighbour and has been attracting visitors since the early nineteenth century, when an enterprising local man advertised warm baths for the "gentry, nobility and public". The town really only comes alive, however, during the four-day Blues on the Bay music **festival** in late May (ⓦbluesonthe bay.com), and for the **Maiden of the Mournes festival** (ⓦmaidenofthemournes.com), which takes place over the first week of August, a local version of the Rose of Tralee (see p.304).

ARRIVAL AND INFORMATION

By bus Buses drop-off on, and depart from, Church St. Destinations Newry (Mon–Sat every 30min–1hr, Sun 11; 15min); Rostrevor (Mon–Sat every 30min–1hr, Sun 7; 10min).

Tourist office Easy to miss, the tourist office is in the town hall on Church St (Mon–Fri 9am–1pm & 2–5pm; ☎028 4175 2256).

ACCOMMODATION AND EATING

The Balmoral Hotel 13 Seaview ☎028 4175 4093, ⓦbalmoralwarrenpoint.com. Bicycle-friendly hotel (bike storage and wash) with nine contemporary rooms, though only the suite has sea views – as well as a very accomplished in-house restaurant called 23; Mourne black lamb, Dromara beef and Kilkeel fish all feature prominently on the menu. Restaurant Mon–Sat 12.30–2.30pm & 5.30–9pm, Sun noon–8pm. **£90**

Whistledown Hotel 6 Seaview ☎028 4175 4174, ⓦthewhistledownhotel.com. Tidy boutique hotel with coloured furnishings, stripey-coloured carpets and regulation mod cons. Grab a gourmet burger from the garishly decorated Fin's Bar, or treat yourself to more refined fare in the bistro. Bar daily noon–11pm (food

12.30–5pm), bistro noon–2.30pm & 6–9.30pm. **£80**
Ye Old Ship Inn 14 The Square ☎028 4175 3125. A venerable – albeit recently modernized – pub with a distinct nautical theme, from the wood-panelled bar to the sweet little table lamps. The beer's top-notch too. Daily 11.30am–midnight.

Newry

Although **Newry**, astride the border of Down and Armagh, is this region's most important commercial centre and bustles with an urban vibrancy, it's worth little more than a short visit. However, its key position means that you're highly likely to pass through here, and it does make a possible base for exploring Slieve Gullion and the south Armagh district.

Newry was founded by Cistercian monks in 1144, but for most of its history has been a **garrison**, guarding the borders of Northern Ireland at the narrow point between hills on either side known as the Gap of the North. There's no trace at all of the bitterly contested early fortresses; what you see dates mostly from the eighteenth and nineteenth centuries, when a canal to Lough Neagh (cut in 1742, the first in the British Isles) brought the produce of the inland towns to the markets here; indeed, **market days** (Thurs & Sat) remain integral to the town.

Catholic Cathedral

Hill St · Daily 8.30am–5pm · Free

One of the most interesting buildings in town is the **Catholic Cathedral**. Constructed in 1829, it was the first such building to be opened following Catholic Emancipation. Despite an unpromising granite exterior, the rich mosaic pattern along its interior walls gives a Byzantine feel, and there's also a striking vaulted ceiling of decorative sweeping plaster arcs and vivid stained-glass windows. Nearby, there's a strange bronze totem pole by sculptor Paddy McElroy, which depicts, in tortured relief, scenes from Newry's past.

Bagenal's Castle

Castle St · Museum Mon–Sat 10am–4.30pm, Sun 1.30–5pm · Free · ☎028 3031 3182, ⓦ bagenalscastle.com

A short walk from the centre of town, **Bagenal's Castle** is a superb example of a fortified house. Located within the environs of a Cistercian abbey, the castle was confiscated during the Reformation of 1548, and the premises were leased to a certain Nicholas Bagenal, who had apparently earlier fled his native Staffordshire to escape indictment for murder. After acting as a secret agent infiltrating the O'Neill clan, he was granted a pardon and subsequently became marshal of the English army in Ireland and established a garrison in Newry. While Bagenal was largely successful in defending the area against the O'Neills, his daughter Mary eloped and married Hugh O'Neill, a story that became the subject of Brian Friel's play *Making History*. The castle functioned as McGann's bakery for more than a century, until its closure in 1996.

The castle is now home to the nicely presented **Newry and Mourne Museum**, where you can inspect some of the building's original elements, most notably a cross section of its sixteenth-century cellar, which contains the original bread oven. Upstairs, in the impressively authentic Great Chamber, you can't miss the crater-like holes along the walls where the joists were removed years ago. There's a fascinating local history exhibition too, with emphasis on the area's strong folk traditions.

ARRIVAL AND INFORMATION

By train The train station (☎ 028 025 6446) is a mile west of town on Millvale Rd and connected to the centre by local bus #41H (free with valid rail ticket).

Destinations Belfast (Mon–Sat 8 daily, Sun 5; 55min–1hr 5min); Drogheda (Mon–Sat 8 daily, Sun 5; 40min); Dublin (Mon–Sat 8 daily, Sun 5; 1hr 10min–1hr 30min).

By bus Newry's bus station (☎ 028 3026 3531) is on The Mall alongside the canal.

Destinations Armagh (Mon–Fri hourly, Sat 7, Sun 3; 35–50min); Belfast (Mon–Fri every 30min, Sat hourly, Sun 10; 1hr 10min); Carlingford (Bus Éireann: Mon–Sat 3 daily;

20min); Crossmaglen (Mon–Sat 5–6 daily; 55min); Downpatrick (6 daily; 1hr 15min); Dublin (hourly; 1hr 45min–2hr); Forkhill (Mon–Sat 4–7 daily; 35min); Mullaghbawn (Mon–Sat 5–6 daily; 30min); Newcastle (6 daily; 50min); Rostrevor (Mon–Sat every 30min–1hr, Sun 6; 25min); Warrenpoint (Mon–Sat every 30min–1hr, Sun 6; 15min).

Tourist office In Bagenal's Castle on Castle St (April, June & Sept Mon–Fri 9am–5pm, Sat 11am–4pm; July & Aug Mon–Fri 9am–6pm, Sat 10am–4pm, Sun 1–4pm; Oct–March Mon–Fri 9am–5pm; ☎ 028 3031 3170, ⓦ visitnewryandmourne.com).

ACCOMMODATION AND EATING

Canal Court Hotel Merchants Quay ☎ 028 3025 1234, ⓦ canalcourthotel.com. On the opposite side of the canal from the bus station, this vast hotel is run through with class, from the opulent reception area to the extravagantly decorated rooms; it's also equipped with a gym and sauna. **£90**

Grounded Monaghan St ☎ 028 3083 3868. There aren't

many places in Newry where you can grab a hearty lunch or a decent cup of coffee, but you can at *Grounded*, an easy-going café just a few paces along from the *Canal Court Hotel*; moreover, the squishy leather sofas and floor-to-ceiling windows are perfect for people-watching. Daily 8am–11pm.

15

South Armagh

Overshadowed by Slieve Gullion, the **South Armagh** (ⓦ south-armagh.com) countryside is among the most attractive in the North. Proximity to the border and a predominantly Catholic population resulted in this once being a nucleus of resistance to British rule. There's much evidence of prehistoric settlement here, important ecclesiastical remains and plenty of traditional music.

The Ring of Gullion

Most of South Armagh's attractions are concentrated in and around the area known as the **Ring of Gullion**, a naturally formed ring-dyke of low-lying hills that encircles (and predates) the mountain at its core. People have lived here for more than six thousand years, and there's a rich heritage of remains and monuments. On the ring's western fringe is the **Dorsey Enclosure**, two huge earthen banks and ditch ramparts dating from the Iron Age, running for a mile either side of the old route to Navan Fort. Elsewhere are numerous dolmens and cairns, Christian relics and monuments from the Plantation era.

Slieve Gullion, which dominates the southeastern corner of County Armagh, is one of the most mysteriously beautiful mountains in the country. A store of romantic legends is attached to it, especially concerning **Cúchulainn**, the hero of the **Táin Bó Cúailnge** (see p.155), who took his name here after slaying the hound (Cú) of the blacksmith Culainn. Due south at Glendhu is where Cúchulainn single-handedly halted the army of Queen Medb of Connaught, who was intent on capturing the great bull of Cooley. **Fionn Mac Cumhaill**, who founded the **Fianna**, a mythical national militia whose adventures are told in the Fenian Cycle, also appears in stories here.

Bessbrook and Killeavy

A scenic way to approach Slieve Gullion is from the north, passing the turning to **BESSBROOK**, a nineteenth-century model village developed by a Quaker linen entrepreneur; the Cadbury family's Bourneville estate in Birmingham, England, followed a very similar layout. After **Camlough** turn off the main road to go down by the eastern slopes of Camlough Mountain and you'll see the beautiful **lake**, set like a jewel within its green banks. A little further on, between Camlough Mountain and Slieve Gullion, are the ruined **Killeavy churches**. Two churches of different periods share the same gable wall: the west church is pre-Romanesque and one of the most important survivors of its kind in the country; the other, larger, church dates from the thirteenth century. A granite slab marks the **grave of St Monenna**, the founder of a fifth-century nunnery sited here – there's a holy well dedicated to her a little further up the slopes of Slieve Gullion, which pilgrims visit on her feast day (the Sunday nearest to July 6).

The official, tarmacked, entrance up into Slieve Gullion is on the mountain's forested southern face, after you've passed through the village of **KILLEAVY**. You'll find a small **forest park** (daily 10am–dusk; free), fronted by the **Courtyard Centre**, where there's a small exhibition on the area, craft workshops and a café. From the centre it's an eight-mile winding drive up to the summit (or you can follow a walking trail), where there's a couple of megalithic **cairns**. Fionn Mac Cumhaill was legendarily bewitched here by Miluchra, and local superstition holds that bathing in the small summit **lake** will turn your hair white; another tale states that under certain conditions a visitor to the site will be given the power to foresee everything that will happen that day. Various vertiginous spots offer spectacular **views** over the Ring of Gullion and the surrounding countryside.

Crossmaglen and around

In the far southwestern corner of Armagh just inside the border, **CROSSMAGLEN** has reputedly the largest market square in Ireland, the scene of a fortnightly Friday **market**. During the Troubles the town's reputation for armed struggle against the British was fearsome, and, in truth, it has been a cauldron of activity ever since Partition. Indeed, had the 1924 Boundary Commission's proposals been fully implemented, the town and surrounding countryside would have been transferred to Dublin rule rather than staying inside the North. All this said, on arrival you'll find the pubs much friendlier than you might have expected.

A couple of miles east of Crossmaglen on the B30 Newry road, **CREGGAN** has a **Poets Graveyard**, so named because three eighteenth-century Gaelic poets are buried here: Art Mac Cooey, Patrick Mac Aliondain and Séamus Mór Mac Murphy (who was also an outlaw of some notoriety). The inscription on Mac Cooey's stone is taken from his most famous poem, "Úr-Chill an Chreagáin" – "That with the fragrant Gaels of Creggan I will be put in clay under the sod".

Crossmaglen is at the forefront of the local revival of interest in Gaelic games, and the town's **Gaelic football** team, Crossmaglen Rangers, has had continued recent success, winning three of the last seven All-Ireland championships, the last of which was in 2012. If you fancy watching a game, their ground is St Oliver Plunkett Park.

ARRIVAL AND INFORMATION

CROSSMAGLEN AND AROUND

By bus Buses drop off on, and depart from, Ó Fiaich Square. Destinations Newry (Mon–Fri 6 daily, Sat 4; 55min).
Tourist office The tourist office is in Ó Fiaich House on

The Square (July & Aug daily 9am–6pm, Sept–June Mon–Fri 9am–5pm; ☎028 3086 8900, ⍉visitsoutharmagh .com).

ACCOMMODATION AND EATING

Cross Square Hotel 4–5 Ó Fiaich Square ☎028 3086 0505, ⍉crosssquarehotel.com. Very amenable accommodation in the centre of town, and though the rooms are slightly on the old-fashioned side, they're immaculately kept, and the staff couldn't be friendlier. The hotel's restaurant, meanwhile, is noted for its superb steaks. **£70**

Keenans Bar Ó Fiaich Square ☎028 3025 2767. The most agreeable of the town's pubs, this place has been around for the best part of eighty years, and hosts a notable traditional music session on Thurs. Mon–Sat 11am–midnight, Sun 4pm–midnight.

Armagh city and around

ARMAGH is one of the most attractive places in the North, and the rich history of the city and its surroundings has plenty to keep you occupied for a day or two. The city offers **cathedrals** and **museums** set in handsome Georgian streets, and two miles west is the ancient site of once-grand **Navan Fort**. Armagh has been the site of the **Catholic** primacy of All Ireland since St Patrick established his church here, and has rather ambitiously adopted the title of the "Irish Rome" for itself – like Rome, it's positioned among seven small hills. Paradoxically, the city is also the seat of the **Protestant** Church of Ireland's archbishop of Armagh.

Armagh has a number of events during the year, and, as you'd expect, the local **St Patrick's Day Parade** (March 17) is one of the largest in the country. Armagh is particularly well known for its **choral music**, and this manifests itself in the annual week-long **Charles Wood Festival of Music and Summer School** in mid-August (⑩charleswoodsummerschool.org), featuring a daily series of recitals in the city's cathedrals and churches. November sees one of Ireland's major *uilleann* piping events (see p.602), the five-day **William Kennedy Piping Festival** (⑩armaghpipers.org/wkpf), and, at the end of the month, the **Bard of Armagh**, a wonderful festival of humorous verse (⑩bardofarmagh.com).

15

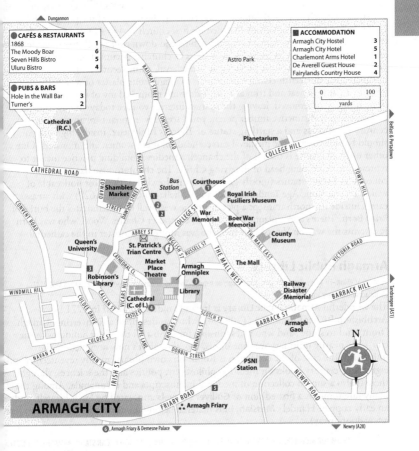

ARMAGH CITY

St Patrick's Roman Catholic Cathedral

Cathedral Rd • Daily: April–Oct 10am–5pm; Nov–March 10am–4pm • Free • ☎ 028 3752 2045, ⓦ armagharchdiocese.org

The best way to get your bearings is to walk up the steps of **St Patrick's Roman Catholic Cathedral**, built on a hillside just northwest of the Shambles Market. The view of the town from here is impressive, and you should be able to identify most of the key sites spread out below. The cathedral's foundation stone was laid in 1840, but completion was delayed by the Famine and a subsequent lack of funding. While the pope and local nobility chipped in, money was also raised by public collections and raffles – one prize of a grandfather clock has still not been claimed. On the outside, the cathedral first appears little different from many of its nineteenth-century Gothic-Revival contemporaries, but it is impressively large and airy. Inside, as befits the seat of the cardinal archbishop, every inch of wall glistens with **mosaics**, in colours ranging from marine- and sky-blue to terracotta pinks and oranges. Other striking pieces include the white-granite "pincer-claw" **tabernacle holder**, reflected in a highly polished marble floor, and a **statue** of the Crucifixion, which suggests (deliberately or otherwise) the old city's division into **Trians**.

St Patrick's Church of Ireland Cathedral

Cathedral Close • Daily: April–Oct 9am–5pm; Nov–March 9am–4pm • £3 donation suggested • ☎ 028 3752 3142, ⓦ stpatricks-cathedral.org

St Patrick's Church of Ireland Cathedral lays claim to the summit of the principal hillock, Drum Saileach, where St Patrick founded his first church in 445 AD. It commands a distinctive Armagh view across to the other hills and down over the clutter of gable walls and pitched roofing on its own slopes. A series of churches occupied the site after 445, and, although the core of the present one is medieval, a nineteenth-century restoration has coated the thirteenth-century outer walls in a sandstone plaster of which Thackeray remarked, "It is as neat and trim as a lady's dressing room." Many of the ancient decorations were removed, leaving the spartan interior you see today. Just as you enter from the highly distinctive timber porch, you'll see a few remnants of an eleventh-century **Celtic cross** and a startling **statue** of Thomas Molyneux. Inside, high up, you should be able to sight the medieval carved heads of men, women and monsters. One other unusual feature is the tilt of the chancel, a medieval building practice meant to represent the slumping head of the dying Christ. The **chapterhouse** has a small collection of stone statues (mostly gathered from elsewhere), the most noticeable of which are the Stone Age **Tandragee Idol** and a Sheila-na-Gig (see p.627) with an ass's ears. Outside the north transept a plaque on the west wall commemorates the burial of **Brian Ború**. There's also a plaque dedicated to composer Charles Wood, who was born just across the way on Vicars' Hill and who was himself a chorister in the cathedral.

Armagh Public Library

43 Abbey St • Mon–Fri 10am–1pm & 2–4pm; guided tours on request • Free, donations welcomed; tours £2 • ☎ 028 3752 3142, ⓦ armaghpubliclibrary.arm.ac.uk

The wonderful **Armagh Public Library** is Ireland's oldest, founded in 1771 by Archbishop Richard Robinson (1708–94), who was described as converting Armagh "from mud to stone" and who is responsible for almost all the older buildings in the city – the nearby infirmary was one of his, too, though it's now occupied by the university. The core of the collection is Robinson's own library, mostly seventeenth-and eighteenth-century books on theology, philosophy, politics and the sciences, though there is also a superb collection of medieval manuscripts and incunabula. Among the many rare tomes is a first edition of **Gulliver's Travels** annotated by Swift himself, and an early copy of Handel's **Messiah**, plus material belonging to Charles Wood (born just a few doors away).

The Mall

The Mall is an elegant tree-lined promenade fringed to the east by two terraces of handsome Georgian houses designed by the Armagh-born architect Francis Johnston, who worked primarily for Archbishop Robinson. Johnston was responsible for many of Dublin's best Georgian buildings, including its GPO (see p.77), and you'll encounter more examples of his work around town, including the classical **courthouse** at The Mall's northern end; the former **jail** occupies the southern end.

The Mall owes its largely oval shape to the fact that it was once a racecourse in the late eighteenth century; nowadays, there's nothing more athletic than the occasional jogger and Saturday cricket matches.

Dotted throughout the park are three **memorials**; at the northern end, you'll find two monuments to those who fell during the Boer War and World War I, while at the southern end is the Railway Disaster Memorial, which remembers the 89 people who were killed in the crash in 1889 (see below); a simple yet affecting piece, it portrays a young girl holding a bucket and spade.

15

Armagh County Museum

The Mall East • Mon–Fri 10am–5pm, Sat 10am–1pm & 2–5pm • Free • ☎ 028 3752 3070, ⓦ armaghcountymuseum.org.uk

A former schoolhouse on the east side of The Mall houses the **County Museum**, a charmingly old-fashioned museum with all the usual local miscellany on display, including an alarmingly vivid collection of stuffed wildlife, plus a little **art gallery** tucked away on the upper floor. Here there are twenty or so mystical pastels, oils and cartoon sketches by the early twentieth-century Irish poet **George Russell**, a much-neglected companion to Yeats, who acquired the alias Æ as a result of a Dublin newspaper misprinting a letter that he had signed "Aeons". The prolific local artist J.B. Vallely is also represented with a superb oil, entitled *The Red Fiddle*, showing five musicians enjoying a session; the theme of traditional music figures in more than three thousand of Vallely's canvases and, with his wife Eithne, he currently runs the town's Armagh Pipers' Club.

Elsewhere, a display devoted to railway history recounts the story of Ireland's worst railway disaster, when two passenger trains collided outside Armagh in 1889, killing 89 people, many of whom are buried in nearby St Mark's churchyard. Along with photos of the wreckage, there's a rather poignant letter, written in 1958, from one of the survivors, in which he recalls the events of that day.

The Royal Irish Fusiliers Museum

The Mall • Mon–Fri 10am–12.30pm & 1.30–4pm • Free • ☎ 028 3752 2911, ⓦ royal-irish.com

Occupying Sovereigns House, the leftovers of the courthouse, is the **Royal Irish Fusiliers Museum**. It's pretty much as you'd expect: tons of weaponry, uniforms, medallions and silverware from the regiment formed in 1793 in response to the Napoleonic crisis and subsequently known as the Faughs, from their battle cry Faugh a Ballagh! ("Clear the way!"). The Fusiliers subsequently fought in the Crimean and Boer wars (where they relieved the Siege of Ladysmith) and in both world wars before amalgamating with the Inniskilling Fusiliers (see p.571) and Ulster Rifles in 1968 to form the Royal Irish Rangers; in 1992, they joined with the Ulster Defence Regiment to form the present-day Royal Irish Regiment.

Armagh Planetarium

College Hill • Mon–Sat 10am–5pm, plus Sun in July & Aug; shows 30–40min each • Adults £6 per show, children 6–15 £5 (pre-booking required); exhibition hall £2; Astropark free • ☎ 028 3752 3689, ⓦ armaghplanet.com

The **Armagh Planetarium** lays claim to "the world's most advanced digital production projection system, Digistar 3", with full animation of the planetarium's dome (and reclining seats to enjoy the full effects), as well as an extraordinarily good sound setup.

arious shows are on offer, including the child-oriented "Secret of the Cardboard Rocket" which explores the solar system; "Pole Position", touring the constellations; nd "Violent Universe", a crash-and-burn account of comets and meteors. Inside here's also an exhibition hall featuring a range of high-tech interactive displays of the osmos, as well as images of deep space and an assortment of meteorite chunks from he Moon and Mars. Outside there's the landscaped Astropark, a series of trails epicting the extent of the solar system in comparison to the known universe – a stroll p the Hill of Infinity leads to its very edge and also offers a glorious view of the city.

Armagh Friary and Demesne Palace

riary Rd · **Armagh Friary ruins** Open access **Demesne Palace** Guided tours July to mid-Sept Thurs–Sat 1.30–2.45pm, Sun 30–4.45pm; pre-booking required · £3 · ☎ 028 3752 1800, ⓦ armagh.co.uk/guidedtours

The ruins of **Armagh Friary**, founded by the Franciscans in 1263, lie within easy walking distance south of the city centre, though they are marred somewhat by the continuous roar of traffic. Nearby is the entrance to the grounds of the Archbishop's Palace, otherwise known as the **Demesne Palace**. Guided tours of the palace (which now houses the District Council offices) take in several of the rooms, as well as the adjacent **Palace Stables**, a well-preserved **ice house**, a curious **tunnel** by which servants accessed the basement kitchens, and a stimulating **sensory garden**. The Palace Stables are also home to a superb restaurant (see p.556).

15

ARRIVAL AND INFORMATION

ARMAGH

By bus The Ulsterbus station (☎ 028 3752 2266) is on Lonsdale Road, just north of the centre.
Destinations Belfast (Mon–Fri hourly, Sat & Sun 7; 1hr 20min); Cavan (Mon–Fri 1 daily; 1hr 30min); Loughgall (Mon–Fri 7 daily; 15min); Markethill (Mon–Fri hourly, Sat 6, Sun 3; 20min); Monaghan (Mon–Fri 10 daily, Sat 7, Sun 3; 30–45min); Navan Fort (Mon–Fri 6 daily; 10min); Newry (Mon–Fri hourly, Sat 7, Sun 3; 35–45min).

Tourist office is in the Old Bank Building, in front of the St Patrick's Trian Centre at 40 English St (April–Sept Mon–Sat 9am–5.30pm, Sun 1–5.30pm; Oct–March Mon–Sat 9am–5pm; ☎ 028 3752 1800, ⓦ www.visitarmagh.com); walking tours of the city operate from here during the summer (June to mid-Sept Thurs–Sat 11.30am–12.45pm, Sun 1.30–2.45pm; 90min; £3; ☎ 028 3752 1800, ⓦ armagh.co.uk/guidedtours).

ACCOMMODATION

Armagh City Hostel 39 Abbey St ☎ 028 3751 1800, ⓦ hini.org.uk. Modern, excellently equipped HINI hostel, superbly situated near the Church of Ireland Cathedral, with small dorms, plus twins and doubles, all en-suite. Lots of good-sized communal areas including a self-catering kitchen, plus laundry and bike storage. March–Oct. Dorms **£19**, doubles **£42**

Armagh City Hotel Friary Rd ☎ 028 3751 8888, ⓦ armaghcityhotel.com. Behind the façade of its soulless exterior, this modern hotel does offer very plush

---

ROAD BOWLS

The sport of **road bowls** is popular in Holland and Germany and was once played throughout Ireland, but is now limited mainly to Cork and Armagh, where it's also known as "road bullets".

The principle of the game is simple: a pair of rival contestants each propels a 28oz (800g) solid-iron ball along a course of country roads (usually about two-and-a-half miles long), the winner being the player who reaches the finishing line with the **fewest number of throws**. In practice, it's a complicated business. The Armagh roads twist and turn, up and down, and bowlers are assisted by a team of camp followers, including managers and road guides who advise on the most advantageous spots to aim for and the force of the throw.

Roads around Armagh where you're likely to catch sight of the game – usually on Sunday afternoons – include Cathedral Road, Knappagh Road, Blackwater Town, Rock, Tassagh, Newtownhamilton and Madden roads. The most reliable information on forthcoming games is probably to be had in local pubs. The **Ulster Finals** are held in the city over two weekends in late June or early July, with the **All-Ireland Road Bowls Final** in early August.

accommodation indeed, but its main business is conferences and weddings, so you'll need to book well in advance. **£80**

Charlemont Arms Hotel 57–65 English St ☎028 3752 2028, ⓦcharlemontarmshotel.com. It doesn't look particularly exciting from the outside, and the rooms are fairly charmless, but this long-established, family-run establishment offers a congenial welcome and it's reasonably priced. **£79**

De Averell Guest House 47 English St ☎028 3751 1213,

ⓦdeaverellhouse.co.uk. The five rooms here don't quite live up to the promise of the building itself – a fine conversion of a town house – but they are restful enough, the hospitality is first rate, and there is also a cosy bar for residents only. **£70**

Fairylands Country House 25 Navan Fort Rd ☎028 3751 0315, ⓦfairylands.net. Very agreeable modern house offering very simply furnished en-suite rooms in a quiet rural setting a mile from the centre. A cracking breakfast is included in what is very reasonably priced accommodation. **£50**

EATING AND DRINKING

1868 2 College Hill ☎028 3751 5353, ⓦ1868restaurant .com. The city's smart option when it comes to eating out is this bare-brick, parquet-floored establishment overlooking The Mall; the creatively thought-out menu features the likes of wild pheasant terrine and timbale of prawn and crab, with perhaps a dessert of toffee apple pie. Tues–Sat noon–3pm & 5–10pm, Sun noon–6pm.

Hole in the Wall Bar 9 Market St ☎028 3752 3515. Dating from the early seventeenth century, this dark, low-beamed inn was the former holding centre for the town's prison. It's the most inviting hostelry around, with great beer, interesting characters and a resident parrot if you're stuck for conversation. Daily 11.30am–11.30pm.

★**The Moody Boar** Palace Stables, Friary Rd ☎028 3752 9678, ⓦthemoodyboar.com. Cleverly integrated within a section of the old stables, this is a super venue, courtesy of its flagstone flooring, alcove seating and floor-to-ceiling windows that open up onto the courtyard. The food is a mix of comfort (herb sausages with mash and creamy peas) and clever (sweet pea panna cotta with crab salad). Tues 10am–4pm, Wed–Sat 10am–4pm &

5–9.30pm, Sun noon–8.30pm.

Seven Hills Bistro 15 Thomas St ☎028 3751 1205. Excellent, three-floored establishment dishing up the city's best coffee, salads and sandwiches, as well as some cracking breakfasts, including pancakes; the retro ground floor is very cool, though for a bit of fun, head to the top floor with its shabby-chic furnishings and chintzy decor. Mon–Sat 8.15am–5pm.

Turner's 57–65 English St ☎028 3752 2719. Attached to the *Charlemont Arms Hotel* (see above), this heavily wooded bar, with snugs and etched-glass partitions, is one of the city's more animated spots, especially on Sat when there's live music. Mon–Thurs & Sun 11.30am–11.30pm, Fri & Sat 11.30am–1am.

Uluru Bistro 16–18 Market St ☎028 3751 8051, ⓦulurubistro.com. The North's only Australian restaurant and a must for anyone keen to explore the delights of marinated kangaroo medallions or various cuts of crocodile and ostrich – the less adventurous will stick with the steaks and seafood. Tues–Sat noon–3pm & 5–10pm, Sun 5–10pm.

ENTERTAINMENT

The Market Place Theatre and Arts Centre Market St ☎028 3752 1820, ⓦmarketplacearmagh.com. A four-hundred-seat auditorium and a smaller studio

theatre, which, between them, host an imaginative programme of theatrical and musical events. There's also a gallery, bar and coffee house.

Navan Fort

2.5 miles west of Armagh • **Fort** Open access • Free **Navan Centre** Daily: April–Sept 10am–6.30pm; Oct–March 10am–4pm • April–Sept £6.20, Oct–March £5.15 • ☎028 3752 9644, ⓦnavan.com • Bus #73 from Armagh (Mon–Fri 6 daily; 10min)

For nearly seven hundred years **Navan Fort** was the great seat of northern power, rivalling Tara in the south. It was here that the kings of Northern Ireland ruled and Queen Macha built her palace on the earthwork's summit. It's a site of deeply mystical significance, but also one of enormous archaeological interest. The court of the **Knights of the Red Branch**, Ireland's most prestigious order of chivalry, was based here too. The knights, like those of the Round Table, are historical figures entirely subsumed into legend, their greatest champion being the legendary defender of Northern Ireland, **Cúchulainn** (see p.155 & p.549). The stories of these warriors' deeds are recited and sung in what's now known as the **Ulster Cycle**. Their dynasty was finally vanquished in 332 AD, when three brothers (the Collas), in a conquest known as the Black Pig's Dyke,

destroyed Navan Fort, razing it to the ground and leaving only the earthen mounds visible today. The defeated Red Branch Knights were driven eastwards into Down and Antrim, and were little heard of again.

The fort stands adjacent to the multimillion-pound **Navan Centre**, which features multimedia displays on archaeology and the legends of the Ulster Cycle. Skirting this building, you'll discover that the site area is defined by a massive bank with a defensive **ditch**. When you reach the fort, you'll find an **earthen mound**, which gives a commanding view but no hint of its past. Excavation of the mound took place over a ten-year period (1961–71) and revealed a peculiar structure, apparently unique in the Celtic world. Archaeologists reckon that around 100 BC the buildings that had existed since the Neolithic period were cleared, and a huge structure 108ft in diameter was constructed. An outer wall of timber surrounded five concentric rings of large posts, 275 in all, with a massive post at the very centre. This was then filled with limestone boulders and **set on fire**, creating a mountain of ash that was then covered with sods of clay to make a high mound. It is anybody's guess what the purpose of the structure was – possibly a temple, or maybe a monumental funeral pyre.

Loughgall and around

LOUGHGALL, a tranquil and pretty estate village about five miles west of Portadown

THE ORANGE ORDER AND THE MARCHING TRADITION

Ireland's oldest political grouping, **The Grand Orange Lodge of Ireland**, was founded in September 1795 following the so-called **Battle of the Diamond**, which took place in or near Dan Winter's farm near **Loughgall**. The skirmish involved the Peep O'Day boys (Protestants) and the Defenders (Catholics) and was the culmination of a long-running dispute about control of the local linen trade. The Defenders attacked an inn, unaware that, inside, the Peep O'Day boys were armed and waiting. A dozen Defenders were killed, and in the glow of victory their opponents formed the Orange Order.

The first Orange Lodge march in celebration of the 1690 **Battle of the Boyne** (see p.585) took place in 1796, and they've been happening ever since. The Boyne is the Loyalist totem, even though the actual battle at Aughter that ended Jacobite rule did not take place until the following year. **William of Orange** is their icon, despite the fact that his campaign was supported by the pope and most of the Catholic rulers of Europe, and that William himself had a noted reputation for religious tolerance. For Protestant Northern Irish, the Boyne came to represent a victory that enshrined Protestant supremacy and liberties, and the Orange Order became the bedrock of Protestant hegemony. Between 1921 and 1969, for example, 51 of the 54 ministers appointed to the Stormont government were members of the Orange Order; at its peak, so were two-thirds of the Protestant male population of the North.

The **Loyalist** "marching season" begins in March and culminates in celebration of the **Battle of the Boyne** on July 12, followed by the **Apprentice Boys'** traditional march around the walls of Derry on August 12. Most Loyalist marches are uncontentious – small church parades, or commemorations of the Somme – but it can't be denied that some of them are something other than a vibrant expression of cultural identity. Marching can be a means by which one community asserts its dominance over the other – Loyalists selecting routes that deliberately pass through Nationalist areas, for instance, or their "Kick the Pope" fife-and-drum bands deliberately playing sectarian tunes and making provocative gestures such as the raising of five fingers on Belfast's **Lower Ormeau Road** (where five Catholics were shot dead in 1992). Though Loyalist marches have tended to be the flashpoints for major disturbances in recent years, not least in the late 1990s at **Drumcree** near Portadown, it shouldn't be forgotten that the marching tradition is common to both communities. Around three thousand marches take place throughout Northern Ireland each year and, although the vast majority are Loyalist parades, a significant number are **Nationalist**. The latter include the St Patrick's Day (March 17) marches of the Ancient Order of Hibernians and the Irish National Foresters, and commemorative parades and wreath-laying ceremonies by Sinn Féin and other Republican bodies on Easter Monday and various anniversaries.

(and the same distance north of Armagh along the B27), lies in the middle of apple-orchard country, beautiful in the spring, and is worth visiting mainly for its historical connections. Like many of its neighbours in Armagh's rural north, Loughgall is strongly **Protestant**. It was three miles northeast of the village at Diamond Hill that the Battle of the Diamond took place in 1795, which led to the foundation of the first Protestant **Orange Order** (see box opposite).

Dan Winter's Cottage

9 Derryloughan Rd • Mon–Sat 10.30am–5.30pm, Sun 2–5.30pm • Voluntary donation • ☎ 028 885 1344, Ⓦ danwinterscottage.com

Located a few miles outside of Loughgall is **Dan Winter's Cottage**, which is where the initial discussions regarding the formation of the Orange Order took place (see box, opposite). The cottage itself – whose roof still contains original lead shot from the Battle of the Diamond – dates from 1703, and has been the ancestral home ever since Dan Winter lived here. Inside, you can see maps and relics from the battle, family photos, and a hoard of banners and sashes. There's some notable seventeenth-century furniture here too, including a remarkable French chair believed to have been here during Winter's time.

Ardress House and The Argory

Ardress House Obligatory guided tours hourly Easter week daily 1–6pm; mid-March to June & Sept Sat, Sun & public hols 1–6pm; July & Aug Thurs–Sun 1–6pm • £5 • ☎ 028 8778 4753, Ⓦ ntni.org.uk • **The Argory** Obligatory guided tours hourly Easter week, July & Aug daily noon–5pm; mid-March to May, Sept & Oct Sat & Sun noon–5pm; June Wed–Sun noon–5pm • £5, including grounds • Ⓦ nationaltrust.org.uk • £3.50

Five miles or so north of Loughgall, two National Trust stately homes lie a few miles apart. **Ardress House** is a seventeenth-century manor house with ornate plasterwork by Michael Stapleton, a good collection of paintings, a sizeable working farmyard and wooded grounds.

More enticing, however, is **The Argory**, a fine Neoclassical building dating from 1824 and set in 350 acres by the River Blackwater. The splendid **grounds** include very pleasant gardens, but it's the house that's the real attraction. Built of Caledon stone, its entrance hall features a fine cantilevered staircase, and the rooms contain Victorian and Edwardian furniture among many other period items, including a fabulous cabinet barrel organ. The house is still lit by an original 1906 acetylene gas plant in the stable yard, and during the summer it stages musical events and organized garden walks. Tours provide entertaining anecdotes about the house's erstwhile owners, the McGeough-Bonds.

15

Tyrone and Fermanagh

BEAGHMORE STONE CIRCLES

Tyrone and Fermanagh

Much of inland Northern Ireland is formed by neighbouring Tyrone and Fermanagh, predominantly rural counties whose few sizeable towns, with the exception of Omagh, lie at the eastern and western fringes of the region. Stretching from the shores of the vast Lough Neagh in the east to the Donegal border in the west, Tyrone is primarily a farming country with little evidence of industrialization apart from the neat planters' villages that grew up with the linen industry and a smattering of heavier industries in the towns near Lough Neagh.

The county's chief scenic attractions can be found in the wild and desolate **Sperrin Mountains** in the north, where the village of **Gortin**, on the Ulster Way footpath, makes a good base. The region's towns hold little of interest, though the largest, **Omagh**, is near the **Ulster American Folk Park**, which explores the connections between the Northern Ireland province and the US.

In contrast to Tyrone, **Fermanagh** attracts plenty of visitors – chiefly for its watersports, boating and fishing. Justly famous for the intense beauty of its lakes, much of the landscape is dominated by their waters, which, along with numerous rivers, constitute more than a third of the county's area. At its core is **Lough Erne**, a huge lake complex dotted with islands and surrounded by richly beautiful countryside. Lower Lough Erne, in the northwest, draws the most visitors, but the Upper Lough in the southeast also has its attractions, its hills wooded with oak, ash and beech. There are plenty of opportunities for watersports, while the less energetic can get onto the lough by renting a boat or taking a cruise. Walkers will find mostly gentle hills and woods which rise to small mountains in the south and west of the county, made accessible by the **Ulster Way**. For cyclists, there are well-surfaced, empty roads, though routes around the Upper Lough are harder to negotiate, with little lanes often leading to the reed-filled shore – an atmospheric spot for a picnic.

At the point where the Upper and Lower loughs meet, the county town of **Enniskillen** has long been a strategic bridging point: today, with more amenities than the rest of Fermanagh put together, it makes an ideal base for touring the area and getting out on the water. With your own transport you can easily access Fermanagh's impressive series of **planters' castles**, while two of the county's stately houses, **Florence Court** and **Castle Coole**, are open to the public.

GETTING AROUND TYRONE AND FERMANAGH

In both Tyrone and Fermanagh, the sights of interest are dispersed, and buses can be very infrequent away from the main routes – you're likely to see little of the most interesting parts of the region without a car or a bike. In the Sperrins, hiking is the best way to get around, although sporadic buses also serve the area.

Omagh and around

The name of Tyrone's largest town, **OMAGH**, is synonymous with the worst single atrocity in the history of the Troubles when, on the afternoon of Saturday August 15,

LOUGH NEAGH

Highlights

❶ The Sperrin Mountains Ruggedly picturesque, the Sperrins offer a splendid variety of hikes and trails. **See p.566**

❷ Beaghmore Stone Circles Seven Bronze Age stone circles and numerous other relics set in a lonely spot with tremendous views. **See p.567**

❸ Lough Neagh Ireland's largest lake – and indeed the biggest in the British Isles – is best viewed from the churchyard at Ardboe. **See p.568**

❹ Castle Coole Perhaps the most magnificent building of its kind in Northern Ireland, this

gorgeous eighteenth-century mansion is richly decorated inside and set in wonderful grounds. **See p.572**

❺ Devenish Island Getting out on the water is an essential part of any trip to Fermanagh, and there's no better place to do it than at this former monastic settlement in Lower Lough Erne. **See p.574**

❻ Marble Arch Caves Take a boat trip along a subterranean river to view these caves filled with stalactites and other marvellous rock formations. **See p.578**

HIGHLIGHTS ARE MARKED ON THE MAP ON P.564

1998, a five-hundred-pound **car bomb**, planted by the dissident Republican group the Real IRA, exploded on Market Street. Twenty-nine people died and more than two hundred were injured. Much of the eastern part of Omagh's main street was devastated by the bombing and has since undergone major reconstruction.

Two sites that recall that day form part of the **Town Trail**, which is well worth an hour or so of your time; a copy of the trail can be picked up at the tourist office. At the bottom of Market Street, a 13ft-high, cenotaph-like **Glass Pillar** – with a three-dimensional heart inside – stands at the point where the bomb exploded, next to a plaque on the wall. From here, head across the Strule Bridge to the **Memorial Garden**.

The area uphill to the west contains two adjacent buildings that would grace any town – the fine classical **courthouse**, adorned with a splendid Tuscan columned portico; and the irregular twin spires of the Catholic **Sacred Heart Church** – inside, take a look at the Rose Window above the high altar. Though there's little else to see in the town itself, it's a useful place to base yourself for exploring the area.

Memorial Garden

Despite the traffic rushing by, the **Memorial Garden** is an affecting place, a beautifully landscaped park with the names of all those who died engraved on a semicircular

granite wall. High above the park, thirty-one pole-mounted mirrors are strategically placed, so that when the sun shines, they direct light on to the glass pillar, a rather ingenious feat of engineering.

ARRIVAL AND INFORMATION

OMAGH AND AROUND

By bus The bus station (☎ 028 8224 2711) is just across the river from the town centre in Mountjoy Road.
Destinations An Creagán Centre (Mon–Fri 2 daily; 40min); Belfast (Mon–Sat hourly, Sun 5; 1hr 50min); Derry (Mon–Sat hourly, Sun 6; 1hr 10min); Dublin (Bus Éireann; 7 daily; 2hr); Enniskillen (Mon–Fri 6–7 daily, Sat 3, Sun 1; 1hr); Gortin (Mon–Fri 9 daily; 25min); Letterkenny (Bus Éireann;

7 daily; 1hr 5min); Monaghan (Bus Éireann; 10 daily; 45min); Ulster American Folk Park (Mon–Sat hourly, Sun 5; 15min).
Tourist office On the ground floor of the riverside Strule Arts Centre on Townhall Square, just west of the bus station (Mon–Sat 10am–5.30pm; ☎ 028 8224 7841, ⓦ omagh .gov.uk).

ACCOMMODATION AND EATING

Bistro 19 19 High St ☎ 028 8225 7772. As good a spot as any in town to stop for a bite to eat (snacks and hot lunches) or a coffee, this popular place has a sunny floral interior with leather couches and big bay windows looking out onto the street. Mon–Sat 8.30am–5pm.

★**Mullaghmore** Old Mountfield Rd ☎ 028 8224 2314, ⓦ mullaghmorehouse. A mile or so down the Cookstown road, this listed Georgian house – birthplace of actor Sam Neill (*Jurassic Park*) – reeks of history and character; the six rooms are packed with some extraordinary features, such as a marble steam room or an Adams fireplace, not to mention some priceless antiques like Meissen porcelain. When you're not enjoying all that, you can make use of the

library, orangery and games room, complete with full-size snooker table. **£80**
The Riverfront Café 38 Market St ☎ 028 8225 0011. Directly opposite the glass pillar memorial, this is a cosy hideaway for a quiet mug of coffee and slice of cake, or perhaps a warming lunch; super homemade ice cream too. Mon–Sat 8.30am–5pm.
Silverbirch Hotel 5 Gortin Rd ☎ 028 8224 2520, ⓦ silverbirchhotel.com. Although aimed largely at the business end of things, this rather ungainly low-rise, out on the Gortin road, is the only hotel in town and the rooms offer a high level of comfort. Some good deals available too. **£79**

ENTERTAINMENT

Dún Úladh Cultural Heritage Centre Drumnakilly Rd, two miles east of town off the B4 ☎ 028 8224 2777, ⓦ dunuladh.ie. Fabulously vibrant regional centre that promotes traditional Irish music and culture, with some big names; there's also a traditional session on Saturday nights.

Strule Arts Centre Townhall Square ☎ 028 8224 7831, ⓦ struleartscentre.co.uk. Stages a lively programme of music, drama and other events, and has a regular roster of excellent touring companies.

16

The Ulster American Folk Park

Mellon Rd, Castletown • March–Sept Tues–Sun & bank holidays 10am–5pm; Oct–Feb Tues–Fri 10am–4pm, Sat & Sun 11am–4pm; last admission 1hr 30min before closing • £9 • ☎ 0845 608 0000, ⓦ nmni.com/uafp • Bus #92 to Strabane or bus #273 Belfast to Derry from Omagh

The most successful of Northern Ireland's American-heritage projects is the wonderful **Ulster American Folk Park**. The first significant emigration from Ireland to North America was that of Northern Irish folk in the early eighteenth century, many of whom were of Scottish Protestant origin. Of all the immigrant communities in the United States, it was the Irish who most quickly – and profoundly – made their mark; the three first-generation US presidents of Irish origin were all of Ulster stock, and thirteen overall could trace their roots to here. Throughout the eighteenth and nineteenth centuries, thousands of people left to establish new lives in North America, a steady flow of emigrants that became a torrent during the Famine years.

You can find detailed information on the causes and patterns of migration in the indoor **gallery** which, regrettably, pays little attention to the Native Americans dispossessed by the Northern Ireland settlers. But the real attractions lie outside in the park itself, where original buildings have been transplanted or replicas constructed to provide a sense of Northern Irish life in the past. The disparity in living conditions in nineteenth-century Ireland is illustrated by the juxtaposition of a typical pre-Famine single-room cabin, from the Sperrins, with the **Mellon Homestead**, a significantly more substantial dwelling from which the local Mellon family migrated in 1818; indeed, it was one of the sons, Thomas, who set up the Mellon Bank in 1869 in Pennsylvania, which now trades as The Bank of New York Mellon. Look out, too, for the **Hughes House**, the one-time home of John Hughes, another successful émigré who became the first Catholic Archbishop of New York in 1842, though if his nickname, "Dagger John", was anything to go by, not a particularly popular one; one peculiar feature of this house is the "jamb" wall, a single brick wall between front door and hearth which prevented draughts, as well as offering a degree of privacy.

A re-created Ulster **street**, including the impressively authentic Reilly's Spirit Grocers, whose shelves are packed with appropriate period stock, leads to the *Union*, a full-sized **brig**, reconstructed to demonstrate the gruelling conditions endured during the voyage across the Atlantic. An American street leads to edifices constructed by the Pennsylvanian settlers, including a massive six-roomed log **farmhouse**. There are plenty of other buildings, and you'll meet costumed guides and craftworkers ready to explain their activities and answer questions, augmenting the folk park's attention to authenticity. One event of note here is the annual **Bluegrass Festival** over the first weekend in September.

ACCOMMODATION AND EATING

ULSTER AMERICAN FOLK PARK

Mellon Country Inn Castletown ☎028 8166 1224, ⓦmelloncountryhotel.com. If you fancy staying in the area, this stylish inn, just a mile away from the Folk Park, has decently priced rooms, including one adapted for disabled guests, as well as a very accomplished restaurant with both grill and à la carte menus. Noon–3pm & 5–10pm. £80

The Sperrin Mountains

The impressive, undulating **Sperrin Mountains** form the northeastern limits of County Tyrone. Wild, empty and beautiful, they reach 680m at their highest point, yet the smooth and gradually curving slopes give them a deceptively low appearance. The covering of bog and heather only adds to this effect, suggesting nothing more than high, open moorland. For all this, views from the summits are panoramic, and the evenness of texture can make the mountains sumptuous when bathed in evening light. It's impossible not to catch sight of **wildlife**, too. Sparrowhawks and kestrels fly above, and you might see buzzards or the rare hen harrier, attracted by a rich range of prey in a landscape mostly undisturbed by development: the Sperrins teem with assorted

---

WALKING THE SPERRINS

The forty-mile-wide range of the Sperrin Mountains offers good long-distance **walking**, without necessarily involving steep inclines. You can ramble wherever you like, but remember that – despite appearances – these are high mountains, and changeable weather makes them potentially dangerous. A map and compass are essential for serious excursions.

The **Central Sperrins Way** (map available from most tourist offices) is a 25-mile waymarked trail which begins and ends at Barnes Gap, halfway between Plumbridge and Cranagh. The two-day walk takes in a variety of countryside with spectacular views of the mountains, moorland and Glenelly Valley. The exposed moorland can often be very wet and boggy underfoot and, as there is no accommodation en route, taking a tent is essential.

For those not equipped for the high ground, the **Glenelly and Owenkillen** river valleys run through the heart of this fine countryside from Plumbridge and Gortin respectively and are particularly enjoyable for cyclists; you can pick up a copy of the Sperrins cycling guide from tourist offices.

The **Sperrins Walking Festival** (☎028 7138 2204, ⓦwalkni.com/festivals/sperrins-walking-festival) is held over the first weekend in August and involves various guided daily walks, graded according to difficulty.

mammals, including even the rare Irish hare. Over the years there's been many a tale about the discovery of "gold in them there hills", and you might encounter the occasional panner testing the story's veracity.

Much depopulated over the years, the local sheep-farming community is now sparsely scattered across the region; there are few **facilities** such as shops or pubs and little accommodation, except in Gortin, so planning ahead is essential if you're intending to walk in the mountains.

Gortin

The best base for exploring the Sperrins is the one-street village of **GORTIN**, ten miles north of Omagh. Three miles south of the village is the **Gortin Glen Forest Park** (daily 10am–dusk; cars £3.50), with a five-mile forest drive and various trails leading to viewpoints of the area. For mountain bikers, there are three variously graded trails in the park's northern reaches, above the Glenpark Road. The park's most popular attraction, however, is its herd of **Sika deer**, which are particularly fun to watch in rutting season, typically from the end of September through to November. Gortin Glen is accessible on any bus between Omagh and Gortin (see below).

Beaghmore Stone Circles

Tyrone is peppered with **archeological remains**: there are more than a thousand standing stones in the Sperrins alone, and the county as a whole boasts numerous chambered graves. The most impressive relics are the Bronze Age **Beaghmore Stone Circles**, in the southeast of the Sperrins. From Gortin, take the B46 east onto the A505, from where they're well signposted up a track 3.5 miles north off the road. Although most of the stones on this lonely site are no more than 3ft high, the complexity of the ritual they suggest is impressive: there are seven stone circles, ten stone rows and a dozen round cairns (burial mounds, some containing cremated human remains). All of the circles stand in pairs, except for one, which is filled with over eight hundred upright stones, known as the **Dragon's Teeth**. The alignments correlate to movements of the sun, moon and stars; two of the rows point to sunrise at the summer solstice.

16

An Creagán Visitor Centre

Daily: April–Sept 11am–6.30pm; Oct–March 11am–4.30pm • Free; bike rental £10 per day • ☎ 028 8076 1112, Ⓦ an-creagan.com

Just off the A505, roughly halfway between Omagh and Cookstown, is the **An Creagán Visitor Centre**, modelled on the many surrounding cairns. The centre explores the rare, raised bog terrain all around with interpretive **displays** and signposted **rambling and cycling routes** over the countryside. The farmers driven to these bogs in the eighteenth century made huge efforts to reclaim the soil: there are limekilns from which they treated the reclaimed land, and you can still see their **potato ridges** – these grassed-over Copney spade ridges point back to the devastating Famine of 1845–51 and illustrate the farmers' desperate attempts to survive.

An Creagán is, however, more of a **cultural centre** than a museum, with locals coming along to occasional traditional music concerts, dancing, storytelling and singing events. There's also a bar and restaurant, with the latter particularly popular for Sunday lunch.

ARRIVAL AND DEPARTURE **THE SPERRINS**

By bus The Central Sperrins are tricky to reach without your own transport, but there is the very useful Sperrin Rambler bus (£9), which runs from Omagh throughout the year (currently Mon–Fri 9.35am & 1.15pm, Sat 10.05am & 1.45pm) via Gortin through the Sperrins to Cranagh and on to Magherafelt in Co. Derry (the return service from Magherafelt operates Mon–Fri 9.40am & 1.20pm, Sat 10.10am & 1.50pm).

Destinations Gortin to Omagh (Mon–Fri 8 daily; 30min); An Creagán Centre to Omagh (Mon–Fri 2 daily; 40min).

ACCOMMODATION AND EATING

An Clachan Cottages An Creagán ☎ 028 8076 1112, ⓦ an-creagan.com. Eight self-catering cottages are available in the traditional *clochán* settlement, each one accommodating either one, two or three bedrooms; the open turf fires are supplemented, fortunately, by central heating. Two-night minimum stay. £180

Foothills 16 Main St, Gortin ☎ 028 8164 8157. You can eat really well at this snug restaurant/bar, where there's contemporary Irish cooking of the highest order; try the

steak with whiskey and blue cheese sauce. Daily noon–10pm.

Gortin Accommodation Suite 62 Main St, Gortin ☎ 028 8164 8346, ⓦ gortincommunity.com. A friendly, multi-functional venue offering a range of self-catering units, six-bed dorms and family rooms sleeping up to four. A variety of on- and off-site activities are available, including canoeing and cycling. Dorms £15, self-catering £75

Eastern Tyrone

The dominant feature in the east of County Tyrone is the western shore of **Lough Neagh**, while there are a number of relics of both the region's historical heritage, such as the high cross at **Ardboe**, and its more recent industrial past at the **Wellbrook Beetling Mill**, close to Cookstown. The village of **Benburb**, to the south, is one of the most attractively situated in the North.

Lough Neagh

According to legend, **Lough Neagh** (pronounced "nay") owes its origins to the mythical giant Fionn Mac Cumhaill, who was so unimpressed by east Tyrone's low-lying terrain that he took a massive lump of land from Ulster and hurled it across the Irish Sea. It landed midway and became the Isle of Man, and the hole it left behind became the lough. Its shores provide excellent fishing and plenty of bird life, though both the surrounding land and lake itself are almost featureless. Small settlements house eel fishermen, whose catches go to the Toome Eel Fishery at **Toome** at the northern tip of the lake.

Ardboe high cross

Slight relief from the featurelessness is to be found at lakeside **Ardboe**, halfway along the lough's western shore, where there's a tenth-century **high cross**. The elements have eroded the various biblical scenes carved onto the sandstone almost beyond recognition, but its exceptional size – almost 20ft high – is impressive. The cross stands in the grounds of an early monastery associated with St Colman, but the ruined church nearby dates from the seventeenth century and is of little interest. On a humid day in early summer, you'll also not fail to be impressed by the swarms of black Lough Neagh mayflies.

Wellbrook Beetling Mill

20 Wellbrook Rd • Mid-March to June & Sept Sat, Sun & public hols 2–6pm; July & Aug Mon–Thurs & Sat 2–6pm • £4 • ☎ 028 8675 1735, ⓦ nationaltrust.org.uk /wellbrook-beetling-mill

Six miles west of Cookstown, on a pretty stretch of the Ballinderry River, stands the **Wellbrook Beetling Mill**, an eighteenth-century water-powered linen mill, and the last functioning one in the country. Harnessing the waters from the river is the superb 16ft waterwheel. "Beetling" was the final stage of production whereby linen was given a sheen and smoothness by hammering with heavy wooden "beetles". Though it ceased operation in 1961, the mill is extremely well preserved, and all the engines still work and can be viewed in action; it's also possible to have a go yourself.

16

Benburb

Seven miles northwest of Armagh (see p.551), the picturesque village of **BENBURB** merits a detour. Main Street's tiny cottages were once apple-peeling sheds, and the parish **church**, dating from 1618, is one of the oldest still in regular use in Ireland. It stands next to the gates of a **Servite priory** – the monastic order of Servants of the Virgin, which, though founded in Florence in 1233, did not establish itself in Ireland until 1948. The priory grounds offer a pleasant stroll, but far better are the walks along the Blackwater River in **Benburb Valley Park** (daily 9am–dusk; free), accessed from Main Street, where, perched on a rock 30m or so above the water, are the substantial remains of a **castle** built by Viscount Powerscourt in 1615, which offer commanding views of the Blackwater valley.

Enniskillen and around

A pleasant, conservative little town, **ENNISKILLEN** sits on an island like an ornamental buckle, the two narrow ribbons of water that pass each side connecting the Lower and Upper lough complexes. The strategic strength of this position has long been recognized – indeed, the town takes its name from Innis Ceithleann, "the island of Kathleen", wife of Balor (see p.443), who sought refuge here after a defeat in battle. Later the island became a Maguire stronghold before William Cole, a planter from Cornwall, was appointed governor in 1607. The town played a major role in the 1641 Rebellion and the later Williamite Wars, the latter leading to the formation of its two famous regiments, the **Inniskilling Dragoons** and the **Royal Inniskilling Fusiliers**, which played a significant role in the victory at the Battle of the Boyne. Much of Enniskillen's character comes from wealth derived from the care of a colonial presence, and evidence of British influence is widespread, not least in the stately **Portora Royal School**, which serves as a reminder of the continued elitism in the social order. Founded by Charles I in 1626, old boys include **Oscar Wilde** – the pride of the school, until his trial for homosexuality – and **Samuel Beckett**, after whom the town's most prestigious festival is named (see p.573).

16

   However, the name Enniskillen is still often associated with one of the most devastating atrocities of the Troubles: on Remembrance Day 1987, an IRA **bomb** killed eleven and injured 61 people as they gathered to commemorate the dead of the two world wars. The resulting widespread outrage was instrumental in directing parts of the Republican movement towards seeking a political solution to the Troubles. Today, Enniskillen is worthy of a day's visit in its own right, with its **castle** and proximity to the elegant **Castle Coole**, plus a town centre relatively unspoilt by shopping developments. It's also ideally situated as a base for exploring Lough Erne and touring the attractive local countryside.

The main street

The centre invites strolling: the main street undulates gently, lined with sturdy Victorian and Edwardian town houses, thriving shops and smart pub fronts, and, clustered together, three fine **church** buildings – Church of Ireland, Catholic and Methodist. This street changes its name five times between the bridges at either end, running from Ann Street to East Bridge Street; to either side, lanes drop down towards the water. On Down Street, just off the High Street, pop your head into the **Buttermarket** (Mon–Sat 10am–5.30pm), a superbly renovated dairy-market dating from 1835 that's now a craft and design centre where a range of artisans – potters, jewellers, woodturners and the like – happily ply their trade.

ENNISKILLEN

CAFÉS & RESTAURANTS

Ardhowen Theatre	7
Café Merlot	2
Dollakis	4
Franco's	3
Jolly Sandwich	1
The Terrace	6

PUBS & BARS

Blakes of the Hollow	2
Corner Bar	5

ACCOMMODATION

Belmore Court and Motel	5
Blaney Caravan and Camping	1
Enniskillen Hotel	2
Lackaboy Farm Guesthouse	3
Westville Hotel	4

Omagh & Trory Point

Forthill Park

Cole's Monument

Erneside Shopping Center

Buttermarket

Bus Station

C. of I. Church

Headhunters

Methodist Church

R. C. Church

Enniskillen Castle & Fermanagh County Museum

River Erne

Castle Island

MILL STREET

IRVINESTOWN ROAD

FORTHILL STREET

BELMORE STREET

WELLINGTON ROAD

DERRY CHARA LINK

DUBLIN ROAD (A4)

TEMPO ROAD

QUEEN ELIZABETH ROAD

EAST BRIDGE STREET

TOWNHALL STREET

WATER STREET

DOWN STREET

HIGH STREET

PAGET LANE

PAGET SQUARE

CHURCH STREET

DARLING STREET

ANN STREET

WELLINGTON ROAD

Donegal, & Round "O" Jetty

Sligo

16

0 yards 100

3 ▲

R.B. Castle Coole

Headhunters

5 Daring St • Tues–Sat 9am–5.30pm • Free • ☎ 028 6632 7488, ⓦ headhuntersmuseum.com

"The Barber Shop with a difference" is how **Headhunters** styles itself – and indeed, this barber shop-cum-railway museum is quite unique. Entering the shop up on the first floor, you'll immediately be struck by the rather surreal sight of customers having a haircut amid a wonderful clutter of **railway memorabilia**, including locomotive nameplates, station signs and photos. Beyond the shop itself, several rooms offer up a voluminous array of exhibits – signalling equipment, lamps, timetables, tickets and so on – that recall the heyday of the long-defunct Great Northern Railway, which closed in 1958; ask, too, to see the fabulous model railway up on the second floor. And if you fancy a trim afterwards…

Enniskillen Castle

Waterways loop their way around the core of Enniskillen, their glassy surfaces imbuing the town with a pervasive sense of calm and in places reflecting the mini-turrets of seventeenth-century **Enniskillen Castle**, which stands next to the island's westerly bridges. The castle was rebuilt by William Cole on the site of an old Maguire fort damaged by siege in 1594, and Cole's additions show obvious Scottish characteristics in the turrets corbelled out from the angles of the main wall.

Fermanagh County Museum

Mon 2–5pm, Tues–Fri 10am–5pm; also April–Oct Sat 2–5pm, plus July & Aug Sun 2–5pm • £4 • ☎ 028 6632 5000, ⓦ enniskillencastle.co.uk

Today, the old barracks house the **Fermanagh County Museum**, which covers in some depth the region's history mainly through agricultural and archaeological displays, though the most worthwhile section is the collection of Belleek pottery (see p.576), starring a terracotta water cooler with gilded ceramic beads.

16

Regimental Museum of the Royal Inniskilling Fusiliers

Same hours and ticket

Occupying the adjacent keep is the more enjoyable **Regimental Museum of the Royal Inniskilling Fusiliers**, a proud and polished display of the uniforms, flags and paraphernalia of the town's historic regiment; formed in 1881 as an Irish infantry regiment of the British Army, the Fusiliers amalgamated with the Royal Ulster Rifles and the Royal Irish Fusiliers to form the Royal Irish Rangers in 1968, before their latest reincarnation, in 1992, as part of the Royal Irish Regiment.

THE KINGFISHER CYCLING TRAIL

Enniskillen is a good starting point for the 300-mile-plus **Kingfisher Cycling Trail** (ⓦ kingfishercycletrail.com), whose circular route skirts Lower Lough Erne to Belleck and then south to Blacklion before running through the Leitrim lakelands to Carrick-on-Shannon (see p.410), then east to Belturbet in County Cavan (see p.160), and back, via Clones in County Monaghan (see p.157), around the Upper Lough to Enniskillen. The route passes through a wonderful variety of countryside, and though some of the hills are pretty steep, they are rarely too arduous to deter cyclists. You can either bring your own bike and plan your own accommodation, or take advantage of various **tour packages** available (visit the website for details). Tours include two- or three-day short breaks and longer six- to eight-day casual, active or challenging rides. Accommodation is usually in B&Bs (though you can choose to stay in hotels or hostels), 18-speed bikes and essential equipment are provided, and your luggage is transported to and from each night's stop.

Castle Coole

House 11am–5pm: mid-March to May & Sept Sat & Sun; Easter week & June–Aug daily; guided tours hourly, last tour starts 1hr before closing; grounds open daily: March–Oct 10am–7pm; Nov–Feb 10am–4pm • House and grounds £5; grounds only £3 per car; Heritage Island • ☎ 028 6632 2690, ⓦ nationaltrust.org.uk/castle-coole • The house can be approached either from the Dublin road (signposted just opposite the Ardhowen Theatre) or across the golf course from the Castlecoole road

Evidence of how the richest of the Enniskillen colonists lived is found about a mile southeast of the town centre at **Castle Coole**, designed by James Wyatt and completed in 1798 as the lakeside home of the Earls of Belmore. A perfect Palladian-fronted building of silver Portland stone, the mansion is part of a huge seven-hundred-acre estate, whose beautiful landscaped **grounds** feature an impressive avenue of stately oak trees and a wealth of woodland walks. Inside, the **house** features scagliola columns, exquisite plasterwork, a cantilevered staircase, a state bedroom decorated for George IV (who didn't actually come – the room was never subsequently used), Hogarth prints and an elegant library boasting Regency furnishings and fireplaces. The informative **guided tour** is well worth taking.

ARRIVAL AND INFORMATION
ENNISKILLEN AND AROUND

By bus Enniskillen's bus station is on Wellington Rd (☎ 028 6632 2633), a block south of the High St.

Destinations Ballyshannon (Bus Éireann; 7 daily; 50min); Belcoo (Mon–Fri 3 daily, Sat 3; 25min); Belfast (Mon–Fri hourly, Sat 7, Sun 4; 2hr 15min); Belleek (Bus Éireann; 7 daily; 35min); Belturbet (Bus Éireann; 8 daily; 30min); Blacklion (Bus Éireann; Mon–Sat 4 daily, Sun 2; 25min); Cavan (Bus Éireann; 8 daily; 50min); Clones (Mon–Sat 5 daily; 55min); Derrygonnelly (Mon–Fri 5 daily, Sat 1; 20min); Donegal town (Bus Éireann; 8 daily; 1hr 10min); Florence Court (Mon–Sat 2–3 daily; 15min); Lisnarick (Mon–Sat 3–4 daily; 20–35mins); Lisnaskea (Mon–Fri 8 daily, Sat 5; 30min); Omagh (Mon–Fri 6 daily, Sat 3, Sun 1; 1hr); Pettigo (Mon–Sat 4–5 daily; 40min–1hr); Sligo (Bus Éireann; Mon–Sat 4 daily, Sun 2; 1hr 25min).

Tourist office The tourist office is across from the bus station on Wellington Rd (all year Mon–Fri 9am–5.30pm, July & Aug to 7pm; also April–Sept Sat 10am–6pm, Sun 11am–5pm; ☎ 028 6632 3110, ⓦ fermanaghlakelands .com). You can get fishing licences and permits here, and book a place on one of the summer guided tours of the town or Lough Erne (May–Sept Thurs–Sat 11am; 1hr; £5). The Round "O" Jetty for lough cruises (see box, p.575) is signposted off the Derrygonnelly road northwest of town.

ACCOMMODATION

★**Belmore Court and Motel** Tempo Rd ☎ 028 6632 6633, ⓦ motel.co.uk. There's a decent choice of different accommodation here in this super-friendly hotel/motel; the original motel building offers doubles, twins and family rooms, all with kitchenettes for self-catering, while the hotel itself has coolly furnished rooms with all mod-cons. Hotel £85, motel £65

Blaney Caravan and Camping Park 8 miles to the northwest off the A46 directly behind the Blaney service station ☎ 028 6864 1634, ⓦ blaneycaravanpark .com. A beautifully situated and well-equipped campsite that's ideal for families. Mid-March to Oct. Tent pitch £22

Enniskillen Hotel 72 Forthill St ☎ 028 6632 1177, ⓦ enniskillenhotel.com The building exterior is unremittingly dull, but the rooms looks fabulous in their various shades of grey, from the carpets and upholstery right down to the light switches; the only exception to the grey is the individually painted wall mural in each room. £85

Lackaboy Farm Guesthouse 51 Old Tempo Rd ☎ 028 6632 2488, ⓦ lackaboyhouse.com. Good-quality B&B in a rural setting a mile northeast of town, whose six florally patterned, en-suite rooms promise a restful stay. Guest lounge with large flatscreen TV and open fire, plus lovely little extras like homemade traybakes upon arrival. £60

Westville Hotel 14–20 Tempo Rd ☎ 028 6632 0033, ⓦ westvillehotel.co.uk. The grey, rough-hewn exterior is far from enticing, but this is actually a sparkling little boutique hotel offering tastefully designed rooms in warming chocolate brown and beige colours; a fine restaurant too (see opposite). £80

EATING AND DRINKING

Enniskillen has a fine coterie of restaurants and cafés, and there's certainly no shortage of cheerful pubs and bars, many of which keep late hours, especially in the summer months.

Ardhowen Theatre Dublin Rd. A mile south of town, this theatre's (see opposite) restaurant and bar are worth a visit for the waterside setting – perfect for a bite after visiting Castle Coole. Mon–Sat 10am–6pm.

Blakes of the Hollow 6 Church St ☎ 028 6632 2143. This agreeably careworn Victorian establishment should be your first port of call for a pint, its dark wooden snugs perfect for cosying up in. Live music on Fridays and

16

ENNISKILLEN FESTIVALS

The town's chief annual event is the Samuel Beckett-inspired **Happy Days Festival** (ⓦ happy-days-enniskillen.com) during the first ten days of August, which celebrates the eponymous novelist and playwright with a fantastic multi-arts programme of theatre, music, talks and readings in venues as diverse as the Buttermarket (see p.569) and the Marble Arch Caves (see p.578). **Fermanagh Live** (ⓦ flive.org.uk), at the end of September, is a vibrant festival of high-class music, drama and visual arts. Otherwise, there's the **Enniskillen Drama festival** in March, hosted by the Ardhowen Theatre, while you should check with the tourist office for dates of the county **Fleadh**, the competitive traditional-music festival, in June (though it sometimes takes place in Derrygonnelly).

Saturdays, which could be either rock and pop or traditional. Daily 11.30am–midnight.

★**Café Merlot** 6 Church St ☎028 6632 0918. Quartered inside the old bottling cellar of the *Blakes of the Hollow* pub, this warm and welcoming white-brick vaulted restaurant is by some distance the town's standout place to eat; fresh and thoughtfully created dishes like smoked Toulouse sausage with sautéed onion and chasseur sauce (£16.95), and white and brown crab pâté with smoked mackerel hummus, ensure that Merlot is always packed to the rafters. Daily noon–3pm & 5.30–9pm.

Corner Bar 22 Townhall St ☎028 6632 6645. Traditional music sessions are few and far between in Enniskillen, but the spirited little *Corner Bar* has a regular Thursday-night session that's one of the best nights in town. Daily 11am–11pm.

Dollakis 2b Cross St ☎028 6634 2616, ⓦ dollakis.com. Three separate menus comprise this brilliantly authentic Greek restaurant's offering: a lunch menu (noon–3pm) followed, between 5 and 7pm, by a meze menu, after which the à la carte menu is wheeled out; expect beautifully prepared classics like lamb moussaka, or a

mixed grill with Greek potatoes and Greek salad (£17.95), then round it off with a glass of Metaxa or frozen ouzo. Tues–Sat noon–3pm & 5–11pm.

Franco's Queen Elizabeth Rd ☎028 6632 4424, ⓦ francosrestaurant.co.uk. With more pizzas (£10.95) than it's possible to contemplate, plus all manner of steak and fish options, you're certainly spoilt for choice at this rustic, wildly colourful restaurant; the three-course early-bird menu (Mon–Fri noon–7pm; £20.95) is good value. Daily noon–11pm.

Jolly Sandwich 3 Darling St ☎028 6632 2277. Jolly by name, jolly by nature, this busy, buzzy daytime café/deli, laid out with dinky tables and bar stools, serves all-day breakfasts, hot wraps, cupcakes and coffee. Mon–Sat 7am–6pm.

The Terrace 14–20 Tempo Rd ☎028 6632 0333. The turquoise and gold furnished interior of the *Westville Hotel*'s sleek restaurant is an appropriately sophisticated setting for dishes such as sea bass with curry foam; the open-plan kitchen is fun too, and the only downside is the restaurant's limited opening times. Fri & Sat 6–11pm.

16

ENTERTAINMENT

Ardhowen Theatre Dublin Rd ☎028 6632 5440, ⓦ ardhowentheatre.com. The hub of Enniskillen's arts scene has a year-round programme of top-quality

drama, film and ballet, and hosts a great range of music events as well as productions by local community groups.

Lough Erne

Lough Erne has a profoundly important place in the history of Fermanagh. The earliest people to settle in the region lived on and around the two lakes, and many of the islands here are in fact *crannógs*. The lough's myriad connecting waterways were impenetrable to outsiders, protecting the settlers from invaders and creating an enduring cultural isolation. Evidence from stone carvings suggests that Christianity was accepted far more slowly here than elsewhere: several **pagan idols** have been found on Christian sites, and the early Christian remains to be found on the islands show the strong influence of pagan culture. Here, Christian carving has something of the stark symmetry, as well as a certain vacancy of facial expression, found in pagan statues. Particularly suggestive of earlier cults is the persistence of the human-head motif in stone carving – in pagan times a symbol of divinity and the most important of religious symbols.

Devenish Island and **White Island**, the most popular of the Erne's ancient sites, are on the Lower Lough, as is **Boa Island** in its far north, which is linked to the mainland by a bridge at each end. The **Upper Lough** is less rewarding, but has interesting spots that repay a leisurely dawdle. Aside from **cruising** the waterways (see box, opposite) and visiting the islands, there are a number of minor attractions around the loughs that are worth dropping into during your stay. Perhaps the most impressive are the early seventeenth-century planters' **castles** scattered around the shoreline.

Devenish Island

Heading around the eastern shores of Lower Lough Erne, **Devenish Island** is the easiest place to visit from Enniskillen without your own transport. A monastic settlement was founded on Devenish by St Molaise in the sixth century and became so important during the early Christian period that it had 1500 novices attached. Though plundered by Vikings in the ninth and twelfth centuries, it continued to be a major religious centre up until the early 1600s. It's a delightful setting, not far from the lough shore, and the **ruins** are considerable, spanning the entire medieval period. Most impressive are the sturdy oratory and perfect round tower, both from the twelfth century; St Molaise's church, a century older; and the ruined Augustinian priory, a fifteenth-century reconstruction of an earlier abbey with a fine Gothic sacristy door decorated with birds and vines. To the south is a superb **high cross**, with highly complex, delicate carving. Other treasures found here – such as an early eleventh-century book shrine, the Soiscel Molaise – are now kept in the National Museum in Dublin (see p.63), while the island's own small **museum** (July & Aug daily 10am–5pm; included in price of ferry) includes other less notable relics and detailed information about Devenish itself.

16

ARRIVAL AND DEPARTURE   DEVENISH ISLAND

Ferries run to the island from Trory Point, around four miles north of Enniskillen off the A32 Irvinestown road (July & Aug daily 10am, 1pm, 3pm & 5pm; May, June & Sept advanced booking is required; £3; ☎028 6862 1588 or ☎077 0205 2873), though it's wise to check times with the tourist office before setting out, as poor weather can sometimes delay or cancel departures. To get to Trory Point from Enniskillen, take the Omagh bus to the Kesh turn-off.

Castle Archdale Country Park

Near Lisnarick, about ten miles north of Enniskillen, off the B82 Kesh road • **Park** Daily: April & May 9am–7pm, June–Sept 9am–9pm, Oct–March 9am–4.30pm; visitor centre April & May Sat & Sun 1–5pm, June–Sept daily 10am–5pm, Oct–March Sat noon–4pm • Free • ☎028 6862 1588 • The only public transport is the Pettigo bus to Lisnarick, two miles away • **Campsite** April–Oct • pitch £20 • ☎028 6862 1333, ⓦ castlearchdale.com **Boat rental** half-day £55, full day £80 • ☎028 6862 1892 • **Bike rental** £12 per day • ☎028 6862 1892

To immerse yourself thoroughly in the beauty of the lough scenery, it's well worth making a trip to **Castle Archdale Country Park**. The eighteenth-century manor house, on which the estate is centred, houses tearooms and a small **visitor centre**, whose exhibits focus on local wildlife and Castle Archdale's role during World War II when flying boats were based here. The park is also perfectly placed for getting out on the lough and has its own **campsite**, which has a small supermarket and a café in high season. The **ferry** to White Island (see below) leaves from the nearby marina, and you can also **rent boats** and **bikes** here between Easter and September.

White Island

A ferry from Castle Archdale Country Park marina runs to White Island July & Aug daily 10.30am, 11.30am, 2.30pm, 3.30pm, 4.30pm; call in advance for travel on the ferry outside these months • £3 • ☎028 6862 1156

Mounted on the wall of a **ruined abbey**, the seven early Christian carvings of **White Island** look eerily pagan. Discovered early in the nineteenth century, they are thought to be caryatids – columns in human form – from a monastic church of the ninth to

---

LOUGH ERNE CRUISES AND RENTALS

The MV *Kestrel*, run by Erne Tours (May, Sept & Oct Tues, Sat & Sun 2.15pm & 4.15pm; June daily 2.15pm & 4.15pm; July & Aug daily 10.30am, 12.15pm, 2.15pm & 4.15pm; 1hr 45min; ☎028 6632 2882, 🌐ernetours.com; £10), sails from the **Round "O" Jetty** northwest of Enniskillen (see opposite) around the Lower Lough, calling at Devenish Island. There are also additional evening **dinner cruises** to the *Killyhevlin Hotel* on the Upper Lough shore (May–Sept Sat 6.30pm, return at 10pm; £25, booking essential). The *Inishcruiser* sails around the Upper Lough from the **Share Discovery Village** (see p.577) at Smith's Strand (Easter–Sept Sun & public holidays 10.30am; 1hr 30min–2hr; ☎028 6722 2122; £10).

Renting your own boat is another possibility, and there are a number of operators. Most offer open rowing boats, with or without outboard motor, though some have larger 20ft boats available. Prices range accordingly from £20 to £150 for a full day, depending on the operator and boat size. The tourist office in Enniskillen (see p.572) has lists of rental companies and cruisers available for rent (weekly prices in high season range from around £600 for smaller boats to £2000 for 8-berth specials). Unless you're going out on a small lake, you should always let the boat owner know where you're heading and ask to borrow navigation charts – Lough Erne can be dangerous, especially outside the summer months.

---

eleventh centuries. The most disconcerting statue is the lewd female figure known as a **Sheila-na-Gig** (see p.627), one of the best preserved in Ireland. Less equivocal figures continue left to right: a seated Christ holding the Gospels on his knees; a hooded ecclesiast with bell and crozier; David carrying a shepherd's staff, his hand towards his mouth showing his role as author and singer; Christ the Warrior holding two griffins by the scruff of their necks; and another Christ figure with a fringe of curly hair wearing a brooch on his left shoulder and carrying a sword and shield – here he is the King of Glory at his Second Coming. There is an unfinished seventh stone and, on the far right, a carved head with a downturned mouth, which is probably of later origin than the other statues. The **church** of White Island also contains eleventh-century gravestones; the large earthworks round the outside date from an earlier monastery.

Boa Island

Six miles west of Kesh at the northern end of the Lower Lough

One of Lough Erne's most evocative carvings is on **Boa Island** (barely an island at all these days, as it's connected to the mainland by bridges), which takes its name from Badhbh, a Celtic war-goddess. The landmark to look out for is **Caldragh cemetery**, signposted off the A47 about a mile west of Lusty Beg Island. Follow the signs down a lane and the graveyard is through a gate to your left. Here in this ancient Christian burial ground of broken, moss-covered tombstones, encircled and shaded by low hazel trees, you'll find a double-faced **Janus figure**. An idol of yellow stone with very bold, symmetrical features, it has the phallus on one side and a belt and crossed limbs on the other. The figure was probably an invocation of fertility and a depiction of a god-hero, the belt being a reference to the bearing of weapons. Alongside it stands the smaller "**Lusty Man**", so called since it was moved here from nearby Lustymore Island. This idol has only one eye fully carved, maybe to indicate blindness – Cúchulainn (see p.549) had a number of encounters with war-goddesses, divine hags described as blind in the left eye.

ACCOMMODATION AND EATING   BOA ISLAND

Lusty Beg Island ☎028 6863 3300, 🌐lustybegisland .com. Set amid beautiful woodland just off Boa Island, this popular weekend retreat (accessible via a free car ferry; 5min) offers B&B accommodation in its *The Courtyard* guesthouse, lakeside cabins and luxury chalets (sleeping 4–6). First-rate spa facilities, a cracking restaurant and canoe rental augment the appeal of the place. Restaurant daily 12.30–9pm. B&B **£95**, cabins (two nights) **£195**, chalets (two nights) **£245**

16

Dreenan Cottage Boa Island ☎028 6863 1951, ✉fisherdavy@aol.com. A restful and tastefully designed riverside bungalow with en-suite rooms. The owners are a mine of information on the area and have fishing boats for rent. £65

Forest of Castle Caldwell

Over towards the western extremity of Lower Lough Erne, the **forest of Castle Caldwell** is formed by two narrow promontories, which make it a natural breeding site for waterfowl and a habitat of rarities such as the hen harrier, peregrine falcon and pine marten. Its seventeenth-century **castle** has long been dilapidated, and the surrounding estate is now a commercial, state-owned forest of spruce, pine and larch. At the castle's entrance, look out for the giant stone fiddle in front of the gate lodge, the sobering memorial to Denis McCabe, a local musician who in 1770 tumbled from the Caldwells' barge while inebriated and drowned. Its inscription "DDD" supposedly stands for "Denis died drunk!".

Belleek

Five miles west of the forest of Castle Caldwell • **Pottery** Mon–Fri 9am–5.30pm, Sat 10am–5.30pm, Sun 2–5pm (July–Sept noon–5.30pm); tours every 30min 9.30am–12.15pm & 1.45–4pm • £4 • ☎028 6865 8501, ⓦbelleek.ie

BELLEEK owes its fame to the local **Belleek Pottery**, Ireland's oldest, which was established in 1857. The enlightening 45-minute **tour** takes in the various stages of production, from mould making and casting through to fettling – the process of sharpening or delineation of the pattern on the pottery – and dipping, where the glaze is added. As informative as the tour is, you'll be far more distracted by watching the craftsmen and women at work, especially the basket-makers – the level of skill required is quite something; indeed, a typical apprenticeship is anywhere between three and five years. The **museum** exhibits numerous pieces, from early hunting bowls and domestic sanitary ware to more recent decorative items, while the **shop** offers up the chance to buy its extraordinary array of products. There's a lovely tea room here too, where you can sit down to a substantial lunch or a cup of tea and one of their home-baked scones – all served, naturally, in the finest Belleek tableware.

ACCOMMODATION AND EATING
BELLEEK

Moohan's Fiddlestone Main St ☎028 6865 8008. Although it's unlikely you'll need to stop over, the village's main pub does have half a dozen solidly old-fashioned rooms, in addition to a little guest lounge. Otherwise, stop by for a pint. Daily 11am–11pm. Rooms £60

Thatch Café Main St ☎028 6865 8181. Sweet little thatched cottage with an inviting, warm interior with thick-set stone fireplace and wood-burning stove – perfect for coffee, or something from the lunch menu like a baked potato with smoked salmon followed by slice of home-baked blueberry pie. Mon–Sat 9am–5pm.

Monea Castle to Lough Navar Forest

Monea Castle free access • **Tully Castle** June–Sept daily 10am–5pm; Oct–May Sun noon–4pm • Free • **Lough Navar Forest** Daily 10am–dusk • car £3.20

In a beautiful setting at the end of a beech-lined lane, **Monea Castle**, seven miles northwest of Enniskillen off the B81, is a particularly fine ruin of a planters' castle. Built around 1618, it bears the signs of Scottish influence in its design, with similar features to the reworked Maguire Castle in Enniskillen (see p.571). It was seriously damaged first by fire in the Great Rebellion of 1641 and later by Jacobite armies in 1689, and was eventually abandoned in 1750 after another fire. Five miles further north, beyond Derrygonnelly, the fortified house and *bawn* of restored **Tully Castle**, itself burned by the Maguires in 1641, sits down by the lough shore. Further to the west, there are tremendous views of the lough and surrounds from **Lough Navar Forest**.

Upper Lough Erne

Upper Lough Erne possesses neither the historic sites nor the scenic splendour of the Lower Lough, but it does have the best preserved of the planters' castles nearby in the **Crom Estate**. There's little to see in the region's main town, **Lisnaskea**, save for the ruins of **Castle Balfour** (free access), which was built for Sir James Balfour, a Scottish planter, in the early seventeenth century; it manifests strong Scottish characteristics in its turrets and parapets, high-pitched gables and tall chimneys.

Crom Estate

Estate daily mid-March to Oct 10am–6pm; June–Aug till 7pm; **visitor centre** daily 11am–5pm • £3.50 • ☎ 028 6773 8118, ⓦ nationaltrust.org.uk/crom • **Cottages** ⓦ nationaltrustcottages.co.uk • £300–840 per week for 2–6 people

The National Trust's **Crom Estate**, three miles west of Newtownbutler on the eastern shore of the lough, has the largest surviving area of **oak woodland** in Northern Ireland, home to rare species such as the purple hairstreak and wood white butterflies. There's a café and interpretive centre here, and you can rent **rowing boats** too. Unfortunately, the modern Crom Castle is privately occupied and not open to the public, though you can visit the ruins of the **old castle**. The estate has renovated courtyard **cottages** to rent.

INFORMATION AND ACTIVITIES UPPER LOUGH ERNE

Tourist office The Upper Lough Erne region's visitor centre is in Lisnaskea, five miles north of Crom Castle, at 113 Main St (Mon–Fri 9am–5pm, plus June–Aug Sat 10am–4pm; ☎ 028 6772 3590, ⓦ upperlougherneregion.com).

Cruises and activities Should you be tempted to venture further into the lough's maze of reeds and water, there are cruises (see box, p.575) from the Share Discovery Village (Easter–Oct; ☎ 028 6772 2122, ⓦ sharevillage.org) at Smith's Strand, signposted off the Lisnaskea–Derrylin road, which offers a host of water-based activity holidays with facilities for disabled travellers.

ACCOMMODATION AND EATING

Donn Carragh Hotel 95–97 Main St, Lisnaskea ☎ 028 6772 1206, ⓦ donncarragh.com. The only hotel hereabouts provides well-equipped en-suite rooms, nearly all of which are triples, albeit with decor stuck somewhere in the 1980s. **£70**

The Kissin Crust 152 Main St, Lisnaskea ☎ 028 6772 2678. Prettily decorated café with chatty staff and a cracking little menu, including a steaming seafood chowder and a mouthwatering selection of home-baked treats like lemon cheesecake. The afternoon tea (3–4.30pm; £12) is great fun, but does need to be pre-booked. Mon–Sat 8.30am–5pm.

Mullynascarthy Caravan Park Gola Rd, two miles north of Lisnaskea ☎ 028 6772 1040. Picturesquely located on the banks of the Colebrook River, this clean and pleasant site has around ten pitches; facilities include showers, laundry and a play area for kids. April–Oct.

Western Fermanagh

The stretch of countryside on the western edge of the county offers some good **walking** opportunities, particularly in the hills to the south. The **Ulster Way** (see box, p.579), which runs northwest from the Upper Lough and east towards Tyrone, makes the riches of the terrain easily accessible.

This region also has two attractions that are well worth seeking out. The magnificent eighteenth-century **Florence Court** is the most assured achievement of the colonists, built 150 years after the initial defensive planters' castles. If you have your own transport, a visit to the house can be combined with an hour or so at the **Marble Arch Caves**, the finest cave system in Northern Ireland. Walkers can reach both along the Ulster Way, accessible from the A4 near **Belcoo**; the path runs four miles south past **Lower Lough Macnean** to the Marble Arch Caves and then a further five miles east to Florence Court.

16

Florence Court

House 11am–5pm: mid-March to April & Oct Sat & Sun; May & Sept daily except Fri; June–Aug daily • £4.50 • **Gardens and park** daily: March–Oct 10am–7pm; Nov–Feb till 4pm • £4.50 • ☎ 028 6634 8249, ⓦ nationaltrust.org.uk/florence-court • To get to the house from Enniskillen, follow the A4 Sligo road for three miles, branching off on the A32 Swanlinbar road and taking the signposted right turn four miles further on. The only public transport from Enniskillen is the infrequent #192 Swanlinbar and #296 Longford services; ask to be dropped off at Creamery Cross whence it's a two-mile walk to the house

The magnificent three-storey mansion of the National Trust-owned **Florence Court**, about eight miles southwest of Enniskillen, was commissioned by John Cole, one of the Earls of Enniskillen, and named after his wife. The house, completed around 1775, is notable for its restored rococo plasterwork and rare Irish furnishings; the **dining room** is especially lavish, its ceiling hosting a cloud of puffing cherubs with Jupiter disguised as an eagle in the centre, all flying out of a duck-egg-blue sky. Unfortunately, the top floor of the house was completely destroyed by a fire in 1955 and has never been renovated internally. The lush walled **gardens**, meanwhile, feature an ice-house, sawmill, and a delightful thatched summer house, though this is currently undergoing restoration following a fire in 2014.

ACCOMMODATION AND EATING   FLORENCE COURT

Arch House 59 Marble Arch Rd, a 10min walk from Florence Court ☎ 028 6634 8452, ⓦ archhouse.com. Award-winning farmhouse accommodation offering six splendid en-suite rooms and a restaurant serving terrific value lunch-time and early evening meals (till 7pm). The house is extremely welcoming to kids. **£70**

Rose Cottage ⓦ nationaltrustcottages.co.uk. In the Florence Court walled garden, you can stay in this pretty cottage which is well equipped with double and twin bedrooms. Sleeps five. Weekly rate **£370**

Marble Arch Caves

Five miles west of Florence Court • Daily: late March to June & Sept 10am–4.30pm; July & Aug 10am–5pm; Oct 11am–4pm • £8.75 • ☎ 028 6634 8855, ⓦ marblearchcavesgeopark.com

Fermanagh's caves are renowned, and while some are for experts only, the most spectacular system of all, the **Marble Arch Caves**, is accessible to anyone of average fitness or above. The caves are one of seven geoparks in the UK (run under the umbrella of UNESCO), although the Marble Arch Caves Global Geopark – to give it its full title – also incorporates Cavan across the border (see p.161), thus making it the first cross-border geopark in the world.

The caves were first discovered in 1895 by a Frenchman, Edouard Martel, and a Dubliner, Lyster Jameson, though it wasn't until nearly a century later, in 1985, that they opened to the public. Following a pleasant little walk down through the reserve, the **tour** (which lasts around an hour and a quarter) begins with an atmospheric boat journey along a **subterranean river**, then on through brilliantly lit chambers, calcite-walled and dripping with stalactites and fragile mineral veils. In a steady Irish downpour, the caves can be flooded, so check weather reports as well. You'll need sturdy walking shoes and warm clothing as the temperature can drop significantly.

From whichever direction you approach the caves, you'll travel along the **Marlbank Scenic Loop**, with tremendous views of Lower Lough Macnean, and on either side you'll see limestone-flagged fields, much like those of the Burren in County Clare. It was fifty thousand years of gentle water seepage through the limestone that deposited the calcite for the amazing stalactite growths in the caves below.

Legnabrocky Trail and Cuilcagh Mountain

Almost opposite the entrance to the Marble Arch Caves is the **Legnabrocky Trail**, which runs through rugged limestone scenery and peatland to the shale-covered slopes of **Cuilcagh Mountain**. This forms part of an environmental conservation area and offers a strenuous six- or seven-hour walk to the mountain's summit and back (be prepared to

THE ULSTER WAY

From Marble Arch Caves the **Ulster Way** heads past Lower and Upper Lough Macnean before traversing the bog and granite heights of the Cuilcagh Mountains to **Ballintempo Forest** with its fabulous views over the loughs. The Way then continues north, through the **Lough Navar Forest**, a well-groomed conifer plantation with tarmacked roads and shorter trails. Although a great deal of fir-plantation walking is dark and frustrating, this forest does, at points, provide some of the most spectacular views in Fermanagh, looking over Lower Lough Erne and the mountains of surrounding counties. The Lough Navar Forest also sustains a small herd of red deer, as well as wild goat, fox, badger, hare and red squirrel.

The **tourist office** in Enniskillen (see p.572) has copies of the very useful *The Ulster Way: Southwest Section*, which describes in detail the five connected trails constituting the Way's route through the county.

ACCOMMODATION AND EATING

Finding somewhere to stay and eat along the Way is fairly tricky, though there are several possibilities near **Belcoo**, two and a half miles west from the trail's ascent to the Ballintempo Forest, plus one or two options in neighbouring Blacklion (see p.161), over the border in County Cavan.

Bella Vista Cottage Drive, Belcoo ☎028 6638 6469, ⓦbellavista-belcoo.co.uk. A few minutes' walk away from *Customs House*, this pretty little guesthouse has just two rooms, both with views of Lough MacNean. **£70**

Customs House Country Inn 25–27 Main St, Belcoo ☎028 6638 6285, ⓦcustomshouseinn.com. The nine rooms in this charming country house are beautifully designed, with all mod cons and luxury features such as Italian marble and handmade pewter tiling. The restaurant, too, is exceptional, with very reasonably priced dishes such as salmon with spring onion mash and sauvignon sauce (£11.95). **£70**

Lough Melvin Holiday Centre ☎028 6865 8142, ⓦmelvinholidaycentre.com. A bit further away from the route of the Way, west near the border at Garrison (take the minor road from Derrygonnelly), this place offers hostel-style accommodation and camping, although you should ring ahead to check on space if you want to stop here. They also have numerous activities, including archery, caving, canoeing and wind-surfing.

Rushin House Caravan Park Holywell ☎028 6638 6519, ⓦrushinhousecaravanpark.com. A mile up the road from Belcoo, this smart caravan park, attractively sited on the shores of Lough MacNean, has comprehensive facilities including barbecue, picnic and play areas, and a service block with kitchen and laundry. March–Oct. Tent pitch **£22**

16

turn back if the weather turns sour). A part of the Marble Arch Caves centre is now devoted to an exhibition describing the restoration of the mountain park's damaged peatland and bogland habitats.

STONE CARVING, JERPOINT ABBEY

Contexts

History

Ireland's history is as rich and colourful as that of any European nation, and comprehending its troubled past is vital to an understanding of its current situation. Though the following pages can merely summarize key events, our book list (see pp.618–622) provides sources of further enlightenment.

Prehistory

Originally connected to mainland Europe, and at times completely glaciated, Ireland's geographical form has developed over the last two million years as a result of global climate change. The end of the last major **Ice Age** saw sea levels rise and the gradual separation of both Britain and Ireland from the European landmass, leaving just a few connections between the two regions. The first plant life is reckoned to have appeared around 12,000 BC, and the first mammals, such as reindeer, arrived a millennium or so later. A subsequent period of glaciation resulted in their extinction in Ireland, though warming again occurred around 9000 BC, at which point the country began its long process of forestation and various animals crossed the last remaining land-bridges.

The **first human settlements** are thought to date from around 8000–7000 BC. These Mesolithic hunter-gatherers, who made various implements and artefacts from flint, lived largely around coastal areas, such as Belfast Lough and the Shannon estuary.

IRELAND'S PREHISTORIC TOMBS

Ireland is sprinkled with an extraordinary number of megalithic tombs, of which more than 1500 examples have been identified, and many are in remarkably fine condition. The oldest tomb-form, dating from around 4000 BC, is the **passage grave**, consisting of a rounded mound or cairn with a stone-lined passage leading from the perimeter to a central chamber. Of the three hundred-plus surviving examples, mostly found in Ireland's north and east, **Newgrange** (see p.142) is the most renowned, remarkable not just because of its intricate construction – and the site's sheer scale – but also for its implicit associations with magic and ritual.

Dating from before 3000 BC, **court tombs** feature an open area beside the entrance, probably used for religious ceremonies. The majority are found in the country's north, **Creevykeel** in County Sligo being the best known (see p.405).

Portal tombs (known as **dolmens**), from around 2500–2000 BC, are the most easily recognizable form, consisting of three or more sturdy upright boulders, dragged into position, on which an often bigger capstone was placed. This tripod-like structure would then have a gallery tomb excavated beneath. Found in the north, west and southeast, a particularly fine example is at **Kilclooney** in County Donegal (see p.438).

Lastly, **wedge tombs** date from the early Bronze Age (around 2000–1500 BC), and are so termed because their burial chamber narrows and decreases in height as one moves inwards. More than a quarter of the recorded four hundred examples are located in **the Burren** in County Clare (see p.334).

---

c. 11,000 BC	c. 8000–7000 BC	c. 4000 BC
The first mammals arrive in Ireland	The first human settlements: Mesolithic hunter-gatherers	The first passage graves appear

Developments elsewhere were slow to reach Ireland and it was not until the **Neolithic** period, around 3500 BC, that people skilled in farming settled here – equipped with stone axes (numerous examples have been found across the country), they were capable of clearing forests for their crops and animals. Subscribing to ritual and magic, notably in their burial ceremonies, they left numerous megalithic monuments across Ireland, including graves and stone circles (see p.581) similar to those found throughout Western Europe's coastal areas, indicating their place in a much broader network. Archaeological discoveries reveal the increasing subtlety of the products of this culture, first in the form of pottery and later, after the arrival of bronze casting techniques around 2000 BC, jewellery.

The Iron Age

Ireland is usually considered a **Celtic** country, one colonized by the Indo-European people who spread rapidly across continental Europe from the East from around 1000 BC onwards. However, while they certainly reached the French coast, recent evidence suggests that far from being Celtic themselves, the peoples of Britain and Ireland gradually became Celticized through contact with traders. As a result, iron reached Ireland around 700 BC and, over the course of the next few centuries, the island's inhabitants adopted the Celtic ritual-based culture and language, though this would diversify significantly over the next millennium.

Other innovations followed, including the development of stone-built ring forts, a response to the need for protection brought about by Celtic systems of land ownership and fealty, which increasingly provoked intertribal warfare. A hierarchical system was gradually established, with individual **kingdoms** forming parts of larger fiefdoms based on the five provinces of Connacht, Leinster, Meath, Munster and Ulster. These fiefdoms in turn supposedly paid homage to a High King (*Ard Rí*) based at Tara, though in fact no such regal figure gained sway over the whole of Ireland until Brian Boru (see opposite). However, like its Norse contemporary, this was also a myth-making culture, based on the cult of the hero. One of these, Cúchulainn, stars in the Irish epic nonpareil, the *Táin Bó Cúailnge*, a bloodthirsty tale of war and revenge whose characters are ever prey to the whims of their gods.

Early Christianity

If the myths are to be believed, Ireland subsequently embraced **Christianity** with remarkable rapidity thanks to the efforts of its patron saint, **St Patrick** (who also eradicated the snakes that had never inhabited the island). Truth be told, the process was far more gradual and never entirely included the abandonment of Celtic pagan beliefs, as proven by the presence of Sheila-na-Gigs (see p.627) in medieval church-building. Missionaries began to arrive from the fourth century AD onwards, though the establishment of monastic settlements did not really begin for another two hundred years. By the eighth and ninth centuries monasteries such as Clonmacnois in County Offaly and Lismore in County Waterford had risen to become major seats of learning in an increasingly church-focused Europe. Extant evidence of such prowess exists in the form of **illuminated manuscripts**, such as the *Book of Durrow* and the renowned *Book of Kells*, on

c. 2000 BC	c. 700 BC	Fourth century AD
The arrival of bronze casting	Iron reaches Ireland	Christian missionaries begin to arrive

show in the Library of Trinity College, Dublin. At this time, using well-established trading routes, the Irish also began to send forth their own missionaries, including **St Columba**, who founded various monasteries in mainland Europe before his death in 615.

The Vikings and the Normans

The **Vikings** reached Ireland towards the end of the eighth century and conducted sporadic raids on coastal areas, usually on monasteries – the defensive round tower dates from this period – before embarking on a more coordinated assault in 914. The upshot was the formation of fortified settlements at places such as Dublin, Cork and Waterford, though one hundred years later the Norsemen were vanquished at the Battle of Clontarf by the *Ard Rí*, Brian Boru.

One branch of the Norsemen, in the shape of the **Normans**, did finally conquer England in 1066, but it was more than a century before a successful Anglo-Norman incursion was made into Ireland, when Irish infighting resulted in Dermot MacMurrough, the dethroned king of Leinster, seeking the support of Henry II to regain his throne. The English king agreed to allow one of his knights, Richard FitzGilbert de Clare ("Strongbow"), to take a contingent of troops across the Irish Sea, but soon became concerned by the extent of Strongbow's success and arrived shortly afterwards to claim sovereignty over Ireland and establish a court in Dublin.

Norman rule over Ireland was largely restricted to the former Viking townships, and attempts to introduce feudalism foundered against the resistance of the Irish chieftains. In reality, the process of assimilation, which saw many of the victors becoming "more Irish than the Irish", resulted in the conquest becoming limited to a small area surrounding Dublin. This became known as the "English Pale" (from the word for an enclosure), and those who lived beyond its bounds were demeaningly described as "beyond the pale", a term which subsequently became synonymous with barbarism.

Attempts to coerce the Irish into submission by force were abandoned, and those Norman settlers who had established themselves gradually became integrated into a society, now usually described as Gaelic, founded on the domains of Irish chieftains. The outcome was a flowering of **Gaelic culture**, with its emphasis on the place of the bard (a court musician-cum-poet) in storytelling and music-making. However, this did not prevent certain Anglo-Norman dynasties from broadening their own power bases, not least the de Burgo family in Ulster and Connacht, and the Fitzgeralds of Kildare.

Tudor and Stuart incursions

The succeeding centuries saw various English interlopers attempting to establish themselves in Ireland, but it was not until **Henry VIII** broke with Rome that a concerted effort to demolish the hegemony of the Irish overlords began, linked to the dissolution of the powerful Irish monasteries with their wealth up for the grabs of any supporter of the Tudor regime. An abortive insurrection in 1534 offered Henry the excuse to send troops to Ireland, quash the revolt and establish himself as both sovereign ruler and ecclesiastical head of his domain.

His daughter **Elizabeth I** continued the process, but adopted much more stringent and far-reaching tactics, geared towards undermining Gaelic authority and its allegiance to

c. 800	795	1169
Production of the magnificent illuminated manuscript, the *Book of Kells*	The Vikings begin their century-long plunder of Irish monasteries, before building fortified settlements	Henry II of England's barons land at Wexford, kicking off the 750-year colonization of southern Ireland

Catholicism while simultaneously reinforcing Ireland's position as an English colony. Taking up her elder sister Mary's policy of **plantation**, which had seen parts of Laois and Offaly sequestered from their Irish owners, Elizabeth unsuccessfully attempted to "plant" colonists from Scotland in the area around Belfast Lough during the 1570s.

The threat of further infiltration provoked Irish offensive reaction, of which the most crucial was the revolt led by **Hugh O'Neill** of Northern Ireland. This chieftain had been deliberately targeted by the Tudors as a potential convert to the Protestant plantation process, but, realizing he had been duped, he took up arms against the Crown. At first successful, his armies were crucially defeated at Kinsale in 1601 and, finally forced into submission by a siege at Mellifont in County Louth in 1603, he signed a treaty granting all his land and that of his underlords to the English, which was leased back to them under an oath of fealty. This opened the door for a flood of "planters", mainly ex-soldiers from England and the Scottish Lowlands who were encouraged to establish themselves in the newly gained territories. Though the Irish chiefs were still ostensibly in control of their land, their power was fatally diminished and a significant number decided to leave their country en masse in 1607, embarking from Rathmullen, County Donegal, in what was later described as the **Flight of the Earls**, heading variously for Flanders and Italy. The power of the old Gaelic kingships was at an end, and the plantation broadened its scale as **James I** urged more Lowland Scots to cross over to Northern Ireland and take over the Earls' impounded lands. This established a significant division between the Protestant planters and the evicted Catholic Irish, the ramifications of which endure to this day.

The 1641 Rebellion and Oliver Cromwell

Concerns about the apparently pro-Catholic religious policies of James I's successor, **Charles I**, resulted in a Scottish rebellion in 1640. Having failed to persuade parliament to vote for taxes to raise new troops to quell the Scots, Charles negotiated a deal with Irish Catholics whereby their troops would be provided to suppress the rising in return for concessions regarding land ownership and religious tolerance. Alarmed that the king might be about to impose Catholicism across his dominion, a Scottish–Parliamentarian alliance proposed invading Ireland to subdue the population. A small group of Irish landowners planned their own rebellion in turn, conspiring to take Dublin Castle, Derry and other northern towns in October 1641. Their assault on Dublin was foiled by an informer, but their Northern Ireland campaign, led by Phelim O'Neill, was initially successful. Charles himself sent an army to put down the rising (and the Scots sent their own to protect Ulster Protestants, four thousand of whom had died in the fighting and a further eight thousand succumbed to the harsh winter conditions after being expelled from their homes by O'Neill's army), but the outbreak of the English Civil War delayed the resolution of the Irish question.

An Irish alliance called the **Catholic Confederation** was created to coordinate attacks on English and Scottish troops in Ireland, though **Oliver Cromwell**'s victory in the Civil War saw the overthrow of the monarchy and a determination to conquer all of Ireland. Cromwell arrived in Dublin with a large contingent of his New Model Army in August 1649 and embarked on a merciless and bitterly fought crusade to establish his authority. His prime targets were those towns occupied by Royalist garrisons, first taking

1534	1601	1607
Henry VIII sends the troops in to establish his hegemony	The Irish chieftains are decisively defeated by Elizabeth I at the Battle of Kinsale	Many of them flee to Europe – the "Flight of the Earls" – opening the way for mass plantation of Ulster

Drogheda, where he massacred the troops and numerous citizens, before sweeping down through the southeast of Ireland and on to Cork and Kinsale. By 1652 all of Ireland was under Cromwell's control, his bloodthirsty troops slaughtering a quarter of the Catholic population in the process and dispatching many others into slavery in the Caribbean. The subsequent **Act of Settlement** saw widespread sequestration of Catholic-held land and all the evictees were instructed to move west of the Shannon River by the beginning of May 1654 or face death – in Cromwell's cold terms, "to Hell or to Connacht". Many more died on the journey to places such as Connemara and the boglands of Mayo, while Cromwell's troops were rewarded with their confiscated land. Unsurprisingly, Cromwell's name remains reviled across much of Ireland.

The Williamite War and the penal laws

Though the monarchy was restored in 1660, Charles II remained in thrall to his Protestant Parliament and it was not until he was succeeded by his brother, the Catholic **James II** in 1685, that Irish hopes were revitalized. However, anti-Catholic concerns, particularly about James's close relationship with Louis XIV of France, led the English Parliament to offer the throne to the Dutch **Prince William of Orange**. James fled to Ireland and enlisted an army to try and overthrow what had become known as the "Glorious Revolution". Though initially successful, the city of **Derry** presented a major stumbling block (see box, p.513), allowing William's forces the time to arrive in Ireland. James was finally defeated at Limerick, though the most celebrated encounter in William's campaign took place earlier, on July 12, 1690, when he was victorious at the **Battle of the Boyne**, an event commemorated as the highpoint of the Loyalist marching season (see box, p.558).

Subsequently, under William, the English Parliament consolidated the legal process (begun under Charles II) of furthering control over Ireland by diminishing the rights of the native Catholic population in terms of land ownership, marriage, religion and enfranchisement. A series of Acts passed between 1695 and 1728, which later became known as the **penal laws**, aimed at safeguarding the Protestant planters while suppressing Irish Catholic identity and culture and dragging the population into penury. Catholics were barred from purchasing land and on a landowner's death his property was split equally between all of his sons, thus incrementally diminishing familial wealth by each generation (an essential factor in the Great Famine of the nineteenth century – see p.587), though any son who converted to Protestantism became entitled to his brothers' inheritance. Catholic priests were banned from practising unless they paid two £50 bonds for registration, and even then were not allowed to say Mass; alternatively, conversion to the Church of Ireland attracted a £20 stipend, levied on their former congregations. Targeting cultural transmission, Catholics were barred from teaching, though some operated surreptitious "hedge schools" in the countryside, using the Irish language as a medium. Despite these exigencies, native Irish culture somehow survived.

Revolution and rebellion

Towards the end of the eighteenth century revolution was in the air throughout much of bourgeois Europe. Its initial catalyst was the **American War of Independence**, which

1649	**1690**	**1695–1728**
Oliver Cromwell descends on Ireland with legendary cruelty	Protestant William of Orange decisively defeats Catholic James II and the French at the Battle of the Boyne	Passage of the penal laws, suppressing Irish Catholics, their culture and identity

saw British troops diverted across the Atlantic from Ireland. The series of laws establishing the primacy of the Anglican Church had not only affected Irish Catholics, but Presbyterian Northern Ireland planters, too, many of whom had emigrated to the Americas (see p.565), bringing about some sympathy among Ireland's burgeoning Protestant mercantile class for Washington's campaign demand of "no taxation without representation". Though not directly taxed by the English Parliament, Ireland was the subject of numerous trade levies and the American war led **Henry Grattan**, leader of the Patriot Party, not only to make increasing demands for proper representation at Westminster and some form of constitutional independence, but to recruit troops to replace the departing English militia in order to defend Ireland against the threat of a French invasion.

More crucially, segments of the Irish middle class saw the **French Revolution** of 1789, with its underlying concepts of liberty, equality and fraternity, reinforced by the publication of Thomas Paine's *Rights of Man* (1792), and the consequent possibility of an invasion from France, as the potential means of securing independence. Formed by Belfast Protestants in 1791, the **Society of United Irishmen** promulgated Nationalist views regarding democratic reform and Catholic emancipation never likely to be taken up by the Grattan Parliament. After the English declaration of war against France in 1793, the Society was forced underground, and adopted agitational policies aimed at severing the link with Britain, linking with militant Catholic agrarian groups in the process. France became the means of breaking the connection with England, and one of the Society's leaders, Theobald **Wolfe Tone**, a Dublin Protestant barrister, was sent there to secure French support for an insurrection. Realizing the possibility of gaining a back-door victory over England, a French army set sail to invade Ireland, but was prevented from landing in Bantry Bay in 1796 by bad weather and indecision (see p.262).

Plans revised, the **Rebellion** took place in 1798 (see p.197), but met brutal English resistance, supported, especially in the North, by Protestant yeomanry (many of whom belonged to the Orange Society (later Orange Order), established in 1795 to oppose Catholic Emancipation – see box, p.558). The French, under General Humbert, finally landed at Killala, Mayo, in late August, by which time much of the uprising had been quelled. Drawing local support, they marched towards Dublin, until defeated at Ballinamuck in Longford. Subsequently, a larger Gallic force, with Tone on board, tried to land in County Donegal, but was intercepted by the British navy. Tone was taken to Dublin and sentenced to death, but slit his own throat before the execution.

As a result, the British enacted the 1801 **Act of Union**, dissolving Dublin's Parliament and ensuring total legislative control over Ireland, which now became part of the United Kingdom. The act did not deter one further Irish revolutionary, **Robert Emmet**, whose wholly ill-planned attempted coup failed ignominiously in 1803.

Catholic Emancipation

The cause of Catholic enfranchisement became the major focus for agitation. Its catalyst was the lawyer **Daniel O'Connell**, who founded the Catholic Association in 1823 to build on successful British popular campaigns to expand the franchise beyond its previously limited bounds, and was returned to the British Parliament as MP for Clare in 1828. Though legislation prevented him from taking up his seat, his

1795	**1798**	**1801**
Northern Protestants found the Orange Society (later Orange Order) to oppose Catholic emancipation	The '98 Rebellion, led by the United Irishmen, is brutally defeated	The Act of Union dissolves the Parliament of Ireland, which becomes part of the United Kingdom

victory played no small part in the subsequent passage of the Catholic Emancipation Act, which, though only enfranchising a tiny number of middle-class voters, had enormous repercussions by making Catholics eligible for a number of previously excluded public offices.

O'Connell was elected as Dublin's first Catholic Lord Mayor in 1841 and subsequently embarked on a campaign to repeal the Union with Britain. Adopting populist techniques acquired from the Chartists, he called a series of "**monster meetings**" across all of Ireland except Ulster, attended on each occasion by as many as 100,000 people. Alarmed, the British government outlawed his October 1843 assembly at Clontarf and jailed him for sedition. More radical supporters of independence, the Young Ireland Movement, attempted their own uprising in 1848, but such was its lack of support that it became known as "The Battle of Widow McCormack's Cabbage Patch".

The Great Famine

The **Great Famine** of 1845 to 1851, during which Ireland's population declined by 1.5 million – almost twenty percent – was one of the most devastating tragedies in human history. In the early 1840s a potato blight spread across Western Europe, and, while resolved reasonably well elsewhere, struck at the core of an Irish peasantry excessively dependent on their potato yields. Britain's laissez-faire economic policy throughout the Famine years allowed continued export from Ireland of other agricultural products, which might have alleviated the situation. By the worst year of the Famine, Black '47, hundreds of thousands faced starvation, a situation exacerbated by mass evictions across Ireland as landlords removed tenants unable to pay their dues. Workhouses were crammed to overcapacity and, while some were fed by soup kitchens or received support from individual landlords, the majority faced death or emigration.

Though Dublin, Belfast and much of the Northern Ireland province remained relatively unscathed, at least a million people died during the Famine and hundreds of thousands migrated to Britain or risked death by travelling on one of the infamous

---

THE IRISH DIASPORA

Even when Ireland's Great Famine was finally quelled, a pattern had been set, with **emigration** becoming regarded as the only means of escaping poverty. Sixty years after the Famine, Ireland's population had sunk to just over half its 1841 level of 8.2 million, and further waves of emigration occurred during the twentieth century. This **diaspora** established large Irish communities in other countries, especially Britain (where ten percent of the population are now thought to have an Irish grandparent) and the USA, where **Irish-Americans** played a major role in supporting moves towards independence and still remain a powerful lobbying group. The list of US presidents with Irish roots now runs into the low twenties (including Ulysses S. Grant, John F. Kennedy, Ronald Reagan, Bill Clinton and perhaps more tenuously Barack Obama), and over forty million Americans, one fifth of the white population, claim Irish descent. Other countries with significant populations of Irish descent include Australia, Canada, South Africa and, perhaps more surprisingly, Mexico and Argentina, the latter explaining how the great Latin American revolutionary Che Guevara came to have an Irish grandmother.

1829	1841	1845–51
The Catholic Emancipation Act gives limited rights to Catholics	Daniel O'Connell is elected as the first Catholic Lord Mayor of Dublin	Around a million people die and hundreds of thousands emigrate in the Great Famine

"coffin ships" to North America or Australasia, which, often crammed beyond capacity, were not fit to sail and floundered en route.

Nationalist action had been fuelled by British policy during the Famine years. The **Irish Republican Brotherhood** (sometimes termed Fenians and funded in part from the US) carried out an abortive uprising in 1867 and incurred a massive backlash, though this failed to destroy the organization. Agrarian groups focused particularly on **absentee English landlords** and those who continued to evict tenants unable to pay their rent – one of the most notorious wide-scale evictions took place at Derryveagh in Donegal (see p.445).

The Home Rule Movement

Over the remaining decades of the nineteenth century the struggles over land and tenants' rights retained pivotal importance and were accelerated by **Michael Davitt**'s formation of the **Land League** in 1879. Its aims, however, became increasingly linked to a concerted campaign to secure independence via parliamentary democracy. The movement's guiding light was **Charles Stewart Parnell** (1846–91), who won County Meath for the **Home Rule Party** in the 1875 election and became its leader two years later. Parnell gained huge popularity in Ireland for his support of the ideal of an Irish Parliament, his use of obstructive tactics in the House of Commons and his full-blooded backing for agrarian action against recalcitrant landlords and their agents, using the tactic of social excommunication. One of the first victims, in 1880, of this device was a Mayo estate factor, Captain Charles Boycott – the action introduced his eponym into the English language.

William Gladstone's government put Parnell, Davitt and other leaders of the Land League on trial for seditious conspiracy in 1881 and, though the jury failed to agree a verdict, Davitt was shortly afterwards re-arrested for breaching his "ticket of leave". A new Land Act, based on the principles of fair rent, fixed tenure and freedom of sale, became law later that year, but was rejected by the Land League which embarked on a new campaign of violence against landowners and thus was declared illegal. On the very day of Davitt's release from prison the following year, the British viceroy Lord Frederick Cavendish and his Under Secretary T.H. Burke were assassinated in Phoenix Park by a Fenian group calling itself "The Invincibles". Parnell denounced the murder in the Commons, but attitudes hardened against the Irish.

Though Gladstone had been persuaded by Parnell's arguments, his first Home Rule Bill failed in 1886 (as did his second in 1893), while Parnell's political career was terminated when his long-term affair with Kitty O'Shea saw him named as co-respondent in a divorce trial launched by her husband.

Towards identity

From the late nineteenth century onwards Nationalist ideas became increasingly intertwined with the concept of cultural revival, especially via the establishment of two new opinion-forming organizations. Founded in 1884, the **Gaelic Athletic Association**'s fundamental aim was to preserve and nurture Irish sports such as Gaelic football and hurling. Avowedly Nationalist, its members were banned from playing foreign games and Crown forces were excluded from membership. The **Gaelic League** was formed in

1848	1867	1877
Unsuccessful uprising in favour of independence by the Young Ireland Movement	Abortive uprising by the Irish Republican Brotherhood	Charles Stewart Parnell, the "uncrowned king of Ireland", becomes leader of the Home Rule Party

1893. While aiming to preserve and maintain the Irish language and native culture, it too became increasingly nationalistic, viewing its goals as central to the "de-Anglicization" of Ireland. At the same time, a group of writers, centred on W.B. Yeats and Lady Gregory, set about establishing a **cultural revival**, based on the creation of distinctly Irish works written in English.

Almost simultaneously, and in response to Parnell's failure to achieve Home Rule via parliamentary means, a current of opinion was developed and promulgated by a Dublin printer, **Arthur Griffith**, in his newspaper *The United Irishman* (established 1898). Initially, this espoused self-determination, involving the withdrawal of Irish MPs from Westminster and the formation of an independent Irish Parliament in Dublin as the only means to achieve economic and political freedom. Supporters of this view coalesced to form the political party **Sinn Féin** in 1905, an organization increasingly influenced by the views expounded by Scotsman **James Connolly**'s Irish Socialist Republican Party, which sought to establish a workers' republic in Ireland. A significant further factor was the rise of the trade-union movement in Ireland, especially the role of the militant workers' leader **James Larkin**, who formed the Irish Transport and General Workers' Union in 1909. Its philosophy was encapsulated in Larkin's slogan, "The land of Ireland for the people of Ireland".

Resistance . . .

The General Election of 1910 resulted in the slimmest of majorities for Asquith's Liberal Party, leaving it utterly reliant on the Irish Nationalist Party to enact legislation. Seizing the moment, the Nationalists pressed for a new Home Rule Bill, which the Commons passed in 1912. This aroused a bitterly intransigent response from Northern Protestants who united under the direction of **Sir Edward Carson**, a Dublin barrister, Tory MP and leader of the Irish Unionists. In September 1911 he and James Craig initiated a campaign to resist Home Rule and any threat of the imposition of Catholicism on Protestant Ulster. More than 200,000 signed up to a covenant pledging to defeat Home Rule by "all means necessary". In readiness for such action, Protestants formed their own militia, the **Ulster Volunteers**, which was armed by munitions from Germany – indeed, Carson went so far as to lunch with the Kaiser in 1913 to discuss German aid for the resistance strategy.

Unsurprisingly, Nationalists and the British responded vigorously. The former founded its own armed force, the **Irish Volunteers**, the second Nationalist militia to form after James Connolly's Irish Citizen Army. The British responded by banning the use of armed weapons in Ireland and went so far as to plan a raid on the Ulster Volunteers, though this was abandoned when troops stationed in Northern Ireland refused to take action against the militia. Lloyd George devised a compromise whereby the province of Northern Ireland would be excluded from the introduction of Home Rule for six years, but the whole issue was deferred when war broke out between Britain and Germany late in the summer of 1914.

. . . and revolt

While Carson and the Irish Nationalist leader **John Redmond** pledged the support of both the Ulster and Irish Volunteers in guarding Ireland from German invasion (and,

1884	1893	1905
Foundation of the Gaelic Athletic Association to nurture Irish sports	Foundation of the Gaelic League to nurture Irish language and culture	Formation of the Sinn Féin ("We Ourselves") political party

indeed, more than 230,000 Irishmen enlisted in the British Army), others saw the war as a fruitful opportunity ripe for the picking. In particular, leaders of the **Irish Republican Brotherhood** (IRB) made preparations for a rising, using the strength of the Irish Volunteers, to be instigated if the Germans entered Ireland or if the British tried to implement conscription. When army and police embarked on a series of raids against Irish Nationalist and revolutionary newspapers in late 1914, plans were made for a rising in September 1915, but were deferred when the Irish Volunteers' leaders declared themselves unready. The IRB sent an envoy to Germany, the former British diplomat **Sir Roger Casement**, who successfully secured German support for the rising.

When it finally occurred on Monday April 24, 1916, the **Easter Rising** (as it became known – see p.78) was a drastically limited affair. The British had already captured the German ship bringing arms and had arrested Casement when he landed from a German submarine in Cork four days earlier. Tipped off by informers, the British had also made plans to arrest all the leaders of the various organizations involved on that Easter Monday (though such action was then largely deferred until the rebels' surrender), and the leader of the Irish Volunteers, Eoin MacNeill, ordered his men not to take part in the rebellion. In the regions, action was limited to the north of County Dublin, Enniscorthy in Wexford and parts of County Galway, while the focus for the rebels' action became the Dublin General Post Office with simultaneous assaults on key targets across the city. Patrick Pearse, a poet and political activist, delivered the **Proclamation of the Irish Republic** from the steps of the GPO, but the rebels were powerless to resist the heavy British bombardment that ensued. After five days of fighting, the leaders surrendered, though it was two more days before combat ended. Over the course of the week, more than 1350 people were killed or wounded and numerous buildings in central Dublin destroyed.

Dubliners were initially aghast at their city's devastation, but public anger turned to outcry when all of the Rising's leaders and numerous other insurgents, with the exception of **Éamon de Valera** who had US citizenship, were executed by the British at Kilmainham Gaol in Dublin after a secret court martial. Connolly himself was so ill from infected wounds that he wouldn't have survived long enough for the planned execution and was shot while tied to a chair. As a consequence of the resulting public revulsion, all other death sentences were commuted, with the exception of Casement, who was hanged in London in August.

The War for Independence

Far from losing support, as the British had hoped, the rebels' ideals were embraced by the next wave of leaders. Key figures were **Michael Collins**, working within the Irish Volunteers, and de Valera, who was elected MP for East Clare in 1916. The Volunteers grew in strength and Sinn Féin achieved a crushing success in the 1918 General Election, though none of its elected members took their seats, instead convening as the Dáil Éireann ("Ireland's Parliament") and issuing a declaration of independence. With de Valera as its leader and Collins as Minister of Finance, the Dáil reorganized the Volunteers and Citizen Army under the new name of the **Irish Republican Army (IRA)**. The British poured troops into Ireland and war effectively began in September 1919, when a soldier was killed in Fermoy, County Cork, and the British subsequently sacked the town.

1912	1912	1913
Home Rule Bill passed by the House of Commons – but deferred with the outbreak of World War I in 1914	Formation of the Ulster Volunteers to oppose home rule	Formation of the Irish Volunteers to oppose the Ulster Volunteers

In consequence, a campaign of guerrilla warfare broke out across most of Ireland which the Royal Irish Constabulary proved powerless to restrain. Irish sentiment was much heightened by the arrival of the **Black and Tans**, British soldiers re-recruited after World War I (and so called because of the colour of their uniforms), whose reprisals were merciless. However, even they were unable to prevent the situation of virtual stalemate, which dragged on until a truce was called in July 1921.

Meanwhile, in 1920 Westminster passed the **Government of Ireland Act**, establishing separate new parliaments for the six counties of "Northern Ireland" and the residual 26 of "Southern Ireland". Elections the following year resulted in a simple reinforcement of the Nationalist majority in the latter, which promptly reconstituted itself as Dáil Éireann, led by de Valera, and demanded independence as a 32-county state. Since Ulster's Protestants clearly held sway in the North and the armed independent struggle had reached deadlock, de Valera sent a delegation to London to negotiate an agreement with Lloyd George (thus absolving himself of any role in the process). In the face of the British prime minister's intransigence regarding the Unionist stand-off, the representatives, who included Michael Collins, agreed to the partition of Ireland as defined by the 1920 legislation, with the South gaining independence as the Irish Free State but retaining allegiance to the Crown through membership of the Commonwealth.

The Irish Civil War

A provisional government was established in the South shortly after the signing of the **Anglo-Irish Treaty** in December 1921, which granted independence at the cost of partition. However, while Collins had signed the treaty on the basis that it was a major leap towards independence and a halfway step towards gaining control of all 32 counties, de Valera rejected the proposals as a diminution of Republicanism and refused to truck with their enactment. By July 1922, pro- and anti-Treaty forces had become embroiled in a bitter **civil war** which would have a lasting impact on Ireland's politics and economy. Though most of the population of the 26 counties supported the "Free Staters", opinion was seriously divided owing to the scale of the fighting and the reprisals taken by the provisional government, not least the execution of the prominent Republican Erskine Childers (who had run guns into the country in 1914) after his arrest for possessing a revolver given him by Collins, and the counter-reprisals that ensued. Eventually, the much weaker Republican forces were restricted to control parts of the southwest and west and were forced to surrender in May 1923. Collins himself died in 1922 in an ambush in County Cork.

The Free State

Since one of the main candidates, Arthur Griffith, had also died (of a brain haemorrhage) during the civil war, leadership of the new government passed on to **William T. Cosgrave**, whose regime set about establishing a new infrastructure for the country's development, including the formation of a civil service and police force. Republicans boycotted the Dáil until 1926 when de Valera formed a new political party, **Fianna Fáil**, drawing members largely from the anti-Treaty element within Sinn

1916	1918	1919–21
The Easter Rising wins widespread sympathy only after the brutal execution of its leaders	The first Dail Éireann ("Ireland's parliament") issues a declaration of independence and forms the Irish Republican Army	The War of Independence

Féin. Cosgrave remained in power until 1932, overseeing the initiation of the Shannon hydroelectric scheme and the foundation of the Electricity Supply Board, but his Cumann na nGaedheal party lost the election that year to Fianna Fáil ushering in de Valera's subsequent sixteen-year reign as Taoiseach. Cumann na nGaedheal itself merged with the National Centre Party and the right-wing Army Comrades Association (known as the "Blueshirts") the following year to form **Fine Gael**.

Throughout this period, the economic situation remained austere, exacerbated first by the Depression after 1929 and then by high British trade-levies on imports from Ireland, a result of de Valera's refusal to repay land annuities to Britain, which forced his government into frugality and self-sufficiency. These stern policies were reflected in Ireland's social and cultural life, and ties with the Catholic Church were reinforced at the time. However, de Valera's government also saw the establishment of state boards for road, rail and air transport (Aer Lingus) and peat production.

De Valera's determination to sever links with Britain resulted in a new **constitution** in 1938 whose central premise was the renunciation of Crown sovereignty and a new system of government for the state henceforth known as **Éire**. The model adopted was bicameral with the Dáil retained, but with a new upper chamber, the Seanad (or Senate), added, and the role of president (Uachtarán) created – the first holder of the office was the Protestant Douglas Hyde (see box, p.419).

Northern Ireland's first decades

Following the enactment of the Anglo-Irish Treaty, Northern Ireland's new-found status as a largely self-governing entity had begun in June 1921 with the establishment of its parliament under James Craig, whose **Ulster Unionist Party (UUP)** would run the mini-state until 1972. Rather than including all nine counties of the Ulster province, leaders of the majority Protestant community had negotiated a settlement for their separation from the Free State on the basis of just six, thus ensuring the retention of a secure mandate which might have been threatened by the inclusion of the largely Catholic counties of Donegal and Cavan. Though a significant and gradually increasing Catholic minority remained, it was largely concentrated on agricultural areas west of the River Bann, plus the city of Derry, while the economically thriving linen and shipbuilding industries east of the river remained almost entirely in Protestant hands.

Britain needed Belfast's industrial strength as much as the UUP wanted Britain's economic and financial support and Unionists quickly set about reinforcing their domination. As well as establishing a largely Protestant police force, the **Royal Ulster Constabulary (RUC)**, and a military adjunct, the B Specials, the new parliament (originally based in Belfast, but moved to Stormont in 1932) strengthened its position by favouring the Protestant population with economic support, housing allocations and gerrymandering (for example, Derry's electoral boundaries were changed to ensure a Protestant council remained in power for decades despite the city's two-thirds Catholic majority).

World War II

As part of the United Kingdom, Northern Ireland was heavily involved in the war effort, particularly Belfast, whose shipyards proved a major target for German bombing

1921	1922–23	1926	1932
Anglo-Irish Treaty signed, setting up the Irish Free State in 26 of Ireland's 32 counties	Civil War between pro- (led by Michael Collins) and anti-treaty (led by Éamon de Valera) forces	De Valera forms a new political party, Fianna Fáil ("Soldiers of Destiny")	De Valera wins the general election, at the start of a sixteen-year reign as prime minister

raids. In contrast, Éire adopted a position of neutrality throughout and negotiated its security with Germany, though it did make certain concessions to the UK regarding flights over its airspace. It also remained utterly dependent on imports from the UK and suffered drastically when British ships carrying goods such as coal and cattle feed were attacked by U-boats. In recent years the Irish Republic's neutral role in World War II has been re-examined to some extent. New estimates suggest that despite the position adopted by de Valera's government during "The Emergency", as it termed World War II, around fifty thousand Irishmen from south of the border volunteered to fight for the British army, roughly the same as those from the north.

The postwar Republic

De Valera lost the 1948 election to a wide-ranging coalition of opposition parties, led by John A. Costello's Fine Gael, which set about the removal of any surviving legislative links with Britain by establishing Éire as the **Republic of Ireland** in 1949. However, the new Republic's economic position remained dire and the early 1950s were characterized by fresh waves of rural depopulation and migration both to Dublin and abroad. De Valera was returned as Taoiseach twice during the decade (in 1951 and 1957), but it was not until his long-serving deputy Seán Lemass took office in 1959 that the policies needed to boost Ireland's stagnant economy began to be enacted. Lemass directed Ireland away from protectionism and firmly towards free trade, drawing foreign investment in the process, and sowed the seeds for membership of the **European Economic Community** in January 1973 – though by this time Jack Lynch's government was fully embroiled in developments in the North (see below).

While the Republic, not least its farmers, initially prospered from EEC membership, the country suffered badly during the recession of the early 1980s, leading to a new wave of emigration. Its remaining population seemed to become increasingly conservative, rejecting referenda to allow abortion and divorce in 1983 and 1986 respectively.

The Troubles and the peace process

Though Northern Ireland had benefited hugely from the social policies begun by the post-World War II Labour government, not least in terms of health and social care, its Catholic population continued to suffer levels of social deprivation far worse than anywhere else in the UK. In 1967 the **Civil Rights Movement**, a nonsectarian coalition demanding equal rights, was formed, promoting its campaign via protest marches. One of these, through Derry in 1968, saw demonstrators attacked by a police baton charge and television pictures of the West Belfast MP Gerry Fitt with blood streaming down his face from a wound – transmitted around the world, these provoked international condemnation of the RUC's tactics. Severe rioting the next year following the Apprentice Boys' August parade led to the barricading of the Bogside area of Derry and Irish Taoiseach Jack Lynch's movement of Irish troops to the border to await developments.

British troops arrived shortly afterwards, ostensibly to keep the peace in Derry and Belfast, where Protestant assaults on West Belfast's Catholics had taken place. Though initially welcomed by Catholics, the army soon shifted its approach in line with the

1933	1938	1939–45	1949
Formation of the Fine Gael ("Tribe of the Irish") political party out of pro-treaty elements in Sinn Féin	Promulgation of a new constitution for the State, henceforth to be known as Éire	Éire remains neutral in World War II, which is known as "The Emergency"	Éire becomes the Republic of Ireland and severs all remaining ties to Britain

laissez-faire and often repressive tactics of the RUC. After years in the wilderness, and bolstered by new recruits, the IRA took up the gauntlet as defenders of the Catholic turf, though its own internal disputes led to the formation of the **Provisional IRA**, which broke away from the Dublin-led Official IRA and began an armed campaign against the army, RUC and Loyalists. As a result, the British introduced **internment without trial**, indiscriminately rounding up any Catholic thought to be linked to the violence. On January 30, 1972, British paratroopers shot and killed thirteen unarmed civil-rights demonstrators in Derry in an incident known ever afterwards as **Bloody Sunday** (see box, p.517). Three days later, the British Embassy in Dublin was burnt down and shortly afterwards Westminster's direct rule was reinstated over Northern Ireland. On **Bloody Friday**, July 21, 1972, the IRA exploded twenty car bombs in Belfast's city centre, killing nine people and injuring 130.

Sunningdale and the mainland bombing campaign

The 1970s were marked by increasing violence and diplomatic attempts to produce a political solution. A first attempt at power-sharing, established by the 1973 **Sunningdale conference**, proved impossible to implement in the face of a massive campaign of disruption led by the **Reverend Ian Paisley** and the strike called by the Ulster Workers Council in May 1974, which paralyzed much of Northern Ireland. During the strike the Loyalist UDA (Ulster Defence Association) detonated three car bombs in central Dublin, killing 33 people. The power-sharing executive was disbanded and direct rule reinstated once again, which continued until 1999.

Meanwhile, the IRA had transferred its bombing campaign to mainland Britain in an attempt to force the reunification of Ireland, and in 1974 set off massive **explosions** in pubs in Birmingham, Woolwich and Guildford, killing 28 people. It declared a ceasefire later that year – subsequently discovered to be a consequence of clandestine negotiations with the British Government – but the failure to secure a lasting agreement led to the resumption of the campaign the following year. In retaliation,

---

THE MAZE HUNGER STRIKES

In the late 1970s IRA inmates at Long Kesh prison (also known as **The Maze**) began a series of protests against the abolition of the Special Category Status they had been granted, which gave them the right to be treated as political prisoners. This began as a "**blanket protest**" in which prisoners refused to wear prison clothes, instead opting to remain naked under a blanket draped over their shoulders, and later moved on to the infamous "**dirty protest**" where the inmates smeared their cell walls with excrement rather than emptying their chamber pots. Despite a 1978 European Court of Human Rights verdict finding the British Government guilty of "inhuman and degrading treatment", the British position remained intransigent, both under the outgoing Labour Government and even more so when a new regime under Conservative leader Margaret Thatcher was elected in 1979. The H-blocks of The Maze had become a hotbed for Republican education and action and, in the early 1980s, a new tactic was employed – the **hunger strike**. The first of these ended ignominiously in 1980, but the second, led by **Bobby Sands**, commander of the Provisional IRA within the prison, who was elected MP for Fermanagh and South Tyrone in the course of the fast, had more effect. The hunger strike resulted in ten deaths, including Sands' own, but Thatcher remained obdurate despite worldwide condemnation of Britain's position.

1959	1967	1972
Sean Lemass succeeds de Valera and begins to stimulate the economy	Formation of the Civil Rights Movement to demand equal rights in the north	Bloody Sunday: British paratroopers kill thirteen unarmed civil rights protestors in Derry

Harold Wilson introduced the **Prevention of Terrorism Act**, allowing extended detention without charge. In two major trials, those found guilty of the Guildford and Birmingham bombings were sentenced to life imprisonment, but increasing concerns about the reliability of the forensic evidence and their confessions led to the release of the Guildford Four in 1989 and the Birmingham Six in 1991.

Though refusing to respond to the Hunger Strikes (see box, opposite) by IRA inmates, Margaret Thatcher's government did attempt another power-sharing initiative with the formation of the **Northern Ireland Assembly** in 1982, but this was shunned by both Nationalists and Republicans. In 1984 the IRA notoriously bombed the Brighton hotel hosting the Tory party conference, in an unsuccessful attempt to kill Thatcher. However, parallel political developments saw a sea change in the form of the Republicans' tactical decision to employ the democratic process alongside the armed campaign. This was encapsulated in Belfast Republican Danny Morrison's famous declaration to the Sinn Féin party's annual conference: "... will anyone here object if, with the ballot box in one hand and the Armalite in the other, we take power in Ireland?" Instrumental in this strategy were two Republican leaders who would become pivotal figures in the peace process: former Maze internee **Gerry Adams**, from 1983 Sinn Féin's party leader and MP for West Belfast, and **Martin McGuinness**, a former member of the Provisional IRA and Sinn Féin's vice president from 1983.

Towards the Good Friday Agreement and the Assembly

The IRA kept up its bombing campaign during the 1990s, beginning with a brazen mortar attack on 10 Downing Street in February 1991 targeting a Cabinet meeting chaired by the new British leader, John Major. Loyalist sectarian attacks on Catholics also continued relentlessly, matching the numbers killed by Republicans. Undeterred, Major concluded an agreement with the Irish Prime Minister Albert Reynolds in December 1993, the **Downing Street Declaration**, largely shaped by the diplomacy of the SDLP's leader, **John Hume**, which sought to bring peace to Northern Ireland by democratic means.

The IRA launched another audacious mortar attack, this time on Heathrow Airport, in March 1994, but after focused lobbying by Dublin and the US vice president Al Gore, announced a ceasefire at the end of August, followed two months later by a similar Loyalist move. The following year witnessed intense negotiations involving the London and Dublin governments and the Republicans, which floundered in the face of the IRA's refusal to decommission its weaponry. Its bombing of Canary Wharf in London's financial centre in February 1996 re-emphasized its determination to continue the armed struggle, but lobbying for all-party talks on a resolution of the settlement intensified further. The key players were John Hume, who repeatedly met Gerry Adams with the intention of restoring the IRA's ceasefire, and the US president **Bill Clinton**, whose involvement and support for change went way beyond any intention to bolster his Irish-American electoral support.

The most significant broker, however, became British Prime Minister **Tony Blair**, the Labour leader elected with a vast majority in 1997, alongside his Northern Ireland Secretary, **Mo Mowlam**. They targeted a solution by diplomatic discussions with Bertie Ahern's government and the securement of the commitment of the **David Trimble**-led Ulster Unionists and Gerry Adams to all-party talks on Northern Ireland's future. The IRA's resumption of a ceasefire in July 1997 eased the process, but continuing violence

1973	**1973**	**1981**
The Sunningdale Agreement, an unsuccessful attempt at power-sharing	The Republic joins the European Economic Community	Bobby Sands and nine other Republican prisoners die on hunger strike; Margaret Thatcher is unmoved

throughout the following months, including the assassination of the LVF leader, Billy Wright, inside The Maze, provided further stumbling blocks.

Blair's commitment to a democratic solution culminated on April 9, 1998. After anxious negotiations late into the night, an accord was somehow agreed, and the **Good Friday Agreement** was signed the following morning. The Agreement committed its signatories "to exclusively democratic and peaceful means of resolving differences on political issues".

More vitally, the agreement laid down the principle that any subsequent changes in the government of Northern Ireland – whether it remained part of the UK or opted to amalgamate with the Republic – relied entirely on the consent of the majority of both the Catholic and Protestant communities. An **Assembly** would be elected, based on proportional representation, with an executive of ministers drawn equally from both camps operating departments previously run by the British. Political prisoners would be rapidly released and an independent commission appointed to determine the future of Northern Ireland's policing.

The agreement was ratified by the North's population in May, and elections in June 1998 saw the UUP's David Trimble returned as First Minister and the SDLP's **Séamus Mallon** as his deputy.

Impasse . . .

Almost as soon as the agreement was signed, however, the new administration, opposed by **Ian Paisley**'s DUP and numerous other Loyalists, became embroiled in debate regarding the right of the Orange Order to march from a Presbyterian church in Drumcree, prior to celebrations of the Battle of the Boyne (see p.585), through Catholic areas of Portadown. Drumcree became a significant annual flashpoint over the next few years and the marching issue remains a significant element in the sectarian divide to this day.

It was not just Loyalist unrest that threatened to derail the peace process, though. A breakaway Republican grouping, the self-styled **Real IRA**, soon perpetrated the most murderous act of the whole history of the Troubles. As part of a campaign of town-centre assaults, it exploded a car bomb in the centre of **Omagh**, County Tyrone, on Saturday August 15, 1998, killing 29 people and injuring hundreds more. In the face of uniform condemnation, the group declared a ceasefire two weeks later.

David Trimble and John Hume were jointly awarded the **1998 Nobel Peace Prize**. However, while general optimism remained in place, the ramifications of parts of the Good Friday Agreement soon became apparent, as the UUP became concerned at the reduction of army numbers. Their worries were exacerbated by the report of the **Patten Commission** into the future of the **Royal Ulster Constabulary**, which proposed the force's abolition and replacement by a new body – with a new name – whose members were to be recruited equally from Catholic and Loyalist communities. The loss of the words "Royal" and "Ulster" from the new organization's title were impossible for Unionists to accept, and the new secretary of state, **Peter Mandelson** (who had replaced Mo Mowlam), bowed to pressure by rejecting many of the Commission's findings, despite strong Nationalist and Republican protest. The new **Police Service of Northern Ireland** (PSNI), however, came into existence in November 2001, but has not yet managed to recruit equally from the two communities.

1983	1991	1993	1994
Gerry Adams and Martin McGuinness take control of Sinn Féin and Adams becomes MP for West Belfast	Mary Robinson becomes Ireland's first woman president	The Downing Street Declaration by the Irish and British prime ministers	Short-lived Republican and Loyalist ceasefires

However, the two key issues, interrelated in the eyes of many Unionists, were the release of political prisoners and the **decommissioning of weaponry**. While the release of prisoners passed relatively smoothly, the operation of the Assembly was thoroughly bedevilled by the decommissioning issue from the day it opened for business on December 1, 1999, and over the next six years its powers were regularly suspended by a succession of different British Northern Ireland Secretaries.

On May 6, 2000, an unexpected and hugely significant **statement from the IRA's leadership** declared that, while they remained committed to a united Ireland, they would "initiate a process that will completely and verifiably put IRA arms beyond use". Neither the UUP nor the DUP, which despite its complete abhorrence of the Good Friday Agreement had taken its seats in the Assembly, would accept that the IRA really meant business, despite the reports of the independent arms inspectorate led by the Canadian General John de Chastelain. In response, Sinn Féin's leadership of Gerry Adams and Martin McGuinness (the latter now MP for Mid Ulster) argued that, as a political party, it had no powers over decommissioning. Many now worried for the future of devolution, fearing that this apparent stalemate would see many IRA members defecting to the reactivated Real IRA (which indeed subsequently began a bombing campaign in London), based on the belief that the Adams–McGuinness strategy for political progress had been a mistake. If Gerry Adams could not persuade the IRA to decommission, they reasoned, then nobody could.

As the impasse continued, conventional crime seemed to hoover up the activities of Loyalist and Republican paramilitaries. The former were involved in a violent feud over the illegal drugs trade, while in December 2004, a staggering £26.5 million **bank raid** of Belfast's Northern Bank had fingers immediately pointing towards the IRA (though so far only a financial adviser has been convicted, of money laundering). In January 2005 the murder of a Catholic from the Short Strand, **Robert McCartney**, allegedly by IRA members, resulted in a huge cover-up and a well-publicized campaign by his bereaved sisters and partner to seek as yet unresolved justice. Later that year, a senior Sinn Féin apparatchik admitted that he had long been paid to spy on the party itself by British Intelligence.

...and resolution

However, local and national **elections** in May 2005 witnessed a sea change in public opinion. The SDLP suffered badly at the hands of Sinn Féin, while the UUP was virtually wiped off the political map by the DUP, leading to Trimble's resignation as minister. The centre ground had now completely disappeared, leaving hardline Republicans and Loyalists as the arbiters of the peace process's continuation. In September 2005 the IRA announced that it was putting all of its weaponry beyond use, thus effectively declaring the end of its armed struggle for unification and against British rule (the UVF would follow suit in 2007).

Assembly elections in early 2007 ratified the DUP's and Sinn Féin's positions as the North's two leading parties. Subsequently, following the ending of a suspension which had begun in late 2005, Ian Paisley and Martin McGuinness took up their positions as, respectively, leader and deputy leader of the Assembly. The DUP's **Peter Robinson** succeeded Paisley (who passed away in 2014) as both DUP leader and the Assembly's First Minister in 2008. Robinson and McGuinness continued their roles after the 2011

1998	1999	2000
The Good Friday Agreement commits all parties to democratic and peaceful solutions	The new Assembly convenes but is bedevilled by the issue of arms decommissioning	The IRA announces that it will initiate a process to put its arms beyond use

Assembly elections, which again returned the DUP and Sinn Féin as the largest parties. Meanwhile, as Sinn Féin attempted to increase their cross-border popularity, Gerry Adams successfully stood in the Republic's 2011 general election as TD for Louth.

Small Republican terrorist groups and splinter groups, such as the **Continuity IRA**, the **Real IRA** (now calling itself just "the IRA") and **Óglaigh na hÉireann** ("soldiers of Ireland"), continue to operate within Northern Ireland, concentrating their attacks upon members (especially Catholics) of the PSNI.

Meanwhile in the Republic

While events in the North had been completely dominated by the peace process, the story of the Republic in the 1990s and 2000s was one of **rapid economic development** (see box, below) and a series of political scandals. The first major event of the new decade was the election of **Mary Robinson** as Ireland's first woman president in 1991. This heralded a more liberal outlook for the country, but her time as head of state was overshadowed by the resignation of two of Ireland's Taoiseachs. **Charles Haughey** was the first to go in 1992, his administration smeared by long-lasting and later substantiated allegations of corruption, and brought down by the revelation that journalists' private telephone calls had been tapped by the Republic's police. In 1994 his successor, **Albert Reynolds**, was also forced to resign after revelations that his government had covered up allegations of paedophilia made against a Catholic priest.

Following a brief interlude of a Fine Gael coalition under **John Bruton**, the Republic was run for fourteen years by a series of Fianna Fáil–headed alliances. The Taoiseach from 1997 until 2008 was **Bertie Ahern**, whose ministries were dogged by further revelations of financial corruption involving key members of his party, resulting in the establishment of the **Flood Commission**'s long-standing investigations into innumerable

---

THE RISE AND FALL OF THE CELTIC TIGER

The 1990s witnessed a remarkable economic boom in the Republic, leading to the country's acquisition of the soubriquet **Celtic Tiger**. Ireland's emergence resulted from a combination of huge European Union subsidies (especially to farmers) and massive tax concessions to multinational companies, encouraging them to site operations in Dublin and elsewhere. For the first time in decades, Irish people actually returned home from abroad to seek work, reinvigorating an economy already bolstered by an increase in the number of graduates emerging from the country's universities. The most visible changes were apparent in the Dublin skyline, where new edifices seemed to emerge almost daily, and in the wave of "mansion" building reflecting the increasing affluence of Ireland's nouveaux riches. Additionally, sparked partly by the redevelopment of Dublin's Temple Bar, the vigorous local music scene (epitomized by the worldwide success of the band U2 and the singer Sinéad O'Connor) and the liberal tax concessions given to artists, writers and musicians, Ireland became for the first time a hip place to visit.

However, as it later emerged, the economy's growth was largely that of a boomtown built on silt, with vast wealth created for a relatively small number of investors in high-tech industries, bankers and property developers, but little legislation to tackle the social deprivation facing those way down the pecking order.

2001	2005	2007
The Royal Ulster Constabulary becomes the Police Service of Northern Ireland	The more extreme DUP and Sinn Féin succeed the UUP and SDLP as the north's major parties	Ian Paisley (succeeded by Peter Robinson) and Martin McGuinness become leader and deputy leader of the Assembly

transactions, as well as major enquiries into the operation of Ireland's police force, centred on various nefarious goings-on in County Donegal.

Ahern's government somehow stumbled on until May 2008, when he resigned following the **Mahon Tribunal**'s investigation into corrupt payments to politicians. He was succeeded by **Brian Cowen**, whose 2007 budget while Minister of Finance was widely regarded as the biggest spending spree in Irish political history. However, the international monetary crisis of 2008–2009 saw all of Ireland's boom-and-bust economic chickens come home to roost in alarming numbers. Cowen's government (forced to enact three budgets within a calendar year) struggled to maintain control of a situation verging upon national insolvency, and enforced austerity measures which cut the salaries of public servants and lowered welfare benefits, while simultaneously attempting to safeguard the Irish banking system. Added to this was the 2009 **Murphy Report** which resulted from investigations into sexual abuse by priests and others within the Catholic archdiocese of Dublin which exposed widespread exploitation of children, numerous cover-ups and a widespread failure to prosecute the perpetrators.

In 2010, the government was forced to turn to the EU and the IMF for an €85 billion bailout to save the banks, which has put the country in hock for generations to come. The unemployment rate rose to a high of over 15 percent in 2012, as the spectre of mass emigration returned. Half-finished, and now unaffordable, housing estates littered the countryside, while among those who already had their own properties, a fifth of all mortgage-holders were in danger of defaulting. Some optimism returned with the success of Fine Gael, led by Mayoman Enda Kenny and in coalition with Labour, in the 2011 election. By 2014, the unemployment rate had fallen to 11 percent and the country recorded a year-on-year economic growth rate of 7.7 percent, the highest in the Eurozone. Seasoned observers of Ireland's boom-and-bust economy, however, could only wince as newspapers coined the term "The Celtic Phoenix".

2008	2010	2011	2014
Fianna Fail's Bertie Ahern resigns after eleven scandal-hit years as prime minister	Ireland accepts an €85 billion bailout to survive the international economic crisis	Enda Kenny of Fine Gael becomes prime minister	President Michael D Higgins makes the first official visit by an Irish head of state to Britain

Traditional music

Ireland and music are as inseparable as fish and chips. Though the country has developed a thriving rock-music scene over the last forty years and artists such as U2, Sinéad O'Connor and Van Morrison have achieved massive international success, it's Ireland's traditional music that in many ways continues to hold centre stage.

The country's musical traditions remain essentially based on the age-old practice of passing down tunes and songs by oral transmission, from generation to generation and from friend to friend. Its core has become the **pub session**, where the richness of the musical tradition can be experienced at first hand, and the *craic* (or crack) – that idiosyncratically Irish, heady combination of drink-fuelled chat, banter and fun – simply takes over.

The best sessions are always the ones you never expected to find, spontaneous and uproarious affairs, and the areas where you'll most likely find them are in the counties along the western and southern seaboards, especially Donegal, Sligo, Galway, Clare, Kerry and Cork, though there are excellent session scenes in Belfast and Dublin. Otherwise, the places to visit are festivals, and we've listed the best of both these and the session pubs throughout the Guide. For more information on the music itself and its instruments, see pp.602–603.

Irish music rediscovered

While the musical traditions of other Western European countries were dissipated by the process of industrialization and political change, Ireland's indigenous music remained at the centre of its people's social life until well into the twentieth century, when its survival became threatened by emigration and governmental controls aimed at curbing dance forms regarded as immoral. It needed two major shots in the arm in the 1960s – the **folk song boom**, which originated in the USA, and the pioneering work of **Seán Ó Riada** in establishing ensemble playing as the new norm – to reinvigorate its existence.

Ireland's greatest musical ambassadors, **The Chieftains**, emerged from Ó Riada's initiative in the 1960s, and the following decade saw the formation of the country's two most influential groups, **Planxty** and **The Bothy Band**. Their performances and recordings effectively laid out the ground for others to tread, not least **De Dannan**, the Donegal-based **Altan**, and, in more recent times, **Lúnasa**, **Danú** and the US-based **Solas**.

The tunes

Almost all of Ireland's traditional-music tunes are based on imported **dance** forms. The only exceptions to this rule are slow airs which largely owe their origins to the song tradition (see p.602), a few special pieces belonging to the *uilleann* piping tradition (such as *The Fox Chase*, in which the instrument mimics the sound of fox, hunters and hounds), and a body of more than two hundred tunes composed by the blind itinerant harper **Turlough O'Carolan** (1680–1738), which carry some influence by Italian classical composers of that era.

There are several thousand reels, jigs (in various formats), hornpipes, barndances, strathspeys, waltzes and numerous other dance tunes, though many are only rarely played. At most sessions it is reels and jigs that predominate. Particular tune forms are favoured in different parts of the country – the polka for example is especially popular in Cork and Kerry. The authors of the vast majority of tunes are unknown, though some do bear their composer's name, such as *Martin Wynne's No. 1*, and many more are added to the canon each year in the form of new compositions. Apart from such eponymous works, tune titles should not be taken as anything more than a labelling device (and some have particularly arcane titles – witness *Wallop the Spot* or *The Cat That Kittled in Jamie's Wig*).

This depth of the tradition owes much to fears at certain times in Ireland's history that it was on the wane, spurring collectors to amass as much information as possible from musicians. The most notable collector was **Captain Francis O'Neill**, erstwhile Chicago police chief, who in the early twentieth century gathered tunes together in publications such as *The Dance Music of Ireland*. Later collectors of note include **Séamus Ennis**, who assiduously accumulated material for Radio Éireann and the BBC, and **Breandán Breathnach**, who published several volumes of material under the title *Ceol Rince na hÉireann* ("Dance Music of Ireland"). Today Dublin's Irish Traditional Music Archive continues the process of storing and cataloguing newly found material.

While these tunes were originally played at house or "crossroads" dances (held in a suitable open space – frequently a road junction), and often at weddings or wakes, they form merely a staging post for skilled traditional musicians, who embellish their renditions with all manner of musical ornamentation, though rarely straying from the essential rhythms of the dance. Nowadays, most dance tunes are played as part of a set, usually consisting of two or three of the same form, each played through a couple of times (or sometimes more) before segueing into the next one.

Sessions

The pub session as we know it today is in fact another import, having emerged in pubs in London and elsewhere where there were plenty of Irish émigrés in the years following World War II. During the folk and ballad boom of the 1960s, led by **The Clancy Brothers and Tommy Makem** and their more raucous contemporaries **The Dubliners**, Ireland's pub landlords began to welcome traditional musicians and the practice continues to this day. The session has become the focal point for the tradition and usually consists of a regular and informal gathering of local musicians on a particular evening, one of whom is usually paid to ensure that it takes place.

The majority of sessions (except some in extremely popular tourist areas) are relatively informal affairs where the musicians play the tunes of their choice, breaking off whenever they feel like doing so for a chat or an outdoor fag-break. Sessions can be found throughout the year in cities such as Belfast, Cork, Dublin and Galway, but in smaller towns and rural areas the months between June and September are usually the best time. Most begin at around 9.30pm, though on the west coast in high summer you'll find plenty not starting until 10.30pm and sometimes later. The lure for the pub's punters is the chance to hear top-class musicianship for the price of a pint or two, as well as participating in the associated *craic*.

Bear in mind that the musicians' seats are sacrosanct, so don't plonk yourself down next to a fiddler to enjoy the music from a closer aspect – the vacant seat you've just occupied was reserved for a musician who might or might not appear later.

You'll only rarely come across dancing at a session (and you'll probably be in Kerry or Clare if you do), thus the best bet, if you want to twirl the light fantastic, is to look out for a **ceili dance**. Plenty of these take place during local festivals, but there are also a number of renowned venues along the west coast that feature regular nights of set dancing to the accompaniment of a ceili band. These bands normally feature just the usual main traditional instruments, though some also include oddities such as the saxophone and accompaniment via piano and/or snare drum.

INSTRUMENTS AND PLAYERS

We've mentioned some of the best instrumentalists on the Irish music scene in this roundup of traditional instruments. If you get the chance to see any of them at the festivals, don't miss it.

UILLEANN PIPES

The English folk singer Martin Carthy once aptly described seeing the renowned **Séamus Ennis** playing the *uilleann* pipes as like "watching a man wrestling an octopus". The world's most complex set of bagpipes (variously pronounced "illun" or "illyun") is an extraordinarily temperamental creature and notoriously hard to master. The instrument has several components, consisting of a nine-holed chanter capable of producing a double-octave range, powered by air squeezed from a bag positioned under the left arm, itself driven by bellows pressed against the player's torso by his or her right elbow. The pipes also come equipped with three drones and a set of three regulators that can be flipped on and off to provide chordal accompaniment. No other instrument in the Irish canon is as capable of replicating the vocal ornamentations of *sean-nós* singers via the playing of slow airs.

Since the late nineteenth century two distinct styles of playing have evolved: one more gentle and ornamentally delicate, exemplified by Séamus Ennis and **Leo Rowsome**; and the other (often termed "open" or "legato") much more intricate, crisp, showy and rhythmically driven, and associated with members of the Traveller community who earned a living playing at country fairs – key protagonists of this style were the late brothers **Johnny and Felix Doran**, and, more recently, **Davy Spillane**.

Pipers have long held a special place in Ireland's musical heritage and among today's virtuosos are **Liam O'Flynn**, famed for his solo recordings, work with the classical composer Shaun Davey and poet Seamus Heaney, and membership of Planxty. **Paddy Keenan**, memorably once described as "the Jimi Hendrix of the *uilleann* pipes", rose to fame via The Bothy Band and continues to produce performances of astonishing majesty. Other pipers of note include **Neillidh Mulligan**, one of the best exponents of slow airs, **Ronan Browne** (also adept on flute and whistles), the Belfast-born **John McSherry** and the phenomenally talented young Dubliner **Seán McKeon**.

FLUTES AND WHISTLES

The flute preferred by Irish musicians is the simple wooden version with fingers used to cover the holes rather than keys as in its classical cousin, though some players do employ semi-keyed instruments. The long-standing hotbed of Irish flute music is North Connacht, famed for its seeming production-line of players incorporating a mellifluous, sometimes flamboyant style, in their music. The best known of these is **Matt Molloy** of The Bothy Band and The Chieftains, but **Séamus Tansey** has also been hugely influential. Belfast too has produced some fine flute players, often influenced by the North Connacht style or that of neighbouring Fermanagh (from which **Cathal McConnell** is a major figure), including **Desi Wilkinson** and **Harry Bradley**, while Dublin's **Paul McGrattan** has drawn much from the Donegal fiddle tradition.

The essential learning instrument of Irish music is the tin whistle, and one is still carried around by many players of other instruments keen to learn new tunes quickly – if you're tempted to buy one, make sure it's a D-whistle, as many tunes are played in this key. In the hands of a skilled operator – such as **Mary Bergin**, **Gavin Whelan** or **Bríd O'Donohue** – the whistle utterly surmounts its apparent technical limitations.

FIDDLES

The fiddle is Ireland's most popular traditional instrument and perhaps the best exemplar of regional musical styles (although these have been undermined as players learn their tunes and

The song tradition

Sadly, unaccompanied songs play little part in today's sessions, despite Ireland's remarkable vocal tradition. Essentially, this falls into two categories: songs in the Irish language and songs in English. Many Irish-language songs are of great antiquity and adaptations from the radio, CDs and MP3s rather than their neighbours). Donegal is famed for its captivating rhythmic style, often referred to as "driving" and best heard in the recordings of **John Doherty** (see p.439) and **Tommy Peoples**. The Sligo style, encapsulated in the recordings of **Michael Coleman** (see p.410) and **James Morrison**, is generally regarded as more ornamented and flashy, but continues to be a major influence. The eastern parts of Galway and Clare are noted for their more lonesome style, produced by a tendency to play in flattened key signatures and exemplified by the playing of **Martin Hayes**, who uses his native tradition as an extraordinary springboard for musical exploration. To the south, in Kerry and Cork, the polka remains the most popular dance tune and much of the most atmospheric playing dates back to the fiddle-master **Pádraig O'Keeffe**, though his enduring influence can be heard in the playing of **Matt Cranitch** and the late **Séamus Creagh**.

MELODEONS, ACCORDIONS AND CONCERTINAS

Squeeze-boxes come in a variety of shapes and sizes in traditional music. The simplest is the one-row button accordion, usually known as a melodeon in Ireland. One of its true masters is the Connemara box-player **Johnny Connolly**, generally regarded as the acme of accompanists for dancing. The far more popular two-row button accordion comes in a range of tunings, usually either B/C (favoured by the highly influential **Joe Burke**), which produces a more rolling and frilly style of play, or the C sharp/D variety (whose well-known exponents include **Dermot Byrne** and **Séamus Begley**). Also well worth seeking out are **Jackie Daly** and **Máirtín O'Connor**, both of whom play boxes in a variety of tunings, while the music of Clare's **Sharon Shannon** continues to attract a global audience. The piano accordion is less well favoured, though there are some cracking musicians using it, including **Alan Kelly**, **Mirella Murray** and **Martin Tourish**.

The smaller concertina was once thought of as primarily a women's instrument and was especially popular in County Clare (for too many reasons to list here). Again, it's ideal for accompanying dancers. Probably the best-known exponents are **Mary Mac Namara**, **Noel Hill**, **Chris Droney** and **Micheál Ó Raghallaigh**.

THE BOUZOUKI AND OTHER STRINGED INSTRUMENTS

The Greek *bouzouki* was first introduced to Ireland by **Johnny Moynihan** of the band Sweeney's Men in the late 1960s and made popular by **Dónal Lunny** of Planxty and The Bothy Band, and **Alec Finn** of De Dannan. Along with the guitar, it's the most common form of stringed accompaniment found at sessions, though, thanks to its open tuning and flat back, it's nowadays more akin to the mandolin than its Greek forebear. As a relatively quiet instrument, the mandolin itself, as played by **Paul Kelly**, is rarely seen at sessions, though you may see a larger version known as the mandola, whose well-known protagonists include **Andy Irvine**. Lastly, there's the banjo, an instrument reviled by many for its "plunker-plunker" sound, but which does have some exceptional exponents, including **Gerry O'Connor** and **Darren Maloney**.

THE BODHRÁN

This goatskin frame drum (pronounced "bore-run" or "bough-ron"), resembling a tambourine without jingles and played with the hand or a wooden beater, divides opinion among Irish sessioneers more than any other instrument. Some musicians appreciate the driving rhythm provided by a good percussionist (such as **John Joe Kelly**), but others regard it as the devil's detritus and sounding, in one fiddler's memorable words, "like a sack of spuds tipped down the stairs". Originally associated with the "wren boys" who went out revelling ("hunting the wren") and playing music on St Stephen's Day (Dec 26), it was adopted for ensemble playing by **Seán Ó Riada** in the 1960s. Many music or souvenir shops sell the drum and, if you're tempted to buy one, do listen to recordings of the best players (**Johnny McDonagh** and **Colm Murphy** with De Dannan or **Donnchadh Gough** with Danú) before even considering whether your own formative skills might be welcome at a session.

together they form part of what has become known as **sean-nós**, which literally means "old style". The tradition is strongest in the Irish-speaking areas of the west coast, particularly in West Kerry (Dingle), Connemara and Donegal, and incorporates an unaccompanied singing style of great emotional intensity when applied to the "big songs" of the tradition – tales of love, loss and longing – or sprightly frivolity when handling more light-hearted matters. Singers essentially construct a soundscape in which their use of vocal ornamentation and changes in tempo and tone lead the listener through the lyrics' twists and turns. Though knowledge of the Irish language is essential to a full understanding of their abilities, even without this it's still possible to appreciate singing that can be very beautiful. Some of the best contemporary members of the tradition, not least **Iarla Ó Lionáird** (from West Cork), well known through his work with the Afro Celts fusion band, and **Lasairfhíona Ní Chonaola** (from the Aran Islands), have produced albums of extraordinary splendour.

Simultaneously, Ireland possesses a vast wealth of traditional songs in English, including many derived from the broadsheet ballad-sellers of the nineteenth and earlier twentieth centuries and others shared with the heritage of England and Scotland, and there are traditional singing clubs in several of Ireland's towns and cities. The country's foremost interpreter of these and many other contemporary songs is unquestionably **Christy Moore.**

DISCOGRAPHY

The following selection of albums provides a solid foundation for investigation of Ireland's musical traditions. They can be purchased at Claddagh Records in Dublin (see p.108), Custy's in Ennis (see p.325), other record stores and online.

Mary Bergin *Feadóga Stáin* (Gael Linn). Marvellously adept whistle-playing.

The Bothy Band *The Bothy Band 1975* (Jasmine). Short-lived but still incredibly influential, this band set the template for so many others to follow.

Cran *Lover's Ghost* (Black Rose Records). A gripping melange of songs and flute/*uilleann* pipes interplay.

Séamus Creagh and Jackie Daly *Same* (Gael Linn). Polkas from the mountains of Sliabh Luachra on the Kerry–Cork–Limerick border and much more on this exhilarating fiddle/accordion album.

Martin Hayes and Dennis Cahill *Live in Seattle* (Green Linnet). Ireland's most soulful and imaginative fiddler, in cahoots with long-time guitarist buddy, produces one of the most invigorating live performances you'll ever hear.

Joe Heaney *The Road from Connemara* (Topic). A double-CD which encapsulates the singing of perhaps Ireland's finest exponent of the *sean-nós* style.

Noel Hill and Tony Linnane *Same* (Tara). Tremendous concertina/fiddle duets from the Clare duo, recorded when both were in their late teens.

Christy Moore *At the Point Live* (Columbia). Captures the singer in his heyday when he was justifiably regarded as a national treasure.

Maighread and Tríona Ní Dhomhnaill *Idir an Dá Sholas* (Gael Linn/Hummingbird). Glorious singing in both Irish and English.

Gerry O'Connor *Journeyman* (Lughnasa Music). One of the finest fiddle albums of recent years.

Planxty *Same* (Shanachie). AKA "*The Black Album*" and featuring a dazzling array of songs and tunes from Christy Moore, Andy Irvine, Liam Ó Flynn and Dónal Lunny, this magical release redefined Ireland's musical landscape.

Sharon Shannon, Frankie Gavin, Michael McGoldrick and Jim Murray *Tunes* (The Daisy Label). A splendid constellation of accordion, fiddle, flute and guitar.

Solas *Reunion* (Compass Records). A fabulous live recording (including film footage on DVD) of a concert reuniting the Irish-US band's former and present members.

Séamus Tansey *King of the Concert Flute* (Sound Records). Outstanding flute-playing from the Sligo master.

Various *The Rough Guide to Irish Folk* and *The Rough Guide to Irish Music* (both World Music Network). Two excellent compilations providing an overview, respectively, of the song and instrumental traditions.

Literature

For an island of fewer than six million people, Ireland has an astonishingly rich **literary tradition**, the oldest in Europe outside of Italy and Greece. While most of this literature up to the seventeenth century was written in Gaelic (usually called Irish in Ireland today), and to a lesser extent Latin, English would become pre-eminent from the eighteenth century onwards and is today the first language not just of most Irish writing but also of the vast majority of Irish people. Ireland's literary tradition has developed over two thousand years from the first markings on rocks around the time of Christ, to the acclaimed poetry, prose and theatre of writers such as W.B. Yeats, James Joyce and Samuel Beckett, producing startling works of originality and influence.

Beginnings

The oldest writing in Ireland was ogham script, a system of parallel notches that survives on standing stones from the fourth century AD, but was likely in existence for several hundred years previous. However, it was the arrival of Christianity in the fifth century that would have the most significant early influence on the emergence of literature in Ireland. With the growth of the monasteries between the seventh and tenth centuries, a rich culture of Latin manuscripts developed, the finest surviving example of which is the *Book of Kells* in Trinity College, Dublin (see p.59).

During the same period, a thriving literary culture in the vernacular of Irish life, Gaelic, began to emerge and develop, too. While the oldest surviving manuscripts in this language date from around the twelfth century, much of the material was copied and recopied for many hundreds of years before that. The oldest datable work of Gaelic literature is **Amra Choluim Chille** (Elegy of St Columba), a poem attributed to the poet Dallán Forgaill and written soon after the death in 597 of one of Ireland's most famous early saints, Colmcille, regarded as the patron saint of Irish poets. The Gaelic manuscripts also incorporated ancient, often fantastic and supernatural tales which had been preserved in a primarily oral culture. One such classic Irish story is the **Táin Bó Cúailnge** (The Cattle Raid of Cooley), which features the legendary figures of Cúchulainn, the larger-than-life Ulster warrior, and Queen Medb of Connaught.

While the manuscript tradition preserved tales concerning Cúchulainn, found in a larger narrative called the Ulster Cycle, a further popular hero in Gaelic oral culture was **Fionn Mac Cumhaill**, the leader of a band of warriors defending Ireland called the Fianna. The stories of Fionn and his men are commonly referred to as the *Fiannaíocht* tales and include the classic *Tóraíocht Dhiarmada agus Gráinne* (The Pursuit of Diarmuid and Gráinne), in which Fionn's intended, Gráinne, seduces one of his handsome warriors, Diarmuid, and elopes across Ireland, chased by Fionn and his men. Another famous early Gaelic tale is **Buile Shuibhne** (The Frenzy of Sweeney), the story of Suibhne Geilt, a king who, after being cursed by a local cleric, is transformed into a bird, banished and condemned to wander through Ireland's most desolate landscapes enduring great hardship and loneliness. These Gaelic legends have provided recurring inspiration for Irish writers, including W.B. Yeats, Synge, Joyce, Beckett, Flann O'Brien and Seamus Heaney.

The arrival of the Anglo-Normans in Ireland in the twelfth century brought another influence to bear on the Irish language and literature, and some of the finest poets of the Middle Ages would descend from Anglo-Norman stock, including in the fourteenth century Gearóid Iarla Fitzgerald, the Third Earl of Desmond. The thirteenth-century version of what is today known as Middle Irish was preserved as a literary language through the **bardic schools** that emerged in this period and continued in Ireland down to the mid-seventeenth century. These provided structured training for the *filí*, or poets, who were both feared and highly respected in a very hierarchical society. One significant aspect of poetry in this period was its close association with music, an association that would continue throughout the history of Irish literature. Surviving records suggest that bardic poetry was always performed with the accompaniment of the harp, the instrument that remains the national emblem of Ireland today. The esteem in which these poets were held is evident from the fact that many examples of this richly ornate and highly sophisticated bardic poetry survive, despite the tumultuous events that would lead to the decline of Gaelic Ireland.

Irish-language works of the seventeenth and eighteenth centuries

With the undermining of the Gaelic order following the Battle of Kinsale in 1601, the structures that had supported indigenous poetic and musical production went into decline. Furthermore, as the power of musicians and poets had been feared by the British establishment throughout the sixteenth century, efforts were made to persecute them and generally limit their influence. Previously exalted *filí* were now often reduced to **sráid-éigse** or "street poetry". The result was to bring the formerly independent professions of musician and poet together in the one performer whose compositions, particularly by the eighteenth century, gradually became more and more associated with the folk tradition of song. The passing on of Irish poetry through song ensured its survival and some songs from the eighteenth century, including *Dónal Óg* and *Úna Bhán*, continue to be sung today in the *sean-nós* or old-style tradition.

The eighteenth century would also witness, inspired by the Jacobite insurrections in Scotland of 1715 and 1745, the emergence of an indigenous, politically engaged poetry, as poets such as Piaras Mac Gearailt, Seán Ó Tuama, Seán Clárach Mac Domhnaill and Eoghan Rua Ó Súilleabháin produced work confident of the return of the Catholic Stuart kings to power and the revival of the Gaelic aristocracy. One of the most popular genres to evolve in this period was the **aisling**, its finest exponent **Aogán Ó Rathaille** in works such as *Mac an Cheannaí* (The Merchant's Son) and *Gile na Gile* (Brightness Most Bright). These "vision poems" feature the poet, on falling asleep, imagining he is visited by a beautiful woman who reveals herself as Ireland and laments her oppression. Such was the popularity of the *aisling* that one of the finest Gaelic poems of the eighteenth century is actually a parody of the genre, **Brian Merriman**'s *Cúirt An Mheán Oíche* (The Midnight Court). Here the poet encounters no beautiful maiden but rather an old hag, who summons him to a court where he witnesses an attack by Queen Aoibheal on the young men of Ireland for their refusal to marry and lack of virility. A ribald and satiric piece, regarded as the greatest comic poem in the language, it was banned in English when translated by Frank O'Connor in 1945, though the Irish-language version remained on the shelves.

Another highly accomplished Gaelic work of the eighteenth century is the *Caoineadh Airt Uí Laoghaire* (Lament for Art Ó Laoghaire), a long, traditional *caoineadh* or lament composed *ex tempore* by **Eibhlín Dhubh Ní Chonaill**, the aunt of Daniel O'Connell. It is a haunting piece lamenting the killing of Eibhlín's husband by the local sheriff, Abraham Morris, for refusing to sell his horse to him for £5, at a time when no Catholic was allowed under the hated penal laws to own a horse worth more than that figure.

The emergence of Irish literature in English

While Irish-language literature took a downturn from the seventeenth century onwards, Irish literature in English began to come to the fore, most importantly in the angry little shape of the poet, essayist and satirist **Jonathan Swift** (see p.75). Other notable writers in English from the eighteenth century include **Laurence Sterne**, the Tipperary-born clergyman and author of the innovative and highly influential satire on the biographical novel, *The Life and Opinions of Tristram Shandy, Gentleman*; the Longford doctor, **Oliver Goldsmith**, best known for his elegy *The Deserted Village*, novel *The Vicar of Wakefield* and play *She Stoops to Conquer*; and **Richard Brinsley Sheridan**, author of *The Rivals* and *The School for Scandal*, one of the first in a long tradition of leading Irish playwrights in the English language.

Despite the decline of Irish language and culture, the late eighteenth and early nineteenth centuries were nonetheless important for the rejuvenation of Irish nationalism, Irish music and the emergence of a distinctive Irish poetry in English. The efforts of primarily Anglo-Irish antiquarians, concerned to promote the distinctiveness of the adopted country of their ancestors, would help to preserve some of the native literature and music. In 1789, the first translations of Gaelic poetry and songs, *Reliques of Irish Poetry*, were published by **Charlotte Brooke**, a pioneering mediator between the Anglo-Irish Ascendancy and the local tradition. Her work would inspire subsequent antiquarians such as **Sir Samuel Ferguson**, the most important collector and translator of Gaelic poetry and mythology in the nineteenth century and a crucial influence on the writers who emerged in the Literary Revival at the end of the century, including W.B. Yeats.

Thomas Moore and the Young Ireland Poets

In the early nineteenth century, "the darling of the London drawing rooms" was **Thomas Moore**, born of a Catholic family in Dublin, whose romantic and nostalgic nationalist compositions – such as the still-popular songs *The Minstrel Boy* and *The Last Rose of Summer* – were included in *Irish Melodies*, published in ten volumes between 1808 and 1834. These poems were set to traditional Irish tunes from Edward Bunting's *General Collection of Ancient Music of Ireland* (1796), a compilation of the airs of some of the few remaining Irish harpists who performed at the Belfast Harpers' Festival of July 1792. Moore's *Melodies* has been called "the secular hymn-book of Irish nationalism" in the nineteenth century and he was regarded by many during his lifetime as Ireland's national poet. He represents the beginnings of the articulation of Irish identity and culture, on a national scale, in the English language.

While Moore had found in Irish music a means of access to what he believed to be the national spirit, the **Young Ireland Poets** associated with the nationalist newspaper, *The Nation* (which began publication in 1842), would find similar sustenance in the ballad. Among the most influential contributors to *The Nation* were **Thomas Davis** and **James Clarence Mangan**, both of whom would be alluded to in the work of W.B. Yeats and Joyce. While Davis's *A Nation Once Again* is still sung and was given serious consideration as the national anthem of Ireland, his emphasis on the importance of literature for national identity would have a vital influence on the Literary Revival. Mangan's free translation of the Gaelic song *Róisín Dubh* (Dark Rosaleen) has been described as the "most widely known nationalist poem" of the nineteenth century, but his overall ambivalence towards the nationalist project would find resonance in the work of Joyce, who wrote an essay on the poet.

Irish playwrights of the nineteenth century

Born in Dublin of Huguenot stock, **Dion Boucicault** found inspiration in Irish history and legend for plays such as *The Colleen Bawn* (1860), *The Shaughran* (1875) and *Robert Emmet* (1884). His work was renowned for its humour and enjoyed considerable popular success in Ireland, Britain and the US during his life, but subsequent Irish writers and commentators would accuse him of perpetuating the figure of the drunken and pugnacious "stage Irishman", a popular stereotype that had gained currency in the early eighteenth century in the work of Irish playwright George Farquhar.

Better known to her readers by her pseudonym **Speranza**, Jane Francesca Wilde was an Anglo-Irish author and literary hostess who contributed nationalist poems and anti-British writings to *The Nation*. While her work was of limited artistic value, her son **Oscar Wilde** would become one of the most famous (and eventually infamous) dramatists of the British stage in the late nineteenth century. Oscar did not share his mother's engagement with Irish politics and left the country for England shortly after graduating from Trinity College, where he was an outstanding student of classics, in 1874. He was awarded a scholarship to Magdalen College, Oxford, where he joined the Aesthetic Movement, a society dedicated to making an art out of life. Although Wilde published prose – his novel *The Picture of Dorian Gray* provoked a storm of protests in Victorian society because of its implied homoerotic theme – and poetry, his dazzling plays, including *Lady Windermere's Fan* and *The Importance of Being Earnest*, enjoyed the most success during his lifetime and continue to be performed today. Wilde managed to satirize the pretensions of the English upper and middle classes with humour and insight in a way that only someone coming from outside this society could. He was respected on both sides of the Atlantic for his work and enthralling lectures, and admired in polite society for his ability as a raconteur – as he said himself, to W.B. Yeats, "we Irish have done nothing, but we are the greatest talkers since the Greeks". However, a homosexual relationship with Lord Alfred Douglas, son of the Marquis of Queensbury, would eventually lead to his demise following a conviction and imprisonment for gross indecency. He was sentenced to two years' hard labour, an experience, given chilling insight by one of his finest works *The Ballad of Reading Gaol*, that would break him both physically and psychologically. Wilde died in Paris on November 30, 1900, a broken man who could never ignite his fires of creativity after prison. He left not just great literature but also some of the most memorable aphorisms in the English language, some of which too sadly described his own fate: "The secret of life is to appreciate the pleasure of being terribly, terribly deceived."

The other major playwright to emerge in England in the late nineteenth century was also Irish, the Dublin-born, life-long socialist, **George Bernard Shaw** (see p.68), whose career and influence extended well into the twentieth century. Shaw's work for the theatre was ground-breaking in bringing his own economic, moral and political concerns to the fore, but like Wilde he was also a legendary wit, combining acerbic humour with potent insights into human nature: "Gambling promises the poor what property performs for the rich – something for nothing." Nothing short of prolific, Shaw wrote over sixty plays, including *Arms and the Man*, *John Bull's Other Island* and *Pygmalion*, as well as five less successful novels and an impressive array of literary criticism and political commentary, before his death at the age of 94 in November 1950.

The emergence of the Irish novel

A relatively new form that was to play an increasingly central part in cultural life in the nineteenth century, the novel in Ireland generally traces its beginnings to *Castle Rackrent* (1800), written by **Maria Edgeworth**. Although from an Anglo-Irish Ascendancy family, who gave their name to Edgeworthstown in County Longford, Edgeworth reveals the inequitable and sometimes abusive treatment estate tenants endured at the hands of their landlords. *Castle Rackrent* began one of the most popular genres in Irish literature, the "Big House" novel, concerning the experiences of the landholding class on an Anglo-Irish estate.

Though dominated by writers from the Ascendancy class in Ireland, the nineteenth century was also important for the emergence of female writers such as Edgeworth. Others include **Lady Morgan** (Sidney Owenson), whose *The Wild Irish Girl* (1806) is regarded as an important early feminist text, and the co-authors Edith Somerville and her cousin Violet Martin, known for works such as *The Irish R.M* written under their pseudonyms **Somerville and Ross**.

Other important writers of fiction to emerge in the nineteenth century include **William Carleton**, whose *Traits and Stories of the Irish Peasantry* would be a very influential text for writers such as Yeats; the brothers **John and Michael Banim**, whose major work is the 24 volumes of *The Tales of the O'Hara Family*; and Limerick-born novelist **Gerald Griffin**, whose *The Collegians* was based on events surrounding a trial in which Daniel O'Connell acted as attorney for the defence. The most popular novel in Ireland of the nineteenth century, however, was *Knocknagown; or The Homes of Tipperary* (1879), a convoluted and sentimental account of Tipperary rural life and critique of landlordism, written by the patriot and Young Irelander, **Charles Kickham**.

The Gothic genre was given much of its shape by Irish writers in this period, including **Charles Robert Maturin**, particularly in his dark tale of a man who sells his soul to the devil, *Melmoth the Wanderer* (1820); and **Joseph Sheridan Le Fanu**, the leading ghost-story writer of the nineteenth century, best known for his novel *Uncle Silas* (1864) and collection of short stories *In a Glass Darkly* (1872). But they pale in comparison to **Bram Stoker**, whose *Dracula* (1897) is still one of the most popular and adapted works of fiction today. Born in Dublin and educated at Trinity College, Stoker spent most of his life in London as manager to the famous Shakespearean actor, Henry Irving. However, in its pseudo-folkloric style and its preoccupations – the nature of the soul set against the temptations of the flesh, the noble serfs against the aristocratic fiend – his most famous novel remains curiously Irish.

The Literary Revival

While Oscar Wilde and George Bernard Shaw were dominating the stage in Britain at the end of the nineteenth century, Irish cultural nationalism was on the rise back home. This period is collectively referred to as the **Irish Literary Revival**, though there were at least two revivals apparent: the Anglo-Irish, concerned with the promotion of Hiberno-English, the English language as sculpted by the particularities of Irish accent and the structures of Gaelic; and the Gaelic Revival, focused on the Irish language, which by now had been devastated by famine, emigration, poverty, lack of support and, indeed, outright discouragement in education. During the Literary Revival, literature in both languages would become a central focus for the revitalization of Irish culture, though attempts were also made through organizations such as Conradh na Gaeilge (the Gaelic League), founded in 1893, to preserve and encourage indigenous musical practices. The League's first president, **Douglas Hyde**, who later became Ireland's first president, would do much to popularize the Gaelic poetic tradition through his translations in *Abhráin Grádh Chúige Connacht* (The Love Songs of Connacht; 1893) and *Abhráin Diadha Chúige Connacht* (The Religious Songs of Connacht; 1905). These collections were an important inspiration for both Irish- and English-language writers, contributing to the idealization of the rural peasantry of the west, particularly in Yeats's work, as the well-spring from which, it was thought, a new, invigorated Irish literature and identity would emerge.

W.B. Yeats

Though **William Butler Yeats** was born in Dublin in 1865 into an aristocratic Protestant family, it was Sligo in the west of Ireland, where he spent a considerable part of his formative years, that would fire his creative imagination. The most important writer of the Revival period, Yeats was in many ways the father of modern Irish literature. One of his major roles was in bringing material in Irish – including elements from the *Táin* and *Fiannaíocht* tales – into mainstream English-language literature through collections such as *The Wanderings of Oisin* (1889). But, more importantly, as a dramatist, essayist and, above all, poet, Yeats brought Irish culture onto a world stage, winning the Nobel Prize for Literature in 1923 and producing some of the finest poetry in any language of that era. While influenced by and commenting on the turbulent years in Ireland of the early twentieth century, his work resonated internationally in a time of calamity and change during and after World War I, with the lines of *The Second Coming*, published in 1921 as the Irish war of independence was coming to an end, still among the most quoted in modern literature:

Things fall apart; the centre cannot hold;
Mere anarchy is loosed upon the world,
The blood-dimmed tide is loosed, and everywhere
The ceremony of innocence is drowned;
The best lack all conviction, while the worst
Are full of passionate intensity.

From his Late Romantic beginnings, Yeats's work developed through the trauma of lost love – Maude Gonne, a recurring presence throughout his work – and the disappointment of the Ireland he saw emerging, more mercantile than artistic, to produce a harder, more realist and direct poetry. Among the best examples of this work are *September 1913, Easter 1916* – his elegy for the executed leaders of the Republican Rising of that year – and *The Fisherman*. But it was in Yeats's last decade that the challenges of ageing and declining health inspired some of the finest moments in modern poetry, including *Among School Children* and *Sailing to Byzantium*. Yeats died in January 1939 in France, with his body returning to Ireland after the war in 1948 to be reburied in Drumcliffe churchyard in County Sligo.

The Abbey and Synge

One of the major ambitions of Yeats, Lady Gregory and other leaders of the Literary Revival was the development of an Irish national theatre, realized with the opening of the **Abbey Theatre** in 1904. The Abbey would define a distinct form of Irish theatre, combining a concern with the English language as spoken in Ireland with an attempt to revive belief in the value of Irish culture. In its early years, its greatest playwright was **John Millington Synge**, whose work would provide some of the most memorable characters and narratives of this period, particularly in his masterpiece *The Playboy of the Western World*, first performed in 1907. This dark and yet at times very humorous play, featuring Christy Mahon who achieves fame in a rural Mayo community by claiming that he killed his father, was more than the nationalist audience of its day could accept and resulted in a riot during its first performance. Synge was not afraid to reveal the full gamut of the rural peasant's language, inflected with the Irish language, in both its vulgarity and wit, and an audience that had been conditioned to view the peasant as the very paragon of pure Irishness could not tolerate such a blasphemy. Synge died all too young at the age of 37 in 1909, but helped to inspire later dramatists to create realistic depictions of Irish life.

Joyce

James Joyce was born in Dublin in 1882 into a middle-class Catholic family, which by his early teens had declined into poverty, due largely to his father's carelessness with money. Joyce's challenging experiences, however, provided considerable material for characters and narratives, giving rise to one of the most innovative and imaginative voices in English literature. Although Joyce began writing when the Literary Revival was at its height, he would become one of its strongest critics: as Stephen Dedalus, the protagonist of his semi-autobiographical *A Portrait of the Artist as a Young Man* (1916), remarks to his nationalist school-friend Davin, "You talk to me of nationality, language, religion. I shall try to fly by those nets." For Joyce, each of these elements placed constraints on the writer that could only limit his creativity and expression, something he could not countenance. In the end, he found Ireland too oppressive socially and culturally for his art and headed for the continent, rarely returning to the country of his birth after 1904, and visiting for the last time in 1912. However, while much of his writing was done in Trieste, Paris and Zürich – the city in which he died in 1941 – Ireland, and particularly Dublin, remained the central locale of his work. Indeed, arguably no other writer in twentieth-century literature mapped a city so effectively, epitomized in his finest work, *Ulysses* (1922), which recounts the happenings of a single day in the life of Dublin. Joyce's partner, and eventual wife, during his years on the continent was Nora Barnacle, and the day on which they first met in Dublin, June 16, 1904, has become immortalized as "Bloomsday" (see also p.80), the day on which all the events of the novel, concerning the life and ruminations of a Jewish advertising canvasser, Leopold Bloom, take place.

Irish fiction after Joyce

The short story, a form pioneered in Ireland by George Moore in *The Untilled Field* (1903) and developed by Joyce in *Dubliners* (1914), has been an important genre for Irish writers ever since. **Liam O'Flaherty**, born in 1896 on the Irish-speaking Aran Islands off Galway, wrote several acclaimed novels, including *The Informer* (1925), a salty tale of an ex-IRA man who betrays an associate to the police and is hunted down by his former colleagues. However, it is his short stories, in both English and his native Irish, including "Going into Exile", "The Shilling" and his Irish-language collection, *Dúil* (1953), that constitute his best work. Two other notable exponents of the short-story form were **Seán Ó Faoláin** and **Frank O'Connor**. Among Ó Faoláin's finest collections are *Midsummer Night Madness and Other Stories* (1932) and *The Man Who Invented Sin* (1948), while his story "Lovers of the Lake" remains a classic in modern Irish writing. Ó Faoláin was also an editor of the seminal literary journal of the 1940s and 1950s, *The Bell*, and an outspoken critic of the anti-intellectualism that characterized Irish society during his life, under the considerable influence of the Catholic Church. While O'Connor also worked as a translator, essayist and biographer, it is for his short stories that he is best remembered, including "The First Confession" and "The Luceys", and the collection *Guests of the Nation* (1931).

One of the most experimental writers of the twentieth century was **Flann O'Brien**, born Brian Ó Núalláin in 1911. While O'Brien's finest work is arguably found in the novel *At Swim-Two-Birds* (1939), his wonderfully surreal and funny *The Third Policeman* (1967) recently enjoyed renewed popularity after its brief appearance in the TV serial *Lost*. O'Brien's first language growing up in Tyrone and later Dublin was Irish, and he also wrote some of the most satirically humorous work in this language, including *An Béal Bocht* (The Poor Mouth; 1941), published under the pseudonym Myles na gCopaleen ("Myles of the little horses"). A parody of the celebrated Blasket Island autobiographies of writers such as Tomás Ó Criomhthain and Peig Sayers, *An Béal Bocht* is an unrestrained attack on the pretensions of the Irish-Ireland movement.

Irish poetry after Yeats

The generation of poets that followed Yeats could not escape the long shadow cast by the Nobel Laureate, but were also concerned to critique the legacies of the Literary Revival, especially its reliance on the idealization of the peasant. While **Austin Clarke** charted the urban experience, Patrick Kavanagh's work provided one of the first authentic catalogues of rural life in twentieth-century poetry. Clarke began writing verse in the 1910s much influenced by early Yeats and concerned with similar goals of bringing Gaelic literature into the English language; for example in his free translations of stories about Fionn Mac Cumhaill in *The Vengeance of Fionn*. As his work matured, he became one of the most consistent and acerbic commentators on Irish life and particularly the suffocating influence of the Church, apparent in one of his finest poems *Martha Blake at 51*, and his short lyric *Penal Law*:

Burn Ovid with the rest. Lovers will find
A hedge-school for themselves and learn by heart
All that the clergy banish from the mind,
When hands are joined and head bows in the dark.

Clarke's legacy has been particularly influential in the work of **Thomas Kinsella**, who continues Clarke's mapping of the urban geography of Dublin. Kinsella has also turned to Gaelic literature and Irish mythology for themes and motifs in his work and, influenced by Jungian psychology, as part of his exploration of his own unconscious, in collections such as *Notes from the Land of the Dead* (1973) and *Fifteen Dead* (1979). Kinsella has also been one of the most important translators of Gaelic literature into English, in works such as *The Táin*, *An Duanaire 1600–1900: Poems of the Dispossessed* and *The New Oxford Book of Irish Verse*.

The poetry of **Patrick Kavanagh**, who was born in 1904 and raised on a small farm near Inniskeen, County Monaghan, revealed the challenges of rural life in a manner that included an implicit, and sometimes explicit, critique of the Revival's pretensions. Though his work also includes striking lyrics recognizing the power and beauty of the natural world – "the spirit-shocking wonder of a black slanting Ulster hill" – for Kavanagh rural life was often characterized by deprivation, both physical and psychological, as demonstrated in *The Great Hunger* and the pounding rhythms of *Stony Grey Soil*:

O stony grey soil of Monaghan
The laugh from my love you thieved;
You took the gay child of my passion
And gave me your clod-conceived.

Kavanagh, who died in 1967, has been arguably the most influential Irish poet after Yeats for contemporary poets such as Seamus Heaney and **John Montague**. Raised in Tyrone, Montague inherited Kavanagh's rural concerns, but added to it a political consciousness focused on the Troubles in Northern Ireland, apparent in the volume *The Rough Field* (1972).

As Montague's work, and that of other Northern poets suggests, the setting-up of Northern Ireland in 1920 created distinct historical and political processes within that region. Issues such as culture, language, history and identity became all the more important to writers attempting to articulate distinctive voices in a contested space, coming to a head with the outbreak of the Troubles in the late 1960s. However, these themes were already apparent in the work of the major writers from Northern Ireland in the early and mid-twentieth century: **John Hewitt** and **Louis MacNeice**. In the work of MacNeice, who is often associated with the British poetry movement of the 1930s that included Cecil Day Lewis, Stephen Spender and W. H. Auden, one finds an ambiguous relationship with the country of his birth, though his focus on the west of Ireland in particular, in poems such as *Galway* and *Western Landscape*, anticipates the concern with this part of the island in the work of the next generation of Protestant poets, Michael Longley and Derek Mahon. Meanwhile Hewitt promoted his belief in cultural regionalism, in writing from and for the community in the North from which he emerged:

I write for my own kind
I do not pitch my voice
that every phrase be heard
by those that have no choice:
their quality of mind
must be withdrawn and still,
as moth that answers moth
across a roaring hill.

Irish-language literature in the twentieth century

The Revival was important for the emergence of prose writers in Irish in the twentieth century, most notably Galway-born **Pádraic Ó Conaire**, the author of over four hundred short stories, several plays, numerous essays and the ground-breaking novel *Deoraíocht* (Exile; 1910), still one of the most remarkable Irish works of fiction and regarded as the first modern novel in the Irish language. Set in London at the beginning of the twentieth century, the narrative concerns an Irish emigrant, who after losing an arm and a leg and being seriously disfigured in an accident shortly after arriving from Galway, ends up working in a travelling circus as a sideshow freak.

Autobiography emerged as an important form in Irish-language literature in the early twentieth century. This was most apparent in the work of writers from the now-uninhabited **Blasket Islands** (see p.298) off the coast of Kerry, including Peig Sayers, Muiris Ó Súilleabháin and Tomás Ó Criomhthain, whose *An tOileánach* (The Islandman; 1929) is probably the most accomplished of all these texts.

The dwindling audience for Irish-language literature would be a matter of concern for writers throughout the twentieth century. As **Máirtín Ó Cadhain**, author of the century's most innovative novel in Irish, *Cré na Cille* (Graveyard Clay; 1948), remarked, "[i]t is hard for a man to give of his best in a language which seems likely to die before himself, if he lives a few years more". Despite the decline in the number of native speakers, however, writers like Eoghan Ó Tuairisc, Bréandán Ó hEithir, Pádraig Standún, Mícheál Ó Siadhail and Pádraig Ó Cíobháin have all produced substantial fiction in Irish, while Pádraic Breathnach, Alan Titley and Micheál Ó Conghaile continue to produce critically acclaimed collections of short stories.

In poetry, the major Irish-language writers to emerge in the mid-twentieth century were **Máirtín Ó Direáin, Máire Mhac an tSaoi** and **Seán Ó Ríordáin**. For Ó Direáin, from his first self-published collection, *Coinnle Geala* (1942), the speech of the Aran Islands where he grew up was an important source, but he would turn, particularly from the collection *Ó Mórna agus Dánta Eile*, to forms apparent in the work of earlier Gaelic poets. Mhac an tSaoi would bring a thorough knowledge of the Gaelic literary tradition to her work, reflected in her use of both bardic and *amhrán*, or Gaelic song, metres in poems such as *Caoineadh* and *Ceathrúintí Mháire Ní Ógáin*. For collections such as *Brosna* (1964), Ó Ríordáin is regarded as the great modernist of Gaelic poetry, whose conscious rearranging of language would produce an original and, for many, controversial, poetics in Irish.

Other accomplished Irish-language poets over the past thirty years have included Michael Hartnett – who was also a major poet in English – Michael Davitt, Gabriel Rosenstock, Liam Ó Muirthile, Nuala Ní Dhomhnaill, Cathal Ó Searcaigh, Gréagóir Ó Dúill, Micheal Ó Siadhail, Áine Ní Ghlinn, Biddy Jenkinson, Colm Breathnach and Louis de Paor. Many of these writers have at some point been associated with **Innti**, an Irish-language poetry movement (and literary journal) that emerged in Cork in the early 1970s, which has been one of the most important initiatives in building a new audience for poetry generally in Ireland, often through public readings.

Irish theatre after Synge

Whereas Synge had focused on rural Ireland, the Abbey's next great dramatist, **Sean O'Casey**, would bring the lives and challenges of the urban poor onto the stage, in some of the theatre's most famous and controversial productions, including *The Shadow of a Gunman* (1923) and *Juno and the Paycock* (1924). As with Synge's *Playboy of the Western World*, O'Casey's next, and arguably finest play, *The Plough and the Stars*, resulted in a riot in the theatre when first staged in 1926. Depicting the events of the 1916 Rising from the perspective of ordinary tenement-dwellers in Dublin, O'Casey cast a critical eye over events considered sacred in Irish nationalist history, regarding the leaders as more concerned with their own egos than with the welfare of the populace. O'Casey, however, felt suffocated as many Irish writers before and after by the oppressive forces of religion and orthodoxy in Ireland. After his subsequent play, the experimental *The Silver Tassie*, dealing with World War I, was rejected by the Abbey, he left Ireland in 1928, spending the remainder of his life in Devon, England.

Among those who assisted James Joyce in his work during his years in Paris was a young writer who had similarly left Ireland in his early twenties, and would himself go on to achieve worldwide fame as a modernist writer: **Samuel Beckett**. While creating some of the century's most memorable dramatic works – including *Waiting for Godot* (1952), *Endgame* (1958) and *Krapp's Last Tape* (1959) – Beckett developed a minimalist and sometimes severe theatre of the absurd, if one relieved by occasional moments of insight and humour. He brought to his writing the attention to detail characteristic of one writing in an acquired tongue (many of his greatest works were written in French) and was awarded the Nobel Prize for Literature in 1968.

Brendan Behan is today unfortunately remembered almost as much for his effusive personality and drunken interviews as for his important literary work, which included the autobiographical *Borstal Boy* (1958) and the plays *The Quare Fellow* (1954) and *The Hostage* (1958; originally produced in Irish as *An Giall*), a piece that in many respects anticipated the narrative of Neil Jordan's Oscar-winning 1992 film, *The Crying Game*. Behan's weakness for alcohol was a major factor in both his small, if accomplished, output as a writer and his early death at the age of 41.

Contemporary theatre

Among the recurring themes of Irish theatre since the middle of the twentieth century has been the legacy of colonialism, including the Troubles in Northern Ireland. Reflecting the nationalist standpoint, **Brian Friel**'s *Translations* (1980) and *Dancing at Lughnasa* (1992) remain modern classics of the Irish stage. One of the most important studies of Unionist identity is found in the Donegal-born **Frank McGuinness**'s *Observe the Sons of Ulster Marching Towards the Somme* (1985). Similar critical acclaim has attended **Thomas Kilroy** (*The Death and Resurrection of Mr Roche*, 1968; *The O'Neill*, 1969; *Sex and Shakespeare*, 1976) and **Tom Murphy** (*Famine*, 1968; *Conversations on a Homecoming*, 1985; *Bailegangaire*, 2001), while **Hugh Leonard** and **John B. Keane** have written some of the most popular dramatic works since the 1960s, several of which have been adapted for film, including Leonard's *Da* (originally produced in 1977) and Keane's *The Field* (1965).

A significant development over the past forty years has been the emergence of new theatre companies to challenge the dominance of the Abbey, including **Field Day**, founded in 1980 in Derry by Seamus Heaney, Brian Friel and Thomas Kilroy, among others. Galway's **Druid Theatre** has produced some of the most important contemporary works on the Irish stage, including the plays of **Martin McDonagh**, born in London of Irish descent. McDonagh, who won an Academy Award for best short film in 2006 and a BAFTA for 2008's *In Bruges*, has garnered widespread critical acclaim for his provocative and violent work, notably *The Beauty Queen of Leenane* (1996). A feature of younger playwrights such as **Conor McPherson**, **Enda Walsh** and **Mark O'Rowe** has been a willingness to bring the vernacular and popular culture onto the stage. Each of these writers has moved between theatre and film, with Walsh's *Disco Pigs* (1996) being adapted for the screen by Kirsten Sheridan in 2001, O'Rowe providing the script for one of the most successful independent Irish films in recent years, *Intermission* (2003), and McPherson going on to direct his own films, including *Saltwater* (2000) and *The Actors* (2003) starring Michael Caine. One of the most significant new voices to have emerged from the North is **Gary Mitchell**, whose plays such as *As the Beast Sleeps* (1998), *The Force of Change* (2000) and *State of Failure* (2006) draw strikingly on his own Belfast working-class Loyalist experience. However, following first threats then full-scale intimidation by the paramilitaries (angered by TV adaptations of his work), Mitchell and his family were forced to flee Belfast in 2005 and live in hiding for five years. Other playwrights of note to emerge in recent years include Paul Mercier, Marina Carr, Christian O'Reilly and Sebastian Barry, who has also achieved recognition for his fiction, including *A Long Long Way* (2005) and *The Secret Scripture* (2008), which were both shortlisted for the Man Booker Prize.

Contemporary Irish poetry

Undoubtedly the leading light of the contemporary poetry scene has been the late Nobel Prize–winner **Seamus Heaney** (see box, p.523), who built on the legacy of Patrick Kavanagh to produce lyrical verse relating the experiences of rural life. Heaney unearthed empowering metaphors in the Irish, and Danish, landscape, particularly bogs, for the Troubles, finding parallels for contemporary violence in ancient ritualistic killings, in poems such as *Bogland*, *Punishment* and *Tollund Man*:

Out here in Jutland
In the old man-killing parishes
I will feel lost,
Unhappy and at home.

  Michael Longley, born in Belfast in 1939, the same year as Heaney, has written some of the most evocative poems of the Troubles, including *Wounds* and *Ceasefire*, which draws on Book XXIV of the *Iliad* and was printed on the front page of the *Irish Times* on the eve of the IRA ceasefire on August 31, 1994. Indeed, Northern Ireland has been a particularly fertile ground for poetry since the 1960s. Other poets of note from the region include **Padraic Fiacc**, **Derek Mahon**, **Paul Muldoon**, the Armagh-born but American-based poet whose collection *Moy Sand and Gravel* won the 2003 Pulitzer Prize for poetry, and **Ciaran Carson**, one of the most distinctive and innovative voices to emerge since the 1970s and also a fiction writer of considerable talent, in novels such as *The Star Factory*, *Fishing for Amber* and *Shamrock Tea*.

  Significant women's voices in Irish poetry have emerged, including **Eavan Boland**, **Eiléan Ní Chuilleanáin**, **Medbh McGuckian**, **Paula Meehan**, **Rita Ann Higgins**, **Mary O'Malley** and **Sinead Morrisey**, each of whom has brought the female experience to the fore, while critiquing previous representations of women in a primarily male-dominated canon. Another important development in recent years has been the growing number of literary festivals – including the Cúirt Festival in Galway, Listowel Writers' Week and the Dublin Writers' Festival – and the increasing engagement of contemporary poets in the performance of their work. Audiences have had many more opportunities to encounter new writers, and poets such as **Paul Durcan**, **Brendan Kennelly** and **Gearóid Mac Lochlainn** have established considerable reputations through performing.

Contemporary Irish prose

Much as in poetry, the North of Ireland has produced some of the most popular and interesting prose writers. One of the most admired since World War II is **Bernard**

MacLaverty, whose most famous novels are *Lamb* and *Cal*, both of which he adapted for the screen. **Eoin McNamee**'s *Resurrection Man* (1994) is a disturbing fictionalized account of the notorious Loyalist paramilitaries, the Shankill Butchers, while **Glenn Patterson** has turned to moments before the Troubles to explore other possibilities that might have emerged, in *Burning Your Own* (1988) and *The International* (1999). One of the North's most innovative voices has been **Robert McLiam Wilson**, notably in his 1996 novel *Eureka Street*, focusing on the relationship between a Catholic and a Protestant before and after the IRA ceasefire in 1994. Meanwhile, Derry-born **Sean O'Reilly** has been compared to Isabel Allende, producing experimental and magical realist prose in works such as the short-story collection *Curfew and Other Stories* (2000) and novel *Watermark* (2005).

The death in 2006 of **John McGahern** robbed contemporary readers of one of the finest Irish writers since Joyce. McGahern had an almost uncanny insight into human nature and rural Irish society – he was born and lived for most of his life in County Leitrim – and rarely has a writer managed to realize as effectively the details of his life experience in literature. From his first novel *The Barracks* (1963) to his final autobiographical work *Memoir* (2005), McGahern's work evinced a deceptively accessible plain technique, which disguised a unique stylistic meticulousness and inner order.

While Wicklow-born **Claire Keegan**'s work – including her acclaimed 2007 short-story collection *Walk the Blue Fields* – has been indebted in style and theme to McGahern, **Colm Tóibín** has also been regarded as the heir to the Leitrim writer in his focus on aspects of the rural Irish experience. Tóibín's childhood town of Enniscorthy provides the setting for some of his most accomplished work, including *The Heather Blazing* (1992), *The Blackwater Lightship* (1999), a novel that explores the theme of homosexuality in contemporary Ireland, and 2014's *Nora Webster*. Fellow Wexford-born novelist **John Banville** has, like many of his contemporaries, moved outside the Irish context, with subjects ranging from eminent European scientists (*Dr Copernicus*, *Kepler* and *The Newton Letter: An Interlude*) to reflections on a European city (*Prague Pictures: Portrait of a City*). He remains the most critically acclaimed of modern Irish authors, winning the Man Booker Prize in 2005 for his novel, *The Sea*.

Colum McCann has also moved outside his Irish roots for inspiration and subject matter, in novels such as *The Dancer* (2003), concerning the Russian ballet legend Rudolf Nureyev, and *Zoli* (2007), focused on the gypsies of Eastern Europe. A key influence on McCann's work was the novelist and short-story writer **Desmond Hogan**, who along with Neil Jordan founded the influential **Irish Writers' Cooperative** in 1974. Hogan focuses repeatedly on the marginalized, isolated and unconventional, in settings that include rural County Galway where he grew up (*The Ikon Maker*) and 1950s Dublin (*The Leaves on Grey*). While **Neil Jordan** is better known today for his Oscar-winning film work, he continues to produce well-crafted and, indeed, powerfully visual literature, including his 2004 gothic tale *Shade*, entirely narrated by a murder victim.

Other members of the Writers' Cooperative include **Ronan Sheehan**, author of *The Tennis Players* and *Foley's Asia*, and **Dermot Bolger**. A poet and dramatist as well as novelist, Bolger has charted Dublin life, especially the Northside, since his first novel *Night Shift* (1985), including reimagining in the context of contemporary working-class Dublin *Caoineadh Airt Uí Laoghaire* (see p.606) as the play *The Lament for Arthur Cleary* (1989). Bolger also founded Raven Arts Press in 1979, one of several Irish publishers, including Dolmen, Gallery, Brandon, Salmon and Arlen House, that have emerged since the 1960s to provide a vital outlet for the work of Irish writers.

Clones-born **Patrick McCabe** has written some of the most provocative and sometimes deeply unsettling fiction of the past twenty years, including *The Butcher Boy* and *Breakfast on Pluto*. Meanwhile, few have managed as successfully to chart the urban experience in contemporary Ireland as **Roddy Doyle**, notably in the Barrytown trilogy (*The Commitments*, *The Snapper* and *The Van*) and the 1993 Booker Prize-winning

Paddy Clarke Ha Ha Ha, an absorbing portrayal of a child's experience growing up in Dublin in the 1960s. His 2007 collection of short stories, *The Deportees*, is just one of a growing number of texts focusing on multicultural Ireland.

Edna O'Brien has remained in the vanguard of Irish novelists since her pioneering work charting the female experience in 1960s Ireland, including the Country Girls trilogy: *The Country Girls, Girl with Green Eyes* and *Girls in Their Married Bliss*. Meanwhile, the award of the 2007 Man Booker Prize to **Anne Enright** for her fourth novel *The Gathering*, a powerful study of the trauma of suicide for those family members left behind, confirmed her position as one of the leading novelists of her generation. Described by John Banville as "one of the subtlest and most penetrating of the latest generation of Irish writers", **Mary Morrissey** has followed Banville in focusing on non-Irish themes, in particular in *The Pretender* (2000), the story of a Polish factory worker who claims to be the daughter of the last tsar of Russia. **Eilis Ní Dhuibne**, who writes in both Irish and English, has also attracted increasing attention for her work internationally, including her 1999 novel *The Dancers Dancing*. One of the most innovative voices to emerge from Northern Ireland in the 1990s was **Antonia Logue**, notably in *Shadow Box*, while **Anne Haverty's** *The Free and Easy* (2006) marked a movement among contemporary novelists to finally explore twenty-first-century Ireland in their work.

In similar vein, Cork-born poet, short-story writer and novelist **William Wall** wrote in 2005 a pointed critique of the Celtic Tiger, *This is the Country*, featuring a man trying to leave a life of drug abuse behind in an increasingly corrupt and uncaring Ireland. **Mike McCormack** also cast a critical eye on the new Ireland, though in a futuristic context, in *Notes from a Coma* (2005), an account of a penal experiment in which five volunteers, including the former Romanian orphan J.J. O'Malley, are kept in a coma for three months aboard a prison ship in Killary Harbour. The academic **Seamus Deane** emerged as one of the most accomplished contemporary writers with the 1996 publication of his semi-autobiographical *Reading in the Dark*. While Deane focused on his formative experiences in the North, one of the most popular recent works of autobiography was **Frank McCourt**'s Pulitzer Prize-winning *Angela's Ashes* (1996), an evocative, and at times deeply moving, account of growing up in poverty in 1930s Limerick. Dublin-born **Keith Ridgway** has also attracted increasing notice since his debut novel *The Long Falling* in 1998. While **Joseph O'Connor** began his career as a journalist and writer of popular nonfiction – including the satirical and insightful *The Secret World of the Irish Male* (1994) – he has turned in recent years to fiction, often informed by a meticulous study of history. His 2002 bestselling novel *Star of the Sea* explored the experiences of travellers on a famine ship sailing to the United States in 1847.

Seán Crosson

Books

Most of the books listed below should be available around the English-speaking world, though you may need to visit one of Ireland's many good bookshops to track down one or two.

CLASSIC FICTION

★**J.P. Donleavy** *The Ginger Man*. Riotous and roguish, this is a semi-autobiographical tale of a Trinity College student, full of energy and humour, which unsurprisingly fell foul of the Irish censor in the 1950s.

★**Myles na gCopaleen** *The Best of Myles*. Funny, quirky collection of *Irish Times* columns, under Flann O'Brien's other pseudonym.

Oliver Goldsmith *The Vicar of Wakefield*. Goldsmith used his experiences as the son of a clergyman to write his most successful novel, a masterpiece of gentle irony, laced with common-sense philosophical reflections.

★**James Joyce** *Portrait of the Artist as a Young Man*; *Ulysses*. A largely autobiographical tale of a claustrophobic religious education and social oppression, *Portrait* is Joyce's most accessible novel, while *Ulysses* is one of the greatest modernist works, a stylistically brilliant parody of Homer's *Odyssey* that roams over Dublin in a single day.

Brian Moore *The Lonely Passion of Judith Hearne*. Set in Moore's native Belfast, a moving tale of a lonely Catholic woman's descent into alcoholism and mental breakdown.

★**Flann O'Brien** *At Swim-Two-Birds*. Hilariously subversive reworking of *Buile Shuibhne*, the medieval saga of the mad King Sweeney, in which the characters try to take control of the story from their "author". *The Third Policeman* is a darkly absurdist vision of Purgatory. See also Myles na gCopaleen.

★**Laurence Sterne** *The Life and Opinions of Tristram Shandy, Gentleman*. An eighteenth-century comic masterpiece, described as "the greatest shaggy-dog story in the English language".

Bram Stoker *Dracula*. Stoker penned his most famous novel as a psychological thriller, though it's taken on a life of its own since then.

★**Jonathan Swift** *Gulliver's Travels*; *The Tale of a Tub and Other Stories*. Glorious satires by the Dean of St Patrick's Cathedral, Dublin (see p.74).

★**Oscar Wilde** *The Picture of Dorian Gray*. Wilde developed similar Gothic themes to his acquaintance Bram Stoker's in this novel, an allusive exploration of "the enemy within".

MODERN FICTION

★**John Banville** *The Sea*. One of Ireland's most innovative stylists, the former literary editor of the *Irish Times* won the 2005 Booker Prize for this tale of a widower returning to the seaside village where he spent a formative childhood summer. Look out also for his superior crime fiction, written under the pen name Benjamin Black.

Kevin Barry *City of Bohane*. High-energy, muscular gangland thriller, set somewhere between Cork and Limerick in the not-too-distant future.

Sebastian Barry *The Secret Scripture*. Perhaps Barry's finest work, this engrossing tale of a woman's mental breakdown and subsequent committal is firmly set within the last century's social and political changes. Beautifully written and observed, it packs a powerful finale.

Dermot Bolger *The Valparaiso Voyage*. A tale of a violent homecoming, dealing with themes of political corruption and alienation in contemporary Ireland. *The Family on Paradise Pier* is a vivid account of an eccentric Protestant Big House family as their world collapses after 1915.

★**Ciaran Carson** *Fishing for Amber*. A "long story" by one of Ireland's most original writers that pulls together Irish fairy tales, Ovid's *Metamorphoses* and the history of the

Dutch Golden Age into the form of a magic alphabet. *Shamrock Tea* is a wildly imaginative fantasy based on a herbal remedy that can cleanse the windows of perception infiltrating a Belfast reservoir.

John Connolly *The Wolf in Winter*. The latest thriller from Ireland's leading crime writer.

Roddy Doyle *Barrytown Trilogy* (*The Commitments*, *The Snapper* and *The Van*). The former Dublin teacher made his name with these humorous tales of the ups and downs of working-class Dublin life, and later won the 1993 Booker Prize for *Paddy Clarke Ha Ha Ha*, which shifted the focus, still laced with comedy, to family breakdown. In 2014, he ghost-wrote a memoir of footballer and manager Roy Keane, *The Second Half*.

Anne Enright *The Pleasure of Eliza Lynch*. Historical novel, based on the true story of the nineteenth-century Irish courtesan, who became the richest woman in the world, and her adventures in Paraguay. In 2007, Enright's *The Gathering*, a bleak, compelling tale of family dysfunction, won the Man Booker Prize.

Dermot Healy *Sudden Times*. A rich tale of paranoia, innocence and the tragedy of the working-class Irish in England.

Gene Kerrigan *Dark Times in the City*. The most famous novel by Ireland's answer to perhaps both Carl Hiaasen and Elmore Leonard is a complex and witty thriller, full of tortuous but believable convolutions, and featuring the kind of snappy dialogue you're only ever likely to encounter in a Dorset Street bar on a very black night.

Patrick McCabe *The Butcher Boy*. Darkly humorous tale of rural Ireland that was nominated for the Booker Prize.

Colum McCann *This Side of Brightness*. McCann's breakthrough novel, a multiracial story set in New York, about survival and redemption, and the rise and fall of America.

John McGahern *The Leavetaking*. Semi-autobiographical tale, in which a teacher at a Clontarf national school reviews his life on the day he expects to be sacked for marrying an American divorcée. One of McGahern's finest works is *Amongst Women*, which details the final years and recollections of a disillusioned former IRA soldier, who dominates the women of his family on a small farm in the west of Ireland. *That They May Face the Rising Sun*, McGahern's last novel, is a dark and elegiac narrative set in rural County Leitrim (published as *By the Lake* in the US).

Bernard MacLaverty *Cal*. The Belfast-born writer's best-known book, which tells of the tragic relationship between a young IRA man and his victim's wife.

Eoin McNamee *The Ultras*. Dark, claustrophobic tale centred on the disappearance of a captain in the British Army Special Forces, employing the film noir and postmodern stylistics found in McNamee's earlier works, *Resurrection Man*, about the Shankill Butchers, and *The Blue Tango*, about a real-life murder.

Deirdre Madden *Authenticity*. Evocative and ambitious novel, both a love story and a reflection on being an artist in contemporary society.

★ **Christopher Nolan** *Under the Eye of the Clock*. Powerful, largely autobiographical story of a severely disabled boy's struggles and joys.

Joseph O'Connor *Star of the Sea*. Rich, tragic historical thriller set on a refugee ship bound for New York in 1847. *Redemption Falls*. A gripping and often graphic tale of the exigencies of life for immigrants, revolutionaries and ne'er-do-wells in the post–Civil War US, given solidity by O'Connor's sure narrative hold and a multiplicity of contemporary cultural references.

Seán O'Reilly *Love and Sleep*. A bleak, distinctive novel set in Derry, blending hard-edged realism with vivid, dream-like qualities.

Keith Ridgway *The Long Falling*. Ridgway's often harrowing debut novel is both a love story and murder story, set in a Dublin that is dangerous and alienating. He followed it up with *The Parts*, a compelling and stylistically inventive mystery, also set in Dublin.

Eamon Sweeney *The Photograph*. Witty and erudite novel that deals with the big issues of religion and politics, and their role in Irish culture.

★ **Colm Tóibín** *The Master*. Moving, beautifully crafted novel, dealing with the sexually repressed life of Henry James. His 2009 novel, *Brooklyn*, is a keenly observed, humane story of 1950s emigration and return.

William Trevor *The Story of Lucy Gault*. Nominated for the Booker Prize, a powerful tale beginning in rural Cork – where Trevor was born – during the troubles of 1921 and telling the story of the disasters that ensued for one family.

POETRY

Samuel Beckett *Poems 1930–1989*. The most complete collection of Beckett's poetry, in both English and French (with his own translations), and including translations of major twentieth-century French poets such as Rimbaud and Eluard.

Eavan Boland *Collected Poems*. Ireland's leading female poet, also a central voice in American poetic circles, explores the boundaries of women's experiences.

★ **Paul Durcan** *Greetings to Our Friends in Brazil*. A good starting point for this accessible Dublin-born poet. Many of the poems centre on a priest who, far from being repressive and hypocritical as in his earlier works, is honourable and truly spiritual.

Michael Hartnett *Collected Poems*. A richly lyrical and rhythmical collection covering Hartnett's forty-year career.

★ **Seamus Heaney** *Opened Ground: Poems 1966–96* is a huge selection of Heaney's work (see p.523), while a new selection of his later work was about to be published as we went to press. *Finders Keepers* is an anthology of his energetic prose, consisting of essays and lectures written

between 1971 and 2001.

★ **Patrick Kavanagh** *Collected Poems*. Ireland's best-loved poet is perhaps most famous for *The Great Hunger*, in which he attacked sexual repression in 1940s Ireland.

Thomas Kinsella *Collected Poems: 1956–2001*. The full variety of Kinsella's work is on display here, employing modernist and traditional elements, on subjects ranging from love to political satire, social commentary and metaphysical speculation.

Michael Longley *Gorse Fires*; *The Ghost Orchid*; *The Weather in Japan*. Three fine collections, which show Longley as a highly skilled poet with a strong moral voice.

Nuala Ní Dhomhnaill *The Astrakhan Cloak*; *The Water Horse*. Good introductions to her work, in Irish and English, with translations in the former by Paul Muldoon, in the latter by Medbh McGuckian and Eileán Ní Chuilleanáin.

★ **William Butler Yeats** *Collected Poems*. Love, anger, meditation and disillusionment from W.B., one of the greatest figures of twentieth-century literature.

GAELIC LITERATURE AND FOLKLORE

Ciaran Carson *The Midnight Court*. Vibrant rendering of Brian Merriman's bawdy, eighteenth-century Gaelic poem, *Cúirt an Mheán Oíche*.

★ **Kevin Danaher** *In Ireland Long Ago*. Vivid and detailed, the classic work on all aspects of Irish folk life.

Seamus Heaney *Sweeney Astray*. The late Nobel laureate's version of *Buile Shuibhne*, the twelfth- or thirteenth-century tale of Sweeney's mad wanderings and healing.

Thomas Kinsella *The Táin*. The best translation of the *Táin*

Bó Cúailnge (The Cattle Raid of Cooley), the heroic centrepiece of the Ulster Cycle.

Tomás Ó Criomhthain (aka Thomas O'Crohan) *An tOileánach* (The Islandman). Vivid insights into the cruelties of life on the Blasket Islands.

Maurice O'Sullivan *Twenty Years A-Growing*. The story of O'Sullivan's youth and the traditional way of life on the Blasket Islands in the early twentieth century, in a style derived from folk tales.

HISTORY AND POLITICS

Jonathan Bardon *A History of Ulster*. A comprehensive account from early settlements to the Troubles.

Angela Bourke *The Burning of Bridget Cleary*. Impeccably researched account of nefarious goings-on in Tipperary in the 1890s, describing the sensational case of a young woman supposedly taken by the fairies, tortured and murdered, and the subsequent trial of her husband, father, aunt and four cousins.

★ **Tim Pat Coogan** *Ireland in the Twentieth Century*. An engrossing account of political and social developments, both North and South, by the former editor of the *Irish Press*, who has written many readable histories that are worth seeking out, notably *The IRA*, *1916: The Easter Rising* and biographies of Michael Collins and Éamon de Valera. His *Wherever Green is Worn: The Story of the Irish Diaspora* is a ground-breaking account of Irish emigration and the impact of the émigrés on culture throughout the world.

Richard English *Irish Freedom: A History of Nationalism in Ireland*. Lucid and fascinating scholarly dissection of Irish nationalism over the last three centuries.

Diarmaid Ferriter *The Transformation of Ireland 1900–2000*. Extensive and insightful account of the making of modern Ireland, combining politics, economics and social history.

Garret FitzGerald *Reflections on the Irish State*. The former Taoiseach offers perceptive insights and challenging theories on the big issues of Irish public life.

★ **R.F. Foster** *Modern Ireland 1600–1972*. The best history of the period, authoritative and comprehensive, though heavy going at times for the lay reader. In contrast, *Luck and the Irish* gambols entertainingly and insightfully through the period from 1970 to 2000, while *The Irish Story: Telling Tales and Making It Up in Ireland* is a provocative, witty deconstruction of myth-making and clichés in Ireland's telling of its own history.

Tom Garvin *Preventing the Future: Why Was Ireland So Poor for So Long?* Perhaps the most important socio-historical analysis of postwar Ireland, not least in terms of the "lost" decades of the 1950s and 1960s. Garvin offers not only an acute analysis of the rotten core of Irish social policy but a persuasive and often witty account of its impact upon future generations.

★ **Robert Kee** *The Green Flag*. Lucid and incisive account of nationalism from the Elizabethan Plantations to "ourselves alone" after Independence.

Conan Kennedy *Ancient Ireland: The User's Guide*. Extremely useful descriptions of Ireland's various types of megalithic field monuments, plus a fascinating account of the place of magic, ritual and mythology.

★ **Declan Kiberd** *Inventing Ireland*. Witty, insightful and thought-provoking re-reading of the literature of the modern nation.

Christine Kinealy *This Great Calamity: The Irish Famine*. Unravels fact from fiction through systematic analysis of primary source material related to the Great Famine.

Henry McDonald *Colours: Ireland from Bombs to Boom*. *The Observer*'s Ireland correspondent takes his Belfast upbringing during the time of the Troubles as a base for a sparkling comparison between Ireland past and present.

Susan McKay *Northern Protestants: An Unsettled People*. Utterly grim but absolutely essential account of the North's Protestant community and its disparate views, based on numerous interviews, simultaneously offering hope for the future and showing sheer desperation.

David McKittrick and David McVea *Making Sense of the Troubles*. Clear, dispassionate and authoritative crash-course on the conflict.

Ed Moloney *A Secret History of the IRA*. Authoritative account, with Gerry Adams as its sinisterly intriguing central character, of the struggle within the Republican movement over the last forty years.

George Morrison *The Irish Civil War*. A powerful collection of photographic images of the Civil War, accompanied by commentary by Tim Pat Coogan.

Breandán Ó hEithir *The Begrudger's Guide to Irish Politics*. Astonishingly funny, acerbic and still relevant account of the Republic's political history, written exclusively from the aspect of the begrudger.

Henry Patterson *Ireland Since 1939: The Persistence of Conflict*. At times iconoclastic, Patterson's account of an Ireland divided not only by boundaries, but by ideologies and class-related interests, breaks new ground and provides utterly stimulating reading.

Peter Taylor *Provos: The IRA and Sinn Féin* (published in the US as *Behind the Mask*); *Loyalists* and *Brits: The War against the IRA*. Accompaniments to three fascinating BBC TV series, shedding welcome light on the mind-sets and development of the three protagonists in Northern Ireland, including eye-opening interviews with leading participants.

★**Colm Tóibín and Diarmaid Ferriter** *The Irish Famine: A Documentary*. Highly readable and thought-provoking analysis of the Great Famine, which takes an incisive look at both the complex issues surrounding the failure of the potato crop, and the inadequacy of previous historical accounts of the crisis.

John Waters *An Intelligent Person's Guide to Modern Ireland*. A controversial book, by the *Irish Times'* gadfly columnist, arguing that the Irish have lost their cohesiveness in the drive for a "perverse and lonely" prosperity.

BIOGRAPHY AND MEMOIRS

Christy Brown *My Left Foot*. Born with cerebral palsy, Brown painstakingly typed out this unsentimental autobiography, published in 1954 when he was 22, focusing on his upbringing in a huge Dublin family, dominated by the remarkable character and endurance of his mother.

Ruth Dudley Edwards *James Connolly*. A short, direct biography of the socialist leader, which gathers pace around the time of his relations with Larkin, the 1913 Lock-Out in Dublin and the 1916 Rising.

★**Richard Ellmann** *James Joyce*; *Oscar Wilde*. Ellmann's wonderful biography of Joyce is a literary masterpiece in its own right. His work on Wilde was, unfortunately, unfinished when he died, but is still an excellent insight into the work of this often misunderstood writer.

Christopher Fitz-Simon *The Boys*. Frank and conscientious biography of the founders of Dublin's Gate Theatre, Micheál Mac Liammóir and his equally mysterious lifelong lover, Hilton Edwards.

★**R.F. Foster** *W.B. Yeats: A Life – Volume I, The Apprentice Mage*; *Volume II, The Arch-poet*. A magisterial work, the first fully authorized biography, incisive, exhaustive and compellingly readable.

James Knowlson *Damned to Fame: The Life of Samuel Beckett*. Excellent biography by one of the world's pre-eminent Beckett experts.

Hugh Leonard *Home before Night*; *Out after Dark*. Beautifully written evocations by the noted playwright of, respectively, his childhood and his adolescence in south Dublin around the 1940s. At times moving, often hilarious.

Antoinette Quinn *Patrick Kavanagh: A Biography*. Astute and often gently paced account of the life and poetry of County Monaghan's favourite son.

MUSIC

★**Helen Brennan** *The Story of Irish Dance*. Not just a fascinating history of the development of traditional dancing in Ireland, but a (literally) step-by-step guide to some of the most popular set-dances.

Victoria Mary Clarke and Shane MacGowan *A Drink with Shane MacGowan*. Shane's long-time – now former – partner takes the singer and songwriter through his personal history and several large martinis on the way.

Colin Harper and Trevor Hodgett *Irish Folk, Trad & Blues: A Secret History*. Fascinating accounts of key figures in Ireland's recent musical history, from Van the Man to Altan.

Colin Irwin *In Search of the Craic*. Wittily written account of a quest to hear some of the best of Ireland's traditional music.

★**Christy Moore** *One Voice*. Not just a scintillating account of Moore's own life through song, but a hard-hitting analysis of Ireland over the last thirty years.

Pádraigín Ní Uallacháin *A Hidden Ulster*. Mammoth and utterly engrossing account of the Irish song tradition, centred on the area known as Oriel (containing parts of Armagh, Monaghan and Louth).

Francis O'Neill *The Dance Music of Ireland*. Known as "O'Neill's 1001" or to some musicians simply as "the book", this compiles 1001 of the best-known traditional tunes.

Tommy Sands *The Songman*. Illuminating, droll and incisive autobiographical account by the singer and broadcaster of growing up in 1950s rural Down, being enticed by and rejecting the idea of the priesthood, and moving on to a musical career whose increasingly sharp-edged political tone saw him play a pivotal role in the peace process.

★**Fintan Vallely** (ed) *The Companion to Irish Traditional Music*. Provides constant delight in its copious accounts of the music's form, style and qualities, and brief biographies of many key participants; required reading.

Fintan Vallely and Charlie Piggott *Blooming Meadows: The World of Irish Traditional Musicians*. The fascinating biographical snapshots of a broad range of singers and musicians are enhanced by evocative photographs of their subjects.

Geoff Wallis and Sue Wilson *The Rough Guide to Irish Music*. A quintessential account of the roots and current state of traditional music in Ireland, containing a comprehensive directory of more than four hundred singers, musicians and groups, and details of the best places to see them in action.

MISCELLANEOUS

★ **Aalen, Stout and Whelan** (eds) *Atlas of the Irish Rural Landscape*. Fascinating, lucid exploration of the geography and history of the Irish landscape, beautifully illustrated with photographs and maps. *Newgrange and the Bend of the Boyne*, by Geraldine Stout, is an offshoot of the atlas.

Rosita Boland *A Secret Map of Ireland*. The *Irish Times* journalist and poet tours the country, exploring a little-known place or story in each of the 32 counties to illuminate the whole.

Deirdre and Laurence Flanagan *Irish Place Names*. Exhaustive guide to the names of over three thousand towns, villages and physical features and their derivations.

★ **Pete McCarthy** *McCarthy's Bar*. Runaway bestseller by the late, former travel-show presenter and stand-up comedian. An extended crawl around the *McCarthy's* bars of Ireland provides occasion for insight and plenty of irresistible humour.

Patrick McKay *A Dictionary of Ulster Place-Names*. Not just a cornucopia of etymological derivations but a veritable treasure-trove of information about almost every single place in the province of Ulster.

Eric Newby *Round Ireland in Low Gear*. Enjoyable account by the doyen of travel writers of a leisurely cycle trip around the country.

Tim Robinson *Connemara: Listening to the Wind*. Fascinating story of the Roundstone area around the author's home, ranging over everything from geology to folklore, written in a deceptively plain, easy style. *Connemara: The Last Pool of Darkness* gives similar treatment to the coast from Killary Harbour to Ballyconneely.

Paul Sterry *Complete Irish Wildlife*. Useful spotter's guide to Ireland's flora and fauna, with over a thousand photographs illustrating every species described.

GUIDES

Georgina Campbell *Ireland*. Hundreds of detailed reviews of cafés, restaurants, pubs, hotels and specialist shops.

Kevin Corcoran *West Cork Walks*, *Kerry Walks* and *West of Ireland Walks* (Counties Clare, Galway and Mayo). Also

Paddy Dillon *The Mournes Walks* and *The Complete Ulster Way Walks*. A series of detailed, easy-to-follow guides published by O'Brien, covering mostly circular day-walks, with lots of information about the wildlife and landscape.

★ **Pat Liddy** *Secret Dublin*; *Walking Dublin*. Two beautifully written walking guides to the city, replete with historical insights and up-to-date information.

★ **Joss Lynam** (ed) *Best Irish Walks*. Authoritative and informative guide to over 75 hill walks all around Ireland. Lynam's *Easy Walks near Dublin* and the more recent *Leisure Walks near Dublin* each cover around forty mostly circular walks of between half an hour and three hours on the city's doorstep, mainly in the Wicklow Mountains.

The Irish language

You're most likely to hear the distinctive sounds of spoken Irish if you travel in the Gaeltacht regions, designated areas of Irish-speakers (*Gaeilgeoirí*), the largest of which are in Kerry, Galway and Donegal. Here in summer, you're likely to come on crowds of teenagers from all over Ireland who are passing through the annual ritual of Irish college, learning the language by immersion. If you're interested in having a go yourself, courses are run by the well-respected Gael Linn, 35 Dame St, Dublin (☏01 675 1200, ⓦgael-linn.ie), whether in Dublin usually over six weeks or in summer staying for a week in the Donegal Gaeltacht; by the excellent Oideas Gael in Glencolmcille, Donegal; and in Connemara, Galway (see p.368). Among language-learning materials, Gael Linn produces *Gaeilge agus Fáilte*, an easy-to-follow combination of book and two CDs aimed at adult beginners.

Some history

Irish is one of the Celtic languages, along with Welsh and Breton, and belongs in particular to the **Gaelic** branch, sometimes known as **Goidelic**, which also includes Scottish Gaelic. Celtic language and culture had become dominant in Ireland by around 300 BC, but **Primitive Irish**, the earliest form known to us, is found only in **ogham** inscriptions on stone monuments, dating from the fifth to seventh centuries AD. This highly unusual script consists of tally-like notches cut along the edge of standing stones, rather than conventional letters.

In the next linguistic phase, **Old Irish** (seventh to ninth centuries), the language changed quickly, as Christian monks, now writing in Latin script, adopted a more colloquial form of Irish; from this period comes a fine body of lyric poetry and the earliest version of the *Táin Bó Cúailnge* ("The Cattle Raid of Cooley"), the central saga of the Ulster Cycle. **Middle Irish** (eleventh to thirteenth centuries) was a phase of linguistic confusion and new grammatical forms, with the language going into a decline after the twelfth-century Anglo-Norman conquest. By the fourteenth century it had recovered, entering the period known as **Early Modern** or **Classical Modern Irish**. The use of the language was now governed by the **filí**, a class of professional scholars and poets, among whom the most respected might have the status of a bishop or minor king. Meanwhile, the Anglo-Norman settlers had mostly integrated with the native population, adopting Irish language and customs.

In the seventeenth and eighteenth centuries, however, with the Flight of the Earls, Cromwell's Act of Settlement and the penal laws, the structures of traditional society were comprehensively destroyed. At the beginning of the nineteenth century, just under half the population was purely Irish-speaking, mostly in poor rural areas. These were the very areas, however, that were decimated by the Great Famine of the 1840s and the mass emigration that followed. As early as 1851, the proportion of Irish speakers had declined to a quarter of the population, and by the end of the century it was down to one percent.

Despite the decline of Irish in the nineteenth century, several organizations dedicated to reviving its use sprang up, most notably the **Gaelic League** (Conradh na Gaeilge), founded in 1893 by Douglas Hyde and others. The League ensured that, after Independence in 1921, Irish was constitutionally recognized as the first official language, and was compulsory in the school system and for entry to the Civil Service.

Today, around fifteen percent of the Republic's population have a good competence in Irish, 92,000 of whom live in the **Gaeltacht** areas, in counties Donegal, Mayo, Galway, Kerry, Cork, Waterford and Meath. A recent decline in the actual use of Irish in the *Gaeltachtaí* can be detected, however: a 1980s survey of schoolchildren there, for example, showed that nearly half of them spoke only English at home, while just twenty percent of them spoke only Irish.

Outside of the *Gaeltachtaí*, however, there's been a remarkable recent growth throughout the island, both North and South, in the number of **Gaelscoileanna**, schools in which every subject is taught in Irish and which are known for their high general standards of education. From just sixteen such schools in 1974, the figure has now risen to over two hundred. In **the North**, where the British government is committed to supporting Irish-medium education, the use of Irish has naturally been more politicized. However, about ten percent of the North's population can now speak Irish, and since the Good Friday Agreement of 1998 there's been an all-Ireland body to promote the language, Foras na Gaeilge (Ⓦgaeilge.ie).

For over forty years now, the **Irish-language radio station**, Raidió na Gaeltachta, which is known especially for its support for traditional music, has been broadcasting all over the country from its base in Connemara; it's now 24-hour, with studios in Donegal, Kerry, Mayo and Dublin. In 1996, it was joined in Connemara by a **national television station**, TG4 (Teilifís na Gaeilge Cathair), which, through its often progressive and upbeat programming, has done much to reinvigorate the language.

Basic pronunciation of Irish

Irish **pronunciation** is notoriously difficult for outsiders, bearing little resemblance to English pronunciation. A few basic, simplified pointers are given below. To complicate things further, Ulster, Connacht and Munster have distinct dialects, with different pronunciations and, to a lesser extent, grammars.

Vowels

Note the acute accent, a *fada*, which is used to lengthen vowels.

a as in "bat", or like the "o" in "slot"	**í** as in "machine"
á as in "paw"	**o** as in "ton"
e as in "bet"	**ó** as in "bone"
é as in "prey"	**u** as in "book"
i as in "bit"	**ú** as in "rule"

Consonants

Irish distinguishes between slender consonants – when beside an "e" or "i" – and broad consonants – when beside an "a", "o" or "u". For many consonants the slender pronunciation is different from the broad one.

bh broad, **mh** broad – "w" or "v"	**g** – always hard, as in "gift"
bh slender, **mh** slender – "v"	**ph** – as in "phone"
c – always hard, as in "cot"	**s** broad – "s" as in "some"
ch – like Scottish "loch"	**s** slender – "sh" as in "sugar"
d broad – "th" as in "this"	**sh, th** – "h" as in "hat"
d slender – sharp "d", almost a "j" as in "jelly"	**t** broad – aspirated, with the tongue against the upper teeth, somewhere between the "t" in "toad" and the
dh broad, **gh** broad – "gh", like a voiced version of "ch" in "Bach"	"th" in "thin"
dh slender, **gh** slender – "y" as in yes	**t** slender – as the "t" in "tin"
fh is silent	

A FEW SIMPLE PHRASES

Hello (lit. "God be with you")	Dia duit	Hello (in reply, lit. "God and Mary be with you")	Dia is Muire duit

Welcome (lit. "a hundred thousand welcomes")	Ceád míle fáilte	much)	maithagat
		I don't understand	Ní thuigim
What is your name?	Cad is ainm duit?	Goodbye (to the person staying)	Slán leat
My name is…	… is ainm dom		
How are you?	Conas atá tú?	Goodbye (to the person leaving)	Slán agat
Well	Go maith		
Please	Más é do thoil é	Bye (more informal)	Slán
Thank you (very	Go raibh (míle)		

SIGNS AND PLACE NAMES: SOME COMMON IRISH TERMS

an lár	city centre	gleann	valley – "glen"
árd	height	go mall	slow down
áth	ford	gort	field
baile	town – often anglicized as "bally"	inis	island – "inish"
		leithreas	toilet
beag	small – "beg"	leitir	hillside – "letter"
bóthar	road	lios	ring fort – "lis"
bun	base	loch	lake – "lough"
caiseal	stone ring fort – "cashel"	mná	women
		mór	big – "more"
caisleán	castle	mullach	summit – "mullagh"
carn	cairn	oileán	island – "illaun"
carraig	rock – "carrick"	páirc	field – "park"
cathair	fort – "caher"	ráth	ring fort
ceann	head, headland – "can" or "ken"	rinn	point – "reen"
		ros	headland – "ross"
cill	church – "kill" or "keel"	sliabh	mountain – "slieve"
cnoc	hill – "knock"	sráid	street
doire	oak wood – "derry" or "derreen"	teach, tí	house, cottage
		teampall	church
dún	fort	tír	country – "tyr"
eaglais	church	tobar	well
fir	men	trá	beach
geill slí	give way		

Glossary

Ascendancy The Protestant aristocracy, whether descended from Anglo-Normans granted land in Ireland or plutocrat planters subsequently installed in the country from the late sixteenth century onwards. Often prefixed by the term "Anglo-Irish".

bawn Fortification around a castle enclosure or cattlefold.

big house Mansion built by the Ascendancy.

bodhrán (pronounced "bore-run" or "bough-ron" depending on the region of Ireland). A shallow, hand-held goatskin-frame drum, played either with a wooden beater or the hand.

B Specials Auxiliary Northern Irish police force formed after Partition and disbanded in 1971.

cashel A stone ring fort.

ceilidh/ceili An evening of Irish traditional dancing usually accompanied by a band.

clochán An early Christian beehive-shaped hut constructed of stones fitted tightly together without the use of mortar.

craic/crack General term for a good time, usually accompanying drinking. "What's the crack?" means "What's going on?"

crannóg A Bronze Age artificial island in a lough, constructed to camouflage an otherwise vulnerable dwelling.

Continuity IRA Irish Republican paramilitary group which claims to be the legitimate continuation of the IRA. Opposed to the Northern Ireland peace process.

Dáil Literally means "meeting", but has come to stand for the lower house of the Republic's parliament.

Diamond A central area in a planned Irish town, sometimes actually diamond-shaped, but often triangular, with streets surrounding an open space where usually some form of memorial is erected.

dolmen Dating from around 2500–2000 BC, a burial chamber set below an often triangular placement of standing stones, surmounted by an impressively weighty capstone. Also called a portal tomb.

drumlin A small oval hummock resulting from Ice Age glacial retreat, found especially in County Monaghan.

DUP The Democratic Unionist Party. A staunchly traditional right-wing Loyalist party, co-founded by Ian Paisley in 1971, opposed to any attempts at loosening Northern Ireland's ties with the United Kingdom.

Éire The Irish name for the island of Ireland; often used to mean the Republic of Ireland.

esker/eskar A ridge of gravel and sand formed by a retreating glacier.

famine wall/famine road An enterprise of local landowners during the Great Famine of 1845–51 whereby starving tenants would be rewarded for work given them to build a wall or road rather than aid through hunger-relieving largesse.

Fenian A member of the nineteenth-century revolutionary organization that fought for an independent Ireland; often used as an anti-Catholic term of abuse by Northern Irish Loyalists.

Fianna Fáil Irish Republic political party that emerged from the Civil War, opposing the partitioning treaty, to become a major force under its long-time leader Éamon de Valera. Still largely conservative in aspect, it has retained governmental control for most of the last eighty years, despite being embroiled in a farrago of financial and political scandals in recent decades.

Fine Gael The Republic's long-term and long-suffering (usually) opposition party, whose origins go back to Michael Collins' support for the Independence Treaty (see p.591). Little distinguishes it from Fianna Fáil, though its social policies seem a little more liberal, and its membership is largely drawn from agricultural areas.

Fleadh Literally meaning a "festival", the term has become associated with the Irish traditional-music organization Comhaltas Ceoltóirí Éireann's music competitions in which musicians and singers compete at county and provincial levels before going on to the annual Fleadh Cheoil na Éireann ("Ireland's music festival"). This also includes the winners of the UK and US *fleadhanna* (the plural of "fleadh").

Gaeltacht Regions of Ireland where the Irish language is the predominant vernacular tongue, mainly in the country's west.

gallowglass An armed mercenary in medieval times (from the Irish for "foreign soldier").

Garda Síochána The police force of the Republic of Ireland.

High cross A tall stone cross in which normally the cross itself is surrounded by a circle. The earliest known Irish examples date from the seventh century and are often richly ornamented with biblical scenes.

IRA Irish Republican Army. Longstanding upholders of the Republican drive to restore a united 32-county Ireland. Particularly from the late 1960s onwards, it embarked on an armed struggle to force the British to withdraw from Ireland, with major bombing campaigns in the UK and Northern Ireland. The IRA unreservedly renounced its military initiatives in late 2005.

lough A commonly used term for lake; also a narrow coastal bay.

Loyalist Hardline Northern Irish Protestant loyal to the British Crown, sometimes linked to paramilitary activity.

LVF Loyalist Volunteer Force. Paramilitary group based around Portadown and founded by Billy Wright.

Martello tower Circular coastal tower built for defence during the Napoleonic Wars.

MLA Member of the (Northern Ireland) Local Assembly.

motte An early medieval fortification, much used by the Normans, consisting of a circular earthwork mound, flattened on top, on which would be sited a primitive form of castle.

Nationalists Those wishing to achieve a united Ireland, usually by peaceful means.

The North Politically neutral euphemism for Northern Ireland.

oghan Ancient twenty-letter alphabet used in both Celtic and Pictish inscriptions on standing stones, comprising parallel carved lines or notches.

Oireachtas The Republic's parliament.

Orange Hall A local building where members of the Orange Order meet.

Orange Order Loyalist Protestant organization founded in 1795. Subdivided into local lodges, it derives its name from William of Orange (see box, p.558) and annually celebrates his victory over Catholic James II at the 1690 Battle of the Boyne on July 12 with parades across Northern Ireland. The majority of Unionist politicians and many Presbyterian clergymen belong to the Order.

Palladian A style of architecture derived from the designs of the Italian Andrea Palladio (1508–80), whose work incorporated a rigid adherence to mathematical proportions, first promulgated by the Roman architect Vitruvius. Among the most stunning examples of Palladian architecture in Ireland are Castletown (see p.132), Russborough House (see p.128) and Florence Court (see p.578).

partition The division of Ireland into the 26 counties of the Republic and six of the North created by the 1921 Government of Ireland Act.

passage grave The oldest form of megalithic tomb, dating from around 4000 BC, consisting of a rounded mound or cairn with a stone-lined passage leading from the perimeter to a central chamber.

plantation The process of colonization of Ireland by the English Crown by which land was confiscated from the indigenous people and given to English and Scottish Protestant settlers.

portal tomb see "dolmen".

PSNI The Police Service of Northern Ireland (see also "RUC").

rath or ring fort The most common form of ancient monument found in Ireland, dating from between the late Neolithic period and early medieval times. Consists of a circular (sometimes oval or D-shaped) enclosure surrounded by an earthen bank rising from a defensive ditch. A roofed dwelling, of stone or timber, would be constructed within the enclosure.

The Real IRA Breakaway political faction which rejects the Northern Ireland political process and maintains the armed struggle. Calls itself simply "the Irish Republican Army" or "IRA"; the media sometimes calls it the "New IRA" after its 2012 merger with Republican Action Against Drugs.

Republicans Supporters of the ideals incorporated in the 1916 Proclamation of the Republic, the overthrow of British rule in Ireland and the promotion of Irish language and culture.

ring fort see "rath".

round tower Usually part of a monastic settlement, these lofty and slenderly tapering, circular stone towers range in height from around 20–35m and were often capped with a conical roof. The earliest examples of this uniquely Irish construction date from around the ninth century. The building would have had a variety of purposes, serving as a belfry, a lookout post and a place for storage of goods and valuables. The entrance was often set some 3–5m above ground level, allowing the means of access, a ladder, to be withdrawn inside the building in case of a Viking raid, some claim.

RUC Royal Ulster Constabulary. The Northern Ireland police force from 1921 until 2001, when it was replaced by the Police Service of Northern Ireland.

SDLP Social Democratic and Labour Party. A left-of-centre Northern Irish Nationalist party.

Sheila-na-gig A carved stone representation of a squatting woman, often displaying an over-large vulva; believed to avert death and prevent evil, they are similar to the carvings of Yoni found on Hindu temples. Many Irish churches once bore these carvings, particularly above doors or windows, but they were often removed during the Victorian era. Well-preserved examples are visible on White Island, Co. Fermanagh, in Boyle Abbey and on the ruined church at Kilnaboy, Co. Clare.

Sinn Féin ("We, Ourselves"). Republican political party opposed to the 1921 political treaty that played a major role in the subsequent civil war. From the late 1970s onwards, and, allegedly, closely linked to the IRA, it rose to electoral prominence among the North's Catholics and achieved significant success in the Republic. Since 1983 its leader has been Gerry Adams, one of the key figures in the gradual move towards peace in Northern Ireland.

The Six Counties Nationalist/Republican euphemism for Northern Ireland.

souterrain Prehistoric underground passage which offered sanctuary for those fleeing their enemies; in some mythical locations, seen as an entry to the otherworld.

sweathouse A small stone-constructed, low-roofed building in which a turf fire was lit. Once sufficient heat had been generated, those suffering from aches and pains or a fever would enter and would stay long enough to generate a sufficient sweat before emerging to take a dip in the nearest cold stream. In other words, an early Irish version of the sauna.

Taoiseach Prime minister of the Republic of Ireland.

TD Teachta Dála. Member of the lower house of the Republic's parliament (see "Dáil").

townland An area of land, similar to a parish, but not necessarily a village.

Troubles Euphemism for the vicious cycle of violence in Northern Ireland from the late 1960s to the announcement of the Good Friday Agreement in 1998.

turlough A lake with a limestone base that causes water to drain away during drier months of the year.

Twenty-six counties Somewhat begrudging Republican description of the Republic of Ireland.

UDA (Ulster Defence Association)/**UFF** (Ulster Freedom Fighters) and **UVF** (Ulster Volunteer Force). Northern Irish Loyalist paramilitary organizations, which now seem more concerned about controlling the Northern Ireland drugs trade.

Ulster One of Ireland's four provinces, comprising Northern Irish counties Antrim, Armagh, Derry, Down, Fermanagh and Tyrone, plus Cavan, Donegal and Monaghan in the Republic. Often erroneously used by Unionists and journalists as a synonym for Northern Ireland.

Unionists A term describing those (mainly Protestant) who wish to maintain Northern Ireland's union with the rest of the UK.

UUP Ulster Unionist Party. The dominant party in Northern Ireland from 1921 to 1972, retaining control of its government for the period's entirety. Though initially retaining ascendancy under David Trimble following the enactment of the Good Friday Agreement in 1998, its support subsequently dwindled and it won no seats in the UK 2010 General Election.

Small print and index

A ROUGH GUIDE TO ROUGH GUIDES

Published in 1982, the first Rough Guide – to Greece – was a student scheme that became a publishing phenomenon. Mark Ellingham, a recent graduate in English from Bristol University, had been travelling in Greece the previous summer and couldn't find the right guidebook. With a small group of friends he wrote his own guide, combining a highly contemporary, journalistic style with a thoroughly practical approach to travellers' needs.

The immediate success of the book spawned a series that rapidly covered dozens of destinations. And, in addition to impecunious backpackers, Rough Guides soon acquired a much broader readership that relished the guides' wit and inquisitiveness as much as their enthusiastic, critical approach and value-for-money ethos.

These days, Rough Guides include recommendations from budget to luxury and cover more than 120 destinations around the globe, as well as producing an ever-growing range of ebooks.

Visit **roughguides.com** to find all our latest books, read articles, get inspired and share travel tips with the Rough Guides community.

Rough Guide credits

Editors: Neil McQuillian, Brendon Griffin, Olivia Rawes, Rachel Mills
Layout: Ankur Guha
Cartography: Deshpal Dabas, James Macdonald
Picture editor: Sarah Ross
Proofreader: Jan McCann
Managing editors: Alice Park, Natasha Foges
Assistant editor: Payal Sharotri

Production: Nicole Landau
Cover design: Nicole Newman, Roger Mapp, Ankur Guha
Editorial assistant: Rebecca Hallett
Senior pre-press designer: Dan May
Programme manager: Gareth Lowe
Publisher: Joanna Kirby
Publishing director: Georgina Dee

Publishing information

This eleventh edition published June 2015 by
Rough Guides Ltd,
80 Strand, London WC2R 0RL
11, Community Centre, Panchsheel Park,
New Delhi 110017, India
Distributed by Penguin Random House
Penguin Books Ltd,
80 Strand, London WC2R 0RL
Penguin Group (USA)
345 Hudson Street, NY 10014, USA
Penguin Group (Australia)
250 Camberwell Road, Camberwell,
Victoria 3124, Australia
Penguin Group (NZ)
67 Apollo Drive, Mairangi Bay, Auckland 1310,
New Zealand
Penguin Group (South Africa)
Block D, Rosebank Office Park, 181 Jan Smuts Avenue,
Parktown North, Gauteng, South Africa 2193
Rough Guides is represented in Canada by Tourmaline
Editions Inc. 662 King Street West, Suite 304, Toronto,
Ontario M5V 1M7
Printed in Singapore

© Rough Guides 2015
Maps © Rough Guides
No part of this book may be reproduced in any form
without permission from the publisher except for the
quotation of brief passages in reviews.
648pp includes index
A catalogue record for this book is available from the
British Library
ISBN: 978-0-24100-975-8
The publishers and authors have done their best to
ensure the accuracy and currency of all the information in
The Rough Guide to Ireland, however, they can accept
no responsibility for any loss, injury, or inconvenience
sustained by any traveller as a result of information or
advice contained in the guide.
1 3 5 7 9 8 6 4 2

MIX
Paper from
responsible sources
FSC www.fsc.org FSC™ C018179

Help us update

We've gone to a lot of effort to ensure that the eleventh
edition of **The Rough Guide to Ireland** is accurate and up-
to-date. However, things change – places get "discovered",
opening hours are notoriously fickle, restaurants and
rooms raise prices or lower standards. If you feel we've got
it wrong or left something out, we'd like to know, and if
you can remember the address, the price, the hours, the
phone number, so much the better.

Please send your comments with the subject
line "Rough Guide Ireland Update" to ✉mail
@uk.roughguides.com. We'll credit all contributions and
send a copy of the next edition (or any other Rough Guide
if you prefer) for the very best emails.
Find more travel information, connect with fellow
travellers and plan your trip on Ⓦroughguides.com.

Acknowledgements

Paul Gray Thanks to Gade and Stella Gray, who make
everything possible; to Joy Bradley at the Irish Hotels
Federation and to all the good folk at Great Island Car
Rentals and at Good Food Ireland; to all the helpful staff
at tourist offices across Ireland; and to our editors, Neil
McQuillian and Brendon Griffin. I'd like to dedicate my
work on this book to my dad, Bill Gray, who was there for
me during the original writing of this guide, giving much-
needed support, encouragement and advice.
Ciara Kenny Special thanks to Nicola Fitzgerald
and Catherine Whelan of Fáilte Ireland for all their advice,
and to the many others who provided updates and
information along the way. Thanks too to friends, family

and colleagues for their suggestions for favourite spots
and hidden gems around Dublin.
Norm Longley Thanks to both Neil and Brendon for their
diligent editing and extreme patience. In Donegal, huge
thanks to Helena O'Brien, Mary Houghton, Rosaleen
Campbell, Mary Dorrian and Kirsty Buchanan; in Down,
Chris and Jenny Mullen, Roy Heaybeard, and everyone at
the *Hutt Hostel*; in Monaghan, Eimear Winters; in Cavan,
Patsy Mooney and Sheila McKiernan; and in Louth, Evelyn
Grills and Grace Kinsella. Most importantly, and as ever,
thank you to Christian, Luka, Anna and Patrick.
Ally Thompson A huge thank you to Steven Cockcroft, my
go-to person when it comes to Irish history.

ABOUT THE AUTHORS

Paul Clements is a journalist, broadcaster and writer based in Belfast. He is the author of a trilogy of travel books about Ireland (*The Height of Nonsense*, *Burren Country* and *Irish Shores*) as well as works of biography and literary criticism. His 2014 biography of the Irish travel writer, Richard Hayward, was adapted for BBC television. He has also written and edited two books about the travel writer and historian Jan Morris.

Paul Gray has been a regular visitor to Ireland since 1990, including a three-year spell living in Dublin. He is also a co-author of *The Rough Guide to Thailand* and has edited and contributed to many other guidebooks, including updating his native Northeast for *The Rough Guide to England*.

Ciara Kenny spent much of her youth dreaming of escaping the Emerald Isle, but after a period of globe-trotting and contributing to her first Rough Guide in Vietnam, she returned to her hometown of Dublin in 2008 full of renewed appreciation for the city. She has since contributed to books on Ireland, Indonesia, Hungary and Slovenia. She still lives in Dublin, where she works as a journalist for *The Irish Times*.

Norm Longley has spent most of his adult life writing Rough Guides to countries in eastern Europe and the Balkans, but has now turned his hand to the UK. He researched guides to Scotland and Wales before working on this current edition to Ireland. He lives in Bath and can occasionally be seen erecting marquees on the Rec.

Ally Thompson lives beside the sea in Bangor, County Down with her husband Stuart and three young children, Libby, Isaac and Molly. She's an ex-BBC Producer turned guidebook author and travel writer. Ally regularly contributes far-flung family travel features to a number of national publications but is never happier than when tootling round Ireland and the UK in her 1972 VW Campervan, Beryl, alongside her brood.

Photo credits

All photos © Rough Guides except the following:
(Key: t-top; c-centre; b-bottom; l-left; r-right)

p.1 Adina Tovy/Robert Harding (t)
p.2 Andreas Secci/Corbis (c)
p.4 Chris Hill/Fáilte Ireland (t)
p.5 Christopher Boisvieux/Robert Harding (b)
p.8 Martin Thomas Photography/Alamy Images (c)
p.9 ImageBROKER/Robert Harding (b)
p.11 Ian Dagnall (tl); ImageBROKER/Robert Harding (tr); Nature Picture Library (bl); Beata Moore/Alamy Images (br)
p.13 Elaine Hill Photography/Titanic Belfast (tr); Blickwinkel (cr); Anne-Marie Palmer/Alamy Images (br)
p.14 Douglas Pearson/Corbis (b)
p.15 Dublin Regional Tourism Authority (tr); Andreas Secci/Corbis (b)
p.16 Fáilte Ireland (t); Eirepix/Alamy Images (cl); Fáilte Ireland (cr); C.Bmke/Corbis (b)
p.17 Fáilte Ireland (tl); Fáilte Ireland (b)
p.18 Design Pics (t); Design Pics (c); age footstock/Corbis (b)
p.19 incamerastock/Alamy Images (tl); ImageBROKER/Robert Harding (b)
p.20 Irish Eye/Alamy Images (t); Design Pics/Corbis (br)
p.21 Destinations/Corbis (t); SPORTSFILE (c); Patrick Frilet/Hemis (c)
p.22 Ian Dagnall/Alamy Images (t); Michael Diggin (br)
p.23 David Lyons/Alamy Images (t); Fáilte Ireland (cl); Kevin Foy (cr); Eye Ubiquitous/Robert Harding (b)
p.24 De Luan/Alamy Images (tl); Nikreates (tc); Marshall Ikonography (tr)
p.26 George Sweeney/Alamy Images (t)
p.48 Eye Ubiquitous/Alamy Images (c)
p.51 National Gallery Ireland (t)
p.65 Fáilte Ireland (t); Fáilte Ireland (bl); Con O'Donoghue/Alamy Images (br)
p.103 Hemis (tl); Tim E White (bl); George Sweeney/Alamy Images (br)
p.110 Gareth McCormack/Alamy Images (c)
p.113 Steve Vidler/Alamy Images (t)
p.117 Gareth Byrne/Alamy Images (t); Phil Crean (bl); Irishphoto.com (br)
p.144 Design Pics/Alamy Images (c)
p.147 Barry Mason/Alamy Images (t)
p.162 Eye Ubiquitous/Robert Harding (c)
p.165 Destinations/Corbis (t); Maurice Savage/Alamy Images (bl); Gerry Browne/Fáilte Ireland (br)
p.178 Thornton Cohen/Alamy Images (c)
p.181 Richard Cummins/Robert Harding (t)
p.195 Ian Dagnall/Alamy Images (t)
p.202 Ian Dagnall/Alamy Images (c)
p.205 Rick Strange/Alamy Images (t)

p.219 ImageBROKER (t); Gareth McCormack/Alamy Images (b)
p.226 Ian Dagnall/Alamy Images (c)
p.229 Design Pics/Alamy Images (t)
p.253 Michael David Murphy/Alamy Images (t); Mira (b)
p.268 David Lyons/Alamy Images (c)
p.271 Fáilte Ireland (t)
p.299 Gareth McCormack/Alamy Images (t); ImageBROKER/Robert Harding (b)
p.306 Westend61 GmbH/Alamy Images (c)
p.309 Stephen Emerson (t); Jon Arnold Images Ltd/Alamy Images (br)
p.323 Hunt Museum (t); Ian Dagnall/Alamy Images (bl); Matthew Fry (br)
p.338 Gabriela Insuratelu/Alamy Images (c)
p.341 Paul Lindsay/Alamy Images (t)
p.355 atlantide Phototravel/Corbis (t); Ian Dagnall (bl); Design Pics/Alamy Images (br)
p.357 BrianIreland/Alamy Images (b)
p.392 Eye Ubiquitous/Alamy Images (c)
p.395 National Geographic Image Collection/Alamy Images (t); Nir Alon/Alamy Images (t); Design Pics/Corbis (bl)
p.409 Ian Dagnall/Alamy Images (c)
p.420 Ian Dagnall/Alamy Images (c)
p.423 Design Pics/Alamy Images (t)
p.437 scenicireland.com/Alamy Images (t); Stephen Emerson (b)
p.460 Peter Muhly/Alamy Images (c)
p.463 Scenicireland.com/Alamy Images (t)
p.479 J Orr/Alamy Images (t); Paul McErlane (bl); Stephen Barnes (br)
p.490 David Lyons/Alamy Images (c)
p.493 Fáilte Ireland (t)
p.511 Design Pics/Alamy Images (t); scenicireland.com (b)
p.524 scenicireland.com/Alamy Images (c)
p.527 Dermot Blackburn/Alamy Images (t)
p.553 Ocean/Chris Hill/167/Corbis (t); LOOK Die Bildagentur der Fotografen GmbH/Alamy Images (b)
p.557 David Lyons/Alamy Images (t)
p.560 Stephen Emerson/Alamy Images (c)
p.563 David Taylor Photography/Alamy Images (t)
p.580 Richard Cummins/Robert Harding (t)

Front cover & spine The Giant's Causeway © SIME/Olimpio Fantuz/4Corners
Back cover Newgrange © Fáilte Ireland (t); Puffin, Country Wexford © Guy Edwardes Photography/Alamy (bl); Cottage in Kinsale © National Geographic Image Collection/Alamy (br)

Index

Maps are marked in grey

Map symbols

The symbols below are used on maps throughout the book

Motorway	★ Transport stop	Waterfall	Lighthouse
Main road	♦ Place of interest	Garden	Bridge
Minor road	⊠ Post office	Ruin/archeological site	Church (regional map)
Pedestrianized road	@ Internet access	Castle	Church (town map)
Steps	✚ Hospital	Tower	Market
Railway	ⓘ Information centre	Stately home	Building
Path	P Parking	Abbey	Stadium
Wall	Viewpoint	Museum	Park
Ferry	Mountain range	Gate	Cemetery
✈ International airport	▲ Mountain peak	Statue	Beach
✗ Domestic airport	Cave		

Listings key

- Accommodation
- Restaurant/café/pub/bar
- Club/music venue
- Shopping

For everyone who simply loves good food

Good Food Ireland is about discovering the best and that requires standards

We select Ireland's best accommodation, pubs, cafés, cookery schools, food shops, producers and farmers' markets, all of them passionately committed to using the highest quality local ingredients. Look out for the Good Food Ireland sign or visit **www.goodfoodireland.ie** for a list of members.

GREAT ISLAND CAR RENTALS

YOUR FRIENDLY CAR RENTAL PARTNER IN CORK

Pick-ups at Cork airport, Cork train station and the Port of Cobh

**Great Island Car Rentals
47 MacCurtain Street
Cork City**

📞 +353 21 481 1609

www.greatislandcarrentals.com

¿QUÉ?

When you need some help with the lingo

OVER 5000 WORDS AND PHRASES

FREE AUDIO DOWNLOAD

ROUGH
GUIDES

SO NOW WE'VE TOLD YOU
HOW TO MAKE THE MOST
OF YOUR TIME, WE WANT
YOU TO STAY SAFE AND
COVERED WITH OUR
FAVOURITE TRAVEL INSURER

 WorldNomads.com
keep travelling safely

GET AN ONLINE QUOTE
roughguides.com/travel-insurance

RECOMMENDED BY

ROUGH
GUIDES

MAKE THE MOST OF YOUR TIME ON EARTH™